D0929295

CHRONOLOGIES
IN OLD WORLD
ARCHAEOLOGY

CHRONOLOGIES IN OLD WORLD ARCHAEOLOGY

Third Edition

Edited by

Robert W. Ehrich

Volume I

The University of Chicago Press / Chicago and London

Robert W. Ehrich is research associate at the Peabody Museum of
Harvard University and professor of anthropology at Brooklyn
College of the City University of New York.

The University of Chicago Press, Chicago 60637
The University of Chicago Press, Ltd., London
© 1992 by The University of Chicago
All rights reserved. Published 1992
Printed in the United States of America

01 00 99 98 97 96 95 94 93 92   54321

Library of Congress Cataloging-in-Publication Data

Chronologies in Old World archaeology / edited by Robert W. Ehrich.—
    3rd ed.
        p.   cm.
    Includes bibliographical references and index.
    ISBN 0-226-19447-7 (set) (cl).—ISBN 0-226-19445-0 (vol. 1)
(cl).—ISBN 0-226-19446-9 (vol. 2) (cl)
    1. History, Ancient—Chronology. 2. Antiquities. 3. Man,
Prehistoric. I. Ehrich, Robert W.
    DS54.5.C48   1992   90-11109
    930′.02′02—dc20

♾The paper used in this publication meets
the minimum requirements of the American National
Standard for Information Sciences—Permanence of
Paper for Printed Library Materials, ANSI Z39.48-1984.

ISBN 0-226-19445-0 (cl) (vol. 1)
ISBN 0-226-19446-9 (cl) (vol. 2)
ISBN 0-226-19447-7 (cl) (set)

Contents

Contents

Introduction

The inception of this edition goes back to 1981. By that time various contributors to the one of 1965 had been telling me that their versions were sadly out of date and that in many cases new work and new data called for drastic revisions and even complete rewriting of what had previously appeared. Other colleagues who had not been participants kept asking for a new edition. Despite its obsolescence, however, there was still considerable demand for the old one, so when an editor of the University of Chicago Press informed me that a reprinting was under consideration, it seemed necessary to act.

There are some differences between this edition and previous ones. *Relative Chronologies in Old World Archeology* of 1954 was based on a symposium held in Philadelphia at the annual meetings of the American Anthropological Association in 1952, the aim of which was to present and coordinate not-so-easily available information after the disrupted communications and hiatus of World War II and the years following it. The volume's focus on a single basic theme was experimental. At that time, as the title indicates, the evidence was limited to relative and historical data and, since the symposium itself occupied only one day, there were only nine papers.

By 1961 demands for a second edition to include the very considerable work of the intervening years resulted in the publication of 1965, after a review meeting of the authors which was graciously supported by the Wenner-Gren Foundation. During the interim the first efforts to accumulate and apply radiocarbon dates for archaeological purposes had been under way and, since some of the contributions included them, the term "relative" was dropped from the title. That volume contained fifteen papers.

This present edition reflects not only the explosion of archaeological activity in the years since then but also the spate of publication, improved communications between archaeologists and scholars in related fields, and the practice of holding focused symposia of general and specific interest attended by specialists from several countries. By now enough information has accumulated to extend the geographical coverage in an attempt to justify the ambitious title. This time, comprising twenty-nine contributions and an appendix, the volume includes several new areas and divisions of some older ones. Unfortunately an article on Japan could not be completed in time to go to press and has been withdrawn.

In this instance all the articles were invited or volunteered and were prepared without benefit of a symposium or special meeting. Several participants with neighboring interests, however, were in communication with each other and did establish, to a greater or lesser extent, some degree of cooperation. Others were obliged to proceed in relative isolation.

Because of the welter of new material, the number of papers, and the size of the publication, it has been necessary to concentrate on four major objectives: (1) sequences, (2) distributions and relationships, (3) calibrated radiocarbon and relative dates, and (4) pertinent bibliographies and sources. For the most part, therefore, we have had to eliminate or reduce descriptive and cultural data that have no direct bearing on interrelationships or cross-dating relative to the building of chronologies. In many ways this has resulted in more of a guidebook and summary than a compendium.

Like its predecessors, this edition primarily covers the period from the earliest settlements down to a natural breaking point somewhere between 2000 and 1500 B.C. However, depending on exigencies, some chapters begin before the settlement period and some either end earlier than the terminal date or carry the coverage down to relatively recent times. Because of the number of contributions we have tried to keep the articles reasonably short, but in some cases, despite drastic cutting, the authors felt that they could not reduce them further. There is thus considerable variation in length.

It is often difficult to discuss in a cultural or historical vacuum the matters we list as our major objectives, and differences in approach and interpretation as well as stated and implicit disagreements as to origins, relationships and processes such as diffusion, migration, local evolution, change or survival and the like do appear. Since our primary aim is to provide the chronological framework and reference materials necessary to answer such questions, it seems premature to deal with most of them here. It does, however, seem healthy to try to bring differing points of view into focus, with the hope that the data here furnished will serve both as summaries of where we stand at present and as a way station for future work. We are all thoroughly aware that we are not dealing with eternal verities, and that any interpretations of individual authors may be less enduring and less significant than the data they furnish.

Since the length of this publication has necessitated its appearance in more than one volume, we have departed from the usual practice of entering the various contributions in sequence as complete units. It has seemed preferable to limit volume 1 to the texts and to present in a different volume the technical data such as drawings, synchronic charts, maps, tables of radiocarbon dates, and bibliographies. Our purpose is to make life easier for the reader, so that one can more easily consult items referred to in the texts of volume 1 without the usual distractions and interruptions caused by flipping the pages backward and forward while trying to follow both text and its documentation.

Several authors have used older administrative units and boundaries rather than more recent ones. These are the ones used in older literature, and to graft the newer districts on older materials would result in greater confusion than tracking down more recent divisions and revised boundaries.

Because of the increased coverage, the ordering of the contributions has been more difficult than in the past; it is now no longer possible to progress in a relatively coherent geographical sequence in which each unit is linked to the preceding one. We begin then with the more closely knit components of Southwest Asia, followed by the Mediterranean, and then move southward across the Sahara-Sudan belt to sub-Saharan Africa. We pick up the trail again with continental Europe and the British Isles, starting in the west and working eastward across central and northern Asia and the Far East. Following the interruption after China, Siberia, and Korea we revert to the path across southern Asia from Baluchistan and the Indus drainage southward through India and Sri Lanka and then eastward to include Southeast Asia.

Rather than attempt to enforce complete uniformity in designations, spellings, and the like from chapter to chapter, and even from language to language within individual papers, such variations are brought together in the index.

Concerning Our Radiocarbon Dates

At the time of the first symposium in 1952 and of its publication in 1954 as *Relative Chronologies in Old World Archeology,* radiocarbon dating was at its earliest beginnings and was not sufficiently developed for any general use. Our avowed major objective then was to attempt the construction of a series of floating chronological networks based on imports and close resemblances that could be moved up and down the time scale as more definitive information should become available.

By 1965, the year of the second edition, many of the discrepancies between laboratory procedures and results had been worked out, and a sufficient corpus of data had not only accumulated but had become reasonably accessible as well. It thus seemed proper to drop the term *relative* from the title. Although the editorial statement of *Radiocarbon* 7 (1965) makes the point that a 5730 half-life date is more accurate than the initial 5568 or 5570 original one, our use of the 5730 figures in the second edition (Ehrich 1965) ran into criticism. However, it is simple to convert 5730 B.P. dates back to the original 5568 B.P. dates by dividing them by 1.03.

In the interests of continuity and consistency of results, the laboratories still report their determinations according to the 5568 half-life, with 1950 as the reference year. This provides a standard for further adjustments and new techniques.

Since 1965, not only have floating dendrochronological systems been extended and anchored, but the calibration of radiocarbon dates to a scale of known dendrochronological years now adjusts radiocarbon dates to variations in the rate of radiocarbon formation (e.g., see Baillie 1982 and Klein et al. 1982).

When we began work on this volume in 1981, the most recent system was that generally agreed upon at the International Workshop on the Calibration of the Radiocarbon Dating Time Scale held at Tucson, Arizona in 1979, the results of which appeared in *Radiocarbon* 24 (Klein et al. 1982) as "Calibrated Radiocarbon Dates," conventionally referred to as CRD. Although this article mentions several other systems, in the interests of compatibility and comparisons, it seemed advisable for all contributors to adhere to the same one, and, since the CRD consensus was the most recent and apparently had the widest sponsorship, the editor, with the advice and agreement of various colleagues, opted to use it.

The tables published in 1982 were for a standard deviation of 2 sigmas with a technical level of confidence of 95 percent. A projected second article with tables of a 1 sigma variability and a confidence level of 67 percent was to appear in a subsequent issue of *Radiocarbon.* Our initial plan was to utilize both the 2 sigma and 1 sigma calibrations for each date, but the 2 sigma ranges were enough greater to make them less adequate for archaeological use.

Jeffrey Klein, of the University of Pennsylvania physics department, who had very kindly furnished us with advance copies of the 2 sigma tables before publication, now made available a set of 1 sigma tables in computer printout. When the preparation of our articles was well advanced, it developed that a minor built-in computer error caused general inaccuracies of individual dates, but in no case of more than fifteen years. Considering the time spans covered, the differences between various calibration systems, and the rounding off of both the determinations and their deviations, such errors are, of course, negligible. Shortly before going to press we learned that the 1 sigma tables would not be published as planned, but by then it was far too late to change either to the 2 sigma tables or to some other published system. Thus all the contributors have continued to use them, and we publish them as an appendix. One can also examine our 1 sigma dates against the 2 sigma tables in *Radiocarbon* 24, 2 (1982) into which they fit.

After our papers had actually been sent to the press, *Radiocarbon* 28, 2b, devoted almost entirely to high-precision radiocarbon calibrations, appeared. For our purposes the most important article is that by Pearson et al. (1986:911–34) which gives calibrations for 5210 B.C. to A.D. 1840 from a dendrochronological series of dates derived from Irish oaks. The results are single dates with very small deviations, but to these one must add the laboratory 1 sigma deviations of the individual radiocarbon determinations. These last are already incorporated in the CRD tables. Generally the high-precision Irish oak dates fit within the spans of the CRD dates which are based on the high-altitude western American bristlecone pine.

The "high precision" designation refers both to the use of special equipment, a relatively large volume of carbon in the sample studied, as well as to a longer period of counting, making this inordinately expensive for direct application to individual archaeological samples. Since these high-precision calibration tables are now easily available, they can be used both as controls for our own dates and for future ones, until some better methods of calibration may be devised. (For a clear, intelligible, and nontechnical discussion see Baillie 1982.) Furthermore, there is significant information in other articles by Becker and Kromer (1986:967) and by Stuiver, Pearson, Vogel, de Jong, Linick, Kromer, Becker, and their associates in varying combinations of authorship in *Radiocarbon* 28, 2b. (For late calibration dating see Stuiver 1982.)

In this volume the radiocarbon data tables uniformly consist of the reported B.P. determinations with a 5568 half-life, a column of B.P. dates with a half-life of 5730 years (converted by multiplying the reported date by 1.03) which are slightly but insignificantly flawed by the computer error mentioned above, and a column of CRD 1 sigma B.C. calibrations. Here we emphasize that, despite the tendency of archaeologists to fasten on the in-

dividual central or reported dates, there is a very good chance that actual dates may fall anywhere within the limits of the CRD ranges or within the given ± deviations of the estimated dates. For these reasons, with a very few exceptions, we have eschewed a common practice of converting initial uncalibrated dates to B.C. and of calculating midpoints of calibrated ranges as misleading and meaningless. Also, we found that the formula for estimating dates that fall earlier than the calibration tables, the 5730 B.P. dates ± 1000 (Klein et al. 1982:116–17), raises problems and does not work well, so we have simply converted the 5730 half-life of such B.P. dates to B.C. by subtracting 1950, and have listed them together with their reported deviations as "estimated" in the hope that some further adjustments in the calibration process can more easily utilize them.

A few of us have averaged certain determinations when pertinent to our discussions. Some of these are included in the radiocarbon tables, others only in the text discussions. For the most part we have limited these to clusters of closely similar dates for which the combined sigmas overlap or approximate the differences between each pair of dates in a stepped series. For calibrated dates we have followed a mimeographed instruction sheet, again kindly furnished by Jeffrey Klein, and have calculated simple arithmetic averages of reported 5568 B.P. dates, and have further divided the averaged standard deviations by the square root of N, before entering them into the 1 sigma calibration tables. This process reduces the size of the laboratory uncertainty and usually brings it into a lower grouping for entry into the calibration tables, thus resulting in a somewhat narrower calibrated range. For the estimated determinations that are older than those in the CRD 1 sigma tables, we have used simple arithmetical averages of the 5730 half-life B.C. dates and of their sigmas.

Although several of the contributors have made their own calibrations and have made their own decisions to include or eliminate certain determinations that are either supernumerary, for example, for France, or are obviously discordant, the editor, who has done the rest, accepts full responsibility for all.

In several cases these procedures have been most helpful in establishing relative positions within sites, the dating of individual deposits, and the establishment or controls of chronological equations between sites and cultures.

In every case, however, tables of individual determinations are reported with each article and are available for any use one wishes to make of them. There are some inconsistencies between the results of different laboratories, and there are sometimes questions as to possible sample contamination and the reliability of cultural or stratification associations attributed to given samples as well as the time interval after a piece of wood was cut prior to its use.

In a preliminary statement (Tite et al. 1987:168) the British Museum Research Laboratory announces that all dates between mid-1980 and the end of 1985 (BM-1700 to BM-2315) were potentially affected by a systematic error. Some of them may be as much as 200 to 300 years too young. If other laboratories find that they too must reassess some of their earlier determinations, further reductions in the discrepancies between their results become probable. However, the calibrated radiocarbon system used here does seem to provide vastly improved consistency over the simple listing of uncorrected reported determinations. Despite the relative paucity of dates for various periods and regions, in most cases we have enough anchor points with which to assess the probable validity of interstitial suggested relative chronological relationships, both synchronic and diachronic, with regard to internal sequences and to broader networks of internal relationships. In general we now have the foundations of a better perspective on which to construct more complete and more accurate chronological pictures in the future.

Summary Statement

Because of the increased number of chapters and regions covered, it has been necessary to develop this volume more as a guide than as a compendium, and to focus primarily on the establishment of sequences, geographic spreads, and relationships as well as radiocarbon dating that might support or negate suggested cultural and chronological equations and other conclusions, and also what might serve as introductory bibliographies from which further sources can be derived. Although the chapters vary markedly in length and in detail, they all more or less meet the above objectives. Despite the numerous discrepancies that remain, one must remember that many points are still arguable and that the interpretations of the various authors are subject to change and thus are of somewhat lesser significance than the basic data involved.

Homer L. Thomas has based his summary text and maps on the dates and fundamental information given in the chapters themselves.

It is too much to hope that this publication will completely please anybody. A specialist's reaction to any composite work of this nature is normally, "useful as a guide to neighboring regions, but for *my* area . . ." We will be pleased to settle for that.

Acknowledgments

Listed alphabetically, the following participants who also contributed to the 1965 edition graciously agreed to reappear in this volume: Donald F. Brown, Kwang-chih Chang, Robert H. Dyson, Robert W. Ehrich, Marija Gimbutas, Donald P. Hansen, Helene J. Kantor, Machteld J. Mellink, Edith Porada, and Homer L. Thomas. Of these only Helene J. Kantor and Robert W. Ehrich appeared in the first edition of 1954.

I wish to thank my fellow contributors for their tolerance of my nagging and for their efforts to comply with my sometimes confusing and sometimes changing requests. In addition to Jeffrey Klein, Henry Michael, and Minze Stuiver for such technical aspects of the radiocarbon calibration as I have been able to understand and utilize, and again to Jeffrey Klein, who authorized the publication of the calibration tables, I am most deeply indebted to Homer L. Thomas not only for the coverage of his own two areas and his preparation of the map summary, but also for his very generous and valuable consistent furnishing of data, hard-to-get sources, criticism and advice, and for his unfailing support.

On behalf of all of us I also express our appreciation to the staff of the University of Chicago Press for their help and cooperation, emphatically to our copyeditor for her meticulous and very thorough work in bringing this volume into a reasonably consistent and acceptable form, and most especially to our particular shepherd, guide, philosopher, and friend at the Press, and to his former assistant, for their many kindnesses and long-suffering patience. Unfortunately they must remain nameless because of Press policy, but we are deeply grateful to them and they know who they are.

Part One

The Near and Middle East

The Relative Chronology of Egypt and Its Foreign Correlations before the First Intermediate Period

Helene J. Kantor, Oriental Institute, University of Chicago

Outline

The Chronological Framework in Egypt

The chronology of ancient Egypt relies on indigenous historical traditions organized in the third century B.C. by the priest Manetho into a framework of thirty-one dynasties stretching from the beginning of historical times through the Persian period (Helck 1956). Absolute dates for the dynastic sequence are based on pharaonic king lists giving the length of reigns, which can be checked by documents dated to specific regnal years of individual kings and correlated with astronomical and calendrical data (Drioton and Vandier 1952:10–13, 156, 159, 627–32, and *passim;* W. S. Smith 1960:193–202; Gardiner 1961:61–68, 429–53, and *passim;* Hayes 1970). The dates for the Twelfth Dynasty and later periods are known with only relatively small margins of error (Parker 1950:63–69, and 1976; Krauss 1985), but the uncertain length of the First Intermediate period entails a greater margin of error for both its own dates and those of the preceding periods.

The contributions of radiocarbon determinations to the absolute chronology of Egypt (table 1), as well as the many problems involved, have been much discussed (for recent articles, see Clark 1978; Derricourt 1971; Hassan 1980b, 1984b, and 1985; Hassan and Robinson 1987; Long 1976; Shaw 1985; Trigger 1983). The dates based on samples from older excavations have been subject to considerable contamination and are unreliable. Some of the absolute dates for the first three dynasties provided by radiocarbon determinations have been too late or too

Final text submitted May 1987

early to match the chronologies established for areas with which Egypt was either directly or indirectly connected (Derricourt 1971:280; Mellaart 1979; Kemp 1980; Hassan 1980b; Shaw 1985). By the use of a refined statistical method of analysis, Hassan and Robinson (1987) have shown that the radiocarbon data currently available for the dynastic period, although insufficient for a detailed and exact chronology, correspond well with the standard historical chronologies and with the early Palestinian and Mesopotamian synchronisms. The method also gives reliable ranges for Dynasty I to Dynasty V, Akhenaten, and Ramesses II (see Dynasty I ranges: Aha = 3023 ± 102; Djer = 3006 ± 85; Den = 2969 ± 80; and Qa = 2868 ± 90; Hassan and Robinson 1987:124, table 1; 125). Hassan and Thompson conclude with the anticipation of more accurate radiocarbon determinations in the future.

Egypt has long provided a chronological yardstick for many other areas, in particular the Levant and the Aegean. Already in the fourth millennium B.C., close con-

The illustrations for Egypt and Palestine have been interleaved to facilitate comparisons and can be found in volume 2 between chapters 1 and 2. I wish to thank Abbas Alizadeh for the care and skill with which he has prepared the figures. During the writing of this chapter, I have profited from discussions with Guillermo Algaze, Lawrence E. Stager, and Bruce Williams. I am much indebted to Th. von der Way for his great courtesy in sending me copies of his 1986 and 1987 reports on the excavations at Tell el-Faraʿin before their publication. I am grateful to Janet Johnson, former director of the Oriental Institute, for permission to publish eight sherds in the Oriental Institute Museum (fig. 8). Finally, I express here my deep appreciation for the much-tried and unending patience of Robert W. Ehrich during the preparation of this chapter.

nections with Palestine and Syria allow the relative chronologies of those areas to be correlated with Egypt. Specific contacts with the Aegean become prominent in the earlier part of the second millennium B.C. In the interval since the 1965 edition of *Chronologies in Old World Archaeology,* a flood of new information has become available for both the earlier periods and the second millennium B.C. From the Twelfth Dynasty there is now a vessel of Middle Minoan Kamares type found at Aswan, and the Minoan sherds from Kahun and other sites have been studied in detail (Kemp, Merrilees, and Edel 1980). The excavations directed by Bietak at Tell ed-Dabʿa have brought a new epoch in our knowledge of foreign elements and immigrants in the eastern Delta in the late Twelfth Dynasty and Second Intermediate Period (Bietak 1975, 1979). Additional information is being provided by the excavations at Tell el-Maskhuta directed by Holladay (1982:44–47, 50, 79) and by the survey of the Wadi Tumilat conducted by Redmount (in preparation). However, a review of the second millennium material would unduly extend the present paper; the end of the early epochs of Egyptian foreign relations at the close of the Old Kingdom provides a natural stopping point.

Except for turmoil in the intermediate periods, when rival dynasties ruled in a divided land, from the beginning of the First Dynasty pharaohs, reigning in each case as a king of Upper and of Lower Egypt, united the two components of the country into a single realm. This political unity was matched to a great extent, aside from the normal contrasts between the capital and the provinces, by cultural unity, despite the emphasis on Lower and Upper Egyptian elements in religion and political administration. Thus, in contrast to western Asia, problems of coordinating several cultural sequences developing alongside one another do not exist during much of Egyptian history. Difficulties arise, however, in correlating nonmonumental remains such as pottery and small objects with the relatively simple historical framework. The limited and continually occupied area of the Nile Valley was not conducive to the preservation of such large numbers of mounds as in other parts of the Near East (for geographical setting, see Butzer 1959, 1961, 1976; Trigger 1983:8ff.). Although stratified sites exist (see Bietak 1979) and can yield highly significant results, as illustrated by the wealth and range of information being recovered for the pharaonic period on the island of Elephantine (Kaiser et al. 1970 onwards), by far the greater part of the nonarchitectural material comes from cemeteries, that is, aggregations of discrete units. Thus, details of cultural development must be worked out either by the association of individual grave groups with demonstrably contemporary inscriptions or by typological and seriation analysis, combined when possible with topographical analysis of the cemeteries (e.g., Kaiser 1957; Kemp 1975).

Only the predynastic period provides major problems of comparative chronology within the borders of Egypt itself. Many sites in Upper Egypt represent a well-defined southern tradition. In contrast, for a long time Lower Egypt has been known from only a few sites at the southern periphery of the Delta: Merimde Beni Salameh north of Abu Roash, small settlement areas in the Fayum, and a few settlements and cemeteries on the east bank in the vicinity of Cairo. The comparison of the two predynastic traditions has been greatly hampered by our uneven knowledge of them, a situation that current excavations and publications are rapidly changing (Kaiser 1985:61–62). Even the limited evidence hitherto available has proved that predynastic Upper and Lower Egypt possessed distinctive cultures, whose political and religious configurations are enshrined in historical times in the separate Lower and Upper Egyptian administrations, the dual northern and southern pantheons, and the great traditional cult centers such as Buto and Hierakonpolis.

The Lower Egyptian sites have been too few and scattered to establish either a continuous chronological sequence or even geographical ranges. They also appear to be outlying rural settlements that do not exemplify the full range of the culture of the predynastic Delta. Funerary and other texts of the pharaonic period suggest that the predynastic centers in the north were as advanced as those in the south (Sethe 1930). It is, therefore, of utmost importance that excavations in progress at Minshat Abu Omar in the east (Kroeper and Wildung 1985) and Tell el-Faraʿin in the north (von der Way and Schmidt 1985) are yielding evidence for the Delta proper.

The origins of agriculture and animal husbandry in Egypt and of the predynastic cultures characterized by them have been the focus of much research. Numerous upper, terminal, or epipaleolithic cultures and taxonomic groups have been distinguished in the western Sahara (Caton-Thompson 1952; Wendorf and Schild 1980), in Nubia and the Sudan (Wendorf 1968), and in Egypt proper (Vermeersch 1978; Wendorf and Schild 1980; P. E. L. Smith 1982:342–77, 346–47, fig. 5.2). Some of these groups were already producing pottery that may be some one thousand years older than the earliest predynastic pottery (western Sahara: Banks 1980 and 1984; Khartoum Neolithic: Arkell 1949 and 1953; Chłodniki 1984; Caneva and Zarattini 1984).

The assumption that domesticated plants and animals were introduced from western Asia remains dominant (Clark 1971; Hassan 1984d; Wendorf and Schild 1976b), although considerable attention is being given to the possible or likely contributions of Africa (Wendorf and Schild 1980:273–80; Clark 1984). Discoveries in the southern Nile Valley, particularly in the Wadi Kubbaniya between Kom Ombo and Aswan, raised the possibility that cereals were already being exploited, perhaps even cultivated, around 16,000 B.C. and somewhat later in the Western Desert (Wendorf and Schild 1980:273–80, 1984). However, radiocarbon determinations have now proven the specimens of grain from Wadi Kubbaniya to be recent and not associable with Late Paleolithic materials (Wendorf and Schild 1984:126–27).

Despite the great accumulation of information, the gap between the epipaleolithic groups and the cultures with which the development of predynastic Egypt begins has not yet been filled (see e.g., Ginter and Kozłowski 1984). However, once the predynastic sequences proper begin, they develop, particularly on the better-known Upper Egyptian side, without a break into the complex culture of the First Dynasty with its monumental funerary complexes and wealth of specialized crafts. The archaeological evidence is providing the basis for the reconstruction of economic, social, and political development (Trigger 1983; Fattovich 1979; Krzyzaniak 1977 and 1979; Endesfelder 1984).

The Predynastic Sites of Lower Egypt

The earliest agricultural communities in the north appear to be those in the Fayum, long known from the surveys and excavations of Caton-Thompson and Gardner (1934). Extensive investigation of the geomorphology and archaeology of the Fayum has been carried out by Wendorf and Schild (1976a). More recent Italian and American surveys directed by S. M. Puglisi (Casini 1984) and R. Wenke (1984) respectively are not yet published in detail. Areas near the temple of Qasr es-Sagha in the southern Fayum are being surveyed and excavated by a joint Polish and German expedition (Ginter et al. 1980; Dagnan-Ginter et al. 1984).

The two sites excavated by Caton-Thompson are low mounds with scattered hearths, settlement debris, and groups of underground granaries lined with matting. The finds include an intact basket and sickle (fig. 4:44, 61), brown or red pottery vessels of simple shapes (fig. 4:46, 51, 55, 60) except for some rectangular troughs (fig. 4:45) and footed bowls (fig. 4:47, 48), as well as an extensive flint inventory (fig. 4:49, 56, 57, 61). Despite the importance of agriculture, the faunal remains indicate that there was still much hunting of wild animals. Caton-Thompson and Gardner carefully traced the relationship of artifacts to the changing shoreline of Lake Moeris. Flints of epipaleolithic type, which they termed Fayum B, occurred consistently on shorelines lower than the agricultural settlements of Fayum A. Their hypothesis that the lake was sinking led them to reconstruct a break in

cultural development in which the Fayum A agriculturalists were succeeded by groups of hunters leading a less sophisticated existence (Caton-Thompson and Gardner 1934). This rather disconcerting cultural throwback has been eliminated by Wendorf and Schild's clarification of the oscillations in the level of the lake; they have shown that during the stretch of time in question the lake was rising, not sinking (Wendorf and Schild 1976:222–26, 317, 319). The chronological position of Fayum B, now frequently termed Qarunian, is thus brought into line with its typological character. It was an epipaleolithic culture of hunters who lived along shorelines that were covered by the waxing lake by the time of the Fayum A inhabitants. There are no satisfactory links between the two groups.

The areas near Qasr es-Sagha yielded hearths, in one case with traces of a screen (Ginter et al. 1980: fig. 22) and debris, but no granaries, and are apparently camp sites. At Site QS XI/81, six stratified hearths and their associated debris suggest that Fayum A should be divided into an earlier phase, characterized by pottery with a considerable amount of quartz tempering and a flake industry, and a later phase in which the pottery has only a little quartz tempering and the lithic assemblage includes blade tools, as well as some bifacial ones (Dagnan-Ginter et al. 1984:33; 34, fig. 1; 35ff.; 55–60, figs. 15–16 [QS X/81]; 60–65; 94–99). So far the Fayum A Neolithic has not appeared outside the Fayum, so that the extent to which it constitutes a general stage of a Lower Egyptian tradition remains uncertain. However, the occurrence at various sites, including Tell el-Fara'in in the Delta, of individual flint tools like those of Fayum A and Merimde levels 3–5 is taken by K. Schmidt as evidence that the two sites in question represent a neolithic culture typical for the Delta as a whole (see Schmidt in von der Way 1987:253).

The importance of Merimde Beni Salameh, located northwest of the Fayum on the western edge of the Delta, as a large predynastic settlement was revealed in 1929–39 by an expedition directed by Junker (1929, 1930, 1932, 1933, 1934, 1940, 1945). Excavations were resumed in 1977 (Eiwanger 1978, 1979, 1980, 1982). They corroborate and greatly amplify the stratification observed toward the end of the earlier excavations (Junker 1945). Five levels exist, but are not evenly present in all parts of the settlement. The special character of the lowest stratum is emphasized by Eiwanger (1982:68–70, 1984:12–14). Its sandy yellowish soil was distinct from the grayish-brown soil of the upper levels, which contained Nile mud. Its assemblage has elements setting it off from that characterizing the four upper levels. A gap in occupation was indicated by an almost sterile level of sand separating Strata I and II in several areas. Throughout the existence of the site flimsy houses supported by posts and possessing hearths and shallow plastered holes in front were standard. Round, partially sunken structures with at least the lower walls made of lumps of Nile clay occur only in the later strata and in limited areas; they are apparently not ordinary houses.

In general, the pottery at Merimde is monochrome, varying in color from red or brown to black, and burnished (Eiwanger 1984 and 1988). That of Stratum I consists of many simple bowl and bag shapes (fig. 4:29, 33). Herringbone patterns incised in a reserved matt band on polished-red vessels are characteristic only in Stratum I (fig. 4:25; Eiwanger 1984: pls. 18–20). Oval bowls are particularly common in Stratum II. Somewhat differentiated shapes occur in the later strata (fig. 4:23, 28), as well as simple appliquéd elements (fig. 4:21, 22). Vessels with fingernail incisions appear in Stratum IV (Eiwanger 1982:37f.). In addition to ceramics and the flint assemblage, Merimde is also yielding specialized small objects such as have been hitherto almost completely missing from Lower Egypt. Probably the most important example of these is a terra-cotta human head 11 cm high with a bore hole for attachment (fig. 4:32). Another is a very schematic figurine (fig. 4:40).

The geographical range of Merimde remains uncertain. It may represent an early stage in the mainstream of Lower Egyptian culture and may have existed in the Delta. The various proposals for the relative chronological position of Merimde have been reviewed by Eiwanger (1984:16–17). The radiocarbon dates so far available are not reliable; dates based on stratified samples from the new excavations should be much more helpful (see table 1). In his publication of Stratum I, Eiwanger emphasizes that not only did a period of abandonment separate it from the later strata, but also that it is culturally distinct from them. He concludes that Stratum I represents the earliest neolithic phase as yet known in northern Egypt, antedating Fayum A (Eiwanger 1984:12–14). The small compass of figure 4 does not permit stratigraphic distinctions within Merimde, but it should be remembered that the objects from Stratum I (fig. 4:25, 29, 30, 33) may actually be earlier than Fayum A. The ware of the pottery of the higher strata at Merimde is essentially the same as that of Fayum A, but more developed in its surface treatment, shapes, accessories, and decoration. It provides some typological evidence for considering Fayum A and standard Merimde as successive northern Egyptian phases rather than contemporary regional variants.

On the eastern side of the Nile a prehistoric settlement at el-Omari near Helwan was briefly excavated in 1934–35; the few details hitherto published (Debono 1945; Hayes 1964) will be superseded by a final report by F. Debono and B. Mortenson. El-Omari has been taken as a possible intermediary between Merimde and the ob-

viously later culture revealed at Maadi in the 1930s by excavations directed by Mustafa Amer and O. Menghin (Menghin 1934; Menghin and Amer 1932, 1936). Work at the site has been renewed by S. M. Puglisi, in association with Cairo University (Leclant 1978:273–74). The preliminary reports do not record any stratification. Simple rounded or rectangular houses of perishable posts and matting (Menghin and Amer 1936: pl. XIII) and installations such as hearths occurred. The pottery shows a much greater variation in ware than does that of Fayum A and Merimde. Alongside the brown fabrics made of Nile mud, a light-faced ware, sometimes with painted decoration, occurs (Rizkana and Seeher 1987:23–29). Vessel shapes are characterized by the presence of differentiated elements such as well-formed necks, rims, and ring bases (Rizkana and Seeher 1987:34–48; pls. 1–29, 37–39). Such characteristics, as well as the excellent synchronisms with the Upper Egyptian sequence to be noted below, clearly place the Maadi culture later than either Fayum A or Merimde. The problems as to possible genetic links between them and Maadi still remain (Rizkana and Seeher 1987:63–66).

In addition to the settlement site at Maadi proper, cemeteries at Wadi Digla near Maadi and at Heliopolis indicate the presence of this culture in the region of modern Cairo (Rizkana 1952; Amer and Rizkana 1953; Rizkana and Seeher 1987:19; Debono and Mortensen 1987). Four jars discovered at Giza probably represent another cemetery of the Maadi culture (Mortensen 1985). Graves with vessels of Maadi types found about 50 km to the south at es-Saff (Habachi and Kaiser 1985) and to the north in the area of Merimde (Badawi 1980) suggest that the culture had a wide distribution (Rizkana and Seeher 1987:63). Various pottery groups of special character found in many round storage pits at Sedment and in two at Harageh are interpreted by Williams (1982), followed by Kaiser (1985:67–71), as representatives of a culture contemporary with and allied to Maadi. These groups are important as indications that a local variant of Lower Egyptian culture existed some 100 km. south of Maadi.

It has been tempting to assume that Maadi represents a developed phase of a Lower Egyptian tradition which also existed in the Delta, but until recently the Delta proper has been blank in the predynastic epoch. Now, excavations at Tell el-Fara'in, the site of Buto, the city prominent in pharaonic texts and funerary representations as the traditional predynastic capital of Lower Egypt, are bringing the first direct evidence for the predynastic period in the central Delta. Borings in many parts of the site revealed the location of early levels concentrated on a slightly sloping sand island (von der Way 1984:271–75 and figs. 1, 2). Initial excavations reached levels dated by sherds ranging from Dynasties IV–V back to Dynasty 0, as indicated by a small fragment of late

Decorated ware and by flints (von der Way 1984:275–91 and fig. 11:5). Subsequent seasons have established the existence of predynastic deposits divisible into upper and lower levels (von der Way 1986:195, fig. 2), the former correlated by von der Way with Naqada II c–d$_1$ and the latter with Naqada II b at the latest (1987:243–46), that is, both contemporary with the Gerzean period in the south. The upper phase had imported Upper Egyptian Wavy-handled (von der Way 1987:243, fig. 1:3; 246, fig. 2:1–5) and Rough (fig. 1:4–6) jars. The Tell el-Fara'in pottery and flint tools are basically identical with those of Maadi, thus establishing Maadian as a widely distributed Lower Egyptian culture (von der Way 1986:197, fig. 3; 203, 205–7, figs. 5–8; and 1987:253). Some local variation is exemplified by vessels with small, neat imprints of a type unknown at Maadi (von der Way 1986:200, fig. 4 a, b; and 1987:243, fig. 1: 2; see also Kaiser 1985:67). In addition to the revelation of Maadian at Tell el-Fara'in, the cemetery and settlement discovered by the Munich East Delta Expedition at Minshat Abu Omar constitutes a substantial Gerzean enclave in Lower Egypt (Wildung 1984:269; Kroeper and Wildung 1985:5, fig. 1). Clearly by the later part of the predynastic period the Delta was already a cultural amalgram of considerable complexity.

The Upper Egyptian Sequence

The predynastic period of Upper Egypt is better known than that of the north, although cemetery sites still far outnumber settlements. In his pioneering example of seriation Petrie used pottery to arrange nine hundred graves from the cemeteries of Naqada and Diospolis Parva (Abadiyeh and Hu) into a relative sequence, the end of which was fixed by vessels from First Dynasty contexts (Petrie 1901a:4–12; see also Baumgartel 1970; Davis 1983). After the various stages of his analysis were completed, he divided the nine hundred grave slips into fifty equal groups. Each of these groups constituted a "sequence date," that is, a unit not of time proper, but of associated tomb groups in a typological sequence. Petrie distinguished three predynastic periods: s.d. 30–39 forming Amratian, s.d. 40–65 Gerzean, and s.d. 65–70 Semainean, as well as the First Dynasty, s.d. 70–80. Brunton added a fourth stage, Badarian, as an antecedent to Amratian (Brunton and Caton-Thompson 1928).

The Petrie-Brunton sequence has long been generally accepted, although there has been increasing unease concerning the validity of individual sequence dates, particularly in view of the occurrence in the same graves of Wavy-handled vessels representing different stages of the degenerative series on which Petrie based his arrangement of Gerzean tomb groups. In an analysis using 170 graves at Armant, Kaiser (1957) worked out a new classification of predynastic phases on the basis of both typology and the location of the graves ("horizontal stratification") within the cemetery. He demonstrated that it grew from south to north, from an area with graves containing mostly Black-topped vessels, through the middle part of the cemetery where the proportion of Black-topped to Polished-red vessels was decreasing, to the northern part where jars of Petrie's "Late" class were dominant. Kaiser concluded with a tripartite sequence fundamentally the same as that of Petrie, but with subdivisions: Naqada I, that is, Amratian, divided into three phases; Naqada II, that is, Gerzean, divided into five phases, the first two of which form a transition from Amratian to Gerzean; and Naqada III, that is, Semainean, divided into three phases. Kaiser rounded out his classification with an analysis of grave groups at Tura and elsewhere representing the predynastic-protodynastic transition (Kaiser 1964; Kaiser and Dreyer 1982:264) and has applied it to graves at various cemeteries, although often assigning individual burials to a range of two phases. His system has been influential and his terminology is widely used (Needler 1984:44). More recently Kemp has analyzed predynastic graves excavated at Armant cemetery 1400–1500, el-Amrah A and B, and Mahasna by means of a computer program developed by D. Kendall of the University of Cambridge (Kemp 1982). The seriation that resulted is essentially in harmony with Petrie's distinction of the Amratian and Gerzean periods and, in addition, with various proposals to place "Semainean" at the beginning of the First Dynasty (Kantor 1944; Case and Payne 1962; Arkell 1975).

In Upper as in Lower Egypt, the problem of the origins of the predynastic tradition proper remains unsolved. In the el-Tarif cemetery at Thebes, Ginter and his colleagues distinguished a flint industry accompanied by fragments of pottery vessels of simple shapes (Ginter, Kozłowski, and Drobniewicz 1979; Ginter et al. 1982; Ginter and Kozłowski 1984). In a survey on the west side of the Nile between Armant and Thebes, five Tarifian sites were located (Ginter, Kozłowski, and Pawlikowski 1985:27–29). Ginter and his co-workers consider the Tarifian to be a late northern variant of the epipaleolithic Shamarkian complex known farther south in the Western Desert and suggest as a possible date the first half of the fifth millennium B.C. (see Ginter, Kozłowski, and Pawlikowski 1985 for a determination of 6310 ± 80 for charcoal from Site 2/83 near Malqata at Thebes). Tarifian is analogous to the Qarunian (Fayum B) in being an epipaleolithic industry without any demonstrable links to the later sequence (Ginter and Kozłowski 1984:257–259).

The string of sites on the east bank of the Nile slightly south of modern Assiut excavated in the 1920s by Brunton provided forty graves and eight town groups near the village of Deir Tasa, as well as other scattered finds in the Qau-Matmar area that Brunton took as representative of an earlier stage than any that had yet been found in Upper Egypt. The graves contained only two or three vessels and a very limited number of objects. The pottery is normally brown or red; the few examples with a narrow black area at the mouth (fig. 4:132) are presumably the beginning of the Black-topped class of pottery, which is such an outstanding characteristic of the Upper Egyptian culture. The shapes are simple, consisting of rounded bowls, bag-shaped containers, and slightly biconical, angled vessels (fig. 4:134). The latter are particularly diagnostic. The most differentiated pottery forms are rectangular bowls in a red-washed ware (fig. 4:130) and beakers in a black incised ware (fig. 4:131). The latter, however, are found only in the town groups attributed to Tasian. Their absence from the Tasian graves is disconcerting, particularly since they are not large domestic vessels that might be expected to occur only in habitation areas. Also found only in the town groups are celts. The discrepancies between the finds from graves and settlement debris and the occurrence of Tasian material only in the Qau-Matmar area (see Kaiser 1985:77–79 for evidence interpreted as support for a much wider distribution of Tasian) make it difficult to consider Tasian a well-established cultural phase. Although in figure 4 it is placed at the beginning of the Upper Egyptian sequence, the uncertainties as to its existence as a separate period should not be forgotten; it may, perhaps, represent the beginning of the Badarian phase.

The earliest major phase of the Upper Egyptian sequence, Badarian, is best known from graves and town groups excavated by Brunton in the Qau-Matmar area. The pottery from both graves and habitation areas is consistent. Black-topped vessels are now prominent (fig. 4: 113–15). A distinctive rippling of the surface produced by combing often appears on both the Black-topped and Polished-red wares (fig. 4:117). Although the shapes are for the most part simple, with bag forms common (fig. 4:114), somewhat more differentiated forms such as carinated bowls occur (fig. 4:112).

In the Qau-Matmar area, in addition to the graves and town groups along the edge of the cultivation, Badarian also appeared in the small low mound of Hemamieh, excavated by Caton-Thompson. There Badarian sherds occurred in both the lowest occupational level, sealed by a layer of breccia, and in the level above the breccia. Above were layers with Amratian sherds and round hut emplacements and, still higher, Gerzean sherds. The Hemamiah stratification has been widely accepted as corroboration of the typological arrangement of graves as established by Petrie and Brunton.

Assessments of the character and chronological position of both Tasian and Badarian widely different from that given here have been proposed. Ginter and his colleagues have, with reservations, suggested the existence of two early local traditions, Tasian, distinguished by a specific stone-tool industry of uncertain chronological position, and Tarifian, representing an epipaleolithic phase possessing pottery in the tradition of northern Shamarkian (Ginter et al. 1982:108). They accept the taxonomic distinctions of the later materials but cite overlapping radiocarbon dates for Badarian, Amratian, and Gerzean as the basis for considering those units as contemporary local traditions, rather than consecutive stages (Ginter et al. 1982:104–6). However, the radiocarbon dates in themselves are hardly sufficient to outweigh sequences established by archaeological evidence. In any case, the most recent review of the radiocarbon evidence supports the consecutivity of Badarian, Amratian, and Gerzean (Hassan and Robinson 1987; see table 1 here).

Kaiser, in a detailed discussion of the character and relationships of Tasian, Badarian, and Amratian, concludes that Tasian was indeed a specific local culture, incorporating considerable Lower Egyptian influence and ancestral to Amratian. Badarian he regards as a culture that was brought in from a probable center in the Eastern Desert and which competed first with Tasian and then with Amratian (1985:80–86, and 86, fig. 10). He challenges the stratification of Badarian-Amratian-Gerzean at Hemamieh, pointing to a few sherds of Amratian type in the breccia-sealed, lowest Badarian level and arguing that Amratian is thinly represented there and in the Qau-Matmar region (Kaiser 1956:96–97, 1985:83–84; see also Hayes 1984:214). As further evidence for Badarian-Amratian contemporaneity he cites three Badarian graves, each containing an object of a type normally considered typical for Amratian (Kaiser 1985:84–85).

The picture of the earlier Upper Egyptian cultures proposed by Kaiser deserves detailed consideration, but the following comments must suffice here. In the area of its first discovery, between Qau and Matmar, Badarian settlement debris and graves occurred immediately adjacent to or even mixed with Tasian, Amratian, and Gerzean town groups and cemeteries (Brunton and Caton-Thompson 1928:3–7, 9, 49f. and pls. I, II; Brunton 1937: 3–4 and pl. II, northernmost cluster of cemeteries; Brunton 1948:3 and pl. I [e.g., Matmar, Badarian Cemetery 2500 separated from Amratian and Gerzean Cemetery 2600–2700 by a wadi only ca. 20 m wide]). In addition to the Qau-Matmar area, Badarian also existed upstream at Armant (Mond and Myers 1937:3, 176, 229), at Hierakonpolis (Brunton 1932:274; Hoffman 1982:40), and, across the river, in the area of el-Kab (Vermeersch 1978). The distribution of Badarian and Amratian implies, if they are considered to be contemporary, a scatter of interspersed local cultures which it is difficult to visualize. Also an early position for Badarian is suggested by the radiocarbon (Hassan 1984c; see table 1 here) and thermoluminescent (Caton-Thompson and

Whittle 1975; Whittle 1975 [on breccia:4690 ± 365 B.C. and 4510 ± 475 B.C.]; below breccia 5580 ± 420 and 5494 ± 405) dates available from Hemamieh. The relationships of pottery types and of such categories of objects as slate palettes, ivory spoons, and figurines are here regarded as too numerous and coherent to be interpreted as other than indications of a consistent cultural development. Accordingly, the compressed predynastic sequence suggested by Kaiser is not followed here (fig. 4). Brunton's dating of Badarian is adhered to, and the denomination of the Upper Egyptian phases after the villages where each was first recognised is continued.

Sites of the Amratian phase are known from Matmar in the north throughout Upper Egypt, and even sporadically in Nubia (see Kaiser 1985:86, n. 106, who sees a "naqadoide Mischkultur" in the area south of Gebel Silseleh to about the First Cataract). Important Amratian materials have been excavated at el-Khattarah near Naqada (Hassan 1984b, 1985). The wares dominant in Badarian continue, although the elaborate rippling of the surface disappears. Some Polished-red vessels were decorated in white paint with representational or simple geometric designs; occasionally animal figures in the round were set on their lips (White Cross-lined ware; fig. 4:88, 89, 92, 93). As a whole, Amratian is characterized by a rich repertory of decorated objects and figurines (fig. 4:94, 95, 108–11).

Gerzean brought some striking innovations, among which the most significant is probably the great shift in representational art from the Amratian preoccupation with wild animals, dogs, and hunters to themes that exemplify dawning social and political concerns: ships with nome standards (fig. 4:74), an organized lion hunt, and fighting and defeated opponents (Kantor 1974). In pottery, light-faced Wavy-handled and Decorated wares appear and coarse, straw-tempered Rough ware increases in frequency. However, the new categories of pottery and new types of stone vessels do not negate the continuity of the culture as a whole. In a few transitional graves, White Cross-lined vessels occur alongside Gerzean types (Brunton and Caton-Thompson 1928: pl. XXXVIII C 17n, 25f, 44t, 70k [Badari]). Polished-red and Black-topped wares are still common; in the latter category, vessels with well-developed rims to a considerable extent displace the simple beakers prevalent in Amratian.

The occurrence together in the same tombs of well-formed squat and debased Wavy-handled types (e.g., Brunton 1937: pl. XXIX, Mostagedda Grave 219; Lythgoe and Dunham 1965:157, fig. 68f [Naga ed-Der Grave 7271], 255, fig. 114a [Naga ed-Der Grave 7271]) indicates that Petrie's individual sequence dates cannot be relied on for a close calibration of the development of Gerzean. For our purposes here, a division of Gerzean into an earlier phase in which the old Black-topped and Polished-red wares are still frequent and the ledge handles still relatively functional, and a later phase characterized by an increasing proportion of Rough and Late vessels at the expense of the Polished-red and Black-topped ones, by a varied array of less functional ledge handles on fairly tall forms, and by elaborate ivory and stone carvings (Bénédite 1916; Boehmer 1974a; Kantor 1974).

Gerzean had a wider geographical distribution than Amratian. To the south it penetrated into Nubia (Trigger 1965:68–73, 1983:42–43). It probably existed throughout the Nile Valley, although because of geophysical conditions, predynastic sites have not been found in the long stretch between Matmar and Harageh near the Fayum (Butzer 1961:65, fig. 1; 66–68). However, in a survey conducted by Kaiser some Gerzean sherds were found on the surface in the vicinity of Minya at Sawada, and a little north of Matmar at Deir el-Gebrawi and Deir Bisra (Kaiser 1961:26, 27, 36, 51, fig. 6). Gerzean is well documented in the northernmost Upper Egyptian nomes, as at the eponymous site of el-Gerzeh. A considerable distance to the northeast, the Munich East Delta Expedition directed by Dietrich Wildung has dug a cemetery at Tell es-Sabaa Banat at the north edge of Minshat Abu Omar, located in spurs of sand rising above the alluvium, which ranges from the Gerzean period through the First Dynasty (Wildung 1981; Kroeper and Wildung 1985:6–7 and fig. 2; for geology of area see Stanley 1988). The Gerzean graves at Minshat Abu Omar may well represent an Upper Egyptian enclave located in a strategic position. However, the existence some 90 km to the southwest of a settlement site, Tell Aga (Kufur Nigm), with three meters of stratified debris ranging from the Gerzean to the end of the Old Kingdom and also of another settlement site, Tell Samara, in the same general area (Wildung 1984:269; Kroeper and Wildung 1985:5, fig. 1) as well as a clandestinely discovered fragment of a slate palette carved in the same style as examples found in Upper Egypt (Fischer 1962) establish a substantial Gerzean presence in the eastern Delta.

Many years ago Scharff suggested connections between Petrie's predynastic periods and the primitive kingdoms of Egypt, the existence of which Sethe had postulated by assuming that the Old Kingdom pyramid texts and other religious documents reflect predynastic political conflicts (Sethe 1930; Scharff 1935:89, table). The discussion thus initiated has continued to the present (see Trigger 1983:2, 44–50). Without doubt in both Upper and Lower Egypt local principalities were struggling among themselves for political and other advantages, but the tenuousness of interpretations derived from the religious texts of later date and the limitations of the archaeological evidence preclude detailed historical reconstruction.

Problems concerning the end of Gerzean and the transition to the First Dynasty still remain. In Petrie's system this range was a third major period, Semainean (Sequence Dates 65–70), established on the basis of tomb cards arranged consecutively by the presumed typological sequence of the degenerate Wavy-handled jars. Since such types form an even more shaky basis for reconstructing successive stages than the still functional wavy handles of Gerzean, Petrie's Semainean sequence dates have been little used. Kaiser retains Semainean or Naqada III as a major period and divides it into two phases on the basis of tomb groups from Armant, Turah, and elsewhere. Here the view is maintained that between standard Gerzean and the First Dynasty proper there was only a short transitional period, to which a term used by Reisner (e.g., 1931:130), Dynasty 0, may be applied. The assumption that a period of some length existed between Gerzean and the First Dynasty would entail impossible extensions of the Mesopotamian and Palestinian sequences which are tightly correlated with Gerzean and the First Dynasty. Dynasty 0 falls into place as the brief initial phase of the First Dynasty. It is characterized by Decorated jars with multiple brush designs (fig. 5:43, 44) or, rarely, important representational motifs (fig. 6:19; Williams 1986:152–56, pls. 84, 88, 93, 95), cylinder jars with lattice painting (fig. 5:48, 52, 53), and early versions of Dynasty I storage (fig. 5:40, 46) and cylinder (fig. 5:56–58) jars.

Along with the problems of delimiting the successive phases of the Upper Egyptian cultural sequence is another problem, the correlation with the archaeological sequence of objects that bear elaborate representations, sometimes clearly commemorative, but that are for the most part without specifically dated archaeological contexts. The carved ivory knife handles can be dated to Gerzean by the ripple-flaked flint blades, which in Dynasty 0 are replaced by irregularly flaked blades. Only one example, that from Abu Zedan now in the Brooklyn Museum, has a grave group that is recorded, albeit sketchily; all the available evidence concerning it has been collected and discussed by Needler, who concludes that it should be assigned to "Naqada III" (Needler 1980; 1984:57–58, 124–25, 268–71). Among the pottery vessels are three that are not extant but that she identifies from descriptions and a sketch of Henri de Morgan, the excavator, as belonging to the group of cylinder jars comprising Petrie's Wavy types 60–80 of Dynasty 0 (see fig. 5:48, 52, 53, 56–58). There thus arises an anomaly between the date of the grave and the date normal for the three ripple-flaked knives found in it. Ripple-flaked flint blades would be atypical for Dynasty 0, if found at all. The iconographic and stylistic evidence of the representations on the Abu Zedan handle indicates a Gerzean date, possibly even somewhat antedating the Gebel Tarif and Gebel el-

Araq knives (Bénédite 1918). The difference between the files of many animals arranged in a specific pattern on the Brooklyn handle and the degenerate files on the Dynasty 0 spoon from Tarkhan (Petrie, Wainwright, and Gardiner 1913: pl. XIII:1–6) or on ivory fragments of the beginning of the First Dynasty from Hierakonpolis (Quibell 1900: pls. XIII, XIV, XV:5, 6, XVI:1, 4) is striking.

The Hierakonpolis painting is dated to Gerzean by the objects found in the tomb and by the close resemblances between the renderings themselves and those on the ordinary painted pots of the Decorated ware (Kantor 1944; Case and Payne 1962). An animal style characterized by patterning specific for individual species and the use of carnivore-ruminant pairs links such objects as the Gebel el-Araq, Carnarvon, and Gebel Tarif ripple-flaked knife handles with carvings such as the Hunters and Small Hierakonpolis palettes, which can accordingly be assigned to standard Gerzean. In the scenes of organized hunting, of war, and of the smiting of prisoners occurring on some of these works a dawning historical consciousness is evident. Since the fragmentary Lion and Bull palettes are characterized by the same animal style, with a few slight modifications of detail, particularly in the rendering of the lions, these carvings can also be claimed as still Gerzean although their iconography is strikingly advanced, including, for example, standards holding the ropes of prisoners. Moreover, hitherto unrecognized antecedents of pharaonic themes have been discerned in the Hierakonpolis painting and on the eroded handle of a ripple-flaked knife in the Metropolitan Museum of Art by Williams and Logan (1987). Nonetheless, the free-field composition of the Lion and Bull palettes distinguishes them sharply from compositions ruled by the ground line, as on the Libyan Booty and Narmer palettes, and the maceheads of Scorpion and Narmer (for the watershed position of the Scorpion macehead in Egyptian spatial composition, see Groenewegen-Frankfort 1957:19f.). Although these carvings are without specifically dated archaeological contexts, on stylistic grounds they are later than the Gerzean representations and fall into place as contemporary with the Dynasty 0 transitional assemblage between Gerzean and the First Dynasty. The development of representational art can thus be followed from Amratian to the threshold of the First Dynasty (Kantor 1974).

It has long been clear that there were important rulers antedating the First Dynasty kings of the official lists compiled by the Egyptians, but known to us from the commemorative maceheads (fig. 5:38) and palette dedicated at the early temple at Hierakonpolis, and from primitive serekhs painted or incised on pottery (fig. 5:37, 39, 40, 46). The latter have now been studied in detail by Kaiser (Kaiser and Dreyer 1982) in connection with the renewed excavations in the Archaic Cemetery at Abydos. He identifies pits B 7 + 9 as the grave of Ka, pits B

1 + 2 as that of Iri-Hor, and pits B 17 + 18 as that of Narmer. These constructions, together with the mace-heads of Scorpion, for whom no evidence has been found at Abydos, document four kings of Dynasty 0, the length of which remains indeterminate. Kaiser suggests that it may have consisted of as many as twelve generations (Kaiser and Dreyer 1982:268), and Baer visualized a considerable number of rulers before the First Dynasty (pers. comm.). If so, some of these generations should be correlated culturally with the Gerzean period and such rulers as those commemorated by the Lion and Bull palettes, since archaeologically Dynasty 0 appears to have been a short transitional phase.

Finally, two important aspects of Dynasty 0 as an archaeological period should be emphasized. It existed in Lower as well as in Upper Egypt. Second, it stands with the First Dynasty when its individual characteristics are considered. Examples in pottery are the absence of Black-topped vessels, the presence of vessel forms such as the wine jars (fig. 5:16, 46), and specific traits such as the predilection for flattening the upper body at the root of the neck (fig. 5:6, 10, 11, 43), and in art the use of pharaonic motifs well known in the historical period. Accordingly, it seems more fitting to consider this cultural phase as a short, initial stage of dynastic Egyptian civilization rather than as the final period of the predynastic sequence. Such a conclusion is corroborated by the foreign connections reviewed below.

The Correlation of the Upper and Lower Egyptian Sequences

The earlier phases of Upper and Lower Egypt are linked only by relatively general typological similarities. Fayum A pottery provides analogies for the angled vessels (fig. 4:46, 134), the varyingly profiled rectangular bowls of Polished-red ware (fig. 4:45 and 130), and the roughly rectangular palettes assigned by Brunton to Tasian (fig. 4:52, 137), as well as for the various bag-shaped vessels (fig. 4:60, 114), the sherds with densely set knobs (fig. 4:50, 119), and the solid-based cups of Badarian (fig. 4:35, 114). Only one of these types, however, the rectangular bowl, is a somewhat specialized form, while the others provide only general similarities which suggest, in the absence of definite evidence for a later date, the likelihood that Fayum A was approximately contemporary with the Tasian-Badarian range.

The later strata at Merimde have a few characters comparable to Upper Egyptian traits. The specialized round structures (Eiwanger 1982:68) are distantly reminiscent of the Amratian hut emplacements at Hemamieh (Brunton and Caton-Thompson 1928: pls. LXIV, LXVI). Carinated bowls resembling those of Badarian and Amratian occur in Strata II–V (Eiwanger 1982:70–72). Fortunately, one highly specialized form, the bowls of

Polished-red ware supported by human feet modeled in the round, appears in Strata II–V (fig. 4:37 and 91; see Eiwanger 1982:70–72). Such footed bowls constitute a rare, but characteristic Amratian type that firmly links part, at least, of the Merimde sequence with Amratian.

With Maadi we reach a period the contemporaneity of which with Gerzean is indicated by general typological similarities such as the use of light-faced ware, sometimes painted (Rizkana and Seeher 1984:248, fig. 6:5; Rizkana and Seeher 1987:43–44; pls. 42–47, 66:5, 67:6, III–V), and the differentiation of pottery bodies and rims. In addition, Upper Egyptian imports are present and have recently been discussed by Rizkana and Seeher: a few Black-topped vessels and local copies (1984:239–43 and figs. 1–2; 1987:51–52, pls. 68:3, 5–10 [imported]; 69–71 [local]); basalt vessels with lugs and sometimes a foot (1984:244–45 and fig. 3); lozenge-shaped slate palettes (1984:244, 247–49 and fig. 5); an Amratian-like comb (1984:248, fig. 6:3); and a fish-tailed knife of the older, Amratian type (Rizkana and Seeher 1985:147, fig. 8:1; 251). Accordingly, they conclude that Maadi was contemporary with Amratian, at least the later part of it, and earlier Gerzean (1984:251–52, 1985:252, 1987:55–73, 66–73). Since the range of some of the Upper Egyptian imports extends into Gerzean (Petrie 1921: pl. LVIII 92 D, F [palettes]; 1920: pl. XL [lugged basalt vessels]; Lythgoe and Dunham 1965:153, fig. 66 h [Amratian-type comb in Gerzean grave Naga ed-Der 7266]; note also that the Maadi maceheads [Rizkana and Seeher 1985:246, fig. 4:7, 8] lack the concave profile typical of the Amratian disk maceheads [fig. 4:104]), the overlap with Amratian was at most slight, and Maadi can be taken as basically contemporary with the earlier part of Gerzean, perhaps before the appearance of that culture in the eastern Delta, well to the northeast of Maadi (Wildung 1981). The existence of connections between Maadi and Gerzean is not surprising, for Gerzeh itself was only about 70 km distant.

Foreign Connections of the Predynastic Period

The evidence for Egyptian foreign relations before the Gerzean period is still tenuous. The problems concerning the origins of the domesticated plants and animals that formed the basis for predynastic economy have been summarized by Clark (1971), Trigger (1983:15–20), and Hassan (1985). The general presumption is that Egypt was indebted to western Asia for the introduction of domesticated grains and for most of the domesticated animals, although the possibility of contributions from the Western Desert (Sahara) and the southern Nile Valley (Nubia and the Sudan) has also been raised (see the data on the early grains collected by Wendorf and Schild 1980:264, 270–80). Thus, underground granaries occur in neolithic sites of the Western Sahara that appear to be two thousand years earlier than the clusters of granaries of the Fayum A sites (Wendorf and Schlid 1980:265, 269f.), but so far it has not been possible to correlate with certainty the introduction of elements of neolithic economy with any specific predynastic culture.

In preliminary reports on his excavations at Merimde, Eiwanger suggested that the culture of the lowest level depended on eastern elements and may represent the time when domesticated plants and animals from Asia reached Egypt; in particular, he compared the bowls decorated by herringbone incision on a reserved matt band with the herringbone incision on vessels of the Yarmoukian Neolithic of the Jordan Valley (Eiwanger 1980:69 and n. 25, 1982:82). In reviewing the question in the final publication of Stratum I, he concluded that, despite a general connection between the herringbone designs of western Asia and Merimde, too little is known to determine directions of influence (Eiwanger 1984:61–62). In fact, the use of herringbone patterns seems too abstract a similarity to outweigh the many specific differences in the wares of the cultures in question. In Stratum II, above the level of sand marking a gap in the occupation of Merimde, Eiwanger sees a new cultural development with an African component as, for example, in the harpoons comparable to those of the Khartoum Neolithic (Eiwanger 1982:82).

In the southern Egyptian cultural sequence the earliest apparently foreign object is a narrow-necked globular jar with four vertical loop handles found in a Badarian grave at the type site. Brunton described its un-Egyptian characteristics, which are paralleled in Palestine by Chalcolithic vessels (Brunton and Caton-Thompson 1928:24; pls. XVI:7, XXVI: Group 569; Kaplan 1959; Perrot 1961:75, fig. 39:7–9). Other comparisons between individual predynastic vessels and Chalcolithic Ghassulian ones have been suggested (Kaplan 1959), but these do not seem to be as secure as in the case of the loop-handled jar.

The evidence from the Chalcolithic period in Palestine, now being recovered in ever-increasing volume, documents a highly developed culture with several regional strains and with outstanding artistic achievements in various media (fig. 3:3, 4, 7–12, 18–22). Some ivory figures from sites in the area of Beersheba were originally compared with those characteristic for Amratian (fig. 4:110, 111) because of shared features such as elongated bodies, peglike feet with slight projections for ankle bones, and the use of drill holes (Perrot 1959:18–19, 1963:93, but see now 1974:192). However, the Egyptian and Palestinian figures differ from each other in more specific stylistic characteristics, with the latter having a bolder stylization of details and a more three-dimensional form (e.g., Perrot 1974: pls. XXII, 124b and c; Amiran and Tadmor

1980: pl. 17A, D). The two series should, therefore, be considered as unrelated. They cannot provide a synchronism between Egypt and Palestine.

In Egypt the presence in Badarian and Amratian contexts of imported raw materials such as Red Sea shells, turquoise and copper, and pine, cedar, and cypress or juniper wood testifies to connections with the east, presumably the Sinai peninsula, southern Palestine, and Lebanon (Brunton and Caton-Thompson 1928:41, 62; Lucas and Harris 1962:430; Meiggs 1982:63). On the Palestinian side the discovery of either definitely or possibly Egyptian objects indicates the existence of at least occasional connections between the Palestinian Chalcolithic and the Badarian-Amratian range in Egypt (Ben-Tor 1982:4; see Stager, this vol., chap. 2). It is particularly significant that at least one sherd of Egyptian Polished-red ware was found in a Chalcolithic context in the north Sinai survey of Eliezer Oren and Isaac Gilead (1981:30–35, fig. 9:10; see Petrie 1921:16, 23b).

Gerzean and Maadi are marked as periods of greatly widening horizons by definite evidence for foreign connections. Three categories can be differentiated: imported objects or materials; imitations of foreign pottery in native wares; and Egyptian works incorporating foreign artistic motifs or other features. However, representatives of the three classes do not all begin at the same time. The earliest in Upper Egypt are imitations of Palestinian wavy-handled jars. Simple ledge handles already appear in Palestine in the Chalcolithic period (see Jericho VIII [Garstang 1936: pl. 32:28, 29A, B]; Beth Shan XVIII [Fitzgerald 1935: pl. 2:13, 14]; North Sinai, Site A 301 [Oren and Gilead 1981:31, fig. 6:8]), and by EB I several types of ledge handles had been developed. Although Upper Egypt has provided no indubitably imported wavy-handled jars, local imitations form one of the main diagnostic criteria for Gerzean. In the absence of foreign prototypes, their appearance provides a problem that can probably be solved by reference to finds at the northern site of Maadi, where the situation is strikingly different from that at the Gerzean sites nearby or farther south. At Maadi an obviously un-Egyptian ware was found (Rizkana and Seeher 1984:238 and 1987:73–77, pls. 72–77, IX, X; Tutundzić 1985). The drab-colored, friable fabric with many grits is fully comparable to the standard EB I ware of Palestine. The shapes are Palestinian and consist of ledge-handled jars (fig. 6:34; see Rizkana and Seeher 1984: pl. 77:1–4), jars with two loop or lug handles (fig. 6:32, 33; see ibid., pls. 72:1, 5–9, 73:1–4, 74:1–8, 75:1–8), jars with knobs (ibid., pl. 76:1, 8 [also imprints]), and those completely without accessories (ibid., pl. 76:3–7). At least one good example of EB I Grain-wash ware was found (ibid., pls. 77:7 = X 4; probably also pl. 77:5, 6, 8; see fig. 7:55 here for Grain-wash on a ledge-handled vessel). The closest Palestinian parallels for the imports at Maadi come from early EB I contexts as at Site H in the Wadi Fara (fig. 7:79, 85). Also pointing to a correlation with early EB I is the appearance at Maadi of several bowls allied to the Esdraelon burnished ware by their ridged shapes and burnish (ibid. pl. 55:1–3; see fig. 7:92 here). Other Palestinian shapes imitated locally at Maadi are small vessels or jars with a large loop-handle (fig. 6:31; see ibid., pl. 32:1–8) and two-lugged pots (ibid., pl. 39:8–10). The vertical bands of paint on a small jar resemble the decoration on EB I one-handled cups and lugged jars (ibid., pl. 42:1; see figs. 6:35, 36, 7:48, 49 here). Rizkana and Seeher suggest that the local imitations of Palestinian pottery at Maadi indicate that contacts were more direct than mere trade (ibid., p. 77).

The large amount and variety of the imported Palestinian pottery at Maadi, as yet unrivaled at any other site, contrast strikingly with the isolated specimens from Upper Egyptian sites. Thus Maadi could easily have been the source for the wavy-handled prototypes that were imitated by Upper Egyptian potters.

The large flint scrapers of rounded or oval shape from Maadi (fig. 4:9; see Rizkana and Seeher 1985:245, fig. 6:3, 4; 246, fig. 7:1–3) are comparable to the types prominent in Palestinian EB I–II sites, where they sometimes appear in large masses and were apparently widely traded (Schmidt 1984). Regular blades with straight sides made from a brown opaque flint similar to that of the tabular scrapers occur occasionally at Maadi and are considered by Rizkana and Seeher to be imported Palestinian blades of Canaanean type (1985:249; 250, fig. 10:1–6; 252–55). In addition to the pottery and flint tools, materials such as copper and bitumen were probably also being imported (Rizkana and Seeher 1985:253). The evidence from Maadi shows that site to have been an Egyptian terminus of early trade routes along which Palestinian commodities reached Egypt.

The Gerzean graves of the Minshat Abu Omar cemetery contained such Palestinian imports as wavy-handled jars (fig. 6:30; see fig. 7:85; Wildung 1984:267), a lug-handled pot (fig. 6:28), a spouted loop-handled jar (fig. 6:29), churns (fig. 6:26; see Kroeper and Wildung 1985:72, fig. 210; Amiran 1985: pl. XLVI 2; see ibid., p. 191, fig. 1 for an EB I parallel from Azor), jars with both horizontal ledge and vertical loop handles (Kroeper and Wildung 1985:71, fig. 208; 72, fig. 209), and two one-handled juglets which approach EB II types in shape and ware (fig. 6:27; Kroeper and Wildung 1985:41, fig. 105; 71, fig. 206). Like Maadi, Minshat Abu Omar was clearly a trade entrepôt. It lay on the eastern bank of the ancient Pelusian branch of the Nile and could have been reached by water (Wildung 1984:269). It was also close to the EB I caravan route from Palestine (fig. 1).

In north Sinai itself the survey conducted by Oren and Gilead recovered direct evidence for a route following the shoreline of the Mediterranean in the form of a line of small settlements characterized by a mixture of Palestinian EB I and Egyptian pottery (Oren 1973; Oren and Gilead 1981). The latter includes a wide range of forms from storage jars to shallow bread bowls, indicating that Egyptians actually lived at the sites and did not merely pass through carrying a limited number of vessel types. Some of the north Sinai sites may overlap at least part of Gerzean, although many belong to the period of Dynasty 0 (E. Oren, pers. comm.). In any case, all the evidence together indicates the existence of a regular caravan trade between Egypt and Palestine passing along the north coast of the Sinai peninsula. This now enables us to visualize a situation in which imported Palestinian ledge-handled vessels reaching such sites as Minshat Abu Omar and Maadi stimulated the Egyptian imitations that are a hallmark of the Upper Egyptian Gerzean period.

In addition to the locally evolving class of ledge-handled jars, there are in the later part of the Gerzean sequence several Palestinian imports and some local imitations of Palestinian types. Jars with both loop and wavy handles occur at Naqada (Petrie 1921: pl. 28: W 2 b) and Gerzeh (fig. 6:47). From the neighboring northern sites of Gerzeh and Abusir el-Meleq come respectively a band-painted one-handled cup (fig. 6:36; cf. fig. 7:48) and a drab-ware bowl with a line of knobs (fig. 6:44; cf. fig. 7:91). The southernmost indubitable Palestinian imports are a band-painted two-lugged pot from Badari (fig. 6:35; see fig. 7:49) and an unpainted one from Mostagedda (fig. 6:37). Two kernos rings, a light-faced one from Naqada (fig. 6:39) and a Polished-red one from Matmar (fig. 6:40), represent a specialized form quite alien to Egyptian ceramic traditions, but known in Palestine (fig. 7:89); it is uncertain whether the two examples are imports or imitations. Mostagedda and Naqada have provided three knobbed bowls, one possibly a red-burnished import (fig. 6:38) and two that are probably imitations of Palestinian prototypes in Egyptian Polished-red ware (fig. 6:45, 46). Stone versions of such vessels come from an "early deposit" at Megiddo (Engberg and Shipton 1934:63, fig. 17) and from the huge stone-vessel deposits in the subterranean western magazines of Djoser's Step Pyramid complex at Saqqara, deposits that included some vessels dating to the First Dynasty or perhaps even earlier (Lauer 1939: pl. 17:10). The southernmost examples of vessels of Palestinian tradition are some jugs from Qustul in Nubia, which are probably copies rather than imports (Williams 1986:78–80; 104, fig. 48). Most of them were found in Grave L 24, which is dated by Williams to Late Gerzean (1986:178–79, table 42).

The general contemporaneity of Gerzean and EB I is clear. In addition, it is practically certain that early and late EB I are approximately equivalent to earlier and later Gerzean. In Egypt the knobbed bowls and the even rarer kernoi, despite some examples without dated contexts, can be safely attributed to the later part of Gerzean. In the Palestinian assemblages of figure 7, both types are assigned to the earlier part of EB I (fig. 7:89, 91), but the likelihood is that the knobbed bowls are actually characteristic of the later part of the period. Their range will be clarified when the excavations of P. P. Delougaz at Beth Yerah are published (Esse, in preparation). The band-painted vessels typical for later EB (fig. 7:48, 49; cf. fig. 6:35, 36) have a considerable temporal range; at Beth Yerah they already occur with an Esdraelon-ware bowl (Esse 1984:328, fig. 4B; 329, fig. 5A).

The geographical distribution of imported Palestinian vessels indicates a significant distinction between Upper and Lower Egypt. There is a concentration of Palestinian pottery in the two northern sites of Minshat Abu Omar and Maadi, in contrast to the sporadic occurrences from Abusir el-Meleq to Badari, and the almost complete absence of demonstrable Palestinian imports in the major Upper Egyptian sites south of Badari. Minshat Abu Omar and Maadi, established by the archaeological evidence as Egyptian termini for caravan routes from southern Palestine, show that already in the predynastic period the eastern Delta and the adjoining east bank of the Memphite area had begun to play their roles as a link between Egypt and Palestine. In historical times the usual route to Palestine, indicated by texts, passed directly by Maadi and across the eastern Delta and Sinai (Rizkana 1952:123). By the Second Intermediate period, Palestinians were living at such Delta sites as Tell el-Jahudiyah, Tell ed-Daba (= Avaris), and Tell el-Maskhuta (Bietak 1975; Holladay 1982), which served as centers for the diffusion of Palestinian products southward, presumably just as the predynastic Delta had done.

Gerzean has long been famous for the appearance of Mesopotamian features in a variety of contexts (Frankfort 1924 and 1951: appendix; Scharff 1935 and 1942). Many are foreign motifs belonging to the period Delougaz termed Protoliterate in order to indicate its crucial importance as the beginning of historical Mesopotamian civilization and to distinguish it from prehistoric periods named after sites (Delougaz and Lloyd 1942:8, n. 10. See the contradiction between the title of Frankfort's posthumous chapter in the *Cambridge Ancient History*, "The Final Prehistoric Period in Mesopotamia," and his text [1971]). Delougaz maintained the fundamental unity of Protoliterate as a single period, despite the existence of successive phases, namely, Protoliterate a (Warka, Eanna VI–VII), and b (Eanna IV–V), replacing the "Uruk period," and Protoliterate c (Khafaje, Sin Temple III, I) and d (Sin Temple V–IV), replacing the "Jamdat Nasr period."

The Egyptian motifs imitating Protoliterate prototypes, as well as some actual imports, belong to the later part of Gerzean. However, one pottery type known from the beginning of Gerzean, the Polished-red jar with a bent spout, both in its general shape and in its distinctive accessory closely resembles standard Early Protoliterate vessels. It seems unlikely that such a specific form would have been invented independently in Egypt, particularly since potters there did not indulge themselves, even in later periods, in any but simple, short spouts. However, the Protoliterate imports with datable contexts belong to later Gerzean, which creates the awkward problem of the apparent imitation of foreign vessels without any imported prototypes. The vessels with bent spouts occurring in the Palestinian EB I likewise do not seem to be part of the indigenous repertory (fig. 7:44). Palestine, unlike Egypt, provides no corpus of Protoliterate connections, only two isolated elements, a four-lugged vessel from Jawa (fig. 7:87) and a cylinder seal impression on a jar from Megiddo (fig. 7:86). The latter belongs to a category typical for Syria, (Amiet 1970–71:131f.) and known also in southern Anatolia (Behm-Blancke et al. 1981: pl. 11:1–4 [Hassek Höyük, EB I]). It is unlikely that the Palestinian bent-spouted jars of EB I were directly inspired by Protoliterate examples; they may have depended on Egyptian versions. In the present state of our knowledge, the link with Mesopotamia remains hypothetical.

In addition to the bent spout, the triangular lug handles on the shoulder of relatively large Decorated jars (Petrie 1921: pl. XXXIV, D 45 B. S.D. 46) are reminiscent of those that characterize a major category of Protoliterate pottery (Delougaz 1952:39; Delougaz and Kantor, forthcoming, Protoliterate Pottery Families CXVII–CXXX). However, the general shape of the Decorated vessels with triangular lugs does not closely resemble specific Protoliterate types, so that a Mesopotamian origin for the lugs is suggested here only with considerable reservation.

The occasional use of lapis lazuli for beads in the earlier part of Gerzean is pertinent to the appearance of features typical for Protoliterate ceramics (Brunton and Caton-Thompson 1928, Badari, Grave 1513 [S.D. 43–46]). Its presence may well indicate contacts with Mesopotamia, which must have been a major intermediary in the diffusion of lapis from Badakshan in northeastern Afghanistan. Certainly the prominence of lapis lazuli in later Gerzean, when we do have Protoliterate imports, is no coincidence (see Petrie 1920:44; Davis 1983:23 [Naqada, T5]; Brunton and Caton-Thompson 1928, Badari, Graves 102 [S.D. 44–61], 1579 [S.D. 48–59], 1629 [S.D. 44–60], 1756 [S.D. 56–58], 3732 [S.D. 52–57], 3827 [S.D. 52–59], 3839 [S.D. 44–64], 3850 [S.D. 53–57], 4602 [S.D. 57–58], 4604 [S.D. 57?]; Brunton 1937, Matmar Grave 1759 [S.D. 57–58]; Lythgoe and Dunham

1965, Graves N 7461, N 7534, N 7540, N 7546 and probably N 7290, N 7378, N 7527, and N 7538. For discussion and additional examples, see Payne 1968 and Needler 1984:311).

Three imported four-lugged jars represent well-known Protoliterate types: a small jar with a line of notches (fig. 6:43; see Delougaz and Kantor, forthcoming: Ch.M.II–404; III–296, 401, 482, 488 [Protoliterate Family CXX]; Ch.M.III–483 [miniature, Protoliterate Family CXVII]); a fragment of an undecorated jar which presumably had a neck (fig. 6:42; see ibid., pl. 110 E [Protoliterate Family CXVIII]), and a more ornate jar between the lugs of which were knobs below a hatched band (fig. 6:41, see ibid., Ch.M.IV–63 and Ch.M. 5.282 [buff slip and red wash respectively, Protoliterate Family CXXIV]).

Other imported objects are seals. An example of a standard type of Protoliterate stamp seal was found at Naga ed-Der (fig. 6:54; see Delougaz and Kantor, forthcoming: Ch.M.III–308; Homes-Frédericq 1970: nos. 416–18, 421 [Nuzi]). More frequent are cylinder seals, three excavated from later Gerzean graves at Naqada (fig. 6:49; Boehmer 1974b:500, fig. 1) and in Nubia (Boehmer 1974b:500, fig. 6) and two without context (fig. 6:51, 52). At Naga ed-Der a rich later Gerzean grave had a cylinder seal deviating in a few details from Protoliterate analogies and hence best considered as an Egyptian imitation of them (fig. 6:55; see Kantor 1952:246; Boehmer 1974b:510–13). Also presumably imitations are three similar seals (fig. 6:50, 53; Boehmer 1974b:501, fig. 11), another with three rows of couchant felines (fig. 6:48), and others with designs distant from Mesopotamian prototypes (Boehmer 1974b:500, figs. 7 and 8 [Nubia]; 501, figs. 12 [Berlin; Dyn. 0 ?], 13 [Cairo], 14 [Ashmolean]; for a hitherto unpublished example see Podzorski 1988:fig. 3). The introduction of Protoliterate cylinder seals in Gerzean had long-term effects. The foreign type of seal was adopted wholeheartedly during the intensive cultural development preluding the crystallization of Egyptian writing and the establishment of pharaonic administration. The imitations of the foreign seals were gradually Egyptianized until by the First Dynasty only the cylindrical shape revealed their foreign ancestry (see Kaplony 1963: pls. 6–127, and 1964: pls. 3–18; for a comprehensive study of the cylinder seals of Gerzean and Dynasty 0, quoting numerous parallels, see Boehmer 1974b; for Nubian cylinders see Williams 1986:157f., 167–71).

The most impressive testimonies to the intensity of relations with the East are the imitations of specific Protoliterate motifs: the serpent-necked panther (fig. 6:58), the horizontal-winged griffin (fig. 6:57), entwined serpents with rosette filling motifs (fig. 6:59), and the master of lions (fig. 6:60, 61). To these we may add the ship with a high prow (fig. 6:62; and Quibell and Green 1902: pl. 2),

although some doubts have been cast on its exclusively Mesopotamian character (for summary and discussion of the evidence, see Boehmer 1974a:32–35). In the Hierakonpolis painting the Mesopotamian master of lions is rendered in the same simple style as the other human figures on the wall (fig. 6:60), but on the Gebel el-Araq knife handle he appears with the headdress and long robe of the Protoliterate city ruler (fig. 6:61). It is striking that an Egyptian ivory carver adopted details of costume and the high modeling of the foreign prototypes although casting the city ruler as the master of animals, a role he did not play in the Protoliterate representations so far known (for the view that wandering Elamite craftsmen in Egypt were responsible for the Gebel el-Araq and Gebel Tarif knife handles see Boehmer 1974a:24, 36f.).

The elements just reviewed indicate the presence of strong Protoliterate influence in Egypt, but the question of the phase within the Protoliterate period during which these contacts occurred remains. Of the four-lugged vessels from Egypt, the two simpler examples represent types known throughout the Protoliterate period, but the example from Badari, red-washed and with a line of pellets between the lugs, is a specialized type known only from Protoliterate B (Delougaz and Kantor, forthcoming: table 11, Protoliterate Family CXXIV). The cylinder seals found in Egypt represent the Jamdet Nasr style that was for many years taken to occur only in the later phases (C and D) of the Protoliterate period. It is now known that such seals were already in use during Protoliterate B. At Chogha Mish, which was deserted after that time, Jamdet Nasr style impressions and seals with simple motifs such as ovals, fish, and crosshatching occurred in the same contexts as impressions of the fully modeled Protoliterate style (see Delougaz and Kantor, forthcoming: Ch. M.II–12, 109, 208, 397; Ch.M. III–71, 110, 111, 165, 306, 829).

Protoliterate B is also the phase in which the motifs adopted by the Egyptians belong. To be sure, the serpent-necked panther survives at Warka on seals rendered in the drill-hole technique of Late Protoliterate. At that time, the personage in chignon and long kilt also continued but not in the full modeling copied on the Gebel el-Araq knife handle. Neither is the motif of the master of animals as yet exemplified in Late Protoliterate. Accordingly, the evidence taken as a whole indicates that the connections between Gerzean and Protoliterate took place during the second phase of the latter period. This conclusion is corroborated if the question is considered in the wider context revealed by recent and current excavations (for discussion and historical interpretation, see Algaze 1986b and forthcoming). On the Euphrates in Syria, far to the west of southern Mesopotamia and Susiana, excavations at Habuba Kabira South (Strommenger 1980), Tell Qannas (Finet 1975 and 1979), and Jebel Aruda (van Driel

1979, 1892, and 1983; van Driel and van Driel-Murray 1983) have revealed Protoliterate cities with city walls, tripartite temples comparable to those at Warka, assemblages of Protoliterate B pottery fully comparable to those of Eanna V–IV at Warka, Susa, and Chogha Mish though with some admixture of local ceramics, and a range of sealings and seal impressions comparable to those of the elaborate style known from the eastern sites. To the north in Anatolia in the province of Urfa at sites such as Kurban Hüyük (Algaze 1986a; Marfoe 1982: 101, 108) and Hassek Höyük (Hoh 1981) good assemblages of Protoliterate pottery occur, as well as the standard Protoliterate tripartite house (at Hassek Höyük only; see Mellink 1982:564, ill. 1). Although the massive Protoliterate presence found farther south in Syria at the Tabqa Dam sites is not matched even at Hassek Höyük, the diffusion of Protoliterate characteristics into Anatolia is striking (Burney 1980; Algaze 1986a). That they reached even farther northwest is exemplified by Arslan Tepe with its examples of Protoliterate pottery and the indigenous variations on Protoliterate themes in a large cache of seal impressions (Palmieri 1973, 1977, 1981). While this tremendous explosion of Protoliterate people and civilization occurred in the west, to the east the Susiana plain had a homogeneous Protoliterate occupation, fully comparable to that of southern Mesopotamia and without any local pottery such as the chaff-tempered western wares found at Habuba Kabira South and the Anatolian sites.

In the late Protoliterate period the situation changed markedly. Even in the Susiana plain, local Proto-Elamite characteristics manifest themselves in the script and the glyptic while in the west the change is much more drastic. Habuba Kabira South and the other Tabqa sites were not occupied in the later part of the Protoliterate period, and Protoliterate influence also disappears from the Anatolian sites. There was clearly a major contraction of connections with the west in the later part of the period. The correlation of late Gerzean with Protoliterate B fits into the allover picture of a tremendous Early Protoliterate expansion. It is almost impossible to visualize the Protoliterate-Gerzean contacts as occurring during the contraction and fragmentation marking the later part of the period, which corresponds to Dynasty 0 and presumably part of the First Dynasty (fig. 6). The archaeological synchronisms are compatible with the radiocarbon ranges given by Hassan and Robinson of ca. 3600–3300 B.C. for Gerzean and "later Uruk" (i.e., PL B), ca. 3500–3261 for the beginning of "Jamdat Nasr" (i.e., Late Protoliterate), ca. 3050–2950 or 3043–2853 for the beginning of the First Dynasty, and ca. 3050–2850 for the transition between "Jamdat Nasr" and Early Dynastic I (Hassan and Robinson 1987:125, 127–28).

The question of the most likely route by which Proto-literate influence reached Egypt has been much discussed. The alternatives are a direct sea route around the Arabian peninsula (Frankfort 1951:110–11; Kantor 1952:250, and 1965) or one primarily by land across northern Mesopotamia to the Syro-Palestinian littoral and thence overland or by trans-shipment to the Delta (Helck 1971:5–11). New support for the latter alternative may be drawn from the revelation of Protoliterate colonies along the Euphrates, establishing the existence of major Protoliterate foci considerably closer to Egypt than hitherto known. From them Protoliterate influence penetrated into Anatolia on the north and into Syria on the west, going inland along the Orontes to Hama and toward the Mediterranean into the Amuq plain. Farther south on the coast, Ras Shamra was temporarily unoccupied (see Contenson 1982:96–97 for gap during Amuq F–G), so that a Protoliterate seal of peripheral execution, if actually from there, must have been secondarily deposited (Amiet 1963:67, fig. 12). It is striking that there are no traces of Protoliterate influence at Byblos or south of it except for the four-lugged jar found in the Jordanian desert at Jawa (fig. 7:87). Palestine remained essentially untouched by the example of Protoliterate glyptic, which was so influential on the periphery of the Protoliterate world. In contrast, in Palestine, aside from the Megiddo impression already mentioned (fig. 7:86), the earliest exemplars of glyptic, the sealings from En Basor, derive from Egypt (fig. 7:65). Thus, despite the existence of the colonies in Syria, Protoliterate influences of the complexity exemplified in Egypt could not have traveled overland from Palestine, and it is unlikely that they could have passed through Byblos. If Protoliterate influences did enter northern Egypt, the exclusion of southern land routes leaves presumptive north Syrian ports as the point of trans-shipment.

Another factor pertinent to the question of routes is the geographical distribution of Protoliterate features in Egypt. Except for a presumably Egyptian-made cylinder seal from Zawiyet el-Aryan in the first Lower Egyptian nome (fig. 6:53), the northernmost examples of Mesopotamian connections have until recently been the imported four-lugged vessels from Matmar, Mostagedda, and Badari, and the cylinder seal from Matmar, all from the tenth Upper Egyptian nome. Found farther south are the Protoliterate stamp and cylinder seals from Naga ed-Der in the eighth Upper Egyptian nome. In the sixth and fifth Upper Egyptian nomes, two cylinder seals from Naqada and the knife handles from Gebel Tarif and Gebel el-Araq on the east side of the river come from sites clustered near the western end of the Wadi Hammamat. In historical times that wadi was the primary route between ports on the Red Sea and the Nile Valley. It is quite possible that the route was already in use before the Dynastic period, although unfortunately the existence of predynastic debris along it referred to by Debono (1951) has never been corroborated. The southernmost evidences of Protoliterate connections are the various motifs on the palettes and paintings from Hierakonpolis in the third Upper Egyptian nome. Although the absence of objects with Protoliterate connections from the northern Gerzean sites could be an accident of discovery, the consistent concentration of Protoliterate features in the south and of Palestinian ones in the north has suggested strongly that the latter arrived in the Delta via the north Sinai land route, possibly also by trans-shipment from Mediterranean ports farther north, and that the extensive and catalytic corpus of Protoliterate features was introduced into Egypt directly by Protoliterate voyagers coming by sea around the Arabian peninsula and then through the Wadi Hammamat.

Additional support for an eastern sea route can be sought in the circumstances that two prominent motifs, the horizontal-winged griffin and the entwined snakes with rosette filling, appear to be at home in the Susiana plain (Amiet 1957:126–29, 1961:38–39) and that renderings of Protoliterate high-hulled ships occur in the Gebel el-Araq knife handle and the Hierakonpolis painting. Representations on Protoliterate cylinder seals show the use of ships for fishing, ritual voyages, and warfare. Voyages around the Arabian peninsula hugging the coastline would have been within the capacity of such ships (Johnstone 1980:10–11, 175). Furthermore, already in the prehistoric period the Haji Mohammed phase of Ubaid was carried to the western side of the Persian Gulf (Burkholder 1972; Oates 1978; Oates et al. 1977), while Jamdet Nasr painted jars of the Late Protoliterate period have been found in Saudi Arabia and Oman (Caspers 1971; Frifelt 1975). Analogies for the hypothetical Protoliterate voyages can be found in the modern Arab trading dhows that range along the Arabian, African, and Indian coasts (Villiers 1940:6–10 and *passim;* "Zanzibar Arabs Shipped to Oman," *New York Times,* 12 April 1964). Such modern ports as Gizan and Jiddah may have had ancient predecessors to serve as revictualing stops.

Until very recently, theories as to the routes by which foreign elements entered Egypt had to be developed in the total absence of reliable evidence from the Delta itself. The discovery of Minshat Abu Omar produced Palestinian connections that fit in well with the reconstruction just suggested. Now, however, the excavations underway at Tell el-Fara'in have begun to produce evidence for Mesopotamian connections (von der Way 1987:247–50, 256–57): two terra-cotta cones as used in Protoliterate monumental buildings for mosaic wall decoration (ibid., 249, fig. 3:5, 6) and a terra-cotta spike as inserted into the walls of Protoliterate structures to protect them (ibid., 249, fig. 3:7). These objects were made of local clay; they imply the presence of individuals who

were constructing buildings of Mesopotamian type at Buto in the later part of the predynastic period. Even though the evidence is still limited, it is no longer possible to regard the Red Sea route as the only avenue of connection with Protoliterate civilization; a second, western, route must be envisioned. Th. von der Way suggests that individuals from such western colonies as Habuba Kebira could have traveled by ship from ports in the Amuq, since Buto has yielded locally made bowls with a reserved slip decoration which he compares with that typical for Amuq F (von der Way 1987:246, fig. 2:6; 247; 249, fig. 3:1–4. Its location suggests that Buto may have been an important trading port in the later predynastic period (Kaiser 1985:62, n. 7).

Although the exact nature of Protoliterate connections with Egypt remains a difficult problem, it appears certain that the contacts must have been direct, not through intermediaries. In the great expansionist phase of the Protoliterate period, exploring ships of intrepid traders and raiders appear to have reached both Red Sea ports of Upper Egypt and the Delta. Perhaps the best analogy is that of the Phoenician ships of the early first millennium B.C., whose activities are vividly described in such stories as the abduction of Eumeus in *The Odyssey.*

The Protodynastic Period

Only scanty evidence for the foreign connections of Dynasty 0 appears in Egypt itself. One Palestinian import, an EB juglet painted with vertical bands, occurred along with five lattice-painted cylinder jars in Grave 1019 at Abusir el-Meleq (fig. 6:21). Another Dynasty 0 grave at that site, 41 a 2, contained a squat wavy-handled jar, also probably imported, which has two subsidiary wavy appliqués on the upper body and is made of rather coarse ware with a black core (Scharff 1926: pl. 45:2). It is, however, the evidence from outside the Nile Valley, discussed in chapter 2 of this volume by Stager, that demonstrates remarkably intensive connections between Egypt, northern Sinai, and southern Palestine during Dynasty 0. The presence abroad of large assemblages of Egyptian vessels, some incised with serekhs of Narmer (Kaiser and Dreyer 1982:263, fig. 14:35, 36, 39, 41, 42), indicates the particularly active, albeit brief, presence of Egyptians who were probably engaged in trade.

Of the Mesopotamian features prominent in Gerzean, the serpent-necked panther survives as a theriomorphic juncture on an ivory spoon found at Tarkhan (fig. 6:24), as part of master-of-animal groups on an incised ivory from Hierakonpolis (fig. 6:20, 22), and as a major theme of the Narmer palette. There two men restrain the panthers by leashes; the foreign motif has been Egyptianized to serve, apparently, as an emblem of the unification of Upper and Lower Egypt (Wolf 1957:86–87). The horizontal-winged griffin makes his appearance in an animal file on an ivory from Hierakonpolis (fig. 6:23). A high-hulled ship is painted on a jar attributable to Dynasty 0 (fig. 6:19).

The Dynasty 0 examples of Protoliterate motifs appear as late representatives of the themes that had reached Egypt in the Gerzean period. With the beginning of the First Dynasty proper they disappear from the known repertory until the Middle Kingdom, when serpent-necked panthers and the horizontal-winged griffin reappear on a large scale in tomb paintings at Beni Hasan (Newberry 1894: pl. IV [Baqt III, late Dynasty XI], and 1893: pl. XXX [Khnumhotep II, reign of Sesostris II]; for detailed drawings see Davies 1933:27, figs. 7, 8) and on a small scale on apotropaic ivory wands (Petrie 1927: pls. XXXVI, XXXVII; Hayes 1953:249, fig. 159). A cylinder seal with animal files illustrates the Egyptianization of the foreign type of seal (fig. 6:25).

In general, Dynasty 0 was archaeologically a short interlude, contemporary with the latest part of EB I, between the Gerzean, with its influential contacts with Protoliterate civilization and Palestinian connections funneled through entrepôts in northeastern Egypt, and the First Dynasty, with its highly organized Levantine trade. Dynasty 0 stands out as a remarkable phase of foreign connections, characterized by the appearance in Sinai and southern Palestine of ordinary Egyptian pottery to an extent only rarely equaled later.

By the First Dynasty only two elements of Protoliterate lineage are recognizable, but both play major roles. The cylinder seal introduced in Gerzean has become a standard administrative adjunct, its designs completely Egyptianized with in most cases hieroglyphic elements predominant over representational ones. Hundreds of sealings of officials occur in the niched-brick tombs that constitute one of the most striking indications of the tremendous consolidation of wealth and political power in the First Dynasty. In their exterior shape and in such a detail of construction as the wooden bars inserted into niches, the elaborately recessed tombs closely resemble Protoliterate temples, as Frankfort demonstrated many years ago (1951: appendix). In Mesopotamia the prototypes of such niched buildings can be traced far back in the prehistoric period (Safar, Mustafa, and Lloyd 1982: 85–111). In Egypt niched structures appear suddenly without any known indigenous antecedents. The earliest known examples, the mastaba of Aha at Saqqara and of his presumed consort at Naqada, belong to the beginning of the dynasty (fig. 6:18). Recent excavations at Hierakonpolis show the use of niched brickwork in a nonfunerary context during the First Dynasty (Weeks 1971–72:229–33). In the absence of any traces of actual structures, the widespread assumption that niched brick construction was standard for palaces, in particular for those of the predynastic Delta kingdoms as opposed to the nomadic huts of Upper Egypt (Ricke 1944, *passim*), has remained theoretical (see Kaiser's discussion in Kaiser and Dreyer 1982:255–60 and his volume in preparation, *Nischenarchitektur und frühe Baukunst Ägyptens*). The scanty evidence available documents only fairly simple indigenous architectural forms in the later part of the predynastic period. Traces of modest post houses have been found at Maadi (Menghin and Amer 1936: pl. XIII) and Hierakonpolis (Hoffman 1980:119–37). Representations of somewhat more elaborate frame-and-matting structures occur on an ivory knife handle in the Metropolitan Museum of Art (Hayes 1953:28, fig. 21; Williams and Logan 1987) and on the Hunters' Palette in the form of the later determinative for Lower Egyptian shrine (Kantor 1974: pl. XI; see Emery 1939:20–25, figs. 13–20; 35, n. 2 and pl. 11 for seal impressions of Aha with renderings of similar structures). The pottery box in the form of a house from el-Amrah represents a pisé or mud-brick building with wooden door and window sills and lintels (Randall-MacIver and Mace 1902: pl. 10:1, 2). The sketchily rendered serekhs of Dynasty 0 (Kaiser and Dreyer 1982:262–69) may, like those of the First Dynasty (Frankfort 1951: pl. XXII 42–44), represent niched-brick buildings.

The example of Mesopotamian niched-brick architecture was available in Egypt at a time when the Egyptians were searching for monumental forms commensurate with the momentous themes and grandeur of the new Egyptian state. The mechanism of transmission, however, has been a difficult problem since the niched mastabas only appeared after the cessation of demonstrable connections with Mesopotamia. Now the cones and spike from the later predynastic level at Tell el-Fara'in can be taken as indications that niched buildings once existed there; in view of the smallness of the cones, von der Way suggests that they probably belonged to modest, fairly thin-walled structures (1987:247–50 and 249, 256–57, fig. 3:5, 6 and accompanying text). Thus, the tradition for niched-brick building may have reached Egypt at the same time as the other Protoliterate features and survived there to provide models for the great monuments of the First Dynasty. Structures with elaborate niches on all four sides, however, left unfulfilled an essential need of Egyptian funerary architecture, that of a focal point for the meeting of the dead and the living. Although the unsuitability of mastabas niched on all sides led to modifications by the close of the First Dynasty, the niched facade never lost the sacrosanct character that it had acquired at the dawn of Egyptian history and remained of tremendous importance in the development of Egyptian architectural forms and ornament. It thus stands as the most long-lived and influential of the innovations that can be attributed to Protoliterate influence.

In contrast to the cessation of connections with Mesopotamia by the First Dynasty, those with Palestine and Syria were greatly intensified under the new centralized government. Large amounts of timber must have been imported for building the monumental tombs (Petrie 1900:8–9; Emery 1961:204) and for making coffins (Lucas and Harris 1962:430, 434). The scale of trade by the early Fourth Dynasty, under Snefru, is indicated on the Palermo Stone by a record of a fleet of forty ships filled with cedar wood (for foreign wood in Egypt see Lucas and Harris 1962:429–39 and Meiggs 1982:59–63). Various kinds of oils were also imported: two alabaster cylinder jars are inscribed with the name of Azib and the words "cedar oil" (Kaplony 1963: 1:306). Beginning with the reign of Djer, imported Syro-Palestinian pottery vessels, presumably oil or wine containers, make their appearance. Found in both royal and private tombs, they provide a splendid correlation between the EB II of Palestine and Syria and the greater part of the First Dynasty.

The vessels in question are often referred to as "Abydos ware," a misnomer as three distinct categories occur. Unfortunately, despite Petrie's initial descriptions in his earliest publications of some of the characteristics of the different foreign wares, they have not been clearly distinguished in later publications. These wares are as follows.

1. *Standard Early Bronze Red-Polished Ware* (see Petrie 1901b:46: "entirely un-Egyptian in the form, the colour and the paste"). The buff or brown paste is gritty and fired at relatively low temperatures; the surface usually has a burnished red wash, but only rarely is the presence of a wash specifically mentioned (fig. 10:15). The forms are mostly flasks, often with one large loop handle (fig. 8:1, 4). Flat and stump bases occur. An EB II pedestal jar was found at Saqqara (fig. 14:19).

2. *Light-Faced Painted Ware*. Vessels similar in paste and low firing to the previous group are distinguished by their light surface, often with a cream slip and paint (see Petrie 1901b:46: "soft light-brown clay decomposing in flakes . . . The face is finished with finer clay. . . . The colouring is the iron oxide, burnt either red or black."). The commonest form is the one-handled flask (fig. 12:1–6, 9–18), but various jars also occur (fig. 12:7, 8; possibly Capart and Werbrouck 1930:199, fig. 192). Designs are simple geometric ones except for an atypical bird (fig. 12:6; see Amiran 1978).

3. *Metallic Ware*. The primarily handmade manufacture, dense paste, and the metallic clink due to high firing differentiate vessels that are often the same in shape as those of Groups 1 and 2 (see fig. 8:2). The well-levigated paste, sometimes with grits, ranges from brown through red to gray (see Petrie et al. 1925:5: "hard grey pottery; remarkably hard, tinkling when struck; wheel-turned inside, diagonal scraping outside" (fig. 14:18). The interior surfaces are usually irregularly dimpled from the shaping by hand. Petrie's wheel-made example (fig. 14:18) is atypical, although a string-cut base in the Oriental Institute Museum indicates that handmade vessels could be finished on a wheel (fig. 8:10). Subcategories of metallic ware can be defined by the surface treatment: (*a*) plain; (*b*) burnished; (*c*) deep burnished, leaving slightly depressed bands (figs. 6:16, 8:5–7); and (*d*) combed (figs. 8:8, 9, 14:17, 18). Flasks with small, nonfunctional loop handles (fig. 8:3, 10:6–8) and two-handled jars (fig. 14:17, 18) are specific for metallic ware. Some previously unpublished sherds of imported vessels, mostly from Petrie's excavation of the tomb of Semerkhet at Abydos, are shown in figure 8. All except two are examples of metallic ware.

The occurrences of imported Syro-Palestinian pottery in the First Dynasty are summarized in the following list.

Reign	Site and Tomb	Publication
Djer	Abydos, Upper Cemetery, Tomb O	Petrie 1902: pl. VIII 1–8, 12
Djet	Abydos, Lower Cemetery, Djet Rectangle, Grave 159	Petrie et al. 1925: pl. IV 9
Djet	Saqqara, Mastaba 3504 (substructure burnt; restored under Qa)	Emery 1954:75; fig. 98 G9–12
Djet	Tarkhan, Mastaba 1060 (probably Djet)	Petrie, Wainwright, and Gardiner 1913: pls. XVI 4; XIX 24; XXX 6, 7
Den	Abydos, Upper Cemetery, Tomb T	Petrie 1901b: pl. LIV 3 sherds top left and 1902: pl. VIII
Den	Saqqara, Mastaba 3035	Emery 1938: pl. 27 12 (= G1), 13 (= G2)
Den	Saqqara, Mastaba 3036	Emery 1949: 81 and 152, fig. 86 G1
Den	Saqqara, Mastaba 3506	Emery 1958: pls. 75 G1–3, G12–16
Semerkhet	Abydos, Upper Cemetery, Tomb U	Petrie 1901b: pl. LIV and 1902: pl. VIII. See also fig. 8:1–3, 5–7, 9, 10 here
Qa	Saqqara, Mastaba 3120	Emery 1949:124, fig. 68
Qa	Saqqara, Mastaba 3500	Emery 1958: pl. 123 G9, G16
Qa	Saqqara, Mastaba 3505	Emery 1958: pl. 31 G1, G6, G11, G12

No specific reign	Saqqara, Cemetery NW of Serapeum, Tomb 38	Macramallah 1940:32, fig. 28 1, 5
No specific reign	Saqqara, Cemetery NW of Serapeum, Tomb 59	Macramallah 1940:36, fig. 29 8, 20
No specific reign	Abusir, no grave number	Bonnet 1928: pl. 27, middle
No specific reign	Lahun, Bashkatib, Grave 71	Petrie et al. 1923: pl. LIII 97 c–e

In Egypt, the foreign one-handled flask was an influential type copied in stone (e.g., Emery 1949:144, fig. 77, DDI; Saqqara 3121, reign of Qa). In the Third Dynasty it appears as a determinative in an offering list (Quibell 1913: pl. XXI).

The rarity of imported Syro-Palestinian pottery from Second and Third Dynasty contexts, in contrast to the imports from First Dynasty tombs, probably mirrors only the relatively limited amount of material available rather than a cessation of actual imports. A Second Dynasty context, a tomb at Helwan, has yielded one flask (fig. 6:9b), and a handleless flask like figure 10:15 appears on a niche stone of the Second Dynasty from Saqqara (fig. 6:9a). There was no interruption in the availability of timber indispensible for building projects. On the Asiatic side, Byblos has yielded a stone vessel fragment with the name of the Second Dynasty king, Khasekhemy, and Egyptian stone vessels occurred in EB II contexts at Ai in Palestine (see Stager, chap. 2). The same context at Ai yielded an ivory knife handle decorated with a pattern well known in Egypt among the matting designs painted on several First Dynasty mastabas and in the Third Dynasty tomb of Hesy at Saqqara (fig. 7:23; see Kantor 1956:157). This particular design does not appear after the Third Dynasty. Thus the knife handle reinforces the synchronism between Dynasties I–III and the EB II of Syria and Palestine.

The Old Kingdom

With the Old Kingdom we have reached a period when state monopolies of trade were well established, carrying on a tradition that probably goes back as far as the First Dynasty (Helck 1971:28). The Palermo stone reports a timber collecting expedition of Sneferu (Helck 1971:26; for political relations see 12–24).

A one-handled flask from Medum belongs to the beginning of the Fourth Dynasty. Although its wide neck distinguishes it from the other flasks found in Egypt, this is a typical feature for EB III (fig. 6:4; cf. fig. 7:12). Tombs at Giza, many dated to an individual reign or phase of a dynasty, provide the major part of the imported Syro-Palestinian pottery of this period (Reisner and Smith 1955:62–65, 73–76; figs. 80, 95–98). However, more modest graves at Saqqara (Jéquier 1929:26, fig. 25

[Dyn. VI]) and upstream at Matmar (fig. 14:13) prove that such goods were not limited to the nobility. No trace remains of the light-faced painted ware prominent in the First Dynasty, and the scene is now dominated by metallic one-handled flasks and two-handled jars, frequently cream-slipped and combed. These types correspond closely to metallic ware vessels from EB III contexts in Palestine and Ras Shamra (Schaeffer 1949:237, fig. 99:8, 9, 12, and 1962:203, fig. 16; Courtois 1962:434, fig. 22 H), even in such details as the cylinder-seal impression on a Giza jar (fig. 14:6) comparable to those found in Palestine (Ben-Tor 1978; Prausnitz 1955) and at Byblos (Dunand 1937: pl. CXXXIII [particularly 3232]; for other references and discussion see Dunand 1945, Reisner and Smith 1955:75, and Ben-Tor 1978:71–75). One flask typical of Cilician Early Bronze III was found at Giza (fig. 6:7; Reisner and Smith 1955:73–74, Type B-LIII a [Khufu to mid-Khafre]; see Goldman 1954:73).

Provenience analyses of the clays of ninety-one standard and metallic ware samples from Egypt and the Levant confirm the importance of Byblos and northern Palestine as trading partners of the Old Kingdom and, in addition, indicate that the connections with southern Palestine that had been so prominent in EB I still existed in EB III (Esse and Hopke 1986).

In addition to the finds of actual vessels there are also representations of foreign jars. In a scene showing the rewarding of weavers in the tomb of Ptahhotep at Giza a Syro-Palestinian two-handled jar stands next to an Egyptian storage jar; nearby a man hands a woman a vessel, saying, "See, the sweet oil" (fig. 6:3; see Junker 1941:49). It seems apparent that the foreign vessels were not imported for their own sake but for their contents, such as wines, oils, and resins (see Stager 1985). Evidence for the importation of commodities is given by reliefs in the late Fifth Dynasty tomb of Niankhkhnum and Khnumhotep at Saqqara, which show fruits not native to Egypt—juniper berries and the unidentified *prt-sni* fruit—being plucked from small trees (fig. 6:1; see Moussa and Altenmüller 1977:111, scene 16.3) and piled in the third and fourth heaps of fruits brought to a store house (ibid., fig. 13, pl. 34; see 102, scene 15:1). The *prt-sni* fruit was obtained from Byblos according to a reference in the medical Papyrus Ebers (ibid., p. 102 and n.

530). These reliefs come as an important addition to the well-known fragments with bears and one-handled flasks from the scene in the funerary temple of Sahure at Abusir depicting the return of Egyptian ships carrying Asiatics (fig. 6:2).

The synchronism between the Old Kingdom and EB III in Syria and Palestine is unquestionable, and the closeness of the contacts is exemplified by the diffusion of Egyptian objects abroad. Fragments of Egyptian stone vessels inscribed with royal names occur on the coast at Byblos (Porter, Moss, and Burney 1951:388–91 [Khufu, Khafre, Sahure, Neferirkare, Neuserre, Isesi, Unis, Teti, Pepi I, Merenre I, Pepi II]) and inland at Ebla (Scandone-Matthiae 1979:33–44 and figs. 11–14, and 1982:125–31; Matthiae 1985: pl. 36 a [Khafre and Pepi I]). Egyptian objects even appear to have penetrated as far afield as Anatolia, the presumed source of a gold cylinder seal inscribed with the names of Menkaure and Djedkare of the Fifth Dynasty (Young 1972:11, fig. 8). The much-debated treasure of Dorak is said to have included the gold overlay of a chair inscribed with the name and titles of Sahure (Mellaart 1966:152; Tomb I). Trade by sea was clearly well organized. Byblos stands out as the great en-trepôt that had been closely linked with Egypt since the Protodynastic period, and in the Old Kingdom it may well have been the primary center for the diffusion of Egyptian objects inland. A prince of Aswan, Khuy, made a journey there during the Sixth Dynasty (Edel 1979:195). Ras Shamra to the north has so far not yielded evidence for comparably close links with Egypt, but such objects as the EB III Cilician jug found at Giza and the inscribed Egyptian gold work said to have been found in Anatolia may have passed through northern ports.

The late third millennium B.C. brought a period of change and turmoil. In Egypt the centralized administration broke down and was replaced by the rival dynasties of the First Intermediate period. In Palestine the fortified cities of EB II and III disappeared, and new cultural elements traceable in pottery by caliciform vessels and associated types are found alongside Early Bronze survivals. The rupturing of trade with Palestine and Syria is shown by the disappearance of foreign pottery from Egyptian tombs. The fall of the Sixth Dynasty ushered in a new phase in Egypt's relations with the East, a phase not documented by archaeological finds from Egypt proper.

Two

The Periodization of Palestine from Neolithic through Early Bronze Times

Lawrence E. Stager, Semitic Museum, Harvard University

Outline

Pre-Pottery Neolithic

About 9000 B.C., toward the end of the Natufian period in Palestine, hunters and gatherers established one of the earliest villages in the Near East, 'Ain Mallaha in the upper Jordan Valley (Perrot 1968). There are no signs that these villagers had begun to domesticate animals or cultivate plants, but they continued to rely on hunting and broad-spectrum food collecting. Shifts toward the first agricultural communities appear in Pre-Pottery Neolithic A (PPNA) settlements, such as Jericho, where domesticated cereals and legumes are attested for the first time.

PPNA sites range in size from 0.20–0.30 ha to 4.00 ha, the largest of which was Jericho, with a population of perhaps as many as one thousand inhabitants. The tell was studded with small circular huts built of "hog-back" mud-bricks, and many of their floors bore impressions of circular mats. A 2.00 m-wide stone wall encircled the village. Inside the wall stood at least one monumental stone tower built to a height of over 9.00 m with a covered interior stairway of twenty-two steps (Kenyon 1979). It makes little military sense to build such a defensive tower inside a fortification line. If the outer wall at Jericho and the later one at Beidha functioned as a barrier against floodwaters and alluvial deposits, the location of these features becomes more understandable (Bar-Yosef 1980; Perrot 1968).

Text submitted March 1986

Many of the Early Neolithic settlements, when not in the Mediterranean zone, were sited on alluvial fans. In the alluvial fields of Jericho, watered and fertilized by seasonal floodwaters and perhaps irrigated by the perennially flowing spring 'Ain es-Sultan, the first farmers cultivated crops of domesticated cereals, such as nonshattering forms of emmer wheat (*Triticum dicoccum*) and hulled two-row barley (*Hordeum distichum*), as well as legumes, such as lentils and chickpeas (Hopf 1983). For meat, however, they relied mainly on gazelle from the hunt, and flint arrowheads still predominated. It was only in PPNB that the transition to a full Neolithic farming economy took place with the domestication of goats, as evidenced by twisted horn cores at Jericho (Clutton-Brock 1979). Complete long bones of goat suggest to Davis (1982) that it was meat rather than bone marrow, indicated by heavily fragmented bones, that prompted early domestication. Sheep were also probably domesticated at PPNB Jericho (Clutton-Brock and Uerpmann 1974). During the Chalcolithic period, it seems that both sheep and goat were exploited for their dairy and fiber products (Levy 1981; Sherratt 1981). However, B. Hesse

The figures for Egypt and Palestine have been interleaved to facilitate comparisons and can be found between chapters 1 and 2 in volume 2.

I wish to thank Abbas Alizadeh for his elegant renditions of artifacts presented in the figures and Helen Dates for typing the manuscript, tables, and charts. I am most indebted to Helene J. Kantor for sharing with me many insights based on her unparalleled knowledge of ancient Near Eastern chronological and cultural interconnections.

(pers. comm.) would question the unilineal sequence from meat to milk and fibers, generalized for the ancient Near East, in which carnivorous pastoralism (Ingold 1980) precedes husbandry for "secondary" products, such as milk and wool. Actually these may have been primary products in the multiple pathways to pastoralism, according to Hesse. Carnivorous pastoralism would then be the result of intensified herding and a shift in the goal of production as herds grew in size.

Whatever the outcome of this debate, the so-called Neolithic Revolution took place over an extensive period of ca. 2,500 years, from mid-ninth to the end of the seventh millennium during Pre-Pottery Neolithic A and B.

PPNA, 8500–7300 B.C.

Crowfoot Payne (1976) has subdivided PPNA into two distinctive lithic industries. The early phase, known as Khiamian, after el-Khiam, a rock shelter in the Judean Desert near Bethlehem, is characterized by a partially microlithic tool kit with a predominance of notched el-Khiam points; the later phase called Sultanian, after Tell es-Sultan subsequently known as biblical Jericho, is characterized by heavy-duty core tools, including tranchet axes. Recent excavations in the central Jordan Valley at Salibiya and Netiv Hagdud tend to confirm this sequence (Bar-Yosef, Gopher, and Goring-Morris 1980).

For PPNA as a whole, innovations in chipped stone included polished axes, baked flints, and obsidian imported from Anatolia. The shift to some domesticated cereals and legumes is reflected in the ground stone industry as mortars and pestles of the Natufian period were replaced by slab querns, grinding stones, and bowls in PPNA (Bar-Yosef 1980, 1981). The earliest clay sculpture, depicting a seated human, appears at Netiv Hagdud.

PPNB, 7300–6300 B.C.

The total number of sites increased dramatically in PPNB: key sites were located in the Jordan Valley at Beisamoun, Munhatta 6–3, and Jericho; in the highlands at Abu Gosh and Khirbet Duma near Hebron; east of the Jordan at ʿAin Ghazal; west of the Dead Sea at Nahal Hemar Cave; in the Arabah at Beidha and Nahal Issaron C; in the Negev at Nahal Divshon, Lavan 109, Boqer, Nizzana, and at several other small sites.

Sites vary in size from 0.30 ha to 12.00 ha, the largest being ʿAin Ghazal located at a spring near Amman and three times the size of Jericho, the next largest contemporary site in Palestine.

Prior to Chalcolithic times, PPNB was the most prosperous period in Palestine. The fully developed Neolithic economy of sheep/goat husbandry and cereal agriculture provided the basis for large settlements with rectangular houses, perhaps even a few public buildings, elaborate weaving and wickerwork, modeled sculpture, plastered skulls and stone masks, and artifacts of wood, bone, and bead (fig. 2).

At Jericho as well as other oases or Mediterranean zone sites, the circle-huts of PPNA were replaced by rectangular houses in PPNB, with thick plaster floors, white-washed, sometimes painted with red ochre, and burnished. Walls probably received the same treatment (Banning and Byrd 1984; Rollefson 1985).

Kenyon (1979:30–40) postulated a lengthy hiatus between the Jerichoan inhabitants of PPNA and the PPNB newcomers, possibly from Syria, who introduced the sophisticated rectangular houses with polished plaster floors and manufactured flints in the Tahunian tradition. However, radiocarbon dates from Jericho (see table 3) do not support such a gap between PPNA and B. Nor does the architectural tradition at Beidha, where round houses in Level VI dated to PPNB but in the PPNA tradition gave way to polygonal houses in Level V to be replaced by rectilinear houses in subsequent strata (Kirkbride 1966).

In the desert of south Sinai, where hunting remained the primary source of procurement throughout the Neolithic period, the tool kits of these hunters consisted mostly of arrowheads and their shelters were circle-huts in the PPNA tradition (Rosen 1988). Contrary to the hypotheses promoted by Binford and Flannery that plant and animal domestication developed first on the fringes of civilization, away from the "natural hearths," there is no evidence from the arid zones of Palestine to support this notion.

In the Mediterranean zone and in oases, naviform cores, with two opposed striking platforms, were new to the chipped stone industry of PPNB (fig. 2:29). Flint tools retouched by pressure flaking took on a finer, more gracile appearance. There was a shift in arrowhead types from Helwan and el-Khiam points to more lanceolate forms, such as Jericho, Byblos, and Amuq points (fig. 2:23, 24, 33). Small quantities of obsidian were imported from Anatolia, Gollu Dag being one of the sources. Double-saddle querns (Kenyon 1979: pl. 19), combining features of mortar and metate, provide the leading type-fossil of the ground stone industry.

Some sort of sewing and weaving industry had been inferred from perforated rib bones presumably used as weaving shuttles (Perrot 1979: pl. 29; for a bone "thimble," see Rollefson 1984: fig. 3). But the extraordinary sophistication of this handicraft has only now been revealed by textiles preserved in the Nahal Hemar Cave. All of the processes for preparing linen from flax fibers and bast from palm fibers were known. Some of the textiles were woven on a loom; most were woven by hand.

Knotted squares for a "bag," spaced twining for a delicate "napkin," tabby weave, and other techniques illustrate the skills of PPNB weavers. They were also making ropes and cordage containers covered inside and out with bitumen (Bar-Yosef 1985; Bar-Yosef and Alon 1988).

Domestic mortuary ritual was linked to hearths at ʿAin Ghazal, where some of the burials were located beneath plaster floors 1.00–1.50 m south of the fireplace (Rollefson 1985). Portrait heads of plaster on human skulls from Jericho, Tell Ramad near Damascus, Beisamoun, and ʿAin Ghazal attest to veneration of ancestors (Kenyon 1979; Lechevallier 1978; Rollefson 1985). At Nahal Hemar, "Bitumen Valley," a skull was found decorated with an elaborate net pattern of bitumen (fig. 2:32). From the same cave, lifesize masks made of limestone with red and green bands of paint radiating from the center of the face (fig. 2:28) might have been worn by ritual dancers, although the masks are rather heavy, or hung on walls or large statues.

At ʿAin Ghazal, spectacular caches of anthropomorphic statues and busts were recently found. The statues, a little less than 1.00 m in height, were made of clay modeled around a core of reeds, twigs, and grasses wrapped in cloth or cords (fig. 2:27). The busts, ca. 0.45 m in height, had modeled heads with eyes outlined in blue-green paint and faces sometimes decorated with red ochre (Rollefson 1985; Tubb 1985; Rollefson and Simmons 1988). Poorly preserved specimens from Nahal Hemar (Bar-Yosef 1985:14) and Jericho (fig. 2:26) resemble statues from ʿAin Ghazal, down to such anatomical anomalies as six-toed individuals, who were obviously endowed with supernatural powers.

In addition to obsidian, a bone belt hook (fig. 2:30) from Nahal Hemar provides a distant link with Anatolia, where similar bone hooks as well as eye-clasps were found at Çatal Hüyük in Level VI A of the "Pottery Neolithic," dated to the early sixth millennium by radiocarbon (P-769 = 5781 ± 96 B.C.; P-772 = 5850 ± 94 B.C.; P-789 = 5800 ± 93 B.C. [half-life 5730]; Mellaart 1964:116, for the belt hooks, see pp. 100–102 and his fig. 44, lower).

We have reluctantly retained the somewhat awkward and misleading nomenclature "Pre-Pottery" and "Pottery" Neolithic because of established usage (cf. Moore 1982). Despite the Pottery Neolithic nomenclature, several desert sites have flint assemblages contemporary with the Pottery Neolithic period, but do not have pottery (Rosen 1985). Despite the Pre-Pottery Neolithic nomenclature, crudely made, low-fired potsherds have appeared for the first time in terminal Pre-Pottery Neolithic contexts at ʿAin Ghazal, a phase tentatively designated PPNC. This pottery and White Ware (Rollefson and Simmons 1985:43–44 and fig. 7) suggest that there was no gap between the end of Pre-Pottery Neolithic and the beginning of the subsequent Pottery Neolithic period in Palestine. The so-called gap completely disappears with the appearance of the Yarmukian Phase, 1.20–1.40 m deep, which overlay the terminal Pre-Pottery Neolithic at ʿAin Ghazal (Rollefson and Simmons 1988).

Pottery Neolithic

The Pottery Neolithic, spanning the early sixth through mid-fifth millennia, can be subdivided roughly into three phases, based on the lengthy stratigraphic sequence at Munhatta, in the Jordan Valley south of the Sea of Galilee (table 1). Following upon the terminal Pre-Pottery Neolithic layers, the earliest pottery-bearing phase is Munhatta $2B_2$, of the Yarmukian culture, first defined by Stekelis at the nearby site of Shaar ha-Golan on the Yarmuk River (Stekelis 1972). The subsequent stratum $2B_1$ was dubbed the Munhatta phase by Perrot (1968). A clear change in building and ceramic tradition, not only at Munhatta but also in other parts of Palestine, occurs in Munhatta $2A_{1-3}$, the Wadi Rabah phase.

Yarmukian Phase

Yarmukian pottery is coarse and handmade, with mat impressions on flat bases. The vessels are often covered with reddish brown slip and decorated with reserved or cream-slipped horizontal and/or zigzag bands which are delineated by parallel incised lines, filled with incised herringbone or diagonal hatching, sometimes burnished (fig. 2:14). Bowls and chalices painted with chevrons are also attested (Perrot 1968: cols. 412–15 and fig. 845, upper).

The globular forms and incised decoration resemble pottery from Early and Middle Neolithic Byblos, although the parallels are far from exact. The hemispherical bowl with lugs below the rim from Early Neolithic Byblos provides a more precise parallel to bowls from Labweh, Jericho PNA, and Munhatta $2B_2$ (fig. 2:18). The rectilinear houses of Early Neolithic Byblos, with polished plaster floors, continue an earlier tradition (PPNB), and the cardium-combed ware represents a decorative technique distinctive of this Syrian coastal enclave (Mellaart 1975:239). Amiran (1970a:20) has suggested a relationship between Yarmukian pottery and the painted-incised ware from the early levels of Hassuna (Ib–IV) in northern Mesopotamia. Although the shapes and fabric of Hassuna pottery are quite different, this decorative parallel seems less tenuous than the one recently drawn to the *Fischgrätkeramik* from Merimde in Egypt. There incised herringbone pattern appears on hemispherical bowls in simple horizontal bands without incised borders (fig. 4:25; cf. Eiwanger 1984:61–62, nn. 253–54, and pls. 18–20).

During the early Pottery Neolithic of Palestine, flint production undergoes some changes: naviform cores disappear; knives and scrapers of tabular flint are introduced. More characteristic, however, are coarse-toothed sickle blade segments made by bifacial retouch, which continue through the middle phase as well. An assemblage from basal Megiddo (sub-Stratum XX) indicates that, when hafted, these sickles were ca. 30 cm long (Crowfoot Payne 1983:714), nearly comparable in length to those found at Byblos and Munhatta (fig. 2:19). Large arrowheads from Shaar ha-Golan may be related to the more elegant leaf-shaped Byblos points with tang and Amuq points without tang (fig. 2:24, 23). In the next phase arrowheads tend to be smaller (fig. 2:20–22; Bar-Yosef 1981). Partly polished ax or adze heads, also known at Byblos, become especially common at Pottery Neolithic sites in Palestine. Their greater frequency in once wooded uplands and highlands suggests uses for cutting timber and working wood (Moore 1973).

More precise links between the Yarmukian and Byblite cultures can be established through stone and clay anthropomorphic figurines. Schematic faces incised on pebble figurines occur in northern Palestine at Shaar ha-Golan and Munhatta (fig. 2:15). These resemble those found at Byblos mostly in the Early Neolithic but continuing into the Middle Neolithic phase (cf. Dunand 1973: pls. 110: 22145, 111:26150 and Stekelis 1972: pl. 48:1–2; cf. Dunand 1973: pl. 111:28710 and Stekelis 1972: pls. 46:4, 47:1, 4, 5). Even more restricted in time are the clay figurines with coneheads and cowrie-shaped eyes, known from Shaar ha-Golan (fig. 2:25), Munhatta 2B$_2$ (Perrot 1968), perhaps Giladi (Kaplan 1966), and Early Neolithic Byblos (Dunand 1973: pl. 113:26160). Also related are the coneheaded figurines from Ramad III and Hassuna figures from Yarim Tepe I (Cauvin 1972:82; Mellaart 1975:239). This type never occurs in later Pottery Neolithic contexts.

Because of the supposed "hiatus" in Palestine, Perrot was led to "delay" the introduction of pottery (Yarmukian phase) until the Middle Neolithic of Byblos, which overlaps Amuq C–D and Ras Shamra IV, when Halafian imported and locally made pottery appears. We are inclined to follow Stekelis (1972:43–44), who suggested the contemporaneity of Shaar ha-Golan and Early Neolithic Byblos, the midpoint of which, Level 43, provides a radiocarbon date of 5630 ± 70 B.C. (GRN 1544; 5730 half-life), which can be bracketed by dates from Ras Shamra VB of 5965 ± 112 B.C. (P-458) and VA of 5450 ± 84 B.C. (P-457). The latter translates into CRD 6310–5690 B.C.

Ras Shamra VA, with Hassuna "husking trays" and pattern-burnished Dark-Faced Burnished Ware, hereafter DFBW, correlates with Amuq B. In addition to White Ware and DFBW, earlier Phase VB at Ras Shamra contains butterfly beads, which provide a nice link with Amuq A (de Contenson 1982).

The home of DFBW was Anatolia. There a continuous tradition of making this handmade lustrous pottery began in early Pottery Neolithic and persisted through the Early Bronze Age, when its last manifestation in the Levant appears in the form of Khirbet Kerak Ware.

For the sixth millennium, DFBW is the hallmark of several sites in Syro-Cilicia and comprises the bulk of the ceramic yield from Amuq A–B. The tradition continued through Amuq C, when Halafian-style pottery first appeared (Braidwood and Braidwood 1960). The earliest phase of DFBW continued down the coast through Tabbat el-Hammam as far south as Byblos, where it became much rarer.

Inland east of Byblos, another production center of DFBW lay in the Beqa Valley, its province extending to the southeast at least as far as Ramad (Str. III). Soundings at Labweh produced the earliest ceramic horizon in the Beqa with White Ware and DFBW; and soundings at Ard Tlaili, a later horizon comparable to Amuq C with DFBW and Halaf painted pottery (Kirkbride 1969; Copeland 1969).

Enclaves of DFBW in its early phase appear at a few sites in northern Palestine: Kefar Giladi IVb (basal level) in Upper Galilee and Abu Zureiq V (Hazorea complex) in the Plain of Esdraelon. Farther south, probably Tuleilat Batashi IVb in the central foothills (Shephelah) should also be included. Later during the Wadi Rabah phase, many more sites were added to this lustrous ware tradition.

Another thin strand of ceramic evidence, Cord-Impressed Ware, links Giladi IVb to Labweh and Tabbat el-Hammam in the early Pottery Neolithic. This rare variant of DFBW was first recorded from the basal layers of Tabbat el-Hammam, which had a pottery assemblage similar to Amuq A (Braidwood 1940:220 and pl. 23:1; Hole 1959: fig. 2:27–29, 33). It was later identified at Giladi, although not illustrated (Kaplan 1966), and at Labweh (Kirkbride 1969:47; Copeland 1969:87). Some of the DFBW from basal Hammam has reserved chevrons and bands incised with herringbone pattern (fig. 2:16), a decorative technique remarkably similar to that used by Yarmukian potters.

From these synchronisms between the early Pottery Neolithic of Syria and northern Palestine, buttressed by radiocarbon dates, it seems clear that the great gap in Palestine after PPNB is illusory, based as it was on undemonstrated interpolations from the geologico-climatological reconstructions of Europe and selectively applied to the steppe zones of Palestine, but not Syria.

Wadi Rabah Phase

Sites represented by the Wadi Rabah culture have architectural, ceramic, and flint traditions sufficiently different from what precedes them to justify a demarcation in the periodization scheme, in what we shall call late Pottery Neolithic. Kaplan (1958), who first recognized this phase at the type site of Wadi Rabah on the Yarkon River, east of Tel Aviv, felt that this assemblage had more in common with Garstang's Jericho VIII (= Kenyon's PNB) and the subsequent Beersheba-Ghassulian horizon than with the preceding Pottery Neolithic of Jericho IX, or PNA; hence, his designation "Early Chalcolithic," although copper does not occur in Wadi Rabah contexts. To the east in the Shephelah, this culture appears in Batashi III. The most completely published assemblage is from ʿEin el-Jarba (Kaplan 1969) in the Esdraelon Plain. Giladi II–III and Kabri in Upper Galilee, Tel Ali and Munhatta 2A$_{1-3}$ in the Jordan Valley, and, to a lesser extent, Jericho PNB (= VIII) bear the imprint of the Wadi Rabah culture.

Biconical sling bullets, of stone or clay, as well as maceheads appear for the first time. They are known from many Halafian sites in northern Mesopotamia and Syria, occurring in Amuq C with imported and locally made Halaf painted pottery (for the weapons and tools, see Kaplan 1969).

Although some of the Wadi Rabah pottery retains the incised techniques known from the Early Neolithic (fig. 2:5), the most common and distinctive vessels have bright red or glossy black, burnished surfaces, thus representing another episode in the DFBW tradition (fig. 2:9–11). Twin, or Siamese, pots make their first appearance, and holemouth jars are common (fig. 2:12). A unique reddish brown, burnished vase has on its shoulder an appliqué of two spread-eagled figures, possibly humans wearing masks (fig. 2:7).

Bowrim jars also appear for the first time during this phase in Palestine. This rim type occurs toward the end of Byblos Middle Neolithic and in Amuq D. Mortuary offerings from a rich grave in Kabri include a bowrim jar made of gypsum (fig. 2:8), a red granite macehead, which is probably from Sinai, a large core of Vannic obsidian, an elegant obsidian mirror (fig. 2:6), and heavy-footed pedestaled stone vessels, similar to a specimen from Late Neolithic Byblos (fig. 2:2; cf. Dunand 1973: pl. 79:31971).

Based on the crisply carinated shoulders and splayed rims of bowls and cups found in the Wadi Rabah and Halafian cultures, Kaplan (1969) proposed an interconnection between the two traditions (fig. 2:9–11). The Siamese vessel (fig. 2:12) further reinforced the links.

Until recently, however, no true imports or local Halaf painted pottery had been found in Palestine. Beyond the primary Halafian sphere, the western periphery of that culture extended to Syro-Cilicia (Amuq C–D, Ras Shamra IV) as far south as Ard Tlaili in the Beqa, where imported and local Halaf painted pottery occurred with DFBW. This area was thought to be the source of direct contact and influence leading to the formation of the Wadi Rabah culture (Mellaart 1975:242–43).

Now the Halafian periphery must be extended at least as far south as the Beth Shan Valley in northern Palestine. Excavations by Gophna (1979) at Tel Tsaf revealed mud-brick walls laid in herringbone pattern, typical of Mesopotamia and Syria but heretofore unknown in Palestine. Alongside DFBW was found Halafian or Halaf-like painted pottery decorated with red and black bichrome, including some examples with net-patterned lozenges against a white-slipped background. This discovery confirms Kaplan's interconnection between the Wadi Rabah and Halafian cultures and suggests a period in the first half of the fifth millennium for the Wadi Rabah phase (a date more in accord with radiocarbon assay GX-787 = CRD 4730–4415 than with GX-786 = CRD 3895–3505; see table 3).

Chalcolithic

Chalcolithic culture is highlighted by a rich repertoire of carved ivories, copper artifacts, terra-cotta figurines, basalt bowls and sculpture, and wall paintings (fig. 3). Amid the unity expressed by shared cultural traits, there is also a diversity of subcultures, or facies, whose variation can be attributed, to some extent, to the different ecological settings in which they flourished; for example, the Beersheba complex in the northern Negev, the Ghassulian aspect north of the Dead Sea, and the newly discovered Golan Heights facies (Perrot 1968, 1984; Levy 1986, 1987; de Vaux 1970; Epstein 1978b, 1979).

The number and size of Chalcolithic settlements in the northern Negev increase dramatically when compared with the preceding Pottery Neolithic period. Fifty-seven Chalcolithic sites, ranging in size from 0.09 to 9.5 ha compare with eleven Pottery Neolithic sites, 0.19 to 3.0 ha in area. Other surveys indicate an increase in Chalcolithic settlements in the Golan and in the northern valleys of Jezreel, Beth Shan, and the Jordan (Levy 1983:20). The central highlands, however, were only sparsely settled before the Early Bronze Age.

Accompanying the demographic increase in these regions were higher degrees of specialization in ivory carving and copper metallurgy; in desert floodwater and runoff farming; in olive and date cultivation; and in animal husbandry, styled the "Secondary Products Revolution," with its emphasis on wool and dairy products (Sherratt 1981). At the same time, interregional exchange of animal products, basalt, copper, and pottery, to name but a few, was more intense than in the Pottery Neolithic. With the domestication of the donkey, low-level long distance trade with Egypt began over the coastal road of north Sinai (Levy 1983; Perrot 1984; Stager 1985; Oren and Gilead 1981).

What we have just summarized pertains to the latter part of the period, which came to an end probably ca. 3500 B.C., a CRD terminus based on radiocarbon dates (I-353, I-285, W-1341) from Nahal Mishmar and the initial phase of EB I, which was contemporary with the Early Gerzean, or Naqada II, of Egypt. How much before ca. 4000 B.C. early Chalcolithic culture begins, its origin, and its relationship, if any, to the terminal Neolithic must remain unanswered questions.

Perrot (1955:185) has emphasized how suddenly the Beersheba culture appears, already well adapted to its semiarid surroundings, and has suggested an immigration of pastoralists from Transjordan or even from Egypt, who had had no contact with the earlier Neolithic inhabitants of Palestine.

A partial solution to the problem of the early Chalcolithic may be forthcoming from Hennessy's excavations at the type-site of Ghassul, long thought to be three small hillocks but now recognized as one site extending over 20 ha, the largest settlement in the country, with 5.00 m of successive occupation prior to its abandonment before the EB I, or Proto-Urban, period. The lowest level has round huts with sunken foundations and pebble floors (Hennessy 1982). These excavations, when published, should provide the missing link between Pottery Neolithic and Chalcolithic cultures at Ghassul.

Metallurgy

Several caves located in steep-sided wadis leading into the Dead Sea were inhabited during the Chalcolithic period. The most famous of these is the "Cave of the Treasure" in Nahal Mishmar, 10 km south of the oasis of ʿEn Gedi.

There Bar-Adon (1980) discovered the earliest known cache of copper objects in the ancient Near East, of a quality and sophistication unmatched until the Bronze Age in Anatolia. The hoard of 442 artifacts had been wrapped in a reed mat and tucked away in a recess of the cave. Most of the objects were made of copper (429), including many ritual items: 240 copper maceheads, 10 "crowns," 138 standards (mostly stylized maces, but also referred to as "sceptres"); a few baskets, jars, and horns;

and 16 tools (axes/adzes and chisels). The copper objects weigh ca. 135 kg (300 lbs.). In addition there were ivory "sickles" made of hippopotamus tusks (fig. 3:10) and an ivory box made from elephant tusk.

A healthy but unwarranted skepticism greeted Bar-Adon's Chalcolithic date for the hoard (e.g., Perrot 1968: cols. 441–42 argued for an EB I, or Proto-Urban, date). But several lines of evidence converge to support Bar-Adon (Ussishkin 1980:39):

1. Radiocarbon dates for the reed mat that held the hoard cluster in early to mid-fourth millennium.
2. Associated pottery is clearly of the Beersheba-Ghassul horizon (see table 2).
3. The ivory "sickles" resemble an example from Beersheba (cf. Perrot 1964: pl. 51:1).
4. The "nose" and "ibex-horn" motifs in metal are attested throughout the Chalcolithic repertoire in several other media (fig. 3; Epstein 1978a).
5. Some of the stylized copper maces (standards/scepters) closely resemble others found in copper-processing contexts at Beersheba and Shiqmim (fig. 3:11 from Abu Matar; Baumgarten and Eldar 1984:54 from Safadi [= Neveh Noy]; Alon and Levy 1983 from Shiqmim).

Even with the Chalcolithic date of the hoard accepted, some scholars have sought foreign origins for such sophisticated metallurgy, although distant parallels as of Luristan are later in date. Undoubtedly part of the reason for foreign ascription comes from a reluctance to believe that the local culture had achieved a degree of civilization much beyond village subsistence levels despite the obvious evidence for local specialized artisans and artists who produced basalt and ivory sculptures as well as brilliant wall paintings.

The ritual copper objects in the Nahal Mishmar hoard and the mace from Abu Matar have a high arsenic content (2–12 percent). In fact arsenical copper artifacts were known in many parts of the Near East in the late fourth through the third millennia (Eaton and McKerrell 1976; Garenne-Marot 1984). Apparently one must look to the distant north, as far away as Anatolia (Perrot 1984:80), Armenia, or Azerbaijan (Key, in Bar-Adon 1980) for the nearest mines with arsenic-rich ores. This may be a better, if not compelling, reason for seeking a foreign source for the objects. But other artifacts in the hoard, such as the tools, were made of "pure" copper. Key suggests that the difference in metal types is according to their function, whether utilitarian or ritualistic. It seems more likely that arsenic was added to the "ritual" artifacts, made by the cire-perdue process, in order to produce a free-flowing melt for more elaborate casting than was required for the axes, adzes, and chisels.

The motifs on the stylized maces and crowns from Nahal Mishmar, the similarity to copper maces found at sites in the northern Negev, and their copper metallurgical installations, complete with crucibles, ores, and slags, clearly indicate that Palestine was the place of manufacture, most probably in the Beersheba region.

A Canaanite jar containing orpiment, a yellow sulfide of arsenic, has recently been discovered in the rich cargo of the fourteenth-century B.C. shipwreck off the Cape of Ulu Burun in Turkey (Bass 1987:713). It never made much sense to suggest that Chalcolithic smiths imported huge quantities of arsenic-rich copper or alloys from such distant sources as Armenia to manufacture the Nahal Mishmar hoard. There was probably a long history of importing arsenic sulfides for various purposes, including medicines, insecticides, and backing mirrors. Because of its low evaporation point, arsenic cannot be added directly to copper. However, through sublimation—a heating and cooling process—arsenic sulfides can be converted to metallic arsenic and alloyed with copper. It seems likely that already by the Chalcolithic period coppersmiths in Palestine had learned how to adapt arsenic for metallurgical purposes without succumbing to its poisonous effects.

Although the Nahal Mishmar treasure might have been manufactured in the northern Negev, where had such a hoard of wealth been accumulated before it was secreted in this remote desert cave? No individuals, families, or even village communities of the period had anything like this concentration of wealth. However, just to the north of the Nahal Mishmar cave, high on a cliff overlooking the Dead Sea at ʿEn Gedi, stood the most impressive Chalcolithic temple yet known (Ussishkin 1980). Since no contemporary settlement in the vicinity has been found, this isolated temple complex may have served as a regional ceremonial center and pilgrimage site, a meeting ground between the desert and the sown.

A large stone temenos wall connected the main broadroom-style temple with subsidiary buildings and gates leading into the central courtyard. The temple interior had once been plastered and painted, perhaps with murals as sumptuous as those at Ghassul, but although most of its contents had been removed in antiquity, hundreds of cornets in fragments, a few ibex and goat horns, a terra-cotta ram (called a "bull" in Ussishkin 1980: fig. 11) with churns on its back, and the base of an Egyptian alabaster jar (fig. 3:5) remained in the building. The cornets probably were drinking or offering vessels (cf. rhyta). Cornets projecting from a terra-cotta ram came from a cultic context, probably a temple, at Gilat. There, too, was found the charming "Lady of Gilat," balancing a churn on her head (fig. 3:3, 18). Dairy products must have figured prominently in the overall economy of the period and, therefore, in ritual offerings as well. In Palestine the alabaster jar fragment is the only known au-

thentic Egyptian import from a Chalcolithic context. It is impossible, however, to date it as late as Dynasty 0 or I, as Baumgartel and a few others have wanted to do (Ussishkin 1980:25), for, as Amiran (1974a) has shown, its best Egyptian parallels belong to the Amratian, or Naqada I, period. This vessel, then, provides the best synchronism between Chalcolithic Palestine and Amratian Egypt. At the same time the north Sinai coastal road became an active caravan route, shortly after the donkey was first domesticated. There, along with Ghassul-Beersheba pottery, Egyptian Polished Red sherds and a grinding palette have appeared (Oren and Gilead 1981).

The copper trove from Nahal Mishmar probably came from the temple precincts of ʿEn Gedi (Ussishkin 1971, 1980; Bar-Adon 1980:202), which provide a plausible institutional context in which a regionally supported priesthood could acquire sufficient wealth to "commission" such a vast array of ritual items in copper and ivory.

More immediately relevant to the question of social organization may be a temple precinct at Ghassul (Hennessy 1982), apparently as impressive as the one in ʿEn Gedi, located in the midst of a comparatively large community of perhaps four thousand to five thousand people. Also in this "urban" context, earlier excavations produced a badly damaged, but very intriguing, mural which depicts at least six individuals in a row or procession, preserved unfortunately only below the knees. The most important person has his feet, clad in laced sandals, planted on a dais and is being served by a small attendant (Mallon, Koeppel, and Neuville 1934: pl. 66). Whether depicting the realm of the gods or human rulers, the hierarchical symbolism of the painting is clear.

These discoveries from ʿEn Gedi, Nahal Mishmar, and Ghassul provide evidence for a religious elite, or priesthood, active in Chalcolithic society.

Early Bronze I

The EB I period, which we shall attempt to subdivide into an "early" and a "late" phase (fig. 16), led to the formation of large EB "city-states," which characterized the settlement pattern of Palestine throughout the subsequent millennium during EB II–III. Like the posturban period of EB IV/MB I, this preurban period of EB I has been shrouded in confusing terminology, which reflects chronological uncertainty; this, in turn, has led to muddled periodization. Regional variation in the ceramics of the post-Ghassul-Beersheba and pre-EB II horizon (Amiran 1970a:41), compounded by the lack of well-stratified deposits containing *all* of the major pottery groups, has complicated the situation. It is clear, however, that such a crucial period in the cultural history of Palestine deserves a more sustained and detailed examination than do most other eras.

There are at least four distinctive ceramic assemblages that can be isolated in the EB I period:

1. *Gray-Burnished Ware* (= GBW, or Proto-Urban C, or "Esdraelon" Ware) (fig. 7:92; Wright 1958) had its production centers in the north, extending down the Jordan Valley: in lower Galilee at Yiftahel; in the Esdraelon Plain at Megiddo Stages VII–V and Strata XX–XIX, Affula, and at Beth Shan XVII–XV; in the Transjordanian plateau at Arqub edh-Dhahr; in the northern coastal plain at Meser II–I and Tell el-Asawir; in the central highlands at Tell Farᶜah (N); in the Jordan Valley from north to south at Beth Yerah or Khirbet Kerak, Sheikh Ali, Munhatta I, Tell es-Shunah II, and Tell Abu Alayik or "Herodian" Jericho.

Although overlapping with but extending later than GBW, knobbed bowls, usually plain or red-slipped, are not Esdraelon Ware in the strict sense (fig. 7:91 and 6:38, 44; cf., however, Hennessy 1967:28; Wright 1958), nor should GBW, with its distinctive repertoire of shapes and gray lustrous surface treatment, be classified as a variant of red-slipped ware or as a mere ceramic imitation of basalt vessels of the Chalcolithic period (cf. Lapp 1970).

The original home of GBW in Anatolia was part of a very long ceramic tradition which began with DFBW and continued, in an unbroken sequence, through Khirbet Kerak Ware (Arsebük 1979; Hennessy 1967:35–36). The sporadic appearance of these Anatolian-type wares, when abundant yet locally made in Syria and Palestine, indicates an influx of new peoples from the north.

The introduction of Esdraelon Ware in northern Palestine and at a few enclaves farther south, such as Tell Farᶜah (N) and Tell Abu Alayik, marked the beginning of EB I in Palestine and the apparently peaceful intermingling of Anatolian peoples with the indigenous population. GBW continued in production throughout some, if not all, of late EB I.

2. *Red-Burnished Ware* (= RBW, or Proto-Urban A) (fig. 7:90; Hennessy 1967:36–40, pl. 31:1–9) had a broad distribution in both the north and the south. During early EB I, RBW appears with Esdraelon Ware at Megiddo, Beth Shan XVII–XV, and Tell Farᶜah (N). At Azor on the coast it occurs in a mid-to-late EB I context (Ben-Tor 1975). Variants of orange-red burnished ware occur in the EB IA shaft tombs at Bâb edh-Dhrâᶜ, where as elsewhere it continued along with Line-Group Painted pottery in late EB I.

3. *Line-Group Painted Ware* (= LGPW, or Proto-Urban B) (fig. 7:45, 46, 50) is marked by groups of parallel lines painted in red or brown over the natural clay surface of bowls and amphoriskoi. Under the rubric "B tradition," Schaub (1982) has included other forms, whether painted or not. LGPW was most frequent in the central highlands and in the south. At Arad it appears in Stratum IV, firmly dated to late EB I and Dynasty 0 in

Egypt, and is clearly later than the Chalcolithic pottery of Stratum V. Stratified tell and tomb deposits from Jericho, where LGPW does not begin before Phase 0, and from Bâb edh-Dhrâᶜ, where it does not appear before EB IB, indicate that an earlier phase of EB I, characterized by GBW, RBW, and ISW (= Impressed-Slashed Ware) as well as ceramics and lithics typical of Gerzean Egypt, as found, for example, in Wadi Ghazzeh Site H, preceded LGPW. Perhaps the "broad-stripe" painted pottery, well known from loop-handled cups and white-slipped store jars, also began somewhat earlier (Lapp 1970; Schaub 1981a:77–78).

The line-group decoration was obviously patterned after basketry and wickerwork (fig. 7:46, 50), such as the multiple-stranded, plaited cordage from EB Bâb edh-Dhrâᶜ (Adovasio and Andrews 1982:60–62 and fig. 3).

4. *Impressed-Slashed Ware* (= ISW, or Proto-Urban D or "Umm Hammad" Ware) (fig. 7:70–74; Glueck 1951:318–29, 505–11, pls. 156–62; Helms 1984; Ussishkin 1961:19–20, figs. 40–51; Miroschedji 1971:38–40, and fig. 14) is characterized by relief decoration on large jars produced by finger indentations on rims in "piecrust" style and on raised bands and by diagonal slashes on rims, necks, and raised bands. This decoration occurs mainly on pithoi, holemouths, and grooved-rim bowls with thickened rim interior, and short-necked, wide-mouthed jars with everted rims. The ware is frequently found in association with corrugated ear handles, grooved loop handles, sometimes corrugated, and spaced conoid projections, often upright, on the shoulders of large jars. Painting is rare or absent in these contexts, and burnishing sometimes occurs on vessels with orange, red, or brown slip, less commonly on white slip.

ISW appears mainly in central and southern Palestine and Transjordan: on the coast at Azor, Installation C; in the central highlands at Tell Farᶜah (N) in de Vaux's "Chalcolithique supérieur"; in the Jordan Valley at Tell Umm Hammad esh-Sherqi and Tell Abu Alayik; on the Kataret es-Samra Plateau; in the Shephelah at Lachish ("North-West Settlement"), Gath Guvrin, and Areini XII–VIII (?); in the Wadi Ghazzeh at Site H; and near Gaza at Taur Ikhbeineh. This ware may be closely related to or identical with some of the impressed and incised ware from Bâb edh-Dhrâᶜ in EB IA and from Beth Shan. Its domestic character has been stressed by Miroschedji (1971) and Leonard (1983). This should not obscure, however, its chronological priority, since both domestic and funerary deposits were found at Jericho, and the nearby Tell Abu Alayik phase of occupation is quite different and antecedent.

ISW has clear affinities with Chalcolithic pottery, especially that from the Golan (Epstein 1978a, 1978b; Amiran 1977; Helms 1986, 1987). However, because of its association with Canaanean blades, slipped and burnished pottery, grooved loop handles, and sometimes Esdraelon Ware as at Tell Farʿah (N), Tell Umm Hammad esh-Sherqi, and Tell Abu Alayik, ISW should herald the earliest phase of EB I in Palestine (cf. Phase I, excluding Ghassul IV A and B, in Miroschedji 1971:74, fig. 19; Gophna 1974); at Tell Farʿah [N] de Vaux's "Chalcolithique" usually corresponds to our early EB I.

Assuming that Palestine was too small an area for contemporary but very different cultural provinces, Albright, followed by Wright (1937), originally considered Esdraelon Ware to be post-Ghassulian and pre-EB I; in Wright's terminology, "Late Chalcolithic." Albright persisted in this opinion (1965); but Wright (1958) changed his mind on the basis of the Tell Farʿah (N) tomb assemblages, in which GBW and RBW were found together with line-group and net-painted pottery. Wright then concluded that Esdraelon Ware belonged with EB I and subdivided the period into three phases: EB IA, his Late Chalcolithic of 1937; IB, his EB Ia of 1937; and IC, his EB Ib of 1937. He thus distributed his four types of Esdraelon Ware throughout the period (for a critique, see Lapp 1968a, 1970).

Because Kenyon found Proto-Urban A and B together with a little C in the Jericho tomb deposits, she concluded that these pottery groups were more or less contemporary (Kenyon 1960:7–9), each group representing a different ethnic or tribal element that congregated around the oasis of Jericho and other centers in Palestine, such as Tell Farʿah (N). According to Kenyon, these newcomers had little in common with their Chalcolithic predecessors.

De Vaux (1970:531–37, 1971:211–12) and Perrot (1968) thought that RBW and GBW of the north overlapped in time with the final Ghassul-Beersheba horizon in the south. Thus GBW and RBW should be classified as "Chalcolithic." According to de Vaux the real Early Bronze Age did not begin until the painted pottery of Proto-Urban B was introduced in the central highlands. Before that time there was nothing that corresponded with what we would call "early EB I" in the south.

M. Dothan (1971), on the other hand, viewed the south as having a gap in occupation after the demise of the Ghassul-Beersheba cultures, while in the north, remnants of this late Chalcolithic culture survived and were augmented with Esdraelon newcomers.

In the periodization that follows, we propose an early EB I culture in the south, heretofore either dimly perceived or completely unrecognized, which would obviate the need for a temporal overlap of the southern Chalcolithic facies with northern Esdraelon or for an occupational hiatus in the south, when the Esdraelon culture was beginning to flourish in the north. (For recent proposals suggesting an equally "long" EB I period, ca. 3500–3100 B.C., see Hanbury-Tenison 1986, and Moorey 1987.)

Early EB I (North)

In very limited exposures at the basal layers of Megiddo XX, Beth Shan XVIII–XVI, and Beth Yerah in the north and as far south as Tell Farʿah (N), the architectural sequence from small circular huts, or *fond de cabane* in the lower levels, to rectilinear and apsidal buildings, in later levels of EB I, is repeated (de Vaux 1961:564–65).

At Beth Yerah, where no Chalcolithic remains were found, the circle-hut phase is characterized by the introduction of GBW and RBW, including knobbed bowls. In the same phase an early form of Grain-Wash Ware appears (Kantor, pers. comm.), followed in the apsidal phase by classic Grain-Wash Ware, introduced in Beth Shan XVI and so-called because the surface of holemouth jars, pithoi, and vats were brushed with a thin red, brown, or black slip, which resembles the texture of stained wood. Although Grain-Wash Ware is extremely rare in the south, it appears at Jericho Square III–IV, Phase N, along with LGPW during the period when an apsidal building was still in use, and pillar-handled store jars were introduced there (see Beth Shan XVI, Megiddo XIX, Areini VI, and fig. 10).

The circular hut phase in the south is present, along with early EB I deposits, at Areini XII (Yeivin 1975:96), Tell el-Hesi (Toombs 1974:31, pl. 5B), Gath-Guvrin (Perrot 1962), and Azor Installation C (Ussishkin 1961:19–20).

In addition to apsidal buildings found at Megiddo Stage IV, Beth Shan XVI, Beth Yerah, and Jericho Phase Q–M (Hennessy 1967:6–9), a new ellipsoidal-type dwelling has recently been discovered in lower Galilee at Yiftahel. Perhaps the partially preserved "apsidal" houses at Meser II were also ellipsoidal (cf. Dothan 1959: figs. 2, 4). The ellipsoidal dwellings of Yiftahel, some 15 m long, with several floors containing GBW, provide an architectural link with the "énéolithique" settlement of Dakerman, south of Sidon (Braun 1983:12–14, 1985–86). The many ellipsoidal buildings, surrounded by an undulating outer wall, at Dakerman resemble "énéolithique final" structures from Byblos farther up the coast (de Contenson 1982; Dunand 1973: pl. 132:1–2, Building 46–18). This phase at Byblos, with its mother-of-pearl pendants from the Red Sea, basket-handled jars, carinated bowls, silver earrings (see Ben-Tor 1975:27–29), and an ivory fiddle figurine (Dunand 1973: figs. 196, 162, 152–53, and frontispiece and pl. 162, respectively), corresponds generally to EB I in Palestine and Amuq F in Syria.

During the apsidal/ellipsoidal phase in the north, utilitarian copper implements, especially adzes and axheads, had become a feature of the tool kits at Meser II, Beth Shan XVI, and Yiftahel.

Although many more details concerning this phase of architecture must await further publication, we would tentatively compare it with the early to mid-EB I sequence in the south of Palestine. Apsidal architecture occurs at about the same time in Troy I in Anatolia and has a long history in the Aegean world (Sinos 1971).

Early EB I (South)

Cave dwellings at Lachish in the "North-West Settlement" in Area 1500, circular huts and other occupation at Azor Installation C and "Crevasse B," and Areini XII–VIII?, rectangular mud-brick houses with a curved corner at Wadi Ghazzeh Site H, surface occupation at Taur Ikhbeineh, and communal shaft tombs at Bâb edh-Dhrâ𝑐 in EB IA currently comprise early EB I deposits in the south. ISW, GBW, RBW, and circle-hut architecture link this culture chronologically to the north. Imported and locally made Egyptian pottery connect it with Gerzean Egypt, and especially with the Deltaic entrepôt at Maadi (Kantor, chap. 1, this vol.). Connections with Protoliterate Mesopotamia and Elam can be made through the eastern entrepôt of Jawa in the basalt desert of Jordan (fig. 7:87). However, the other few but vital chronological links with the East in late EB I, such as cylinder seals (see the Gezer impression, fig. 7:65), did not arrive through direct trade or diffusion but were mediated via Egypt. Consequently, the search for Sumerian stimuli which led to state formation in EB II Palestine as well as its city-state religion seems misdirected.

The best stratigraphic evidence for distinguishing early from late Early Bronze I in the south comes from the huge cemeteries of Bâb edh-Dhrâ𝑐, which span the EB I–IV periods and, except for EB IA, have contemporary settlement stratigraphy on the mound. The tomb and occupational sequences first outlined by Lapp (1968b, 1970) have been considerably refined and augmented during subsequent excavations by Rast and Schaub (1978, 1980, 1981).

From the Bâb edh-Dhrâ𝑐 tomb sequence, it is now possible to place the Proto-Urban A, B, and C tombs of Jericho in proper chronological perspective. The earliest Proto-Urban A tomb (A 94) belongs not at the beginning, but midway, in the EB I period (Schaub 1981). Prior to the earliest EB occupation at Jericho, the "Esdraelon" enclave 2 km to the south at Tell Abu Alayik was established, with its GBW, ISW, and grooved loop handles (Pritchard 1958; Miroschedji 1971:59).

Contemporary with the EB IA pastoralists at Bâb edh-Dhrâ𝑐 were the Lachish cave dwellers, who, as Tufnell (1958:29–30) correctly recognized, shared a common ceramic tradition with the inhabitants of Site H in the Wadi Ghazzeh, now known to have occupied a settlement extending over 5 ha, one of the largest of this period (Gophna 1976a).

From his prescient analysis of surveyed and partially excavated sites in the Wadi Ghazzeh, MacDonald (1932) concluded that Site H was the latest in the sequence of mainly Chalcolithic settlements there. This has been confirmed by the absence at Site H of such distinctive Ghassul-Beersheba type fossils as cornets and churns and the presence of red- and brown-burnished wares, which place Site H early in EB I.

That Site H, however, should not begin too much later than the end of the Ghassul-Beersheba horizon is evident from the presence of straight-handled spoons, fiddle figurines, and piecrust rims (MacDonald 1932: pls. 31–37, lower right). The LGPW of late EB I has not yet appeared, but Canaanean flint blade segments have. Canaanean blades appear only in Early Bronze Age Palestine (Rosen 1983).

Imported or locally made Egyptian pottery in the form of Polished Red Ware (e.g., MacDonald 1932: pl. 36, lower register, upper right, with rouletting) and small drop pots (MacDonald 1932: pl. 40:44, 59), with parallels at Lachish, Areini, and Taur Ikhbeineh (fig. 7), appear alongside twisted blades and bladelets, known only from contemporary Early Gerzean (= Naqada II a–b) Egypt (Roshwalb 1981:332, 379).

With these several direct connections with Egypt, it is not so surprising to find at Site H the closest ceramic parallels to the long-recognized "Palestinian" pottery at Maadi in the Delta. These include the wide-mouthed jar with loop handles (fig. 7:79 and 6:33), the tall-necked jar with ledge handles (fig. 7:85 and 6:34), and grooved loop handles (see Menghin and Amer 1936: pl. 38:4; Rizkana and Seeher 1987). These pottery types as well as similar copper fishhooks (fig. 7:84) and the chipped stone industry (Rizkana and Seeher 1985) indubitably link Maadi with southern Palestine in the overland trade network, beginning in early EB I (not EB IC, as in Lapp 1970).

Long before Dynasty 0, when the mixed Palestinian and Egyptian settlement at Areini V and the Egyptian outpost at the perennially flowing spring of 𝑐En Besor III were established, it seems likely that Egyptians were already living with Palestinians near this spring at Site H (note the concentration of Egyptian artifacts in Dwelling I, Roshwalb 1981:332).

During this early phase of EB I, the trail of Egyptian imports led north to Gaza (Taur Ikhbeineh; Amiran 1976b: fig. 1) and on to Azor (Perrot 1961: fig. 40:14–15). One branch of this route forked east along the Wadi Ghazzeh to Site H; and another, along the Nahal Lachish to Areini and Lachish (Yeivin 1961: pl. 8: upper right, Stratum IX, lower left, Stratum X; pl. 7: upper, middle, Stratum VIII; Tufnell 1958:274–75, pl. 57:74).

It was probably along this north Sinai coastal route, the "Ways of Horus" and later known as the "Way of the Philistines," that coniferous wood and tree resins, bitumen from the Dead Sea, copper ingots, artifacts, ores probably from Feinan, and the wavy ledge handle first made their way into Egypt.

Middle and Late EB I

Unlike the Chalcolithic period, during EB I settlements proliferated throughout the Mediterranean zone, especially in the foothills and highlands. In Galilee and in the central highlands, on both sides of the Jordan River, recent surveys have revealed numerous new foundations of open agricultural villages and pastoral encampments (Miroschedji 1971; Kochavi 1972; Esse 1982; Ibrahim, Sauer, and Yassine 1976; Schaub 1982). Although the overall size of the population remained the same or even grew during EB II, many of these smaller communities decreased in number as they were taken over by or incorporated into the larger heavily fortified centers of the EB II city-states (Kempinski 1978; Esse 1982).

Beginning with EB I, when the grape and the plow were introduced, Palestine completed its "Mediterranean revolution" in agriculture, during which horticulture, cereals, and sheep and goat husbandry became established as the distinctive triad of its Mediterranean-type economy (Stager 1976, 1985; Amiran, in press).

The fairly rapid transformation from rural late EB I to urban EB II environments can be documented at the excavated sites of Ai from village in Stratum I–II to city in Stratum III, Arad from caves in Stratum IV to city in Stratum III, and Bâb edh-Dhrâ° from tombs in EB IA and from village in EB IB to city in EB II. At these three southern sites, LGPW precedes the standardized pottery of EB II. Along the coast, in the northern Negev and the Shephelah, Egyptian contacts not only continued from early EB I but also intensified in the latter part of the period.

North of Gaza the EB I coastal route has been traced in surveys by Gophna (1978a). This line of ephemeral settlements disappears by EB II. The best example of Egyptian contacts and actual presence during mid to late EB I (= Late Gerzean and Dynasty 0) comes from the Azor tombs, where, according to skeletal evidence, a mixed population of Egyptians and Palestinians was buried (Ben-Tor 1975, 1981). The tomb offerings include stone palettes, Egyptian drop pots, a copper mid-rib dagger with parallels at Naqada, Site H, and Amuq F, and a ripple-flaked knife with an exact parallel at Minshat Abu Omar, a Late Gerzean settlement, near Maadi (see fig. 7:69), which was importing EB I churns similar to those from Azor (Amiran 1985). Comparisons with the one-handled jug with ear handle on the shoulder extend as far

south as Qustul in Nubia (fig. 7:53; see Williams 1980). In Egypt these artifacts date to Late Gerzean. However, it is clear that the *latest* tomb deposits from Azor, containing a "proto-Abydos" jug (fig. 7:52), can be dated no earlier than Dynasty 0 or very late EB I.

The clearest synchronisms with Dynasty 0 in Egypt appear at Arad in Stratum IV, in context with LGPW (Amiran 1965; Amiran and Baumgartel 1969). In addition to a lattice-painted cylindrical jar (fig. 7:62), characteristic of Dynasty 0 through the reign of Ka, a sherd engraved with the *serekh* of Narmer (fig. 7:60) was found. The inventory of late EB I sites in southern Palestine with Dynasty 0 *serekh*s, often accompanied with substantial amounts of Egyptian pottery, continues to grow as at Areini, Ma°ahaz, the Tell Halif terrace, and small Malhata (Amiran, Ilon, and Arnon 1983:82).

Egyptian pottery constitutes almost half of the assemblage in Areini V (Yeivin 1960; Kempinski 1978), which was preceded by many Egyptian imports already in early to middle EB I. Areini, beginning in Stratum VI, would be the earliest fortified city in Palestine, if the very fragmentary preliminary reports can be believed (Yeivin 1960; Ciasca 1962; cf. Weinstein 1985). In a recent reassessment of the stratigraphy of Areini, Brandl (forthcoming) suggests a more plausible date for the fortifications in EB III. Whatever the case, in Areini V, and probably even earlier, there was a sizable Egyptian "colony" living there alongside the local EB I inhabitants. This settlement, perhaps extending over more than 20 ha, must have stood in sharp contrast to the much less developed cave and hut dwellings at neighboring Lachish and Arad (Amiran 1978b:17).

In the Wadi Ghazzeh at °En Besor near Site H, Gophna has excavated a mud-brick building that surely served as an Egyptian outpost in late EB I or at the very beginning of EB II (Gophna 1976a, 1978b, 1980). °En Besor III was sandwiched between EB I, Stratum IV, and EB II, Stratum II, settlements, both characterized by typical local pottery, including Metallic Combed Ware with white lime wash in Stratum II (Gophna 1976a: pl. 1:4–5). Most remarkable, however, was the preeminence of Egyptian artifacts which made up over 90 percent of the assemblage in Stratum III. These finds included bread moulds, flint knives, a bucranium amulet, and cylindrical jars, common in Dynasty 0 (fig. 7). Most important, however, were the dozens of clay sealings impressed with elegantly carved cylinder seals, rich with early Egyptian motifs and designs (e.g., fig. 7:63). Schulman (1976, 1980) has dated these sealings to the reign of Den of mid-Dynasty I or well into EB II, according to our terminology. But this has been done largely on the basis of a dubious attribution of a largely reconstructed incised *serekh* to the reign of Den (Schulman 1976:11, 25, fig. 2). Other scholars have preferred an earlier date for the *serekh* (Mittmann 1981 and Helck 1979, to the reign of Aha; and Kaiser and Dreyer 1982:263–66, in Dyn. 0). An early date for this short-lived site seems more in accord with the style of the bulk of the sealings, the bucranium amulet, which has parallels in an EB I tomb at Tell el-Asawir and in Egypt (figs. 7:68 and 5:54), and the Egyptian pottery, especially the cylindrical jars. This pottery dovetails nicely with the end of the sequence of settlements along the Sinai coastal route.

Claims have been made on the basis of the Narmer palette (Yadin 1955), Areini V (Yeivin 1960, 1963, 1968), ʿEn Besor III (Gophna 1976b, 1978b), and the Sinai coastal sites (Oren 1973, 1979:184–85) that the Egyptians had begun to establish military control over southern Palestine as early as the reign of Narmer (cf., however, Smith 1965, Ward 1969, and Helck 1979). This interpretation has been repeatedly criticized by Amiran (1970d, 1978b, 1985) and evidence against this viewpoint has been marshaled by Ben-Tor (1982). Both scholars make a strong case for viewing the Egyptian presence in Palestine in the context of a commercial rather than a military network. We would support this position, but perhaps allow for a greater degree of Egyptian control over the trade network by the time of Narmer and Aha, when the trading post or "clearing house" found at ʿEn Besor in Stratum III, at a critical junction on the old EB I caravan route, was built.

Whichever interpretation is to be preferred, one should not forget that Palestinian pottery found in Egypt increases during the Late Gerzean phase and then decreases markedly during the subsequent Dynasty 0 period (fig. 6, and Kroeper, forthcoming), at a time when the Egyptian evidence in southern Palestine is most abundant.

EB I: Sinai

Coastal Road

Oren and his survey team have discovered the missing link between Palestine and the Egyptian Delta in a series of more than a hundred EB I small, short-lived campsites located along the north Sinai coast between Gaza and the Suez Canal. These were recognized from sherd scatters, bread moulds, clay ovens, bitumen, copper ore, and implements (Oren 1973:198–205, 1979:183), but were clustered in groups of from five to ten sherd scatters, without any signs of permanent architecture. Located on sand dunes or in depressions, they resemble the present-day pattern of encampment by the Sinai Bedouin and may reflect a similar organization in "tent-groups" or large "families" by their EB I predecessors (see the *nawamis* builders, below and Miroschedji 1976).

At many of these coastal encampments Egyptian pottery outnumbered Palestinian pottery 5:1; while at a few

sites, particularly those east of Wadi el-Arish, Palestinian vessels predominated (Oren 1979:184).

Typical Egyptian pottery from the coastal survey included Polished Red Wares, bread moulds, and cylindrical jars decorated with scallops, lattice painting, single incised bands, and rouletting. Much of this can be firmly fixed in Dynasty 0, but a double falcon *serekh*, incised on a sherd from a wine jar, suggests an even earlier date in EB I (Oren 1979:184, fig. 32; Kaiser and Dreyer's "Horizon A," 1982:263, fig. 14:5).

Most of the Palestinian pottery dates toward the latter part of EB I, when pillar-handled store jars and white-slipped store jars painted with broad vertical stripes were in vogue. Whether occupation along the Sinai coast should be extended as late as the beginning of EB II remains moot. It is not certain, for example, whether a few pieces of metallic red ware should be classified under Red-Polished flasks, in which case they would be EB II, or identified with an EB I form known from the Azor tombs (see Ben-Tor 1975: fig. 6).

Several of the coastal sites yielded copper ore and artifacts. The source of this copper is unknown, although metallurgical analyses have apparently eliminated the south Sinai mines, a copper-producing area in EB II. Perhaps Wadi Feinan, or biblical Punon, Perrot's putative source for Chalcolithic copper, should be considered (Glueck 1970:80–86; Weisgerber and Hauptmann 1988). But wherever the source proves to be, it seems unlikely that the coastal route was active in EB II, when we know that copper ores were coming from south-central Sinai and the Arabah.

South-Central Sinai

Evidence for copper mining in this region does not appear before EB II. That for turquoise extraction and processing is earlier: EB I, in our opinion.

Near Serabit el-Khadim, Beit-Arieh (1980) excavated a "Chalcolithic" settlement, which specialized in turquoise production. Thus far the site is unique. Its inhabitants lived in ellipsoidal houses (see EB I Yiftahel, above). (For their workshops see Beit-Arieh 1980:56–59, fig. 10:14–15.)

Most of the pottery consisted of Palestinian holemouth jars and simple bowls, usually too fragmentary to provide a conclusive date. The same can be said for the supposed "churn" fragments used to date the assemblage to the Chalcolithic period. What is clear is the date of an Egyptian cream-slipped cylindrical jar (Beit-Arieh 1980: fig. 7:14–15, pl. 18:1–2), similar to those from Areini V, which in Egypt cannot be earlier than Dynasty 0, a probable date for the Palestinian pottery as well.

There can be little doubt that the mines in Wadi Maghareh provided the turquoise used in Egyptian jewelry from Badarian times onward (Beit-Arieh 1980:58), but it was not until Dynasty III that they came under the direct supervision of the Egyptians (fig. 9:5).

The only other archaeological evidence for an EB I presence in south-central Sinai comes from the twenty-one *nawamis* fields, or burial grounds, marked by hundreds of aboveground beehive tombs, dated broadly to the fourth millennium.

A few *nawamis* have been excavated (Bar-Yosef et al. 1977, 1983). There was very little pottery. According to the excavators, the *nawamis* builders were a tribally organized society of indigenous pastoralists.

To judge by the number of flint transverse arrowheads in the tomb offerings, these desert tribesmen were also hunters, and such arrowheads have also been found along the EB I coastal route of N. Sinai (Oren 1973:203). This weapon was much more common in Egypt and Nubia than in Palestine, and complete arrows of this type were discovered in early Dynastic tombs. Hunters, holding bows and arrows tipped with transverse arrowheads, are depicted on the Hunter's Palette, a well-known example of Gerzean art (Kantor 1974:248–49 and pl. 211; Yadin 1963:118–19; and Bar-Yosef et al. 1977:76–77).

Bracelets fashioned from the Red Sea mollusk *Lambis truncata* provide further help in dating *nawamis*. *Lambis* bracelets occur already in pre-Dynastic Egypt and then become a very popular ornament in tomb deposits of Dynasty 0 (e.g., at Tarkhan [T. 702], Petrie 1914: pl. 3:8; Bar-Yosef et al. 1977:75–76). In Palestine, *Lambis* bracelets appeared first in the Beersheba region at Abu Matar, Shiqmim, and Gilat in the Chalcolithic (Levy and Alon 1983:135). By EB I they became frequent in the tomb offerings at Tell Far°ah (N) (Tombs 5, 8, and 14), along with typical EB I pottery, fan scrapers, and other shell pendants (de Vaux and Stève 1949: pl. 6; de Vaux 1951: pl. 17). During the EB IA at Bâb edh-Dhrâ°, *Lambis* bracelets were also included in the grave goods (fig. 7).

Later, in EB IB and EB II a unique tomb type appears at Bâb edh-Dhrâ°: the so-called round charnel house, or *tholos*, made of mud-bricks with corbeled walls. These beehive tombs have their exact desert counterparts among the stone-corbeled *nawamis* of the Sinai (see Bâb edh-Dhrâ°, tombs G 1, A 53, and A 56 in Schaub 1981b:62–68, figs. 23:24, 26–27, and in Lapp 1968b, 1968a: pl. 3.) The keyhole plan of Chalcolithic tombs recently excavated near Shiqmim also resembles *nawamis* (Levy and Alon 1982:37–41, figs. 2, 4).

The *nawamis* may span the Chalcolithic and EB I periods. However, the recent attribution of two unpublished Egyptian juglets to Naqada I (Bar Yosef et al. 1983:56) is uncertain and, therefore, should not be used to indicate a clear Chalcolithic date. Amiran (pers. comm.) has examined the vessels and prefers a later date in Naqada I–

II, or EB I. This would also seem to be a more probable date for the raisins found there (Bar Yosef et al. 1983:57), since the grape is nowhere attested in Egypt or the Levant before EB I (Stager 1985).

EB II: Sinai

During the *floruit* of early urban settlement in Palestine and of early dynastic rule in Egypt, new settlements sprang up in the Sinai and Negev deserts in response to developments in these core civilizations. In contrast, however, to the predominance of Egyptian sources for the material culture characterizing the north Sinai coastal encampments of EB I, the arid zone settlements of EB II were indebted mainly to their connections with southern Palestine.

Intensive surveys by Beit-Arieh and others during the past decade have revealed hundreds of these new settlements, a few of which have been excavated. These are located in the granite massif of south-central Sinai, north of St. Catherine's monastery (Beit-Arieh 1974, 1980, 1981a, 1981b); to the west around the Feiran Oasis (Beit-Arieh 1982, 1983); farther north near the oasis of Kadesh-Barnea (Beit-Arieh and Gophna 1976, 1981); in the Negev central highlands and in the southern Arabah (Cohen 1978).

The type site for determining the period when these desert sites flourished is Arad, Strata III–II, that is, EB II, although the precise moment when urban Arad disappeared is a matter of some controversy (Amiran 1978a; cf. Dever 1982).

Exchange networks, linking Arad with the south Sinai settlements, have also been proposed on the basis of ceramic comparisons between the two regions, for example, Red-Polished juglets and "cup-bowls" (fig. 7:31). These links have been further reinforced by petrographic analyses, which indicate the high-necked store jars found in Sinai were imported from the Arad region, whereas holemouth cooking pots came from areas rich in granitic clays, such as south Sinai, the southern Arabah, or Transjordan (Glass, in Amiran 1978b:50; Amiran, Beit-Arieh, and Glass 1973).

Other items procured or produced by the Sinai inhabitants and traded as far north as Arad, more than 300 km away, included fan scrapers on tabular flint and Red Sea shell pendants, beads, and rhomboid spacer beads. More important than this trinket trade, however, were the raw copper and copper products supplied to the Palestinians. The Sinai side of this network is attested by the copper ore, slags, crucibles, tuyeres, stone casting moulds, and copper prills as well as such finished products as copper awls, adzes, and axes (fig. 7:34) found in their desert settlements.

This trade network may also have had an influence on

the Sinai inhabitants whose domestic housing in EB II resembles somewhat the broadroom houses known from many sites in Palestine. Such architectural details as a central pillar for a roof support, benches along the wall interior, and door sockets on the left side of the entrance may suggest southern Palestine and Arad, in particular, as the source of the template, then adapted, with slightly rounded corners, to the building materials available and the family arrangements prevailing in the desert environment (Beit-Arieh 1981b).

These many connections have led to the general consensus that the Sinai settlers were "Canaanite colonists," who came from southern Palestine, many of them directly from Arad to the Sinai in order to exploit the copper resources there (Ben-Tor 1982:8; Beit-Arieh 1974, 1977, 1981b; Amiran, Beit-Arieh, and Glass 1973:197). These prospectors vanished from the Sinai during the "copper bust" at the end of EB II, when Arad and a few other city-states were abandoned.

This interpretation falters, however, when one considers the widespread distribution of comparable EB II settlements in desert areas where copper and turquoise sources did not exist (note Beit-Arieh's dilemma in 1982:155; 1983:47–48).

One key to arid zone settlement appears in the intrasite settlement patterns themselves, especially in their housing arrangements. Rectilinear to curvilinear houses and auxiliary rooms, including animal pens, form a circular or oval "chain" around an open-air courtyard (e.g., Beit-Arieh 1981b, 1982). Again, in layout and orientation these configurations resemble modern Bedouin encampments in the Sinai and elsewhere, and probably reflect the residential patterns of small lineage groups living and working together in the same compounds (for continuities into the EB IV period, see Dever 1985). In addition to their mining activities, the Sinai tribesmen hunted gazelle and mountain goat and herded flocks of desert goat as well as some sheep.

It seems preferable, therefore, to view these people not as outsiders who colonized the desert and adapted very quickly to its constraints, but as part of the indigenous population who adjusted its strategies to the needs of the core areas. When relying more on metal and mineral resources than on their flocks for their livelihood, they settled into more or less permanent quarters which they might have occupied only seasonally, but became, nevertheless, more "visible" to the archaeologist than when they were more mobile and predominantly pastoralist.

During EB II when large quantities of "foreign ware," such as Red-Polished and EB II Painted wares and combed oil jars, were reaching Egypt in Dynasty I, turquoise and especially copper were also in greater demand there than ever before. Nowhere is this increase in wealth and status among the early pharaohs better exemplified

than in the turquoise and gold bracelets from Djer's "tomb" at Abydos and in the huge cache of copper objects in his mastaba at Saqqara (Emery 1949:20–57, pls. 4–6, 8–10). The turquoise and copper were probably produced by the Sinai tribesmen.

Trade with Egypt, however, was most likely not carried on directly between the Egyptian court and the desert merchants. Given the overwhelming Palestinian character of the latter's material culture (fig. 7:30–37), their trade links were to the north. Arad and probably other settlements in southern Palestine served as a "gateway" to the Sinai and to the central and northern areas of Palestine where cereals, olive oil, and wine could be traded for the resources of the Sinai and the Red Sea. The "gate" was slammed shut on these lucrative enterprises in the Sinai, however, when the Egyptians took over direct control of the copper and turquoise mines during Dynasty III (Smith 1965:9; Giveon 1974; Drower 1971:356).

These state-sponsored expeditions to Sinai continued throughout the Old Kingdom until the reign of Pepi II, when decentralization began in Egypt. Under the supervision of the navy, Egyptian mining expeditions included naval officers, scribes, stonecutters, scorpion charmers, coppersmiths, and interpreters (Gardiner, Peet, and Černy 1955:14–15).

Already by Dynasties I and II a few pharaohs recorded skirmishes in the Sinai with the *Setjet* and *Iwntiw* (literally, "pillar-folk"; fig. 9:3, see Helck 1971:13–16; Drower 1971; Edwards 1971:23; and Ben-Tor 1982). Perhaps they were given this name by the Egyptians because of the central pillar that characterized their houses. None of these early encounters seems to have dissuaded the Sinai tribesmen from pursuing their mining activities. However, their independent status changed dramatically after the navy arrived in force, when these same "Asiatics" are shown being smitten by Egyptian kings of Dynasties III and IV in reliefs carved on the spot at the Wadi Maghareh mines (fig. 9:5).

Early Bronze II–III

The continuity and basic unity of EB II–III culture in Palestine has been highlighted by many scholars (e.g., Wright 1937, 1965; Lapp 1970; de Vaux 1971), although the degree of change at the end of EB I and the rapidity with which urbanization advanced throughout the area have been somewhat obscured by faulty periodization caused by the insertion of a spurious phase designated "EB IC" by Americans (Wright 1958; Lapp 1970; Callaway 1972, 1980) and "EB I" by the British (Kenyon 1979; Hennessy 1967). Various assemblages, such as Ai III and a few Bâb edh-Dhrâ' tomb groups, have been assigned to this phase, but most of them belong to the EB II period. Internal typological and stratigraphic evidence alone indicates little or no time for such an intervening phase (Esse 1984; Stager, in Brinkman 1979–80:60–61), and the precise external synchronisms between Egypt and Palestine at the end of Dynasty 0 and EB I (Narmer) and the beginning of Dynasty I and EB II (Djer) allow, at most, for the reign of one king (Aha) during EB IC. Even if the *serekh* from ʿEn Besor III could be attributed to Aha, there are no distinctive local Palestinian wares from that stratum which can be assigned unequivocally to EB I or EB II.

If by periodization we refer to deep change in a society, or to use D. H. Fischer's definition, "how and when to draw the line across the flow of time," we are left with no chronological peg on which to hang EB IC and demarcate systemic change such as occurred in Palestinian society ca. 3150–3100 B.C., during the shift from village to city life. EB IC, then, provides no more basis for a large periodization scheme than that used by Michelet to divide the reign of Louis XIV into two periods: "*avant la fistule, and aprés la fistule*—a great epoch in the history of a great nation, and periodized by a painful anal fistula on the bottom of the man at the top" (Fischer 1970:146).

By these same criteria for detecting deep or systemic change in a society, it could be argued that the appearance of Khirbet Kerak Ware, the leading chronological indicator for EB III, had an insufficient impact on local societies to warrant a major change in periodization, even when we link it to an influx of foreigners into northern Palestine. This is especially clear in southern Palestine, the Negev, and the Sinai, where the virtual absence of Khirbet Kerak Ware, makes it extremely difficult to gauge when EB II ends and EB III begins; however, the local pottery sequence, EB II, EB IIIA and IIIB, is being refined and defined by the excavations at Yarmuth (Miroschedji 1988). Whereas, the post–EB III period, variously designated EB IV, MB I, EB–MB, or "Calciform culture," like EB I, is marked by a decisive shift in settlement patterns throughout the country as ruralization set in.

Early Bronze II heralds the growth of large fortified centers, usually from 5 to 20 ha in area (Gophna 1974)—the largest mean size for settlements in pre-Hellenistic Palestine. The overall size of the settled population reached a peak during EB II–III of perhaps as many as 150,000 people (Broshi and Gophna 1984, computing 250 persons/ha from an inventory of 260 sites)—the largest aggregate prior to the Iron II period. For the first time the major valleys, foothills, and highlands of the Mediterranean zone were cultivated (Stager 1976).

Every major site excavated has a fortification wall (Ross 1980), sometimes of enormous proportions, for example, as at Yarmuth and Tell Farʿah (N), with external bastions of rectangular or semicircular design (cf. fig. 9).

To prevent undermining by erosion or enemy sappers, an earth and chalk *glacis* was sometimes laid up against the base of the fortifications as in Taanach (Lapp 1969), Areini (Ciasca 1962; see Brandl, forthcoming, for possible EB III date), Yarmuth (Ben-Tor 1975 and Miroschedji 1985), Tell Halif (Seger 1983), and Tell el-Hesi (Toombs 1974).

Only a few EB II–III city sites have been extensively excavated: Ai (EB I–III: Marquet-Krause 1949 and Callaway 1972, 1980), Tell Farʿah (N) (de Vaux 1976, for summary and bibliography), Yarmuth (EB II–III: Ben-Tor 1975; Miroschedji 1985, 1988, whose excavations in progress are revealing a formidable EB III city with fortifications standing to a height of 7 m), Numeira (EB III: Coogan 1984), and Arad (Amiran 1970b, 1978b, whose long-term excavations are providing the most spectacular overall view of an EB II city).

Although most of the populace living within the ramparts were involved in agrarian activities, bureaucratic elites also played a dominant role in shaping the community, as seen in the ramparts, central water systems (Ai and Arad), palaces (perhaps Arad), and temples (Ai: Marquet-Krause's "palais" 1949; Wright 1970; Callaway's "Temple A" 1972; Arad: twin-temples, Amiran and Cohen 1978:108, fig. 1; Yarmuth: Miroschedji's "White Building" 1985, 1988). In all of these cases the royal and religious quarters reflect the domestic ones "writ large," in that the broadroom-style house provides the template, best illustrated at Arad, where single- and multiple-house compounds reflect nuclear, extended, and joint family arrangements within walled-off compounds (Amiran 1978b; Marfoe 1980; Stager 1985).

With the advance of urbanism throughout Palestine in EB II, the detached curvilinear buildings of EB I—whether circular huts, apsidal/ellipsoidal buildings, or modified caves—gave way to more standardized, rectangular house forms. This rectilinear module provided an attachable unit for expanding and organizing both public and domestic space more efficiently within a fairly compact urban environment.

The ceramic repertoire develops out of EB I, but displays much less variation than in earlier periods. Grain-Wash Ware, ISW, and GBW disappear, as do forms with trumpet and bent spouts, high loop-handled cups, and omphalos bowls. Pottery types become more uniform, certain storage vessels perhaps even standardized, and are definitely being produced on a larger scale than ever before. Potter's marks appear frequently and may indicate specific workshops and centers of production.

The earliest examples of stone tournettes, the slow potter's wheel, appear in late EB I contexts at Megiddo Stage IV (Engberg and Shipton 1934b:40) and Beth Yerah level II (Mazar [Maisler], Stekelis, and Avi-Yonah 1952:170);

EB II–III tournettes come from Megiddo Stratum XVIII–XV (Loud 1948: pl. 268:1–3) and Tell Farʿah (N) (de Vaux and Stève 1947:405).

For foreign trade and chronological synchronisms in EB II–III, the most important new ceramics are those included under the general rubric "metallic" wares: some red-polished jars and flasks, lattice-burnished jars, and combed store jars. The most outstanding quality of metallic ware is its near impermeability to liquids that results from high-firing techniques achieved through the use of closed kilns, such as the two-chambered updraft kiln discovered at Tell Farʿah (N) (de Vaux 1955:558–63). Combing, slipping, and burnishing the exterior surface of metallic ware vessels also helped reduce their porosity. For wine jars, quartz-tempered clays were preferred over calcium clays because the silicates were more resistant to the effects of acidity (Ben-Tor 1986; note the tempering material found in the potter's workshop at Tell Farʿah [N] in de Vaux and Stève 1948:551; de Vaux 1961:582). Form followed function in the closed vessels used for the long-distance transport of wine, olive oil, and tree resins. The flasks and jars have high, narrow necks, which could have been more easily stoppered than earlier types. Loop-handled store jars were much better suited for loading and stowing on ships than ledge-handled jars (Raban 1980).

Nearly two hundred examples of "foreign ware" have been found in Egyptian tombs of Dynasties I–VI, the vast majority of which were metallic ware types made in Palestine and Syria. These provide invaluable synchronisms with Egypt, which have been recognized for some time and are by now well established (Petrie 1900; Frankfort 1924; Albright 1932:4; Kantor 1942).

The four main categories of "foreign ware" in Egypt are the following:

I. *Red-Polished Ware* (= RPW, so-called "Abydos" Ware) (figs. 10, 11, and 14)
Red- or brown-slipped surface, usually highly burnished, over brown fabric, highly fired. The form is limited to one-handled flasks, small bottles without handles, and small two-handled jars.
A. *One-handled flasks* (fig. 11)
Time range: Palestine and Syria, EB II–III; Egypt, Dynasties I–V.
1. *Rim-to-shoulder handle.* Flat-based flasks have a late EB I "prototype" in Azor (fig. 7:52); somewhat later in early EB II contexts they appear in Palestine at Jericho (fig. 11:8; Kenyon and Hennessy's "EB I") and Bâb edh-Dhrâʿ (fig. 11:10), in Lebanon at Lebea (Tomb 6, fig. 11: 16). When EB II was fully developed, RPW

flasks were widespread in the Levant, from Arad (fig. 11:11) in the south to Byblos (fig. 11:1–2, 5–7), Tell Sukas, and Qaalat er-Rus in the north (Ehrich 1939).

By the time these flasks were being exported to Egypt, some of them already had a small vestigial "handle" attached to the shoulder (e.g., fig. 10, from Djer's tomb; cf. fig. 11:1, 11). Since the earliest Palestinian examples lack such an appendage (see fig. 11:8, 10), perhaps this type of flask was being manufactured even prior to Djer's reign. Already by the reign of Den the Egyptians imitated the one-handled flask in stone (e.g., at Saqqara; Emery 1954:144, fig. 77, Type DD 1; Amiran 1970c:172). The manufacture of stone imitations continued during Dynasties III and later (e.g., Lauer 1939: pls. 17:12, 18:6). Thus far only one RPW flask, with rim-to-shoulder handle, is known from Dynasty II. The latest representation of this type can be seen on reliefs of Sahure in Dynasty V, where a (Byblos?) ship is seen docking, with Asiatics, bears, and one-handled flasks on board (fig. 6:2).

2. *Neck-to-shoulder handle variant.* In the Giza necropolis this flask becomes a popular item in the Dynasties IV–V tombs (fig. 14). The Levantine examples range in date from early EB II (fig. 11:3) through early EB III (Miroschedji 1988: pls. 27:4, 38:12) and do not exactly duplicate the specimens found in Egypt. The time range precludes the use of neck-handled flasks as a precise chronological indicator for "late" EB II or "early" EB III assemblages in Palestine (cf. Amiran 1978a).

Another variant of the single-handled flask appearing in the Giza necropolis has a small band or collar around the neck. In Palestine and Syria collared flasks are known mostly from EB II contexts (see fig. 11:5–6), but this subtype continues into EB III, for example, at Jericho (Tomb A, Garstang 1932: pl. 27:10) and Beth Yerah (Esse 1982: 253–54).

B. *Small bottles without handles* (fig. 11:17)
Time range: Palestine, EB II; Egypt, Dynasty I (Djer-Qaa).
A rare RPW bottle found in EB II contexts only at Jericho (fig. 11:17), Beit Sahur, and

Tell Far'ah (N). In Egypt this type is limited to Dynasty I tombs from Abydos.

C. *Two-handled jars* (fig. 11:14–15)

Time range: Palestine, EB II; Egypt, Dynasty I (Den-Qaa).

A rare RPW jar with two small loop handles on the shoulder limited to EB II in Palestine. Precise parallels to the Egyptian examples have been found at Arad, Str. II (fig. 11:14; and Amiran 1978b:46 and pl. 27:1–4). The type is known from EB Jericho (fig. 11:15) and perhaps from EB II Tell Far'ah (N), if the reconstructed loop handle at the rim is discounted. It was imported into Egypt, probably from southern Palestine, by the time of Den. A larger and possibly related version of the two-handled jar already appears in Djer's tomb (fig. 10:13).

D. *One-handled, wide-mouth flask* (fig. 7:12)

Time range: Palestine-Syria, EB III; Egypt, Dynasty IV.

A fairly rare RPW flask found only in EB III contexts in Palestine, for example at Jericho (Hennessey 1967: pl. 59), and in coastal Syria at Byblos (fig. 7:12). Only one example of this type has been found in Egypt at Medum (fig. 6:4) and was probably imported from Byblos. The Egyptian context is clearly Dynasty IV, not Dynasty III as usually asserted (see Kantor, chap. 1, this vol.). The proper attribution of this vessel to the beginning of Dynasty IV then removes the only "synchronism" supposedly linking Dynasty III with the beginning of EB III in the Levant. It seems preferable to keep Dynasty III contemporary with the latter part of EB II and begin EB III with Dynasty IV.

II. *Deep-Grooved Lattice Burnished Ware*

Time range: Palestine and Syria EB II; Egypt, Dynasty I (probably Djet).

In Palestine deep lattice burnishing occurs on RPW one-handled flasks, in metallic ware(?), at Beth Yerah in EB II contexts (Esse and Hopke, 1986) and at Tell Umm Hammad esh-Sherqi (fig. 7:38; probably EB II). In coastal Syria similar metallic ware flasks appear in Amuq G-H (Braidwood and Braidwood 1960: figs. 217:3–5, 233:11, 272, 288; the Phase "H" examples may be survival sherds from EB II, Phase "G") and at Byblos (fig. 11:5–7; however, there is no adequate description of the ware). Rare examples of this metallic ware import have been recognized in

Egypt at Abydos and Tarkhan in early Dynasty I contexts (fig. 8). The source of this ware could have been either coastal Syria or Palestine in early EB II.

III. *EB II Painted Ware* (or "Light-Faced Painted Ware") (figs. 12, 13)

Time range: Palestine and Syria, EB II; Egypt, Dynasty I (Den-Qaa).

Flaring-rim jars, with loop or vestigial handles, and small one-handled flasks or juglets similar in shape to red-polished ones, painted with brown or red geometric designs, most notably the dotted triangle and lozenge, over a light mat or cream-slipped surface, constitute this small but very important group of vessels.

In Palestine this painted style of pottery is known only from EB II contexts. It is most abundant at Arad, undoubtedly a center of production for the painted jars (fig. 13:12–18; see Amiran 1974b), but probably not for the flasks and juglets. The latter forms occur rarely, at Ai in the central highlands (fig. 13:1), at Jericho in the lower Jordan Valley (fig. 13:2), at Beth Shan (fig. 13:3) and at Beth Yerah (fig. 13:4–5) in the north. A painted sherd comes from the temple area at Megiddo (Dunayevesky and Kempinski 1973). EB II Painted Ware is unknown in Syria, except for a few sherds from Amuq G and possibly H. The Amuq cannot be ruled out completely as a source for some of the painted flasks found in Egypt. EB II Painted Ware has been found in tombs at Saqqara, Abydos, and Abusir el-Meleq, dated to Dynasty I, beginning with the reign of Den.

IV. *Metallic Combed Ware* (= MCW) (figs. 14:6–14, 15, and 6:15)

Time range: Syria and Palestine, EB II–III; Egypt, Dynasties I–VI.

Store jars occur in metallic ware, although this quality is frequently not mentioned in the pottery descriptions, with horizontal combing on the jar exterior done while leather-hard. Usually a multi-toothed instrument was used for this effect. Frequently "pattern combing" was produced by short diagonal strokes with the same tool. The difference between patterned combed oil jars in EB II–III and MB IIA is that the former were handmade and the latter wheelmade.

Combed ware store jars appear on the Syrian coast, in the Orontes Valley, and in northern and southern Palestine. The earliest examples, dating to EB II, are squat and globular (fig. 15:2–3). In

EB III, when combed ware store jars are most abundant, they become more slender and ovoid (e.g., fig. 15:6–7, 9–11).

Contemporary with the EB II jars at Dan in northern Palestine and Lebea in coastal Syria are the Dynasty I examples imported into Egypt (fig. 6:15). Most of MCW found in Egypt was shipped there in the Old Kingdom, especially during Dynasties V–VI, precisely when the bulk of Egyptian royal inscriptions appears at Byblos. The form and reddish brown fabric of the Old Kingdom jars most closely resemble the few whole vessels published from Byblos (see fig. 15:6) and sherds in the Oriental Institute collection from Byblos, the probable source for many of Egypt's MCW imports. Several of the Dynasties IV–VI jars were coated with a thin lime wash, a surface treatment popular in southern Palestine in EB III but found on vessels with lighter colored fabric than those in Egypt. Lime wash is much rarer on combed ware jars in northern Palestine and Syria, but it is found at Byblos and Beth Yerah.

The primary commodity transported in MCW store jars was probably olive oil and tree resins. Combed bowls used in the olive oil separating process were found together with MCW store jars in an EB III oil press excavated at Ras Shamra (Schaeffer 1962:420–24 and figs. 6–13; see Stager 1985). Large combed separator vats (e.g., fig. 15:12–13) made of coarse ware can be found from Ras Shamra in the north to Tell el-Hesi in the south.

Most of the EB cylinder seal impressions (e.g., fig. 15:5, 8) from Palestine occur on combed ware jars and cluster at EB II–III sites in the Jezreel Valley and in Galilee, both centers of olive oil production.

The latest MCW store jars in Egypt date to the reign of Pepi II, ca. 2350–2260, according to Klaus Baer's Old Kingdom chronology (Baer, in Brinkman 1979–80:58–59). This provides the best evidence for dating the end of EB III in Palestine and Syria.

Khirbet Kerak Ware (= KKW) (fig. 7:1–6, 8, 10)

Time range: Palestine, EB III; Syria, EB III (–IV/MB I?).

KKW, named after the type-site Khirbet Kerak, also known as Beth Yerah, south of the Sea of Galilee, is found in abundance in northern Palestine in the Jezreel Valley, the Galilee, and the upper Jordan Valley at such sites as Megiddo, Af-

fula, Beth Shan Strata XII–XI (early), Beth Yerah, Tell Qishyon, Khirbet Quneitra, Qadesh Naphtali, Hazor Strata XX–XIX, and Tell esh-Shunah V.

The assemblage of KKW from northern Palestine bears a striking resemblance to that from the Amuq Phases H–I, where it is known as Red-Black Burnished Ware and when it comprised nearly half of the ceramic repertoire. KKW comprised almost a third of the ceramic yield excavated by the Oriental Institute at Beth Yerah where it continued to appear along with local Palestinian pottery throughout the EB III period (Esse 1982).

Neutron activation analyses suggest that KKW was manufactured locally at the Amuq sites, Beth Yerah, and Hazor (Esse and Hopke, 1986). Beth Shan may also prove to be a local production center. The few examples of KKW found south of the Jezreel Valley were likely interregional trade items. In the north the abundance of KKW, including portable hearths or "andirons," and its manufacture from local clays, strongly suggest that it was migrations of peoples, not trade or diffusion, that brought this alien potting tradition to certain enclaves in Syria and Palestine.

In the Altinova-Elâzig region of Turkey, DFBW and KKW (locally known as Karaz ware) occurred together throughout the Chalcolithic period, with Karaz ware continuing alone in Early Bronze Age deposits. The close association and resemblance of these two wares suggest eastern Anatolia as a center for the more or less continuous production of lustrous wares (Arsebük 1979); the KKW tradition may have ultimately originated in the Kura-Araxes basin of southern Russia. This potting tradition was introduced sporadically in the Levant during the pottery Neolithic, EB I, and EB III periods by new peoples migrating south, usually no farther than the Jezreel Valley.

The exotic "green stone" hammer ax and crescentic axhead (fig. 7:9, 7) may also have been introduced from Anatolia. Less compelling is the architectural comparison frequently made between a granary from Melos and the large public building with circular compartments from Beth Yerah. The most striking parallel to this unique EB III structure comes from Egyptian model granaries with dome-shaped silos found at el-Kab and dated to Dynasty IV (Quibell 1898: pl. 6:2).

The Periodization of International Trade: A Synopsis

In terms of F. Braudel's *la longue durée,* we can recognize some recurrent patterns or trends of trade between Egypt and the Levant during the fifteen hundred years that separated the end of the Chalcolithic from the beginning of the Middle Bronze period.

These patterns are most evident in the alternate use of two important trade routes: (1) the overland trail along the north Sinai coast and farther north, known as the "Ways of Horus" and much later as the "Way of the Philistines"; (2) the sea route from the Nile Delta to coastal Palestine and Syria, which we shall call the "Byblos Run."

As the table at the bottom of this page illustrates, the use of the overland trail correlates with periods of decentralized, often rural, polities, and the use of Mediterranean shipping lanes with periods of state governments (cf. Oren 1979; + = in use, − = not in use).

The reasons for these correlations are fairly straightforward. The small donkey caravans operated by Bedouin families could not compete with the volume, variety, and price of goods delivered by the large merchantmen. However, the initial outlay of capital to build and outfit a fleet required substantial accumulations of wealth. Elite groups with these resources were more likely to arise in more highly stratified, hierarchical societies such as dynastic Egypt and the more prosperous EB II–III Levantine city-states.

Phase IA (Chalcolithic in Palestine; Amratian and Naqada I in Egypt)

Small-scale, sporadic trade began between Egypt and Palestine along the overland trail. Domesticated donkey made its first appearance in the Near East at Beersheba. Olives and dates were first cultivated in Palestine.

Phase IB (EB I in Palestine and coastal Syria; ca. 3500–3100 B.C.; Gerzean–Dynasty 0 and Naqada II–III in Egypt)

Donkey caravaneering intensified between Egypt, Palestine, and coastal Syria, as far north as Byblos (see Amiran 1985: pl. 46:3–4 for EB I donkey figurines laden with panniers; Stager 1985). Small caravans transported copper ores probably from Feinan near the Arabah, bitumen

from the Dead Sea, tree resins and manufactured products, to Egypt from Palestine. The middlemen of this entrepreneurial trade were the Bedouins, who had a mixed material culture derived from Egyptian and Palestinian sources.

The grape was first domesticated in the Levant. Wine and olive oil were introduced into Egypt for the first time. The earliest wood exported from Palestine or Syria to Egypt was small enough to be carried by donkey caravan, whereas the large timbers of Phase II required transportation by ship (see Lucas and Harris 1962:429–48).

As political unification proceeded in Egypt during Dynasty 0 (= Naqada III), the Egyptian presence in coastal and southern Palestine became more pronounced as trading posts like ʿEn Besor III and mercantile colonies such as Areini V and possibly Azor were established.

Egyptian unification at home accompanied by more highly organized trade abroad provided a powerful impetus toward city-state formation in parts of Palestine, the so-called urbanization of EB II (see Esse, forthcoming). The impact, if any, on city-state development in northern Palestine by those who brought Esdraelon culture from farther north remains unclear.

Phase II (EB II in Palestine and coastal Syria; ca. 3100–2650 B.C.; Dynasties I–III in Egypt)

Mediterranean shipping superseded overland transport. Donkey caravans ceased to operate along the coastal road. Alternate overland trails between Palestine and Egypt, if they existed, have not been located.

Eastern Mediterranean shipping can be inferred from the first appearance in Egypt of large coniferous timbers used in Dynasty I tomb construction at Abydos (see Petrie 1900:9–13, 1901:8–10), and from pottery containers designed for sea transport of wine, olive oil, and tree resins to Egypt from Palestine (RPW flasks as in fig. 11:8–15, 17; EB II painted flasks and jars as in fig. 13; combed jars as in fig. 15:3; and pillar-handle jars as in fig. 7:40) and from coastal Syria (RPW flasks as in fig. 11:1–2, 5–7).

A cache of alabaster vessels and a dagger handle, originally from the great temple at Ai, comprised the Egyptian imports preserved in Palestine (fig. 7:21–29). A fragment of a stone bowl bearing the name of the Dynasty II pharaoh Khasekhemy was exported to Byblos, already an active port in Phase II. Although the oldest known sea-

Levant	Chalco-lithic	EB I	EB II	EB III	EB IV/MB I	MB IIA	MB IIB–C 2d Inter. Period ("Hyksos")
Egypt	Amratian	Gerzean Dyn. 0	Dyn. I–III	Dyn. IV–VI	1st Inter. Period	Middle Kingdom	
Overland	+	+	−	−	+	+	−
Sea	−	−	+	+	−	+	+

ports in Palestine date to MB II, it seems unlikely that the week-long journey by ship from the Nile Delta to Byblos was made nonstop. The 1986 excavations of the Leon Levy Expedition to Ashkelon, under the direction of the author, produced the first clear examples of EB II–III pottery, including Metallic Combed Ware, found on the coast of Palestine. This discovery makes Ashkelon a likely candidate for an EB port.

Desert tribesmen at this time no longer functioned as middlemen in Egyptian-Levantine trade. They responded to core area needs, however, by trading copper for pottery and other commodities produced in southern Palestine whence raw and processed copper was transported to Egypt.

Phase III (EB III in Palestine and coastal Syria; ca. 2650–2250 B.C.; Dynasties IV–VI in Egypt)

Byblos became the oil, resin, and timber emporium of the period and the leading seaport of Syria, lending its name to a type of merchantman known as the "Byblos" ship, which transported goods, animals, and people (see fig. 6:2) between Egypt and the Levant. The bulk of MCW oil jars and some, if not all, of the RPW flasks (e.g., fig. 7:12) were imported into Egypt, most probably from Byblos. The reserved-slip flasks (figs. 6:7–8, 7:18) came from farther north in Syro-Cilicia. The large number of Egyptian royal inscriptions found at Byblos suggests some degree of pharaonic control over shipping at both ends of the Byblos Run during the Old Kingdom.

Trade between Palestine and Egypt dropped off sharply during the EB III period. Only one Egyptian import, a drop pot (fig. 7:13), has been found. However, the absence of distinctively Palestinian wares in Egypt, such as those known from Phase II, does not rule out the possibility that some of the MCW with reddish brown fabric and lime wash from northern Palestine and RPW collared flasks might have reached Egypt from Palestine during Phase III. The peoples from the Syro-Anatolian sphere, who brought the Khirbet Kerak culture to northern Palestine, exported none of their wares to Egypt.

Phase IV (EB IV/MB I in Palestine and Syria; ca. 2250–2000 (?) B.C.; First Intermediate period in Egypt)

As city-states disappeared, more and more of the population of Palestine moved into the pastoralist mode, settling in large encampments or villages in the steppe, where they raised sheep and goats and worked in copper

metallurgy for part of the year (Dever 1973, 1980, 1985; cf. Prag 1974, 1985). Settlement throughout the Early Bronze period at Bab edh-Dhrâ' and its environs indicates that the exploitation of Dead Sea resources, such as salt, sulfur, and bitumen, continued during Phase IV.

It is probably not fortuitous that the recent discovery of the first strongly fortified settlement of the EB IV/MB I period is located on the "King's Highway," a major Transjordanian trade route leading to Damascus, at the site of Khirbet Iskander (Richard and Boraas 1988; Dever 1985:27, n. 4).

Donkey caravaneers were now peddling their wares over great distances into Syria and Egypt (cf. fig. 9:6 for such a Middle Kingdom caravan). The north Sinai overland trail was marked once again with encampments that yield not only local Palestinian MB I "calciform" pottery but also, for the first time, Red Sealing-Wax Ware known from Medum in Egypt (E. Oren, pers. comm.).

In Egypt itself this was a time of decentralization designated the First Intermediate period. From a dynastic perspective, conditions there were as lamentable as those mentioned in the "Admonitions of Ipuwer," when oil for embalming and "pine trees for the mummies" were no longer available and when "no one really sails north to Byblos" (see Wilson 1950:441; Lichtheim 1973:152).

Addendum

Since this chapter was written, new data have been published indicating that there was a Mesopotamian mercantile enclave at Tell Fara'in (ancient Buto; Kantor, chap. 1) in the western Nile Delta, established during the Uruk IV/V or Protoliterate B period (contemporary with mid-EB I of Palestine and Late Gerzean/Naqada IIc–d of Egypt), that is, ca. 3300–3200 B.C. Tell Fara'in was probably linked directly by sea to an unknown EB I port in Syro-Cilicia which transhipped goods from Amuq F and from a trading diaspora along the Euphrates, which included such colonies as Jebel Aruda and Habuba Kabira (South), with a home base in southern Mesopotamia or Sumer. This Euphratean-Egyptian maritime trade network was active in the eastern Mediterranean at the same time as the EB I Palestinian-Egyptian caravan network, which served the eastern Delta as well as coastal and southern Palestine. These two trade networks were probably complementary rather than competitive. The position of Buto with a Mesopotamian mercantile enclave connected by sea to Syro-Cilicia is analogous to that of Naucratis, with its Greek trading colony, and its links to the north Syrian port of Al Mina during the Iron Age II and Persian period.

Three

Archaeological and Chronological Problems within the Greater Southwest Asian Arid Zone, 8500–1850 B.C.

Juris Zarins, Southwest Missouri State University

Outline

The Ecology: Some Basic Considerations
The Pre-Pottery and Pottery Neolithic: The Early
  Pastoral Phase

The Cultural Climax: The Chalcolithic–Early Bronze
  Age
Decline and Change: EB IVA–C (2200–1850 B.C.)

Almost two decades have passed since the appearance of *Chronologies in Old World Archaeology* (Ehrich 1965). During the intervening years, our understanding of the Neolithic and the sedentarization process in the Near East has accelerated greatly, and questions about these issues have become evermore sophisticated and complex. During this same period, great strides have been made in a different area of the Middle East—an area that has been neglected, but that nonetheless has always been inextricably linked to our understanding of cultural process in the region. We refer here to human adaptation within the arid zone of the Near East. Due to increased interest within the last two decades, we believe that arid zone archaeology soon will take its place alongside the "Fertile Crescent" in terms of emphasis and study, particularly with reference to pastoralism. (For latest apologia, see Garrard et al. 1985).

We propose a provisional chronological framework for the arid zone covering a time span of slightly less than seven millennia. Since the arid zone today is characterized primarily by the presence of pastoral peoples, we emphasize the archaeological record in relation to possible traces of pastoralism. Recent studies on the question of agriculture and animal domestication have suggested that a trend may well have begun by ca. 10,000 B.P. A major break in the cultural process apparently occurred in the arid zone in the EB IV–MB I period, ca. 1850 B.C., and it is here that we conclude our discussion. In some cases, the material for selected periods is abundant and supported by radiocarbon dates (Henry and Servello 1974; Weinstein 1984). In others, we are struggling to provide an initial assessment of the materials present.

Submitted September 1985

This disparity is due to both politico-historical and ecological reasons, and thus a preliminary report serves as a first step in emphasizing and highlighting the archaeology of the arid zone. It also suggests the direction future research should take.

One of our first problems is to describe the geography of the area. Our first goal in defining the area of study is noting the line between the farming and pastoral zones, the 250 mm isohyet. In geographical studies, a steppe is described as a region that receives 200–350 mm of rainfall and a desert as one that receives less than 150 mm (Clawson, Landsberg, and Alexander 1971:172). This northern dividing line in the "western branch" of the Fertile Crescent applies only to the period of the Neolithic and later.

Following the 250 mm isohyet along its northern path, the demarcation line includes the Negev south of Beersheba, virtually the entire Sinai, and the Arabah rift val-

The author thanks and acknowledges the following persons for their assistance in completing this research. First, Robert Ehrich provided much direction and guidance in the course of researching this topic. David Massey drafted the maps and chart. Specific details from the western zone which have not yet been published were provided by Uzi Avner, B. Kozloff, and Benno Rothenberg. A special mention of thanks to Ofer Bar-Yosef for reading the manuscript, providing many comments and corrections, and adding unpublished radiocarbon dates. For the eastern zone, the author thanks Abdullah H. Masry for providing the opportunity for field work in Saudi Arabia, where many of the ideas expressed here originated. Don Henry, Alison Betts, Svend Helms, and Andrew Garrard provided much valuable information on the eastern zone in Jordan. The manuscript owes much to Marsha Bolstad, who not only avoided the pitfalls of the author's English but revised the manuscript into its current format. To all a grateful thanks. Finally, the author dedicates this research to the memory of Michael B. Rowton, who stimulated the author's interest in prehistoric pastoralism.

ley (Bar-Yosef 1981c:56). We have labeled this our "western" zone. Moving east and north, approximately four-fifths of Jordan, about half of Syria, the western desert of Iraq, and a third of Saudi Arabia constitute the "eastern" sector. To the north, the farthest extent of applicable material is in the Jebel Bishri/Jebel Sinjar area, although generally speaking, the Tigris-Euphrates basin limits the eastern boundaries. The southern borders are very vague and, based on cultural material assigned to the early Neolithic tradition, we suggest a demarcation following the western lava fields of central-western Saudi Arabia, just south of Taif. Similarly, the western boundary is difficult to assess clearly, especially since the Sinai was a traditional land bridge between Africa and Southwest Asia. In certain respects, particularly for 6000–2000 B.C., the Southwest Asian arid zone is merely the eastern arm of the much greater Saharan Neolithic. Questions tangential to our study involve the archaeological materials from the Nile Valley, the Eastern Desert of Egypt, and the Red Sea littorals (see fig. 1).

The Ecology: Some Basic Considerations

The archaeology of the arid zone (see fig. 2) involves some peculiar difficulties which separate it from the study of more fertile areas. Thus the recognition of certain geomorphological and phyto-zoological patterns is of extreme importance. With the exception of the Sinai/Negev, the area is a vast tableland which slopes west to east, draining into the Euphrates basin and the Arabian Gulf. The bulk of the region is extremely arid today, with 80 percent receiving 50–250 mm of rainfall. However, plant life responds not merely to rainfall, but to the type of rainfall, soil type, and dew nights (Zohary 1952:204; Schyfsma 1978; Thompson 1975:1–23). The zone is thus characterized by intermittent wadi flow given to sheet and flash flooding, and by local depressions such as the Dead Sea, Wadi Sirhan, and the Azraq, Jafr, and the Jowf-Sakaka basins. A few sheer, local elevations are present. High points include the Edom Mountains, Midian, Jebel Druze, and the Sinai ranges. Basalt lava fields cover portions of Syria, Jordan, and Saudi Arabia. Thus, the present-day landscape is dominated by features typical of such an arid area: exposed rock formations, abrupt scarps, mesas, and pinnacle rocks with intervening flat-floored wadis filled with detritus, open plains, gravel flats, dune formations, and pans. (For the three major zones of Sinai, see Bar-Yosef 1981c:35.)

The varied topography has a decisive influence on the salinity, moisture, and soil formation, as well as on vegetation. A number of studies have isolated six basic soil classes for the region: hammadas (gravel plains), loess, sand plains/fields, salines such as salt deserts/saline plains/sabkhas, gray calcareous soils, and alluvium (see

Zohary 1952:205–7, and 1962; Clawson, Landsberg, and Alexander 1971). It appears that vegetation useful for grazing animals currently grows only in the wadi bottoms and other drainage areas where there is some accumulation of rainfall runoff from high ground. Other soils with potential for grazing and agriculture occur in areas of derivative basalt (Clawson, Landsberg, and Alexander 1971:172).

Zohary has recognized two major phyto-geographical zones: the Irano-Turanian and the Saharo-Arabian. The majority of archaeological sites fall within the latter and cover three-fourths of our area. The two zones differ from each other in climate, soil, flora, and fauna. The Irano-Turanian is more continental and receives a greater rainfall of over 300 mm. Its soils are gray calcareous, and most of the loess soils fall within this zone. The hammadas are not saline, and the flora is rich in species and genera which are generally lacking in the drier Saharo-Arabian zone. Although vegetation is denser, agriculture is still unreliable and hazardous. By contrast, the Saharo-Arabian zone has usually less than 200 mm of rainfall, typical desert soils, saline hammadas, dune fields, and is floristically poor, with vegetal cover generally under 50 percent of the land surface. (For the list of characteristic plants in these regions, see Zohary 1952:21–114, 1962; Allred 1968:Appendix 2; Baron 1981:table 1.)

Recent reevaluations of the fauna suggest that a complex mixing of Paleartic, Saharo-Arabian, and Ethiopic elements occurred in the arid zone during the mid to late Pleistocene (see Harrison 1964–72; Tchernov 1982:127, fig. 4.7).

The Pre-Pottery and Pottery Neolithic: The Early Pastoral Phase

Toward the end of the ninth millennium B.C., a basic change of life took place with the gradual development of the Neolithic period, which first appeared at such sites as Jericho, Nahal Oren III/II, Mureybet, El Khiam, and Gilgal (see fig. 3). (For Jericho radiocarbon dates and interpretation, see Henry and Servello 1974:37; Weinstein 1984:304, 326–27, 329–31.) According to Kenyon, the earliest phase, the Proto-Neolithic, was succeeded by the Pre-Pottery Neolithic A (PPNA), 8300–7300 B.C., and the later Pre-Pottery Neolithic B (PPNB), 7300–5800 B.C. (For radiocarbon dates and summaries see Henry and Servello 1974; Weinstein 1984:304–5; Bar-Yosef 1980:127–30; Bar-Yosef and Mintz 1979:314ff. For general overviews of the Near Eastern Neolithic see Mellaart 1975; Baron 1981:64; Singh 1974; Redman 1978; Çambel and Braidwood 1980; Braidwood and Braidwood 1982; J. Cauvin 1978.)

The number of PPNA sites, while rare, suggests a basic Natufian tradition with round structures, now developed into well-defined villages. However, at other Natufian sites (Beidha, Abu Hureyra), periods of abandonment separate the Natufian from the PPNB. Increasing population is clearly indicated, and structures such as the Jericho tower suggest a well-coordinated hierarchy. The lithic industry, while of Natufian tradition, is dominated by flaked axes, adzes, sickle blades, blades produced for burins, scrapers, and El Khiam points. Polished axes appear as well as grinding slabs and handstone querns which replace mortars and pestles (Moore 1982:2–9). The question of plant domestication is still an unsettled issue, but the Jericho materials clearly suggest that cultivation was practiced in the PPNA (Hopf 1969; Moore 1982:9; for Abu Hureyra see Moore 1979:66). Animal domestication may have begun by the end of the PPNA (Clutton-Brock 1978; Clutton-Brock and Uerpmann 1974). Moore, in a recent review, has suggested a revision of the Levantine Neolithic, labeling the periods 1–4. His "Archaic Neolithic," periods 1–2, corresponds roughly with the PPNA and PPNB. He suggests that during this period the inhabitants, grouped in large sedentary sites, had an economy based in part on the cultivation of cereals and pulses as well as on gathering wild plants and the selective exploitation of wild animals (Moore 1982:fig. 3).

Having briefly commented on the heartland of the Early Neolithic, we must ask how the sites of the arid region correspond to this development. In the western zone, we note the development of the Harifian industry in the Negev-Sinai. A number of radiocarbon dates from Abu Salem clearly suggest that the sites are contemporary with the Early Neolithic of Palestine. Bar-Yosef suggests that the settlement pattern consisted of larger base camps in the central Negev alternating with smaller seasonal camps. The lithic industry is dominated by the Harif point, but the remainder is essentially a development of the Geometric Kebaran/Natufian (Bar-Yosef 1980:125–26; Moore 1982:9; Marks and Scott 1976:50–55). The type site of Abu Salem is similar in layout to that at Nahal Oren, and Moore regards the Harifian as a variant of the Neolithic 1 complex to the north (Moore 1982:9 and fig. 3). The excavators of the Abu Salem site note the extreme high density of lithic artifacts in selected structures and compare them with the site of Rosh Horesha, a Late Natufian base camp. They conclude that hunting played a large role, with gazelles and wild goats of equal importance; Tchernov observes that gazelles dominate the faunal remains from Gilgal in the north (Tchernov 1980:80). Although it has been debated, cereal exploitation has been suggested based on scarce cereal pollen, ground stone artifacts, cup marks, and a few sickle blades (Bar-Yosef and Mintz 1979:313). However likely this may seem, the excavators stress that a wide-spectrum approach was necessitated until the arrival of

domestic animals (Marks and Scott 1976:59). The issue is further complicated by the presence of sites in the Negev/Sinai which are classified as PPNA, such as Nahal Lavan 108 on the Negev fringes (Noy, Schuldenrein, and Tchernov 1980:69) and the site of Abu Madi in the southern Sinai. At the latter site, a radiocarbon date has been reported (table 1), and the basic microlithic tradition included the El Khiam point (Bar-Yosef 1980:126).

In the eastern zone, the presence of PPNA horizon sites is strictly limited. In the Azraq area, the site of Uweinid 6B/6A has yielded surface projectile points which are of the PPNA type and comparable to Tell Aswad and Mureybit (Garrard and Stanley-Price 1975–77:118; cf. Mortensen 1970:fig. 13a–c; Mellaart 1975:44–45). A similar site may be the stratified locale of Kharaneh 4 which also has tanged points of the PPNA type (Garrard and Stanley-Price 1975–77:120). In the Ras en Naqb area, the site of Jebel Queisa (J24) proved to have a short three-level chronological sequence. A and B were assigned to the Chalcolithic and C to the PPNA Aceramic Neolithic based on diagnostic tanged points of the Mureybit II type (Cauvin's A26 type; see M.-C. Cauvin 1974) and limited numbers of the El Khiam point (Henry 1982:438). Most recently, the site of Wadi el Jilat 7, southwest of Azraq, Waechter's Wadi Dhobai C, may also date in part to the PPNA by virtue of the El Khiam point, microlithic tools, and Ouchtata retouch (Garrard et al. 1985). In both the eastern and western zones this cultural manifestation remains rare, and the relationship of this material to the sedentary culture of the PPNA (Sultanian) Levant is unclear. Little is known in terms of datable sites (see table 1), and the faunal/floral preferences remain tentative. (For dates of the sedentary zone see Mellaart 1975:45; Weinstein 1984:326–31.) It seems debatable that, as suggested by Goldberg and Bar-Yosef (1982:403), the arid zone remained the sole prerogative of the hunters and gatherers to the exclusion of a fledgling change to pastoralism. In terms of the environmental setting, the period including the PPNB was "slightly wetter" for the western region (Goldberg and Bar-Yosef 1982:403 and table 1). We also note the rarity of PPNA horizon sites in contrast with the earlier Epipaleolithic tradition in the arid zone.

The succeeding PPNB culture and period (Moore's Neolithic 2), again in the arid zone, contrasts strongly with the preceding phase (fig. 3; see Moore 1982:14, fig. 8). Sites like Mureybit, Tell Aswad, and Nahal Oren show a strong resurgence, and others which were abandoned in the Natufian such as Abu Hureyra and Beidha were reoccupied. In the Levantine settled zones, sites are large with complex circular structural remains replacing rectilinear types. (For burial customs, see Moore 1982:11; Rollefson 1983; for radiocarbon dates see Mellaart 1975; Henry and Servello 1974; Weinstein 1984.)

The common lithic types diverge from the earlier PPNA types dominated by distinctive tanged arrowheads. Specialization in craft production, long-distance trade in exotics such as turquoise and obsidian (see Perlman and Yellin 1980:84), and the threshhold of ceramics by 6000 B.C. also characterize the period (Moore 1982:15; Bar-Yosef 1980:126–30).

Within the western zone of our arid region, a substantial number of sites have been recorded, and this has allowed some internal chronological work to be developed for the Negev. The Early PPNB, as typified by Nahal Boqer, Nahal Lavan 109 (Noy 1976; Noy and Cohen 1974; Noy et al. n.d.; Bar-Yosef 1981b:226 and fig. 1; Cohen 1979:250–51), may be characterized by projectile points that are tanged, notched, as well as tanged/winged. The Middle PPNB is marked by retouched tangs, as well as by tanged and shouldered points (Mortensen 1970:A6–A7). The Late PPNB, ca. 6500 B.C., represented by Nahal Divshon and Mushabi VI, have points that are pressure-flaked, tanged, shouldered, and leaf-shaped (Mortensen 1970:A14–A16; Bar-Yosef 1981b:221). Radiocarbon dates for the Negev have traditionally been tied to the sequence from Beida (table 1) covering levels VI–II. The dates suggest a basic seventh millennium B.C. development. More recent sites of the PPNB period have furnished additional radiocarbon dates. (See table 1 for dates from Nahal Issaron, Nahal Divshon, Massad Mazzal.) Finally, future dates from Ain Ghazzal may add considerably to our data base (Rollefson 1984).

From an ecological and archaeological standpoint, a number of summary studies have appeared. Simmons (1981:32ff.) suggests that the Negev PPNB sites fall into two major groupings: larger sites with base camp attributes, and more numerous smaller ones, considered "satellites," used principally for hunting. The larger base camp sites, with or without architecture, such as Nahal Divshon, Nahal Boqer, Nitzana, Nahal Issaron, and Masad Mazzal, suggest a significant advance over the preceding periods in sophistication and sedentarization. The smaller sites have a preponderance of specialized projectile points and open fire-pits (Servello 1976). The question of human activity and settlement pattern is crucial in light of the role of wild versus domestic flora and fauna. Simmons has suggested that seasonal transhumance was the norm for the period and that there was no reliance on animal husbandry or food production (Simmons 1981:47). Sites such as Nahal Divshon confirm this assumption, for only wild megafauna have been found (Servello 1976:369). However, it seems difficult to reconcile this view with sites having grinding stones and identified cereal pollen (Baron 1981:65). At Nahal Issaron, Goring-Morris and Gopher suggest that the recovered data from the site, particularly the faunal remains

dominated by *Capra* sp., suggest the development of animal husbandry as well as the practice of hunting (Goring-Morris and Gopher 1983:162). Baron also suggests that both hunting and herding were possible during this period in the Negev (Baron 1981:61).

In the Sinai, a number of sites for the period have been reported. At Kadesh Barnea two PPNB sites lay on terraces above the Wadi el Quderat (Gilead and Goldberg 1976:137). In the jebel massifs of northern Sinai, the smaller satellite sites, as in the Negev, are represented by Mushabi VI and Lagami II. Tanged points of both the Jericho and Amuq types are prevalent. Hunting camps are suggested by the dominance of projectile points and end scrapers and a lack of hoes and sickles (Mintz and Ben Ami 1977:242–43; Bar-Yosef 1981b:222).

In the southern Sinai, PPNB sites tend to be larger and greater in number than those in the north. Sites with PPNB affinities have been reported as far west as the banks of the Bitter Lake on the Suez Canal (Copeland and Hours 1971:17), and a large number seem to cluster in the southern tip of Sinai. There are no PPNB sites in the central Sinai region, including the Tih plateau. The earliest reported southern site was in the Wadi Ahmar (Currelly 1906:229–44; Rothenberg's site no. 590). Recent work has shown that most sites of the period are generally small, under 500 m², and characterized by oval structures built of rock slabs, and often semisubterranean. (For similar construction technique in the MB I period see Cohen and Dever 1978.) Some sites appear to have attached silos with burials. Lithic materials include the well-known projectile points of the tanged and leafed types (Mortensen 1970:A6–A7, A11–A14), and their implements are also present in varying degrees. Ground stone artifacts also are found in varying amounts while shell beads suggest primary sources from the Red Sea. Reported sites to date include Wadi Tbeik, Igrat el Mihad, Wadi Feiran, Wadi Jibba I–II, Jebel Rubshah, Abu Madi I–II, Sheikh Faranje, Tarfat el Kudrin, and Watiyah Pass. (See Goring-Morris and Mintz 1976:138; Bar-Yosef 1981c: 45–47, 1981b:218, 224–26; Goldberg and Bar-Yosef 1982:fig. 19.5.)

For the entire Sinai, we have only one date from Igrat el Mihad (table 1). Based on the Negev subchronology, it appears that many sites belong to the Late PPNB, and analysis of the ecology by Bar-Yosef suggests distinctions between winter and summer camps (1981c:45). The climatic optimum continued throughout the PPNB in the Negev/Sinai. Pollen studies from Currelly's site in the Wadi Ahmar, from Igrat el Mihad, and from Wadi Tbeik suggest the presence of oaks, olives, umbelliferae, and cultivated cereals (Horowitz, quoted in Bar-Yosef 1981a:226).

In a series of reports, Bar-Yosef suggests that the Negev/Sinai PPNB people were hunters and gatherers, but he leaves open the question of ovicaprid domestication. Others have concluded that these sites suggest that pastoralism was practiced (Moore 1982:16; Baron 1981:65). This may have occurred due to the lack of game animals in the region and may be confirmed by the discovery of domestication in the sedentary Levantine zone (Bar-Yosef 1981a:403). We know that many sites report a preponderance of *Capra ibex*, such as at Wadi Tbeik, Igrat el Mihad, and Rothenberg 590, but the difficulties in separating these remains from domestic goat, *Capra aegagrus*, require caution. Perhaps not all remains are those of wild animals. Domestic goat has been identified at Beidha in the PPNB context (Perkins 1966), and possibly the domestic goat was brought south into the Negev/Sinai by PPNB times (Clutton-Brock 1982:131; Uerpmann 1982a, 1982b). Thus in light of the burgeoning sites of the PPNB period in the Negev/Sinai, the initial stages of pastoralism may have already begun by 7000 B.C.

Prior to World War II, we were faced with a profusion of names such as Wualian, Dhobaian, and Kilwan/Horsfieldberg for isolated and not very well understood sites of the arid facies (see fig. 3; Horsfield and Horsfield 1933; Waechter and Seton-Williams 1938; Rhotert 1938; Garrod 1960). During the 1960s it required detailed concentrated work at PPNB sites within the eastern zone to define the nature of the complex. The sequence at Beidha with its corresponding stratigraphy and radiocarbon dates furnishes the backbone of the PPNB complex in the eastern zone (see table 1; Kirkbride 1966). As in the western zone, large "base camps" with stratigraphy, structures, and a wide assortment of cultural materials are now known in the western and eastern Wadi Arabah (Taute 1981; Raikes 1980:53). To the northeast, the discovery of Ain Ghazzal in the Amman area promises another well-stratified PPNB site (Rollefson 1983, 1984). The large base camp sites apparently also continued farther to the southeast. In the Wadi el-Hasa and Wadi Rumm, the sites of Khirbet Hammam (Rollefson and Kafafi 1985), and Ain Abu Nekheleh resemble Beidha (Kirkbride 1978). The southernmost of these camps is located in northwestern Saudi Arabia. Site 200–104, Al Aynah, located by a deflated marsh lake in the Tabuk basin, also has the structural remains and artifacts of a PPNB base camp (Ingraham et al. 1981:67). (Farther to the east, the site of 206–36 in the Kuhayfiyah basin, east of Hail, may also resemble a similar PPNB camp with structures, lithics, mortar holes, and grinding slabs (Parr et al. 1978:39, and pls. 20, 27b–c).

As sedentary sites such as Jericho define the PPNB materials found in the Negev and Sinai, in the east, Beidha and other more recent sites have defined the facies variation of this region. We have no similar site for Jordan, Saudi Arabia, Syria, or Iraq. In the Azraq basin, a number of PPNB sites have either a stratigraphical sequence or large surface concentration (see Garrard and Stanley-Price 1975–77; Garrard 1984:v; Garrard et al. 1985). Recent work at Ain al Assad, within the immediate Azraq Lake, also revealed PPNB material in possible stratification (Layer 2A; see Rollefson 1982:26–27). Work by Betts in a three-season survey and excavation in the eastern "arm" of Jordan have tied together much of the material labeled Wualian/Dhobaian/Kilwan or "burin sites." Working principally along the lava field stretching from Syria to Saudi Arabia, Betts has noted a large number of site assemblages dominated by blade burins on concave truncations (Betts 1982:27ff.). Other lithic material includes the typical PPNB tanged projectile points. Betts has classed her sites in broad structural groupings which we can use to describe a much larger complex covering the entire eastern zone in which stone circles are widely scattered and may even stretch as far south as the Asir in Saudi Arabia. Their specific and sole association with the PPNB is, of course, debatable (Betts 1984a:29–31, 1984b:78). (For a more complete discussion see the Chalcolithic/EB period below.) Other circle complexes which Betts calls "jellyfish" have interlocking circles and outer defensive walls (Betts 1982:25). Kites, so called because they were discovered by early RAF pilots who saw them from the air, are very common in the eastern zone (for a recent distribution study see Betts 1985:fig. 19). But, again, a direct association with the PPNB is difficult. Several kites found in 1981 may have had broken Amuq PPNB projectile points directly associated (Betts 1983:9–10, 1985:39). In Saudi Arabia, several kites in the northern Wadi Sirhan also had apparently associated PPNB blades and points (Parr et al. 1978:36–37).

The burin sites have not yet been securely dated, although Betts suggests that burins date Syrian sites around Kowm to the second half of the seventh millennium B.C. (Betts 1984a:29, citing M.-C. Cauvin 1981; for similar dates for many of the western zone sites see above). Other recent surveys in southern Jordan have revealed additional burin sites (Rollefson and Frohlich 1982). The southern extent of the PPNB associated with either structures or simple lithic scatters now appears to be in north central Saudi Arabia and includes the previously named Wualian and Kilwan traditions. In 1977, a small site (201–42) was found on a limestone ridge in the Wadi Arar, northeast of Jowf-Sakaka. About 50 m², the site contained the usual lithic forms. The flint is identical with that found at Umm Wual and Dawqira, some 250 km to the north (Parr et al. 1978:36). The typical burin PPNB assemblage occurred also at a smaller site (202–4) possibly associated with a small stone circle at Hadhilul north of Linah (Gilmore, al-Ibrahim, and Murad 1982:13). The easternmost recorded PPNB sites are in the vicinity of Rutba (western Iraq) and lie in the wadi drainage system of the Euphrates basin (Garrod 1960). The most recent discovery of the PPNB burin complex was in the Wadi Hauran drainage northeast of Rutba (Tyraček and Amin 1981:147). Along the northern fringe of the eastern zone, we may note the Kowm materials. Poidebard's aerial survey of this critical region suggests that identifiable architectural remains such as stone circle complexes and kites follow the 250 mm isohyet. The northeastern limit seems to cross the Euphrates in the Jebel Sinjar. A number of sites cluster around the well-known Jebel Bishri (Poidebard 1934). In the Doura basin, we again encounter the typical PPNB burin sites, for example, site 79 (Hanihara and Akazawa 1979:159). (For the Doura Cave excavations into the wadi fan [fan gravel I and II], see Endo et al. 1978:96–97.)

Radiocarbon dates are noticeably lacking for the eastern zone, although recent work by Garrard in the Azraq basin and Betts in eastern Jordan may soon rectify this. For now, we are faced with relying mainly on typological studies and comparisons to the better-dated western zone sites and to the Wadi Arabah in general. Ecologically, climatic amelioration is suggested for the eastern zone based on geomorphological observations within the Doura basin and the isotopic dating of groundwater in eastern Jordan (Lloyd 1980:196, table 1). What little we have in floral/faunal remains suggests some differences from the western zone in exploitative patterns. In the Wadi Arabah itself, at Masad Mazzal, Taute suggests that domestic cattle, hitherto rarely identified in the western zone, were present (Taute 1981:249). (For ecological interpretation of the presence of *Bos primigenius*, see Bökönyi 1982:150; Clutton-Brock 1982:131, 140–41; Uerpmann 1982a.) Bates mentions the dominance of hares and gazelles in the faunal remains from Wadi Dhobai B but does not include either domestic or wild goats. Rock art attributed to the Kilwan period depicts the spearing of ibex, gazelles, and oryx (Rhotert 1938:pls. 10–17). Betts may substantiate the contemporaneity of the burin sites and rock art in several recent excavations at Dhuweila (22/2), and Ibn al Ghazzi (3133) (Betts 1984b, 1985:33ff., and fig. 10; for fauna see Garrard 1985:43–49).

Thus, the PPNB is extremely well represented throughout the arid zone and represents a very large complex both spatially and temporally. The remaining question is one of interrelationship with the Fertile Crescent. It appears that while agriculture was being fully established in the sedentary area by the middle of the seventh millennium B.C., herding or pastoralism based on ovicaprids and bovids(?) was only nascent. However, ibex remains are dominant in the western part, and ibex are shown in rock art in the eastern zone. While hunting and gathering retained its importance, incipient transhumant herding was probably present as people shifted from dependence on wild species to dependence on the same domestic species (from *Capra ibex* to *Capra aegragrus*). (For comment on this transition see Garrard 1985:45.) It also follows that the PPNB represents an interaction between the arid and sedentary zones, thus setting the pattern for later cultures. We should also note that while in the preceding periods the Harifian/Natufian/Hamran and PPNA sites tended to be small or absent, during the PPNB they multiplied dramatically and became larger. (For a similar argument for the settled zone see Hours 1982:427–28.) This change reflects the increase in population brought about by pastoralism.

The succeeding period, the Pottery Neolithic (PN) or Developed Neolithic, can be dated to 5800–3750 B.C. (fig. 3). This period, poorly known in Palestine, is better represented in Syria and Lebanon. Sedentary zone sites such as Abu Hureyra and Bouqras continued after the PPNB but were later abandoned. Initial settlement at Byblos and Tell Judedieh began at this time. In Palestine, the early part of the PN seems absent, although sites such as Jericho, Munhatta, and Shar Hagolan were established later. (For site distribution in Palestine, see Moore 1973:fig. 1; for a recent summary see McConaughy 1979:131–43.) The introduction of ceramics marks this period as distinct from the preceding PPNB, and many sites throughout the Levant appear to have had ceramics shortly after 6000 B.C. (For summaries of vessel types see Mellaart 1975:238–43; Moore 1973:figs. 6–9, 1932:17–20; Bar-Yosef and Mintz 1979:316.) While some carryover from the PPNB lithic tradition continued, the number of types decreased (Moore 1975:figs. 2–4). Buildings tend to be rectilinear with several rooms, and in Palestine pit dwellings are usual (Moore 1973, 1978, 1982). Moore suggests that during the PN, the population abandoned the arid south and the steppelike interior, moving westward almost entirely into the sedentary, coastal Mediterranean zone. It is thought that this was partly because man had become more reliant on domesticated ovicaprids, cattle, pigs, and plant cultivation, and partly because of climatic deterioration which significantly affected the steppe zone (Mellaart 1975:68–69; Moore 1982:25; Baron 1981:65).

Although it seems correct that a greater dichotomy between the settled lands and arid zone occurred at this time, the reasons stated above can be modified by recent work. It seems paradoxical that occupation in the sedentary Levantine zone declined, while in the greater Arabian peninsula many regions appear to have been occupied for the first time since the Middle Paleolithic. For example, the entire eastern Arabian littoral from Kuwait to Oman was settled during 6000–4500 B.C. (see Potts, this vol., chap. 4), and many early sites in southern Arabia and the Yemen belong to this period as well.

Glueck's findings in regard to this period are rather

limited. In Vogel's reevaluation, Pre-Ceramic and PN period materials are simply labeled "flints" or "Neolithic" and thus do not allow for inclusion in the chronology suggested above. (Cf. the southern Jordan survey of MacDonald, Rollefson, and Roller 1982:40–41 for similar problems.) The recent Negev Archaeological Emergency Project recovered and recorded several thousand new sites—1,300 in one six-month period alone. In the western Negev, only a few surface sites of the period have been noted (Bar-Yosef 1981b:227). Most recently, the Wadi Arabah site of Nahal Issaron was found to have three occupation levels, with the PN level (layer B) overlying the PPNB occupation (layer C) and underlying the EB II of layer A. Lithics from the PN level include the typical bifacially worked projectile points with both tanged and winged/leaf-shaped types present. Rare transverse points were also found (Goring-Morris and Gopher 1983:156 and fig. 4). The diagnostic types found in the Negev are named after sites found along the southern Levantine coast. (For range and review see Bar-Yosef and Mintz 1979:315, fig. 8.24; Olami, Burian, and Friedmann 1977:34–47; for a report of excavations of the PN site at Tel Qatif on the Gaza Strip, see Epstein 1984; for its radiocarbon date see table 1). Abundant ground stone was also present at the Nahal Issaron site, although ceramic materials were absent.

The northern Sinai site of Kadesh Barnea 3 belongs to the PN period. Here the excavators located circular structures, silos, fire pits, at least one hearth, and numerous installations that had been dug into the sandy terrace. In addition to the usual stone inventory dominated by pressure-flaked projectile points, a few sherds with large grits were also found (Bar-Yosef 1981b:227–29 and fig. 4). Several similar sites in the Wadi Luzan, although containing architecture, appear to be surface sites only. A date of the late PN or ca. 5000 B.C. is suggested (Bar-Yosef 1981b:228–29, 231). In the southern Sinai, site 383 in the Wadi Zaghara is the only one listed by Rothenberg as associating rough stone circles with projectile points of the PN type (Rothenberg 1970:27). Thus in the western zone, it seems that PN sites are rare and often linked to sedentary occupation. The majority are unaccompanied by ceramics. Tile flint knives and bifacial tanged, winged projectile points are the most representative objects. The relationship of this material to the Elatian of Rothenberg remains enigmatic.

Radiocarbon dates for the period are rare (Weinstein 1984:305, 333–34). For the characteristic projectile point sites of the southern coast, we have the date from Nissanim (table 1) of ca. 5500 B.C. or early PN. The latest comes from Ein el Jarba, Phase IV, ca. 4500 B.C. Two dates associated with the PN layer at Nahal Issaron (table 1) indicate a fairly early date. From site G9 in the Har Harif comes a date of ca. 5000 B.C. (table 1). A final determination from the northern Sinai site of Kadesh Barnea 3 suggests a very early PN of ca. 5800 B.C. (table 1). In addition, little can be deduced from the scarce environmental data. If current data are suggestive, it appears that during the period 5800–4500 B.C. inhospitable ecological conditions predominated in this western zone, particularly in its southern reaches.

In the eastern zone, we have a much more dramatic situation. In the greater Azraq basin survey, a number of sites were defined by the presence of the distinctive tanged projectile points with bifacial pressure-flaking—Azraq 1, 2, 4 ("minute winged arrowheads"), Uweinid 5 (segmented sickle blades), Uweinid 9, Kharaneh 2, and Kharaneh 7 (Garrard and Stanley-Price 1975–77:fig. 2:11–15). The uppermost layer from the spring area at Ain el Assad (2B) revealed points of the Late Neolithic type (Rollefson 1982:26 and fig. 4). Curiously, while this period is well represented in the Azraq basin, material from it has not been reported from the lava area of East Jordan surveyed by Betts (1982, 1984a). However, in northern Saudi Arabia, sites are well known, most often without associated structural remains. In the Mudawwara region stretching south to the Tabuk basin, tanged, winged, and leaf-shaped points are found in small concentrations, occasionally with hearths and with oval structures, as, for example, at Wadi Akhdar and 200–90 in the Tabuk area (Ingraham et al. 1981:67). In the dunes of the Nafud, sites consisted of debitage, small sandstone blocks, fire hearths, calcified rootlets suggestive of weak pedogenesis, and a lithic tradition dominated by the diagnostic projectile points as at site 205–13 (Parr et al. 1978:36). In the southern Nafud, at the lake bed of Jubba, a number of these surface sites were found along the shore at 201–25e–j and 201–27a–b. Characterized by the presence of the tanged and winged points, several of them also produced sherds of a rough handmade, nondescript pottery. Farther to the south, at Majmah, south of the Nafud, clearing impressions on the ground suggest an encampment with hearths and lithics of the type described above, including scrapers, discs, and denticulates (site 207–5; Parr et al. 1978:36). In the Riyadh area, a large number of such sites have been found on lake shores, wadi terraces, sand dunes, and high terraces. A number of small sites yielded hearths and ground stone tools in addition to the usual lithic repertoire dominated by the distinctive projectile points. Imported dentalium and connus shells were also found (Zarins, Rihbini, and Kamal 1982:32). The largest site to date, Thamamah, is on a wadi terrace in the region of the Irq al Banban sands just northeast of Riyadh. This site with a large number of circular stone structures may hold the key to the development of this culture in central Arabia.

In western Arabia, sites of this period are often associated with similar structures and/or tumuli (Zarins et al.

1980:19–20; e.g., 210–49, 210–76A). Additional sites like this are found south of Riyadh in the Khamasin and Wadi Dawasir areas (Zarins et al. 1979:19–21), the most spectacular and best known of which come from the Rub al Khali and are usually associated with lake beds. A number of these have been investigated and suggest that the bifacially knapped points and blades form the nucleus of lithic material (for a recent summary and preliminary typology of the Rub^c al Khali Neolithic, see Edens 1982). The region's obsidian has a southwest Yemen source (Zarins, Murad, and al-Yish 1981:20 and pl. 5c). Hearths and ground stone implements are also very common, but structural remains have yet to be reported. Finally, this cultural phenomenon is also widespread in the Eastern Province of Saudi Arabia (Potts et al. 1978:8, pl. 18; Potts, this volume, chap. 4). We should note here that there seems to be no simple borderline concerning introduction and spread of the "Neolithic" in Arabia. Sites have now been found all the way into southern Yemen (Hermens 1976), the Hadramaut (Crowfoot Payne 1963), and the Red Sea coastal Tihama (Zarins and Zahrani 1985; Zarins and Badr 1986).

Radiocarbon dating and a discussion of the ecological conditions go hand in hand in this region. The weak soil pedogenesis as represented by calcified rootlets in the Nafud sites such as 205–13 suggests a moister environment. At Jubba Lake in the Nafud, a radiocarbon date of ca. 5500 B.C. associated with layer 3 is described as a paleosol or swamp deposit (Garrard, Harvey, and Switsur 1981). The sites in the Riyadh region cluster around lake and wadi deposits (for a typical example see 207–89, Zarins, Rihbini, and Kamal 1982:pl. 34b). In the Wadi Dawasir/Khamasin region south of Riyadh, the reported radiocarbon dates, associated with active lake and stream flow, appear somewhat high (table 1) and may be contaminated by resurgent groundwater. Within broad parameters, however, based on aquifer groundwater studies, it seems clear that a Holocene moist interval persisted in the Nejd from ca. 10,000 to 4500 B.P. (see summary in Zarins et al. 1979; Zarins, Rihbini, and Kamal 1982). This assumption is also supported by a date from the Wadi Luhiy south of Riyadh, a number of Tihama dates, and a long series of dates from the Rub al Khali and Mundafan ranging from 6800–4100 B.C. (table 1). A single date directly associated with cultural materials, but taken on ostrich shell, seems slightly later (table 1). *Bos* sp. remains from the Mundafan lake beds also suggest a moister phase (McClure 1978:262); but the rather limited materials from the Rub al Khali sites themselves only confirm the animal types known from earlier sites in the western zone: abundant gazelles, *Equus* sp., and occasional *Capra* sp. (summarized by Edens 1982:119).

The question that concludes this section centers around the relationship between the settled Levantine sites and the arid zones. As one proceeds south toward the Arabian interior, the sites become more numerous. Did these people inherit incipient herding from the PPNB tradition and practice pastoral nomadism? The distribution of these sites and their relationship to the Fertile Crescent sedentary sites require intense examination (see Mellaart 1975:140–41). Also note that at Umm Dabaghayah, while animal domestication was practiced, it was insignificant as compared with hunting activities (Bökönyi 1973:9–10). Finally, in terms of the cultural sequence, the PN (or perhaps the earlier PPNB) marks the end of an era in the Levantine sequence which began with the Epipaleolithic/Natufian. In the arid zone, however, we tend to see the PPNB as the beginning of an era passing into the PN, but reaching a cultural climax only in the succeeding Chalcolithic-EB period. What seems to be crucial to our understanding is the relationship between the arid zone sites occupied in the PPNB/PN periods and the later ones dubbed Chalcolithic-EB in these same zones.

The Cultural Climax: The Chalcolithic–Early Bronze Age

During the long Chalcolithic–Early Bronze Age period, ca. 3750–2200 B.C., the number of recoverable sites increases dramatically in certain areas, and we suggest that the period represents the climax in the development of early pastoralism (fig. 3). In the settled zones, the Chalcolithic begins in the early fourth millennium B.C. and is widespread in the northern Levant (Epstein 1978). In Syria and Anatolia it bears different names. For our purposes, the Ghassulian of the southern Levant can be subsumed under the term Chalcolithic (Perrot 1968; DeVaux 1970; Moore 1973:65–68). The introduction of smelted copper seems to be an innovation of the period, and the ceramics are distinctive (Baron 1978:152–60; Moore 1973:64; Amiran 1969:22–33). (For the standard lithic repertoire including the characteristic fan scrapers of tabular flint, see Moore 1973:65; McConaughay 1979:170–86; Lee 1973.) The absence of typical PN points should be noted. Footed basalt dishes, shell inlay, ivory carvings, and other exotica constitute other aspects of the culture. Copper, though rare, is known, and the hoard from Nahal Mishmar, for which a number of associated dates are reported (table 1), is noteworthy (Bar-Adon 1980).

In the Chalcolithic there was a great expansion of culture into both western and eastern zones of the arid lands. One of the keys is the Beersheba area and the Wadi Besor, which are marginal to both the northern sedentary zone and the southern arid lands. Large, rich Chalcolithic sites were excavated here during the 1950s—Horvat Beter (Dothan 1959), Tell Abu Matar (Perrot 1955), and Bir es Safadi (Perrot 1959). Similar material was discovered later at Arad in level V (Amiran 1978:4–9). In 1977–79, a survey of 380 km² in this loess area revealed fifty-four settlement sites (Levy and Alon 1983a:107). These distinctive assemblages were labeled the Beersheba culture and seem related to the Ghassulian. (For the distinctive ceramic tradition see Perrot 1955:8–83; de Contenson 1956:163–79, 226–38.) Here, Chalcolithic farming practices differed from the earlier Neolithic fixed plot cultivation as the latter expanded into the foothill zones. Innovative floodwater and runoff irrigation practices became important (Levy and Alon 1983a:107; for Jawa and the eastern zone see Helms 1981:135ff.). It appears that both microcatchments and large-scale diversion systems were in use. Finally, Levy and Alon concluded that during the Chalcolithic, specialized pastoralism developed in areas around nucleated Chalcolithic village settlements in the northern Negev. It seems, then, that pastoralism dependent on sedentary populations developed here in conjunction with specialized farming practices.

Because of inherent difficulties in determining whether sites are Chalcolithic or EB, particularly in the eastern zone, we shall examine some of the basic characteristics of the arid zone as a "pastoral nomad technocomplex," a single entity that covers the period 3750–2200 B.C. (Clarke 1968:338–43). While we have seen that the transition from a hunting and gathering way of life had already begun by the PPNB period, its apparent peak was not reached until this time. Before we examine internal differences with regard to areas and chronology, we shall give a brief summary of the main features of the technocomplex here.

Stone circles are the first characteristic element. As would be expected from such a large area, diversity in type and construction is great, but several basic elements are common to all sites. The circles may be simple or complex, incorporating internal subdivisions and/or external attached lines. They can be part of larger, designed, interlocking structures such as an integrated circle or form very large isolated circles of more than 60 m in diameter. In their smallest configuration they form a "homestead" in which two or three joined circles form the basis of a site. At the other extreme, elements can stretch in one seemingly coherent archaeological site for over 4 km. Individual circles are generally 3–5 m in diameter, with walls composed of from two to ten courses of stone, depending on rock type, state of preservation, and construction technique. With very few of the structures excavated it is difficult to judge absolute wall height, especially since in some cases there is a semisubterranean effect. In the reported examples, wall height has ranged from 70 cm at Nabi Salah or 30 cm at Wadi el Quderat to 1 m at Bir Resisim. In all cases, the stones were laid in a dry-wall technique and vary from being well made to having been hastily built. Vertical slabs

were also used in outer wall construction for the definition of the doorway, threshold, and for internal subdivisions. Stone slabs in the center of the circle suggest a base for a pole or the support of a superstructure. The large adjoining stone walls emanating from the central structure have usually been interpreted as corrals or courtyards where human and/or herding activities took place as part of a larger residence unit.

Tumuli are the second major component of the technocomplex, occurring both as isolated tomb fields and as integral parts of the stone circle complexes. Many tumuli are placed on convenient stone outcrop plateaus where tabular, blocky sandstone or limestone is available for easy construction. In other cases, they are on prominent ridgelines visible for great distances. Their typology can be broken down into several conventional types (see Parr et al. 1978:40). First, simple circular structures built in a dry-wall fashion are common and widespread. Variants in Sinai and Arabia appear to have well-designed doorways with lintels, and weathered examples on occasion reveal an internal rectangular cist grave. Tumuli of a second type often have associated appendages, referred to as "tails" in Saudi Arabia, and can be circular or rectangular in shape. Regardless of shape, the appendages are discrete, often no more than 1 m in diameter or length, and thus form part of a larger straight or curvilinear line often stretching for great distances. Several examined in Saudi Arabia exceed 1 km in length. Numerous explanations have been traditionally attached to the significance of the tail. (For an early descriptive typology in the Negev, see Woolley and Lawrence 1914–15:21–23.)

Perhaps the most spectacular aspect of the technocomplex is the large-scale structures called kites, so named because their configuration appears to most closely resemble a flying kite with a tail. While the earlier evidence suggested that they first occurred in the PPNB, the majority apparently served in the Chalcolithic. For eastern Jordan, Maitland described them as "rose-shaped enclosures connected together by a series of single walls or fan walls" (Maitland 1927:200 and pl. 3). The kite structures with walls over 1,000 m long and with small loops attached to the outside of the "head" were on occasion incorporated in chains or series of attached kites which could be 20 m to 50 km in total length (Rees 1929:397). These structures have been identified on recent pilot maps (e.g., TCP H-5B 1969) and cover a wide area of the eastern arid zone. Poidebard's aerial survey illustrates examples that he calls "enceintes fortifées indigènes" in the area of Dmeyr, northeast of Damascus (Poidebard 1934:pl. XIV), on the jebel tops northeast of Palmyra (Poidebard 1934:pl. LXVIII), in the Jebel Bishri at Oruba south of Kowm, and even east of the Jebel Sinjar and Khabur River across the Euphrates in the vicinity of Al Khan and Haseke (Poidebard 1934:pl. CXL). In the western zone, kites are rare (Thompson 1975:67, site no. 1002.13; Rothenberg 1972:53 and fig. 13; for Sinai examples see Meshel 1974:fig. 12). To the south, numerous kite complexes are known from Saudi Arabia north of the Nafud, but rarer examples come from western Arabia (Ryckmans 1976:162) and central Arabia (205–8 in the Hail area, Parr et al. 1978:pl. 22b). Maitland and Rees suggested that kites were defensive structures used to protect domestic herds (Maitland 1927:202; Rees 1929:395–96), Poidebard that they were defensive forts used by armies and refugee populations to ward off cavalry raids (Poidebard 1934:193), and Helms that they were game traps (1975:36, 1976:19). However, based on the water retention system at Jawa, Helms later thought they were constructed as water and soil traps for increasing potential grass for grazing. The long chains of kites such as at Tulul Ashaqif might be such an attempt (Helms 1976:20 and fig. 14). Rothenberg agreed that they represented game traps (1972:53 and fig. 13). The best evidence marshaled to date by Meshel also suggests that they were game traps (1974:134–35). The differences in kite size and construction details may possibly hint at the hunting of diverse gazelle species (Meshel 1974:139).

A more exotic aspect of this technocomplex includes the "pillars and platforms." Palmer, traversing the Negev in 1871, remarked on "pillars of stone accompanying the cairns and circles" (Palmer 1871:357). These structures, well known from Arad, may symbolize the Hebrew bamah/maṣṣebot idea. The most dramatic of the pillar sites is Rajajil in northern Saudi Arabia where isolated and grouped pillars were found (Parr et al. 1978:pl. 23; Zarins 1979). Similar pillar sites are also reported from Sinai (Rothenberg 1973) and the Negev (Cohen 1979:251; Avner, pers. comm.). These pillars and platforms are not to be confused with the dolmens found in northern and central Jordan and the Golan Heights (Swauger 1966; Epstein 1975). While dolmens may be indirectly related and dated to the Chalcolithic-EB period, they do not appear to form an integral part of the technocomplex described here. Stone-built platforms filled with stones and cleared pavements may also be related to this grouping.

Within the Negev, Glueck was the first to attempt a systematic approach to recording the sites found within the western arid zone (summaries in Glueck 1955a–1958b, 1960, 1965). He described them as cultural entities with assignable periods based on diagnostic ceramic remains (Glueck 1955a:11–22). He recognized the stone circle complexes and described them with their distinctive associated features. At the conclusion of his surveys he had reported over 150 such complexes in the Negev and northern Sinai (for a summary and update by Holladay and Dever, see Vogel 1975). Glueck's pioneering work in the Negev was followed by others including Aharoni (Evenari et al. 1958; Aharoni et al. 1960), Roth-

enberg (1961, 1968), and Kochavi (1963, 1967). Rothenberg's work in particular opened wider horizons. While the sites had hitherto been described as in the central Negev south of Beersheba, Rothenberg located sites in the southern Negev, Wadi Arabah, and the Kadesh-Barnea area (Rothenberg 1961, 1970, 1972). More recently, work has proceeded in the central and southern Sinai (Rothenberg 1970) and northern Sinai (Oren and Gilead 1981). As a result, we know of well over four hundred stone circle sites within the region of the Negev and Sinai (Cohen and Dever 1978:29; Thompson 1974:65, 1975; Beit-Arieh 1984a:35–36). These figures will change markedly with the publication of the Negev Archaeological Emergency Project (see Cohen 1979:250) and the publications of the Sinai investigations. For example, in the Shivta-Nissava area alone, ten Chalcolithic sites without architecture were reported.

The lack of major excavations at these Negev sites has caused confusion as to the specific affinities of many of them. Juli in 1973 (1978:183–86) investigated and tested three stone circle sites in the central Negev: Im Zin, Dahak Zin, and Ramat Zin in the Ein Avdat region near the large wadi of Nahal Zin (for site plans see Juli 1978:191–99). The lithic collection consisted of retouched flakes and blades, end, side and fan scrapers, perforators, notches, denticulates, retouched blades, and abrupt retouched blades (Juli 1978:203–13). The ceramic remains were very limited and highly fragmentary. Since the deposits were very shallow, only a few small bowl fragments were recovered (Juli 1978:213; for microscopic examination by Kozloff see Juli 1978:table 35, pl. 214; for the use of rounded quartz and crushed calcite as in the Arad Chalcolithic samples see Glass 1978:8–9). Based on these characteristics and the fan-shaped tabular flint scrapers, Juli suggested the sites were of the Ghassul-Beersheba tradition of southern Palestine.

Over the last two decades, survey and excavation by Rothenberg in the Wadi Arabah have yielded a number of Chalcolithic sites (Rothenberg 1966, 1968). In the Timna area was a Chalcolithic settlement and evidence that smelting camps (Rothenberg site 29) had already been established by the fourth millennium B.C. Rothenberg's site 42 was classified as a copper mine where copper nodules were extracted by irregular trenching and pitting (Rothenberg 1978:1). The lithic material from site 39, identified as a Chalcolithic smelter, consisted of picks, end/side scrapers, burins, awls, and adzes (Bercovici 1978). These are related to the Ghassul/Beersheba culture and classed as Timnian I (see below; Rothenberg 1978:nn. 23, 30). A concentration of stone circle sites with ceramics and lithics is reported from Yotvata (Rothenberg 1972:51–52). Rothenberg suggests that desert kites from the Nahal Quleb may be contemporaneous (Rothenberg 1972:53–54). Finally, Timna site 200 (the "sanctuary") had several sherds of Chalcolithic type including a holemouth fragment with appliqué (Rothenberg 1978:13).

From the Timna and Eilat areas, stretching westward into the Sinai, Rothenberg (1970:30–31, 1978:fig. 1, 1980:12) identified a number of Chalcolithic sites, with forty-eight listed for the Eilat area alone (1970:fig. 1). Based principally on lithic material, Rothenberg proposed two cultural terms for these sites, the Elatian and Timnian. The earliest phase, the Elatian, he dates to ca. 4500–3500 B.C. (see distribution map of Beit-Arieh 1984a:33 where they are listed as "local culture" sites). Elatian sites occur on both the eastern and western sides of the Tih plateau and in southern Sinai (Rothenberg 1980:112, distribution map). The architectural remains suggest a direct relationship with the earlier PPNB/PN sites of rough stone circle complexes (1980: figs. 17–18). Distinctive elements of the lithic industry are large hand-ax-like choppers, picks, planes, hoes, flakes with the distinctive side-struck bulbs, possible T-shaped implements, and the ubiquitous tabular flint scrapers. Minor components include raclettes, denticulates, and blades (Ronen 1970:30–37 and fig. 45, citing primarily site 372 near Eilat; Kozloff 1974). While the lithic component is well defined, Ronen and Kozloff suggest that ceramics are also present (Ronen 1970:38). However, neither Rothenberg (1980:114) nor Beit-Arieh (1984a:36) mention them. This poses an intriguing question between the well-defined PPNB and the less-well-known PN of the Sinai region. Nevertheless, from sites such as Kadesh Barnea 3, ceramic material from the PN is reported, and with later Chalcolithic ceramics well attested from the Sinai (ca. 3500–3000 B.C.), the question remains as to the ceramic development in the region during the Elatian.

The Timnian, typified by Rothenberg's site 310, Negev/Arabah 39 and 200, is divided into two subperiods of which Timnian I succeeds the Elatian and is described as covering the Late Chalcolithic and continuing into the EB I (ca. 3500–2925 B.C.). Geographically, the sites are reported on both sides of the Tih, but especially in the Eilat range on the east. Sites extend to the edge of the Suez Canal and on the isthmus between the small Bitter Lake and the Gulf of Suez (Rothenberg 1973:31–32, 1980:114–15). Architecturally, the complex continues the basic stone circles of the Elatian with some modification, especially of offshoot corrals (Rothenberg 1980:fig. 19). Lithic material suggests a trend toward smaller flake implements, and the large-tool component found in the Elatian is largely absent. The side-struck element is also rare. Tabular flint scrapers, burins, raclettes, borers, truncated tools, notches, and retouched blades are characteristic (Ronen 1970:38–39; Bercovici 1978:18; Kozloff 1974). The ceramics reported to date from Timnian I exhibit the typical Chalcolithic/EB I

holemouths, lugs, and appliqué decoration (Rothenberg 1970:fig. 9, 1973:23–33). Rothenberg has also suggested that at least some of the Elatian I period ceramics show closer affinities with Egyptian types of the "Proto-Dynastic," or the First Dynasty (Rothenberg 1973:24, 27). Microscopic analysis of certain small vessels from the central Sinai showed them to be made of Nile Valley clay (Rothenberg 1980:114), again suggesting a close relationship to the Archaic period in Egypt (see below). The largest and most compact of the Timnian I sites is no. 688 found in Wadi Fogeiya (Rothenberg 1973:25ff., 1980:117–19 and fig. 22). This site, measuring 100 × 75 m, is a complex of stone circles which also include a number of adjacent tumuli. Rothenberg suggests a Timnian I date based on the presence of Egyptian Nagada II ceramics and lithics (1973:27). Beit-Arieh gives this an EB I date (1984a:39), while Cohen states it belongs to MB I (1983:20).

Mining in the Sinai is also known from at least the late Chalcolithic/Timnian I. At site 688 a quantity of slag, crucible parts, and metallic prills indicates copper casting operations (Rothenberg 1973:27, 1980:114, 138–39). While malachite may have been extracted as early as the PPNB in the Sinai (Rothenberg 1980:138), present evidence suggests that smelting operations had actually begun possibly as early as ca. 3800 B.C. (For the developmental phases of copper smelting see Rothenberg 1980:139; for a comparison with the copper mining and smelting of the Wadi Arabah in the same period see Rothenberg 1978.) Turquoise mines principally in the Maghara area of western Sinai may also have been exploited as early as the PPNB (Rothenberg 1980:138), although the best evidence for concentrated activity comes from the Timnian I period (Rothenberg 1980:114). Site 1105 excavated by Beit-Arieh in the vicinity of Serabit el Khadim has a number of lithic items called blades and hammerstones apparently used to mine turquoise (Beit-Arieh 1980:53 and fig. 10). (For turquoise fragments from the site itself see Beit-Arieh 1980:56, 1984a:44.)

The prominent tumuli of southern Sinai called nawamis, known since the nineteenth century, were examined by Currelly at the turn of the century (Currelly 1906:chaps. 15–18). More recently, a series of tumuli fields has been examined (Goren, pers. comm.; Beit-Arieh 1984a:35). In the Ein Huderah area, twenty-four tombs were investigated during a two-season campaign (Rothenberg's site 388). The excavations suggested that the burials were principally secondary ones (Bar-Yosef et al. 1977:72, 87), similar to burials reported from the Beersheba area (Levy and Alon 1982) and Bab ed Dhra (Frohlich and Ortner 1982). (For skeletal attributes of the burial population and comparisons see P. Smith *apud* Bar Yosef et al. 1977:80–84; Hershkovitz, Kobyliansky, and Arensburg 1982.) Funerary gifts from the tumuli point to certain chronological ties. Shell bracelets suggest a tie with both Egypt and Palestine during the Nagada II/First Dynasty and Chalcolithic/EB I periods. The transverse projectile points and fan scrapers indicate a peak fourth and an early third millennium B.C. date (Bar-Yosef et al. 1977:76–77). In addition, Beit-Arieh states that two juglets from a nawami may belong to a Nagada I/Chalcolithic date ca. 3400–3100 B.C. (1984a:36). Rothenberg assigns the nawamis to the Timnian I period (1980:119–20).

Other features suggestive of the Chalcolithic/Timnian I complex in Sinai are kites, according to Rothenberg, who found Timnian I ceramics and lithics apparently associated with them (Rothenberg 1980:116–17). Pillars and platforms have also been reported from the Sinai as well as from the Negev. At site 676, nine pillars were found, possibly associated with two large enclosures (Rothenberg 1973:21, figs. 7–8). Recent work by Goren reveals packed platforms and cleared rectangular areas as well as pillars (Goren, pers. comm.).

While this sequence of the Elatian and Timnian has been accepted for the Arabah/Sinai, others have seen material from Sinai as being contemporary and related to the Beersheba-Ghassulian. In north Sinai, over one hundred sites without structural remains represent the Chalcolithic (Oren and Gilead 1981). Here again, ceramic material suggests ties with both Palestine and Egypt. One site near Serabit el Khadim is identified as having a distinct Ghassulian complexion (site 1105, Beit-Arieh 1980:45), but Beit-Arieh, on a recent map, shows at least twelve sites in southern Sinai as belonging to the Ghassulian (Beit-Arieh 1984a:33). The ceramic repertoire includes the usual Chalcolithic types (Beit-Arieh 1980:fig. 7). Sherds with distinctive pink clay covered with a burnished cream-colored slip may be Egyptian jars, and have been attributed to early First Dynasty or Late Nagada II and thus contemporary with the Beersheba Ghassulian tradition or with early EB I (Beit-Arieh 1980:50–53 and n. 2). The lithics are perhaps associated with the turquoise mining attributed to the site (Beit-Arieh 1980:35). To what extent this and other sites labeled "Ghassulian Chalcolithic" in the southern Sinai belong to the Timnian I must await further research in classification studies.

Radiocarbon determinations for the western zone during the Chalcolithic are rare (for discussion see Weinstein 1984:305–6, 334–36). A series of dates is available from Nahal Mishmar (table 1) and a few from elsewhere, for example, Shiqmim. We have a series of twenty-one radiocarbon determinations from five carefully examined Timnian sites in the Tih plateau of central Sinai. Two clusters have appeared, one at 5000 B.C. and the other at 3400 B.C. (Kozloff, pers. comm.). For the Elatian, no ceramics have been reported and the lithic material is associated with the Early Chalcolithic ca. 4500–3500 B.C.

Ronen suggests that the material has connection with the Kharga industry of Egypt (Ronen 1970:37), but these ties are quite vague. Current research in the Eastern Desert of Egypt holds promise in linking the Nile Valley, the Arabian coast, and the Sinai during this period. Equally uncertain are the relationships between sites labeled Elatian and the traditional ones dubbed PN at Kadesh Barnea 3, Nahal Issaron, and the like. Some of the radiocarbon dates from the pillar/cultic sites suggest a fifth millennium B.C. and therefore an Elatian date (Avner, pers. comm.), but these have not yet been published. Timnian I is better documented because of Egyptian/Palestinian synchronisms. (For radiocarbon dates from Bir Safadi and Horvat Beter see Baron 1978:162; Weinstein 1984:334.) Ceramics from the Sinai sites suggest close Egyptian ties with the Nagada I = Early Chalcolithic/Timnian I, and Nagada II/First Dynasty = Late Chalcolithic/EB I. At site 1105, Beit-Arieh suggests that the Egyptian jar, which is later than the bulk of the Chalcolithic ceramics, has parallels with the early First Dynasty and Stratum IV at Arad (1980:50–51). (For other references to Nagada II/First Dynasty sherds in southern Sinai see Rothenberg 1973:24ff.)

The paleoecology of the western zone during this period is beginning to receive some attention. The Early Chalcolithic falls within the Atlantic phase, and several researchers have suggested increases in moisture and in vegetation density (Raikes 1967; Neev and Emery 1967; Butzer 1966; Goldberg and Bar-Yosef 1982:403–4; Bintliff 1982:506–7). This evidence is based on Lake Lisan levels, pollen cores, and wadi alluviation associated principally with the Chalcolithic, although some think these conditions persisted well into the EB I period. Others suggest that even with major moisture accumulations, the basic focus of human adaptation in the Negev/Sinai would not have changed. What must be recognized is that the indigenous populations pursued a pastoral life augmented by mining, long-distance trade, and some agriculture. It seems ill advised to insist that structures such as the nawamis could not have been built by local people (Beit-Arieh 1984a:36) or that the stone circles are those of Palestinian pioneers who settled in Sinai (Beit-Arieh 1980:61, 1984b:22). Neither does it seem plausible that people were in the Negev/Sinai for special mining activities only (Amiran, Beit-Arieh, and Glass 1973:197; Rothenberg 1978:2–3) and that these were replaced by "metal-hungry Canaanite intruders" of the EB II period (Rothenberg 1980:150), nor were the local people in fact Israelites creating the first Exodus (Cohen 1983:16).

With regard to human adaptation, we would rather emphasize that the Elatian/Timnian I represents the peak period of a process begun in the Epipaleolithic and accelerated during the PPNB period. Thus, the indigenous populations were more adept at practicing pastoralism, together with some hunting-gathering and agriculture, mining and trading (Bar-Yosef et al. 1977: 87). The people of the Beersheba culture (based on faunal/floral remains from Bir es Safadi and Abu Matar) herded *Capra hircus, Ovis aries, Bos taurus, E. asinus*(?), and *Canis fam.* (Josien 1955:356). The ovicaprids dominated, representing 77 percent of the sample. Domestic crops are also known from Abu Matar (Negbi 1955), Horvat Beter (Zaitschek 1959), and Ghassul (Lee 1973). From the Chalcolithic site 1105 in the Serabit el Khadim area as described above, Tchernov states that ovicaprid remains again dominate with a minor bovid component (quoted in Beit-Arieh 1980:61). Similarly, at the Timnian sites in the Sinai Tih, Kozloff reports excavating goat dung inside stone circles (Kozloff, pers. comm.). From the nawamis at Ein el Hudereh, a *Bos* pelvis bone tablet was reported (Bar-Yosef et al. 1977:78). It seems plausible, then, that the local inhabitants existed principally by herding caprids (Rothenberg 1973:51–54, 1980:114) and that they engaged in copper and turquoise mining, with their principal markets in Egypt.

The transition from the Chalcolithic to the Early Bronze Age in the southern Levant is complicated by a welter of terms that refer to a number of chronological problems (for a summary of conflicting views see Baron 1978:174). Again, because of a major change through EB I–EB IV, as small villages became towns and cities, we see a different relationship between the arid and fertile zones and also possible changes in the ecology of the arid zone itself. The key to the chronology of the western zone is Arad (table 2), with additional material from Bab ed Dhra/Numeira and the crucial dates of the First Dynasty in Egypt (see Callaway and Weinstein 1977:table 4; Derricourt 1971; Hassan 1980; Amiran 1978:119, n. 68). At Arad level V, the Chalcolithic is separated from the EB development by a period of abandonment. Level IV, which is assigned to EB IB, begins a different cultural sequence. The major occupation of the site spans level III (either EB IC or EB II) and level II (Later EB II) (Callaway 1982:71ff.; Amiran 1978, 1965, 1969; for the view that the occupation at Arad spans the EB II–III periods see Cohen 1983:26–28). Level I at Arad is considered a squatters' camp belonging to the end of the First Dynasty or early Second Dynasty ca. 2700 B.C. (For the radiocarbon dates to be used at Arad see table 1; for comments on another relevant site, Tel Esdar, south of Arad, see Cohen 1978.) The chronology and ceramic materials of the southern Levant, and particularly of Arad, have allowed archaeologists to make finer distinctions within the chronological sequence, which are not yet achievable in the arid zones due to a lack of ceramics and/or poorly represented types. (For the EB ceramic chronology in Palestine, see summaries by Kenyon 1979:66ff.; Amiran 1969:41ff.; Baron 1978:176ff.; DeVaux 1971:208ff.).

This period, spanning roughly 3200–2200 B.C., is here dealt with as a unit in the arid zone with the conventional subdivisions integrated into Rothenberg's schema.

Unfortunately, one of the problems with the picture in the Negev/Sinai is the lack of agreement on the nature of settlement within any one given period. For example, the term *Chalcolithic* has often been a catch-all to define vaguely held notions of settlement in the fourth millennium B.C. In the Wadi Arabah surveys, the stone circles are dated to the Chalcolithic by Rothenberg as "Chalcolithic-EB" (1972:51–52). In the Eilat survey, forty-eight sites are listed as Chalcolithic but only four as EB (Rothenberg 1970:30–31). In the central Sinai, Rothenberg suggests that thirty sites belonged to the Chalcolithic, only two to the EB, and three to EB IV (see 1970: figs. 3–4). It appears from these data that a vast population in the Chalcolithic period disappeared from the peninsula during the entire EB period, which ended ca. 2000 B.C. Other scholars have contrasting views. In the Negev at Nahal Boqer, Noy describes the site stratigraphy as PPNB succeeded by EB and MB I, with no Chalcolithic mentioned (Noy 1976:48). In the southern Sinai, the structures are assigned exclusively to the EB II sites in the Serabit el Khadim, Feiran, and St. Catherine's areas (Beit-Arieh 1979:256–57). In discussing the nawamis, Bar-Yosef concludes that they predate EB II and may belong to the very late Chalcolithic and very early EB I periods (Bar-Yosef et al. 1977:87–88). (For another view, which dates the tombs to the EB III period, see Ritter-Kaplan 1979.) Taking Bar-Yosef's statement and Beit-Arieh's conclusions as to the age of the settlements, it seems that no contemporary stone circle settlements can be attributed to the makers of the nawamis. This problem is graphically defined by Beit-Arieh in 1984 maps listing numerous sites for the southern Sinai as "Local Culture site" dated to the fifth–fourth millennia B.C., and only a few as "Chalcolithic" also of the fourth millennium B.C. Fairly numerous EB II sites of 2850–2650 B.C. succeed them. Finally, following a gap of 450 years, a few sites dated 2200–2000 B.C. are classed as MB I (Beit-Arieh 1984a:maps 33, 49). It appears that the answer lies in adapting Rothenberg's proposals. Thus, the Elatian and Timnian I represent cultural phases that smooth over these disjunctures in cultural chronology and allow the archaeologist to see continuous occupation in the region from the fifth millennium B.C. to the end of EB I.

The Negev data gathered by Glueck also illustrate this. He suggested that the bulk of his sites belonged to the MB I period (Glueck 1968:97–101). A 1970 reevaluation by Holladay and Dever confirms this. A compilation of the material in Vogel (1975) shows 11 sites as Chalcolithic, 10 grouped under EB I, 7 under EB II, none under EB III, 25 under EB IV, and a startling 157 under the MB I period. This pattern, of course, is very striking, and we shall discuss the MB I problem in the last section of this study. More recent work has amended this picture considerably. Based on Thompson's compilation (1975:201–5), we class 229 sites as Chalcolithic/EB I, 88 as EB, presumably EB II–III, and 455 as EB IV/MB I. In the latest work in the Negev, it appears that many MB I sites do contain traces of earlier occupation in the EB sequence, often mentioned as EB II (Cohen and Dever 1978:42), but it remains unclear why the ceramics must be placed specifically as EB II when Cohen and Dever (1975), in discussing the Negev, suggest that a "Late Chalcolithic–EB I/II" horizon existed. In the Emergency Survey, Cohen reports that of the 10 Chalcolithic sites in the Shivta/Nissana area of the Negev, 2 sites were also EB I, and 5 sites also yielded EB II sherds. (For the EB II of the Beersheba region, see Cohen 1978:185, n. 4, and 189.) In the Uvda Valley, of some 180 EB sites, about 50 were modified in MB I (Cohen 1979:250–51). With regard to the Negev distribution, Cohen correctly observes that in the south, EB II ceramics continued until the end of the EB period (1983:26).

The excavations at Arad provide the base for the chronological argument already outlined, and also for comparing the ceramic, lithic, and other finds from the Negev/Sinai EB sites. We can thus briefly mention some of the relevant points of comparison. Local ceramics of the EB period are categorized by two studies of stratum IV and III–I. Most are handmade, with some evidence of the use of the wheel on selected types (Amiran 1978:49). The level IV assemblage includes small bowls of various shapes as a popular type, as well as holemouth vessels including deep bowls, jars, and cooking pots. Amphoriskoi, jars with spouts, necked jars with ledge handles, round out the main corpus. From levels III–I, Amiran labels four series that dominate the corpus (Amiran 1978:42ff.). Glass's petrographic analysis suggests that from strata III–II, arkose temper was imported to finish the holemouth globular cooking pots (Glass 1978:48, 50) (for the Sinai origin, see below). Egyptian imports, confined to cylindrical or ovoid sealed jars all from levels IV–II, belong to the First Dynasty (Amiran 1978:51). Subsequent to her final report of the first five seasons, Amiran talks of a vessel with the serekh of Narmer from level IV (Amiran 1974; for the serekh of other First Dynasty examples in southern Canaan, see Yeivin 1960; for the latest discussion, see Schulman and Gophna 1981). The Abydos painted ware examples from Arad belong to the EB II period (Amiran 1978:51–52).

The lithic material from Arad consists of several key types. Fan scrapers of tabular flint with cortex, some with luster, follow the Canaanean type. Scrapers, denticulated and notched tools, retouched flakes and blades, awls, cores, and ground stone celts round out the picture. Since only fan scrapers and blades are present in quantity,

Schick suggests that specialized craftsmen were in charge of production. With sedentarization and the introduction of more copper implements, lithic tools were in permanent decline (Schick 1978:58–63). Copper smelting appeared at Arad in the Chalcolithic period and is well known in the EB levels (Amiran 1978:55ff.; Fuchs 1978:56).

The Sinai gives important synchronisms and archaeological evidence concerning the EB occupation. The transition from the earlier Timnian I to Timnian II took place during this period (Rothenberg and Ordentlich 1979: 234). Timnian I corresponds to both the Late Chalcolithic of Arad V and the EB I of Arad IV. Rothenberg suggests that the end of Timnian I coincides with the subjugation of the Sinai by Hor-Aha (2955–2925 B.C.) and finally Den (2870–2820 B.C.). On the Palermo stone, Djer has a year date labeled the "year of smiting the land of Setjet," probably Sinai, and his tomb at Abydos has yielded turquoise (see Edwards 1971:23). From an ivory docket found at Abydos, Den is shown smiting the kneeling Asiatic with a mace. The inscription says, "the first time of smiting the east(erners)," which may also refer to Sinai (Edwards 1971:27). An ivory baton from the tomb of Qa'a, the last king of the First Dynasty, depicts a captive Asiatic interpreted as a nomad from Sinai (DeVaux 1971:225).

The Timnian II phase, which Rothenberg notes as the final phase, is most often equated with the Nabi Salah site in southern Sinai and is usually interpreted as representing the EB II period (Rothenberg 1980:150–51). However, in accordance with Cohen's caveat, it appears likely that EB II–style ceramics from the southern Levant continued in use throughout the succeeding EB III period. This can be shown at Wadi Mughara, where a number of Egyptian pharaohs left behind inscriptions and stelae recording their activities.

From table 3 we see that Egyptian pharaohs apparently encountered local populations in the Sinai continuously from the Third Dynasty to the end of the Sixth (2686–2181 B.C.) with no real gaps in the evidence. This historical material thus seems to support Cohen's suggestion.

In northern Sinai, of several Timnian II stone circle sites, those at Kadesh Barnea had circular courtyards surrounded by oval or rectangular rooms (Beit-Arieh and Gophna 1976:144 and figs. 3–7). These yielded fragments of holemouth jars (fig. 8), red-slipped juglets, and an Egyptian jar (p. 143). The lithic industry is dominated by fan-shaped tile scrapers, Canaanean blades, and polished black celts (fig. 9). Beit-Arieh suggests that the Negev sites, the northern Sinai material, and the southern Sinai data all point to one large interacting network in the EB II–III (Beit-Arieh and Gophna 1976:148).

From central Sinai, Rothenberg reports similar sites, suggesting that structures tended to become rectangular with attached smaller units (Rothenberg 1980:114; see site N. 691, fig. 20). (For additional sites, see Rothenberg 1973:20.) From southern Sinai, at least fifteen EB II sites are known (Beit-Arieh 1984a:map, pl. 49), continuing the tradition of courtyards surrounded by peripheral units (Beit-Arieh 1974: figs. 3–8, 1981:37ff.). The best known of these is Nabi Salah (Rothenberg survey, N. 380) just north of St. Catherine's. Others include Sheikh Muhsein (Beit-Arieh 1981: figs. 12–13), Watia (fig. 19), Wadi Umm Tumur (fig. 20), and Sheikh 'Awad (figs. 21–23). The ceramic collection, with a majority of parallels with Arad III–I, includes familiar types, some with the potter's mark (Beit-Arieh 1974:fig. 9), and Abydos red-burnished ware (Beit-Arieh 1974:fig. 9, 1983:fig. 3). Fragments of an Egyptian jug duplicate the Arad Egyptian combed jar (Beit-Arieh 1974:151; Amiran 1978: pls. 55–56). Similar ceramic material now comes from other south Sinai sites, including Sheikh Muhsein and Watia Pass (Beit-Arieh and Gophna 1976:148), sites in the Wadi Tamile region near Serabit el Khadim (Beit-Arieh 1979:257), and others in south Sinai (Goring-Morris and Mintz 1976:138). The ceramic material from south Sinai has striking similarities with Arad pottery, and petrographical analyses have shown that arkose-tempered cooking wares in Arad came from south Sinai, and that other small, red-slipped and burnished vessels in south Sinai came from Arad (Rothenberg 1978:14, n. 15; Amiran, Beit-Arieh, and Glass 1973:194–97).

Also from these sites are the well-known tabular flint fan scrapers (Beit-Arieh 1974:pl. 28:1–2; 1983:fig. 4), as well as a small number of blades, arrowheads, and a black diorite ax from Nabi Salah (for other miscellaneous small objects including Red Sea shell varieties, see Beit-Arieh 1974:153, 1983:46).

Copper implements were also abundant. From Nabi Salah came flat axes, picks, square-cut awls, chisels, and other assorted objects (Beit-Arieh 1974:153 and pls. 28:4, 29:1–3; 1983:44). Rothenberg, who has studied extensively the mining activities of the Timnian period, has suggested that the evidence for mining activity comes from the Timna area in northeast Sinai, Wadis Riqeita, Wadi Shellal and Gebel Samra in southern Sinai, and Wadi Nasib/Maghara in western Sinai (Rothenberg 1980:139). Rothenberg believes that during the Timnian I phase, bowl-shaped smelting pits were replaced by stone-lined furnaces. It was not until Timnian II that bellows, tuyeres, and lined furnaces were introduced by Egyptian metal workers. (For examples of Timnian II sites exhibiting these activities, see N. 229 in the Timna Valley and N. 701 in the Wadi Ahmar, Rothenberg 1980:pl. 149.) Turquoise mining seems to have continued at a number of sites (Rothenberg 1980:139).

From the ecological-climatological evidence, the Chalcolithic falls within the Atlantic optimum in the Levant. Concerning the Timnian II or EB II period, it seems that the climatic amelioration continued throughout the period, but that deterioration began by the mid-third millennium B.C. (Butzer 1976:32). Pollen studies in the Negev during both the Atlantic and post-Atlantic suggest that chemopods heavily dominated at the expense of arboreal pollen. Horowitz concludes that through EB II, some summer and mild brief winter rains contributed to a richer vegetation (Horowitz 1980:343). Pollen studies in the Nabi Salah area show a significant percentage of Compositae present, thus supporting the idea that there was a greater rainfall and more moisture in EB II (Beit-Arieh 1983:46).

The inhabitants of the Timnian II period continued the pastoral life of the earlier Elatian/Timnian I. Domestic goats formed the backbone of the economy, and there was apparently some reliance on sheep (Beit-Arieh 1974: 153–54, and n. 5 quoting Hakker). Hunting continued to be important, as suggested by remains of wild goats and gazelles at Nabi Salah (Beit-Arieh 1983:46). Cereal pollen suggests continuing limited farming, a tradition carried on from at least the Natufian (Beit-Arieh 1983:46).

The most difficult aspect of the chronological problems, and for the Negev and Sinai specifically, is that investigators have insisted that Timnian II/EB II sites could be limited to that period alone. Rothenberg states that the end of Timnian II coincides with the demise of the "Nabi Salah phase" and the rise of the Egyptian Third Dynasty: "under the reign of Nebka (ca. 2635–2620 B.C.), the first king of the Third Dynasty, the local Timnian population of Sinai—and their Canaanite guests—finally vanished from the annals of Sinai history" (Rothenberg 1980:151). The question then becomes what to do with a gap of some four hundred years before the appearance of EB IV/MB I sites in the area. We believe that several explanations are possible. First, from the Arad sequence, we agree with Cohen that contrary to currently-held ideas, the ceramics and artifacts identified as solely EB II actually stretch through the EB III period. (For confirmation, see discussion of Bab edh-Dhra below.) This is possible if the Khirbet Kerak culture of Palestine, which dominated the EB III period, did not penetrate south and the local EB II culture of the area continued essentially without interruption (Cohen 1983:26–28). If this is the case, the Glueck evidence for the Negev occupational patterns then covers the EB III period, now seen as a void. In addition, the Nabi Salah sites would thus include both the EB II and EB III periods. This, we believe, is demonstrated by the record of Old Kingdom kings at the Serabit el Khadim site as outlined in table 3. Pharaohs of the Third Dynasty equated to the EB II period are succeeded by those of Dynasties IV–VI, who mention their activities in the Sinai. Thus, in their dealings with local populations, they confirm that the Sinai settlements continued uninterrupted through the EB III and EB IVB periods. In fact, Rothenberg himself finds that despite the end of the "Nabi Salah invasion," the Egyptian pharaohs continued to describe "Bedouin of the East," "local Semitic inhabitants," and "Asian nomads" in the Sinai (Rothenberg 1980:151). Would not these people have left an archaeological record?

The eastern zone during the Chalcolithic/EB period (ca. 3700–2200 B.C.) cannot be as readily divided into subphases as the western. First, there has been less exploration in the area, although recent work, particularly in Jordan and Saudi Arabia, has somewhat alleviated this problem. Second, fewer historical data are available. Mesopotamian cuneiform sources do not mention people of this zone until ca. 2500 B.C. Similarly, Syrian Ebla texts cannot be dated much earlier than 2400 B.C. Third, ceramic remains, particularly from the southern part of the zone, are scarce or unknown. Fourth, critical ecotonal sites similar to Arad remain unreported for much of the eastern zone. Finally, there is a dearth of radiocarbon dates for much of the period.

Two key excavated sites stand out for the eastern zone to date—Jawa in eastern Jordan, and the Bab edh Dhra complex in the Jordanian Ghor. Jawa is the earlier and suggests a bridge between the Palestinian cultures and the lesser-known Syrian sites. Jawa, located in the Harrat Rajil basalt zone (Helms 1975:fig. 1), is a large complex of almost urban proportions, with population estimates for the Late Chalcolithic period ranging from three thousand to five thousand people (Helms 1977:24, 30). Of four phases that Helms recognized at the site, I–III belong to the Ghassulian/Late Chalcolithic and EB I periods and suggest parallels to the Amuq G, Hama K, and Habuba Kebira (Helms 1982:102, and n. 1). The site has a number of components: houses, fortifications, and water installations (for the latest site plan, see Helms 1982:103). The Jawa house plans have a number of features similar to those at Arad, and other parallels with the Negev and Sinai sites are suggested (Helms 1976:10). (For the water installations and parallels to EB Arad, Bab edh Dhra, Jericho, and Ai, see Helms 1982:109ff., 1981:fig. 4.)

The ceramic corpus from Jawa strongly points to both Palestinian and Syrian/Mesopotamian connections. The earliest houses at the site (Helms 1976:12) have Ghassulian-type vessels. Ceramics from the fortification areas suggest parallels to Ghassul, Hama K, and the Amuq F–G (Helms 1975:fig. 13 and pl. 36). A date of 3750–3350 B.C. is offered. Vessels from the later houses point to both Syrian/Mesopotamian and Palestinian Late Chalcolithic EB I examples (Helms 1975:fig. 9, pl. 31; 1976:11 and fig. 8; 1981:B2–B5; for specific parallels, see Helms 1981:table B1). The lithics from Jawa parallel the reported material from Bab edh Dhra (see below), and

include Canaanean blades and the distinctive Ghassul-like tabular flint fan scrapers (Duckworth 1976:31–35; Duckworth, in Helms 1981:229–34). (For Jawa ground stone bowls and mortars, see Duckworth, in Helms 1981:240; Helms 1976:13, 1975:fig. 10.)

The Jordanian southern Ghor complex yields a number of sites that enhance our understanding of the eastern zone, particularly southern Jordan and northwest Saudi Arabia. At Bab edh Dhra, a long-range study has produced the history of a town and cemetery complex beginning in the EB IA period and concluding with the enigmatic EB IV period (Rast and Schaub 1980, 1981, 1984). The earliest occupation of the site was apparently by pastoral people who constructed the first shaft tombs in the EB IA period, ca. 3150–3050 B.C. (Frolich and Ortner 1982:264 for the physical evidence; Rast and Schaub 1980:21, 40; for location of this and four other related EB sites see Rast and Schaub 1980:fig. 1). A small village was built in the succeeding EB IB period (Rast and Schaub 1980:24–31). EB IB shaft tombs at the site are replaced by the EB II–III charnel houses (Rast and Schaub 1980:37ff.) (for EB IV see below).

The ceramic material from Bab edh Dhra cemetery, noteworthy for its complete state and its long sequence, largely confirms our opinion that EB IB–II types continued throughout the EB III period (Schaub 1981:77–78; for the EB IA–II types see Schaub 1981:69–118; also Lapp 1968, Schaub 1973; for parallels from Jericho, see Kenyon 1979:74–75, 109–17). The charnel house A22, of late EB III date, has one Egyptian-type vessel attributed to Dynasties III–VI (Rast and Schaub 1980:39).

The lithic material from Bab edh Dhra includes only a few basic types again characterized by the familiar Ghassulian-like tabular flint fan scrapers (McConaughy 1980:53–58, 1979:41ff.).

These two key sites permit a brief look at the stone circle complexes in the eastern zone. In Henry's survey in the Ras en Naqb area of southern Jordan, some 25 percent of his sites had a "Chalcolithic" component. As in the Sinai, most have a small number of stone circles often accompanied by ash lenses and refuse pits. At J14 (Jebel el Jill) on the terrace complexes of a wadi system, test excavations yielded an archaeological assemblage strongly suggestive of the Timnian I of the Sinai (Henry et al. 1983:15; Henry 1982:443). In light of its location in southern Jordan, this suggestion is probably correct. Surveys in the Ma'an Aqaba area have also reported similar stone circle sites, such as Hebeib el Fala, east of Aqaba (Jobling 1982:201).

Farther to the east in the Azraq basin, identification is more difficult as the small bifacial points are associated with the PN of the Levant and not the Chalcolithic, with perhaps the exception of two dubious ones. Aseikhim 5 is reported to have the tabular flint fan scrapers, a tile flint knife fragment, and a bifacial adze (Garrard and Stanley-Price 1975–77:table 119). Similarly in eastern Jordan, little is known that is attributable to the Jawan period. Although Helms suggests that the countryside around Jawa was inhabited (Helms 1982:102), little has been published on stone circle complexes with associated ceramics and lithics in the region. His suggestion that some of the kite structures were utilized in the Jawan period also remains tentative (Helms 1975:36, citing Rothenberg).

Farther to the south, numerous sites have been found that may date to the fourth–third millennia B.C., although they cannot be placed too precisely within the Chalcolithic/EB framework. One of the most productive areas is the Jowf-Sakaka basin, delimited on the south by the Nafud Desert and on the north by the Wadi Sirhan. First, within the Jowf basin, the most interesting of the sites is the Rajajil complex. Located on a prominent sandstone terrace just south of Sakaka is a complex of standing sandstone pillars. Discrete clusters, ranging from three to nineteen pillars, have approximately thirty-five different combinations (for the site plan, see Parr et al. 1978:pl. 23). Upon examination, the pillars appear to have been originally aligned along a north-south axis facing east. Small, associated structures are also visible on the surface. Excavation of one such complex (no. 18) confirmed the alignment of the original pillars, and it became obvious that the associated structure had been deliberately filled with rock to create a "platform" for the pillars. The excavation also confirmed that these structures were not burial tumuli or habitations (Parr et al. 1978:pl. 24). Found scattered among them on the terrace, not covered by sand, were badly worn and eroded micaceous ceramic vessel fragments identified as simple bowls, holemouths, ledge handles, and vertical-loop handles for jars (see Parr et al. 1978:40–42). Lithic material included the now well-known tabular flint fan scrapers and other forms (Zarins 1979:74–75). The pillars and platforms suggest parallels with the western zone as described above (Cohen 1979:250–51; Rothenberg 1973:20–21 and pls. 7–8; Avner, pers. comm.).

Surrounding the Rajajil site are isolated sandstone jebels on which we find a series of small settlements. The majority have three to four simple stone circles with a few partitions. Tumuli are often directly associated. Some fifty handmade, micaceous tempered sherds of Rajajil type come from 201–12. The shapes included simple bowls and holemouth fragments. Ground stone fragments and a sandstone bowl were also found (for a similar example from Jawa see Helms 1975:fig. 10). The lithics included the usual forms, rare side-struck flakes (see Ronen 1970), and the larger component of hoe fragments and picks (Zarins 1979:76).

Larger site complexes resembling western zone sites are also known from the Jowf-Sakaka region. Some 20 km northeast of Sakaka along the shores of a large fossil lake, site 201–15 stretches in complexity for over 2.5 km (Adams et al. 1977:37 and pl. 18C). Structural remains include both the simple and interlocking types made of local limestone. Such sites, although usually on a much smaller scale (e.g., 201–22), are numerous in the area on the northern edge of the Nafud Desert. The eastern limits of these sites of the Chalcolithic/EB tradition are important in light of the Tigris-Euphrates basin and Mesopotamian civilization. It now appears that the sites in the Arar basin on this limestone fringe some 150–200 km west of the Euphrates were the closest "pastoral belt." This belt stretched from the northeast borders of the Nafud north to the Wadi Hauran and beyond, perhaps as far north as the great bend in the Euphrates (Poidebard 1934; Zarins 1986). Two sites in the Arar basin can be considered typical with the usual lithic assemblages. Site 201–37, consisting of sixteen structures, primarily simple circles, lies on a low sandstone ridge. At 201–39, the ceramic material indicates a tie to Rajajil some 90 km to the west.

Sites south of the Nafud in the Hail region include the lone kite, site 205–8 (Parr et al. 1978:pl. 22B), but are generally aceramic (for sites 206–32, 206–34, 206–36, and 206–4 see Parr et al. 1978:pl. 27A–C). Lithic material is somewhat similar to that found north of the Nafud (Parr et al. 1978:nos. 128–35), but in contrast to the northern assemblages, few tabular flint scrapers or, in fact, few flint tools occur. Instead the local population utilized quartzite, green obsidian, metamorphic materials, and ferruginous quartzite. No sites have been found south of Hail although Chalcolithic ceramics may be present in the Gasim oasis (Parr and Gazdar 1980).

Larger and more complex sites lie west of Jowf. In the basal Sirhan, site 201–54, al Adani (Parr et al. 1978:38 and pls. 25B, 28A) is located on top of an isolated jebel with sheer sides. In layout and position it is similar to examples cited by Maitland (1927:pl. 2) and Helms (1977:23) in the Jordanian Harrat al Rajil. Some fifty structures are arranged over the summit and are mostly of the simple type without interconnections. The presence of entry foyers may ally the plan to Jawa houses (for site plan, see Parr et al. 1978:pl. 22A; Helms 1976:7–10). Lithics are again typical but include a significantly larger component of hoes, adzes, chisels, choppers, and prepared platform cores. Several unique spear points with notched tangs were also found (Parr et al. 1978:38 and pls. 35–36/nos. 90–106). Site 201–56 in the basal Sirhan is probably the largest site discovered to date and lies on three limestone ridges overlooking the Wadi Sirhan to the west. Many of the well over three hundred structures resemble those found in the western zone, for example, interlocking circles, corrals, and courtyards surrounded by smaller rooms. Ceramics from this site are rare and are entirely absent from al Adani, with only nine sherds having been recovered from a simple bowl (Parr et al. 1978:pl. 32:1). Lithic remains are similar to those at al Adani. At the northern end of the Wadi Sirhan, similar but much smaller sites have been reported (Ingraham et al. 1981:79–80 for sites 200–118,-119,-129,-126).

In northwest Arabia, we have clear links between sites in the western zone in the Sinai and those described for southern Jordan. At least twenty datable sites have been found within the larger Tabuk basin. Northwest of Tabuk in the Wadi Damm, sites 200–98,-100,-101,-102, and in Wadi Tamra are loosely clustered settlements (Ingraham et al. 1981:68–69). Southwest of Tabuk in the Wadis Baqqar, Asafir, and Fuha, are sites 200–95,-96,-112, and 200–108 (Ingraham et al. 1981:pl. 91c–d). The Wadi Fuha site is very close to Beit-Arieh's type I village layout at Nabi Salah (1981:fig. 8). Large circular rooms are attached around the large central courtyard. Prominent monoliths mark the center post and the lintels/doorways. Southeast of Tabuk in the Wadi Akhdar are additional sites numbered 200–90,-129,-130 (for locations, see Ingraham et al. 1981:68 and pl. 68, map 6). The basic structural remains range from stone circles to pillar and tumuli structures. Ceramics are rare and the lithics are of the usual types (Ingraham et al. 1981:pl. 69c).

In the western Hisma, site 204–101, over 2 km long, lies in the Wadi Shakri and is reminiscent of those already described from the Sirhan and Arar regions. Along the Red Sea coast, at the confluence of the Wadis Sharmah and Arnab, site 200–47, Jebel Arrayiq al Yusri, belongs to this complex (Ingraham et al. 1981:67) and indicates a maritime orientation, perhaps participating in the Red Sea shell network of inland sites.

The southwestern boundary of the complex is less well defined than it is in the Nafud-Hail region. Stone circle sites have been reported from the Nejd and the southern Hejaz (Zarins et al. 1980:17–20; Zarins, Murad, and al-Yish 1981:19–23), but their basic affinities remain unclear. Many characteristics of the northern regions are clearly absent.

The chronology of the eastern sites is still tied to the better-defined western zone and to the two key sites of the eastern zone described above. Few have yet been sounded or excavated. For J24, a key site in southern Jordan, Henry reports three levels. The lower was aceramic (Neolithic?) and the upper two, A and B, belonged to the Chalcolithic. A radiocarbon date (see table 1) of 3770 B.C. implies a fairly early Chalcolithic date, and reference to other Timnian I dates suggests a fairly close correlation. The problem lies with the Saudi Arabian

sites to the south and future sites to be found farther to the east. As for the preceding periods, we are reluctant to adopt western zone terminology for sites in the eastern zone. Hence we suggest keeping the basic term *Chalcolithic/EB* until further excavations elucidate the phases more clearly. That such subphases may be present is suggested by the Wadi Sirhan material, where the al Adani and 201–56 site materials may be contemporaneous with the imperfectly known Elatian of the west. Similarly, we have real problems in trying to establish the end of the Timnian II equivalent in the east. The EB III horizon at Bab edh Dhra was badly disturbed, and Jawa was abandoned well before then. From evidence presented below, however, it seems clear that the "new" EB IV cultures in the western zone actually came from the eastern one. Thus, again we should be cautious about proposing any clear-cut break. The Mesopotamian evidence suggests that the MAR.TU, mentioned apparently for the first time ca. 2500 B.C. in Fara texts, show no break in subsequent periods. They are increasingly described in the ED III, the Old Akkadian, Ur III, and Isin-Larsa periods (2400–1900 B.C.).

Climatic conditions are again imperfectly known for the eastern zone. Henry suggests that the final moist phase occurred during the Chalcolithic in southern Jordan (Henry et al. 1983:23). Additional work on lakes should clarify the matter. At Rajajil the structures were built in a red sand before the latest sand mantle formed on the terrace (Parr et al. 1978:41).

Mesopotamian cuneiform texts (ca. 2400–1900 B.C.) independently confirm a pastoral life-style for this later phase. From the Chalcolithic at Jawa, Kohler reports that the assemblage is 87 percent domestic ovicaprids and only 8.5 percent domestic cattle (Kohler 1981:249–52). A minor component includes hunted animals such as gazelles and *E. hemionus*. These percentages are nearly the same as those found at Arad during the EB I–III periods, where ovicaprids constituted 87 percent and cattle 7.4 percent (Lernau 1978:83). Similarly at EB Bab edh Dhra, sheep-goats dominate the identified species by percentage, with a smaller amount of cattle and pigs. Wild gazelles may also be present (Finnegan 1981:177–78 and fig. 1). The only site that has been examined for these periods in the eastern zone is J24. Here Henry reports that, as expected, ovicaprid remains dominate (pers. comm.; Turnbull, pers. comm.). (For the presence of domestic animals based on texts, see the following section.) At Rajajil, the faunal remains included *Capra, E. hemionus,* and *Bos* sp. Although the data are meager, it appears that caprids, with the addition of sheep and cattle in selected areas, constituted the herded animals. Hunting remained important, with possibly some localized agriculture. Mining for copper may be indicated in the Midian area. (For the EB mining site of Funon in south Jordan, see Beit-Arieh 1984b.)

Decline and Change: EB IVA–C (2200–1850 B.C.)

Between the twenty-third and nineteenth centuries B.C., life in the Levant underwent radical change. EB III society, based on walled towns, declined and collapsed. Non-walled villages, cave occupation, and campsites appeared (Prag 1984:59). (For suggested reasons, for the decline of EB towns see Richard 1980:23–24.) There is a clash of opinions as to the nature of society in this period, particularly in Palestine, and this is evident by the welter of terms used (Richard 1980:6–8; for recent summaries, overviews, and studies see Prag 1984, Richard 1980, Dever 1980, and Gerstenblith 1980). A basic question involves the reported archaeological assemblages. Authorities seem divided not only on the terminology of the period, but also on the relative merits of its subdivisions during 2200–1900 B.C. (see summation by Prag 1984:66–68). With regard to the ceramics, some stress the continuity of the tradition from EB III (Richard 1980:12–20; Dever 1971:209, n. 28); others suggest a dramatic break (fig. 3; Kochavi, in Cohen 1983:19).

Studies up to the 1970s were based on Palestinian material principally from transitory and tomb sites (Dever 1971:197; Baron 1978:196–202; Kenyon 1979:119ff.). Accordingly, Dever has suggested that the ceramics from the southern Levant be classified into six "Geographic-Cultural Families." Of these, the southern one (S) stretches south from Hebron well into the Sinai (Dever 1971:203). In accordance with his analysis of the data, Dever has proposed the term EB IV, with subphases A–C stretching from EB IVA (2300–2200 B.C.), EB IVB (2200–2100 B.C.), to EB IVC (2100–2000/1900 B.C.) (Dever 1980:fig. 1). In light of the recent evidence from Jordan and the eastern zone (summary by Prag 1984:66ff.), it is difficult to resist the notion that in the arid zone and perhaps in Jordan, EB IV follows as a logical and uninterrupted cultural phase from earlier periods. How it should be viewed in Palestine, however, is a different matter and one that cannot be solved here. For our purposes and in line with Dever and Cohen, we use the term EB IV for the period 2200–1900 B.C. Finally, a related question is whether EB IV in the Levant represents an "intrusion" of Amorite pastoral peoples. This remains under discussion and relates to our treatment of the arid zone (Rothenberg 1980:120; Dever 1980: 53–58; Prag 1984:59; Kenyon 1971:594ff.; Mazar 1968).

The specific ceramic assemblage for the S Family is quite uniform, with ample use of the simple comb-and-banding technique. (For recent additions see Gitin 1975:

60–62; for burial practices and evidence of secondary burial see Smith 1982:66–67.)

Based on Glueck's work in the Negev, 157 EB IV (MB I) sites were cataloged, as opposed to only 10 EB I and 7 EB II. In Thompson's catalog emendations, 229 sites were considered Chalcolithic/EB I, 88 EB II, and 455 EB IV. Dever has suggested that in combined surveys, over 300 sites belonged to the EB IV period (Cohen and Dever 1978:29; for EB IV sites in the Negev see Cohen and Dever 1978:fig. 1.) More recent surveys in the central Negev suggest that fully half of the recovered 243 sites belong to EB IV (Cohen 1979:250–51, 1980:231–34; also see Cohen 1983:19 and nn. 10–11). Similarly, in the Bir Resisim area, the survey indicates that the sites are overwhelmingly Late EB or EB IV (Cohen and Dever 1979:42). In the Uvda Valley, fully 20 percent of the sites are EB IV (Cohen 1979:251). Any interpretation of this striking pattern must take into account the ecology of the western arid zone, the conditions of the settled zone alluded to above, and the sociopolitical conditions affecting Egypt, Syria, and Mesopotamia.

The Negev EB IV sites have been described as forming a three-tiered site hierarchy of large central sites, intermediate ones, and small ones (Cohen 1983:19, citing Kochavi). Horvat Nahal Nissana (see photo and plan, Cohen 1983:20), the largest EB IV site in the Negev, covers 1 ha and exhibits the usual concentration of circular or rectangular structures interlocking around courtyards. Har Yeruham, excavated and studied in 1963 and 1973, represents a similar pattern (Kochavi 1967; Cohen 1974, 1983:20). (For site plan and photos of Bir Resisim, another large site, see Cohen and Dever 1979:41, 1981:59.) These structures are fairly substantial, with central pillars, well-defined doorways, and beamed roofs. Intermediate sites such as Nahal Boqer and Horvat Har Harif are much smaller with fewer structures (Cohen 1983:22). The largest number of sites by far are the small sites, with only two to three structures and associated animal pens.

The ceramic material from the sites, exemplified by that from Bir Resisim (Cohen and Dever 1978:40 and fig. 10, 1979:fig. 17, 1981:67 and figs. 10–11) covers 250 years and is typical of Family S but shows some contact with Syria (Cohen and Dever 1981:64). The main influence comes from Jordanian EB IV sites such as Bab edh Dhra, Iktanu, Aroer, and Ader (Dever's earlier Family TR, 1971, 1973; Cohen and Dever 1979:54, 57, 1981:64). Lithic material, simplified from the earlier EB tradition, is confined to a few standard types (Cohen and Dever 1979:54, 57; Cohen 1983:photo, pl. 16). Copper ingots and a dagger were recovered from Bir Resisim (Cohen and Dever 1979:48, 51; see GÍR MAR.TU, Amorite daggers, mentioned in the Ebla texts, Pettinato 1980:9). Red Sea shells support the earlier patterns of shell trade (Cohen and Dever 1979:51). Disarticulated burials again point to earlier parallels (Cohen and Dever 1979:59, n. 13) and to contemporary material from the Levant (Smith 1982).

In northern Sinai, a number of EB IV settlements occur in the Kudeirat oasis and the Gebel Halal (Rothenberg 1961, 1980:120). Small homesteads have been reported in the Jebel Lagama area. At Mushabi 103, the ceramic corpus included an unusual mat-impressed/moulded ware (Clamer and Sass 1977:249–51 and fig. 112). In central Sinai, a number of EB IV sites have been identified (Rothenberg 1973, sites 699, 676, 692, 677; Beit-Arieh 1979:256–57). However, to date no EB IV sites are reported from the Wadi Arabah (Rothenberg 1970:fig. 1). In sum, the extensive EB IV period in Sinai is well represented in all regions of the peninsula (see summary by Rothenberg 1980:121). The majority apparently belong to the small settlement type.

Since these EB IV sites were abandoned and not destroyed (e.g., Bir Resisim, Cohen and Dever 1978:35), questions of ecological adaptation and chronology arise. A radiocarbon date of 1850 B.C. from Mushabi 103 in the north Sinai suggests a lower limit of ca. 1900–1850 B.C. (table 1). Cohen and Dever have suggested that the peak occupation at Bir Resisim took place during 2100–2000 B.C., but radiocarbon dates from the site, although collected, are not yet available. In his geomorphological study at the site, Gerson concluded that EB IV was already in the post-Atlantic optimum; however, conditions were certainly still more favorable than at present, with shrub vegetation more abundant and with hillsides covered by a loess blanket (Cohen and Dever 1981:73). Nevertheless, the climatic optimum is seen by most authorities as having ended both in Egypt and the Levant (summary by Richard 1980:25), with increasing aridity setting in by this time. One interpretation of this dramatic increase of sites in the western arid zone could thus be that the arid conditions required greater pastoral foraging and seasonal movement. Bir Resisim may have been occupied only in the winter (Cohen and Dever 1981:74). However, the same reliance on domestic ovicaprids at Bir Resisim as in earlier EB periods gives no evidence of this (Cohen and Dever 1978:37). Perhaps this emphasis on ovicaprids, subsequent overgrazing, and the greater aridity, in addition to declining urban patterns, contributed to both an absolute increase in the number of people in the arid zone and the dissolution of larger bands into much smaller units. In sum, it appears that EB IV represents the last major archaeologically attested period in the western arid zone until the Iron Age/Romano-Nabatean period. This occupation gap may hold clues to the transition from a way of life beginning in the PPNB to the modern pastoral life-style. While these events were oc-

curring during the EB IV period, it is not necessary to view the pastoral elements in the zone as "Amorite shepherd warriors" who saw the Sinai purely as a "transit country on their way to Egypt" (Rothenberg 1980:120–21) or simply as a new ethnic group moving from Sinai to the Negev in a proto-Exodus (Cohen 1983:19). Rather, as the Twelfth Dynasty stelae on the Serabit el Khadim site mention, the local inhabitants were the archaeological and historical heirs of a long tradition in the region's pastoral nomadism (for Semitic names on stelae and their relationship to West Semitic, see Černy 1935 and Gelb 1980).

The eastern zone has little in the way of EB IV material to match that found in the west, but this may be due merely to a lack of detailed exploration. Within the settled zone on the eastern bank of the Jordan, a number of surveys and excavated sites suggest a fairly substantial presence of people in EB IV. In addition to the Glueck survey (see Dever 1970), recent surveys have added new sites of the period (Ibrahim, Sauer, and Yassine 1976; Prag 1971:158–206; Dever 1980:36). Preliminary work at Iktanu (Prag 1974), Aro'er, Iskander, and Ader (Richard 1980:27, n. 3) promise to add considerably to our knowledge of the period in Jordan. At Bab edh Dhra, the excavations have revealed that EB III tombs were used in EB IV and new ones were built (Schaub 1973; Rast and Schaub 1980:39–40). Most interesting are the insubstantial remains of the EB IV settlement. The excavators note that on the remains of the destroyed EB III town, EB IV structures were restricted to a few areas, and that the general concentration was outside of the main EB III site (Rast and Schaub 1980:32). A date of ca. 2200 B.C. is suggested for the phase occupation. Jawa, our other key site, was reoccupied during EB IV after an apparent millennium of abandonment. Here broad-roomed houses and forecourts surrounded a formal, central, rectangular structure (see plan, Helms 1976:figs. 3–4, 1981:fig. B1 and pl. 222). Helms sees this as a caravanserai and as a focal point for people in the surrounding eastern Jordanian desert (Helms 1976:7, 1981:34).

For the arid zone sites of this area, Dever has suggested that the EB IV of Jordan gave rise to the arid EB IV phase in the western zone (Dever 1973:56–57). However, the actual surveys in south Jordan have provided very little evidence. MacDonald's work in the transition zone of southern Jordan, north of At Tafila, suggests that agricultural communities such as Mashmil existed there during the EB IVA–B period (ca. 2300–2100 B.C.), but little is available from later periods (MacDonald, Rollefson, and Roller 1982:38 and fig. 3). The Ma'an-Aqaba survey may produce some EB IV stone circle sites in the area (Jobling 1981:108, 1982:201).

To the northeast, no specific evidence of the EB IV

period in northern Saudi Arabia has yet appeared, but this is probably due to a lack of detailed survey work. Similarly, in western Iraq, especially in the Wadi Hauran area, more detailed work is necessary to establish the sequence of the EB I–IV periods. About 100 km southeast of Damascus in the Syrian Hauran, the stone circles of Hebariye are typical examples of those already described from Bir Resisim in the western zone, and are characterized by interlocking circles and prominent central pillar (Dubertret and Dunand 1954–55:74 fig. 7). The ceramics may suggest an EB IV date (Dubertret and Dunand 1954–55:pl. 7), and lithics are typical (Dubertret and Dunand 1954–55:pl. 7 bis/2). Furthermore, stone circle complexes in the Jebel Bishri area may represent the EB IV period. Survey work in 1967 confirmed the location of sites that were neither excavated nor closely examined (Buccellati and Kelly-Buccellati 1977 and pers. comm.). Also the excavations at Terqa suggest that this town, as well as Mari, functioned in the early second millennium B.C. as a focal point for nomadic populations (for Terqa, see Buccellati and Kelly-Buccellati 1977; Galvin 1981; for the voluminous historical analysis of the Mari pastoralists see Luke 1965; Kupper 1957; Rowton 1973; Matthews 1978; for the equivalent role in central Mesopotamia, refer to Sippar, in Harris 1975). However, these nomads, so vividly described in the historical record of the early second millennium B.C., have so far not been attested by archaeological evidence (Prag 1985).

It is our contention that the identification of the EB IV period with the MAR.TU in the western zone may be premature, particularly if we do not accept the western Semitic pastoral nomads as already present in the region. However, for the eastern zone, especially in western Iraq, southern Syria, and northeastern Saudi Arabia, the MAR.TU seem to be the people described with increasing frequency in the Mesopotamian records beginning in EB III (Buccellati 1966). Their activities, both in the arid zone and in the Mesopotamian valley, are well documented through the Ur III period until ca. 2000/1980 B.C., when they managed to found several dynasties in the southern alluvium (Isin-Larsa). The reorganization of the southern Mesopotamian alluvium at this time also extended to the less-known eastern Arabian littoral known as Dilmun (Zarins, 1986) where sites after ca. 1850 B.C. are difficult to recognize. Surely, as others have argued, these pastoral people, faced with similar declining resources in the arid zones during this period, created new urban-arid zone interactions in the Levant as well as in Egypt (Prag 1984:68; Kenyon 1979:145–46; Dever 1971:216ff., 1980:53–55; for divergent views see Cohen 1983; Kamp and Yoffee 1980).

The chronology of the eastern arid zone is still in its infancy, and the only available radiocarbon dates are those from the Syrian Harrat al Rajil basalt site of Hebariye (see table 1). The date of 2125 B.C. seems to fit the accepted range of the EB IV period. It is clear, however, that our reference point must remain with the settled zone sites. Further refinements in the categorization of the period's subphases will be welcome (for recent work in the Levant, see Gerstenblith 1980).

Although it is difficult to assess the ecological material because of its paucity, the southern fringes of the region seem to have been abandoned already by 2200 B.C. and the EB IV materials have been restricted to the more northerly region, where greater reliable moisture was available. The historical Mari nomads, relying on seasonal transhumance during ca. 1850–1790 B.C., may represent the last examples in our arid zone. What precisely led to the MAR.TU increase in the southern Mesopotamian basin and the subsequent militarism during the Ur III period remains unknown; but certainly, ecological factors such as increasing aridity, partly caused by overgrazing, must have played a significant role. The faunal analysis of Gaillard from Hebariye confirms the presence of sheep, goats, and cattle (Dubertret and Dunand 1954–55). The Ur III texts from Drehem record that the MAR.TU bring in various varieties of sheep, including fat-tailed, goats, equids, probably *E. asinus* and hybrids, and cattle (Buccellati 1966:282ff., esp. charts A and B).

Finally, there is the question as to the fate of the people who had developed this technocomplex from its early beginnings in the Epipaleolithic. As we have remarked, the sites constructed of fairly permanent materials in sometimes large conglomerations were abandoned at the end of EB IV. It appears that a gradual change took place in the life-style, brought about by new ecological and sociopolitical circumstances. The critical factor of increased mobility apparently stimulated both the development of the goat-hair tent and an increased reliance on the domesticated camel. But surely human occupation did not cease in the arid zones in the succeeding periods. From Palestine and Jordan we have evidence of the Shosu from the first half of the Eighteenth Dynasty well through the reign of Ramses II (Giveon 1971:1). Similarly, nomadic populations are mentioned in the Tell el Amarna correspondence. (For the Proto-Sinaitic script of Sinai, see Albright 1969.) In the literature we see the replacement of the Amorites and Mari nomads by the Ahlamu/Aramu and finally by the Arabi (Cornwall 1952; Brinkman 1968; Eph'al 1982). (For the second millennium B.C. and for later archaeological remains in the Arabian peninsula, see Zarins et al. 1980:20–23; Zarins, Murad, and al-Yish 1981:28–31; and Zarins, Rihbini, and Kamal 1982: 32–34.)

Four

The Chronology of the Archaeological Assemblages from the Head of the Arabian Gulf to the Arabian Sea, 8000–1750 B.C.

Daniel T. Potts, Carsten Niebuhr Institute of Ancient
Near Eastern Studies, University of Copenhagen

Outline

The areas discussed in this chapter (fig. 4) border the western Arabian Gulf (Kuwait, eastern Saudi Arabia, Qatar, Bahrain, and the United Arab Emirates), the Gulf of Oman (northern Oman), and the Arabian Sea (southern Oman and Dhofar). Due to their geographical location and to the fact that much of what is known here has been discovered only in the past few years, there is a tendency to mix local chronological nomenclature with that of southern Mesopotamia. Since many artifactual parallels have been drawn between our area and southern Mesopotamia, this practice is both convenient and appropriate. However, Mesopotamian terms are used purely as "flags" to signal a particular chronological message to all familiar with the standard southern Mesopotamian chronological terminology. Unless otherwise stated, they should not be taken as indicators of political, economic, or cultural relationships.

The Early Holocene (8000–5000 B.C.)

The geomorphological setting of the Early Holocene is now fairly well understood, but it will not be treated here (see Kassler 1973; McClure 1976, 1978; al-Sayari and Zötl 1978; Vita-Finzi 1978; McClure and Vita-Finzi 1982; Perthuisot 1980; and Larsen 1980, 1983a, 1983b, 1986). Work on the chipped stone industries of the Arabian Gulf began with the first Danish reconnaissance of Bahrain (Glob 1954a:112–15), but concentrated subsequently on Qatar (Glob 1957, 1958a, 1959b, 1960; Madsen 1961; Nielsen 1961). In 1965 H. Kapel published a

Text submitted September 1984
Final revision April 1987

preliminary typology and chronology of the Qatar industries (Kapel 1965, cf. 1967). His schema of groups A (Palaeolithic), B and C (Mesolithic), and D (Neolithic) was called into question in 1976–77 by a new program of French excavations in Qatar (Tixier 1977:8–9), which subsequently revealed A, C, and D types in situ with Ubaid 3–4 pottery (Inizan 1980a:197). The B group, however, characterized by blade arrowheads, is chronologically earlier and may form a point of departure for our discussion of the period ca. 8000–5000 B.C.

A radiocarbon date of 6970 ± 130 B.P. (table 1) comes from a surface sample collected at the B group site of Shagra (Kapel 1967:17). Moreover, typological similarities with Pre-Pottery Neolithic assemblages of the Levant and Syria, datable to the eighth and seventh millennia B.C., have long been noted. P. Mortensen pointed to connections between arrowheads, awls, and backed blades with triangular section of the B group, and material from Beidha and Tell Ramad (Kapel 1967:18). Similar observations were subsequently made by L. Copeland, who constructed a chronological chart for "arrowhead and foliate sites in the Near East" (ca. 8000–

The author thanks the following scholars who kindly placed new or unpublished information at his disposal, or made helpful comments on earlier drafts of this chapter: Pierre Amiet, Paris; Serge Cleuziou, Paris; Lorraine Copeland, Oxford; E. C. L. During Caspers, Leiden; S. A. El-Dabi El-Darmaki, Al Ain; Karen Frifelt, Moesgaard; H.-G. Gebel, Berlin; the late Marny Golding, Dhahran; Flemming Højlund, Moesgaard; M.-L. Inizan, Valbonne; Poul Kjaerum, Moesgaard; C. C. Lamberg-Karlovsky, Cambridge; L. de Meyer, Gent; P. R. S. Moorey, Oxford; Peder Mortensen, Moesgaard; Timothy Potts, Oxford; J.-F. Salles, Lyon; Maurizio Tosi, Naples; B. Vogt, Sanaa; and G. Weisgerber, Bochum.

5000 B.C.) which placed the Qatar B group near the end of those sites exhibiting the blade arrowhead tradition beginning with Mureybit 2 (ca. 8056 B.C.), and ending with the Yarmukian culture, around 5000 B.C. (Copeland and Bergne 1976:51, table 2). Other scholars, too, have drawn parallels between Qatar B and Levantine or Syrian assemblages (e.g., Smith 1978:36; Pullar 1974:44). "Armatures perçantes," similar to those from the B site Al Bahath on Qatar, appeared at Ramlat Fasad in northern Dhofar (Inizan 1980c:234; cf. Pullar 1974:fig. 9A–B), and sites in southern Dhofar also seem related to the Qatar B group (Smith 1977:74). F. Hours et al. place the B group in the range of 7600–5000 B.C. (Hours et al., in press).

Turning to the interior, Arabian sites located in the Wadi Al-Fau (Kapel 1973:63), the Wadi Dawasir (Zarins et al. 1979:18), and at Jebel Daba, ca. 30 km south of the Yabrin oasis (Masry 1974:91), have yielded comparable material. The alleged presence of Qatar B–type material in the early levels at Ain Qannas (Masry 1974:113–14) is, however, disputed (Copeland and Bergne 1976:51, table 2).

A contemporary occupation of fishers is also known at Ra's al-Hamra 10 (Biagi et al. 1984:table 2) on the Batinah coast of Oman, where two corrected radiocarbon dates (table 1) fall squarely in the sixth millennium B.C.

At Mazyad, near Jabal Hafit, an early flint industry has recently been identified which appears to predate the fifth millennium B.C. (Gebel 1982:16).

We add a final brief word on early ground stone. Thirteen red granite handstone grinders, found on the surface of sites along the northern edge of the Rubʿ al-Khali, have been compared with PPNB types from Jericho (Sordinas 1978:25, pl. 16/6, 7).

In sum, the typological comparisons drawn suggest a time range of ca. 8000–5000 B.C. for Qatar B and related assemblages, while the radiocarbon date from one Qatar B site falls near the very end of this range.

The Middle Holocene (5000–3600 B.C.)

Important discoveries have been made within the time range of the Middle Holocene in recent years. Certainly the most noteworthy has been that of painted and plain pottery in the southern Mesopotamian Ubaid tradition on the surface of about forty sites in eastern Arabia (Burkholder and Golding 1971; Burkholder 1972, 1984:17–21 and pls. 7–9c; Mitchell 1972:137 and pl. LVIb; Bibby 1973b:64, 1973a), five on the Qatar peninsula (de Cardi 1974; Oates 1978:42; Inizan 1980b:219), and two on Bahrain (Roaf 1974; Larsen 1980:39). To date it has appeared in excavations at Ain Qannas, al-Dosariyah, and Abu Khamis in Saudi Arabia (Masry 1974); al-Daasa, Ras Abaruk, and Khor in Qatar (Oates 1978:39–52; Inizan 1980b:95); and al-Markh on Bahrain (Roaf 1974, 1976).

Neutron activation and petrographic and electron microprobe analyses have shown that nearly every sherd of painted and plain Ubaid-style pottery from the Arabian Gulf originated in southern Mesopotamia, most probably at Ur, Eridu, and al-ʿUbaid, whereas a chaff-tempered, handmade, coarse redware that occurs alongside the imported ware seems to be of local manufacture (Oates et al. 1977:232; cf. Potts 1978:34; Oates 1986; de Cardi 1986).

Bowl fragments from the surface of Ain Qannas (Masry 1974:fig. 18) and level 8 at Abu Khamis (Masry 1974:fig. 90/1), as well as a possible "tortoise vase" sherd from the surface of Dosariyah (Masry 1974:fig. 39/2), show parallels to Ubaid 2 (Hajji Muhammad) types, according to J. Oates (1986:84–85), who also notes that the latter type continues into Eridu Temple VIII, of Ubaid 3 date. A straight-sided bowl fragment from level 2 at Abu Khamis can also be compared with a piece from Temple VIII. Thus, Oates concludes that "Ain Qannas, Abu Khamis and Dosariyah were all certainly occupied during ʿUbaid 3 and conceivably as early as late ʿUbaid 2," while noting that "there is no published pottery from these sites necessarily later than ʿUbaid 3" (Oates 1986:85).

A temporally more varied collection comes from the Qatar and Bahrain sites. According to Oates, two sherds from al-Daasa are Hajji Muhammad types, dating to either Ubaid 2 or early Ubaid 3, while the majority of the painted, albeit poorly preserved, Ubaid pottery from that site would be either Ubaid 3 or 4 (Oates 1978:43–44). The material from Khor has also been dated to Ubaid 3–4 (Inizan 1980b:218). Ra's Abaruk, on the other hand, as well as al-Markh show parallels with Woolley's Ur-Ubaid II and Warka XVIII–XVI, and would therefore be Ubaid 4 at the very earliest (Oates 1978:44), or what has been referred to variously as Late Ubaid, post-Ubaid, terminal Ubaid, or Early Uruk (Oates 1976:28). Oates proposes a date of ca. 3800 B.C. for this material (Roaf 1976:151).

The flint tool type most often associated with the Ubaid pottery is the tanged and/or barbed arrowhead of tabular or tile flint with fine pressure flaking. This is characteristic of Kapel's D group (Kapel 1967:20, pls. 47–49). It is, for example, well represented in levels 12–4 at Ain Qannas, and in level 4 at Dosariyah (Masry 1974:figs. 23/2–5, 25/1 and 5, 27/2, 28/1–3, and 64/5); throughout the sounding at al-Markh (Roaf 1976:151, pl. 2/B–E); at Ra's Abaruk (Smith 1978:96, pl. C, fig. 9/4, 5); at al-Daasa (Smith 1978:66, pl. B, fig. 9); and at Khor (Inizan 1980b:218, fig. 6).

Sites with characteristic Qatar D–type arrowheads but *without* Ubaid pottery were once abundant in eastern Arabia. The published material now available comes from the eastern coastal strip (Masry 1974:92–93); the area east of Abqayq near Ayn Dar (Potts et al. 1978:8); in and around the Hofuf oasis (Sordinas 1973:fig. 9; Golding 1974:19, fig. 2; Adams et al. 1977:31; Burkholder 1984:11); and around the Yabrin oasis (Sordinas 1973:fig. 9; Masry 1974:91–92). An awl and six pieces of debitage from an exposed layer of the tell on Tarut may also belong to this period (Bibby 1973b:31, fig. 24). In addition, we note that five pieces of obsidian from surface sites near Dhahran, including a blade found in association with Ubaid pottery, all came originally from the Lake Van-Azerbaijan-Armenia area (Renfrew and Dixon 1976:141).

On Bahrain, Qatar D arrowheads, awls, and scrapers have been found at seven sites (Larsen 1980:38, cf. 1983b:29). Qatar D types and techniques, with the notable exception of barbed and tanged arrowheads, are also present in a collection from Jabal Huwaya, Abu Dhabi (Copeland and Bergne 1976:53). H.-G. Gebel has recently suggested, however, that the "Huwayan" industry, which he dates from the fifth to mid-fourth millennium B.C., may precede and then overlap with the purer Qatar D components known elsewhere in Abu Dhabi (e.g., Tarif, Habshan, Ghiati, Quasiawira, Al Ain Hilton) and Oman (e.g., Sohar, Sayq, Lizq 2) (Gebel 1982:16, Abb. A). Smith has pointed to "fine foliate points" at Sayq in central Oman, and an ovate from al-Mays, about halfway between Bahla and Ibri, which are comparable to material from al-Jubeijib and Ra's Abaruk in Qatar (Smith 1977:72, fig. 4; cf. Kapel 1967:pls. 51–54; Smith 1976:189, fig. 2/3; cf. Smith 1978:88, fig. 5/4, 5). J. Pullar has recently published some heterogeneous surface collections from Kadusah, near Ibri, and Fahud, south of Natih, in the interior of Oman which include bifacially and unifacially retouched arrowheads (Pullar 1985:fig. 3/7 = pl. 1/4, fig. 9/4). Farther south in Dhofar, material which shows connections to the Qatar D tradition also exists. This is well illustrated by the bifacially retouched tools of Bir Khasfa on the Wadi Arar (Pullar 1974:36). The misleading term "Akhdar-Obed," once given to the Qatar D–related assemblages of the Oman peninsula (Weisgerber 1980b:99, n. 37–39, 1981:256), has since given way to "Qatar D" (Gebel 1982:16).

Elements characteristic of Qatar C have been found with Ubaid pottery at Ain Qannas in levels 11–6 (Masry 1974:114); at Abu Khamis in levels 3, 4, and 6, where awls were common (Masry 1974:figs. 81/2–8, 84/2–4, 86/1–3); throughout the al-Markh sequence (Roaf 1976:151); at al-Daasa and Ra's Abaruk (Smith 1978:37); and at Khor (Inizan 1980a:217).

Khor is also important in providing a link between Kapel's A group and both the C and D industries. Inizan interprets the A material from Khor as "an original Neo-

lithic facies," and the C and D types as "perhaps the expression of the different activities or local groups" in contact with Ubaid Mesopotamia (Inizan 1980a:197). Both hypotheses are debatable. We also note that material has recently been published from Qaharir in Oman which appears to belong to the Qatar A tradition (Pullar and Jäckli 1978:54).

Let us turn now to the absolute chronology of the Ubaid and Qatar A, C, and D assemblages. The Arabian and Qatar Ubaid sites provide dates that range from 7265 to 5515 B.P. (table 1). Yet, al-Markh, from which unfortunately we have no radiocarbon dates, shows that the Qatar C and D materials continued in use for an indeterminate length of time *after* the disappearance of Ubaid pottery. Thus, the dates from levels with Ubaid pottery should not be used indiscriminately to date all aceramic Qatar A, C, and D surface sites. This point is further emphasized by several related industries found in the interior of the Arabian peninsula. Here, a number of distinctive chipped stone assemblages share the characteristic tanged or barbed arrowhead as a common bond with the Ubaid/Qatar C–D sites. These include the "Rub al-Khali Neolithic" (Zeuner 1954; Field 1960; Smith and Maranjian 1962; Drechou, Hivernel, and Karpoff 1968; McClure 1971; Gramley 1971; Sordinas 1973, 1978; Edens 1982), one of whose "hallmarks" is the tanged and barbed arrowhead, and the "Nejd Neolithic" (Edens, in Zarins et al. 1979:19–21), while in the Nefud (Parr et al. 1978:36) and the Taif area (Zarins et al. 1980:19–20), comparable material has also been found.

The dates for this material range from ca. 5235 B.P. (Zeuner 1954; Field 1960) to 9790 ± 250 B.P. (McClure 1978:262; Zarins et al. 1979:20), and taken together, suggest the need for extreme caution in attempting to date Aceramic Qatar C–D or related surface assemblages.

The Mid-Fourth through Early Third Millennium (3600–2500 B.C.)

Excavated material for the earlier part of this period is available from Bahrain and from the northern coast of Oman, while for the later part our best evidence comes from inner Oman and Tarut.

Although we have already discussed al-Markh, we note that it probably remained occupied into the second half of the fourth millennium B.C. Most of the settlement and graves in shell middens 3, 4, 5, and 10 at Ra's al-Hamra date to the fourth millennium (Durante and Tosi 1977:137–62; Biagi et al. 1984:60; cf. now Phillips and Wilkinson 1982), although parts of the site are both older and younger (table 1). Several sherds of dark gray-black burnished ware found in the 1982 and 1983 seasons of excavation are reminiscent of late fourth or early third millennium burnished grayware from Iran (Biagi et al.

1984:53, n. 4). It was once suggested that the chipped stone industry of the middens, known as "Ra's al-Hamrian," followed and overlapped with the Qatar D–related assemblages of Oman (Gebel 1980:99, 1981:256). It now appears, however, that the "Ra's al-Hamrian" lithic technology may have been in use from the late sixth through the mid-third millennium B.C. (Gebel 1982:16). The most common artifacts at Ra's al-Hamra are notched or violin-shaped net weights made of limestone river cobbles (Durante and Tosi 1977:147). Simple subterranean pit graves, in which the body was covered with stone boulders and sometimes accompanied by a few shell beads, also occur (Durante and Tosi 1977:pl. XLVIIa–c; cf. Weisgerber 1981:181–82).

Aside from Ra's al-Hamra 5, no other ceramic sites of this period have been positively identified anywhere in the Arabian Gulf region. Claims have been made for the possible "Late Uruk" date of types present at sites in eastern Saudi Arabia such as Sabkhah Hamman, al-Rufayah, Umm ar-Ramadh, and Umm an-Nussi (Piesinger 1983:409–31, 469–504). Most of these types span a longer period of time in the Mesopotamian sequence and, as they are associated in Arabia with types of indubitable ED I–II affinity, should certainly be dated there to the early third millennium. Serrated sickle blades (Golding 1974:25; cf. Raikes 1967:28, fig. 3/1–15) found in eastern Arabia and on Bahrain (Larsen 1980:103, 1983a:29) could date to this time but may be later, for they are well represented at Kish and Abu Salabikh in ED III levels (Payne 1980:103). The same applies to several archaic-looking alabaster and travertine bowls from Tarut (Burkholder 1984:pls. 16a–c, 18a,c).

For the latter part of the period we have more material. Excavations on the Oman peninsula have concentrated on a number of cairn fields at Jabal Hafit, Qarn Bint Sa'ud, Ibri, Bat, and Siya, while the only excavated settlement from this period is Hili 8, period I (building III). However, the single-chambered cairn with southerly entrance, constructed of two concentric ringwalls of unmodified stones heaped up to form a domed chamber (Bibby 1965:109), is the dominant architectural feature of the period. The cairns normally contain a "family," who were "laid on their side with the hands in front of the face and the knees drawn up" (Frifelt 1975b:67).

The most diagnostic artifact found in the cairns is a small, biconical jar with everted rim, often with a painted panel in plum-red and black on the shoulder (fig. 1/1). Vessels still bearing traces of paint from Jabal Hafit cairns (Frifelt 1971b:figs. 1, 5, 12, 13, 17, 18, 19B, 20, 21A, 21B; During Caspers 1971b:figs. 5–6 = Mitchell 1972:pl. LVId, right), and similar, unpainted, or badly weathered vessels from Hafit (Frifelt 1971b:figs. 19D, 21C, 22A, 22B; During Caspers 1971b:figs. 3–

4 = Mitchell 1972:pl. LVId, left), Ibri (Frifelt 1975b:fig. 1), Mazyad (Frifelt 1975b:figs. 7, 9), and Tawi Silaim (de Cardi, Bell, and Starling 1982:fig. 7/9–10), once incorrectly dated to the fourteenth–thirteenth centuries B.C. (Bibby 1965:109), have been compared since 1970 (During Caspers 1970:250) by most scholars to jars excavated in Jamdat Nasr or Protoliterate c–d contexts in southern Mesopotamia. This led to the period of the graves' original construction being called "the Jemdet Nasr horizon" (Frifelt 1975a:391; cf. Doe 1984:43, 46), now more commonly known as the "Jabal Hafit horizon" (Cleuziou 1984:371), or "Hafit-Zeit" (Weisgerber 1981:179).

In fact, there is significant typological variation in the corpus of so-called Jamdat Nasr jars from the Oman peninsula (cf. Potts 1986b:figs. 1, 2). Parallels with stratified pieces from the Diyala area suggest a time range from Protoliterate c through ED III. Parallels can be cited as follows: *Protoliterate c:* Delougaz 1952:pl. 186[C.603.270]; cf. Frifelt 1971b:fig. 19D; Delougaz 1952:pl. 18c[B.513.170]; cf. Frifelt 1971b:fig. 19B; Delougaz 1952:pl. 18b[C.516.270]; cf. Frifelt 1980:fig. 1; *Protoliterate d:* Delougaz 1952:pl. 154[B.454.270]; cf. Frifelt 1971b:fig. 21C; Delougaz 1952:pl. 33, left[C.604.370]; cf. Frifelt 1971b:figs. 12, 18, and 1975b:fig. 1; Delougaz 1952:pl. 36d[C.604.370]; cf. Frifelt 1975b:fig. 9; *ED I:* Delougaz 1952:pl. 155[B.514.270]; cf. Frifelt 1971b:fig. 21C; *ED I–II:* Delougaz 1952:pls. 178[C.514.370a] and 180[C.525.370b]; cf. Frifelt 1971b:fig. 21A; *ED II:* Delougaz 1952:pl. 73f[C.515.270]; cf. Frifelt 1975b:fig. 7; and *ED III:* Delougaz 1952:pl. 102f[B.545.540]; cf. Frifelt 1971b:fig. 22B.

A Jamdat Nasr–ED III date for the Hafit horizon is also reflected in the types of faience beads found at Tawi Silaim when compared with Mesopotamian examples (de Cardi, Bell, and Starling 1982:84).

Several finds from Umm an-Nar island also fall in this time range. A collared jar (fig. 1/5) with ovoid body from cairn 1 (Thorvildsen 1963:fig. 24), unknown in the interior of Oman (Cleuziou 1984:19), can be paralleled with Woolley's type 61 (fig. 1/6) from the Royal Cemetery at Ur (Frifelt 1971b:373, n. 13), and with jar type XXXIII from the al-'Ubaid cemetery (Hall and Woolley 1927:pls. LIII, LVII). The Ur type is found most frequently in graves of ED III date, although it appears right down to the Late Akkadian period, sometimes in association with other ceramic types whose life span may run from ED III to Ur III (e.g., in PG 38, Woolley 1934:413, Nissen 1966:164). The al-'Ubaid type is of ED III date.

Contemporary with the earlier Hafit horizon is the earliest occupation at the settlement of Hili 8. Building III (period Ia–c) at Hili 8 is a 16 m² tower which appears ancestral to the later and better-known round towers of the Umm an-Nar period (Frifelt 1976:fig. 3, 1975a:figs. 3, 52–55, 1985b:fig. 3, pl. 2). Cleuziou considers this structure contemporary with Jamdat Nasr and ED I in Mesopotamia (Cleuziou 1982:3, 1986:144). A high-necked, buff-ware jar (fig. 1/2) with everted rim, shoulder ridge, and crude shoulder lugs from period Ib at Hili 8 can be compared to a Diyala type of ED I–II date (Delougaz 1952:pl. 192[D.515.370]) and a late ED I–ED II type from Tell Razuk in the Hamrin basin (Gibson et al. 1981:pl. 70/20). Black-painted redware suspension jars with pierced shoulder lugs, perforated ring base, and plastic shoulder ridge from Hili 1 have been compared with ED I suspension vessels from Tell Agrab (Frifelt 1971b:359, fig. 4), but as these occur throughout the Hili 8 sequence, it appears that they span the entire third millennium and are not to be relied on as a fossil index for the earliest part of the third millennium (Cleuziou 1980a:36; cf. de Cardi, Collier, and Doe 1976:128).

Cleuziou equates his period II, phases IIa–c, with ED II and III (Cleuziou 1986:145). It is interesting that plano-convex bricks ($50 \times 30 \times 12$ cm) appear at this time (Cleuziou 1984:12, 1986:145), and although they are not set in the herringbone pattern so typical of Mesopotamia, the mere occurrence of so typical an Early Dynastic building material in the Oman peninsula is unlikely to be entirely without significance. Pottery is rare in IIa and IIb, consisting largely of a fine black-on-red ware. Black on sand-tempered orange-buff, appearing for the first time in IIb, is dominant in IIc, and remains the common "domestic" ware throughout the entirety of period II, that is, down to the end of the third millennium (Cleuzou 1986:145). A single sherd from a hollow-footed pedestal chalice made of a red-slipped micaceous redware found in a IIc context (Cleuziou 1984:32, fig. 28/3) can be compared with sherds occurring at Tepe Yahya in all levels of IVB (Potts, in press:257; Lamberg-Karlovsky 1970:fig. 26N, O, P), and elsewhere in eastern Iran, Baluchistan, and the Indus Valley. These are also known later on Bahrain in City II levels on the Qal'at (Larsen 1980 and 1983b:fig. 51m, n), and in a grave at Sar (Ibrahim 1982:fig. 38/3). Painted black-on-red variants of the same type have been found in a "royal" tomb at 'Ali (Bibby 1965:103 and fig. 3, 1969:pl. XVI, above; cf. Frifelt 1986:133, fig. 33), and in a tomb in Dhahran (Piesinger 1983:390 and fig. 139).

Beehive graves, examples of which are known at Qarn Kabsh, Al Banah, Bat, Al 'Ayn, 'Ablah, Saih Bureid, Ba'id, Izki, Zukayt, Maysar, Fath, Gerran Amr, Tawi Silaim, Jabal al Hammah, and Aflaj, are considered by K. Frifelt to represent a transitional grave type, falling chronologically between the Hafit and Umm an-Nar types (Frifelt 1975b:69). She describes the beehive graves near Bat as consisting of "two or three curtain walls with hand-sized stones between . . . built of the brownish limestone that dominate the surrounding country and which flake in brick-like shapes ready for use . . . a low plinth, about half a meter wide, runs all the way round on the outside" (Frifelt 1975b:67). The material basis for the tentative dating of this grave type, however, is one sherd, one black-on-buff jar, and one serpentine bead from two graves at Bat (1137, 1138). While the date suggested is not necessarily wrong, it is, in our opinion, hardly substantiated by the three artifacts just cited. Furthermore, if the Hafit period is extended down to ED III, then there is no longer a gap between it and the Umm an-Nar period. The absence of a gap between the two periods is also suggested by the apparent contemporaneity of the Umm an-Nar–type tomb M at Hili and phase IIa–c (Cleuziou 1986:145).

Tombs excavated at Sabkha Hammam southeast of Abqayq (Burkholder 1974, 1984:25–29) in eastern Saudi Arabia have yielded tall, plain, buff-ware jars, often with narrow, collared rims and occasionally with straight spouts (Department of Antiquities and Museums 1975b:150; Piesinger 1983:figs. 56 and 65), showing an unmistakable similarity to types 42 (Jamdat Nasr through ED I) and 164 (early ED I) in the Jamdat Nasr cemetery at Ur (Woolley 1956:pls. 57, 64; Kolbus 1981:124, 137); Khafajah types C.525.362b (ED I and II) and D.566.370 (ED II) (Delougaz 1952:pls. 180, 195); jar type 6A at Tell Razuk in the Hamrin of late ED I–II (Gibson et al. 1981:pl. 68/16); and a straight-spouted jar of ED I date from Planquadrat I XIII at Warka (Nissen 1972: Taf. 62/5).

In 1965, during earth-moving operations on Tarut, 314 published, undecorated chlorite vessels and vessel fragments were found, mostly at al-Rufayah (Golding 1974:26; Zarins 1978; Potts 1986b:Appendix 2, pl. 5, fig. 7/2; Burkholder 1984:pls. 15a, d, 18a, 19b, c, 20b, 22c, 28a). The Jamdat Nasr cemetery at Ur contained stone bowls which Golding used as a point of reference for dating the Tarut material, specifically Woolley's type 31 (fig. 1/4). According to Kolbus, type 31 is restricted to vessels of steatite or chlorite, and these occur only in the ED II graves in the Jamdat Nasr cemetery (Kolbus 1981:82). Also of probable ED II date is a broken male figurine of lapis lazuli from Tarut (Golding 1974:fig. 4/11). An unpainted, globular jar with everted rim from Tarut (Department of Antiquities and Museums 1975a:6; Potts 1986b:pl. 4, fig. 7/1) is similar to one from Hafit cairn 23 (Frifelt 1971b:fig. 22B), to Jamdat Nasr cemetery type 56 of ED I date (Kolbus 1981:142), and to Diyala type B.545.540 of ED II–III date (Delougaz 1952:pl. 102f). A crude limestone statue of a naked male, hands clasped in a devotional attitude, which S. A.

Rashid has dated to the Fara period, that is, ED II–III (Rashid 1972:162; Department of Antiquities and Museums 1975b:149; Potts 1986b:pl. 6a, b), was also found on Tarut.

Also datable to this time are about 323 carved soft stone vessel fragments which belong to the *série ancienne* defined by de Miroschedji (de Miroschedji 1973) or to Kohl's "Intercultural Style" (Kohl 1974). Until recently (Zarins 1978; cf. Burkholder 1984:pls. 10, 11, 13, 27a, b), only a small selection of these had been published (Burkholder 1971; Golding 1974). We have tabulated the Tarut material following the stylistic categories defined by Kohl (Kohl 1974:150–218) and find the following distribution: *representational designs:* combatant snakes, felines, or eagles, 93; date palms, 11; scorpions, 5; figured, 56; Imdugud, 15; guilloche, 3; rosettes, 2; total = 185, *nonrepresentational designs:* huts, 41; mats, 34; whirls, 2; imbricates, 6; bevelled squares, 55; total = 138. In addition, eight fragments of bell-shaped bowls were also found on Tarut (Zarins 1978:cat. nos. 5, 91, 334, 417, 497, 585, 587, and 593).

The variety of stone colors in the Tarut corpus, ranging from almost black to green to pale gray, suggests multiple sources, an assumption substantiated by the findings of a variety of analyses to which a portion of the Tarut material was subjected (Kohl, Harbottle, and Sayre 1979). Pieces made of a talc (true "steatite") or talc-chlorite, possibly made of stone quarried about 150–200 miles southwest of Riyadh, show a strong compositional similarity to pieces from Mari, Bismaya, and Failaka. Chlorite-quartz, chlorite-andradite mixtures, and pieces made of a rare phlogopite also occur in the Tarut corpus. These come from at least two clearly separate chlorite sources (Arabian groups A and B). A third group of Tarut finds is compositionally very similar to pieces from Kish, Khafajah, Nippur, and Ur (Kohl, Harbottle, and Sayre 1979). In addition, about half a dozen pieces of carved muscovite schist included portions of two large canisters with combatant snakes (Zarins 1978:cat. nos. 544, 545; Burkholder 1984:pl. 23). Muscovite schist occurs in limited quantities over a wide area in western Arabia (M. Golding and R. L. Maby, Jr., pers. comm.).

At Khafajah, Mari, Nippur, and Ur, stratified examples of similar chlorite are mostly of ED II and IIIa date (Kohl 1974:243–52; al-Gailani 1975:47). De Miroschedji has listed three pieces (U. 7072, 231, and 224) as coming from Akkadian contexts at Ur, and pointed to a piece from Tello depicting a motif (the dragon as symbol of the god Ningishzidda) not found prior to the Akkadian period (de Miroschedji 1973:25, fig. 3), as two pieces of evidence for extending the life of the style into the Akkadian era (cf. Sürenhagen 1977:169). In fact U. 7072 is a surface find, while U. 231 and 224 both come from the E-nun-maḫ destruction level sealed beneath a floor dating

to the time of Kurigalzu (information kindly provided by Timothy Potts, Oxford).

Outside of Tarut, carved soft stone in the *série ancienne* is known in much smaller quantities on Failaka, where examples of the figured, mat weave, and hut motives occur (Kohl 1974:148, 149, maps 4, 5). These, however, are chronologically anomalous, since the colonization of Failaka does not appear to have taken place until the twentieth century B.C. (see below). No *série ancienne* chlorite has appeared on Bahrain, a point in favor of dating the beginning of City 1 there to ED IIIb at the earliest. One decorated sherd with the mat motif was found during the Iraqi excavations at Umm an-Nar (Cleuziou 1980a:43, center right), while an undecorated canister of the type normally covered with the hut motif came from cairn 1 on Umm an-Nar (Thorvildsen 1963:fig. 21). A beaker from tomb A at Hili North is said to recall the *série ancienne* (Cleuziou and Vogt 1983:41, fig. 10/5), but in fact finds no parallel in that corpus.

On Bahrain, a badly worn, recut Jamdat Nasr–style stamp seal is known from grave 1, mound 1, near al-Hajjar (Al-Tarawneh n.d.; Porada 1970; Rice 1972:68). A single Jamdat Nasr polychrome sherd from a temple I layer at Barbar (Mortensen 1971:395) may perhaps be attributable to "an earlier activity at the site" (Mortensen 1986:181).

The Late Third Millennium (2500–1950 B.C.)

Our principal stratified sources of information for this period are the sites of Umm an-Nar, Hili 8, and Maysar on the Oman peninsula, and the North Wall Sounding (hereafter NWS) on Ras al-Qalaʿat, Bahrain.

On the Oman peninsula the period ca. 2500–2000 B.C. (see table 1 for radiocarbon determinations from Hili 1, Hili 8, Bat, and Maysar) is known as the Umm an-Nar period, taking its name from an island off the coast of Abu Dhabi. Here elements of a distinctive culture complex were recognized for the first time in the late 1950s (Glob 1959c:164–65, 1959b:239; Bibby 1965:108, 1966:148–49, 1967:93–94). Since that time much work has been done on sites of this period (Frifelt 1971a, 1971b, 1975a, 1976, 1979, 1985; de Cardi, Collier, and Doe 1976; de Cardi, Doe, and Roskams 1977; de Cardi, Bell, and Starling 1982; Cleuziou, Pottier, and Salles 1978; Cleuziou 1980a, 1980b, 1982, 1984, 1986; Cleuziou and Costantini 1980; Cleuziou and Vogt 1983; Berthoud and Cleuziou 1983; Weisgerber 1980a, 1980b, 1981), and a plethora of recent articles deal with the copper resources and bronze metallurgy of late third millennium Oman (e.g., Berthoud 1980; Berthoud et al. 1978, 1982; Franklin, Grosjean, and Tinkler 1976; Goettler, Firth, and Huston 1976; Hassan and al-Sulaimi 1979;

Hauptmann and Weisgerber 1981; Meadow, Humphries, and Hastings 1976; Kroll 1984; Weisgerber 1983, 1984).

The ceramics of this period comprise three separate, if not mutually exclusive, groups belonging to the area of primary coastal settlement, that is, Umm an-Nar itself; the settlements of the interior, for example, Hili 8, Bat, Amlah, and Maysar; and the graves, respectively.

The pottery of the Umm an-Nar settlement consists mainly of plain wares, usually buff-colored, sand-tempered, and gray-slipped. Sherds with meandering ridges, often ending in snakes heads, also occur here (Frifelt 1971b:361, fig. 7). These are also known, inter alia, in nearly all levels of period IV at Tepe Yahya in Iran (Lamberg-Karlovsky 1970:figs. 28Q, R, 32G; Potts, in press:47, fig. 33), where they are perhaps most plentiful in early IVB; in the City I levels of the NWS at Ras al-Qalʿat (Larsen 1980:figs. 42b, 46g); and in Proto-Imperial levels at Susa (Stève and Gasche 1971:pl. 73/1–4), all contexts datable roughly to ca. 2350–2100 B.C. A cylinder seal-impressed, buff-ware sherd (fig. 1/3) from the settlement (Bibby 1969:362) has recently been compared by P. Amiet (Amiet 1985:9–10) to impressed sherds from Tell Mardikh Palace G (Mazzoni 1984), which he dates to ca. 2400–2250 B.C., thus reversing the ED I date which he had formerly proposed (Amiet 1975:426).

The Hili 8 excavations continue to provide the best stratified ceramic sequence for the interior of the Oman peninsula in the later third millennium. The pottery of period IIe–g (IId has been omitted from the sequence; see Cleuziou 1986:145) is quite homogeneous, consisting of a variety of holemouth jars and bowls, normally made of a reddish buff or orange, fine grit-tempered ware, occasionally slipped in buff, gray, or red. The vast majority of the pottery is made of this ware (said to differ from the "domestic ware" of IIc mentioned above; Cleuziou 1986:145) and is generally decorated in black with painted wavy and occasionally intersecting lines, or very rarely with spirals (Cleuziou 1980a:36). Minor variations in decoration occur from phase to phase in period II, but vessel form appears constant throughout the sequence. Small numbers of this type (fig. 1/7, 8) appear in all phases of period IV at Tepe Yahya (Potts, in press: fig. 37/A1, 2, 4; figs. 42F, 49K, 53B; Lamberg-Karlovsky 1970:fig. 16D).

The fine wares, which have been compared with "Kulli" pottery from Pakistan and eastern Iran (Thorvildsen 1963:219; Bibby 1969:278–80; Frifelt 1971b:374), number only in the dozens in the Hili settlement levels, but represent about 50 percent of the total ceramic inventory in the Hili graves. They are also common at other Umm an-Nar period grave sites (Frifelt 1975a:32, 33, 59, 81; de Cardi, Collier, and Doe 1976:122; Weisgerber 1980b:Abb. 73). The principal types are black-on-gray ware, incised grayware, black-on-red ware, black-on-red slipped buff ware, and brown- or black-painted buff wares.

The black-on-gray ware is best known in the form of a round jar with short neck, or in the shape of a canister. Characteristic are friezes of stylized running caprids between registers of parallel lines. Intervening bands of geometric decoration and of stylized palm trees also occur. The appearance of this type of pottery at Bampur in periods IVc–VI, and at Shahr-i Sokhta in period IV, where it is well dated to ca. 2200–1800 B.C., is generally known (cf. Lamberg-Karlovsky and Tosi 1973:fig. 64; Tosi 1974:fig. 10, 1976:85). Its presence at Shahr-i Sokhta in period IV does not serve to date the entirety of the Umm an-Nar period on the Oman peninsula (cf. Potts 1978:39), but rather, in light of the presence in Umm an-Nar cairn 1 of a jar (probably imported) of ED III type (discussed above), suggests a synchronism between *late* Umm an-Nar and *early* Shahr-i Sokhta IV. Black-on-gray ware has been found in at least four contexts in the Gulf outside of the Oman peninsula. On Bahrain, a single sherd came from a site near Horat Unqa (Larsen 1980:96), and on Tarut, a nearly complete, short-necked, round-bodied jar with a frieze of running caprids was found during construction activities there in the 1960s (Department of Antiquities and Museums 1975b:148). Another nearly complete example of similar description was found in a Sabkhah Hammam tomb near Abqayq (Piesinger 1983:fig. 61, type 51; cf. Thorvildsen 1963:fig. 23, upper). In addition, a single black-on-gray sherd is reported from a location south of Dhahran (Golding 1974:29).

The incised grayware of Oman, eastern Iran, and Pakistan has recently been reviewed by de Cardi (de Cardi, Collier, and Doe 1976:118–22, figs. 15, 16). At Shahr-i Sokhta, both the incised grayware and painted black-on-gray occur in the so-called Burnt Building of Shahr-i Sokhta IV (Biscione 1979:293–94). However, the argument against dating all of Umm an-Nar by the occurrence of black-on-gray ware in period IV applies equally in the case of the incised grayware. In addition to the fifteen sites with incised grayware listed by de Cardi (de Cardi, Collier, and Doe 1976:118–22), we can add Tarut (fig. 1/9), where two pieces with the hut motif were found (Zarins 1978:77, cat. nos. 198, 201); and Umm ar-Ramadh, where a single piece was found on the surface (Piesinger 1983:486).

Parallels between black-on-red ware from Umm an-Nar funerary contexts and settlement pottery from Tepe Yahya IVB and Mundigak IV3 have sometimes been overemphasized (e.g., Frifelt 1975a:369–71). Black/brown-on-red/buff suspension vessels (fig. 1/10) with lattice decoration (Frifelt 1975a:fig. 29b; Cleuziou, Pottier, and Salles 1978:38, fig. 5/8) do not occur at Tepe Yahya.

However, a black-on-orange beaker (fig. 1/11) on which two humped bulls are shown beneath a metope of parallel, zigzag lines (Potts, in press:fig. 51L) from an early IVA context at Tepe Yahya is similar to a globular jar (fig. 1/12) from cairn 5 at Umm an-Nar (Thorvildsen 1963:fig. 23). In addition, a small, variegated assemblage of black-on-orange/buff sherds with irregular, geometric designs, found in IVC and early IVB contexts at Tepe Yahya (e.g., fig. 1/14), is comparable to material (fig. 1/13) from the Bat graves (Potts, in press:fig. 37/D2; cf. Frifelt 1975a:fig. 32a). Parallels in black-on-red ware, said to link Umm an-Nar sites with Mundigak IV3 (Frifelt 1976a:371, n. 21), in fact relate more to IV1 and IV2 than to IV3 and are more general than those drawn between Tepe Yahya or Shahr-i Sokhta and the Omani sites. In eastern Saudi Arabia, black-on-red ware of Umm an-Nar type has been found on Tarut (Golding 1974:26, fig. 5/2; Burkholder 1984:190 and pl. 17b).

Parallels between the streak-burnished grayware of the Umm an-Nar period in Oman (Frifelt 1975a:369, fig. 18a) and that of Tepe Yahya are too general to be of real chronological value, for neither the vessel forms nor the burnishing patterns are comparable (Potts, in press:251).

Brief mention should also be made of thumbnail-impressed sherds. These have been reported from the second period of Hili 8, where they are dated to ca. 2500 B.C. and believed to be of Harappan inspiration if not manufacture (Cleuziou 1984:390, fig. 41.28/1–2). Similar sherds are also known from Maysar 1 (Weisgerber 1984:fig. 3); al-Rufayah on Tarut (Piesinger 1983:292, fig. 83/15); and a site in the Abqayq area (Piesinger 1983:499, fig. 148/2–3).

Carved chlorite in the *série récente* (de Miroschedji 1973) is common on Umm an-Nar period sites, such as Amlah 1 and 2a (de Cardi, Collier, and Doe 1976:139–40); Bat (Frifelt 1975a:fig. 28a); Bilad al-Maaidin (Weisgerber 1981:211, Abb. 43/1, 3); Hili 1 (Frifelt 1975a:fig. 17d); Hili 8, period IIf (Cleuziou 1980a:fig. 41/1, 2); Hili North, Tomb A (Cleuziou and Vogt 1983:fig. 10); Maysar 1 (Weisgerber 1980a:83, Abb. 39, 40; 1981:213, Abb. 46); Samad (de Cardi, Collier, and Doe 1976:156; Cleuziou 1980a:41); and Tawi Silaim (de Cardi, Doe, and Roskams 1977:23, fig. 4). Maysar 1 was a production site, at which shallow and deep bowls (fig. 1/15); small cups with and without a lip for a lid; and rectangular, compartmented vessels were produced during the Umm an-Nar period (Weisgerber 1981:212,Abb. 46). These were decorated with simple, incised lines, and one or more rows of the dot-in-circle motif (also called the concentric circle motif, or the dotted double circle), produced by a tube or compass drill. Thanks to the Maysar excavations we can now state that the types just described represent the *early* phase of dot-in-circle decorated chlor-

ite, for which the original name *série récente* may be retained, whereas a later phase of early second millennium date, in which the dot-in-circle is used on vessels of differing type (see below), may be most appropriately called *série tardive*, as recently suggested by Cleuziou (1986:155, n. 6).

Three *série récente* bowls from Mesopotamia are important for the dating of this group. The earliest two come from graves (PG 473 and 899) of Middle Akkadian date (reigns of Maništušu, 2269–2255 B.C., and Naram-sin, 2254–2218 B.C.) at Ur (Nissen 1966:170, 177). A third example from Tello (Cros 1910:250; cf. Amiet 1979: pl.XXIa) bears a dedication in standard Neo-Sumerian by one Ur-Baba, son of Šeš-šeš, to an unnamed *ensi*. The dedicant cannot, as M. Lambert claimed (*apud* de Miroschedji 1973:28, n. 116), be identified unequivocally with an Ur-Baba who lived during the reign of Amar-Suen (2046–2038 B.C.), since both Ur-Baba and Šeš-Šeš were among the most common names in the Lagaš onomasticon (J.-P. Grégoire, pers. comm.; cf. Limet 1968:530, 537; for a list of the texts mentioning merchants by the names of Šeš-Šeš and Ur-Baba at Lagaš and Girsu, see Neumann 1979:23, 24). The most one can say, therefore, is that, in view of the Neo-Sumerian inscription on the bowl in question, it must date to the period of the Second Dynasty of Lagaš (ca. 2164–2112 B.C.) or the Third Dynasty of Ur (2112–2004 B.C.). This is of obvious significance for the relative chronology of the Umm an-Nar period, especially when one considers that, notwithstanding the mat-weave sherd from the settlement on Umm an-Nar mentioned above, *série récente* chlorite is a *fossil directeur* of Umm an-Nar period graves in the Oman peninsula.

Série récente material is also known from Tarut (fig. 1/ 16), where about fifty-seven pieces have been designated as "Omani" imports (Zarins 1978:66; cf. Piesinger 1983:fig. 183/12). At least eleven pieces can be compared with virtually identical types from Maysar 1 (lids, Zarins 1978:pl. 71/37; cf. Weisgerber 1981:Abb. 46/8; bowls, pl. 71/104, 384, 565, 586; cf. Abb. 46/4, 6, 9; cups, pl. 71/107, 331, 332, 547; cf. Abb. 46/11; and compartmented vessels, pl. 71/551; cf. Abb. 46/13).

The typical cairn of the Umm an-Nar period is multi-chambered, containing between two and ten separate chambers, and the remains of up to two hundred individuals (see now Cleuziou and Vogt 1983 on "Umm an-Nar burial customs"). The outer wall is constructed of large, "sugar lump" limestone blocks, sometimes faced with smaller pieces of limestone (Frifelt 1975b:69). The cairns vary from 3 m to 15 m in diameter.

Finally, two seals of the Umm an-Nar period should be mentioned. The first, from House 4 at Maysar 1, is a three-sided prism, drilled longitudinally, and depicts animals such as wild sheep(?), ibex, zebu, scorpions, and dogs (Weisgerber 1980b:105–6, photo Abb. 77; Weisgerber 1980a:86, drawing Abb. 15). Triangular prism seals are known in the late third millennium on Crete, in Syria, and in Egypt. During Caspers considers the prism-shaped "sealing amulets" of the Harappan civilization comparable to the Maysar seal (*apud* Weisgerber 1980a:86, n. 17; 1983:661–70). Better comparanda can be found in central Asia, however, including a prism seal showing a lion, a man, and a griffin, from Anau in Turkmenistan (Pumpelly 1908:text fig. 400, pls. 41, 45); and a broken prism seal depicting a winged creature from Dashly in northern Afghanistan (Sarianidi 1976:fig. 28/2). A four-sided prism seal in the Ashmolean, said to be Iranian, should also be noted in this connection (Buchanan 1984:36 and pl. XVI:246). The second seal to be mentioned is a pear-shaped stamp seal, also from Maysar 1, bearing an incised stick figure which may be a character in the Indus script (Weisgerber 1981:218, Abb. 53; cf. Brunswig, Parpola, and Potts 1983:101).

The contemporary sequences from the NWS at Ras al-Qalʿat and the temples at Barbar on Bahrain have recently been thoroughly revised (Andersen 1986; Bibby 1986; Højlund 1986; Mortensen 1986). The changes entailed are so great that the older reports on these excavations should no longer be consulted for either the assignment of specific levels to particular periods or phases in the NWS (e.g., Bibby 1969; Larsen 1980, 1983b) or for the periodization of the temple sequence at Barbar (e.g., Mortensen 1971).

Let us turn first to the NWS (see fig. 2). The idea of a "pre-Barbar" settlement prior to City 1 (Bibby 1969:356, 360; Larsen 1980:269, 1983b:217ff.) has now been abandoned. Levels 30–22 in the NWS represent the earliest period on the Qalʿat, known as City 1. Chain-ridged pottery of red "Barbar" ware, a "thin, red, hard-fired, grit-tempered ware with small lime-particles" (Højlund 1981:37), is characteristic. Tall jars with ovoid bodies and short-necked storage jars with meandering ridges, normally made of a sand-tempered orange or buff ware, from the lowest four levels, can be compared with pottery from Umm an-Nar (Bibby 1969:360; cf. Larsen 1980:figs. 42/b, e, g, 43/d, e, f) and contemporary, late third millennium levels at Tepe Yahya (Potts, in press: fig. 33/F1). Larsen has also pointed to parallels between ring-based jars from early City 1 levels, and material of late Early Dynastic and Akkadian date from Nippur (Larsen 1980:275); storage jars with rims similar to the triple-grooved rim of Akkadian and Ur III date (Larsen 1980:278, fig. 45f–l, o) are also present. Comb-incised buff ware, present in levels 25–19, can be compared with finds from late third millennium Tepe Yahya (Potts, in press:fig. 49q), contemporary Bampur V–VI (de Cardi

1970:figs. 32/12, 41/473), and Ur III Susa (Stève and Gasche 1971:pl. 66/9–10).

This being the case, one could comfortably begin level 30 of the NWS sequence at ca. 2400 B.C., dating levels 27–22 to ca. 2350–2100 B.C. on the basis of Umm an-Nar black-on-red/orange fine ware found there, although Cleuziou has stressed the difficulty of making exact comparisons with Umm an-Nar types in the Oman peninsula (Cleuziou 1986:149). Furthermore, the occurrence of *série récente* chlorite as early as level 26 suggests a date of perhaps 2300 B.C. for that level, which would allow for the appearance of the earliest examples of this type in Mesopotamia (discussed above) slightly later. Once again, it should be stressed that the absence of *série ancienne* chlorite, as in Oman, suggests that the NWS sequence postdates ED IIIA, if we accept ED II–IIIA as the date for the floruit of this style. All in all, a date of ca. 2400–2100 B.C. can be suggested for City 1.

Contemporary material is also known from eastern Saudi Arabia. Both surface survey and sondage in the main tell on Tarut recovered City 1 chain-ridged sherds (Bibby 1966:150, 1967:95, 1973b:29–31; Masry 1974: 143–45). These have also appeared along the entire coastal strip from Jinnah Island southward to Dhahran (Golding 1974:29). Among the unstratified finds from Tarut are vessels similar to Diyala types B.556.540 of Akkadian date, and C.565.540 of ED III/Proto-Imperial and later date (Delougaz 1952:pls. 160 bottom, 185 bottom). Also comparable are Royal Cemetery types 44a and 44b, 46, and 48 (Woolley 1934:pl. 253), the former two dating to Akkadian and Ur III times, the latter two concentrated in the Akkadian period (Nissen 1966: Taf. 5).

The end of the Umm an-Nar period in the Oman peninsula is put at ca. 2000 B.C. by most researchers working in the area, and this date receives support not only from the ceramic parallels cited above, but from the association of *série récente* chlorite with Umm an-Nar period sites, an artifact group whose life span in Babylonia seems to run through the Ur III period. With this in mind, it is interesting to note that, on the Qalʿat, Umm an-Nar sherds do not appear in the NWS after level 22, that is, they are present only in City 1 and not in the following City 2A phase. This suggests that the dividing line between City 1 and City 2 be placed around 2000 B.C., a date corroborated by a cuneiform text (Brunswig, Parpola, and Potts 1983:107–8,pl. III, fig. 12) written in early Isin-Larsa style found 7 m to the north of the NWS in a layer Bibby equates to NWS 21–19 (Bibby 1986:114), that is, City 2A. As we shall see, however, the associated seals call for a slight adjustment to this date.

The first seals in the NWS, the "Persian Gulf" seals as

Sir Mortimer Wheeler called them (Wheeler 1958:246; cf. Bibby 1958a, Hallo and Buchanan 1965:206), also appear in NWS 21, lasting through level 18 (City 2B). These are circular stamp seals, with a high, pierced boss bearing one or occasionally two grooves on the top. Animals (predominantly bulls) and abstract motifs, but generally no humans (but note Golding 1974:29), are used in the design. Roughly thirty seals can, with reasonable confidence, be assigned to this group. These come from the following sites or areas: *Qalᶜat al-Bahrain* (Bibby 1958a:fig. 13b, c, 1967:fig. 4b, c, d, e, g; Brunswig, Parpola, and Potts 1983:figs. 8a–b, 9?); *Sar el-Jisr* (Ibrahim 1982:figs. 49/4, 50/3; Mughal 1983:pl. XLV/1–5); *Dhahran* (Barger 1969:139; Golding 1974:29; Piesinger 1983:fig. 186/11); *Tarut* (this vol., fig. 1/20; Zarins 1978:pl. 70/583 = Burkholder 1984:pl. 32a); *Failaka* (Bibby 1969:253 = Brunswig, Parpola, and Potts 1983:fig. 6); *Luristan* (Amiet 1973:pl. 23a–b = Brunswig, Parpola, and Potts 1983:fig. 3); *Ur and environs* (Gadd 1932:pls. I/2–5, II/10–11?, III/15–17); and *Babylonia, unspecified* (Gadd 1932:pl. III/18).

Persian Gulf seals have been dated cautiously to the Akkadian period (e.g., Bibby 1986:115), and to the Early Dynastic era (e.g., Porada 1971:331ff.). Yet the only reasonably datable examples from Ur are U.17649 (Gadd 1932:pl. III/16) from a grave (PG 1847) of early Ur III date (Nissen 1966:106), and U.8685 (Gadd 1932:pl. III/15) from a grave (PG 401) that can be considered generally Neo-Sumerian (Nissen 1966:54). A date slightly before ca. 2100 B.C. is therefore proposed for the appearance of the Persian Gulf–style seals, and with them for the beginning of City 2A. As the Persian Gulf seals appear to have been superseded by the Dilmun seal group, whose beginnings date to the Isin-Larsa period (see below), a terminus of ca. 1950 B.C. for both the Persian Gulf group and City 2B, or NWS level 18, the last stratum in which seals of this type are not found on the Qalᶜat, seems in order. This would mean that the early Isin-Larsa-type text mentioned above would date to the latter part of City 2A.

In connection with the chronology proposed here, note that Buchanan drew attention to the similarity in the depiction of the scorpion on U.16397 (Gadd 1932:pl. II/11), and on Mesopotamian stamp seals of Neo-Sumerian and Larsa date (Hallo and Buchanan 1965:206).

The fact that no fewer than twelve of the Persian Gulf seals listed above bear Indus inscriptions (Gadd 1932: pls. I/2–5, III/15–18; Brunswig, Parpola, and Potts 1983:figs. 3, 6, 8, 9) is also chronologically significant. The two Ur exemplars from Ur III and Neo-Sumerian graves fall into this group, incidentally representing the earliest Indus inscriptions found anywhere in Mesopotamia. Also, the Ur III period is precisely the time in which

people from Meluḫḫa, normally identified with the Harappan area, are thought to have resided in the territory of Lagaš (Parpola, Parpola, and Brunswig 1977:129ff.; Brunswig, Parpola, and Potts 1983:104). Seals found in Mesopotamia or the Arabian Gulf with Indus inscriptions may have been used by Meluḫḫans at this time. The presence of Indus-type stone weights (Bibby 1986:110–11) in late City 1 (NWS 23–22) and City 2A (NWS 21–19) also attests to contact with the Harappan area at this time.

With the start of City 2A we also see the introduction of a new common ware, the so-called red-ridged ware, which eventually replaces chain-ridged pottery as the main ceramic type in City 2. Levels 21–20 attest to the brief coexistence of chain-ridged and red-ridged pottery, and this is significant for the date of the earliest temple (Ia–b) at Barbar (Glob 1954b:149–53, 1955:178–93, 1958b:126–27, 1959a:144–45, 1959b:233–39; Andersen 1956:175–88; Andersen 1986; Bibby 1965:101–2, 1969:69–75; Mortensen 1956:189–98, 1971:393–97; During Caspers 1971a:223, 1973:132; for the latest plan, see Bahrain, Ministry of Information 1983:26; Andersen 1986:169), where both types also occur. Temple Ia–b also contained sherds of Umm an-Nar fine ware (e.g., Mortensen 1971:fig. 6, bottom right), which Cleuziou considers "very clearly late" (Cleuziou 1986:150). This may mean that, contrary to Mortensen (1986:183) who has equated Temple Ia–b solely with Qalᶜat NWS 21, Temple Ia must have been founded at least as early as late City 1, NWS 22, when Umm an-Nar ware is last seen in the NWS, or else it is just chance that none has been found in NWS 21–20 when, as in Temple Ia–b, both chain-ridged and red-ridged pottery are present. A link between NWS 20, mid-City 2A, and Temple Ia–b is the presence of a goblet in the former of a type found in the foundation deposit of the latter (Larsen 1980:313, 1983b:247).

Mortensen and Højlund compare the pottery of Barbar Temple IIa with that of City 2B (NWS 18) on the Qalᶜat (Mortensen 1986:183). Objects from the foundation deposit of Temple IIa all cluster in date between ca. 2200–1800 B.C. These include a copper bull's head (Glob 1955:178; During Caspers 1971a:217–224; Braun-Holzinger 1984:33, Taf. 25/96) with horns curved in a style reminiscent of horn-crowns on late Akkadian cylinder seals (Mortensen 1986:184; see Boehmer 1967:table IV, J23 bottom); tall, cylindrical alabaster jars (Glob 1959a:figs. 2–4; Mortensen 1971:fig. 7) of a type well known in the Indo-Iranian borderlands in the late third and early second millennium B.C. (Amiet 1977:96–99; Potts 1983a:129–31, 1986a); and an anthropomorphic bronze mirror handle (Rao 1969; During Caspers 1973) belonging to a genre well known in late third and early second millennium B.C. Baluchistan, Uzbekistan, and Afghanistan (Potts 1983a:131–32). Since these finds come from a foundation deposit, however, they must not be given undue weight for dating purposes.

The Early Second Millennium (1950–1750 B.C.)

The remainder of the City 2 sequence on Bahrain, that is, phases 2C (NWS 17), 2D (NWS 16–10), and 2F (NWS 9–8), can be dated to the Isin-Larsa and early Old Babylonian periods. The later style Gulf seals, normally known as "Dilmun" seals (Hallo and Buchanan 1965:206; cf. Kjaerum 1980:45), occur in levels 17–9. They are characterized by a low boss decorated with three parallel incised lines flanked by four dots-in-circles. The motif repertoire of the Dilmun seals includes human as well as animal figures. "Hybrids" combining the iconography of the Persian Gulf seals with the boss of the Dilmun seals (e.g., Bibby 1967:fig. 4f; Ibrahim 1982:fig. 49/6) or Dilmun seal iconography with the simpler Persian Gulf boss (e.g., Ibrahim 1982:fig. 50/2; Mughal 1983:pl. XLVIII/4a) are also known. Perhaps these are chronologically transitional.

The dating of the earliest seals of Dilmun type was first established by B. Buchanan, who pointed to the presence of an impression of a Dilmun seal on the text YBC 5447, dating to the tenth year of Gungunum of Larsa, ca. 1923 B.C. (Hallo and Buchanan 1965:203). A text from Susa (Sb 11221 + 12404), bearing the impression of a Dilmun seal, has been dated (palaeographically) by M. Lambert to the early Isin-Larsa period (Lambert 1976:71, cf. Amiet 1986:265), but most of the Old Babylonian texts from Susa, including one (TS.A/XV.46) that books the receipt of 12.5 minas of silver from a Dilmunite (de Meyer 1966:116), date from the period of Hammurabi (1792–1750 B.C.) down to ca. 1500 B.C. (Salonen 1962:9). Both of these impressions were made with seals belonging to P. Kjaerum's earliest type IA (Kjaerum 1980:46).

An Isin-Larsa date for the IA seals is important, since examples of this type were also found in Barbar Temple IIb (Mortensen 1986:184). On the other hand, an example of Kjaerum's IB seal type, datable to the Old Babylonian period (Mortensen 1986:185), was found in a Temple III context. In addition, a "sherd identical to black on red painted graveware from the Wadi Suq in Oman" (Larsen 1980:311, 1983b:247; cf. Frifelt 1975a:fig. 22d) was found in a Temple III context, albeit north of the temple itself (Mortensen 1986:181). As we shall see, this type of pottery also dates to the first half of the second millennium in the Oman peninsula.

Before leaving the subject of Bahrain, we should briefly mention the dating of the famous tombs there (for bibliography, see Potts 1983b). Chain-ridged pottery is not found in the tombs (Bibby 1954:132–41, 1969:147; Frifelt 1986:129), and therefore the earliest graves may only date to ca. 2100 B.C., or the beginning of City 2A in the NWS. Many tombs, however, date to the Kassite, Neo-Babylonian, Seleucid, or Parthian periods (e.g., Rice 1972; Al-Tarawneh n.d.). One of the most common pottery types found in graves is a fine red- or buff-ware jar with "screw top" and round base which can be closely compared to examples from the Apadana at Susa, probably datable to the Ur III and Isin-Larsa periods (de Mecquenem 1924:fig. 7). A number of important new publications now provide a large body of tomb material with which to work (During Caspers 1980; Cleuziou, Lombard, and Salles 1981; Reade and Burleigh 1978:75–83; Ibrahim 1982; Mughal 1983; Frifelt 1986; Potts 1985:688–95).

Sometime shortly after 2000 B.C. the island of Failaka was colonized, probably by people from Bahrain. The Danish excavations conducted there between 1958 and 1963 brought to light a sizable quantity of Bronze Age material which is gradually being published (e.g., Kjaerum 1980, 1983; Højlund 1981; Glassner 1984). In addition, brief investigations by an American team (Carter 1972, 1983) and new work since 1983 by a French mission (Salles 1984) have contributed more information.

A date of ca. 2000 B.C. for the foundation of the settlements on the F3 and F6 tells has been proposed (Kjaerum 1983:8; Højlund 1986:chart), based on the presence of two Neo-Sumerian cylinder seals, one of which is inscribed (Glassner 1984:35), just above virgin soil in the Danish trenches on F3 and F6, respectively (Kjaerum 1983:154–55, nos. 368–69). Dilmun seals were "completely dominant" here (Kjaerum 1980:45), however, and can be no earlier than the Isin-Larsa period as shown above, while an Old Babylonian cylinder seal was found in the lowest meter of deposit on F6. A date of ca. 1950 B.C. is therefore suggested here for the beginning of the Failaka sequence. The two Neo-Sumerian seals could easily have been old by the time of their arrival on Failaka. An analogous case which could be cited is that of the kārum at Kültepe, where the presence of at least a dozen Ur III seal impressions in level II does not alter the fact that this level should be dated to ca. 1900–1824 B.C. on the basis of references to Irišum I, Puzur-Aššur II, and perhaps Sargon I in texts and seal impressions also found there (Orlin 1970:208–9).

This chronology would also be supported by ceramic parallels between Failaka and southern Babylonia. Højlund now divides the Failaka sequence into four periods, Ia–b, 2, 3a–c, and 4a–b (Højlund 1983, 1986, contra 1981). Of interest for us is the presence of Barbar red-ridged ware and the complete absence of chain-ridged sherds in periods 1–3, coupled with the rare occurrence in periods 1–2 (ca. 3 percent) of sherds showing "a slender, flaring band rim with a short vertical neck and a round-bottomed, oval body," most common in Isin-Larsa contexts in Mesopotamia (Højlund 1983:2). In period 3 as much as 60 percent of the Failaka pottery is considered Mesopotamian, including "a jar with ring base, thick oval body and simple rim . . . sloping inward with an everted lip." A very similar jar from the recent Isin excavations contained a tablet dated in the thirty-ninth year of Hammurabi (Højlund 1983:2). Thus, period 3 is dated generally to the Old Babylonian period, a date fully consistent with the evidence of the seals. Højlund also draws close parallels between the pottery of Failaka and the Qal'at as follows: Failaka 1A:City 2C–D, Failaka 3A:City 2F, Failaka 3B:City 3A. He has dated the pottery of the latter complex, also comparable to that of Barbar Temple III, to the late Old Babylonian and early Kassite period, but this will not be dealt with in any further detail here as it brings us to the end of the time span with which we are concerned.

"Wadi Suq" is the name given in the Oman peninsula to a period of ca. 700 years which begins in the early second millennium. Several settlements are known, including Hili 8, in Al-Ain (Cleuziou 1981:280–81); Shimal, on the coast of northern Ras al-Khaimah (de Cardi 1971); and possibly Tawi Sa'id, in the Omani Sharqiyah (de Cardi, Bell, and Starling 1982:85–86). Graves of the period are of various types. Long, collective burials consisting of an oval enclosure of rough stone slabs with a flat or saddle-back roof have been excavated at Qattarah, in Al-Ain (al-Naimi n.d.; Cleuziou 1981:284), Al-Qusais, in Dubai ("Archaeological Excavations" n.d.), and Shimal (Donaldson 1984:19–220, figs. 2–15). Single graves have been excavated in the Wadi Suq, above Sohar, and the Wadi Sunaysl, near Ibri (Frifelt 1975a:377–78), and at Maysar 9, in the Wadi Samad (Weisgerber 1981:219–29).

Cleuziou has stressed the disjuncture between period II (Umm an-Nar) and III (Wadi Suq) in the Hili 8 sequence (Cleuziou 1981:281, 1986:146), particularly with regard to pottery. Spouted, globular pots appear, covered with a pattern of large, parallel, zigzag lines. The ware most commonly encountered is a porous, red-slipped, grit-tempered redware. A fine, well-fired redware, often in the form of a beaker painted with horizontal parallel lines, chevrons, and geometric patterns, also occurs. At Ra's al-Junayz, 11 km south of Ra's al-Hadd on the east coast of Oman, a sherd incised with four Harappan signs recalling incised sherds from Kalibangan has recently been found on the surface of a site with remains of about twenty stone structures (Tosi 1982).

Wadi Suq period chlorite consists of round-bodied suspension vessels with four vertically pierced suspension lugs (fig. 1/21), and conical bowls, often with simple incised parallel strokes all along the rim (Cleuziou 1981:287; cf. Weisgerber 1981:212, 214, Abb. 47). Such material is known also at Hili 3 and 8, period III (Cleuziou 1980a: fig. 41/5, 6); Maysar 9 (Weisgerber 1981:214, Abb. 47); Qattarah (Cleuziou 1981:287); Qusais (Cleuziou 1980a:40); Shimal (de Cardi 1971:fig. 52; Donaldson 1984:fig. 11/4); Wadi Sunaysl grave 1112 (Frifelt 1975a:figs. 25b, 72, 73); and Wadi Suq graves 1122, 1123, and 1126 (Frifelt 1975a:figs. 24a–c, 72, 73). This late genre of dot-in-circle decorated chlorite can be called *série tardive* to distinguish it from the *série récente*, where different vessel forms prevail.

Série tardive chlorite is present on Failaka (Kuwait n.d.; cf. Frifelt 1975a:380) and may be dated therefore to the Isin-Larsa and Old Babylonian periods at the earliest. A Dilmun seal (fig. 1/18) in a reused cairn grave at Mazyad (Cleuziou 1981:285), along the eastern side of Jabal Hafit, certainly dates to this period as well. Also remember that a Wadi Suq sherd was found in a context associated with Temple III at Barbar, again datable to the Old Babylonian period. Also present in Hili 8 at this time are thumbnail-impressed sherds of Harappan type (Cleuziou 1984:32).

Finds from this period are also known in eastern Arabia. Very significant, but rarely mentioned (Cornwall 1946:36–37; Potts et al. 1978:9, 18; Piesinger 1983:388–402), are the burial tumuli of "Bahrain" type south of Dhahran which once must have numbered in the thousands. Red-ridged pottery has been found in and among the Dhahran tumuli (Bibby 1965:104; Piesinger 1983:411, 416, 503–4, fig. 145/33–39), along the coast (Potts et al. 1978:9, pl. II/65–66), and on Tarut (Golding 1974:29; Bibby 1973b:29–37). Three Dilmun seals were found near Nadqan (Golding 1974:29), and an Isin-Larsa-style hematite cylinder seal was picked up on the surface of Thaj (Barger 1965:231). In addition, at least six pieces of *série tardive* chlorite (fig. 1/22) are known from Tarut, including fragments of globular suspension vessels (Zarins 1978:pl. 71/40 and 594; cf. Cleuziou 1981:fig. 9 upper; Weisgerber 1981:214, Abb. 47/1); deep bowls with hatching along the rim (Zarins 1978:pl. 71/129, 252, and 300; cf. Weisgerber 1981:214, Abb. 47/2); and shallow bowls or suspension jars with bands of parallel, diagonal lines between bands of horizontal lines and rows of dots-in-circles (Zarins 1978:pl. 71/136 and 246; cf. Cleuziou 1981:fig. 9 bottom, fig. 10 top).

On Qatar several red-ridged sherds have been found at the site of Khor-Ile Nord (Tixier 1978:43, fig. 3; Edens and Tixier 1980:35; Edens 1981:11; Inizan 1979:280); at Khor-Ile Sud (Edens 1981:20), where they do not appear to belong to the main occupation; in small quantities in a sounding at Bir Abaruk 3; and on the surface of the Howar Islands ca. 9 km west of Ras Abaruk (de Cardi 1978:33).

In conclusion, note that little has been said of the historical foundations for the artifactual parallels often cited between the Arabian Gulf area and Mesopotamia. This has been necessary due to lack of space, for to deal adequately with questions such as the identity of ancient Dilmun, or the changing picture of southern Mesopotamia's cultural and economic relations with the countries of the "Lower Sea," would require another chapter. Therefore, in an abbreviated version, some of these problems are indicated in the summary chart (fig. 3) of correlations between southern Mesopotamia and the Arabian Gulf from Late Uruk through Isin-Larsa times as seen in both the archaeological and historical records.

Addendum

Without going into detail, a number of recent works and the subjects to which they pertain are noted here.

On the paleoenvironment of eastern Arabia, with a table of fifty-six radiocarbon dates from "lake bed and associated material," see H. A. McClure, "Late Quaternary Palaeoenvironments of the Rub‘ Al Khali," Ph.D. dissertation, University of London, 1984; cf. "Late Quaternary Palaeogeography and Landscape Evolution of the Rub‘ Al Khali," in D. T. Potts, ed., *Araby the Blest,* Copenhagen: Carsten Niebuhr Institute, 1988. For the most recent discussion of the "Rub Al-Khali Neolithic," see C. E. Edens, "The Rub al-Khali 'Neolithic' Revisited: The View from Nadqan," in Potts, *Araby the Blest.*

A new Middle Holocene stone tool assemblage, including flakes, blades, bladelets, scrapers, and bifaces, has been discovered in the emirate of Sharjah. The material collected on the coast is dated post-6000 B.P. on geomorphological grounds, while some of the inland material came from the section of a terrace datable to between 8000 and 6000 B.P. None of the Sharjah material resembles contemporary industries found elsewhere in the Oman peninsula or in Qatar. See, A. Minzoni Déroche, "The Prehistoric Periods: The Artefacts," and "Survey on Prehistoric Sites," in R. Boucharlat, ed., *Second Archaeological Survey in the Sharjah Emirate, 1985: A Preliminary Report,* French Archaeological Mission in Sharjah, Lyon, 1985, pp. 21–26, 53–61. Cf. S. Calley and M.-A. Santoni, "Sounding at the Prehistoric Site Al Qassimiya," and S. Calley, R. Dalongeville, P. Sanlaville, and M.-A. Santoni, "The Dhaid-Fili Plain: Geomorphology and Prehistory," in R. Boucharlat, ed., *Archaeological Surveys and Excavations in the Sharjah Emirate, 1986: A Third Preliminary Report,* French Archaeological Mission in Sharjah, Lyon, 1986, pp. 13–27.

A new Ubaid site has been discovered in the emirate of Umm al-Qaiwain. Painted sherds and characteristic lithics were collected in October 1986 by R. Boucharlat, E. Haerinck, C. Phillips, and the author. Comparable sites have also been located now by B. Vogt at Jazirat al-Hamra in the emirate of Ras al-Khaimah.

For a new, general overview of Arabian prehistory, encompassing the Arabian Gulf area as well, see M. Tosi, "The Emerging Picture of Prehistoric Arabia," *Annual Review of Anthropology* 15(1986):1–20.

For the graves at Ra's al-Hamra, as well as those of Hafit, Umm an-Nar, and Wadi Suq type, see B. Vogt, "Zur Chronologie und Entwicklung der Gräber des späten 4.–2.Jtsd.v.Chr. auf der Halbinsel Oman: Zusammenfassung, Analyse und Würdigung publizierter wie auch unveröffentlichter Grabungsergebnisse," Ph.D. dissertation, Georg-August-Univ. zu Göttingen, 1985.

For the 1981–82, 1982–83, and 1983–84 seasons at Ra's al-Hamra, see "IsMEO Activities: Oman," in *EW* 31(1981):182–95, *EW* 32(1982):223–30, and *EW* 33(1983):330–40 (no author given); and A. Coppa, R. Macchiarelli, S. Salvatori, and G. Santini, "The Prehistoric Graveyard of Ra's al-Hamra (RH5): (A Short Preliminary Report on the 1981–83 Excavations)," *JOS* 8/1(1985):97–102.

For a new coastal site of Umm an-Nar type, see W. Y. al-Tikriti, "The Archaeological Investigations on Ghanadha Island, 1982–1984: Further Evidence for the Coastal Umm an-Nar Culture," *AUAE* 4(1985):9–19. Tomb A at Hili North is now published in full; see B. Vogt, "The Umm an-Nar Tomb A at Hili North: A Preliminary Report on Three Seasons of Excavation, 1982–1984," *AUAE* 4(1985):20–37. A rich tomb of Umm an-Nar type has also just been excavated in the emirate of Ajman by al-Tikriti, while farther north at Shimal, in Ras al-Khaimah, the German mission has excavated one as well.

On metallurgy and copper resources in Oman, see A. Hauptmann, *Die Entwicklung der Kupfermetallurgie vom 3. Jahrtausend bis zur Neuzeit,* 5000 Jahre Kupfer in Oman, Bd. 1 [= Der Anschnitt, Beiheft 4], Bochum 1985.

On Gulf glyptic, see D. Beyer, "Les sceaux," in Y. Calvet and J.-F. Salles, eds., *Failaka, fouilles françaises 1984–85,* Travaux de la Maison de l'Orient No. 12, Lyon, 1986, pp. 89–103; L. Al-Gailani Werr, "Gulf (Dilmun)-style Cylinder Seals," *PSAS* 16(1986):99–101; and R. M. Boehmer, "Einflüsse der Golfglyptik auf die anatolische Stempelglyptik zur Zeit der assyrischen Handelsniederlassungen," *Baghdader Mitteilungen* 17(1986):1–5. For the pear-shaped seal from Maysar 1, see E. C. L. During Caspers, "A Note on Two Stamp

Seals from the Arabian Gulf Area," *Annali dell'Istituto Universitario Orientale* 45(1985):313–15.

For a recent overview of the architecture and stratigraphy of the early second millennium sites on Failaka excavated by the Danish expedition, see P. Kjaerum, "Architecture and Settlement Patterns in 2nd Mill. Failaka," *PSAS* 16(1986):77–88. For the pottery from the Danish excavations, see F. Højlund, *The Bronze Age Pottery,* Failaka/Dilmun, *JASP* 17:2. On the 1984 season of French excavations on Failaka, see Y. Calvet, A. Caubet, and J.-F. Salles, "French Excavations at Failaka, 1984," *PSAS* 15(1985):11–26; for the report on the 1985 season, see Calvet and Salles, *Failaka, fouilles françaises.*

Late third and early second millennium graves recently excavated on Bahrain are discussed in A. Lowe, "Bronze Age Burial Mounds on Bahrain," *Iraq* 48(1986):73–84.

For the finds from the Wadi Suq period Tomb 6 at Shimal in Ras al-Khaimah, which include a cubical Indus-type weight and a painted jar said to be Harappan, see B. de Cardi, "Harappan Finds in a Tomb at Ras al-Khaimah, U.A.E.," *PSAS* 16(1986):23–24, and her more detailed contribution on the same subject in Potts, *Araby the Blest.* The entire sequence from the Umm an-Nar period through the Iron Age is now represented in the excavations of the German mission at Shimal; for a preliminary report see B. Vogt and U. Franke-Vogt, eds., *Shimal 1985/1986,* Berliner Beiträge zum Vorderen Orient 8, Berlin, 1987.

The sherd from Ra's al-Junayz with incised Harappan signs is published in "IsMEO Activities: Oman," *EW* 31(1981):195–98, fig. 39. No author given.

Finally, for a very useful bibliography of Arabian Gulf archaeology, see E. Haerinck and K. G. Stevens, *Pre-Islamic Archaeology of Kuwait, Northeastern Arabia, Bahrain, Qatar, United Arab Emirates and Oman: A Bibliography,* Gent, 1985.

Postscript

Since April, 1987, when the addendum was written, several important publications have appeared and a considerable amount of new fieldwork has been carried out in the region. Volumes 8 and 9 of *Atlal,* which appeared in 1988 and 1989, contain reports by J. Zarins and B. Fröhlich on excavations in the tombfield at Dhahran. Fieldwork in the Oman peninsula has been particularly fruitful of late. An aceramic site has been excavated on the coast of Oman at Quriyat by H.-P. and M. Uerpmann. A large mudbrick building is under excavation at Ra's al-Junayz by a Franco-Italian team directed by S. Cleuziou and M. Tosi. In southern Ras al-Khaimah, C. S. Phillips has excavated an Umm an-Nar tomb, as well as graves containing Wadi Suq and Iron Age material, and the important Iron Age settlement of Rafaq. In Fujairah, W. Y. al-Tikriti has uncovered an Umm an-Nar round building and a ca. 30 m. long Wadi Suq tomb at Badiya, while a Swiss team led by P. Corboud has excavated an important T-shaped tomb containing Wadi Suq and Iron Age material at Bithna. B. Vogt has carried out investigations at Asima, in northern Ra's al-Khaimah. In Umm al-Qaiwain, the author has begun excavations at Tell Abraq, a stratified mound with an uninterrupted sequence extending from the early third millennium through the Iron Age. Full bibliography and discussion of these finds together with a more up-to-date version of the region's chronology can be found in my synthesis of Arabian Gulf archaeology and history, entitled *The Arabian Gulf in Antiquity,* Clarendon Press, Oxford, 1990. Finally, note that a journal devoted to the archaeology of the Arabian peninsula, called *Arabian Archaeology and Epigraphy,* has been founded by the author and will begin appearing in the spring of 1990.

Five

The Chronology of Mesopotamia, ca. 7000–1600 B.C.

Edith Porada, Columbia University
Donald P. Hansen, New York University
Sally Dunham, Sidney H. Babcock,
Columbia University

Outline

The chronological divisions used in the 1965 edition of *Chronologies of Old World Archaeology* are retained here and only changes necessitated by new information were made. Restrictions of space imposed limitations on the selection of sites and bibliographical references. Unless otherwise indicated, radiocarbon dates cited in the text are based on the most recent calibrations, as described in the introduction to this book.

The dates for the historical periods are dependent on the so-called Middle Chronology, which is retained here in favor of the chronology suggested by Huber based on new computations concerning the text recording observations of the Venus star and dated in the reign of the next to last Babylonian king, Ammiṣaduqa (Huber 1982). About this text Pingree said that it "has undergone a considerable process of expansion and corruption, prior to its being inscribed on the tablets available to us" (Reiner and Pingree 1975:25). Therefore, the text does not appear to us to be sufficiently reliable for adopting the "Huber dates" for this book, which anyhow aims at relative rather than absolute dates.

Introduction

Geography

Mesopotamia—modern Iraq—may be divided into the mountains, foothills, and steppes of the northeast, gen-

Text submitted June 1986

erally referred to here as the north, and the central and southern lowland, here called the south (see fig. 1). The mountains are a part of the belt that extends from the Zagros to the Taurus and rises to its highest points along the frontiers of Iraq with Iran and with Turkey. The mountain ridges with narrow valleys between them decrease in height, whereas the distance between them increases as one moves south from the frontier, so that the Assyrian piedmont consists of widely separated ridges or hills.

The Mesopotamian Plain is composed of several regions; the northern one consists of good rain-fed farming land, while the central and southern sectors receive very little rainfall. Here agriculture is possible only by irrigation, for which the topography presents severe limitations. The central plain is an undulating steppe through which the rivers have cut deep troughlike valleys, three or four miles wide at most. These can be irrigated, but a wider expansion of irrigation would necessitate large dams, long canals, or an elaborate lifting system (Oates and Oates 1976:15) Finally, the alluvial plain of the south is flat land and irrigation with the waters of the two rivers is possible, but there are major difficulties: the flooding of the rivers follows the planting season and endangers

The radiocarbon dates are the work of Sally Dunham; the chronological charts have been compiled and executed by Sidney H. Babcock; Elisabeth Ustinoff typed the manuscript. The authors are indebted to a host of scholars and friends for important corrections and suggestions, who are in no way responsible for the ideas expressed here.

the seedlings, and the large quantities of silt carried and deposited by the rivers result in clogging canals and riverbeds (Oates and Oates 1976:124).

The enormous amount of silt brought down by the two rivers may have also affected the coastline at the head of the gulf. The suggestion made by Lees and Falcon (1952), that the ancient coastline was never very much farther north than today, has been challenged. Recent investigations have shown that around 14,000 B.C. the level of the gulf was some 110 m below present and that it was actually a dry bed through which the original Euphrates and Tigris rivers ran to the Gulf of Oman (Nützel 1978, 1979). Then the sea level rose until it reached its present level around 4000 B.C., after which it continued to rise until around 3500 B.C. to about 3 m above its present level (ibid.). Some researchers have argued for at least 150–200 km of progradation since that time, thus suggesting that the coastline was not far south of Ur-Nasiriya in the fourth and third millennia (Nützel 1978; C. Larsen 1975; Larsen and Evans 1978). However, others cite evidence supporting the Lees and Falcon theory of the balance of subsidence and alluviation (Brice 1978:275). Thus, whether such sites as Ur and Eridu were situated on the sea or not is still uncertain (see discussion by Adams 1981:14–19).

The geography of the country is reflected in its ancient history. Paleolithic man found natural shelters in the caves of the mountains of the northeast; sufficient rainfall made early farming possible in the piedmont foothills of what was later Assyria. These foothills belong to a wide arc reaching from Iran to Turkey and Syria; in their valleys farming produced a livelihood for small communities for which pastoralism provided additional sustenance.

Mesopotamian urbanism, the country's most distinctive social achievement, was viewed by Adams as a directly adaptive feature in an ecological sense. He pointed out that cities made possible a greater measure of stability for their dependencies and for their own population than would have been possible otherwise.

Trade and Trade Routes

In the south, the lack of any raw materials needed for the manufacture of items above the mere level of subsistence—suitable timber, building stone, and metals—stimulated economic activity to provide such items by means of surplus goods for barter and organized trade. In the past three decades the investigation of such trade has been a favored topic of research and discussion. "Trade in the Ancient Near East" (Oppenheim 1970), "Anthropological Perspectives on Ancient Trade" (Adams 1974), and "A Review of Interregional Exchange in Southwest Asia: The Neolithic Obsidian Network, the Assyrian

Trading Colonies and a Case for Third Millennium B.C. Trade" (Yener 1982) are among the most informative and thoughtful. The *Rencontre Assyriologique* XXIII, 1976, was also devoted to trade (*Iraq* XXXIX, 1977).

Several land routes were important for Mesopotamian trade to the west. Two routes went north, one along the Diyala River, which then followed the line of the Jebel Himrin to cross the Tigris at Assur (D. Oates, 1968b:5–8). The other route went north along the Tigris to the Mosul area, the onetime heartland of Assyria, and from there across the Sinjar to the Syrian towns of Harran or Aleppo and the sea. During dry, hot months the route moved as far north as Mardin-Urfa, and even Diabekr. Klengel (1977:163–64) stressed especially the route from the middle Euphrates valley near Mari along the oases with groundwater to Tadmor-Palmyra and from there to the middle Syrian agricultural area near Qatna. The central caravan route went from Iran through the east Tigris area, especially through the Diyala region (Klengel 1977:164). Along these routes traveled the objects that indicate contact between regions and suggest contemporareneity which serves as an aid to chronological determinations.

Shipping was the preferred means of transportation of goods destined not only for southern Mesopotamia but also as much as possible for the north (Hallo 1964: *passim;* De Graeve 1981; Qualls 1981). Salonen called the Euphrates and the Tigris the main arteries of Mesopotamia (Salonen 1939: foreword). By the middle of the third millennium B.C. seafaring in the Persian-Arabian Gulf and the Arabian Sea seems to have extended to the coast of Oman, ancient Magan, and perhaps to Baluchistan, ancient Melukha (Oppenheim 1954:14–15). By the end of the third and beginning of the second millennium B.C. the distance covered by Mesopotamian ships seems to have been reduced. Merchant ships from Ur went to Dilmun, modern Bahrain. Dilmun appears as the mercantile emporium of that period, with commodities from farther east reaching Mesopotamia and perhaps even Egypt via the sea route (Porada 1982:291).

The earliest recognizable import in the north was obsidian, volcanic glass, which was used for tools. Large amounts were found at the Pre-Pottery Neolithic site of Maghzaliyah on the southern slopes of the Sinjar spurs. The sources of this obsidian were several sites in Anatolia hundreds of kilometers northwest of Maghzaliyah and Umm Dabaghiyah where some obsidian tools were found (Kirkbride 1982:18).

Imports also comprised metals (Moorey 1985), mainly copper (Muhly 1973:1977), and stone-worked artifacts. A more detailed and focused analysis carried out with early copper objects from Iran and Mesopotamia (Berthoud 1979) indicates different ore sources for Mesopotamian sites, specifically Oman, as a source for the copper found at Ur, and sources on the Iranian plateau, such as probably Anarak, for the copper of the sites in the Himrin.

Judging from Sargonid texts, trade may have been organized by persons from the receiving point. Thus, the trade between Umma in Mesopotamia and Susa in southwest Iran was carried out by people from Umma residing at Susa. Later, Lagash assumed Umma's position as Mesopotamia's entrepôt with southern Iran (Foster 1977:39).

Most of what is known about large-scale and long-distance commercial undertakings was learned from tablets that record the activities of the Old Assyrian merchant colonies in Anatolia (Garelli 1963, 1977; M. T. Larsen 1967, 1976, 1977; Orlin 1970; Veenhof 1972, 1977).

Although Sumerian, Babylonian, and Assyrian merchants nominally paid for goods in silver, Oppenheim pointed out that "silver as a means of exchange was hardly changing hands outside the context of the palace and the overland trade" (1970:21). But payments could be made with such commodities as dates, oil, and grain, or with textiles such as those produced by the flourishing wool industry of Sippar (Leemans 1950:3, 103) or Tell al-Rimah (Dalley 1977, 1984:51–54). Such cuneiform texts help to determine some of the commercial contacts and activities dimly perceived in the archaeological material.

The different environments of north and south in Mesopotamia did not prevent the two regions from being allied culturally, especially in historical times, and from showing greater similarity with each other than either had with any other land. "The central part of the country—notably the Diyala region—often showed a transitional character, although more closely tied to the south. In discussing the problems of relative chronology in Mesopotamia, therefore, there are always two aspects: the relation of the material from north and south and the relation of materials from either or both areas to those of other countries" (Perkins 1954:43).

Theory and Science

In the decades since the publication of *Chronologies* (Ehrich 1965), the results of excavation have been submitted more consistently than before to theoretical and scientific examination. An excellent summary of the state of the theory and method in the United States and Europe was given by J.-C. Gardin (1980).

Major contributions to the knowledge of the early periods of the Mesopotamian development resulted from international cooperation organized for the Himrin Salvage Project of which some of the reports have appeared (*Sumer* XXXV, 1979; XL, special issue, 1984; *Paléorient* 6,

1980, etc.) and are beginning to be integrated in the overall development of the ancient Near East. The Haditha Dam Salvage Project and the Eski Mosul, now called Saddam Dam Salvage Project, are also beginning to produce important results (Killick and Roaf 1983; Killick and Black 1985).

Problems of economy and population distribution were discussed in a review by H. Weiss (1985a) of the survey of the work from 1933 to 1982 of the British School of Archaeology in Iraq (Curtis 1982).

The Prehistoric Periods

The Early Prehistoric Periods in the North

The Pre-Pottery Neolithic Period

In recent years the image of the Late Neolithic phase of northern Iraq has changed dramatically. In 1965 the earliest known village was Jarmo in the hill country of northeastern Iraq, consisting of *tauf*-built houses (for an explanation of the term *tauf* see Braidwood and Howe 1960:40). The site mainly was distinguished by its numerous clay figurines of animals and humans. Now it is realized that there existed at the same time, and earlier than Jarmo, the impressive settlement of Maghzaliyah, excavated by Bader, Merpert, and Munchaev of the Soviet project, and located 7.5 km to the northwest of that project's excavation at Yarim Tepe.

Maghzaliyah lies on the southern slopes of the Sinjar hilly spurs on the west bank of the Wadi Ibra (Postgate and Watson 1979:152; Bader 179:131; Merpert, Munchaev, and Bader 1981:29). The settlement seems to have been built on the bank of the river in a north-south direction down the slope of a mound, referred to by the excavators as the northern mound. A southern mound emerged in the excavation of 1980. This preference of the first settlers for slight elevations seems to have been shared with the—probably somewhat later—settlers of ʿOueili in the south.

In the excavation of 1979–80 (Munchaev, Merpert, and Bader 1984:45–53), fifteen building levels were distinguished, which were divided into four major periods. On the northern mound lay levels 15 to 9. Above them a new settlement was built consisting of levels 8 to 5. In level 5 the buildings of the northern slope were enclosed by a massive defensive wall, which stood as high as 2 m in places and was traced for a length of over 60 m (Postgate and Roaf 1981:181). The wall was twice rebuilt in levels 4 and 3. In one place it describes a U-shaped curve which has been tentatively interpreted as the foundation of a tower. No defensive wall was found in levels 2 and 1 in which the settlement became smaller and may have ceased to exist at the end of level 1. During the entire period covered by the fifteen levels the material culture remained homogenous.

An example of one of the surprisingly large structures covering about 50 m² was excavated in level 2; it had been rebuilt twice. The structure was raised on a stone socle. The foundations of its walls, about 80 cm wide, were made of closely fitted blocks of limestone on the inner and outer face, whereas the inside was filled by small stones. These foundation walls were 40 to 50 cm high; above them *tauf* walls were raised. *Tauf* was a rather fluid mixture of mud containing straw or grass to prevent cracking, and was moulded with the builder's hands with a vertical face on either side to a height of about 7–10 cm, after which the section of the wall was left to dry completely for a day or so until the next layer was raised above the first (see Braidwood and Howe 1960:40). The walls at Maghzaliyah seem to have been related to those of Jarmo, where rough fieldstone foundations often preceded the building of the *tauf* walls. Photographs of the foundation walls of Maghzaliyah, however, show rather carefully selected stones creating in one case the impression of a regular wall face (Munchaev, Merpert, and Bader 1984:49, fig. 31, upper left).

The floors were made of a layer of small stones which was covered with a layer of packed clay and plastered with gypsum. Presumably, reed mats protected the white floors. The walls were also plastered with gypsum, which was often renewed, reaching a thickness of 2–3 cm in some places. Architectural modifications for the convenience of the inhabitants of these houses included hearths, benches, storage niches, and troughs.

The high quality of the artifacts of Maghzaliyah conforms to the elaborate architecture of the site. Relations with Jarmo are claimed for the figurine repertory of which human examples of clay and stone are mentioned (Merpert, Munchaev, and Bader 1981:54, fig. XXV/17 [here, fig. 2/1]). Some beautifully worked small conical objects (Bader 1979:126–27 in reference to fig. 7/8–12; Merpert, Munchaev, and Bader 1981: 54, fig. XXV/8 [here, fig. 2/2]) perhaps similar in shape to a group of twenty from Çayönü, referred to as pestles in the report (Çambel and Braidwood 1981:48, pl. 46/6 and 9), suggest a relation with the polished stonework of Umm Dabaghiyah and with the perhaps later polished stonework found at Tell es-Sawwan. Connections with bone carving of Bouqras, in the middle Euphrates valley, are suggested by the remarkable carved head of a gazelle (Merpert, Munchaev, and Bader 1981:62, and pl. XXXIII, second row, right side).

The lithic industries were rich with good blades, serrated sickle blades with sheen and tanged lanceolate arrowheads with retouch (here, fig. 2/3). In the upper layers, flint and obsidian occurred roughly in equal quantities, but lower down 80 percent of the tools were of obsidian. This suggests links in the obsidian trade with Anatolia and Iran. The site appears to have been an eastern exponent of the "Pre-Pottery Neolithic B–related" tradition which has been documented as extending from Beidha in Jordan to Çayönü near Diabekr in the north, with Gritille and Çafer Harabesi among the upper Euphrates area salvage excavations situated between them.

The absolute chronology of Maghzaliyah is still uncertain. Radiocarbon dates are published for Çayönü, Turkey (Çambel 1981), and for Bouqras, Syria (Akkermans, Fokkens, and Waterbolk 1981), which has clear affinities to "PPN-B final" complexes at such sites as Abu Hureyra, Syria (ibid.). Both sets of dates, Çayönü and Bouqras, are beyond the range of the most current calibration tables, so one must use the 5730 h.l. B.C., which seems to be usually about five hundred years later than the calibrated dates in instances where the two can be compared for the same determination. Tentatively, then, one might say that the Çayönü dates suggest an eighth to early seventh millennium range for "PPN-B related" sites and an early to mid-seventh millennium range for Bouqras.

Jarmo, which may in part be approximately contemporary with Bouqras, has been classed with the "Zagros Neolithic" sites on the basis of its chipped flint and the pottery of its upper levels (J. Oates 1973; Hole in Braidwood et al. 1983; Voigt and Dyson, this volume chap. 6). However, certain stone bowl shapes and obsidian tools, steeply retouched obsidian blades, suggest connections with western sites as well (Voigt, pers. comm., December 1985).

The Proto-Hassuna Phase

The new area of settlements, somewhat later than Maghzaliyah, was in the central northern plain of Mesopotamia, the north central Jezireh, where the site of Umm Dabaghiyah was discovered about 20 km west of Hatra (Kirkbride 1972, 1973a, 1973b, 1975), as well as farther north in the Sinjar Plain at Yarim Tepe I (level XII) and at tells explored in connection with it: Tell Sotto and Kül Tepe (Bader 1983; Merpert and Munchaev 1971a, 1971b; Merpert, Munchaev, and Bader 1981:27–29), and Telul eth-Thalathat (Fukai, Horiuchi, and Matsutani 1970; Fukai and Matsutani 1981). This phase of development can be correlated with the long-known so-called camp site of Hassuna (Lloyd and Safar 1945:271–72) on the basis of pottery similarities. The earlier levels of the developmental phase are called here Proto-Hassuna culture to distinguish them from the fully developed Hassuna period known in the literature as the earliest developed village of Mesopotamia and whose name was therefore retained.

The Proto-Hassuna pottery, some fine but mostly thick medium coarse, heavily straw- and chaff-tempered, has the distinguishing shape of the large vessels, a carination low on the body profile, with the outline of the lower part of the body becoming a double curve or a concave curve, while the upper part of the body describes a convex curve (here, fig. 2/4). The most distinctive feature of the pottery is the applied clay decoration of small pellets and short rolls. In the early levels, these features often suggest breasts, horns, or eyes (Lloyd and Safar 1945: fig. 6/15–22 [here, fig. 2/5, 6]; Kirkbride 1972:pl. XI/1–17 [here, fig. 2/7]; Bashilov, Bolshakov, and Kouza 1980:60, fig. 9) and, in the later levels, full animal and even human forms appear to have developed (Kirkbride 1973a:pl. X/a, b [here, fig. 2/8] and pl. XI; Fukai and Matsutani 1981:pl. 14/1). However, this progression is not fully demonstrable stratigraphically.

In addition to the applied decoration there seem to have been experiments in painting in the earliest levels at Umm Dabaghiyah, which were freer in design than at a later stage (Kirkbride 1972:9). Dots, circles, and snakelike squiggles were tried out as well as a variety of linear effects with straight lines (here, fig. 2/9, 10).

Some sherds of another kind of pottery which appears to have been shared by several sites of this period were found in the lowest levels of Umm Dabaghiyah of "almost pure, pinkish-brown clay, with light grit temper in some cases, extremely well-fired, hard, thin and with good burnish" (Kirkbride 1972:9). Similar pottery was found at Tell Sotto (Postgate 1973:203 [red burnished]), in the earliest strata of Yarim Tepe I (Bashilov, Bolshakov, and Kouza 1980:50, Group 4 [dark gray and brightly burnished]), and at Telul eth-Thalathat (Fukai and Matsutani 1981:37 [red slipped and burnished]).

The earliest occupation at Umm Dabaghiyah is represented by some small irregularly curved bins or basins, with which as yet no buildings have been associated. To the same phase appears to belong a set of pits in stratum 1 at Yarim Tepe I (Bashilov, Bolshakov, and Kouza 1980:45), layer XVI of Telul eth-Thalathat with its "pit dwellings" (Hori, p. 22, and Furuyama, pp. 29–30, in Fukai and Matsutani 1981), as well as the Hassuna camp sites.

The later development of the Proto-Hassuna culture at Umm Dabaghiyah showed elaborate *tauf*—walled storage blocks (Kirkbride 1973b:206). The domestic buildings have surprisingly sophisticated features such as outside ovens and inside hearths and chimneys. Traces of mural paintings were found in levels IV and III (Kirkbride 1975:pls. VI–VIII). One house has an onager hunt, reflecting the purpose of what is taken to have been an industrial community founded to obtain various onager products, principally the hides (Kirkbride 1982:19–21). The most general color in the painting was red ocher, but both black and yellow were also used, although more sparingly (Kirkbride 1975:7).

The use of well-built rectangular storage blocks, like those of Umm Dabaghiyah, continued in the Hassuna-

Samarra period as is shown by examples at Yarim Tepe I, levels XI–VII. Whether such buildings also existed at Telul eth-Thalathat in the contemporary level XV is not known because the architecture of the site is difficult to ascertain from the publication.

The easternmost site of this phase was Gird ali Agha, which lacked the substantial architecture of Umm Dabaghiyah (J. R. Caldwell 1983: 649).

The chronological precedence of the finds of Umm Dabaghiyah over those of Hassuna is indicated by the appearance of the "husking tray," a type of tray with corrugation inside the bottom, perhaps for baking (Voigt 1983:159). It has been a favored criterion for comparisons among early farming communities since its discovery in level II of Hassuna (Lloyd and Safar 1945:277 [here, fig. 2/11]). At Umm Dabaghiyah such a husking tray appears only in the "later levels" (Kirkbride 1972:9).

Of three female figurines found at Umm Dabaghiyah, one is "the most elegant yet recovered among the early cultures of Iraq" (Kirkbride 1972:8, pls. VII/1, VIII [here, fig. 2/12]).

At the sites of Tell Sotto (levels 3–4), Kül Tepe (level 1), Yarim Tepe I (levels XII–IX), and Tell Hassuna (level Ia), the Proto-Hassuna materials are succeeded by those of the Hassuna culture proper (Bader 1983). Thus, radiocarbon dates for Hassuna levels at Yarim Tepe I (LE 1086: 6275–5660; LE 1070: 6260–5665 B.C.) suggest ca. 6200–6000 B.C. for the end of Proto-Hassuna. Similarities between the fine stone bowls of the latest level of Umm Dabaghiyah and those of the earliest level at Tell es-Sawwan support this, since radiocarbon dates from Tell es-Sawwan level I are 5720 plus/minus 73 (P-855)* and 5860–5455 (P-857). Ceramic affinities suggest that the latest levels of Bouqras may slightly overlap with the earliest of Umm Dabaghiyah (Kirkbride 1972:14; Akkermans, Fokkens, and Waterbolk 1981; Akkermans, pers. comm., November 1983). Since the Bouqras dates allow an early to middle seventh millennium range, one can suggest the second half of the seventh millennium for Proto-Hassuna.

The Hassuna and the Samarra Periods

To this phase of early village culture belongs sites that range from the modest beginning with level Ib at Hassuna to the substantial houses with rectangular rooms grouped around a courtyard in which there were ovens, grain bins, and the like in Hassuna, level III.

The principal criterion of the Hassuna period is the Hassuna standard incised ware (here, fig. 2/13), which began at Hassuna in levels Ib–c and was widely distributed in northern Iraq (J. Oates 1973:163). There is a wide range of sizes, from storage jars nearly a meter high to tiny carinated bowls (for the pottery from Hassuna see

Lloyd and Safar 1945: 276ff.). The Hassuna standard vessels were covered with a thin cream slip, and while the slip was still wet the patterns were drawn with a pointed tool both in the incised and in the incised-and-painted standard wares. The earliest painted pottery, called "archaic painted ware," is characterized by the almost uniform red color of the paint and a glossy surface finish. Standard painted jars are squatter and have shorter necks than those of the archaic painted ware. Hassuna standard ware is most frequently decorated on the shoulder of the jar with crosshatched triangles or groups of opposed oblique lines painted in mat color on a mat background (here, fig. 2/14).

In addition to the local pottery at Hassuna, an imported one was in use. It was called Samarra after the central Mesopotamian site where it was discovered in graves (Herzfeld 1930). Samarra pottery manifests a distinct culture at the sites of Samarra, nearby Tell es-Sawwan, Choga Mami near Mandali, Mattarah, and Baghouz, where it is not accompanied by Hassuna ware.

Samarra pottery is exceptionally fine, mat painted, usually in strong black color, but sometimes in red. Distinctive ornaments are painted in narrow bands one above the other, each running in an opposite direction (here, fig. 2/15). Occasionally, figured designs are used. One vase from Hassuna, several fragmentary ones from Tell es-Sawwan, and two fragments from Choga Mami have the neck of a jar ornamented with painted and appliquéd female faces (here, fig. 2/16). Previous to producing elaborate pottery, the people of Tell es-Sawwan had manufactured hundreds of finely ground stone objects, in particular, female statuettes (here, fig. 2/7) and elegantly shaped bowls (here, fig. 2/18). These objects were also found in graves clearly associated with several unusually large buildings attributed to the earliest level (J. Oates 1973:170). This stonework of Tell es-Sawwan is reminiscent of the fine stonework of the aceramic levels of Maghzaliyah, Çayönü, and Bouqras, and of the beautiful stone bowls of Umm Dabaghiyah and Jarmo. Eva Strommenger noted this relationship of excellent craftmanship about 6000 B.C. at widely separated sites in south Anatolia, north Mesopotamia, and the areas on the middle courses of the Euphrates and Tigris (Kohlmeyer and Strommenger 1982:20).

The stately multiroom rectangular buildings of Tell es-Sawwan are constructed of very large mud-bricks with buttresses at wall junctions. There were five levels distinguished in all, of which T-shaped buildings could be recognized. In level III the settlement was surrounded on at least three sides by a defensive wall and a ditch 3 m wide. At Choga Mami, the structures were erected with long cigar-shaped mud-bricks, a rectangular plan was used, and buttresses were placed at the junctions of walls. Rooms were small, square, and frequently opened into

each other along the long axis of the building. New houses were built on top of the older ones but within the walls of the earlier buildings, perhaps indicating property rights (J. Oates 1973:169). At Choga Mami there may have also been some evidence of walls surrounding a group of smaller buildings (ibid.). J. Oates associated the suggestion about property rights of house owners with the contemporary appearance of stamp seals as perhaps reflecting the recognition of private ownership.

The stone stamp seals so far published share a roughly rectangular sealing surface and a handle, which may be ridge-shaped or knob-shaped. Only the seal from Yarim Tepe I (Merpert, Munchaev, and Bader 1978:pl. VIII/5, lower right) is photographed with the handle, but not enough is shown to be certain of the shape. In all of the published seals the sealing surface is marked by rather crude, oblique crosshatching. In an example from Hassuna, level II (Lloyd and Safar 1945:pl. XI/2, top row, right end [here, fig. 6/1]), the handle had been broken and a suspension hole had been drilled through the middle of the sealing surface. The same can be observed in an almost identical example from Matarrah (Braidwood et al. 1952: fig. 20/10). In later seals a small cup-shaped hollow appears as part of the design.

It is curious that no seals have been published from several of the Samarra sites, for example, Tell es-Sawwan or Choga Mami. Most characteristic of Choga Mami are the elegant, painted figurines (here, fig. 2/19, 20), which prefigure in several features those from Ubaid, Ur, and ʿOueili of the Late Ubaid phase.

Further north, at Yarim Tepe I, the upper six levels also show rectangular multiroom houses, frequently with buttresses at wall junctions. The distinctive building material consists of compact blocks of clay, apparently of uniform size and often laid in regular patterns (Merpert and Munchaev 1973:101). As stated by Oates, Samarra sites occur "in a band across Mesopotamia north of Baghdad and south of the rainfed lands generally occupied by the 'Hassuna' peoples. Samarra penetrates also into the hills to the north-east; the bulk of the prehistoric pottery from Shemshara in the Rania plain would appear to be Samarran, and it has been noted that no ceramics earlier than Samarra have been found in this area" (J. Oates 1973:171).

Recently, Samarra occupation has been reported for the Himrin basin at mound A of Tell Songor (Fujii 1981:169–70, 173–75; Postgate and Watson 1979:179) and at Tell Rihan (Postgate and Roaf 1981:186; Gibson 1979). Both sites are said to have material similar to that of Choga Mami (Postgate and Watson 1979:178; Postgate and Roaf 1981:189; Fujii 1981:180). One building at Songor has two rows of square rooms with buttresses at wall junctions (Matsumoto 1979: fig. 2) and is similar to Samarra house plans published from Choga Mami (J.

Oates 1969:pl. XXIV). The figurines from this site are also somewhat related to those of Choga Mami (compare Matsumoto 1979, fig. 3, lower right, with J. Oates 1969:pls. XXVIII/c–d, XXIX/c–e).

From the available radiocarbon dates both the Hassuna and Samarra cultures would appear to have flourished in the first half of the sixth millennium, though perhaps beginning late in the seventh (see table 1). At Yarim Tepe II the earliest Halaf levels overlie an already abandoned Hassuna settlement (Munchaev and Merpert 1981:277). Since Early Halaf may have overlapped with Late Samarra (Hijara et al. 1980:151), the Hassuna culture may not have lasted as late as the Samarra.

At Choga Mami the levels with Samarran-type pottery were overlaid with one not known before, which has affinities with Early Ubaid materials of the south and with Iranian materials to the west (see Voigt and Dyson, this vol., chap. 6), but which developed at Choga Mami out of the Samarran levels without a break. Oates called this pottery "Transitional Ware" to emphasize its place between Samarra and the early southern material (here, fig. 2/21). While "Transitional Ware" is better fired and harder than Samarra pottery and there is much less tendency for the paint to flake off, many of the shapes and decorations are so close to the preceding Samarra pottery that out of context it would be indistinguishable. A radiocarbon determination for the site suggests the mid-sixth millennium as a reasonable date for Choga Mami Transitional (BM-483; 5965–5410 B.C.).

The Halaf Period

Following the Hassuna and Samarra periods the appearance of a new pottery initiated a new period in the Mosul and Sinjar regions of Iraq. The pottery was called Halaf after the site in the northern half of the Khabur headwaters region in north Syria, where it was first discovered.

Halaf pottery is a lustrous burnished pottery with static compositional schemes and, from about the middle of the period onward, with a measure of polychromy. The perfection in the technique of painting pottery in this phase consisted in the homogeneity, density, absence of bubbles, and consistency of the surface. Although there were great differences in quality, some Halaf vessels approached the technique of Attic vase painting.

Some of the finest Halaf pottery was discovered at Arpachiyah in the Mosul area. This site, which is the most extensively published Halaf site so far, was excavated by Mallowan in the 1930s (Mallowan and Rose 1935) and by Hijara in 1976 (Hijara et al. 1980). Hijara paid closer attention to the stratigraphic relations between the various parts of the mound than had Mallowan, hence he was better able to define the ceramic sequence (for a correlation of these reports see Dunham 1983:22, table I [here, fig. 9]).

There is obvious agreement between Hijara and Mallowan on the earliest Halaf pottery. Characteristic of this pottery is that the paint and slip easily separate. Mallowan's "Early Halaf Pottery" seems to correlate with Hijara's pottery Phases H1 and H2 (here, fig. 9/1, 4).

The Middle Halaf phase is difficult to determine from the published material. Mallowan's "Middle Halaf Pottery" may fit into Hijara's pottery Phases H3 and H4. Middle Halaf pottery can, however, be visualized from the finds from Tell Aqab in the Khabur headwaters region of north Syria by Davidson and Watkins (1981). These show a development from early pottery with simple forms of straight-sided bowls with limited geometric decoration in bands or alternating panels, which introduce the static Halaf-type composition, to more complicated forms in the middle period, in which also the earliest polychromy occurred. However, none of the animal forms of Mallowan's Early Halaf, or the bucrania, so common in the Middle and Late Halaf at Arpachiyah, occurs at Aqab. Arpachiyah cream bowls (here, fig. 9/1, 2) and squat jars with flaring necks (here, fig. 9/3–5) had occurred early at Aqab, but the cream bowl disappeared in the middle period at Aqab (ibid., p. 7).

The latest group of pottery from Arpachiyah with its magnificent polychrome plates (here, fig. 2/22), the aesthetic quality of which is due to the selectivity of pattern and spacing, is represented by only two examples from Aqab. Polychrome painting was also used on small shallow hemispherical bowls, which resemble what Mallowan called "saucers" at Arpachiyah. But the majority of the vessels at Aqab were painted in one color. Polychrome plates are also reported from Choga Mami, where they were locally made, and from the Himrin (Oates, pers. comm.).

The new excavations at Arpachiyah yielded two architectural phases which preceded those determined by Mallowan. The first, Hijara's Phase A1, his levels XI–IX, had village debris with rectangular rooms. However, the lack of round structures, the so-called "tholoi," in this phase could be due to chance, since Hijara's trenches were only 2–3 m wide. At Yarim Tepe II, round and rectangular buildings occurred from the earliest levels on (see below). In Hijara's Phase A2 (levels VIII–VI, layers 22–11), "tholoi" with walls 35–30 cm thick without stone foundations were found. A thick mass of *tauf* apparently originating late in level VII or level VI has been interpreted by Hijara as the remains of an enclosure wall surrounding the upper part of the mound (Hijara et al. 1980:132–34). Phases A3 and A4 were found only inside this enclosure wall. Phase A3a (levels V–IV, layers 10–8 = Mallowan's TT 10–9) had larger "tholoi" with thicker walls and stone foundations; while Phase A3b (levels III–II = Mallowan's TT 8–7) had large "tholoi" with adjoining rectangular chambers. Indeed, the "tholoi" in these levels are some of the largest known anywhere, having diameters of 9–10 m, with attached rooms 7–9 m long. So far, the only other equally large "tholos" is one in the uppermost level at Tell es-Sawwan (ca. 12 m diameter; al-Soof 1971:4). Finally, in Hijara's Phase A4, equivalent to Mallowan's TT 6, these large "tholoi" are replaced by the rectangular building in which Mallowan found the large hoard of Late Halaf pottery.

Hijara suggested that in Phases A2 and A3 the tholos area was a ritual center, walled and having graves adjoining but not containing any settlement debris. In Phase A4 the artisan's rectangular house in which the contents had been preserved by a fire indicates the character of the village as producing pottery and other artifacts.

Another important site in the Mosul region is Tepe Gawra, the lowest levels of which contain Halaf pottery and round structures (Tobler 1950). Neutron activation analysis has demonstrated that some of this Halaf pottery was imported from Arpachiyah, a fact that bears out the pottery-producing function of Arpachiyah in this period (Davidson and McKerrell 1980). Watson reports that although Davidson thinks the Halaf pottery from Gawra belongs to his Late (comparable to Arpachiyah TT 6) and Transitional (to Ubaid) phases, "Hijara finds pottery at Gawra that fits his Phases One and Two (pre-TT 10)" (Watson 1983a:234).

At the small site of Banahilk near Rowanduz (Watson 1983b), the painted pottery from all levels appears to be "Late Halaf" (but cf. Hijara, in Watson 1983a: 233). The chipped stone industry comprises chert flakes and obsidian blades in similar proportions as at Girikihaciyan, Turkey. The chert industry continues earlier Hassunan traditions and is quite different from the contemporary chipped stone industries in the Amuq Plain in north Syria. Hence, the homogeneity demonstrated for the painted pottery across north Syria and north Mesopotamia may not extend to all aspects of technology (Watson 1983a:239–40; LeBlanc and Watson 1973).

West of the Halaf sites of the Mosul region lie those of the Sinjar region, Yarim Tepe II and III (Merpert and Munchaev 1973:108–13; Merpert and Munchaev 1984; Munchaev and Merpert 1981; Munchaev, Merpert, and Bader 1984). At Yarim Tepe II there were two uppermost levels greatly disturbed by grave pits of Hellenistic and Assyrian times; below these were seven levels of Halaf settlement. In the southeastern part of the mound were "remains of a destroyed stratum of a small Hassuna settlement which undoubtedly preceded the foundation of the Halaf settlement" (Munchaev and Merpert 1981:277).

The earliest excavated levels at the site contained nar-

row, rectangular structures interpreted as having been for domestic use "with many rooms and walls made of yellow-brownish loam slabs" (Munchaev and Merpert 1981:278). The slabs are probably the same "compact clay blocks" described in the buildings of the Hassuna period structures on Yarim Tepe I (Merpert and Munchaev 1973:101) of which it is said that they were approximately uniform in size and were laid in a regular pattern in some individual buildings (ibid.). Coating the walls with clay plaster was also continued from the earlier period. Adjoining the houses were hearths in pits and domed ovens. West of that functional sector were the main dwelling structures, the tholoi. Their shapes differed—one had vertical walls and a flat roof, another was domed, and inside the latter was a domed oven. The sizes were modest, with diameters ranging from 4.5 m to 3 m. A somewhat later tholos was bigger, having a diameter of 5.3 m. Its massive walls (up to 40 cm thick) rested on a special platform. With the foundation of the big structure are connected ritual pits with marks of fires and a number of finds that include painted vessels, microlithic tools, anthropomorphic figurines, and a unique copper seal, all of which were discovered under the floor of the tholos (Munchaev and Merpert 1981:278).

The largest tholos discovered by the Soviet expedition was excavated on Yarim Tepe III. It had a diameter of 5.85 m and the walls are 30 cm thick, standing to a height of 2 m. They were built of unbaked clay, with mud plaster on each face. Inside the tholos were four symmetrically placed corner-shaped buttresses to strengthen the walls (Munchaev, Merpert, and Bader 1984: 33–35). The bins created by the corner buttresses appear to have been used for objects that were meant to be kept together in one place, such as the seven hundred so-called clay slingballs. Although the remains of broken pots were also thrown into the bins, there were obsidian plates (not defined as to their shape), pieces of flint, part of a broken rose-colored marble cup, beads, two of which were of white stone, and painted clay rings, about 3 cm in diameter. These rings are a distinctive object of the Halaf period at Yarim Tepe II and III. Neither Arpachiyah nor Tepe Gawra has yielded that type of artifact. There were also numerous anthropomorphic and animal figurines in the bins.

The most extraordinary figurine comes from Yarim Tepe II (here, fig. 2/24). It is hollow, forming a vessel in the shape of a headless female figurine, with the open neck serving as the spout, and represented with small breasts, a slender body in profile, and long strands of hair painted down its back (Munchaev and Merpert 1981:pl. opp. p. 137, and p. 252, fig. 98; Russian text pp. 251–52, and English, p. 281). Corresponding female torsos have been found at Arpachiyah (Mallowan and Rose

1935: fig. 45/10–12). The figurine-shaped vessel from Yarim Tepe II has halterlike bands which come together and run parallel between the breasts and then spread widely at the hips, prefiguring the painted bands known until now only from Ubaid figurines from Gawra (Tobler 1950, pl. LXXXI/c, d).

The more common Halaf period female figurine is heavy bodied and heavy breasted, and is seated supporting her breasts with her arms (Merpert and Munchaev 1973:pl. XLIII/12 [here, fig. 2/25]; Munchaev, Merpert, and Bader 1984:43, fig. 21). Another type from Yarim Tepe II (Munchaev and Merpert 1981:205, fig. 64/9), in which the upper part is reduced to a peg, has only the lower part of the body preserved like the almost identical figurine from Arpachiyah (Mallowan and Rose 1935: fig. 47/2, 3 [here, fig. 2/26]).

In the excavations at Yarim Tepe III even more abbreviated forms were found. They consist of triangular lumps of clay that have the female triangle incised above the bottom (Munchaev, Merpert, and Bader 1984:44, fig. 22). Others have the top pinched to suggest the presence of the head (ibid., fig. 23).

The excavators of Yarim Tepe III stressed the fact that the big tholos and the entire level belonged to the Late Halaf period. This is also confirmed by the pottery which has geometric and zoomorphic designs including snakes, leopards, birds, and fish (Postgate and Watson 1979:159). Sherds with long-legged birds from Yarim Tepe II, levels 4 and 3 (Merpert and Munchaev 1973:pl. XLVI/4, 5), can be compared to such Late Halaf pottery as sherds from Chagar Bazar in a "post level 12" context, which means Late Halaf (Mallowan 1936: fig. 27/8), as well as to examples from Gawra (Tobler 1950:pls. CXVI/59, CXVII/61, CXVIII/62) and from Choga Mami (J. Oates 1969:138 [from a well containing Late Halaf pottery]).

Somewhat earlier may be a sherd with horizontal grooves all over from level 4 of Yarim Tepe II (Merpert and Munchaev 1973:pl. XLVI/1), which may be of the same "painted and incised ware" that occurs at Arpachiyah TT 6 (Mallowan and Rose 1935:pl. XX/a).

Early Halaf pottery corresponding to Hijara's pottery Phase H1 is represented at Yarim Tepe by the numerous sherds with the "huts and flowers" motif (here, fig. 2/23) from levels 9 and 8 of Yarim Tepe II (Munchaev and Merpert 1981:243, fig. 90; 247, fig. 93; Merpert, Munchaev, and Bader 1978:pl. XX/1–10).

In the Late Halaf level III at Yarim Tepe III was found a seal in the shape of a flattened drop, suggesting the haunches of a female and resembling the abbreviated anthropomorphic clay figurines from the same site. The design of two animals on the flat side of the pendant indicates its possible use as a seal. The seal form is well known from the Late Halaf level, Area A, at Tepe Gawra (Tobler 1950:pl. CLXXII/19 [here, fig. 6/22]). Three such seal pendants were reproduced from Yarim Tepe II (Munchaev and Merpert 1981:213, fig. 71/7, 8, 11).

Seals with geometric shapes, circular or rectangular, were engraved with the same delicate and distinctive pattern of squares with crossed diagonals, known from Halaf pottery designs. The impression of a pendant with such a pattern was found at Tepe Gawra in Area A, the Late Halaf level just mentioned (Tobler 1950:pl. CLVIII/11). The earliest occurrence of the pattern on seals is in Phase B of the Amuq (Braidwood and Braidwood 1960:95, fig. 68/2), where it is somewhat coarser and reminiscent of the crosshatching on seals of the Hassuna-Samarra period of Mesopotamia.

Area A of Tepe Gawra also yielded the impression of a small rectangular seal, engraved with an antelope in a natural pose with lowered head, which fits well into the available space (Tobler 1950:CLXVI/123 [here, fig. 6/3]). The refined style of this minute design and the excellent workmanship are characteristic of the Halaf period. The animal motif may be a Mesopotamian innovation, for animals are not represented on seals of the Amuq C and D phases, which are contemporary with the Halaf and earlier periods of Mesopotamia.

The fine workmanship in seal pendants, figurines, and pottery manifested at Yarim Tepe II and III, comparable to the workmanship at Arpachiyah and, to a lesser degree, at Tepe Gawra, may be considered a criterion of the period.

One of the several sites in the Himrin basin with Halaf materials, Tell Hasan (Watson 1983a:237; Jasim 1985:164–65), shows the combination of round and rectangular buildings observed at Yarim Tepe II and III. At Tell Hasan the Halaf occupation was situated on the western part of the tell, while on the eastern part was a small settlement of the Ubaid 4 phase. Nowhere on the site did Halaf and Ubaid sherds occur together in a stratified context (Jasim 1985:165).

However, at another Himrin site, Tell Songor B (level II), Late Halaf pottery appears to have been in some contact with Early Ubaid pottery (Fujii 1981:185–86, 193). Watson reports that Hijara noted several other Halafian sites in the region between the Jebel Himrin and the Iranian border, most of which are known only from surface collections. The most important of these may be the partially excavated site of Bagum near the Darbendi Khan reservoir (Watson 1983a:237), which is said to have yielded some red-burnished pottery, perhaps comparable to that at Choga Mami (J. Oates 1969:122, 138–39). All these Late Halaf occurrences are classed by Watson in her "Halafian Periphery: East," along with Halaf-influenced pottery found in Iran (Watson 1983a:237–38), and must represent an expansion of Halafian influences outside the "heartland" of the culture in north Syria and north Mesopotamia.

Available radiocarbon dates suggest that the Halaf culture should be dated to the second half of the sixth millennium (see table 1). The one date from Hijara's excavations at Arpachiyah, BM-1531 from Phase H2, 5985–5495 B.C. (for details see table 1), suggests some contemporaneity with Choga Mami Transitional. This date does not represent the earliest Halaf material since that material had overlapped a little with Samarra. Given the Samarra radiocarbon dates, the Halaf period of Mesopotamia may have begun about the middle of the sixth millennium. If one accepts Hijara's judgment that the lowest Halaf levels at Yarim Tepe II and at Arpachiyah were roughly contemporary, then the radiocarbon dates of levels 7 and 6 of Yarim Tepe II (LE 1212, LE 1211: 5455–5210 B.C. and 5555–5257 B.C. [for details see table 1]) may suggest that these belonged to Middle Halaf, Hijara's pottery Phases H3 to early H4.

The integration of these finds with those of recent excavations of Halaf sites in the west, like Shams ed-Din Tannira, the Euphrates Dam project of the American University of Beirut (al-Radi and Seeden 1980; Azoury and Bergman 1980), and the most promising site in Turkey, Çavi Tarlasi (see Mellink, this vol., chap. 9), remains a task for the future.

The Ubaid Period

For most of the time during which the present version of *Chronologies* was assembled, the period called Ubaid, after a site near Ur in southern Mesopotamia, was considered to have begun somewhat later than the end of the Samarra period in central Mesopotamia and also after the end of the Halaf period in the north. This chronological assumption was reinforced by the fact that Ubaid pottery, made of hard-fired buff or red paste with small geometric designs in black paint, was found at northern sites like Arpachiyah as the last period of occupation, following the Halaf period (Mallowan and Rose 1935:20, and passim). The structure of the present section of this book was planned accordingly.

In 1985, results of a deep sounding at Tell el-'Oueili near Larsa have yielded information concerning periods preceding the earliest Ubaid phase from Eridu. Twenty levels were distinguished in the sounding; however, the groundwater level prevented full exploration to virgin soil. The term *Ubaid 0* was used for levels thirteen to twenty which show relations with Samarra pottery designs and, in at least one case, a resemblance to an early Hassuna coarse-ware shape. At this writing no radiocarbon date is available; however, the pottery and brick types (see below) are related to those at Choga Mami Transitional sites and suggest a likely contemporaneity. Now, it is not surprising that the chemical composition of the Ubaid pottery was closely related to that of Samarra pottery, but different from Halaf pottery (Noll 1976–77: 32, 34).

The Ubaid Period in Southern Mesopotamia

The excavations of the deep levels at 'Oueili have shown that the first settlers built on an elevation, probably to protect themselves against yearly flooding (Calvet 1985:257). Calvet pointed out that the great alluvial deposits of several meters depth, which can be observed at the site, would prevent the discovery of any but the largest of the Early Ubaid settlements (Calvet 1985:255). These observations were made tentatively in amplification of the work of Adams, Nissen, and Wright, who suggested that the earliest phases of the Ubaid period were characterized by small sedentary communities, fairly widely and evenly dispersed in the Eridu region (Adams 1981:59). They thought that they could discern some suggestion of a two-level settlement hierarchy, especially in the Ur-Eridu region, toward the end of the Ubaid period. Here, a variety of smaller settlements of ca. 2–5 ha extension can be seen as subsidiary to a few larger sites covering about 10 or more ha each, for example, Ur and Eridu (Wright in Adams 1981:325).

The Ubaid 0 Phase (The 'Oueili Phase)

The deep levels of 'Oueili have architectural remains showing building techniques for permanent structures (Calvet 1985:259). Huot (1985a:122) describes the material as "loaves" of clay up to 60 cm long, flattened on both sides by boards between which they must have been formed. The upper surface has two long parallel furrows. In their flatness, these large loaves or bricks differ from the otherwise related "cigar-shaped" bricks described by Joan Oates in the buildings of the Samarra houses at Choga Mami (J. Oates 1969:117–21).

The pottery of Ubaid 0 is often painted, except for the earliest levels in which the number of potsherds collected is also very limited. One finds bowls the sides of which are more or less widened toward the top. There were large bowls, footed bowls, closed jars, and jars with convex-concave profiles. Decoration is often produced by parallel lines forming zigzags, large cross-shaped forms, parallel vertical lines, parallel festoons, and superimposed chevrons. On the basis of several items one can suggest a continuity between Ubaid 0 and Ubaid 1, and the overall phase can be considered a direct predecessor of Ubaid 1; however, the repertory of Ubaid 1 is far more sophisticated and the execution closer and tighter. Several morphological and decorative parallels exist with the repertory of the so-called Choga Mami Transitional as it is known from Choga Mami and from Choga Sefid in Iran; moreover, there are relations with the material of Baghouz and Songor A. However, the culture of the ʿOueili phase is not a simple local variant of Choga Mami Transitional but shares with it the horizon of the Samarra period which needs to be further elucidated (Huot 1985a:122–23).

One of the two jars reproduced by Huot (1985b:305, fig. 3) resembles in its lower part a large flat "bowl, upon whose rim was built an upper structure, which . . . curves sharply inward [then rises in the neck] to make a squat . . . vessel." This description was given by Lloyd (Lloyd and Safar 1945:277) for coarse-ware jars of the coarse, straw-tempered vessels of the first, second, and third camp sites in level Ia at Hassuna (for the type, see here, fig. 2/4). Aside from the neck, the description also applies to the shape of the jar from ʿOueili. The painted decoration of the jar from ʿOueili indicates, of course, a somewhat later stage of development. In the second vessel reproduced by Huot (1985b:306, fig. 4), the regular parallel lines suggest the use of a multiple brush, a rather sophisticated technical device that appears to have been used in the subsequent Eridu phase.

The Ubaid 1 Phase (The Eridu Phase)

This phase is named after the ware found in levels XIX–XIV at Eridu in a sounding made near the south corner of the ziggurat. The pottery is fine to extremely fine and covered inside and out with a slip of the same clay. The paint varies from black to red and was normally laid on thickly. One of the most common forms is a broad, either flat or shallow, dish or plate (here, fig. 2/27), occasionally provided with a ring base. Also common are jars with short or long vertical necks, or with flared necks rising from a curve (here, fig. 2/28). A distinctive type is a tall goblet with ogee-shaped sides, occasionally with a carination near a flat bottom (Safar, Mustafa, and Lloyd 1981:174–75, and fig. 96/20 [here, fig. 2/29]).

The painted designs are elaborate, delicately applied, small, and varied. Each type of vessel has its own characteristic repertory of designs. Thus, the shallow dishes have the maximum decoration on the central ground and border of the inner face. The usual type of border pattern is a wide band filled with double crosshatching or diaper pattern, sometimes elaborated by the intermittent solid filling of the checks, giving an extremely rich effect. The central ground is decorated with an allover pattern (checks, opposed triangles, etc.), or with a centrifugal design reminiscent of Samarra wares. From a mere medallion in levels XVIII and XVII the decoration develops into an elaborate design covering the whole ground, usually with some sort of cross as a basis (Safar, Mustafa, and Lloyd 1981:174, and fig. 99/5, 8; J. Oates 1960:35,

and pl. V/24). Another distinctive motif on the inside of shallow bowls is a small tassel of varying form pendent from a sweeping triangle (here, fig. 2/30). Various forms of running ornament between horizontal bands are preferred for jars and are usually limited to the rim and shoulder of the pot (Safar, Mustafa, and Lloyd 1981:175; fig. 98/29–32). Tall goblets are decorated on the outside only, often with bands of solid color beneath the rim, alternating with running patterns. Usually these are balanced by a single heavy band near the bottom (ibid., p. 175; fig. 96/20 [here, fig. 2/29]).

The earliest architecture found at Eridu, levels XVIII–XVI, is characterized by large flat bricks, ca. 50–54 cm × 20–26 cm × 6–7 cm, laid as stretchers in thin walls only one brick thick. In level XVI there was a small building, 2.10 × 3.10 m, with a deep niche containing a small mud-brick pedestal on one side. Opposite the pedestal in the middle of the room was another pedestal which bore clear traces of burning. The doorway was slightly off center with another small mud-brick pedestal outside it. These elements, essential to later Sumerian temples, plus the placement of the building underneath of what was later clearly a sacred area, form the basis for the convincing interpretation of this building as a temple (Safar, Mustafa, and Lloyd 1981:111). Level XV contained a larger rectangular building of less distinct character and built of a clearly different kind of brick: handmade, without any kind of mould, 40 × 14 × 8 cm, and having deep finger grooves on one side. This type of brick was also used "to pack out" the ruins of Temple XV in order to provide an emplacement for a new building, of which no traces remain. The filling was designated as Temple XIV (Safar, Mustafa, and Lloyd 1981:90).

The remains of level 10 at ʿOueili, which was contemporary with Ubaid 1, as shown by relations in the potteries of the two sites (compare Calvet 1983a:*passim*, with Safar, Mustafa, and Lloyd 1981:*passim*), are not yet fully published. They contained several floors, although no walls were found. Level 9 lacked all architecture as such; however, there was some modification of the ground descending toward the south. Part of the pottery of this level was of Ubaid 3 type.

In level 9 was found a pendant of clay (Huot 1985b:309, fig. 6) resembling the shape of the Halaf pendants in the form of an abbreviated female body (here, fig. 6/2). The fact that the ʿOueili pendant is made of clay is unparalleled among the pendants of the Late Halaf and Ubaid periods of Tepe Gawra and Yarim Tepe II and III. Moreover, the motif engraved on the pendant, which the excavators compared to the Late Ubaid subject of an animal-headed demon between two animals or humans, is equally unique on this type of pendant and shows the earliest local glyptic endeavor so far known from the south.

The site of ʿOueili was abandoned after this level and covered by sand until it was reoccupied in Ubaid 4 (Calvet 1985:258).

In the Himrin basin, at Tell Abada, Ubaid 1 material was found in the lowest level, level III, together with "a few apparently genuine Samarra sherds," and associated with "a type closely related to both and reminiscent of Choga Mami 'Transitional'" (Jasim 1983a:184, 1985:90–96). The association of these potteries indicates that they are probably also to be considered chronologically close. Relations of decorative patterns on Eridu phase pots, especially of groups of juxtaposed parallel lines, often with a solid or reserved triangle between them (e.g., Safar, Mustafa, and Lloyd 1981:figs. 94, 97–100, levels XIX–XVI), can be compared to a characteristic external motif of "Transitional Ware" bowls at Choga Mami (J. Oates 1969:pl. XXXII/2–8, 10–12 [here, fig. 2/31]). The radiocarbon date for the Choga Mami Transitional (BM-483) may indicate about 5500 B.C. for the beginning of Ubaid 1. How long it lasted is uncertain, as is the duration of the rest of the Ubaid period. Thus, discussion of absolute chronology will be deferred until the end of the section on northern Ubaid.

The Ubaid 2 Phase (The Hajji Muhammed Phase)

Hajji Muhammed ware, first recognized in the excavations at the Qalʿat Hajji Muhammed (Ziegler 1953), is characteristic of levels XIV–XII at Eridu and continues as well into some later levels. The ware usually has dark purplish black paint, often thickly applied, resulting in a metallic luster. Patterns are often close and create dark zones on the light buff pottery. Wide bowls are usually painted on the interior wall with an oblique grid pattern, leaving a regular scatter of tiny squares in reserve (here, fig. 2/32); the center of the bowls frequently has a radial pattern. Three sherds of Hajji Muhammed pottery examined by Noll showed relations with the painting techniques of Halaf ware (Noll 1976–77:40).

Hajji Muhammed pottery had as wide a distribution as that of Ubaid 1. While it appears to have been most concentrated in the area of Uruk and Ur, it was also found in the excavations at Ras al-ʿAmiya, near Kish, although most of the pottery there belonged to Ubaid 3 (Stronach 1961; Adams 1981). Farther north in the Himrin, Late Ubaid 2 materials, mixed with Ubaid 3, have been found at Tell Abada in levels II–I, Tell Songor B and C, Tell ʿAyash, and Tell Rashid. At Tell Abada above level III was 50–70 cm of fill in which no buildings were found. Level II above this contained Late Ubaid 2 and Ubaid 3 pottery, but Ubaid 2 types predominated (Jasim 1985:98). This level also contained an extensive settlement of well-built mud-brick buildings having a T-

shaped central hall, or court, flanked to either side by smaller rooms or more T-shaped rooms. This is the earliest occurrence of a type of plan that will continue in both north and south in the later Ubaid and Uruk periods. At Choga Mami the Ubaid levels had been heavily eroded, but the sherds collected on the surface of the mound included a number in the Ubaid 1 and 2 styles which predated the Late Halaf material in the vicinity (J. Oates 1983:256).

In this phase Ubaid pottery begins at sites along and behind the Saudi Arabian shoreline of the Persian-Arabian Gulf, more than 600 km south of Eridu, although most of the Ubaid pottery is Ubaid 3 or 4 (J. Oates 1978:1983). Neutron activation analysis has shown this pottery to be of Mesopotamian manufacture (Oates et al. 1977). Potts stresses the likelihood of Mesopotamian fishermen exploiting not only the rich fishing banks off the Arabian coast, but also those of the coast on the opposite side at Bender Boucher (Potts 1978), whereas J. Oates also considered that trading ventures might have played a role (J. Oates 1978; Adams 1981).

The Ubaid 3 and 4 Phases (Former Ubaid I–II Periods)

In levels XI–VI at Eridu (corresponding to the architectural phases of the temple) occur the typical features of the Late Ubaid period, known from several sites: bent clay nails or mullers, clay sickles (here, fig. 3/1,2), and, in pottery painting, simple, often bold curvilinear designs with frequent use of negative space (here, fig. 3/5–6). A clear division between Ubaid 3 and 4 is not possible, therefore the phases are treated together.

One of the links between Ubaid 3 and the foregoing phase 2 is formed by "tortoise jars" (here, fig. 3/4), first found at Eridu in level XIII, but lasting until level VIII. At Gawra the type was found in the Early Ubaid strata XIX–XVII (Tobler 1950:136), and a better, more regularly painted example of similar type was found at Songor B in a grave; it "rested against the grave hole with its spout upside down" (Fujii 1981:171; fig. 36/1; pl. 19/4). A fine example was also found at Tell Abada in level I (Jasim 1985:119; fig. 192). Transitional types were found at the Ubaid 2–3 site of Ras al-ʿAmiya, north of Kish (Stronach 1961:116).

Connections with areas outside southern Mesopotamia appear to have been extensive in Ubaid 3. They are chiefly demonstrated by pottery from Mehmeh in the Deh Luran Plain in Khuzestan, Iran (Hole, Flannery, and Neely 1969:361), namely, Mehmeh red-on-red ware with geometrical designs in a red paint that is darker than the reddish color of the vessel. It was found at Ras al-ʿAmiya (Stronach 1961:121–22) and also occurred at Choga Mami and in the Himrin at Songor C, level 1, Songor B, level 2 and Tell Abada, levels II–I (J. Oates 1983:258–59, and fig. 6/2–4; Jasim 1985:168, and fig. 159).

Toward the end of the Ubaid period in the south, pottery painting became careless and uninspired, and even at Eridu the later wares are "less skillfully painted" (J. Oates 1960:39; also Safar, Mustafa, and Lloyd 1981:160). In Temple VI only 76 painted sherds were found in contrast to 579 unpainted ones (Safar, Mustafa, and Lloyd 1981:160). Some of the grave pottery (here, fig. 3/5, 6), however, has simple bold designs as pleasing as those of Gawra XIII, which are probably contemporary.

Criteria of the Ubaid 4 phase are (1) bowls with flattened inverted rims, occasionally with a ring base, mostly in greenish ware and scratched inside with a blunt, comblike instrument, and (2) bowls with the same kind of rim and painted black inside (Safar, Mustafa, and Lloyd 1981:262, and fig. 127/types 6–8 [here, fig. 3/7, 8]; cf. J. Oates 1983:260). The types were found in the Hut Sounding, but not in the temple or the cemetery. They are found at Warka in both the Eanna and Anu soundings, at Ur, and at ʿOueili, but have not been found so far in the Himrin (J. Oates 1983:260; Adams and Nissen 1972:99).

The architecture of the Ubaid 3 phase is only known from the temple sequence at Eridu. The thin-walled Temples XI–IX have mud-bricks of new proportions, clearly defined regular buttresses, a platform on which the temples are raised, and a plan in which the principal unit is a cella with an altar at one end behind which is a passage. Annexed to the sanctuary chamber on the side were two smaller rooms, one of which contained an offering table.

Temple VIII contained Ubaid 3 pottery but the plan is closely related to that of Temples VII and VI. The walls have greater thickness than before, and the buttresses seem to have become decorative pilasters as in the later temples. The impressive plans of Temples VIII–VI at Eridu agree with the general character of the Ubaid 4 phase. They have often been compared to the public buildings of Gawra XIII. More specifically, comparison has centered on the so-called Northern Temple, built in the middle of the period covered by stratum XIII at Gawra (Tobler 1950:35), which was compared to Temple VII at Eridu (Lloyd and Safar 1947:93). Both structures are identically oriented and seem to be based on a plan that had a cella flanked by four corner rooms. There is a major recess in the facade, decorated like most other outer walls by stepped buttresses. Despite these similarities, which suggest that the buildings were contemporary, there are important differences between them, especially in the position of the entrances, probably owing to different ritual requirements.

The chronological division between Ubaid 4 and the following Uruk period is difficult to discern because of the gradual pace of the transition which can be observed in recent excavations at Warka. These have revealed an Ubaid 4 to Early Uruk settlement in the area of the northwest side of the later Anu ziggurat. Levels 5–6 of *Schnitt* I and 6–7 of *Schnitt* II, the lowest Ubaid levels reached, appear to be approximately contemporary with levels XVII–XVI of the Eanna sounding and seem to be the only Ubaid levels not disturbed by later building activity, that is, the digging of the foundation trench of the *Steingebäude* (for the pottery see Boehmer, in *UVB* 26–27:31–42). In these Ubaid levels of Uruk, two temples prefigure architectural characteristics of the Uruk period as noted by J. Oates (1983:251). Both temples are raised on a mud-brick platform, have a tripartite plan and facades elaborately recessed and plastered. Moreover, one temple was carefully whitewashed like the White Temple on the Anu ziggurat.

Further evidence for the continuity from the Ubaid to the Uruk period may be indicated by the evidence from the small site of Tell Mismar (Schmidt 1978), where numerous clay cones were found in a building with some cone ornament in situ. If this site can be considered terminal Ubaid, the cone mosaic as well as the large size of the rooms precede similar features in the architecture of the Uruk period.

To about the same period belong the Ubaid 4 levels of ʿOueili in which Lebeau has pointed out close relations of the pottery with that of the Late Ubaid-Uruk settlement at Uruk-Warka in K XVII (Lebeau 1983a, 1983c). In these late levels of ʿOueili, three architectural phases can be accommodated within Ubaid 4 (Forest 1983a, 1983c). In the earliest of these phases, the third, was found a well-built, large construction, in which the differences of the terrain had been evened out by a substructure of small boxlike chambers on which a floor had been laid. Opposite the construction were "annexes" in which similar boxlike chambers seem to have been built as support for storage above. Such relatively large storage installations herald the transition to an urban economy as does the mass production of pottery.

In this last phase of the Ubaid development were also found clay figurines of animals, mostly bovine, and of humans, mostly female. Dales distinguished an Ur-Eridu naturalistic style with reptilian heads and natural legs (here, fig. 3/9) and at Warka a pillar style that is paralleled by figurines from Gawra XVI–XV (Dales 1960:182). The Warka examples have the typical "coffee bean" eyes, while the Gawra ones do not (Tobler 1950:pl. LXXXIV/b; Heinrich, in *UVB* 8:pl. 47/h). Figurines from Tell es-Sawwan and Choga Mami with a tall headgear, or hairstyle, covered with bitumen, and slender, small-breasted female figurines with coffee-bean eyes furnish prototypes for the Ubaid figures of the south. This can be assumed despite the gap in time which seems to separate the earlier figures from the later ones. Examples of these later ones found in the surface layer of Tell el-ʿOueili (Lebeau 1983b:133) indicate a date at the end of Ubaid 4. They show that influences not only went from south to north in the middle of the Ubaid period, as suggested by the pottery, but that important cultural traits at an earlier period had traveled south from northern sites.

The first period in which stamp seals were found in the south is Ubaid 3–4, but the number was small. The most characteristic type is exemplified by one seal from Uqair (here, fig. 6/4, drawing after Buchanan), which has a raised back and slightly raised, oval base. The base is engraved with a symmetrical pattern of parallel lines in different directions, interspersed with small, shallow drillings. The seal was found in a level preceding the end of the Ubaid period (Lloyd and Safar 1943:149), presumably Ubaid 3 to 4. To the same type belongs a stamp from Tello (Buchanan 1967:528, pl. I/13).

A symmetrical pattern created by groups of parallel lines in different directions was a device favored by Ubaid-period seal carvers. Several seals with such patterns and the shape of the seal from Uqair were found at Uruk (Jakob-Rost 1975:pl. 1/5–7) and can be ascribed to the Ubaid period on the basis of their type, although they were not so recorded stratigraphically. The same applies to a pink stamp seal from Ur (Woolley 1955:pl. 28/U.17923).

Characteristic of Ubaid 4 are several types of small engraved terra-cotta and stone beads, examples of which were found well stratified at ʿOueili (Lebeau 1983b:pl. B/2, 3, and pl. D/5, 6; text, p. 134). The same types have been found at Ur (here, fig. 6/5, 6) and doubtless at other sites from which they were not published. The same type of object, though with a rhomboid shape and made of terra-cotta, was found in Gawra XIII, supporting the contemporaneity of Gawra XIII and Ubaid 4.

No seal impressions or figured designs have so far been discovered in the south in Ubaid levels.

The Ubaid Period in Northern Mesopotamia

The Early Northern Ubaid Phase (Ubaid 3)

The transition from Halaf to Ubaid culture as reflected in the pottery of the northern sites of Tepe Gawra, levels XX–XVI, Telul eth-Thalathat XIV and XIII, and Qalinj Agha, located within the city limits of Erbil, was gradual (Dunham 1983). To these northern sites should also be added Tell Aqab in Syria, which shows in its latest levels a very close relation to the pattern of Halaf and Early Ubaid elements seen in the pottery of Gawra XX–XVI (Davidson and Watkins 1981:9). The transition from Halaf to Ubaid has also been found at Yarim Tepe III, where a small Early Ubaid settlement overlay a more ex-

tensive Halaf occupation. In the Himrin basin, early northern materials appear at nine sites, the most important of which are Tell Abada (II–I), Kheit Qasim III, Tell Rashid, and Tell ʿAyash.

Certain types are characteristic of this Early Ubaid phase. Small bell-shaped bowls with hatching between solid lines near the rim, hemispherical bowls with scalloped lines or hatched triangles near the rim, and globular-bodied jars with constricted neck and hatched decoration on the shoulder (here, fig. 10/4, 6, 8). The patterns are continuous and rapidly executed. A type of vessel often found in Thalathat XIV, less frequently in XIII and XII, is a large globular-bodied jar with a very short neck and a ledge inside the rim (here, fig. 3/10). The ledge is often perforated in four places. This is a very rare type at Gawra, but a rim sherd of this vessel type occurred at Qalinj Agha in level X of sounding I (al-Soof and es-Siwwani 1967:70) and at other sites of the north as well as south (Dunham 1983). The occurrence of the ledge-rim jars in north and south parallels the long-known situation concerning the so-called tortoise or trumpet jars in level XI of Eridu and XIX–XVII at Tepe Gawra (Porada 1965:142). No tortoise jars are reported from Thalathat but a trumpet-shaped spout was found at Qalinj Agha, in sounding 1, level X. Moreover, examples were found at Tell Abada in the Himrin and at Tell Brak far to the northwest (Jasim 1983a:179, fig. 12/1; Jasim 1985:fig. 192; D. Oates 1982b:64).

At Tell Abada in levels II–I a large amount of incised pottery was found (Jasim 1985:130–38; pl. 9/a, b). Similar pottery is reported from Kheit Qasim III (Forest-Foucault 1980:224) and Tell Rashid (Jasim 1985:150). Some of this is similar to incised ware excavated long ago at Kudish Saghir and Nuzi (Starr 1937:pls. 44–46; J. Oates 1983:254). This type of pottery appears to continue into the Late Northern Ubaid period in the Himrin, at Tell Madhhur and Abu Husaini, and at Tepe Gawra, level XIII (J. Oates. 1983:254; Tusa 1980:227; Tobler 1950:141; Jasim 1985:159–61). At Abada and Kheit Qasim III some of the incised ware is said to be Dalma impressed ware, such as was found at Dalma Tepe in western Azerbaijan (Hamlin 1975). One Dalma-like painted bowl occurs in Abada level II (Jasim 1985:167; fig. 125/d). Also to be noted is a large bowl with flaring sides found at Dalma Tepe and said to be an import (Hamlin 1975: fig. 10/i). This is decorated in a bold sweeping design of a type found in Abada level I and in the Ubaid levels at Arpachiyah (Jasim 1985:35, and fig. 164; Mallowan and Rose 1935:fig. 32). At both sites such bowls were associated only with burial urns (Mallowan and Rose 1935:46; Jasim 1985:114–15).

Links between north and south in the Ubaid period are also obvious in the so-called mullers or bent clay nails. Examples come from all the Ubaid levels (except level

XV) of Tepe Gawra after level XX (Tobler 1950:169), from Telul eth-Thalathat levels XIV and XIII, from Tell Aqab, where it first appeared in the uppermost level of trench 1 (Davidson and Watkins 1981:10), and from southern sites like Tell Uqair (Lloyd and Safar 1943:pl. XVI, "a group of objects from houses in the Ubaid settlement") and ʿOueili (Lebeau 1983c:135). At Tell Abada II–I, some were decorated with paint or attached pellets of clay at the curved end and one was shaped into a simplified human torso (Jasim 1985:63; fig. 57).

The glyptic development of the Early Ubaid period, however, seems to have been limited to the north. A lentoid seal shape engraved with a delicate, single antelope, like the earliest imprint (Tobler 1950:pl. CLXVI/123 [here, fig. 6/3]), was found in Gawra XVIII and again in XV (ibid., pls. CLXIV/103, CLXV/104). In the latter level an imprint was also found that shows human figures and animals in a coherent composition (Tobler 1950:pl. CLXIV/98 [here, fig. 6/7]). The thin, linear figures seem to float in the space which they fill with their dovetailing forms. Legs of both the humans and animals are bent. Seal impressions found in the well of Gawra XIII of the Late Northern Ubaid period (Tobler 1950:pls. CLXIV/100–102, CLXIX/162) as well as a seal from Tell Gomel in northern Iraq (Frankfort 1935:29, fig. 31) also belong to this style. Often the figures stand on the circumference of the seal, causing something of a rotational movement in the design.

Female figurines of the Early Ubaid period are simplified in comparison with Halaf figurines. Especially characteristic are stumps for arms (Tobler 1950:pls. LXXXI/c, CLIII/4 [here, fig. 3/11]) and painted bands on the body crossed or converging at the breast and forming a girdle below (ibid., pl. LXXXI/c, d). The ornamentation of the crossed bands survived in later periods from the Mediterranean to India.

In the architecture of this period at Tepe Gawra the survival of Halaf round structures can be observed in levels XX and XVII. Round buildings like those at Gawra with interior wall projections were also found at Thalathat in level XIII (Egami 1959:3; figs. 9, 10). However, these are single structures of which at most two occurred in one level, while rectangular buildings predominated.

The important new type of the period is a tripartite house, "consisting of a roofed central room, either rectangular or cruciform, running the length of the house and two rows of smaller rooms on each side" (Roaf 1984b:88).

The interpretation as temples of the buildings of Gawra XIX and XVIII, with a plain rectangular central room in which there was a rectangular podium slightly to the rear of the room, was rejected by Roaf (1984b:82), who considered only the extraordinary buildings of the Late Ubaid period, Gawra XIII, to have been temples. Their

plans resemble those of the temples of Eridu and make southern influence seem very likely (Roaf 1984b:83).

The characteristic Ubaid-period house with cruciform or plain rectangular room has a stepped facade "where an internal wall meets the outside wall, and the staircase unit consists of two narrow, parallel rooms" (Roaf 1984b:88). Examples of this occurred in Gawra and later, at Thalathat (Egami 1959:fig. 47), and in the Himrin—at Tell Songor B (Matsumoto 1979:524; fig. 4), at Abada, level II (Jasim 1983a:figs. 7–9), and an almost identical plan at Kheit Qasim III (Forest-Foucault 1980:222) and Madhhur II (Roaf 1984b:82–88; figs. 7, 12, 14, 17–19, 21, and 23).

The Late Northern Ubaid Phase (Ubaid 4)

In levels XVI–XIII of Tepe Gawra, the acropolis of XIII, crowned by three elaborate temples, built of excellent, well-bonded mud-brick with complex stepped piers and niches, probably indicates that Gawra was the most important place of the entire region. The pottery of other sites more recently excavated can therefore be keyed into the Gawra sequence. Bold designs on pottery with much use of negative space are found on beakers with gently curved sides and slightly flaring rims, characteristic of level XIII (here, fig. 3/12). Pottery comparisons between Thalathat IX and VIIb cluster around Gawra XIII. The most striking comparisons are with the corrugated jar with flat base, round body, and high cylindrical neck, a distinctive type at Gawra XIII that can be compared to fragments of level IX from Thalathat. The distribution of the type into the Sinjar region is documented by the excavations of S. Lloyd at Grai Resh (Lloyd 1940:pl. II, fig. 5/29). Another widely distributed type is the plain globular jar with incised herringbone pattern on the body, with a usually short out-turned rim. The rim is either plain or has the incised herringbone pattern on only the inside or the outside, and, in an example from Gawra XIII, although the rim is slightly taller, the rim has the pattern on both sides (Tobler 1950:pl. CXXXI/217). Comparisons come from Thalathat VIIb (Egami 1959:fig. 53/3), Nuzi (Starr 1937–39:599; pl. 46/C, D, E, G) and from Tell Abu Husaini in the Himrin (Invernizzi 1980:fig. 84). In general, pottery from that site, if decorated at all, is more frequently incised than painted. The same is true at Tell Madhhur, another Late Ubaid site in the Himrin. However, here the rarer painted pots have parallels in the Ubaid pottery at Tell Uqair, especially in the use of a "goat" motif (Jasim 1985:160, and fig. 261/8–10; Lloyd and Safar 1943:pl. XIX/a). A jar with comparable decoration was found at Tell Hasan, a third Late Ubaid site in the Himrin (Jasim 1985:pl. 19/b). A fourth Late Ubaid site, Tell ʿAyash, is said to have parallels with Nuzi, Telul eth-Thalathat, and Gawra, although illustrations are not yet published. A vessel in the form of a hoof from 'Ayash can be compared to ones from Gawra XIII and XII (al-Jadir 1980:179, fig. 12; 1979:565, fig. 7; Tobler 1950:pls. CXXXII/231, CXL/326). Among the plain pottery from Tell Madhhur one might mention deep U-shaped vessels (Jasim 1985:fig. 258/4, 5), which are a type seen in Gawra level XII, where it was used for burials, and in Thalathat level VIIa (here, fig. 12/1).

An incense burner with architectural decoration (Tobler 1950:pls. LXXVIII/d, CXXXII/228) may indicate the type of object to which belonged a cylindrical ceramic object from Thalathat with perforated triangles (Egami 1959:fig. 54/8). The incense burner from Gawra (here, fig. 3/13) may also be compared to a painted one of the Ubaid 4 phase from Eridu with related architectural decoration (Safar, Mustafa, and Lloyd 1981:160; figs. 74, 81). In general, however, ceramic correlations between north and south are only about half as numerous as those that could be established for the Early Northern Ubaid period (Perkins 1949:90–93, passim).

In the well of Gawra XIII, the contents of which preceded at least the building of the so-called Northern Temple of XIII (Tobler 1950:31–32, 35), were found stamp seal impressions of distinctive design, which must belong to the first part of the period, if not to the preceding level XIV. One group continues the dovetailing, rotating composition of thin figures found first in Stratum XV (ibid., pl. CLXIV/100–102). Others show increasingly substantial figures concentrated in the lower part of the seal as on a base (pl. CLXX/173). In an imprint with a gazelle-horned demon (pl. CLXIV/94 [here, fig. 6/8]), a more vertically directed composition is found, perhaps even an axial one, if the seal is correctly reconstructed.

Most of the ornamental seal designs from the well of Gawra XIII have patterns of parallel lines in different directions but related to a median axis (Tobler 1950:pl. CLX/38, 39, 43, [here, fig. 6/9]; pl. CLXI/48). Some of the designs of imprints found in the well and elsewhere in stratum XIII suggest vegetal forms like leaves, marked by short parallel lines (pl. CLXI/62, 64). This type of seal design lasted into the Gawra period since some examples are known from Gawra XI and XI-A (pl. CLXI/59, 60, 61). A seal of this type was found at Qalinj Agha (Erbil) (al-Soof 1969:33, pl. XX [here, fig. 6/10], compare to Tobler 1950:pl. CLXI/60), a site that seems to be contemporary with Gawra XII to XI-A (see below).

The Absolute Chronology of the Ubaid Period

Since very few radiocarbon dates from Mesopotamia are available, one has to keep in mind the relations between the north and the south and the connections with areas outside Mesopotamia. As stated above, the date for

Choga Mami Transitional may indicate that Ubaid 1 started around 5500 B.C. How long it lasted is uncertain since there are no radiocarbon dates for Ubaid 2. For Ubaid 3 and Early Northern Ubaid, synchronisms occur between Ras al-'Amiya, Early Ubaid 3, and the Mehmeh Phase of Tepe Sabz in Iran and between Himrin sites with Dalma impressed ware and the Dalma culture of Iran. Also, the end of Halaf seems to overlap slightly with Early Northern Ubaid. A date for the Mehmeh phase, when calibrated, falls in the second half of the sixth millennium (Hole, Flannery, and Neely 1969:333, No. I-1493; cf. Voigt and Dyson, this vol., chap. 6), while one for the Dalma culture suggests early fifth (P-503: 5100–4835 B.C.; Voigt and Dyson, this vol., chap. 6). These, coupled with Hole's observation that Halaf ended ca. 5000 B.C. (see above), suggest that Ubaid 3 belongs in the first half of the fifth millennium. Dates for Ubaid 4 and Late Northern Ubaid are also somewhat uncertain. Radiocarbon determinations from the uppermost Ubaid levels at Tell 'Oueili fall in the first half to third quarter of the fifth millennium (see table 1; Huot 1983:201). A date from Tell Madhur points to the middle of the fifth millennium (BM-1458:4460–4400 B.C.; see table 1), while dates for the Pisdeli culture in Iran suggest the second half of the fifth millennium (see Voigt and Dyson, this vol., chap. 6):

P-1841	4430–4115 B.C.
P-1842	4410–3930 B.C.
P-157	4440–4085 B.C.
P-504	4450–4335 B.C.
P-505	4565–4414 B.C.

The Madhur date probably does not come at the end of Ubaid 4, since there are said to be "four main building levels with numerous phases" above the level from which the radiocarbon sample came (Roaf 1982:43). Thus, perhaps Ubaid 4 (which here includes Oates's "Terminal Ubaid"; (J. Oates 1983:263) dates to the last half of the fifth millennium, ca. 4500–4000 B.C. Until more is known about the absolute chronology of the Early Uruk period (see below), this is, of course, very tentative, especially in light of the 'Oueili dates.

The Gawra Period in the North and the Uruk and Jamdat Nasr Periods in the South

The Gawra Period

This period, roughly equivalent to the Uruk and Jamdat Nasr periods in the south, is named for the site that has provided the longest stratified sequence in north Mesopotamia. The term was retained despite the fact pointed out by Roaf in his discussion of the Uruk levels at Tell Muhammed 'Arab in the Eski Mosul region that the

Gawra assemblage is not found at other sites of the area since in northern Mesopotamia "the results at different sites do not appear to repeat" (Roaf 1984a:154). As an example he cited the absence of beveled-rim bowls from the Gawra publication, whereas at Nineveh, only a few kilometers away, they are characteristic of level 4. However, some connections with the sites of Telul eth-Thalathat and Qalinj Agha and others can be established, as pointed out below.

The Early Gawra Phase

The most striking feature of this phase is the replacement of the stately structures of stratum XIII by the crowded buildings of a town in Gawra XII. Forest convincingly suggests that this stratum also comprises the hardly recognizable stratum XII-A (Forest 1983b:27). Forest also stressed the large number of burials in XII and suggests that a new social structure in the settlement can be deduced for this period (Forest 1983b: *passim,* especially p. 110). In the pottery the tournette was widely employed, and sand appears to have been the tempering material. There is a notable increase in undecorated pottery, although decorated vessels were by far the larger group in publication. The outstanding feature of the level is the ring base, which appears on all types of vessels (Perkins 1949:51 [here, fig. 3/14, 15]). Green wares were most common in stratum XII, but some light brown and reddish brown persisted (Tobler 1950:147). Pottery from Thalathat VIIa, which is said to be mostly of reddish or greenish brown ware (Egami 1959:7), fits in with this description. Furthermore, several shapes have parallels with Gawra XII (see here, fig. 12). A squat pot with flared rim in Uruk grayware as well as several examples of jars in Uruk redware, all in the Iraq Museum, are said to have come from Gawra stratum XII (Safar, Mustafa, and Lloyd 1981:150–51).

A new type of pottery in stratum XII, although a single example was found in stratum XIII, is the "sprig ware," painted black on a thick brown or red slip (Tobler 1950:pl. CXXXIII/243 [here, fig. 3/16], 245; pl. CXXXVII/294, 295; pl. CXXXIX/310, 311). Some pottery from Thalathat, published as coming from "Strata 4b and 10b," appears to be that ware, characterized by its branchlike decoration (Egami 1959:fig. 20/13–21 and p. 3). "Sprig ware" has been reported from several sites farther west, in the Sinjar district, where it occurs at one site with a number of Uruk sherds (J. Oates 1983:262). It has also been found at Norsun Tepe in the Keban region of east Turkey in a context containing stamp seals comparable to some of Gawra XI–IX and greenish grayware like that mentioned below (Hauptmann 1976:85–87; pls. 48, 50).

A few sherds of a hard-fired greenish gray pottery with incised, applied, and stamped decoration, which became more plentiful in the following strata (Tobler 1950:pls. LXXIX/a–d, LXXX/a), are in the University Museum, Philadelphia, clearly marked "12." They were not mentioned in Tobler's publication. About ten probably similar sherds described as greenish buff, highly fired with incised and stamped decoration, were found at Qalinj Agha in level III (al-Soof 1969:22).

Double-horned, large clay objects were found at Gawra in stratum XII, XI-A, XI, and IX (here, fig. 3/17). In one instance in stratum XI, such an object was found in association with a heap of ovoid sling pellets. Examples of such objects were found in all three levels at Qalinj Agha (al-Soof 1969:4–7) and in the west, at Brak (Mallowan 1947:pl. XXXIX/2). So-called hut symbols, another new and perhaps symbolic form, which began at Gawra in stratum XII—one sun-dried and fragmentary example from stratum XV may not belong to the group— were also found in all three levels of Qalinj Agha (al-Soof 1969:pl. XI). Also spindle whorls, plain and decorated, especially with incisions, which were numerous in levels XII–XI at Gawra, were found in all three levels at Qalinj Agha.

In the seals of Gawra XII all ornamental designs are simplified. There are many small seals with simple geometric decoration based on the division of the circle (Tobler 1950:pl. CLVIII/14; pl. CLIX/16, 17, 24, 25, 27; pl. CLIX/26 [here, fig. 6/11] was found "below XII"). Most of these seals are hemispheroids ranging from low to high and from small to medium sized. Many of the geometrically decorated ones are said to be of white paste.

A few seals of this stratum have a single horned animal figure engraved on the base, usually with forelegs bent or stretched out obliquely (Tobler 1950:pl. CLXV/109 [here, fig. 6/12], 110, 111). Two of these seals also have holes or grooves in the back for inlay, a new feature that also occurs on stone studs in Amuq Phases F and G (Braidwood and Braidwood 1960:254, fig. 192/2; p. 333, fig. 255/2) and in kidney-shaped seal amulets from Brak, three of which were found in the Gray Brick Stratum (Mallowan 1947:pl. XVII/9, 13, 23).

Ritual and other scenes with more than one figure seem to have had their inception in seals of stratum XII and continued into XI. In general, glyptic art fails to show the abrupt change from some painted to almost completely monochrome pottery between strata XII and XI-A. In fact, two imprints of the same seal (Tobler 1950:pl. CLXIII/82, 83) were found in strata XII and XI-A respectively (Amiet 1980:pl. 2/44 shows a combined drawing). Although this may be an accidental division into levels at the time of the excavation, the general continuity in the seals from one level to the other is interesting, in view of the violent end of stratum XII (Tobler 1950: 25–26).

The Middle Gawra Phase

Strata XI-A–X are here joined in a Middle Gawra unit, which partially corresponds to the amalgamation of these strata suggested by Forest on the basis of a reevaluation of their architectural plans (Forest 1983b:26–27), although he would link the early phase of stratum XI-A with stratum XII. The character of this Middle Gawra period is marked architecturally by the fact that XI-A was a fortified town with a strong inner citadel, the Round House (Tobler 1950:18). Possibly "sling balls" in heaps found throughout strata XI-A and XI at Gawra (ibid., p. 173), Thalathat (Egami 1959:4), and Qalinj Agha (al-Soof 1969:4) reinforce the impression of latent warfare, although Jasim has recently questioned their practicality in such a function (Jasim 1985:62).

Tombs, in which were buried persons probably of higher status than those in simpler inhumations (Forest 1983b:69ff. and passim), were built of stone or mud-brick and were placed in a cemetery or within the grounds of a habitation or a temple (in stratum XII, tombs had been built of pisé). For the rich tomb of a child, locus 181 (Tobler 1950:101, 116–17), which Tobler assigned to stratum XI and was dug into XI-A, Forest prefers a date in stratum VIII, a suggestion supported by parallels for the gold objects, like the rosette in tombs of the later stratum (Forest 1983b:53, n. 178 [here, fig. 3/18]).

In Gawra XI-A the first of a series of temples was built, which continued with minor variations through stratum VIII. These have the tripartite plan of the earlier temples at Gawra, with a long central chamber flanked by subsidiary rooms. The corners are oriented to the cardinal points as in the south (see below), however, a portico entrance in Temple XI, which became even more accentuated in strata IX and VIII (Perkins 1949: 174–75), seems to be a distinctive northern feature, as is its entrance in a short wall, opposite the podium (Tobler 1950:pls. II, V, XXII).

At Thalathat was found a related type of building in which smaller rooms of various sizes and plans were arranged along the long sides of a central rectangular room. Two such buildings were found at the site, one in "C-Period Layer" which equals VIIa, probably contemporary with Gawra XII, but the central room had two phases of which the second belonged to "B-Period Layer," which equals VI/V, probably contemporary with Gawra XI-A–XI. The large size of the building and hoard of sling pellets on the floor of B, as well as a strikingly niched buttress on the southern wall of the central room, mark the building as something more important than a private dwelling. A second building of this type with a more compact plan, found in Trench IX, was said to be of Uruk date but no specific level was given. On the basis of an altarlike mud brick pier, the building was thought to be a temple. Related types of buildings at Thalathat and Qalinj Agha are discussed by Dunham (1983:35–38).

The pottery of Qalinj Agha levels III and II corresponds to that of Gawra in the lack of painted decoration and in having among its most prevalent forms a flat-based bowl with flaring sides, either buff or reddish in color and of coarse or semicoarse ware (al-Soof 1969:8 and passim; Tobler 1950:pl. CXLI/328 [here, fig. 12/6]). Important in these levels is a specific type of double-mouthed pot with the necks close together and set more vertically on the vessel than in earlier examples from Gawra XI-A (Tobler 1950:pl. CXLIII/356 [here, figs. 3/19, 12/5]), the Himrin (Jasim 1983a: fig. 12/7), and Thalathat level XIV (Fukai, Horiuchi, and Matsutani 1970:pl. LXXV/19). A fragment of such a pot was found at Qalinj Agha (al-Soof 1969:15), and a fine example comes from Thalathat level VI–V (Egami 1959:pl. XIX/1). Double-mouthed jars are also reported from Early Uruk pottery at Eridu (al-Soof 1973:18, 1967:pl. XLVII, type 41; Lloyd 1948:50). Lloyd suggested that the earlier pottery phase at Eridu is contemporary with Uruk-Eanna XIV–VII (Lloyd 1948:51).

Seals from Qalinj Agha support the correspondences so far established with Gawra XI-A and XI. One of the seals shows several animals, specifically a goat and above it a small dog with a disembodied horned head in the field (al-Soof 1969:pl. XX, upper right), which can be paralleled by several sealings from Gawra XI-A and XI for which such designs are characteristic (Tobler 1950:pl. CLXIX/163, 166, 169, pl. CLXX/170 [here, fig. 6/13]). Even the simple geometric designs of two stamps from Qalinj Agha (al-Soof 1969:pl. XX, lower left and middle) correspond in the central hollow of the rayed design to an example from Gawra XI-A (Tobler 1950:pl. CLX/36).

Gawra, however, has a number of other important innovations among the seal designs of strata XI-A and XI. The human and demonic figures are now often completely upright and have a human gait (Tobler 1950:pl. CLXIII/81, 89). A significant motif is the demon with human body and the head of a mountain goat holding a serpent (pl. CLXIII/81 [here, fig. 6/14]), comparable to a seal impression of layer 25 at Susa (Amiet 1971:fig. 35/2, text, pp. 219–20), and to another example on a sealing from Susa B, the earlier chronological determination for levels 27–23 (Amiet 1980:pl. 6/118). Connections between Gawra, Susa, and Giyan on the basis of these and other motifs have been frequently made (D. H. Caldwell 1976). Another characteristic motif of this period is that of a couple in an erotic scene, either seated and represented identically or bending over (Tobler 1950:pl.

CLXIII/86, 87); the latter rendering may be paralleled in a seal from the end of Giyan V with horned figures (Contenau and Ghirshman 1935:pl. 38/24; perhaps pl. 38/22 represents a related motif).

Designs composed entirely of disembodied heads of horned animals are another feature of the period (Tobler 1950:pl. CLXIX/168, 169; pl. CLXX/170 [here, fig. 6/13]). Susa has intricate geometric patterns produced by heads of horned animals arranged on a cross within a circle, closely related in style to a purely geometric design found in level 25 (Amiet 1971:fig. 35, 3), and therefore probably contemporary. With this group might be associated the large stamp impression of Uruk XII (Jordan, in *UVB* 3, pl. 19/a).

Syro-Cilician connections in Gawra XI-A are manifested by the rectangular imprint of what must have been a gable-shaped stamp seal with three large horned animals (Tobler 1950:pl. CLXVIII/155 [here, fig. 7/1]) engraved on the rectangular sealing surface in the manner of numerous gables from Syro-Cilicia (e.g., Hogarth 1920:pl. IV/90, 91, 93), the precise date of which in Phase F or late E of the Amuq remains to be established.

The typical seal designs of Gawra XI-A and XI, with numerous animals, especially saluki dogs, pursuing horned animals or standing above or below them (Tobler 1950:pl. CLXVIII/157 [here, fig. 7/2]), of which the sealing from Qalinj Agha is an example, are also paralleled at Arpachiyah in "Superficial strata" (Mallowan and Rose 1935:pl. IX/605, 612) and in the "early series" at Nineveh (Mallowan 1933:pl. LXIV/13, 14).

The Late Gawra Phase

The Late Gawra phase, strata IX–VIII-c, is here taken to be contemporary with the Late Uruk and Jamdat Nasr periods in the south. This correlation is shown mainly but rather tenuously in the seal designs; architecture does not permit any specific correlations between levels, and pottery manifests only the general feature of the wheel-made technique beginning in stratum IX and becoming common in VIII. The fabric is light buff, which is the characteristic color of the pottery in this period. Beveled-rim bowls, the hallmark of the Uruk period, were not illustrated among Gawra pottery drawings and photographs, nor at Qalinj Agha or Thalathat, although they were recorded from Nineveh, levels 3 and 4, Nuzi IX and VIII, from Grai Resh and Gerdi Resh (Perkins 1949:57, 163, 165, 170, 199; Hijara 1976:59ff.), from Tell Brak and Tell Leilan.

A tie with the south is stressed even more strongly by the few seal impressions found in stratum IX which indicate a relation with the massive modeled forms of the imprints found in Uruk IV. The closest parallel for the example here given (Tobler 1950:pl. CLXIX/165 [here,

fig. 7/3]) seems to come from Uruk IVb (Lenzen 1950:pl. 4/8 [here, fig. 7/5]; note especially the stylization of the animal's legs). In a second imprint from Gawra IX (here, fig. 7/4), two human figures are shown in profile instead of with the earlier convention of a triangular frontal thorax. Such profile renderings are again related to the glyptic style of Uruk IV, although other details are unparalleled there.

The animals with crossed horns and necks on the stamp sealings of stratum VIII at Gawra (Speiser 1935:pl. LVIII/31 [here, fig., 7/6], 32, 33) are somewhat reminiscent of cylinder seal impressions from Habuba Kabira, north Syria, where birds are seen with entwined necks and horned animals with entwined tails (Sürenhagen and Töpperwein 1973:28, Abb. 6/a and p. 30, Abb. 8/a, b). The principal parallels for the new small- and medium-sized seals of Gawra VIII, engraved with one or at most two horned animals or felines (Speiser 1935:pl. LVI/8–14; pl. LVII/15–27), can, however, be found in Brak in seals from the Gray Brick Stratum (Mallowan 1947:pls. XVIII–XX, *passim*), assigned to the earlier Jamdat Nasr period, and in examples from the Amuq sites from Phase G (Braidwood and Braidwood 1960:330, fig. 253/8–11), equated with the later Protoliterate and Early Dynastic I ranges (ibid., p. 516).

Especially striking at Gawra, Habuba Kabira, and Brak is the placing of animals tête-bêche (here, fig. 7/7) and of showing horned animals with three legs (here, fig. 7/8). Opposed pairs of volutes are also seen at all three sites. The example with volutes from Gawra is on a terracotta seal cursorily made and actually found in stratum VII (Speiser 1935:pl. LVI/6), where it is one of the few survivals of stamp seals in a level otherwise characterized by cylinder seals. West-east influences indicated by these stamp seals are further documented by an impression of a large plaque or gable found in Gawra VIII (Speiser 1935:pl. LVII/28) and by actual plaques of the same group from strata VIII and VII (pl. LVII/29, 30). Relations with Syro-Cilician gables are suggested by the size of the designs and by similarities, in the rendering of the animals and fillers, to gables from various sites in Syro-Cilicia (see especially a gable of "bronze" bought near Antioch: Hogarth 1920:pl. IV/103). While stamp seals remained as the seal form of Gawra VIII, cylinder seals appeared at Thalathat (Fukai, Horiuchi, and Matsutani 1974:pl. XXXVIII/6–9; Egami 1959:fig. 38/8). Conceivably these cylinders, although said to be of Jamdat Nasr type because of their resemblance to some from Sin Temple IV at Khafaje, which was formerly assigned to the Jamdat Nasr period, belong already to the transition to Early Dynastic I, a period in which various seal types and styles were used concurrently in different regions. Publication of the excavations of Early Dynastic I levels in the Himrin area will probably provide some approximate dates for a period which is as yet insufficiently known.

In the Himrin basin very little evidence has been found for the Uruk and Jamdat Nasr periods. In a small sounding at Tell Rubeidheh a large quantity of beveled-rim bowl fragments was recovered along with pottery similar to that found at Gerdi Resh in the Shahrazor Plain to the northeast (Postgate 1979:591; Postgate 1972:141; Hijara 1976). At Tell Gubba, a round building with eight concentric walls was excavated by the Japanese expedition to the Himrin working at Gubba and Songor (Fujii 1981: 141–47). The earliest levels are said to be "Protoliterate" (Postgate and Roaf 1981:176).

The largest area of remains of the Uruk period in the north, contemporary with the Gawra period, was uncovered at the huge site of Tell Brak (D. Oates 1985a). The intermediate position of Brak between the cultures of north and south in Mesopotamia is revealed in the plan of the Eye Temple. It shows "an adaptation of the cruciform tripartite plan, known already in the Hamrin and at Gawra in the 'Ubaid period" (J. Oates 1985a:179). Plans of this type of building have been conveniently collected by Roaf (1984b). Characteristic of the north are the storage areas guarded by massive walls; however, the decorative articulation of the walls by niches and salients, and the use of stone mosaics and rosettes (here, fig. 3/20), are features comparable to buildings at Uruk and at other sites in the south. There exists no parallel, however, for the rich decoration of the altar in the Eye Temple, which had strips of gold sheathing over wood, together with strips of white and blue limestone and shale (Mallowan 1947:93–94).

In recent excavations at Brak a series of Jamdat Nasr platforms of the Eye Temple has been noted, but the date of the earliest Eye Temple has not yet been determined. However, the appearance of a human eye as a conspicuous decorative motif on Late Ubaid pottery from levels below the earliest Uruk ones (which were found 14 m below the surface of the tell) indicates an early inception of the cult represented by this symbol (D. Oates 1987:176).

In connection with the Late Ubaid painted ware of Brak, attention should be drawn to the pair of clay horns found near the Eye Temple platform (Mallowan 1947:184; pl. XXXIX:2). Similar finds were made at Gawra and Qalinj Agha.

The Uruk sequence at Brak is said to be the fullest yet known; especially important is the evidence for an Early Uruk phase, some characteristics of which, as given by Joan Oates, are "burnished red ware, hole mouth vessels (both red and grey), bowls with criss-cross incised bases, very distinctive stamped and incised pottery, and large numbers of 'wide flower pots' " (J. Oates 1985a:178).

For the Late Uruk–"Jamdat Nasr" levels 9–13, Joan

Oates cites the following characteristic types (J. Oates 1985a:176–77): crudely finished platters and a wide "flower pot"—flat-based coarse vessels of a type known at Tepe Gawra; some beveled-rim bowl sherds; casseroles and finely corrugated rim interiors; and eggshell-quality bowls. Also characteristic are a stone bear and an alabaster spectacle idol (D. Oates 1985a pp. 163, 173; pl. XXV/a–c, e), the latter related to the "Hut Symbol" from Tepe Gawra (Speiser 1935:pl. XLIV/c, probably from stratum IX). There was also "a particularly fine bulla (Pl. XXX, a), in conventional typology Warka V–IV . . . found unequivocally stratified beneath level 12 (immediately below the lowest of the upper levels)" (J. Oates 1985a:176). The most striking feature of the cylinder seal impression on the bulla is a delicately engraved vulture, probably of the gigantic type seen paired on a cylinder seal impression from Habuba Kabira (Sürenhagen and Töpperwein 1972:28, Abb. 6/a). The relationship may serve to confirm the date of the Brak impression within the Late Uruk period.

Joan Oates states that Brak lacks "the agreed southern criteria for 'Jamdat Nasr', i.e. the polychrome pottery, which so far has not been found in the north, and the Warka III type of tablet" (J. Oates 1985a:176).

The Uruk and Jamdat Nasr Periods

The Uruk Period

The Uruk period derives its name from the great Sumerian town of southern Mesopotamia. Only a series of magnificent buildings, interpreted as temples and their subsidiary structures, has been excavated; nevertheless, these remains indicate the stage of urban development that had been reached in Mesopotamia. The period has been variously named and subdivided (Johnson 1973:52, table 12). In the present chapter the division into an Early, Middle and, Late phase, made in the 1965 edition of *Chronologies,* is retained. The division follows the strata observed in the Eanna precinct of Uruk. Early Uruk corresponds to Eanna XIV–IX, Middle Uruk to Eanna VIII–VI, and Late Uruk to Eanna V to IV/III. These divisions are tentative and subject to change as are all of the periods before the end of the Early Dynastic period, and even thereafter.

The Uruk period is marked in the archaeological remains of southern Mesopotamia and in the areas to which the Uruk culture extended by a light-colored, unpainted, but significantly often wheel-made ware. The early phase of this pottery was first recognized in the excavations at Uruk, the modern Warka, in the deep sounding of the precinct known as the location of the later Eanna sanctuary of the goddess Inanna (Jordan, in *UVB* 3: pl. 10, plan 1, pp. 18–19; Nöldeke, in *UVB* 4: pls. 17D–20, text, pp. 31–47). While the pottery of the period can be divided into Early, Middle, and Late Uruk, most of the other artifacts cannot be assigned with any certainty to a time before the Late Uruk phase.

Pottery surveys were made to determine the settlement patterns of the "Uruk Countryside" (Adams and Nissen 1972). In the Early-Middle phases of the Uruk period the focus of settlement appears to have been in the Nippur-Adab region, but in the Late Uruk period this had shifted southward toward the environs of Uruk. Indeed, Uruk appears to have been the single large center in the south, apparently dominating a surrounding area of much smaller "rural" communities (Adams and Nissen 1972:18). The hierarchy of settlement sizes, which was to be apparent in the Jamdat Nasr and Early Dynastic periods, began in the Late Uruk phase. In contrast to the situation around Uruk, the Nippur-Adab area had several large sites, perhaps contending centers, with fewer smaller settlements in their environments. Adams suggested that this may have been a prototype of the later pattern of contending city-states (Adams 1981:75). In the Ur-Eridu area of the extreme south, settlement apparently declined. During the Early Uruk phase, Eridu seems to have increased its size, while smaller surrounding sites were abandoned. Ur seems to have been a small town throughout the period. In the Late Uruk phase several small settlements to the northwest of Ur were also occupied (Wright, in Adams 1981:325–26).

The Early Uruk Phase

The unpainted plain ware of the Early Uruk phase at Eridu, originally examined by Seton Lloyd (1948), yielded straight-spouted jars with the spout placed high on the shoulder (here, fig. 3/22). A variation of this type, characteristic of the earlier Eridu group, has the spout placed directly beneath and sometimes touching the rim, corresponding to vessels from Uruk-Inanna XIII; these spouts are often false (here, fig. 3/23). Double-mouthed jars usually had globular bodies, perhaps comparable to those of Gawra XI-A (Tobler 1950:pl. CXLIII/356 [here, fig. 3/19]). There were also many fragments of open bowls, each bearing a ledge or lug handle directly beneath the rim. A redware, common in the early group, may have had its origins in the Ubaid period, since fragments were found in Eridu XI. As summarized by al-Soof (1973), four types of redware vessels occurred in the early group (here, fig. 3/24–27), with some analogies from Uruk, Eanna XIII–XII. The gray Uruk ware seen at Warka from levels XIV–VI is said to have a fine gray slip applied to both the interior and the exterior. The beveled-rim bowl (here, fig. 3/28), is one of the guiding fossils of the Uruk period, beginning in Uruk-Eanna XII and lasting into the successive period. It spread from southwest Iran to Syria in great quantities, the reasons for which

have been debated but not fully explained. In level XII of the deep sounding in the Eanna precinct was found an imprint of a large stamp with flat sealing surface (Jordan, in *UVB* 3:pl. 19/a). Engraved on it are animal heads with sinuously carved horns, symmetrically disposed on either side of what could be the vertebral column of an animal. The design has been compared to a stamp seal impression from Susa B (Nagel 1963:46, Abb. 95) and to an extant seal from the same level (Amiet 1980:23; pl. 7, fig. 140), with both of which it may be contemporary as well as with a group of seals from Gawra XI-A and XI (Tobler 1950:pl. CLXIX/168–69; pl. CLXX/170–72.

The Middle and Late Uruk Phases

The Middle Uruk phase, corresponding to Eanna VIII–VI, was paralleled at Nippur in Inanna levels XX–XVIII. Hence the Nippur sequence as published in the 1965 edition of *Chronologies* illustrates the pottery development and correlations in the south. For the sequence in the north after the Gawra period, see G. Schwartz and H. Weiss in connection with the sequence at Leilan (this vol., chap. 10).

At Uruk little is known about the architecture of the Middle Uruk phase. In Eanna, levels VIII–VI were excavated only in the sounding of 1932. No further buildings have been stratigraphically linked with these levels, although on the basis of glyptic styles the *Kleinfunde-schicht* of the Anu Ziggurat may go back that early, and consequently levels D–E may be Middle Uruk. Schmidt's analysis of the levels northwest of the Stone Cone Temple suggests that the valuable limestone and concrete of that temple were first removed sometime between levels VI and IV, so that the temple could have been erected in level V or VI, and levels below it could have belonged to Middle Uruk times (Schmid 1977). The use of *Riemchen* bricks may have started in Eanna VI and lasted through Eanna III (Lenzen, *UVB* 20:6, n. 2).

The architecture of the Late Uruk levels of Eanna, levels V–IVa, is better known. These levels show rather elaborate layouts of monumental buildings in relation to courts and subsidiary buildings, all enclosed by a precinct wall. While the outer wall of the precinct and, hence, its boundaries may have remained relatively unchanged from level IVc up through level I (Schmid 1977:47; Lenzen, in *UVB* 20:11), the buildings within it were constantly rebuilt, and every rebuilding involved significant changes in plan (Lenzen, in *UVB* 25:14–22, *passim;* Dunham 1980:72–102). The most common type was that of a tripartite plan with large rectangular central room, either straight or T-shaped, flanked on both sides by symmetrically planned smaller rooms. None of the buildings in Eanna contained an "altar" or any unequivocal furnishings of a sanctuary, although many of them had the niched and buttressed walls characteristic of Mesopotamian temple architecture. The tripartite plan is called that of a *Mittelsaalhaus* by Heinrich (1982:7–14; Ludwig 1980:64) and has been found in Uruk period settlements in north Syria in houses as well as in buildings that seem to have been temples (Habuba Kabira Süd, Tell Qannas, Jebel Aruda, in Strommenger 1980b; van Driel and van Driel-Murray 1979; Finet 1975). This type of plan, the predecessors of which can be seen at Eridu in levels VI–XI, may be considered, perhaps, as a southern development of the "common Ubaid house plan" mentioned above for the Himrin and the north. A similar suggestion was made by Heinrich (1982:8–9) in relation to the plans of Gawra.

Although the Late Uruk period is divided into four levels in the Eanna precinct, levels V, IVc, IVb, IVa, these are all quite interrelated, since often a building would last from one level to another, for example, the Limestone Temple. Especially closely related are levels IVb and IVa since several buildings of IVb lasted into IVa for a time (Lenzen, in *UVB* 24:13–18). The use of cone mosaics for wall decoration, which may have started as early as Late Ubaid times (Schmidt 1978:12), achieves its greatest development in these levels (here, fig. 3/29). The buildings of level IVa appear to have all been destroyed about the same time and, indeed, rather suddenly, since some structures seem unfinished (Lenzen 1975:169).

Southwest of the Eanna precinct is the Anu Ziggurat complex which involves three parts: an ancient artificial hill of mud-bricks, forming the ziggurat; a huge terrace on the northeast under the Seleucid "Bit Resh" temple; and a curious subterranean stone building, the *Steingebäude,* on the northwest. The earliest levels of the ziggurat probably date back to Late Ubaid times, but these are not yet coordinated with the twelve levels identified counting down from the surface. Of these twelve, only the top five, A–E, have been explored enough to yield comprehensible plans. Temples of the *Mittelsaalhaus* plan stood on top of the ziggurat in levels E–D and B— the White Temple—and probably also in C, although only the outlines of buildings in postholes, C2, or red lines, C1, were found in this level. Convincing arguments that there was only one surrounding state (*Ummantelung*) instead of two, D and E, below the C and B states on the Anu Ziggurat, were set down by Margueron (1986). Between C and D an intermediary level of rubble contained many small finds, the *Kleinfundeschicht*. Level A actually includes three separate mud-brick encasings of the ziggurat, A1, the earliest, to A3. By the time of the second of these, A2, a huge terrace was made to adjoin the ziggurat on the northeast (Schmidt, in *UVB* 28:13–23). In 1936–37 Heinrich found an earlier phase of this terrace which may be contemporary with level C on the basis of the seals in the rubble overlying this ter-

race (Behm-Blancke 1979:54–55; Heinrich, in *UVB* 9:23–24). Attempts to correlate the Anu Ziggurat levels with those of the Eanna precinct are based on the most diagnostic specimens among the small quantities of pottery and small finds found on the ziggurat and the northeast terrace. The most recent evaluations indicate that while there is nothing from the A-levels that can definitely be said to be later than Eanna level III, there are finds from the earliest A-level, A1, which could be as early as Eanna IV; seal impressions from the postholes of level C and the earlier phase of the northeast terrace have closer stylistic similarities to seal impressions from Eanna IV than to those from Eanna III (Behm-Blanke 1979:54–55, 60f.; Dunham 1980:131–45). The context of the Jamdat Nasr sherd by which Lenzen dated all levels from level L to the Jamdat Nasr period seems questionable and may be disregarded. Hence, level B and the White Temple would be contemporary with Eanna level IV. The finds from the *Kleinfundeschicht* might be dated earlier on the basis of the glyptic remains (see below). The *Steingebäude* probably dates somewhere in the range of levels E–B, or A1. A tall jar with a narrow neck, folded-over rim, and drooping spout, which comes from the foundation trench of the *Steingebäude* (*UVB* 26–27:28; pl. 30b), is similar to some from the A1-level of the ziggurat and the destruction levels of the Stone Cone Temple. This type of jar has not been found elsewhere in the Eanna precinct, although short, narrow necks with folded-over rims are illustrated for Eanna levels VII–IV (Haller, in *UVB* 4:pls. 18D/a′, 19B/p″, 19D/v, 20A/n,o) and bent spouts begin in Eanna level VII (pl. 18D/u′). Tall jars with foldover rims and bent spouts are known from Susa in Le Breton's Cb phase and level 17a of the new excavations and from Habuba Kabira (Le Breton 1957:101; fig. 12/5b, 6b, 7b; Le Brun 1971:fig. 52/5; Sürenhagen 1978:Taf. 17/102 [here, fig. 3/30]), which implies that the type is Late Uruk in date.

New work at Uruk, begun in 1982, was a systematic survey of the area within the city wall (Finkbeiner 1983). In the second campaign the fields in front of the city wall were included (Finkbeiner 1984). The most important result for the Uruk period was the discovery of a settlement on a hill, unusual for that period, which contained typical Late Uruk pottery (Finkbeiner 1985:30–42). Most characteristic were (1) bellied closed vessels with straight or slightly inverted neck and plain rim; (2) bellied jars with short,straight spouts, often with low, inverted neck; and (3) jars with strap handles. On the shoulders, many jars had incised patterns or other decoration. The pottery corresponded to that previously found in Uruk K/L XII in the Late Uruk levels 38–42 (Nissen 1970).

The latest temple platforms of levels I–II at Eridu may date to the Late Uruk period, since they both made use of limestone set in gypsum mortar (Safar, Mustafa, and

Lloyd 1981:78–82), and at Warka both limestone and gypsum seem to have been used extensively in the Late Uruk period buildings: the Limestone Temple, the Stone Cone Temple, and the *Steingebäude*. Furthermore, in Temple I at Eridu, circular or part-circular columns were incorporated in the architectural treatment paralleling the use of columns and engaged half columns in the Mosaic Court of Eanna IVb (ibid., p. 80). Finally, the occurrence of gypsum bricks and stone cones in the debris of Temple I also suggests a Late Uruk date.

At Uqair the Painted Temple probably belongs to this same period, as is suggested by its many similarities with the White Temple and the finding of gypsum cement bricks with a trident mark on them in the debris of its filling (Lloyd and Safar 1943:149; pl. XVI/a). Gypsum cement bricks with incised symbols on them have been found in the *Steingebäude* (*UVB* 29–30:15–16). The "Archaic III and IV" levels of the ziggurat terrace at Ur probably also belong here, based on the association of *Riemchen* walls with small or large cones and limestone paving.

In addition to the archaeological reexamination of the evidence concerning the tablets (here, fig. 3/31), the paleographic work on the script promises new insights and criteria for dating texts. As yet, these firmly dated tablets do not seem to have been examined for dating the seal impressions more reliably than has been possible before. Therefore, the stratigraphic evidence of the Anu Ziggurat is still the best means of arriving at some chronological determination of the development of seal engraving at Uruk. A cylinder found in the intermediate level D–C on the Anu Ziggurat (*UVB* 8:pl. 49a), primarily carved with a mechanical drill, belongs to this initial stage of cylinder seal engraving. It is characterized by very baggy figures, aligned in rows, the simplest composition for a cylindrical object. At the same time, the seal from the Anu Ziggurat has the field filled by various animals as in a stamp seal. Another example (*UVB* 16:47; pl. 25a), the largest cylinder known, is said to come from the rubble of the Jamdat Nasr period kilns in Me XV, but in the same area there had been some structures older than the Stone Cone Temple (*UVB* 17:13, and pl. 29; Schmid 1977: 43–44). It is possible that the cylinder derives from that early level, especially since it was found in the same square as a female torso (*UVB* 16:pl. 16), possibly equally early. Baggy figures and excessive drilling, such as were found on the two cylinders just mentioned, are also characteristic of Middle Uruk period sealings from Sharaffabad in Khuzestan (Wright, Miller, and Redding 1980:279, fig. 6). Similar figures are also said to have been found on sealings from Susa in excavations of the Acropolis I, level 20 (unpublished).

Better-worked forms appear in the sealings on the clay balls found in a hole in a *Riemchen* wall of stratum IV.

However, they may have been earlier than their findspot, especially if they contained records from the Stone Cone Temple, which may put them into IVc or V (Brandes 1979:68–69). The earlier ones among the scenes on sealings of cylinder seals showing prisoners (*UVB* 15:pl. 28/c, and pl. 30/a, b [here, partly copied in fig. 8/2]), belong to the same stage (Brandes 1979:pls. 4–11). The subsequent stylistic development toward the fine style of Uruk IVb is not reflected in the stratigraphic evidence. Thus the impression of a fine cylinder seal with the scene of prisoners before a ruler (here, fig. 8/3) had an earlier findspot than the baggy-style prisoner scene above.

At the same time as the fine cylinder seals of the Uruk impressions were being carved, the drilled technique continued on squat, mostly rather small cylinders with certain distinctive motifs, such as pigtailed figures in various actions of which several examples were found in Late Uruk levels in widely distant places. The seal type was extensively discussed by Asher-Greve (1985:12–61, *passim*). The example here reproduced (fig. 8/1) is one of several from the Inanna Temple at Nippur. This one was found in level XV. Other motifs also existed in this strongly drilled, simple style. But it is often difficult to determine the date of such cylinders because their findspot could have been assigned by earlier excavators to the Jamdat Nasr period on the basis of their style.

Like the cylinders, the sculptures of the Late Uruk phase at Uruk, though small in number, present distinctive stylistic characteristics that have value for chronological determinations. These characteristics have been summarized on the basis of small animal figurines (Behm-Blancke 1979). The two figures from the Middle Uruk levels D–C of the Anu Ziggurat (Behm-Blancke 1979:pls. 2/3 [here, fig. 3/32] and 4/18) were not clearly set off as a chronologically distinct group, probably because their number was too small. Nevertheless, their baggy appearance and simple, heavy forms relate them to the cylinders of the period. The criteria of the fully developed style of level IVb are illustrated by a figure from the *Sammelfund* of stratum III, which also contained earlier material (Behm-Blancke 1979:52–53; pl. 2/5 [here, fig. 3/33]). They are plastic definition, stress on the mass and volume, and observation of natural features such as the veins of the face. The same criteria can be applied to some of the major sculptures discovered at Uruk out of context, not one of them in stratum IV. From that phase come objects that convey an idea of the high level of craftsmanship available in Uruk at this age and at the same time convey "indications of wealth, religious complexity, and centralization of political power, with at least partial control over labor" (Perkins 1954:47).

From the *Riemchengebäude* also come "various copper vessels and spearheads as well as animal horns" (Lenzen, in *UVB*, 14:24–25; Lenzen, in *UVB* 15:9–10; pls. 17,

39b). The Uruk excavation reports rarely detail more mundane copper finds. Between levels C and D of the Anu ziggurat were an "astonishing" number of completely oxydized lumps of copper, some as large as a man's fist (Nöldecke, in *UVB* 9:25). Worked copper was also noted in levels of Eanna XI (Jordan, in *UVB* 3: 30). Objects of copper are noted in levels D and E of the Anu Ziggurat (Nöldecke, in *UVB* 8:53, references given by Moorey 1985:24–25).

The Absolute Chronology of the Uruk Period

Since there are no reliable radiocarbon dates for the Uruk period in southern Mesopotamia, one has to look at connections with other areas. The problem here is that although correlations with Late Uruk are fairly clear, sometimes those with Early and Middle Uruk are not. For the Late Uruk there are series of dates from Jebel Aruda, Syria (GrN 7989, 8463, 8464—van Driel and van Driel-Murray 1979; Schwartz and Weiss, this vol., chap. 10), and Period V at Godin Tepe, Iran (Voigt and Dyson, this vol., chap. 6). These all point to the last half of the fourth millennium for Late Uruk, probably ca. 3500–3100 B.C. Since the Ubaid period seems to end ca. 4000 B.C. (see above), Early and Middle Uruk should date to the first half of the fourth millennium. For Middle Uruk a series from Arslan Tepe, Anatolia, discussed by Wright (Wright 1980), suggests the second quarter of the fourth millennium, but a radiocarbon date from Sharaffabad, Iran, is a little earlier: P-2210, 3970–3850 B.C. (Voigt and Dyson, this vol., chap. 6). For Early Uruk there are no available reliable radiocarbon dates. Hence the suggestions on figure 3 for Early and Middle Uruk are tentative (Early ca. 4000–3750 B.C.; Middle ca. 3750–3500 B.C.).

The Jamdat Nasr Period

The name of this period derives from a site seventeen miles northeast of Kish excavated by S. Langdon in 1925–26 and by L. Watelin in 1928. Langdon's excavations, published by E. Mackay (1931), yielded what was called "a Late Prehistoric Administrative Building" (Moorey 1976). The most distinctive finds in the building were polychrome-painted pottery, semipictographic inscribed tablets, and cylinder seals primarily engraved with a drill. These finds were recognized as being later than the Uruk period but earlier than the subsequent Early Dynastic period. In 1930 the directors of the principal excavations in Iraq agreed on the names for a sequence of four periods in the early development of Mesopotmia: Ubaid, Uruk, Jamdat Nasr, and Early Dynastic. The validity of this terminology was confirmed by the excavations at Nippur, where the finds of the levels of the Inanna Temple XIV–XII, following upon the Uruk levels XX–XV, and preceding the Early Dynastic levels XI–VI,

yielded material comparable to that of Jamdat Nasr itself. The following material with the accompanying table of criteria attempts to point out some of the salient pottery features of these levels, some of which have already been given in the previous edition of *Chronologies*. A fuller presentation of the pottery is given by Wilson (1980), who notes that "monochrome and polychrome painted vessels, which are considered the primary distinguishing characteristics of the Jamdat Nasr period . . . appear first in Late Uruk and continue sporadically into the early part of Early Dynastic I. Therefore at Nippur, the presence of painted sherds of the Jamdat Nasr type is not an *a priori* indication of a Jamdat Nasr date." To frame the Jamdat Nasr period, some pottery of the last Late Uruk period levels and the earliest Early Dynastic I level at Nippur are given below.

Table of Criteria from Late Uruk to Early Dynastic I at Nippur

Late Uruk Period

XVI–XV   Beveled-rim bowls are common. Redware and grayware are prevalent, but reserved slip is evident. The first plum-red slip and monochrome and polychrome painting appears. Bottlenecks with folded-over rim are prevalent, but no flowerpots with folded-over or beveled rims are found in these levels.

Jamdat Nasr Period

XIV   Beveled-rim bowls are less common. Redware, but no grayware or reserved slip is present. There is a heavy increase in plum-red slip as well as in polychrome (here, fig. 3/34) and monochrome painting (here, fig. 3/35), and there is an increase in the number of bottlenecks with folded-over rim. Jamdat Nasr types now appear and include flowerpots (here, fig. 3/36) and other conical bowls (here, fig. 3/37) and goblet-type, shallow open bowls (here, fig. 3/38) and trays, low-necked jars, jar caps with plum-red slip (here fig. 5/1), ovoid jars with beveled-edge rims (here, fig. 5/2), and spouted vessels (here, fig. 5/3).

XIII   Beveled-rim bowls continue, but there is no reserved slip or grayware or redware. Plum-red slip and monochrome and polychrome pottery continue as before, as do the Jamdat Nasr types.

XII   The beveled-rim bowls continue, but now the grayware and reserved slip reappear; the quantity of plum-red slip remains unchanged, but there is a reduction of polychrome and monochrome painting. The Jamdat Nasr types continue as well as bottlenecks with folded-over rim. A rim-lugged vessel and a tray type, both characteristic of Early Dynastic I, first appear.

Early Dynastic I

XI   This level finds the end of beveled-rim bowls and plum-red slip. Although the grayware continues, and the amount of reserved slip increases, plum-red slip ends. There is a sharp reduction of monochrome and polychrome painting. The number of the rim-lugged vessel and tray types increases. Solid-foot chalices occur and other Early Dynastic I types appear, including wing-lugged vessels, elaborate incised wares, fenestrated stands, top-shaped hollow stoppers, and theriomorphic vessels.

In the south, such pottery is found in quantity at the site of Jamdat Nasr itself (Mackay 1931), but unfortunately the material is not stratified. There is some meager evidence for a slightly earlier and slightly later occupation. At Kish the material is negligible. Jamdat Nasr levels are present in Pit "F" at Ur, and in the so-called Jamdat Nasr Cemetery perhaps a few graves predate Early Dynastic I (Kolbus 1983). There is very little Jamdat Nasr material from either Fara or al-Ubaid (Martin 1982:147, 150, 1983:24–25). Farther north the period is well represented in the Diyala region by Protoliterate "c," yet the continuation of the Jamdat Nasr "culture" into Protoliterate "d" is chronologically speaking the equivalent of Early Dynastic I at Nippur (Wilson 1986:63–66). Thus far, in the adjacent Himrin region, Jamdat Nasr has been found, for example, in level VII of Tell Gubba (Fujii 1979:517, 1981:153–55, 1984) and might well belong to the Protoliterate "d" phase of the lower Diyala. At Habuba Kabira only Late Uruk pottery is recorded, and the characteristic painted Jamdat Nasr wares are absent in both Syria and northern Mesopotamia; however, Joan Oates has suggested that the recently excavated levels 9–12 in the CH sequence at Tell Brak postdate the "Late Uruk" material and are the equivalent of the Jamdat Nasr period of the south (J. Oates 1985a:176–79). For an example, the tray from CH 591, level 9 (J. Oates 1985a:181, fig. I/10), is of a type known from Inanna XIV at Nippur (Wilson 1986:fig. 5/11). In the Acropolis sounding of Susa in Iran, strata 18 and 19 are Late Uruk while the position of stratum 17 is chronologically difficult. Strata 16–14B, the Proto-Elamite period, seem to equate with the Jamdat Nasr period (i.e., Nippur XIV–XII), but the span of time probably extends into the early part of the southern Mesopotamian Early Dynastic I.

Jamdat Nasr pottery is reported from the Gulf within the Hafit "horizon," but chronologically this may also extend into the Early Dynastic period (Potts, this vol., chap. 4).

At Uruk, Eanna level III belongs to this phase and represents a break in the architectural sequence within the precinct. None of the level IV buildings survived, and, of those assigned to level III by the excavators, not even the so-called labyrinth and the building in which the *Sammelfund* was discovered can be considered to belong to Eanna III with any certainty (Finkbeiner 1986). Carefully laid out pits containing evidence of burning were found in an intermediate layer between levels IVa and III, and were interpreted by the excavator (Lenzen 1955:13) as the remains of a ritual purification of the area, and by M. T. Barrelet (1974) as pits primarily used for the preparation of food but not necessarily excluding ritual purposes.

Observations made by the excavators concerning architectural features of Eanna III are cited here with the understanding that the date of the buildings is uncertain. Thus Lenzen pointed out that cone mosaics continued in use for wall decoration, but now only in panels as, for example, between the buttresses of the court wall to the southwest of the high terrace in levels IIIc and IIIb (Lenzen 1975:174 and references given there).

The latest encasings of the Anu Ziggurat, A1–A3, must belong, in part at least, to the Jamdat Nasr period. A1 probably belongs to the very beginning of the period (see above). The latest encasing, A3, rose in steps, and at the upper edge of one step a band of cone mosaics was found in situ (Schmidt, in *UVB* 26–27:16; pl. 2b). Many more fallen cones were found associated with A2 and A3. Although some cone mosaics were found in situ in Eanna level I[6] (Lenzen 1941:16–17), they are much more chracteristic of Eanna levels IV and III.

With the negative result of the reexamination of the evidence from Uruk, the only major building of the Jamdat Nasr period so far known in the south is the one at the type site mentioned above. Finds of the Early Dynastic I period made there (Moorey 1976:pl. XVc) indicate only that the site was occupied after the conflagration that destroyed the large building. The latter's most distinctive feature is a chain of rectangular rooms, some of which are of equal size and which communicate through doors that were occasionally blocked. These room chains seem to surround courtyards and complexes of rooms. Margueron took issue with Moorey's interpretation of the building and its use in the discussion of early official Mesopotamian architecture (Margueron 1982: 23–34). It is undeniable, however, that this was an important building of the Jamdat Nasr period. It was constructed of *Riemchen* bricks, also used at Nippur for the series of houses of Inanna XIV–XII, and hence it cannot be ignored.

At Tell Uqair the building of a terrace of large mud-bricks, filling the Painted Temple (Lloyd and Safar 1943:145–46), probably occurred during the Jamdat Nasr period. A second filling, traced only in places, but made of similar mud-bricks, may also belong to this period. On the northeast side of the temple platform the "first filling" extended outward to form a terrace about 50 cm high on which were three levels of buildings of *Riemchen* bricks containing Jamdat Nasr painted ware and tablets. The uppermost level contained "painted Jamdat Nasr and a little Scarlet Ware and had *Riemchen* laid in the manner of plano-convex bricks" (Lloyd and Safar 1943:147), thus probably dating to Early Dynastic I. This evidence indicates the gradual transition from Jamdat Nasr to Early Dynastic in contrast to the more sudden break between the Uruk and the Jamdat Nasr period observed at several sites.

An important change in the chronology of the Jamdat Nasr period was suggested by Wilson (1986:64–66) for the sequence of the Sin Temple at Khafajah, where only Sin I–III corresponds in pottery forms and decoration to Nippur, Inanna XIV–XII, whereas Sin IV already belongs to Early Dynastic I, despite the fact that *Riemchen* were still in use instead of the plano-convex bricks characteristic of the Early Dynastic age.

This change is particularly important for the classification of the glazed, ornamentally decorated beadlike cylinder seals (here, fig. 4/1) which constitute a new glyptic type that is closer in shape to Early Dynastic beads than to the small, squat cylinders of the Jamdat Nasr period, the diameters of which are often equal to the height. The technique in which these common Jamdat Nasr cylinders were engraved consisted mostly in an unmitigated use of the drill, a technique probably inherited from the Middle Uruk period. It seems likely, however, that the development within this group was iconographical rather than technological. Pigtailed figures in varying activities (here, fig. 8/1), for example, are represented in five examples from stratified contexts of the Late Uruk period: at Nippur (Wilson 1986:60), at Habuba Kabira (Sürenhagen und Töpperwein 1973:31, Abb. 9), and at Chogha Mish (Delougaz and Kantor 1972: 32/a). One cylinder of this type was found at Uruk in a grave under the skull of the skeleton in Ne XVI 2 (Lenzen, in *UVB* 21:pl. 20/c), which is actually another Late Uruk locus although the date of graves without supporting finds is uncertain. Among the 17 cylinder seals found at Jamdat Nasr, only one has pigtailed figures, and among 1002 cylinders of the Diyala sites (Frankfort 1955:17) only 14 are of this type, and even those are not all good representatives of the group. Other themes among seals of Jamdat Nasr style from the Diyala sites, such as animals before a byre (here, fig. 4/2), are more numerous, as are plain animal rows. It seems likely, therefore, that such seals

actually derive from the Jamdat Nasr period, whereas pigtailed figures and other themes such as spiderlike designs belong to the earlier age.

The style of the cylinder seal impressions on tablets of the Jamdat Nasr period differs radically from that of the common cylinders. The impressions continue the style observed on the tablets of Uruk-Eanna IVb–a. The most distinctive of these sealings are narrative scenes with human and animal figures given ample, carefully executed forms. The differentiation between the styles of Uruk-Eanna IV and III noted many years ago by Ann Farkas as consisting of greater detail in the later cylinders (Farkas 1963:26ff.) is supported by the evidence of numerous impressions of a richly varied seal design found in square Ne XVII 1 of Eanna, level III and convincingly interpreted by Boehmer as the seal of an administrative official in charge of work and of the reception of deliveries for the temple (Boehmer, in *UVB* 26–27:71–72; pls. 18–19). Another demonstration that elaborately engraved cylinders continued in the Jamdat Nasr period is provided by impressions on tablets from the building at Jamdat Nasr. The original cylinders with which such impressions were made were generally large, with a diameter about a fifth less than the height. The finest of this type of cylinder (Moortgat 1940:pl. 5/29) has a copper handle in the form of a reclining ram, which was surely made at the same time as the engraving of the cylinder (here, fig. 4/3). The style of the figurine was classified as *Stilgruppe* IIA by Behm-Blancke (1979:24, s.v.2.2.2.), which implies a Jamdat Nasr date for the cylinder. The style of this group has been characterized by Behm-Blancke as retaining the voluminous and massive earlier forms with plastically rounded contours but showing at the same time an excessive stress on some parts of the body either by strong modeling or linear means. Observation of natural features was no longer as precise as in the animal figurines of Uruk-Eanna IVb–a (Behm-Blancke 1979:32). However, the engraving of the cylinder design shows great care in the execution of details and has achieved an extraordinarily pleasing composition. The difference between these rare fine cylinders used on tablets and the common, squat, drilled cylinders, earlier considered to have been a chronological one, was interpreted by Nissen as individual versus collective seals, and their differences to have been caused by the purposes for which they were used (Nissen 1983:86). Collon, reviewing Brandes (Collon 1981–82), also discussed the significance of the differences between these early seal styles.

The classification of larger sculptural works in the Uruk IVb–a or in the Jamdat Nasr period is far more difficult, therefore a partial acceptance of Delougaz's term "Protoliterate," namely, his subdivisions a–c for both periods, may be preferable to assigning an insufficiently supported classification to one or the other period. However, on evidence available at present, the appearance of the nude bearded hero with curls as a conqueror of animals (here, fig. 5/4) who replaces the priestly ruler figure of Uruk IVb–a and who may have had a more specific local and temporal meaning can be set in the Jamdat Nasr period.

The absolute chronology of the Jamdat Nasr period is suggested by the series of radiocarbon determinations from the Banesh period at Tepe Malyan, Iran (Voigt and Dyson, this vol., chap. 6). These indicate a late fourth to early third millennium range, ca. 3100–2900 B.C.

As repeatedly stated here, the inventory of seals and other objects associated with Jamdat Nasr pottery at various sites in Mesopotamia can be established on the basis of the pottery of Nippur XIV–XII. In sum, the Jamdat Nasr period is definable in Sumer and in the Diyala; outside these areas its presence may be felt, even though it is not as yet recognizable as a distinct entity. Its absence as a unit in surrounding regions is not a reason for denying its existence as a period in the south.

The Historic Periods

The Early Dynastic Period

The Early Dynastic period represents the time of the city-states of Sumer. For the growth of the cities and the distribution patterns of settlement see the works of Adams and Nissen in the reference list. Although the survey method of defining the periods of occupation at given sites undoubtedly elicits results that are basically correct, some caution must be exercised when the diagnostic pottery types are not neatly confined to a specific period (e.g., Martin 1982:155, n. 25; for a critique of the method, see Kohlmeyer 1981).

For absolute dates of the period we depend on a complicated series of calculations based on archaeological evidence and the estimated lengths of rulers' reigns in early historic times. Often, dates derived from the radiocarbon method yield only very general indications and are not specific enough for the determination of the subperiods involved. Nevertheless, samples from Mari, Nippur, and Tell Abu Salabikh, leaving aside obviously contaminated samples, strongly suggest a date of the twenty-sixth century B.C. for the Early Dynastic IIIa period (Wright 1980:95–96). Furthermore, a recent reworking of the published Early Dynastic dates (Hassan and Robinson 1978) neatly confirms the suggested traditional dates for this period as given in *Chronologies* (Ehrich 1965:178).

In recent years many details of the systems proposed for classifying the phases of the Early Dynastic period have been questioned. Frankfort's scheme of Early Dynastic I, II, IIIa and IIIb is based on his excavations in the region of the lower Diyala, while Moortgat's system is basically "art historical" in conception. Frankfort's terms are used in this chapter, although it is now clear that the results of the excavations in the Diyala region cannot be used as the main guide for determining the development of the entire period over all of Mesopotamia. In this presentation we have virtually abandoned the term Early Dynastic II except for its use in the Diyala region.

For indicating the upper and lower chronological limits of the whole period or for defining its subphases, no single cultural feature or trait should be used by itself. For example, since Riemchen bricks continued in sporadic use during the earlier part of the period, and since plano-convex bricks were still employed in the early part of the following Akkadian period (Gibson 1982:533, n. 22), architectural changes alone can not characterize the subperiods. Likewise, an art style manifest in sculpture or glyptic, important as it may be in the history of art, is not always the best indicator of an archaeological phase. In the Early Dynastic period, pottery is the most ubiquitous of the archaeological remains, and it is used here predominantly in conjunction with architecture, art, and other artifacts to aid in delineating for discussion the parts of an uninterrupted cultural sequence.

Early Dynastic I: The South

This phase of the Early Dynastic period has come to be recognized as one of great importance in the development of Mesopotamia. Although table 2 details some major sites of Early Dynastic I in the south, the relationship between their various levels is only approximate and schematic.

At Nippur the period comprises levels XI–IX A of the Inanna Temple. Architecturally the successive buildings follow one another in general form, but only in level IX does the furniture within the rooms allow for the clear identification of the building as a temple. (For a simplified plan of level IX B, see Hansen 1971:48, fig. 1.) With the destruction of level IX and the filling in of the rooms to form a platform comes the major break in the Inanna architectural sequence. Thereafter, the temple is built with a completely different plan beginning in level VIII (Hansen and Dales 1962:80–82). The pottery from these levels accords well with the comparable Early Dynastic I levels of the Diyala (Hansen 1965:209). The solid-foot chalice (here, fig. 5/5) and the jar with a single triangular lug (here, fig. 5/6) are characteristic of the period, but the scarlet ware so prevalent in the lower and upper Diyala region is definitely lacking, except for the appearance of a few sporadic sherds (e.g., Postgate and Moorey 1976:165). In the recent excavations at Mari only one possible sherd is reported from level 9, a late level in the Early Dynastic I sequence of levels 9–13 (Lebeau 1985:94; pl. XXI/5). Also of interest at Mari is burnished grayware in levels 10 and 11 equivalent to Early Dynastic I examples from Nippur and the lower Diyala (ibid., p. 94; pls. XXV/40, XXIV/22, 24; Hansen 1965:209).

Chronologically important are a group of cylinder sealings found in a work area within the Inanna precinct but separated from the main temple by a narrow corridor or street (Hansen 1971:47–48). Although there are two sealings from level XI, one of which is from a geometric seal of early "piedmont" style, the majority came from level IX B and A. Those of IX B are comparable to sealings from Ur, Kish, and Fara (see below), while those from level IX A display a stylistic change from a heavy figure style characterizing the earlier level to a slighter, more elegant one (here, fig. 4/4). The later sealings are similar to some from Fara that are generally called the "Fara" or Early Dynastic II style (Hansen 1971:54; Amiet 1980:204–5).

At Ur, sealings comparable to those from level IX B at Nippur come from the Seal Impression Strata (SIS) 4 and 5. These are layers of dumped debris into which the Royal Cemetery was later sunk, and by their very nature they are difficult to assess. A summary of various opinions concerning the dating of these strata is given by Karg (1984:6–10). SIS 4 and 5 are the equivalent of the building strata C and D of pit "F" (Moorey 1979b:117–18), which are preceded by levels E–G roughly equating with SIS 6–8 and the underlying cemetery, and thus date to the earlier part of Early Dynastic I. Level B, above level C, contains Fara-type texts and hence postdates Early Dynastic I and is in part contemporary with the Royal Cemetery. There is apparently no real break in the sequence, and there is no evidence of material dating to Early Dynastic II as defined by the chronology of the Diyala (Moorey 1979b:117–18).

The "archaic" texts from Ur were also found in the Seal Impression Strata. Three tablets from level IX A at Nippur (Buccellati and Biggs 1969:5) are clearly comparable to the Ur texts.

The cemetery termed "Jamdat Nasr" by Woolley is basically Early Dynastic I in date, with a few of the earliest graves containing polychrome pottery probably belonging to the preceding Jamdat Nasr period. The grave material has recently been studied by Kolbus (1983), who finds much of it comparable to that of the building strata H–E in pit "F." These strata in the mind of the present writer belong to the early part of Early Dynastic I.

The meticulously detailed work of H. Martin (1972, 1975, 1982, 1983) has greatly clarified the results of the expeditions in 1902–3 and 1931 at Fara. Early Dynastic I material, including pottery and sealings, has been found in I d–e of the German excavations and in four of the five Early Dynastic levels of the American excavations. Precise stratification is lacking. As expected, the pottery of Fara displays a continuous evolution, and according to

Martin, "clearly ED II, when judged by its pottery, does not stand out as a distinct period in its own right; it is much more a period of gradual transition from ED I to ED III" (Martin 1982:166; see also p. 151). It seems wrong to force the data into the Diyala chronological framework.

Besides some large geometric sealings dated to the early part of Early Dynastic I, most of those from the Early Dynastic I context I d–e, fall into two groups or styles (Martin 1975:180–82; pl. XXXIX, fig. 6). The first of these (here, fig. 4/5) is stylistically comparable to the well-stratified sealings of level IX B of the Inanna Temple at Nippur, while the second group (here, fig. 4/6) seems to equate with the tenuous and delicate figure style that characterizes the fragmentary seals of the later level IX A. This second style is dated by Martin to *early* Early Dynastic II (ibid.) and by Amiet (1980:54–55) to a Fara *série archaique* of Early Dynastic II. It seems preferable to consider this second style as falling at the very end of Early Dynastic I.

Rich Early Dynastic I material was found at Kish in the so-called Y sounding of Tell Ingharra (Moorey 1979a:99–115; Gibson 1972a:83–86, 1980b:616–17). Painted pottery in the earliest strata indicates probable occupation in the Jamdat Nasr period. These are followed by settlements constructed of plano-convex bricks which must date to the early part of Early Dynastic I (Early Houses Stratum). Intrusive in these levels are graves displaying advanced metalworking exemplified by two copper stands, one of which has a frog cast in the round (Moorey 1982:26 [here, fig. 5/7]). These graves lack the solid-foot chalices and jars with incised decoration that are found outside of them, and Moorey, therefore, suggests that the graves date late in the Early Dynastic I period (1979a:110–11), but he includes the Early Dynastic II of the Diyala within their time span. In terms of absolute dates this may indeed be correct, but in terms of a relative chronology it is highly dubious. The argument seems to rest on the association of the typical Early Dynastic I single-lugged jars with jars with upright handles (here, fig. 5/8). The latter is also an Early Dynastic I type, but on the evidence of Khafajah it is also found in graves dug from Houses 6, the very earliest level of Early Dynastic II in the Diyala chronological system. It seems unnecessary to force an Early Dynastic II date based on such slim evidence. (For the Flood Stratum, the chariot or cart burials, the Red Stratum, and the A Cemetery, see below.)

Besides the rather extensive Early Dynastic I cemeteries of Ur and Kish, a third one was excavated at al-Ubaid. Wright considers that most of the graves belong to Early Dynastic I (1969:79), while Martin interprets the evidence differently and assigns only sixteen graves to Early Dynastic I (1982:147–49), 165). Fifty-nine graves are assigned to Early Dynastic II–IIIa and more specifically to the early part of IIIa since the tall conical bowls found in these graves seem absent in the Royal Cemetery at Ur. In a detailed analysis of the pottery, Martin stresses the continuity of the pottery types of the Early Dynastic II–IIIa graves and suggests that only certain ones may be dated to Early Dynastic II while others belong to Early Dynastic IIIa (1982:166; p. 179, table 6). Since there are really two different groups of graves among the ninety-six burials, it is doubtful that a truly definable group from Early Dynastic II exists. The difficulties of providing a proper definition for a series of Early Dynastic II graves at al-Ubaid are emphasized by Gockel's quite different conclusions in his analysis of the same material (Gockel 1983:40–41).

Although many scholars have used paleography to suggest the date of a specific inscribed object, difficulties arise when inscriptions on clay tablets are compared with inscribed texts on stone. The Archaic Texts from Ur come mostly from Seal Impression Strata 4 and 5, which at present seems fairly well dated to the later part of Early Dynastic I. They do not help much, however, in dating accurately the few stone objects that should belong in this period. (For a discussion of the problems involved in early paleography see R. Biggs 1973.) Nevertheless the so-called *figure aux plumes* (here, fig. 5/9) and the Metropolitan Museum *kudurru* of Ushumgal must be early (Hansen 1975a:pls. 75, 74/b and c; Braun-Holzinger 1977:21–22) and must date to the Early Dynastic I period. The former is closer in certain stylistic and iconographic details to the preceding Jamdat Nasr period than is the *kudurru*. The latter has many of the characteristics used to define the art of Early Dynastic II in terms of the Diyala chronology. Also dating to Early Dynastic I on the basis of the inscription is the lion-headed bird from Khafajah found in Sin Temple VIII, the earliest of the Sin Temple levels assigned to Early Dynastic II in the Diyala system.

Uninscribed works of art, either incised or in relief, may also be attributed to Early Dynastic I on stylistic grounds, such as several votive plaques found in level VIII of the Inanna Temple at Nippur (Hansen 1971:54 [here, fig. 5/10]) as well as comparable pieces from Susa (Pelzel 1977).

Like relief, the rich tradition of sculpture in the round of the Uruk and Jamdat Nasr periods continues in Early Dynastic I. The female figurine from Sin Temple IV at Khafajah (Protoliterate d = ED I in the south, see above) is best seen as either a holdover from the previous Jamdat Nasr period or as a continuation of the Jamdat Nasr style in the Diyala during a period chronologically equivalent to Early Dynastic I in the south.

A prime example of Early Dynastic I sculpture is the limestone figure from the Shara Temple at Tell Agrab of a male resting on one knee and holding a large vessel by two hands on the top of his head (Hansen 1975b:pl. 36/a [here, fig. 5/11]). The form of the vessel is distinctive and is of a type characteristic of Early Dynastic I in the Diyala region (Delougaz 1952:pl. 48/c–d) and of level X of the Inanna Temple at Nippur. Porada has pointed to the early date of the sculpture (Porada, Hansen, and von Beckerath 1968:303) and commented on the implicit naturalism in the style of the body even though the head is executed in a more severe or geometric fashion. The continuation of the earlier naturalistic style of the Jamdat Nasr and Uruk periods into the Early Dynastic period was suggested long ago by Porada (1956). Stylistically comparable to the limestone figure is a standing, belted, nude figure in copper from Temple Oval I at Khafajah. Although the dating of these figurines is reasonably clear, that of their contexts is far from precise. Stylistically related to the preceding sculptures are two alabaster statues supposedly from Umma which represent bull-men (Hansen 1975b:pl. 16). Only the stone portion of the figures is preserved, but originally some features—the legs and horns, and the like—were made of different materials such as silver and lapis lazuli. This use of composite materials in sculpture was a favored one in the preceding period.

Probably to be included with these few statues in the round of the Early Dynastic I period is the famed hoard from the Square Temple of Tell Asmar, executed in the severe style (Frankfort 1939). The nude kneeling worshiper, although less finely executed than the Shara Temple figure, is certainly related in style. Hrouda has suggested that the findspot of the hoard may well predate the construction of Square Temple I and has pointed out that some of the figures carry a vessel resembling the solid-foot chalice of Early Dynastic I (1971:112). Of the extant relief sculpture of this period, the *kudurru* of Ushumgal would be the closest stylistically to some of the pieces from the hoard. There is little if anything from the level of the Square Temple assigned to the sculpture hoard which would necessitate a date in Early Dynastic II. Indeed, those levels in the Diyala sites which contained sculptures of the clearly definable styles, *Stilstufe* Ia–Ib of Braun-Holzinger (1977)—Square Temple I (Asmar), Sin VIII (Khafajah), Nintu V (Khafajah), the Shara Temple excluding the Latest Building (Agrab), and probably Temple Oval I (Khafajah)—should be dated late in Early Dynastic I. Braun-Holzinger considers her *Stilstufe* I to be the equivalent of the Mesalim style as defined by Strommenger (Braun-Holzinger 1977:15).

The style called "Mesalim" by many scholars is characterized by the earlier group of sealings of the "Fara Style." In light of the above discussion of the seals, the Mesalim style should be dated to the last phase of Early Dynastic I. King Mesalim, himself, and the inscribed macehead from Tello bearing his name have led to some rather tortuous argumentation (e.g., Börker-Klähn 1980). The king is best dated in Early Dynastic IIIa, and the style of the macehead does not argue against such a date (Porada 1965:162; Pelzel 1977:9, n. 64; Braun-Holzinger 1977:14–15).

Early Dynastic I: The Diyala, the Himrin, and the Northern Regions

Although the pottery development in the lower Diyala and in the south shows a continuous evolution throughout the course of the Early Dynastic period, the pottery assigned to the first part of this long period is readily definable in the Diyala (Delougaz 1952:135–41) and is closely related to that from the south. Very characteristic of Early Dynastic I are the jars with a wing-tip handle and elaborate fenestrated stands. The hallmark of the period seems to be the solid-foot chalice which practically disappears before the end of Early Dynastic I. Although chalices are reported from the settlement, but not from the cemetery, of Ahmad al-Hattu (Sürenhagen 1983–84:194), this distinct type is not found in most of the Himrin sites which might mean that these date late in Early Dynastic I. Also distinctive for the Diyala region is the painted pottery known as Scarlet Ware, a phenomenon of Early Dynastic I which develops out of the painted wares of the preceding period. It is thought that a late phase of Scarlet Ware lasted into Early Dynastic II; however, this is based on only two examples, neither with a proper context (Delougaz 1952:69). Scarlet Ware appears in abundance in the Himrin, where it shows some regional variations (see, for example, Fujii 1981:figs. 13–18 [here, fig. 5/12]).

A style of cylinder seal carving aptly called "Brocade" by Frankfort seems to be dominant in the Diyala during Early Dynastic I (Frankfort 1955:21–24). Indeed, Frankfort saw it as prevalent during the period in all of southern Mesopotamia. Occasional examples of "Brocade" cylinders do appear in the south, as in level VIII of the Inanna Temple at Nippur, but they are probably imports from more northern regions.

Gubba, Ahmad al-Hattu, Madhhur, Kheit Qasim, Abu Qassem, and Razuk all show an Early Dynastic I occupation. The sites may have grown up in Early Dynastic I due to their important geographical situation on the way to Iran. It is suggested that Razuk belongs at the end of the period, and there is some evidence that its occupation lasted into Early Dynastic II in terms of the Diyala chronology (Gibson 1981:159–60). Most remarkable are the round buildings excavated at Tell Gubba (Fujii 1979, 1981, 1984), Tell Razuk (Gibson 1981), and Tell Madhhur (Roaf 1982, 1984bc). The level VII structure at Tell Gubba was built during Protoliterate "d" of the Di-

yala chronology but lasted into Early Dynastic times. Only a portion of an extremely large rounded building of Early Dynastic I was excavated at Tell Madhhur, while a very well preserved circular structure with an open central court appeared at Tell Razuk. The building at Razuk is believed by the excavators to have been erected with rather large-scale simple vaulting. There is a long tradition of round buildings in the Halaf and Ubaid periods in northern Mesopotamia and Syria as well as in the later building of level XI-A at Tepe Gawra of the Middle Gawra period (Tobler 1950:pls. VI–VIII). Whether this northern round building tradition was in any way connected with the temple ovals of the lower Diyala and the south is as yet unclear. The Temple Oval at Khafajah and a briefly tested building, probably a temple, with a curving exterior wall in Area G at al-Hiba may extend back into the Early Dynastic I period.

In the north during this period a distinctive type of pottery, including plain, incised, and painted wares (here, fig. 5/13, 14) has been called "Ninevite 5" after the site where it was excavated in a semistratified context (Mallowan 1964). Sites at which this pottery has been found seem to be concentrated in the Mosul region and in the west, with only rare occurrences eastward toward Iran (al-Soof 1968:75–76). The incised variety has recently been reported from the Early Dynastic I levels 10 and 12 at Mari (Lebeau 1985:94, pls. XXIV/23, XXVII/10, XXVIII/12). Although at Qalinj Agha, Gawra, and Telul eth-Thalathat these wares are said to be found in association with Late Uruk pottery (al-Soof 1968:75), in the region of Eski Mosul at Tell Mohammed ʿArab where the painted wares are earlier than the incised, the Ninevite 5 levels follow what is called a Late Uruk deposit (Roaf 1983:71, 1984a:150–55, 1987). In northeastern Syria at Tell Brak, the Ninevite 5 material succeeds what has tentatively been called the "Latest Uruk" or Jamdat Nasr phase (J. Oates 1985a:178; see the Jamdat Nasr Period, above). At Tell Leilan in the Khabur region, a sequence of some twenty-four strata of Ninevite 5 wares comprises Period III (Weiss 1983, 1985a, 1985c; Schwartz 1985). Period III is considered to span the entire range of time when Ninevite 5 ware was produced. Weiss sees "Ninevite 5/Leilan III" lasting some eight hundred years, beginning with the end of the Late Uruk period (Weiss 1985c). Such a span of time seems excessive, especially since, on the basis of Tell Mohammed ʿArab, Roaf (1987) considers that the strata of Leilan Period III represent only a portion of the entire Ninevite 5 sequence, and that there is a gap between Leilan III and the earlier Leilan IV. Period IV has three strata containing beveled-rim bowls and is characterized as "a kind of settlement differentiation within the late Uruk period on the Habur plains" (Weiss 1983:44). The occurrence of beveled-rim bowls does not necessarily signify the Uruk period. In the south they last, albeit in reduced numbers, throughout the Jamdat Nasr period and even into the transitional Early Dynastic I. There is no reason to assume that the production of beveled-rim bowls in the north ceases with the end of Late Uruk in the south.

The span of time represented by the Jamdat Nasr period of southern Mesopotamia must be accommodated in the north. Tell Brak now seems to show such a phase, and Period IV of Leilan may fall into a similar stage. Ninevite 5 would appear to begin after this, approximately with Early Dynastic I in the south, and last into Early Dynastic III. A group of cylinder seals with geometric designs from some Ninevite 5 sites, cited as partial evidence for indicating that Ninevite 5 begins in Jamdat Nasr, has been compared with the many seals from Sin IV at Khafajah dated to the Protoliterate "d" of the Diyala region (Schwartz 1985:58); however, Protoliterate "d" has now been shown to date to Early Dynastic I of the south.

The possible relationships between the northern and southern glyptic developments during this period have been outlined by Porada (1965:160). Of interest is the republication of a cylinder seal impression found at Nineveh which depicts a row of linked, stooping, skirted figures separated by oval-shaped filling motifs (Collon and Reade 1983:39–40; fig. 6 [here, fig. 4/7]). The style of the seal is certainly reminiscent of sealings from Ur and Susa.

Early Dynastic II

The chronological system developed for the Diyala region to trace archaeological development during the Early Dynastic period is primarily architectural. The tripartite division of the successive levels of the Abu Temple at Tell Asmar into the Archaic Shrine, the Square Temple, and the Single Shrine, all built of plano-convex bricks, played a considerable role in determining the chronological framework. In table 3 the levels of some of the major areas of excavations are given with the period sequence for the Diyala, that is, Protoliterate d, Early Dynastic I, Early Dynastic II, and Early Dynastic III indicated in the second column on the left.

Unlike the cylinder seals (Frankfort 1955), which are illuminatingly presented by findspot, the pottery (Delougaz 1952) is published by period so that it is often difficult to "see" the sequence as it develops. Furthermore, the lack of pottery in a given level is difficult to ascertain. The present writer, for example, can find relatively little pottery for the Shara Temple and only one curious vessel (Delougaz 1952:pl. 71/c) for the crucially important level VIII of the Sin Temple. The pottery of Early Dynastic II is a compilation of those pots from building levels assigned to Early Dynastic II on the basis of architectural considerations. When this material is plotted, it is clear

that the pottery for the period consists of three kinds: (1) types that run the gamut from Early Dynastic I through or into Early Dynastic III; (2) types that begin in Early Dynastic I and continue into Early Dynastic II; and (3) types that begin in Early Dynastic II and last into Early Dynastic III. Only two types are considered as solely representative of Early Dynastic II, namely, a type of flask and a particular type of stand (Delougaz 1952:141–42). Perhaps with a large assemblage of pottery from other comparable sites in the Diyala region one could determine a phase that could be set off from a preceding Early Dynastic I and a succeeding Early Dynastic IIIa, yet when dealing with the south and the rest of Mesopotamia it seems next to impossible to define archaeologically such a period with any precision. Attempting to fill a time span represented by Early Dynastic II in the Diyala with a comparable period in the south by means of a few rather slim individual references to the Diyala seems doubtful and even more dubious as the geographical distance between the southern sites and the Diyala increases. A dotted line about 2600 in table 3 suggests where the break between Early Dynastic I and Early Dynastic IIIa in the south might occur with reference to the Diyala system. In regard to the development of sculpture in the round as defined by Braun-Holzinger (1977), this would place her *Stilstufe* I and the Mesalim style in the end of Early Dynastic I of the south, along with the relevant seals mentioned above. It was suggested some time ago that the Mesalim style of Moortgat corresponds only to the earlier part of the Diyala Early Dynastic II (Strommenger 1960:4–6). At present, the continued use of the designations Early Dynastic II and *Mesilim-Zeit* in the south can only refer to a specific phase in the art historical evolution of early Sumerian art which archaeologically is best accommodated in the end of Early Dynastic I.

In the south the Inanna Temple at Nippur furnishes an archaeological sequence covering the range from Early Dynastic I through Early Dynastic IIIa. In very preliminary reports (e.g., Hansen and Dales 1962:76–80) and in the chart in *Chronologies* (Porada 1965:178), level VIII of that temple is labeled as Early Dynastic II. A few comments are in order.

During the excavations of the Inanna Temple it became apparent that level IX should date to Early Dynastic I and that Fara-type texts found in level VII B should date that level to Early Dynastic IIIa. In attempting to fit this sequence into the system of the Diyala region, then prevalent for all of Mesopotamia, level VIII was assigned to the intervening period of Early Dynastic II, essentially by default.

The pottery from level VIII is not extensive, but besides the ubiquitous conical bowls a few rather distinctive types were found. Some parallels with pottery from the Diyala (Delougaz 1952) are as follows:

1. Spouted jars with ring bases and a plastic ridge at the juncture of the shoulder and body.
   D.525.362, Khafajah, Houses 3–6.
   D.515.362 with double plastic ridge, Khafajah, Houses 4, 6, and 11[?].
   C.515.362 As a general type, jars with a ring base, spout, and a plastic ridge begin in Early Dynastic I, Khafajah, Houses 8, 10, 11.
   C.525.362 b is closest in shape but without the plastic ridge, Khafajah, Houses 6 and 10.
2. Four elaborately decorated stands, three of which have triangular fenestrations.
   Three stands are of type C.3—.0—, Tell Asmar, Archaic Shrine IV. The type is also found in Inanna IX as well as in 6G54c, level II of Tell Abu Salabikh (Postgate 1977a:281; p. 290, fig. 5/11), a level that may well date to the end of Early Dynastic I. The fourth stand lacks the fenestration and has wavy lines of appliqué.
3. Bowl rim from a "fruit stand."
   C.365.810 c, Khafajah, Houses 2–3.
   C.365.810 d, Khafajah, Houses 2–3 and Oval II. A practically identical example comes from Inanna VII and from Tell Abu Salabikh (Postgate and Moorey 1976:148, fig. 7/5).
4. Shallow bowl with sharply inturned shoulder.
   B.601.530, Khafajah, Houses 3 and Oval I–II.

The late types, namely, the "fruit stand" bowl rim and the bowl with sharply inturned shoulder are both from fills outside the main temple walls and thus are not well stratified. If these types are accepted as dating criteria, then the pottery from Inanna level VIII, according to the Diyala system, would range from Early Dynastic I into Early Dynastic III.

Only one very fragmentary sealing with a partially preserved animal in an abstract style reminiscent of Early Dynastic I glyptic was found as well as five cylinder seals. One of these is clearly a Jamdat Nasr type; two are of the "Brocade Style"; and two show geometric patterns related to the "Brocade Style."

A single tablet of the Early Dynastic IIIa Fara type (see below) is recorded as found in level VIII (Buccellati and Biggs 1969:5). The locus IT397, however, is not secure and contained a mixture of materials from levels VII and VIII.

The finds of sculpture in the round are negligible and include a small head of a man with a peaked cap, and the lower part of the skirt and feet of a small votive figurine. Both are stylistically indistinct and afford no chronological indications. Several examples of votive plaques (Hansen 1963) and a fine example of a steatite or chlorite vessel with scorpion decoration appeared. It has been suggested that several of these plaques actually were created in the Early Dynastic I period (Hansen 1971:54).

A group of small votive vessels which formed part of the original temple inventory have either square or round holes in the top and are of an unknown purpose. A few have a border of inlay composed of tiny pieces of shell set in bitumen. They are like some of the objects used in level VII B of the Inanna Temple or found as grave goods in the Royal Cemetery at Ur. Two of the small limestone vessels have the sharp shoulder carination found on Early Dynastic I vessels of level X mentioned above.

In sum, the materials from level VIII of the Inanna Temple do not allow for the definition of a distinct period in the south of Mesopotamia that equates with the Early Dynastic II of the Diyala. At best, it is a transitional phase between Early Dynastic I and III of Nippur, just as level XII in the Inanna sequence is a transitional phase between Jamdat Nasr and Early Dynastic I and not a period in its own right. Reports of the excavations at Tell Abu Salabikh refer to graves and houses dated by the excavators to Early Dynastic II (for example: Martin, Moon, and Postgate 1985:2–17, particularly p. 17, n. 2; Postgate 1984:101–11). It is not evident as yet if a distinct period can be defined; however, a clearer picture may emerge as excavations continue and more material becomes available.

Early Dynastic IIIa: The South

With the first part of the Third Early Dynastic period we enter the historical age of Sumer, exemplified, for example, by a recently found account at al-Hiba enumerating the military triumphs of Urnanshe of Lagash (Crawford 1977:192–97; Cooper 1983:13, 46, 1986:24–25). Fundamental to the reconstruction of the Third Early Dynastic period is the place of the kings of the First Dynasty of Ur in their relation to the rulers of Lagash. Nissen has argued that Mesannepada of Ur and Eannatum of Lagash are in part contemporary, and that the Royal Cemetery of Ur dates between the Fara texts and Eannatum (Nissen 1966:135–41). In dealing with the glyptic, Boehmer (1969:271–78) has followed Nissen, and Cooper (1983:chart on p. 60) has advanced a similar construct. Such an assumption would place Urnanshe and Akurgal roughly contemporary with Meskalamdug and Akalamdug who are known archaeologically to have preceded Mesannepada of Ur (see below). Recently a new reading by Boese of the inscribed bead from the Early Dynastic treasure of Mari indicates that Meskalamdug is indeed the father of Mesannapada (Boese 1978; Cooper 1986:98). This important fact seems to have received general acceptance and fixes historically the so-called *Kalam* dynasty. (See table 4 for a schematic chart of Early Dynastic IIIa.)

Crucial to Early Dynastic IIIa are texts from the site of Fara of a type also found at other sites. The use of the term *Fara* has led to some confusion since the name has been employed in a least four different ways. It refers to (1) the site of ancient Shuruppak and the material excavated therein; (2) a style of glyptic usually the equivalent of Early Dynastic II or the Mesalim period; (3) the stage in the development of writing synonymous with the Fara tablets; (4) the Fara period which in the German system comprises the later part of Early Dynastic II of the Diyala and Early Dynastic IIIa. It is obvious that the term should be abandoned, yet it is difficult to do so since the name is so deeply embedded in the literature. Hence, for clarity it is absolutely essential to specify the sense in which one uses it.

The texts from Fara itself are essentially unstratified, and many come from house XIII f–i along with a great quantity of sealings. For the most part, their original dating to the period following Moortgat's Mesalim phase is stiil maintained (Falkenstein 1936:22), and they have been linked to a stage in the development of glyptic termed the *Imdugud-Sukurru-Gruppe* in Moortgat's system of classification. This name, Imdugud-Sukurru, has been read by some in recent years as *Anzu-[d]Sud*. Although none of the tablets from Fara bore impressions of cylinder seals, the name of the priest Imdugud-Sukurru was found on an impression as well as in a text, but not both on the same document. The assumption is that they are the same person.

At present it is difficult to ascertain with precision the span of time in absolute terms covered by this phase in the development of writing. Falkenstein (1936:22) considered that the texts dated to about one hundred years before Urnanshe, while Hallo, on the basis of onomastica, dates them into the time of Urnanshe and perhaps even slightly later (Hallo 1973:235). Another group of texts comparable both in size and content to the tablets from Fara have been found at Tell Abu Salabikh, a site some 25 km to the northwest of Nippur. These have been published by R. Biggs who suggests that they "antedate the reign of Ur-Nanse by one or two generations" (1974:26). Nevertheless, Biggs implies, although he does not as yet explicitly state, that it is possible to discern an earlier and a later stage of development (see Gibson 1972a:79). At this point one does not known whether such a developmental sequence has true chronological significance. It seems best to assume at present that the stage in the development of writing represented by the texts of Fara, Tell Abu Salabikh, Kish, and Ur extends well into the time of Urnanshe and thus covers the major part of Early Dynastic IIIa. In any case, it seems clear that the glyptic phase associated with the name of Imdugud-Sukurru is not the sole style represented in this period (see Braun-Holzinger 1977:13, n. 34.).

In western Syria at Tell Mardikh, ancient Ebla, a royal archive was discovered in level IIB1 of palace G. The texts are related to those of Tell Abu Salabikh and even share common geographical and word lists with them (Biggs 1980). If, as is claimed (Matthiae 1978, 1982b:111–12, 1982a), this palace was destroyed early in the Akkadian period by Sargon or perhaps Naram-Sin himself, there seems to be a chronological problem. Assuming that there is a time lag between the production of the Tell Abu Salabikh texts in Sumer and those in the city-state of Ebla in Syria at the end of the Early Dynastic period, a difference of over one hundred years might seem excessive. The Ebla archive represents a collection of texts, including perhaps some three generations of rulers according to Archi (1985:140). Michalowski offers a different opinion and considers that the archive consists of texts of "no more than one generation" (1985:296). Indeed, a reevaluation of the Mardikh evidence may well indicate that the palace was destroyed before the Akkadian period; however, the find with the tablets of an alabaster jar lid inscribed with the name of Pepy I may argue, at present, for an Akkadian destruction.

Unfortunately the ancient name of Tell Abu Salabikh is not yet certain, although Biggs and Postgate have suggested ancient Eresh (Postgate 1982:54). For the Early Dynastic IIIa period in southern Mesopotamia, the site might well serve almost as a paradigm for the archaeology of the period. As stated above, the texts come from Area E, a complex of buildings that are probably part of a large temple precinct (see the plan of the "Burned building" and the "Southern Unit" in Biggs 1974:4, fig. 1; and Postgate 1982:53, fig. 40). The curious long corridor leading from the entrance to the central court of the "Southern Unit" is not unique but is paralleled in house XIII f–i of Fara and also in house "D" in the Temple Oval at Khafajah (Heinrich and Andrae 1931:14, fig. 12; Delougaz 1940:pl. 4.).

In preliminary reports Postgate has already published a considerable portion of the corpus of the Salabikh ceramics for Early Dynastic IIIa (see the references cited under Postgate) as well as some from Early Dynastic IIIb when the site appears to have been less extensively inhabited. He has pointed to connections up the Euphrates to Mari and farther west for Early Dynastic IIIa during a time when Tell Abu Salabikh might well have been under the political domination of Kish (Postgate 1982:50–51). For example, from graves 100 and 176 came ovoid jars with small ring bases and orange-painted horizontal stripes on their shoulders which have western connections as far as Tell Khuera in northern Syria (Postgate 1977a:295; Postgate and Moon 1982:131).

Important is burial 162 found in room 59. The shaft had been dug after the erection of the building in phase IB, and the grave contained the skeletons of at least five equids (Postgate and Moon 1982:135; Postgate 1984:95–97), indicating that this practice of burying animals was much more widespread than suggested by the famous graves of Ur and Kish. Other recently found equid burials of Early Dynastic IIIb and Akkadian date are now known from the Himrin in the upper Diyala and from al-Hiba in the south (for equids and equid burials see Postgate 1986, and Zarins 1986).

The date of the cart or chariot burials of Kish has always been problematic. They were found in the Y sounding at a depth of 1–2.5 m below the Flood Stratum (Moorey 1979a:104). Thus, other than considering the comparative material for the objects from the graves themselves, the basic questions concern (1) the date of the surrounding context in which they were found, (2) whether or not they were sunk from above or below the higher Flood Stratum, (3) the date of the Flood Stratum, and (4) the date of the Red Stratum and the intermediate layer between it and the Flood Stratum. Although it is difficult to be precise or conclusive on any of these matters, a few observations are in order. (1) The Y Cemetery and the building strata are here considered as Early Dynastic I, a date that for all intents and purposes has now been proved by Algaze (1984). (2) Both Moorey (1979a:106) and Gibson (1972a:84, 1980b:616) think that the burials were dug from above Flood Stratum. No evidence argues against this most reasonable assumption. (3) Materials are lacking for the date of the Flood Stratum itself, but Moorey and Gibson claim to have seen Early Dynastic II and Early Dynastic III sherds in the level during a visit to the site. To the present writer this observation seems overly astute. The crux of the matter lies in the sealings and tablets said to have been found immediately below the Flood Stratum in YW, which according to Moorey (1979a:99, 115) would provide a *terminus post quem* for the level. Having noted the recording difficulties, Algaze dismisses this material and argues for intrusions from above (1984:143 and n. 35, 146, n. 46). (4) The graves were dug before the time of the Red Stratum, the debris of which must have been deposited before or at the beginning of Early Dynastic IIIb, for private graves of the A Cemetery type were dug into it. The stratum contained tablets said to be of the Fara type, hence, Early Dynastic IIIa (Moorey 1979a:97). Since none of this is overwhelmingly clear, Algaze's conclusion that the "lack of adequate records as to the stratigraphic position of the Chariot Burials at Kish precludes a definitive solution to the question of their date" (1984:154) seems most reasonable. The present writer would opt for a date in the first half of the Early Dynastic IIIa period, earlier than the graves of the Royal Cemetery at Ur.

Certainly postdating the time of the chariot burials at Kish are the graves from mound A where some 150 were excavated from the so-called A Cemetery (Mackay 1925). Discussions concerning the chronology of this cemetery are extensive, with dates ranging from late

Early Dynastic II into Akkadian. That it was in use in both Early Dynastic IIIb and Akkadian times seems to be without question (see the discussions of Moorey 1979a:61–75; Gibson 1972a:78–80; Moon 1982:44–46); however, the date of the earliest graves has proven more problematic. Whelan's (1978) early date for some of the pottery has been contested by Moon (1982:45–46). Fundamental to any discussion of the cemetery is the fact that it was dug into the destroyed or abandoned remains of the palace of mound A and the fact that a tablet of the Fara type was found beneath a bench in room 31 of the palace. No matter how one attempts to dispose of the importance of this tablet, it is clear that the palace lasted into the early part of Early Dynastic IIIa, so the A Cemetery at its earliest could only have begun in the latter part of Early Dynastic IIIa, the period to which most of the seals from the cemetery may be dated (Porada 1965:164n; Moorey 1979a:66).

The most impressive of all the monumental buildings of the Early Dynastic period is the palace of mound A with its grand pillared "loggia." Although the plan of the building as presented is undoubtedly overly simplified and regularized, the scale and arrangement of the parts show a sense of design (for a full description see Margueron 1982:35–70; figs. 12–34). A distinctive feature of the north wing is a long surrounding corridor separating the exterior wall from the inner complex of chambers. Although the function of such a corridor is not readily understood, its purpose may well have been defensive. As stated above, the date of the palace during this phase is Early Dynastic IIIa as established by the Fara-type tablet found in one of the rooms. Porada (1965:161n) would date the building on the basis of some shell inlays found within the palace to Early Dynastic II. This proposal is essentially followed by Dolce (1978) who concludes from a study of the inlays that the palace was founded in Early Dynastic II or late Early Dynastic I, but she admits to the building's continued existence. The palace may well have had earlier phases to which the inlays originally belonged, but only reexcavation of the entire complex including earlier levels would help to solve many of the problems (Gibson 1980b:617).

Besides Palace A at Kish, the large, so-called Plano-Convex Building is also dated to Early Dynastic IIIa (Moorey 1979a:41–44), and like the palace, it has a long narrow surrounding corridor. This architectural feature relates the buildings of Kish to the two "palaces" of Eridu (Safar, Mustafa, and Lloyd 1981:273–87) which may well belong to the same period even though nothing that provides a secure dating was found in them. The function of the Eridu buildings is not yet ascertainable, but they were perhaps temple dependencies like the complex of Abu Salabikh, the *giparu,* for example, rather than the actual seat of a *lugal.* The A Palace of Kish may well have been a residence of the ruler, as were the Early Dynastic palaces of Mari which lay below the monumental one of Zimri-lim of the Old Babylonian period (Margueron 1982:86–106; figs. 46–56). It is difficult to date precisely the Early Dynastic remains at Mari in terms of the chronology of southern Mesopotamia, but an early phase of the Early Dynastic palace sequence, *palais présargonique* 2, must have existed during at least part of Early Dynastic IIIa, for a bead inscribed with the name of Mesannepada of Ur was found in the latest Early Dynastic construction, that of the *palais présargonique* 1 (Parrot 1968:44, 53–59; pls. XXI–XXII [here, fig. 5/15]).

The archaeological remains at Fara during Early Dynastic IIIa have been well studied by Martin (1972, 1975). The Imdugud-Sukkuru phase of the glyptic development, so well represented at the site of Fara itself, is probably confined to the earlier part of Early Dynastic IIIa and is only one of a series of styles recognized in such other cities and areas as Ur and the Diyala region (here, fig. 4/8). Boehmer has divided the seals for Early Dynastic IIIa into an ED IIIa[1] and an ED IIIa[2] (1969; see also Porada 1980b:8). The second stage of this development is probably contemporary with the later phase of the Fara writing pointed to by Biggs, and which at Ur is represented by the Royal Cemetery and the sealings of Meskalamdug and Akalamdug, contemporary with Urnanshe and Akurgal of Lagash.

Probably the most important find of the entire Early Dynastic period is the Royal Cemetery of Ur (Woolley 1934). One of the arguments proposed for the dating of a large part of the cemetery to the Early Dynastic IIIa period is that stylistically the seals of Meskalamdug and Akalamdug are clearly earlier than the seals of Mesannepada and his wife Ninbanda, who date to the beginning of Early Dynastic IIIb (Porada 1965:162–63; Boehmer 1969). The graves of the cemetery have been analyzed and put in order by Nissen (1966), with further commentaries provided by Gockel (1982) and Pollock (1985). Many of the objects found in the Royal Cemetery can be connected with artifacts found in regions far outside of Mesopotamia proper. Various stones, jewelry types, weapons, and so forth have been discussed (Porada 1965:164), but the chronological implications of these relationships can be stated only in very broad terms. One class of artifact, the carved chlorite vessels executed in a style and displaying an iconography not purely Sumerian, are found in the Royal Cemetery as well as in other areas that extend from Syria to Pakistan (Kohl 1975). Based on the archaeological context of a few Mesopotamian examples, these have been dated to the mid-third millennium (Kohl 1982:24), but, because of stylistic considerations, some should date as early as Early Dynastic I, as, for example, the vessel from the Sin Temple at Khafajah (Hansen 1975a:185–86; pl. 77).

One of the most magnificent of all the chlorite vessels is a painted fragmentary vase or stand with a depiction in relief of a panther and a toothed serpent that came from level VII B of the Inanna Temple at Nippur (Hansen 1975a:184–85; pl. 76/a [here, fig. 5/16]). Although this vessel may well be earlier than its findspot, the temple of level VII B contained a series of deposits rich in temple furnishings, some of which are comparable to finds from the Royal Cemetery at Ur (see for example, Hansen 1975a:187–88; pl. 83). Much of the sculpture from this temple belongs to the stylistic grouping called *Stilstufe* II (ED IIIa) of Braun-Holzinger (1977:50). The date of level VII B of the Inanna temple is arrived at from a group of tablets found in a street to the west in a stratum securely linked to level VII B of the temple proper. Biggs (pers. comm.) has indicated that these tablets belong to the more developed phase of writing of the Fara-type texts, which here is considered as lasting to the time of Urnanshe. Thus, level VII B must be contemporary at least in part with the Royal Cemetery of Ur.

At Tello, ancient Girsu, several important inscribed stone objects of Urnanshe, including the "family reliefs," were recovered in Tell "K" (Parrot 1948:55–63). How these objects relate to the remains of what must have been part of a large complex built after the so-called *construction inférieure* remains unclear.

Early Dynastic IIIb: The South

In absolute terms the period of Early Dynastic IIIb must comprise some 150 years before Sargon of Akkad, whose dates are ca. 2334–2279 B.C. There is no clearly defined archaeological break between this period and the previous one, but historically Early Dynastic IIIb is taken here to begin with Mesannepada and A'annepada of the First Dynasty of Ur and with Eannatum of Lagash. Although the names of many of the rulers of the dynasties of Ur, Uruk, Umma, and Lagash are known, up to the present time the entire period is not well represented archaeologically.

At Ur, in the area of and below the ziggurat of the Third Dynasty of Ur, Woolley's "Archaic II" would in part correspond to the time of the First Dynasty (Woolley 1955:1ff.). In the soundings, Seal Impression Strata 1 and 2 which overlay the debris into which the Royal Cemetery was dug (Moorey 1979b:117–18) must belong to the First Dynasty since sealings of Mesannepada (here, fig. 4/9) and his wife Ninbanda were found in these strata. Stylistically they date after the seals and sealings of the Royal Cemetery (Porada 1965:162; Boehmer 1969:271ff.). Furthermore, the style of the sealing of Mesannepada is closely related to that of the sealing of Eannatum of Lagash (Amiet 1980:206 [here, fig. 4/10]).

Although the temple of Inanna at Nippur was for the

most part rebuilt and expanded in design, there is no evidence for a lapse of time between levels VII B and VII A. The accumulation of level VII A may well have begun in Early Dynastic IIIa and continued into Early Dynastic IIIb, but the rare finds from the level VII A temple allow for little comparison with materials from other sites. The temple must have continued to the end of Early Dynastic IIIb, but only scrappy walls remain, for the entire area was razed during the preparations for a subsequent building by Shulgi of the Third Dynasty of Ur.

The A Cemetery at Kish, which may have begun in Early Dynastic IIIa, continued in use throughout Early Dynastic IIIb and lasted into the Akkadian period (Moorey 1979a:61–75; Gibson 1982:532). The distribution of two of the characteristic pottery types, stemmed dishes and jars with upright handles, has been studied by Moon, who notes that the latter form tends to be concentrated north of Nippur (Moon 1982).

Extensive remains from the first half of Early Dynastic IIIb have been uncovered at al-Hiba, the site of the ancient capital city of Lagash. For this period, excavations have concentrated on the Ibgal of Inanna (Area A), the Bagara of Ningirsu (Area B), and a large administrative complex (Area C). For the first time in Early Dynastic Sumerian archaeology, specific building levels may be linked chronologically to individually known historical rulers: Area A, level I = Enannatum I; Area B, level III = Eannatum; Area C, level IB = Eannatum and Enannatum I (Hansen 1983). The present lack of archaeological building remains for the later part of Early Dynastic IIIb at Lagash (Enannatum II–Uruꞌinimgina) may be due to the fact that after Eannatum II and an Elamite invasion, the state of Lagash was administered from Girsu, the modern site of Tello (Bauer 1983:420). Unfortunately, at Tello there is nothing architectural that can be associated with the late rulers. Due to a current archaeological reevaluation of the Akkadian period, this portion of Early Dynastic IIIb, once called Proto-Imperial by the excavators of the Diyala, may need extensive revision.

The glyptic of Lagash during the time of Eannatum, Enannatum, and perhaps Entemena displays a wide variety of styles and iconographic elements (Hansen 1987), suggesting that the work of individual seal cutters may have been influenced by several external sources. A distinct royal style, exemplified by the sealing of Eannatum, is comparable to the royal style of the First Dynasty of Ur and to the sealing of Mesannapada. Toward the end of Early Dynastic IIIb at Lagash, in sealings from Tello associated with Lugalanda, his wife Barnamtara, and Uruꞌinimgina, the composition of the frieze tends to become tighter and employs more marked vertical accents (Amiet 1980:pl. 83,figs. 1098, 1100–1103).

The pottery of the temples and of the administrative building is similar to some from the A Cemetery of Kish.

The Early Dynastic IIIb pottery types are varied and include a few rare painted sherds of Susa IV A style, with very specific parallels to painted wares from Godin III 5/6 in Iran (Henrickson 1987).

A singular find at al-Hiba was a grave located to the south of the administrative complex of Area C, which contained the skeleton of a man buried with his mount (Hansen 1973:70; fig. 26). This might well have taken place after the destruction of Lagash by Lugalzagesi of Umma, who was probably responsible for the extensive burning evidenced in both Areas C and B. As noted above, the elaborate equid burials in southern Mesopotamia of Early Dynastic IIIa at Ur, Kish, Abu Salabikh, and at Susa in Khuzestan are now supplemented by other burials from the Himrin region of the upper Diyala at sites such as Tell Razuk (Gibson 1981:73, 1982:532) and Tell Madhhur (Roaf 1982:45–46), where they are dated by the excavators to the Akkadian period.

The Ibgal of Inanna built by Enannatum at Lagash was in the form of a temple oval with antecedents at least as early as Urnanshe. Probably contemporary with Enannatum's temple was the richly decorated temple oval at al-Ubaid (Hall and Woolley 1927; Delougaz 1938). Although a stone foundation tablet bearing the name of Aꞌannepada of Ur, not found in situ, may have come originally from the temple, it may just as well have belonged to an earlier, as yet unexcavated level.

At Tell al-Wilayah another monumental building was partially excavated (Madhlum 1960; S. A. Rashid 1963). A long narrow corridor suggests that the excavated part is related to the type of "palace" known from earlier Kish and Eridu. The fact that the building was constructed of plano-convex bricks and contained material of both the Early Dynastic and the Akkadian periods dates the level to the end of Early Dynastic IIIb, with occupation lasting into Akkadian times.

Early Dynastic IIIa and IIIb: The Diyala and the North

For the upper and lower Diyala region and the north, the periods equivalent to Early Dynastic IIIa and IIIb of the south, comprising some 250 years, are discussed together.

As indicated in table 3, Early Dynastic IIIa in the lower Diyala includes at Khafajah levels IX and X of the Sin Temple, Houses 5–3, Temple Oval II, and Nintu VI–VII, and at Tell Asmar, Square Temple III. From the sculpture, Braun-Holzinger would date Nintu VII and Oval II into the equivalent of Early Dynastic IIIb (1977:63; table 2). For Early Dynastic IIIb and what was termed Proto-Imperial by the excavators, the archaeological remains are meager, but in a preliminary study of the relevant material, Gibson (1982) has made important observations and suggestions. Based on a reexamination of the tablets, sealings, and pottery, he reassigns Temple Oval III as well as Houses 1 of Khafajah and Houses V*b* and V*a* of Tell Asmar to the Early Akkadian period (Sargon to Naram-Sin), while he relegates Single Shrine II, III, and IV of the Abu Temple at Tell Asmar to a Late Akkadian period. Such considerations argue for an elimination of the Proto-Imperial period (from Entemena to Sargon) of the Diyala excavators and for a very much shortened ED IIIb period, if indeed, the latter exists at all. Gibson points out that at Tell Abu Salabikh and in the Inanna Temple at Nippur, Early Dynastic IIIb is scarcely attested. While this seems to be true, its absence at these sites cannot be justifiably used in support of extending the argument to the south, for at Salabikh there was extensive erosion of the late remains, and at Nippur late rebuildings extensively destroyed levels VI and V. The fact that at al-Hiba (Lagash) Early Dynastic IIIb after Entemena so far is absent is perhaps more telling, but only future excavation can assist in solving these problems. Somehow, the period from Enannatum II through Uruʿinimgina must be accounted for archaeologically beyond the seal impressions of Lugalanda and Uruʿinimgina, though the time involved is probably less than one hundred years. If the historical situation were unknown, one would probably be unaware of any difficulty.

The monumental plano-convex brick buildings at Tell Asmar known as the Earlier Northern Palace and the Northern Palace were originally dated to Early Dynastic IIIb and the Proto-Imperial period. However, Gibson (1982) has now justifiably assigned them to the Early and Late Akkadian periods respectively.

In the Himrin basin of the upper Diyala region, excavated sites have produced material dated to Early Dynastic III as, for example, some graves from Tell Madhhur (Roaf 1982:45, 1984b:133–35) and some pottery from the settlement of Tell Abqaʿ (Trümpelmann 1982), but thus far such remains seem sporadic. The glyptic style for Early Dynastic III is represented by a group of fine cylinders from Tell Sleimah, which for the most part are executed in a style identical to that of Sumer (al-Gailani Werr 1982). The fact that level IV of Sleimah produced seals of Early Dynastic III style as well as others of the classic Akkadian style remains to be explained.

In the north at Assur, level G of the Ishtar Temple corresponds to Early Dynastic IIIb. The votive statuettes from here show a close resemblance to contemporary works from the south (Braun-Holzinger 1977:52, 61), but with a marked dependence on the sculptural style of the Mari school. In general, the art of the Mari school in both sculpture in the round and in other media such as carved shell inlays shows a marked refinement frequently verging on a mannerism, in comparison with the works

of art from the south. A counterpart is found in Ebla in the beautifully carved stone wigs apparently dating to the end of the Early Dynastic III period (Matthiae 1980). Undoubtedly the arts of Mari and farther west formed a major component of the developed Akkadian style of southern Mesopotamia.

The archaeological phase in the north called "Ninevite 5" seems to end during the time of Early Dynastic III. At Tell Taya in northwestern Iraq, the pottery of level 9 (Early Dynastic III) continues certain Ninevite 5 traditions but nonetheless is distinctly different from it (Reade 1982:74). Ninevite 5 ware is also absent in the Early Dynastic III level of Tell Brak (J. Oates 1985a:175), a level destroyed perhaps by Sargon before Naram-Sin's palace was constructed (D. Oates 1985a:160; J. Oates 1985b:143).

The Period of Akkad

The period of Akkad was named by modern scholars after the capital of the Semitic ruler, Sargon. Akkad had been a new city, probably fairly close to the ancient town of Kish. The title "king of Kish" assumed by Sargon after his defeat of Ur-Zababa of Kish may have indicated his claim to domination of the north as had been made by several Early Dynastic rulers before him (Edzard 1980:608). The dates of Sargon and his successors given by Brinkman (in Oppenheim 1977:335–36) are as follows: Sargon, 2334–2279 B.C., which may include a period during which he was a dependent prince before his victory over Lugalzagesi; Rimush, 2278–2270 B.C.; Manishtushu, 2269–2255 B.C.; Naram-Sin, 2254–2218 B.C.; Shar-kali-sharri, 2217–2193 B.C.; Igigi, Nanijum, Imi, Elulu, 2192–2190 B.C.; Dudu, 2189–2169 B.C.; Shu-Turul, 2168–2154 B.C.

Little is known about the sequence of events that led to the emergence of Sargon as a ruler of all of Mesopotamia and, subsequently, as the overlord of the first documented empire in western Asia.

Brinkman pointed out (in Oppenheim 1977:346, n.1) that Hallo had suggested a shortening to about five or four decades of the period in which the Guti, who put an end to the Akkad dynasty, actually ruled over the north (Hallo 1971:713–14). Boese has taken up Hallo's suggestions and tried to support them with textual and archaeological references (Boese 1983:33–35). In the present state of uncertainty, however, the tentative dates suggested by Brinkman are retained here.

At the major sites of Mesopotamia, like Ur, Uruk-Warka, Nippur, and Mari, inscriptional evidence documents the rule of the Akkad dynasty, but few archaeological remains of the period have been preserved. Near Kish the sites of Umm al-Jir and Ishan Mizyad have Akkadian levels, as does the recently investigated site of Umm al-

Hafriyat near Nippur. The publication of the latter two should enhance the meager evidence currently available for the south (Gibson 1972b, 1978; Postgate and Roaf 1981:184). The possible identification of Ishan Mizyad with the city of Akkad had been suggested by Weiss (1975:442–51). However, at present most of the archaeological evidence comes from the north; only al-Wilayah lies in the south. There a palace was excavated (Madhlum 1960) that was compared to the palaces at Kish and Eridu not only on the basis of plano-convex bricks, which may be less decisive, but also on the basis of a surrounding uninterrupted corridor (S. A. Rashid 1963:85). Despite the pottery and cylinder seals of Akkadian style found in the palace, it may have been built in the preceding period since it also fails to show the regularity and nearly symmetrical arrangement of rectangular rooms characteristic of Akkadian palace plans such as that of Naram-Sin at Brak (Mallowan 1947:pl. LX) or the reconstructed plan of the so-called Old Palace at Assur (Preusser 1955:3), of which only foundation trenches were completed. Moreover, the use of rooms arranged around a courtyard increased in this period. A large house at Assur (Preusser 1954:pl. 2), perhaps a private dwelling, gives the same impression and probably belonged to this period, although the excavator thought a date in Ur III to be a possibility. A room, interpreted as a bath, witnesses the elaborate sanitary installations introduced at this period. These are especially striking in the Northern Palace of Tell Asmar-Eshnunna (Delougaz, Hill, and Lloyd 1967:187–89), a building called Pre-Sargonid and Proto-Imperial in the publications of the excavations but assigned by Gibson to the Akkad period (Gibson 1982:533–35).

Sargonic tablets found in looters' holes in the area around the main court of the "palace" provide information on a large establishment, with hundreds of women employed in making textiles. The sanitary installations, which had been introduced in the northern part of the "palace" along the eastern row of rooms, may have served the needs of such an establishment. Gibson pointed out that his dating of the "palace" in the Akkad period makes it seem possible that the tablets were connected with the activities in that building (Gibson 1982:534). The assumed organization in the "palace" of the space and appointments for industrial purposes would conform with organizational measures undertaken by Sargon and his successors according to their inscriptions.

The interpretation by Heinrich (1984:32–35) of part of the "Akkadian Foundations" at Khafajah as a large and presumably luxurious house adds another spacious building (which could have only been erected by persons of wealth and power), to the ground plans of the period.

In the north, distinctive architectural features of the

Akkad period are seen in the buildings of level VIII at Tell Taya, where the foundations and lower walls in this period and in the preceding late Early Dynastic level IX were built of stone and are therefore in a remarkable state of visible preservation. On the central mound are a gatehouse and two monumental buildings, one of which is probably a shrine, which faced each other across a large open space in the middle (Reade 1982:73). The mound is surrounded by a fortified circuit wall which was probably built in level IX. It rested on bedrock and had its lower 3 m constructed of crude limestone masonry. The stones were largely unworked, apparently as they came from the quarry. On top of the stones a layer of large sherds was spread, and the wall then continued upward in mudbrick. The average dimension of the bricks was $32 \times 36 \times 10$ cm. The shrine, built in the same technique as the circuit wall, had less crude stonework to a height of 1.20 m, with at least 3 m of mud-brick above (Reade 1968:241–42).

Reade compared Tell Taya to Tell Jidle in the Balih Valley, where a large mound was also ringed with a wall partly built of stone (Reade 1968:243). He also compared a hoard of jewelery, found in a pot buried in the center of a room in the house west of the shrine, to hoards found at Brak and Jidle, suggesting that they were all buried simultaneously (Reade 1968:248).

In the Himrin basin Akkadian remains have been found at several sites, of which the most important for the period under consideration are Tell Atiqeh and Tell Sleima, formerly written Tell Suleimah. At Tell Atiqeh, a large well-preserved house or administrative building was excavated (Gibson 1979:467; Postgate and Watson 179:169). Tell Sleima yielded residential buildings with characteristic pottery and metalwork of great interest (Rmaidh 1984).

Old Akkadian tablets found at the site may indicate that the town should be identified with Awal (F. Rashid 1984:55–56; Gibson 1980a:178–81).

At Tell Madhhur and Tell Razuk, rich graves with equid burials date to either late Early Dynastic III or early Akkadian times (Killick and Roaf 1979:540; Gibson 1980a:25).

Brak, which D. Oates called "essentially a Mesopotamian site" (1982a:196), contains the chronologically most significant building of the Akkad period, the palace of Naram-Sin, built with bricks stamped with that king's name. The regularity of the building's courts and long storage rooms shows a characteristic trait of Akkadian architecture which also distinguishes another Akkadian building at Brak. It was discovered in the northeast corner of the mound in area FS. Its south facade was ornamented with deep rectangular niches, suggesting that it was a public, possibly a religious, building. Inside the building was a rectangular court (D. Oates 1987:178, fig. 2). "It represents the latest of three distinct levels of Akkadian occupation of which the earliest is represented by a substantial building with finely plastered walls, doorways with reveals and benches around the sides of the room" (D. Oates 1987:177–78). It was thought to belong to the earliest Akkadian occupation under Naram-Sin, and the destruction of the building may have occurred at the end of that king's reign (ibid.).

D. Oates identified two destruction levels at Brak "both earlier than the construction of the palace and separated by a relatively short interval" (D. Oates 1985a:160). He suggested that the first destruction was due either to Sargon or to Lugalzagesi, the second conceivably to Naram-Sin, before the erection of his storage "palace." A more extensive treatment of the problem concerning the date of the destructions and their likely connection with destructions at Mari and Ebla was given by J. Oates (1985b).

With the drawings of Late Early Dynastic III pottery, stoneware, and stone vessels from Brak, J. Oates included some "Agade" types (J. Oates 1982:fig. 1/4, 11–13; fig. 6/91, 93). A "rectangular pottery vessel with appliqué snakes" was one of two such vessels found on an Agade floor in area ST (D. Oates 1982a:195, 199; pl. XII/c).

For the pottery of the Akkad period in general, Adams listed the following items as most characteristic: ribbed ware, either on the shoulders of large storage jars (here, fig. 5/17) or on large ledge-rim bowls (here, fig. 5/18), which apparently began to be made at the end of the Early Dynastic III period. Large spouted bowls were also distinctive (here, fig. 5/19); the spout had a beaded rim and was set immediately below the down-flaring rim of the bowl. Broad incised meanders on large bowl and jar sherds were also noted (Adams 1965: p. 128: 4B.d). Gibson added that at Akkadian Nippur and Umm al-Hafriyat, large jars with a single ridge at the shoulder were the predominant jar type (Gibson 1982:537). At Tell Taya, herringbone patterns below the rim were frequent as were incised circles and crescents, and rows of small dots produced with a comblike instrument (Reade 1968:pl. LXXXIV/9, 12, 13).

Gibson pointed out several pottery types that appear to mark the transition from Early Dynastic III to Akkadian: fruit stands (also called stemmed dishes); upright handled (or goddess-handled) jars; vessels with knoblike feet and/or vertically pierced lugs, along with jars that have applied knobs on the body; and large bowls (Gibson 1982:536–37).

Abundance of metal in the Akkad period, level VIII, at Tell Taya indicates both prosperity and connections with the southeast. Reade pointed to the relation of bronzes in the vicinity of the shrine at Taya to those of an Akkad hoard at Brak: a sickle, a dagger, a chisel, and a typical spearhead (Mallowan 1947:pl. XXXI/1, 2, 9, 11). These metal types are said to have continued from late Early Dynastic ones to judge by their resemblance to examples from the Royal Cemetery at Ur. Shaft-hole adzes, corresponding to examples from Ur (Woolley 1934:pl. 229, type 3 [here, fig. 5/20]) were found at Gawra (Speiser 1935:pl. XLIX/5 [here, fig. 5/21]) and Billa (Speiser 1931:21). The miniature pickax found at Gawra (Speiser 1935:pl. XLIX/3), however, was in its proper context in the Akkadian stratum VI for a pickax from Ur (Woolley 1934:pl. 224/U.9680 [here, fig. 5/22]) came from grave 689, together with cylinder seals of mature Akkad style. A shaft-hole axhead with lateral ribs on the socket, found in a "Late Agade context" at Brak (D. Oates 1985a:165), determines an early date for this type of socket.

Reade did not mention pins among the finds from Taya, although many toggle pins with simple head and upper shank flattened for piercing were found at Gawra in stratum VI, Chagar Bazar III, Brak Sargonid (Speiser 1935:pl. L/8; Mallowan 1937:fig. 12/5, 1947:pl. XXXI/3, 4) and are related to pins in the Royal Cemetery of Ur (Woolley 1934:pl. 231, type 3b [here, fig. 5/23]) all mentioned by Perkins (1954:49). She also cited a hairpin with spatulate head of which rare examples were found at Ur, including one of gold (Woolley 1934:pl. 159/a) and which is represented in Brak Sargonid, Tell Aswad (Mallowan 1947:pl. LIII/32 [here, fig. 5/24]), in Billa 5 (Speiser 1932–33:268), and in forked form in Gawra VI (Speiser 1935:pl. L/4).

One may finally quote Perkins (1954:49) for the relation of the lunate gold earrings of Nuzi and Brak Sargonid (Starr 1937–39:pl. 55/I; Mallowan 1947:pl. XXXVI, *passim*) to those from the Royal Cemetery (Woolley 1934:pl. 219, types 2–7 [here, fig. 5/25]). (For a detailed discussion of the Sargonid lunate earrings, see Maxwell-Hyslop 1971:22–24, *passim*.)

Chipped flint and occasionally obsidian arrowheads of lanceolate shape were in use in the Akkad to the Ur III periods in Gawra VI (Speiser 1935:84), at Brak (Mallowan 1947:180–82; pl. XXXVII), in the Diyala, and at Susa. At Tell Taya, Reade was able to identify an area on the outskirts of the late Early Dynastic to Early Akkad period town with an industry of flint knapping (Reade 1973:161).

The cylinder seals of the fully developed Akkad style are easily recognized by the carefully modeled bodies of men and animals as well as by the rich repertory of mythological figures, gods, hybrids, animals, and human worshipers. A chronological differentiation of the Akkad cylinders was proposed by R. M. Boehmer (1965) on the basis of the development of the friezes depicting contesting heroes and animals, inherited from the Early Dynastic period and gradually broken up into two pairs of contestants.

The first group that showed the new style was Boehmer's group Ib, dated in the time of Sargon's daughter Enheduanna on the basis of seal inscriptions of her officials. Boehmer's group II is dated in the time of Rimush and Manishtusu, group III in that of Naram-Sin to the end of the dynasty. The fluid limits of these stylistic groups were pointed out in a review by Nagel and Strommenger (1968). They stated their own views of the general chronology of the glyptic development which are summarized here. An early phase Ib, which is already clearly within the framework of Akkadian style, was followed by group Ic, in which the style is fully developed and extends without major changes to groups II and III. In group III, works of extraordinary balance and artistic quality were produced, which transcended the achievements of groups I and II.

The linear style of the Akkad period, which prevailed in the Diyala region and other peripheral areas with a limited repertory of themes, was explored by M. Laird (1985). Some groups, which had been thought to belong to the post-Akkad period, were shown to be regionally, not chronologically, different.

The monumental art of the period was assembled by Pierre Amiet (1976) around the long-known dated monuments discovered at Susa and preserved in the Louvre. An important addition with significant chronological implications was the discovery at Bassetki, near Dohak in northeast Iraq, of the lower part of a cast copper, crouching nude man clasping the base of a standard or gatepost, and set on a circular podium bearing an inscription of Naram-Sin (al-Fouadi 1976; Moorey 1985:30).

Nude female figures of ivory, wood, or clay emerge as a criterion of the period on the basis of excavations at Umm al-Hafriyat (Gibson 1983). Gibson compared the naturalistically modeled clay figurines, all of which have their hair gathered in a bun at the back, to the ivory figurine from Tell al-Wilaya (Madhlum 1960:pl. 7 [here, fig. 5/26]) and to the ivory figurines from the floor of level G at Assur (Andrae 1922:pl. 57/44–47). There are also stylistically comparable clay figurines from Assur (Andrae 1922: pls. 54/u, 55/y–aa).

An ivory statuette of a nude female found in an Akkad period building at Brak has her right arm hanging down at the side and the left laid across her waist, an Egyptian posture noted by D. Oates (1982a:135, 198; pl. XI). Most of the other figures cited have both elbows bent and hands clasped in front. The ivory figurine from the Treasure of Mari (Moortgat and Moortgat-Correns 1974:157) is the best executed and preserved of this type of object. Since it is part of an Early Dynastic assemblage, it sup-

ports the contention that the Akkad style was stimulated by the stylistic developments in Syria.

The Post-Akkadian Period and the Third Dynasty of Ur

The Post-Akkadian Period

The period between the end of the Akkad Dynasty, ca. 2150 B.C., and the beginning of the reign of Ur-Nammu, set at present in 2112 B.C., the first ruler of the Third Dynasty of Ur, has been called the Post-Akkadian period by historians of ancient art, especially as a term for the sculptures of Gudea of Lagash and for cylinder seals of the period. However, recent research has shown that Gudea was a contemporary of Ur-Nammu's and may have been an ally in Ur-Nammu's successful struggle against the Elamites to wrest Babylonia from their control (Steinkeller 1988:52–53). Steinkeller added that "one could imagine that Gudea took part in that conflict as an ally of Ur-Nammu, in their common quest to reopen the trade routes, 'from the lower to the upper sea'" (Steinkeller 1988:53).

One of the possibilities considered by Steinkeller of placing Gudea chronologically in relation to Ur-Nammu is that the early years of Gudea fell into pre-Ur III times. Gudea was followed by his son, Ur-Ningirsu, and his grandson, Pirigme. While the chronological positions of the two other rulers of Lagash, Ur-Gar and Nammahani, are uncertain, it seems most likely that Lagash lost its independence to Ur-Nammu under Nammahani (Steinkeller 1988:52). The code of Ur-Nammu, in which Nammahani was mentioned (and which was almost certainly authored by Shulgi, Ur-Nammu's son; Steinkeller 1988: n. 2), was written in Sumerian, like all other inscriptions of the period. Such texts are called Neo-Sumerian to distinguish them from those of the Early Dynastic age.

Archaeologically, little can be said about the period after the Akkad Dynasty in the north. The major structures, such as the Northern Palace at Tell Asmar-Eshnunna and the shrine and large building at Tell Taya, were destroyed, no doubt by the Guti tribes, on whom the writers of the Third Dynasty heaped invectives.

Of the architecture of Gudea at Girsu, there remains only a small part of a building that was not connected with the rest of the "palace" drawn by de Sarzec, who did not recognize that he had three different building periods, which he combined in one and ascribed to Gudea. The small remains of a beautifully niched wall built of Gudea's bricks with asphalt and clay was marked by Koldewey in his reproduction of the plan of "Telloh" (Koldewey 1925:287, Abb. 242). The account of the excavations at Lagash (al-Hiba) summarizes the limited information available for the architecture of Gudea and the Third Dynasty of Ur (Hansen 1983). However, aspects of the decoration of Gudea's architecture can be pictured from the beautiful poetic account of the construction of the Eninnu of Ningirsu, the major deity of Lagash, which was recorded on the cylinders buried in the foundations of the temple at Girsu.

Gudea mentioned copper and exotic woods, which he obtained from regions that participated in the trade of the Persian Gulf. The same trade probably provided diorite from Magan, and lapis lazuli, carnelian, and gold from Meluhha. From east Syria Gudea received copper, from the Middle Euphrates area he received stones and wooden beams for rafts, and from north Syria he obtained cedars (Falkenstein 1966:46–54).

The magnificent sculptures of Gudea and some of the members of his family, as well as his stelae, convey the high level of art and culture at his court. Whether that court created a fashion in its time or merely continued one common in the Akkad Dynasty cannot be determined on present evidence.

Work on the sequence of the *shakkanakku,* rulers of Mari, by J.-M. Durand (1985), has revealed that the statue of a ruler called Ishtup-ilum by Parrot (1959:2–5, pls. I–III) and Ishdub-El by Durand (1985:156–57) is contemporary with the reign of Gudea, indicating the existence of one or more interdependent sculptural styles within the areas of greater Mesopotamia.

The seal style that appears to have developed at the court of Gudea is very delicately executed and maintains a tripartite scheme of composition in contests of heroes with animals (Porada 1968:142). A tripartite scheme is seen on a late Akkad-style sealing that shows the small figure of a nude bearded hero who grasps the tails of two rampant bulls which flank a tree in a second tripartite motif. The inscription on the seal names Shu-Turul, the last king of the Akkad Dynasty (Frankfort 1955:pl. 65/701). Therefore, the tripartite scheme is an indication of a date in the end of the Akkad period, but it is more commonly seen in the time of Gudea and the Third Dynasty of Ur. A large number of such cylinders in the British Museum come from Ur (Collon 1982:nos. 254–75).

A second, less common theme, often with sharply gouged forms, is derived from the linear style of the north in the Akkad age. Frequently, a standing or enthroned female figure without divine attributes, though probably a goddess, is the principal figure of the scene. Again, several examples in the British Museum come from Ur (Collon 1982:nos. 286, 290–99).

In the pottery, Akkad period types continue with only slight modification into the Ur III period.

The Third Dynasty of Ur

The Third Dynasty of Ur was formed of the following rulers: Ur-Nammu, 2112–2095 B.C.; his son, Shulgi,

2094–2047 B.C.; Shulgi's son, Amar-Suen, who was formerly called Bur-Sin or Amar-Sin and ruled in 2046–2038 B.C.; Amar-Suen's brother, Shu-Sin, who was formerly called Gimil-Sin, and who ruled in 2037–2029 B.C.; and Shu-Sin's son, Ibbi-Sin, 2028–2004 B.C. It was suggested that Ur-Nammu, who had been military governor of Ur for the king of Uruk, Utuhegal, was the latter's son (Sollberger 1954–55:12, n. 8).

Ur-Nammu erected temple towers, called ziggurats, in the major towns of the south: Ur, Nippur, Eridu, and Uruk, which provided the most striking architectural monuments. A new unit in the plan of a site was the sacred precinct surrounding a large open space with a temple or ziggurat in the center (D. Oates, cited in Hansen, Mellink, and Porada 1973:142). At Ur the *giparu,* the official dwelling of the *entu* priestess, was built and rebuilt during the periods with which the present section is concerned. The earliest remains are those of the Early Dynastic period. That building was used until the Ur III period when Ur-Nammu seems to have rebuilt the structure, which, subsequently, Shulgi elaborated and Amar-Suen repaired. The building was destroyed by the Elamites with the rest of Ur in 2004 B.C. and restored by the *entu* priestess, daughter of Ishme-Dagan, king of Isin (1953–1935 B.C.) in the Isin-Larsa period (Weadock 1975:105–8).

Royal apartments at Ur with the niched decoration of the walls, a characteristic of sacred architecture, probably served for a limited religious function, to be performed by the king (Heinrich 1984:43–44).

A provincial palace that contained a temple for the ruling king of the Third Dynasty was excavated at Tell Asmar-Eshnunna (Frankfort, Lloyd, and Jacobsen 1940).

The most common plan for private houses was an arrangement of rooms around a central court, usually within a square or rectangular outer wall. Lateral extensions of such houses to form a block in which the main room would have been flanked by smaller side rooms—Heinrich's *Mittelsaalhaus*—appeared at Nippur in the Scribal Quarter in level VIII (McCown, Haines, and Hansen 1967:pl. 55/B).

In the north, level F at Assur has fragmentary remains of houses with crude stone foundations (Andrae 1922:22 and 95), which may be related to those of Tell Taya. Level E, with an impressive stairway and gate towers at the entrance to the Ishtar Temple, was assigned to the Third Dynasty of Ur on the basis of an inscription of a vassal of king Amar-Suen. This was built into the pavement of a sideroom of the Ishtar Temple of the Middle Assyrian king Tukulti-Ninurta I (1243–1207 B.C.). The sealings found in level E, in an ash layer in the court before the temple, include a variety of styles from Late Akkad to one inscribed for a *shakkanakku* of Mari (Andrae

1922:103, fig. 76/b). The seal probably dates from the time of Sumuabum of Babylon (1894–1881 B.C.) because on the sealing of that ruler two male worshipers appear before a deity (Legrain 1925:pl. XX, no. 326), a motif for which we have no parallels from the time of the Third Dynasty of Ur. The subsequent level D of the Ishtar Temple was thought to be earlier than Shamshi-Adad because its remains were more modest than those ascribed to that king at Assur. However, this evidence is tenuous and the temple of Assur E, together with the related temple of stratum V at Gawra, may have been built after the time of the Third Dynasty of Ur, in the Isin-Larsa period, a period of provincial wealth and expansion in northern Mesopotamia.

Pottery from Ur III to the end of the Old Babylonian period shows a large number of types, which increase and decrease within the period without sharply determined breaks at the beginning or the end. This is amply illustrated by a study of the pottery from Ur III to the end of the Kassite period (Ayoub 1982). Ayoub noted 32 types that can be traced from before Ur III down to the end of the Old Babylonian period, 10 of which continue into Kassite times (Ayoub 1982:35–36); of the 52 he identified as first appearing in the Ur III period, 35 continue into the Old Babylonian period, 17 of which last into Kassite times (ibid., pp. 36–37). Within each type he observes small changes and developments over time, representing a gradual evolution (Ayoub 1982:45–63). A similar situation was found by Woolley at Ur (Woolley 1974:82).

Criteria for a more restricted dating are provided by the cylinder seals of the Ur III period. The most characteristic are those showing a scene of presentation to an enthroned king (Franke 1977). Presentations to an enthroned deity carved in the Ur III period are recognizable by the inscription, the frequent occurrences of goddesses as recipients of worship (Buchanan 1981:214–25, nos. 562–93), and, in the best-made cylinders, the delicate detailed and still naturalistic style of engraving as in the cylinder of Hašḫamer, servant of Ur-Nammu (Collon 1982:pl. LII/469 [here, fig. 4/11]; Wiseman 1959:40). In scenes of conflict between heroes and a lion or a lion griffin, the tripartite composition prevails (Collon 1982:pl. XXXV/246–pl. XXXVI/269; pl. XXXVII, *passim*).

Monumental sculpture of the time of the Third Dynasty of Ur, hitherto limited to the badly battered torso of Shulgi (Orthmann 1975:pl. 63/a, b) and to the foundation figurines of Ur-Nammu and his successors, has been enriched by the statues of two rulers of Mari: Parrot's Idi-Ilum (Parrot 1959:16–22; pls. IX–XI), the Iddin-El of Durand (1985:156–57), who is now known to have been a contemporary of King Shulgi; and Puzur-Eshtar (Parrot 1959:16, fig. 12), who was a contemporary of King

Amar-Suen (2046–2038 B.C.). Both Iddin-El and Puzur-Eshtar had been dated in the Isin-Larsa period by Frankfort (1954:58), who has been followed in this view by most scholars in the field. "The elegance and fineness of the figurine" of Iddin-El and the "broad but sensitive treatment of the bare parts of the body with an extraordinary elaboration of all those details of dress and hair which are capable of ornamental treatment" (Frankfort 1954:58) in the figure of Puzur-Eshtar, must now be ascribed to the Third Dynasty of Ur.

A criterion of Ur III date is a type of clay figurine (Dales 1960:112) that is modeled in one piece with the chair on which it sits. Relations of these chair figurines with those of Assur were pointed out by Dales (1960:215–18). The Diyala figurines assigned stratigraphically to Ur III are pleasingly modeled with large lunate earrings and extended arms (Frankfort, Lloyd, and Jacobsen 1940:221, fig. 109/c [here, fig. 5/27]). The influence of the central administration on the outlying areas of the Ur III empire can be observed in the finds of the period made in the Himrin. Especially the cylinder seals, of which a fair number was found at the site of Sleima (al-Gailani Werr 1982:82–84, nos. 45–50), may have been owned by officials working for the southern administration. It is noteworthy, however, that the majority of the seals show the crude cutting of provincial work, and the seal that has the finest engraving, which could have been made in the south, has the inscription rubbed off to eliminate the name of the original owner.

There is no indication concerning the findspot of these seals. However, copper ceremonial axes were found in graves (Rmaidh 1984:57). One of these, a crescentic, fenestrated ax with opposed animals on the socket, reproduced in a photograph (Rmaidh 1984:49, fig. 8/1 [Arabic section]), had not been found previously in a datable context (Maxwell-Hyslop 1949:119–20, type B3; pl. XXVI/7 [here, fig. 5/28]). These axes had been assigned to the period between the Akkad and Old Babylonian periods (Calmeyer 1969:45 s.v., Abb. 46). It is therefore important to learn the precise context of the axe from Sleima. Another fine axe has a lion-head finial on the lower edge of the socket, facing downward in the direction of the handle. Still another has curving projections above and below the socket (Rmaidh 1984:54, fig. 18/2 [here, fig. 5/29]). This last-mentioned type was assigned by Calmeyer to the Third Dynasty of Ur (Calmeyer 1969:42). Perhaps such axes found in graves had belonged to military officers stationed at Sleima in the Himrin which belonged to the periphery of the Ur III empire.

The Isin-Larsa and Old Babylonian Periods

The centrally administered empire of Ur III was followed by a number of active urban centers, each of which dominated its surrounding area. They had far-flung trade relations with other centers and occasionally attempted to extend boundaries by warfare. The literacy of a relatively large number of "scribes," for which a good equivalent is our word *secretary,* which applies to as high an official as the secretary of the treasury and to the lowliest typists, resulted in a mass of records from which the political, economic, and, in some cases, personal history of the leaders of these centers can be reconstructed.

The kings of the First Dynasty of Isin, whose authority extended over Ur, Eridu, and Uruk, were the successors to the kings of Ur in their tenets of administration and general policies. With the capture of Ur by Gungunum of Larsa, 1932–1906 B.C., Isin lost its preeminence in the south. Although Ur came again briefly under the suzerainty of Isin, Larsa remained the greater power in the south until the advent of Hammurabi of Babylon, who aimed for, and achieved, the domination of all of Babylonia with his victory over Rim-Sin of Larsa in about 1783 and Mari in 1759 B.C..

The period demonstrates the fusion, which Oppenheim saw as part of the Mesopotamian pattern: "a fusion was achieved between the native legacy with its inherent traditionalism and the political drive of the sheikhs experienced in trade, warfare, and plundering, who were open to innovations and experiments but sufficiently awed by the cultural supremacy of the old cities to assume the politically advantageous role of guardians of Mesopotamian traditions" (Oppenheim 1967:32).

Most of the dynasties of Mesopotamia in the Isin-Larsa and Old Babylonian periods had descended from Amorite tribal chiefs, as could be determined, for example, from the names of the predecessors of Sumuabum, 1894–1881 B.C., the first king of the First Dynasty of Babylon (Finkelstein 1966; Lambert 1968).

The archaeological evidence is rather limited for this period of intellectual activity and material wealth, which was brought about by trade and industry. Much of what is known about the layout of a town and its buildings in the Isin-Larsa period is due to the excavations by Woolley and Mallowan (Woolley and Mallowan 1976). An Old Babylonian town with a remarkably regular plan was discovered at the site of Haradum on the Euphrates, south of Mari, and dated between Samsuiluna and Ammiṣaduqa (Joannes 1985; Kepinski and Lecomte 1985). Current excavations at Isin have shown that the site was inhabited in the Akkad period and may go back to Ubaid times (Hrouda 1977). So far, the most important pre-Kassite discoveries in the southern part of the eastern sector of Isin have yielded Old Babylonian houses and a street. One of the houses, in which tablets were prepared and written and scribes were instructed, was either part of a public archive or the office of a scribe who also lived there (Hrouda 1977, 1981:49). In the campaigns of

spring 1983 and autumn 1984, a public building was excavated in the southeast area, which, according to the report by Killick and Black (1985:221), resembles the Southern Building of Tell Asmar, which the excavator ascribed to Ipiq-Adad II (Frankfort 1933:30), whom Hallo dated ca. 1860 (Hallo 1971:99). In the northeast area of Isin a brick-built tomb and private houses, which contained a number of tablets of extraordinary interest from the early second millennium B.C., were found. Northeast of the temple of Gula was a large enclosure wall with some clay cones of Ishme-Dagan which mentioned work on the "Great Wall."

At Larsa, excavations have centered on the sanctuary of the sun god Shamash, the Ebabbar, now thought to have originally been two sanctuaries, the ziggurat and the Ebabbar as such, a temple situated on a tell, today hidden by the Neo-Babylonian constructions and sand dunes (Calvet 1984:20). Hammurabi is thought to have rebuilt these structures into a single great complex, shortly after his conquest of Larsa (Huot 1985b:311–12). In the walls of the large courts I and III, Hammurabi's architects created a magnificent decoration of engaged spiral columns comparable to those of Tell al-Rimah (D. Oates 1967:pl. XXXII–XXXIII) and Leilan (Weiss 1985c:8).

Due to the high water table, excavations at Babylon are prevented from descending much deeper than the level of the Neo-Babylonian period. However, there are numerous inscriptions and texts, which Renger used to give some idea of the building activities of the rulers of the First Dynasty of Babylon (Renger 1979).

At Nippur, private houses of the Isin-Larsa period were smaller and more cheaply built than the earlier ones that had stood in the same places in the time of the Third Dynasty of Ur; however, there had been a marked change of property lines after the fall of the Ur Dynasty. Once the houses of the Isin-Larsa period had been built, there was no radical alteration in the character of the area or in the general level of prosperity (McCown, Haines, and Hansen 1967:145). Chapels for the worship of the family god or the personal god of the householder appear to have been planned for most houses of the period at Nippur (McCown, Haines, and Hansen 1967:146).

The site of Tell ed-Der, close to Sippar, yielded houses like those of Nippur and of other sites of the period (Gasche, in De Meyer 1978:78–85). Other investigations at Tell ed-Der, including Abu Habbah, ancient Sippar, have focused on the dating of various canal systems and flood deposits. The result is that there was a major flood phase in this area during the second millennium B.C. and that the high embankments surrounding Tell ed-Der and Sippar, formerly thought to have been defensive walls, were dikes, originally built in late Old Babylonian times to protect each city from floods (De Meyer 1978:1–35, 1980:37–52).

Returning to the architecture of the period, elaborate temples were still built, though on a smaller scale than in the Ur III period. The most innovative plan appeared to be that of Tell al-Rimah, ancient Karana, north of the approximate border of the Jezireh, a steppe area in northwest Iraq, and south of Tell Afar (D. Oates 1965:66). There a small ziggurat was combined with a temple (D. Oates 1967:pl. XXX, 1968a:pl. XXVIII). The temple had the southern plan with a broad cella and resembles the Ebabbar of Larsa in the way the ziggurat was surrounded by a court (Huot 1983:293, fig. 1). Another link between Tell al-Rimah and Larsa concerns the use in the temple facade of engaged columns built of bricks in such a manner as to suggest spiral torsion of the shaft. At Larsa this feature was dated to the time of Hammurabi (Calvet et al. 1976:24; pl. III/3, 4). At Tell al-Rimah the decoration of the shafts included patterns suggestive of palm trunks, and similarly decorated columns were found at Leilan (Weiss 1985b:289, pl. 1) and at Ur (Woolley 1939:42–45). At Tell al-Rimah the decoration of the columns was not used in the royal palace, a necessary ceremonial structure in this period reflecting the great representational and administrative needs of the rulers of the period. This is most evident in the palace of Mari, famous already in its own time (Kupper 1973:13), and also that of Sinkashid at Uruk (Lenzen, in *UVB* 19:pl. 49; Heinrich 1984:63–66).

The importance of the palace at Karana, aside from its architectural interest, lies in its yield of tablets of which the earliest were dated to the first part of the reign of Shamshi-Adad (Dalley, Hawkins, and Walker 1976:202) and the principal archive, that of Iltani, wife of the ruler of Karana, dated in and shortly after the last years of Hammurabi of Babylon, 1792–1750 B.C. (Dalley, Hawkins, and Walker 1976:32). The archive contains letters from Zimrilim of Mari and mentions Ibalpiel of Eshnunna among the rulers involved in the complicated political situation after the death of Shamshi-Adad.

Under the influence of Shamshi-Adad, the dating at Tell Rimah, as at Mari, was by *limu* or year eponyms. These officials and their dates have been most recently discussed by Veenhof (1985), who suggested several revised dates for the events at Mari and a date of 1760 for the latest group of texts of Tell al-Rimah.

Changes have also occurred in the dates for Zimrilim at Mari, whose reign was probably much shorter than the thirty-five years assigned to him previously (Charpin and Durand 1985:337).

At all the sites mentioned, a great deal of pottery was discovered. One type characteristic of central and southern Mesopotamia during the Isin-Larsa period has simple linear designs in black on a background of the natural clay color, crosshatchings, diagonals, mostly between

broad, horizontal bands, are a characteristic decoration of small bottles, bowls and storage vessels. Ayoub illustrates numerous examples under his types 25 and 63 (Ayoub 1982:95, 112–13 [here, fig. 5/30, 31]).

In the north the so-called Khabur ware was widely distributed. It is characterized by rounded forms (here, fig. 5/32), especially jars with narrow or wide necks and high bowls with strongly marked rims. The color is buff and the decoration consists of simple bands or zones of simple designs, such as linear triangles, crosshatched triangles, or other plain geometric forms. The distribution and chronology of this pottery were the subject of several studies; the most extensive is Hamlin's (1974; but for a recent discussion, see Stein 1984).

Toward the end of the Larsa rule, small vessels of grayware with incised, pricked, and impressed decoration and remains of white incrustation and red paint were found at several sites (here, fig. 5/33), especially at Telloh, Tell Asmar, and Susa. These were set by Börker-Klähn between the time of Urningizida and Ibiq-Adad II of Eshnunna, or about 1840–1770 B.C. (Börker-Klähn 1970).

Most characteristic among the remains of the Isin-Larsa period are the terra-cotta plaques with figures in relief (here, fig. 5/34), which provide some insight into the popular iconography of the period (Moorey 1975:79). They are generally found in private houses. Since the appearance of the books by Opificius (1961) and Barrelet (1968), groups from several sites have been published: Nippur (McCown, Haines, and Hansen 1967:pls. 125ff.), Larsa (Calvet et al. 1976:20–21, pl. IV/1–5), Der (De Meyer, Gasche, and Paepe 1971:pls. 27–29, *passim;* De Meyer 1978:pls. 26–28, 1984:pl. 11/6–7, pl. 12/11–13, pl. 13/1–2, 10–12, pl. 16/3, pl. 17/4, pl. 21/11), Kish (Moorey 1975:79–99), and Isin (Hrouda 1977:47–51, pls. 23–24).

The cylinder seals of the officials at the courts of the Isin and Larsa periods continued the delicate, carefully modeled seal style of Ur III with the favored motif of an enthroned figure which may represent a king or a deity. From about the time of Abishare of Larsa (1905–1895 B.C.) onward, figures of deities, largely derived from Akkadian prototypes, appear in multifigured scenes on the seals (al-Gailani Werr 1980). A most refined style prevailed at Sippar; other local styles existed which are still to be fully defined (al-Gailani Werr 1988). Some simplification of the elaborate style began in the time of Hammurabi and continued in that of Samsuiluna. The use of a mechanical drill increased until the end of the First Dynasty of Babylon. A thorough study of the 656 Old Babylonian cylinder seals in the British Museum (Collon 1986) shows that there was a somewhat impoverished linear style with a tendency to show minor rather than major gods. The type of cylinder was surely cheaper and more easily available than the better products. It appeared in seal impressions from the time of Hammurabi (Figulla 1967:pl. 25).

A predominantly linear, angular style that used many Babylonian figures, called Late Old Assyrian, was found to the north of Babylonia, at Assur (Moortgat 1940:pl. 61/505, 516) and to the northwest at Kültepe-Kanish in level Ib, dated from the time of Shamshi-Adad (1809–1776 B.C.) to that of Samsuiluna (1749–1712 B.C.) (Özgüç 1968:pl. XV/B; pl. XVII/A; pl. XIX/A). Characteristics of the style are frequent use of hatching by thin short lines, especially on the brim of the hats of the worshipers; garments with shoulder straps, which converge at the waist, and are worn by gods and worshipers; and stress on the eye by a diminutive, usually horizontal line.

Several of the Himrin sites had their best period in the time of the Isin-Larsa dynasties, though the area was under the rule of the kings of Eshnunna who held the key to the major land routes connecting Sumer, Akkad, and Elam with the north. This advantage was to pass to Hammurabi after his conquest of the region (Postgate 1979).

Tell Sleima is said to have continued in this period, Tell Yelki to have had a prominent building of the Isin-Larsa period, and Tell Genj, carefully described and well illustrated (Wilson Briggs, Heim, and Meighan 1984), also seems to have belonged mainly to that period. The most interesting find at Tell Genj is the impression of a cylindrical object, ca. 6 cm high on a potsherd (here, fig. 4/12). Hitherto, the practice of decorating pots with cylindrical objects had been known in Syria, but not in Mesopotamia.

The superior craftsmanship that existed in the major centers of the early second millennium B.C. in Mesopotamia and elsewhere in the Near East is exemplified by the treasure discovered at Larsa in a room of the Ebabbar temple of Shamash (Huot et al. 1978). Contained in a jar was the raw material, the finished products, and the weights and tools of a goldsmith. The tools consisted of a pair of tweezers, a little anvil, and a lode stone (Arnaud, Calvet, and Huot 1979:7, figs. 8–9, 12). In another, related deposit was a cylinder seal that bore the name Ilshu-ibnishu, taken to be that of the goldsmith, and a tablet providing a date in the time of Samsuiluna (Arnaud, Calvet, and Huot 1979:51–53).

The treasure doubtless belonged to the temple, not to a wealthy individual. A tendency to curtail the activities of the rich Babylonian merchants had already made itself felt in the time of Rimsin of Larsa (Leemans 1950:113–19), and continued under the Babylonian rulers so that "no more great and wealthy businessmen are found during the reigns of Hammurabi and his successors" (Leemans 1950:121). Together with the impoverishment of the south caused by salinization of the soil (Jacobsen 1957:139), this policy of the rulers had probably strangled the importation of luxury goods by a relatively large number of persons, and, as a result, Babylonian influence abroad had ceased long before the destructive raid of Murshilish of Hatti and before the resulting conflagration sealed the Old Babylonian level of the capital about 1595 B.C. (Koldewey 1925:234).

Postscript

The writing and subsequent updating of this section of *Chronologies* extended from 1975 to the end of the academic year 1985/6. After the delivery of the manuscript to the editor, no more additions and changes were made. The present version of this section is therefore already out of date in view of the rapid changes in the chronological estimations of the prehistory and early history of Mesopotamia, caused in part by the new insights acquired as a result of the rescue excavations in the reservoir areas such as the Hamrin or the Saddam Dam Basin.

Readers are therefore urgently advised to add to the information contained in this section of COWA, summaries of current work such as those provided in *Iraq* XLIX (1987):231–251 to XLIX (1989), in press.

Publications of major significance for the prehistoric periods are *Chronologies du Proche Orient; Chronologies in the Near East: Relative chronologies and absolute chronology 16,000–4,000 B.P.* C.N.R.S. International Symposium, Lyon (France) BAR International Series 379 (1987). Especially J. Oates, "Ubaid Chronology," 473–82, with a chart on p. 479, also *Colloques internationaux, Préhistoire de la Mésopotamie,* CNRS, Paris, 1986; J. Oates, "The Choga Mami Transitional": 163–80, and "Le Choga Mami Transitional et l'Obeid 1," 199–206.

For publications concerning the Early Dynastic and later periods: H. P. Martin, *Fara: A Reconstruction of the Ancient City of Shuruppak,* Birmingham, UK, 1988. E. Porada, "Review of Martin, 'Fara' and N. Karg, 'Untersuchungen zur älteren frühdynastischen Glyptik Babyloniens.'" in *American Journal of Archaeology* 94 (forthcoming 1990). D. and J. Oates, "Brak in the Third Millennium B.C.: The Akkadian Empire" *Archéologia* (in press).

Six

The Chronology of Iran, ca. 8000–2000 B.C.

Mary M. Voigt
Robert H. Dyson, Jr., University Museum, University of Pennsylvania

Outline

In the 1965 edition of *Chronologies* the chapter on Iran was dependent on a small number of excavations, most of them carried out before 1950 (Dyson 1965). Although many of these were well done for their day, they cannot compare in terms of stratigraphic control and efficiency of recovery to standards established since then. Some parts of Iran were completely unstudied or only partially explored by archaeologists. A chronology for the prehistoric periods in Iran was, therefore, necessarily based for the most part on comparisons with better-known Mesopotamia. Since then, twenty-five years of intensive excavation supplemented by surface surveys and radiocarbon dates have produced reliable regional sequences. Thus it is now possible to construct a chronology of Iran based primarily on internal evidence. This chapter focuses on information acquired since 1950 and does not repeat the material discussed by Dyson in 1965.

Unlike Mesopotamia with its open plains and great river valleys, Iran is a complex geographical area broken up into deserts, mountain valleys, and coastal plains. This diversity of environment led to multiple cultural adaptations in prehistoric times, making cultural generalizations difficult. For this reason, archaeologists working in the area have concentrated on the development of strat-

Text submitted February–March 1986
Final revisions May 1986

ified regional sequences before undertaking studies of major time periods as such. In constructing a general chronology for prehistoric Iran we have focused on the regional sequences, linking them through the traditional archaeological method of artifact comparisons.

Broadly speaking, Iran is shaed like a saucer, with two great central deserts encircled by mountains that are in turn bordered by lowland plains such as Khuzistan, Sistan, and Gurgan. During most periods, these lowlands, as well as mountainous border regions such as Azerbaijan and Kurdistan, were in contact with the geographically adjacent areas: Turkmenistan, Afghanistan, Pakistan, Mesopotamia, Anatolia, and the Caucasus. We have, therefore, outlined the relationship between our regions and adjacent sequences reported in this volume.

We emphasize that the length of the discussion of a specific site or phase is not directly proportionate to its

While writing this chapter we received help from the following scholars who provided comments on earlier drafts and/or unpublished data: Genevieve Dollfus, Elizabeth Henrickson, Robert Henrickson, Frank Hole, C. C. Lamberg-Karlovsky, Louis D. Levine, Richard Meadow, Ezat Negahban, Edith Porada, Martha Prickett, Philip E. L. Smith, William Sumner, Henry Wright, T. Cuyler Young, Jr., and Allen Zagarell. We thank them for their generosity. A special debt is owed to Robert Ehrich, whose patience and editorial suggestions helped us produce a clearer and more economical synthesis.

importance. Some of the most significant sites and chronological units are only briefly discussed due to high-quality description and documentation in readily available publications. Poorly known assemblages on the other hand frequently require extended discussion in order to evaluate ambiguities or conflicting evidence.

This chapter has a strong focus on ceramics, which is a result of three factors. First, after ca. 6500 B.C., pottery is well represented in the archaeological record, and has been described and illustrated even in very brief preliminary reports. Second, ceramic industries generally change more rapidly than other artifact categories. Third, we have in many cases firsthand knowledge of the ceramics derived from the study of the extensive pottery collections from Iran in the University Museum; the generosity of colleagues who showed us unpublished materials in museum collections or in Iran during visits to sites or surveys in progress; and our own research.

Once our relative sequence was completed, we used radiocarbon evidence to establish fixed points in time, providing information on the span of specific chronological units as well as on the rate of change within sequences. This was done by averaging fifteen sets of tightly clustered determinations, spread through eight geographic regions (table 1). With rare exceptions discussed in the text, the grid derived from the averaged samples was compatible with that derived from artifact comparisons.

Table 2 contains a list of all radiocarbon samples from Iranian sites known to us. This list does not exclude determinations "rejected by the excavator," since new data have sometimes resulted in the rehabilitation of dates rejected at an earlier stage of study. We have not attempted to evaluate individual dates. To do so would usually require extensive discussion, often of stratigraphic information that is not yet published in final form.

In describing the stratigraphically-based regional sequences we have chosen to proceed along two major traverses from west to east (fig. 1). The first traverse begins in Khuzistan and moves across the southern half of Iran to its eastern border. The second begins in the central Zagros and proceeds along the northern edge of the great central deserts. The northwestern corner of the country, Azerbaijan, stands alone, often as part of a cultural zone that extends beyond Iran to the north or west. To avoid redundancies, the artifact parallels cited for each regional sequence are usually limited to those that link it to the previously described adjacent region. Thus a reader interested only in one specific regional sequence must also consult the sections on adjacent geographical zones to obtain full documentation of interregional relationships and their chronological implications. A summary of the relationship of regional sequences is presented in figure 2.

Southwestern Lowlands (Khuzistan)

Deh Luran

The Deh Luran Plain Sequence

Deh Luran in the northwest corner of Khuzistan lies on a traditional route between Mesopotamia and the Susiana Plain. The sequence is based on excavations at Tepes Ali Kosh and Sabz by Frank Hole, Kent Flannery, and James Neely (1969; Hole 1977); at Chagha Sefid by Frank Hole (1977); and at Farukhabad by Henry Wright (1981); supplemented by surface survey (Neely 1969; Hole 1987a:figs. 7–8). The first eleven phases (Bus Mordeh to Farukh) are named locally while the remaining periods use Mesopotamian terminology (Uruk to Early Dynastic I/II), and conclude with the Elamite/Shimashki phase defined at Susa (Wright 1981:10, table 2). A unique assemblage known from surface survey, Sargarab, is placed between the Farukh and Early Uruk phases (Wright 1981:168).

A. *The Bus Mordeh phase* represents the earliest settlement in the area and is defined at Tepe Ali Kosh (Hole, Flannery, and Neely 1969:34–40, fig. 9). In assessing its chronological position, the excavators cite general resemblances to highland sites such as Zawi Chemi and Karim Shahir in Iraq and Ganj Dareh and Asiab in Iran (Hole, Flannery, and Neely 1969:333, 345). In a detailed analysis of aceramic Neolithic sites in Mesopotamia and Iran, Howe (1983:120) states that the Bus Mordeh chipped stone industry does indeed resemble that of Karim Shahir "quite closely in typology and morphology as well as in technological caliber." Unfortunately, this does not establish a precise relative date for the Bus Mordeh phase, since such tools were used over a long time span. Considering all of the archaeological evidence, including architecture and floral and faunal remains as well as artifacts, Howe dates the Bus Mordeh phase as "well subsequent to the horizons of Karim Shahir and similar sites and closer to the time and cultural phase of Jarmo" (1983:122). Given the parallels linking the succeeding Ali Kosh phase to lower Jarmo, we would place Bus Mordeh between the Karim Shahir/Zawi Chemi/Asiab/Ganj Dareh E horizon as established by Howe (1983: 111–32), and earliest Jarmo.

B. *The Ali Kosh phase* was defined at Ali Kosh, and also appears at Chagha Sefid (Hole, Flannery, and Neely 1969:40–45, fig. 10; Hole 1977:47–50, figs. 5–8). The chipped stone industry is very similar to that of the preceding phase. Potentially useful for chronology is a single "reamer" of unspecified material (Hole, Flannery, and Neely 1969:fig. 251) which is morphologically similar to steeply retouched obsidian tools found at aceramic Neolithic sites from the Zagros to the Euphrates. These include lower Jarmo (Hole 1983a:241, n. 5 [by L. Braidwood], fig. 122:11, 13–21, table 22); Magzaliya (Bader 1979:pl. 6:3–7, 10); Çayönü (Redman 1982:42–44, figs. 2.14:1–2, 2.15:1–3, pl. 2.II:15–18); Cafer (Cauvin and Aurenche 1982:fig. 10:1, 3–4, 6–7); and Gritille (Voigt 1985:fig. 17s). However, even if the Ali Kosh tool is also of obsidian and has the requisite longitudinal striations, it does not necessarily indicate an early date. This same type also occurs at later, ceramic sites in the Zagros: at Shimshara, where it is most common in levels 12–10 (Mortensen 1970:43, figs. 24d, 25f–h, 29a, e–f, 30–31, 36–37); in upper/ceramic Jarmo (Hole 1983a:table 22); and at Hajji Firuz (Voigt 1983: 236–37, pl. 33, fig. 111n–o).

Better evidence for the contemporaneity of Ali Kosh with the earlier aceramic settlements is provided by the stratigraphic distribution of stone bowls. Vessels with a flat base, flaring sides, and beaded rim are the most popular form in the earliest levels at Jarmo, continuing in much reduced numbers to the end of the sequence (type A; Adams 1983:210, 212–13, fig. 101:1–3, chart 2). In Deh Luran, their initial appearance and greatest popularity is in the Ali Kosh phase, but a substantial number were also found in Mohammad Jaffar contexts (Hole, Flannery, and Neely 1969:107, fig. 42a–k, table 10; two Sabz examples are presumably out of context). Also supporting this dating is the presence of two sherds identified as *vaisselle blanche* in Ali Kosh deposits at Chagha Sefid (Hole 1977:145–47, fig. 55j–k). This distinctive material is characteristic of PPNB and PPNB-related sites in the Levant and Turkey (Mellaart 1975:62; Hours and Copeland 1983). Ties between the Ali Kosh phase and Zagros sites other than Jarmo cannot be established until sites such as Tepe Guran, Ganj Dareh, and Abdul Hosein have been published.

To summarize, the Ali Kosh phase is apparently contemporary with aceramic Neolithic sites in the northern Mesopotamian steppe, and therefore predates the early Hassuna occupation in the latter area at least in part. However, the duration of this phase is not known. Given the evidence for a correlation of the succeeding Mohammad Jaffar phase with early Samarra in Mesopotamia and later Zagros Neolithic sites (see "Central Western Iran"), late Ali Kosh settlements may have been contemporary with the earliest ceramic settlements in these regions. If so, Ali Kosh would be analogous to Shimshara, where an aceramic assemblage apparently coexisted with Early Hassuna settlements in the adjoining lowlands.

C. *The Mohammad Jaffar phase* is defined at Ali Kosh and is also known from Chagha Sefid (Hole 1977:82–86). The excavator considers the material from Chagha Sefid to be somewhat later than that from Tepe Ali Kosh (Hole 1977:31). Chaff-tempered buff pottery sometimes painted in fugitive red (Hole, Flannery, and Neely 1969:114–20, figs. 43–44; Hole 1977:101–3, fig. 37)

appears in quantity for the first time. Based on the published material from Khuzistan, only one motif links Mohammad Jaffar with Chogha Mish Archaic 1 (Hole, Flannery, and Neely 1969:fig. 44f; Kantor 1974:fig. 5:"Painted Burnished Ware" 3264). The fabric and vessel forms of Mohammad Jaffar pottery are generally compared with those of ceramic industries found at Zagros sites such as Jarmo, Sarab, and Guran (e.g., Hole, Flannery, and Neely 1969:115–17). Change within the Zagros sequence, however, is most evident in painted design, as well as in a few diagnostic forms (see "Central Western Iran"). The best parallels for Mohammad Jaffar Painted Ware occur in late Zagros Neolithic industries: the Guran Standard Painted Ware of levels J–D at Tepe Guran (Hole 1977:fig. 37a, v; Mortensen 1963:fig. 17g), and the linear style found in Late Sarab and upper Jarmo (see "Mahidasht Sequence"). The Mohammad Jaffar painted style also has parallels with chaff-tempered pottery from Qal'eh Rostam I in the Bakhtiari Mountains (Hole, Flannery, and Neely 1969:fig. 44a–c, f–g; Hole 1977:fig. 37c, e, aa; Nissen and Zagarell 1976:figs. 3:11, 13, 4:10); however the necked jars and elaborate designs of Qaleh Rostam I suggest a later date (see also McDonald 1979:530).

Within the chipped stone industry, geometric microliths, trapezes, and triangles appear first in the Mohammad Jaffar phase in Deh Luran (Hole 1977:fig. 56a–c, tables 37, 42); at Jarmo, four trapezes were found in Op. I:7–8 or lower Jarmo. They are apparently absent in the middle of the sequence and then reappear in large numbers in Op. II or upper Jarmo, with the greatest number in the latest levels (Hole 1983a:237–38, table 22, fig. 112:1–18). More important, however, is a highly distinctive stone artifact called a "phallus" (Hole, Flannery, and Neely 1969:203, pl. 38a, fig. 87a) which connects Mohammad Jaffar A_2 with two Mesopotamian assemblages: level I at Tell es-Sawwan, and latest Jarmo (Wailly and Soof 1965:22, fig. 66, center; Moholy-Nagy 1983:figs. 137:5, 142:32). This unique type supports the ceramic and chipped stone parallels with upper Jarmo and also establishes a link with early Samarra.

To summarize, Mohammad Jaffar is weakly linked to Late Neolithic sites in the Zagros and Samarran sites in Mesopotamia. The succeeding Sefid phase is more strongly linked to the same sites and periods, but in some cases to slightly later levels within the sites (see below). We would therefore place Mohammad Jaffar contemporary with the end of the Zagros Standard Painted Ware tradition and the beginning of the Linear Painted tradition as seen at late Guran, Sarab and Jarmo, and with early Samarra.

D. *The Sefid phase* is defined at Chagha Sefid (Hole 1977:50–59, figs. 9–14). Continuity between Mohammad Jaffar and Sefid, as well as between Sefid and Surkh, is evident in small artifacts such as domed or cuff link–shaped labrets (Hole 1977:table 76) and T-shaped figurines (Hole 1977:table 67).

Ceramic comparisons indicate that Sefid Painted Ware is part of a widespread ceramic horizon, with linkages to the Late Sarab, Archaic Zagheh, and Hajji Firuz periods (Hole 1977:fig. 43; Malek Shahmirzadi 1977b:pls. XI:20–27, XII:levels IX–X). A trade sherd of classic Samarra type from a Sefid context (Hole 1977:138, fig. 51g) establishes a relationship with the Mesopotamian sequence and reinforces the link with Zagros "linear-painted" sites, since rare Samarran sherds also occur in late Hajji Firuz contexts (Voigt 1983:101–2). Two other types have a limited chronological distribution at Chagha Sefid. T-shaped figurines, which initially occur in the Ali Kosh phase, appear in large quantities in the Sefid phase (Hole 1977:229–32, tables 67, 72, fig. 91g–n); in upper Jarmo, where they were called "double-wing-based objects" (Morales 1983:385–86, figs. 164:8–10, 165:2, 4–5, 8–11, 166:5–7); and in the West Mound at Sang-i Chakhmaq in northeastern Iran (Masuda 1974a:fig. 3:10, 12). Nail-shaped objects or "mullers" of stone and clay (Hole 1977:234, fig. 87e–h; table 75, pl. 54b–c) also occur in Mushki period deposits in Fars, associated with small stone and clay "mortars" (Fukai, Horiuchi, and Matsutani 1973:pls. XXXIX:2, LIV:1–24, LV:9–11). Both nails and mortars with a pronounced flange on the base are found across the Iranian Plateau to Central Asia. Sites include Sialk I (Ghirshman 1938:pl. LII:26–31, 37–39, fig. 2), the East Mound at Sang-i Chakhmaq (Masuda 1974a:fig. 4:15, 16), and Djeitun (Masson 1971:pls. XL:1–5, 15, XLI:5–6, 16–17).

Labrets with a domed upper surface are most popular in the Sefid and succeeding Surkh phases, but extend from the Mohammad Jaffar into the Choga Mami Transitional phase (Hole 1977:236, table 76, pl. 54n–r, t–bb, fig. 92o, q–t). Reflecting this wide time span is their occurrence at Tepe Guran (Mortensen 1963:fig. 20c) and Choga Mami (Oates 1969:pl. XXX:b, middle row). Although not reported from sites on the Iranian plateau, they are also found at Djeitun in Turkmenistan (Masson 1971:pls. XXXVII:10, XXXVIII:13).

E. *The Surkh phase* is defined at Chagha Sefid (Hole 1977:59–75, figs. 15–26). The definition of this phase is based on ceramics, specifically on changes in frequencies rather than the occurrence of new types (Hole 1977:34, 107, tables 9–10). The artifacts and architecture of this assemblage are basically continuations from the Sefid phase, and similar parallels apply (Hole 1977:33–34 and above). Within Khuzistan, the Surkh phase is apparently contemporary with Chogha Mish Archaic 1 (see "Eastern Susiana Sequence"). One common Surkh type, the Black-on-Red Ware hemispherical bowl with incurved rim, occurs in Hulailan during the Red Burnished Ware

phase and in the Mahidasht during the Late Sarab phase (Hole 1977:125, figs. 41b, 48c–h; Mortensen 1963:fig. 16i; McDonald 1979:fig. 14y). Given the predominance of Khazineh Red Ware in Surkh contexts, a relationship with Latest Guran and/or slightly later sites in the Hulailan Valley such as Sar Arsiaban seems likely (Mortensen 1974b:26, 41). The presence of Sialk Black-on-Red Ware in late Surkh deposits links this portion of the phase to Sialk I$^{3-4}$ (see "Qazvin/Kashan Sequence").

F. *The Chogha Mami Transitional (CMT) phase* is defined at Chagha Sefid (Hole 1977:75–79, figs. 26–29). The pottery begins the hard-fired, grit-tempered buff ware tradition characteristic of later Susiana. It compares closely in technology, shape, and painted designs with that from the type site, Chogha Mami in Mesopotamia (Hole 1977:pls. 34–44, figs. 50, 51a–b, d; Oates 1968:pl. IV; 1969:pls. XXXI:b, XXXII:2–8, 10–12). Within Khuzistan, CMT Ware is also found at Chogha Mish in Archaic 3 as "Close-line Ware" (Kantor 1974:fig. 4) and in Jaffarabad 6 (Dollfus 1983:table 42). Its chronological relationship to the northern and central Mesopotamian sequence is established at Chogha Mami, where it is stratified above Samarran deposits. In the south, the CMT phase is often correlated with Ubaid 1/2 (Porada et al., this vol., chap. 5; Oates 1969:138). However, a limited deep sounding at Tell el-Ouilli near Larsa produced sherds within the range of the CMT industries from Iran, stratified below pottery comparable to that from the lowest level at Eridu (Calvet 1983:pls. I–VII; Safar, Mustafa, and Lloyd 1981:fig. 100).

Ties to the Iranian plateau are provided by imported vessels of Sialk I Black-on-Red Ware (Hole 1977:134–38, figs. 52–53, tables 9–10). Pottery of this type first appears in the Deh Luran sequence during late Surkh and amounts to 4 percent of the sherd sample in the CMT phase (Hole 1977:134–38, figs. 52–53, tables 9–10). Sherds like those at Chagha Sefid were collected from the North Mound at Sialk by Hole (1977:135), and a few are published in the Sialk report. Although Hole assigns the Deh Luran sherds to Sialk I$_2$, the earliest stylistic parallels documented in the site report are with Sialk I$_{3-4}$ (compare Hole 1977:figs. 52a, 52e, 53f with Ghirshman 1938:pls. XLIV:A:2, XLI:A:11). The designs on thin-walled sherds with fine-line motifs (e.g., Hole 1977:figs. 52d, h, k, 53b, e, g) are comparable to Cheshmeh Ali/Sialk II Ware in the collection of the University Museum (Hole 1977:figs. 52d, h, k, 53g; R. H. Dyson, unpublished notes). Confirmation of the technological as well as stylistic identity of the Chagha Sefid and Cheshmeh Ali sherds has been provided by Dollfus (pers. comm. 1985). Other artifact types that occur in Sialk I$_{3-4}$ and in late Surkh and CMT, as well as in later deposits, are spindle whorls with an ovoid section and short linear incisions around the outer edge (Ghirshman 1938:pl.

LII:19; Hole 1977:217, fig. 87a), and chipped stone hoes with pear-shaped or subrectangular outlines (Ghirshman 1938:pl. LVI:2, 4; Hole 1977:209, pl. 49f–g, j).

The following phases are represented by small artifact samples, and are more completely documented at sites in the Susiana Plain (see below).

G. *The Sabz phase* is defined at Tepe Sabz (Hole, Flannery, and Neely 1969:55–57, figs. 15–16) and also appeared in a very limited test at Chagha Sefid (Hole 1977:79–82, figs. 30–32). Although the ceramic styles are quite distinct, the Sabz phase has been compared to Jaffarabad 6–4, Jowi 17, and Chogha Mish Early Susiana by Dollfus (1983:165, table 42). At present, we have no convincing parallels between Sabz and Ubaid 1 at Eridu (Porada et al., this vol., chap. 5; Oates 1983). Links with the Iranian plateau are also rare, although wide bangles with grooves morphologically similar to those from Tepe Sabz do occur in Sialk I_{4-5} (Ghirshman 1938:pl. LII:15, 22).

H. *The Khazineh phase* is defined at Tepe Sabz (Hole, Flannery, and Neely 1969:57–58, figs. 15–16). It is closely related to Jowi 16–13 and Chogha Mish Middle Susiana 1 in Susiana (Dollfus 1983:165, table 42). Black-on-Buff vessels of this phase are also clearly similar in form and design to pottery from (1) Eridu levels XVI–XV (Hole, Flannery, and Neely 1969:fig. 56d–e; Safar et al. 1981:figs. 90:3, 5, 92:2, 90:5; Hole, Flannery, and Neely 1969:fig. 54c, d–f; Safar et al. 1981:fig. 91:18, 28; Hole, Flannery, and Neely 1969:fig. 56b, d; Safar et al. 1981:figs. 90:20, 91:7, 9, 96:11; Hole, Flannery, and Neely 1969:fig. 57c, f; Safar et al. 1981:figs. 90:24, 91:6); (2) Ras al'Amiya (Hole, Flannery, and Neely 1969:fig. 61a–b; Stronach 1961:pl. XLVII:5; Hole, Flannery, and Neely 1969:fig. 52b; Stronach 1961:pl. XLIV:5; Hole, Flannery, and Neely 1969:figs. 54g, 55b; Stronach 1961:pl. XLIV:3–4; Hole, Flannery, and Neely 1969:figs. 56b, d, 57f; Stronach 1961:pls. XLVIII–XLIX); and (3) Hajji Mohammad (Hole, Flannery, and Neely 1969:fig. 56; Ziegler 1953:pl. 11, 14). Parallels with Halaf pottery from Banahilk and Gawra (Hole, Flannery, and Neely 1969:141, 144) are very general, limited to simple shapes and motifs used over long time spans; examples of the latter are central rosettes or wheels, hatching between opposed scalloped lines and bands of solid diamonds (Hole, Flannery, and Neely 1969:figs. 54g–h, 56b; Tobler 1950:pls. CXI:15; CXIV:38; Watson 1983b:fig. 199:2, 8).

I. *The Mehmeh phase* is defined at Tepe Sabz and also documented in a small test at Musiyan "E" (Hole, Flannery, and Neely 1969:58–61, 65–72, fig. 17). Within Khuzistan, Mehmeh is most closely related stylistically to the Transitional phase at Jowi, levels 12–11, and to Bendebal 28–27; imported Mehmeh Red-on-Red sherds have also been found in Jowi 12 (Dollfus 1983:166, fig.

26:15, table 42). Strong ties with Mesopotamia are also evident. Large carinated bowls with painted interiors of the type generally associated with Hajji Mohammad Ware continue to be abundant in the early part of the Mehmeh phase (Hole, Flannery, and Neely 1969:144). Ledge-rim jars link Mehmeh with Eridu XIII–IX (Safar, Mustafa, and Lloyd 1981:154–56, figs. 84–89). Parallels to Gawra XX–XVI dated to Ubaid 3 include not only forms such as ledge-rim jars, but also painted style (Hole, Flannery, and Neely 1969:fig. 58; Tobler 1950:pl. CXXII). However, the greatest number of comparisons are with Ras al'Amiya. In addition to large carinated "Type 14" painted bowls, which continue from the Khazineh phase, and ledge-rim jars (Stronach 1961:pl. LIV:1–3), both assemblages contain large open bowls with scallops painted on the interior, at the rim (Hole, Flannery, and Neely 1969:fig. 60a–g; Stronach 1961:pl. LI:9). Imports from Deh Luran have also appeared in central Mesopotamian sites. Sherds tentatively identified as Mehmeh Red-on-Red Ware were found in small quantities at Ras al'Amiya (Hole, Flannery, and Neely 1969:159; Stronach 1961:107, 121–22, pls. XLVI:8, LI:7; Porada et al., this vol., chap. 5), and a spouted holemouth jar of Mehmeh Red-on-Red Ware was found at Choga Mami in a "Late Ubaid" well (Oates 1969:128, 139). Bent clay nails, common in Mehmeh deposits (Hole, Flannery, and Neely 1969:210, fig. 91a, table 42), are considered diagnostic of Ubaid 3 (e.g., Stronach 1961:107; Oates 1969:139; Safar, Mustafa, and Lloyd 1981:fig. 72; Tobler 1950:169, pl. LXXXIII:f–g). Although the excavators of Tepe Sabz stress ties with plateau settlements such as Sialk III, Hissar IA, and Giyan, based on the occurrence of animal and human motifs (Hole, Flannery, and Neely 1969:362), such motifs occur over a long time span in Khuzistan.

J. *The Bayat phase* is documented at Tepe Sabz and Farukhabad, with the Farukhabad material slightly later (Hole, Flannery, and Neely 1969:61–64, figs. 18–19; Wright 1981:58–59). The Bayat assemblage is very similar to Jaffarabad 3m–n, Jowi 10–5/4, Bendebal 26–13 and Chogha Mish Middle Susiana 3, and is equivalent to Le Breton's Susiana c (Dollfus 1983:166, tables 41–42; Wright 1981:59). Thin-walled bell-shaped bowls from the Bayat phase are paralleled in Eridu IX–VIII (Hole, Flannery, and Neely 1969:fig. 62e, k, m; Safar, Mustafa, and Lloyd 1981:fig. 84:6, 7, 10; H. Wright, pers. comm. 1986). There are also numerous parallels between early Bayat and Gawra XVIII–XVII (Hole, Flannery, and Neely 1969:figs. 58f–g, q, 61k–l, 62e; Tobler 1950: pls. LXXII:a–c, CXXII:104, CXX:88, CXXI:95, LXXIV:b1–2; see also Wright 1981:68–69). Thus Bayat, like the preceding Mehmeh phase, is related to Ubaid 3 settlements in Mesopotamia (see also Dollfus 1983:166; Wright 1981:68–69).

K. *The Farukh phase* is defined at Farukhabad by Excavation A:layers 31–23 and Excavation B:layers 47–37 (Wright 1981:12–22, figs. 4–9). Surface remains indicate that at this time the major center in Deh Luran was at Musiyan (Wright 1981:66). According to Dollfus, the only excavated assemblage in Susiana comparable stylistically with Farukh comes from Bendebal levels 12–11 and Qabr Sheykheyn 3–2, or Susiana d (Dollfus 1983:166–67, tables 41–42; Wright 1981:59). Individual pottery types, however, have a longer time span, with conical goblets occurring at Bendebal as early as level 21 (Dollfus 1983:figs. 58:5, 66:1, 83:2), and design parallels with the Farukh phase occurring from Bendebal 16 on (compare Wright 1981:fig. 24a with Dollfus 1983:fig. 77:8–9; Wright 1981:fig. 17b with Dollfus 1983:fig. 83:8). Two sherds of impressed pottery classified as Khazineh Red Ware were found in the earliest Farukh level (Wright 1981:fig. 10d–e). They appear to be examples of Dalma Impressed Ware, contemporary with Ubaid 3 or perhaps early 4 (E. Henrickson 1983:196, fig. 50; see "Mahidasht" and "Godin").

The excavator divides this phase into Early, Middle and Late subphases, based on changes in the frequencies of ceramic attributes (Wright 1981:57–58, tables 8–10). Although the sample is small, these subphases do have chronological significance in relating the Deh Luran and Southwestern Zagros sequences (q.v.).

L. *The Post-Farukh phase* is represented by surface remains that fall into two groups: (1) Tepe Musiyan and one or two other sites that produced Black-on-Buff Ware apparently related to Susa A ceramics in Susiana; and (2) Sargarab and Chakali with unpainted pottery closely related to sites in the highlands (Wright 1981:70, fig. 33). Sargarab and Chakali are both located on the piedmont slopes at the foot of the mountains, near a pass leading to high pastures in the Kabir Kuh.

The predominant ceramic type within the Sargarab "assemblage" is Sargarab Ware, which differs from Susiana wares in the use of a mixture of grass and crushed calcareous rock as temper, as well as in vessel forms and decoration (Wright et al. 1975:135–36, figs. 7–8). Also found at Sargarab were a basin of the type found in Terminal Susa A and very early Uruk levels at sites in Susiana (Wright et al. 1975:fig. 9f; unpublished data from KS-34 and Susa Acropole III, H. Wright, pers. comm. 1986) and four ledge-rim jars with a fine sand temper that have been tentatively identified as Uruk Ware and dated to Early Uruk (Wright et al. 1975:136–37).

Wright states that "almost every feature" of the Sargarab pottery is paralleled in ceramic industries in central Luristan, at sites such as Kunji Cave, Baba Jan, Godin and in the Hulailan Middle Chalcolithic (Wright et al. 1975:133; Wright 1978:233). There seems to be little question that the technology of Sargarab Ware is indige-nous to sites in the highlands. Vessel forms and decoration indicate that Kunji, Baba Jan V, Godin VII–VI/V, and unexcavated sites in Luristan form a ceramic group that can be differentiated from Sargarab, but that a range of stylistic attributes are also shared. These include (1) bowl and jar forms (compare Wright et al. 1975:figs. 6c–e, 8b–c; Goff 1971:fig. 7:14–15; Young and Levine 1974:fig. 13:6; Wright et al. 1975:figs. 6n, 7f–g; Goff 1971:figs. 6:28, 30, 7:10–12; Mortensen 1976:figs. 8, 9d, f; Wright et al. 1975:134, figs. 6j, m, 7d; Goff 1971:figs. 5:12–13, 20–21, 26, 6:15, 17, 7:2–6, 19; Mortensen 1976:fig. 7a; Young 1969:figs. 6:8, 9:5, 16, 24; Wright et al. 1975:fig. 8h–j; Goff 1971:fig. 5:22, 25; Mortensen 1974b:fig. 38g–h; Young 1969:figs. 7:16, 24, 9:7) and (2) the use of appliquéd strips bearing round or oval impressions (Wright et al. 1975:figs. 7e, h, j, 8a; Goff 1971:figs. 5:40₁, 6:25–27, 7:9, 17–18, 21–22; Mortensen 1976:figs. 6h, 8f; Young and Levine 1974:fig. 13:14). Some of these forms also occur at sites much farther to the north in the Zagros, around Bukan (Swiny 1975:fig. 1:3, 11–12, 14, and survey collections in the University Museum). Red-slipped vessels with black-painted bands from Sargarab (Wright et al. 1975:fig. 8e, h) have been identified with the distinctive Black-on-Plum Ware found at Susa A and sites in the Zagros by E. Henrickson (1985b:table 5; see "Susiana" and "Central Western Iran"); however both Dollfus and Wright state that the Sargarab vessels are unlike Susa A Black-on-Plum in form, design, and surface finish (pers. comm. 1985, 1986).

Wright interprets the data from Sargarab and Chakali as possible evidence for settlement on the Deh Luran Plain by groups moving down from the highlands, perhaps transhumants (Wright et al. 1975:137, 140; Wright 1981:70). The ceramic evidence supports this hypothesis, but the chronological placement of these settlements remains problematic. Wright assigns the Sargarab material to a separate cultural phase and places it within the "Terminal Ubaid period." Also placed within this chronological unit is the "Terminal Susa A phase" in Susiana (Wright 1981:167–69; Wright et al. 1975; Wright and Johnson 1975).

Given the similarity of the Sargarab assemblage to Early Uruk pottery at Farukhabad (compare Wright et al. 1975:figs. 7–8; Wright 1981:figs. 41, 43a) and the occurrence of Uruk Ware at Sargarab itself (Wright et al. 1975:137, fig. 8k), it is unclear whether Sargarab and Chakali represent an occupation of the plain during a hiatus at Farukhabad or whether these sites are in fact contemporary with the Early Uruk at Farukhabad. The predominance of Sargarab Ware in the Early Uruk deposits at Farukhabad and its subsequent decline in popularity (Wright 1981:table 36) could be used to support either position. If we assume that the frequency of all artifact classes in an ongoing sequence takes the form of a battle-ship curve, then Sargarab should be earlier than the Early Uruk levels at Farukhabad, representing a phase before Uruk wares gained popularity. However, if Sargarab represents a small number of highland groups with a distinct ceramic technology moving down onto the plain, then the relative frequencies of Sargarab and Uruk wares at Farukhabad may document exchange, with the "new" or exotic ware gradually disappearing as the immigrants adopted new styles and technologies from their neighbors.

Both a rectangular stamp seal with dogs and caprids paralleled in Gawra XI (Tobler 1950:pl. CLXIX:158) and the ceramic comparisons with other regions favor a date for the Sargarab assemblage within the Uruk period. The only well-dated pottery comparable to Sargarab comes from Godin VII to VI/V, contemporary with Early to Late Uruk (see "Mahidasht" and "Godin"). Pending the complete analysis and publication of Seh Gabi and Godin and the excavation of a Sargarab assemblage, we can place Sargarab after the Farukh/Late Ubaid occupation of Deh Luran, but cannot determine whether it is contemporary with Susa A, Early Uruk, or perhaps both. We urge in any case that the term *Terminal Ubaid* as applied to Sargarab be discontinued. Sargarab is not only non-Ubaid in technology and style, but is closely linked with Uruk, with diagnostic Uruk elements of form occurring in Sargarab Ware at Farukhabad (Wright 1981:165–72, tables 38–41, fig. 44).

M. *The Uruk phase* has been documented at Farukhabad where it follows a stratigraphic hiatus (Wright 1981:167). It has been divided into three phases by the excavator.

1. *Early Uruk* occurs only in Excavation B and consists of two strata, layers 36 and 35, excavated over an area that never exceeded ca. 25 m² (Wright 1981:73–74, table 2, figs. 8, 36a). The pottery consists of chaff- and grit-tempered Sargarab Ware, with the addition of some characteristic sand-tempered Uruk wares and a special chaff-tempered form—the beveled-rim bowl (Wright 1981:168–69). Reasonable comparisons of the Uruk forms can be made with Warka-Eanna XIII or XII and Susa Acropole I:23 or 22 (Wright 1981:169). Links between the Sargarab vessels and highland sites (Wright 1981:91) have been discussed above.

2. *Middle Uruk* material comes from Excavation A:layers 22–21 and Excavation B:34–32 (Wright 1981:table 2). Definition of the Middle Uruk is based on an increasing frequency of standard Uruk forms, especially beveled-rim bowls, and the appearance of new elements including crosshatched incised bands on jar shoulders, small conical spouts, conical cups, and low expanded band rim jars (Wright 1981:169, tables 35–41,

figs. 45a, 48a–c, e–h, j, 50e, i–j, 51a, c–e, 52i, l, 55a, 56o, 57a–b, e–f, i–k; see also fig. 40). Although the Middle Uruk at Farukhabad has many local features, it can be compared to Middle Uruk levels in the Innana sounding at Nippur, and correlated "by interpolation" with Warka-Eanna XI–VII and Susa Acropole I:21–20 (Wright 1981:172; pers. comm. 1986).

3. In *Late Uruk* there is a further expansion of the settlement at Farukhabad, with excavated material from all three major soundings: Excavation A:layers 20–18, Excavation B:31–28, and Excavation C:33–32). The initial occurrence of polychrome painting is in this phase (Wright 1981:111, fig. 58a, g–i). The Farukhabad Late Uruk "shares many features" with Warka-Eanna VII–IV and Susa Acropole I:19–17, including twisted handles, grooved and oblique shoulder decorations, bottles, and droop spouts (Wright 1981:172; see "Susa Area").

N. *The Jemdet Nasr phase* at Farukhabad has been redefined following the Tübingen Conference as those levels called "Early Jemdet Nasr" in the site report: Excavation A:17–13, B:27–24, and C:31–27 (Wright, pers. comm.). The pottery is "in many respects, a simplified version of the Late Uruk assemblage" (Wright 1981:172). Again, the distinctive local character of the plain wares within this assemblage makes it difficult to establish correlations with other regions (Wright 1981:173–74). The dating of this phase within the Jemdet Nasr period is, therefore, based on comparisons of the polychrome vessels (H. Wright, pers. comm. 1986).

O. *The Early Dynastic phase* is known from Farukhabad and has been subdivided into two chronological units. Early Dynastic I includes what was called "Late Jemdet Nasr" in the site report, Excavation A:12–6, B:23–21, and C:26–24 (Wright, pers. comm.; Dittmann 1986(b)). Early Dynastic II–III is defined by material from Excavation A:5–1, Excavation B:20–19, and Excavation C:23–9 (Wright 1981:table 2, figs. 34–35; pers. comm.). A Late Polychrome style with complex designs composed of fine parallel oblique lines and crosshatching appears in Farukhabad EDII–III (Wright 1981:173, figs. 58a, c, 59e, 1, 61c, e, i–k). Similar vessels are found in the Hamrin, the Diyala, and at cemetery sites in the Pusht-i Kuh (Carter 1987).

P. *The Elamite phase* pottery sample is small but useful because of its geographical position between the better-known sites in Mesopotamia and Susa (Carter 1981:200–209). The early Elamite ceramics from Excavation B:18–15 date to the Shimashki period (ca. 2100–1900 B.C.), and may be compared to Susa Ville Royale BVI and levels 3–4 in Carter's Ville Royale 1 sounding. In Mesopotamia these forms have a range from Akkadian to Isin-Larsa but are concentrated in the late Ur III and early Larsa levels at Nippur (Carter 1981:202).

Susiana

From Deh Luran, a route leads along the foothills to the southeast. The earliest farmers in Susiana seem to have settled within this zone, moving east of the River Dez before colonizing the rolling gravel plains to the south. In relating the regional sequences within Khuzistan, it is convenient to move from Deh Luran to eastern Susiana where there is a long history of settlement prior to that in western Susiana. This violation of our west-to-east rule is also advantageous in that it allows an immediate comparison between the better-published sites in western Susiana and Fars.

The Eastern Susiana Sequence

The major excavated site east of the River Dez is Chogha Mish, located on the edge of the Susiana Plain only a few miles from the Zagros foothills. Excavations were carried out from 1967 to 1978 under the direction of P. Delougaz and H. Kantor (Delougaz 1967, 1976; Delougaz and Kantor 1971, 1972a, 1972b, 1975a, 1975b; Kantor 1974, 1976a, 1976b, 1976c, 1978, 1979). Additional soundings by the Chogha Mish team, aimed at the recovery of early material, were made at Chogha Bonut-i Moezi (Kantor 1978) and Boneh Fazili (Delougaz and Kantor 1972b). Later prehistoric and protohistoric material was recovered through area excavations conducted by H. Weiss at Qabr Sheykheyn (Weiss 1972, 1976) and stratigraphic soundings by D. McCown and J. Caldwell at Tal-i Ghazir (Caldwell 1968; Whitcomb 1971). Surface surveys in western Susiana for the period before 2000 B.C. were conducted by R. McC. Adams (1962), F. Hole (1969, 1987a:figs. 9–10), G. Johnson, and H. Wright (Johnson 1973, 1976, 1987; Wright and Johnson 1975; Wright 1987; see also Weiss 1976, 1978).

A. *The Aceramic Susiana period* has been documented only in a 2 m deposit of ashy trash and earth floors at the bottom of a "small stratigraphic trench" at Choga Bonut (Kantor 1978:191). The presence of stone vessel fragments in this small sample suggests that Aceramic Susiana is contemporary with the Ali Kosh phase in Deh Luran, rather than with the earlier Bus Mordeh phase in which stone vessels were rare (see Hole, Flannery, and Neely 1969:table 10).

B. *The Formative Susiana period* is defined by 1.5 m of deposit stratified above the Aceramic at Chogha Bonut, and by deposits stratified below the Archaic at Boneh Fazili (Delougaz and Kantor 1972b:96; Kantor 1978:191). It is characterized by a chaff-tempered pottery with a bright red-to-plum wash or filmy paint. A group of sherds with simple geometric designs "can be considered ancestral to Painted Burnished Ware of Archaic [Su-

siana] 1" (Kantor 1978:191, fig. 2). Stacked triangles and wide plain bands at the rim provide a tentative link between the Formative Susiana pottery and the Sefid phase in Deh Luran (compare Kantor 1978:fig. 2 with Hole 1977:figs. 43r, v, w, 44z–aa).

C. *The Archaic Susiana period* occurs at Chogha Bonut (Kantor 1978) and Boneh Fazili (Delougaz and Kantor 1972b) as well as at Chogha Mish (Delougaz and Kantor 1972a:16). Buildings constructed of long, finger-impressed bricks were found at Chogha Mish and Boneh Fazili (Delougaz 1976:35–38, figs. 9, 13–20). Three ceramic phases were defined based on painted wares from the Gulley Cut at Chogha Mish (Delougaz and Kantor 1972b; Kantor 1976b:25–27).

1. *The Archaic Susiana 1 phase* is characterized by Painted Burnished Ware (Kantor 1974:fig. 5, 1976c:184, figs. 28–30), which indicates strong ties with sites to the west and north. Pottery from Tepe Tula'i near Jaffarabad that can be identified as Archaic 1 Painted Burnished Ware is also said to be "nearly indistinguishable" in attributes of fabric and shape from Deh Luran types dating to the Mohammad Jaffar through Surkh phases (Hole 1974:228, figs. 11–14; see also Hole 1977:table 8). T-shaped figurines, common in the later part of the deposit at Tula'i and also present at Chogha Mish (H. Kantor, pers. comm. 1985), provide a second link to the Sefid and Surkh phases (Hole 1974:fig. 15f–g, i–k; see also Hole 1977:table 72, 1978:table 4; Dollfus 1983:table 42). A more specific link between Archaic 1 and Deh Luran is a single unusual vessel from a Surkh context at Chagha Sefid which is closely comparable in style as well as technology to a large group of sherds from Archaic 1 (compare Kantor 1976c:fig. 28 lower right, fig. 30, with Hole 1977:fig. 44bb). Taking the evidence as a whole, we suggest that Archaic 1 is contemporary with late(?) Sefid and Surkh in Deh Luran.

Chogha Mish Archaic 1 sherds in the collection of the Oriental Institute are virtually identical to Late Sarab wares, including Sarab Linear Painted and Sarab Black-Slipped (L. Levine and E. Henrickson, pers. comm. 1985; see also McDonald 1979:fig 14y). Ties between Archaic 1 and the plateau are more tenuous. The fabric of some Archaic 1 sherds is reminiscent of Mushki pottery from Fars recovered by the Sumner survey (M. Voigt observation), and a similarity between Archaic 1 designs and Jari lattice and meander patterns has also been suggested (Delougaz and Kantor 1972a:23).

2. *The Archaic Susiana 2 phase* is characterized by Red-line Ware (Kantor 1974:fig. 4, 1976c:fig. 27), originally called "Chevron Ware." The painted ceramics of Archaic 2 are closely related to Archaic 3, and represent a break from Archaic 1 in temper, surface finish, and painted design. There are no good parallels for this phase

within the Deh Luran sequence, but given the relationships between Archaic 1 and 3 and Deh Luran (q.v.), Chogha Mish Archaic 2 should be contemporary with the Surkh phase, and probably only the latest part of Surkh. There is some stylistic similarity between this phase and ceramic industries in the central Zagros, consisting of hourglass motifs and nested zigzags or chevrons, present on Zagheh Archaic and Sarab Linear Wares as well as in Archaic 2 (Kantor 1976c:fig. 27; Levine and McDonald 1977:pl. Ia; Malek Shahmirzadi 1977b:pls. IX:20–33, XIII:Z40246).

3. *The Archaic Susiana 3 phase* is characterized by Close-line Ware, formerly "X Ware," and Mat-painted Ware (Delougaz and Kantor 1972a:pl. VIa; Kantor 1974:fig. 4, 1976c:183–84, fig. 25). Mat-painted Ware has no good parallels. Close-line Ware, however, is very similar to the Chogha Mami Transitional pottery of Chagha Sefid and Choga Mami itself (see "Deh Luran") and provides a good relative date. Kantor considers Chogha Mish Archaic 3 to be significantly earlier than its Mesopotamian analogues (1976c:184), but others working with related assemblages disagree (Dollfus 1983:table 42; Hole 1978:table 4).

D. *The Early Susiana period* has been found at Chogha Mish and Boneh Fazili (Delougaz and Kantor 1972b:96). Close and identical parallels for Early Susiana painted pottery lie in Eridu levels XVIII–XV, or the Late Eridu and Hajji Mohammad periods (compare Kantor 1976c:fig. 19 with Safar, Mustafa, and Lloyd 1981:figs. 92:18–19, 99:15; Kantor 1976c:fig. 20 with Safar, Mustafa, and Lloyd 1981:figs. 90:5, 92:2, 4–5, 7–8, 94:6, 8–9, 12, 14, 96:4, 1; Kantor 1976c:fig. 17 with Safar, Mustafa, and Lloyd 1981:figs. 91:14, 97:6). Vessel forms and some designs characteristic of the Chogha Mish Early Susiana period are found in the Sabz phase in Deh Luran (compare Kantor 1980:18 with Hole, Flannery, and Neely 1969:fig. 50). Within the Susiana Plain, Chogha Mish Early Susiana is contemporary with Jaffarabad level 5, formerly Susiana a (Dollfus 1983:165, table 41). Parallels include figurines as well as ceramics (Kantor 1979:38; Dollfus 1975a:fig. 32:1, pl. XVIII:1). Nearly identical figurines are found in Eridu level XVI (Safar, Mustafa, and Lloyd 1981:fig. 116:8).

E. *The Middle Susiana period* has been recovered at Chogha Mish, Chogha Bonut, Boneh Fazili, and Qabr Sheykheyn. Pottery form and design have been used to define a break between the Early and Middle Susiana periods, as well as to divide the Middle Susiana period into three phases (Kantor 1976c:179–81).

1. *The Middle Susiana 1 phase* has many similarities to Early Susiana and seems to be a "true intermediate phase" (Kantor 1976c:181). The pottery is part of a horizon usually referred to as "Hajji Mohammad," which extends throughout southern Mesopotamia and along the

shores of the Persian/Arabian Gulf (Kantor 1976c:180–81, figs. 10, 12–14). Within Khuzistan, the distinctive bowls of this style/phase illustrated from Middle Susiana 1 are also found in the Khazineh phase of Deh Luran and in Jowi level 15 (compare Kantor 1976c:fig. 10 with Hole, Flannery, and Neely 1969:fig. 56a; Dollfus 1983:fig. 13:8; for additional parallels between Jowi 17–13 and unpublished Middle Susiana 1 material see Dollfus 1983:figs. 11–23).

2. *The Middle Susiana 2 phase* pottery shows a great range of vessel shapes and motifs. Painted designs are "bold" and "provide some striking antecedents for characteristic Late Susiana features" (Kantor 1976c:178, figs. 1–9, 11). Within Khuzistan, one bowl type characteristic of this phase is paralleled in the Khazineh phase in Deh Luran (Kantor 1976c:fig. 11; Hole, Flannery, and Neely 1969:fig. 56g), but representational motifs are shared with the succeeding Mehmeh phase (Kantor 1976c:figs. 1, 7–8; Hole, Flannery, and Neely 1969:figs. 59d, 62c, 63l–m). Dollfus compares Middle Susiana 2 with Jowi 11–12, contexts that also produced sherds of Mehmeh Red-on-Red (1983:166, table 41; pers. comm. 1985).

3. *The Middle Susiana 3 phase* is defined by a large ceramic sample from the Burned Building in the East Area of Chogha Mish (Kantor 1976b:27–28). Also dating to this phase is the lowest part of the deposit at Qabr Sheykheyn (5 and below; Dollfus 1983:166, fig. 41). Good ceramic parallels link Middle Susiana 3 with the Mehmeh phase in Deh Luran with its distinctive goat bowls (compare Kantor 1976b:fig. 14 with Hole, Flannery, and Neely 1969:fig. 58e–f; Kantor 1976b:fig. 13 top with Hole, Flannery, and Neely 1969:fig. 60a, g). According to Dollfus, some of the Middle Susiana 3 material is also contemporary with the Bayat phase (1983:table 42). Within Susiana, Chogha Mish Middle Susiana 3 is equivalent to Jaffarabad 3m–n, Jowi 10–4, and Bendebal 27–17 (Dollfus 1983:table 41).

F. *The Late Susiana period* has been excavated at Chogha Mish (Delougaz and Kantor 1972a:21–22; Kantor 1976a:28). Based on ceramic parallels, Chogha Mish Late Susiana is considered contemporary with Susa A settlements such as Jaffarabad 3–1, Bendebal 10, and Susa Acropole I:27–25 (Delougaz and Kantor 1972a:16, pl. IVa–c; Dollfus 1983:table 41; Hole 1978:table 4). The correlation of Middle Susiana 3 and the Mehmeh phase in Deh Luran (q.v.) indicates that at Chogha Mish there must be a gap between Middle Susiana 3 and Late Susiana. Dollfus places Qabr Shekheyn 4–1 within this gap (1983:166–67, table 41; see also Weiss 1972, 1976).

G. *The Protoliterate (Uruk) period* has been documented at Chogha Mish, in a carefully excavated pit at Sharafabad (Wright, Miller, and Redding 1980), and in the "Early Proto-Elamite"/Uruk deposits within the Step trench at Tal-i Ghazir (levels 11–38; Caldwell 1968:350–

51, figs. 11–38; Carter 1984:115, 121–22, figs. 7, 15; Whitcomb 1971:13–14, fig. 4; Wright 1978:table 5). At this time Chogha Mish was a major settlement with a city wall and imposing buildings as well as houses (Delougaz 1967:148, 1976:32; Johnson 1973:71–73; Delougaz and Kantor 1973:189). Pottery forms included hundreds of types, "many of them new" (Delougaz and Kantor 1972a:26). The most important were beveled-rim bowls, squat jars with four lugs, and a great variety of spouted bottles (Delougaz and Kantor 1972a:pls. VIIb, d, f, VIII). Based on the published seals (Delougaz and Kantor 1972a:30–31, pl. X; Kantor 1979:34) and the presence of numerical tablets (Kantor 1976b:24–25, figs. 5–6), the Chogha Mish Protoliterate period should be contemporary with Susa II, or Acropole I:18–17 (Le Brun 1978a; Le Brun and Vallat 1978; Wright 1978:table 5).

H. *The Proto-Elamite period.* After the Protoliterate occupation Chogha Mish was abandoned until the second millennium, but the Tal-i Ghazir "Stake [Trench] 10 rooms" apparently fall within this time range (Caldwell 1968:355, fig. 39; Whitcomb 1971:16–17, fig. 5). The Stake 10 rooms are probably contemporary with Proto-Elamite settlements such as Susa III, Malyan Middle Banesh, and Yahya IVC (Carter 1984:122, fig. 15; Wright 1978:table 5).

Western Susiana: The Susa Area Sequence

The modern stratigraphic sequence in the Susa area has been established primarily through recent excavations by the French Archaeological Mission at Jaffarabad (Dollfus 1971, 1973, 1975a, 1975b, 1978b), Jowi (Dollfus 1977, 1978b, 1983), Bendebal (Dollfus 1978a, 1978b, 1983), and Susa. At Susa, the key areas are Acropole I levels 27–13 (Le Brun 1971, 1978b, 1978c) and Ville Royale I levels 18–3 (Carter 1976, 1978, 1980). The Acropole I sounding is augmented by work on the High Terrace by Perrot and Canal (Canal 1978a, 1978b); a sounding on the east side of Morgan's Grande Tranchée (Dyson 1966); Wright's Acropole III sounding at the north end of the mound, on the western edge of the Sondage Nord of Mecquenem (Wright 1985); and by general excavations on the Acropole by Stève and Gasche (their 1965 Sondage, loci 374, 376; Chantier Ouest 1966 and 1968, loci 101, 102; Chantier de la Terrasse 1968, loci 266, 267, 282, 332, 334; see Alden 1982b:table 1; Stève and Gasche 1971). Additional information for the earliest part of the sequence was obtained through salvage excavations conducted by Frank Hole at Tepe Tula'i (Hole 1974, 1975). Surface surveys aimed at the recovery of sites that existed before 2000 B.C. were conducted by R. McC. Adams (1962), J. Alden (1987), F. Hole (1969, 1987a), G. Johnson (1973, 1976, 1987), and H. Wright (unpublished; see Hole 1987a:39).

A. *The Archaic period* is defined by excavations at Tepe Tula'i (Hole 1974, 1975). The ceramics were so similar in technological attributes to pottery from Deh Luran that they were sorted using the following Deh Luran types: Jaffar Painted and Plain, Khazineh Red, and three varieties of Sefid Painted Ware (Hole 1974:235–36). Based on a comparison of type frequencies Hole (1974:235) has suggested that Tula'i is contemporary with late Mohammad Jaffar and early Sefid. Stylistic attributes, however, indicate that Tula'i is more closely linked to Chogha Mish than to Deh Luran, specifically to Chogha Mish Archaic 1 Archaic Burnished Ware (Hole 1974:235, figs. 11–14; Delougaz and Kantor 1972a:pl. VIb–i; Kantor 1974:fig. 5).

B. *The Jaffarabad period* was defined by large-area clearances in levels 6–4 at Jaffarabad and includes related material from smaller excavations at Jowi levels 17–13 and Bendebal levels 28 and below (Dollfus 1975a:16–22; figs. 6–8; 1978b:158, fig. 13; 1983:20–21, 137, fig. 5–7; pers. comm. 1983). Chaff-tempered Plain Buff Ware makes up 62 percent of the sample at Jaffarabad (Dollfus 1975a:23–24, figs. 10–15; 1978b:fig. 12; 1983:24–25,figs. 11:15–16, 12:3–4, 13:1–2, 8–10). It is, however, at this time that grit-tempered ceramics appear in Susiana (Dollfus 1975a:23–25). Painted Buff Ware vessels are often so heavily painted that designs appear in reserve (Dollfus 1975a:25–30, figs. 16–30; 1978b:figs. 13–14; 1983:26–28, figs. 12–18, 21–23).

Based on firsthand knowledge of the material, Dollfus places the earliest part of the Jaffarabad period (Jaffarabad 6) contemporary with the latest part of Chogha Mish Archaic 3, and the rest of the period parallel to the Chogha Mish Early Susiana and Middle Susiana 1 periods (Dollfus 1983:tables 41–42, figs. 17–30 with refs.). Within the Deh Luran sequence, parallels for most of the Jaffarabad period are with the Sabz and Khazineh phases (Dollfus 1983:tables 41–42). In the Mesopotamian sequence, this period corresponds to the Eridu and Hajji Mohammad periods (Dollfus 1983:table 42; see also "Deh Luran"; and Porada, Hansen, Dunham, and Babcock, this vol., chap. 5). A striking nonceramic parallel linking Jaffarabad with Eridu XVI occurs in the form of columnar human figurines that have been incised to indicate legs and pubic triangle, and painted to indicate clothing (Dollfus 1975a:fig. 32:1, pl. XVIII:1; Kantor 1979:38; Safar, Mustafa, and Lloyd 1981, fig. 116:8).

C. A short *Transitional phase* represented by Jowi levels 12–11 and Bendebal 28 is approximately equivalent to Chogha Mish Middle Susiana 2 (Dollfus 1983:table 41).

D. *The Chogha Mish period* was originally defined as levels 3 m–n at Jaffarabad (200 m² cleared), and later extended to include Jowi 10–4 and Bendebal 27–11 (Dollfus 1975a, 1978b, 1983:table 41, pers. comm. 1983).

The duration of this period has been estimated at up to 750 years based on the depth of deposit at Bendebal (Dollfus 1983:table 41). The ceramic industry (Dollfus 1975a:figs. 47–53; 1978b:16, figs. 15–17; 1983:figs. 32–38, 54–87) is virtually identical to that from Chogha Mish Middle Susiana 3. It is also related to Qabr Sheykheyn 4–2 and to the Mehmeh, Bayat, and Farukh periods in Deh Luran (Dollfus 1983:166, figs. 33–38, 56–87 with refs.). Within the Mesopotamian sequence it is therefore contemporary with both Ubaid 3 and 4 (see Parada et al., this vol., chap. 5). Ties to ceramic industries in Fars are also present (see "Southwestern Zagros"). A button seal with an incised quadrat design from Bendebal 15 is paralleled on a hemispherical seal with a tang from Sialk III, and on a hemispherical seal from Gawra described as coming from "below XII" (Dollfus 1983:fig. 95:5; Ghirshman 1938:pl. LXXXVI:S117; Tobler 1950:pl. CLIX:26).

E. *The Susa A/Susa I period* is defined by Jaffarabad levels 3d–1, Bendebal level 10, and Susa Acropole Sounding I, levels 27–24 (Dollfus 1971, 1978b, 1983:table 41, pers. comm. 1983; Le Brun 1978c:190). The large and well-controlled ceramic sample from Jaffarabad includes Plain Buff Ware, Painted Buff Ware, and Red Burnished Ware; Burnished Gray Ware and Black-on-Plum Ware are rare (Dollfus 1971:30–51, figs. 9–20; 1978b:165, figs. 18–19). At Susa, Plain Buff, Painted, and Red Wares have been recovered from a much smaller excavated area, ca. 100 m² (Le Brun 1971:206, figs. 31, 36–39; 1978c:fig. 30). The painted pottery of this period is elaborate, with representations of horned animals, dogs, birds, snakes, snails, and people in what appear to be "scenes" (Amiet 1966:figs. 11–16; Hole 1983b).

The ceramics from Jaffarabad levels 2–1, Bendebal 10, and Susa Acropole 27–25 correlate with those from Qabr Sheykheyn 1 and Chogha Mish Late Susiana (Dollfus 1983:167–68, table 41; pers. comm. 1983). The Black-on-Plum Ware found at Jaffarabad, which may be imported, provides a valuable synchronism with Zagros sites (Dollfus 1971:47–48, fig. 12:16–24; 1978b:fig. 19:17, 19–22). In the Mahidasht, it is found at Chogha Maran in Middle to Late Chalcolithic contexts; in the Hulailan Valley it occurs at Hakalan and Parchinah in Luristan (E. Henrickson 1983:491–92, 506, 509–10, 517, tables 69–70; see also "Western Luristan"). Wright (1978:233) states that the minority red wares of Susa 25–24 "duplicate in form and fabric the ceramics of the Lapui period of the Marv Dasht" (see "Southwestern Zagros").

The chronological relationship of Susa A/Susa I to sites in Mesopotamia rests primarily on glyptic evidence. A stamp seal impression showing an ibex-headed man holding two snakes (Amiet 1971:218–19, fig. 35:1–3; Dollfus 1971:fig. 23: 3–5) found in Acropole I:25 has direct counterparts in Gawra XIII–XI (Tobler 1950:pls.

CLXII:76–80, CLXIII:81, CLXIV:94–96, 100, 101). Ties with Luristan are so numerous that Amiet groups the Luristan and Susa A material as part of a single glyptic tradition (1972:5–32, 1979:196). The form of a hemispherical seal from Acropole I:23 is paralleled in Sialk III₅, (Amiet 1971:fig. 35:7; Ghirshman 1938:pl. LXXXVI:S172) and in the Uruk period at Telloh (Buchanan 1967:528, 533–34). The latter is significant in that it suggests that late Susa A may have been contemporary with the Early Uruk period in Mesopotamia (Amiet 1971:220). Deposits assigned to the "Terminal Susa A" phase, or the transition between Susa A and Uruk at Susa, produced sherds from basins with thumb-impressed strips that are paralleled in levels II–IV of the Hut Sounding at Eridu and at sites near Nippur assigned to Early Uruk (H. Wright, pers. comm. 1986; see also Stève 1968:131).

F. *The Susa II (Uruk) period* marks a cultural break, with the disappearance of the Susiana painted pottery tradition and the appearance of ceramics and other artifacts very similar to Uruk materials found in Deh Luran and Mesopotamia (Amiet 1979:196; Wright 1981:181–84). At Susa, this period is defined by Acropole I:levels 22–17 (Le Brun 1978b:58–71, pls. XI–XIII, figs. 14–18; 1978c:180–83, figs. 31, 33). Other recently excavated material dated to this period comes from Acropole II:levels 6–1, Acropole III:10–1, and Apadana Trench 1038 (Canal 1978a:173; Miroschedji 1976; Wright 1985; for a summary of Susa II–III material from earlier excavations see Dittmann 1986b).

Pottery consists of typical Uruk fabrics and vessel forms: chaff-tempered Coarse Ware storage jars and beveled-rim bowls; buff, grit-tempered Common and Fine Ware jars and bottles with drooping spouts, shouldered jars with four vertical nose lugs and incised designs on the shoulder, squat jars with handles, cylindrical jars and open bowls; and beginning in Acropole I:18, Red-Slipped Ware (Le Brun 1971:figs. 45–53; 1978b:73–82, figs. 19–33; 1978c:figs. 32, 34). Within Khuzistan, ceramic parallels for Susa Period II occur at Chogha Mish in the Protoliterate period (Le Brun 1978b), in the early Proto-Elamite levels at Tal-i Ghazir (Carter 1984:121–22, figs. 2, 15), and in the "Uruk pit" at Sharafabad (Wright, Miller, and Redding 1980). Based on Le Brun's plates illustrating typical vessel types, Acropole I:18 pottery is comparable to Nippur Inanna XX–XVII or the Middle Uruk period in Mesopotamia (compare Le Brun 1978c:fig. 32:1, 2, 10, 11, 15 with Hansen 1965:203–4, figs. 10, 16, 12, 11a, 17, 18), and level 17 is related to Inanna XVII–XVI or Late Uruk (compare Le Brun 1978c:fig. 34:8, 11, 3, 2, 14 with Hansen 1965:204–6, figs. 17, 27, 34, 35, 21; see also Johnson 1973:tables 7, 11). The ceramic sample from Acropole I:22–19 is small and has not yet been described in detail, so whether the cultural correlation is between Susa II and Early to Late Uruk, or only Middle and Late Uruk, remains to be seen.

Glyptic evidence for the relationship between Susa II and Mesopotamia is difficult to interpret due to a dependence on style rather than on stratigraphic context and artifact association for the dating of seals from Mesopotamian sites. The earliest cylinder seal, decorated with two rows of fish, occurs in Acropole I:21 (Amiet 1971:221, fig. 43:10). It is a "well known Jemdet Nasr type" according to Amiet (1971:221); however, he points out that the motif occurs at Telloh in a context earlier than the Jemdet Nasr period. Glyptic materials from Acropole I:18–17B include geometric patterns, rows of animals, humans engaged in a variety of activities, and humans or animals associated with buildings (Le Brun 1978a; Le Brun and Vallat 1978:figs. 5–7; Vallat 1973:fig. 14; see also Dittmann 1986a). They are paralleled in Warka IV (Amiet 1971:222–23, 1979:199), dated to the Late Uruk period (Hansen 1965:204; Porada et al., this vol., chap. 5).

At a greater distance, there are strong ceramic parallels between Acropole I:17 and sites on the Euphrates such as Habuba Kabira and Kurban Hüyük VIII (Le Brun 1978b; Algaze 1986). Within Iran, ceramic links to the Zagros are found in Godin VI/V (Weiss and Young 1975; see also "Mahidasht" and "Godin") and in the Early Banesh period in the Marv Dasht (Alden 1979:60, fig. 12; see also "Southwestern Zagros"). Ceramic evidence for contact between Susa and settlements on the central plateau is found in Sialk IV$_1$ (Ghirshman 1938:pls. XXVI, LXXXVIII–XCV); see also Carter 1984:115, fig. 7; Dyson 1965:225). The Godin VI/V tablets are probably related to those from Susa II, and there are also parallels between the numerical tablets of I:17 and fragments from Sialk IV$_1$ (Stolper 1984:6; Vallat 1971:243; Weiss and Young 1975:11, figs. 4–5). At the end of the period, contacts between Susa and Godin VI/V cease, and Chogha Mish is abandoned (Amiet 1979:199).

G. *The Susa III period* is documented by Acropole I levels 16–14B and Ville Royale sounding I levels 18–13 (Le Brun 1978c:190; Carter 1978:table 1; Perrot 1978:fig. b; note that the Carter and Perrot charts just cited contain an error, reversing the position of Acropole I levels 14B and 14A as defined by Le Brun in 1971:fig. 32, 1978c:table I, fig. 29). Additional material from the Acropole was obtained in a 1965 Sondage and the 1968 Chantier de la Terrasse excavated by Stève and Gasche (1971:9–11, 25–41; see also Alden 1982b:table 1; Dittmann 1986b). Carter has divided the period into three phases, based on internal stratigraphy, ceramic typology, and external relationships (1978:198, 202, 211).

1. *The Susa IIIA phase* is defined as Acropole I:16–14B (Carter 1978:202; Le Brun 1971:189–202). It follows a short hiatus and marks the reoccupation of the

Acropole by a group with close links to Fars (see Carter 1984:117 with refs.). There is a complete break in ceramic fabric and form between levels 17 and 16 (Le Brun 1978c:183, 190, 192). The chaff- and grit-tempered plain wares are joined in Acropole I:15 by Gray Ware with encrusted white decoration, Red-Slipped Ware, and black-and-red-painted Bichrome Ware (Le Brun 1971: 192–94, 199–201, fig. 64; 1978c:190, 192, fig. 36). Common shapes are footed goblets, jars with everted rims, trays and squat sinuous-sided bowls (Le Brun 1971:figs. 60–63, 1978c:fig. 36). Dittmann, in a paper given at the 1983 Tübingen Conference, discusses the difficulty of linking the ceramics of Susa IIIA to Deh Luran, much less to Mesopotamia. However, using a few well-dated types he compares I:16–14B with the Jemdet Nasr levels at Farukhabad, and with Nippur Inanna XIV–XI (1986b:table 2). On the plateau, Susa IIIA is comparable to the Middle and Late Banesh phases in the Kur River Basin (see "Southwestern Zagros"; Alden 1979:60, fig. 12; 1982b:fig. 2).

Glyptic evidence includes "glazed steatite"/chlorite cylinder seals and sealings with geometric patterns (also referred to as "schematic" seals by Amiet 1971:figs. 43:10, 44:20?, 59:3–4, 9, 17) and sealings on tablets in the distinctive Proto-Elamite style (Amiet 1971:225, figs. 59, 67:12; 1979:197). Amiet (1971:218, 227) says that this material corresponds to Le Breton's Cb–Cc and is "Jemdet Nasr" in style, with marked local originality (see also Amiet 1979:196–97).

2. *The Susa IIIB phase* is defined by the lowest levels (18–16) in the Ville Royale I sounding and Acropole I levels 14A–13 (Carter 1978:202, table 1). In Ville Royale I:18–17, over 220 m² has been cleared for this period (Carter 1978:197, figs. 38–39; 1980:13–15, figs. 2–3). Characteristic of the ceramic industry are plain grit-tempered Common Ware and Chaff-Tempered Ware (Carter 1978:202, fig. 41; 1980:16–17, 20, figs. 9–13). Decorative elements include plastic finger-impressed bands shaped to form triangles and semicircles, and incised decoration (Carter 1978:202, figs. 40–41; 1980:17).

Ceramic parallels may be drawn with the Early Dynastic I period in Mesopotamia, as at Nippur Inanna ED I and Sin Temple VI at Tell Asmar (Carter 1980:21). A Proto-Elamite tablet, sealings, and two frit cylinder seals were found; designs are limited to animals and linear patterns (Carter 1980:19, fig. 17). The designs on the frit cylinder seals are also related to those from Sin Temple VI or ED I (Carter 1980:19). A conical jar stopper from Ville Royale I:18 bears the impression of a seal with a row of horned goats and a pair of kneeling animals facing one another; similar impressions are dated by Amiet to ED II (Carter 1980:19, fig. 17:1).

Relationships with sites on the plateau form a consistent pattern. Carter considers the pottery to be contemporary with the latest Banesh at Malyan and with Yahya IV-B (1980:20–21, 1984:fig. 8). The geometric style seals of Ville Royale I:18–17 compare with sealings from the Banesh period at Tepe Malyan, Yahya IVC, and Shahr-i Sokhta I (Carter 1980:19, fig. 17:3–5, 7 with refs.). Amiet considers the glyptic material from Susa IIIB to be contemporary with Sialk IV$_2$ (1979:195).

3. *The Susa IIIC phase* comprises Ville Royale I levels 15–13 (Carter 1978:table 1). The area cleared was less than 20 m² (Carter 1980:fig. 4), and the artifact sample was correspondingly small. In I:13, rare sherds of Monochrome Painted Ware with simple geometric designs, the Susa "second style," first occur (Carter 1980:20–21). Carter correlates the end of Susa III with the end of Early Dynastic II, since in Mesopotamia "wares of the second style date approximately to ED III" (1980:21; see also Dittmann 1986b). Amiet (1979:200) suggests that the end of this phase was due "not to an inner crisis, but rather to a defeat such as the one that the Sumerian King List ascribes to Mebaragesi from Kish."

H. *The Susa IV period* is defined by Ville Royale I levels 12–7 and also includes material excavated by Stève and Gasche on the Acropole (Carter 1978:table 1). Level 12 rests on an erosion surface which caps level 13, indicating some kind of local hiatus. The period has been subdivided by Carter.

1. *The Susa IVA phase* is equated with Ville Royale I:12–9, and with "Early Dynastic" couche 4 and "Proto-Imperial" couche 3 on the Acropole (Carter 1978:table 1; Stève and Gasche 1971). Plain buff Common Ware vessels decorated with incised wavy lines or finger-impressed appliqué (Carter 1978:fig. 43:3–8, 1980:figs. 25–27) and "significant numbers" of Monochrome Painted Ware sherds of the "Susa second style" now occur (Carter 1978:207–9, fig. 44; 1980:23, figs. 28, 29:1–10; see also Amiet 1966:figs. 108–9). Both the painted and plain wares of Susa IVA closely resemble pottery from Zagros sites (Carter 1980:25–26, figs. 25–29 with references; 1984:fig. 9); in fact the Monochrome Painted Ware can now be identified as imported Godin III:6 Painted Buff Ware (compare Carter 1978:fig. 44; 1980:23, figs. 25–29, 34–35 with R. Henrickson 1984a:figs. 51–52, 91). Direct ceramic parallels between Susa IVA and Mesopotamia are rare, but include conical cups, and conical bowls typical of ED III–Akkadian times (Carter 1980:24).

Not found in controlled contexts but assigned to Susa IVA because of their ED II–III date in Mesopotamia are an "Early Group" of steatite/chlorite vessels of intricate style and their bitumen copies (Carter 1980:31; Miroschedji 1973:9–25, figs. 4–5, pls. I–V; Amiet 1966:fig. 124, 1979:199, 200). The geographical distribution of such vessels demonstrates the existence of an important trade network linking Susa, the Persian Gulf, and south-

eastern Iran in this period (Amiet 1979:200; Carter 1984:134; Kohl 1975; Miroschedji 1973).

2. *The Susa IVB (Akkadian) phase* is documented by levels 8–7 of Ville Royale I as well as by levels on the Acropole (Carter 1978:table 1; Stève and Gashe 1971). As implied by the name, there is a shift back to Mesopotamian styles throughout the assemblage, presumably a result of the conquest of Elam by Sargon and his successors (Carter 1984:135; Stolper 1984:11–16). Within the ceramic industry Mesopotamian influence can be seen in a modeled "goddess handle" (Carter 1978:fig. 45:4; Delougaz 1952:pl. 87k–q) and the continuation of conical bowls (Carter 1980:24). During this phase, cuneiform script is adopted at Susa for the first time in the Treaty of Naram Sin (ca. 2291–2255 B.C.), but the Proto-Elamite script may also have continued in use (Vallat 1978:194).

I. *The Susa V (Shimashki) period* is defined by levels 6–3 in Ville Royale I, the contents of which closely correspond to Ghirshman's Ville Royale B:VI–VII (Carter 1978:211, 1984:146; Ghirshman 1970; see also Stève, Gasche, and de Meyer 1980). Because the Ville Royale I sample is very small, the division between period IV and V is arbitrary (Carter 1980:30). Based on minor ceramic changes, the period has been subdivided (Carter 1978:211).

1. *The Susa VA phase* is defined by Ville Royale I levels 6–5 (Carter 1978:table 1, 1980:26, fig. 37). Common Ware vessels are abundant, and Fine Ware largely replaces painted pottery (Carter 1978:fig. 46, 1980:figs. 38–39). Susa VA probably represents the brief period of Elamite independence between the Mesopotamian Akkadian (Susa IVB) and Ur III (Susa VB) ascendency. During this period Puzur/Kutik Inshushinak adopted linear script for the national Elamite language, replacing the older Proto-Elamite script (Vallat 1978:194). Examples of the linear script occur in the highlands on an unstratified silver vase said to come from Fars, and on a pottery vessel at Shahdad (Hinz 1969:11ff., 1971:21–24).

2. *The Susa VB phase* is defined by Ville Royale I:levels 4–3. Ceramic markers are "upright-indented-band-rim" bowls and ridged-shouldered jars (Carter 1978:211, 1980:figs. 41, 49–51). Inscribed material consisted of a cone of Puzur/Kutik Inshushinak redeposited[?] in level 4 along with a brick of Shu Shin of Ur III (Carter 1980:28; Vallat 1980). It is to this period that Miroschedji's "Late Group" of serpentine vessels with concentric circle decoration belongs (1973:26–42, figs. 7–12, pls. VI–VIII).

This period probably represents Susa after its annexation by the Ur III empire and the construction of the Ninhursag Temple on the Acropole (Amiet 1979:201). The dating of Susa VB contemporary with the Ur III period in Mesopotamia is secure, suggested by the inscriptional evidence, and confirmed by two cylinder seals and seal-ings that are well-known Mesopotamian types assigned to Ur III (Carter 1980:28–29, fig. 52). A serpentine ves-sel with concentric circles is dated by an inscription at Telloh to the reign of Amar Sin, King of Ur (Amiet 1979:202). These vessels as well as square-based cos-metic bottles decorated with concentric circles occur along the Persian/Arabian Gulf and across the Iranian plateau at Shahdad, Yahya IV, Hissar IIIC, and in Bactria at the end of the third millennium (Amiet 1979:202; see also "Shahdad"; and Potts, this vol., chap. 4).

Surveys in Adjacent River Valleys

Information on the relationship of Khuzistan to adjacent mountain zones comes from surface surveys, with lim-ited tests carried out on the Izeh Plain (Wright 1979). On the Behbehan and Zureh Plains along the southeastern edge of Khuzistan, the survey was complemented by soundings made in Tepe Sohz and Do Tulune (Dittman 1984; Nissen 1976, 1973). These plains are important due to their geographic location, linking lowland Khuzis-tan and highland Fars (Dittmann 1984:64–71, tables 11–12; Dollfus 1983:table 42).

The Radiocarbon Evidence for the Southwestern Lowlands

Only two clusters of consistent dates have been obtained from sites in Khuzistan. These are for the Bayat period in Deh Luran, with a calibrated average date of 5080–4880 B.C. obtained from eight samples recovered from Tepe Sabz, and for the Susa A/Susa I period, with a cali-brated range of 4115–3880 B.C. obtained from ten samples from Jaffarabad and Susa (table 1). Major incon-sistencies in the radiocarbon record from other contexts (table 2) are probably due to the common use of bitumen by the early inhabitants and contamination of charcoal samples by this material. As a result, dates frequently are "too old" (see, for example, the dates from Qabr Shey-kheyn, *RC* 19:204).

There is some reason to treat the Bayat dates with cau-tion, since they necessitate a long span of time for the archaeological material that falls between the Bayat and Susa A analyzed samples, which is assigned to the Fa-rukh period in Deh Luran and the latter portion of the Chogha Mish period in Susiana. On the other hand, if the Bayat samples came from contexts within the early part of the phase, and/or were obtained from long-lived samples, this span of seven hundred years or more is compatible with the estimates based on depth of deposit provided by Dollfus (1983:table 41).

The chronometric dates for the earlier part of the se-quence have been established by using the synchronism

between Tell es-Sawwan I and the Mohammad Jaffar pe-riod in Deh Luran. Although there are only two carbon samples for Sawwan I, a cluster of dates for Sawwan III with a calibrated average range of 6100–5570 B.C. (Oates 1983:271; Porada et al., this vol., chap. 5) suggests that Sawwan I and hence the Mohammad Jaffar period should fall in the second half of the seventh millennium.

Southwestern Zagros (Fars)

The Marv Dasht (Kur River Basin) Sequence

The areas within the Kur drainage investigated most in-tensively by archaeologists are the Baiza and Marv Dasht or Persepolis Plains. The prehistoric sequence relies heavily on test excavations carried out at a number of sites during the 1950s by Vanden Berghe (1952, 1954, 1959, 1968c; see also Sumner 1972a:294–96) and on surface surveys (Sumner 1972a, 1977a; see also Alden 1979; Gotch 1968, 1969; Jacobs 1980; Rosenberg 1980; Stein 1936; Vanden Berghe 1952, 1954). The key exca-vated sites are Tal-i Mushki (Fukai, Horiuchi, and Mat-sutani 1973; Sono 1967; Sumner 1977a:293–94, 1980); Tal-i Jari A and B (Egami 1967; Egami Masuda, and Go-toh 1977; Sumner 1977a, 1980); Tal-i Bakun A and B (Egami and Masuda 1962; Langsdorff and McCown 1942; Schmidt 1939a, 1939b; Sumner 1972a, 1980); Tal-i Gap (Egami and Sono 1962; Sono 1967); Tal-i Nok-hodi (Goff 1963, 1964; Sumner 1977a); Tal-i Kureh (Al-den 1977, 1979); and Tal-i Malyan (Sumner 1972b, 1974, 1976, 1980, 1985; Nicholas 1980; Nickerson 1977).

A. *The Mushki period* is defined at Tal-i Mushki. Ini-tially tested by Vanden Berghe (1952:214), it was more extensively excavated by the Tokyo University Iraq-Iran Archaeological Expedition under Namio Egami (Fukai, Horiuchi, and Matsutani 1973:2). The placement of the Mushki assemblage at the beginning of the Marv Dasht sequence has been the subject of controversy. Character-istic of Tal-i Mushki is Red-Slipped (Mushki) Ware, usu-ally decorated with dark-painted linear designs on a bur-nished, red-slipped surface. Less common Buff-Slipped Ware with painted designs on a mat or (rarely) burnished surface is related to Jari Ware (see below). Based on his excavations and ceramic parallels with other regions, Vanden Berghe concluded that the Mushki "culture"/ware *followed* the Jari "culture"/ware. The stratigraphic basis for this conclusion is not known, since none of Van-den Berghe's tests has been fully reported (1952, 1954; see also Fukai, Horiuchi, and Matsutani 1973:76–79 for translations). Subsequent excavations by the Japanese did not actually document the superposition of Jari over Mushki (Fukai, Horiuchi, and Matsutani 1973:4, 31–34, 76–79, pls. XLII, XLVI); they did provide stratigraphic information that leads Sumner to conclude that the evidence for the priority of Mushki is "unequivocal" (pers. comm. 1985).

Ceramic parallels with other regions are only suggestive. Sumner sees a "generalized resemblance" between Mushki and Archaic Wares at Chogha Mish in Khuzistan (1977a:299). There is some stylistic similarity between Mushki and Chogha Mish Archaic 1 Painted Burnished Ware, including shared motifs, such as interlocking linear patterns, and the placement of designs on the upper body wall of carinated vessels (Fukai, Horiuchi, and Matsutani 1973:pls. IIIj, XLVII:10; Delougaz and Kantor 1972b:pl. VI:i; Kantor 1976c:fig. 30).

A Mushki design composed of Y figures strung together in parallel rows (pattern p-24 or Y2; Fukai, Horiuchi, and Matsutani 1973:pls. L, XLVII:6) also occurs in red-on-buff at Qal^{c}eh Rostam II in the Bakhtiari Mountains (Zagarell 1982:fig. 9:1) and Tepe Guran R-O (Archaic Painted Ware; Mortensen 1963:fig. 15). Matsutani (Fukai, Horiuchi, and Matsutani 1973:82) draws attention also to the tendency toward diagonal patterning shared by Mushki, Jarmo, Sarab, and Guran. But while Mushki and Qal^{c}eh Rostam II may be related to the Zagros group ceramic tradition, it is highly unlikely that they are contemporary with the early part of the Zagros sequence. Vessel forms, the burnished red slip, and painted linear designs with crosshatching all suggest that Mushki and Qal^{c}eh Rostam II are contemporary with the latest part of the Zagros Neolithic tradition, including the Red Burnished Ware phase in Hulailan, Late Sarab, and the Zagheh Archaic (see "Central Western Iran").

The relationship between Mushki ceramics and Tepe Sialk is a key issue in previous discussions (Fukai, Horiuchi, and Matsutani 1973:74–83). While there are stylistic links between Jari Ware and Sialk I$_{3-5}$ (see below, "Jari Period"), there are good reasons for placing this deposit at Sialk contemporary with the Mushki period. First, Jari Ware does occur in small quantities in the strata dominated by Mushki Ware (Fukai et al. 1973:32, 78); thus the excavated Mushki period deposits, containing the earliest Jari Ware, could be contemporary with Sialk I$_3$. Second, a single specialized design, a reserved zigzag in a crosshatched band, also links Mushki and Sialk I$_3$ (Fukai, Horiuchi, and Matsutani 1973:pl. XX:4; Ghirshman 1938:pl. XLI:A11). Third, Mushki pottery is generally quite different in shape and design from Sialk I$_{1-2}$, an exception being a carinated bowl from Sialk I$_2$ (Ghirshman 1938:pl. XXXIX:S1517). If we consider that there are no more than 2 m of Mushki deposit at the type site, and that Sialk I$_3$ is nearly 3 m in depth, an equation of the two is reasonable (Fukai, Horiuchi, and Matsutani 1973:pl. XLVI; Ghirshman 1938:pl. XXXVI).

The high frequency of geometric microliths (crescents and trapezes) at Mushki (Fukai, Horiuchi, and Matsutani 1973:pls. XXXII, XXXIII:1, LII:31–45, LIII:1–7) is du-

plicated within the Deh Luran sequence only during the Sefid and Surkh phases (Hole 1977:table 40; Hole, Flannery, and Neely 1969:table 5). To the northeast, geometrics are reported from Sang-i Chakhmaq East (Masuda 1974a:fig. 4:10) and Djeitun (Masson 1971:pls. XVIII–XX). "Cosmetic mortars" that appear in Sialk I$_3$, Sang-i Chakhmaq East, and Djeitun occur at Mushki, where they have been called "ear plugs" (Fukai, Horiuchi, and Matsutani 1973:pls. LIV:1–24, LV:7–8; Ghirshman 1938:pl. LII:37–39; Masuda 1974a:fig. 4:11; Masson 1971:pls. XL:13–15, XLI:5–6). The clay and stone cones from Mushki, elsewhere referred to as "miniature pestles or mullers" or "nail-shaped labrets," occur in Sialk I, Sang-i Chakhmaq East, and Djeitun (Fukai, Horiuchi, and Matsutani 1973:pl. LV:10–14; Ghirshman 1938:pl. LII:26–31; Masuda 1974a:fig. 4:16; Masson 1971:figs. XL:1–5, XLI:16–17). In Deh Luran, mullers/labrets occur at Chagha Sefid primarily in the Sefid phase, but have a second peak of popularity in the Sabz and Khazineh phases at Tepe Sabz (Hole 1977:234, fig. 87e–h, pl. 54b–c, table 74; Hole, Flannery, and Neely 1969:237, fig. 102h). Concave-sided or spool-shaped labrets/ear plugs (Fukai, Horiuchi, and Matsutani 1973:pls. LIV:27–66, LV:5, 60) fall within the range of variation illustrated for "stud-shaped labrets" at Chagha Sefid (Hole 1977:pl. 54d); they may also be related to the oval, concave-sided "cuff link" labrets in Deh Luran, common from the Mohammad Jaffar to the Chogha Mami Transitional phases, but most frequent in the Sefid and Surkh phases (Hole, Flannery, and Neely 1969:237, fig. 102a; Hole 1977:237, fig. 92m; compare Fukai, Horiuchi, and Matsutani 1973:fig. LIV:61–64). Another widespread artifact type with a long history is the "grooved polisher" or grooved stone; these occur in Mushki (Fukai, Horiuchi, and Matsutani 1977:pl. LV:65–66), the Sefid and Surkh phases (Hole 1977:211, pl. 50p–r, fig. 86i), and Sialk II$_1$ (Ghirshman 1938:pl. LIII:16). Similar objects occur much earlier at Zarzi, Zawi Chemi, Shanidar, Jarmo, Asiab, and Guran (Hole 1977:211–12; see also Solecki and Solecki 1970; Voigt 1983:203). The bone sickle haft from Mushki (Fukai, Horiuchi, and Matsutani 1973:pls. XXXVI:1, LVI:1) is closely paralleled at Sang-i Chakhmaq East (Masuda 1974a:fig. 4:3; see also fig. 4:1–2, 4) and bears a general resemblance to those from Sialk I$_1$ (Ghirshman 1938:pls. LIV:I–III) and Djeitun (Masson 1971:pl. XIV top).

To summarize, a series of nonceramic artifacts from Mushki are paralleled in the Sefid-Surkh phases in Deh Luran. These support the relatively weak ceramic evidence linking Mushki and Chogha Mish Archaic 1, since the contemporaneity of Surkh and Chogha Mish Archaic 1–2 has been independently established (see "Deh Luran" and "Eastern Susiana"). Given the argument above for the contemporaneity of Mushki and Sialk I$_3$, and the presence of imported sherds of Sialk I$_{3-4}$ and perhaps Sialk II sherds in the Surkh and Chogha Mami Transitional periods at Chagha Sefid (see "Deh Luran"), it seems likely that Mushki is contemporary with the Sefid phase, and the early part of Chogha Mish Archaic 1. The ground stone, clay, and bone artifacts provide direct evidence relating Mushki to sites on the plateau, including Sialk I, Sang-i Chakhmaq East, and distant Djeitun.

B. *The Jari period* is defined by Jari Mound B, and Jari Mound A:level AIII (Egami et al. 1977:1). Jari Painted Ware has red, black, or brown designs on a smooth surface that has sometimes been coated with a thin white slip (Sumner 1972a:37, 1977a:295; see also Egami, Masuda, and Gotoh 1977:pl. V; Egami and Masuda 1962:fig. 22; Fukai, Horiuchi, and Matsutani 1973:33–34, pls. XXIII–XXIV; Sumner 1972a:pl. IV). Sherds of unpainted, "roughly made" jars and basins also occurred (Egami 1967:2938; Egami, Masuda, and Gotoh 1977:pl. V:33, 38–39).

Sumner sees "generalized parallels" for Jari pottery in the Susiana Archaic period and at Qal'eh Rostam (Sumner 1980:2). Most scholars have compared Jari Painted Ware with Sialk I (Mellaart 1975:190; Sumner 1972a:56; Vanden Berghe 1954:400). Although the number of shared motifs is not large, some are unusual and cluster in Sialk I$_4$: parallel lines joined by short cross bars and arranged diagonally or in chevrons (Egami, Masuda, Gotoh 1977:pl. V:12, 19, 22; Fukai, Horiuchi, and Matsutani 1973:pl. XXIV; Ghirshman 1938:pl. XLIV:A5, B4; Sumner 1972a:pl. IV:H–J); diagonal hatching cut by irregularly spaced crosshatch (Fukai, Horiuchi, and Matsutani 1973:pl. XXIII:2:11; Ghirshman 1938:pls. XLII:D13, XLIII:A14); and thick annular bands at the rim (Egami, Masuda, and Gotoh 1977:pl. V:30; Ghirshman 1938:pl. XLIV:B18; Sumner 1972a:pl. IV:D, K).

Small finds are similar to those of the Mushki period (Egami 1967:2939; Egami, Masuda, and Gotoh 1977:pl. VI:7–14). A domed "stud-shaped" labret (Egami, Masuda, and Gotoh 1977:pl. VI:12) finds an exact parallel in the Surkh phase at Chagha Sefid (Hole 1977:237, pl. 54d–e, fig. 92k–l), but is also found in a later Susa A context at Jaffarabad 3 (Dollfus 1971:fig. 21:19). Given the artifact comparisons presented here, it seems likely that the Mushki and Jari periods followed one another closely in time and were of short duration.

C. *The Shamsabad (Bakun BI) period* is defined by excavations at Tal-i Bakun Mound B by the Oriental Institute of Chicago (Schmidt 1937:27, 1939b:124; McCown 1942:23) and the Tokyo University Expedition (Egami and Masuda 1962). The 1937–39 Chicago excavation at Bakun B found a small number of sherds of a coarse, plain pottery in the strata from virgin soil to a thick layer of ash; above the ash, painted pottery appeared (McCown comments, 1941; documented in files

of R. H. Dyson). The Chicago expedition called the lower or earlier part of the deposit level BI, and the term Bakun BI was later used for the entire phase within the Fars sequence. The Japanese excavation of 1956, however, *reversed* the numbering of stratigraphic units, naming as "Level I" the upper or painted pottery phase and referring to the lower phase as "Level II" (Egami and Masuda 1962:fig. 4). This chapter uses the original Chicago numbering for the levels at the site and adopts the name "Shamsabad" for the phase within the Fars sequence as suggested by Sumner (1972a, 1980). Shamsabad occupations have also been documented at Tal-i Jari A in level AII (Egami, Masuda, and Gotoh 1977:7, pl. II; see also Sumner 1977a:300, 1980:2–3).

Shamsabad Ware, Pottery Group B2 of the Japanese excavators and formerly referred to as "Bakun BI Plain Ware," is tempered with large pieces of chaff and is poorly fired to a light brown (Egami, Masuda, and Gotoh 1977:2–3, pl. IV:5–8; Egami and Masuda 1962:fig. 18; Sumner 1972a:37, 1980:2). Forms of decoration include a single incised line around the rim (Sumner 1972a:pl. V:R), application of knobs or wavy lines (Egami, Masuda, and Gotoh 1977:pl. IV:1–2), and painting with a "purple" or "fugitive red" paint (Egami and Masuda 1962:4–5; Egami, Masuda, and Gotoh 1977:pl. IV:3; Sumner 1972a:38, pl. III:L).

There are no good parallels in the lowlands for Shamsabad Ware, although a general relationship can be cited with the chaff-tempered plain wares that are associated with Susiana Black-on-Buff painted wares in Khuzistan (Sumner 1980:3; see "Susiana"). Plain large bowls in *pâte grossière* similar to those typical of Shamsabad are found in Jaffarabad 6–4 (Dollfus 1975a:figs. 10, 12:1–2; Egami and Masuda 1962:fig. 18; Egami, Masuda, and Gotoh 1977:2, pl. IV). The plan of a three-room building in Jari AII has been compared with the Eridu XVI temple (Egami, Masuda, and Gotoh 1977:7; Safar, Mustafa, and Lloyd 1981:fig. 39), which is contemporary with the Jaffarabad period (Dollfus 1983:table 42). Ties between the Shamsabad period and Kirman also occur (see "Southeastern Iran").

D. *The Bakun period* is characterized by the distinctive painted pottery originally found in Tal-i Bakun A (Langsdorff and McCown 1942). Well known from surface survey (Kole 1980; Sumner 1972a:39; see also Stein 1936, 1937, 1940; Vanden Berghe 1959:37–42), Bakun material has been excavated at Tal-i Bakun (Egami and Masuda 1962; Herzfeld 1932; Langsdorff and McCown 1942; Schmidt 1939b), Tal-i Gap (Egami and Sono 1962), Tal-i Jari A (Egami, Masuda, and Gotoh 1977), and Tal-i Nokhodi (Goff 1963, 1964). The period is very long as indicted by deposits of 10 m or more at some sites (Kole 1980). It can be subdivided into three subphases based on ceramic attributes (Dyson 1965), but the boundaries between these phases are not clear-cut. For example, the Middle Bakun phase is based primarily on changing design frequencies at Gap (Egami and Sono 1962:table 1), but the conclusions drawn from the frequency chart do not match those that can be drawn from an examination of the published line drawings and plates, which are highly selective. Moreover, very few designs are sufficiently limited in their chronological distribution within the Bakun period to be useful for interregional comparison. A truly satisfactory distinction between Early and Middle Bakun must eventually be based on a study of changes in vessel forms and the grammar of designs, as well as design frequencies. The following discussion is therefore tentative.

1. *The Early Bakun phase* is defined by Tal-i Bakun BII (Schmidt 1939b; McCown 1942; Egami and Masuda 1962, where these deposits are referred to as "Bakun B level I") and Tal-i Jari AI (Egami, Masuda, and Gotoh 1977). The latest part of this phase is represented by Tal-i Gap Ia–b, and perhaps the beginning of II (Egami and Sono 1962; Dyson 1965:243). Deposits of this phase contain the coarse, chaff-tempered Shamsabad Ware characteristic of the preceding period (Egami and Masuda 1962:4–5, fig. 19: Pottery Group B2; Egami, Masuda, and Gotoh 1977:1, pl. III:21–33; Egami and Sono 1962:fig. 11:6), accompanied by a variant of Bakun Painted Ware, buff-slipped with a burnished or brush-marked surface (Pottery Group B1: Egami and Masuda 1962:4–5, pls. II, V, figs. 13–17; Egami, Masuda, and Gotoh 1977:pl. III; see also McCown 1942:23).

Although many of the designs and vessel forms of Early Bakun continue in Middle Bakun, at least one ceramic parallel relates the Early Bakun phase to the Early and Middle Chogha Mish phases in Susiana. Large jars with ovoid bodies that are often decorated with isolated motifs on the shoulder and with straight everted necks painted as a solid zone occur in Gap Ia–b (Egami and Sono 1962:fig. 25:2–3) and in Jowi 11–12 (Dollfus 1983:figs. 28:3, 30:13, 33:17), Bendebal 21–16 (Dollfus 1983:figs. 61:13, 76:11, 14–15, 78:1–4), and Jaffarabad 3m–n (Dollfus 1975a:fig. 52:14–18). Also popular at Gap in I–IIa, Jowi 11, and Bendebal 24–22 were deep bowls decorated in a wide zone composed of thick and thin annular bands with a central band of geometrical elements (Egami and Sono 1962:figs. 21:1, 7, 22:3, 5–6, table 1; Dollfus 1983:figs. 31:3, 8–11, 56:4–5, 12, 60:12).

Concave-based whorls with bold painted designs link Early/Middle Bakun and the Chogha Mish period (Gap I–II: Egami and Sono 1962:pl. XL:10–15, fig. 32:1–6; Jowi 13, 7, Bendebal 17b, 16: Dollfus 1983:figs. 43:5–6, 93:2–6). Similar but not identical whorls were found in Deh Luran from Mehmeh through Bayat (Hole, Flan-

nery, and Neely 1969:205, fig. 89a–d). Biconical whorls with notched edges occur in Gap I–II (Egami and Sono 1962:pl. XL:2–3, fig. 32:8–10), Jowi 10 (Dollfus 1983:fig. 43:4), Bendebal 27–11 (Dollfus 1983:fig. 93:1, 94:6), and in the Bayat phase at Tepe Sabz (Hole, Flannery, and Neely 1969:fig. 90e).

2. *The Middle Bakun phase* is defined by the earliest deposits in the Chicago excavations at Bakun A, levels AI–II (Langsdorff and McCown 1942), and by Tal-i Gap IIa, levels 12–10 (Egami and Sono 1962). The Japanese excavation in Bakun A was located on the lower edge of the mound (Egami and Masuda 1962:1, fig. 3; Langsdorff and McCown 1942:fig. 2); the excavated strata were numbered I–IV, with I at the top of the deposit, again *reversing* the sequence established by Chicago. On the basis of painted walls and the orientation of a building found in his level IV or the earliest deposit excavated, Egami correlates it with level AIII of the Chicago excavation, located 50 m away and at a higher absolute level (Egami and Masuda 1962:1). The published pottery, however, is more directly related to Chicago's Bakun AI and AII; we therefore include the Japanese Mound A excavation within the Middle Bakun phase.

The handmade Buff-Slipped Ware of Bakun A, or Pottery Group A-1 in the Japanese report, is a continuation of the painted ware present in Early Bakun (Egami and Masuda 1962:2–3, figs. 6–11; Langsdorff and McCown 1942:pls. 15:1, 17:10, 76:16). Painted Buff-Slipped vessels carry designs composed of motifs set in one to three horizontal registers, covering one-half or more of the exterior (Langsdorff and McCown 1942:59–60, pls. 35:5, 36:4, 37:12, 43:14, 45:2, 47:9, 48:12–13, 49:1, 53:14, 59:13, 67:7, 68:1, 70:15, 72:18, 73:7, 76:16, 78:27). Motifs characteristic of Middle Bakun are mainly geometric, but highly stylized humans, caprines, ticks, flying birds, fish, and plants also occur (Egami and Masuda 1962:fig. 9; Egami and Sono 1962:table 1:designs Ig, XIII; Langsdorff and McCown 1942:pls. 67:4–5, 69:15, 71:7, 9, 76:9, 15, 78:2–4, 6–9). Found in Bakun AI–II, and characteristic of Gap IIa, is a variety of circular Maltese cross patterns (Egami and Masuda 1962:figs. 6:8, 7:17; Egami and Sono 1962:table 1:designs IIb, IIc, fig. XXXIII:6; Langsdorff and McCown 1942:pls. 42:9, 43:4, 48:15, 55:14, 72:4, 78:26–27).

Middle Bakun pottery has specific parallels with the middle and late Chogha Mish period at Bendebal and Jowi: large jars with straight or ridged high collars and isolated swastika motifs on the body (Langsdorff and McCown 1942:pl. 44:7; Dollfus 1983:fig. 78); deep bowls with flaring sinuous sides (Egami and Sono 1962:fig. 14:7; Langsdorff and McCown 1942:pl. 76:16; Dollfus 1983:fig. 36:7); and lines of painted dots (Langs-

The Chronology of Iran

dorff and McCown 1942:figs. 42:5, 48:12, 49:11, 62:7; Dollfus 1983:fig. 82:2). Dotted motifs also occur in Early and Middle Farukh (Wright 1981:fig. 17, table 8) and are considered a particularly useful chronological marker within Khuzistan by Dollfus (pers. comm. 1985). An identical and complex design composed of annular bands and alternating solid and dash-filled rectangles that has its greatest frequency in Gap IIA also occurs in Middle Farukh (Egami and Sono 1962:table 1, design Ic5; Wright 1981:fig. 18f). A second complex design links Gap IIa and Bendebal 14 (Egami and Sono 1962:fig. 14:7; Dollfus 1983:fig. 82:8). The conical-based bowls that begin in Bakun AI (Langsdorff and McCown 1942:pl. 71:7) may be related to conical bowls at Faru-khabad (Wright 1981:table 8, fig. 13–14), but the relatively narrow Farukh vessels have better parallels in Late Bakun. To the east, Middle Bakun is firmly linked to Tal-i Iblis II (see "Southeastern Iran").

3. *The Late Bakun phase* is defined by Bakun Mound A levels III–IV (Langsdorff and McCown 1942) and Tal-i Gap IIb–c (Egami and Sono 1962). Late Bakun Painted Buff Ware is elaborately decorated with geometric and representational designs that often cover the entire vessel and sometimes appear as negative patterns. Carefully formed by hand, they are sometimes extremely thin walled (Langsdorff and McCown 1942:24–25, 60–61, pls. 1–4, 9–80). At Bakun a Red Burnished Coarse Ware that is chaff-tempered and poorly fired also occurs (Langsdorff and McCown 1942:26, pls. 17:24–28, 18:1, 4, 13).

A number of ceramic parallels link the Late Bakun phase to Middle and Late Farukh in Deh Luran: an open bowl with incurved rim decorated with spiral ibex horns and maltese cross (Langsdorff and McCown 1942:pl. 71:7; Wright 1981:fig. 22f, Late Farukh); tall, narrow conical cups with rounded bases (Langsdorff and Mc-Cown 1942:pl. 2:7, 16:7; Wright 1981:fig. 14a–b, Middle Farukh);* open bowls with low ring bases painted with a bands or straight and/or wavy lines (Langsdorff and McCown 1942:pls. 52:3, 61:1, and Wright 1981:fig. 12c–d; Egami and Sono 1962:pl. XXIII:5, table 1:design Ia2, and Wright 1981:fig. 15h, table 8; Egami and Sono

1962:fig. 18:1–2, table 1:design IXc, and Wright 1981:fig. 22a, table 8); and holemouth jars, sometimes with applied knobs (Egami and Sono 1962:pl. XX:5; Langsdorff and McCown 1942:pl. 12:5–7, 17:27; Wright 1981:fig. 10a–c, f, h, Middle Farukh). Within Susiana, some of the same or related forms are found in middle and late Chogha Mish contexts at Bendebal and Jaffara-bad: tall conical cups (Langsdorff and McCown 1942:pl. 16:6; Dollfus 1975a:fig. 47:7, 12; 1983:fig. 83:2), open bowls with ring bases and painted band (Dollfus 1975a:fig. 47:19–22; 1983:figs. 74:8, 82:1, 84:3); and holemouth vessels (Dollfus 1975a:fig. 53:1). In addition, necked jars with out-turned rims occur in Jaffarabad 3 m–n (Dollfus 1975a:fig. 53:5) as well as Bakun AIV (Langs-dorff and McCown 1942:pl. 12:13). A highly stylized representation of a mouflon head from a Susiana d/late Chogha Mish context at Tepe Bouhallan is very like one from Bakun A III (Langsdorff and McCown 1942:pl. 71:15; Amiet 1966:fig. 10). Although the painting styles are quite different, some parallels link Late Bakun and Susa A: tall goblets with a decorated zone extending over the entire vessel (Langsdorff and McCown 1942:pls. 40:6, 54:15, 67:13; Amiet 1966:fig. 13; Dollfus 1971:fig. 14; Canal 1978a:fig. 25:1) and snake motifs, including snakes bordered with dots (Langsdorff and McCown 1942:pls. 77:6–7, 9; Amiet 1966:fig. 11).

Evidence for the contemporaneity of Late Bakun with Middle-Late Farukh and late Chogha Mish–Susa A also comes from other artifacts. A relatively large sample of stamp seals recovered from Bakun A III–IV (Langsdorff and McCown 1942:65–68, pls. 7:11–19, 8:1–11, 81:15–33, 82:1–26; Schmidt 1939b:fig. 93) includes low and high hemispheres with pierced tabs, hemispherical and lenticular seals pierced longitudinally, and conical seals with convex faces. The shape of the seal face is highly variable and may be round, oval, subrectangular, trian-gular, or fan-shaped; designs tend to be quartered pat-terns and may be deeply cut. Hemispherical seals with tab handles and quartered patterns like those in Late Bakun occur in the Middle Farukh at Farukhabad (Wright 1981:fig. 29d; see Langsdorff and McCown 1942:pl. 81:17–18) and in Susa Acropole I:25 (Le Brun 1971:fig. 35:6; see also Amiet 1972:5–32). Longitudinally pierced lenticular and hemispherical seals with incised quartered patterns are found in Susa A (Dollfus 1971:fig. 23:3, 1978b:fig. 20), as well as sites in the Zagros (see "Central Western Iran") and in Sialk III$_{1-7}$, especially III$_{4-6}$ (Ghirshman 1938:pl. LXXXVI). At Tepe Gawra they are found in levels XIX to X-A, with a cluster in XI-A that includes tanged and longitudinally pierced seals with a wide range of patterns comparable to those in Bakun AIII–IV (Tobler 1950:pls. CLVIII:1, 8, 12–15, CLX:31–33). Clay labels and jar stoppers appear in Fars during

---

*Some vessel forms of the Late Bakun phase have a long duration in the lowlands. For example, a variant of the conical cup with rounded base continues into the Early Dynastic period in the Diyala (Langsdorff and McCown 1942:pl. 15:8; Delougaz 1952:pl. 50b); bell-shaped cups (Langsdorff and McCown 1942:pl. 12:3–4) occur at Eridu from Ubaid 2 through 4 (Oates 1960:Type 13a); high-collared jars with globular bodies, present throughout the Bakun period, also occur throughout the Chogha Mish and Susa A periods in Khuzistan (Dollfus 1978b:figs. 16–19; Le Brun 1978c:fig. 30:12) and in Ubaid 1–3 (Oates 1960:type 5). Such forms have limited value for chronology and are cited here only when the parallel involves a combination of form and painted de-sign.

Bakun AIII–IV (Langsdorff and McCown 1942:66–67, 72, pls. 7:13, 15–19, 83:8–9, 12). At Jaffarabad, jar stoppers appear in Susa A (Dollfus 1971:fig. 27:6), while in Deh Luran they do not occur before the Bayat phase (Hole, Flannery, and Neely 1969:247, fig. 103p).

Plain and painted clay figurines from Late Bakun contexts include representations of animals and humans, primarily females with small conical breasts (Langsdorff and McCown 1942:61–65, pls. 5:4–19, 6:1–27, 7:1–10). Several heads in the form of elongated cones with pinched faces and slanted incised eyes found in Bakun AIII (Langsdorff and McCown 1942:pl. 7:24–27; Schmidt 1939b:129, fig. 94:top, TBA 68) have been compared to Ubaid figurines from Ur and Eridu (Schmidt 1939b:129). Although this comparison is very generalized, it is supported by body fragments from standing figures with separately modeled legs and a fragment with broad shoulders decorated with applied pellets that are similar to the Ubaid standing figurines (Langsdorff and McCown 1942:pl. 6:18, 21, 24–26, 7:1; see Safar, Mustafa, and Lloyd 1981:fig. 116:3–4; Woolley 1955:pl. 20). Parallels for columnar, stub-armed figurines from Bakun are found in Susa A (Langsdorff and McCown 1942:pls. 6:17, 7:7, 10; see Amiet 1966:figs. 18–19; Dollfus 1971:pl. IX:5, fig. 22:2). Also making their initial appearance in Susa A and Late Bakun are figurines of birds (Langsdorff and McCown 1942:pl. 5:4–6; see Dollfus 1971:fig. 22:4, 6–7, 9, 12; 1978b:fig. 20).

Biconical whorls with notches or incisions around their edges link Bakun and the Bayat period at Tepe Sabz (Egami and Sono 1962:fig. 32:8, 12; Langsdorff and McCown 1942:69, pls. 8:16, 82:28–31, 34–36; Hole, Flannery, and Neely 1969:fig. 90d–e). In Susiana they occur in the Chogha Mish period at Jowi and Bendebal (Dollfus 1983:figs. 43:4, 94:2–4, 6), and in the Susa A period at Jaffarabad (Dollfus 1971:fig. 21:2, 4, 6; see Langsdorff and McCown 1942:pls. 8:16, 82:29, 30, 35; Egami and Sono 1962:fig. 32:8–9, pl. XL:2–4).

To summarize, a series of diverse parallels can be drawn between the Late Bakun phase, the Middle-Late Farukh phase in Deh Luran, and the Middle to Late Chogha Mish and Susa A periods in Khuzistan. The comparisons that are most specific and limited in time, however, suggest that Late Bakun is contemporary with Middle and/or Late Farukh and Susa A.

E. *The Lapui period* was defined by Sumner (1972a:40–42, pls. XII–XVIII) based on survey material from the Marv Dasht; a small sample of sherds from the surface of Bakun A and from the latest excavated deposit, AV (Langsdorff and McCown 1942:32–33; McCown 1942:48–49; Schmidt 1939b:123; Sumner 1972a:40); and sherds from Mounds C to G in the Tal-i Gap group (Sono 1967:2940). Material stratified beneath Banesh deposits at Tal-i Kureh, assigned to a "Terminal Lapui

phase" by Alden (1979:154–56, fig. 52), is better treated as Early Banesh (Sumner 1986).

Lapui Fine Ware, equivalent to typical Bakun AV Red Ware, is smoothed or roughly burnished; it sometimes has a red slip over a buff paste. Lapui Common Ware has a red paste; the smoothed or burnished surface is frequently crazed or pitted (Sumner 1972a:41–42). Vessel forms include beakers, open bowls, incurved bowls, holemouth vessels, and jars with sharply everted rims (Egami and Masuda 1962:fig. 12:14–19; Langsdorff and McCown 1942:pls. 20–21; Sumner 1972a:41–42, pls. XII–XVI, XVII:J, L–N, XVIII:G–J). Incised or painted sherds are extremely rare (Langsdorff and McCown 1942:pl. 21:13; Sumner 1972a:pls. XV:M–N, XVI:I). On one site Lapui Ware was found associated with pottery that had red, brown, or black painted designs on a buff paste, designated as Asupas Ware (Sumner 1972a:42, pl. XVII:A–F, O–R).

Strong parallels in vessel form occur between Lapui and Susa Acropole I:25–24, the late Susa A Period (Sumner 1980; compare Langsdorff and McCown 1942:pl. 20:13, and Le Brun 1971:fig. 39:10; Langsdorff and McCown 1942:pl. 20:8, and Le Brun 1971:fig. 39:3–5). Wright states that "the minority redwares of Susa 24–25 duplicate in form and fabric the ceramics of the Lapui Phase" (1978:233); he places late Lapui contemporary with Early Uruk in Khuzistan (Susa Acropole I:22; pers. comm. 1984; 1978:fig. 5). Related material has also been recovered from the surface of sites in the Bakhtiari Mountains (Sumner 1980; see Zagarell 1982:50, figs. 29:1–7, 30). Continuing to the northwest, a tall Red Ware vessel from an unknown provenience at Bakun (Langsdorff and McCown 1942:pl. 20:21) is identical in form to the red-slipped and burnished S-walled jars of Godin VII (Levine and Young 1987:35, fig. 16:5; see also Young and Levine 1974:fig. 13:6). To the east, Lapui ware occurs at Iblis in periods I–II, and in Yahya VI–VA2 (see "Southeastern Iran").

F. *The Banesh period,* originally defined on the basis of surface material collected by Sumner (1972a:40–41, 42), has now been firmly established by excavations at Tal-i Kureh (Alden 1977) and at Tal-i Malyan or ancient Anshan (Sumner 1974, 1976, 1985; Nicholas 1980). It can be divided into three phases based on ceramics within which two major groups have been distinguished: Banesh Chaff-Tempered Ware, dominant throughout the period (Alden 1979:211; Nicholas 1980:486); and Banesh Grit-Tempered Ware (Alden 1979:209; see also Nicholas 1980:555–57, tables 79–80). The latter may be slipped and decorated with black, white, and/or red paint (Alden 1979:209–10; Sumner 1972a:42–44).

1. *The Early Banesh phase,* which includes Alden's "Terminal Lapui," "Initial Banesh," and Early Banesh phases (Sumner 1986), is defined by a small sounding at

Tal-i Kureh (site 7F1; Alden 1977, 1979:50, 155–56). Ceramic parallels strongly relate Early Banesh to Susa II, or Acropole I:18–17 (Alden 1979:60). These include two variants of "pinched-rim bowls" (Alden 1979:fig. 36:3–23; Le Brun 1971:fig. 45:11, 1978b:fig. 19:10); Banesh trays (Alden 1979:fig. 33; Le Brun 1978b:fig. 23:7–9); folded-rim jars (Alden 1979:fig. 31:17–20; Le Brun 1978b:fig. 25:2, 8, 11–13); straight-sided goblets and flat goblet bases (Alden 1979:figs. 31: 31–47, 32:1–9; Le Brun 1971:fig. 47:6-7, 1978:fig. 20:9); straight-sided open bowls with incised wavy line below the rim (Alden 1979:fig. 40:15; Le Brun 1971:fig.46:11); and black-on-white painted bands (Le Brun 1971:fig. 53:4). Nonceramic parallels between Early Banesh and Khuzistan are limited to a stone macehead with four grooves from the surface of Site 10I3L that is duplicated in Susa Acropole I:17A (Alden 1979:fig. 57:21; Le Brun 1971:fig. 55:2).

2. *The Middle Banesh phase* includes material designated by Alden as Early-Middle and Late-Middle Banesh; it is defined by building levels TUV:1–3 and ABC:2–5 at Tal-i Malyan (Nicholas 1980, 1981; Sumner 1974, 1976, 1986). Area TUV and ABC 4 were the locus of domestic and craft activities, while in ABC 2–3 there were large-scale formal structures (Nicholas 1980; Sumner 1976, 1986). Malyan was at this time a small city of ca. 45 ha (Sumner 1986).

Middle Banesh ceramics have parallels with both Susa II (Acropole I:18–17) and Susa III (Acropole I:16–14B; Ville Royale I:18–13). In use at Malyan were several variants of jars with four nose lugs, also found in Acropole I:17–18 (Nicholas 1980:508, 558, fig. 159; Sumner 1976:fig. 7a; see Le Brun 1971: figs. 50:1, 3–4, 51, 53:1, 3–4; 1978b:figs. 24:4, 12, 32, 33:4, 7; 1978c:figs. 32:10–11, 14, 34:9–10, 14); at Farukhabad vessels combining four nose lugs with painted triangles on the shoulder occur in both Middle and Late Uruk contexts (Wright 1981:111, fig. 57d, h). Deep beveled-rim bowls first appear in the Fars sequence during Early Banesh, already established as contemporary with Susa II (see above); they have their maximum popularity during the Middle Banesh phase, with a decline from TUV level III to I (Nicholas 1980:361, 364, table 82, fig. 154c). In Khuzistan, beveled-rim bowls are most frequent in Susa II (Le Brun 1978b:fig. 20:8, 1978c:fig. 34:1); Le Brun (1978c:192) implies that these do not occur after Acropole I:level 17 (i.e., after Susa II), but according to Carter this type is still "relatively common" in Ville Royale I:18–16 or Susa IIIB (1978:fig. 40:2–3; see also *grossen blumentöpfe* type 8a from Warka; Nissen 1970:table 104). At Farukhabad, beveled-rim bowls are common in Middle Uruk and remain so in Late Uruk, declining in frequency in the Jemdet Nasr phase (Wright 1981:tables 40–41). Late occurrences of beveled-rim bowls are re-

ported for at least one Mesopotamian site: at Nippur they survive into Jemdet Nasr and the transition into Early Dynastic I (Hansen 1965:202, 208). Finally, low-rimmed trays continue as common forms in Middle Banesh (see Early Banesh above), but at Susa they are common only in Susa II, Acropole I:18–17, and all but disappear by Acropole I:14A-13 (Le Brun 1971:203; see also *blumentöpfe* type 2 at Warka; Nissen 1970:table 104).

Characteristic of Middle Banesh and Susa Acropole I:16–14B are pedestal-based goblets (Nicholas 1980:fig. 155 [hollow-based], fig. 156a–b [solid-based]; see Le Brun 1971:192, 199, 203, fig. 60:1–4; 1978c:fig. 36:4). The chronological distribution of these goblets is apparently linked to that of beveled-rim bowls (see Nicholas 1980:561, 564, 568, 581): in TUV, goblets increase in frequency from level III–I, as BRBs decline; at Farukhabad, the pattern is repeated, with solid-footed goblets becoming common in the Jemdet Nasr period and persisting into Early Dynastic I (Wright 1981:169, tables 40–41). Also occurring in Susa I:16–14A are jars with rolled or expanded rim (Nicholas 1980:figs. 164, 165a; Le Brun 1971:fig. 61:11–13); flaring-sided bowl/cups (Nicholas 1980:fig. 166a–d; Le Brun 1971:figs. 60:7–9, 65:9; see also *blumentöpfe* types 3–5 at Warka, Nissen 1970:table 104); horizontal bar lugs (Nicholas 1980:89; Le Brun 1971:fig. 65:14); and crescent lugs placed at the rim or lower on the body (Le Brun 1971:figs. 60:21, 65:13).

To summarize, while some ceramic forms characteristic of Susa II occur in the Middle Banesh phase of Fars, associated Middle Banesh forms are found only in Susa IIIA. Given the entire pattern of ceramic distribution, an equation of Middle Banesh and Susa III is quite convincing. Using the Farukhabad material to link Middle Banesh with the Mesopotamian sequence, it is contemporary with Jemdet Nasr and may last into the Early Dynastic period (Alden 1979:fig. 12; Nicholas 1980:86–96; Sumner 1986). This dating is strongly supported by both tablets and glyptic evidence. The signs on the Malyan tablets are comparable to the Proto-Elamite A script from Susa found in Acropole I:16–14B, and the Malyan glyptic is closely paralleled stylistically in the same levels (Carter 1984:119, with refs., 1980:fig. 17:3, 7; Pittman 1980; Sumner 1986).

3. *The Late Banesh phase* is known from surface survey (Alden 1979:51–52), from Malyan test H5, and from Malyan By8 along the southern city wall. It is also possible that TUV level I should be placed in this phase. The fortification of Malyan during Late Banesh is interesting in light of the intrusion of Mesopotamian rulers into Elam during the Early Dynastic Period. Indeed Gudea boasts of having "conquered with weapons the town of Anshan (Kerd Malyan) in Elam" (Hinz 1972:70).

Although a low percentage of Chaff-Tempered Ware vessels including standard Middle Banesh forms were found in the Malyan city wall sounding By8, diagnostic types for Late Banesh are of Grit-Tempered Ware (Alden 1979:51, fig. 42; Sumner 1985:156, figs. 3–4, pl. Ib). Ceramic parallels occur in Susa Acropole I:15–14A and Ville Royale I:18–13, dated to Susa III (Alden 1979:60, fig. 12). These include bowls with flattened rims decorated with simple incised lines (Alden 1979:fig. 42:9–10; Sumner 1985:fig. 4g–i; Carter 1980:fig. 10; Le Brun 1971:figs. 60:20, 65:15) and a painted carinated bowl with everted rim (Alden 1979:fig. 51:12; Carter 1980:fig. 15:12). Carinated vessels with painted bands from Malyan By8 are duplicated in Ville Royale I:12–10 (Sumner 1985:fig. 3l–n; Carter 1980:figs. 28:4, 29:1–3). Given the evidence relating Middle Banesh to Susa IIIA, a correlation of Late Banesh with Susa IIIB–IVA and by extension Early Dynastic I–III is suggested.

G. *The Kaftari period* is defined by excavations at Malyan and at Tal-i Nokhodi I–II (Goff 1964, pottery mistakenly identified with Bakun AV or Lapui Red Ware; Sumner 1972a:44, 1980:table I; see also Nickerson 1983:8; Stein 1936; Vanden Berghe 1954). The most common ceramic group is Kaftari Buff Ware, which occurs in plain and painted variants (Nickerson 1983:132; Sumner 1974:167). Designs include banded motifs and the famous fat Kaftari birds, which always fly left (Nickerson 1983:figs. 39–40; Sumner 1972a:pls. XXIII–XXV, 1974:167, figs. 6–7, pl. IVc–d). Kaftari Plain Buff Ware may be decorated with incised wavy lines, comb incision or finger impressions (Nickerson 1983:fig. 41; Sumner 1972a:pl. XXXI:A, D, 1974:167, fig. 8). Kaftari Red-Slipped Ware also occurs in both a plain and painted variety, and sometimes has plastic decoration (Nickerson 1983:134–35, figs. 39–41; Sumner 1972a:pls. XXVII:G, P, Q–R, XXVIII–XXIX, 1974:167, fig. 9c–f).

Artifact parallels linking Kaftari and Susa span a long period. Painted Buff Wares with geometric motifs and left-flying birds appear in Susa IVA or Early Dynastic III, and there is a general stylistic similarity to Kaftari (e.g., Carter 1980:fig. 28; Nickerson 1983:fig. 58a–i). Vessel forms differ, however, with the best parallels for the Kaftari forms occurring later in the Susa sequence. Low tripod bowls similar to those found at Malyan are found at Susa in the Shimashki period, which postdates the Ur III period in Mesopotamia (compare Sumner 1972a:fig. XXIX:O–P, 1974:fig. 8d; Carter 1984:fig. 10:4). Bowls with sharply incurved rims (Sumner 1972a:pl. XXVII:G, P–R) occur in Ville Royal I:4–3 or Susa VB, also dated to the Shimashki period (Carter 1980:fig. 45:1–3); similar examples are found at Tell Asmar in the Larsa period (Delougaz 1952:pl. 120c). Large storage vessels with impressed ridges and incised decoration are found in Ville Royale I:5–3 (Sumner 1972a:pl. XXXI:A–D, 1974:fig. 8g–h; Carter 1980:figs. 39:17, 49:18, 50:14–21). Sherds

of Fine Gray Ware with "drilled and incised, sometimes white filled decoration" (Sumner 1974:170, fig. 10:a–c) have been identified as Isin-Larsa imports by Carter (1984:152; see Delougaz 1952:pl. 123). Tall sinuous-sided jars with pronounced ridges on the interior were found in Kaftari and in the Sukkalmah period at Susa, ca. 1900–1600 B.C. (Sumner 1974:fig. 8a–b; Carter 1984:fig. 10:9). This form also occurs at Tell Asmar in a Larsa context (Delougaz 1952:pl. 121e), as do shallow bowls with flat bases and wide ledge rims (Sumner 1974:fig. 8k; Delougaz 1952:pl. 148:B.061.210). One of the mold-made female figurine fragments from Malyan appears to duplicate a typical Sukkalmah figure (Sumner 1974:fig. 11o; Carter 1984:fig. 10:8).

Other evidence confirms a long duration for Kaftari. Although early reports based on the evidence from Operation ABC suggested a hiatus of unknown length, parallels with Susa IVA found in both Late Banesh and Kaftari (see above) suggest a gradual transition between phases (Alden 1979:51–52, n. 2). A *terminus post quem* for most of the excavated Kaftari material is provided by sealings with cuneiform inscriptions (Stolper 1976; Sumner 1977b:178), which indicate a date sometime after the ascendance of Sumerian influence at Susa and the introduction of cuneiform as the written script during period IVB ca. 2400 B.C. (Carter 1984:134; Vallat 1978:194). The cluster of strong parallels with the Susa Sukkalmah period indicate that Kaftari lasted well into the second millennium (see also R. Henrickson 1986b:fig. 3).

The Fasa-Darab Valley Sequence

Surveys carried out in the Fasa and Darab valleys to the southeast of Shiraz by Piere de Miroschedji (1971, 1972, 1974), supplemented by the earlier work of Aurel Stein (1936) and unpublished excavations by M. F. Tavallali of the Iranian Archaeological Service, document settlements contemporary with the Mushki/Jari, Bakun, Lapui, and Kaftari periods in the Marv Dasht (Miroschedji 1972; Sumner 1977a).

The Radiocarbon Evidence for the Southwestern Zagros

Only scattered dates are available for the early portion of the Kur River Basin sequence. The Banesh period, however, is dated by a large and consistent cluster of dates from Malyan. A total of twelve samples from Middle Banesh deposits in Operations ABC and TUV provides an average calibrated date of 3370–3050 B.C. This overlaps with the range suggested by two dates from contexts in the sounding at Tal-e Kure assigned to the Early Banesh phase on the basis of ceramics (table 2). Three more dates from Late Banesh deposits within the city wall also overlap. Thus the radiocarbon evidence for Banesh firmly dates this period to the late fourth millennium, but does not provide good evidence for its precise duration.

Another large suite of determinations from Kaftari deposits provides an average corrected range of 2120–1880 B.C. This is within the time period suggested by correlations with the historical sequence from Mesopotamia if the high chronology is adopted (Porada et al., this vol., chap. 5).

Southeastern Iran

Kirman: The Iblis Sequence

A study of the remains of the largely destroyed mound of Tal-i Iblis, located in the Bard Sir Valley south of Kirman, was undertaken by Joseph R. Caldwell in 1964 and 1966 (Caldwell 1967a, 1967b, 1967c; Caldwell and Malek Shahmirzadi 1966; Caldwell and Sarraf 1967; Chase, Caldwell, and Fehervari 1967; Evett 1967). The 1964 study collected a small sample of sherds and associated radiocarbon samples (table 2:P-924 through P-929) from a stratigraphic column; it defined a series of Iblis *levels 0–6*, with 0 at the bottom (Caldwell 1967a; Caldwell and Malek Shahmirzadi 1966). Excavations in 1966 using arbitrary digging units produced new Iblis *periods 0–VI*, each characterized by a "pottery complex" (Caldwell 1967b:32; Chase, Caldwell, and Fehervari 1967:112, fig. 1, table 1). This new, typologically oriented sequence is not interchangeable with that from 1964 (Caldwell 1967b:30–32; Chase, Caldwell, and Fehervari 1967:112). In the following discussion, each phase is strictly defined by those excavated units that seem most coherent. Even allowing for gaps, the sequence as presently known does not appear to represent any great length of time, since the total depth of deposit for Iblis I–IV is less than 4.5 m (Chase, Caldwell, and Fehervari 1967:fig. 1).

A. *The "Iblis 0 period"* was defined by the lowest 40–50 cm of excavation Area A:sections A and B (Caldwell 1967b:fig. 3; Chase, Caldwell, and Fehervari 1967:fig. 1). In this small test area, only Lalehzar Coarse Ware sherds were found. The absence of painted fine wares in this deposit was used by Chase to establish a "pure Lalehzar Coarse Ware horizon" (Chase, Caldwell, and Fehervari 1967:149–51). The other excavators, however, had reservations about the reality of Iblis 0, pointing out the strong possibility of sampling error given the volume of deposit excavated and the very small number of decorated sherds in Iblis I strata (Caldwell 1967b:32; Chase, Caldwell, and Fehervari 1967:149–50); for example, within the 96 m² of Iblis I floor deposits cleared in Area D, only one Bard Sir sherd was associated with 275 Lalehzar Coarse Ware sherds (Evett 1967:table 2). Based on the available evidence we conclude that Iblis 0 cannot stand as a time unit distinct from Iblis I, and this "period" should be rejected.

B. *The Iblis I period* is best documented by material on the floors of buildings in Areas B, D, F, and G (Caldwell 1967b:fig. 3). Up to 99 percent of the pottery sample from Iblis I consists of Lalehzar Coarse Ware, with very rare sherds of Bard Sir fine wares (Caldwell and Sarraf 1967:306; Evett 1967:table 8, 15; for Bard Sir, see below). Lalehzar Coarse Ware is a thick, heavily chaff-tempered ware covered with a slip (Chase, Caldwell, and Fehervari 1967:150, citing F. Matson).

In Kirman, Lalehzar Coarse Ware is paralleled in Yahya VIB to V (see "Southeastern Iran"). Martha Prickett (1986) points out that the Lalehzar Coarse Ware at Iblis is of the porous variety designated as Type 2 in her Rud-i Gushk survey and found at Tepe Yahya in periods VIB–VB. It is quite different from the dense Rud-i Gushk Type 1 which is found in Yahya VII. Common Iblis I forms are large storage vessels with undercut lower bodies and concave bases, pear-shaped vessels, and simple bowls (Caldwell and Sarraf 1967:pl. 2:lower left, figs. 6–7, pl. 7:lower left; Chase, Caldwell, and Fehervari 1967:150; Evett 1967:fig. 1:1–3). At Yahya, large storage jars with undercut lower bodies and flat bases are characteristic of Yahya VI–VA.2.

The best ceramic parallels to the west are with the Shamsabad period in Fars. The fabric of Lalehzar Coarse Ware is similar to Shamsabad Ware (Chase, Caldwell, and Fehervari 1967:150), and coarse ware vessels with concave bases are relatively common in the Shamsabad assemblage (Egami and Masuda 1962:5, fig. 18; Egami, Masuda, and Gotoh 1977:pls. III:31–33, IV:10, 14; Sumner 1972a:pl. V:E–F). The use of applied elements on Shamsabad Coarse Ware sherds (Jari AII, Egami, Masuda, and Gotoh 1977:2, pl. IV:1–2) is paralleled by large storage vessels on Iblis I house floors (Evett 1967:203). A small number of Lalehzar sherds from Iblis I are painted with broad red bands and simple designs (Caldwell and Sarraf 1967:fig. 6:3; Chase, Caldwell, and Fehervari 1967:fig. 3, bottom); painted Coarse Ware sherds occur at the beginning of the Early Bakun phase in Fars (Egami and Masuda 1962:fig. 19:36) as well as in Yahya VIB.2–VC (Beale 1978:27–28, 34, fig. 3:lower right). Farther to the west, very good parallel storage vessels with concave bases occur in Jowi 14, or the end of the Jaffarabad period (Dollfus 1983:fig. 19:10), where they represent a development of forms found at the beginning of this period (Dollfus 1971:fig. 30:8, 1975a:figs. 14–15, 1983:fig. 11:13–15, 17–18).

Parallels for Iblis I small finds also occur in Shamsabad and Early Bakun. Conical concave-based spindle whorls similar to those in Iblis I occur in Bakun deposits at Jari AI and Bakun BII (Caldwell and Sarraf 1967:fig. 10:3; Evett 1967:fig. 8:8; Egami and Masuda 1962:fig. 21:20, pl. IV:3; Egami, Masuda, and Gotoh 1977:pl. VI:15). They are found in somewhat later contexts at Bendebal 16–20 or the middle of the Chogha Mish Phase (Dollfus 1983:fig. 93:2–5). A fragment from the floor of House F appears to be the incised base of a seated figurine (Evett 1967:fig. 8:2), similar to one from Jari A (Egami, Masuda, and Gotoh 1977:pl. VI:2).

The buildings of Iblis I are made of mud-bricks, with four to eight thumb impressions arranged in two rows (Caldwell and Sarraf 1967:pl. 7, lower). Similar bricks appear within Kirman in Yahya VIIC and go out of use during Yahya VB (Beale 1978:494). Thumb-impressed bricks with four depressions occur in Sialk II, and in slightly variant form in the Cheshmeh Ali period at Zagheh (Ghirshman 1938:pl. LVIII; Malek Shahmirzadi 1977b:fig. 11, 1979b:184). In Mesopotamia they occur in the Transitional levels at Chogha Mami (Oates 1973:175) and in Temple XV at Eridu (Lloyd and Safar 1948:121). The Iblis I long bricks are similar in size to finger-grooved bricks found in the Archaic Susiana period at Chogha Mish (Delougaz 1976:35) and in the Cheshmeh Ali period at Zagheh (Malek Shahmirzadi 1979b:184, fig. 3). Long bricks occur in the Jaffarabad period at Bendebal 28 (Dollfus 1983:137–38), Jowi 16 (Dollfus 1983:22), and in the Susa A Phase at Jaffarabad (Dollfus 1971:28).

Thus ceramic parallels link Iblis I with Yahya VI and early V, a range that is supported by the architectural evidence; however, the presence of strong ties between Early Iblis II and Yahya VC–B (see below) suggests that Iblis I is contemporary Yahya VI. Farther west, Iblis I can be placed contemporary with Shamsabad and Early Bakun in Fars.

C. *The Iblis II period* is defined by the appearance of large quantities of fine ware (Chase, Caldwell, and Fehervari 1967:154; Evett 1967:tables 2, 8, 15). It can be divided into two stratigraphic phases, characterized by different frequencies of the major decorated wares. Although comparisons with other regions are not always clear-cut due to the overlap in ceramic types between phases, the chronological pattern that emerges is consistent and useful.

1. *The Early Iblis II (Bard Sir) phase* is represented by "fill" inside the houses of Areas D, F, and G (Evett 1967:table 8), and by the lowest levels of a trash dump in Area E, ca. 60 m away from the mound (Chase, Caldwell, and Fehervari 1967:155–58; Caldwell 1967b:fig. 1). Lalehzar Coarse Ware continues, but Bard Sir and Iblis Wares also occur in some quantity (Chase, Caldwell, and Fehervari 1967: tables IV–VIII; Evett 1967:tables 2–4).

Bard Sir Painted Ware is decorated with black, maroon, or fugitive red painted designs which are arranged in bands on bowls (Chase, Caldwell, and Fehervari

1967:151, fig. 4:middle and bottom, 5–10; Evett 1967:203, figs. 3–4; Sarraf 1981:fig. 5:73, pl. 7:2–3). Prickett (1986) compares this pottery with her Rud-i Gushk survey Types 4 and 5 or Yahya Black-on-Buff Ware, as does Beale (1978:126; see also Lamberg-Karlovsky 1970a:figs. 39–40, 42–43); this places Early Iblis II contemporary with Yahya VC–B (see Yahya sequence). The only illustrated example of Iblis Painted Ware from Early II, a small sinuous-sided beaker with a band of nested chevrons running around the rim (Evett 1967:fig. 5), is exactly paralleled in Yahya VB (Lamberg-Karlovsky 1970a:fig. 29b–c).

To the west, a group of unique and complex design elements links the Bard Sir Painted Ware of Early Iblis II to Middle-Late Bakun in Fars: a "tick" or insect motif (Chase, Caldwell, and Fehervari 1967:fig. 6:center right, 10:lower; Egami and Sono 1962:fig. 20:12, Gap I, 12:6, Gap II; Egami and Masuda 1962:fig. 15:2, Chicago Bakun BII; Miroschedji 1973:fig. 4:19, Fasa); flying birds with "comb" wings (Chase, Caldwell, and Fehervari 1967:fig. 5:upper right, fig. 6:upper left; Langsdorff and McCown 1942:pl. 76:11, 14, Bakun AIII; Miroschedji 1973:fig. 4:6, Fasa); triangular-bodied figures lined up end to end (Chase, Caldwell, and Fehervari 1967:fig. 6:upper right; compare with Langsdorff and McCown 1942:pl. 47:11, Bakun AII; Miroschedji 1972:fig. 4:6, Fasa); a zigzag pattern alternating with vertical combs (Chase, Caldwell, and Fehervari 1967:fig. 6:lower left, fig. 11:center right; Egami and Sono 1962:fig. 23:2–4, Gap I and II); a Maltese cross with combs on four sides (Chase, Caldwell, and Fehervari 1967:fig. 7, bottom; Egami and Sono 1962:fig. 31:1, Gap I; variants in Bakun AI, III and IV: Langsdorff and McCown 1942:pls. 44:10, 45:5, 48:15; Gap II: Egami and Sono 1962:fig. 30:2); a lozenge or square (Chase, Caldwell, and Fehervari 1967: fig. 4, center; Langsdorff and McCown 1942:pls. 61:2, 49:4, Bakun AI; Egami and Masuda 1962:fig. 17:4); bands of solid black triangles bordered on each side by a line (Chase, Caldwell, and Fehervari 1967:fig. 6, center right; Langsdorff and McCown 1942:pls. 32:8, 35:6, Bakun AIII); and a multiple-lined swastika (Chase, Caldwell, and Fehervari 1967:fig. 5, above center; Langsdorff and McCown 1942:pls. 78:32, 80:21). Designs composed of zigzags with solid apices and combs (Chase, Caldwell, and Fehervari 1967:fig. 6:lower left, 11:top and center; Evett 1967:fig. 3, top right) occur in a variant form in Chicago Bakun BII (Egami and Masuda 1962:fig. 15:7), Tal-i Gap Ia (Egami and Sono 1962: fig. 23:3–4), and Bakun AIII (Langsdorff and McCown 1942:pl. 57:6–7). An incised artifact in a crosslike form with crosshatched incision on one face and with a lenticular cross section is generally comparable to lenticular and button seals with notches cut into the sides found in Middle and Late Bakun contexts (Chase, Caldwell, and Fehervari 1967:fig. 36:11; Egami and Masuda 1962:fig. 20:2,pl. IV:1; Langsdorff and McCown 1942:pl. 8:6–7).

To summarize, the numerous and specific parallels in painted design suggest that the Early Iblis II Bard Sir Painted Ware is an eastern variant of the Middle to Late Bakun phase ceramic tradition of Fars. They also provide a strong link to Yahya VB–C. If we accept these correlations, the chronological distribution of Bard Sir Red-Slipped Ware, common in Iblis II, is particularly interesting (see Chase, Caldwell, and Fehervari 1967:152, 154, fig. 12, pl. 6, tables V–VIII; Evett 1967:203, tables 2–4). Prickett equates Bard Sir Red-Slipped with the Soghun Wares characteristic of Yahya VI and VC–B (1986; see "Yahya"). Parallels in vessel form link Bard Sir Red-Slipped Ware to the Lapui period in Fars: holemouth jars (Chase, Caldwell, and Fehervari 1967:fig. 12; Sumner 1972a:pl. XV:A–C) and flared-rim bowls with flat bases (Chase, Caldwell, and Fehervari 1967: pls. 4:7–8, 6; Sumner 1972a:pl. XIV:A, G, J–L, N). The Lapui period succeeds Bakun and is therefore later than Iblis II. Thus the technological tradition represented by this group of red-slipped wares seems to have begun in the east and gradually spread to the west.

2. *The Late Iblis II phase* is defined by level 1 of Area E:sections A–B, and by the deposit from 260 cm to 200 cm in Area A:section C (Chase, Caldwell, and Fehervari 1967:157, 170, tables V–IX. Note that most of the illustrated pottery comes from Area C, a unit assigned by the excavators to Iblis II but never analyzed; Chase, Caldwell, and Fehervari 1967:174). While Bard Sir Painted is still present, Iblis Painted Ware is now the most common fine ware (Chase, Caldwell, and Fehervari 1967:154, figs. 13–17). Parallels between Iblis Painted ceramic industries in Fars are less striking than those for Bard Sir Painted, but they cluster in the Late Bakun phase. They include painted zigzags on sinuous-sided beakers found in Gap IIa–b (Chase, Caldwell, and Fehervari 1967:fig. 13; Egami and Sono 1962:fig. 82:5, 8, table 1:designs Ic3) and painted potters marks on the base of vessels in Bakun AIII–IV (Chase, Caldwell, and Fehervari 1967:fig. 15, bottom; Langsdorff and McCown 1942:pl. 80:25–26).

D. *The Iblis III (Dashkar) period* is defined by level 3 of the 1964 test block, supplemented by material from the 150–200 cm level in Area A:section C (Chase, Caldwell, and Fehervari 1967:177, table IX). This sample, which consists almost entirely of ceramics, is further enlarged by material found in the Gypsum Burning Furnace (Caldwell 1967b:fig. 3; Chase, Caldwell, and Fehervari 1967:112, 117, pls. 7, 9, figs. 18–20, tables IX, XII; see also Sarraf 1981:pl. 8:126–31, figs. 44:79, 46:117–18). During Iblis III, Lalehzar Coarse Ware and associated painted wares have become rare, replaced by three types

of red-to-buff pottery: Dashkar Plain, Dashkar Brushed, and Dashkar Painted Wares (Chase, Caldwell, and Fehervari 1967:177, pl. 7,figs. 18–20). Prickett (pers. comm. 1984) equates Dashkar Plain and Painted Wares with Rud-i Gushk survey types 7, 7A, 8, and 8A, and Dashkar Brushed with her type 6. The same pottery is found in Yahya VA (q.v.). The marked break noted at Iblis between periods II and III (Caldwell 1967b:36) appears to be a local phenomenon, since the Rud-i Gushk survey produced transitional pottery (Prickett 1986). Fabric and simple vessel forms suggest a link between Dashkar Wares and Lapui Wares from Fars; common forms include jars with short everted rims (Chase, Caldwell, and Fehervari 1967:fig. 18:top, 19:top; Langsdorff and McCown 1942:pl. 20:11, 15; Sumner 1972a:pls. XII:K, M, XIII:K–Q) and hemispherical bowls (Chase, Caldwell, and Fehervari 1967:pl. 7:2; Langsdorff and McCown 1942:pl. 20:10, 14, 19; Sumner 1972a:pl. XIV:D, M).

E. *The Iblis IV (Aliabad) period* is defined by levels 4–5 in the 1964 cut, supplemented by material stratified above Dashkar Ware sherds at the site of Aliabad (Chase, Fehervari,Caldwell 1967:75–79). The only other area where this ceramic assemblage has been found is in the Soghun Valley, where it occurs only in surface contexts (see below). Since Iblis IV represents the only stratified occurrence of Aliabad pottery, it is described in some detail here.

The ceramic "complex" includes Aliabad Plain, Painted, Bichrome, Brushed, and Ridged Wares (Chase, Fehervari, and Caldwell 1967:79; Chase, Caldwell, and Fehervari 1967:pl. 10, figs. 23–27). With the exception of Ridged Ware, the Aliabad pottery is handmade; fired from pink to red, it is frequently buff-slipped (Caldwell 1967b:37; Chase, Caldwell, and Fehervari 1967:79, 184, fig. 21:right, 27; Sarraf 1981:figs. 1:2, 26:291–92, 41:33–45, 45:98, 100–108, 46:109–16, 119–26, 47:127–36, 48–50, 51:183–87, 59:511–16, pl. 12:1, 16). Large and "carelessly drawn" geometric designs are characteristic of Aliabad Painted Ware (Chase, Caldwell, and Fehervari 1967:figs. 21–26; Chase, Fehervari, and Caldwell 1967:79, pls. 1–2; Sarraf 1981:figs. 1:2–6, 11–15, 3:41–47, 4:50–54, 6:75–81, 9:108, 116, 10:118–26, 11, 12:140–41, 144–45, 14–15, 16:181–85, 17–19, 20:215–18, 222–24, 23:265–67, 24, 26–30, 31:345–48, 32–34, pls. 9–23). Aliabad Bichrome Ware has black and red, brown and green, or black and green paint on a buff slip (Caldwell 1967b:37; Chase, Caldwell, and Fehervari 1967:79, pls. 1–2; Chase, Caldwell, and Fehervari 1967:pl. 10, figs. 21–23, 25–28). Vessels classified as Aliabad Ridged Ware have string-cut bases (Chase, Caldwell, and Fehervari 1967:fig. 24; Chase, Fehervari, Caldwell 1967:pl. 7; Sarraf 1981:fig. 48:149–50). Beveled-rim bowls were sometimes associated with Aliabad wares

(Caldwell and Malek Shahmirzadi 1966:16, fig. 4; Chase, Caldwell, and Fehervari 1967:tables XIII, XVI).

Sites with Aliabad wares have been identified in the Soghun Valley, and dated to a hiatus in the Yahya sequence between periods VA and IVC. The following ceramic parallels suggest that the Aliabad period is contemporary with the Early(?) Banesh period in Fars: rare beveled-rim bowls, trays (Chase, Caldwell, and Fehervari 1967:fig. 24, bottom; Alden 1979:fig. 33:28), and squat, sinuous-sided vessels with strongly everted rims (Chase, Caldwell, and Fehervari 1967:fig. 22, center; Nicholas 1980:fig. 170).

F. *The Iblis V (Mashiz) period* is defined by geometric painted sherds found in stratigraphically mixed contexts on the mound; in addition, surface sherds extend for several hectares around Tal-i Iblis (Chase, Caldwell, and Fehervari 1967:188). Mashiz Wares are grit-tempered and extremely hard, described by the excavators as "stone ware" (Chase, Fehervari, and Caldwell 1967:84–85, pls. 4:2–3, 8:2–3). The only similar pottery reported is from unstratified contexts at Shahdad; so at present this material appears to be a local development within Kirman. If the Mashiz ceramic complex has been placed correctly, and we emphasize that its position relative to the Najaferabad complex (see below) has not been established stratigraphically, this "period" must have been of brief duration, interpolated between two periods characterized by ceramics related to Early Banesh.

G. *The Iblis VI (Najafarabad) period* is here defined as the upper levels of Test II, 0 to −60 cm (Chase, Caldwell, and Fehervari 1967:188–89). The pottery assigned to the Najafarabad complex (Chase, Caldwell, and Fehervari 1967:figs. 39–40; Sarraf 1981:fig. 60:525–28) is generally paralleled in Sialk IV (Caldwell 1967b:38; Ghirshman 1938:pls. LXXXVIII, XC:S.537). In addition to beveled-rim bowls, there are two parallels in vessel form between the Najafarabad period and the Banesh period in Fars: trough spouts (Chase, Caldwell, and Fehervari 1967:fig. 40:1–2; Alden 1979:fig. 47, top) and sinuous-sided bowls with a flattened, everted rim (Chase, Caldwell, and Fehervari 1967:fig. 39, top; Alden 1979:fig. 50:7). This bowl form is also found in Susa Acropole I:17 (Le Brun 1971:fig. 46:16–17) and in Godin VI/V (V. Badler, pers. comm.).

The Central Desert: Shahdad

Ancient Khabis or Shahdad lies east of Kirman on the edge of the Dasht-i Lut. Excavations from 1969 to 1977 by the Archaeological Service of Iran under the direction of Ali Hakemi revealed an extensive necropolis (Hakemi 1970, 1972, 1973a, 1973b, 1976a, 1976b; Amiet 1973a, 1974, 1976). In 1977 a systematic surface survey of the area around the necropolis was carried out by S. Salvatori

and M. Vidale (Salvatori 1978a, 1978b; Salvatori and Vidale 1982). The "points" sampled by the survey provide evidence that Shahdad is a horizontal rather than a vertical site, resulting from a movement of the settlement from east to west following the retreat of water sources toward the adjacent mountain (Meder 1979). Complete publication of the survey data should make it possible to document the cultural sequence at the site; meanwhile, it seems wiser to simply present a brief summary of the results without attempting to define descrete chronological units.

A. *The Shahdad Survey* sherds can be dated by comparisons with the Iblis and Yahya sequences. They indicate an occupation contemporary with Yahya VB–A and Iblis I–II at Shahdad Point 2; Iblis IV at Point 4; Yahya VA–IVC at Point 5; and Yahya IVA at Point 6 (Salvatori and Vidale 1982).

B. *The Shahdad Cemetery* was divided into four areas labeled A through D. Area A was the main necropolis, and most of the published artifacts come from this zone; two zones within it, areas AT1 and AT2, reflect distinct periods of use (Hakemi 1972, 1973b, 1976a).

1. *Area AT1* contained graves with Black-Painted Red, or Buff pottery decorated with motifs such as loops, lines, stylized birds, and trees. On overfired greenish pottery, motifs include suns and date palm leaves (Hakemi 1976a:fig. 2). Hakemi (1976a:136) compares this pottery to that from Bampur, Yahya, Khurab, Damin, and Deh-Qazi and suggests a general date at the beginning of the third millennium.

2. *Area AT2* is much larger than AT1. Although no bones remained, the graves were very rich, containing artifacts that have wide-ranging parallels. Unfortunately, grave groups have not been published; so speculation on dating has centered around individual objects.

The wheel-made pottery includes plain and painted buff wares, the latter decorated with animal and floral motifs (Hakemi 1976a:fig. 4, 1972:pls. I–VII). More common, however, is Black-Painted or Plain Red Ware (e.g., Amiet 1973a:23, top left; Hakemi 1972:pls. IV:C, VII:B; 1982:4, top left; Salvatori and Vidale 1982:fig. 12). Over eleven hundred Red Ware vessels bore pictographs that were incised or stamped with compartmented bronze seals (Hakemi 1976a:137; Amiet 1973a:24, 1974:figs. 2–4; Hakemi 1972:pls. XXII:B, XXIII:B, XXIV:B–C; 1973a:pl. X). Lamberg-Karlovsky states that the painted wares of Yahya IVB and the incised and stamped pottery of Yahya IVA are virtually identical to material at Shahdad (1973:41, n. 3, 1977:41–42). Of the 348 signs recorded at Shahdad (Hakemi 1973a, 1973b), 16 were also found at Yahya, primarily in IVB and IVA (Potts 1981:figs. 3, 5, tables 3, 5; Lamberg-Karlovsky and Tosi 1973:fig. 49; for earlier marks in Susiana see Dollfus and Encrevé 1982).

Bronze compartmented seals provide an excellent horizon marker (Amiet 1974:fig. 1; Hakemi 1972:pl. XXI:B, 1976a:138a, fig. 8; Salvatori and Vidale 1982: fig. 6:5–6). They also occur at Susa (Amiet 1974:97ff.); in Yahya IVB (Lamberg-Karlovsky 1971a:91, fig. 2c; see also Amiet 1974:fig. 3); in Bampur IV (de Cardi 1970: fig. 47:15, 51); in Shahr-i Sokhta II–III (Lamberg-Karlovsky and Tosi 1973:figs. 41–49; Tosi 1968:figs. 99–100, 1969a:fig. 276); in Mundigak IV–V (Casal 1961:pl. XLV); in Hissar III (Schmidt 1937:figs. 118:H2697 and 2698); and in the Namazga V period in Turkmenistan where such seals apparently originated (Pittman 1984:53–56).

Additional links to Hissar III are minicolumns of Hissar IIIC type (Deshayes 1977:101, n. 10; Hakemi, pers. comm.; Schmidt 1937:pl. LXI); flat copper dishes decorated with repoussé figures in the base (Amiet 1973a:27, top, 1976:fig. 9; Hakemi 1972:no. 253 opp. p. 17, 1976a:figs. 5–6; Schmidt 1937:fig. 112:H2252); and the use of incised concentric circles to decorate steatite/chlorite vessels (Hakemi 1972:pl. IX:C–D; Schmidt 1937:pl. LX:H3494, 3495, 3498, figs. 128, 130). Alabaster/"marble" vessels that are carinated or cylindrical with everted rims have good parallels in Hissar IIIC (Hakemi 1972:pls. XII–XIII; Schmidt 1937:fig. 125, pls. LIX:H3615, 3523), as do rectangular white stone beads with notched sides (Hakemi 1976a:fig. 12; Schmidt 1937:pl. LXIX:H2856).

Other steatite vessels include plain bowls, compartmented boxes, cosmetic jars, models of buildings, and bowls with incised floral and animal representations, including serpents, bulls, and felids (Amiet 1973a: 24:lower, 1976:fig. 8; Hakemi 1969:fig. 9, 1972:pls. IX–XI, XIV–XV, no. 166 opposite p. 16, 1976a:fig. 10). Both the *ancienne* and the *récente* styles delineated by Miroschedji (1973) are found in the excavated sample (see "Western Susiana"). Although some of the decorated Shahdad vessels can be assigned to the Intercultural Style characteristic of Yahya IVB, most are closer to the chlorite found in Yahya IVA and later (Kohl 1974:75, 338–40; Lamberg-Karlovsky 1973:41, n. 3).

Important cylinder seals are an alabaster seal with seated vegetation goddess (Hakemi 1972:pl. XXVI, 1973:pl. XC, 1976a:fig. 11; Amiet 1973a:25:upper, 1974:fig. 9); a less well preserved alabaster/calcite seal with vegetation deities (Amiet 1973a:25:middle, 1974:fig. 10; Hakemi 1976a:140); and a silver seal with two women flanking a tree (Hakemi 1972:no. 325, 1976a:140, not illustrated). Amiet compares the iconography of the vegetation goddess seals with some from Yahya IVB and IVA as well as from late Early Dynastic Susa and Early Dynastic and Akkadian Mesopotamia (Amiet 1973a:23–24); but as is so often the case with seals, these examples may well be older than the contexts in which they are found. The only historical date comes from an Elamite inscription on a small red vase that may belong to the time of Puzar-Inshushinak around 2330 B.C. (Amiet 1973a:23).

Amiet (1973a:22–23) believes that within Area AT2 there is an early series of graves with carinated vessels of alabaster and copper (see above and Hakemi 1969:fig. 13:1–7, 1972:pls. XVI–XIX, XX:B, XXI:A) which he equates with the terminal Early Dynastic period at Susa (IVA), and a second or more recent series containing the red pottery with stamped and incised signs. The range of parallels documented certainly suggests that the graves from Area A span a good deal of the third millennium B.C.; however, much of the published material shows strong ties with Hissar III and Yahya IVB–A, or the second half of the third millennium.

Soghun Valley: The Yahya Sequence

The Soghun Valley is located approximately 200 km south of Kirman. Routes lead 150 km farther south to the Persian Gulf, 350 km east to Bampur, and 180 km north to Tal-i Iblis and Kirman. Tepe Yahya, the largest mound in the area, has been the major focus of research. Excavations carried out from 1967 to 1975 by the Harvard University Yahya Project were under the direction of C. C. Lamberg-Karlovsky (1968, 1969, 1970a, 1970b, 1971a, 1971b, 1972a, 1972b, 1973, 1974, 1976a, 1976b, 1977; Lamberg-Karlovsky and Tosi 1973; dissertations on file at Harvard University: Beale 1978; Kohl 1974; Potts 1980). Surveys were carried out in the Soghun Valley, and the adjacent Shah Maran-Dolatabad Basin which includes the upper Rud-i Gushk drainage 25 km west of Yahya (Lamberg-Karlovsky 1968, 1974, 1976a; Beale 1976; Vidali, Vidali, and Lamberg-Karlovsky 1976; Prickett 1976, 1979).

At Yahya, excavation was confined to two large step trenches down the northern and southern slopes of the mound. The South Trench, which established the primary sequence, was composed of 10 × 10 m areas labeled from A at the top through E (Lamberg-Karlovsky 1976a:fig. 1). The strata excavated in the North Trench, in areas XA through XE, were correlated with the main South Trench by means of ceramics (Beale 1976:9, 12, map 3; Lamberg-Karlovsky 1976a:fig. 1). The sequence was ultimately divided into seven periods, designated Yahya VII–I from the bottom up (Beale 1978; Potts 1980; Lamberg-Karlovsky 1977). This system replaces and alters the designations published between 1969 and 1976. An earlier phase of Yahya VII was found in a stratigraphic test at Tepe Gaz Tavila in the Upper Rud-i Gushk drainage (Prickett 1979, 1986).

A. *The Muradabad (Early Yahya VII?) period* is defined by five phases of mud-brick architecture at Tepe

Gaz Tavila, R37 in the Rud-i Gushk survey (Prickett 1979, 1986). The occupation is characterized by Vegetal-Tempered Dense Coarse Ware, or Rud-i Gushk survey Type 1. Comparable pottery at Yahya, called Early Coarse Ware, was used to separate period VII—which it characterizes—from period VI (Beale 1978:8). Radiocarbon dates (table 2) seem to indicate that the Gaz Tavila material is somewhat earlier than the period VII material at Yahya.

B. *The Yahya VII (Baghin) period* is defined in the South Trench by areas C, D, E, and CDE. It is divided into subperiods VIID, VIIC, VIIB6–1, and VIIA on the basis of building remains and surfaces, with a total depth of deposit of about 5.5–6 m (Beale 1978:138ff., 289, plans 1–10, 20, sections 2, 4). The predominant pottery is Early Chaff-Tempered Coarse Ware which is handmade and often burnished (Beale 1978:fig. 2). Prickett (1986) notes that this pottery has a dense fabric and bears little resemblance to the porous variety characteristic of Yahya VIB–VB and Iblis I–II.

Yahya VII Coarse Ware does resemble the plain chaff-tempered pottery characteristic of the Shamsabad period in Fars (Beale 1978:125, 127), and also associated with Jari Painted Ware in the preceding period (W. Sumner, pers. comm. 1985; see "Southwestern Zagros"). A group of artifact parallels suggest a correlation of Yahya VII and the Mushki period in Fars: two-holed bone ornaments (Beale 1978:356–57, fig. 32; Fukai, Horiuchi, and Matsutani 1973:pl. LV:39–40, 42), concave-sided labrets/ear plugs (Beale 1978:358, fig. 33; Fukai, Horiuchi, and Matsutani 1973:pl. LV:33), clay cones (Beale 1978:40; Fukai, Horiuchi, and Matsutani 1973:pl. LV:11–14), grooved stones (Beale 1978:375, fig. 38; Fukai, Horiuchi, and Matsutani 1973:pl. LV:65–66), stone bangles (Beale 1978:361; Fukai, Horiuchi, and Matsutani 1973:pl. LV:33), and bone sickle handles (Beale 1978:385; Fukai, Horiuchi, and Matsutani 1973:pl. VI:1). There is, however, great continuity both at Yahya (see below) and in the Fars sequence, so clay cones, grooved stones, and labrets/ear plugs also occur in Jari contexts (see "Southwestern Zagros"). Given the probable correlation of Yahya VI with Shamsabad to Early Bakun and the parallels listed above, Yahya VII can only be placed contemporary with some part of the Mushki to Shamsabad range in Fars.

C. *The Yahya VI (Soghun) period* is defined by ca. 2.2 m of deposits in the South Trench (Areas B, BW, C, CW, CDE, and D; Beale 1978:section 2). Beale divides Yahya VI into building stages VIA and B, with VIB subdivided into VIB1 and VIB2 (1978:217, 228, 237, plans 13–15). Since most of the small object types are very long-lived, continuing from periods VII to V, it is the ceramics and architecture of these periods that change and provide evidence for relative chronology. The major ceramic group

in Yahya VI, Late Chaff-Tempered Coarse Ware, is lighter and less dense than the Early Coarse Ware of VII, and is rarely burnished. A very small number of fine ware sherds with varying surface treatments are designated as Soghun Wares (Beale 1978:43–44, figs. 5, 7–8, 10).

Prickett compares all of the Lalehzar Coarse Ware from Iblis I–II to the porous Late Chaff-Tempered Coarse Ware of Yahya VIB to VB. Yahya VI straight-sided carinated vessels with undercut lower body (Beale 1978:25–26, fig. 3, top center) are also typical of Iblis I Lalehzar Coarse Ware (Caldwell and Sarraf 1967:pl. 2 lower left, fig. 7; Evett 1967:fig. 1:1). From Yahya VIB2–VC comes rare Coarse Ware rims or body sherds painted in red with broad meandering patterns on the exterior (Beale 1978:27–28, 34, fig. 3); they are comparable to Coarse Ware with red geometric designs found in Iblis I (Caldwell and Sarraf 1967:figs. 3, 6) and in Early Bakun in Fars (Egami and Masuda 1962:fig. 19:36). Rare pedestal bases from Yahya VI are also paralleled in Early Bakun (Egami and Masuda 1962:fig. 19:36). In Yahya VIB the first stamp seal occurs, made of lightly fired clay. With crosshatched incised lines on a rectangular face and a tabular stem, it recalls a seal from the Early Bakun phase at Jari AI (Beale 1978:366; Egami, Masuda, and Gotoh 1977:pl. VI:4).

Prickett (1986) compares the fabric of Soghun Wares to the Bard Sir Plain and Red-Slipped Wares found at Iblis. Holemouth jars, characteristic of Soghun Mottled Purple, occur in rare Bard Sir Red-Slipped Ware in Iblis I (Beale 1978:41; Chase, Caldwell, and Fehevari 1967:fig. 12; note that the jar illustrated is from Iblis II). Beale (1978:123) has suggested the possibility that some Bard Sir Painted at Iblis, occasionally decorated with a faded/fugitive red (Chase, Caldwell, and Fehervari 1967:152), could be Soghun Red Painted; Bard Sir Painted is rare in Iblis I, common in Early Iblis II, and declines in Late Iblis II. The only design parallel for Red-Painted Soghun Ware is a single Bard Sir Painted sherd with triangles filled with diagonal lines at the rim from a Late Iblis II deposit, and therefore later than the rest of the parallels (Chase, Caldwell, and Fehervari 1967:fig. 4, upper right).

Thumb-impressed bricks, which began at Yahya in VIIB, are now found in walls supported by buttresses placed at corners and other strategic points; carefully plastered semicircular hearths were placed in room corners (Beale 1978:218, plans 13, 16). These attributes, which continue through period VC at Yahya, are paralleled in Iblis I buildings (Caldwell and Sarraf 1967:306, fig. 18, pl. 7 bottom; Evett 1967:figs. 9–18).

In general, ceramic correlations would appear to place Yahya VI contemporary with Iblis I and perhaps Early II. Ceramic ties to Fars are limited to the Early Bakun phase. Specialized architectural features support a correlation of

Yahya VI with Iblis I, the latter independently linked to the Shamsabad to Early Bakun phases (see "Iblis"). Given the strong ties between Iblis II and Middle to Late Bakun, we suggest a correlation of Yahya VI with Iblis I and Early Bakun.

D. *The Yahya V (Yahya) period* is divided into three major phases, VC, VB, and VA2–1. These deposits are defined in the South Trench in Areas B, BW, C, CW, CDE, and D (Beale 1976:sec. 3, plans 16–17, 19).

1. *The Yahya VC phase* consists of perhaps two building levels totaling about 1.25 m in depth (Beale 1976:248–250, sec. 3, plan 16). The architecture of Yahya VC, which includes a large residential complex consisting of a "central core of small square rooms surrounded by several larger rectangular 'living' rooms" (Beale 1978:250, plan 16), is virtually identical in plan and construction to that of Iblis I. Black-on-Buff Ware, some of which has been established by mineralogical analysis as imported from the west (Kamilli and Lamberg-Karlovsky 1979), is rare as is Bichrome and Red-Painted Ware. The repertoire of painted designs includes "ticks" and reversing crosshatched triangles or torsos linked by arms, in a style that is quite different from that in Yahya VB–A (compare Beale 1978:fig. 14 with figs. 13, 16), but is characteristic of Iblis II Bard Sir Painted Ware and the Middle to Late Bakun phases (Beale 1978:123, 321–25; Lamberg-Karlovsky 1971a:88; see also "Southwestern Zagros"). Limited to Yahya VC is the occurrence of painted bands on the interior of bowls, similar to those found in Gap I or Early Bakun. A correlation of Yahya VC with the earliest part of Iblis II, and with the Early to Middle Bakun period seems indicated. Farther to the east, Dollfus considers the best parallels for the VI–VC Black-on-Buff ceramics to be with Bendebal 14–12 at the end of the Susiana sequence (pers. comm. to Martha Prickett), which would be compatible with a Middle Bakun correlation. Note that the presence of significant quantities of Lapui-related pottery in Yahya VC (Beale 1978:53–55, fig. 11) provides evidence that the ceramics characteristic of the period following Bakun in Fars originated in eastern Iran (see "Southwestern Zagros").

2. *The Yahya VB phase* is defined by a single building level about 1.10 m deep (Beale 1978:268, plan 17, sec. 3). The highest percentage of Lapui Ware occurs in this phase. Black-on-Buff Ware is now common and is manufactured of local clay. Late Coarse Ware continues as does rare Red-Painted Coarse Ware (Beale 1978:figs. 13, 16–17, 28).

The dating of this phase is difficult. Beale (1978:126) compares the Yahya VB Black-on-Buff Ware, also designated as Rud-i Gushk survey Types 4 and 5, with Bard Sir Painted Ware at Tal-i Iblis. This places Yahya VB contemporary with our Early Iblis II phase, the period in which Bard Sir Ware is most common. On independent evidence, Early and Late Iblis II are contemporary with Middle and Late Bakun (see "Iblis"). A correlation with Middle Bakun for Yahya VB seems indicated.

3. *The Yahya VA phase* is divided into two subphases, VA1–VA2, defined in Areas B, BW, C, CW, and CDE in the South Trench (Beale 1978:279, 282, plan 19). The total depth in square C is about 2.35 m (Beale 1978:sec. 3). During Yahya VA2, Plain Coarse Ware replaces Late Chaff-Tempered Coarse Ware as the dominant ceramic group (Beale 1978:fig. 25), while in VA1, Black-on-Red Ware or Plain Coarse Ware with paint increases to 40 percent of the ceramic sample (Beale 1978:21, figs. 18–22, 26). Prickett (1986) equates the pottery of Yahya VA, her Rud-i Gushk survey Types 7, 7A, 8, and 8A, with the Dashkar wares of Iblis III. A deep-cut stamp seal–like artifact made of lapis lazuli, which has a subrectangular incised upper surface and is perforated in the center at a right angle to the decorated surface (Beale 1978:350, fig. 31), is closely comparable in design and method of cutting to a Late Bakun stamp seal from Fars (Langsdorff and McCown 1942:pl. 82:2).

Thus the few parallels available suggest a linkage between Yahya VA and Late Iblis II and Iblis III, as well as with the Late Bakun phase and possibly Lapui period in Fars. This is supported by an independent set of parallels that correlate Iblis II–III with Late Bakun and Lapui (see "Iblis").

E. *The Aliabad Period (Yahya VA–IVC hiatus)* is represented at Yahya by "erosion deposits" in the South Trench (Beale 1978: secs. 1–3) and is defined by surface remains from sites in the Dolatabad and Soghun Valleys, including Tepe Yahya (Prickett 1979:54, 1986). Aliabad ceramics are characteristic of Iblis IV (q.v.) and are said to occur at Shahdad (Potts 1980:430).

F. *The Yahya IVC (Proto-Elamite) period* is defined by a building in the South Trench that may have been laid out to a standard unit of measure close to that used in the Late Uruk period at Habuba Kabira in Syria (Beale and Carter 1983; Potts 1980:8–45, figs. 1–2). This period is securely tied by artifact parallels to sites in the west (Lamberg-Karlovsky and Tosi 1973, with refs.). Beveled-rim bowls, trays, and numerous conical cups may be compared to pottery from Middle Banesh Malyan (Potts 1980:426; Nicholas 1980; see "Southwestern Zagros"). Ceramic parallels also occur between Yahya IVC and Ville Royale I:18–17 or Susa IIIB (Potts 1980:429, n. 2 with refs.; see also Carter 1980). Kohl (1974), using chlorite artifacts, also ties Yahya IVC to the Proto-Elamite/"Jemdet Nasr" horizon (Potts 1980:570). Paleographic evidence links the tablets from Yahya IVC with those from Susa Acropole I:16 or Susa IIIA, as well as with Malyan (Potts 1980:381–82, 425–26, fig. 67; Lamberg-Karlovsky 1976a:73, fig. 3, pl. 7; Le Brun and

Vallat 1978:39–40; Vallat 1971:243). Cylinder seals and sealings from the IVC building have clear-cut affinities to Susa Proto-Elamite glyptic of Acropole I:16–14b (Amiet 1972:34, 71; Potts 1980:437) and with Sin Temple I–V at Khafaje (Amiet 1972:34ff.; Potts 1980:365–66, 369–73, figs. 61–64). Carter (1980:19, fig. 17:3–5, 7 with refs.) presents specific comparisons of sealings from Yahya IVC with Middle Banesh and Ville Royale I:18–17 to the west, and Shahr-i Sokhta I to the east. Black-on-Red-on-Orange Ware provides close parallels between Yahya IVC and Bampur II–III in Baluchistan (Potts 1980:519 with refs.).

Thus evidence from a variety of artifact types suggests that the Yahya IVC occupation was contemporary with Susa IIIA–B, the Middle and Late Banesh phases in Fars, and with the Jemdet-Nasr to Early Dynastic I period in Mesopotamia (Potts 1980:427; see also Carter 1984:127–28).

G. *The Yahya IVB period* is subdivided into six building phases delineated in the South Trench. In 1970 these levels were presented as two units: phase IVB2, the "Persian Gulf Room," containing Persian/Arabian Gulf pottery types, cylinder seals, and Gulf-type stamp seals; and phase IVB1 with little architecture and much chlorite evidence. Potts (1980) revises this sequence to include six subphases: IVB6; IVB5, formerly IVB2; and IVB4–1, formerly IVB1.

Some of the ceramic types have a long duration and pertain to the period as a whole rather than to individual subphases. Much of the pottery with black-painted designs on an orange surface can be linked with Bampur V–VI to the southeast; common motifs include palm fronds, meandering crosshatched parallel lines, and humped bulls (Lamberg-Karlovsky and Tosi 1973:fig. 126; de Cardi 1970:figs. 34–41). At Yahya these occur from IVC through IVA, but are most common in the IVB strata (Potts 1980:519). Burnished Gray Ware in forms that include a pedestal base is also found in Yahya IVB and Bampur IV–VI (Lamberg-Karlovsky and Tosi 1973:41, figs. 110, 129–30; de Cardi 1970:fig. 43). Lamberg-Karlovsky and Tosi (1973:39–40) point out that Black-on-Gray Ware is a useful horizon style linking southeastern Iran, Pakistan, and sites on the Arabian penninsula. It occurs at Yahya from IVC through IVB5, and is also found in Bampur IV–V, Shahr-i Sokhta I–III, and as "Faiz Mohammed Gray Ware" at sites in Pakistan including Damb Sadaat III–II, sites in the Zhob and Lorelai valleys, and Mundigak III–IV2 (Lamberg-Karlovsky and Tosi 1973:40, chart I with refs.; Potts 1980:516–17). Similar pottery occurs in the Umm an-Nar culture of Oman and Abu Dhabi (Potts 1980:516) and in Mehrgarh VII (Jarrige and Lechevallier 1979:519ff.). Comb-incised ware, which occurs in limited quantities, is found throughout IVB and perhaps in IVC (Potts 1980:520) and

is found in Bampur V and VI (de Cardi 1970:figs. 41:473, 32:12), at Bahrain in pre-Barbar and City I deposits (Potts, this vol., chap. 4), and in Ur III deposits on the Acropole at Susa (Stève and Gasche 1971:pl. 66:9–10). Based on style, Amiet considers the Yahya IVB glyptic to be Akkadian in date (1976).

1. *The Yahya IVB6 phase* follows a major cultural break in the sequence (Potts 1980:499ff.). The IVC building stood abandoned for some time, was leveled, and was eventually sealed by a floor level representing a reoccupation. At a slightly higher level several wall stubs occur below the floors of the IVB5 "Persian Gulf Room" (Potts 1980:508). This deposit, from the end of IVC to the construction of the "Persian Gulf Room," is defined as IVB6 by Potts (1980:509); it can only be considered as mixed fill and should not be used to bolster arguments about the degree of continuity between IVC and IVB.

Two unique finds from this context deserve mention. A stamp seal has a high back boss of Early Gulf type. Unfortunately the seal is broken and cannot be further identified with any certainty (Potts 1980:527–28, fig. 66B). Amiet (1976:20) considers it Akkadian in date, in which case it is probably intrusive from a later level. A sherd of brown-buff ware with applied bosses is closely paralleled in Ville Royale I:18–17 and in Early Dynastic II–III contexts in Mesopotamia (Potts 1980:211; Carter 1980:fig. 14:13–14); it may, however, be derived from a lower stratum, as several sherds of this type occur in IVC (Potts 1980:211: Lamberg-Karlovsky and Tosi 1973:fig. 89:4).

2. *The Yahya IVB5 phase* is defined by the "Persian Gulf Room" (Potts 1980:62–72, fig. 10). Ceramics provide good evidence of contact with sites to the east (see above), and a few parallels to the west. Forms continuing from IVC and IVB6 are beveled-rim bowls and a vessel resembling the "conical cup" of southwest Iran and Mesopotamia (Potts 1980:512–14; the latter is referred to as "conical solid-footed goblets" by Lamberg-Karlovsky and Tosi 1973:37, fig. 114 and "solid-footed chalices" by Kohl 1974:240). The "conical cups" occur in Banesh contexts in Fars (Potts 1980:514, citing I. Nicholas and W. Sumner), and in Jemdet Nasr through Early Dynastic II levels at Warka (Adams and Nissen 1972:99); Potts considers the Yahya conical cups closer to Mesopotamian than to Proto-Elamite forms.

A vessel type that appears in quantity in the Persian Gulf room as well as in later Yahya IV deposits is a large, orange storage vessel with applied meandering snakes or snakelike ridges (Potts 1980:190, 517–18; Lamberg-Karlovsky and Tosi 1973:fig. 113). Similar vessels occur in Mundigak IV and Anjira IV (Lamberg-Karlovsky and Tosi 1973:41), and in the Umm an-Nar culture of Oman (Potts, this vol., chap. 4). They are also found in "Proto-Imperial" levels on the Acropole at Susa (Stève and

Gasche 1971:pl. 73:1–4). This vessel form was not found in the Ville Royale I sounding, but applied snakes do occur in Ville Royale I:18 (Carter 1980:14:11).

Kohl dates the "Persian Gulf Room" to Early Dynastic II/IIIA based on the presence of chlorite vessels assigned to the International Style (Potts 1980:510–11; Kohl 1974:235–45). A stamp seal with caprid, bull(?), and crescent moon from just above the floor of the IVB5 Persian Gulf Room is considered an early example of the Persian Gulf style, dated from Early Dynastic to late Akkadian/Ur III times in Mesopotamia (Potts 1980:403, 528–29, 536, fig. 66C).

To summarize, the most diagnostic artifacts within Yayha IVB5 suggest a range from Early Dynastic III through Akkadian times. If so, the beveled-rim bowls and conical cups, dated to Early Dynastic II at the latest, may be derived from earlier contexts; quantitative data on their distribution are needed to resolve this question.

3. *The Yahya IVB4–1 phase* is defined by four occupational strata which Potts thinks lead directly to IVA, in contrast to the initial interpretation of a discontinuity between IVB and IVA (Potts 1980:572–79; Lamberg-Karlovsky 1970a:34, 1974:39). A stamp seal with two feet on one side and a scorpion(?) on the other is now assigned to Yahya IVB2, rather than to the Persian Gulf Room as originally reported (Potts 1980:527, fig. 66a; see also Lamberg-Karlovsky 1971a:92). Given the degree of continuity in the ceramics, a general date of Early Dynastic II/III to Akkadian must also be applied to Yahya IVB4–1.

H. *The Yahya IVA (Elamite) period* is defined in Areas A, B, and BW of the South Trench (Potts 1980:575). The Black-on-Red-on-Orange Ware that indicated a relationship between Yahya IVB and sites in Baluchistan continues. Incised or stamped potters' marks are now common and can be related by morphology as well as by associated vessel shapes to Shahdad, where both are characteristic of the later cemetery area (Potts 1981; see also "Shahdad"). Artifacts of "probable Indus origin or style" found in IVA contexts are not considered useful for dating (Potts 1980:586–87).

Specific parallels with the west are few. A single sherd of Kaftari Ware from Fars was found, and Yahya VA Brown Banded Ware "bears a very general resemblance to some examples of the Kaftari Painted Buff Ware of Malyan" (Potts 1980:570–71; Sumner 1974:173, figs. 7, 9). Chlorite bowls with a dot-in-circle motif can be assigned to Miroschedji's Late Group; they provide a correlation with Susa VB and by extension, the Ur III period (Potts 1980:581; see "Western Susiana"). On Failaka Island such bowls are associated with nearly five hundred Late Gulf Seals, dated by epigraphic evidence to the Old Babylonian period (Potts 1980:582–84). These and other parallels support a date somewhere within the range

spanned by Ur III to the Old Babylonian period (Potts 1980:579, 583–86).

The Bampur Sequence

The Bampur Valley in Persian Baluchistan lies on a route linking central Iran to southern Baluchistan and Pakistan. In 1932 Sir Aurel Stein conducted a surface survey and test excavations at the sites of Bampur, Chah Huseini, and Khurab (Stein 1937:104–31). The mound at Bampur was again excavated in 1966 by Beatrice de Cardi under the sponsorship of the Royal Asiatic Society and the British Academy (de Cardi 1967a, 1967b, 1968, 1970). De Cardi cleared a total area of 24 m² in two trenches, Y and Z. The latter reached virgin soil at −7 m below the mound surface (de Cardi 1970:fig. 6); this depth was divided into 6 "periods"/levels, numbered I–VI from bottom to top.

A. *The Chah Husseini period* is defined by stratigraphically mixed and surface material (Lamberg-Karlovsky and Schmandt-Besserat 1977:130; Stein 1937; Tosi 1974). A Black-on-Red-Slipped sherd and a chevron-painted beaker excavated by Stein at Chah Husseini are paralleled in pottery of Yahya V (Lamberg-Karlovsky 1969:186; Stein 1937:pls. XXV, XXIX, XXXIV:18; see also Lamberg-Karlovsky and Schmandt-Besserat 1977:fig. 8:1–5; Tosi 1974: 31). Chevron-painted beakers are also characteristic of Iblis II (see "Iblis"). De Cardi (cited in Tosi 1979:31) relates this material to the Geoksiur culture of southern Turkmenia.

B. *The Early Bampur period* is defined by levels I–IV of the de Cardi excavation at Bampur (de Cardi 1970; see also Tosi 1974). Caprid heads painted in bands below the rims of small Gray Ware bowls are related to vessels found in burials excavated by Stein at nearby Khurab (de Cardi 1970:294, 297, figs. 28:269, 29:300; Lamberg-Karlovsky and Schmandt-Besserat 1977:127, fig. 7:13; Stein 1937:pl. XXXIV:15). The position of the site as a crossroads is reflected by ceramic comparisons. Tosi links Bampur I–IV to Shahr-i Sokhta II–III and Mundigak IV$_{1-2}$ (1974:32, figs. 4, 13, table 1 with comparanda). Bampur II–III is firmly tied to Yahya IVC (Lamberg-Karlovsky 1971a, 1972a; Potts 1980:519). Incised Gray Ware vessels have parallels in Kulli 460 km to the east (de Cardi 1970: 324–25).

C. *The Later Bampur period* is defined by levels V–VI in de Cardi's excavation at Bampur (1970). Ties with the east and Sistan do not cease, since numerous sherds of Bampur VI pottery occur in the Burnt Building of Shahr-i Sokhta IV as well as on the surface of sites in the Rud-i Biyaban (Tosi 1974:33, fig. 4). Contacts with the west and with sites across the Persian/Arabian Gulf, however, appear to be more important. To the west, Bampur V–VI designs and shapes in Black-on-Red Ware are most similar to those of Yahya IVB (Potts 1980: 519; Lamberg-

Karlovsky 1971a:80, 1977; Tosi 1974:33). The distinctive Black-on-Gray Ware of VI provides a link to the Umm an-Nar culture of Oman (de Cardi 1970:268–69, 318, fig. 43:475–84, table 5; Tosi 1974:36, fig. 4). Finally, ceramic copies of chlorite vessels, designated as Incised Gray Ware, are common in Bampur V–VI (de Cardi 1970:320–25, figs. 54–46). Rare parallels for these vessels occur in Yahya IVB4–1 (Lamberg-Karlovsky 1977; Lamberg-Karlovsky and Tosi 1973:figs. 97, 99), and they are also found at Hilli and Umm an-Nar on the Gulf (de Cardi 1970:325). Tosi (1974:33, fig. 3; see also de Cardi 1970:266) has suggested a correlation of Bampur VI with the Qaleh/Shogha period in Fars, but the latter is much later, securely dated to the mid and late second millennium (Jacobs 1980).

The Hilmand Basin Sequence

Sistan provides a long-distance link between southern Iran and the Turkmenistan-Afghanistan area. The key site is Shahr-i Sokhta, a large, well-preserved settlement that provides a well-stratified sequence. It was excavated by the Italian Archaeological Mission of IsMEO from 1967 to 1978 under the direction of M. Tosi (1968, 1969a, 1970, 1972a, 1976a, 1976c, 1983a, 1983b; Lamberg-Karlovsky and Tosi 1973; Tosi and Piperno 1975; Amiet and Tosi 1978; Piperno 1977, 1978; Salvatori 1979). Additional information was obtained from a pottery-manufacturing site called Rud-i Biyaban (Tosi 1972b).

A. *The Shahri-Sokhta I period (phases 10–8)* is defined by limited test trenches (Amiet and Tosi 1978:9–10, 20; Tosi 1976a). The ceramics, predominantly buff wares, have paneled designs similar to those found in Mundigak III, and on Quetta Ware in Baluchistan (Amiet and Tosi 1978:22, figs. 12–14; Lamberg-Karlovsky and Tosi 1973:26, figs. 6, 14; Casal 1961:figs. 53–59). Imports include two sherds of Gray Streak-Burnished Ware of Yahya IVC–IVB5 type (Amiet and Tosi 1978:fig. 3; Lamberg-Karlovsky and Tosi 1973:fig. 10) and three sherds of Nal Polychrome (Amiet and Tosi 1978:22–23, fig. 4a–c; see also Shaffer, this vol., chap. 26). The pottery also shows strong connections to Namazga III in southern Turkmenistan (Amiet and Tosi 1978:10–11; Biscione 1973; Lamberg-Karlovsky and Tosi 1973:24, figs. 4–13; Sarianidi 1983:figs. 1–7); this evidence supports a correlation of Shahr-i Sokhta I and Yahya IVC, where Namazga III pottery was also found (R. Biscione, cited by Lamberg-Karlovsky in pers. comm. 1971).

Seals and sealings excavated from Shahr-i Sokhta I are stylistically related to Proto-Elamite settlements (Amiet and Tosi 1978:24–25). A cylinder seal fragment is similar to examples found at Susa in Acropole I:16–14 (Amiet and Tosi 1978:28, fig. 35). Other seals of period I are of Early Dynastic I type in Mesopotamia (Amiet

and Tosi 1978:207–8). A Proto-Elamite tablet from the earliest phase is also related to Susa Acropole I:16–13 (Amiet and Tosi 1978:24, fig. 16; Tosi 1976a:168).

B. *The Shahr-i Sokhta II period (phases 7–5,)* defined primarily in the East Residential Area, is the best preserved and most widely exposed occupation at the site (Biscione, Salvatori, and Tosi 1977; Tosi 1983b:103–19, figs. 8–10, 14–16). The pottery is simply a standardized version of period I forms and decoration (Lamberg-Karlovsky and Tosi 1973:54, figs. 21–27). In this and the following period, parallels between Shahr-i Sokhta, Bampur III–IV, and Mundigak IV$_{1-2}$ are sufficient to lead Tosi to conclude that they are "one culture" (Tosi 1974:32; see also Lamberg-Karlovsky and Tosi 1973; de Cardi 1968:144). Much copper metalworking is evidenced at Shahr-i Sokhta, and compartmented copper or bronze stamp seals appear; a flat, square stamp seal is a type known in Mundigak III and IV in Afghanistan (Amiet and Tosi 1978:22–28, fig. 24). A figurine of Namazga III type comes from the upper levels of Shahr-i Sokhta II (Tosi 1972b:175).

C. *The Shahr-i Sokhta III period (phases 4–3)* is defined by structural remains in the central part of the site (Tosi 1976c:142, table 1; 1983b:119–21, fig. 17), supplemented by evidence from the Rud-i Biyaban kilns (Tosi 1970:189, 1972b:175). Pottery, lithics, metalworking, building techniques, brick typometry, figurines, and seals provide a close identity with Mundigak IV$_{1-2}$ (Lamberg-Karlovsky and Tosi 1973:26). Fine Black-on-Gray Ware, already present in Shahr-i Sokhta I, becomes common in periods II/III, permitting a correlation with Bampur IV–V and Yahya IVC–B (Lamberg-Karlovsky and Tosi 1973:39–41, figs. 107, 143–46; (see "Yahya"). Copper or bronze stamp seals are similar to those found at Namazga IV–V in Turkmenia, and in Hissar III (Lamberg-Karlovsky and Tosi 1973:figs. 41–49; see "Damghan/Khorasan"; see also Kohl, this vol., chap. 7).

D. *The Shahr-i Sokhta IV period (phases 2–1)* is defined by burned structures on the southeast corner of the mound (Lamberg-Karlovsky and Tosi 1973:28, figs. 71–72; Tosi 1983b). Sherds of Incised Gray Ware, found only in period IV at Shahr-i Sokhta (Lamberg-Karlovsky and Tosi 1973:figs. 147–50), provide a direct correlation with Shahdad (Lamberg-Karlovsky and Tosi 1973:43, n. 100, 44), Late Bampur, and Yahya IVB (see "Yahya"). Black-on-Red Ware with appliquéd "snakes" also links Shahr-i Sokhta IV with Yahya IVB (Lamberg-Karlovsky and Tosi 1973:28, 43, fig. 65), and "numerous finds of Bampur VI pottery" from the Burned Building indicate contact with Late Bampur and sites such as Hili in Oman (Tosi 1974:33, fig. 4). A shallow dish with painted interior, again from the Burned Building, closely parallels one from Mundigak IV$_3$ (Lamberg-Karlovsky and Tosi 1973:figs. 67–68).

Radiocarbon Evidence for Southeastern Iran

The earliest radiocarbon determinations for this region are from deposits at Tepe Gaz Tavila which is contemporary with or earlier than Yahya VII. They form a consistent series, dating the initial settlements in Kirman to the middle of the sixth millennium (table 2). This is compatible with the relative dating that correlates Yahya VII with the Mushki to Shamsabad range in Fars, and two dates for Shamsabad at the end of the sixth millennium (table 2). The next cluster of dates comes from Yahya VI and Iblis I, placed contemporary with one another on ceramic grounds. Although there is a considerable range in the Iblis dates, a general date for this material in the middle of the fifth millennium is suggested.

The radiocarbon dates for later periods at Yahya are highly inconsistent, with the exception of four samples from period IVC or the Proto-Elamite period, which overlap within the last quarter of the fourth millennium. This is compatible with the large series from the closely related Middle Banesh assemblage at Malyan (tables 1–2). The long series of dates from Shahr-i Sokhta begins with a single date for phase 10 (Tunc-61), which places it contemporary with other Proto-Elamite settlements. Large clusters of samples from Shahr-i Sokhta II and III overlap, with a CRD average at the middle of the third millennium. A cluster from period IV produced a corrected average range from 2405–2180 B.C. (table 1). Artifact parallels place Shahr-i Sokhta II–IV roughly parallel to Yahya IVB, which is in turn linked to the Early Dynastic II to Akkadian periods in Mesopotamia. Thus the Shahr-i Sokhta radiocarbon evidence supports the long span suggested for Yahya IVB by artifact parallels (see "Yahya").

Central Western Iran

Western Luristan

Recent excavations within the regularly folded mountain zone of western Luristan are limited to the Pusht-i Kuh in the south and the Hulailan Valley in the north. Investigation of the prehistory of other valleys has been less intense, but some information is available from a survey with limited soundings by Sir Aurel Stein (1940) and surveys conducted by Clare Goff (1971). These studies have been integrated with the major sequences by E. Henrickson (1985b) and R. Henrickson (1984b, 1986b, 1987) and will not be discussed here.

The Pusht-i Kuh Cemetery Sequence

This region has contact with Mesopotamia via the Diyala, and with Susiana via Deh Luran. Excavations have been carried out by Louis Vanden Berghe at Dum Gar Parchinah (1975a, 1975b); Hakalan (1973b, 1973c,

1974); Bani Surmah (1968b); War Kabud (1967, 1973c); and Kalleh Nissar (1970a, 1971a, 1973a). He also surveyed the region for eleven seasons between 1965 and 1975 (Vanden Berghe 1967, 1968b, 1970a, 1970b, 1971b, 1972a, 1972b, 1973b, 1975b; see also Vanden Berghe 1973c, 1979). Apart from a small area of domestic architecture at Kalleh Nissar, all of the excavated material comes from graves. The chronological ordering of this material into three major units is thus based entirely on artifact comparisons with other regions rather than on stratigraphy.

A. *The Chalcolithic period* is defined by excavations in the cemeteries at Dum Gar Parchinah and Hakalan on the Mehmeh River. At Hakalan 35 large rectangular tombs constructed of stone slabs contained single inhumations and a few multiple burials (Vanden Berghe 1973b, 1974:figs. 1–2). At Dum Gar Parchinah, 156 tombs similar to those at Hakalan were opened (Vanden Berghe 1975a:46–47, figs. 1–3; 1975b:49–54; 1976:165). The only settlement data for this period come from Area C at Kalleh Nissar (Vanden Berghe 1970a:67 lower left, 70, 73 bottom; 1973a:fig. 1, pl. 22). It has been suggested that the cemeteries were constructed by pastoral nomads (Vanden Berghe 1975b:60–61; E. Henrickson 1985a).

Rare Black-on-Plum Ware vessels from these cemeteries (Vanden Berghe 1973b:51:vessel 3, 52:vessels 2–3; 1974:figs. 3:3, 4:2–3; 1975a:47) are similar to pottery found at sites in Susiana dated to the Susa A/Susa I period (Dollfus 1971:fig. 12:16–24; pers. comm. 1985) and have been identified with the "Black-on-Red" Ware found in the Maran phase in the Mahidasht (E. Henrickson 1985a:33–34, 1985b:79, table 5). Hakalan and Parchinah Black-on-Buff Slipped Ware bearing geometric, vegetation, and animal motifs (Vanden Berghe 1973b:51–56, 1974:figs. 3–6, 1975a:figs. 5–7, 1975b:51–52) is similar but not identical in fabric to the "Red-White-and-Black Ware" characteristic of the Maran phase (E. Henrickson 1985b:73, 79, n. 31); strong stylistic parallels can also be drawn between these ceramic groups (E. Henrickson 1983:fig. 108:7; Vanden Berghe 1974:fig. 6, 1975a:fig. 6:10–11; E. Henrickson 1983:109:1; Vanden Berghe 1975a:fig. 5:10; E. Henrickson 1983:fig. 103:3, 7, 11; Vanden Berghe 1975a:fig. 5:1). Stylistic parallels with Susa A Black-on-Buff Ware are less precise, but include high ring or pedestal bases (Dollfus 1971:fig. 9:9, 12; Vanden Berghe 1975a:fig. 6:19) and squat jugs with small lugs, decorated with panels on the shoulders (Dollfus 1971:fig. 16:10, 17:6; Vanden Berghe 1975a:fig. 6:15–16, 18).

A comparison of ceramic forms and designs from the Pusht-i Kuh cemeteries with those from Deh Luran and Mesopotamia suggests that some graves are earlier than the horizon represented by Susa A and the Maran phase.

Rare parallels are found in the Farukh phase in Deh Luran (Vanden Berghe 1975a:fig. 6:15; Wright 1981:fig. 24h–j). There are also overall similarities in style, especially the use of unusual combinations of complex motifs and of overall designs, which link Hakalan/Parchinah and Gawra XIII or Ubaid 4 (Tobler 1950:pls. CXXVII–CXXX). Globular pots with spouts and/or basket handles are found in the Eridu cemetery (Safar, Mustafa, and Lloyd 1981:pl. 5:3; Vanden Berghe 1974:fig. 3:1), also assigned to late Ubaid 4 (Porada, et al., this vol., chap. 5; for additional Ubaid 4 parallels see Zagarell 1982:70–72).

Other artifacts repeat the pattern. Animal figurines with fused legs are found in Susa A contexts at Jaffarabad levels 3–1 and Parchinah (Dollfus 1971:fig. 22:5, 8, 10–11, 13; Vanden Berghe 1975b:58; see also Amiet 1966:fig. 5). A standing female figurine from Parchinah (Vanden Berghe 1975a:fig. 8, 1975b:46, 57–58) duplicates in form and posture late Ubaid 4 figures from cemeteries in Mesopotamia (Porada et al., this vol., chap. 5; Safar, Mustafa, and Lloyd 1981:fig. 115; Woolley 1955:pls. 20–22). Stamp seals from Hakalan and Parchinah have good parallels in Gawra XIII–XII (Vanden Berghe 1975b:59; see Tobler 1950:pls. CLX:35, CLXI:48, CLXIX:168; Vanden Berghe 1973b:57, 1975b:59). Round, pear-shaped, and ridged maceheads are paralleled in Gawra XII–IX (Vanden Berghe 1973b:57–58; 1974:70–71, fig. 9; 1975a:fig. 3:6–7, fig. 10; 1975b:59, lower; Tobler 1950:pl. CLXXVII:30–35).

B. *The Early Bronze I period* is defined by excavations at the cemetery sites of Bani Surmah, Kalleh Nissar, Dar Tanha, War Kabud (Mihr), Takht-i Khan, and Qabr Nahi (Vanden Berghe 1972a:2, 1973c:208). Characteristic are large collective tombs made of stone (Vanden Berghe 1968b:54, 60–61, 1970b:figs. 9–10) which contained plain, painted monochrome and polychrome pottery (Vanden Berghe 1968b:59, 1970a:69, 1970b:fig. 11) and numerous metal artifacts (Vanden Berghe 1968b:58, 59:bottom, 1970b:figs. 12–13, 1972a:2, fig. 3).

The polychrome pottery is described as a "late and provincial variety" of Diyala "Scarlet Ware" (Vanden Berghe 1973c:208). The arrangement of motifs in horizontal bands suggests a closer relationship to Deh Luran than to the Diyala (see also Carter 1987); a more precise relative date may emerge when specific designs from the Pusht-i Kuh are compared with stratified examples from Farukhabad (see Wright 1981:115–25). Calcite and serpentine cylinder seals, including scenes of diagonal animal fights, appear to be Early Dynastic II–III in date (Vanden Berghe 1972a:2, 1968b:56). Socketed axes are paralleled in Susa IV(A?), independently correlated with Early Dynastic II–III (Carter 1980:fig. 22c; Vanden Berghe 1968b:58, upper; see also "Western Susiana"; Carter 1984:141).

C. *The Early Bronze II period* is defined by Kalleh Nissar Area AII, with additional information from Darwand, Kazab, Gululali Galbi, and Sardant (Vanden Berghe 1972a:3, 1973c:208). Kalleh Nissar AII produced individual stone tombs (Vanden Berghe 1972a:fig. 4; 1973a:27, 29, figs. 6–11, pls. 12–21). Plain Ware vessels occur in forms typical of the Akkadian to Ur III period in Mesopotamia (Vanden Berghe 1970a:71 lower right; 1973a:27, pl. 15, figs. 7, 9, 11–12). Goblets with pointed base and flared, grooved rims (Vanden Berghe 1973a:fig. 12) are most common in Ur III levels at Nippur (McGuire Gibson, pers. comm. 1984) and are characteristic of the Susa VB or Shimashki period, also dated to Ur III (see "Western Susiana"; Carter 1984:fig. 10). Monochrome Painted Ware with simple geometric designs seems to be local (Vanden Berghe 1973a:fig. 9:2, pl. 14). Two cylinder seals have crudely cut designs paralleled in the Diyala at the end of the Akkadian and Post-Akkadian periods (Vanden Berghe 1973a:28, fig. 14, pl. 21).

The Hulailan Sequence

An intensive survey of the Hulailan Valley was conducted from 1962 to 1974 by the Danish Archaeological Mission under the directorship of Jørgen Meldgaard and Peder Mortensen (Meldgaard, Mortensen, and Thrane 1963; Mortensen 1974a, 1974b, 1975a, 1975b, 1976, 1979). These data were augmented by a deep sounding (Trench GI) cut into Neolithic deposits at Tepe Guran. Twenty-one "main" strata were distinguished, with levels A–C dating to post-Neolithic periods and with V resting on virgin soil (Meldgaard, Mortensen, and Thrane 1963:fig. 9; Mortensen 1963:110). Surveys specifically aimed at late prehistoric material were conducted by Thrane (1964) and Goff (1966, 1971).

A. *The Early (Aceramic) Neolithic period* is defined by Guran GI:levels V to T, the lowest 1.5 m of the mound. Until the final report is published, there is no means of determining the date of this occupation relative to other aceramic sites in the region. Mortensen (1974b:25) has suggested that basal Guran is contemporary with the latest levels at Ganj Dareh. A multiple secondary burial cut into virgin soil may indicate a relationship between Aceramic Guran and the late Bus Mordeh/early Ali Kosh period at Tepe Ali Kosh, which contained a similar grave (Hole, Flannery, and Neely 1969:248; Mortensen 1963:112).

B. *The Middle to Late Neolithic period* is defined by Guran GI:levels S to D. This sequence provides evidence of change in the ceramic industry which is of critical importance for the relative chronology of the Neolithic in the Zagros (Mortensen 1962, 1964). To simplify discussion and facilitate comparisons we have divided Guran into ceramic phases. These are tentative and will bear revision when the complete assemblage is published.

1. *The Guran Archaic phase* is defined by levels S to P. Level S marks the appearance of Undecorated Grayish Brown Ware, lightly fired with a wet-smoothed or burnished surface (Mortensen 1963:113, fig. 14). The photographs and published description of a vessel from Ganj Dareh D (Smith and Crépeau 1983) appear similar to Undecorated Grayish Brown Ware. In levels R to P Undecorated Grayish Brown Ware continues, but more characteristic is better-fired Undecorated Buff Ware which appears in Level R and continues through the rest of the sequence (Mortensen 1963: 114, fig. 16g–h).

Also found in R are very small quantities of Archaic Painted Ware, decorated with red motifs including reversing Y's in a zone immediately above the base, and triangles or Y's at the rim (Mortensen 1963:114–16, figs. 15, 16a–b). Archaic Painted Ware has not been reported from any other site in the central Zagros. Farther east, chaff-tempered pottery with a Y design has been found at Qal'eh Rostam II (Nissen and Zagarell 1976:162–63; Zagarell 1982:22, 25, fig. 9:1). Although the excavators relate this material to Guran Archaic Painted Ware, both vessel form and the placement of designs on the vessel differ; moreover, most of the unpainted Qal'eh Rostam II pottery has a highly polished red slip, suggesting a date at the end of the Hulailan Neolithic sequence for this assemblage.

2. *The Zagros Standard Painted Ware phase* is defined by Guran levels O to E. Characterized by red designs on a buff ground, it has four variants with differing chronological distributions: Jarmo Tadpole Ware (O–H, with its greatest frequency in M); Sarab Tadpole and Sarab Geometric Wares (L–D, with frequency peaks in levels L and D); and Guran Close-Patterned Ware (K–D, with a peak in H–F)(Mortensen 1964:fig. 7). The Jarmo, Sarab Tadpole, and Guran variants have dense, often negative designs composed of small geometric elements repeated along diagonal lines (Mortensen 1963:116–17, figs. 16c–f, 17; Oates 1973:pl. XVII:A). Sarab Geometric Ware is unusual, with bands of negative lozenges or zigzags at the rim and carination (Mortensen 1963:fig. 18).

Although Mortensen originally lumped Sarab Tadpole and Sarab Geometric Wares, a more recent assessment indicates that Sarab Tadpole appears before Sarab Geometric in the Guran sequence (Levine and McDonald 1977:43, based on a communication from Mortensen). Survey data also indicate that these wares have slightly different chronological distributions: in Hulailan, Tepe Faisala produced Sarab Geometric without Sarab Tadpole (Mortensen 1974b:fig. 22); in the Mahidasht, Sarab Tadpole and Geometric co-occur only at Tepe Sarab, while at four other sites they occur separately (Levine and McDonald 1977:43, fig. 3).

Zagros Standard Painted Ware is widely distributed. Jarmo Tadpole was found in the lower pottery-bearing deposits at Jarmo (Op. II:5–3; Adams 1983:215–17). The illustrations in the final report show only this motif in the earliest ceramic level, II:5, suggesting that it is contemporary with Guran N–O. At Tepe Sarab, Jarmo Tadpole is found with Sarab Tadpole and Sarab Geometric Wares in the early or SI deposit (McDonald 1979: 141, table 5; see also "Mahidasht" and "Godin"); since Guran Close-Patterned is not present, SI is probably contemporary with the middle of the Neolithic deposit at Guran.

Relationships with the Mandali area in central Mesopotamia are documented by surface remains from Tamarkhan and a few sherds similar to Guran Close-Patterned Ware in a late Samarran context at Chogha Mami (Mortensen 1974b:25; Oates 1973:pl. XVIIB:3, 6; Oates and Oates 1976:63, lower, row 1:2, row 2:2). Tamarkhan represents a lowland settlement within the Zagros Neolithic tradition (Oates 1968:3–4). The recovery of a small number of sherds of Tadpole Ware indicates that at least part of the Tamarkhan deposit must be contemporary with the Zagros Painted Ware phase at Guran, although numerous highly burnished red to orange chaff-tempered sherds suggest that the occupation continues somewhat later. The latter possibility, plus the presence of middle/late Samarran trade sherds at Late Neolithic sites in the Zagros (q.v.), implies that the Zagros Painted sherds from Chogha Mami were derived from an earlier context. This is supported by evidence from Deh Luran: the Mohammad Jaffar phase, probably contemporary with the latest Zagros Standard Painted Wares, is also correlated with early Samarra (see "Deh Luran").

3. *The Red-Burnished Ware phase* is defined by the latest Neolithic deposit at Guran, and by survey material. Red-Burnished Ware appears in Guran H and increases rapidly in popularity, becoming dominant by level D (Mortensen 1964:fig. 7, 1963:117–18, fig. 16i–k). Sar Arsiaban, a site discovered by the Hulailan survey, produced only Guran Buff Ware and Red-Slipped Ware (Mortensen 1974b:25–26, fig. 24); Mortensen places it slightly later than Guran, representing a period during which Zagros Standard Painted Wares are rare or absent (1974a:fig. 35). The Guran Red-Burnished Ware phase is contemporary with Late Sarab (see below), and by extension with the linear painted pottery of Sefid and Surkh in Deh Luran and Hajji Firuz in Azerbaijan (see "Hasanlu").

C. *The Early Chalcolithic period* is defined by surface material. Probably transitional from the Neolithic is Tepe Chena A, which produced chaff- and sand-tempered pottery that was often burnished and rarely decorated with black and/or red paint (Mortensen 1974b:28, fig. 29; 1976:43). This Chena Buff Ware is similar to pottery from Chogha Mish Archaic 2–3 (Mortensen 1976:43). More typical of the Early Chalcolithic were sites with grit-tempered "Susiana Black-on-Buff" sherds, such as the Kazabad mounds and Sil Kuska (Mortensen 1974b:28–29, figs. 31–33; 1976:43, figs. 2–3). Although this material has been compared to Hakalan and Parchinah by Mortensen (1976: 43), this dating is rejected here because of synchronisms between the Pusht-i Kuh Chalcolithic and the Hulailan Middle Chalcolithic (see below). E. Henrickson (1985b:83) considers the designs on published sherds of Hulailan Early Chalcolithic Black-on-Buff to be more closely related to Seh Gabi and Late Siahbid (see "Mahidasht" and "Godin"). This earlier dating is supported by a series of vague but clustered design parallels with Bendebal 14–12 which tie the Early Chalcolithic to the latest part of the Chogha Mish period (Dollfus 1983:figs. 81:15, 82:8; Mortensen 1976:fig. 2h; Dollfus 1983:83:9, 86:10; Mortensen 1976:fig. 2b), and by parallels with Gawra XIII (Mortensen 1976:fig. 2e; Tobler 1950:pl. CXXVII:173; Mortensen 1976:fig. 2d; Tobler 1950:pl. CXXX:207).

D. *The Middle Chalcolithic period* is defined by survey material from sites such as Kahreh Tappeh, War Cheshmeh C, Tepe Cheshmeh Mahi, and Mina Khan Kushia (Mortensen 1976:44). Imported sherds of Susa A Black-on-Buff Ware established a relative date for the Hulailan Middle Chalcolithic. For example, a beaker with a row of long-necked birds from War Cheshmeh C is duplicated in Bendebal 10 (Dollfus 1983:fig. 88:12; Mortensen 1976:fig. 4a); a large jar with solid painted neck and bands with triangles from Mina Khan Kushia (Mortensen 1976:fig. 5a) is found in Jaffarabad 3 (Dollfus 1971:fig. 17:3, 6). Sherds of Black-on-Plum Ware (Mortensen 1976:fig. 5) link the Hulailan Middle Chalcolithic not only to Susa A, but also to sites throughout the Zagros, including Hakalan and Parchinah, and the Maran phase in the Mahidasht (E. Henrickson 1985b:74, 87–88, table 5 with refs.; see also "Mahidasht" and "Godin"). Middle Chalcolithic Coarse Ware from Mina Khan Kushia (Mortensen 1976:44–45, fig. 6) is related to the Sargarab Horizon, and may represent a transition to the Hulailan Late Chalcolithic (see below).

E. *The Late Chalcolithic period* is defined by surface material from Chia Fatela Bosurk and Cheshmeh Sardeh (Mortensen 1974b:figs. 38–39, 1976:45, figs. 7–9). Excellent parallels for this ceramic assemblage can be found in the pottery of Godin VI and VI/V (Mortensen 1976:45, fig. 7a; Young 1969:fig. 8:12, 9:6; Mortensen 1976:fig. 7g; Young 1969:fig. 9:1, 3, 10; Mortensen 1976:figs. 8, 9d, f; Young 1969:fig. 8:4), Kunji Cave (Wright et al. 1975:fig. 6i–j, n–o), Baba Jan V (Goff 1971:fig. 7), and Sargarab ("Deh Luran," with refs.). The presence of beveled-rim bowls (Mortensen 1976:figs. 7f, 9e) firmly links part of the Hulailan Late Chalcolithic to Godin VI/

V and Late Uruk (see "Mahidasht" and "Godin"; see also Mortensen 1974b:32).

F. *The Bronze Age* is poorly known in Hulailan. There is apparently a hiatus after the Late Chalcolithic (Mortensen 1976:45–46). The next period to be identified has been equated with Godin III (R. Henrickson 1984a:770–71, table 25; Mortensen 1974b:33–45); published sherds indicate that some survey material is contemporary with Godin III:5 (Goff 1966; R. Henrickson 1984a:table 35).

The High Road and Eastern Luristan

The northern part of the region designated here as Central Western Iran consists of a series of valley systems running roughly east and west. These formed a segment of the great trade route or High Road that crossed from the vicinity of Baghdad through the Zagros to the central plateau. In discussing the archaeology of this large area, it is convenient to break it into large zones: the western end of the High Road or the Kermanshah region, and the eastern end of the High Road or the Kangavar region. Eastern Luristan lying to the south of the Kangavar region is less known, but seems generally to have formed part of a culture area that included the eastern segment of the High Road. Sites in eastern Luristan will therefore be incorporated within the description of the Kangavar regional sequence.

Kermanshah Region: The Mahidasht Sequence

Most studies of the archaeology of the western end of the High Road have focused on the broad Mahidasht, Kermanshah, and Bisitun Plains, and smaller immediately adjacent valleys. The first systematic research was conducted by the Iranian Prehistoric Project of the Oriental Institute of Chicago under the direction of Robert J. Braidwood in 1959–60 (Braidwood 1960a, 1960b, 1961; Braidwood, Howe, and Reed 1961). In addition to surface survey in the Kermanshah, Mahidasht, and adjacent western valleys, small-scale excavations were carried out at Asiab, Sarab, Siahbid, and Deh Savar Tepes. A specific investigation of the Early Neolithic period was undertaken in valleys to the south of Bisitun by Philip E. L. Smith for the Université de Montréal. Excavations at the site of Ganj Dareh were carried out from 1967 to 1974 (Smith 1967, 1968, 1970, 1972a, 1972b, 1974, 1975, 1976), followed by an intensive survey with Peder Mortensen (Smith and Mortensen 1980; Smith and Young 1983). Building on the Chicago team's work, a large-scale program of research covering all periods of occupation has been carried out by the Mahidasht Project of the Royal Ontario Museum under the direction of Louis D. Levine in 1975 and 1978. In addition to a systematic surface survey of the Kermanshah and Mahidasht

Plains, it included soundings at Sarab, Siahbid, and Chogha Maran (E. Henrickson 1983, 1985b; McDonald 1979; Levine 1974, 1976a, 1976b; Levine and McDonald 1977).

A. *The Early Neolithic (Ganj Dareh) period* is defined by excavations at Tepe Ganj Dareh, supplemented by a test at Tepe Asiab and survey data (Smith and Young 1983:146–48, fig. 2) Ganj Dareh is a village site located in a small side valley between Bisitun and Harsin. The earliest of five phases of occupation (level E) is interpreted as a camp; well-preserved mud-built buildings were recovered in level D, which was destroyed by fire (Smith 1975, 1976). Asiab is a low mound on the Kermanshah Plain which contained a large circular depression interpreted as a pit house (Braidwood 1960b; Braidwood, Howe, and Reed 1961; Flannery 1983:170–71; Howe 1983:115–17, 126–28; Smith and Young 1983:fig. 2); the associated chipped stone industry is considered very similar to that from Ganj Dareh E (Howe 1983:115, 118).

The relative dating of Ganj Dareh and Asiab must at present rest on preliminary statements by scholars who have firsthand knowledge of one or both sites. Howe states that the earliest material, from Asiab and Ganj Dareh E, includes chipped stone industries "strikingly like" those from Karim Shahir and Zawi Chemi Shanidar (Howe 1983:118, 129–32). Within Luristan, the chipped stone industry from Abdul Hosein is said to be "fairly close" to that from both Mahidasht sites (Pullar 1979:154). Smith (1976:13) considers Asiab and Ganj Dareh to be contemporary with the Bus Mordeh phase at Ali Kosh.

B. *The Middle to Late Neolithic period* has been defined at Tepe Sarab, a very low mound, with two "lobes" separated by a central north-south depression. In 1960 the Iranian Prehistoric Project placed a major excavation unit on each lobe: SI on the west, and SV on the east (Braidwood 1960a; McDonald 1979:131–33; 216–20, pls. VI–IX, figs. 15–19). Although Braidwood considered Sarab to be a single-period site, an analysis of the pottery led Mary McDonald to conclude that the ceramic assemblages represented in SV and SI differed significantly (McDonald 1979:133 and following). In 1978 the Royal Ontario Museum made additional soundings, Operations 1–3, adjacent to the 1960 trenches; these indicated that there were two distinct phases of occupation lying side by side, and the Sarab period has accordingly been divided into two phases (McDonald 1979:311–12).

1. *The Early Sarab phase* is documented by Area SI and Operation 2 (McDonald 1979:197, 311). In Operation 2, almost all of the sherds were of chaff-tempered Buff Ware and of Sarab Standard Painted Ware, including both Tadpole and Geometric variants (McDonald 1979:311; Levine and Young 1987:fig. 1, upper; for ware descriptions see Levine and McDonald 1977:40). In the larger SI sample of decorated vessels, tadpole motifs predominated, with the Jarmo style much more common than the more densely painted Sarab style (McDonald 1979:141, 144, fig. 11, pls. I–II). The Early Sarab phase is therefore approximately contemporary with the Zagros Standard Painted Ware phase in Hulailan, especially the time before the introduction of Red-Slipped Ware (Guran H; see "Western Luristan"). Tadpole Wares also link it to the earliest ceramic levels at Jarmo, J–II:5–4? (McDonald 1979:195–98).

2. *The Late Sarab phase* is documented by Area SV and Operations 1 and 3 (McDonald 1979:312). It has also been found in test excavations conducted at two sites by the Mahidasht Project: Tepe Siahbid, Operation I:levels 106–3; and Chogha Maran, Operation III: below 306 (E. Henrickson 1985b:figs. 4, 21; McDonald 1979:516, 519; see also Smith and Young 1983:fig. 3). It is characterized by Red-Slipped Ware, Sarab Linear Painted Ware, and Black-Slipped Ware (McDonald 1979:197–202, tables 5–6; Levine and Young 1987:fig. 1, lower).

Late Sarab is linked by technology and form with the Red-Burnished Ware phase in Hulailan (McDonald 1979:138–39, 173–87, 195–204 with refs., figs. 13, 14s–x). Sarab Linear Painted Ware, with red- or black-painted chevrons, zigzags, and crosshatching, is part of a horizon style present throughout the Zagros. It is documented at Zagros Group sites such as upper ceramic Jarmo, Operation II:3–1 (McDonald 1979:198; Adams 1983:fig. 105:1–3, 107), at Zagheh in the Archaic period (Malek Shahmirzadi 1977b:pl. XII; Levine and McDonald 1977:pl. Ia), at Hajji Firuz period sites in Azerbaijan (Voigt 1983:161–63, 168 with refs.). The use of black and white pigments and specific linear motifs links Late Sarab with the Sefid period in Deh Luran (Hole 1977:112; compare Hole 1977:fig. 43s; McDonald 1979:pl. V:1, bottom).

C. *The Early Chalcolithic (J Ware) period* is defined by the earliest excavated deposits in Chogha Maran Operation 3:306 and by Tepe Siahbid Operation 2:206 to 203 (E. Henrickson 1985b: fig. 21). At Siahbid, J Ware is stratified above Late Sarab material and below an eroded level dated to Early Siahbid; at Maran, it also underlies Early Siahbid material (E. Henrickson 1983:305–16, 479–80, 1985b:figs. 4–5). J Ware has red, black, or white paint on a plain buff or red- and/or black-slipped surface, creating a bichrome or polychrome effect (E. Henrickson 1983:330–32, tables 44–45, figs. 97–99; 1985b:69, fig. 6 poorly reproduced; Levine and McDonald 1977:42, pl. Ib, fig. 1). It is similar in fabric, vessel form, and decorative style to lowland Halaf pottery; however, the design repertoire on J Ware is more limited, and complex Halaf motifs do not occur. The closest Halaf assemblage is that from Banahilk in Iraq, which apparently dates to the end of the Halaf period (E. Henrickson 1985b:69; Watson 1983a:233–34, 238, 1983b:figs. 197–200). To the south of the Mahidasht, J Ware occurs on the surface of sites in Hulailan, and perhaps in the Kuh-i Dasht (E. Henrickson 1986:89–90). It does not occur in the valleys to the north and east of the Mahidasht, and E. Henrickson has raised the possibility that J Ware may be partially contemporary with early Dalma occupations in these regions (1985b:101).

D. *The Middle Chalcolithic period* is divided into three phases.

1. *The Siahbid phase* is known from Tepe Siahbid and Chogha Maran. The deposit at Siahbid has been separated into two chronological units on the basis of stratigraphy and the occurrence of minor wares in the ceramic industry; a statistical analysis of motifs supports this division (see E. Henrickson 1985b:93–94, fig. 22). Early Siahbid is defined by Operation 2:202–201 at Siahbid and Maran Operation 3:305–304; Late Siahbid is defined by Siahbid Operation 1:102–101 (E. Henrickson 1983:481–88, 1985b:93–94, fig. 21).

At Chogha Maran, diagnostic Early Siahbid phase Black-on-Buff Ware is accompanied by Dalma "Ubaid" Painted Ware identical to sherds found in Dalma contexts in Kangavar (E. Henrickson 1983:333, 337–38, tables 46–47, 50, 58, figs. 101–3, 106; 1985b:figs. 12–15; see also "Godin"). A small quantity of Dalma Impressed Ware, again duplicated at Dalma period sites in Kangavar, occurs during the Early Siahbid phase but is absent from Late Siahbid deposits (E. Henrickson 1983:338–40, figs. 104–5, tables 51–52; 1985b:73, figs. 4–5, 9). By extension from Dalma parallels, Early Siahbid is contemporary with Ubaid 3 in Mesopotamia (see "Hasanlu").

Chronological placement of the Late Siahbid phase is based primarily on a computerized quantitative analysis of style, ALSCAL A, which indicates a strong relationship between Late Siahbid pottery from Siahbid and Maran phase pottery from Chogha Maran (for ALSCAL, see E. Henrickson 1985b:88, 1986 with refs.). The distribution of wares as well as stylistic evidence indicates that this pattern is most plausibly interpreted as the result of the continuation of a tradition in successive phases (E. Henrickson 1985b:74). The distance between them in time is not known, but a substantial gap may be indicated by the fact that ALSCAL A shows no stylistic relationship between Late Siahbid and Tell Madhhur in the Hamrin, a site strongly linked to the Maran phase by both ALSCAL A and ware comparisons (E. Henrickson 1985b:94, but see also p. 73). Late Siahbid is not linked stylistically to the Seh Gabi phase in Kangavar (E. Henrickson 1985b:93–94), nor is it similar to Pisdeli pottery from Azerbaijan (Voigt, in prep.). In the end, therefore, the chronological placement of Late Siahbid rests on in-direct rather than direct evidence (see also E. Henrickson 1983:486–87).

2. *The Maran phase* is defined at Chogha Maran in Operation 1:levels 116–105 and Operation 3:levels 303–302 (E. Henrickson 1985b:fig. 21). Characteristic are Red-White-and-Black Ware, with a reddish-buff fabric covered with a thin white wash and decorated with a gray-black paint (E. Henrickson 1983:340–42, tables 53, 58, figs. 107–10; 1985b:figs. 18–19); and "Black-on-Red Ware," with black paint on a plum slip (E. Henrickson 1983:344–45, fig. 111, table 55; 1985a; 1985b:74, fig. 20).

Two of these ceramic types are widely distributed in western Iran and thus provide important evidence for relative chronology. "Black-on-Red Ware" is identified with pottery referred to here as "Black-on-Plum Ware," found in excavated contexts at Hakalan and Parchinah in Luristan, and in Susa A contexts in Khuzistan (E. Henrickson 1985b:74, 95–96, tables 2–5; see also "Western Luristan" and "Western Susiana"). E. Henrickson (1985b:95, table 5) also assigns sherds from Madhhur and Tell ᶜUqair to Black-on-Red/Plum Ware, but these seem to be different in form and decoration from any of the published examples from Iran. Sherds that match the description of Red-White-and-Black Ware are characteristic of most of the deposit at Pisdeli Tepe in northwest Iran (Voigt, in prep.). Related material has been identified to the south in Luristan at Hakalan and Parchinah, and in survey collections (E. Henrickson 1985b:tables 2, 4).

A rare type in the Maran phase, Black-on-Buff Painted-and-Incised Ware, occurs at Tell Madhhur and other late Ubaid assemblages in the Hamrin, and is probably imported (E. Henrickson 1983:345). An independent link to Madhhur is established by an ALSCAL A test which shows a close stylistic relationship between Madhhur and the Maran phase (E. Henrickson 1985b:94, fig. 22).

E. *The Late Chalcolithic (Deh Savar) period* is defined by excavations at Deh Savar Tepe and has been documented at additional sites through survey. The Deh Savar assemblage is said to contain both Godin VI plain wares and beveled-rim bowls, the diagnostic type for Godin Period VI/V (E. Henrickson 1985b:74; see below).

F. *The Bronze Age,* known from limited soundings and surface survey, has been divided into two broad phases.

1. *The Maran Red-Slip phase* is defined by Operation 1:levels 104–101 and Operation 3:level 301 at Chogha Maran (E. Henrickson 1983:313–14, figs. 76–77, table 37). There is a complete break between the plain Red-Slipped and Gray-Slipped Wares characteristic of these deposits and the pottery from the underlying Chalcolithic levels (E. Henrickson 1983:490, 1985b:73–74).

The Maran Red-Slip phase is most closely related to

Godin III:6. At Chogha Maran a dozen sherds of Godin III Painted Ware were found through excavation, one of which was identified as Godin III:6 (R. Henrickson 1984a:708). Ceramic parallels with Godin III:6 include "slosh-proof jars"; Red-Slipped pots with an everted rim; and Gray-Slipped "carinated cuplets," small bowls with a row of white-filled incisions at the carination (R. Henrickson 1984a:figs. 72:1–2, 4–7, 79:12, table 23). A chronological link to Mesopotamia is provided by a few of the almost two hundred sealings found at Maran; most were in "an unfamiliar, probably local style," but some have close parallels in Early Dynastic II–III contexts in the Sin temple at Khafajeh (H. Pittman, cited in R. Henrickson 1984a:709). This comparison suggests that the Maran Red-Slip phase may begin earlier than Godin III:6 (see "Godin"; R. Henrickson 1984a:709, fig. 173). Finally, this phase is linked to Susa IVA by bowls with impressed ridge decoration (R. Henrickson 1984a:724; Carter 1980:fig. 25:5–9; see also Stève and Gasche 1971:pls. 14:6, 12:30).

2. *The Godin III phase* in the Kermanshah region is known only from surface material (Levine 1976a:160). A comparison of the Kermanshah pottery with that from the type site suggests an occupation equivalent to Godin III:5 to III:2 (R. Henrickson 1984a:table 23, 1986b:table 2).

The Kangavar Region and Eastern Luristan: The Godin Sequence

The sequence for the Kangavar Valley 90 km east of Kermanshah has been documented by the Godin Project of the Royal Ontario Museum under the general direction of T. Cuyler Young, Jr. Area clearances as well as a deep sounding were carried out at the large mound of Godin Tepe between 1967 and 1973 (R. Henrickson 1984a; Weiss and Young 1975; Young 1969; Young and Levine 1974). To obtain a larger sample for the early periods, excavations were undertaken at a group of small mounds collectively known as Seh Gabi in 1971 and 1973, under the direction of Louis D. Levine (Hamlin 1974b; E. Henrickson 1983, 1985b; Levine 1972, 1975; Levine and Hamlin 1974; McDonald 1979; Young and Levine 1974; Young and Weiss 1974:fig. 1). Surface surveys were carried out in 1961, 1965, and 1974 (Young 1966, 1975a, 1975b).

Adjacent valleys to the south seem to contain archaeological material closely related to that in Kangavar. The following research has therefore been incorporated into the discussion of the Kangavar sequence: excavations at Tepe Giyan carried out in 1931–32 by Georges Contenau and Roman Ghirshman (1935); a sounding at Tepe Abdul Hosein carried out in 1978 by Judith Pullar (1979); a deep sounding at Baba Jan carried out by Clare Goff (1968a, 1968b) in 1966 and 1967; a survey of the Malayer Plain

in 1977 and 1978 by Rosalind Howell (1979); and soundings at Kunji Cave carried out by Frank Hole in 1963 and John Speth in 1969 (Speth 1971; Wright et al. 1975).

A. *The Early Neolithic (Abdul Hosein) period* is defined at Tepe Abdul Hosein in the Khawa Valley (Pullar 1979). The earliest occupation consists of features cut into virgin soil; this is succeeded by levels containing the remains of mud architecture. The chipped stone industry is said to be generally similar to that from Ganj Dareh and Asiab; it differs from that of Sarab in that the tools are smaller and better made (Pullar 1979:154). In a recent synthesis, Smith and Young have suggested that the aceramic levels at Abdul Hosein are contemporary with Zagros Ceramic Neolithic sites such as Jarmo, Sarab, and Guran (Smith and Young 1983:148); however, the basis for this statement is not clear, and both the excavator's relative dating and a large suite of radiocarbon dates suggest that Abdul Hosein is more likely to be contemporary with Ganj Dareh (see "Mahi Dasht"; McDonald 1979:512).

B. *The Middle to Late Neolithic (Sarab) period* is known from surface survey in the Malayer Plain, where White-on-Black Ware like that found in the Mahidasht Late Sarab phase has been reported (Howell 1979:157). In Kangavar, a small number of sherds including some identical to Sarab White-on-Black Ware from a tertiary deposit at Seh Gabi Mound C suggests the presence of a nearby buried site, perhaps a camp (McDonald 1979:404–5, 413, 496, 522; but see also Smith and Young 1983:150, n. 7).

C. *The Early Chalcolithic (Shanabad) period* is defined by Seh Gabi Mound C:levels 1–5 (McDonald 1979:317–52, figs. 24–29; Levine 1975:fig. 3; note that Shanabad has also been referred to as Godin XII and as Kangavar XI). Obtaining a relative date for this assemblage is difficult. The buff chaff-tempered pottery, sometimes decorated with rows of red or black triangles (Hamlin 1974b:275; Levine 1975:fig. 4; Levine and Hamlin 1974:212, pl. IIc; McDonald 1979:360–405, pls. X–XI, figs. 30–39), is technologically similar to pottery from Sarab; however, the chipped stone industries are "strikingly different," with Shanabad lacking the formal blade technology characteristic of Sarab (McDonald 1979:410–18, 449–51). Shanabad is clearly later than Sarab, but its placement immediately prior to Godin X is based on a consistent set of radiocarbon dates rather than on stratigraphic position (see below, "Radiocarbon Evidence"). Shanabad pottery has been found at sites in Malayer (Howell 1979:157) and in the latest level at Tepe Abdul Hosein (one sherd; Levine and Young 1987, citing J. Pullar Humphries). There are "pre-Dalma" levels in Godin's Operation XYZ:spits 78–76 containing sherds described as "soft-ware," but little is known about this "Godin XI" assemblage (E. Henrickson 1983:478).

D. *The Middle Chalcolithic period* is divided into three phases based on the stratigraphic sequences at Godin Tepe and at Seh Gabi Mound B (Levine and Young 1987).

1. *The Godin X (Dalma) phase* is defined by spits 63–50 in Operation XYZ at Godin Tepe (E. Henrickson 1983:170–72, fig. 37; Young and Weiss 1974:210) and the lower part of the deposit at Seh Gabi Mound B (levels 5–7; Hamlin 1974b:275; E. Henrickson 1983:158–61; Young and Levine 1974:2–4). This phase is characterized by a series of unusual ceramic types: Dalma Painted, which includes Monochrome and rare Bichrome; Dalma Impressed Ware; and Dalma Double-Slipped Ware (E. Henrickson 1983:196–203, figs. 50–51, 55–64, tables 34–35; 1985b:69, figs. 7–8; Young and Levine 1974:3–4, figs. 9–10). Present in smaller quantities are Black-on-Buff and Dalma "Ubaid" Painted Ware (E. Henrickson 1983:203–6, tables 34–35; 1985b:69, fig. 10).

Although the ceramic samples from each 20-cm deep arbitrary level or spit in the 6–8 m² area of Godin Operation XYZ are small, they can be used to subdivide the period into three subphases that are potentially useful for chronology (E. Henrickson 1983:173–74, fig. 37). Early Dalma has a high frequency of Dalma Streaky Ware. Dalma Monochrome with simple linear decoration slowly increases and is characteristic of Middle Dalma. Dalma Impressed Ware appears near the end of Middle Dalma and increases significantly during Late Dalma. The Seh Gabi Dalma occupation appears to cover a much smaller period of time, probably contemporary with Middle or Late Dalma at Godin (E. Henrickson 1983:174, figs. 38–39).

The Kangavar Dalma assemblage is very similar to that at the type site in Azerbaijan (E. Henrickson 1985b:101; see also "Hasanlu"). Dalma pottery has been recovered from Tepe Giyan, and through surface survey in the Nehavand, Khawa, and Kakavandi Valleys to the south, but not from Malayer (E. Henrickson 1985b:tables 1, 4; see also Goff 1971:134, figs. 2:23–28, 3:32–45). To the west, Dalma Impressed Ware links Middle and/or Late Dalma with the Early Siahbid phase in the Mahidasht (q.v.). Sherds of "Dalma-like Impressed Ware," interpreted by E. Henrickson as local copies, are found at Ubaid sites such as Abada and Kheit Qasim in the Hamrin and Yorgan Tepe near Kirkuk (E. Henrickson 1986) and in a Bayat context in Deh Luran (Wright 1981:fig. 10 d–e).

Sherds from Abada I/II, identified as Dalma Painted Ware (Oates 1983:253; Yasim 1983:181), are significantly different from Kangavar Dalma pottery (E. Henrickson and L. D. Levine, pers. comm. 1985). Nevertheless, Henrickson's ALSCAL analysis found that the designs on Dalma painted wares from Seh Gabi B level 7 are "fairly close" to those of Ubaid 3 Gawra XIX–XVII (E. Henrickson 1983:667–68, figs. 131–32), a correla-

tion supported by the presence at Dalma Tepe of sherds at home in Gawra XVI (see "Hasanlu"; Porada et al., this vol., chap. 5).

2. *The Godin IX (Seh Gabi) phase* is defined by Godin Tepe Operation XYZ:spits 48–42 (Young and Weiss 1974:210; E. Henrickson 1983:172), and Seh Gabi Mound B:levels 2–4 (Young and Levine 1974:figs. 4–6, levels A1–B; E. Henrickson 1983:161–69). Seh Gabi Painted Ware, with a shiny black vitrified paint on a mat oxidized surface (E. Henrickson 1983:203, 204, figs. 65–71, tables 27–28, 32; Young and Levine 1974:fig. 11), occurs at Giyan and at sites in the Malayer Plain (E. Henrickson 1983:494–95, table 65; 1985b:table 1, 4; Howell 1979:157). This period is technologically and stylistically isolated from sites in the nearby Mahidasht (see "Mahidasht"). There are, however, stylistic similarities between Seh Gabi Painted and Pisdeli Painted Ware recovered from Hajji Firuz Tepe Trench F10, dated to the middle of the Pisdeli period and contemporary with Gawra XIII (see "Hasanlu"; E. Henrickson 1983:484–85). Seh Gabi Red-Slipped Ware (E. Henrickson 1983:187–90, figs. 37, 39–43, tables 34–35; Young and Levine 1974:fig. 12) is comparable in form and fabric to Pisdeli Red-Slipped and Burnished Ware (Voigt, in prep.).

3. *The Godin VIII (Teherabad) phase* is defined by Godin Operation XYZ:spits 40–29 (E. Henrickson 1983:174–75, fig. 37). Pottery related to Godin VIII from the surface of Seh Gabi B may have originated from an eroded deposit (E. Henrickson 1983:175, 205). The predominant ceramic group is Seh Gabi Red-Slipped Ware, accompanied by a Black-on-Buff Ware that is very different from the Seh Gabi Painted Ware stratified below it in Operation XYZ (E. Henrickson 1983:174–75, 204–5, table 27).

Comparisons with material from the Mahidasht are very general and link Godin VIII with the Black-on-Buff Ware found in earlier, Middle Chalcolithic contexts at Tepe Siahbid and Chogha Maran (E. Henrickson 1985b:70). Because Godin IX is correlated with the Late Siahbid phase, E. Henrickson places Godin VIII contemporary with the Maran phase in the Mahidasht (1985b:fig. 21). This dating is supported by similarities in form and some painted designs between sherds from late Godin VIII and the late Pisdeli period (Voigt, in prep.). Relative to the Mesopotamian sequence, both the comparison with Maran and with late Pisdeli indicate a correlation of Godin VIII with the end of Ubaid and the beginning of Uruk.

E. The *Late Chalcolithic period* is divided into three phases that are stratigraphically related at Godin Tepe.

i. *The Godin VII (Hoseinabad) phase* is defined by Operation XYZ:spits 26–13 and Operation B:levels 49–35 at Godin (Young 1969:3, fig. 5; Young and Levine

1974:17), and Seh Gabi Mounds A, E:levels 3–4, and F (E. Henrickson 1983:172; Young and Levine 1974:13–15). The ceramic industry includes highly distinctive S-shaped jars and squat concave-based vessels with finger-impressed handles (E. Henrickson, pers. comm. 1984; Levine and Young, 1987:fig. 16; Young 1969:fig. 6; Young and Levine 1974:fig. 13). Godin VII pottery is apparently not present in the Mahidasht (Levine and Young 1987), but has been found at sites to the east including Malayer (Howell 1979:157), and Avaj in the pass to the east of the Hamadan Plain, as well as to the south at Tepe Giyan and sites in Harsin (L. D. Levine, pers. comm.). Farther east, there are excellent parallels between Godin VII and Ghabristan I (see "Qazvin/Kashan"). These include jars with molded decoration on the rim (Young 1969:fig. 6:3; Young and Levine 1974:fig. 13:1–5, 7; Majidzadeh 1977:pls. 79:1–4, 80:3) that are virtually identical in fabric as well as style to the Godin vessels (Dyson and Voigt, observation).

Stamp seals found in Godin VII contexts at Seh Gabi have good parallels in other regions (see Hamlin 1974b:276 top right; unpublished drawings and information on context from E. Henrickson, 1985). Two seals, one hemispherical and a second with a pierced tang, have an incised design with chevrons filling the area between the arms of a central cross that is duplicated on a tanged seal from Sialk III$_1$ (Ghirshman 1938:pl. LXXXVI:S417), and on a seal and a sealing from Gawra XI (Tobler 1950:pls. LXXXVIII:4, CLIX:20–21). The same design occurs on an ovoid hemispherical seal pierced longitudinally; this seal form also occurs in Gawra XI and "before XII" (Tobler 1950:pl. CLIX:26, 28). A second design with straight lines filling each quadrant occurs on a seal with a tang tentatively assigned to Godin VII. It is duplicated on a seal from Sialk III$_5$ (Ghirshman 1938:pl. LXXXVI:S117); a second Sialk example from III$_4$ is slightly smaller and has a proportionately larger tang (Ghirshman 1938:pl. LXXXVI: S.259). A round-faced hemispherical seal with schematic figures may be related to seals of the same form, with animals and linear fill found in Gawra XII (Tobler 1950:CLXVII:139) and in Susa A at Jaffarabad (Dollfus 1971:fig. 23:5).

2. *The Godin VI (Cheshmeh Nush) phase* is defined by Godin Operation XYZ spits 12–5, a single building level; Operation B strata 34–19; the Brick Kiln Cut; and Seh Gabi Mound E levels 2–1 as well as tests in Mounds F and G (E. Henrickson 1983:172; Levine and Hamlin 1974:211; Young 1969:4; Young and Levine 1974:17; Young and Weiss 1974:210). The largest exposed area at Godin comes from the Brick Kiln Cut on the lower slopes of the Citadel, where 5 phases of architecture rest on virgin soil (Young and Weiss 1974:210–11). Characteristic of Godin VI is Buff Fine Ware, some-

times white-slipped and/or decorated with fine incisions or painted designs (E. Henrickson, pers. comm. 1984; Levine and Young 1987:fig. 17; Young 1969:5, fig. 7; Young and Levine 1974:fig. 14). The Godin VI ceramic assemblage is found at sites in Malayer (Howell 1979:157), in Baba Jan V (Goff 1971:145, fig. 7; 1976:pl. VIII:c–d), and at Tepe Giyan (E. Henrickson 1985b:table 1; L. D. Levine, pers. comm. 1985). Painted Ware and some vessel forms from Kunji Cave are said to be most similar to the latest Godin VI levels in Operation B (Wright et al. 1975:132–33, fig. 6). Farther east, vessels identical to VI Painted Ware were found in Ghabristan IV, levels 6–4 (Majidzadeh 1977:pls. 95–96, 1978:fig. 3:8), with a smaller number of parallels to Ghabristan II (e.g., Majidzadeh 1977:pl. 91:2, and Young 1969:fig. 7:1; Majidzadeh 1977:pl. 89:1, and Young 1969:fig. 7:10; Majidzadeh 1977:pl. 84; E. Henrickson, pers. comm.). Godin VI plain wares are also present at Ghabristan (Levine and Young, pers. comm.), suggesting a relatively close relationship between these settlements. Some of the same forms and designs are found at Tepe Sialk in Period III$_{3-7}$, with the majority in Sialk III$_{6-7}$ (E. Henrickson 1985b:74, pers. comm. 1985; Majidzadeh 1978).

Bowls with punctate decoration identical to Godin VI Buff Fine Ware have been found as far north as Bukan (Swiny 1975:82, fig. 1:11–14; unpublished collections in the University Museum). To the west and south, plain wares with fabric and vessel forms related to Godin VI occur in the Mahidasht (E. Henrickson 1985b:74) and a few sherds of Painted Ware were also found in the sounding at Deh Savar (Levine and Young 1987). Plain wares occur to the south in Hulailan, and in Deh Luran at Sargarab and Farukhabad, the latter in Early Uruk contexts (see "Western Luristan" and "Deh Luran"). A second tie to the Uruk period is provided by a stamp seal impression from a Godin VI context at Seh Gabi E (Hamlin 1974b:276) that shows a squatting human. The pointed head and posture of this figure are found on a seal impression from Susa assigned to period II (Amiet 1972:38, 44, pl. 3:239); related to the Susa example is a sealing from the Uruk pit at Sharafabad, suggesting a date within Middle Uruk for the entire group (Wright, Miller, and Redding 1980:fig. 6:3).

3. *The Godin VI/V (Late Uruk) phase* has been defined in the Godin Tepe Deep Sounding, with additional material from Operation B:17–11, XYZ:4–0, the Brick Kiln Cut, and small tests (E. Henrickson 1983:172; Weiss and Young 1975; Young 1969:6–7, figs. 4–5; Young and Levine 1974:17; Young and Weiss 1974:208–11). Near the end of Godin VI, an oval-walled compound containing a series of small buildings around a court was built at the top of the citadel (Weiss and Young 1975:fig. 2). Within the oval compound, about a third of the pottery recovered

is characteristic of Godin VI as described above, but the rest is "exotic," related to lowland Late Uruk (Young and Weiss 1974:209; Weiss and Young 1975:5–6); elsewhere on the mound the only Late Uruk types associated with VI pottery are beveled-rim bowls and trays (Levine and Young 1987). Although the compound had been used to establish a separate period, it is now apparent that Godin V consists of an architectural unit and some diagnostic ceramic types within a typical Godin VI occupation (Levine and Young 1987). To emphasize the continuity of the Godin VI assemblage within the settlement as a whole and still recognize a significant historical event, this short phase has been renamed "Godin VI/V."

Lowland parallels for the pottery of VI/V include four-lugged pots with rope appliqué on the shoulder from Warka Eanna IV, Nippur Inanna XIX, and later, and Susa Acropole I:17 (Weiss and Young 1975:6, n. 6, fig. 3:1, 2a with refs.; Le Brun 1978c:fig. 34); four-lugged pots with incised shoulder triangles from Warka Eanna IV, Nippur Inanna XVI, and Susa Acropole I:17a (Weiss and Young 1975:6, n. 7, fig. 3:1a); red-slipped vessels with nose lugs and bands of black paint from Susa Acropole I:17 and Middle Uruk Farukhabad (Weiss and Young 1975:6, n. 8, fig. 3:2; see also Wright 1981:fig. 57:a); and beveled-rim bowls from Warka Eanna IV, Susa Acropole I:17–16, and Early to Late Uruk contexts at Farukhabad (Weiss and Young 1975:fig. 3:3–5; Wright 1981:128–29). Also recovered were droopy spouts, rolled-rim jars, and trays paralleled in Susa Acropole I:17 and 16 (Levine and Young 1987:fig. 22:2–5; Le Brun 1971:fig. 52, 1978c:fig. 36), as well as bowl forms characteristic of Susa Acropole I:17 (V. Badler, pers. comm.; see Le Brun 1971:fig. 46:17). Missing at Godin are ceramic types characteristic only of Proto-Elamite sites such as Susa Acropole I:16–14C and Jemdet Nasr sites in Mesopotamia (Weiss and Young 1975:6, nn. 9–10).

Clay tablets, which bore numerical signs or in one case a pictograph and numbers, are paralleled in Susa Acropole I:17 (Weiss and Young 1975:11, figs. 4, 5:1–2, 4–5; Amiet 1972: nos. 602, 604, 629, 657; Le Brun 1971: fig. 44.8; see also Le Brun 1978a). The seals and seal impressions also find parallels in Acropole I:17 as well as in Warka V–IV (compare Weiss and Young 1975:fig. 5:8, with Le Brun 1971:fig. 44:5; see also Le Brun 1978a). Thus ceramic, epigraphic, and glyptic evidence all points toward a correlation with Susa Acropole I:17.

Beveled-rim bowls document contemporary settlements during the Deh Savar period in the Mahidasht (Levine and Young 1987), at Tepe Giyan (L. D. Levine, pers. comm. 1985), and in Malayer (Howell 1979:157). They are associated with Godin VI pottery in Ghabristan IV:levels 3–1 (Majidzadeh 1981:146, 1977:pl. 96), and at Sharak in the Bakhtiari Mountains (Zagarell 1982:figs. 23–25). There are also ceramic parallels between Godin

VI/V and Sialk IV (see "Qazvin/Kashan") and Early and Middle Banesh in Fars (W. Sumner, pers. comm.).

F. *The Godin IV (Yanik) period* is defined at Godin Tepe in the Deep Sounding, with additional material from the Brick Kiln Cut and Operations A:28–31, B:10–3, F:10–1, and small tests around the perimeter of the mound (Young 1969:9; Young and Levine 1974:fig. 17). There seems to have been a hiatus between Godin VI/V and IV, but the excavators think it was probably brief (Weiss and Young 1975:2).

The diagnostic ceramic group is Gray-Black Burnished Ware, which is sometimes decorated with small angular motifs that have been excised and filled with white paste (Young 1969:fig. 11; Young and Levine 1974:fig. 19:1–6). As the name of the period implies, closely related pottery was first excavated in the Early Bronze Age I deposit at Yanik Tepe in Azerbaijan (see "Northwestern Iran"; Young 1969:10); the characteristic round buildings of Yanik Early Bronze I are not, however, found at Godin. Related assemblages occur in the following regions to the east and north of Kangavar, providing a more or less continuous distribution between Godin and Yanik: Malayer (Howell 1979:157); the Hamadan Plain (Young 1966:232, 235); and the Bijar and Mianduab areas (Swiney 1975:82–83, fig. 5). At least one site is known on the Qazvin Plain 1 km southwest of Sagzabad (E. Negahban, pers. comm.).

White-Filled Black-Burnished Ware has also been recovered from sites to the south, usually in quantities suggesting imports rather than settlements. Several sherds have been picked up at Tepe Giyan (L. Levine, pers. comm.), and Goff (1966:82–83) reports a stratum of this material underlying sherds of "Susa D type" at Chia Zand in the Pusht-i Kuh. A sherd of the excised type occurs in the Susa D sherd collection of the Musée des Antiquités Nationales, St. Germain (Dyson 1973a:698, n. 7). Finally, two sealings now assigned to Godin IV are paralleled in the "late Proto-Literate or ED I" period in Mesopotamia (R. Henrickson 1984a:724, n. 4, citing E. Forte; Young and Levine 1974:fig. 34:3).

G. *The Godin III period* is defined by stratified building remains in the Deep Sounding, with additional material from numerous small trenches (R. Henrickson 1984a:tables 4–5, fig. 3). The original description (Young 1969:11–23; Young and Levine 1974:18–29) has been superseded by R. Henrickson (1984a, 1984b, 1986b, 1987). In Henrickson's study the earlier published levels are modified, so Young and Levine's levels "III$_{5-7}$" are all now subsumed under III:6 (R. Henrickson 1984a:103). The sequence has seven stratigraphic units labeled as levels III:6 to III:2, Post-III:2, and III:1, each characterized by a ceramic assemblage with distinctive vessel forms and painted style (R. Henrickson 1984a:5–7). Only levels III:6 to III:4 date before 2000 B.C. and are relevant here. This sequence provides for the first time a relatively well-documented description of the time range formerly represented in this area by Tepes Giyan, Jamshidi, and Bad Hora; it replaces former attempts to define a sequence from this inadequately documented material (Dyson 1965, 1973a; R. Henrickson 1984a:746–824, fig. 173, table 17–35, with refs.).

1. *The Godin III:6 phase* has a series of architectural sublevels (R. Henrickson 1984a:114–94, figs. 7–18, 37–39); but although the stratigraphy indicates a long duration for Godin III:6, the pottery is "quite homogeneous" (R. Henrickson 1984a:387). Painted Buff Ware includes restricted, carinated vessels and ovoid jars with ridges at the neck and a design zone at the shoulder (R. Henrickson 1984a:388–92, figs. 46–90). Motifs in the main register include bull's-eyes, nested triangles, lozenges, "shark's teeth" or "flames," abstract birds' wings, "tufts," animals, and arcs with pendant lines (R. Henrickson 1986b:figs. 4–5). Rare (Burnished) Gray-Black Ware may represent a continuation of the Godin IV ceramic tradition (R. Henrickson 1986b:fig. 6:4–7, 9–10; pers. comm. 1985).

In the Mahidasht, Godin III:6 is contemporary with the Maran Red-Slip Phase, correlated through glyptic evidence with Early Dynastic II–III in Mesopotamia (see "Mahidasht"). At al-Hiba in southern Iraq, sherds comparable to Godin III:6 Painted Buff Ware were associated with sealings and tablets dated to late Early Dynastic III (R. Henrickson 1984a:707, n. 2, with refs.).

There are numerous parallels between Godin III:6 and material from recent excavations at Susa assigned to period IVA (Ville Royale I:9–13; R. Henrickson 1984a:table 33, 1986b:table 2). In addition to imported sherds of Godin III:6 Painted Buff Ware (see "Western Susiana"), parallels include bowl forms (R. Henrickson 1984a:figs. 80:5–6, 81:19, 82–84; Carter 1980:figs. 15:7–8, 11, 25:1–3, 10); large pithoi with cable decoration (R. Henrickson 1984a:figs. 65–68; Carter 1980:figs. 24:1, 26:2, 27:2); "pie-crust" bases (R. Henrickson 1984a:figs. 65, 67–68; Carter 1980:fig. 27, 3–4, 5–7); and ovoid jars with ridges (R. Henrickson 1984a:figs. 59–62; Stève and Gasche 1971:figs. 17:1, 5, 18:15–16, 22:1–2, 4). Vessels from some of the Pusht-i Kuh tombs dated to Early Bronze I are comparable in shape and painted design to Godin III:6 pottery (R. Henrickson 1984a:table 30, 1986b:table 2). Both Susa IVA and Pusht-i Kuh Early Bronze I have been independently correlated with Early Dynastic III and the early Akkadian period (see "Western Susiana" and "Western Luristan").

2. *The Godin III:5 phase* appears to have developed from III:6, but the two phases are sufficiently distinct stylistically to suggest a short hiatus between them (R. Henrickson 1984a:417, 847). Godin III:5 at Godin Tepe represents a short occupation, ending when the settlement was suddenly destroyed, perhaps by an earthquake (R. Henrickson 1984a:195–96). Large quantities of pottery were found in situ on the floors. Painted Buff Ware motifs include eagles, goats, waterfowl, nested diamonds, zigzags, vertical chains, the "sting-ray," and the lozenge (R. Henrickson 1984a:396–97, figs. 91–104; 1986b:figs. 8–10).

Exact ceramic parallels lie primarily in adjacent valleys along the High Road and in the south (R. Henrickson 1984a:878, fig. 179; 1984b:fig. 2). In the Khawa-Harsin area, Godin III:5 sites are known from surface survey (R. Henrickson 1986b:table 2 with refs.) and from excavated contexts at Tepe Giyan, formerly assigned to Early Giyan IV (Contenau and Ghirshman 1933; R. Henrickson 1986b:table 2). At Baba Jan, architectural remains in level 5 of the deep sounding on the Central Mound correspond to Godin III:5, as do two graves dug beneath the Painted Chamber on the East Mound (Goff 1976:21–26, figs. 1–4, 5b:1; R. Henrickson 1986b:table 2). Settlements related to Godin III:5 were also found at sites in the Mahidasht, Kamtarlan, and Chigha Sabz in the Rumishgan Valley (R. Henrickson 1986b:table 2). In Khuzistan, recent excavations at Susa found an imported III:5 sherd in deposits with monochrome painted wares (R. Henrickson 1984a:711, n. 6 on 724–25; Stève and Gasche 1971:pl. 16:12), assigned to Susa IVA by Carter (1978:table I; see also R. Henrickson 1986b:table 3).

A few parallels can be drawn with Hasanlu VII to the north, which is contemporary with Early Dynastic III and the Early Akkadian period (see "Hasanlu"). A globular jar of Painted Orange Ware from Hasanlu (Dyson 1967b:pl. 1483A) follows the stylistic canon of Godin III:5 as set forth by Henrickson, and a small carinated bowl in Unpainted Orange Ware (Dyson 1967b:fig. 1027, center) is paralleled in form by Red-Slipped Ware bowls from Godin III:5 (R. Henrickson 1984a:fig. 108:8–10).

To summarize, links to the Mesopotamian sequence via both the southern lowlands and the northern Zagros indicate that Godin III:5 is approximately contemporary with the Early Dynastic III to Akkadian periods. Since Godin III:6 is correlated with Early Dynastic IIIB, Godin III:5 should date to the Proto-Imperial/Akkadian period (R. Henrickson 1984a:710, fig. 173).

3. *The Godin III:4 phase* buildings were constructed while some III:5 wall stubs were still visible and could be used as foundations (R. Henrickson 1984a:209–50, figs. 22–26, 37–39, 41); it ended with burned debris and what seems to have been a general destruction (R. Henrickson 1984a:244). Carinated vessels continue as the major Painted Buff Ware form; ridges frequently appear at the carination on larger vessels, while on smaller vessels the carination may be reduced to a slight break in the shoulder curve. Painted designs executed with fine lines are predominantly geometric (R. Henrickson

1984a:404–7, figs. 110–21, 128, 130, 132; 1986b:figs. 11–13). New is a complex "sun" motif, and pairs of waterfowl with long beaks are common.

Closely related sites within the highlands are found in the same areas occupied in Godin III:5. At Tepe Giyan, material from "Classic Giyan IV" is considered contemporary with Godin III:4 as is Jamshidi IV (R. Henrickson 1986b:table 2, fig. 3). Survey sherds dated to III:4 have been found in the Mahidasht, Kuh-i Dasht, and Alishtar valleys; the southernmost occurrence is from an excavated context at Chigha Sabz in Rumishgan (R. Henrickson 1984b:fig. 3, 1986b:table 2).

Sherds of Burnished Gray Ware tentatively identified as imports (R. Henrickson 1984a:403) provide some evidence for the dating of Godin III:4 relative to the Mesopotamian sequence. Fragments of a fenestrated base decorated with a band of incised or impressed bull's-eyes bordered by a series of fine bands (R. Henrickson 1986b:fig. 13:14) find a close parallel in a Gray Ware vessel from a "Gutium-Ur III?" context at Tell Asmar in the Diyala; related sherds are of Larsa date (Delougaz 1952:pl. 123c). A second Godin III:4 sherd has an incised design tentatively identified as a bird, another popular motif in the Larsa period (R. Henrickson 1986b:fig. 13:16; Delougaz 1952:pl. 124a–a′, 125c). A Gray Ware bowl decorated with a band of concentric circles and incised bands, together with the fenestrated base mentioned above, may imitate the "late group" of chlorite bowls at Susa (Miroschedji 1973:26–79), dated to Susa VB and contemporary with Isin-Larsa (see "Western Susiana"). Since most of the Godin III:4 Gray Ware was found in tertiary contexts and therefore provides a *terminus post quem,* it can be argued that this level is contemporary with or later than Isin-Larsa.

Internal dating for this phase provides chronological boundaries. Godin III:5 is dated to the Akkadian period (see above). Following the destruction of III:4, there is a hiatus; Godin III:3 is represented only by pits and architectural fragments, which were then filled and leveled for phase III:2 construction, and is of indeterminate duration. Godin III:2 is dated by parallels that generally date to the late Larsa and Old Babylonian periods (R. Henrickson 1984a:712–18,fig. 173). Thus the correlation of III:4 with Isin-Larsa, and perhaps Ur III, is upheld (R. Henrickson 1986b:fig. 3).

Radiocarbon Evidence for West Central Iran

All of the dates for the Neolithic are beyond the range of the CRD tables and are quoted here with the 5730 half-life. Absolute dates for the Early Neolithic have been obtained from Ganj Dareh and Abdul Hosein. The determinations from Ganj Dareh are inconsistent but suggest that the occupation begins by ca. 7000 and had a duration of several hundred years (table 2). This conforms with the single date from Aceramic Guran. However, the determinations from Abdul Hosein are stratigraphically inverted—two of three samples from "just above virgin soil" dating to ca. 7000, while two of three from overlying deposits dated to ca. 7250 B.C. (table 2). Dates for Zagros Standard ceramic assemblages at Sarab and Guran indicate that they were well established by ca. 6000 B.C.

All other dates lie within the range of the CRD tables. The Early Chalcolithic Shanabad phase has three dates, suggesting that this unique assemblage dates ca. 5000 B.C. (table 2). The next cluster of five dates comes from late(?) Godin IX, the Seh Gabi phase, with a corrected average range of 4160–3905 B.C. (table 1). This range seems too late for two reasons. First, it would place Godin IX contemporary with Susa A, which is incompatible with a network of relative dates documented for the Middle Chalcolithic in the Mahidasht and Kangavar (see "Mahidasht" and "Godin"). Second, an average date for the middle of the Pisdeli period, which provides the only direct artifact parallels for Godin IX (see "Hasanlu"), ranges 4540–4405 B.C. A comparison of individual dates shows that a single date for the early part of Godin IX (SI-4913) overlaps with the Pisdeli range.

The only other large group of dates for this region comes from Godin VI/V. Reasonably consistent, the group has a corrected average range of 3190–2960 B.C. (tables 1–2). This again seems too late since artifact parallels suggest that Malyan Middle Banesh should be later than Godin VI/V; however, a large cluster of dates places Middle Banesh within the range 3370–3050 B.C. Removing the two dates at Godin which appear to be possibly from intrusive samples (SI 2674 and SI 2675) (see Dyson 1987) would leave an average of the remaining five in the same range as the average for Middle Banesh. This is probably closer to reality but still does not resolve the descrepancy with the artifact parallels. Possibly confirming what may be a late bias within the Godin series, two consistent dates for Godin IV ca. 2400 B.C. are significantly later than the culturally related assemblage from Yanik Tepe Early Bronze I dated near the beginning of the third millennium by a cluster of four samples (table 2).

Central Northern Iran

The Qazvin/Kashan Sequence

The Qazvin Plain lies at the western end of a strip of agricultural land that stretches eastward along the foot of the Elburz Mountains from Azerbaijan to Khorasan; along this strip runs the continuation of the High Road. Kashan, one of a series of oasis cities along the western edge of the Dasht-i Kavir, also lies on a major trade route running from Qazvin in the northwest to Kirman in the southeast. The Qazvin Plain Project of the University of Tehran carried out systematic research from 1970 to 1978 under the direction of Ezat O. Negahban (1981). Survey of the plain was combined with excavations at the sites of Zagheh (Negahban 1973, 1977, 1979, 1984; Malek Shahmirzadi 1977b, 1979b), Ghabristan (Negahban 1973, 1977; Majidzadeh 1976, 1977, 1978, 1979, 1981), and Sagzabad (Negahban 1973, 1974a, 1974b, 1976, 1977; Malek Shahmirzadi 1977a, 1979a). The resulting sequence extends and partly replaces that from Tepe Sialk, excavated in 1933–37 by Roman Ghirshman (1938) for the French Archaeological Mission in Iran.

The earliest periods are documented at Zagheh, in very limited tests taken to virgin soil (FX: Malek Shahmirzadi 1977b:52; Negahban 1973:6, 1974a:216; TTFGX, Malek Shahmirzadi 1977b:55, 65–66, 84, chart I, map 9). Other excavations include an area of over 1,000 m², sometimes referred to as "the Village" (Malek Shahmirzadi 1977b:97–115, chart IV, figs. 8–45; 1979), and an area of ca. 600 m² to the north of the Village Trench which contained the "Painted Building" (Malek Shahmirzadi 1979b:191–92, map 2; Negahban 1979). Malek Shahmirzadi used his excavations in the deep sounding FGX and the Village Trench to construct an overall sequence for the site (Malek Shahmirzadi 1977b:chart I): Zagheh levels IX–XIII are assigned to the Archaic period and Zagheh VIII–I to the Cheshmeh Ali period, based on the presence of Cheshmeh Ali Ware (Malek Shahmirzadi 1977b:table 8). This phasing, which involves the correlation of distant probes based on absolute depth, is not accepted by Negahban; based on his own excavations he would assign only levels III–I to the Cheshmeh Ali period, and level IV and below to the Archaic (Negahban 1979, 1981:9–10). The critical issue for chronology is not just the assignment of individual stratigraphic units to a specific time unit, but a determination of the total depth of the Zagheh Archaic deposit and thus some estimate of its duration. While the Malek Shahmirzadi sequence cannot be accepted for the site as a whole without serious reservations, it is used here because it is the only published account of Zagheh with named stratigraphic units and associated ceramic types.

The middle portion of the Qazvin sequence is known from Ghabristan, the western portion of the mound of Sagzabad (Negahban 1973:5, Plan VI). The sequence, which does not overlap with that from Zagheh, is based primarily on Trench A/AEE (Majidzadeh 1977:45–46). In using the preliminary reports for this site, note that the numbering system for the major occupation phases has been reversed: in early reports (Negahban 1973, 1974a, 1974b; Majidzadeh 1977) periods are numbered I to IV from the top down; in later reports Majidzadeh has

switched the order; so Ghabristan I is the earliest period and IV the latest (Majidzadeh 1976, 1978, 1979, 1981).

A. *The Zagheh period* is defined by TTGFX levels IX–VI, or Zagheh "phases" XII–IX (Malek Shahmirzadi 1977b:84–92, fig. 5, chart I; 1979:fig. 2). Characteristic of the Zagheh period are two types of chaff-tempered decorated wares: Crusted Ware, coated on the exterior with a thin layer of fine sand and highly burnished on the interior (Malek Shahmirzadi 1977b:286, pls. XIIA:8–9, XIIB:7, XIID:1–2); and Zagheh Archaic Painted Ware, with red geometric designs applied to a burnished red-to-buff chaff-tempered fabric. Common motifs in the Zagheh period are nested zigzags, crosshatched bands, diagonal lines with pendant loops, and hatched or crosshatched triangles (Malek Shahmirzadi 1977b:286, pl. XIIA–D). Very similar sherds were recovered from Sialk I_{1-2} (Ghirshman 1938:pl. XL). Parallels to the west are with Late Sarab Linear Ware found at Mahidasht sites (see "Mahidasht"; Levine and McDonald 1977:pl. Ia) and with painted pottery from Hajji Firuz in Azerbaijan (Voigt 1983:figs. 92–94, 97). More distant ties for this entire group can be found in painted Samarra and Hassuna pottery (Dyson 1965:236; Levine and McDonald 1977:44; Voigt 1983:163–68).

Parallels for clay figurines are more widely distributed in time, but conform to the spatial pattern found for ceramics. Thirty-nine female figurines from the Painted Building include realistic portrayals of pregnant, seated females with spread legs and stalklike upper bodies that are similar to figures throughout the Jarmo sequence and in the early Hassuna period at Telul eth-Thalathat (Negahban 1984:pls. II, III:a–b; Broman 1983:figs. 156:1–4, 7, 9, 157:3a–b; Fukai and Matsutani 1981:pls. 20:4, 21:1–2); and seated figures with heavy legs but no indication of pregnancy, similar to figures from Umm Dabaghiyah (Kirkbride 1972:pl. VII:2–3; Negahban 1984:pl. VI:a–b). More stylized seated forms with fingernail-impressed bodies resemble figures from the Surkh and Chogha Mami Transitional Phases at Chagha Sefid (Negahban 1984:pl. VII; Hole 1977:229, fig. 90d). Highly abstract "boot-shaped" or triangular objects with heavy fused legs tapering to a conical foot are nearly identical to figures from aceramic Neolithic deposits at Gritille on the Euphrates (Negahban 1984:pls. VI:e, VII:g–h, VIII; Voigt, unpublished field data); a variant of this form occurs in Iblis I (Negahban 1984:pl. IX:a, f; Evett 1967: fig. 2).

B. *The Sialk I_{3-5} period* is not documented at Zagheh, but is defined by the upper six meters of the deposit in Trench I on the North Mound at Tepe Sialk (Ghirshman 1938:pls. XXXV–XXXVI). Painted designs include hatched motifs similar to those in the Archaic, with new elements such as stacked solid triangles, panels of thin horizontal lines bordered by large solid triangles, and net patterns. Particularly popular in I$_{4-5}$ is a series of motifs that seems derived from basketry (Ghirshman 1938:pls. XXXVIII, XLI–XLIV).

There are good parallels for this period in the Mushki and Jari phases in Fars (see "Southwestern Iran"). Ties to the Deh Luran sequence are diverse, but form a consistent pattern: sling missiles (Ghirshman 1938:pl. LII:35) occur only in the Sefid and Surkh phases at Chagha Sefid; miniature mullers (Ghirshman 1938:pl. LII:37–39) occur from Mohammad Jaffar to Surkh, with a large group in the Sefid phase (Hole 1977:fig. 87e–h, table 74). Although somewhat vague, stylistic similarities occur between Sefid Red-on-Cream Ware and sherds from Sialk I$_3$ with boldly painted designs (Ghirshman 1938:pls. XXXIX:S1274, XLI–XLII; Hole 1977:fig. 43). To the east, Sialk I$_{3-5}$ is linked to the Djeitun Phase at Sang-i Chakhmaq East (see "Damghan/Khorasan").

C. *The Cheshmeh Ali period* is defined at Zagheh by TTFGX V–0, and by large area clearances in the Village Trench; in Malek Shahmirzadi's sequence this is Zagheh VIII–0 (Malek Shahmirzadi 1977b:chart I, 97–245, figs. 8–53; 1979b). Unpublished strata above the Painted Building also date to this period (E. Negahban, pers. comm.). Other Cheshmeh Ali sites include Sialk II, excavated in Trenches 2 and 3 on the North Mound (Ghirshman 1938:24–27, pls. XI, XXXV, XXXVII, LVIII), and three sites near Tehran: the type site Cheshmeh Ali (Malek Shahmirzadi 1977b:427–31; Schmidt 1940:pls. 37–38; unpublished collections in the University Museum); Kara Tepe (Burton-Brown 1962); and Ismailabad or Tepe Moushelan (Navai 1976; Tala'i 1984). The depth of deposit assigned to Sialk II is 7.0 m, suggesting that the period is of some duration, at least in that part of the region. At present, however, there is not enough published data to warrant a formal division into phases here (but see Majidzadeh 1981:141).

At Zagheh, Crusted and Archaic Painted Wares continue throughout this period (Malek Shahmirzadi 1977b:280, table 8, pl. XIII), but there are significant changes in the latter. The Archaic Painted Ware of the Cheshmeh Ali period tends to have more complex painted designs, with several registers and more elaborate motifs (Malek Shahmirzadi 1977b:pls. VI:7–17, VII:11–22, VIII:13–26, IX:19–34, X:19–29, XI:14–27, XIII:Z40503, Z40246, Z40249, Z40247). Beginning in Zagheh VIII are Cheshmeh Ali or Sialk II Painted Wares. These are grit- or chaff-tempered, with a red surface that is usually slipped and smoothed before decoration with a black paint (Malek Shahmirzadi 1977b:279, 281–84, pls. V, VI:1–6, VII:1–10, VIII:1–11, IX:1–16, XIII–XVI; see also Ghirshman 1938:pls. IX, XLV–LI).

Cheshmeh Ali Painted Fine Ware is highly distinctive and can be used to establish a horizon style within western and northern Iran. Thin walled, it is fired so hard that it "clinks" when struck; the orange-to-red surface is painted in black with fine line motifs, including stylized birds and animals (e.g., Malek Shahmirzadi 1977b:pls. V:11, 19, 24, 28, 30–31, XIII:Z40239, Z40228). It occurs in quantity in Sialk II$_{1-2}$ (e.g., Ghirshman 1938:pls. IX:1, 3, XLV:S1603, S1394; XLVII:B:11, 13, C:8, 13, 15, XLVIII:A:13, 15, 16, C:6–8, 10, 12, 15–17, D:4–5, 8–11, XLIX:A:13, 15, 17, 22–23, B:14–15, 18–20) and in the later part of the deposit at Cheshmeh Ali Tepe (McCown 1942:3, 7; Schmidt 1937:298–99, 319, n. 1). At Zagheh, it also appears in the topmost levels assigned to the Cheshmeh Ali period (Malek Shahmirzadi 1977b:430; Negahban 1973:7). At Chagha Sefid, it has been tentatively identified in late Surkh and Chogha Mami Transitional deposits, where it is called "Sialk Black-on-Red" (Hole 1977:134–33, figs. 52d, h, 53g; see also "Deh Luran"). To the east, it is found on sites between Qazvin and Tehran (Malek Shahmirzadi 1977b:406; Maléki 1968; Negahban 1981:13–14 with refs.), extending along the Elburz to Shahrud where it is known from excavations at Sang-i Chakhmaq East (Masuda 1974a:26, 1976:64). On the Gurgan Plain, Cheshmeh Ali Painted Fine Ware occurs at Hotu Cave and Tureng Tepe (see "Mazandaran/Gurgan").

Ceramic parallels for the Zagheh Archaic Painted Ware of the Cheshmeh Ali period lie along the western border of Iran. An unstratified sherd from Tepe Sarab is decorated with a motif characteristic of Zagheh—a narrow band or reserve lozenges (Malek Shahmirzadi 1977b:pls. VI:14–15, VIII:20–22, IX:32–33; Negahban 1976:fig. 30; McDonald 1979:148, pl. V); the collections from Sarab in the Royal Ontario Museum also contain sherds with small triangles at the rim that are duplicated by sherds of Zagheh Archaic Painted Ware in the collections of the University Museum (Voigt, unpublished notes; Malek Shahmirzadi 1977b:pls. IV:A, VIII:25). In Azerbaijan the latest Hajji Firuz pottery is decorated with nested lozenges and black-painted checkerboards (Malek Shahmirzadi 1977b:pls. VI:9, VII:20, XI:24; Voigt, in prep.).

Bricks used for domestic structures in the Zagheh Village sounding have four finger impressions at each end, and long grooves on the sides apparently made by drawing fingers along the clay (Malek Shahmirzadi 1979b:184, fig. 3). Long bricks with longitudinal grooves were used during the latter part of the Archaic period at Chogha Mish (Delougaz 1976:fig. 17; Delougaz and Kantor 1971:41, 1973:191). Sialk II walls were built of shorter bricks with two finger impressions at either end (Ghirshman 1938:26–27, pls. XI:4–5, LVIII); these are similar to bricks with rows of finger impressions along the sides from Iblis I and Yahya VII–VI (see "Southeastern Iran").

D. *The Ghabristan I (Plum Ware) period* is defined by

levels 19–13 at Ghabristan (Majidzadeh 1977:48, 1981:142). Handmade Plum Ware has been coated with a brown-to-plum slip; vessels are sometimes decorated with applied or incised decoration at or below the rim (Majidzadeh 1977:54–56, pls. 76:2, 79–80). Excellent parallels for the fabric and molded decoration of Plum Ware vessels from late Ghabristan I occur in Godin VII (see "Godin"). Relationships with sites to the east are based on painted pottery and are somewhat more tenuous. Exact parallels for a bowl of Black-Painted Fine Ware with a zone of nested zigzags (Majidzadeh 1977:55, pls. 76:3, 80:1) are found in the sherd collections from Cheshmeh Ali and Murteza Gird at the Oriental Institute (Majidzadeh 1976:figs. 8:2, 5, 11:2).

Majidzadeh also identifies small cups and sherds from the Chicago collections as Plum Ware. Using some shape and design parallels between Cheshmeh Ali and Murteza Gird sherds, and published vessels from Sialk III_{1-2} (Majidzadeh 1976:figs. 7, 8:1; Ghirshman 1938:pls. XLII:S393, 1811a, LXIII:S382, 1806), he postulates Plum Ware at Sialk and places a hypothetical Plum Ware phase at both Cheshmeh Ali and Sialk contemporary with the earliest part of Ghabristan I; Sialk III_{1-3} is correlated with the rest of Ghabristan I (Majidzadeh 1981:142–43). Majidzadeh has documented no direct ties between Ghabristan I and Sialk III_{1-3}, and the two ceramic industries are very different in style, if not in technology. Nevertheless, given the strong relationship between Ghabristan II and Sialk III_{4-5} (see below), an indirect argument can be made for the complete or partial contemporaneity of Ghabristan I and Sialk III_{1-3}. An evaluation of the chronology of upper Cheshmeh Ali (McCown 1942:7) and an evaluation of Majidzadeh's "Middle Plateau A–B" horizon (1981:142–44) must await complete publication of Schmidt's excavations at Cheshmeh Ali and Murteza Gird.

E. *The Ghabristan II period* is defined by levels 10–9 at Ghabristan (Majidzadeh 1981:142, 1977; Negahban 1974a:216). Buff Ware vessels are usually plain, while all vessels classified as Red Ware are decorated with brown-painted geometric and naturalistic motifs (Majidzadeh 1977:56–59, pls. 77–78, 81–93). Characteristic are spiral plant and comb designs, leopards, ibex, bulls, birds, and reptiles (Majidzadeh 1977:58–59, 1978:98). At Sialk, many of the motifs of Ghabristan II are found in early period III; however, the animal motifs characteristic of Ghabristan II first occur in Sialk III_{4-5} (Majidzadeh 1978:96; compare Majidzadeh 1977:pls. 84–89 with Ghirshman 1938:pls. LXV:S1292, 260, LXVI:S1769, LXXVIII:B:4, 6, 7–8, LXXIX–LXXX). Related material also is found at Hissar IB (see "Damghan/Khorasan").

There are few ties between the ceramics of Ghabristan II and sites immediately to the west. One distinctive design is shared by Sialk III_{4-7}, Ghabristan II, and Godin VI: a band of thin vertical chevrons or zigzags below the rim, resting on a checkerboard band (Ghirshman 1938:pls. LXIV:S228, LXVI:S1400, LXIX:S1695, LXXIII:S1688). Given the close ties between Godin VI and Ghabristan IV (see "Godin"), we suggest that Ghabristan II is contemporary with Sialk III_{4-5} (Majidzadeh 1978:101) and is earlier than Godin VI. If the link between Ghabristan III and Godin VII proposed here is valid, Ghabristan II would by default fall into the chronological range of Godin VII. Note that seals found in Godin VII contexts provide independent evidence for a correlation of this period and Sialk III_{4-5} (see "Godin").

F. *The Ghabristan III (Gray Ware) period* is defined by Ghabristan levels 8–7, with a total depth of ca. 0.5 m (Majidzadeh 1981:142, 145). Given this shallow deposit, the period is likely to have been of short duration (but see Majidzadeh 1978). Majidzadeh has suggested that Ghabristan III represents a gap in the Sialk sequence between Periods III_5 and III_6. This is compatible with the links between Ghabristan II and Sialk III_{4-5}, and between Ghabristan IV and Sialk III_{6-7} documented here.

Unique to Ghabristan III are bell-shaped bowls, sometimes decorated with incised bands of geometric elements such as hatched triangles or chevrons (Majidzadeh 1976:figs. 35:1, 36; 1977:59–60). The only potential dating evidence is provided by distinctive squat vessels with projecting hooklike handles and concave bases (Majidzadeh 1977:60, pls. 76:5, 94:2) that are very similar to containers for extramural burials assigned to Godin VII (E. Henrickson, pers. comm. 1984; Young and Levine 1974:13–14, fig. 16:1a, 4a).

G. *The Ghabristan IV period* is defined by Ghabristan Trench E levels 6–1 and Trench A:5–3 (Majidzadeh 1977:60; Malekzadeh 1977). The pottery from the two excavated trenches differs somewhat in vessel form and painted style. Beveled-rim bowls appear in quantity in Trench A:5–3, together with a conical cup (Majidzadeh 1981:146; see also 1976:fig. 37:1, 3, 4; 1977:61, pls. 96:6–7). Based on the presence of these forms, Trench A:5–3 is placed later than Trench E and designated as Ghabristan levels 3–1. The Trench E material is designated as Ghabristan 6–4 (Majidzadeh 1976:figs. 37:7, 9–11, 38:2, 4, 8, 44:1; Malekzadeh 1977:pls. 109–27). Ghabristan 6–4 corresponds to Sialk III_{6-7} (Majidzadeh 1981:142). Sialk III_{7b} was destroyed by fire, and the site was apparently unoccupied during part or all of the period corresponding to Ghabristan 3–1; stratigraphic evidence for this abandonment comes from what seems to be an erosion surface, on which the Sialk IV_1 deposits rest (Dyson 1965:237; Ghirshman 1938:pl. LIX).

Close ceramic parallels link Ghabristan IV with Godin VI and VI/V (see "Godin"). Characteristic of these occupations are plain incurved bowls (Majidzadeh

1976:fig. 37:10–11; Young 1969:fig. 8:24); incurved bowls with beaded rims (Majidzadeh 1976:fig. 38:2; Young 1969:fig. 8:6, 8); and pedestal-based bowls (Majidzadeh 1976:fig. 38:4, 6–7; Young 1969:fig. 7:22, 27–28). Painted designs shared by Ghabristan IV, Godin VI, and Sialk III$_{6-7}$ include leopards (Ghirshman 1938:pls. XVII:3, LXVII:S152, 137; Majidzadeh 1976:fig. 41:1, 1977:pl. 95:1–2; Young and Levine 1974:fig. 14:14); bulls in a "skid" position with S-curved horns (Ghirshman 1938:pls. XX:4, LXX:top row; Majidzadeh 1976:fig. 8, 1978:100; Levine and Young 1987:fig. 17:1, 4); vertical combs (Majidzadeh 1977:fig. 95:3; Young and Levine 1974:fig. 14:10, 20); clusters of three thin crosshatched triangles resting on annular bands (Ghirshman 1938:pl. LXXX:B:15; Majidzadeh 1977:pl. 95:4; Young and Levine 1974:fig. 14:9); and net patterns with dots at each juncture (Ghirshman 1938:pls. LXXII:S154, LXXXII:D:2, LXXXIII:A:19; Majidzadeh 1977:fig. 96:1–2; Young 1969:fig. 7:14).

H. *The Sialk IV (Proto-Elamite) period* is defined by the upper portion of the South Mound at Tepe Sialk (Ghirshman 1938:58–61, pls. LIX, LX). No other related sites are known in this region, although there may be some overlap in time with the latest part of Ghabristan IV. At Sialk, two stratigraphic units were distinguished: IV$_1$, which contained mud-walled structures and apparently produced most of the artifacts, and IV$_2$, a badly disturbed deposit above the brick walls (Ghirshman 1938:58–59, pls. LIX, LXXXVII). Two tombs containing the bodies of adults accompanied by rich grave goods were cut beneath the floors of IV$_1$, and two jar burials containing infants were dug into IV$_2$ (Ghirshman 1938:59–61, fig. 9, pl. XXXII). A large hoard of jewelry in a painted jar found beneath the floor of IV$_1$ is also associated with this period (Ghirshman 1938:pls. XXX:1, XC:S1689). The form and painted design of the jar are matched by a vessel assigned to Sialk III$_7$ (Ghirshman 1938:pl. LXXIV), suggesting that it may be an heirloom or that the hoard actually dates to III$_7$. Although hoards are notoriously difficult to date, there is no internal evidence to suggest that this material postdates Sialk IV.

Similarities in ceramic forms link Sialk IV with Susa Acropole I:17–17B and Tal-i Ghazir "Early Proto-Elamite" contexts (see "Susiana"). Parallels include beveled-rim bowls (Ghirshman 1938:pl. XC:S537, 34; Le Brun 1971:fig. 47; Whitcomb 1971:pl. VIII:J); bottles (Ghirshman 1938:pl. LXXXIX:S1645b, 1608; Le Brun 1971:fig. 17:5; Whitcomb 1971:pl. V:G–H; also Ghirshman 1938:pl. LXXXIX:S80, 2, 483; Le Brun 1978b:fig. 29:5); droopy or straight tube spouts on globular jars with everted necks (Ghirshman 1938:pl. LXXXIX, top 2 rows; Le Brun 1971:fig. 52, 1978b:fig. 31:4, 6, 10; Whitcomb 1971:pl. IV:A, D); carinated jars with trough

spouts, and in some cases painted bands (Ghirshman 1938:pl. LXXXVIII:bottom 2 rows, XC:S7; Le Brun 1978b:fig. 24:9–10; Whitcomb 1971:pls. IV:J, VI:C, F); goblets (Ghirshman 1938:pl. XC:S244; Whitcomb 1971:pl. VI: B); and open bowls with lip spouts (Ghirshman 1938:pl. LXXXIX:S1645a; Whitcomb 1971:pl. VIII:D).

Nonceramic evidence provides better evidence for the duration of Sialk IV. Tablets attributed to Sialk IV$_1$, with numbers and only a few signs (Ghirshman 1938:pls. XXXI:2–7, XCII–XCIII), are comparable to those from Acropole I:17 or late Susa II (Carter 1984:129; Vallat 1971:243). Glyptic attributes shared with Acropole I:17–17B include animals with drilled eyes (Ghirshman 1938:pl. S1628; Le Brun 1971:fig. 44:2) and seated humans in front of vases with tall loop handles (Ghirshman 1938:pl. XCIV:S79; Le Brun 1978a:fig. 8:5). Amiet considers the Sialk IV$_1$ corpus stylistically transitional between the Susa II and III glyptic (1961; see also Carter 1984:129). A horn or antler from Sialk IV with an incised crosshatched band at the large or "head" end (Ghirshman 1938:pl. XXIX:5) appears to be paralleled by a bronze artifact from Susa I:17B (Le Brun 1978b:fig. 40:8). To the west, a seal and at least one sealing are very similar in content and style to a seal from Godin VI/V (Ghirshman 1938:pl. XCIV:S48, 1614; Weiss and Young 1975:fig. 5:8, pl. IVa). Some Sialk IV$_1$ tablets also resemble those from Godin VI/V (Weiss and Young 1975:11). Although there are few ceramic parallels between Sialk IV$_1$ and Godin VI/V, the latter does have an independent set of ceramic ties to Susa 17 (see "Susa Area").

A single tablet assigned to Sialk IV$_2$ (Ghirshman 1938:pls. XXXI:1, XCII:S28) has a variety of signs and is similar to those from Susa III, the Banesh phase in Fars and Yahya IVC (Vallat 1971:243; see "Southwestern Iran," "Yahya"). Parallels for unusual metal artifacts suggest that the end of Sialk IV$_2$ may be as late as the Early Dynastic III period (Dyson 1965:226 with refs.). After this period, Tepe Sialk is abandoned until the late Iron Age.

I. *The Early Bronze period* is known only from surface remains: a single site with Yanik Early Bronze/Godin IV pottery located on the Qazvin Plain 1 km southwest of Sagzabad (E. Negahban, pers. comm.).

J. *The Sagzabad or Middle Bronze period* is defined by the basal levels of Trench A and Trench OXX levels 1–4, or Sagzabad period I (Negahban 1976; Malek Shahmirzadi 1977a:67–76). Dominating the ceramic industry is Sagzabad Polychrome Ware which employs red and/or black paint on red and buff or orange slips applied to a handmade grit-tempered fabric of red, orange, or buff (Malek Shahmirzadi 1977a:pls. 136–40; see also Negahban 1976:pl. 139:8–9). There is little evidence for the dating of this period. Ceramic parallels from far distant Kansu Province in China suggest that it may begin in the late third millennium B.C. (Egami 1972:305 with comparanda). Small quantities of pottery similar in fabric to rare Fine Gray-Burnished Ware (Malek Shahmirzadi 1977a:76, pls. 141:1–2, 4–9, 10–13, 142:1, 5) occur in the Late Bronze Age assemblage at Dinkha Tepe in Azerbaijan, which dates to the earlier half of the second millennium B.C. (Hamlin 1974a). The form of a grayware cup from the top of the Sagzabad I deposit is common in Iron Age I contexts (Malek Shahmirzadi 1977a:pl. 142:1; Young 1965:fig. 8:1), perhaps indicating that Sagzabad I ends in the middle of the second millennium.

Northeastern Iran

The Damghan/Khorasan Sequence

Information for the prehistoric period comes primarily from the Damghan Plain south of the Elburz Mountains and the Atrek and Darreh Gaz Valleys which lead north toward Turkmenistan. The Neolithic sequence is based on excavations carried out by the Japanese-Iranian Joint Archaeological Mission at the double mound of Sang-i Chakhmaq, just to the east of the Damghan Plain (Masuda 1972, 1974a, 1974b, 1976). The Bronze Age is known from excavations at Tepe Hissar conducted by Erich Schmidt for the University Museum during 1931–32 (Schmidt 1937) and from a 1976 restudy by a team from the Iran Center for Archaeological Research, the University of Turin and the University Museum, under the direction of Robert H. Dyson, Jr., and Maurizio Tosi (Dyson and Howard, 1989). In addition to a reexamination of Schmidt's trenches and limited excavation, the Hissar Restudy Project made a survey of the Damghan Plain (Trinkaus 1981) and a surface study of the site aimed at the identification of functionality specialized areas (Bulgarelli 1977). Surveys in the Darreh Gaz (Kohl and Heskel 1980, 1982) and Atrek (Ricciardi 1980) Valleys, which recovered pottery assigned to Namazga periods I and III–IV, provide a direct link between Iran and Turkmenistan.

Schmidt's Hissar sequence, a major building block for this as well as previous chronologies, relied heavily on a stylistic analysis of grave goods rather than stratigraphic data (1937:39). A study of the Hissar archives indicates that in a number of instances interpretations of field data proved correct by the restudy project were either ignored or reversed by Schmidt (1937). During the restudy, areas on the North Flat, Main Mound, South Hill, and Twins were examined (Schmidt 1937:fig. 16). These produced consistent chronological, typological, and stratigraphic results. The key to the revised sequence was developed in the Main Mound, where Schmidt (1937:155–57, fig. 19) had provided an outline of his assigned phases for a

7-m deep exposure. Howard's revision breaks the sequence into six phases, A to F from the top down, that apply to the occupational stratigraphy of the site as opposed to Schmidt's burial seriation (Dyson and Howard, 1989; Howard 1982). Because much of the material in Schmidt's broad chronological units, Hissar I–III, can be related to the stratigraphic phases worked out in 1976, we have retained those terms here. The A, B, C subdivisions within Schmidt's periods have been abandoned since they are artificial stylistic constructs unsupported by the stratigraphy.

A. *The Sang-i Chakhmaq period* is defined by levels V–I in the West Tepe, with V at the base (Masuda 1972:2). Pottery is extremely rare, and no vessel forms could be reconstructed (Masuda 1976:65). The only published evidence useful for dating is clay figurines (Masuda 1974a:25, fig. 3:10–13). T-shaped figurines resembling those from Sang-i Chakhmaq West are common from the Mohammad Jaffar to Surkh phases in Deh Luran, with the highest frequency in Surkh (Masuda 1974a:fig. 3:12; Hole 1977:fig. 91h–n, table 67), and in the Archaic phase in Susiana (Hole 1974:fig. 15f–k). At Jarmo this figurine type is restricted to the upper levels ("double wing-based objects," Morales 1983:385, figs. 164:7–11, 165). Animals with legs extended to the front and rear were also found at Chagha Sefid in the Sefid and Surkh phases (Masuda 1974a:fig. 3:13; Hole 1977:fig. 89d, i, table 67), and in contemporary or slightly earlier contexts at Tepe Tula'i (Hole 1974:fig. 15a). At Jarmo they occur in Op. II:2–4 or the upper levels, contemporary with the Sefid phase (see "Deh Luran"; Jarmo types D-2, E–H, N, Morales 1983:figs. 150:1, 8, 151:1–6, 152:1, 5–7, 153:3, 154:9–13).

B. *The Djeitun period* is defined by the lower strata at Sang-i Chakhmaq East, levels VI–III (Masuda 1976:63–64). These deposits contained hard, dense, chaff-tempered pottery, with an orange-to-buff surface and gray core; decorated sherds are burnished and have brown-painted geometric designs (Masuda 1972:fig. 6, 1974a:fig. 5, 1976:63). The Painted Ware is virtually identical to that found at Djeitun sites in Turkmenia (Masuda 1976:63; compare Masuda 1972:fig. 6; 1974a:fig. 5; Masson 1971:pls. XXIX–XXXI, fig. 13; Masson and Sarianidi 1972:fig. 7) as well as at geographically intermediate sites in Gurgan (see "Mazandaran/Gurgan"). Other industries are equally similar, with similarities in geometric microliths and borers (Masuda 1972:fig. 7:6, 1974a:fig. 4:6–10, 1976:63, fig. 7:9–10; Masson 1971:pls. X–XI, XVI, XVIII–XIX); rich bone industries with bone sickle hafts, needles, and awls (Masuda 1972:fig. 7:9–13, 1974a:fig. 4:1–5); clay "cosmetic objects"/mini-mortars (Masuda 1972:fig. 7:1–3; Masson 1971:pls. XL:13–15, XLI:5–6); flat, square, or round whorls (Masuda 1972:fig. 7:8, 1974a:fig. 4:13–14, Masson 1971:pl. XXXIX); and carved figurines of horned animals (Masuda 1972:fig. 7:5; Masson 1971:pl. XXXVIII:11). In fact, the only major difference between the assemblages from Djeitun and Sang-i Chakhmaq East VI–III is the architecture (Masuda 1972:fig. 4–5, 1974a:26, fig. 1, 9; Masson 1971:fig. 19). Although only a small sample from Sang-i Chakhmaq has been published, it appears to span the entire time range represented at Djeitun (Masson and Sarianidi 1972:fig. 7).

Numerous artifact parallels relate this period to sequences in the west. Painted designs and motifs link the Djeitun period to Sialk I: stacked inverted triangles (Masuda 1972:fig. 7:6; Ghirshman 1938:pls. XLII:B, 7, XLIII:D, 2); open crosshatching over the entire exterior surface (Masuda 1972:fig. 6; Ghirshman 1938:pl. XXXIX:S1274); dots (Masuda 1974a:fig. 5:4; Ghirshman 1938:pls. XL:C, 5, XLI:B, 3); vertical nested zigzags (Masuda 1976:fig. 7:2; Ghirshman 1938:pl. XL:A. 10); nested regular or irregular wavy lines (Masuda 1974a:fig. 5:6–8; Ghirshman 1938:pls. XL:C, 2, XLI:B, 7, XLIII:A, 3, 5, 10; see also Masson 1971:fig. 16). Black burnished sherds (Masuda 1976:63) may be related to black pottery from Sialk I (Ghirshman 1938:16) and from the early deposit at Cheshmeh Ali (collections of the University Museum). Other Djeitun types in Sialk I are clay "cosmetic objects" (Ghirshman 1938:pl. LII:37–39) and bone sickle hafts with animal heads (Ghirshman 1938: pls. VIII:2, LIV:II), types also found in the Mushki period in Fars (see "Marv Dasht"). A few isolated but striking ceramic parallels in design, vessel form, and technology link Djeitun and Tepe Tula'i or the Archaic period in Khuzistan (Masuda 1974a:fig. 5:6–7; Hole 1974:figs. 11j–q, 14a–b); also reported at Tula'i is "gray ware" (Hole 1974:228). Further evidence to support this correlation is the presence of cosmetic objects and geometric microliths in the Sefid and Surkh phases in Deh Luran, independently linked to Chogha Mish Archaic 1 (see "Deh Luran" and "Eastern Susiana").

C. *The Cheshmeh Ali period* is defined by levels II–I at the top of the East Mound at Sang-i Chakhmaq (Masuda 1976:64). Buildings are generally similar in plan to those of the preceding levels (Masuda 1976:63, figs. 1–2, 6; note that the captions of figs. 5–6 are reversed), but a new element is the use of "stamp-impressed" mudbricks of the type found in Sialk II (Masuda 1976:63; see "Qazvin/Kashan"). Painted pottery included a mixture of Djeitun Painted Ware and Cheshmeh Ali Ware (see "Qazvin/Kashan"). The hard, thin Cheshmeh Ali Ware, which predominates in level I (Masuda 1976:64), links Sang-i Chakhmaq East I–II to sites in the Qazvin/Kashan area, and to the Surkh and CMT phases in Deh Luran (q.v.). A vessel from an unspecified context in the East Tepe has a design that is common on Archaic Painted Ware from the Cheshmeh Ali period at Zagheh (Masuda 1976:

fig. 7:3; see Malek Shahmirzadi 1977b:pls. VII:17, XIII:Z40503, 40246).

D. *The Hissar IA/B period* is defined by Schmidt's excavations in the Painted Pottery Flat, in the Main Mound, and in the North Flat (Schmidt 1937:21–39, fig. 21); the restudy project did not reach these phases. Hissar IA/B Painted Ware is decorated with geometric, plant, and animal motifs, primarily gazelles and birds (Schmidt 1937:40, figs. 32–36, pls. III–VI; see also Yule 1982:fig. 4). Close parallels occur in Sialk III$_{1-5}$ (McCown 1942:7, figs. 2–3), including deep, small-based bowls with a row of chevrons on a checkerboard band (Schmidt 1937:pl. IV:H2060; Ghirshman 1938:pl. LXIV:S228); pedestal-based bowls and jars (Schmidt 1937:pls. III, top, IV; Ghirshman 1938:pl. LXIII); coiled plants and arrow-headed snakes with hatched bodies (Schmidt 1937:pl. V, bottom left; Ghirshman 1938:pl. LXII:S1693); rows of dancers (Schmidt 1933:pl. LXXXVIII:Hd23; Ghirshman 1938:pl. LXXV:1, 7); ibex with a star inside curving horns (Schmidt 1937:pl. V:H2063; Ghirshman 1938:pl. LXXIX:A:13, B:7); rows or files of stacked birds (Schmidt 1937:pls. VI:DH34, 10, 31, DH44, 10, 3; Ghirshman 1938:pls. LXXX:A:7, B:5). The form and complex pattern on a round and a square seal from Hissar IB are nearly identical to seals found in Sialk III$_{4-5}$ (Schmidt 1937:pl. XV:H4708, 3829; Ghirshman 1938: pl. LXXXVI:S246, 232).

E. *The Hissar IC/IIA period* is now defined by the lowest levels reached in 1976 on the Main Mound E and F, and North Flat, corresponding to Schmidt's IC/IIA assemblages (Dyson and Howard 1989). In the 1976 stratigraphic sample, Buff Ware predominates, with lesser amounts of Red Ware. Burnished Gray Ware bowls on tall-pedestal bases, deep bowls with flaring rims, and short- and long-necked bottles are already in use as shown from closed excavation contexts. Mineralogical analyses indicate that the same local sources of clay were used for all three wares (Dyson 1983b; Dyson and Howard 1989).

A limited number of very close parallels in Painted Ware forms and design links this period to Sialk III$_{6-7}$. Examples include deep bowls on high ring bases with bands of leopards (Schmidt 1937:pl. VIII:H4479; Ghirshman 1938:pl. LXVII:S152); shallow open bowls with a zone below the rim filled with panels of vertical lines and a pedestal base decorated with annular bands (Schmidt 1937:pl. IX:H3421; Ghirshman 1938:pl. LXX:S116, 9bis); and high ring-based jars with panels of vertical wavy lines and "trees" (Schmidt 1937:pl. X:H4637; Ghirshman 1938:pl. LXVII:S69, 1810; for additional parallels see Dyson 1965:238–39).

F. *The Hissar II period* is defined by phases C–D in the 1976 sequence, which includes Buildings 1–3 on the Main Mound assigned by Schmidt to period III (1937:fig.

86) and graves assigned by Schmidt to Hissar IIB (Dyson and Howard 1989). The working of lapis, evident in small quantities at the end of the preceding period, now becomes extensive, and a massive local production of copper is attested by copper ore, slag, and furnace fragments (Pigott, Howard, and Epstein 1982).

The only closely related ceramic industries are in Gurgan. Parallels between Hissar II and Tureng Tepe IIB include a fine, thin black pottery bowl decorated with parallel incised lines from just below Building 3 at Hissar (Dyson 1983b:fig. 18a; Deshayes 1965:88, pl. XXVIII:18); pedestaled bowls (Schmidt 1937: pls. XXV:H4767, XXVI:H5153; Deshayes 1965:pl. XXVIII:20); and pattern burnishing (Dyson and Howard 1989, contra Schmidt 1937:308; Deshayes 1965:pl. XXVII:17). The surface-manipulated Gray Ware of Tureng Tepe IIB (see "Mazandaran/Gurgan") is rare at Hissar.

Ties to other sites depend on parallels in the stone and metal industries. Hissar II and Sialk IV_1 share copper pins with double spiral heads (Schmidt 1937:pl. XXIX:H4856; Ghirshman 1938:pl. XCV:S1602e) and a teardrop-shaped pendant (Schmidt 1937:pl. XXXII:H2187; Ghirshman 1938:fig. 9). Square beads pierced diagonally across two corners (Schmidt 1933:pl. CVIII:H1202) are found in Yahya IVC (Potts 1980:fig. 57a), Susa Acropole I:14B–15 (Le Brun 1971:fig. 70:2, 4), and in Mesopotamia from Jemdet Nast to Early Dynastic II times (McCown 1942:51, fig. 14). Also linking Hissar II and Proto-Elamite Susa is a copper spiral bracelet (Schmidt 1937:pl. XXVIII:H2170, 2194; Le Brun 1971:fig. 67:18). Flat trapezoidal stone beads pierced perpendicular to the parallel sides occur in Hissar II (Schmidt 1937:231, pl. LXVIII:H2107, redated by 1976 study), Shah Tepe AIII (Arne 1945:pl. XCII, fig. 611b), and the Sialk IV_2 hoard (Ghirshman 1938:pl. XXX:1; see also McCown 1942:fig. 15). A crescent-shaped lapis bead associated with the trapezoidal bead (Schmidt 1937:H2107) is paralleled in Gawra VIII (Speiser 1935:pl. LXXXIII:4) and Mundigak I (Casal 1961:fig. 138:3). Eight pillow-shaped tablet blanks excavated from Hissar II context in 1976 are comparable to those from Sialk IV_1 (see Dyson 1987).

Thus numerous artifact parallels indicate a correlation of Hissar II with Proto-Elamite sites in Iran, and with Jemdet Nasr to Early Dynastic II settlements in Mesopotamia. How long the period lasted into the third millennium remains problematic, since Schmidt's period IIIA lacks stratigraphic definition.

G. *The Hissar III (Middle Bronze Age) period* is defined by phases B–A of 1976 (Schmidt 1937:157–71, figs. 90–92; revised plan in Dyson 1977:420). Based on stratigraphy, our Hissar III can be divided into two phases. Early III consists of the Burned Building, which

is roughly equivalent in time to Schmidt's IIIB graves. Late Hissar III is documented by levels overlying the Burned Building which contain clusters of artifacts, including a large number made of alabaster. This material is augmented by graves and hoards elsewhere in the upper levels of the site assigned by Schmidt to IIIC (see Dyson and Howard). Schmidt's Hissar IIIA has no stratigraphic definition and is therefore not usable for chronology. Within the ceramic industry, the tall pedestal bowls, goblets, and chalices characteristic of Hissar II have now disappeared, leaving pear-shaped bottles and canteen jars as typical forms (Schmidt 1937:pls. XXXVII–XLIII). Spouted vessels occur in pottery, metal, and alabaster (Schmidt 1937:catalog).

Both architecture and artifacts link Hissar III to Altyn-Depe in Central Asia. Five insets into a plastered wall of the Burned Building that Schmidt interpreted as female figures (1937:fig. 93; Dyson 1977) are more likely related to the stepped niches found at Altyn-Depe and dated to the Middle Bronze Age or Namazga V period (Masson 1981a:pl. I:1). Other parallels with Namazga V settlements include compartmented bronze seals (Schmidt 1937:fig. 118:H2697, 2698; Masson and Kiiatkina 1981:fig. 2, lower left); beads in the form of a stepped square (Schmidt 1937:pl. LV:H2365, fig. 35; Masson 1981a:pl. XXII:4); and large alabaster discs with handles (Schmidt 1937:pl. LXIII:H3492, 2895; Masson 1981a:fig. 22:1). Flat oval gold beads with raised medial perforation (Schmidt 1937:fig. 138, pl. LXVI:H2360, 2361) occur in the funerary complex at Altyn-Depe (Masson and Kiiatkina 1981:fig. 11) and in Troy IIg (Blegen et al. 1950:illus. 356:17, 357, 37–712) and Mohenjo-Daro (Wheeler 1968:pl. XXVI). Alabaster minicolumns from graves stratified above the Hissar III Burned Building (Schmidt 1937:fig. 132, pl. LXI) are similar to those found in Tureng Tepe IIIC1 and other sites to the east and south, again indicating influence from Central Asia and Sistan (See "Hilmand Basin"; Masson 1981b:fig. 3). Since there is no evidence of alabaster working at Hissar, and since these items appear abruptly in the sequence, we conclude that they were imported.

There are numerous parallels between Hissar III and Shahdad (q.v.). To the west, McCown (1942:table 1) documents parallels with the Mesopotamian sequence ranging in time from Early Dynastic III to Ur III. Metal parallels with the Levant (Dyson 1965:242) suggest that Hissar III continued into the beginning of the second millennium B.C. (see also Carter 1984:139 with additional refs.).

The Mazandaran/Gurgan Sequence

This region consists of the Caspian coastal plain at the southeastern corner of that sea and the adjacent plain liest part of the Gurgan sequence is known from excavations at Belt and Hotu Caves carried out for the University Museum by Carleton S. Coon (1951, 1952, 1957; Dupree 1952). The later Neolithic to Bronze Age sequence is stratigraphically related at Yarim Tepe, known from incompletely published excavations directed by David Stronach for the British Institute of Persian Studies (Crawford 1963; Stronach 1972). More complete information on the Bronze Age comes from Tureng Tepe, a cluster of mounds initially tested by Wulsin for the University Museum (Daher 1969; Wulsin 1932) and recently subjected to intensive investigation by the French Archaeological Mission under the direction of Jean Deshayes (1963, 1965, 1966, 1968a, 1968b, 1969a, 1969b, 1970, 1972, 1973a, 1973b, 1974a, 1974b, 1976a, 1976b). Additional Bronze Age material was obtained from Shah Tepe, excavated by T. J. Arne (1945) for the Sino-Swedish Expedition.

A. *The Aceramic Neolithic period* is defined by material from Hotu Cave labeled "Sub-Neolithic" and by Belt Cave levels 10–8 (Coon 1951:30–31, 1957:149–51, 211, 215). The small sample of chipped stone from Hotu includes blades and microblade cores, but consists predominantly of flake and pebble tools (Dupree 1952:250–53, 257, figs. 9–36). Its stratigraphic position, beneath levels assigned to the Djeitun horizon, indicates that it is probably contemporary with or earlier than the Sang-i Chakhmaq Neolithic.

B. *The Software Neolithic period* is defined by upper Belt Cave, levels 7–4, and by Hotu −8 to −6.2 m, stratified below levels with painted pottery (Coon 1951:41, table 2A, 16; 1957:185, 209, 211). These deposits produced a soft, thick, chaff-tempered pottery. The surface was often burnished and in some cases had been rubbed with red ochre; a few pieces from Hotu had a rich chocolate brown slip or a fugitive red paint (Dyson notes on sherds in the University Museum Collection; see also Coon 1951:78; Matson 1951). Pottery technologically similar occurs in the Yahya VII–VI, Iblis 0–I and Shamsabad periods in the southern plateau (See "Yahya" and "Marv Dasht"). However, since deposits with Djeitun and Cheshmeh Ali Wares are stratified above those with Software at Hotu, and since the relative chronology for the west and south places Shamsabad and related assemblages later than the Cheshmeh Ali horizon, the Caspian Software Neolithic must be part of a tradition earlier than the porous chaff-tempered wares of Yahya VI, Iblis I, and Shamsabad. It may be contemporary with Yahya VII, but a comparison of the dense fabric from the latter site and the Belt/Hotu software has not yet been made.

C. *The Djeitun period* is defined by the lowest strata at Yarim Tepe, or the Yarim "Early Chalcolithic" (Crawford 1963:272–73). Sherds from this deposit in the University

Museum collections include chaff-tempered pottery with geometric designs comparable to that at Djeitun in Turkmenistan, and at Sang-i Chakhmaq East (see "Damghan/ Khorasan"). Within Gurgan, Djeitun sherds also occur at Tureng Tepe, incorporated in bricks made in later periods; they are assigned to Tureng "Period IA" which is assumed to lie below the water table (Deshayes 1967:123–25, pl. Ia, d, fig. 1a–c; 1969a:12).

D. *The Cheshmeh Ali period* is defined by Hotu Cave Trench B, the 560 and 580 cm strata (Coon 1952:243; Dyson notes based on a study of the University Museum collection and archives). Sherds of classic Cheshmeh Ali Painted Fine Ware place this occupation within a widespread horizon on the plateau (see "Qazvin/Kashan"). At Tureng Tepe, Cheshmeh Ali Painted Ware is assigned to Period IB, again presumably below the water table ("Ismailabad" Ware, Deshayes 1967:fig. 2d–e, 1970:207, 1973b:fig. 8).

E. *The Tureng IIA period* is defined by Tureng Tepe Sondage A:levels 26–20 (Deshayes 1966, 1967:125). The same assemblage is found at Yarim Tepe in period II, where it was originally designated as the "Late Chalcolithic" (Crawford 1963:272–73; Stronach 1972:22), and in Shah Tepe III (Arne 1945). The ceramic industry includes Black-Painted Red-Slipped Ware (Arne 1945:164–67,figs. 276, 278, 281–98, pls. XLI, XC–XCI; Deshayes 1967:pls. Ib–c, II–III, fig. 1d–j) and Burnished Gray Ware (Arne 1945:171–80, 236, figs. 301a–12, pls. XXI:fig. 167–68, XXII:170a–73, XLIII–XLVIII; Daher 1969:68–69, fig. 1; Deshayes 1966:pl. I:3, 1969a:12, top, 13).

Based on the presence of both painted and gray wares, the Gurgan Late Chalcolithic has been placed contemporary with Hissar IC/IIA (Arne 1945:307; Deshayes 1966:3, 1970:208). There are, however, major differences in the ceramic traditions of the two regions. The Gurgan Painted Red Ware differs from that of Hissar IC/ IIA in technology (Boucher et al. 1976), form, and decoration (e.g., Arne 1945:pl. XC, fig. 664; Schmidt 1937:pls. VII–XIII, XX–XXII; see also Yule 1982:fig. 5). Moreover, the basic Gray Ware of the two regions differs in surface treatment: incised and appliquéd decoration on Gray Ware is common in Tureng IIA and Shah III, but virtually absent from The Gray Ware of Hissar IC/IIA. The range of vessel forms also differs (Arne 1945:fig. 664; Yule 1982:fig. 6B). Pedestaled bowls occur in Tureng IIA and Hissar IIA, but also in Hissar IIB (Deshayes 1966:pl. I:3; Schmidt 1937:pls. XXIII: H. 2998, XXVI:H.5119). A trapezoidal lapis bead from Shah III is paralleled in Hissar II or later (see "Damghan/ Khorasan"). The best evidence for contemporaneity comes from the appearance of small items of jewelry, such as double spiral wire pendants (Deshayes 1966; Schmidt 1937:pl. XXX:A, H2982), which occur at both sites. There is also a single brown-on-buff sherd with a sloppily painted ibex and star motif found in Shah III which appears to be a Hissar IC import (Arne 1945:fig. 299a; Schmidt 1937:pl. X:H802). We conclude that the exact correlation of this period relative to Hissar should be left open, pending the complete publication of Tureng IIA and Yarim II.

F. *The Tureng IIB period* is defined by Tureng Tepe Sondage A:levels 18–12 (Deshayes 1965:86–89). During this period, only Burnished Gray Ware is in use. Incised and grooved decoration continues, and pattern burnishing makes its initial appearance (Arne 1945:178–80; Deshayes 1965:pls. XXVII:17, XXVIII:18–19; 1969a: 12–13). A "goblet" from Tureng IIB (Deshayes 1965:pl. XXVIII:20) is not the bowl-on-pedestal of Hissar I, but is of the type found in Hissar II (Deshayes 1965:pl. XXVIII:20; Schmidt 1937:pls. XXV:H4767, XXVI:H5153). Although Schmidt (1937:308) states that at Hissar "definite burnished designs were not found prior to Hissar IIIB," the 1976 restudy found such sherds in a closed context firmly dated to Hissar II (Dyson 1983b).

G. *The Tureng Tepe III period* is defined by Tureng Sondage A:levels 11–2, Sondage C:3–1, Sondage D:9–2, Sondage E:5, and the High Terrace excavations (Deshayes 1965:84, 1969b:140, fig. 1, 1976a). Other occupations in this period are Yarim Tepe III (Crawford 1963:273) and Shah Tepe IIB–A (Arne 1945). Deshayes has delineated four phases for Tureng III: IIIA, IIIB, and IIIB–IIIC1 transition, and IIIC1 (Deshayes 1970, pers. comm. 1976). While these phases are significant in the history of the site and region, the brief preliminary reports available at present indicate that there is a great deal of continuity between them, and it is sometimes necessary to discuss the period as a whole for comparative purposes.

A series of ceramic parallels links Tureng IIIA with Hissar II. Deep bowls with slightly flaring rims (Deshayes 1965:pl. XXV:8) are characteristic of Hissar graves assigned by Schmidt to IIB (Schmidt 1937:pl. XXV:H4838), and tall pedestals with a conical base (Deshayes 1965:pl. XXIV:7) were found in a sealed Hissar II occupation level (Dyson 1983b). A long-necked, pattern-burnished bottle from Tureng IIIA is duplicated in graves assigned by Schmidt to Hissar IIIB (Deshayes 1965:pl. XXIII:3; Schmidt 1937:307, fig. 105, pl. XXXVII:H2227). It is also found in habitation debris excavated in 1976b and dated to Hissar II (Dyson and Howard, 1989).

Other peculiar ceramic forms link Tureng III with Hissar III. Dippers or cylindrical vessels with a loop handle extending vertically from the rim were found in Tureng IIIC1–2 (Deshayes 1969b:147–49, fig. 69; 1973b:fig. 7), Shah II (Arne 1945:209, fig. 420a, pl. LIII), and Hissar IIIB (Schmidt 1937:pl. XXXIX:H1734) as well as Troy IId and IIg (Blegen et al. 1950:289, fig. 406). Jars in the form of a female torso are found in Shah IIa (Arne 1945:fig. 412) and Hissar IIIC (Schmidt 1937:fig. 115, pl. XLVI:H2790). Canteens with pattern-burnished ovoid bodies, tall necks and tiny loop handles at the base of the neck are found in Shah IIa (Arne 1945:fig. 408), Tureng III (Deshayes 1968b:pl. 48), and Hissar IIIC (Schmidt 1937:pl. XL:H4219). Squat concave-sided vessels with flat bases and pattern-burnished bands on the side are found in Tureng IIIB–IIIC2 (Deshayes 1969b:144, fig. 12), Shah II (Arne 1945:figs. 367, 368), and Hissar IIIC (Schmidt 1937:pl. XLII:H3483 from the "Hoard" on Treasure Hill).

Miniature "columns" of limestone from the massive brick Terrace building of Tureng Tepe IIIC1 (Deshayes 1976a:fig. 1, 1976b:pl.II:f) are duplicated in Hissar IIIC (Schmidt 1937:pl. LXI, fig. 132), the Cult Building at Altyn-Depe (Masson 1968:191, pl. XXV), and at other sites in Bactria (Amiet 1977:fig. 10) and Sistan (Dales 1977). Bands of crosshatched pattern burnishing of Tureng III type (Deshayes 1969a:14, 15 top; Crawford 1963:fig. 14) also occur at Dashly 3 in Bactria, which is contemporary with Namazga V in Turkmenistan (See Kohl 1984:166–69); note that Namazga V is independently linked to Hissar III (see "Damghan/Khorasan"). Lapis rhomboidal beads from Tureng IIIA are found in Namazga V at Altyn-Depe and also provide a direct tie between Tureng III and Mesopotamia since they occur in the Royal Cemetery at Ur (Deshayes 1969a:14; Woolley 1934:pl. 143c–d; see also Dyson 1965:240–41). Finally, Deshayes (1977:100–101) notes the presence of high-terraced structures similar to that of Tureng IIIC1 in Altyn-Depe 7 or the Namazga V period, and in Mundigak IV ("Monument Massif"; Casal 1961).

Thus artifact parallels indicate a relatively long span of time for Tureng III, parallel to both Hissar II and III. The links to Hissar III and sites in Turkmenistan are striking. Those to Hissar II are difficult to interpret given the problems with Schmidt's sequence and a lack of information on the span of time represented by ceramic forms at both Tureng and Hissar. We therefore place Tureng IIIC contemporary with Hissar III and leave open the question of the relationship of Tureng IIIA–B and Hissar II/III.

Radiocarbon Evidence for Northeastern Iran

The earliest well-dated chronological unit in the northeast is Hissar IC/IIA, with a cluster of six radiocarbon determinations yielding an average corrected range of 3980–3865 B.C. Relative dates indicate that Hissar IC/IIA and the closely related ceramic assemblage of Sialk III_{6-7} are somewhat later than Susa A, which has a corrected average range of 4115–3880 B.C. A cluster of twenty determinates places the 1976 sample from Hissar

II within the range from 3365–3030 B.C. (tables 1–2). This is fully compatible with the relative chronological evidence that places Hissar II contemporary with the Proto-Elamite horizon, dated at Malyan to the late fourth millennium (see "Marv Dasht"). Clusters from Hissar III and Tureng Tepe IIIC place these related assemblages from 2400–2170 and 2170–1900 B.C. respectively. This conforms with historical dates from Mesopotamia: based on artifact parallels, Hissar III is correlated with the time spanned by Early Dynastic III to Ur III, ca. 2600–2000 B.C. (Porada et al., this vol., chap. 5).

Northwestern Iran (Azerbaijan)

Southern Urmia Basin: The Hasanlu Sequence

South of Lake Urmia lies the Ushnu-Solduz Valley. This rich, well-watered plain forms a crossroad, with routes leading west through the Keleshin Pass into northern Mesopotamia, east onto the plateau, and north into the Caucasus. Research in this area has been carried out from 1956 to 1977 by the University Museum of the University of Pennsylvania, under the general direction of R. H. Dyson, Jr. (Dyson 1969, 1972, 1983a with refs; see also Levine and Young 1977:399–405). Information on the early part of the regional sequence, Hasanlu periods X–VII, comes primarily from excavations at Hajji Firuz, Dalma, and Pisdeli Tepes, and from a well dug through the citadel mound at Hasanlu (Dyson 1967b, 1969, 1983a; Dyson and Young 1960; Hamlin 1975; Voigt 1983; Young 1962).

A. *The Hasanlu X (Hajji Firuz) period* is defined by excavations at Hajji Firuz Tepe. Thirteen phases of the occupation labeled L through A were distinguished, with most of the excavated material coming from the latter part of the occupation, phases D–A (Voigt 1983:18–30). In addition, a few Hajji Firuz sherds were also found in a mixed wash layer at the base of Dalma Tepe (Hamlin 1975: 113). To the east of Lake Urmia, the Neolithic assemblage from Yanik Tepe is sufficiently similar to be considered part of the same tradition (Burney 1964; Voigt 1983:95).

Hajji Firuz Ware is chaff-tempered and poorly fired; decorative techniques include the use of a red or brown slip, painted designs, and (rarely) incision (Voigt 1983:figs. 92–98). These characteristics, plus vessel forms such as husking trays, carinated bowls, and collared jars with ovoid or carinated bodies, link the Hajji Firuz ceramics to early Hassuna sites such as Umm Dabaghiyah, Telul eth-Thalathat XVI–XV, and to a lesser extent Hassuna levels I–II. However, the presence of imported sherds as well as columnar or skirted figurines with high-domed heads indicates that Hajji Firuz phases D–A are contemporary with the later part of the Hassuna period and with "classic" Samarra (Voigt 1983:101–2,

163–67, 178–81, with refs.). The pattern of Hassuna/Samarra parallels has led Voigt to speculate that the Hajji Firuz farmers migrated into Solduz from northern Mesopotamia in the latter part of the seventh millennium.

Although Young (1962) originally saw a close relationship between Hajji Firuz and sites within the Zagros Group, there are only general technological and stylistic similarities between Hajji Firuz and late Zagros Group ceramics, specifically Sarab Linear Ware. On the other hand, there are good parallels in ceramic form and decoration between Hajji Firuz and Jarmo Operation II:4–1 (Adams 1983:figs. 105:1–4, 107:1, 3–4, 108:1–5, 109:1–8; Voigt 1983:figs. 82, 84:i, 92–93). A few sherds with linear painting from the upper levels at Jarmo are indistinguishable from Hajji Firuz D–A pottery (Voigt 1983:160–63).

Several of the chipped stone types are very distinctive and have limited occurrence in adjacent regions. Thin sections or "side-blow blade-flakes" (Voigt 1983:231–35, pl. 32c, g, i, fig. 111c–d) have been found in the upper levels at Jarmo (Hole 1983a: 247–48, table 10, fig. 122:1–10); the early Hassuna sites of Ali Agha (Braidwood et al. 1983:669); Telul-eth Thalathat (Fukai and Matsutani 1977:54, fig. 3:1–3); Umm Dabaghiyah (Kirkbride 1972:11, pl. XVII:3–5); and a series of sites lying just south of the Taurus, stretching from the Mosul area to Gritille on the Euphrates (Kirkbride 1972:11; Oates 1969:132, n. 33; Copeland 1979:254, 267–68, fig. 2:14, 16; Voigt, unpublished). Obsidian blades with steep lammelar flaking (Voigt 1983:236–37, pl. 33, fig. 111n–o) also occur at sites in the Zagros including both Aceramic and Samarran levels at Shimshara (Mortensen 1970:43, figs. 24d, 25f–h, 29a, e–f, 30–31, 36–37), the lower levels at Jarmo (Hole 1983a:241, n. 5, fig. 122:11, 13–21), and a large number of Aceramic Neolithic sites stretching across Anatolia from Çayönü ("backed blades," Redman 1982:42–44, fig. 2.14:1–2, 2.15:1–3, pl. 2.II:15–18) to Gritille (Voigt 1985:fig. 17s).

B. *The Hasanlu IX (Dalma) period* is known primarily from excavations at Dalma Tepe (Hamlin 1975), but also from Hajji Firuz and Pisdeli Tepes in Solduz (Voigt, in prep.; 1983:7–8, 17–18, figs. 4, 8) and from Tepe Seavan in the Mergavar Valley to the north of Ushnu (Solecki and Solecki 1973). At Pisdeli Tepe, several strata assigned to the Dalma period contain pottery that is transitional between typical Dalma wares and the succeeding Pisdeli ceramic industry (Voigt, in prep.).

Dalma material has been found all along the western side of the Urmia basin (see "Salmas" and "Urmia Plain"; Solecki and Solecki 1973; Kearton 1970). To the south, painted and impressed pottery very similar to that from Dalma Tepe has been recovered in the Kangavar Valley and designated as Godin X (see "Godin"; E. Henrickson 1985b), and survey data document the presence of the

Dalma assemblage at sites in the area between Solduz and Kangavar (Dyson 1967b:2955; Stein 1940, collections of the British Museum; Swiny 1975:79–81, fig. 1:4–8; Young 1966). Dalma Impressed Ware provides a chronological link to the Early Siahbid phase in the Kermanshah region, and perhaps to the Bayat phase in Deh Luran (q.v.; Wright 1981:fig. 10e).

Imports found at Dalma Tepe establish the chronological relationship between Hasanlu IX and sites to the west. Several sherds and one complete vessel are closely paralleled to Tepe Gawra XVI, or the Ubaid 3 period (Hamlin 1975:fig. 10:I; Tobler 1950:pl. LXXVII:b:13, 15). Independent parallels for the Dalma period in Kangavar also indicate an Ubaid 3 date (see "Godin").

C. *The Hasanlu VIII (Pisdeli) period* is defined by soundings at Pisdeli Tepe (Dyson and Young 1960; Young 1962), and is also known from Hajji Firuz and Hasanlu Tepes (Voigt 1983:8, 16–17, figs. 4, 8). An 8-m thick deposit at Pisdeli Tepe, and 6.5 m in the Hasanlu Well Sounding, suggests a long duration for this period. There are many parallels between the chaff-tempered Pisdeli Painted vessels and sherds from Gawra XIII–XII (Voigt, in prep.; e.g., Tobler 1950:pls. CXXVII:167–73, CXXXI:224, CXXXV:262–64, CXL:320), and a sealing showing a man with a shield(?) found eroded out of Hasanlu VIII deposits at Hajji Firuz Tepe is nearly identical to a stamp seal from Gawra XIA (Tobler 1950:pls. LXXXVIIIa:10, CLXII:77). Thus Pisdeli is equivalent to both Ubaid 4 and the Gawra or Early Uruk period in Mesopotamia. To the south, red-slipped fingertip-impressed sherds from Pisdeli contexts are paralleled in the Godin IX/Seh Gabi period in Kangavar (E. Henrickson 1983:196–98, figs. 52–54), and some Pisdeli Painted pottery is apparently related to the "Red, White, and Black Ware" characteristic of the Maran period in the Kermanshah region and Luristan (see "Mahidasht" and "Godin").

D. *The Hasanlu VII (Painted Orange Ware) period* is defined by excavations on the Citadel and in the Lower Town at Hasanlu Tepe (Dyson 1967b, 1969) and is also known from a tomb at Hajji Firuz Tepe (Voigt 1976:805–10, fig. 115). The period has been divided into phases VIIA–C based on changes in the ceramics found in the U22 sounding on the citadel (Dyson 1973b; Dyson and Pigott 1975:182). The ceramic industry includes Painted Orange Ware, a thin, grit-tempered ware that is sometimes decorated with black-painted geometric motifs or birds, and rare Burnished Gray Ware vessels.

Sherds of Painted Orange Ware have been found on the surface of sites in eastern Azerbaijan; one of these, Gol Tepe, has an area of ca. 12 ha (Tala'i 1984:figs. 1–2). A boundary between the northern and southern portions of the Urmia basin developed after the Pisdeli period, which dates no later than Gawra XI. In the Urmia Plain this division is represented first by Geoy M, a late Chalcolithic assemblege that can be correlated with Gawra XI–IX, and then by Geoy K, and Early Trans-Caucasian I and II occupation (see "Urmia Plain"). A small number of sherds testify to contacts between Hasanlu VII and Early Trans-Caucasian groups to the north: (1) At Hasanlu Tepe, a single sherd of Graphite-Burnished Black Ware with a "dimple" of Early Trans-Caucasian II–III type was found in a level assigned to Hasanlu VIIA–B; the sherd was eroded and could have been derived from an earlier context. (2) At Geoy Tepe, Hasanlu VII–like painted sherds occur in level K3, or Early Trans-Caucasian III context (Burton Brown 1951:fig. 12:1249). Although this scanty evidence cannot be used to determine the precise relationship between the Hasanlu and Early Trans-Caucasian sequence, it strongly suggests that Hasanlu VII is contemporary with the latter part of Geoy K or Early Trans-Caucasian (II)–III. The radiocarbon evidence supports this conclusion (see below). The recovery at Gol Tepe of a small number of burnished black sherds, some of which are incised, indicates an occupation dated to Yanik Early Bronze I or Early Trans-Caucasian II (Tala'i 1984:151, fig. 3: a–i). Given the evidence for the precedence of Yanik Early Bronze I over Hasanlu VII, it is possible that these incised Early Trans-Caucasian sherds represent an occupation at Gol Tepe predating the Hasanlu VII settlements in Solduz.

A date in the second half of the third millennium for Hasanlu VII is also indicated by parallels outside the region. Hasanlu VII shares some distinctive vessel forms with Early Dynastic III and Akkadian pottery in Mesopotamia. For example, jars with ovoid or "bag-shaped" bodies, straight necks, and everted beveled rims are found both at Hasanlu and in the Diyala (Dyson 1967b:fig. 1027, lower left; Delougaz 1952:pls. 185:C.556.540, 188:C.6566.540). The most common form of Hasanlu VII jar, with a globular body, strongly angled shoulder, and everted beveled rim, occurs in Akkadian levels at Nippur (M. Gibson, pers. comm. 1984) as well as at Godin in period III:5 (see "Godin"). Although the Godin III:5 painted designs are more diverse and intricate than those of Hasanlu VII, the motifs employed are similar; more important, the way in which designs are placed on jars is very close (Dyson 1967b:pl. 1483a; R. Henrickson 1984a:fig. 93:2, 5; Dyson 1967b:fig. 1027; R. Henrickson 1984a:fig. 92).

Northeastern Urmia Basin: The Yanik Sequence

Most of the archaeological information for this area comes from excavations at Yanik Tepe under the direction of Charles Burney (1962, 1964; Burney and Lang 1972), supplemented by surface surveys carried out by Stuart

Swiny (1975) and Hasan Tala'i (1984). Although the mountainous area around Ardebil has been surveyed, few sites predating the Iron Age were recorded (Burney 1979b; Ingraham and Summers 1979).

A. *The Yanik Late Neolithic period,* defined in Trench P on the small mound at Yanik Tepe (Burney 1964), is closely related to Hasanlu X or the Hajji Firuz period (Voigt 1983:95, 167–68, 204–5). Ceramic parallels link the Yanik Neolithic pottery with Hassuna/Samarra sites to the west and Sialk I₃ to the east (Burney 1964:56–57, pl. 15:3–4; Voigt 1983:167–68). Alabaster artifacts, including bangle fragments and a bowl, suggest a relationship with Zagros sites such as Jarmo, Sarab, and Shimshara. An alabaster head, probably from a figure modeled of clay or an organic material, is very similar to that of a seated male from Tell es-Sawwan level I (Burney 1964:57, pl. 15:11; Oates 1966:pl. 38; Voigt 1983:178). In general, the occupation at Yanik seems to be contemporary with that at Hajji Firuz; however, much of the excavated Yanik Neolithic sample may be earlier than the best-known Hajji Firuz phases (D–A). This tentative conclusion is based on the scarcity of painted pottery at Yanik and on the presence of simple intramural pit graves which at Hajji Firuz fall in the early part of the sequence (Burney 1964:56; Voigt 1983:70–71). The radiocarbon dates from Yanik and Hajji Firuz support this interpretation (see below).

B. *The Yanik Chalcolithic period* is defined by 9 m of deposit in Trench M, a deep sounding in the Main Mound at Yanik Tepe (Burney 1962, 1964). Burney stresses continuity within what must be a long time span, but also indicates that there are significant differences within the ceramic industry, with implications for chronology. A few sherds from the early levels identified as Dalma Painted and Dalma Impressed Ware place the beginning of this period contemporary with Hasanlu IX (Burney 1964:58; Burney and Lang 1972:37). The burnished Red-Slipped Ware that predominates in the Yanik Chalcolithic is paralleled in technology and vessel form by Pisdeli Red Ware. Also found in the latest Yanik levels were "finely burnished relatively thin wares" and painted pottery which Burney compares to that of the Pisdeli period, and one sherd is identified as a Pisdeli import (Burney 1962:137, pl. 43; 1964:58). Based on the published material, however, closer parallels for the Yanik Painted pottery are found at sites such as Geoy M (Burney 1962:pl. XLIII:10; Burton Brown 1951:fig. 7:1), Gawra XII (Tobler 1950:pl. CXXXIX:307), and Norşuntepe (Hauptmann 1976:fig. 50:8, 1979:fig. 30:10; see also "Urmia Plain"). A painted human figure with upraised arm and open hand from Yanik (Burney 1962:pl. XLIII:9) is similar to one from Gawra level X (Tobler 1950:pl. CXLV:398). Finally, Red-Slipped Ware "fruitstands" (Burney 1962:pl. XLIII:5) have analogues in

Gawra XI–IX (Tobler 1950:pl. CXLVI:400–401). All of this evidence indicates that the later part of the Yanik Chalcolithic deposit postdates the Pisdeli period in Ushnu and Solduz, and is instead contemporary with Middle to Late Gawra material in northern Mesopotamia and Late Chalcolithic deposits in the Keban.

C. *The Yanik Early Bronze I period* is defined by nine major building levels containing round mud-brick buildings (Burney 1961:141–47, 1962:139–41, 1964:59). The assemblage is that of the Early Trans-Caucasian culture, found at sites throughout the Caucasus, eastern Anatolia, the Levant, and portions of western Iran (Burney and Lang 1972:43–85). Yanik Early Bronze I has been assigned to the Early Trans-Caucasian II period, contemporary with settlements such as Shengavit III in the Caucasus, Geoy K2 in the western Urmia Basin, and numerous sites in eastern Anatolia (Mellink, this vol., chap. 9). Early Trans-Caucasian I pottery is well burnished, and fired from red to black. The use of incised and white-filled geometric elements arranged in bands or long rectangular panels seems to be a local development in Iran, found not only in Yanik Early Bronze I, but also at settlements located along the eastern side of the Alvand alignment within the Zagros, the best known of which is Godin IV (Burney and Lang 1972:61–62; Young 1969:10, figs. 11–12; see "Godin").

D. *The Yanik Early Bronze II period* is defined by rectangular houses in Area J/K/L on the Main Mound at Yanik Tepe (Burney 1962:142–45, pls. XL, XLI:b–c, XLII: a–b, fig. 2). Within the ceramic industry, the plain burnished wares found in the latest levels with round houses continue into those with rectangular houses, indicating a gradual transition between the two periods (Burney 1962:142). Jar and bowl forms are similar to those in Early Bronze I, but a new element is the presence of pointed bases (Burney 1962:pl. XLIV:17–19).

The Yanik Early Bronze II pottery, which includes sherds with a metallic sheen produced through the application of graphite, is assigned to the Early Trans-Caucasian III period (Burney and Lang 1972:65–66). It is contemporary with the related sites of Geoy K.3 and Haftavan VII in the Urmia basin (Burney and Lang 1972:65–66), and thus by extension with Hasanlu VII and other "Painted Orange Ware" sites (see "Hasanlu"). Outside of Iran, Early Transcaucasian III sites include Kavatskhelebi B and Shengavit IV in the Soviet Union (Burney and Lang 1972:64–73), and "Early Bronze III" levels at sites in the Keban area of eastern Turkey (Mellink, this vol., chap. 9; Sagona 1984).

Northwest Urmia Basin: The Salmas Sequence

For the prehistoric period, the best-known area to the north of the lake is the Salmas Plain, surrounding the towns of Shahpur and Khoy. A major program of excavation was carried out at Haftavan Tepe under the direction of Charles Burney (1970a, 1970b, 1972, 1973, 1974, 1975, 1976a, 1976b, 1979a; Edwards 1983). As part of this research Regnar Kearton (1969, 1970) conducted a surface survey of the Salmas Valley. Surface surveys of the extreme northwestern part of the region by the German Archaeological Institute in Iran have provided additional information on the Early Bronze Age (Kleiss and Kroll 1975, 1979).

A. *The Neolithic period* is documented by the presence of thick-walled, poorly fired, chaff-tempered pottery on the surface of four sites (Kearton 1970:267, figs. 27–28). The technology employed, as well as painted motifs such as nested chevrons and diagonal lines below an annular band, links this industry to the Hajji Firuz period (Hasanlu X) in Ushnu and Solduz.

B. *The Early Chalcolithic period* is defined by surface material, painted pottery very similar to that of the Dalma period in Solduz (Kearton 1970:116, fig. 26:2, 5). Although only two impressed sherds are illustrated (Kearton 1970:fig. 26:1, 4), one is typical of the Dalma assemblage both in Solduz (Hamlin 1975:pl. IIa) and Kangavar (E. Henrickson 1983:fig. 50:3, 9; Young and Levine 1974:fig. 10:8).

C. *The Late Chalcolithic period* is again defined by surface material very similar to that of Hasanlu VIII in Solduz (Kearton 1970:112–13, figs. 23–24). Most of the painted ware illustrated by Kearton seems to date to the middle and later part of the Pisdeli sequence in Solduz; however, bowls decorated with scallops below the rim on the vessel interior are best paralleled in Geoy M (see "Urmia Plain"). The red-slipped and the burnished wares so typical of this period at sites to the south have not been reported in Salmas (Kearton 1970:112).

D. *The Haftavan VIII (Early Transcaucasian II) period* is defined by deposits in trench TT9 on the citadel mound at Haftavan Tepe (Burney 1974:102, 1976a:258–59). The settlement was made up of round structures similar to those of Yanik Tepe Early Bronze I (Burney 1975:150, fig. 1; 1976a:fig. 1; 1976b:157). This link is confirmed by the Haftavan VIII ceramics, which include a plain Burnished Gray Ware and some Graphite-Burnished Ware, decorated with "dimples" and Nakhichevan lugs. Burney, who excavated both sites, considers Haftavan VIII to be contemporary with the latest of the twelve levels assigned to Early Bronze I at Yanik Tepe (1975:150, 1976b:157).

E. *The Haftavan VII (Early Transcaucasian III) period* is defined by material from trenches on the citadel mound (Burney 1970a:164, 1970b:182, 1973, 1974). The ceramic industry is characterized by Graphite-Burnished Ware of the type found in Yanik Early Bronze II and at Early Trans-Caucasian sites in the Caucasus

(Burney 1973:159; Burney and Lang 1972:66–67).

F. *Haftavan period VIC,* defined by a robbed-out building and pits in trench C2 at Haftavan Tepe (Burney 1976b:157; Edwards 1981:102), represents a stratigraphic and cultural break from Haftavan Period VII. It is characterized by rare sherds of incised ware, Brown-on-Buff Painted Ware and Black-on-Red Ware (Burney 1983:ix; Edwards 1983:12–13, figs. 10–15). Burney (1976b:157) has suggested a possible relationship between the Haftavan VIC Black-on-Red Ware and Hasanlu VII Painted Orange Ware (1973:159, 1976b:157) as well as a tie between Haftavan VIC and Godin III. However, vessel forms are different, and the painted designs of both Red-on-Black Ware and Brown-on-Buff Ware seem more closely related to the succeeding Haftavan VIB period than to sites in the south. Continuing relationships between Haftavan and areas to the north are indicated by the presence of sherds from a burnished black vessel with fine herringbone incision that is "typical of the Early Trans-Caucasian III period" (Edwards 1983:13, fig. 15:13) with parallels at Trialeti (Burney 1973:159).

The Urmia Plain Sequence

Along the western side of Lake Urmia lies a large flat plain, surrounding the town of Urmia. Two major mounds have been investigated: Geoy Tepe, by T. Burton Brown (1951); and Kordlar Tepe, by a team from the University of Innsbruck under the direction of Andreas Lippert (Kromer and Lippert 1976; Lippert 1976). At both sites the bulk of the excavated material dates to the Iron Age, and earlier periods are known only from limited exposures in deep soundings that did not reach virgin soil.

A. *The Chalcolithic period* is defined by level 1 of the Profile Cut at Kordlar Tepe, and by Geoy periods N and M. The published material from Kordlar (Kromer and Lippert 1976:80–81, pl. VI), as well as sherds collected from Kush Ali Tepe near Geoy, dates to the middle and late portion of the Pisdeli sequence in Ushnu-Solduz. Although little is known about Geoy N, sherds of a "well-polished red ware" may be related to Pisdeli Red Ware and/or the Yanik Chalcolithic Red Ware (Burton Brown 1951:16, fig. 5:674).

On typological grounds, Geoy M (Burton Brown 1951:17–33) is later than any of the Pisdeli material recovered from Ushnu-Solduz; moreover, although it may be derived from the Pisdeli tradition, the painted pottery from Geoy M seems to be part of a new ceramic assemblage that is found in "Late Chalcolithic" levels at sites in the Keban region of eastern Turkey, including Norşuntepe and Tepecik, as well as in the Gawra period in Mesopotamia. Shared items include open bowls with pinched rims, low ring bases, and painted scallops at the rim (Burton Brown 1951: fig. 4:43, 351, fig. 5:632, pls.

I:12, II:635, 623, 632, III:43; Tobler 1950:pls. CXXXIV:248–49); open bowls with incurved rims beveled to the inside, sometimes decorated with thick drips of paint descending from the rim (Burton Brown 1951:figs. 4:355, 5:634, 46, 1127, pl. II:634; Tobler 1950:pl. CXLIV:375, 383, from level X-A; Hauptmann 1972:pl. 71:5–6; Esin 1972:pl. 112:2); large jars or "pithoi" with short strongly everted necks and globular bodies, decorated with bands of crosshatched triangles on the shoulder and short vertical lines on the interior of the rim (Burton Brown 1951:fig. 7:1, 97, pls. I:11, III:97; Tobler 1950:pls. CXXXIX:307, CLII:525; Hauptmann 1976:pl. 50:8, 1979:pl. 30:10). A distinctive design element shared by Geoy M and Gawra XI-A is the use of rows or bands of squiggles as a painted motif (Burton Brown 1951:pl. I, fig. 4; Tobler 1950:pl. CXLI:339). Finally, a clay stamp seal impression from the top of Geoy M that portrays a stag with comblike horns above a caprine(?) has its closest parallels in Gawra XII and XI-A (Burton Brown 1951:pl. VIII:1646; Tobler 1950:pl. CLXVI:126–27).

B. *The Geoy K (Early Trans-Caucasian I–III) period* is defined by deposits at Geoy Tepe that have been divided into three phases based on absolute depth. The pottery is the best-published example of the Early Trans-Caucasian ceramic industry within Azerbaijan (Burton Brown 1951:34–62, figs. 7–12, pls. III–VII).

The earliest levels, Geoy K.1, apparently represent the initial occupation of the Urmia Basin by Early Trans-Caucasian I groups (Burney and Lang 1972:59; Sagona 1984:60–61). A small number of decorative techniques link this assemblage to sites in eastern Turkey. A checkerboard design incised on a potlid (Burton Brown 1951:pl. IV:35) is paralleled on bowls from Late Chalcolithic/Early Bronze I Tepecik (Esin 1970:168, pl. 15:1–2; 1976:115, pl. 72:2). A second lid from Geoy was decorated with a cylinder seal impression with hatched lozenges (Burton Brown 1951:pl. V:34); this is very similar to an impression on a jar found in an Early Bronze I context at Han Ibrahim Şah (Ertem 1974:pl. 61:5).

The pottery of Geoy K.2 and K.3, decorated only with round or lenticular "dimples" and in Geoy K.3 round or oval knobs on vessel bodies (Burton Brown 1951: pls. III:958, 39, 3, V:586, 342, VI:449, 385, VII), is dated to Early Trans-Caucasian II and III, contemporary with such closely related sites as Yanik Tepe Early Bronze Age I–II and Ḥaftavan periods VIII–VII (Burney 1975:

150; Burney and Lang 1972:59; Sagona 1984:50–65).

Isolated sherds provide some evidence of contact between Geoy K and groups occupying the southern half of the Urmia Basin. Two that can be identified as Hasanlu VII painted ware were recovered from near the top of K.2 and from K.3 (Burton Brown 1951:fig. 12:1249/50; inventory no. 1251), and a rolled sherd of Graphite-Burnished Ware was found in a period VII deposit at Hasanlu.

Radiocarbon Evidence for Northwestern Iran

Calibrated radiocarbon determinations from the upper part of the Neolithic deposit at Hajji Firuz, and from comparable Late Neolithic levels at Yanik Tepe, all fall within the first half of the sixth millennium (table 2). Dates from earlier levels at Hajji Firuz and Baranu, which are beyond the range of the CRD tables, suggest that the initial colonization of the Urmia Basin took place approximately five hundred years earlier, or in the middle of the seventh millennium.

The next time range for which a cluster of absolute dates is available can be broadly termed the Middle and Late Chalcolithic. A consistent series of radiocarbon determinations which produced an average range of 4540–4405 B.C. (table 1) has been obtained from the Hasanlu VIII levels at Pisdeli, Hajji Firuz, and Kush Ali Tepes. Analysis of the individual dates suggests that the transition from Hasanlu IX to VIII took place in the first half of the fifth millennium, and that Hasanlu VIII/Pisdeli sites in Solduz may have been abandoned before 4000 B.C. Two dates for the Yanik Chalcolithic period suggest late fifth to early fourth millennium occupation (table 2).

Five dates for Yanik Early Bronze I firmly place this material within the latter part of the fourth millennium/ first half of the third millennium. A single carbon sample for Geoy Tepe taken from the exposed side of Pit I within K.1 dates between 3365 to 2890 B.C. Given the range for Yanik Early Bronze I, the earlier part of the range seems more likely. A series of six dates from Hasanlu VII produced an average date of 2650–2415 B.C. (table 1); two dates for Yanik Early Bronze II which equates with Early Trans-Caucasian III also fall within the second half of the third millennium. A *terminus ante quem* of ca. 2000 B.C. for the Early Trans-Caucasian III/Hasanlu VII horizon is provided by dates for early Hasanlu VI deposits excavated at Dinkha Tepe (Hamlin 1974a:table I).

Seven

Central Asia (Western Turkestan):
Neolithic to the Early Iron Age

Philip L. Kohl, Wellesley College

Outline

The area covered in this chapter stretches from the Caspian Sea in the west to the Fergana Valley in the east and from the Aral Sea in the north to the Hindu Kush and Atrek Valley of northeastern Iran in the south. It is simply the vast area of interior drainage formed by the streams draining the Kopet Dagh and northern Hindu Kush mountains and by the Atrek, Tedjen, Murghab, Amu Darya, Zeravshan, and Syr Darya rivers and their tributaries (fig. 1). Today, western Turkestan is divided among three nation-states: Iran; Afghanistan; and the republics of Turkmenistan, Uzbekistan, Tadjikistan, and part of Kirghizia in the Soviet Union. The boundaries of prehistoric culture areas and modern political borders rarely coincide, but the existence of the latter usually implies a different history of archaeological investigations and research for regions separated by the borders, and this fact affects the interpretation of the archaeological evidence or, in this case, the attempt to make a chronological reconstruction. Specifically, little prehistoric work has been undertaken in Iranian Khorassan; while northern Afghanistan is known through the efforts of American and, particularly, French and Soviet archaeologists, important regions, such as the foothills of the northwestern Hindu Kush, remain ill explored. Consequently, most of the data summarized in this chapter come from Soviet central Asia, particularly southern Turkmenistan, where

the most detailed prehistoric sequences have been established.

The land itself consists of largely uninhabited deserts (Kara Kum and Kyzyl Kum, in particular), rugged mountain ranges, lowland alluvial plains, watered piedmont zones, and intermontane valleys. Important rivers, such as the Amu Darya and Zeravshan, that rise in the high eastern mountain ranges are fed largely by melting snows, while those to the west, such as the Murghab, Tedjen, or numerous streams of the Kopet Dagh, rely more on rainfall or, in some cases, tap groundwater sources (Dolukhanov 1981). Southern central Asia is a landlocked basin with a sharply continental climate and is very arid, particularly throughout its low-lying plains. While Soviet specialists disagree on the extent of environmental change during the Holocene (contrast Lisitsina 1978:189–93 with Vinogradov and Mamedov 1975:234–55), a longer term pattern of general desiccation is clear, and Neolithic archaeological remains in the inner Kyzyl Kum and Bronze Age settlements in an area formerly watered by the lower Murghab suggest that waters at least flowed farther into the deserts during the period of our concern, ca. 6500–1500 B.C., than they do today. Part of the retraction of rivers terminating in the desert was human-induced in the sense that the establish-

Submitted January 1983
Addenda submitted May 1984, September 1985

The author wishes to thank P. Dolukhanov and L. Kircho for kindly providing him with the additional radiocarbon determinations reported in the appendix. Robert W. Ehrich kindly calibrated these new dates.

ment of settlements upstream siphoned off water for the construction of irrigation works (Masson 1959:90–91), and the determination of cultural factors involved in settlement-pattern shifts from the Late Eneolithic through the Late Bronze periods remains an important problem for future investigations.

The Neolithic Period

The most complete Neolithic sequence for southern central Asia has been defined as the Djeitun culture of southern Turkmenistan and northern Iran (see table 1). Soviet archaeologists divide the culture into three phases—Early, Middle, and Late—which were distinguished initially by changes in the forms and decorations of pottery. Recent work in Iran, particularly at the sites known as Sang-e Caxmaq (Masuda 1974, 1976), suggest that an even earlier phase may have developed on the Iranian plateau.

In the Kopet Dagh piedmont strip of southern Turkmenistan the Early Djeitun phase appears particularly at the type site of Djeitun, a small village (.7 ha) located on the first sand ridges of the Kara Kum near Geok Tepe, and is characterized by crude handmade bowls, 12 percent of which are painted with a dominant vertical wavy line motif. Blade tools dominate the flint assemblage, and numerous bone scrapers were made from the shoulder blades of animals. Bone piercers and awls also occur, though their frequency increases greatly in the Middle and Late phases of the culture (Berdiev 1969:42). In the Early phase, one-room houses, made of long "protobricks" (60–70 cm) with an oval cross section, are scattered almost randomly over unplanned villages, while in the Middle phase, as represented in the upper levels at Chopan-depe, the houses were set in a line and shared walls, suggesting a higher degree of planning than at Djeitun. A large (64 m²) public building or "clubhouse" with geometric and naturalistic wall paintings was excavated at the Middle Djeitun site of Pessedjik-depe, and recent excavations have shown that storage areas or granaries abutted this structure, possibly indicative of an early centralized institution or cult center (Lollekova 1979:80). The Middle phase, known also from sites farther east in the Meana-Chaacha region, such as the lower levels at Chagylly-depe, is characterized by a sharp increase in the number of forms of vessels, flint knives, and grinding stones and a corresponding decrease in the percentage of painted wares, bone scrapers, and geometric flint tools. Excavations of the upper levels of Chagylly-depe defined the Late Djeitun phase (Berdiev 1966) and uncovered a series of one-room houses, made both of oval "protobricks" and of long rectangular bricks (60 × 20 × 10 cm). The houses often had stone door-sockets and were densely packed together, sharing common courtyards. Earlier trends for the frequency of stone and bone tools continued, although bone tools in general formed a much higher percentage of the total tool industry (ca. 23 percent), and pottery designs now included naturalistic representations of trees. Small copper fragments also occurred for the first time in the Late phase of the Djeitun culture. In short, the three phases of the Djeitun culture are characterized by distinct features of material culture which are reasonably interpreted as forming a continuous evolutionary or chronological sequence, although no single site contains all three phases (those showing internal development are Bami, Togolok, Chopan, and Chagylly), and none are known from the central piedmont or Kara-depe, Namazga-depe region, thus leaving open the possibility that chronological development may in part be confused with regional variation.

The subsequent transitional period from the Neolithic to the Early Eneolithic in southern Turkmenistan is known as Anau IA, which, following Berdiev (1972), overlaps with Late Djeitun. Anau IA is divided into two subphases, Chakmakli and Mondjukli, named after two sites located in the southeastern piedmont or Meana-Chaacha region. Pottery from levels II–IV at Chakmakli-depe is much better made than the contemporary or perhaps slightly earlier Late Djeitun ware; it is sand-tempered, thin-walled, frequently slipped, and sometimes burnished. Forms also are different, consisting mainly of cups with concave and occasionally flat bases, and a common motif on painted ware consists of lightly hatched triangles which become darker at Anau and Mondjukli. A stone hoe, the first recorded example from southern Turkmenistan and similar to those from Sialk, was found at Chakmakli, and copper tools, such as pins, awls, and chisels, were much more common here than at Chagylly-depe, located 1 km to the west. The houses from Chakmakli II were made of mud bricks with standard dimensions (40 × 20 × 10 cm), and more than thirty rooms were uncovered that appeared to form four complexes, separated from one another by a central street and two alleys (Berdiev 1968:28, illus. 1). Mondjukli is distinguished from Chakmakli by having Late Djeitun materials stratified beneath its Anau IA levels and contains numerous spindle whorls—attesting to a development in weaving—polished stone chisels, pierced circular stones interpreted as digging stick weights, grinding tools, and handled stone objects similar to later cult "weights." Semiprecious materials include alabaster, shell, and lapis lazuli, and metal artifacts again consist primarily of tools, including rectangular-sectioned punches, awls, and needles. A lump of unworked copper ore also was found, suggesting local production. Culture appears to have developed rapidly during the Anau IA period, and Soviet archaeologists stress increased interaction with the Iranian plateau, including possible movements of people, to explain this evolution.

It is extremely difficult to date precisely the Djeitun and Anau IA periods not only because radiocarbon determinations (table 3) are few and dendrochronological corrections for such early periods are unavailable, but also because the beginnings of this culture are poorly understood, with the earliest stages possibly developing on the Iranian plateau beyond the borders of Soviet central Asia. All investigators (e.g., Berdiev 1969:55) note that the earliest Djeitun sites in southern Turkmenistan appear as relatively well-developed food-producing settlements, and recent work in the basal levels of Sang-e Caxmaq West near Shahrud suggests the presence of an earlier aceramic phase which, on the basis of one presumably uncorrected radiocarbon determination from the third of five levels of ca. 7800 B.P. (Masuda 1976:65), would push such a phase back to the first half of the seventh millennium. The duration of the Djeitun period is equally uncertain, but the total depth of deposit should be at least 9.5 m since the sites of Djeitun with 3 m of deposit and Chagylly with 6.5 m do not seem to have overlapped chronologically. The same two sites contain a total of seventeen building levels, and it is further claimed that such levels in these small villages that lack monumental architecture should have existed for approximately fifty years each, making the duration of the period as known from Soviet central Asia slightly less than a millennium (see Masson 1971:59–60). Such calculations, of course, rest on numerous assumptions but may represent a minimal estimate since an interval of unknown duration could have separated the abandonment of Djeitun with the founding of Chagylly. The duration of the Anau IA period is equally difficult to assess, although the Anau IA levels at Mondjukli, the only site to witness the transition from Djeitun to Anau IA and probably to Namazga I, are 3 m thick. As noted, Berdiev favored an overlap between the earlier Anau IA levels at Chakmakli with the Late Djeitun levels at Chagylly. Summarizing this admittedly unclear picture, the following sequence emerges:

pre-6500 B.C.—aceramic phase, possibly represented in basal levels at Sang-e Caxmaq West

6500–6200 B.C.—an Iranian or piedmont-highland initial that predates settlements in the Kopet Dagh strip

6200–5800 B.C.—Early Djeitun

5800–5400 B.C.—Middle Djeitun

5400–5000 B.C.—Late Djeitun

5200–4800 B.C.—Anau IA

Beyond the piedmont strip of the Kopet Dagh, the Neolithic of the other regions of southern central Asia is less well known, for the materials are more fragmentary

and more difficult to interpret and date. Most importantly, relatively primitive food-producing cultures appear to continue later in regions outside of southern Turkmenistan, in some cases apparently coexisting with Bronze Age developments to the south. We consider briefly the archaeological remains from three regions: the middle course of the Murghab and northwestern Afghanistan; northeastern Afghanistan; and southern Tadjikistan; and the inner Kyzyl Kum and Khoresmia.

On the right bank of the Murghab River nearly opposite the town of Takhta Bazar, five stations or scatters of lithic tools (Takhta Bazar 1, 2, 3, 3/4, and 4) have been found which have been dated Early Djeitun on the basis of a high percentage of geometric microliths (Korobkova and Yusupov 1979:80); no evidence for mud-brick architecture appeared at any of these stations, suggesting that such a development was limited to the Kopet Dagh strip immediately to the west. In the late seventies Vinogradov (1979) found over 150 points or lithic scatters in northwestern Afghanistan in the contact zone of the *takyrs* (alkaline soil formations generally containing only algae and lichens which are formed by the accumulation of elutriated dry alluvium) and desert dunes ca. 10–30 km south of the Amu Darya. In other words, these sites were not associated with the Amu Darya but with rivers that flowed down from the Hindu Kush and ran much farther to the north than they do today. The sites date to both the Mesolithic and Neolithic periods, with most located north of Akcha, and, on the basis of morphological similarities, particularly the presence of symmetrical trapezoids and so-called horned trapezoids, are related to the Early Neolithic and such sites as Djeitun, Tutkaul 2, Djebel 5 and 5a, and Uchashchi 131. Although an Early Neolithic date is favored, Vinogradov (1979:56) notes that such trapezoids occasionally occur in later fifth and fourth millennia contexts in other areas of central Asia, suggesting a possible later date that would partially bridge the long chronological gap between these stations and the Bactrian Bronze Age settlements immediately to the south. It remains puzzling, however, that no Eneolithic sites are yet known for northwestern Afghanistan, an absence perhaps best explained by the lack of systematic survey work in the piedmont zone of the western Hindu Kush. On the other hand, earlier work by Dupree (1972) at the Epi-Palaeolithic and Neolithic Aq Kupruk sites in the piedmont zone watered by the Balkh Ab revealed surprisingly early evidence for sheep domestication (a single uncorrected radiocarbon date of 10,210 + 234 B.C., see table 3) but did not find later Neolithic Djeitun-like sites with mud-brick architecture or Eneolithic settlements. On present evidence it is at least equally possible that the western Hindu Kush, which lacks numerous terminal streams like those that empty into the Kara Kum from the Kopet Dagh, experienced a fundamentally different developmental sequence from that documented in southern Turkmenistan.

A relatively long-lived and primitive Neolithic period known as the Hissar culture characterizes the narrow mountainous valleys of northeastern Afghanistan and southern Tadjikistan. Its chronological limits are difficult to define because of its apparent lack of development. Masson and Sarianidi (1972:74) suggest a range from the sixth to the early second millennia B.C., although radiocarbon determinations (table 3) suggest a slightly earlier beginning date. The basis for the lower limit is unclear but presumably relates to the presence of better-known "steppe" and Late Bronze elements in association with Hissar-like features. This culture has been documented at several sites and is defined by the continued presence of pebble tools with microlithic tools, polished stone axes, grinding stones, and on later sites, crude ceramics with pointed bases. Mud-brick architecture is lacking, but some sites, such as Tutkaul 2, could have been permanently occupied. The wear patterns on blade tools, the grinding stones, and the location of sites on the terraces of large rivers suggest food production, both agriculture and stockbreeding. A Hissar station, Akli Mamai, is reported from northeastern Afghanistan along the Kokcha River, and Vinogradov (1979:58) emphasizes the difference between the Hissar lithic materials and those from the stations found in northwestern Afghanistan, thus implying an earlier cultural separation between western and eastern Bactria, a division characteristic of certain later prehistoric and historic periods. Moreover, systematic French surveys in eastern Bactria have not revealed food-producing sites earlier than the possibly early third millennium Late Eneolithic to Early Bronze settlements in the Taluqan area, the surface pottery of which can be compared to materials and sequences established south of the Hindu Kush, such as Mundigak III, Amri, and Kot Diji (Lyonnet 1981; Gardin n.d.).

Today the most complete Neolithic sequence for the inner Kyzyl Kum and Khoresmia comes from the former Lake Lyavlyakan region near the small mountains that rise 500–700 m above the desert enclosing the Karakatinskaya basin (see map 1 in Vinogradov and Mamedov 1975:5). In addition to the possible presence of Middle and Upper Palaeolithic remains, five chronological stages for this region have been defined, the last four of which date from the Early Neolithic through the Bronze Age. In the lower Zeravshan along the Daryasai extension the station of Uchashchi 131 contained trapezoids similar to those from northwestern Afghanistan north of Akcha that were stratified beneath a peat horizon yielding uncorrected radiocarbon determinations dating to the mid-fifth millennium B.C. (table 3), while in the Akcha Darya delta of Khoresmia, settlements of the Kelteminar culture,

which is divided into three chronological stages, appear to get underway slightly later. The earliest group includes such sites as Djanbas 4 and Kavat 5 and is dated particularly by the presence of distinctive Kelteminar arrowheads, which, according to Vinogradov (1968:135–43), occur subsequent to sites dominated first by asymmetrical then by symmetrical trapezoids. These latter are attested at Djeitun and in levels 6–5 of the Caspian Djebel cave, while the earliest Kelteminar arrowheads are recorded in the upper levels at Chopan-depe, together with a sharply reduced number of symmetrical trapezoids. The basic equation for the beginning of the Kelteminar culture of Khoresmia is with Djebel 4, which lacked the trapezoids but contained the Kelteminar arrowheads and which an uncorrected radiocarbon determination dates to the end of the fifth millennium. Sites in both Khoresmia (Djanbas 4) and the inner Kyzyl Kum (L 26) contained large wooden and reed oval huts, enclosing areas ranging roughly from 100 to 350 m², that can be sharply distinguished from the characteristic one-room mud-brick houses of the Djeitun culture, possibly suggesting a different organizational base to the society. Agriculture is not directly attested for the early stages, but stockbreeding is assumed to have supplemented the primary subsistence activities of hunting, gathering, and fishing.

The Eneolithic of Southern Turkmenistan

In 1952, B. A. Kuftin established the primary sequence for Eneolithic (Chalcolithic in Western terminology) and Bronze Age developments in southern central Asia on the basis of five stratigraphic soundings, excavated in 50 cm arbitrary levels, sunk into Namazga-depe, the largest known prehistoric mound in the Kopet Dagh piedmont strip. Although this sequence, itself a refinement and extension of the earlier one devised by Pumpelly (1908) at Anau, has been subdivided by later work, particularly at Altyn-depe (Masson 1981b), it is well established and still used for the relative dating of material from all of southern central Asia, a practice that has created chronological problems for newer materials excavated beyond the Kopet Dagh piedmont strip. The point is not that the sequence is not reliable but that several transitions to new periods are based almost exclusively on changes in the ceramic assemblages and that earlier periods in the piedmont zone are known from limited stratigraphic soundings. In other words, like most archaeological sequences, the unconscious assumption is made that certain motives, shapes, or fossil indexes are exclusively the property of one chronological period and have little reference to functional or regional variation. As noted below, this tendency is particularly problematic in dating the new Bronze Age materials from Bactria.

Direct stratigraphic continuity between Anau IA and

Namazga I (4800–4000 B.C.) appears at nine sites: Mondjukli; a settlement at Serakhs; Til'kin-depe; Dashli-depe at Izgant; Ekin-depe; Ovadan-depe; Anau northern mound; a mound near Beurme; and Chuli upstream of the Ashkhabad and Geok-depe oases (Lisitsina 1978:fig. 3). Internal subdivisions within the Namazga I (NMG I) period, which encompasses most of the fifth millennium, are less clear, and this lack of refinement is unfortunate in that the number of known settlements sharply increases during Namazga I times, with nearly thirty NMG I sites alone recorded for southern Turkmenistan. Some of these, such as Namazga (ca. 15 ha), Kara-depe (ca. 15 ha), and Altyn and Ilginli (both estimated at ca. 6–7 ha), appear to have been larger than the majority of sites and correspondingly may already have experienced some internal social differentiation or development from Neolithic times. Interestingly, the NMG I levels at Anau (Anau IB) are thicker than those at Namazga and Kara (respectively, ca. 12 m, 7+ m, 6.5 m), which in turn are thicker than those at Altyn (ca. 5.5 m) and in the Geoksyur oasis (ca. 2+ m). The significance of this west-to-east gradient is unclear but may imply earlier and longer-lived NMG I settlements in the western and central piedmont than farther east. Given NMG I remains from Mondjukli, such an interpretation does not mean that southeastern Turkmenistan was unoccupied during early NMG I times, although careful comparative analysis of materials (Khlopin 1963:20) suggests that the initial settlement of the Geoksyur oasis occurred late in the NMG I period. Internal differentiation of NMG I levels comes only from soundings at Kara-depe, where a tripartite division was based on a 12.5 m sounding placed in the center of the settlement: (a) Early NMG I or levels XXVII–XXIII are characterized by dark-on-red wares with contoured or tapering triangles as a common motif; (b) Middle NMG I or levels XXII–XIX contain dark brown paint on yellow-to-white cylindrical bowls (korchagi), with triangles and horizontal bands of rhomboids; and (c) Late NMG I or levels XVIII–XVI have dark-brown-on-red designs on thin-walled cups and goblets, some of which have chevrons and triangles painted on their interiors. The earliest building level, 3, at Dashlidji-depe, a small village site (.5 ha) in the Geoksyur oasis, equates with the beginning of the Late NMG I period as defined at Kara-depe. Given the overburden of deposits on larger sites, this small and possibly unrepresentative settlement has received the most extensive horizontal exposure, revealing evidence for local ceramic production in relatively unsophisticated open-air kilns and a large rectangular domestic building (rm. 1), occupied for two consecutive building levels, which is interpreted as the home of the village chief or leader of the community (see Khlopin 1964). Two radiocarbon dates are not helpful (table 3) but, from the thickness of the levels at Kara-

depe and the possible presence of an earlier NMG I occupation at Anau, one could *tentatively* redate this long and poorly understood Early Eneolithic period as Early NMG I = ca. 4800–4500 B.C.; Middle NMG I = ca. 4500–4250 B.C.; and Late NMG I = ca. 4250–4000 B.C.

The Middle Eneolithic or NMG II period (ca. 4000–3500 B.C.) is better documented both in the piedmont zone and in the Geoksyur oasis. NMG II levels in the piedmont are roughly 2.5–3 m thick, while in Geoksyur, which sees a maximum extension of settlement with eight of nine prehistoric sites in the oasis occupied during this period, they are somewhat thicker. One can detect regional differences in ceramic assemblages for the piedmont strip, with polychrome red and brown on buff wares appearing first in the central piedmont zone at Kara-depe and Namazga-depe, while monochrome black-on-red ware marks the eastern piedmont (Altyn) and the Geoksyur oasis. Similarly, the association of NMG II painted wares with graywares at Ak-depe immediately southwest of Ashkhabad suggests that the western piedmont already formed part of a grayware province stretching into the Gorgan plain and northern Iran. The Middle Eneolithic period is divided into Early and Late subperiods in both the central piedmont and the Geoksyur oasis. The Early NMG II or Yalangach period of the Geoksyur oasis is characterized by fortification walls, "shrines," or substantial buildings, usually in the center of the settlements, with their corners oriented to the cardinal directions and containing raised rectangular podium-altars, and circular towers or rooms set at the end of sections of the fortification walls. Ceramics for this Early NMG II period are very diagnostic and consist chiefly of open pots with parallel annular bands beneath the rim, occasionally connected by thin triangles, an obvious degeneration of the NMG I common motif. Numerous bent-legged or sitting figurines with emphasized sexual organs, thighs, and buttocks came from Yalangach-depe. The Late NMG II or Mullali-depe period in the Geoksyur oasis continues the architectural innovations of the Yalangach period, together with, possibly, an increase in the number of multiroom living complexes. A characteristic type of ceramic is an irregularly black-mottled, unpainted red-slipped ware, occasionally burnished. The Early NMG II of the central piedmont zone is best represented in levels 4–6 at Kara-depe. These levels have a dominance of polychrome painted ware, which does not continue into the subsequent Late NMG II period or Kara 2–3. There is a clear architectural break between Kara 3 and 4 in the orientation of structures, but the types of multiroom complexes and the practice of burying the dead in abandoned parts of the settlement continue until the site itself is abandoned in NMG III times. Children's burials at Kara-depe are as wealthy as, if not wealthier than, adult burials, possibly indicating that status was ascribed not achieved, and the frequent presence of nonindigenous semiprecious materials, such as carnelian and lapis lazuli, argues for regular access to the sources supplying them. The settlements at both Altyn-depe and Ilginli-depe in the southeastern piedmont grew to ca. 12 ha during this period, and a relatively large (3500 m³) "reservoir" near Mullali-depe in the Geoksyur oasis suggests technological improvements concerning water management on the lowland plains during NMG II. When corrected, only one of three radiocarbon determinations for NMG II from Geoksyur makes sense (table 3); in fact, the entire series of dates from the oasis is problematic, with most dates being far too young, perhaps resulting from a systematic error of sample collection or calculation.

The NMG III period (ca. 3500–3000 B.C.) generally continues trends observable during the Middle Eneolithic. Regionalism persists within southern Turkmenistan: the western zone characterized by the dominant presence of graywares; the central piedmont distinguished by the appearance of dark-on-light monochrome wares frequently depicting zoomorphic motives; and the eastern zone and the Geoksyur oasis marked by a polychrome ware on a red background with dominant geometric motives, particularly stepped and cruciform designs. The major sites tend to increase in size, with few small ones known. A process of nucleation is clearly documented in the Geoksyur oasis, where the type site of Geoksyur 1 incorporates all but one of the previous settlements during the Geoksyur period or late NMG II/NMG III times and also seems to have occurred in the eastern piedmont zone where Ilginli-depe appears to have been abandoned and Altyn appears to have expanded roughly to its final size of ca. 26 ha. Judging by the thickness of the Late Eneolithic deposits—ca. 2.5 m in sounding 1 at Namazga (but with a reported and clearly mistaken or anomalous 8.5-m NMG III deposit in sounding 5), 2–2.5 m at Kara, 3 + m at Altyn—and given roughly the same number of building horizons in the Geoksyur period as in the preceding Yalangach-Mullali periods combined, it is likely that the NMG III period was approximately of the same duration as NMG II or just slightly longer, a problem in the calculations being the exact relation of the Geoksyur sequence to that obtained from Kara-depe and Namazga-depe. If the early Geoksyur period is equated to late NMG II (or Kara 2–3), then the middle and late Geoksyur periods, as represented particularly at Chong-depe, are equivalent to NMG III or Kara 1b and 1a (see Khlopin 1964:64–66). Masson's recent chart on stratigraphic correlations of the Eneolithic to Bronze levels at Altyn-depe (1981a:19, fig. 5) seems to support a much deeper deposit and presumably longer duration for NMG II than NMG III, although the terminological confusion

is resolved if Altyn levels 9–14, which are characterized by the presence of Geoksyur-like ceramics and are roughly as thick as those characterized by Yalangach-like wares (Altyn 15 and cuts XXXVI–XXXIX), are considered Late Eneolithic. Thickness of deposit, of course, can never be precisely equated with temporal duration, but when the stratigraphic soundings show no evidence for platforming or for monumental architecture and reveal approximately the same number of building levels for NMG II as for NMG III, the case for a roughly equal duration for the periods is strengthened. Calibrated radiocarbon determinations (table 3) suggest possibly an even earlier beginning date for NMG III of ca. 3600 B.C., but it seems preferable to equate the period with the second half of the fourth millennium in order to avoid a spurious sense of accuracy and to correlate better the NMG III materials with similar remains recovered outside of southern central Asia, as well as to support a roughly equal duration for NMG II and III.

In the Geoksyur oasis, shrines, which now have circular altars with central holes giving evidence for controlled or slow burning, continue to appear in multiroom living complexes, but a major change seems represented by the presence of a separate cemetery at Geoksyur 1 with collective "tholoi" burial structures, the latter also occurring in Late Eneolithic levels at Altyn-depe. This collective burial tradition was not common at Kara-depe, where extensive excavations of NMG III levels revealed the continuation of the earlier pattern of contracted individual interments, though now oriented to both the north and south. Multiroom living complexes, separated by alleys or streets, containing evidence for local domestic pottery production but lacking shrines of the Geoksyur 1 and Chong-depe type, characterized the domestic architecture in Kara 1b and 1a. Important technological and economic developments occurred during NMG III times as seen in more advanced partitioned ceramic kilns, the possible introduction of a slow-turning device for the production of Geoksyur wares (Khlopin 1964:122), and the construction of fairly large irrigation canals. The canals have been documented at Geoksyur 1 and seem securely dated to the period through the discovery of a Geoksyur female figurine found in sectioning one canal. Aerial photographs and excavations over a ca. 400 km² area surrounding the site have shown that two major canals ran parallel to each other in a W/SW to E/NE direction for ca. 3 km, and small irrigation ditches or *arykhs,* running off these canals at sharp angles, have been traced. Calculations of agricultural productivity based on this data (Lisitsina 1969:284–86, 1978:211–12) and comparisons made with estimates on yields in Neolithic Djeitun times show a considerable increase, suggesting the creation of a substantial food surplus.

The traditional Soviet interpretation of the NMG III

period is one of intensive contact with and tribal migration from Iran, an interpretation heavily dependent on general similarities in zoomorphic motives between Kara 1b and 1a and with Hissar IB–IIA and Sialk III4–7, IV. Large-scale movements into southern Turkmenistan are not supported by a comparison of known estimated areas of occupation for the NMG II and NMG III periods, and, when closely examined, the resemblances in zoomorphic motives are of a very general nature, useful at best for establishing chronological correspondences but hardly indicative of mass migrations. In addition, some of the zoomorphic motives derive from earlier designs present in the NMG II levels at Kara-depe (e.g., Masson 1960:tables V, VII). Similarities with the geometric Geoksyur style, on the other hand, have been detected outside of southern Turkmenistan, notably as a component of the so-called Quetta ware from the Quetta Valley, in the Shahr-i Sokhta I assemblage from Iranian Seistan, and at Sarazm along the middle Zeravshan. The latter two regions lack prehistoric sequences prior to levels containing Geoksyur-related elements, while the Quetta Valley and, more significantly, the region at the foot of the Bolan pass, as documented by materials from Mehrgarh, have long sequences that antedate the appearance of Quetta ware in Damb Sadaat II. In short, while NMG III chronological correspondences can be made with areas outside of southern Turkmenistan, its stronger and perhaps historically more important links are with regions to the southeast and east and not with the Iranian plateau.

The sequence from Mundigak in southwestern Afghanistan also provides parallels and some discrepancies with the NMG III corpus. The late radiocarbon dates from this site (see Agrawal and Kusumgar 1974:87); the indisputable earlier introduction of wheel-turned pottery at Mundigak; the occurrence of stone seal-amulets beginning as early as Mundigak II, 2; the presence of metal shaft-hole axes and adzes in Mundigak III, 6 or in the same level with collective rectangular graves; and the continued occurrence of Geoksyur-inspired stepped designs (e.g., Casal 1961:tome II, fig. 91) in Mundigak IV, 2—all make precise chronological correlations with the Namazga sequence difficult. The Geoksyur-related motives found outside southern Turkmenistan are not exact duplicates of those found in the Geoksyur oasis and can most reasonably be interpreted as a development or degeneration from those found at Geoksyur 1 and Chong-depe. From this perspective, it seems possible to equate the end of Mundigak II and the first four phases of Mundigak III with NMG III and the end of Mundigak III (5–6) and perhaps IV, 1 with the subsequent Early Bronze or NMG IV period. Damb Sadaat II would largely overlap with this latter period, while Shahr-i Sokhta I, which has definite links with the Jemdet Nasr and Proto-Elamite ho-

rizons of Mesopotamia and southern Iran, would bridge the transition between NMG III and early NMG IV.

The degree of correspondence between the Shahr-i Sokhta I and NMG III assemblages has been greatly exaggerated in the literature, for the total number of painted sherds with southern Turkmenian affinities barely exceeds fifty (Biscione n.d.). The NMG III correspondences with the site of Sarazm east of Samarkand are also real but rare, although the isolated polychrome sherds are found here in association with a major building that exhibits features of a Geoksyur shrine in its orientation of corners to the cardinal directions and in the presence of circular altars with burnt holes. Thus, Sarazm could have been occupied as early as NMG III, although the polychrome pottery (see Isaakov 1981:279, fig. 3) clearly represents a degeneration from classic Geoksyur ware, and the occurrence of fairly sophisticated metal artifacts, including a shaft-hole axe-adze, suggests a slightly later date, possibly beginning in the Early Bronze or NMG IV period. Finally, an incised grayware sherd of a type familiar to the Bampur Valley and southern Iran (see Masson 1960:377), as well as a miniature grooved stone column ca. 5 cm. high (Masson 1960:437, table XVIII, 12) and numerous marble and alabaster objects, including handled weight-shaped ones, from the topmost "level of the bull" at Kara-depe, suggest that there may have been a later unrecognized terminal or squatter occupation at the site. In the recent Altyn-depe monograph Masson (1981a:94) reports in a footnote that a gray-decorated vessel from the topmost level at Kara-depe was identical with one labeled as coming from Hissar IIIA that he examined in the University Museum in Philadelphia. While the status of Schmidt's IIIA at Hissar is now open to question (Dyson, pers. comm.), this parallel, if exact, again suggests some later (NMG IV ?) terminal occupation at Kara-depe.

The Early Bronze Age of Southern Turkmenistan

Many important technological and social developments seem to have occurred during the Early Bronze or NMG IV period in southern Turkmenistan (3000–2500 B.C.). Most major sites appear to have attained their maximum size in the NMG IV period, with the total known estimated site area for the Kopet Dagh piedmont strip likewise reaching its greatest extent during prehistoric times. Depth of NMG IV deposits varies from site to site and even within sites. The following figures are derived from Masson (1981a:28): Namazga—4 m in sounding 1, 1 m in sounding 4, and 6.5 m in sounding 2; Altyn—excavation 1, levels 4–8, less than 4 m; excavation 5, three levels, not more than 2.5 m; and on the "hill of the wall" (i.e., a monumental structure) possibly up to 9 m;

Khapuz-depe—5 m; Ulug-depe—4–6 building levels; and Ak-depe near Ashkhabad—9 levels, 7 m (although this last figure may not be reliable). The questionable practice of estimating duration on the basis of number and thickness of levels becomes even more dubious in the Early Bronze Age since the presence of monumental structures, like the fortification wall at Altyn, can distort the calculations and cause inflated estimates (Masson 1981a:28). Most scholars favor a subdivision of NMG IV into earlier and later subperiods: the former, which Masson (1981a:28; see also Tosi 1973–74:61; Gupta 1979:136–39) terms Khapuz, is equivalent to Altyn, excavation 1, levels 6–8; and the latter, which is characterized by intricate tapestry or detailed carpet designs on pottery, comes from Altyn, excavation 1, levels 4–5. Kircho's (1980:11–13) complete study of Early Bronze remains, however, distinguishes three subperiods on the basis of ceramic designs, relating Altyn excavation 1, level 4, and Altyn excavation 5, levels 4–5, to a final period. Three corrected radiocarbon determinations (table 3) are consistent with a date relating NMG IV to the first half of the third millennium.

Most of the information on domestic architecture in the Early Bronze period comes from Altyn-depe, excavation 5, level 5. Multiroom dwelling complexes are characteristic, although they now also include series of rooms with apparently only a single living area and a separate courtyard (excv. 5, level 6, complex 1). These latter can possibly be interpreted as complexes for relatively prosperous nuclear, as opposed to extended, families (see Kircho 1980:6–7, 14). The period is marked by technological advances in pottery production, including the introduction and dominant utilization of the fast wheel and the appearance of efficient, two-tiered pottery kilns; metallurgy (Terekhova 1981:321–22) with deliberate alloying and evidence for local production in the form of copper smelting furnaces on the outskirts of Khapuz-depe; stone working; and a development of wheeled vehicles drawn by Bactrian camels and possibly bulls as indicated by terra-cotta models (see Kuzmina 1980). Figurines foreshadow the famous flattened NMG V types with characteristic incised designs, and Masson (1981a:27) suggests that part of excavation 5 near the "hill of the wall" at Altyn-depe represented the remains of an early cult center, the functions of which were expanded and transferred to the location of excavation 7 in NMG V times. While this interpretation is based primarily on the occurrence of distinctively decorated rooms with stepped niches and can be questioned, nearly all indexes of material culture, such as monumental architecture, craft specialization, and differentiation of domestic structures, suggest that the "urban revolution" was well underway during the Early Bronze period. Unfortunately, at most of the sites in the Kopet Dagh piedmont strip, NMG V remains

overlie earlier levels and thus hinder extensive exposure of the Early Bronze period.

A major division between a western grayware province, stretching roughly west of Ashkhabad to the Gorgan plain, and an eastern painted and plain buff-ware zone, extending from the central piedmont east to Khapuz-depe, is evident in the distribution of NMG IV remains and is supported by the materials from Ak-depe and by the recent discovery and excavations of the Early Bronze Age cemetery of Parkhai II in the middle Sumbar Valley (see Khlopin 1981; Kohl, Biscione, and Ingraham 1982). Finally and most importantly, carinated graywares, tentatively dated to late NMG IV–early NMG V, recently were discovered in the lower building level at Kelleli 1 in Margiana (Masimov 1981b:466). Note that graywares constitute a minor proportion of the Late Bronze ceramic assemblages of Margiana and Bactria (e.g., at Sapalli), and, given the absence of more complete documentation and illustration of the materials, it is currently impossible to determine whether or not these ceramics provide absolutely secure chronological links to the late Early Bronze period. Their discovery seems to indicate that the earliest known settlements, as opposed to surface scatters, in the northernmost Kelleli oasis overlap completely with the so-called urban phase or florescence of cities, like Altyn and Namazga, in the Kopet Dagh piedmont strip.

The Middle Bronze Age or "Urban Phase"

While the documented occupation of the piedmont strip during the Early Bronze period is greater, the subsequent NMG V period (ca. 2500–2200 B.C.) is much better known and is emphasized in the literature as the period that witnesses a transformation of society and the appearance of cities. Such emphasis may be misleading and is primarily due to the extensive excavations of the topmost NMG V levels at Altyn-depe. With the advent of the Middle Bronze period, use of the Namazga sequence terminology becomes more problematic since materials from beyond the Kopet Dagh piedmont strip are not necessarily or are only indirectly related to southern Turkmenistan. It now becomes necessary to consider at least seven major regions separately (table 2): (a) central Kopet Dagh piedmont strip and Iranian Khorassan; (b) southwestern Turkmenistan and the Gorgan and Damghan plains; (c) southeastern Turkmenistan; (d) Margiana or the Lower Murghab; (e) the Bactrian plain of northwestern Afghanistan and southern Uzbekistan; (f) eastern Bactria or southern Tadjikistan and northeastern Afghanistan; and (g) a northern zone consisting of Khoresmia, the inner Kyzyl Kum, and the Fergana and Zeravshan valleys.

In the central piedmont strip, Namazga V remains are

best known from the ca. 50-ha site of Namazga-depe (2–2.5 m of deposit), but much smaller sites, such as Shor (3 ha), Taichanak (1.1 ha), Kosha (.6 ha), and the stations referred to as the Shabalinskii complex (Shchetenko 1979:84–85), have been recorded and partially excavated, revealing surprisingly rich remains, such as a silver cross-shaped seal from Taichanak (Shchetenko 1968) and a bronze seal fragment and a metal spiral-headed pin from Shor. Shchetenko (1970:50) comments:

> The form of the material culture of these settlements (Taichanak, Kosha, and Shor) is similar in its basic features and strongly recalls [the culture of] the large centers of the Bronze Age, Altyn-depe and Namazga-depe, which are distinguished from them by their large dimensions. However, in all basic features—craft development, trading ties with separate regions, the development of proto-writing (as suggested by the signs on the female figurines)—it is apparent that there existed a sufficiently high level of development of the small villages of the Bronze Age. (Trans. by the author)

The fact that these sites ceased to exist when the nearby metropolis of Namazga-depe collapsed at the beginning of NMG VI may refute the notion of the independence of these settlements, but the quality of their remains, which also include evidence for local ceramic and metallurgical production, suggests some degree of autonomy and is perhaps best paralleled by the relative wealth of remains found in villages of the Indus Valley, such as Allahdino (see Fairservis 1982; Shaffer 1982). The absence of an absolute urban/rural dichotomy for both areas is noteworthy and possibly indicates the presence of elites in the countryside. In any event, the concept of an overly nucleated or completely urbanized NMG V settlement pattern is mistaken (contrast Shchetenko 1979:85 with Biscione 1977) and fails to consider sufficiently the problem of locating small sites in the heavily alluviated piedmont zone.

The dominant surface material at Namazga-depe (Litvinskii 1952) consists of unpainted, wheel-made, thin-walled, elegant NMG V vessels which are grouped into about thirty standardized types. Grayware generally is absent in the central piedmont zone during NMG V times. Large-scale excavations on the site were impeded by the presence of an Islamic cemetery and remain incompletely published (see Masson 1956b:307), but we are told that multiroom houses with open courtyards were separated from neighboring complexes by narrow streets. A ceramic trough or drain, presumably for water runoff or sewage purposes, and ladles, slag, and production debris indicating local metallurgical and ceramic production were also recorded. Finally, NMG V sites have not yet been located in the upper Atrek Valley (Ricciardi 1980:57), while only the site of Yarim Tepe on the Darreh Gaz plain of northeastern Iran contained NMG V materials on its surface (Kohl and Heskel 1980).

With the exception of the southern mound at Anau, no NMG V sites are known in southern Turkmenistan from the Ashkhabad oasis westward to the Iranian border. This absence is surprising since earlier related settlements on the Gorgan and Damghan plains of north central Iran, such as Tureng, Shah, and Hissar, appear to have been large and flourishing during the third quarter of the third millennium. The occurrence of monumental architecture in the form of the "high terrace" at Tureng Tepe IIIC1 and the presence of objects, such as miniature stone columns, at Tureng and in the terminal levels at Hissar seem to link these sites chronologically to the NMG V levels at Altyn, although they could as well equate with the subsequent transitional Kelleli period. The 1976 reexcavations at Hissar seem to present one additional anomaly with the southern Turkmenian sequence in that the site appears to have reached its maximal dimensions not during its terminal occupation but earlier in the third or in the late fourth millennium, then shrinking during Hissar III times.

The Middle Bronze levels from Altyn-depe have been extensively excavated and provide the most complete record of a complex urban social formation in central Asia. Evidence for monumental architecture in the form of a 55-m-long stepped structure and adjacent funerary complex clearly related to cult practices (excv. 7), craft specialization documented by an extensive potters' quarter essentially occupying the northern part of the mound (excvs. 10, 6, and 12), and elite (excvs. 9 and 13) and less elaborate residential areas (excv. 5)—all attest to the site's urban status in the second half of the third millennium. Here, we reiterate that, despite the relatively limited exposure of Early Bronze levels at the site, much of the social differentiation attested in NMG V levels at Altyn begins earlier as indicated by the monumental fortification wall and gate (excv. 8) and the elaborately decorated structures of NMG IV rooms in excavation 5. Similarly, while the work at Altyn-depe is most impressive particularly in terms of the scale of the excavations (excv. unit 9 alone has exposed more than 6,000 m^2), numerous areas of the site, including nearly the entire western half of the mound and other places where metalworking activities and possible grain-processing and storage activities might have taken place, remain to be systematically investigated. Despite this limited understanding, Masson (1981a:92) argues on the basis of a sounding in the western half of the mound for a final restricted occupation at Altyn during a period contemporary with the Kelleli settlements in Margiana, an equation that now seems too conservative given the evidence for earlier materials in the lower building level of Kelleli 1. While earlier discussions of NMG V ceramics from Altyn-depe divided the material into earlier and later sub-periods (cf. Masson 1970:11–20; and Askarov 1973:105, 115–16), Masson (1981a:82–83) now refers to three stages of NMG V ceramic evolution at Altyn-depe. The earliest stage is marked by light-slipped biconical vessels with a sharp carination in the lower third of the body; cups, small vases, teapots with a biconical or carinated shape and short, stubby spouts, and large, thick-walled pots with large, everted bell-shaped throats also occur. Ceramics of the second stage include biconical vessels with raised bases and long necks, pots with tall swelling throats and raised bases, and pear-shaped pots. In general, ceramics of the earliest stage exhibit the "elegant" features first observed in NMG V levels at Namazga-depe and are particularly characterized by sharp carinations; ceramics of the second stage exhibit more rounded, drawn-out forms. The third-stage forms, which Masson considers identical with ceramics from the Kelleli sites in Margiana, are found only in isolated burials in excavation 13 (and presumably 9) and in the northern (excv. 1 and presumably 10) and western (sounding 1) parts of the mound during the final period of supposed decay and re-stricted occupation. Most characteristic are ceramic sup-ports (or "chucks" used in the production of large storage jars), some of which have incised designs and are consid-ered a classic NMG VI trait; jars with cylindrical bodies, pot-shaped vessels with relatively short throats, squat goblets with straight rims, deep basins with raised coni-cal bases, and cups with spouts similar to ones from a later site in Margiana, Auchin-depe, are clearly related to NMG VI forms, as originally defined in the "tower" se-quence at Namazga-depe. However, no burnished red-wares occur at Altyn, although they do appear in the NMG VI levels of the "tower" excavations at Namazga. Unfortunately, the internal evolution of NMG V ceramics at Altyn-depe is described but not illustrated, and it is unclear where materials from the latest hoards, particu-larly those excavated by Ganyalin (1967) immediately beneath the surface on the highest part of Altyn-depe, and rich tombs, like burials 252 (Gul'muradov 1978) and 362 (Alyekshin 1979) with clear Indus and Bactrian parallels, such as ivory, an etched carnelian bead, a grooved mini-ature column, and a long stone staff, actually fit within this sequence. The vessels from Ganyalin's hoards, which include an apparently imported gray carafe or decanter-shaped vessel of Hissar III type, a large jar with a slightly inverted or concave rise above the base (a more typical NMG VI feature), a pedestaled chalice, and deep cups with flaring sides (see Ganyalin 1967:217, fig. 7, nos. 5, 8, 10), seem to correspond with the final stage as defined in the Altyn-depe monograph, though this attri-bution needs independent confirmation from the Soviet specialists.

Assuming that the carinated graywares from the lower building level at Kelleli 1 date to the late NMG IV or early NMG V period, it becomes likely that the subse-quent major occupation of the Kelleli oasis is contempo-raneous with the "urban phase" at Altyn-depe, the differ-ences in the assemblages being explained as regional variants. From this perspective, the final restricted occu-pation at Altyn-depe, characterized by the presence of Kelleli-like forms, indicates that occupation in the Kel-leli oasis continued after the collapse of the NMG V city of Altyn-depe and might even suggest some movement from Margiana to the piedmont strip or just the opposite of the traditionally argued expansion from the piedmont onto the lowland plains. Mid-third millennium remains on the Bactrian plain of northwestern Afghanistan and southern Uzbekistan are more problematic in that clearly Harappan-related remains of this period exist farther east in northeastern Afghanistan at Shortugai I and one of the earliest manifestations of the Bactrian Bronze Age, the Dashli 3 palace, level 1, shows unmistakable Harappan influence in the form of mosaic trefoil patterns and bull designs (Sarianidi 1977:47). It is clear from the super-positioning of graves and other evidence from the Dashli sites, as well as from the excavations of a 7-m cultural deposit at Hirdai-depe in the Daulatabad oasis, that the Bactrian Bronze Age sites were occupied for a reasonably long period. Given the Harappan connections at Shortu-gai I, which corrected radiocarbon determinations place in the mid to second half of the third millennium (table 3), and the fact that even the early NMG V levels at Altyn of the funerary complex (excv. 7, rm. 7) contain materi-als of probable Harappan origin, such as an alabaster seal with swastika motif, it seems likely that the fertile Bac-trian plain was occupied in the mid-third millennium and that the earliest known Bactrian Bronze remains date to this period. Alternatively, the size and general planning of the early Dashli 3 palace (84 × 88 m) recall features of the Dashli 1 palace and Sapalli-tepe, which, on the basis of ceramics and other materials, relate to the major occupation of the Kelleli oasis, possibly continuing after the collapse of Altyn-depe (see below and Askarov 1973:105).

The eastern Bactrian plain, the area stretching from the Kunduz Valley east to the Pamirs, sees the establishment of Harappan-like settlements sometime near the middle of the third millennium (Francfort and Pottier 1978). The development leading up to Shortugai I is unclear, al-though earlier, possibly Late Eneolithic (i.e., contempo-raneous with NMG III) remains may have been found farther west near Taluqan. Intriguingly, surface ceramics from these sites may relate more to wares defining prehistoric sequences established south of the Hindu Kush—Mundigak III, Amri, Kot Diji—than to those from southern Turkmenistan (Lyonnet 1981; Gardin n.d.). Shortugai I materials include classic mature Harappan pottery, both painted and unpainted, Harappan-like brick architecture, and small finds, such as an Indus seal depicting a rhinoceros. A consistent series of more than sixteen corrected radiocarbon determinations supports a mid-third millennium date for the beginning of the Shortugai settlements, which is in accord with the early part of the Mature Harappan period. No similar evidence has yet come from southern Tadjikistan, where the primitive Hissar Neolithic culture seems to have continued.

No dramatic changes in material culture are recorded in Khoresmia, the Kyzyl Kum, or the Zeravshan and Fergana valleys during the middle to the third quarter of the third millennium. At this time, turquoise working presumably was still carried out on a relatively large scale in the inner Kyzyl Kum on sites like Lyavlyakan 26. A chlorite stone weight with projecting snake heads and drilled and inlaid bodies was found near the Soch River which flows north into the Fergana Valley (Brentjes 1971). While this object relates stylistically to the widely distributed corpus of carved "Intercultural Style" stone objects that date to the middle of the third millennium (Kohl 1979), it lacks context and at present must be treated as a stray find.

Farther south the Middle Bronze phase probably corresponds to Shahr-i Sokhta III, the period of maximum settlement (ca. 80 ha) of the site. Pear-shaped vessels with raised bases and long necks similar to those of the middle NMG V assemblage at Altyn-depe (see Lamberg-Karlovsky and Tosi 1973:fig. 58) occur, and the general decline in painted forms and an increase in compartmented bronze seals during Shahr-i Sokhta III seem to link the site with the NMG V "urban phase" sites of southern Turkmenistan. The recently defined period VIIC at Mehrgarh contains forms, such as red-slipped bowls with nail-shaped rims, characteristic of Amri IIB and Early Harappan levels at Kot Diji, together with ceramics, such as circle-stamped wet wares, which are more characteristic of Mature Harappan forms and are also found in Mundigak IV, 3. Possibly, period VIIC at Mehrgarh overlaps the Middle Bronze phase of southern central Asia and is followed by a short gap (or occupation of the Mature Harappan mound at Nowsharo ?) before the appearance of central Asian Bactria-Margiana-like materials in the Mehrgarh VIII cemetery. Alternatively, Mature Harappan settlements, such as Nowsharo immediately south of Mehrgarh, coexisted with Mehrgarh VIIC, a period that shows many aspects of continuity with the earlier Mehrgarh VIIB community (Jarrige n.d.).

Terminal Middle Bronze or Kelleli Phase

Materials from the final occupation at Altyn-depe, when settlement apparently was restricted largely to the western half of the mound, resemble those found on the surface and, presumably, in the upper levels of the Kelleli settlements. Data thus suggest that occupation in the Kelleli oasis continued after the collapse of the city of Altyn-depe. While it must be emphasized that the tripartite chronological division of the Bronze Age of Margiana proposed by Sarianidi (1981a) demands stratigraphic documentation, differences in materials distinguish the northwesternmost Kelleli oasis, and a chronological gradient of settlement from northwest to southeast is consistent with the later pattern observed in Margiana through to the end of the Iron Age. Deep, truncated conical bowls or basins with clipped rims and vases on stands sometimes having crimped or goffered feet have parallels in the late NMG V assemblages of the piedmont strip (see Masson 1981a:91, fig. 27). The absence of graywares and classic footed goblets, which occur at Sapalli and other Bactrian sites, is noteworthy; such forms only appear in the presumably later Gonur phase settlements farther south. Perforated jars, possibly of Harappan inspiration, occur as do flat NMG V-like terra-cotta violin-shaped figurines with incised lines. The absence in the Kelleli sites of the so-called Murghab style (Sarianidi 1981b) stone stamp seals, handled cylinder seals similar to those found to the south at Taip-depe 1 (Masimov 1981a), and incised steppe-bronze ceramics found on oases south of Kelleli also argues for the chronological priority of the Kelleli settlements. The piedmont strip may have been largely abandoned at the end of the third millennium as suggested by the absence of building remains in the basal NMG VI levels of the "tower" excavation at Namazga-depe (Shchetenko and Dolukhanov 1976), although NMG V levels at Namazga-depe have not received the extensive exposure that they have at Altyn-depe and that some final restricted NMG V or Kelleli phase occupation at Namazga might parallel that postulated for Altyn. Farther west, the site of Anau (southern mound) seems to witness the transition from Middle to Late Bronze, but the present, more precise excavations at Anau will have to document whether this was a continuous or interrupted process. The cemetery in the upper Sumbar Valley of Daina, which contained both a miniature stone column and a shaft-hole ax-adze, could date to this period, although neither of the objects alone is diagnostic. Similarly, the rich and still enigmatic Hissar IIIC period contains materials, such as the stone columns, bronze flagons, and elaborate alabaster vessels, that occur at Altyn-depe (except for the pedestaled and thin alabaster vessels), Sapalli-depe, and pillaged Bactrian tombs. Stone columns occur at the NMG VI and presumably later site of Tekkem-depe in the piedmont strip and at Gonur-depe 1; consequently, these objects are relatively long-lived, with an earlier prototype known from the final, presumably Late Eneolithic level at Kara-depe (1A), while the bronze flagons are also found in the terminal Bronze Sumbar cemeteries, which should date roughly to the middle of the second millennium B.C. (Khlopin 1977).

In general, the rich Hissar IIIC tombs and the Hissar IIIC settlement (Schmidt's terminology), if continuous with the earlier IIIB occupation, should relate to this transitional phase or possibly to the beginning of the subsequent Gonur phase, which in turn can be equated with the florescence of the currently documented Bactrian Bronze settlements of northwestern Afghanistan and southern Uzbekistan. Architectural correspondences of small, planned fortified settlements or centers of ca. 1 ha, at Dashli 1, Sapalli, and possibly the Dashli 3 palace site, as well as ceramic similarities with the final NMG V assemblage at Altyn and now the Kelleli settlements, clearly demonstrate that the intensive settlement of the Bactrian plain began during the final centuries of the third millennium. Sapalli, the most thoroughly investigated of these settlements (Askarov 1973, 1977), consists of a central fortified area (82 × 82 m) surrounded by a ca. 4-ha zone with cultural remains. Most of the Bactrian settlements are smaller than their Margiana counterparts (Kelleli 1 is ca. 5–6 ha), but show evidence of local self-sufficiency, including ceramic production, particularly at Sapalli. One hundred and twenty-five single and thirteen collective burials, together representing the remains of 158 individuals, lay under the floors and in the walls of the Sapalli houses. The preservation was excellent, and wooden plates, skins, textiles, straw, matting, caches of carbonized millet seeds, and—in four cases—silk clothing were recovered. Little social differentiation appeared in these tombs, and children's graves were relatively poor. With regard to the Dashli 1 palace site in southern Bactria, the excavator (Sarianidi 1977:32) emphasizes the similarity in materials from the fortified "palace" (99 × 85 m) with those from nine graves excavated at the site, but notes that the latter, unlike those at Sapalli, were dug into the abandoned remains, including the top of the fortification wall, thus implying some time lapse between the occupation of the settlement and its later use as a cemetery. The burials, consequently, may belong to the subsequent Gonur phase. Alabaster column(s), one of which is said to have been 36 cm high, were found at Dashli 1, but, as noted, unfortunately, do not provide precise chronological correlations. Pottery from Sapalli and Dashli 1 is closely similar, consisting dominantly of finely made wheel-turned ware, including footed vases and flower stands—some with sharply angled inverted

rims, sauceboats, teapots, footed goblets, deep conical cups with broad clipped or bordered rims, storage jars characteristically concave above the base, and ceramic supports or "chucks" used in the production of the jars. Minor proportions of streak-burnished grayware (3 percent at Sapalli) occur on the Bactrian sites but hardly provide evidence of massive west-to-east migrations. Correspondences with the Kelleli and final Altyn assemblages are close, but differences include the lack of footed goblets in the Kelleli oasis and the broader clipped or bordered rims on the deep conical bowls from Sapalli. Most significantly perhaps, practically no terra-cotta figurines have been found on the Bactrian plain. The presence of late NMG V–like figurines at Sibri, located ca. 8 km southwest of Mehrgarh, suggests possibly closer relationships between the Bolan area and Margiana than Bactria. The individual graves in both northern and southern Bactria often contained the bones of a young animal, and rich burials of young rams with numerous ceramic vessels and other offerings were found both at Sapalli and Dashli 1. A very well-developed chipped stone industry, including symmetrical flint arrow and lance heads, also characterizes both sites and argues for close cultural affinity and chronological contemporaneity.

Farther east the Shortugai II period, which on the basis of the corrected radiocarbon dates seems to follow directly after period I, no longer exhibits classic Harappan features but shows some similarities to cemetery sites in southwestern Tadjikistan, termed the Beshkent culture. Bronze objects from the Khaka hoard (see Zadneprovsky 1962:52–55) of the northern Fergana Valley, including an elaborately figured pin, have been compared both stylistically and compositionally with metals from Hissar IIIC but now may also relate to those of Bactria for this or for the subsequent Gonur period. Perhaps more significantly, it is roughly at the end of the third or the beginning of the second millennium that Vinogradov and Mamedov (1975:225–28) see a major change in materials from the inner Kyzyl Kum, with the presence of steppe-bronze ceramics, a reduction, if not cessation, of turquoise production, and intensive metallurgical activities. This pattern, marking a sharp break with the earlier tradition, presumably continued throughout the first half of the second millennium. Unfortunately, the sequence of radiocarbon dates from Bactria and southern Turkmenistan for the Middle and Late Bronze is not consistent and must be interpreted from other sequences, particularly those from Hissar and from Shortugai (table 3).

Initial Late Bronze or Gonur Phase, ca. 2100–1800 B.C.

The Late Bronze Age shows a sharp shift in settlement location from previous periods. Most strikingly, the Kopet Dagh piedmont strip appears to have been largely abandoned or to have had sharply restricted occupations of what had once been major sites (e.g., Namazga-depe). Since the earlier investigations took place in the Kopet Dagh piedmont strip, the abandonment of these sites was interpreted as indicating a decline in the development of complex "urban" or "proto-urban" society in the area. Unlike other nuclear areas, the Bronze Age civilization of central Asia was viewed as an experiment that failed, and the Late Bronze period was described as a period of degeneration and decay (Masson and Sarianidi 1972:137; Gupta 1979:175–76). Given recent discoveries in Margiana and Bactria of large urban sites like Gonur-depe 1 or Djarkutan and the wealth of Late Bronze materials, particularly metal artifacts from Bactrian tombs, this view has to be radically modified or altogether abandoned. Today, it seems more accurate to speak of a shift in settlements, rather than their decline. In particular, lowland areas, such as the Lower Murghab delta and the Bactrian plain, were then occupied on an intensive scale.

Our knowledge of settlements in Margiana has increased dramatically over the last ten years, and it is now one of the most systematically and carefully surveyed areas of southern central Asia. Most of the Margiana sites appear to be small and to have been occupied for a single period, contrasting sharply with the multiperiod settlements in the Kopet Dagh piedmont strip and even with the earlier lowland sites along the Tedjen river in the Geoksyur oasis. Even the larger sites in Margiana have relatively shallow deposits, which never exceed 4 m (and that figure is exceptional and only reached at a few sites, such as Gonur 1 and Taip 1), and have a maximum of two to three building levels. Depth-of-deposit calculations roughly estimating the duration of settlement are particularly misleading for the Margiana sites in that the major ones were obviously planned and fortified with massive structures built during a single period of occupation. In other words, although extensive excavations of Margiana sites are just beginning and although our understanding might change as a result of this work, preliminary investigations suggest a striking contrast with the more organically or gradually developed settlements of the piedmont zone. The tripartite (Kelleli-Gonur-Togolok) chronological division proposed by Sarianidi (1981a) seems sensible, although given the nature of the deposits, it will prove difficult to confirm through stratigraphic superpositioning. The Gonur phase is distinguished by the presence of stamp seal-amulets in a distinctive iconographic Murghab style (Sarianidi 1981b), handled cylinder seals at Taip-depe 1 (Masimov 1981a), the relatively common occurrence of potters' marks on vessels, the presence in minor proportions of gray and red burnished wares, a rough, heavily chaff-tempered handmade ware, the occurrence of steppe-bronze-incised vessels, the absence of

footed vessels with crimped or goffered feet and perforated wares, and the occurrence of biconical chlorite whorls with dot-in-circle designs. New features, such as bridged spouts at Gonur 1, also separate these materials from those found in the Kelleli oasis. Terra-cotta figurines continue but are heavier and coarser than those from Altyn or Kelleli and lack elaborate hairdos. There are suggestions, such as the cylinder seals from Taip-depe 1, that it may be possible to subdivide this phase into earlier Taip and later Gonur subphases, although on present evidence it is premature to do so.

Comparisons of the Margiana materials of the Gonur phase with remains from north Bactrian sites yield many parallels to both Sapalli and Djarkutan. The obvious continuity in the ceramic assemblages from these latter two sites (cf. Askarov 1977:65, fig. 32) renders precise chronological correlation with Margiana difficult, although the appearance of pots with complex spouts and the general heavier form of the Djarkutan wares make the synchronism between Gonur and Djarkutan most likely. In southern Bactria the best evidence for some duration of settlement comes from Hirdai-depe in the Daulatabad oasis and from the Dashli 3 site in the Dashli oasis. This latter site is difficult to interpret because it includes both the early palace, then fortress structure, and the so-called circular temple and because no general plan for the entire settlement has been published. A kidney-shaped chlorite vessel with incised design came from level 2 of the Dashli 3 fortress and another came from room 10 in the circular temple. Such objects, however, are also known from the presumably later Farukhabad and Nichkin oases and from Togolok 2, and a similarly shaped frit example was found in cenotaph 6 of the Mehrgarh VIII cemetery (Santoni n.d.:pl. IC). What is noteworthy is that the Dashli 3 palace site was seemingly abandoned and then reoccupied on a smaller scale (Sarianidi 1977:33), and it is during these later periods, particularly level 3, that evidence for local metallurgical production in association with graves containing metal artifacts has been recorded. In general, Dashli 1 ceramics compare closely with those at Sapalli and those at Dashli 3 with the Djarkutan and Molali stages of southern Uzbekistan (Askarov 1977:89–90). Although there are distinctions, such as the absence of grayware cups on slightly raised bases (Askarov 1977:179, table XV, 13–16) and short-necked spherical-shaped pots with everted rims (ibid., table XXIII, 1–9) on the Dashli sites, the assemblages of northern and southern Bactria are remarkably similar.

The excavation of over seven hundred graves from Djarkutan shows little evidence for sharp social distinctions, a fact that must be borne in mind when interpreting the wealth of materials from plundered tombs in northwestern Afghanistan. That is, while our conceptions may change with the excavation of other areas at Djarkutan and related sites in the Sherabad region of southern Uzbekistan, the scientifically excavated materials to date show relatively little differentiation with numbers of accompanying vessels ranging from 1 to 40 and bronze objects from 1 to 7 in Djarkutan phase burials. A similar picture seems to hold for the earlier Shahr-i Sokhta cemetery in Iranian Seistan, while evidence for differentiation from the roughly contemporaneous burials with elaborate remains found farther west at Shah-dad near Kerman is unclear. The apparent richness of the Bactrian Bronze Age is partly explained by the fact that thousands, if not tens of thousands, of tombs have been plundered over the past decade and scores of beautifully crafted metal artifacts, in particular, have been unearthed and removed from their original context. One possibly important distinction between northern and southern Bactrian burials is that in the former region males lay exclusively contracted on their right sides and females on their left, while at Dashli 3 the pattern may have been the reverse (Khlopina 1980). Although no accurate mapping of the southern Bactrian sites has been undertaken, most of the settlements are apparently small and not comparable in size to settlements in Margiana, like Taip-depe 1 (12 ha) or, particularly, Gonur-depe 1 (50 ha; Sarianidi, pers. comm.).

Radiocarbon evidence from Shortugai suggests that Beshkent-related materials follow directly on the earlier Harappan occupation of the plain, which, if correct, makes them earlier than those from the original Late Bronze Beshkent cemetery remains from southern Tadjikistan (Mandel'shtam 1968). It is possible to distinguish between the Beshkent cemetery remains on the basis of tomb construction, for the more elaborate catacomb type is later and presumably contemporary with the Vakhsh culture originally defined by Litvinskii (see Pᶜiankova 1981). Most of the wheel-thrown diagnostic ceramics from the Beshkent tombs are related to the later Molali phase of southern Uzbekistan. Finally, the Shortugai evidence also suggests that the Beshkent and later Vakhsh peoples may not have been exclusively pastoralists or herdsmen but lived in settlements and practiced agriculture (Francfort 1981), while the northern zone of Khoresmia, the Zeravshan Valley, and Fergana show increasing contact with or movement from the steppes of Kazakhstan and greater metallurgical activity at sites, such as L506 in the inner Kyzyl Kum (Vinogradov and Mamedov 1975).

Terminal Late Bronze or Togolok Phase, ca. 1800–1500 B.C.

In a general summary of materials from Margiana, Sarianidi (1981a:186) implies the possibility of distinguishing an earlier Togolok subphase from a later Takhirbai subphase, both of which were associated with the progressive retraction or movement of the Murghab River southward. Whether or not this distinction is valid, most of the Bronze Age sites in the two southernmost oases of Margiana contain Iron Age materials in their topmost levels and on their surfaces, suggesting a direct continuity with the beginnings of the Iron Age. Some of these Late Bronze settlements, such as Takhirbai 3 (22.5 ha), continue to be fairly large, although there does appear to be a general reduction in known settlement size from the Gonur phase. Incised steppe-bronze ceramics and handmade wares become more common, though wheel-thrown vessels with incised designs, including wavy lines, are also characteristic and constitute one of the distinguishing wares from the topmost levels at Tikar 1 and 2 in the Daulatabad oasis of northwestern Afghanistan, which also presumably represent a terminal Bronze Age occupation. An irrigation canal 20–25 m wide and traceable for 3 km was constructed near the largest Takhirbai 3 settlement, and definite local ceramic and metallurgical production is attested for the Margiana sites of this final phase. Aspects of continuity with the Gonur phase are strong and include continued production of stone stamp seals with distinctive naturalistic iconography; leaf-shaped tanged flint arrowheads; biconical chlorite whorls or ornaments with dot-in-circle designs; miniature stone columns; and numerous ceramic parallels, such as footed goblets, flower stands, raised deep bowls, and conical basins. Ceramic developments in northwestern Afghanistan seem to follow a pattern first observed for southern Uzbekistan at Djarkutan and in sites of northern Surkhandarya province, namely, two subphases, Kuzali and Molali, have been defined (Askarov 1977; Abdullaev, pers. comm.). The former is characterized by the appearance of finer ware than is typical for the preceding Djarkutan stage and by the presence of incised wavy-line designs and complex spouts, while the latter is distinguished by swelling or bulbous feet on the fruit stands and on raised vessels and by conical elongated pots on slightly raised bases. Sarianidi (1977) divides the sites of the Dashli oasis into an earlier western and later eastern group, largely on the frequency of incised wares on the surfaces of sites in the eastern half of the oasis, but it must be emphasized that the eastern group has received little systematic investigation. Similarly, materials from the Farukhabad and Nichkin oases even farther to the east, which include steppe-bronze ceramics and so-called Achaemenian wares found together with Bactrian Bronze pottery, are interpreted as terminal Late Bronze settlements that reflect a general west-to-east pattern of settlement or colonization. Here again, however, these sites have been only cursorily examined, and the west-to-east gradient argued for Bactria is far less clear than the north-to-south retraction of the Murghab in Margiana, since later Iron Age sites, such as the principal settlement of Dal'verzin, are scattered from the Dashli to the Farukhabad oases (see Sarianidi 1977:29, illus. 7). Ceramics from the large urban Farukhabad 1 site (1100 × 800 m or ca. 90 ha) are said to consist largely of light-slipped wares, but red-slipped footed bases and goblets, teapots, and spouted vessels also occur.

Farther east in southern Tadjikistan the later Beshkent, Vakhsh, and Hissar Valley cemetery sites, as well as the settlements of Kangurt Tut and Teguzak (Vinogradova et. al. 1979), have ceramic parallels with the northern Surkhandarya sites of Molali and presumably Buirachi-tepe 1 (Sagdullaev 1978:8) and with plundered cemetery sites in southern Bactria, such as Dashli 17 and 19. The Vakhsh catacomb burials, noteworthy for their elaborate construction with *dromoi* entrances and ritual use of fire, also contain metal artifacts, including knives and "razor"-type cutters, similar to objects found on the northern steppes. Karasuk-like materials (Askarov and Masson, pers. comm.) found on the Middle Zeravshan site of Sarazm may suggest that it was occupied either throughout a long period from late NMG III or NMG IV times to the end of the Bronze Age or perhaps in distinct periods, while the Andronovo-related Tazabagyab sites occur in Khoresmia as well as in the former extension of the Lower Zeravshan in direct proximity to the Zamanbaba sites and cemeteries. The presence on Zamanbaba sites of censers (*kormushki* or rectangular forms with pointed corners and an internal partition in one corner), cross-shaped beads, straight-sided vessels with holes beneath the rims, and numerous ceramic parallels to the southern Tadjikistan cemetery sites has lowered the relative date of the Zamanbaba culture (Sarianidi 1979; Askarov 1981) and proves that it was closely related to the Late Bronze Age sites in Bactria. The lower date for Zamanbaba also is in accord with the occasional presence of Tazabagyab materials (Gudzhaili variant) at the Zamanbaba settlements.

To the west of Margiana, the Kopet Dagh piedmont strip was now definitely reoccupied on a relatively substantial scale, as witnessed by remains from El'ken I (Marushchenko 1959), the Namazga-depe "tower," Tekkem-depe, Anau southern mound, and Ekin-depe and the Yangi-Q'ala cemetery site. While most of these sites appear small, some, such as Ekin-depe (see Ganyalin 1956:375–76) and possibly El'ken I, may have been reasonably large, perhaps approaching the size of Takhirbai 3 of ca. 22.5 ha. The new materials from Bactria and Margiana suggest that the so-called NMG VI wares of the piedmont may represent less a local evolution from earlier NMG V wares than a movement east to west of ce-

ramic forms initially produced in Bactria and Margiana (Alyekshin 1980). Finally, the Sumbar cemetery materials from the Middle Sumbar Valley of southwestern Turkmenistan clearly overlap in time both the Yangi Q'ala materials and the beginnings of the ancient Dakhistan culture. Khlopin (1977) likens certain forms with handles and/or complex spouts to those from necropolis A at Sialk and to Khurvin but claims that there are eight vessels identical in form to those from NMG VI contexts in the piedmont strip, including a storage jar with a characteristic concave rise above the base. The small finds from the Late Bronze tombs include small bronze flagons of the type known from Hissar III, Altyn, and Sapalli and southern Bactrian tombs; pins with vertically set cross-shaped tops like those from the Yangi Q'ala cemetery; and extremely well-made ribbed bronze arrow or lance heads which have parallels at Sialk VI and Hissar III. It is clear that these Sumbar tombs should date to the very end of the Bronze Age, ca. 1500 B.C. (see the arguments for relative dating of this material in Khlopina 1981).

Conclusion: Transition to the Iron Age

In Soviet central Asia one of the most significant findings of recent years is the clear evidence of continuity between Late Bronze Age sites and, despite the general absence of iron, what have come to be called Early Iron Age cultures that were first defined at Yaz-tepe in Margiana and on the Meshed-Missrian plain east of the Caspian (ancient Dakhistan). Continuity is manifest in the ceramics from the Sumbar cemeteries and the Parkhai Iron Age settlement (Khlopin 1975) and probably could be documented for small settlements east and west of Kyzyl Arvat in the western Kopet Dagh piedmont strip (see Masson 1956a:423–24). Similarly, chronological continuity with Yaz I culture sites in Margiana is evident, particularly in the southernmost Takhirbai and Togolok oases. Stratigraphic superpositioning of handmade painted Yaz I ware has been demonstrated on many sites of these two oases. While such superpositioning does not necessarily imply direct chronological continuity and while clear architectural features, such as the characteristic Early Iron construction of citadels on brick platforms, distinguish Iron Age from earlier sites, continuity is clear from the recent excavations at Kuchuk-tepe in southern Uzbekistan not far from Sapalli. Kuchuk-tepe shows a constellation of Early Iron architectural features, including a fortified core of rooms erected on a 4-m thick platform, associated with the ceramics of the terminal Bronze period as documented at Djarkutan. In other words, the excavators (Askarov and Al'baum 1979) argue convincingly for direct continuity with the gradual introduction and then disappearance of characteristic handmade wares. Ceramic correspondences, bronze sickles or knives with a hole at one end possibly used in carpet production (Khlopin 1980), and smoothed stone sickles link Kuchuk and other Yaz I–related sites to the beginnings of the amorphous Chust culture in the Fergana Valley, and architectural and ceramic parallels also link Chust and Yaz I sites with Mundigak V in southwestern Afghanistan and with Yam Tepe in the Upper Atrek Valley of Iranian Khorassan (Ricciardi 1980:58–60). In short, strong evidence for continuity from Bronze to Iron settlements seriously vitiates recent attempts (see Francfort n.d.) to extend back even further the dates for the initial Bronze settlements in Bactria and Margiana as compared with those from the earlier documented sites in the Kopet Dagh piedmont strip.

In ancient Dakhistan, sites on the Meshed-Missrian plain are impressively large and supported by extensive irrigation works that have recently been painstakingly mapped and studied (Lisitsina 1978, particularly figs. 12 and 15). While the major sites are scattered over broad areas, precluding exact population estimates (Lisitsina 1978:73–74), their dimensions are noteworthy: Madau, 224 ha; Izat Kuli, 180 ha; Tangsikildzha, 180 ha; Chialik, 36 ha; and Benguvan, 35 ha. Substages of this large and obviously complex culture have yet to be established, but two uncorrected radiocarbon dates (old half-life) of 1280 + 150 B.C. (LE 1052 from a lower level at Benguvan) and 590 + 150 B.C. (LE 1051 from an upper level at Tangsilkildzha, see table 3) suggest that the culture may have extended for ca. 700 years or well into the first millennium B.C. Farther east, the irrigation constructions in Margiana are also impressive, but the Yaz I–related settlements tend to be smaller than those of the preceding Bronze Age, with the 22-ha site of Kyzyl-tepe (Sagdullaev 1978) in northern Surkhandarya province of southern Uzbekistan noteworthy for its size. The material culture inventory of the Yaz I–related sites, which stretch from the Upper Atrek Valley possibly to Fergana, also seems impoverished as compared with the Late Bronze materials; elaborate metal objects, compartmented and figured stamp seals, and finely made, wheel-turned mass-produced ceramics no longer appear. In general, the remains east of the Dakhistan area exhibit a fairly dispersed settlement pattern with regional peculiarities that possibly represent a decentralized political order (Masson and Sarianidi 1972:162).

Addendum 1—May 15, 1984

The dates in tables 4 and 5 were obtained from P. M. Dolukhanov and L. B. Kircho when the author visited the Soviet Union in September 1983. The dates from Namazga-depe, which were analyzed in Rome, will be published in *Sovyetskaya Arkheologiya* in an article by P. M. Dolukhanov, M. Tosi, and A. Ya. Shchetenko entitled "Absolutnaya khronologiya eneolita: Epokhi bronzi Yuzhnoi Turkmenii." In a comment on the Namazga dates from the Rome laboratory, Dolukhanov suggests that dates R1303, R1306a, R1309, and R1310 were partially contaminated for a variety of contextual reasons. Also, the late R1305 sample came from the bottom of the stratigraphic hiatus in building levels separating Namazga V from Namazga VI. That is, this date apparently could relate either to the upper Namazga V or lowermost Namazga VI period. The rest of the dates follow a fairly precise stratigraphic sequence. He concludes: "Judging from the[se] dates obtained, the transition Namazga V/Namazga VI occurred between 3800–3500 B.P. [1850–1550 B.C.; 2330–2160/2110–2000 B.C. MASCA corr.]" or 2395–2165 and 1945–1745 B.C. CRD 1σ. His corrected date for this transition at Namazga-depe agrees remarkably well with the date argued for in this chapter and provides a reasonably secure, independent confirmation of the higher chronology.

The dates for Namazga IV levels at Altyn-depe were presented by L. B. Kircho in her paper "Kul'turnaya evolutsiya v epokhu formirovaniya rannegorodskoi tsivilizatsii (po materialam raskopok Altyn-depe)" at the second U.S.-USSR archaeological symposium, Arkheologiya Srednei Azii i Blizhnego Vostoka, in Samarkand, Uzbekistan, September 1983. The discrepant CRD 1σ calibrated date of 1995–1765 B.C. (3540 ± 60 B.C. date) from excavation 5, level 8 room, apparently consisted of a very minute sample of charcoal. The differences in the dates from the yards and pits compared with those from rooms cannot yet be explained (Kircho, pers. comm.); hopefully, future determinations will help solve this problem. In any event, when corrected, the three relatively consistent dates from the level 5 or latest NMG IV level rooms again strongly support the chronology suggested in this chapter.

Addendum 2—September 26, 1985

A. Isakov, director of the ongoing excavations at the important site of Sarazm, 45 km east of Samarkand in the Zeravshan Valley, has kindly provided the following uncorrected dates and their periodization.

We have converted the furnished B.C. dates back to what must have been the original 5568 B.P. half-life determinations by adding 1950. We then calibrated them, to the CRD 1σ B.C. dates, as shown.

Sarazm			*As furnished*	*5568 Half-life*	*CRD 1σ B.C.*
Period I	(excv. 4, level 1)	LE 2172	3100 ± 60 BC	5050 ± 60	3905–3775
Period I	(excv. 4, level 1)	LE 2173	2930 ± 30 BC	4880 ± 30	3790–3645
Period I	(excv. 2, level 1)	LE 2174	2990 ± 30 BC	4940 ± 30	3870–3660
Period II	(excv. 3, level 1)	LE 1806	2510 ± 50 BC	4460 ± 50	3365–3020
Period II	(excv. 3, level 2)	LE 1808	2280 ± 40 BC	4230 ± 40	2970–2795
Period III	(excv. 2, level 3)	LE 1807	1890 ± 40 BC	3840 ± 40	2415–2185
Period III	(excv. 3, level 2)	LE 1420	1840 ± 80 BC	3790 ± 80	2410–2115

The calibrations seem to indicate that Sarazm I dates to the early fourth and Sarazm II to the late fourth, early third millennium. The dates for Sarazm III suggest that some occupation at the site may have lasted into the last half of the third millennium.

Finally, the following surprising and discrepant dates (given as CRD 1σ) for the Late Bronze Sumbar cemetery in southwestern Turkmenistan and the Djebel Cave in northern Turkmenistan were reported in *Radiocarbon* 26, 2 (1984): 224–25:

			5568 Half-life	*CRD 1σs*
Sumbar cemetery		P-3079	4860 ± 60	3790–3555 B.C.
Djebel Cave	(depth .2–25 m)	P-3080	2170 ± 210	420 B.C.–20 A.D.
Djebel Cave	(depth .3 m)	P-3083	1360 ± 180	450–880 A.D.
Djebel Cave	(depth .4 m)	P-3082	4520 ± 240	3405–2925 B.C.
Djebel Cave	(depth .8–.85 m)	P-3081	6140 ± 80	5250–4935 B.C.

Addendum 3—January 3, 1990

Professor C. C. Lamberg-Karlovsky, director of the Peabody Museum, Harvard University has kindly allowed me to publish the following dates from Margiana and southern Uzbekistan. The samples brought back from the Soviet Union by Mr. F. Hiebert, a graduate student at Harvard, were processed by Beta Analytic Lab in October 1989 and have been calibrated with the CALIB program.

Southern Uzbekistan			
Djarkutan	Beta-33557	1888 B.C.	(2125–1695 B.C.)
Margiana			
Togolok 21	Beta-33564	1846 B.C.	(1920–1680 B.C.)
Gonur South	Beta-33562	2067 B.C.	(2290–1930 B.C.)
Gonur Krem'l	Beta-33563	2334 B.C.	(2490–2140 B.C.)
Gonur North	Beta-33558	2921 B.C.	(3035–2902 B.C.
Gonur North	Beta-33559	1554 B.C.	(1685–1585 B.C.)
Gonur North	Beta-33560	1936 B.C.	(2032–1883 B.C.)
Gonur North	Beta-33561	1883 B.C.	(2030–1694 B.C.)
Yaz-4	Beta-33565	276 B.C.	(400–123 B.C.)
Yaz-19	Beta-33566	1415 B.C.	(1512–1309 B.C.)

These dates clearly support a late third to early second millennium B.C. date for the Margiana and, correspondingly, Bactrian Bronze Age sites. Mr. Hiebert, who has studied recently excavated Bronze Age materials from Margiana, and Professor Lamberg-Karlovsky believe that the Margiana materials fall into two basic periods, the earlier of which overlaps completely with the Namazga V materials as documented at Altyn-depe. At Gonur, they date the earlier period roughly 2400–2200 B.C., followed by a short break, and then a reoccupation extending roughly from 2000 to 1800 B.C. (personal communication).

Eight

Culture and Environment in the Prehistoric Caucasus: The Neolithic through the Early Bronze Age

Petar Glumac, Department of Materials Science, University of Southern California
David Anthony, Hartwick College

Outline

Background to the Present Study

In the decade between 1965 and 1975, the study of Caucasian archaeology was greatly advanced by the publication of a series of regional syntheses. Among the most important were Khanzadyan (1967), Sardaryan (1967), Kushnareva and Chubinishvili (1970), Burney and Lang (1971), and Munchaev (1975). A detailed review of Munchaev's synthesis by Kushnareva and Dzhaparidze (1978) is very useful. Subsequently, these syntheses have been added to substantially through important studies by Kiguradze (1976), Lordkipanidze (1977), Andreeva (1977), Munchaev (1982), Korobkova and Gadzhiev (1983), Kavtaradze (1983), and Sagona (1984).

Physical and Cultural Geography

The Caucasian region (fig. 1) is linked both culturally and geologically with eastern Anatolia and northwestern Iran. Through its fertile valleys run the routes that connect the Iranian plateau with the seaports and settlements of Asia Minor, and nations have contended from the remote past for its temporary possession. It is at the same time a region of inaccessible defiles, arid plateaus, and forbidding mountains, among which a multitude of isolated populations have made their homes. In the first cen-

Text initially submitted February 1986

tury A.D. Pliny noted that Greek traders seeking to deal with the merchants of Colchis at Dioscurias, near the mouth of the Rioni on the Black Sea, required 130 interpreters (*Natural History* VI.5.15). The broken nature of the terrain has nurtured regionalization and prevented cultural or political unification through all but a few brief periods. A description of the major territorial/administrative units follows.

The Greater Caucasus, the highest and most impassable mountain system west of the Pamirs, extends some 1,100 km southeastward from the Black Sea to the Caspian, effectively limiting cultural exchange between the Eurasian steppes and the territories to the south. The peaks rise to elevations of 16,000 to 18,000 feet. The Greater Caucasus is pierced by only two year-round passes in its central portion on the headwaters of the Terek; only one of these (the Darial) was usable by wheeled vehicles prior to the improvement of the other (the Mamison) in 1874. Alternate passes were open only to horses, and only for a few summer months. The eastern end of the system is passable along the Caspian shore by the Derbent Gate, but the Black Sea shore is broken, remote, and difficult.

We thank K. Rubinson and P. Kohl for providing us with several key Russian sources. Part of this research was done with the assistance of NSF grant BNS-8712070.

The north-facing north Caucasian piedmont is fertile, copper-rich, and bubbling with mineral springs. The western Kuban region is the most productive and overlooks what was once the vast delta of the meandering Kuban River, beyond which lie arid steppes. The Stavropol watershed is an upland separating the Kuban from the Terek drainages. The Terek flows eastward into the Caspian, fed by tributaries that drain the intermontane Chechen-Ingushesht valleys. At the broad eastern end of the Greater Caucasus, east of the latter region, lies Daghestan, divided into a lowland portion that overlooks the Caspian shore and a much greater upland portion that consists of high limestone tablelands cut by deep valleys and broken by high peaks. All of these regions, particularly the latter two, were united to Transcaucasian cultures through the central passes, but they also exhibited many divergent local traits. In these regions stylistic/typological links with the south are not reliable chronological indicators, for considerable lag in transmission and local conservatism might have occurred. This uncertainty in distinguishing regional from chronological variation is in fact symptomatic of the Caucasus area as a whole and greatly increases the difficulty of constructing a reliable general chronology.

South of the glaciated Greater Caucasus ridge lies the transverse trough of the Rioni and Kura River valleys, providing a corridor that passes from the Black Sea to the Caspian. The southern slopes of the mountains, the Rioni watershed, and the upper and middle Kura watershed are contained in Georgia, which is, accordingly, a region of great ecological diversity. The Rioni drains ancient Colchis, a semitropical, luxuriantly forested (beech, oak, walnut, citrus) land open to humid winds from the Black Sea. The Surami Range separates the Rioni and Kura drainages and creates a rainshadow to its east, so the valley of the Kura, though fertile, is increasingly dry and steppelike as one moves to the east. The capital of Georgia, Tbilisi, lies near the juncture of the major east-west and north-south communication routes passing through the province. The dry, open steppes of the lower Kura Valley are contained within Azerbaijan.

South of the Kura-Rioni depression the Lesser Caucasus rises toward the Armenian plateau. The Lesser Caucasus range with a maximum elevation of 10,000–12,000 feet is a buttress that marks the northern limit of the high volcanic plateau of Armenia where the average elevation is 6,000 feet, a region of wide tablelands underlain by andesites and basalts. While the majority of the plateau is relatively level, the terrain is broken by isolated volcanic peaks, interior ridges, down-folded lake basins, and deeply eroded river valleys. The Araxes curves across the plateau from the folded mountains at the junction of the Lesser Caucasus and the east Anatolian systems, flows through the Nakhichevan region toward the

Urmia basin, then returns northward to water the Mil'sk steppe before joining the Kura in Azerbaijan.

All of the region within the USSR south of the Greater Caucasus ridge is referred to as Transcaucasia. Several important communication routes cross and unite Transcaucasia. The primary north-south routes follow the central passes through the Greater Caucasus, branching south of the primary ridge to lead southwestward to ancient Colchis and the Black Sea coast via the Mamison Pass or southeastward to Tbilisi via the Darial Pass. From Tbilisi the traditional route led southward up onto the Armenian plateau, to Erevan on the Araxes. Below Erevan this north-south route met one of the primary east-west routes and, therefore, branched either southeastward down the Araxes to Tabriz on Lake Urmia or westward to Erzerum and eastern Anatolia. Both of the primary east-west routes pass through Tabriz or the Urmia basin, which was why Tabriz was, for centuries until the construction of the Suez Canal, the principal market of the European-Persian trade. The northern route from Tabriz led north out of the Urmia basin up onto the Armenian plateau, then passed northwestward by Mt. Ararat to Erzerum and eastern Anatolia or to the Black Sea port of Trebizond. The southern route passed west out of the Urmia basin by Lake Van to Elazig and Malatya, where it met the great highway leading from central Anatolia to Diyarbakir and northern Syria. Productive territories near nodes on these routes—Tbilisi, Erevan, Urmia, Malatya/Elazig—became pockets of relatively dense settlement separated by large areas that were lightly or seasonally settled.

Neolithic

The Neolithic period in the Caucasus is poorly understood, tenuously documented, and has produced little or no evidence of domesticated plants or animals. It is possible that many of the sites attributed to the Neolithic were in fact contemporary with the Eneolithic. The absence of radiocarbon dates, direct artifactual links to the Near East, or multiperiod stratified open-air sites inhibits our ability to construct a regional chronology or even to provide a precise chronological placement for individual sites.

Soviet archaeologists divide the Neolithic into an Early and Late phase, both of which are thought to span the ninth to the seventh millennia B.C. (Formozov 1973; Nebieridze 1972). Sites of the Early Neolithic are said to exhibit strong links to local Upper Paleolithic and Mesolithic cultures (Kushnareva and Dzhaparidze 1978:270) based on the predominance of microlithic stone tools. These sites represent hunting/gathering societies and lack ceramics. Changes in the relative proportion of microlithic to macrolithic flaked stone tools and in the proportion of local or nonlocal lithic resources are thought to reflect a shift from mobile hunting/gathering to increased sedentism and initial attempts at food production. In sites attributed to the Late Neolithic phase there are proportionately more macrolithic chipped stone tools and more local lithic materials, as well as new types such as hoes, querns, axes, and adzes with ground and polished surfaces or working edges, and crude ceramic vessels.

There are, of course, serious limitations to the use of microlithic versus macrolithic chipped stone tools as chronological indicators. In many parts of the Caucasus, particularly in Colchis and the Kuban, microlithic technologies continued in use from the Mesolithic through the Early Bronze Age (Korobkova and Gadzhiev 1983:134). This distinction might well be functional rather than chronological.

The majority of the sites attributed to the Neolithic period in the Caucasus are surface collections located during areal surveys, but there are a few excavated stone tool workshops, settlements, and even burials. None of these is firmly dated.

Georgia

All of the Neolithic sites reported in Georgia occur in the western part of the region, in the Colchis lowland and along the Black Sea littoral. Early Neolithic assemblages occur in southern Colchis in the Makharadze-Kobuleti region, at the interior site of Anaseuli I and the estuarine site of Kobuleti at the mouth of the Kintrishi River (Nebieridze 1972). Microliths made of obsidian predominate at both sites, as do axes and adzes with polished working edges. A similar assemblage was recovered from Khupynipshakva cave on the river Kodori 30 km south of Sukhumi in northern Colchis. Munchaev (1975:66) has interpreted this site as a specialized fishing station, implying increased sedentism and economic specialization.

The Late Neolithic phase of Georgia is represented by a larger number of sites. They include Anaseuli II, the cave site of Samele-klde on the river Dzhruchula in Imereti, and four sites located on the Black Sea littoral—Odishi near Zugdidi, Kistrik near Gudauti in Abkhaz, Nizhne-Shilovskaya near the town of Adler, and Chkhortoli. This last is a unique open-air site on a river terrace and has deep undisturbed layers of cultural deposit (Kushnareva and Dzhaparidze 1978:270).

All of the sites ascribed to the Late Neolithic phase have yielded ceramic sherds which derive from crude, handmade wares tempered with grit, sand, and shell. The pottery from sites in the Black Sea littoral, such as Nizhne-Shilovskaya and Kistrik, is undecorated, whereas that from the Colchis region of western Georgia,

such as Samele-klde cave, Anaseuli II, and Odishi, has ornamentation in the form of zigzag lines and round external extrusions (Nebieridze 1972:116).

In Late Neolithic sites local flint replaces nonlocal obsidian as the predominantly used raw material, perhaps implying a diminution in exchange or movement. The predominance of microlithic forms continues in the Late Neolithic phase. The majority of these are geometric, with bifacial retouch. Formozov's (1962:38) attempt to correlate these chronologically with Natufian types is unconvincing. Late Neolithic sites have yielded triangular projectile points at Nizhne-Shilovskaya, Kistrik, Anaseuli II, and Odishi.

Architecture is rare in Neolithic sites from the Caucasus. A portion of a house floor in which a grinding stone was embedded and an associated one-meter-deep storage pit appeared at Kistrik. There is some debate over the interpretation of some features at Nizhne-Shilovskaya as pit houses.

There is some divergence of opinion concerning the subsistence economy of the Late Neolithic phase in the western Caucasus, but there is little direct evidence. Burnt grain, too charred to identify, was found at Kistrik. Because there is an overall increase in the number of types of microlithic tools as well as in the introduction of new types such as hoes, sickle blades, mortars, and grinding stones, Nebieridze (1972:116) feels that sedentary horticulture was the mainstay of the economy. Munchaev (1975:71), on the other hand, feels that during the Late Neolithic phase there was a growing reliance on agriculture and stockbreeding but that the mode of subsistence and settlement was not yet fully sedentary.

Armenia

Sardaryan (1967:277) reports two "preceramic neolithic" sites at Zaghe and Barozhi, as well as a series of settlements in the Ararat plain, which he attributes to the ceramic Neolithic. These are Mashtots-blur, Khzyak-blur, Terteri-dzor, St. Tapa, and Agvesi-bner (Sardaryan 1967:278–79; Kushnareva and Chubinishvili 1970:42, fig. 15).

The hilltop settlement of Berin-Khatunarkh in the Echmiadzin region is 150 m in diameter and had two separate culture layers. The upper strata contained medieval material, but below this were seven superimposed strata attributed to the Neolithic (Torosyan, Mikaelyan, and Dabedzhyan 1970:386–87). The stone tools include nuclei cores, blades, scrapers, microlithic tool forms, mortars, grinding stones, hoes, and axes. Bone awls and sickle handles were found as well as three sherds of a flat-bottomed vessel. Many animal bones are said to have been recovered but they are not described.

Azerbaijan

Stratified rock shelters containing Mesolithic and Neolithic materials are reported from the Beyuk-dash area of Kobistan on the Caspian near the Baku peninsula (Formozov 1969, 1973). The excavations revealed geometric forms of flint tools in all of the layers documenting technological continuity between the Mesolithic and Neolithic. Sherds of coarse pottery with conical bottoms occurred in the Neolithic levels. Neolithic sites are also reported from the Gandzha-chay basin. The most important of these is a lithic workshop near Kilikdage where 6 m of deposit revealed three distinct levels of the Neolithic, Eneolithic, and Early Bronze Age. The stratigraphic positioning of tool types made it possible to date other sites and single finds in the area. Kilkidage is one of the few sites in the Caucasus where Neolithic strata are overlaid by Eneolithic strata.

Several burials, including some under kurgans, have been ascribed to the Neolithic period in Azerbaijan. In the Kichikdash region the site of Firuz (Muradova and Rustamov 1972:477–78) revealed Early Bronze Age material stratified over a Neolithic layer that was 15–20 cm thick and devoid of pottery. The lithics from the Neolithic layer consisted of geometric and trapezoidal microliths in the form of blades and scrapers. The excavators recognized a burial platform near the site which they attributed to the Neolithic occupants. Below the platform were eleven skulls and some disarticulated bones. The burial goods consisted of several necklaces with different types of beads and adornments made of paste, animal teeth, stone pendants, and shells. Implements of stone and bone were also buried with the dead. Formozov (1973:38) has classified Firuz and other sites in this area as Early Neolithic, based on the fact that the lithic industries associated with them were "archaic" type having close affinities to those of the local Upper Paleolithic. There are, however, no other data indicating a chronological placement for these sites, which might, therefore, date to any period preceding the later Early Bronze Age. The Firuz grave goods resemble those at Nalchik in the north Caucasus in a cemetery dated broadly to the fourth millennium B.C.

Two other burials found beneath Early Bronze Age tumuli, or kurgans, at Stepanakert, kurgans 119 and 125, have been attributed to the Neolithic (Munchaev 1975:64). In fact, there are no artifactual or stratigraphic data suggesting a placement earlier than the Eneolithic, and if it were not for the few ceramic sherds from 119 (which do not conform to documented Kura-Araxes types), these burials might be placed in the Early Bronze Age with others from this site.

Daghestan and the West Caspian

Most sites in Daghestan, except Tarnair and Buynask, are known only from surface collections (Kotovich 1964). These two sites are thought to be single-period ones, the stone tool assemblage of which largely consists of microlithic blades, scrapers, and pencil-like nuclei. Wedge-shaped axes-adzes with polished working edges were also present. Kotovich thinks that the chipped stone tool industry resembles "Tardenoisian" forms, and he therefore dates the sites to the Early Neolithic phase.

Pottery, described only as "archaic," has appeared at several sites in the vicinity of the town of Rugudzha in Upper Daghestan. The ceramics from Malin-karat consisted of red-ochre-colored sherds of a pot and a cup. Similar crude ceramic sherds came from Arkhinda and Muchu-bakh-bakli. The clay was tempered with coarse grit, and some of the surfaces had a slip. The stone tool industry is macrolithic, based on large blades and scrapers with unifacial retouch (Kotovich 1964:203–11).

In the west Caspian area, all of the settlements are located on the shores of lakes or on the banks of rivers flowing into the Caspian. None of the sites was excavated but intense surface collecting trips were made to the sites of Achikulak, Makhmud-mektep, Yestak-huduk, and Terekli-mektep, as well as to a site on the collective farm Bozhigan. All of the sites are ascribed a Neolithic date. The stone tool assemblages consist of microlithic blades from flint and obsidian, as well as segmented geometric microblades with secondary retouch (Munchaev 1975:58). The obsidian came from the north-central Caucasus.

Eneolithic

Currently, more than seventy settlements attributed to the Eneolithic periods are reported from the Caucasus, the majority of which are located in Transcaucasia, especially in Georgia and Azerbaijan (see table 1 and fig. 2). A thorough survey of the Eneolithic sites in the Caucasus was published by Munchaev in 1975 and again in 1982. These two studies, incorporating a great quantity of archaeological detail and containing exhaustive bibliographies, provide the basic background for studying Eneolithic economy and chronology.

Based on a large amount of settlement data and a scatter of radiocarbon dates, Munchaev (1982) has delineated two major regional and chronological groups in Transcaucasia: the "Central Transcaucasian" or "Shulaveris/ Shomu-tepe" group and the "Southern Transcaucasian" or "Nakhichevan-Mil'sk-Mugani" group. In addition to these, there are a few contemporary sites known from elsewhere in the Caucasus, such as the settlement of Ginchi in Upper Daghestan, the settlement of Agubekovo and the Nalchik cemetery in north-central Caucasus, and the Macharskoe settlement on the Black Sea littoral.

Central Transcaucasian Group

The Central Transcaucasian group consists of three distinct geographic clusters of sites as follows: (1) several settlements located on the banks of the Khrami River (Shulaveris-gora, Dangreuli-gora, Gadachrili-gora, and Imiris-gora). These occupy a total area of 500 ha and are all located within 0.5–1.7 km of each other. (2) At the confluence of the Khrami and Mashavera rivers, 8 km west of the first group, a group of five eroded tells occupies an area of 800 ha. Three of these have been excavated (Arukhlo I, II, III). Collectively, these two sets of sites are known as the Kvemo-Kvartli sites of Georgia. (3) The third group is 50 km east of the Kvemo-Kvartli sites in the Akstafi River valley of west Azerbaijan, near its confluence with the Kura River.

There is almost universal agreement among Soviet archaeologists that the "Central Transcaucasian" group consists of chronologically the oldest Eneolithic sites in Transcaucasia. All of the sites in this group are tells, many of which have been impacted by erosion and modern land use. They are of variable height and have up to 10 m of cultural deposits incorporating several building levels. All of the houses are circular or oval in plan, made of plano-convex bricks, and the diameter of the dwellings ranged from 2.5 to 5.0 m while the storage structures ranged from 0.75 to 2.0 m in diameter. These circular, one-room dwellings resemble the "keyhole plan" dwellings of the Middle Halaf period in Mesopotamia. Some authors speculate that the round house tradition of Halaf may have originated in Transcaucasia (Dzhavahishvili 1973; Mellaart 1975:205).

A single flexed burial was found at Baba-dervish and is the only known burial from the Central Transcaucasian group.

These sites are thought to represent fully food-producing settlements based on irrigation (Munchaev 1982:107; Kushnareva and Dzhaparidze 1978; Kushnareva and Lisitsina 1979) and possibly incorporating the use of light plows (Kushnareva and Lisitsina 1979). Many types of cultigens have been recovered from Eneolithic sites in Transcaucasia, including five types of wheat and four types of barley, millet, rye, oats, peas, lentils, and grapes (Lisitsina and Prishchepenko 1977:47). No local developmental phase is documented for the domestic plants and animals that characterize the Eneolithic economy.

Large numbers of flint and obsidian tools are the most common artifacts. These are typologically quite diverse, including microliths. A great number of sickle blades have been found, some still in their wooden or bone hafts

and others still having bitumen adhering to them. These are the oldest sickles in Transcaucasia. The obsidian came from the Parvan site in Georgia and Atis in Armenia.

No stone arrowheads were found. The sites yielded many bone implements but these are not chronologically sensitive. Bits of copper are also present.

Sherds from ceramic vessels occur on all Central Transcaucasian sites, but not in great numbers (Kushnareva and Chubinishvili 1970: fig. 4B, 8–10). Thus, only seventy-five sherds were recovered from all nine building levels at Shulaveris-gora. Clay anthropomorphic figurines and sling ammunition are also encountered. The ceramics from this group are almost exclusively plain, crude, poorly fired, tempered with straw, sand, and crushed obsidian. They are predominantly jar forms with flat bottoms and usually without handles. The surface is fired to black, gray, or yellow color and there is little decoration. At Shomu-tepe there are black and drab-red vessels with wide bases and ornaments of circles and dots that were impressed using a stick. Decoration in the form of conical appliqué in rows near the top of the vessel, curvilinear appliqué in the shape of bars and crescents, or incised chevron and zigzag ornamentation is also encountered. Similar incised decoration and conical appliqué are known from Neolithic sites in western Georgia such as Idishi and Anaseuli II (Kiguradze 1976:157), as well as at the Eneolithic site of Ginchi in Upper Daghestan (Munchaev 1982:112).

There is considerable debate about the nomenclature and internal chronology of the Central Transcaucasian group of sites. The issue boils down to one of "lumpers" and "splitters." Radiocarbon dates, while few in number and of little use for a precise internal chronology, help us to place this group and the Eneolithic period generally in absolute terms as having lasted through the late sixth and fifth millennia B.C.

Kiguradze used the artifactual data from stratified sequences of the sites in Kvemo-Kvartli to establish a relative chronology for the sites in this group. The author is the first to admit that the available radiocarbon dates do not support his scheme. Others have criticized the methodology and the applicability of the scheme to sites outside of Kvemo-Kvartli (Munchaev 1982:103; Chubinishvili and Chelidze 1978:64–66). Most scholars do agree that the single radiocarbon date from Shomu-tepe is aberrant and that the settlement of Shulaveris-gora is typologically older. Munchaev states that, despite the radiocarbon dates, Shulaveris-gora is the oldest site and that the west Azerbaijan sites of Shomu-tepe and Toiyre-tepe are chronologically contemporary with Imiris-gora, Khramis-didi-gora, and Arukhlo I in Kvemo-Kartli (1982:113). He further states that there are no direct ceramic parallels with Mesopotamian materials. It seems that many of the impressed wares of the Central Transcaucasian group have vague similarities to those found in the Urmia basin of northwest Iran (Mellaart 1975:204; Kushnareva and Dzhaparidze 1978:272).

The sudden appearance here without precedent of a fully food-producing economy must be explained by contacts and immigration from other parts of the Near East, as can be seen from some common artifact categories (architecture, plano-convex bricks, ceramic stamp seals, etc.). Most Western archaeologists would see the adoption of food production as due to density-dependent demographic stresses. In Transcaucasia there is not sufficient site density in the Neolithic to cause stresses of the type that might warrant the adoption of a food-producing economy. Therefore, until more data come to light, the possibility that the Eneolithic economy and technology were brought from elsewhere remains a strong one.

Southern Transcaucasian Group

The first known Eneolithic site in the Caucasus was Kyul-tepe, located 8 km northeast of Nakhichevan. The whole tell was excavated and was shown to have 22 m of deposit with four distinct cultural strata. The bottom layer, 9 m thick, was Eneolithic and was separated by a 20–40 cm sterile layer from the 9.5 m of deposit above that belongs to the Kura-Araxes culture of the Early Bronze Age (Abibulaev 1965).

Toward the top of the Eneolithic deposit the excavators found the poorly preserved remains of thirteen round and rectilinear dwellings. In between the dwellings and under house floors were seventy-three flexed burials, twenty-five of which contained burial goods (ceramics, beads, obsidian).

Most of the chipped stone tools were made from obsidian from the Atis and Sisian sources in Armenia. The basic forms were prismatic blades up to 10–15 cm long, scrapers, and sickle blades. Also found were stone querns, hoes, polished ax-adzes, and maces, as well as seven pieces of arsenical copper, including an awl and some beads. Copper artifacts have also appeared on sites of the Central Transcaucasian group, at Gargalar-tepesi and Khramis-didi-gora. No ceramic figurines were encountered but there was abundant clay sling ammunition.

The crude ceramics are similar to those of the Central Transcaucasian group except that the wares from Kul-tepe I exhibit a greater range of forms and have no decoration (Kushnareva and Chubinishvili 1970:37, fig. 11; Munchaev 1975:103, fig. 10; Munchaev 1982:155, fig. XLIII). Most common were sherds of a light-colored, crude, poorly fired fabric with straw and occasionally with sand temper. The variety of forms includes pots, bowls, and cups, all of which have flat bottoms with occasional lug handles but no decoration. Twenty painted

sherds and one complete painted vessel were found at Kul-tepe I. This small pot (Munchaev 1982:117, fig. XLIV, no. 1) is a Halaf import. The painted sherds were divided into two groups. The first consisted of well-fired wares having a burnished surface on which are painted geometric motifs. These are also said to have been imported, and Kearton (1970:124) has compared them to the ceramics from Hajji Firuz (Voigt 1983) in the Urmia basin. The sherds of the second group were well fired and had vegetable temper. Geometric motifs were applied with black, red, and yellow paint. These are thought to have been locally made (Munchaev 1982).

Coarse as well as painted ceramic sherds similar to those of Kul-tepe I have been recovered from unexcavated sites in the Mil'sk steppe at Shakh-tepe, Bezymyanoe-tepe, and Kyamil-tepe (Kushnareva and Chubinishvili 1970:pl. 12). The majority of these sherds were of crude wares, but twenty of them were painted. These were of a buff-colored background with simple geometric patterns such as stripes and chevrons applied with a purplish brown to black paint. Munchaev states that they do not resemble Halafian pottery (1982:120).

Eneolithic painted ceramics also came from sites in the Karanbakh and Mugani steppes (Kushnareva and Chubinishvili 1970:39, fig. 13). Surface collections from the sites of Misharchai II, IV–VI and Gurudere 1–6 produced sherds similar to those from Kyul-tepe I and the sites in the Mil'sk steppe (Munchaev 1982:118; Kushnareva and Chubinishvili 1970:39, fig. 13).

Alikemek-tepesi, located on the bank of the Inchenchai River, is the only excavated Eneolithic site in the Mugani steppe. Four meters of cultural deposit occupying one hectare contained six building horizons. There was a progressive change in the architecture from circular to rectilinear dwellings. In the uppermost strata, ten burials in between the homes and under house floors were all flexed, covered with red ochre, and each individual had a ceramic cup placed next to the head.

The chipped stone tools were predominantly of flint and less so of obsidian which came from the Kelbadzharskoe source, some 300 km away. Bitumen was found adhering to some of the sickle blades. As was the case at Kul-tepe I, there were no ceramic figurines, but there were many clay balls for slings, of which as many as 70 to 130 were found together.

Three distinct types of ceramics were identified at Alikemek-tepesi. The first group appeared only in the topmost strata and consists of sherds whose surface had impressed vertical lines made with a comb. This type is not limited to the South Transcaucasian group but is found in the central Transcaucasian region at the site of Kechili III in Azerbaijan southeast of the Shulaveris/Shomu-tepe sites, and at the site of Rioni in the Marneuli region of Georgia. The second group occurs in all of the strata and consists of light buff-colored undecorated pottery similar to that from Kul-tepe I. More than two hundred sherds of painted pottery appeared here, more than at any other Eneolithic site. Many of these are similar to the sherds from Kul-tepe I and the sites in the Mil'sk steppe (Munchaev 1982:157, fig. XLV; 158, fig. XLVI).

The majority of the ceramics of the South Transcaucasian group have parallels in technology and style of painting closer to the ceramics from sites in the Urmia basin than to Halafian ceramics (Munchaev 1975:125–28). Thus, for example, sherds from vessels that were painted on the inside and outside of the upper surface and those with a red slip and jabbed decoration from the Karanbakh steppe sites of Ilanli-tepe, Geoy-tepe, and Kul-tepe are said to have direct analogies to the painted vessels from Dalma-tepe in northwest Iran. The finger-impressed wares from Alikemek-tepesi and other Mugani sites are said to have exact parallels in the lower strata at Dalma-tepe.

Armenia

The best-known excavated site is the settlement of Tekhuta located 3 km south of Echmiadzin. There was a single 1.6 m stratum of Eneolithic deposit consisting of round dwellings that had open hearths in the floors. Tekhuta is the only Eneolithic site having portable clay braziers, which is a characteristic feature of the subsequent Kura-Araxes culture.

The stone industry consists of macrolithic blades, but no microblades, of flint and obsidian (Torosyan 1976). The 3a obsidian source at Mt. Ararat is located across the river from the site and has been exploited since the Halaf period. Obsidian from this source came from the contemporary settlement of Tilki-tepe in the Lake Van region of eastern Anatolia (Mellaart 1975:205). A knife and two awls made of arsenical copper were also found at Tekhuta.

Two types of ceramic sherds appeared at Tekhuta (Kushnareva and Chubinishvili 1970:40, fig. 14; Munchaev 1975:109, fig. 12). The first and most numerous type was a coarse ware similar to that from Kul-tepe I and Alikemek-tepesi, although here there is a greater variety of forms. Among the undecorated wares was a yellow, well-fired one with a burnished surface, usually with small forms such as cups. The second group had black or red paint on a yellow background with vertical lines from the neck down. Munchaev (1975:122; 1982:123) says that they are north Ubaid-like, and he draws a parallel with the ceramics from the top layer (III) at Tilki-tepe, which are said to postdate Halaf, an opinion also held by Kushnareva and Dzhaparidze (1978:272). Munchaev also equates Tekhuta with the north Ubaid aspect of Pisdeli-tepe in the Urmia basin.

Daghestan

The settlement of Ginchi, located at 1,600 m elevation on a terrace of the Giderilor River in Upper Daghestan is the only Eneolithic site of the Transcaucasian type so far found in the northeastern Caucasus, across the Greater Caucasus range. Here, as at many sites in Transcaucasia, the 1.2 m Eneolithic layer was overlaid by an Early Bronze Age Kuro-Araxes culture layer. The architecture consisted predominantly of one-room rectilinear houses made of stone, although there were several circular dwellings and a semisubterranean one as well. The settlement was defended by a stone wall 2 m thick and 1.15 m high. Korobkova and Gadzhiev (1983) state that cattle breeding played a preeminent role in the economy, but finds of sickles, grindstones, and cereal grain impressions in pottery indicate that agriculture was also an aspect.

There are no good local lithic resources. The majority of the chipped stone tools were of flint, and less than 2 percent were of obsidian which came from either Transcaucasia or the north-central Caucasus. The industry is characterized by large prismatic blades and by an absence of microblades or geometric microliths. This stone tool assemblage has parallels with the Neolithic Rugadzha settlements (Malin-karat, Arkhinda, Muchu-bakh-bakli) in Daghestan and with that of the Agubekovo settlement in north-central Caucasus (Korobkova and Gadzhiev 1983:134). Overall, the stone industry at Ginchi is more like the Southern Transcaucasian group than the Shulaveris/Shomu-tepe one (Munchaev 1982:125).

The majority of the ceramics were thick-walled, tempered with sand and gravel, and fired to a red or brown color. Some vessels had a clay slip on the exterior surface which was occasionally polished or highly burnished. There is a large variety of forms including colanders (Munchaev 1975:122, fig. 13). Twelve sherds from small pots with painted decoration were similar to some from Alikemek-tepesi (Munchaev 1982:126). Decoration in the form of incised herringbone was also encountered.

The stone tool and ceramic evidence, as well as the fact that copper was also found, all point to a fifth millennium B.C. date for this site (Munchaev 1982:126).

North-Central Caucasus

Thus far, only two sites attributed to the Eneolithic period are known from this area—the settlement of Agubekovo and the Nalchik cemetery, both located in the Kabardino-Balkaria area near the town of Nalchik. The Agubekovo settlement was excavated during the 1930s and the 0.4–0.6 m thick cultural deposit contained stone, ceramics, and fragments of wattle and daub. In technology and morphology the stone tool industry is similar to that of

Ginchi in Daghestan. Over one thousand sherds of a light-colored, poorly fired, densely tempered fabric in the form of flat-bottomed vessels without decoration were recorded. They have no direct parallels to ceramics of any specific region anywhere else in the Caucasus. Munchaev dates the site to the end of the fifth millennium B.C.

Based on the orientation and location of the burials at Nalchik, two chronological groups were delineated. Burials attributed to the Eneolithic periods were in flexed position and covered with red ochre, with the females lying on their left side and the males on their right. Only a few contained grave goods, which were mostly ornaments such as stone beads, bracelets, and copper rings, as well as stone blades with lateral and terminal retouch. Munchaev (1982:130) equates with the Nalchik burials two other kurgan burials in Chechen-Ingushesht: the No. 6 kurgan at Bamut (Munchaev 1961:139–40), and another in the town of Grozni. Both were flexed, covered with red ochre, and each contained a chipped stone blade with lateral and terminal retouch and stone beads.

The data available are imprecise for dating purposes. Munchaev (1982:130) places all of them in the second half of the fifth millennium B.C.

Black Sea Littoral

The settlement of Tetrametsa, located on a hill on the bank of the Riono River, near the town of Kutais, has been assigned to the early phase of the Eneolithic. The stone tools are like those of the preceding Neolithic period of the area and lack geometric microliths. A few sherds of crude, densely tempered ceramics were found (Munchaev 1982:162, fig. L).

Eneolithic settlements are known in the Abkhaz region, including the settlements at Guad-ikhu and Macharskoe. The only known architecture is a semisubterranean dwelling at Macharskoe. Here were twelve sherds of crude, highly fired, unornamented, flat-bottomed vessels. Two small lead ingots came from Guad-ikhu (Bzhaniya 1966:8). Macharskoe has a single radiocarbon date which falls in the middle of the fifth millennium B.C.

Early Bronze Age

The Kura-Araxes Culture

The Caucasian Early Bronze Age begins about 3600 B.C. with the appearance of the Kura-Araxes culture (Burney and Lang's 1971 "Early Transcaucasian" culture). Kura-Araxes settlements occur over a wider range of topographic/ecological settings, including for the first time high upland river terraces, and three times as many of them as Eneolithic sites are reported. At most sites in which a Kura-Araxes component has been found strati-

fied above an Eneolithic component, as at Geoy-tepe in northwest Iran, Kyul-tepe in Nakhichevan, Misarchai, and Shengavit, there is an intervening sterile layer. Kura-Araxes ceramics are distinctly different from those of the Eneolithic, but there are a few antecedents in shape and decoration for the black-burnished wares of the Kura-Araxes period (Kushnareva and Chubinishvili 1970:145). Burney and Lang (1971:54) considered the Erevan region with Shresh-blur II and Shengavit II a likely homeland for the earliest development of the Kura-Araxes tradition, while admitting that a continuous evolution from the local Eneolithic could not be demonstrated. Many Soviet scholars have tended to seek an origin in the middle Kura Valley in southern Georgia, where, at settlements such as Abelia, Tsopi, and Tetritskaro, they have identified Kura-Araxes ceramic assemblages that display some similarities in shape to Eneolithic ceramic types (Munchaev 1975:194–95; Chubinishvili 1971:161). Kura-Araxes traditions apparently emerged during a rapid burst of cultural evolution, the early stages of which remain undocumented or unrecognized.

Unlike the other Caucasian cultural divisions considered in this chapter, the Kura-Araxes culture has been the subject of several excellent studies in English. We therefore discuss it only briefly here. Kura-Araxes components in the Urmia region are well described in Burton-Brown (1951) and Burney (1958); east Anatolian sites studied in conjunction with the Keban Dam Project and elsewhere are discussed in a thorough review by Sagona (1984). Burney and Lang's (1971) general study is useful and is still largely accurate. The most recent general study in Russian remains that of Munchaev (1975).

The earliest period in the development of the culture, Kura-Araxes I, begins at 3700–3600 B.C. or earlier. A date of 4880 ± 90 B.P. (3625–3800 B.C.) from Kultepe II in Nakhichevan, taken from the middle portion of a Kura-Araxes zone some 9 m thick, is supported by dates from early Kura-Araxes components at Kvatskhelebi CL 4760 ± 90 B.P. (3490–3680 B.C.) and Amiranis-gora 4835 ± 180 B.P. (3490–3790/3890 B.C.). Despite some confusion concerning the stratigraphy of the latter site, and the conflicting radiocarbon evidence from other sites processed over a decade after the samples were collected (LJ-3272 and TB-29), the three readings just cited can be accepted as indicating a date of around 3700–3500 B.C. for an already well-established aspect of Kura-Araxes I. The territory embraced by these sites extends from the mountainous upper course of the Kura through its fertile middle valley, and reaches across the Armenian plateau to the middle Araxes. Typologically related sites expand this early territory westward to eastern Anatolia in the Erzerum region (Karaz) and to the Mingechaur region at the point where the Kura enters the wide steppes of its lower valley in northwestern Azerbaijan.

Within this broad region the early Kura-Araxes tradition developed. In many respects it exhibited continuity with aspects of the preceding Eneolithic such as round houses, crowded and unplanned settlements, elaborate ceramic braziers and hearth accessories, a few ceramic forms, copper metallurgy, basic subsistence economy, and a few decorative techniques including rare Eneolithic examples of burnishing. Kura-Araxes societies, however, greatly increased their investment in technically and aesthetically sophisticated ceramics, and even more so in metallurgy. An increase in the relative importance of short-horned cattle and sheep over long-horned cattle and swine may indicate a greater emphasis on transhumant stockbreeding, a suggestion possibly supported by the initial appearance of domesticated (?) horses in Kura-Araxes sites across Transcaucasia. Horses were apparently exploited during the Eneolithic only on the steppes of the lower Kura drainage. The more important settlements were defended by stone walls up to 5 m thick, and covered areas of 3,500 m² at Kvatskhelebi to 10,000 m² at Amiranis-gora. At Shengavit, near Erevan, a tunnel passed beneath the defensive wall and provided a secure access or a sally port to the river.

Kura-Araxes II began by 3300 B.C. as is firmly indicated by the occurrence of Uruk IV and Jemdet Nasr imports in Kura-Araxes II components at sites near Elazig, and by their correlation with the well-dated Arslantepe VI A deposits. These contained similar imports but no Kura-Araxes ceramics. Arslantepe VI A is dated by ten radiocarbon dates to a period around 3300 B.C. Kura-Araxes ceramics of this period exhibited marked technical and aesthetic improvements, with a continued elaboration of relief spirals and of incised geometric ornament. Kura-Araxes traditions were diffused or adopted over most of the Caucasus, and although there were clear regional groups, there was also a remarkable degree of linkage between them, presumably reflecting the operation of active communication networks. Munchaev (1975) devoted much of his synthesis to a description of the Daghestan and Chechen-Ingushesht variants that appeared during this period in the eastern north Caucasus at sites such as Kayakent and Velikent in the Caspian lowlands, and later Period III sites that were established in the neighboring uplands such as Lugovo, Mekeginskoe, and Galgalatli. Period II sites are also found in the Urmia basin at Geoy-tepe K and Yanik-tepe XXVI–XVI, and southeastward down the north face of the Zagros to Godin-tepe IV and as far as Hamadan. Western expansion reached as far as the Sivas region on the upper Halys in eastern Anatolia.

Period III apparently began much earlier in the Urmia region and perhaps also in Armenia and Georgia than in eastern Anatolia. In the latter region, Period III was marked by a well-documented and much-discussed expansion indicated by the appearance of Khirbet Kerak ware in Palestine at about 2500 B.C. (Sagona 1984:126; Burney and Lang 1971:50–51; Maisler, Stekeus, and Yohah 1952; Kenyon 1970). In the Urmia region Period III levels can be assigned starting dates of 2800 B.C., and perhaps earlier, as is indicated by the radiocarbon dates from Yanik-tepe XIII–VII and Hasanlu VII. Shengavit IV in Armenia yielded a comparable date of ca. 2500 B.C. Period III probably lasted until about 2000 B.C.

During this final period regional variants became strongly expressed, particularly in eastern Anatolia. Metallurgical production reached new peaks in Georgia and the Kura Valley, and a series of metal-rich tumulus cemeteries appeared, from Sachkhere in west-central Georgia to Uch-tepe in Soviet Azerbaijan. Marked social differentiation can be inferred from the structure and content of these graves. Rectangular domestic architecture, which had existed in some areas since the Eneolithic, became more widely established. Decoration and form became simplified in ceramic assemblages, and a new attractive technique of silvery graphite burnishing suggests the extent to which metal vessels were now emulated. Sumerian Early Dynastic metal types such as socketed pickaxes appear in Kura-Araxes III contexts, and some reached as far north as Ciscaucasia, appearing in the Maikop culture. Kura-Araxes II settlements such as Lugovo and Mekeginskoe in the eastern north Caucasus might well have played a role in the formation of the Maikop culture.

The Maikop Culture

Fairly reliable accounts of the Maikop culture have been published in Western languages by Childe (1936), Tallgren (1933), Gimbutas (1956), Sulimirski (1970), and Burney and Lang (1971). The Maikop culture first became known during the final decade of the nineteenth century through the opening of the rich "royal" tumulus graves at Maikop and Tsarskaya, now known as Novosvobodnaya, on the Belaya and Farsa River drainages in the Kuban region of the north Caucasus. In a study that still forms the basis for Maikop chronology, Iessen (1950) established that these two sites represented two successive periods: early Maikop (Maikop) and late Maikop (Novosvobdnaya). Subsequently, a survey program in the Kuban directed by A. A. Formozov, and lasting eight years (1957–64), led to the discovery and excavation of ten Maikop settlements on the upper Belaya and Farsa rivers (Formozov 1965). A "royal" tumulus at Nalchik coeval with Novosvobdnaya was reported by Chechenov (1970), and a similarly well-endowed grave was discovered near Stavropol (Korenevski and Petrenko

1982). An overall review by Munchaev (1975) added much to, and occasionally disputed, Formozov's study. Recent studies (Nechitailo 1984; Andreeva 1977) have sought to establish a very early date for the beginning of the Maikop period.

The chronology of early Maikop rests today, as it has for decades, on the contents of the original Maikop "chieftain's grave," and on the parallels between these objects and similar ones from the Near East in Early Dynastic III contexts and from Alaca Hüyük in Anatolia. The copper transverse ax from Maikop is still a unique find in all of the north Caucasus, and is typologically identical with the shaft-hole transverse axes wielded by the armies of ED III in Mesopotamia. The grave canopy, with fully three-dimensional cast golden bulls mounted on silver support rods, is likewise still unique here and can be paralleled only in the royal tombs of Alaca Hüyük, which are themselves not tightly dated, but are also likely to belong within a period equivalent to ED III and Troy II. These parallels make it very probable that the Maikop "chieftain's grave" dates to a period between 2500 and 2300 B.C. From this grave the silver vases with decorative motifs, including a goat climbing a "tree of life," reinforce the Near Eastern connections of the Maikop chieftain but have only general parallels (Rostovtzeff 1922:22–29; Andreeva 1977).

Three radiocarbon dates have been reported from Maikop-related tumulus graves at Ust-Dzhegutinskaya in the upper Kuban Valley (see table 2). This extensive tumulus cemetery contains inhumations dating from the middle Maikop period, between the Maikop "chieftain's grave" and Novosvobodnaya, through the Late Bronze Age (Munchaev and Nechitailo 1966). The dated graves are said to belong to the late Maikop or perhaps even the immediately post-Maikop period (Munchaev 1975:335). The radiocarbon determinations from the Uch-tepe tumulus cemetery in the Mil'sk steppe in Soviet Azerbaijan are earlier, but this site is quite distant from and has no direct connection with the Maikop culture (Kushnareva and Dzhaparidze 1978:275). In fact, Uch-tepe would fit most comfortably within a series of late Kura-Araxes tumulus cemeteries such as Sachkere, Bedenski, and Tsnori, located in Georgia and Azerbaijan, that are generally dated 2300–2000 B.C., implying that the reported Uch-tepe radiocarbon dates are significantly too early, particularly when recalibrated.

The Maikop culture occupies a transitional geographic position between the Pontic-Caspian steppes to the north and the Caucasus and Anatolia to the south. The scholars who have studied the Maikop culture tend to be similarly divided. Those who have attempted to establish synchronisms with the Pontic-Caspian steppes have suggested correlations that imply an extremely early dating for early Maikop, as far back as Dnieper-Donets II, ca.

4000 B.C. (Danilenko 1969:50–51), or the more generally accepted early Yamna/late Sredni Stog/Mikhailovka I correlation of ca. 3500–3200 B.C. (Nechitailo 1984; Gimbutas 1977; Telegin 1973:24). Even the latter correlation implies a date that is perhaps one thousand years earlier than that suggested by those scholars whose interest lies primarily in the southern connections of the Maikop culture (Burney and Lang 1971:80–82; Munchaev 1975:335). Recently, an attempt has been made to bridge the gap by denying the validity of the traditionally cited ED III and Alaca Hüyük parallels for the Maikop "chieftain's grave," while suggesting a new correlation with Amuq F based on a stylistic interpretation of the decorative motifs on the engraved Maikop vessels (Andreeva 1979).

It is true that some details of these motifs have parallels in proto-Dynastic Egyptian art or in objects of the Uruk IV period, but such styles can be and were retained over long periods. The transverse ax and the burial canopy rods, on the other hand, offer specific parallels and have no earlier prototypes in the Kuban region. They are almost unique, although two copper rods reported from another tumulus 5 km north of Maikop *might* represent a poorer version of the chieftain's canopy (Munchaev 1975:225). These objects cannot be assigned a date earlier than 2500 B.C. in their area of origin unless Mellaart's (1979) widely criticized recalibration-adjusted high chronology be invoked, in which case a *terminus post quem* of 2800 B.C. might be acceptable. Even so, they would be much more recent than the 3500–3200 B.C. period suggested by the north Pontic correlations.

The correlation of early Maikop with early Yamna/late Sredni Stog/Mikhailovka I is, moreover, based on a tenuous array of evidence, most of which consists of small, well-fired sherds of a red fabric, occasionally burnished, that appear sporadically in late Sredni Stog and Mikhailovka I sites such as Konstantinovka on the lower Don (Telegin 1973:23–25) and Mikhailovka I on the lower Dnieper (Nechitailo 1984). Late Sredni Stog cannot be assigned to a period later than ca. 3500–2900 B.C.; the Mikhailovka I group of sites on the lower Dnieper emerged from and overlapped chronologically with late Sredni Stog, but continued to ca. 2800–2400 B.C. The latest expression of the Mikhailovka I tradition might therefore have been coeval with early Maikop; this explains the presence of an entire Maikop vessel, perhaps early Maikop, in the Mikhailovka I–style burial 6a of Kurgan I at Sokolovka on the Ingul River, between the Dnieper and the Southern Bug (Nechitailo 1984:127, 130). The sporadic appearance in the earlier north Pontic sites of red fabric, highly fired ceramic sherds that are technologically unrelated to the locally made shell-tempered wares might be attributed to an early phase of contact and trade between the late Sredni Stog culture and middle Kura-Araxes settlements in Daghestan and the eastern north Caucasus, prior to the evolution of the Maikop culture. In fact, such early commerce might help explain the poorly understood rapid evolution of the early Maikop culture in the Kuban region.

The early Maikop period cannot begin very much earlier than 2600–2500 B.C., if the Alaca Hüyük and ED III imports in the "chieftain's grave" are considered valid chronological indicators (this statement supersedes a slightly earlier placement in Anthony 1986). A hypothetical developmental period preceding the "chieftain's grave," not recognized in the existing data, might be given an additional century. The north Pontic correlations would then be with the earlier part of the late Yamna or Pit-grave horizon (see Anthony 1986) and the latest monuments of the Mikhailovka I group. The latest stage of the Usatovo culture on the northwestern Pontic coast might overlap with the earliest stage of the Maikop culture around 2800–2400 B.C.

The period between early and late Maikop might have been relatively brief, for late Maikop also correlates with Troy II and the later part of the Yamna horizon. The late Maikop exchange network reached farther and was even more active than that of early Maikop; indeed, this seems to have represented a peak period of wealth and prosperity in the north Caucasus. A series of very rich, gigantic tumulus graves are known, containing stone "dolmens" or wooden enclosures built on the original ground surface, but not in a burial pit as during the early Maikop period. The richest are the type site of Novosvobodnaya on the Farsa River, in the Kuban region (Munchaev 1975:241–53; Gimbutas 1956:59–62); a grave near Nalchik, on the headwaters of the Terek River (Chechenov 1970); and a grave at Inozemtsevo near Stavropol (Korenevski and Petrenko 1982). Less spectacular, but still very well-endowed graves dating to the end of this period have been opened at Bamut, in the Sundzha River valley of eastern north Caucasus (Munchaev and Nechitailo 1966).

A variety of distinctive artifact types identify monuments of the late Maikop period. Principal among these are the hammer-headed pin, the cast copper bident/ "fork," the sleeved shaft-hole ax, the long-tanged, shouldered dagger with a broad, stout midrib, elongated biconical beads, and the rectangular-tanged metal spearhead. Wheel-made ceramics also made their appearance, as they did in the contemporary site of Troy II; the late Maikop examples exhibit the impression of the spindle in the pot base (Bobrinskii and Munchaev 1966). The peculiar

late Maikop bidents/"forks" are paralleled only at Tepe Hissar IIIc, on the Iranian plateau at the entrance to the Shahrud pass which leads down to the south Caspian shore.

Amber, presumed to be Baltic, also occurs in the same Tepe Hissar levels (Dyson 1968:5). The sleeved shaft-hole axe, which was essentially a Kura-Araxes weapon type, became widespread during the late Maikop period not only in the north Caucasus, but throughout the Aegean. Chernykh (1977) has identified sixty-two subtly different types of this ax from the Black Sea region.

During the late Maikop period the central focus of power at Usatovo on the northwest Pontic coast was eclipsed. No late Maikop artifact types occur at Usatovo. The Pontic focus shifted eastward, to the Crimea with the Kemi-Oba culture, the eastern Azov steppes with late Yamna/Catacomb, and to the north Caucasus with Maikop.

Most settlements seem to have consisted of seven to ten rectangular houses, occasionally semisubterranean, with dimensions of 8–10 m by 4–5 m. Timber post, wattle and daub construction was used in some areas such as Uruk and Dolinskoe, and stone foundation walls were combined with timber or wattle and daub in others as at Meshoko and Yasenova Polyana. Houses were scattered and unaligned in some settlements like Dolinskoe, or were arranged in a linear fashion along a terrace edge in others, as at Uruk, and in two cases, were arranged in a circle within a stone defensive wall around an interior plaza at Meshoko and Yasenova Polyana. Meshoko, the largest documented settlement, covered approximately 1.5 ha. No Maikop settlement overlies an earlier occupation, and thus the local antecedents of the Maikop culture are virtually undocumented. Ceramic technology and some lithic traits such as denticulate-edged blades and asymmetrically tanged triangular arrowheads link the Maikop assemblages to Kura-Araxes prototypes, while mortuary rites appear to have been derived from the steppe cultures to the north. The opening of maritime trade with north-central Anatolia, perhaps encouraged by the appearance of new boat technologies like the high-prowed rowing vessels of Early Cycladic II, might have played a role in the evolution of the Maikop culture. The late Maikop "dolmen" tombs display a restricted distribution that may reflect the emergence of a coastal trade, for they are found in the western Kuban region and along the northeastern Pontic coast, with similar grave types reported for the Kemi-Oba culture on the Crimea (Shchepinski 1968).

Nine

Anatolian Chronology

Machteld J. Mellink, Bryn Mawr College

Outline

Introduction

Ancient Anatolia is here taken as the territory about equivalent to that of modern Turkey. In its eastern extension it overlaps with north Mesopotamia and Transcaucasia, to the southeast with north Syria, and to the west with the Aegean zone. The connection with southeastern Europe is important for northwest Anatolia from the Hellespont to the Bosporus and for the adjoining Pontic zone. The core area is the Anatolian plateau.

The chronology of Anatolia is determined by methods familiar to the archaeologist and historian of the Near East. To a large extent the material is prehistoric and datable only in a relative sequence. Scientific age determinations such as radiocarbon and dendrochronology may ultimately provide a reliable absolute time scale for the archaeological stages of development. At present the archaeologist is responsible for his own interpretation of the relative order of data gathered from a great many, but

Text submitted October 1985
Final draft June 1986

still rather disparate sites, and for the construction of a network of probable interconnections and synchronisms.

This network is more easily constructed in the areas adjoining Mesopotamia and Syria than in central and west Anatolia. The nature of the contact with the Near Eastern neighbors of Anatolia varies from technical and cultural borrowings to regular trade, political connections, and military conflicts. Coordination with Mesopotamian historical chronology becomes potentially possible from the Late Uruk period on. By the time of Old Assyrian trade, early in the second millennium B.C., when merchants from Assur resided and pursued their enterprises in Anatolian cities in cooperation with Anatolian merchants and officials, we are entering the era of precise absolute chronology based on documents found in stratified Anatolian context.

The Old Assyrian trade network extended at least as far west as the later Hittite capital Hattusha and the Halys River. It brought central Anatolia into history. Before the twentieth century B.C., central and west Anatolia are prehistoric to the archaeologist, with some expectation that

Akkadian enterprise may in the near future be identified in archaeological remains on the plateau, and with some reason to believe that the Old Assyrian traders had Mesopotamian predecessors.

The relationship of west Anatolian chronology to Aegean chronology is peculiar. Although Anatolia is often considered a bridge, the known link with historical chronology is weaker in west Anatolia during the third millennium B.C. than it is in Crete, and even second millennium dates for west Anatolia, including Troy, are often derived from Aegean timetables. The Aegean situation emphasizes the importance of overseas contacts with the Levant and Egypt as more beneficial, at least to the student of chronology, than the long land routes from the west Anatolian coastal cities and river valleys to the plateau and across the Taurus and anti-Taurus to Mesopotamia.

In this survey of the status quo and problems of Anatolian archaeological chronology we use the traditional terminology of Stone and Bronze Ages as a general frame of reference. The broad divisions are agreed on by most scholars, but when it comes to subdivisions, interpretations differ because the facts are few and the gaps are large. If some of the order suggested below is controversial, the evidence is presented in more detail than is the case for zones of general agreement.

The Earliest Stages

Palaeolithic remains have been found in many Anatolian sites from Thrace to Kars and from Antalya to the Euphrates (Yalçınkaya 1981; Özdoğan 1984a). The extensive presence of Palaeolithic communities in southwestern Anatolia, as attested by the stratified deposits in the Karain cave, 27 km northwest of Antalya, must be taken into account for an understanding of the early development of regional traditions (Kökten 1963 and 1967). Mesolithic remains, such as microlithic flint tools, are recorded for the rock shelters of Beldibi and Belbaşı on the east coast of Lycia, ca. 45 km south of Antalya (Bostancı 1968). The sites of Karain and Beldibi-Belbaşı were also in use during the aceramic and ceramic Neolithic periods.

Aceramic Neolithic

The aceramic Neolithic (see table 1) villages recently discovered along the Euphrates at Cafer Hüyük, 40 km northeast of Malatya (Cauvin and Aurenche 1982), and Gritille, 10 km north of Samsat (Ellis and Voigt 1981 and 1982), along with the flint workshop at Hayaz south of Samsat (Roodenberg 1979–80), represent a stage of settled communities with established technologies and some practice of agriculture. Houses consist of small rectangular units, built of long mud-bricks measuring 70–80 × 33 × 8–9 cm. Pebble or stone foundations occur under walls and floors; floor and wall surfaces are finished in plaster. The tool tradition, predominantly obsidian at Cafer, flint at Gritille, is related to that of the north Syrian variant of PPNB. These aceramic sites along the Turkish Euphrates can be correlated typologically with north Syrian sites like Mureybet IV and Abu Hureyra. We are beginning to see a continuum of early food-producing villages in the Euphrates Valley. The chronological range of these sites, which to judge by their compact stratification must have lasted through many centuries, is estimated at ca. 7000–6500 B.C. on the basis of radiocarbon dates from north Syria. Dates for Turkey are listed below.

The site of Çayönü in the upper Tigris area, 20 km south of the copper mines at Ergani, presents a different aspect of aceramic settled communities. Large rectangular houses were built on fieldstone or river-stone foundations, which at basement level form parallel narrow spaces or cubicles (Braidwood and Braidwood 1982; Braidwood, Çambel, and Schirmer 1981). The houses are freestanding and measure up to 6.20 m in width and 13.50 m in length. The superstructure of mud-brick is rarely preserved. The so-called terrazzo building (later phase) has a 7.50 × 9.80 m main room with a floor of pink limestone chips set in a hard lime paste, polished and finished to a smooth hard surface. Two white stripes were inlaid, marking the lines between pairs of pilasters. All levels except the lowest show this advanced stage of building tradition and community organization. The privileged position of Çayönü near the copper resources of Ergani is evident in the use of metallic copper for a reamer, an awl, and a pin in the grill plan houses (Muhly 1983:350). Chipped stone tools are increasingly of obsidian in the upper levels, as trade with obsidian-bearing centers of east Anatolia, the Bingöl area, and the central Anatolian Göllü Dağ–Çiftlik district is being developed (Braidwood 1979). Çayönü has early domestication of cereals and later of sheep and goat. The earliest phases remain to be investigated, but excavated remnants show a construction of posts and wattle-and-daub. The village tradition in the upper Tigris area must have several stages antedating Çayönü. A related architectural development may be emerging from new excavations at Nevalla Çori, in the Kantara Valley east of the Euphrates in the Lidar area (Hauptmann 1984b).

The Southern Plateau

An unexcavated aceramic site is Aşıklı Hüyük, 25 km southeast of Aksaray on the right bank of the Melendiz River. Close to the central Anatolian sources of obsidian, the site's chipped stone industry is almost exclusively of obsidian (Todd 1966, 1980:59). Characteristically, the architecture shows the use of long and wide mud-bricks, at least 60 cm long, hard lime plaster and red color for floors. Can Hasan III, 13 km northeast of Karaman, sampled by excavation (French 1972; Hillman 1978; Todd 1980), is a farming village with domesticated sheep, goats, cattle, and pigs (Payne 1972). The houses are built of pisé slabs without stone foundations and form tightly adjoining units of small size; larger courtyards can also be recognized. The tools are predominantly of obsidian. More intensive work has been done at Suberde, 13 km southeast of Seydişehir in the Suğla Lake district (Bordaz 1969, 1973). Mud-brick houses without stone foundations, with the usual plaster floors, characterize the nearly aceramic level III. The chipped stone industry is 90 percent obsidian. The fauna seems not to be domesticated, whereas agriculture may have been practiced. This site is not among the earliest aceramic communities, as is also evident from the sherds in the upper level III, but it may be typical of the various transitional stages of adaptation along the south edge of the Anatolian plateau. Aceramic Hacılar (Mellaart 1970b:3–7, 1961:70–75), south of Burdur Lake, also shows the use of long mud-bricks (72 cm), red-painted floors, as well as fixed hearths and ovens. There is some obsidian and flint, but the sample is very small. Many such aceramic villages must have existed in the region of the Beyşehir and Burdur lakes, and most of them were ultimately abandoned. The most successful experiments in settled living are probably hidden under the large mounds of ceramic Neolithic and later periods, as must be true of the other regions discussed above, and of Cilicia, where no aceramic levels have been identified so far.

In summary, the Euphrates region of southeast Anatolia can be correlated with, but is not totally dependent on, the development in the Levant and north Mesopotamia. In the upper Tigris area, Çayönü-Ergani signals considerable and prolonged regional development in the aceramic, incipient food-producing stage. Experiments with copper are earlier than elsewhere. The sites along the southern edge of the plateau rely on obsidian technology in the Konya-Aksaray region. The southwest may have its own flint tradition connected with the Mesolithic hunters and gatherers of the Beldibi Belbaşı stage, which some day may be clearly connected with the aceramic Neolithic sequence. Central Anatolia proper and the Pontic zones are terrae incognitae at this stage of exploration.

Radiocarbon dates for Çayönü run from the eighth millennium to the seventh. Cafer and Aşıklı seem to antedate Can Hasan III and Suberde III in the seventh.

Ceramic Neolithic

Euphrates

The salvage digging in the Keban area reached levels of the developed ceramic Neolithic stage at Tepecik and elsewhere (Esin 1982a:13–14). Current work in the Adıyaman-Urfa region has identified a ceramic site of this period at Kumartepe, which differs from the Amuq A–B tradition in its pottery types (Roodenberg 1984). The affinities are with north Syria. Gelinciktepe-Malatya also starts in this period (Palmieri 1976:122–23).

Cilicia

Well known among the various regional zones of Anatolia is the complex of Syro-Cilician sites of the Amuq A–B stage to which the lower levels of Mersin (XXXII–XXVI) and Tarsus, along with a good many other sites in Cilicia, belong (Garstang 1953:11–26; Goldman 1956:65–72). Their affinities are with the Amuq as well as with Ugarit VB–A and Levantine coastal sites as far south as Byblos. The food-producing, settled communities of this era are fully ceramic in technology; the dark-faced burnished ware common to the Cilician and the Amuq sites has become a hallmark for the period. An obsidian industry is flourishing in Cilicia, and trade with the plateau sources of obsidian is established. The architecture of Cilicia is ill known, but plastered and burnished floors are characteristic. The mound at Mersin contains a long development of well-built levels.

In 1983, Neolithic levels were found under the Bronze and Iron Age fortress of Domuztepe on the east bank of the Ceyhan River, northwest of the Amanus passes (Özdoğan 1984b). The relevant pottery resembles that of Tarsus and Mersin. So far, there are no such data from the Islahiye-Gaziantep area, where Sakça Gözü seems to start in the Chalcolithic era (du Plat Taylor, Seton Williams, and Waechter 1950:83).

The Southern Plateau

The Anatolian development in its local cultural aspects is best known from Çatal Hüyük which remains the outstanding representative of an early ceramic Neolithic community with its architecture, wall reliefs and wall paintings, burial customs, obsidian, stone and bone technology, and its diversified minor arts. The excavated material gives ample information on cultural traits and economy (Mellaart 1967:1970a; Todd 1976). Correlation in precise chronological terms is still difficult, because crossing the Taurus Mountains means entering a different province of material culture, although generic resemblances in ceramic and obsidian technology point to contemporaneity between Çatal Hüyük's best-known upper levels and Cilician ceramic Neolithic.

North of the Cilician Gates we have a number of less extensively excavated but related sites. Close to the obsidian sources are Pınarbaşı-Bor and Köşk Hüyük southeast of Bor (Todd 1980:41–43; Silistreli 1984); soundings here have yielded obsidian cores and tools, and dark burnished pottery with relief ornamentation of remarkable variety in representation. Surface exploration and chance finds suggest an extensive distribution of ceramic early Neolithic sites in southwest Anatolia and the south plateau zones near the obsidian centers of Çiftlik-Göllüdağ and the Acıgöl district (Todd 1980:109). To the west, the Beyşehir area sites of Suberde levels I–II and Erbaba III must overlap with Çatal Hüyük (Bordaz and Bordaz 1982; Bordaz 1973). Erbaba has houses built of stones with mud mortar; rectangular units are closely clustered.

The developed aspect of ceramic Neolithic ("Late Neolithic") is also widely represented, but no extensive excavations have taken place at sites of this period. Hacılar IX–VA is best known (Mellaart 1970b:8–22). The chipped stone industry declines, and copper working increases. The artistic modeling of clay and stone figurines continues through Neolithic. Can Hasan I has lower levels of Late Neolithic (French 1967:176–77). The sites in the Bor area continue, as do those in the Beyşehir district, such as Erbaba I–II. Some sites have been identified in the Elmalı plain, notably Gökpınar and Akçay (Eslick 1980b). Aphrodisias VIII C (Joukowsky 1982:732–39, 1986:59, 348, 521) in the upper Maeander Valley belongs to this phase. It seems possible that a Late Neolithic ceramic tradition will be identified along the west coast of Anatolia and as far north as the Thracian Chersonesus and the Asiatic shores of the Sea of Marmara, with echoes of the Syro-Cilician dark-faced burnished ware (Özdoğan 1982a).

Northwest Anatolia

The date of the prehistoric settlements at Fikirtepe and Pendik on the east coast of the Sea of Marmara is Late Neolithic (Özdoğan 1979, 1983). With these sites, consisting of simple huts built of wattle-and-daub walls, we reach the counterpart of the European village tradition, as suggested also by the mixed economy of fishing, hunting, and stock breeding, with some agriculture. Yet there seems to be little connection with contemporary Thrace. More durable agricultural communities of this stage existed in the region of Iznik, Yenişehir, and Demirci Hüyük (Korfmann 1980:9; Özdoğan 1985).

Radiocarbon Dates for Ceramic Neolithic

Çatal Hüyük has a good number of determinations for level VI which cluster in the 6000–5800 B.C. era; levels IX–XII perhaps belong to ca. 6300–6000 B.C. Hacılar IX–VI may reach ca. 5600 B.C. Erbaba III seems to parallel Çatal Hüyük from level VIII on, ca. 6000 B.C. All these dates are best estimates and may need considerable revision.

Early and Middle Chalcolithic

The nomenclature of Early and Middle Chalcolithic (see table 2) is debatable, but it is current in the excavation reports of Anatolian sites. We note a continuation of the Late Neolithic tradition. Copper technology, which had been increasing during all Neolithic phases, becomes gradually more prominent, with a considerable upsurge in the final Chalcolithic phase.

We must keep the geographical zones of Anatolia grouped according to their contacts. In the east we can follow the Mesopotamian and Syrian tempo with the aid of cultural, principally ceramic, borrowings, so that a sequence correlated with the Halaf and Ubaid periods can be recognized. The Taurus Mountains continue to form a barrier between the zone of Mesopotamian affinities and the Anatolian plateau; the coastal southwest and west are beginning to show increasing interaction with the Aegean islands.

Euphrates Valley and East Anatolia

Through the series of recent salvage excavations along the Euphrates it has become evident that many sites in the Keban area and as far south as Samsat were adopting and following recognizable Mesopotamian fashions in pottery, as previously known from Carchemish (Woolley 1934a)".

The Halaf tradition is ceramically, but not architecturally, noticeable at Tülintepe (Esin 1982c:130; Arsebük 1983), at Korucutepe (Van Loon 1978:7) and Çayboyu (Aksoy and Diamant 1973) in the Keban, and at Samsat Hüyük (Mellink 1983b:432) in the Samsat-Urfa districts. At Cavi Tarlası near Hassek Hüyük, a site of the Halaf period contains tholoi as well as characteristic pottery (Von Wickede 1984). Kurban Hüyük has yielded similar evidence. Other villages have rectangular mud-brick houses continuing into the phase associated with northern Ubaid-Gawra ceramics. The Amuq correlations of the Halaf traits are with phases C and D; phase E is of regional Ubaid character. Ubaid material appears in the Keban at Norşuntepe, Korucutepe and Tepecik, but more clearly at Değirmentepe in the Malatya zone (Esin 1982a:16, 1983, 1984). Here the characteristic pottery categories are painted and monochrome wares, among which scraped bowls are prominent. At Değirmentepe, stamp seals and bullae show the regional use of seals for the marking of merchandise or property. Architecture becomes complex, and the main room of a Değirmentepe building of level III had wall paintings (Esin 1983: 180–81).

Both Halaf and Ubaid traits appear widely in east Anatolia and in Cilicia, thus providing chronological links with the north Mesopotamian sequence, and suggestions of intensive cultural and technical interaction which need to be analyzed in other contexts.

The diffusion of Halaf pottery is noticeable at the site of Girikihaciyan 60 km north of Diyarbakır (LeBlanc and Watson 1973) and as far east as Tilkitepe near Van (Korfmann 1982:phase III). West of the Euphrates, Halaf and Halafian wares occur at Sakçagözü (du Plat Taylor, Seton Williams, and Waechter 1950:87–94), which also has a clear representation of northern Ubaid features. Scraped bowls were nicknamed Coba bowls at this site (du Plat Taylor, Seton Williams, and Waechter 1950:94). Gedikli to the northwest of Sakçagözü also has extensive deposits of local Ubaid type (H. Alkım 1979:137, pls. 85–86).

The phase of the Coba bowls is also recognizable at Göksün in the Antitaurus, along the road up to the plateau from the Gedikli-Maraş area (Brown 1967:132, 139) and at Tilkitepe (Korfmann 1982:67; the distribution is also discussed by Mellaart 1981 and Palmieri 1985).

Cilicia

The Halaf and Ubaid diffusion reach as far as Cilicia. The best examples of pottery resembling Halaf wares in fabric and decoration come from Mersin (Garstang 1953:114–19), levels XIX–XVII. There is an older tradition of pot painting in Cilicia, notable in Mersin levels XXIV–XX, which may have developed independently. During the Halaf phase, and in the following phases which run parallel with Amuq D and E, much local pot painting continues. In level XVI, Mersin was fortified in what seems an Anatolian system (Garstang 1953:130–37). This fortress was captured and burnt; in the debris were copper tools and pins. The level is dated by the clear Amuq E affinities of some of the pottery (Garstang 1953:147, fig. 91:4–6; 149, fig. 92:5), which continued in the following levels XV–XIIB. Tarsus has a feebler representation of all this (Goldman 1956:figs. 219–24) but then appears with a strong counterpart of Amuq phase F which so far is lacking at Mersin.

The Southern Plateau

Crossing the Taurus Mountains means losing the thread of Halaf and Ubaid chronology, even if we follow the easy way up onto the plateau through the Göksu Valley to Karaman and the site of Can Hasan (French 1962–68). The main mound, Can Hasan I, starts in Late Neolithic and develops into a well-built village with mud-brick houses, tightly grouped, the basements of which are well preserved after a conflagration of the Early to Middle Chalcolithic level IIB. The mud-bricks are long (80 × 40 × 10 cm), and timber was used to reinforce the walls. Some of the fallen plaster of the upper storey had geometric ornament painted in red (French 1962:33). Copper working is attested by a macehead (Muhly 1983:352). The painted pottery shows a clearly independent development; a generic resemblance to the Mersin sequence ca. XXIV–XX has been suggested, but there is no unmistakable set of precise correlations. Can Hasan IIB also has its own style in the making of seated clay figurines and large masks (French 1963:36). Çatal Hüyük West, by comparison of its painted pottery, must belong in Can Hasan phase IIB (French 1966:118; Mellaart 1965). We can call this Early Chalcolithic and assume that it runs parallel with Mersin ca. XXIV–XX, before the Halaf infiltration.

Another strong regional development of painted pottery styles characterizes Chalcolithic Hacılar (Mellaart 1970b). This material is quite difficult to place because it is so local in technique and style. There seems to be a gap between the latest Neolithic level VI and the Early Chalcolithic levels V–III, which are poorly represented, and it is not until levels IIA–B and I that we have good architectural evidence for habitation and organization. The painted pottery is typically Anatolian, using the red ochre that so often appears as a solid slip on pottery, to make red patterns on a light ground or vice versa, by reserving the decoration. Style, repertoire, and technique are southwest Anatolian. We now know that Early Chalcolithic pottery of Hacılar type occurs on other sites in the Burdur area such as Kuruçay (Duru 1983:42). Here and there in the Elmalı plain, sherds of Hacılar I type have come to light, and related wares appear as far to the northwest as the Demirci Hüyük area.

The sites of the painted pottery phase in southwest Anatolia do not seem to last into the final phase of Chalcolithic. Hacılar II and I show attempts at fortification: the houses or parts of the main establishment join their outer walls to make a compound. Both levels end in destruction by conflagration, as did Kuruçay 7 which seems roughly of Hacılar I date.

We cannot claim to know much about the sites that run parallel with the Halaf and Ubaid phases in central and west Anatolia. Many sites may look Late Neolithic to us because they do not share in a painted pottery tradition, and the beginnings of the Late Chalcolithic phase cannot be pinpointed chronologically. Perhaps we may discern a

Middle Chalcolithic phase in material from the Elmalı plain that seems to have affinity to the Aegean coast and islands (Eslick 1980a). This would help fill the gap between Hacılar I and west Anatolian Late Chalcolithic of the Beycesultan variety.

Radiocarbon Dates for Early and Middle Chalcolithic

The best series of dates for Early Chalcolithic is available for Can Hasan II B, which stays roughly in the first half of the sixth millennium, not too far from Late Neolithic. Hacılar II–I and Kuruçay may be close followers. The dates for the Euphrates sites are lower, but few and erratic.

Late Chalcolithic

Euphrates Area

In the Keban region the ceramic material associated with the Late Ubaid tradition is succeeded by that of Amuq F type, with the leading ware a chaff-faced light fabric used for pots of handmade and tournette-made types. Most of this ware is light to orange-slipped, as it is in the Amuq. Korucutepe XLIV–XXX (Brandt, in Van Loon 1978:58–60), Tepecik below level 14 (Esin 1972:157), Norşuntepe West Slope level 7 (Hauptmann 1976:86), Tülintepe (Esin 1982a:14), and Çayboyu (Aksoy and Diamant 1973:105–7) all have characteristic pottery.

In the course of the Late Chalcolithic period (see table 2) the Turkish Euphrates area below the Taurus mountain gorge experiences intensive contact with the Late Uruk expansion and trade outposts of the Habuba Kabira type (see Schwartz and Weiss, this vol., chap. 10). Level 5 of Hassek Hüyük has architectural and ceramic features that link it with Habuba Kabira South (Behm-Blancke 1981). Its ceramic inventory is close to that of the Syrian site, and the building in the center of the mound has a layout worthy of the "colonial" Late Uruk period. Tablets have not yet been found; scattered cones remain as fragments of mosaic. Similar conditions must exist in the lower levels of Samsat Hüyük (surface observations and finds by Nimet Özgüç; Özdoğan 1977:133). At Hassek Hüyük, the relevant level 5 was destroyed by conflagration. Beveled-rim bowls occur in the level 5 building. These provide a synchronism with Habuba Kabira South as well as Amuq F–G transitional from Late Chalcolithic to EB I. Beveled-rim bowls also are well represented at Carchemish (Woolley and Barnett 1952:217, pl. 52b). In the Keban region, they appear at Tepecik (Esin 1974:134, 1979:110, 1982a:14–16, 1982b:115) and even in the Malatya area; Arslantepe has a few specimens in what may be a phase between Late Chalcolithic level VII and

VIA, the temple level, which has an Amuq G inventory, EB I in Anatolian terms (Palmieri 1981:106, 1985)

West of the Euphrates, Amuq F–type Late Chalcolithic material is represented at Gedikli (H. Alkım 1979:138–39), Sakçagözü V (du Plat Taylor, Seton Williams, and Waechter 1950:102–7), and Domuztepe (Özdoğan 1984b) on the upper Ceyhan east bank.

Cilicia

Tarsus has about three meters of stratified deposit of Late Chalcolithic type as well as a cemetery of extramural pithos burials (Goldman 1956:5–7, 82–91). Ceramically, the Amuq F imprint is unmistakable from Tarsus to the Euphrates and into North Syria (Braidwood and Braidwood 1960:513–16). In the Amuq, beveled-rim bowls occur toward the very end of F and at the beginning of phase G (Braidwood and Braidwood 1960:234, n. 10, 516). This would provide a correlation of the end of Amuq F with the Late Uruk period and with the occurrences of beveled-rim bowls in Hassek, Tepecik, and Malatya.

At Tarsus, beveled-rim bowls do not seem to occur. They are of chronological as well as cultural significance as an indicator of specific Mesopotamian contact. At the end of Amuq F, and before the beveled-rim bowls begin to appear in the Amuq, the contact between the Amuq and Cilicia is interrupted by Anatolian interference. Amuq G and Cilician EB I have much less in common, archaeologically, than do Tarsus Late Chalcolithic and Amuq F.

Southwest Anatolia

The areas known to have been active in Neolithic and Early Chalcolithic times continue to yield evidence for agricultural and trading communities. Many of the known old sites are abandoned and new settlements arise, some of which are short lived.

As in the earlier periods, we cannot apply the criteria of exact correlation with Cilicia or the Euphrates area through recognizable imports or cultural borrowings.

The longest sequence on the southern plateau is that of Beycesultan in the upper reaches of the Maeander. Levels XL–XX, starting from virgin soil, offered a stratified sample of southwest Anatolian material evidence for rectangular mud-brick houses with fixed hearths, bins, and platforms and an inventory of pottery. There is continuity of building and ceramic traditions (Lloyd and Mellaart 1962:17–26, 70–115). The pottery is locally made dark burnished ware with some white-painted decoration and conservative shapes. Contemporary sites have been widely identified by surface exploration in southwest Anatolia. Excavated overlapping material comes from Aphrodisias (Joukowsky 1982:756–59, 1986:60–72,

349–55), south of the Maeander Valley, and from Kuruçay south of Burdur, where in levels 6A and B (Duru 1983) are rectangular houses, typical pottery, and some copper tools. Bağbaşı and other sites in the Elmalı plain (Eslick 1980a, 1980b) show the diffusion of Late Chalcolithic habitation in northern Lycia. It is clear that all of this material postdates Hacılar I by some interval and antedates EB I, which shows clear changes in ceramic evidence. Among the latest Chalcolithic material is the cemetery of period A at Kusura (Lamb 1937:54–64), some 60 km east northeast of Beycesultan in the plain of Sandıklı.

Northwest Anatolia, the Pontic Zone

Surface exploration suggests some diffusion of Beycesultan-type material to the regions of Manisa and Balıkesir (French 1961:99–104). In the Troad, Kumtepe has material antedating Troy I (Sperling 1976), but barely of Chalcolithic character. Sites of the Kumtepe variety exist also along the coasts of the Gelibolu Peninsula and the north coast of the Sea of Marmara (Özdoğan 1982a:44, 1982b:10–11). At Beşiktepe, Chalcolithic material is recognizable in the form of pattern-burnished ware. An idol of the so-called Kilia type confirms the Late Chalcolithic date (Korfmann 1984). Idols of this kind have been found on the Gelibolu Peninsula and as far inland as Aphrodisias, where a fragment was embedded in level VIIA of Pekmez (Kadish 1971:129–31; Joukowsky 1982: 608–13; Caskey 1972, 192–93).

The Pontic sites will gradually become better known. At Ikiztepe near Bafra, Late Chalcolithic levels III.1–7 have timber or wattle-and-daub houses, some with fixed round hearths (U. B. Alkım 1978:544–46, 1979b:890–93). The pottery is of gray and mottled ware and may, in shape and incised or relief decoration, have affinities with Balkan wares or pottery from the Yarımburgaz cave 30 km west of Istanbul (Özdoğan 1982a:44–45). Copper artifacts are found in most of the relevant levels of Ikiztepe, and obsidian also occurs, showing that contact with the copper and obsidian trade channels exists from the beginning. Dündartepe near Samsun has similar pottery, but a steatopygous idol fragment seems to be even earlier than most of the stratified Late Chalcolithic artifacts (Kökten, Özgüç, and Özgüç 1945: 367–69).

Central Anatolia

One stage of Late Chalcolithic on the Anatolian plateau is recognizable in material from Büyük Güllücek, a small settlement 15 km north of Alaca Hüyük (Koşay and Akok 1957). The simple pottery with its knobbed handles, and white-painted and incised or impressed decoration, has parallels among early wares from Alaca Hüyük (Orthmann 1963b:66–67). It also has affinities with the lower level of Yazır Hüyük in the upper Sakarya bend (Temizer 1960) and to Ikiztepe and Dündartepe.

Levels 19–12 of the citadel mound at Alişar Hüyük in the Halys bend were labeled Chalcolithic by the excavators (Von der Osten 1937: 1: 28–109). The upper levels, 14–12, of this 12-m deep deposit run parallel with the developed EBI period in Cilician terms. Stratified material contemporary with Alişar 14–12M occurs also at Alaca Hüyük, at Yarıkkaya near Boğazköy (Hauptmann 1969:69), where it is preceded by building levels with a regional type of pottery, and at Çengeltepe east of Yozgat (Ünal 1966). Some of Alişar levels 19–15M could belong to a stage immediately antecedent to EB I.

The excavators of Tepecik in the Keban area have characterized a group of red-and-black burnished wares as having affinities with central Anatolian ones (Esin 1982b:107–17). If the pedestaled bowls from layer 3 in Tepecik West are indeed relevant parallels to the fruit stands from Alişar (Von der Osten 1937: vol. 1, figs. 75–76), we would have a valuable synchronism. Tepecik material of this type belongs to the period of Uruk expansion of Habuba Kabira type, Amuq F–G transitional. The affinities of these central Anatolian and Keban wares remain to be studied in further detail.

Radiocarbon Dates for Late Chalcolithic

Korucutepe phase B is in an early bracket, still in the second half of the fifth millennium. Dates for Arslantepe VII belong in the first half of the fourth. The entire Late Chalcolithic would seem to range from ca. 4500–3500 B.C., with early representatives also in the west (Kuruçay? Aphrodisias?) and north (Ikiztepe?). The later group includes Beycesultan.

Early Bronze Age
Euphrates Area and East Anatolia

The current excavations south of the Taurus mountain barrier show that the strong Syro-Mesopotamian contacts lasted through the third (and second) millennium B.C., with special affinities to the Syrian middle Euphrates area. The labeling may still have to be expressed in terms of EB I–III (–IV), or Amuq G–J, rather than historical terms, but correlation and relative chronology will present no basic puzzles. For the Early Bronze Age, the relatively unencumbered site of Kurban Hüyük on the east side of the Euphrates (Marfoe 1983), and Lidar, a major site upstream, will provide extensive sequences. Lidar has solid habitation levels of EB. The pottery sequence can be studied through a series of stratified kilns which produced all variants of Syrian wheel-made wares locally.

Built tombs and cist graves provide another set of closely datable EB I–III contexts (Hauptmann 1982b,

1983, 1984a). The sequence of metallic ware and corrugated, smeared, and combed ware is amply documented and can serve as a guide to the identification of the exports taken to the areas west of the Euphrates including Cilicia and the plateau.

EB cemeteries were also found at Hassek Hüyük, a pithos cemetery, and at Titriş 7 km east of Lidar. Cylinder seals from the tombs and impressions on reserved-slip ware provide correlations with Mesopotamian Early Dynastic (Behm-Blancke 1981, 1983).

The Malatya region and the sites in the Keban area demonstrate more complex cultural interrelations at the beginning of EB I. Several Keban sites and Arslantepe enjoyed Late Uruk contacts with Mesopotamia and Syria and went into a phase of EB I which initially was closely related to the Euphrates and Amuq sites of phase G. Cylinder seals were locally made and served commercial and decorative purposes, as at Hassek. A large group of bullae came to light at Arslantepe period VIA. One impression reveals Uruk iconography (Palmieri 1981:pl. XVa). A group of weapons from the same level has parallels in spearheads from graves near Carchemish (Palmieri 1981:109; Woolley 1914:pl. XIX).

Arslantepe period VI B betrays the presence of cultural elements of East Anatolian origin (Palmieri 1985), which are clearest in the temporary monopoly of red-black burnished, handmade pottery (Palmieri 1973:165–71). Later in the period, but not consistently, wheel-made Syrian wares and local reserved-slip ware are again in evidence. The "Transcaucasian" influx at Arslantepe is clear and datable, in relative terms, to a later phase of EB I and of Amuq G. It ties in with the diffusion of the handmade red-black polished ware and its concomitant architectural features, such as new building techniques, new forms, and decorated, elaborate hearths, to sites in the Keban area, especially Sakyol-Pulur (Koşay 1976), Korucutepe (Van Loon 1978:13, 71–75), Norşuntepe (Hauptmann 1979:69–73), and Tepecik (Esin 1979:108, 111–12, 1982b:104, 112). These elements come from the north and east, arriving early in the third millennium B.C. at the stage when in the Malatya and Keban zones connections with the Amuq G phase prevail, corroborated by wheel-made plain simple wares, reserved-slip jars, cylinder seal impressions on pottery, and rectangular mud-brick architecture. We do not yet know the Anatolian sources of the influx in full geographical and chronological detail, but connections with the EB Age sites in the Erzurum area, Karaz, Pulur, and Güzelova (Koşay and Turfan 1959; Koşay and Vary 1964 and 1967) are evident in their general traits, if not as yet with stratigraphic precision. In the Van area, ceramic traces occur at Tilkitepe phase I (Korfmann 1982:175–78). The affinities with the Transcaucasian Kur-Araxes complex have been sufficiently studied (Burney and Lang 1972:43–85; Burney 1977:128–32; Sagona

1984) to show the wide extension of a northeastern cultural continuum that forms the counterpart of the Syro-Mesopotamian cultural world. The two meet in the Malatya region. Elements of the Transcaucasian culture intrude into sites of the Amuq and coastal Syria, and into Palestine in the form of the Khirbet Kerak phenomenon. Without interpreting the ethnic and linguistic components of this penetration, we can here simply point to its chronological benefits, such as the synchronism of a recognizable intrusive stage of the Transcaucasian complex with Mesopotamian and Syrian EB I in Malatya, and its selective diffusion to the south in the Amuq H phase.

The Syrian contacts of the Anatolian upper Euphrates area are not completely blocked by the Transcaucasian influx. This is evident not only at Arslantepe, but also in the steady trickle of north Syrian imported pottery that appears in the Keban sites in the course of EB I–III. The local sequence of subdivisions, with deposits of 18 m at Norşuntepe, will become a time scale to be applied to neighbors in all directions. The Syrian ware consists principally of buff simple wheel-made pottery, datable by profile development, and in EB I recognizable by its reserved-slip surface treatment (Hauptmann 1982a:53–54; Norşuntepe West Slope XXV–XXIV). The change to Transcaucasian handmade dark wares takes place in XXIV, along with architectural changes (Hauptmann 1982a:55). Painted pottery of a simple red-on-light kind starts in XXIII and continues through the EB levels, with a fine-painted style of handmade EB III ware in levels VIII–VI (Hauptmann 1976:79). Wheel-made corrugated gray goblets and bottles of Syrian make occur sporadically in the Transcaucasian levels XXIII and above (Hauptmann 1982a:56–57, 1979:72).

It is clear, therefore, that in the Euphrates area below the Taurus gorge we shall be able to correlate the sequence readily with that of the Syrian Middle Euphrates. North of the gorge, in the Malatya-Elazığ region, a limited contact with Syria is maintained even after the change of cultural orientation in EB I. The east Anatolian culture is best represented in the dominant, palatial complex of Norşuntepe VI, which was destroyed at the end of EB III. Historical interpretation of these destructions in relation to Akkadian campaigns may yield a tie-in with Mesopotamian chronology.

Cilicia

The excavated sequence of EB I-II-III at Gözlü Kule, Tarsus, is a mainstay for chronological coordination of Anatolian material with that of Syria and the Near East. The close ties with Late Chalcolithic Amuq F are interrupted in Cilicia by a cultural volte-face in the direction of the south Anatolian plateau and the vigorous opening of the Taurus passes at the start of EB I (Amuq G), comparable to the east Anatolian influx in the Malatya-Keban region at about this time. In Cilicia, as in Malatya and the Keban region, the ties with Syria are not completely cut off, and indeed in EB Tarsus we note a mingling of connections, perhaps concomitant with the developing exploitation of metal ores in the Taurus Mountains.

The clearest indicator of the variety of Cilician contacts is the pottery, although metal objects, the development of seals and sealings, and architectural traits can also be considered diagnostic. In EB I, Tarsus continues a small-scale production of buff wheel-made wares (Goldman 1956:fig. 236) and some chaff-faced ware (figs. 234–35), enough to prove contact with the Amuq G and North Syrian sequence. The bulk of the pottery is now of Anatolian handmade wares, with the first beak-spouted pitchers turning up at the start of EB I (Goldman 1956:fig. 237:53–56).

Tarsus EB II still has buff wheel-made Syrian wares (Goldman 1956:fig. 245:178–87) in specimens imported or made by resident potters; it also has spiral-burnished wheel-made jars (fig. 263:369–70), some with red bands of the type known from the Gaziantep region, from the Amarna cemetery near Carchemish (Woolley 1914:pl. XXII), from Chuera (Kühne 1976:68–70), and from Mari (Parrot 1956:221–22, M1548–1549). A bottle of this period (Goldman 1956:114, no. 154) resembles one from tomb PG 1273 at Ur (Woolley 1934b:466–67; Kühne 1976:69, pl. 42:7), a similar piece from Fara (Istanbul Museum 5926), as well as bottles from the Amarna cemetery (Woolley 1914:pl. XXII) and Mari (Aleppo M3016). The date of PG 1273 is Early Dynastic III, "Meskalamdug period." A strong link of Tarsus EB II is with the Zincirli-Gedikli Hüyük area just across the Amanus, attested by the presence of brick-red incised ware (Goldman 1956:figs. 255, 278–83; U. B. Alkım 1968:84–96; H. Alkım 1979). This ware starts to appear at the beginning of EB II in Tarsus and continues into EB III. It is equally long lasting at Gedikli, with a gradual change of shapes. Early wheel-made goblet fragments of reddish ware (Goldman 1956:fig. 248, no. 240) are also paralleled at Gedikli (H. Alkım 1979:pl. 89:17–18). The Tarsus pieces are imports. The range of such wares in the Amuq, brittle orange ware, is phases H–early J.

Cyprus is connected with EB II Tarsus through the red-and-black streak-burnished ware (Goldman 1956:figs. 263, 371–78, pp. 112–13) which is known from Kyra-Alonia and Philia (Dikaios 1962:201–3; Watkins 1981:18–19; Peltenburg 1981:36).

An Egyptian connection of long-range trade and exchange is proved by the presence of a Cilician reserved-slip pitcher in an annex to mastaba G 1233 at Giza, dated before the end of Cheops' life (Goldman 1956:60; Reisner and Smith 1955:73, early Dynasty IV, before 2566 B.C. by *Cambridge Ancient History* chronology). The

specific kind of reserved slip represented here is not of north Syrian type, but is typical of Tarsus (Goldman 1956:fig. 248, no. 204, *pace* Huot 1982:1069). For EB II then, Tarsus has an absolute date from Egyptian historical chronology; the range of the reserved-slip ware is fairly early in the development of the EB II town. In Goldman (1956), plan 4, room 115 is a prominent find-spot of this ware.

The connection with the south Anatolian plateau is most clearly marked by the presence in Tarsus of a peculiar handmade painted ware that is a subgroup of the handmade "metallic" ware of the Konya and Aksaray-Niğde plains. The ware in question (Goldman 1956:fig. 247) is buff-yellowish slipped and painted in a purplish, sometimes shining paint. Shapes are pitchers with rising spouts, two-handled jars, and bowls. Jars and pitchers tend to have tiny pierced lugs added below rim or spout. The fabric is imported in Tarsus. It was found in Mellaart's 1951–52 survey (Mellaart 1954:191) especially near the northern entrance to the Cilician Gates. Examples of complete vessels come from Konya Karahüyük level 7 (Alp 1968:pl. 10:19), from Bolgarmaden, from a plundered cemetery near Dar Boğaz in the Ulukışla area, and from Acemhüyük in level 10 of the deep sounding (N. Özgüç 1983a:110). This ware may be especially at home in the region of the metal trading communities of the Taurus Mountains and their associates during the period of Tarsus EB II, starting at least as early as 2600 B.C., if we use the Egyptian synchronism.

A considerable change takes place in the EB III contacts of Cilicia. West Anatolian communications have been opened forcefully and make themselves known in the ceramic repertoire without cutting off the Syrian interaction. As before, the Syrian synchronisms of Tarsus EB III are in the ceramic categories of wheel-made goblets and bottles (Goldman 1956:fig. 268). Wheel-made plain-ware cups and goblets are always present in small quantities, but these become more elegantly profiled in the last phase of EB III (Goldman 1956:144–45). Here they correlate with Amuq J.

The bottles attest a trade perhaps of a perfumed commodity. Some of the containers are buff and smooth, others gray and ribbed or spiral-burnished. All imported specimens are wheel-made (Goldman 1956:154, fig. 268). The North Mesopotamian and Syrian series continues from Early Dynastic III into Akkadian; the slender gray bottles with double-profiled rim (shaped like Goldman 1956:fig. 286:617) and rather pointed base are recognizable also in the Amarna cemetery (Woolley 1914:pl. XXIII, 12) and at Tilmen Hüyük level IIId in the Islahiye area (U. B. Alkım 1964:505, fig. 9); at Chuera the types differ slightly (Kühne 1976:37–38, pls. 7 and 42). At Kültepe these bottles turn up in mound levels 12 and 11 (see below). The synchronisms of the Tarsus EB

III late sublevels are indicative of increasing export from north Syria and north Mesopotamia in the second half of EB III, EB IIIb.

The major change in Anatolian connections of Tarsus EB III is in its interaction with southwest and west Anatolia. Contacts now clearly extend as far as Troy to the northwest, although one hesitates to call the initiatives for the new era Trojan. Several ceramic innovations appear in Troy and in southwest Anatolia (Aphrodisias, Karataş) and Cilicia, with wide-ranging side effects.

The principal innovations in Tarsus are one- and two-handled tankards with globular lower bodies and flaring rims; bell-shaped two-handled cups; depa with two bold handles on a narrow body, initially handmade and coiled, later wheel-made; one- and two-handled bowls of articulated profiles; wheel-made buff plates, large red-slipped and polished platters. Technically the wheel is introduced for more and more shapes. The finish of much of the pottery is red, with a striking use of interior rim bands and careful polishing (Goldman 1956:figs. 264–67 for general survey).

At Tarsus these innovations appear suddenly and en masse at the beginning of a period clearly to be separated chronologically as EB III. The final EB II building level had ended in conflagration (Goldman 1956:plan 9). The next habitation phase is poorly preserved, but the first construction on top of the burnt level and the numerous bothroi have all the telltale features. The better-preserved succeeding phases have megaroid plans (Goldman 1956:34) which gradually disappear in EB IIIb.

The west Anatolian depas and tankard forms became known as far east as Gedikli in the Islahiye plain, where a cremation cemetery of the EB III phase has tomb gifts in the shape of depa (U. B. Alkım 1968:pl. 40, p. 96) and two-handled tankards (H. Alkım 1979:140–41, pls. 91:28, 92:29 and 30; Exhibition 1983, I, A 453, p. 172, cf. depas A 454, p. 107, A 455). Some of these are imports; other pieces have been locally manufactured in brick-red ware. They are associated with lentoid pilgrim flasks with cutaway spouts (H. Alkım 1979:pl. 92:31, p. 140; Bilgi 1982:6) which also coexist with depa and tankards in southwest Anatolia. The Gedikli context moreover has gray bottles with double-profiled rims along with the reddish orange ware which continues to develop during the EB III period. The range of this large cemetery is EB IIIa–b. An EB IIIb–type depas occurs at Tell Tainat in Amuq phase J (Braidwood and Braidwood 1960:450–51). Another depas variant of curvaceous profile came from a tomb at Selenkahiye on the Euphrates (Van Loon 1968:21), with goblets of Hama J6 type in a context judged to be Late Akkadian.

The west Anatolian traits will allow a stratigraphic coordination of sites and sublevels of the EB III period from Gedikli and Tarsus to west and central Anatolia. We review the EB I–III developments regionally.

West Anatolia

The exact coordination of the Troy I sequence with sites outside of the Troad proper is difficult because of the parochial nature of the handmade pottery traditions and the scarcity of imports. Typologically it is clear that the newly excavated fortified establishment of Demirci Hüyük (Korfmann 1983) runs parallel with Troy I; Demirci Hüyük has earlier, Chalcolithic levels which are not easily accessible. Another larger fortress is that of Klazomenai-Limantepe (Erkanal and Erkanal 1983), which has architectural as well as ceramic parallels with Troy I. The earliest known occupation of Old Smyrna-Bayraklı also dates back to this period (Akurgal 1950:54). Cemeteries of the Troy I era, but of slightly different ceramic traditions, are found inland in the Yortan-Soma area (Bittel 1941; Kamil 1982).

The debate concerning the chronology of Troy I and its subphases (Blegen et al. 1950) is continuing without agreement (Podzuweit 1979; Easton 1976). The transition to Troy II is judged differently by various analysts. Wherever the exact dividing line may be drawn, there are signs of destruction at the end of I and signs of innovation in II. The ceramic innovations, starting in Blegen's phases II b–c, are largely although not completely identical with those seen at Tarsus in Cilician EB IIIa: depa, tankards, wheelmade plates, red platters, new shapes of bowls, buff fabrics, introduction of the wheel, reddish surface finishes. There is no slow development of these shapes and traits at Troy, or at Tarsus; the real center of these ceramic fashions is presumably elsewhere in the west.

A candidate for analysis in this context is Aphrodisias (Kadish 1969:61, 1971:137), where a good stratification contains levels corresponding to Troy II and Tarsus EB IIIA, which yield the one-handled sharply profiled red tankards that are atypical in the Troad, and stacks of wheel-made plates (Kadish 1971:complex VI, pl. 25:4; pl. 30:39, p. 137; Joukowsky 1986:389–92). Beycesultan has a solid EB I and II development of regional type, but a destruction at the end of level XIII seems to cut off the introduction of the west Anatolian ceramic traits so evident at Aphrodisias; the beginnings of the red-slipped bell-shaped cups and tankards may be just detected in XIIIa (Lloyd and Mellaart 1962:56, 190, fig. P46, 1–5, wheel-made plate in 6). What appears to be lacking is Troy II material; levels XII–VIII run parallel with Troy III–IV (Lloyd and Mellaart 1962:264).

The development at Karataş in the Elmalı plain of north Lycia is represented in the central mansion, the village houses, and the tombs of EB I and II, Karataş levels

I–V. At the end of the Karataş series of pithos burials we note the appearance of one-handled tankards, lentoid flasks with cutaway spouts, and basket-handled spouted jars of "teapot" type (Mellink 1964: figs. 14, 18, 20, 29), still mostly handmade, but with an occasional wheel-made piece, such as a gray one-handled jar (fig. 15). This material is also found in the latest houses of level V, which reach the transitional stage EB II–III. In the EB IIIa houses of trenches 31, 35–37, and 66, the new-style pottery appears with two-handled tankards, depa, and wheel-made plates and platters (Mellink 1967: figs. 42, 46, 1968:259).

The transitional EB II–III material from Karataş is also represented in unstratified material now housed in the museums at Burdur, Uşak, and Eskişehir, presumably from looted cemeteries. It is noteworthy that no depa and two-handled tankards have been found in tombs at Karataş. In the Yortan cemetery, the very latest tombs may have had lentoid flasks, small teapots, and tankards, but no depa, although the record can only be hypothetically reconstructed (Kamil 1982:49–52, Class B and C pottery). In faraway Gedikli, cremation burials were provided with depa, tankards, and lentoid flasks (see above).

The debate over the relative placement of the regional EB II–III sequences in west Anatolia has a bearing on the coordination with the Aegean chronology of Early Helladic and Early Cycladic II–III (see Coleman, this vol., chap. 11). An intrusion of west Anatolian ceramic material is discernible in the Cyclades, on Euboea, and in central Greece. Its clearest symptoms are tomb gifts in the Cyclades, in the cemetery at Manika, which has one-handled tankards, lentoid pitchers with cutaway spouts, beaked pitchers (Papavasiliou 1910), and pottery from Lefkandi habitation level I (Popham and Sackett 1968:6, 8). It is possible to interpret the first manifestations of this intrusion as west Anatolian transitional EB II–III, regionally not Trojan but rather southwest Anatolian on the strength of the present indications from Aphrodisias and Karataş, and as probably antedating the appearance of the developed Troy II features at Troy itself (Mellink 1986). The occurrence of fragments of EH II sauceboats in late Troy I levels (Blegen et al. 1950:186, 193) would support an overlap of Troy I and EH II, and a start of Troy II very late in EH II or early in EH III. Troy II is here classified in west Anatolian terms as EB IIIa. Troy III–IV can be seen as regional aspects of EB IIIb, and Troy V as the start of a new era on the verge of MB.

Cilicia may be responsible for the redistribution of some Syrian wares in west Anatolia. The occurrence of Syrian or pseudo-Syrian bottles in Troy IIIa (Blegen, Caskey, and Rawson 1951:58, shape B5; cf. p. 27; SS 1823–24; Kühne 1976:50–51) and perhaps in Troy IIg (Schliemann's Burnt City) may be best explained as a result of Cilician contacts by coastal navigation. The wheel-made jar with vertical double tubular lug handles SS 2081 from Troy I (Schliemann) or II–V (Schmidt) is aptly compared to a metallic ware counterpart from Tell Chuera by Kühne (1976:49–50, pl. 40). The jar must have been imported, again most likely via Cilicia, in early Troy II rather than in late Troy I. A similar handle fragment from Tarsus is of EB IIIa context (Goldman 1956:161, no. 699), while a miniature counterpart from Tell Brak is unstratified (Fielden 1977:247, pl. XIII, 14). Halawa on the Syrian Euphrates yielded a gray jar of this kind in a semirobbed EB tomb (Orthmann 1981:58, pl. 58:10).

Such occasional pottery imports must be incidental to a much greater volume of metal trade and exchange. The metal tools, weapons, and jewelry from the hoards at Troy are referred to below in a central Anatolian context.

The Western and Southern Zone of the Plateau

Contact with the west Anatolian zone is evident at Polatlı, 75 km west of Ankara, with depa and tankard rims in levels 7–10, some wheel-made (Lloyd and Gökçe 1951:45–46), and at Karaoğlan, 25 km south of Ankara, which has a local EB I–II tradition but EB IIIa material of good west Anatolian type, including depa and tankards (Arık 1939; Exhibition 1983:107, A234). In the Phrygian highlands, the cemetery of Yazılıkaya yielded EB IIIa material of fine quality, now in the Afyon Museum. In the Konya plain, the large mound of Karahüyük shows the transition from EB II handmade wares of level 7, discussed above for its Cilician connections, to the EB III wares of level 6, in which thin-walled buff goblets of conical or curved profile appear as variants of the depas types seen in the middle phase of Tarsus EB III. The Karahüyük cups do not yet have offset bases in Amuq J fashion (Alp 1973).

At Acemhüyük, EB II levels have been reached in the sounding on the south slope of the mound (N. Özgüç 1980a). EB III wares begin to appear in levels 10 and 9, some of west Anatolian character, along with fine wheel-made, red-painted local pottery, and an occasional Syrian bottle. One- and two-handled red-slipped tankards of EB IIIa type appeared in a tomb found to the south of the mound. At Karahüyük and Acemhüyük, contacts with Cilicia must be responsible for the EB IIIa imports or imitations, as they were for the EB II appearances of the painted ware of "metallic," lug-handled type in all three regions.

Central Anatolia

The early levels of the mound at Alişar, as noted above, may just barely start in Late Chalcolithic. Part of the "Copper Age," levels 11–8M, 14–13 T, runs into Cilician EB IIIa, to judge by ceramic symptoms of central Anatolian Copper Age ware in EB III Tarsus (Goldman 1956:134–35). A sign of indirect Syrian contact is the presence of a small Syrian bottle in jar burial d X46 below the floor level 13T (Von der Osten 1937:1:147, fig. 168; cf. 1:176; Orthmann 1963b:86). The development of the EB III levels at Ališar is articulated by the presence of intermediate ware in 7M (13T) and 6M, along with red-burnished monochrome wares, and the appearance of Ališar III ("Cappadocian") ware as an addition to the old repertoire in 6M. Ališar III ware survives in the setting of a new repertoire of wheel-made ware in 5M (12T). In a pit belonging to early EB III, alongside an early intermediate-ware cup (b 2537, Öktü 1973:209, IIA/06), was a one-handled red tankard of typical southwest Anatolian profile (Schmidt 1932:116, fig. 134 and pl. XII), suggesting a synchronism with Acemhüyük level 9 within the EBIIIa range.

Kültepe is the site with the best potential synchronisms, given its historical development. The city mound in level 14 has corrugated buff ware cups of Tarsus EB II and of north Syrian type (Öktü 1973:103). Simple buff wheel-made ware cups also begin to appear, as do wheel-made Syrian jars. The EB III levels of the mound are 13, 12 and 11; level 10 is the beginning of MB and Karum IV (T. Özgüç 1986). In 13, corrugated cups and conical buff cups continue. Level 12 has the large building with central hearth and column supports resembling the main room of a west Anatolian megaron (T. Özgüç 1963:13–14). In this building and level were found samples of wheel-made plates of Troy II–Cilician EB IIIa type (Öktü 1973: pl. 59, I-m/01), a rather simple version of the Syrian bottle (Öktü 1973: pl. 58, I-k/01), as well as a number of local imitations and variants of the depas shape executed in intermediate ware, handmade and painted with red stripes (Öktü 1973:45–46; Spanos 1972:107–8). The cross-painted depas cups are technically similar to red-cross bowl variants occurring in the same level. Similar cross-painted depa are known from Ališar levels 7–6M (Öktü 1973:63; Orthmann 1963b:19). A more complicated variant, also made in intermediate ware, is provided with tubular sipping spouts and decorated with chevron patterns (Öktü 1973:pl. 36, II-C/03, Ališar 6M, and pl. 17, I-C/07, Kültepe, level 12). At Kültepe, plain wheel-made depas cups also occur in level 12 (Öktü 1973:pl. 54). An occasional tall depas finds its way to Kültepe (De Genouillac 1926:pl. 49, no. 112) or to Hacıbektaş in the Halys bend (Exhibition 1983:107, A 276, wheel-made red depas, tall), but note that neither the original depas form nor the tankard has a career in Cappadocia. A variant of the tankard shape was found in Kültepe level 12 (T. Özgüç 1963: pl. X.3; Spanos 1972:73, BI/31), with the handles moved up to the neck and shoulders, in contrast to a tall-necked tankard from Karaoğlan

(T. Özgüç 1963:pl. X.2). The Cappadocian relationship to the west Anatolian Troy II–Tarsus EB IIIA complex is not strong. The wheel-made depas cups from Kültepe level 12 look as if they belong in the middle range of the Cilician EB III period, which is confirmed by the appearance in Kultepe level 11 of Syrian bottles with a double-profiled rim, by now also imitated locally (Öktü 1973:pl. 58, I-k/03 and 02), while the Syrian handleless wheel-made cups become more elegant in profile (Öktü 1973:pl. 59, I-1/02 and 03).

One Tarsus sherd (Goldman 1956:163, no. 744), a fragment of a handmade painted cup, is now classified as Çıradere ware, after an unexcavated site near Boğazköy. This ware occurs in level 13 at Kültepe (Öktü 1973:132, n. 2). The Tarsus sherd comes from an early EB III context, a cup that may have been imported from Kültepe or from a site in the Halys bend. It is notable that exports of Intermediate or Ališar III ware have not been identified in Cilicia.

The EB levels of Alaca Hüyük are only sketchily known. The major find groups come from the Royal Tombs, which, with their profusion of ceremonial and ritual metal objects, have revealed aspects of technology and religion not surmised from the habitation levels. The tombs, in an area on the edge of the EB habitation site, have no clear stratigraphic position in the record of levels 5–7; the burnt stratum 5 is late in the EB sequence, and some of the tombs may have cut into it (T. Özgüç 1948:51–59; Koşay 1951:59; Orthmann 1963b:32–34; Bittel 1959:28–30). Ceramically the tombs are old-fashioned, without Syrian or west Anatolian imports, but with some painted Çıradere-ware sherds in the fill of tombs S, D, and T (Öktü 1973:130, 238–43). If these sherds belong to the original fill of the tombs, they provide a synchronism for the latest Alaca tombs with the first stage of EB III at Kültepe, level 13. None of the metal tomb gifts has a sufficiently restricted chronological range to allow precise synchronisms with sites to the south or west, but there are important similarities.

Fragments of a bronze basket-handled spouted jar from Alaca tomb T, and of similar copper attachments of a silver jar from tomb K, are closely related to spouted vessels from Schliemann's hoards B and S from Troy IIg and another hoard found in the Troad. A related vessel comes from Kayapınar in the Tokat region (Bittel 1959). The rough synchronism again points to EB IIIA for the diffusion of the peculiar mechanism and shape of the handle attachments.

Akkadian reliefs may have historical references to precious metal vessels of Anatolian EB IIIA type. The disc of Sargon's daughter Enheduanna illustrates a presumably metal basket-handled jar of the Anatolian shape attested at Troy and Alaca (Öktü 1973:110–11; Spanos 1977:101–2). A metal vessel with depas handles is carried as booty on the stela fragment from Nasariya (Mellink 1963; Öktü 1973:110).

Other metal forms characteristic of the period are slotted spearheads with bent tangs, known from Alaca Tomb T, Horoztepe in the Tokat-Erbaa area (Özgüç and Akok 1958:pl. XIX) and various cemeteries in the Çorum-Amasya district (T. Özgüç 1978:91–93, 1980:473), Troy II hoard A (SS 5842–44), and Tarsus EB III (Goldman 1956:fig. 428:93).

Jewelry comparable to that of Alaca has come from a hoard in Eskiyapar (Temizer 1969, 1981:54). In this site close to Alaca Hüyük the jewelry was associated with a silver bottle of Syrian profile of early EBIII type, ribbed on the shoulder but with a simple rim. Basket-shaped earrings from Eskiyapar in turn have parallels in Troy II hoards and in contemporary jewelry molds (Canby 1965:pl. XI, 7).

The animal figurines and standards from Alaca Hüyük are comparable to more modest metal work from Horoztepe (T. Özgüç 1964b; Özgüç and Akok 1958) and from plundered tombs in the region of Merzifon and Oymaağaç (T. Özgüç 1978:89–99, 1980). A large metallurgical and cultural complex probably developed in this northern plateau zone in EB II and III, with some interaction to the west (Troy, Poliochni) and east (Transcaucasia).

The site that was to become the Hittite capital in the seventeenth century B.C., Boğazköy-Hattusha, did not have a strong occupation in the EB Age, although settlement has been noted at Büyükkaya to the north of the main site, at Yarıkkaya farther north, and at Çıradere to the southeast. At Boğazköy the earliest occupation on the citadel and in the lower city belongs to the very beginning of MB, Büyükkale level Vf and NW-slope level 9 (Neve 1982:7–20; Orthmann 1984:9–10). A typical ceramic innovation of NW-slope 9 is the wheel-made small cup or bowl (Orthmann 1963a:pl. I, 1–9) also known at Kültepe in levels 13–11 (Öktü 1973:pl. 59), at Alişar, at Ikiztepe (U. Alkım 1979a:pl. 103, 5–6) in the EB-MB transitional level, and also at Polatlı and as far to the southwest as Beycesultan level VIa, EB IIIb (Lloyd and Mellaart 1962:fig. P. 64, 1–5). These are the first experiments with the wheel on the plateau and signs of technical contact with Syria or Cilicia, where simple wheel-made bowls and cups date back to Late Chalcolithic.

At Maşat, ca. 120 km east northeast of Boğazköy, EB settlement is well attested, ending in a conflagration of the upper level on the citadel and lower terraces. This stage is dated to EB III by means of cross-painted depas goblet fragments and some wheel-made ware (Emre 1979:25–27).

The Pontic Coast

The site of Ikiztepe near the mouth of the Halys River has begun to yield a repertoire of EB culture different from that of the plateau and its northern fringes. The architecture is of timber and wattle-and-daub, and the stratification of the several mounds that make up the site runs from EB I to III. Metallurgy flourished, as is evident from the tomb gifts (U. B. Alkım 1978, 1979b, 1983). The correlation with central Anatolia can be made only on general grounds because of regional differences in material culture. Affinities in terra-cotta figurines point west to Europe (U. B. Alkım 1979a:155–56, pl. 115) as do occurrences of gold flat ring-shaped pendants with tabs also known from Varna and other Balkan sites. The end of the EB development is clear because of the central Anatolian links of the following MB culture (U. B. Alkım 1979a:pls. 103–9).

Radiocarbon Dates for the Early Bronze Age

The general range for radiocarbon dates for the Early Bronze Age is from 3400 to 1900 B.C. Arslantepe VI A with its Late Uruk connections still seems to belong mostly to the late fourth millennium, ca. 3350–2900 B.C., as may Korucu phase C, Norşuntepe EB I, and Sakyol-Pulur levels V–XI. The EB I levels of Ikiztepe, Demirci Hüyük, and Karataş clearly cluster in the early third millennium B.C., ca. 3000–2650. Korucu phase D still overlaps with this, but phase E shifts to the 2650–2500 bracket, as does Tepecik EB III A.

For the EB III period we have a series of dates for complex II of Aphrodisias, running from ca. 2400–2000, and the new determinations for Troy II which are in about the same range. This set of dates would agree with the historical estimates suggested by archaeological parallels, Akkadian and post-Akkadian third millennium developments, Amuq I and J.

Postscript on the Middle and Late Bronze Ages

Correlations in the second millennium B.C. become much clearer in the light of historical connections with Assur, Mari, and other cities engaged in Anatolian trade. The Karum of Kanish-Kültepe is the hub of the trade system and best known through excavations (T. Özgüç 1950, 1959, 1964a; Özgüç and Özgüç 1953). The archives of the merchants in the Karum, both native and Assyrian, and of the officials and rulers living in the upper citadel are providing the elements of history in two distinct phases from ca. 1950–1850 B.C., Karum level II, and ca. 1850–1750 B.C., Karum level Ib. These levels will gradually be more precisely coordinated with the historical chronologies of Assur and Mari with the aid of the Assyrian eponym system.

Correlation within Anatolia has been established with two other trade centers datable through tablets of the Ib period, Alişar levels T11–10 (Von der Osten 1937:2:108; Gelb 1935), and Boğazköy-Hattush(a) lower city level 4 (Bittel 1970:41–47). In turn, these sites can be internally coordinated, especially Boğazköy level 4 with citadel Büyükkale level IVd (Orthmann 1984:9; Neve 1982:21–33; Fischer 1963:101). The Old Assyrian period settlement at Boğazköy is large; its burnt remains have also been noted in the area northwest of temple I.

Local Anatolian history is becoming known in political and economic as well as in cultural terms. Names of kings and queens of Kanish are taking their places in the dynastic framework of the Near East. Anitta of Kuššara, a founder of a proto-Hittite kingdom in the Karum Ib era, appears in contemporary records at Kanish and Alişar, and survives in the historical record at Boğazköy.

Acemhüyük is also beginning to yield information on its network of trade with Šamši-Adad I of Assur, and with rulers of Carchemish and Mari (N. Özgüç 1980b, 1983b). Relevant seal-impressed bullae were found in the burnt palaces of Acemhüyük whose rulers were contemporaneous with Kanish Karum level Ib.

A close relative is the large city at Karahüyük near Konya, which was destroyed at the end of the Karum Ib level or slightly later (Alp 1968). Both Karahüyük and Acemhüyük have yielded large quantities of bullae impressed with stamp seals displaying the regional Anatolian variety of iconography and trade centers. Minor arts, such as metalwork and ivory carving, flourish, and trade with north Syria is very active.

The pottery tradition of the Karum Ib era, wheel-made and simpler than its predecessors in Karum Kanish II (Emre 1963), allows wide-ranging coordination of Anatolian plateau sites maintaining contact or being politically annexed in this period of Anatolian strength, for example, Alaca Hüyük, Eskiyapar, Maşat (T. Özgüç 1982:85–89), Polatlı, Gordion, Yanarlar near Afyon (Emre 1978), as well as sites in the Pontic zone, Dündartepe near Samsun and Ikiztepe (U. B. Alkım 1979a). In Cilicia (Goldman 1956:183–202) and in the west, Beycesultan IV (Lloyd and Mellaart 1965:73) and Aphrodisias (Marchese 1976), the ties are less close, but can be discerned.

It is a bit more difficult to coordinate Troy on this ceramic basis, but the continuing study of the western variants of Hittite monochrome pottery from the Karum Ib to the Old Hittite and Middle Hittite periods (ca. 1700–1400 B.C.) will make it possible to create a framework in which the levels of Troy VI will fit as well as the second millennium levels of Aphrodisias, Miletus, Klazomenai-Limantepe, Bayraklı, and Demircihüyük.

For the Late Bronze Age, absolute chronological support is furnished by the Hittite archives of Boğazköy-Hattusha and Maşat-Tapigga, as well as their extensive connections with the literate world of western Asia and Egypt, as with Ugarit, Carchemish, Meskene, and Amarna. In the west, another chronological link is provided by the increasing evidence for Minoan and Mycenaean contacts (Mellink 1983a), providing separate access to the network of Egyptian and Levantine synchronisms.

In the east, Hittite administrative efforts extended to and across the Euphrates. Archaeological evidence for Hittite contacts has come to light in Korucutepe, Norşuntepe, Tepecik in the Keban area, and in sites being excavated in the Malatya zone of current rescue operations. There the central Anatolian expansion meets with the second millennium survivors of the Transcaucasian EB tradition as well as with the strong continuity of north Syrian involvement, which is better known in this stage for its Hurrian components. Historians and linguists are working with archaeologists to clarify the chronology as well as the lively cultural interaction that extends from the Hittite centers on the plateau to Tarsus, Alalakh, Carchemish, Ugarit, Aleppo, Emar, Mitanni, Assur, Babylon, Alashiya, and Egypt.

Ten

Syria, ca. 10,000–2000 B.C.

Glenn M. Schwartz, The Johns Hopkins University
Harvey Weiss, Yale University

Outline

Introduction

The pace of archaeological research in Syria has accelerated significantly since the 1965 publication of *Chronologies in Old World Archaeology,* permitting the refinement of existing regional chronologies and the consideration of sequences from newly investigated areas. Preeminently, the salvage operations of the Tabqa Dam Project on the middle Euphrates have provided a wealth of new evidence from a broad range of periods, and excavations at Tell Mardikh, ancient Ebla, have raised important new questions on third millennium Syrian history and have provided an epigraphically dated chronological sequence. Other regions that have seen a proliferation of research include the upper Habur, with excavations at such sites as Chuera, Brak, Leilan, Aqab, Barri, and Mozan; the Balikh, with excavations at Hammam-et-Turkman and neighboring sites; the middle Euphrates sites of Bouqras and Terqa; and the el-Kowm oasis sites. The long-running excavations at Mari and Ras Shamra have also continued to furnish valuable evidence

for a diversity of periods, and salvage operations on the middle Habur are now beginning to contribute data from a hitherto ill-documented area.

Physical Background

Our geographic concentration in this chapter is the area encompassed by modern Syria. Moving from west to east, this area includes (1) the Mediterranean coastal strip and the parallel mountain ranges of the Jebel Ansariyah, (2) the Aleppo/Qoueiq Plains, the Orontes basin, and the Damascus oasis, fertile agricultural zones, (3) the barren, dry steppe to the east, with its occasional oases such as Palmyra and el-Kowm, and (4) the "Jezireh," the Syrian segment of northern Mesopotamia, to the northeast, with the valley and floodplain of the Euphrates, its two tributaries the Balikh and Habur, and the fertile rain-fed plains of the upper Habur triangle. We occasionally venture into neighboring regions to discuss related material culture assemblages.

The most exhaustive treatment of Syrian geography is by Wirth (1971), who includes an extensive bibliography. Useful geomorphological references are de Vaumas

Submitted 1986
Partially revised 1988

(1957), who covers northwest Syria, and de Heinzelin (1967), Besançon and Sanlaville (1981), and Geyer (1985), who treat the Euphrates Valley. Data on modern seasonality and climate are available from SAR Military maps and FAO/UNESCO (1966); soil data appear in van Liere (1960–61, 1963, 1964), FAO/UNESCO (1966), and Galactinov, Demidov, and Katkova (1966); and information on agricultural conditions and productivity is available in USDA et al. (1980). A summary of the state of knowledge on Pleistocene and Early Holocene environmental conditions appears in Bottema and van Zeist (1981).

Periodizations

General overviews of Syrian archaeology appear in four catalogs of the Directorate-General of Antiquities and Museums's archaeological loan exhibition (Strommenger and Kohlmeyer 1982; Amiet 1983; Matthiae, Archi, and Matthiae 1985; Weiss 1985a). Matthiae (1981a) succinctly recounts the history of late prehistoric–early historic Syrian archaeological research.

Aurenche et al. (1981) provide a synthetic periodization of the Near East for 12,000–5600 B.C. Earlier periodizations of late prehistoric–early historic Syrian archaeology include Watson (1965), who utilized the Amuq sequence as a framework, and, more recently, Matthiae (1981a:52), Mellaart (1981), and Kühne (1980:15).

For the period 10,000–3700 B.C., the periodization presented here reflects the collective work in progress of Hours et al. (Aurenche et al. 1981: 572), first outlined for the period 10,000–6000 B.C. by Cauvin (1978:143), as well as the synthesis presented by Mellaart (1981: fig. 202).

Relative Chronology

Relative chronology for the preceramic periods depends on lithic type comparisons, using either presence/absence or relative frequencies of artifact occurrence. For pottery-producing periods through the middle of the third millennium, chronological weight is assigned to ceramics, frequently produced artifacts whose attributes change more quickly than those of more rarely produced artifacts like metal tools or cylinder seals, which may attain heirloom status. In the early historic periods, a more precise relative chronology can often be determined through the use of year names, royal names, and paleography.

Absolute Chronology

Even for the early historic periods, a fine-grain absolute chronology is difficult to achieve because of doubt as to the veracity of any of the chronologies that have been proposed. The "middle chronology" (Brinkman 1977, and nn. 1–4) is used here for the later third millennium.

The use of tree-ring calibrated radiocarbon dates raises the absolute chronology for later prehistoric periods, lends general support to the high chronology proposed by Huber (1982) and Mellaart (1979), and lengthens the periods that immediately precede the Sargonic period, the first "historically dated" period. Therefore, the Early Dynastic period in southern Mesopotamia, the Ninevite V period in northeastern Syria and northern Iraq, and the Amuq H period in northwestern Syria are each lengthened because of the "high" chronology that results from calibrated radiocarbon dates, while the Sargonic period is fixed, in this chapter, within the "middle chronology."

Paleolithic

Recent summaries for the Paleolithic period in Syria include Copeland and Hours (1981), Copeland (1981a, 1981b), Sanlaville (1979), Hanihara and Akazawa (1979), and Hours, Copeland, and Aurenche (1973); for the Acheulean see Mohesen (1985).

Natufian, ca. 10,000–8300 B.C.

Natufian assemblages succeed Geometric Kebaran A assemblages at Yabrud, Nahr el-Homr, and el-Kowm (see figs. 2 and 3) and are characterized by lunates, pounding tools, and bone industries (Valla 1975; Bar-Yosef and Valla 1979; Bar Yosef 1980), which, with radiocarbon dates, have permitted the division of the period into early and late subperiods (Aurenche et al. 1981:574). Bar Yosef and Valla (1979; Bar-Yosef 1983:17–21) have attempted to distinguish Early and Late Natufian assemblages by both the relative frequencies of bifacial retouch on lunates and their mean length. Stratigraphically superimposed Early and Late Natufian assemblages have not yet been retrieved.

The Early Natufian, which probably spans the tenth millennium and can be identified from Palestine to the middle Euphrates, has a Syrian facies on the middle Euphrates at Dibsi Faraj and Nahr el-Homr (Boerma and Roodenberg 1977) and in the el-Kowm oasis (Cauvin, Cauvin, and Stordeur 1979:92; M.-C. Cauvin 1981a). Microliths with Helwan retouch, also known from Yabrud (Rust 1950) and Beidha (Kirkbride 1966), characterize the Early Natufian (Cauvin and Cauvin 1983).

The Natufian levels of Abu Hureyra on the middle Euphrates, retrieved from Trench E (49 m²), constitute a deposit one meter deep. The flint industry consists of large core tools (hammerstones), flake- and core-scrapers, and microliths. Steep-backed lunate bladelets lacking Helwan retouch dominate the microlithic component

(Moore, Hillman, and Legge 1975:56–58). Three radiocarbon dates are available from these levels (see Table 1); two (BM-1121, -1718) suggest a later tenth millennium date for the settlement.

The Late Natufian of the ninth millennium is documented at Mureybet IA on the middle Euphrates (35 m² excavated), founded on virgin soil. The tool assemblage is characterized by small "segments à retouches abruptés" and microborers (Aurenche et al. 1981). Specific to the late Euphrates Natufian are the "erminette de Mureybet" and polished stone ornaments (J. Cauvin 1978:89). Radiocarbon dates from Mureybet IA suggest that the transition between IA and IB falls at ca. 8300 B.C. (J. Cauvin 1977).

Other Natufian assemblages in Syria have been identified at Qornet Rharra (de Contenson 1966) and Jayroud (M.-C. Cauvin et al. 1982) near Damascus and Taibe in the Hauran (M.-C. Cauvin 1973).

Pre-Pottery Neolithic, ca. 8300–6000 B.C.

Pre-Pottery Neolithic A, ca. 8300–7600 B.C.

Early PPNA, ca. 8300–8000 B.C.

The Mureybet IB and II (van Loon levels I–VIII) lithic assemblages feature a Khiamian facies, also known from Palestine (Cauvin and Cauvin 1983:47). An abundance of borers and microborers is a characteristic shared with the Palestinian Khiamian, and erminettes and baton polis also distinguish the Mureybet assemblage. Most tools were made from small blades and flakes struck from prismatic cores. Microliths, especially lunates and microborers, and Khiamian points, abundant in Mureybet IB and II, disappear in Mureybet III (J. Cauvin 1977:23, 26, 34; M.-C. Cauvin 1974:317), but other notched and tanged arrowheads are also common in II and increase in popularity in III (J. Cauvin 1977:28, 34). Mureybet II has "round-house" architecture with pisé walls and floors of stones set in red clay (ca. 70 m² excavated).

Cauvin suggests a date ca. 8300–8000 B.C. for this Khiamian phase of the PPNA on the Euphrates, accepting the van Loon excavation radiocarbon dates (P-1215, P-1217) from Mureybet and rejecting the three dates (Gilot and Cauvin 1973) available from his excavations (Cauvin 1986; see table 1).

Late PPNA, ca. 8000–7600 B.C.

Mureybet IIIA and IIIB

Mureybet IIIA (van Loon levels IX–XIV) (150 m² excavated) has the first rectilinear architecture at the site, which consists of orthogonal divisions within round houses (J. Cauvin 1978:38). There are several changes in the lithic assemblage: microborers and retouched blade-

lets make their final appearance, arrowheads, including tanged examples, increase in number, the first polished stone axes appear, and naviform cores are utilized to manufacture long-blade tools (J. Cauvin 1977:34). The "erminette de Mureybet" continues to be used here and at the contemporaneous site of Cheikh Hassan (J. Cauvin 1980b). The first baked clay objects are small vases, unique for this early period, and female figurines (J. Cauvin 1978:91). Four radiocarbon dates imply a late ninth/ early eighth millennium date (P-1220, MC-616, -734, -735).

Mureybet IIIB (van Loon levels XV–XVII) continues the previous lithic tradition, with the addition of the new hafting of sickle blades and the appearance of digging stick weights and polished axes. Seven radiocarbon dates (P-1222, -1224, MC-611, -612, -613, -614, -615) suggest an early to middle eighth millennium date.

Tell Aswad

Tell Aswad is located in the Damascus basin, east of the Ghuta and between the Hijjane and Ateibe lakes. The Aswad IA assemblage has long, retouched sickle blades and tanged Khiamian facies arrowheads. The best connections are with Mureybet IIIB. Two radiocarbon dates (GiF-2633, -2372) place this occupation ca. 8000 B.C. (M.-C. Cauvin 1974:435; de Contenson 1983:58; J. Cauvin 1986).

Pre-Pottery Neolithic B, ca. 7600–6600 B.C.

The Pre-Pottery Neolithic B period is characterized by fully developed agriculture, rectangular houses, and a lithic assemblage featuring Byblos points.

Mureybet IVA and IVB

Mureybet IVA (16 m² excavated) has no architectural remains, but IVB provides some evidence for a large rectangular house with several rooms (J. Cauvin 1978:48). Continuity with phase III is evident within the lithic assemblage (ibid., 94), now with characteristic large Byblos points and naviform cores. The three radiocarbon dates available for Mureybet IVA (MC-861, -862, -863) and the two from IVB (MC-736, -737) suggest a middle eighth millennium date for IVA and a late eighth–early seventh millennium date for IVB (J. Cauvin 1977:48, 1986).

Abu Hureyra Early Aceramic Neolithic

Trenches B and C exposed a small area of an "early aceramic" occupation with rectilinear multiroomed structures. The tool kit includes long, irregular blades, tanged points with retouch, end scrapers, and borers on flakes

(Moore, Hillman, and Legge 1975:58–60) similar to Mureybet IV. The radiocarbon dates from this period at Abu Hureyra are derived from undefined stratigraphic contexts (Moore 1982:8) but imply an early seventh millennium date.

Tell Aswad

Aswad IB is dated by four radiocarbon dates (GiF-2370, -2371, GrN-6678, -6679) to the mid-to-late eighth millennium. The lithic assemblage is similar to that of Mureybet IVA, with the first appearance of numerous pressure-flaked, narrow-tanged Byblos arrowheads (de Contenson 1983:58).

In Aswad II, the lithic assemblage consists of flint sickles with serrated blades, often truncated and pressure-flaked, retouched blades, diverse arrowheads, and burins. Five radiocarbon dates are available and cluster in the first half of the seventh millennium B.C. "Connections are patent both northward with Mureybet IV and southward with PPNB culture" (de Contenson 1983:59). The lithic assemblage at Ghoraife I, near Aswad, is very similar to that of Aswad II. Three radiocarbon dates (GiF-3376, -3375, -3374) from this level fall in the first half of the seventh millennium (de Contenson 1983:59).

Keeled cores found at Slenfe in the Jebel Alawiye 50 km east of Lattaqia were identified by J. Cauvin (1968:227) as contemporary with Palestinian PPNB.

Pre-Pottery Neolithic B Final,
ca. 6600–6000 B.C.

Ras Shamra

The Neolithic component at Ras Shamra, on the coast north of Lattaqia, is known from five separate deep soundings conducted in diverse areas of the acropolis (Schaeffer 1935, 1936, 1962a; Kuschke 1962; de Contenson 1962, 1977). Percentage figures for the lithic finds of the most recent sondage, SH, are provided, although the raw counts are not.

Ras Shamra VC

The earliest phase at Ras Shamra, VC, *Néolithique ancien,* comprises a deposit 2 m thick in at least two soundings (SC and SH). The chipped stone assemblage is considerable (19,500 pieces in SH). Tools from SH included scrapers (25 percent), end-scrapers (22 percent), notched, tanged arrowheads including Byblos points (20 percent), sickle blades (15 percent), and burins (9 percent). Unretouched debitage consisted of flakes (68 percent) and blades (25 percent); several naviform cores were recovered (de Contenson 1977:13). Two steatite

stamp seals resemble Amuq A examples. The VC architecture was of stone with plastered floors. Four radiocarbon dates delineate a later seventh millennium dating for this assemblage.

Ramad

Ramad, located 15 km southwest of Damascus at the base of Mount Hermon, was first settled with round semisubterranean buildings featuring plastered hearths and stone platforms. The tool kit of Ramad I includes pressure-flaked Byblos points, naviform cores, and scrapers. Plastered skulls were found, as at PPNB Jericho. Three Ramad I radiocarbon dates (GrN-4426, GrN-4428, GrN-4821) fall in the mid-to-late seventh millennium (de Contenson 1983:60). Ghoraife II, with a similar assemblage, has provided one radiocarbon date from the second half of the seventh millennium (de Contenson 1983:60). Tell Aatne, 60 km northeast of Damascus, has a contemporaneous assemblage with Byblos and Amuq points, sickles, racloirs, and white plastered floors (Coqueugniot 1981).

Bouqras

Bouqras is a "one period" site of ca. 2.5 ha situated on the right bank of the Euphrates 35 km south of Deir ez-Zor. The initial three-week 1965 sounding at Bouqras (de Contenson and van Liere 1966; de Contenson 1985) was supplemented by the 1976–78 University of Amsterdam excavations (Akkermans et al. 1978–79). The latter supply data from (1) the cleaning of the section remaining from original test excavations, (2) a set of five 7.5-m squares excavated to virgin soil, providing a sequence of ten architectural levels and a series of radiocarbon dates (GrN-8258 through Grn-8264), and (3) extensive horizontal excavations at the southwest corner of the site (Akkermans et al. 1983).

The ten levels of the five deep squares included segments of one to three adjacent large houses with a courtyard area, horse-shoe-shaped oven, small side rooms with an oven or bin, and a side broad room with square hearth. The southwest quarter of the site, with more than 3,000 m² excavated, provided ca. 25 houses.

Roodenberg's analysis of the lithic assemblage from three of the five deep squares reveals that of ca. 14,000 pieces retrieved, 4.5 percent of the tools were arrowheads and spearheads of Byblos type, 11 percent were scrapers, and 17 percent burins. Sickle blades were rare, while 54 percent of the tools comprised retouched blades and bladelets. Larger axes, chisels, and paring chisels were also recovered. For the 1965 sounding lithics, see de Contenson (1985:341–46).

The retrieved ceramic assemblage consists of more

than seven thousand sherds, most with vegetable inclusions, beige- or sometimes pink-fired, with smoothed or occasionally burnished surfaces. Five percent of the ceramics have red paint and burnish, while a few red-slipped and burnished sherds also appear. Incised white-filled sherds are rare. The shapes and decorations of these ceramics resemble those of Yarim Tepe I, Tell Sotto, and especially Umm Dabaghiyah levels III and IV in northern Iraq. More than fifty stone vessels of limestone, basalt, and granite occur as little cups, four-legged vase models, and dishes.

The Bouqras ceramics were found in mixed deposits, never in situ on the floors of rooms. Within the deep sounding of five trenches, pottery was found within levels 1–6 and was absent from the earliest four levels. The fourteen sherds from the 1965 excavations were retrieved from level III, the latest occupation in that sounding. The relatively sophisticated Bouqras ceramics do not seem to represent the earliest attempts at pottery manufacture.

Of the approximately 150 "White-Ware" sherds, none occurred in the lowest levels of the site and did not, therefore, precede the introduction of pottery at Bouqras. White Ware vessels (vaisselles blanches) consist of lime plaster, sand, and gravel, and resemble limestone after firing; examples are found over a broad expanse of sites including Ramad II, lower Labweh, Beisamoun, el-Kowm, Byblos Neolithique Ancien, Hama M, Sukas N11-4, and Ras Shamra VB (see Frierman 1971; de Contenson and Courtois 1979; Marechal 1981; Hours and Copeland 1983:76 and carte 1).

Four radiocarbon dates from the 1965 sounding (GrN-4818, -4819, -4820, -4852) and seven from the 1976–78 excavations (GrN-8258–8264) are internally consistent and suggest that the site was occupied throughout the second half of the seventh millennium B.C.

A brief sounding at Tell es-Sinn, south of Deir ez-Zor on the left bank of the Euphrates, produced houses with plastered floors and assemblages very similar to those of Bouqras. Three radiocarbon dates from Tell es-Sinn also complement those from Bouqras. Indications are that this region was densely occupied in the later seventh millennium (Roodenberg 1979–80). Roodenberg compares the Tell es-Sinn lithics with Abu Hureyra, Tell Assouad, el-Kowm, and surface material from Tulul Breilat and Mafraq Slouq on the Balikh and from Palmyra.

Abu Hureyra Late Aceramic Neolithic

After a long abandonment, a resettlement at Abu Hureyra grew to ca. 11.5 ha, the largest village known for this time period. A 300 m² excavation yielded portions of a cell-plan rectangular house. The lithic assemblage is made up of bipolar cores and arrowheads with squared tangs; side and disc scrapers are more common than in the "early aceramic" period (Moore, Hillman, and Legge 1975). Burins and Byblos points are similar to those at Bouqras (de Contenson 1985:342, 344). A White Ware vessel parallels those known from el-Kowm, Bouqras, and Umm Dabaghiyah (de Contenson 1985:342, 344, 349), and stone bowls appear along with fired clay stamp seals. Three widely divergent radiocarbon dates come from this settlement, which may have been abandoned in the early sixth millennium.

Tell Assouad

Tell Assouad is situated on the Nahr et-Turkman, a tributary of the Balikh, twenty kilometers from the Turkish border. Mallowan first sounded Tell Assouad in 1948, uncovering a Halafian settlement, to be succeeded by Cauvin in 1969, whose step trench revealed earlier occupation (Cauvin and Cauvin 1972). The lowest levels (VIII–VII) contained low-fired plain coarse pottery, sometimes burnished (LeMiere 1979), which is not present in later levels (VI–I). The homogeneous lithic assemblage resembles that from Bouqras. Copeland (1979) assigns the surface collections from Breilat, Hammam, and Mafraq Slouq to the same period. Two of three radiocarbon dates from Tell Assouad, from levels VIII and III (Mc-864 and Mc-865), suggest an early to middle seventh millennium date for the occupation and are probably too early (J. Cauvin 1986).

Final PPNB contexts have been excavated in soundings at Damishliyya I–II (strata 1–7) on the upper Balikh near Hammam-et-Turkman (Akkermans 1988d). Ceramics were found in the later strata 3–7. These were low-fired and undecorated except for frequent burnishing and are comparable to the ceramics from Assouad. Lithics included several Byblos points but few burins, in contrast to the abundance of burins at Assouad. Survey results for aceramic Neolithic sites in the Balikh Valley are discussed by Copeland (1979) and Akkermans (1984).

In the el-Kowm oasis, el-Kowm 2 had an aceramic assemblage with burins and Byblos points in the Euphrates PPNB final tradition (J. Cauvin 1986). The radiocarbon dates cluster around 6000 B.C. El-Kowm 1 also included PPNB final occupation (Dornemann 1969) with White Ware and an early sixth millennium radiocarbon date. Qdeir 1, with a different lithic tradition (J. Cauvin 1986), may be later in date (see radiocarbon date Ly-2578).

Summary of PPNB Final

PPNB final sites share such characteristics as Byblos points, burins, scrapers, and sickles. Lime is now used for walls, floors, and the fabrication of White Ware, and an early ceramic ware appears at Bouqras, Assouad, and

Damishliyya. Regional relationships are discussed at length by Hours and Copeland (1983). The PPNB final, with the exception of some outliers, has radiocarbon dates clustering ca. 6600–6000 B.C. (J. Cauvin 1978).

PPNB final sites such as el-Kowm and Bouqras were apparently deserted at the end of the seventh millennium, as were contemporaneous sites in Palestine. Successor settlements are found in the coastal region, the Beqaʿa, and the Damascus basin and share the continued manufacture of White Ware, the PPNB chipped stone industry, and the introduction of Dark-faced Burnished Ware.

Ras Shamra VB–VA/Amuq A–B, ca. 6000–5500 B.C.

The earliest pottery in western Syria is Dark-faced Burnished Ware (Braidwood and Braidwood 1960). A Syro-Cilician *oikoumene* characterized by Dark-faced Burnished Ware and comparable lithic and architectural assemblages has been postulated (Braidwood and Braidwood 1960:500), but regional differences are now apparent (Matthers et al. 1978:122).

Ras Shamra VB

Ras Shamra VB, *Néolithique moyen,* a deposit of about one meter (Schaeffer 1962; de Contenson 1977), is characterized by a prevalence of Dark-faced Burnished Ware (93 percent in SH), which is occasionally impressed or incised with lunate designs or other motifs. Horizontal ledge handles are common on bowls of Dark-faced Burnished Ware. White Ware is also present in small quantity.

The quantity of chipped stone is considerably smaller in VB than in VC (19,500 pieces in VC, 1,800 in VB in the SH sounding). Blades are now more common than flakes, and denticulated sickle blades, relatively rare in VC, comprise 38 percent of the VB tools in the SH sounding. Also common are burins, scrapers, and tanged arrowheads of Byblos and Amuq type. Architecture in VB includes buildings with plaster floors (de Contenson 1963). Polished stone "butterfly beads" are comparable to Amuq A examples. One early sixth millennium radiocarbon date is available from Ras Shamra VB (see table 1).

Ras Shamra VA

Ras Shamra VA, *Néolithique recent,* with deposits one to two meters thick, is again characterized by Dark-faced Burnished Ware, often impressed or incised (de Contenson 1977:12). Dark-faced burnished pottery declines in popularity from early to late VA and is replaced by an unburnished simple ware. Occasional examples of Dark-faced Burnished Ware were decorated with pattern burnish (de Contenson 1962: figs. 26, 27; Schaeffer 1935:164). White Ware and a plaster-coated ware often painted with red stripes are present (de Contenson 1977:10–12). "Husking trays" from VA (de Contenson 1962:503, 1977:11) are remarkably similar to examples from Hassuna II–VI in northern Mesopotamia and provide a link to that region. Flint tools, 9 percent of the lithics, are similar to those of VB and are dominated by burins, sickle blades, projectile points, and *couteaux.* The VA architecture is of stone, with lime-plastered floors. One radiocarbon date from the end of VA assigns the period to the early sixth millennium B.C.

Amuq Plain

The Pre-Halafian deposits from the Amuq sites are grouped into two phases, A and B, on the basis of ceramic typological criteria (Braidwood and Braidwood 1960). The stratigraphically retrieved samples are from Tell el-Judeideh in an area of no more than 72.25 m², with the A and B deposits in level XIV both below the water table. All three operations on Tell Dhahab, 130 m² in area, contained A and B material assigned on typological grounds. A selective field sample of pottery was quantified.

Amuq A, a deposit of 1.75 m at Tell el-Judeideh, is dominated by Dark-faced Burnished Ware (79–84 percent of the selective sample), often with ledge handles under the rims. Bowls are sometimes impressed with lunate, elliptical, squarish, or other varieties of motifs. Other common wares were Coarse Simple Ware and Washed Impressed Ware, the latter found only on the Amuq plain. The lithic remains of Amuq A and B, though mixed, are held to have been homogeneous. Characteristic tools are finely retouched, tanged projectile points ("Amuq points") and sickle blades, as in Ras Shamra VB and VA. The six greenstone stamp seals of Amuq A recall examples from Early Halaf Arpachiyah and Hassuna II. The presence of Dark-faced Burnished Ware and similarities of the chipped stone industries indicate a correspondence of Amuq A with Ras Shamra VB.

Amuq B, a 1.9-m thick deposit at Tell el-Judeideh, saw a continuation of the dominance of Dark-faced Burnished Ware on a somewhat less pervasive basis (52–57 percent). The ware is better fired in Amuq B and for the first time exhibits occasional evidence of pattern burnish. Other important wares were Washed Impressed Ware and Coarse Simple Ware, already known in Amuq A, and the new Brittle Painted Ware. A Dark-faced Unburnished Ware also makes its appearance. The lithics of Amuq B are said to be virtually identical to those of A. Two stamp seals differ in shape and decoration from the Amuq A examples. Amuq B is approximately contemporary with Ras Shamra VA, given the appearance of pattern burnish in both strata, their shared ceramic and lithic attributes, architectural similarities, and position directly below Halaf assemblages. Elsewhere in the Amuq, a deep shelter in the Wadi Hammam yielded a Neolithic occupation which included Dark-faced Burnished Ware and tanged projectile points (O'Brien 1933:174).

Survey data for Amuq A–B sites are available from the Amuq plain (Braidwood 1937:59) and the Qoueiq Valley (Matthers 1981).

The assemblage from Tell-esh-Sheikh XII, near Tell Atchana in the Hatay, is said to include Dark-faced Burnished Ware (Woolley 1953:26) and is probably contemporary with Amuq B and Ras Shamra VA, since level XI, which followed, yielded more of the same ware together with Halaf pottery. The flint and obsidian assemblage included tanged projectile points, sickle blades, burins, and end-scrapers (Moore 1978:314).

Coastal Sites

Tell Sukas, on the Syrian coast 6 km south of Jeble, yielded a 3-m thick deposit of ceramic Neolithic material in a 25 m² area (Riis and Thrane 1974). Quantified data are provided for all artifact remains. The Neolithic levels, N11–N4, were characterized by Dark-faced Burnished Ware and White Ware throughout. White Ware is occasionally as common as Dark-faced Burnished Ware in the earlier levels, then declines in popularity while remaining present until N1. Dark-faced Burnished Ware, comprising roughly half of the pottery in the early levels, predominates in the middle and later levels. The sherds of this ware are from bowls or collared jars and are sometimes incised or impressed; horizontal ledge handles are common. One example of a pattern-burnished sherd was retrieved from N11, the earliest level. The flints, which are relatively few, include tanged projectile points, sickle blades, burins, and scrapers. The architecture of N11–N4 consists of rectilinear mud-brick walls with stone foundations and often plastered floors. Tell Sukas N11–N4 clearly shares many attributes with Ras Shamra VB and VA; the pattern-burnished sherd in N11 suggests a VA dating, but the prevalence of White Ware, usually considered a relatively early phenomenon, might indicate a VB equivalence.

Qalʿat er-Rus, 6 km north of Jeble, may have also been occupied in the Ras Shamra VB–VA period, since Dark-faced Burnished Ware and pattern-burnished vessels were reported from the lower levels of the site (A. Ehrich 1939: 10, 18).

Basal Tabbat al-Hammam was a 50-cm thick deposit excavated in an area of ca. 25 m² (Hole 1959). The site is located 45 km north of Tripoli. The published pottery consists of a quantified analysis of a representative sample sent to the United States. The assemblage included Dark-faced Burnished Ware, often with ledge handles and decorated occasionally with incised motifs, as well as a cord-marked ware and a coarse jar ware. Since no pattern burnish appeared with the Dark-faced Burnished Ware, Hole suggested a contemporaneity with Amuq A, but pattern burnish is present on only a "small quantity of sherds" in Amuq B (Braidwood and Braidwood 1960:77), so the absence of the technique in Tabbat al-Hammam may not necessitate a pre-Amuq B date.

Other Sites

Surface finds from Tell Janoudiyeh, on the Orontes north of Jisr-esh-Shughur, include Dark-faced Burnished Ware, occasionally incised, and Amuq points (de Contenson 1969). Moore (1978:306) suggests an equivalence with Ras Shamra VB for this assemblage.

A ceramic Neolithic assemblage was present in Hama M, including Dark-faced Burnished Ware and White Ware. In the Hama deep sounding, a circular excavation 1.5 m in diameter at its deepest point (Fugmann 1958:13), level M is a 5.5-m thick deposit above virgin soil. Dark-faced Burnished examples are sometimes decorated with vertical incisions (Ingholt 1940:11). The thickness of the deposit may signify a contemporaneity with both Ras Shamra VB and VA.

Ramad II, with rectangular mud-brick houses, is characterized by coarse-denticulated sickle blade sections, White Ware, and a "Soft Ware." Three radiocarbon dates from Ramad II (GrN-4427, -4822, -4823) cluster at the end of the seventh millennium (de Contenson 1967, 1983). Ramad III continues the Ramad II tool tradition, and Dark-faced Burnished Ware appears.

Contemporary with early Amuq A and Ramad II are the lower levels at Labweh in the northern Beqaʿa Valley of Lebanon (Kirkbride 1969); upper levels at Labweh are probably contemporary with later Amuq A or early Amuq B (Kirkbride 1969). Nebaʿa Faour in the southern Beqaʿa, surveyed by Copeland (1969), belongs in the same period. Byblos Néolithique ancien 1, with Dark-faced Burnished Ware, is equivalent to Amuq A, and Néolithique ancien 2 to Amuq B (Dunand 1973).

At Abu Hureyra, the "ceramic Neolithic" occupation is also Amuq A–related. Chaff-tempered burnished vessels appear, some with collared necks and a few with red paint (Moore, Hillman, and Legge 1975:63, fig. 8). The lithic tool kit continues earlier traditions, although squamous pressure retouch is more common, and Amuq points now appear (Moore, Hillman, and Legge 1975:fig 6:9–10).

Recent excavations at Tell Sabi Abyad on the upper Balikh near Hammam et-Turkman have identified a ceramic Neolithic occupation with grit-tempered painted pottery, Samarran-related sherds, and "husking trays" (cf. Ras Shamra VA) but no Dark-faced Burnished Ware (Akkermans 1987). A tentative Amuq B equivalence is suggested.

Ras Shamra VB–VA/Amuq A–B Summary

The predominant ceramic diagnostic of the Ras Shamra VB–VA/Amuq A–B period is Dark-faced Burnished Ware, which continues on a reduced basis in succeeding phases. Lunate incision and horizontal ledge handles on Dark-faced Burnished Ware are particularly characteristic. White Ware and plaster-coated red-painted pottery are found in both Ras Shamra VB and VA and can serve as chronological diagnostics, declining in use by the end of VA. Flint tool types of the period include denticulated sickle blades and tanged "Amuq" projectile points. Lime-plastered floors are characteristic on the Levantine coast but are found earlier as well. The second half of the period, Ras Shamra VA/Amuq B, is distinguished by the use of pattern burnish on Dark-faced Burnished Pottery.

Halaf Period, ca. 5500–5000 B.C.

In the mid-to-late sixth millennium B.C., Halaf painted pottery serves as the major artifactual diagnostic for Syria and north Mesopotamia. Halaf sequences are available from Aqab, Chagar Bazar, Ras Shamra, and the Amuq plain and can be linked to northern Iraq via the Arpachiyah sequence. While distinctions between "true" (i.e., imported) Halaf and "Halaf-influenced" pottery in western Syria have often been drawn, it is now known that at least some of the "true" Halaf material in the west was locally made (de Contenson 1982).

A Halaf sequence from the Habur triangle has been retrieved from Tell Aqab, 6 km south of Amouda. The Aqab data come from four trenches with a total area of 152 m² which, considered together, provide a sequence from Early Halaf to Ubaid (Davidson and Watkins 1981).

Aqab Early Halaf is characterized by painted wares with simple geometric designs on deep straight-sided bowls, round-based hemispherical bowls, and Arpachiyah-style "cream bowls." These early levels also included plain straw-tempered burnished wares comparable to "altmonochrom" pottery at Tell Halaf and one sherd with pattern burnish. Middle Halaf is marked by new shapes such as the *Trichterrandbecher* and by new complex painted motifs, while straight-sided bowls decline and "cream bowls" disappear. Late Halaf includes poly-chrome plates and shallow flat-based bowls with everted rims. "Mother goddess" seated clay figurines, sometimes painted, appeared in Late Halaf levels, as did stone seal pendants with incised linear designs. The Transitional phase, following Late Halaf, includes jars with bow-rims, disc-based deep bowls with S-profiles comparable to Gawra XX–XVII examples, and Ubaid motifs in the painted ware. More "mother goddess" figurines and stone seal pendants were recovered from this phase.

The Early Halaf pottery at Aqab is correlated to Arpachiyah pre-TT 10 (Arpachiyah "Early Halaf"), Middle Halaf to TT 10–8 (Arpachiyah "Middle Halaf"), and Late Halaf to TT 7–6 (Arpachiyah "Late Halaf"); the entire sequence is contemporary with Hijara's pottery phase 4 (Hijara 1980; Watson 1983a). The chipped stone industry at Aqab is 80 percent obsidian and is said to remain uniform throughout Halaf and Ubaid levels (Davidson and Watkins 1981:10); tools include retouched and unretouched blades, burins, and end scrapers made on blades. The Halaf period architecture consisted of circular tholoi.

Tell Halaf itself, on the Habur near Ras-al-Ain, yielded an abundance of its eponymous pottery from unstratified contexts above levels of "altmonochrom" pottery, a gray-ware with simple shapes, often burnished, perhaps datable to Amuq B or earlier. Seated clay female figurines with painted stripes also occurred (von Oppenheim 1943: pl. CV).

In 1935, Sir Max Mallowan excavated a sequence of Halaf levels at Chagar Bazar on the Wadi Dara in the Habur triangle. Halaf pottery was found in levels 15–6 of the Area M Prehistoric Pit (Mallowan 1936:fig. 2). Although Halaf painted pottery was retrieved from levels 15–13 and included characteristic motifs such as bucrania comparable to Aqab Early Halaf, the majority of the pottery of the three levels was said to be Samarran painted ware (Mallowan 1936:10). Also present were Dark-faced Burnished Ware with occasional pattern burnish and Ninevite 1–type incised sherds. No arrowheads were reported, while clay sling missiles were abundant. Halaf painted pottery dominated in levels 12–6 with such forms as straight-sided and carinated bowls. Level 12 is compared to Aqab Middle Halaf (Davidson and Watkins 1981); some polychrome pottery appeared in level 12 and in levels 8–6. Three clay "mother goddess" figurines, two with red-painted decoration, came from Chagar Bazar 8 (Mallowan 1936: fig. 5:3, 4, pl. I:1, 2); a stone seal pendant with linear incising was associated with level 7 (Mallowan 1936:23, fig. 7:12). One radiocarbon date is available from Chagar Bazar 11–12, suggesting a middle sixth millennium dating (see table 1). Tell Brak, southeast of Chagar Bazar on the Wadi Jaghjagh, was said to yield Halaf and Samarra painted pottery, but no information on their provenience was provided (Mallowan

1947:45, 245). An assemblage of Samarran pottery was also recovered from Baghouz on the Euphrates (du Mesnil du Buisson 1948).

Mallowan conducted brief soundings at two Halaf sites on the Balikh, Tell Assouad (Mallowan 1946:123) and Tell Mefesh, 40 km south of Tell Abyad (Mallowan 1946:126). Halaf painted pottery was retrieved from pits dug into the Neolithic levels at Damishliyya on the upper Balikh (Akkermans 1988d), comparable to Aqab Middle and possibly Early Halaf. Another upper Balikh site, Sabi Abyad, had five levels with both rectilinear architecture and tholoi and a Halaf painted pottery assemblage with deep straight-sided flat-based bowls and "cream bowls" contemporary to Aqab Early Halaf (Akkermans 1987). Akkermans (1984) and Copeland (1979) discuss the Halaf survey data from the Balikh.

Shams-ed-din Tannira is a one-period Halaf site on the middle Euphrates in the Tabqa Dam region, with an exposed area of 175 m². The pottery is suggested to be contemporary with the Aqab Middle and Late phases (Gustavson-Gaube 1981). The lithic assemblage included end-scrapers, piercers, burins, and sickles (Azoury and Bergman 1980). A sounding to virgin soil at Tell Ahmar on the middle Euphrates, ancient Til-Barsib, identified an early occupation with Halaf pottery (Thureau-Dangin and Dunand 1936).

Excavations at Tell Rifaat in the Qoueiq Valley recovered Halaf painted pottery and Dark-faced Burnished pottery in lower level VI, with a chipped stone assemblage including scrapers, sickle blades, and small blade cores (Seton-Williams 1961:87). At Tell Maled, 35 km north of Aleppo, lower levels had a Halaf assemblage comparable to Amuq C, while higher levels had Red Wash Ware, found in Amuq D and Ras Shamra IVC–A (Gustavson-Gaube 1981–82). Survey data are available from the Qoueiq (Mellaart 1981) and from the Jabboul plain (Maxwell Hyslop et al. 1942:24).

Ras Shamra IV

The period of Halaf painted pottery at Ras Shamra is divided into three phases. Ras Shamra IVC is characterized by painted pottery, including bucrania motifs, comparable to the Mesopotamian Halaf. This pottery, which constitutes no more than 6 percent of the SH ceramics, was previously considered an import from the east but has recently been shown to be locally manufactured (de Contenson 1982:96). Other wares were orange pottery with painted chevrons resembling Amuq B Brittle Painted Ware (cf. also Mersin XXIV) (Schaeffer 1962a:168; de Contenson 1982), Dark-faced Burnished Ware, sometimes with pattern burnish, and Red Wash Ware, which continues at Ras Shamra until the end of

IIIB. In Sounding SH, Halaf painted pottery rises in popularity as the use of pattern burnish decreases (de Contenson 1973b:23). The architecture of IVC consists of rectilinear stone foundations.

Ras Shamra IVB contains painted Halaf-style pottery with motifs comparable to Arpachiyah Late Halaf, constituting 20 percent of the SH assemblage. The predominant pottery is Red Wash Ware, used for bow-rim jars, a new shape, and pedestal-based bowls, sometimes with lug handles. Baked clay "sling balls" are reported to be characteristic of IVB (de Contenson 1963:38), as is rectilinear stone architecture.

The end of Halaf pottery occurs in Ras Shamra IVA. Halaf-style painted ware comprises 7 percent of the SH assemblage, and the predominant ware remains Red Wash Ware (80 percent). The chipped stone industry of Ras Shamra IV includes backed, denticulated sickle blades, diamond-shaped arrowheads with short tangs, bifacially worked axheads, borers, burins, grattoirs, and racloirs (de Contenson 1973b:27).

Amuq C–D

Stratified Halaf-period remains from the Amuq sites derive from Tell Kurdu Trenches I and IV, constituting an exposed area of 43 m². These contexts were excavated without respect to floors, and no architectural data are available. The First Mixed Range at Tell el-Judeideh also contains pottery datable to this period (Braidwood and Braidwood 1960:100).

The beginning of Amuq C is defined typologically by the appearance of Halaf painted ware. Since no transitional period is evident between Amuq B and C, it is possible that a gap representing the end of Amuq B and the beginning of C is present at Kurdu. Halaf painted pottery, 9 percent of the Amuq C selected sherd sample, includes bowls with everted collars (*Trichterrandbecher*), holemouth vessels, and collared jars, and such motifs as bucrania, plain bands, and chain bands with dot filling. This pottery parallels the Mesopotamian Halaf and was previously considered imported (de Contenson 1982:95–96). Another Halaf-related painted ware comprised 31–36 percent of the assemblage and included bowls with everted collars and collared jars, with simple geometric motifs such as plain bands and vertical or oblique line groups between wavy bands. The most popular ware of Amuq C is still Dark-face Burnished Ware but now with thicker walls than in Amuq B. The most common shape is a jar with a high flared collar; the bowls are now often burnished only about the rim. The ledge handles, incised decoration, and holemouth shapes common in Amuq B are absent in C. Likewise, pattern burnish is attested but is not as common as in B. The chipped stone assemblage from Amuq C differs distinctly from the preceding Amuq A and B assemblages: sickle blades are now retouched on the backs and ends as well as on the denticulated edge and are broader and longer, and the abundant projectile points of Amuq A and B are absent. Clay sling balls now appear, perhaps as the replacement of the projectile points (Braidwood and Braidwood 1960:150).

Amuq D is present only in Trench I of Kurdu. In this phase, Halaf painted ware and Halaf-like painted ware persist in reduced numbers. The prevailing ware is Wiped Burnish Ware, a variation of Dark-faced Burnished Ware present in such shapes as bowls with inverted rims and bow-rim jars, a new form in Amuq D. Dark-faced Burnished Ware proper is also still present, and Red Wash Ware makes its first appearance in the Amuq in collared and bow-rim jars. Braidwood and Braidwood (1960:164ff.) identify the presence of several "transitional painted wares" which include Ubaid-like motifs. The chipped stone assemblage resembles that of Amuq C, and one clay sling ball was retrieved. The excavations at Tell esh-Sheikh yielded Halaf painted pottery together with Dark-faced Burnished Ware from level XI up, but this assemblage has yet to be published (see Woolley 1953:29).

Hama L

Hama L was present in Sondage G11 and in Sq. H-I11, which constituted three levels with stone foundations of rectilinear architecture. The pottery from these contexts included Halaf painted ware as well as Ubaid-like painted pottery and may belong in a Late Halaf/Early Ubaid transitional phase (Ingholt 1940:12–13; Fugmann 1958:14, 17). Excavations at Arjoune, southwest of Homs, have recovered an assemblage with Dark-faced Burnished Ware, pattern burnish, and Halaf painted ware (Marfoe and Parr 1981–82c).

Ard Tlaili in the Beqa'a Valley of Lebanon had an Amuq C occupation in its lower levels with Dark-faced Burnished Ware and Halaf painted pottery, while an Amuq D presence was apparent at the very top with bow rims and Red Wash Ware (Kirkbride 1969). Byblos Néolithique moyen is approximately equivalent to Amuq C, and Néolithique récent, with Red Wash Ware and bow rims, is equivalent to Amuq D (Dunand 1973).

Halaf Summary

Reviewing the evidence, we may correlate Amuq C with Ras Shamra IVC because of the presence of Halaf painted ware, Dark-faced Burnished Ware, and pattern burnish. Middle Halaf levels at Aqab and Chagar Bazar are roughly contemporary with Amuq C and Ras Shamra IVC, while Aqab Early Halaf and Chagar Bazar 15–13 must be somewhat earlier.

Amuq D can be chronologically linked to Ras Shamra IVB and IVA, the later Halaf levels at Chagar Bazar, and probably Aqab Late Halaf and Transitional levels, on the basis of the presence of Red Wash Ware in the Amuq and Ras Shamra and the bow-rim jar in the Amuq, Ras Shamra, and Aqab.

In the earlier part of the Halaf period in north Syria, Dark-faced Burnished Ware and pattern burnish decline and disappear, while Red Wash Ware emerges and becomes popular by the end of the period. In northern Mesopotamia, seated clay female figurines often decorated with painted stripes ("mother goddesses") are a Halaf period diagnostic, as are stone seal pendants with incised linear decoration. The lithic assemblages are characterized by sickle blades retouched on the back and end as well as on the denticulated edge. Projectile points, very common in the preceding Amuq A–B/Ras Shamra VB–A period, no longer appear and are evidently replaced by baked clay sling missiles.

Ubaid Period, ca. 5000–4000 B.C.

Ubaid painted pottery serves as the major chronological diagnostic for the fifth millennium B.C. In western Syria, motifs and shapes can be of a markedly local character and are often described as "Ubaid-related" (Mellaart 1981), in contrast to the northern Ubaid tradition of northern Mesopotamia.

Tell Leilan, Period VI

Operation 1, a stratigraphic sounding at Tell Leilan in the Habur triangle, east of Qamishli, provides an early fifth through late third millennium sequence. Schwartz (1982, 1988b) presents a quantitative analysis of all Operation 1 diagnostic sherds. Virgin soil was not reached, and it is possible that earlier Ubaid occupation preceded the lowest stratum excavated. The ten Ubaid strata, designated Period VI, were excavated in an area of about 25–40 m² and entailed some 3 m of deposit. Painted ware comprised 43 percent of the total sherdage of Period VI and was usually buff with vegetal temper and black paint. The Period VI strata were divided into two subperiods on the basis of significant change in the relative frequencies of ceramic traits.

Leilan VIa (Strata 61–58, ca. 1 m thick, 13.5 m³) is characterized by hemispherical painted bowls with flat or pinched rims, often with undulating line motifs, bowls with sharply inverted rims and diagonal slash motifs (cf. Abada I-Ubaid 3 in the Hamrin), and painted horizontal stripes above the vessel base. A contemporaneity with early Gawra Ubaid levels, perhaps XVII–XVI, is indicated. Leilan VIb (Strata 57–52a, ca. 2 m thick, 30 m³) includes jars with very long flaring necks, bowls with slightly inverted sides and ledge rims, painted motifs of undulating lines or bands on the necks of everted neck jars, solid triangles, chains, and "grain" motifs. A contemporaneity with Gawra XIII–XII is probable. "Chaff-faced" vessels later to dominate Periods V and IV (see below) first appear in VIb, and pinched-rim bowls with exterior scraping comparable to "Coba bowls" (see Hammam VA) are also characteristic of VIb. The architectural remains from Leilan VI consisted of rectilinear mud-brick structures of probable domestic function. One radiocarbon date from Stratum 58 suggests a late sixth millennium date for Leilan VIa and is probably too early (see table 1)

Tell Aqab

The excavations at Tell Aqab in the Habur triangle uncovered Ubaid levels above the Halaf and Transitional levels, including hemispherical bowls with simple and incurving rims, bell-shaped bowls, jars with flaring necks, and bent clay nails (Davidson and Watkins 1980:10). The lithic assemblage is said to resemble the Halaf lithic assemblage (see above). Ubaid pottery occurred at Brak but no details of its provenience are available (Mallowan 1947:45, 245), and similarly, unstratified Ubaid painted pottery is recognizable in the Tell Halaf reports (von Oppenheim 1943). Survey data are now available from the lower Jaghjagh (Fielden 1981a), where 6 Ubaid sites of the 116 surveyed were identifiable.

In the Balikh, Mallowan's excavations at Tell Mefesh yielded a burned mud-brick house with Ubaid painted pottery comparable to Leilan VIa, VIb, and Gawra XX–XVII (Mallowan 1946:126, figs. 7:1–4, 8, 8: 3, 8). Halaf pottery was also recovered in this sounding, and some of the pottery from the Ubaid house has a Halaf appearance as well.

Hammam et-Turkman

A prehistoric sequence at Hammam et-Turkman on the upper Balikh included eleven strata with painted Ubaid pottery, designated Period IV and divided into phases A–D (Akkermans 1988b). The trench measured 2 m wide and yielded 15 m of Period IV deposit. The earliest phase, IVA, is compared to Amuq E and Gawra XIX–XVIII. Hammam IVB is linked to Gawra XVI–XV, Leilan VIa, and Thalathat XIV–XIII; IVC equates with Gawra XIII, Leilan VIb, and Thalathat XIII; and IVD is linked to Gawra XIIA–XII and later Leilan VIb. Painted pottery, never more than 18 percent of the assemblage, is mainly restricted to small simple-rim bowls. Three carbon dates from IVB indicate an early to middle fifth millennium date (GrN-13038, -13040, -13041). Sixteen Ubaid sites were identified in a survey of the Balikh Valley (Akkermans 1984).

The 1939 Jabbul survey also noted sites with Ubaid painted ware (Maxwell Hyslop et al. 1942:25). Soundings conducted in 1971–72 at Anab as-Safinah, south of Tell al-Abd on the middle Euphrates, recovered Ubaid painted pottery (Bounni et al. 1974). Level VI at Tell Rifaat yielded Halaf sherds in its lower portions and Ubaid painted sherds in the upper reaches of the Trench F I–II sounding (Seton-Williams 1961:87). The pottery retrieved from Hama L included Halaf (see above) and Ubaid-style painted sherds (Fugmann 1958:17) and can perhaps be assigned an approximate contemporaneity with Ras Shamra IIIC. The survey of the Qoueiq Valley located twenty-one sites with Ubaid pottery (Mellaart 1981).

Ras Shamra IIIC and IIIB

After the decline of Halaf painted ceramics in Ras Shamra IVA, an intermediate phase exists before the full-scale appearance of Ubaid-style painted ware. Phase IIIC is dominated by Red Wash Ware with hemispherical or carinated bowls and bow-rim jars (de Contenson 1970:17). A painted ware, in bowl and handled-jar shapes, was also in use, with motifs of wavy lines and parallel bands. Chipped stone tools, not abundant, included sickle blades, couteaux, axes, and bifacially retouched projectile points. Sling missiles are common. The architecture of IIIC is described as of "miserable" pisé and stone remains. One radiocarbon date from this level (P-389) indicates a late sixth to early fifth millennium dating.

Ras Shamra IIIB is best typified by Ubaid-style painted pottery (de Contenson 1970:9; Schaeffer 1962a:191). Bichrome pottery, with black and red paint, also appears. Red Wash Ware remains in use, although not as frequently as in IIIC. The most common lithic tool of IIIB is the Canaanean sickle blade, along with retouched projectile points and axes, and sling missiles are still frequent. The architecture is of rectangular stone and pisé.

Amuq E

Amuq E was dominated by Ubaid-style painted pottery, retrieved from Trenches I–III at Tell Kurdu (Braidwood and Braidwood 1960:175). Ubaid-like monochrome painted ware, 72–77 percent of selected sherds, appears with hemispherical bowls, usually somewhat flared at the lip, holemouth vessels, and jars with everted necks. Motifs include straight and wavy bands and chains, and an Ubaid-like bichrome ware is also present. Dark-face Burnish Ware finally falls out of fashion in E, and Red Wash Ware is completely absent. The lithic assemblage is again characterized by retouched sickle blades. Clay sling missiles continued in use.

Ubaid-like monochrome painted ware was surface collected from the Amuq site of Karaca Khirbat Ali (Braid-wood and Braidwood 1960:201). Recognized motifs included not only many Amuq E patterns but others as well, and this could represent a missing period on Kurdu, or a local or functional variation. Akkermans (1988b) suggests a contemporaneity with Hammam IVC.

Level VII, the lowest in Trench A (100 m²) at Tabara el-Akrad near Atchana, contained Ubaid painted sherds and pottery said to resemble that of Tell esh-Sheikh I–IV, the latter part of the Tell esh-Sheikh Halaf-to-Ubaid sequence (Hood 1951; Woolley 1953:29, 1955:7). An Ubaid-related assemblage has also been excavated at Qal'at el-Mudiq IV near Apamea on the Orontes (Collon 1975); flint-scraped bowls (cf. "Coba bowls") and other ceramic elements suggest a date near the end of the Ubaid period, a date borne out by the radiocarbon evidence (IRPA-168). Byblos Énéolithique ancien on the Lebanese coast is roughly equivalent to Amuq E (Dunand 1973).

Ubaid Period Summary

The primary diagnostic of the period is Ubaid painted pottery, whose changes through time are observable in the sequences from Hammam et-Turkman and Leilan in the east and the Amuq and Ras Shamra in the west. A correlation with northern Iraq is provided by the Tepe Gawra sequence.

Uruk Period, ca. 4000–3300 B.C.

Uruk Period along the Euphrates and in the Northwest

Along the Euphrates River, within the area now flooded by the Tabqa Dam, south Mesopotamian Late Uruk period "colony" settlements are known at Habuba Kabira South and Tell Qannas (a single site), Jebel Aruda (van Driel 1982), Tell Hadidi (surface collections, D. Süren-hagen, pers. comm.), and Tell Hajj (Stucky 1971, 1974) on the west bank, and Cheikh Hassan and Mureybet (surface collections, D. Sürenhagen, pers. comm.) on the east bank. Together these sites form a line of settlement 30 km long. Farther to the south, other settlements with southern Mesopotamian material culture have been identified at Qrayya, near Tell Ashara (S. Reimer, pers. comm.) and el-Kowm 2–Caracol (Cauvin and Stordeur 1985) in the el-Kowm oasis.

The characteristics shared by Habuba Kabira South and Jebel Aruda that allow them to be considered "genuine" Uruk-period settlements (i.e., sites occupied by southern Mesopotamians) are southern Mesopotamian ceramics, glyptic, and architecture, all recently reviewed by Sürenhagen (1986).

Habuba Kabira South/Tell Qannas are situated on the

west bank of the Euphrates, 15 km north of Meskene, and comprise a large town of ca. 8.5 ha protected by a city wall with towers, gates, and an outer wall constructed of *riemchen* bricks. The southern administrative quarter of the town is designated Tell Qannas (Finet 1975, 1979, 1980). The town underwent at least two successive rebuildings or renovations, but ceramic or other artifact distinctions between these construction phases have not been detected. The entire settlement may have been occupied for no more than 150 years and perhaps considerably less (Strommenger 1980:65). Jebel Aruda, the mountaintop settlement 8 km upstream from Habuba Kabira, appears to have been the administrative and religious center for the nexus of Uruk "colony" settlements in this region (van Driel 1979, 1980, 1982, 1983, 1984; van Driel and van Driel-Murray 1983).

The ceramic assemblages shared by Habuba Kabira South and Jebel Aruda include beveled-rim bowls, flower pots, conical cups with string-cut bases, water bottles with bent spouts, red-slipped four-lugged jars, reserved-slip pottery generated by water burnishing, four-lugged jars with shoulder incising, and miniature vessels. At Habuba Kabira South there are also local ceramic vessels of Amuq F chaff-faced ware (Sürenhagen 1974–75).

The common glyptic materials include drill-bored cylinder seals, jar sealings with cylinder seal impressions of Susa 18B and 17A style, numerical notation tablets, baked clay tokens with string holes, clay balls with tokens, and clay bullae (Strommenger 1980:64). Domestic residences follow the *mittelsaal*-type plan (Strommenger 1980:figs. 15, 16), and public structures show typical southern Mesopotamian niched facades and clay-cone mosaic decoration. Many Jebel Aruda seal impressions are of drill-bored types with figurative and geometric designs, rather than the "international"-style examples with large human and animal figures from Habuba (van Driel 1983:57–58), and baked clay tokens, common at Habuba, are rare at Aruda (van Driel 1979:26; Sürenhagen 1986).

Sürenhagen (1986) has reanalyzed the evidence for the appearance of many of the "colonies'" ceramic traits within the archaic Eanna sounding at Warka: mass-produced beveled-rim bowls appear as early as level IX and probably earlier, red-slipped pottery was produced from at least as early as level XVI, and conical cups with string-cut bases at least as early as level VIII. Ubaid pottery disappears after level XII.

The first settlement of the Uruk "colonies" on the Euphrates may be determined through six common ceramic types which occur together in Uruk Archaic Eanna VII and VI and Susa Acropolis 18 and 17B: mass-produced beveled-rim bowls, reserved-slip ware, water bottles with bent spouts, straight- or sinuous-sided conical cups, conical bowls with pouring lips, and large ovoid storage jars with rounded bases and cylindrical necks (Sürenhagen 1986). Note however that numerical notation tablets and writing do not occur at Warka until Uruk Eanna Archaic IV.

The Amuq F ceramic and lithic assemblages, retrieved from Judeideh JK3 and Chatal Hüyük, represent a substantial break from Amuq E. The pottery is dominated by Chaff-faced Simple Ware, incompletely oxidized, handmade, and manufactured in plain rim bowls and large collared jars (Braidwood and Braidwood 1960:234, 264–75). Beveled-rim bowls are associated with late Amuq F and early Amuq G. The lithics include sickle flints with Canaanean blade sections. Comparable assemblages (without beveled-rim bowls) exist at Tabara el-Akrad VI–V (Hood 1951), Abou Danne VII (Tefnin 1980), Qal'at el-Mudiq (Collon 1975), and the Qoueiq (Matthers 1981b). Hama K8–6 includes beveled-rim bowls and "eye idols" (Fugmann 1958).

Chaff-faced Simple Ware disappears in Amuq G, excavated at Judeideh, where wheel-made, mineral-tempered Plain Simple Ware dominates. Reserved-Slip and Multiple-Brush Painted Wares also appear. Another new artifact type is the cylinder seal, with southern Mesopotamian Late Uruk/Jemdet Nasr parallels, also found in Hama K (Ingholt 1940:22–23).

Uruk Period in the Northeast

Leilan V

At Tell Leilan, Operation 1, Period V (Strata 52–45, ca. 1 m deposit, 19.5 m³, exposed in an area of ca. 20–25 m²) sees the decline of painted pottery, which was only 6 percent of the total diagnostic sherdage, and the predominance of plain buff "chaff-faced" ware. This ware is usually pinkish brown, vegetal-tempered, and incompletely oxidized. The most common shapes include a carinated bowl ("casserole") with an everted or beaded rim, concave upper body, and rounded base, a hammerheaded shallow bowl, and a jar with a short neck and a rim triangular in section. Examples of these ceramics first appeared together with the Ubaid painted pottery of VIb. A few examples of flint-scraped bowls may correspond to the "Coba bowls" of Sakçe Gözü IVA–C and Hammam VA.

Leilan IV

Leilan IV (Operation 1, Strata 44–41, ca. 1.5 m deposit, 27 m³, in an exposed area of 20–40 m²), contains a ceramic assemblage very little changed from Period V, except for the appearance of beveled-rim bowls, which comprise only 1 percent of the sherds. More fine ware appears in this period, 19 percent as opposed to 9 percent

in V, in the form of simple cups and small bowls with simple incised horizontal ribs or lines. Wheel-made examples begin to appear in these strata as well. One radiocarbon date from Stratum 44 in Period IV and two from the succeeding IIIa indicate a mid-fourth millennium dating of Leilan IV.

The handmade "chaff-faced" assemblage of Leilan V–IV is attested at Tell Halaf (von Oppenheim 1943:Tafel IV) and Tell Brak CH 9–12 (see below) in the Habur triangle and also appears well to the west at Kurban Höyük VI (Algaze 1986) and Karatut Mevkii (Schwartz, 1988a) in the Karababa basin of the Turkish lower Euphrates. The Chaff-Faced Simple Ware of Amuq F is virtually identical in paste and temper but does not have the most typical shapes of the Leilan V–IV assemblage.

Tell Brak

At Tell Brak, Mallowan (1947:33–35, 40ff.) recovered Uruk period remains associated with the various Eye Temples. Numerous animal-shaped stamp seals and at least one "Jemdet Nasr" geometric design cylinder seal are attributed to the Gray Temple stratum, as are the alabaster "eye symbols." The earliest structure, the Red Temple, was apparently associated with beveled-rim bowls and Uruk red-slip "sealing wax" ware, and from underneath it came red slip and painted sherds (Mallowan 1947:44, 192).

Since 1976, excavations at Brak directed by David Oates have also retrieved evidence of Uruk-period occupation. Levels 13 and 14 of Area CH, an area of 2 m², yielded clay "hut symbols" and stamped and incised pottery comparable to that of Gawra XI (J. Oates 1985b). Levels 9–12 had a conspicuously different assemblage which included flower pots and beveled-rim bowl sherds; chaff-faced pottery in these levels is equivalent to that of Leilan V–IV and includes carinated bowls with concave upper bodies ("casseroles"). The chaff-faced examples published by Fielden (1981b) are said to belong to the same occupation phase (J. Oates 1985b:176). Joan Oates (1985b) suggests, on the basis of eggshell pottery, a miniature stone bear, and an alabaster eye idol, that the assemblage from levels 9–12 is contemporary with the Jemdet Nasr period in southern Mesopotamia. Possible support for this dating is available from Karatut Mevkii in the Karababa basin, where a comparable chaff-faced assemblage includes sherds diagnostic of Jemdet Nasr levels at Nippur and Abu Salabikh (Schwartz, 1988a). However, the Leilan chaff-faced assemblage is found as early as Late Ubaid times (Period VIb) and continues through the period of beveled-rim bowls (Period IV). Further, stone animal figurines similar to the Brak bear are known from Late Uruk Habuba Kabira South (Strommenger 1976:MDOG 108:22, fig. 11), and Late Uruk eye idols appear at Hassek Höyük (Behm-Blancke 1981: pl. 12:5). In addition to the results from Area CH, many examples of southern Mesopotamian Uruk pottery, as well as clay wall cones, one numerical and two pictographic tablets, have been found out of context at Brak (D. Oates 1985; J. Oates 1985b). Not including Brak itself, Fielden's lower Jaghjagh survey (1981a) noted 11 Uruk sites out of the 116 surveyed and 21 "Uruk or Third Millennium" sites. Farther south, excavations at the middle Habur site of Oum Qseir have recovered an assemblage with both south Mesopotamian Uruk ceramics and local pottery (F. Hole, pers. comm.).

Hammam et-Turkman

Seven building levels excavated in the step trench at Hammam et-Turkman are assigned to Hammam V and divided into two phases. The earlier phase, VA, includes the remains of a burned building and a ceramic assemblage characterized by a profusion of coarse, flint-scraped "Coba bowls" (Akkermans 1988c) similar to those found at Sakçe Gözü IVA–C. Hammam VB, in which bead-rim bowls replace Coba bowls, includes a monumental building with plastered niches (van Loon 1983:3). The Hammam V pottery assemblage is not easily compared to assemblages either east or west, and no south Mesopotamian Uruk pottery is attested. Glyptic remains include "provincial" Uruk cylinder sealings (ibid.). Five radiocarbon dates indicate an early fourth millennium dating (GrN-11909–13).

Tell Jidle on the Balikh was sounded briefly by Mallowan. Levels 8–7 included an assemblage comparable to Ninevite III and beads and amulets similar to examples from the Brak Eye Temples (Mallowan 1946).

Summary

The available evidence for the Uruk period in Syria and northern Mesopotamia indicates the presence of local assemblages at Leilan V, Brak CH 13–14, Amuq F, and Hammam V, and the subsequent intrusion of south Mesopotamian material culture, either at "colonies" such as Habuba Kabira/Tell Qannas or at sites where indigenous material culture also remained in use such as Leilan IV and Brak CH 9–12.

The calibrated radiocarbon dates for the end of the Uruk period (see table 1) are

1. Leilan IIIa dates (UM-1815, UM-1813) which cluster around 3400–3500 B.C.;
2. Leilan IV date (stratum 44) (UM-1812), ca. 3400–3500 B.C.;
3. Jebel Aruda dates which cluster around 3370–3050 B.C.;

4. Habuba Kabira, one date, context unspecified, ca. 3900 B.C.;
5. Hammam et-Turkman V dates, presenting a range 4160–3875 B.C.

Given the relatively wide range of corrected radiocarbon dates, a central date around 3300 B.C. for the end of the Late Uruk period in the north can be used for present purposes. These dates suggest a span between ca. 3500–3300 for the Uruk colonies in Syria. See Mellaart (1979) for similar conclusions.

Ninevite V Period, ca. 3300–2500 B.C.

A variety of fine incised pottery and a new type of painted pottery succeed Uruk period assemblages at sites from the Habur to the Assyrian plain in northern Iraq. First identified in level V of the prehistoric sounding at Nineveh, this pottery has traditionally been designated "Ninevite V" (Mallowan 1964; Schwartz 1985).

Habur Triangle

At Tell Leilan Period III, characterized by Ninevite V pottery (strata 40–16 in Operation 1, exposed area ca. 15–40 m²), fine ware constitutes over half of the assemblage, usually in the form of small buff cups without visible temper, often incised, with slightly inverted beaded or simple rims and pointed bases. Painted decoration is relatively rare, with a frequency of 1–14 percent per stratum. Other Period III characteristics include holemouth handmade cooking pots with crescent or horizontal lugs below the rim, plain, incised, or painted "chalices" with pedestal bases, and coarse straw-tempered disc-shaped lids.

Period III is divided into three subperiods on the basis of quantified ceramic change. The earliest division, IIIa (Strata 40–35, ca. 1.5 m deposit, 15.5 m³), differs from IIIb and IIIc by the presence of vegetal-tempered buff bowls with pinched or ledge rims, specific incised designs (dotted triangles with rows of many dots, simple incision below the rim with many notched bands beneath, crude horizontal lines), and a larger proportion of painted Ninevite V sherds. Subperiod IIIb (Strata 34–21, ca. 1.75 m deposit, 41 m³) is marked by the appearance of thin vertical applied bands on incised ware and the apex in popularity of pointed base cups with slightly inverted bead rims, of pedestal bases, and of horizontal rib incision. Subperiod IIIc (Strata 20–16, ca. 2.5 m deposit, 29 m³) sees the appearance of fine cups with slightly inverted simple rims, everted simple-rim jars, and incised (or "excised") motifs of slashed, panel, lined zigzag, and vertical groove patterns.

In Leilan III, Ninevite V painted ware is contemporary with incised ware but decreases in abundance through time. Its continued use is particularly attested by thirty-two painted, incised, and plain Ninevite V vessels found in a pit associated with a Stratum 19 burial, subperiod IIIc. The eight radiocarbon dates from Leilan suggest that the period lasted from the mid-fourth to the mid-third millennium.

Incised pottery from Leilan IIa, known from the Leilan Lower Town soundings (Nicholas n.d.), is similar to that of Leilan IIIc and may represent a very late stage of incised Ninevite V, if in context.

Chagar Bazar levels 5 and 4 succeed a 2-m gap overlying the Halaf deposit of level 6 (Mallowan 1936). Most of the published pottery is from graves. Painted and incised Ninevite V ceramics are characteristic of these levels. Chagar Bazar 5 is probably equivalent to Leilan IIIa or b, given the incised motifs present, while Chagar Bazar 4 is probably contemporary with Leilan IIIc, given its everted simple-rim jars and incised panel motifs (Schwartz 1985). A connection to Amuq H is supplied by "cyma-profile" cups (Mallowan 1936: fig. 10:16, 17).

Incised Ninevite V sherds were excavated in areas TW and ST at Tell Brak and in unclear contexts in area CH (J. Oates 1985), where later intrusive leveling appears to have removed the strata between the Uruk and late Early Dynastic III levels. "Unequivocal evidence for the association of bevelled rim bowls and incised Ninevite V" is attested at ST (D. Oates 1982b:68), but "no Ninevite V pottery of any type has been found in the well-stratified Uruk deposits in CH" (J. Oates 1985b:178).

The upper levels of the Ninevite V sequence at Tell Barri (Pecorella and Salvini 1982) include sherds with incised motifs comparable to Leilan IIIc examples; lower levels are presumably contemporary with Leilan IIIb or earlier.

For survey data, see the recent work by Fielden (1981a) in the lower Jaghjagh, Meijer (1986) and Weiss (1986b) around Tell Leilan, and Kühne (1979) on the middle Habur where he found a Leilan IIIc–type incised sherd with lined zigzags at Tell Gabi.

Northern Iraq

Nineveh V, the latest level in the Nineveh prehistoric sounding, was troubled by later intrusions which required stylistic rather than stratigraphic division of the artifacts. The deposit is about 2 m deep and covers an area of some 300 m² at the top. The pottery included incised or painted "chalices," painted carinated jars, fine incised cups with pointed bases, incised or painted four-lug jars, and miniature suspension pots. Glyptic evidence included examples of "Piedmont Jemdet Nasr" geometric seals and impressions (Mallowan 1933:141), also found at Leilan IIIc, Billa 6, Gawra VII, Thalathat Tell V, and Eski Mosul sites (Schwartz 1985, 1986). These seals are

associated with Early Dynastic I contexts in the Hamrin (Roaf 1984).

Tepe Gawra VIIIA is said to differ from VIIIB and C in the presence of fine flat-based bowls and jars, painted and ribbed "chalices" with pedestal bases, and jars with painted shoulders. The chalices indicate a contemporaneity with Ninevite V. Gawra VII has one clear illustrated example of Ninevite V painted pottery—a pedestal-based chalice retrieved from a test trench "at the level of Stratum VII" (Speiser 1935: pl. XXIXa). Otherwise, the Gawra VII pottery is not easily correlated with the pottery of any other site of this period. There are some examples of a well-fired dark blue-gray ware often approaching vitrification, reminiscent of "Metallic ware," for which see below. Incision is common but in simple linear designs, not with the Ninevite V repertoire. Applied animal-shaped designs, including snakes, are said to be numerous in this level.

Elsewhere in the Mosul region, excavations at Tell Billa recovered an assemblage of plain and painted Ninevite V pottery above virgin soil in level 7 and an assemblage of plain and incised Ninevite V pottery in level 6 (Speiser 1933). The incised motifs of Billa 6 include Leilan IIIc designs, suggesting an equivalence of Billa 7 with Leilan IIIa or b and Billa 6 with IIIc. The distribution of sites with Ninevite V pottery in the Dokan and the Assyrian Plain is discussed by Abu al-Soof (1964, 1968), who notes that Ninevite V is usually found with Uruk pottery (but see Weiss 1985b:329) and that incised pottery is more common than painted.

In the Sinjar, excavations at Telul-eth-Thalathat Tell V have brought to light a granary with an extensive Ninevite V assemblage (Fukai, Horiuchi, and Matsutani 1974) of painted and incised pottery together. Two radiocarbon determinations suggest an early third millennium date for the component. Survey data on Ninevite V occupation in the Sinjar is provided by Lloyd (1938), Reade (1968:235–36), and Abu al-Soof (1975).

Excavations at Mohammed Arab in the Eski Mosul region have exposed a Late Uruk to Ninevite V sequence (Roaf 1984). Painted Ninevite V appears together with sherds with simple incised motifs; after a hiatus, incised pottery similar to Leilan IIIc occurs in levels with only rare examples of painted sherds. A similar sequence of Late Uruk deposits followed by Ninevite V levels with a predominance of painted over incised pottery occurs at the nearby site of Karrana 3 (Fales et al. 1984). Other excavated Ninevite V components reported from Eski Mosul include Rijim, Kutan, Jikan, Fisna, and Selal (*Iraq* 47(1985):215–39).

The evidence from Billa and Mohammed Arab has implied a sequence of painted Ninevite V pottery preceding incised, but the contemporaneity of the two types is attested at Leilan III and Telul-eth-Thalathat Tell V. Because of the contemporaneity of incised and painted pottery throughout the Leilan III sequence, Roaf (1984) dates Leilan III to a 150-year time span between the painted and incised periods at Mohammed Arab. The 5-m thick deposit, twenty-five strata, and broad range of radiocarbon dates from Leilan III render this relative dating unlikely, however. The association of incised Ninevite V pottery with Late Uruk beveled-rim bowls at Tell Brak Area ST further complicates the picture. Differences between the evidence from the Habur and Assyria may indicate the existence of regional variation in the Ninevite V sequence, particularly with regard to the popularity of painted pottery (Schwartz 1985). Painted ware aside, one can observe that incised pottery follows a similar course of evolution both at Tell Leilan and Mohammed Arab: the simpler motifs of Leilan IIIa–b and the Mohammed Arab Painted period are supplanted by the more complex and "excised" designs of Leilan IIIc and the Mohammed Arab Incised period.

Mari

Evidence for the earliest occupation of Mari, apart from a possible numerical notation tablet of uncertain context (Parrot 1965: fig. 10), is now available from Chantier B, where two sherds of incised Ninevite V appear in level 14 with a sherd of Diyala ED I "cut ware." Level 18, resting on virgin soil, provided a few sherds with shapes similar to Ninevite V shapes (Lebeau 1987a:416–18).

Elsewhere at Mari, a Ninevite V fine pointed-base incised cup with a slightly inverted beaded rim was found in the pre-Sargonic Shamash temple sounding (Parrot 1954:165, fig. 7). The sequence of Ishtar Temple rebuildings is difficult to assign to subperiods, but a late Early Dynastic III cylinder seal under the pavement of "level a" remains one possible guide to the relative chronology of the sequence (Porada 1961:162). The corbeled tombs within the Ishtar Temple precinct include one tomb, 300, which was reported to contain Scarlet Ware, later than that of the Diyala, and an ED III Diyala pot stand, suggesting that these tombs might fall within the Early Dynastic II or even Early Dynastic III period (Porada 1961:161). These tombs might be contemporary with the Nineveh tombs (Campbell Thompson and Hamilton 1932:78–80; Weiss 1985).

Absolute Chronology

The radiocarbon data for this period come from Tell Leilan and Telul-eth-Thalathat Tell V (see table 1). The two Leilan IIIa dates and the one Leilan IV date indicate a mid-fourth millennium beginning of Leilan III; the two IIIb dates suggest an early third millennium dating of that subperiod, and the six from IIIc place IIIc in the second quarter of the millennium. The two Telul-eth-Thalathat

dates suggest an early to mid-third millennium occupation of Tell V. The radiocarbon evidence, the absence of any obvious southern Mesopotamian Jemdet Nasr material in the region, and the apparently continuous occupation between "Late Uruk" and early Ninevite V strata at Tell Leilan and elsewhere (e.g., Mohammed Arab, Karrana 3, and Tell Brak) suggest that the early Ninevite V period was contemporary with the Jemdet Nasr period in the south. These data, therefore, call for an equivalence of Ninevite V with the Jemdet Nasr period and Early Dynastic I and II (and probably the beginning of III) in southern Mesopotamia. The most useful diagnostics of the period are the incised and painted pottery first recognized at Nineveh V and now stratigraphically defined by the Leilan III and Eski Mosul sequences. Holemouth cooking pots with crescent lugs are another characteristic, as are cylinder seals with "Piedmont Jemdet Nasr" geometric motifs.

Amuq H–J, ca. 2900–2000 B.C.*

Amuq H/Mardikh IIA/Ras Shamra IIIA1 (ca. 2900–2400 B.C.)

The ceramic assemblage of Amuq H, retrieved from Chatal Hüyük, Judeideh, Tayinat, and Dhahab, sees the introduction of Red-Black Burnished Ware, also called Khirbet Kerak Ware, from eastern Anatolia (Braidwood and Braidwood 1960:397–419). Khirbet Kerak Ware coexists with the older, probably local traditions of Amuq G ceramic manufacture across northwestern Syria. Brittle Orange Ware, originating in the Islahiye region, also appears in Amuq H. Amuq H Plain Simple Ware includes the "cyma recta" cup with small ring base also found at Chagar Bazar 5 (Mallowan 1936: fig. 10:16–17) and at Kurban Höyük V (Marfoe et al. 1986) and Gritille in the Karababa basin.

At Tell Mardikh, the Period IIA assemblage has been retrieved from deposits cut by the foundations of the Period IIB1 Palace G on the southwest side of the Acropolis (Mazzoni 1985a) and from another palace below Palace G. The latter structure has at least three building levels, with a ceramic assemblage comparable to Hama K5–1 and Amuq H, with goblets, Reserved-Slip Ware, and a few sherds of Khirbet Kerak Ware (S. Mazzoni, pers. comm.). The period IIA assemblage is characterized by plain "Simple Ware" used for angular carinated bowls (Mazzoni 1985a: fig. 7:3,6) and high-shouldered jars with sharply flared and channeled rims (Mazzoni 1985a: fig. 7:7,12–13, 15–21), and by cooking pot wares used

*Chronological subdivisions such as Early Bronze III, IVa and IVb are sometimes imposed on the third millennium west Syrian data, but since they are not explicitly linked to stratified Syrian sequences, their use is avoided here.

for bowls and high-shouldered jars with flaring collars (Mazzoni 1985a: fig. 7:14, 8–10).

Khirbet Kerak Ware is present at Ras Shamra IIIA.1, where it appears together with local wares (de Contenson 1979, 1982:96). Khirbet Kerak Ware is also typical of Tabara el-Akrad I–IV (Hood 1951). Inland, the ware appears only rarely in the Qoueiq (Matthers 1981b) but spreads within the valley of the Orontes through Hama K 5–1 down to Palestine (de Contenson 1982:96). Matthiae (1981a) and Mazzoni (1985a:9) suggest that Khirbet Kerak Ware did not penetrate to the Madekh swamp region, heartland of the Eblaite kingdom, accounting for its limited appearance in Mardikh IIA and its absence from the IIB1 assemblage. Mellaart believes that the distributions of Khirbet Kerak Ware and Brittle Orange Ware are essentially complementary: Brittle Orange was imported from the Islahiye region during Amuq H and I (Braidwood 1960: figs. 286–87, 310–11) and was widely distributed in the Qoueiq (13 sites), while Khirbet Kerak Ware appeared in the Amuq and Ras Shamra (Mellaart 1981:158–59). For the distribution and date of Khirbet Kerak Ware, see Sagona (1984) and Watson (1965:78) for Syria and Todd (1973) and Hauptmann (1982) for Khirbet Kerak Ware in Anatolia. In Palestine, Khirbet Kerak Ware defines "Early Bronze 3" (see Amiran 1968; Stager, this vol., chap. 2).

Amuq I/Mardikh IIB1/Ras Shamra IIIA2 (ca. 2400–2250 B.C.)

During the mid-to-late third millennium, northwestern Syria is characterized by "caliciform" ceramic assemblages, with mass-produced plain and corrugated goblets (for description see Matthers 1981a:329; Matthiae 1981a:figs. 15–17; Mazzoni 1985a). The temporal and spatial distributions of this assemblage have been refined through the excavations at Tell Mardikh, Amuq plain, Ras Shamra, the Orontes Valley, the Qoueiq Valley, and the Tabqa Dam salvage sites along the middle Euphrates.

Two periods have been distinguished: early, equivalent to Amuq I and Mardikh IIB1, and late, equivalent to Amuq J and Mardikh IIB2. These assemblages are also documented at Hama J (Ingholt 1940), Mishrifeh-Qatna and nearby sites (du Mesnil du Buisson 1935), Munbatah (de Maigret 1974), Ansari (Suleiman 1984), the Qoueiq Valley (especially Tell Kadrich) (Matthers 1981a:329), Selenkahiyeh (van Loon 1979; Schwartz n.d.), Halawa (Orthmann 1981), Tawi (Kampschulte and Orthmann 1984), Hadidi (Dornemann 1977), Til-Barsib (Thureau-Dangin and Dunand 1936), Habuba Kabira, and Mumbaqat (see *Mitteilungen der Deutschen Orient-Gesellschaft* 101–3, 105–8, 110, 114, 116, 118 for the latter two sites). For the spatial distribution of the Mar-

dikh caliciform assemblage, see Mazzoni (1985a, 1985b) and Schwartz (n.d.).

Amuq I

Phase I is defined ceramically, rather than stratigraphically, from two limited soundings totaling 78 m² at Tell Ta'yinat. Similar ceramics, however, also occurred within the Chatal Hüyük and Judeideh soundings (Braidwood and Braidwood 1960:396–98). The assemblage includes three wares which continue from phase H (Red-Black Burnished, Brittle Orange, Reserved-Slip) and three new wares (Simple Ware with "caliciform" shapes, Painted Simple Ware with linear designs, crosshatching, and wavy vertical lines, and Smeared-Wash Ware) (Braidwood and Braidwood 1960:396–98).

Ras Shamra IIIA2

These strata have such Amuq I characteristics as storage jars with horizontal combed decoration, Brittle Orange Ware, pithoi of "Scrabbled Ware," Khirbet Kerak Ware, and Simple Ware. Reserved-Slip Ware is absent. Also absent are "gobelets pansus à bord renflé, paroi cannelée et base évasée" (de Contenson 1982:96), known from Amuq I and Mardikh IIB1.

Selenkahiyeh

Two ceramic periods, Early and Late, can be distinguished at Selenkahiyeh on the middle Euphrates, and these correspond to Mardikh IIB1/Amuq I and Mardikh IIB2/Amuq J (Schwartz n.d.). The early strata feature a deep pointed-bead-rim bowl with ring base, also found at Hama J7-5 and Amuq I, a small globular goblet, spiral-burnished ware with painted horizontal stripes ("Early Habur ware") as at Hama J6, and large handmade vessels with painted wavy vertical bands as at Hama J6, Amuq I, and Mardikh IIB1.

Mardikh IIB1

The IIB1 Palace G ceramic assemblage is characterized by the prevalence of plain and corrugated caliciform pottery and by small amounts of Painted Simple Ware, including jugs with wavy vertical lines and jars with horizontal stripes, Reserved-Slip Ware, and Pattern-combed Ware (Mazzoni 1985a, 1985b, 1982). Except for the absence of Khirbet Kerak Ware, the Mardikh IIB1 assemblage is quite like that of Amuq I and Hama J8–5 (see Matthiae 1981a: figs. 15–17; Mazzoni 1985a, 1982; Fugmann 1958; de Contenson 1982:97). (For Amuq I and J see the recent studies of Kühne 1976:113, Hama J = end of Gudea period; Wäfler 1979:788, 794, end of Hama J = late Larsa period; and de Contenson 1979.)

Date of Destruction of Mardikh IIB1

The archives of Palace G in Mardikh IIB1 provide the earliest historical data for northwestern Syria and historical linkages with Egypt, Mari, and southern Iraq. Palace G was ruled by five kings—Igrish-Halam, Irkab-Damu, Ar-Ennum, Ibrium, and Ibbi-Zikir. The last was certainly the ruler of Ebla at the time of the destruction: tablets with his name appear within the Palace G archives; the archive was on the floor of the Palace G and was "alive" up to the time of the destruction (Matthiae 1984). The duration of Mardikh IIB1 (see fig. 1) was probably less than 150 years, perhaps only about 100 years, or the reigns of the five kings whose names occur in the royal palace archive (Matthiae 1980a).

The destruction of Palace G has been attributed to Sargon of Akkad or his grandson, Naram-Sin. The epigraphic documentation naming Sargon is an Old Babylonian bilingual inscription from Nippur (Kupper and Sollberger 1971:IIA1b). The documentation that the palace was destroyed by Naram-Sin is (1) an Akkadian inscription from Tello (Kupper and Sollberger 1971:IIA4b); (2) an Akkadian copy of a monumental inscription from Ur (Kupper and Sollberger 1971:IIA4e); and (3) an Akkadian inscription on a macehead, perhaps from Luristan (Kupper and Sollberger 1971:IIA4q).

The Sargon inscription is not an explicit reference to conquest (Liverani 1966:12–13), but Sargon campaigned against the "West" at least twice, in his third and eleventh regnal years, according to the later omen tradition and "The King of Battle" (Gadd 1971:422–24). Hallo (1971: 56, and n. 52) suggests that Sargon first campaigned in the west and only later in his reign conquered Sumer and Akkad. Kupper (1971) and Gadd (1971:424), however, date Sargon's Syrian campaigns to late in his reign, after his consolidation of control over Sumer and Akkad. This chronological issue remains unresolved: "upon the chronology of Sargon's reign and the order of its events, we are hardly at all informed, and can be guided only by what seems the natural progression" (Gadd 1971:420). The use of the divine determinative and the titulary "the strong" and "king of the four quarters" suggests that the Naram-Sin inscriptions date to a period late in that king's thirty-seven-year reign (Hallo 1957), but does not provide a date for the events reflected in the inscriptions.

An absolute date for the reign of Ibbi-Zikir and the destruction of Palace G is not available directly. The relative date of the Palace G destruction, the Ebla rulers, and their archives might be determined from the following:

1. The synchronism Ar-Ennum–Enna-Dagan and the destruction of the Ninni-zaza Temple at Mari
2. The relative dating of the contents and ductus of the Ebla texts

3. The relative dating of other artifact assemblages (cylinder seal impressions, furniture) retrieved from the Palace G floors
4. An Egyptian synchronism which provides a *terminus post quem* for the Palace G destruction

1. The Mari king Iblul-il is mentioned in the letter of Enna-Dagan of Mari (TM.75.G2367) to, probably, Ar-Ennum of Ebla, as well as in Ebla economic texts (with a possible reference to his death) and in another text of the period of Enna-Dagan. From the Enna-Dagan letter, it appears that Iblul-il is Enna-Dagan's second predecessor (Edzard 1981:89–97; Archi 1985). Iblul-il is known from four inscriptions on statue fragments from the Temple of Ninni-zaza at Mari. Other pre-Sargonic Mari rulers include Ilshu, Ishqi (Lamgi)-Mari, Ikun-Shamash, and Ikun-Shamagan, apart from the x-zi and x-lugal of the Sumerian King List (Dossin 1967; Kupper and Sollberger 1971:87–90). Iblul-il must have reigned after these other pre-Sargonic kings because they are not mentioned in Ebla texts (Archi 1985). A date for Iblul-il and a date for the destruction of the Temple of Ninni-zaza would therefore provide a *terminus post quem* for the reigns of Ibrium and Ibbi-Zikir, and the destruction of Ebla. Iblul-il may be dated by the style of the statue bearing his inscription or by the inscription itself.

Stylistically, the assemblage of statues from the Temple of Ninni-zaza (and the Ishtar Temple) has been dated to the Fara period (Strommenger 1960:27–29) or the latest part of the Early Dynastic period (Braun-Holzinger 1977:59–60; Matthiae 1980a:102, n. 11; Spycket 1981:97, n. 279). This period may include the reign of Sargon.

Paleographically, some of these statue inscriptions date to the period after Ur-Nanshe of Lagash; others (nos. 11, 17, 69) have possibly early Akkadian period features (Dossin 1967: 307ff.). The use of the verbal prefix *i-* (rather than *e-*) in inscription number 12 suggests a date after Entemena (Lambert 1970:169); this usage also appears in the Tagge inscription (Edzard 1984). A tendency, however, to change *e-* to *i-*, whenever possible, can be documented even at Lagash (Hallo, pers. comm.).

The destruction of the Temple of Ninni-zaza might be associated with the conquest(s) and/or destruction(s) of Mari, difficult to date (Moorey 1981) but known epigraphically from the following sources:

1. Two year names from Nippur: the king is not named, but is "certainly Sargon" (Westenholz 1975:115) or conceivably Enna-Dagan (Pettinato 1977:24)
2. Two year names from Ebla, in one of which an Uti, probably the son of Ibrium, is mentioned (Fronzaroli 1980:33–36; Archi 1985)
3. Sargon's claim to the subjugation of Mari (Kupper and Sollberger 1971:IIA1b)

238

4. Eanatum's claim to the conquest of Mari (Kupper and Sollberger 1971:IC5b).

Enna-Dagan was able to muster considerable forces at Mari, which suggests that the destruction of the Ninni-zaza Temple could not have occurred during the reign of his predecessor, Iblul-il. Thus, the destruction probably took place during the reign of Enna-Dagan. Possibly synchronous Mari destructions occurred at the Ishtar Temple a, Temple of Ishtarat, Ninhursag Temple, and Shamash Temple. The destruction of Ebla, therefore, occurred after the period composed of part of the reigns of Ibrium and Ibbi-Zikir (at least twenty-six annual tributes recorded for them), that is, at least twenty-six years, and probably more than thirty years, after the destruction of the Temple of Ninni-zaza (Archi 1985).

A *terminus ante quem* for the destruction of the Ninni-zaza Temple, and thereby the destruction of Mardikh Palace G as well, is now provided by two Mari documents which provide a complete list of *shakkanakku*s and regnal years extending back into the Sargonic period (Durand 1985). Two Ur III period synchronisms fix the *shakkanakku* succession beginning with the reign of Ididish (2266–2206 B.C.). The middle chronology and the assumption of a more than hundred-year span for the Gutian period make Ididish a contemporary of Naram-Sin (2254–2218). However, using the middle chronology and a reduced forty-year span for the Gutian period (Hallo 1971:714), the reign of Ididish begins in the middle of the reign of Sargon (2293–2237) and terminates with the first years of Naram-Sin (2210–2173). This list of *shakkanakku*s, therefore, may set the middle of Sargon's reign as a *terminus ante quem* for the destruction of the Ninni-zaza Temple. The equivocal historical record for the Gutian period, Naram-Sin's reign, Sargon's reign, and the stereotypical length of founding dynasts' reigns (e.g., Ididish and Sargon) preclude chronological precision.

2. Cuneiform texts from Ebla and Early Dynastic III Abu Salabikh share identical month names and regnal-year numeration, tablet forms, and in some cases identical number of lines and cases per line. Most Abu Salabikh lexical texts are, in fact, also found at Ebla (Biggs 1981:129). The absence of any reference to Sargon or Akkad within the Ebla archive might also provide a *terminus ante quem* for the destruction of Palace G (Archi 1985:51). The probable contemporaneity of Enshaku-shanna and Sargon would reduce the span of the ED IIIb period to as few as fifty years; that is, the Abu Salabikh texts may only be fifty years earlier than the accession of Sargon (Westenholz 1975:4).

The paleography of the archive provides only an ambiguous frame for the date of the archive. Gelb has stated that "the majority of Ibla features fit the system of writing of Abu Salabikh, pre-Sargonic and the time of Sargon,

and that none fits the classical Sargonic period, as we know it from the time of Naram-Sin on" (1977:8). Note, however, that "palaeographically 'Pre-Sargonic' extends to include the reign of Sargon" (1981:57). Edzard (1981:122) concurs with Sollberger's dating of the scribal ductus: "malgré un bon nombre de traits sargoniques, l'écriture d'Ebla ignore d'un façon générale l'un des traits les plus caractéristiques du cuneiforme sargonique classique, la multiplication des clous parallèles très fins qui lui donne une élégance toute particuliere. L'époque de Lugal-zage-si et des premiers dynastes sargoniques donnerait une date des plus plausibles pour les archives d'Ebla" (Sollberger 1982:225).

3. The seal impressions on the floor of Palace G provide a linkage to southern Mesopotamian chronology. More than one hundred seal impressions on bullae, mostly applied to shoulders of jars, or on lids of wooden boxes, have been retrieved from Palace G. At least some of these impressions were made during a final phase of Palace G occupation, for at least three belong to two high dignitaries mentioned in texts of Ibbi-Zikir. "The composite character of these seal impressions is typical of the late phase of ED IIIb tradition . . . the friezes of animals represented in close proximity to each other are of the Lugalanda style . . . minor details of the representations of bulls and lions are equivalent to the first and second generations of Akkad" (Matthiae 1982c:115–16).

Although Moorey (1981) states that there are no traces of Akkadian period styles within the Palace G artifacts, Matthiae has noted some motifs contemporary with the Akkad dynasty within the wood furniture carvings; the composite panels with relief figures of royalty are, however, similar to ED II and ED III votive plaques and ED III panels of incised inlay (Matthiae 1982c:114–15).

4. A *terminus post quem* for the destruction of Palace G is provided by diorite and alabaster vessels of Egyptian manufacture found on the floors of the palace. The Egyptian parallels for these vessels are all of the Fourth through Sixth dynasties. One type, Bg, has a precise parallel in a vase lid from the tomb of Henut, a contemporary of Pepi II (Sixth Dynasty) (Scandone Matthiae 1981:99–127). Two sherds bear inscriptions with two names from the titles of Chefren (Fourth Dynasty). An alabaster jar lid is inscribed with titles of Pepi I (Sixth Dynasty) that were only used during the first thirty years of his reign. The lid was inscribed, therefore, between 2290 and 2263 B.C. (Scandone Matthiae 1979:37–43, using Hornung and Straehlin 1975:53, 86), possibly, therefore, early in the reign of Sargon. Absolute dates for Sargonic dynasts still cannot be tied to Old Kingdom reigns (Gelb 1981:58–59).

The date of the destruction of the Temple of Ninni-zaza, the reigns of the Mari rulers documented there and at Ebla, the reign of Ibbi-Zikir, and the destruction of

Ebla are probably late Early Dynastic III–early reign of Sargon.

Amuq J/Mardikh IIB2/Ras Shamra IIIA3 (ca. 2250–2000 B.C.)

Amuq J, retrieved almost completely from Tayinat, saw the continuation of "caliciform" Plain Simple Ware and the appearance of Painted Simple Ware goblets with designs incised through dark paint to the light clay beneath. Smeared-Wash Ware increased significantly in abundance (Braidwood and Braidwood 1960). Comparable ceramics are found at Hama J4–1 (Fugmann 1958).

At Tell Mardikh, the IIB1 deposits are stratigraphically sealed by a destruction level which is capped in some areas by strata containing the Mardikh IIB2 ceramic assemblage. Royal Palace G was not rebuilt, the destroyed audience court was walled off, and a stairway to the IIB2 period Temple D was built over the ruins of the Palace G guardhouse. A Mardikh IIB2 palace may have been created in the northern area of the Acropolis under Palace E of Mardikh IIIA–B (Matthiae 1981a).

The Mardikh IIB2 assemblage contains Painted Simple Ware ceramics, often with bell-shaped bases, and Smeared-Wash Ware (Matthiae 1981a:109–11; Mazzoni 1985a, 1985b). The multiple grooved-rim bowl, a new feature of Mardikh IIB2, also appears within the hypogeum of Til Barsip and the Euphrates sites from Tell Haddi to Tell Sweyhat (see Mazzoni 1985a:9).

The late period at Selenkahiyeh features shallow vertical-rim bowls (as at Hama J4, J1, H5, Mardikh IIB2, Sweyhat), a collared-rim goblet, also from Sweyhat, a coarse-ware pitted tray, also at Hama J6–J2 and Amuq J, Smeared-Wash Ware also at Amuq J and Mardikh IIB2, and Painted Simple Ware, also from Hama J5–1, Amuq J, and Mardikh IIB2. Common to both ceramic periods at Selenkahiyeh are plain and corrugated Simple Ware, grooved-rim tall-neck jars, Coarse Ware with triangular rim lugs, and Orange Spiral-Burnished Ware. Gray Spiral-Burnished pottery and other Metallic Ware variants (see below) are found in abundance in both the Early and Late periods at Selenkahiyeh.

An extensive occupation at Sweyhat on the middle Euphrates appears to be contemporary with Late Selenkahiyeh and is dated to the Ur III period by a 1-mina cuneiform weight (Holland 1975).

At Ras Shamra IIIA3, Khirbet Kerak Ware, poorly made, begins to disappear, while Simple Ware continues to be used for the manufacture of large jars with combed decoration, and "Scrabbled Ware" is used for red pithoi with white slip. The Painted Simple Ware of Amuq J and Mardikh IIB2 is unknown at Ras Shamra (de Contenson 1982:98).

Summary

The assemblages of mid-to-late third millennium western Syria are first typified by Khirbet Kerak or Red-Black Burnished Ware, which is superseded but not completely displaced by the mass-produced caliciform Simple Ware ceramics of Mardikh IIB1–2 and Amuq I–J. The later caliciform period is particularly distinguished by the use of Painted Simple Ware goblets.

Violent destruction appears to separate Hama J6 from J5 and Hama J5 from J4, Amuq I from Amuq J, and phases of Selenkahiyeh (Matthiae 1981a:111; Mazzoni 1985a:12; van Loon 1979). Mardikh IIB2 constructions also seem to have been destroyed by fire wherever they have been retrieved, and a date ca. 2050–1950 for this destruction is plausible (Matthiae 1981a:111; see table 1 for the radiocarbon dates for the early second millennium assemblages at Leilan, Terqa, Nebi Mend, and Taya). Mardikh IIB2 is therefore roughly equivalent to the Ur III period in southern Mesopotamia. Tell Touqan, which continues the occupation of the Madekh swamp region after the destruction of Tell Mardikh, exemplifies the IIB2 ceramic tradition (Matthiae 1982a, 1983).

Later Third Millennium Northeastern Syria, ca. 2500–2000 B.C.

The second half of the third millennium is distinguished in the northeast, as in the west, by the appearance of cuneiform documentation and by the military incursions of the late Early Dynastic, Sargonic, and possibly Ur III rulers of southern Mesopotamia.

In the Habur triangle, the excavations at Tell Brak have recovered ample evidence of later third millennium occupation, most dramatically represented by the massive "palace" excavated by Mallowan and dated to the reign of Naram-Sin by inscribed bricks found in the building (Finkel 1985). The characteristic pottery of the Sargonic contexts at Brak excavated by Mallowan was Metallic Ware (Mallowan 1947). This pottery, also known as Stoneware, is usually gray-black, highly fired, dense and hard, with little temper, and is sometimes decorated with spiral burnishing or painted horizontal bands ("Early Habur Ware" or "Eggshell Habur Ware"; see Postgate and Moon 1982:131; Prag 1970); sherds make a metallic clink when knocked together (Kühne 1976; Fitz 1984). Simple rim cups are reported to be the most common pottery form from Sargonic Brak. An example of a *Schultervase* (see Gawra VI, Ashur E, Nuzi L4 VI) came from a Sargonic house (Mallowan 1947: pl. LXV 14), and four Smeared-Wash Ware sherds are published (Mallowan 1947: pl. XLIII 1–4). Ur III contexts include vessels with snake appliqué, impressed circles, and incised plant designs (Mallowan 1947: pl. LXX).

Recent excavations at Tell Brak have recognized two destruction levels (7 and 6) and a reoccupation (level 5) prior to the construction of the Naram-Sin "palace" (level 4). The level 6 destruction, preceding the Naram-Sin palace by a generation or more, is termed late Early Dynastic III by the excavators (D. Oates 1985; J. Oates 1985b), although they admit that a date well into the Sargonic period is also possible (J. Oates 1985a). Suggested authors of these destructions include Lugalzaggesi and Sargon. The pottery of the "Late Early Dynastic III" and Naram-Sin levels consists of mineral-tempered Simple Ware with such shapes as flat-based bowls with straight slanting sides and collared-rim jars. Metallic Ware is not as common as in Mallowan's excavations. Cooking pots with triangular lugs at the rim, also common at Chuera and other north Syrian/southeast Anatolian sites, are reported (Fielden 1977: pl. XIII 8–10). A set of radiocarbon dates from the level 6 destruction proved to be disturbingly divergent from expected dates (see table 1).

At Tell Leilan, the construction of the city wall is associated with the beginning of period IIa, documented in three soundings on the Lower Town (Nicholas n.d.); there is a gap in the Operation 1 sequence at this point. The Leilan IIa and b pottery corresponds to the late Early Dynastic III and Sargonic material from Tell Brak. Leilan IIa includes fine incised sherds which may represent a Late Ninevite V stage, if in context (Schwartz 1985). IIb includes snake and scorpion appliqué, impressed circles, and incised plant designs.

Chagar Bazar 2–3 are described as homogeneous and succeed the Ninevite V ceramics of 4–5. As at Brak, the characteristic ware was gray-and-black burnished Metallic Ware (Mallowan 1937:95, for shapes see fig. 18). The metal objects from graves dated to levels 2–3 are comparable to examples from the Ur Royal Cemetery. One inscribed clay bulla dated to the Sargonic period was retrieved from early level 2.

To the west of Chagar Bazar, Tell Germayir, sounded briefly in 1936, yielded pottery similar to Chagar Bazar 2–3 (Mallowan 1937), with Metallic Ware and Simple Ware globular jars, a flat-based bowl with slanting straight sides, a sherd with snake appliqué, and miniature bottles. Tell Arbit, east of Chagar Bazar, was sounded by Mallowan (1937), who excavated two rich graves with gray burnished Metallic Ware. The deeper levels at the site yielded fine incised ceramics with designs common in Leilan IIIc or IIa, including lined zigzags, slashed designs, and panels (Schwartz 1985). A socketed copper adze and fluted spherical ball beads resemble specimens from the Ur Royal Cemetery.

Tell Chuera

The date of the assemblage from Tell Chuera, a large site east of the Balikh excavated by Moortgat and later

Moortgat-Correns and Orthmann, has been the subject of debate (Kühne 1976; Zettler 1978; Fielden 1981a). Kühne preferred an Early Dynastic synchronism because of the alabaster "Mesilim-zeit" statuettes, seals, and bent pins with spherical heads which compare well with Early Dynastic examples in the south. The Chuera pottery, however, is most like Chagar Bazar 2–3, Brak late Early Dynastic III and Agade, Leilan II and Selenkahiyeh, implying a middle third millennium date for the assemblage, probably extending into the Sargonic period. Fine incised sherds from deep soundings in Steinbau I and III have excised panel and lined zigzag patterns from Leilan IIIc and do not contradict a late Early Dynastic–Sargonic dating (Kühne 1976: Abb. 404, 405). The ceramics include Simple Ware forms such as globular jars, bowls with simple rims, and occasional examples of snake appliqué, impressed circles, and incised plant designs. Metallic Ware is present in considerable numbers, including examples with spiral burnishing and with painted horizontal stripes. Although Kühne dated Metallic Ware to the Early Dynastic period, the ware is found in Brak Sargonic contexts (J. Oates 1982) and in late third millennium contexts at Selenkahiyeh (Schwartz n.d.). Also present are cooking pots with triangular lugs at the rim, Smeared-Wash Ware, and miniature bottles.

A large number of clay bullae with seal impressions datable to ED II and possibly ED I were retrieved from the Kleiner Antentempel area. These seal impressions cannot, however, be used to date this building level because they "come from debris that was deposited over the ruined buildings. . . . The only thing these bullae can prove is that somewhere on the site there are levels of ED II and ED I date which remain to be discovered *in situ*" (Orthmann 1986:59).

At Moortgat's soundings at Tell Ailun, near Derbassiyeh, levels with Metallic Ware lay above contexts with fine incised Ninevite V pottery. Occasional incised sherds were mixed with the Metallic Ware. Ailun incised Ninevite V sherds have lined zigzag and panel motifs characteristic of Leilan IIIc or IIa (Moortgat 1957: Abb. 11, 12; Schwartz 1985). Excavations at Tell Mozan near Amouda have recently been initiated (M. Kelly-Buccellati, pers. comm.) and have revealed extensive occupation of the middle third millennium as well as evidence of Ninevite V period settlement.

The colossal basalt statues excavated by von Oppenheim in 1927 at Ras et-Tell on the Jebeleh el-Beidha have recently been dated to the beginning of the Early Dynastic III period (Moortgat-Correns 1972:24) and are probably associated with the same cultural phenomena as the circumvallation of large city sites, the destruction levels at Brak, the intrusions of southern Mesopotamian armies, and the emergence of indigenous, Hurrian-speaking dynastic polities.

Recent excavations at Melebiya on the middle Habur have exposed an occupation with a ceramic assemblage that includes cooking pots with triangular lugs, Metallic Ware, incised plant and circle motifs, and many other parallels to Chagar Bazar 2–3, Brak late Early Dynastic III/Sargonic, Chuera, and Leilan II (Lebeau 1987b: pls. X–XVII). A contemporaneous occupation with Metallic Ware and other mid-third millennium diagnostics is also apparent at Mashnaqa on the middle Habur (Monchambert 1985) and may extend back earlier in the millennium.

Third millennium remains were identified at Jidle in the Balikh (Mallowan 1946). Level 6 contained plano-convex bricks, suggesting an Early Dynastic date, and Metallic Ware, implying a middle to late third millennium date. Jidle 5 also included Metallic Ware, including gray spiral-burnished examples, and Smeared-Wash Ware (1946:135). Hammam et-Turkman VI West yielded a sequence of caliciform ceramics comparable to Amuq I and J (Curvers 1988).

Among the third millennium material published from the Mari Ishtar temple sequence is some Metallic Ware (Parrot 1956:209) and two examples of "Early Habur Ware" fine jars with painted horizontal stripes (Parrot 1956:fig. 107). The Mari "Trésor d'Ur," with its Mesannepada bead, provides a link with the First Dynasty of Ur but is of little use for dating because it is probably an heirloom, retrieved between the "enceinte sacrée" and "palais présargonique 1" (Boese 1978; Parrot 1968; Margueron, pers. comm.). After the burning of "palais présargonique 1," the "enceinte sacrée," a rebuilding of palais 1, and the "salle aux pilers" were constructed. The "salle aux piliers" was used into Sargonic times, to judge from the cups and footed jars with Diyala ED III–Akkadian parallels (Lebeau 1985b:135). See also Tunça (1984) for a discussion of the chronology of pre-Sargonic Mari.

Metallic Ware is also identified in the third millennium contexts from Tell Ashara, ancient Terqa (Kelly-Buccellati and Shelby 1977). A grave in SG 5 yielded painted "Early Habur Ware" jars (Kelly-Buccellati and Shelby 1977: fig. 25:62, 63); cooking pots with triangular lugs at the rim (Kelly-Buccellati 1979: fig. 23:1) were also recovered.

Northern Iraq: Related Assemblages

On the Assyrian plain, the Tepe Gawra VI assemblage includes such shapes as a globular pot with incised shoulders and a flat base, carinated bowls with flat bases, and a ring-based bowl with slightly inverted sides (Speiser 1935: pl. LXVII 84, 86, 87). Also present were large collared jars (Speiser 1935: pl. LXVIII 106, 107) and high-shouldered carinated pots with ring bases, equivalent to the *Schultervasen* of Ashur E (Speiser 1935: pl. LXX 143). A distinctive high-necked jar with a ridged, everted rim parallels examples from the Diyala Agade levels (Speiser 1935: pl. LXIX 130; Delougaz 1952:111). Cylinder seals from VI resemble Ur Royal Cemetery examples. Billa 5 pottery is called the equivalent of that from Gawra VI (Speiser 1935: 158, 1933: pl. LIV 4, 8).

A sequence of rebuildings of the Ishtar temple at Ashur, levels H–A, are dated to the later third millennium (Andrae 1922). The pottery is only minimally published. Level H includes model houses with snake appliqué and offering stands, also found in level G, where incised plant designs appear as well. Incised motifs in F include wavy lines and herringbone (Andrae 1922: Tafel 26). Level E includes a new form, the *Schultervase* (Andrae 1922: Tafel 60). Since this level is dated to the Ur III period by a tablet of Amar-Sin, the lower levels are earlier in the second half of the third millennium. Ashur G is equated with Taya VIII by Reade (1968:244).

Later third millennium remains from Nuzi are mainly attested from the L4 sounding, although model houses and offering stands with snake appliqué and incised plant motifs as at Ashur were present in Temples G and F. Nuzi L4 level VI includes one published *Schultervase* (Starr 1939: pl. 53A), and another may derive from level V also (Starr 1939: pl. 52H). Examples of ring-based bowls with slightly inverted rims occur in level III and between level III and IIB (Starr 1939: pls. 5O, 50M). The distinctive high-necked carinated jar with an everted ridged rim also appears in the latter context (Starr 1939: pl. 52G). Old Akkadian tablets were retrieved from levels V–III, dating those contexts to the Sargonic period.

On the Sinjar plain, Tell Taya provides the most useful sequence for this period. A deep sounding on the citadel encountered nine levels of occupation, the earliest of which (IX–VI) included fine incised pottery reminiscent of Ninevite V but later in date and with different shapes and motifs (Reade 1968:244, 1982). Taya VII included a high-necked ridged-rim jar known from Diyala Akkadian levels (Reade 1968: pl. LXXXV 15, 17). Reade equates Taya VIII with Brak Sargonic levels as well as with Ashur G. Correspondingly, Taya IX is presumed to be late Early Dynastic III, and Taya VII and VI Late Sargonic to Ur III.

A deep sounding at Tell Rimah Area AS unearthed late third millennium material, but it is as yet only minimally published. Incised sherds from the deeper levels of the sounding included late third millennium designs (D. Oates 1970: pl. X). Third millennium material was also identified at Telul-eth-Thalathat Tell I (Fukai and Matsutani 1977), where level III yielded pottery said to resemble that of Taya IX–VI. Lloyd's excavation of a shrine at Tell Khoshi identified two building levels (Lloyd 1940). Khoshi 2 is said to include plain and fine "Ninevite V" pottery, but this material may actually correspond to the Taya IX–VI ceramics (Reade 1968:237, n. 6). Khoshi level 1 included gray-burnished pottery, probably equivalent to Metallic Ware. Both levels 1 and 2 yielded numerous sherds with appliqué snakes and scorpions, and impressed circles and incised plant designs appeared in level 1 (Lloyd 1940: pl. III, fig. 6).

The extant evidence indicates that a large number of diagnostic attributes are available for mid-to-late third millennium north Mesopotamia, but few of them indicate a specific moment in time within that era. Metallic Ware is the most widespread diagnostic of the period, found throughout northern Mesopotamia and Syria, but it seems to have had a relatively long period of use. Other ceramic diagnostics of the later third millennium include flat-based bowls with straight slanting sides, *Schulterva-*

sen, collared-rim jars, Smeared-Wash Ware, and cooking pots with triangular lugs at the rim.

Bibliographic Addendum

New research on the chronology of the Neolithic and subsequent periods appears in Aurenche et al. (1987). Akkermans (1988a) discusses fifth–fourth millennium relative chronology in the light of the Hammam et-Turkman sequence, Dornemann (1988) details the fourth–third millennium sequence from Tell Hadidi, and final reports for el-Kowm 1 (Dornemann 1986) and Hama phases M–K (Thuesen 1988) are now available.

The papers in Weiss (in press) provide new data for the Uruk to Ninevite V transition, the Ninevite V to Leilan II transition, mid-third-millennium radiocarbon calendar; Pfälzner (1988) and Curvers and Schwartz (in press) also treat middle Habur chronology. For the chronology of the third millennium Ebla archives, see now Archi (1987, in press).

Part Two

The Mediterranean

Eleven

Greece, the Aegean, and Cyprus

John E. Coleman, Cornell University

Part 1
Greece and the Aegean from the Mesolithic
to the End of the Early Bronze Age

Outline

Introduction
Mesolithic
Aceramic Neolithic
Ceramic Neolithic
Early Bronze Age
    Early Cycladic

Early Minoan
Early Helladic
Early Bronze Age in Thessaly, Macedonia, Thrace,
    the Eastern Aegean, and Anatolia
"Absolute Chronology"
Addendum

Introduction

Part 1 of this chapter considers Aegean chronology from the Mesolithic period, beginning probably in the ninth millennium B.C., to the end of the Early Bronze Age ca. 2100 B.C. The most important cultural changes during this time are those connected with the adoption of a food-producing economy at or near the beginning of the Neolithic Age about 7000 B.C., and with the gradual adoption of copper metallurgy beginning in the fifth millennium B.C. At the outset I acknowledge with gratitude my dependence on the basic and enduring contributions of Saul Weinberg, author of the chapters on Aegean chronology in the two previous editions of this work and on the Stone Age in the Aegean in the *Cambridge Ancient History* (Weinberg 1970).

The absolute datings given here are based almost exclusively on radiocarbon determinations as calibrated according to the recently developed CRD system (table 1). Unless otherwise stated, all determinations are calibrated with a standard deviation of 1σ (see the notes in table 1 for more complete information). Such determinations

Text submitted February 1984
Addendum submitted September 1987

have a considerable range, particularly those that fall earlier than ca. 4500 B.C. in uncalibrated terms, and no time within this range is at present to be preferred over any other. Hence, although absolute dates may now be given with greater confidence, they are also necessarily somewhat imprecise. Calibrations are so far available only for determinations that fall later than ca. 5300 B.C. by the 5568 half-life. Determinations and dating for periods earlier than this are noted here as uncalibrated and given in terms of a half-life of 5730 years. These are fairly conservative in the sense of being low, or recent, and some

Many people have helped me during the writing of this chapter. In particular, I express heartfelt thanks to the following for reading and commenting on one or another of the many drafts this chapter has gone through during the past three years and/or for other useful and sometimes unpublished information: Robin L. N. Barber, Philip P. Betancourt, Jack L. Davis, Oliver T. P. K. Dickinson, Noël H. Gale, Marija Gimbutas, Dhimitrios V. Grammenos, Harald Hauptmann, Sinclair Hood, Thomas W. Jacobsen, John C. Lavezzi, Marcia K. Mogelonsky, Colin Renfrew, Jeremy B. Rutter, John A. Sakellarakis, Adamantios Sampson, René Treuil, Saul S. Weinberg, James M. Weinstein, Hans-Joachim Weisshaar, and David G. Zanotti. Machteld Mellink kindly made her chapter in this volume available to me in advance of publication. Very special thanks are also due Robert Ehrich, who was extraordinarily helpful and conscientious at all times.

scholars may prefer earlier dates. Although dating of pottery by thermoluminescence is not specifically cited, the few available determinations (e.g., Gale and Stos-Gale 1981a:201) are in keeping with radiocarbon dating. A dendrochronology project is also under way for the Aegean, and "floating" sequences have been recorded for some Bronze Age sites (Kuniholm and Striker 1983:420); absolute dendrochronological dating is not yet possible, however, before about A.D. 1100.

In arriving at estimates of absolute dating, I have not undertaken statistical analysis of the radiocarbon determinations. Although Treuil (1983:115–39) has taken the first steps in such analysis for the Aegean by focusing on the interquartile values for groups of determinations representing the beginning and end of the Late Neolithic and the first two phases of the Early Bronze Age, the determinations currently available seem to me too few and many of them too imprecisely attributed in relative terms to warrant such analysis in this chapter. Since detailed information about the nature of many of the carbon samples is lacking, it has not been possible to make systematic adjustments for potentially long-lived samples, such as those of wood, which may have been dead some time before the material reached its final archaeological context. On the other hand, determinations that deviate significantly from the range suggested by other radiocarbon determinations for the same period or phase have been disregarded. There is a helpful discussion of some of the problems of radiocarbon dating from the perspective of Aegean archaeology in Betancourt and Weinstein (1976). A recent summary of Aegean Bronze Age radiocarbon chronology by Betancourt and Lawn (1984), which includes only those determinations belonging to a group of at least three from a given period at a given site, proposes somewhat later datings for the Early Bronze Age than are here suggested.

The terminological system used here is that in which past time is divided into discrete periods, such as Late Neolithic or Early Cycladic, which may in turn be subdivided into numerical phases where appropriate, such as Middle Neolithic I–III, Early Helladic I–III, and the like (figs. 2–5). This simple chronological system seems to me more reasonable and practical than recent alternative proposals, notably the "groups" of French (1972:1–3) and the "cultures" of Renfrew (1972), which require that we deal with ancient people and their material culture in a more abstract way; since it is also still the most widely recognized system, it should, in my view, be retained. The terminology is not entirely consistent for the whole span of time considered in this chapter. The Neolithic phases are generally taken to extend throughout the Aegean, except for Crete. The terms used in the Bronze Age, on the other hand, are more limited geographically: periods and phases in the southern part of the mainland

of Greece are described as Helladic, those in the Cycladic islands as Cycladic, and those in Crete as Minoan. The Early Bronze Age in the more northern parts of Greece has recently been subdivided into Thessalian and Macedonian sequences. The islands of the eastern Aegean tend to be closely related culturally to western Anatolia, and both are therefore usually discussed in terms of the Anatolian sequence. Since Anatolia itself is treated separately in this volume by M. J. Mellink, it is mentioned here only when necessary for an understanding of events within the Aegean.

Opinions apparently vary somewhat about the implications of the terminology, and participants at a recent workshop on chronology (MacGillivray and Barber 1984) noted that misunderstandings and disagreements would be fewer if underlying assumptions about terminology and chronology were made more explicit. My own (see Coleman 1979a, 1979b), which I think are widely shared, are that the periods and phases into which the time span considered in this chapter is subdivided are artificial concepts, imposed on the past as a matter of scholarly convenience. They are essentially chronological and in themselves imply nothing further about the nature or development of the cultures to which they refer. They should, in short, be considered mere blocks of time to which archaeological material has been and continues to be assigned.

Periods, and the phases into which they are subdivided, follow in chronological order within a given geographical region, and they cannot by definition overlap in time. Although many periods and phases cannot yet be closely dated, current research may soon make it possible to delineate them precisely in absolute, calendrical years.

It is appropriate, if not strictly necessary, that we designate the phases and periods by the terms that have proved useful in the past, such as "Middle Neolithic" or "Early Minoan I." The terms must be understood, however, to refer primarily to blocks of time and only secondarily to individual artifacts and assemblages; in other words, their chronological significance takes precedence over their use in designating styles.

The stratigraphy of specific archaeological contexts, particularly habitation deposits, is the primary basis by which archaeological material may be assigned to appropriate chronological subdivisions. These in turn provide a chronological scale against which the stylistic development of pottery may be measured, and the pottery in turn provides a practical means by which less well-stratified or unstratified archaeological material can been ascribed to particular chronological phases. The relationship between particular pottery styles and phases is thus not immutable, but rather subject to change as further discoveries and studies permit styles to be more precisely defined in terms of physical description and chronological duration. It is therefore possible without contradiction or paradox to make adjustments in the assignment of material to particular phases as our knowledge of chronological relationships becomes more precise. Specific questions pertaining to the Late Neolithic and Early Cycladic periods are taken up below.

Research since the previous edition of this work has not led to major changes in the larger picture, although there has recently been an explosion of scholarly activity whereby details have been much enhanced. The many more radiocarbon determinations now available for the Neolithic help fill out the relative sequences and put absolute dates on a much firmer footing. The extensive new sequence of phases and determinations from Jacobsen's excavations at the Franchthi cave in the Northeast Peloponnese, though as yet published only in preliminary reports, has cast much light on the transition in Greece from Palaeolithic to Neolithic ways of life. New information is now also available for the Neolithic and Early Bronze Age Cyclades, and, thanks especially to the work of Milojčić and Theochares, many more details are now known concerning prehistoric Thessaly.

Geographically the Aegean is highly complex, and the natural divisions that were to play such an important role in classical times were also clearly significant in the development of the earliest cultures and civilizations. For our purposes these geographical divisions are in simplified form (fig. 1): the *Peloponnese; Central Greece,* including the Megarid, Attica, Boeotia, Phocis, Eastern Locris, Phthiotis, Euboea, and Skyros; *Thessaly* and the islands of the Northern Sporades; *Northwest Greece,* including Aetolia, Akarnania, Epirus, and the Ionian islands; *Western and Central Macedonia,* bordered to the east approximately by the Strymon River; *Eastern Macedonia* and *Thrace,* south of the Rhodope Mountains; the *Cycladic Islands;* the islands of the *Eastern Aegean,* principally Lemnos, Lesbos, Chios, Samos, Cos and Rhodes; *Western Anatolia;* and *Crete.*

Routes of internal communication by land within the Aegean basin tend to follow the coastline, although there are notable inland routes such as those from Thessaly to Central Greece, from Corinth to the Argolid, and possibly also from Thessaly to Northwest Greece across the Pindus Mountains near Metsovo (Hammond 1976:31). The principal external land approaches are to Aegean Thrace from Western Anatolia via the northern Aegean coast and from Bulgaria via the valleys of the Maritsa-Hebros and Mesta-Nestos rivers; to Greek Macedonia from Yugoslavia via the river valleys of the Struma-Strymon and Vardar-Axios and from Albania via the Haliakmon Valley; and to Northwest Greece via the Adriatic coastline. In view of the mountainous nature of much of the terrain, however, communication by sea may have been at least as important as that by land from very early

times. Seafaring is attested already in the Palaeolithic period by finds of obsidian from the Cycladic island of Melos in Upper Palaeolithic contexts at the Franchthi cave (Perlès 1979; cf. Cherry 1981:45).

A very skeptical view is taken here about the various immigrations into and invasions of Greece postulated by scholars such as Weinberg (e.g., 1970), Gimbutas (e.g., 1974b), and Hammond (e.g., 1976). In my opinion, no changes in material culture during the time here considered were sufficiently widespread or abrupt to support the claims made for invasion or immigration with any reasonable degree of confidence. The Northern, Anatolian, and Near Eastern characteristics usually cited to support these claims generally represent only one element of the material culture and rarely, if ever, constitute a wholesale replacement of preceding elements. An alternative and, in my view, more convincing explanation of the means by which many of these changes took place is provided by the ever-increasing evidence for contacts between the Aegean and neighboring regions, particularly Southeastern Europe (Bulgaria, Yugoslavia, Albania) and Anatolia. The Aegean, for all the glories of Thessalian Late Neolithic pottery and other moments of artistic brilliance peculiar to itself, clearly belonged at all times to a broader cultural continuum and cannot be considered in isolation. The early development of seafaring and trade was surely an important factor promoting such cultural contacts and continuity. Hence, although the nature of archaeological evidence makes it difficult to rule out completely the possibility of invasion or immigration at any particular time, we should hypothesize such events, in my view, only when the supporting evidence is very strong. According to such a stringent stipulation, the only likely occasion for large-scale immigration to Greece was at the beginning of the Neolithic period, and even then the evidence is ambiguous.

Mesolithic

The existence of a Mesolithic period between the Upper Palaeolithic and Neolithic periods had been surmised on the basis of poorly dated material from the Seidi cave in Boeotia, the island of Skyros just off Euboea, the Zaimis cave in the Megarid, the Ulbrich cave in the Argolid, and the Ionian islands of Zakynthos, Cephallenia, and Corfu (Weinberg 1965:285–86, 1970:557–65; Sordinas 1970). Work at the Franchthi cave has now made this period a stratigraphic reality (for summaries see Jacobsen 1973–74:274–75, 1976:78–82, 1981). A Mesolithic deposit some 3 m deep, which intervenes between layers representing the Palaeolithic and Neolithic periods, has produced twenty-four radiocarbon determinations with uncalibrated means ranging from 7811 B.C. to 6184 B.C. (5730 half-life); a representative sample of these is listed in table 1. On the basis of these, and an uncalibrated determination of 8824 B.C. (I-6139; 5730 half-life) from a layer near the Palaeolithic/Mesolithic interface, the excavator has suggested 8300–6000 B.C. as the uncalibrated chronological limits of the Mesolithic deposit (e.g., Jacobsen 1976: charts on pp. 80, 82). The Franchthi deposit appears to be truly "Mesolithic" in that it is characterized by microlithic tools comparable to those of other Mesolithic groups in Europe (Clark 1980) and Palestine (e.g., Kenyon 1979:19–25) and gives evidence, in diet at least, of adaptation to the new warmer and wetter conditions of the Postglacial epoch.

Two phases have been distinguished. The first, or "Lower Mesolithic," appears to follow fairly directly on the Palaeolithic, although there may have been a brief period when the cave was not used (Jacobsen 1981:307). It differs from the Palaeolithic in the character of the stone tools and in a change of diet. Wild ass and wild goat disappear, and red deer, already present in the Palaeolithic, become the predominant prey. Many of the same plants utilized in the Palaeolithic, such as pistachios and almonds, were still gathered. In the second, or "Upper Mesolithic," there are striking changes that attest to more extensive ventures into deep-sea waters than earlier. Melian obsidian occurs, perhaps after a hiatus, and becomes increasingly common, and large fish vertebrae are found in quantity for the first time. The possibility has also been suggested of experimental agriculture in the Upper Mesolithic (Jacobsen 1981:308 and work by Hansen and others there cited). A contracted pit burial without grave goods was found close to the boundary between the two Mesolithic phases, to judge from radiocarbon determination P-1595 from the same excavation unit (Jacobsen 1969:374; Jacobsen and Cullen 1981). This is the earliest deliberate burial yet known in Greece.

The excavator dates the first phase of the Mesolithic period at the Franchthi cave in uncalibrated terms to ca. 8300–7250 B.C. and the second to ca. 7250–6000 B.C. (Jacobsen 1976: chart on p. 80). A Mesolithic determination from Sidari in Corfu (Sordinas 1970:7), although later, has a standard deviation which overlaps that of the Upper Mesolithic at Franchthi. There is also a similar determination for Maroula in the island of Kythnos (GX-2837; Honea 1975), although there are doubts that the site is truly Mesolithic (Cherry 1979:28–32; Cherry and Torrence 1982:34, n. 1). To judge by the dating of the later periods in the Aegean, the end of the Mesolithic period will probably be dated no later than ca. 7000 B.C. when radiocarbon calibrations are eventually carried back far enough.

Although the Mesolithic can now be accepted as a genuine stage in Aegean prehistory, the task of defining it more closely both culturally and chronologically is a formidable one (see Jacobsen 1981). An important step has been taken by a recent restudy of the chipped stone tools from Argissa, the Zaimis cave, and other sites. This distinguishes two phases immediately preceding the Aceramic Neolithic (Tellenbach 1983: esp. 89, fig. 9) which correspond roughly with the Upper and Lower Mesolithic in the Franchthi cave. There are similar developments in the Balkan countries to the north of the Aegean (see Tellenbach 1983:95–122 and fig. 12).

Aceramic Neolithic

The Aceramic Neolithic has so far been claimed as a definite stratigraphic reality only in Thessaly and Crete, and doubts are sometimes expressed as to its existence as a separate chronological period in Thessaly (e.g., Gimbutas 1974a:282–83). Since a few objects of terra-cotta probably occurred in the levels in question, the term "Pre-Pottery" might be more appropriate, but "Aceramic," or "Preceramic," is now in widespread use. The best documented sites in Thessaly are Argissa (Milojčić, Boessneck, and Hopf 1962) and Sesklo (Theochares 1958, 1963), and the period is also said to be attested in test excavations at Souphli Magoula (Theochares 1958) and Gediki (Theochares 1962). Aceramic Neolithic finds were also reported at Achilleion by Theochares (1962), but no such layer was represented in soundings conducted subsequently (Gimbutas 1974a:282), and Theochares was evidently in error. Evidence of emmer and einkorn wheat, barley, sheep, goats, pigs, and cattle (Milojčić, Boessneck, and Hopf 1962; J. Renfrew 1966) shows unequivocally that the people represented by the relevant levels had entered a food-producing stage. That their life was entirely nonmigratory is less clear. Pits with a maximum diameter of ca. 4 m, postholes, and remains of clay daub at Argissa and foundation trenches at Sesklo (Theochares 1973:35) indicate simple huts. The rare artifacts other than tools of bone and chipped stone include studs (small elongated objects of stone and clay sometimes called "earplugs"; e.g., Theochares 1973: pl. XXII, 3, 2d row), two clay sling bullets, both of which are somewhat doubtfully attributed to this period (see Milojčić, Boessneck, and Hopf 1962: 15; Theochares 1958:82), bone hooks (e.g., Theochares 1958: pls. 14, 15, 1970:53), and, from Sesklo, clay figurines (Theochares 1973:36 and pl. XXII, 4, d). As in the Mesolithic, the use of obsidian implies seafaring, but the simple nature of the finds gives little other evidence for interconnections. The studs have parallels in Late Paleolithic Europe (Theochares 1973: pl. XXII, fig. 3), and bone hooks are like those of belt buckles from Çatal Hüyük (cf. Theochares 1958: figs. 14, 15, with Mellaart 1967: pl. 100).

That these levels stand at the beginning of the Neolithic sequence in Thessaly is clear from the fact that they are followed by strata indisputably assignable to the

Early Ceramic Neolithic. Whether they are truly Aceramic, however, is in some doubt. The Aceramic strata at Argissa, for instance, produced some potsherds, and it is not entirely certain that all these were later intrusions, despite the views expressed by the excavator (Milojčić, Boessneck, and Hopf 1962:18–23).

Five radiocarbon determinations from Argissa and three from Sesklo suggest that the levels in question may have been deposited in the first half of the seventh millennium B.C. in actual calendar years; the two earliest determinations from Argissa (UCLA-1657A and UCLA-1567), which might indicate a still earlier dating for the beginning of this occupation, were run on samples of bone and should probably be discounted. The putative Aceramic deposits probably gave way to the earliest certainly identifiable Early Ceramic Neolithic deposits about the middle of the seventh millennium B.C.

At Knossos in Crete, level X, the lowest Neolithic stratum, is truly Aceramic, and both the finds and the three radiocarbon determinations (BM-124, BM-278, BM-436) suggest that it was roughly contemporary with the Aceramic levels claimed for Thessaly (Evans 1964, 1968, 1971). The Aceramic at Knossos was probably followed closely by strata of the Ceramic Neolithic, despite Weinberg's views to the contrary (1970:616–17; see below).

The only other site of significance for this period is the Franchthi cave, where the evidence is equivocal. Although the excavators originally mentioned the existence of an Aceramic layer, subsequent reports (e.g., Jacobsen 1973–74:275–76) have left the question open, inasmuch as such a layer cannot be identified in every trench. Three radiocarbon determinations from this ambiguous "Aceramic" layer (P-1392, P-2094, P-2095) will probably fall in the first half of the seventh millennium B.C. when calibrations are eventually possible.

Questions of definition remain which can only be solved by further evidence. Was there truly an Aceramic period common to most of Greece, or were Aceramic levels as restricted geographically as the present evidence suggests? How widespread were the new means of food production (cf. Tellenbach 1983:124)? In any case, if the Aceramic Neolithic really existed as a widespread and separate chronological stage, the radiocarbon determinations now available for the Mesolithic and Early Ceramic Neolithic suggest that it must have been of relatively short duration. The range of determinations for the putative Aceramic period overlaps somewhat with those for the Early Ceramic Neolithic. However we may define the Aceramic Neolithic period in Greece, it cannot correspond closely to the Aceramic or Pre-Pottery Neolithic of the Near East, for it did not represent a long period of time during which there was a gradual transition to a Neolithic way of life (Nandris 1970). The new plants and

animals appear to have entered Greece from abroad at about the same time, presumably from more advanced centers of the Near East. At present it appears doubtful that there was an Aceramic period elsewhere in Southeastern Europe (Ehrich and Bankoff, this vol., chap. 21).

Ceramic Neolithic

Weinberg's tripartite division of the Aegean Ceramic Neolithic into Early, Middle, and Late periods has come into widespread use and serves here as a basic chronological yardstick for the region as a whole (figs. 2–5). One of the several advantages of this division is that it focuses on common cultural developments rather than on small scale divergences and thus makes the Neolithic Aegean more accessible to nonspecialists. The calibration of radiocarbon necessitates some adjustment in previous assumptions about these periods. It is now clear, for instance, that they are not of roughly equal duration, as had earlier been supposed, but rather that the Late Neolithic is by far the longest and the Middle Neolithic by far the shortest (figs. 2, 4). It is also important to note that the chronological divisions have no historical implications and do not necessarily imply discontinuity, or even rapid change, from period to period. In fact, though the three periods accord well with the general trends observable in the archaeological record, there were probably no sharp breaks in most parts of Greece during the whole of the Ceramic Neolithic. One should also note that the chronological divisions of the Cretan Neolithic do not correspond with the general system. This presents no real difficulty, however, for Crete had few close contacts with the rest of Greece until near the end of the Neolithic.

Each period represents a substantial length of time, and subdivisions are gradually coming into use. Weinberg (1970), for instance, distinguished three phases of the Early Neolithic period, and subdivisions of regional application have been proposed by Milojčić and Theochares for Thessaly. The attempts made in this chapter to define further such subdivisions and to equate them from one region to another are tentative, but the introduction of such "working hypotheses" seems appropriate in view of the great mass of material now available.

The chronology of the later part of the Late Neolithic and the earliest stages of the Early Bronze Age is still not well known, although recent publications (e.g., Hauptmann 1981; Lambert 1981; Sampson 1980) have greatly helped to clarify the local sequences. Differences in terminology have led to much confusion. A site like Tharounia in Euboea, for instance, which is classified as "Final Neolithic II" by Sampson (1980:143–45 and figs. 114–21), is probably contemporary with what has been described as Late Neolithic at Kephala in Keos (Coleman 1977), and with the earliest stage of the so-called Chalcolithic (or *kupferzeitlich*) Rachmani period in Thessaly (Weisshaar 1979a, 1979b). In the interests of a uniform terminology it is here proposed to refer the later group of Late Neolithic finds which may be tentatively recognized in Thessaly, Central Greece, the Peloponnese, and the Cyclades to a Late Neolithic II phase. Late Neolithic II is entirely consistent with the usual numerical system of phases within each period and therefore easily understandable, even by nonspecialists.

Alternative terms for the later part of the Late Neolithic include *Final Neolithic* and *Chalcolithic*. Such terms tend to imply a cultural uniformity for a time in the Aegean when there was instead great diversity, as Treuil notes in a recent book on the change from Neolithic to Early Bronze Age in the Aegean (1983:517–18). *Final Neolithic,* although admittedly widely used since its introduction by Renfrew (1972: 68–80), has not won universal acceptance; it is not used by the German scholars working in Thessaly, for instance, nor by Treuil (1983: see esp. pp. 2–3), and Lavezzi (1983) has recommended that it be avoided. *Final Neolithic* has the further disadvantage that its relationship to Late Neolithic is not immediately obvious. Also, since it may be taken by many to have some significance other than merely chronological, it may raise additional and unnecessary problems of definition. *Chalcolithic* is, in my view, best avoided because of its vagueness. The use of *Chalcolithic* in the Aegean has been so far mostly confined to Thessaly, and it is generally applied there to finds that are here assigned to Late Neolithic II (Theochares 1973:103; cf. Hauptmann 1981: fig. 7), although it also appears sometimes to include the early part of the Early Bronze Age. The fact that metallurgy occurs on a limited scale before the end of Late Neolithic (see below) is hardly a problem, since few would now insist that *Neolithic* must be used in a literal sense.

Pottery continues to be the most convenient and widely used chronological indicator, although chipped stone tools are lately beginning to receive appropriate attention (e.g., Cherry and Torrence 1984). In general, the earliest wares are exclusively monochrome from Thessaly to the Peloponnese and occur in a limited range of shapes and surface treatments. The earliest shapes are simple, although ring bases and everted lips may occur (Milojčić -v. Zumbusch and Milojčić 1971:141; Jacobsen 1969: 362, 1973:262). Simple painted decoration is introduced before the end of the Early Neolithic period, and several local painted styles flourish in the Middle Neolithic period, including "Sesklo" or "Thessaly A" wares in Thessaly, "Chaironeia" ware in Phocis, and *Urfirnis* ware in South and Central Greece. Late Neolithic I is represented by "Dimini" or "Thessaly B" painted wares in Thessaly and by Matt Painted ware in the southern parts of Greece. Although the pottery of Late Neolithic II carries on the traditions of the preceding phase, painted decoration is almost completely absent and its place is taken by incision and plastic decoration; the variety of local styles and techniques includes Pattern Burnished and Crusted wares and, in Thrace and Macedonia, Black-on-Red and Graphite Painted wares.

A slight disagreement over how to define precisely the boundary between Middle and Late Neolithic may here be mentioned. The question hinges on the distinctive Black Burnished wares which are found throughout Greece. These differ from earlier black burnished pottery in that they often occur in carinated shapes and are occasionally decorated with patterns in white paint. On the basis of his observations at Elateia, Weinberg (1962, 1965:297–99, 1970:597–99) argued that these wares occurred already before the end of the Middle Neolithic, and this view has also been adopted by Jacobsen (1973:266–69) with respect to the Franchthi cave. Others (Holmberg 1964; Hauptmann and Milojčić 1969:41–42; Lavezzi 1978:429–30; Hauptmann 1981:38, n. 183) have questioned such a dating and have suggested that the appearance of the Black Burnished wares might better be taken to signal the beginning of the Late Neolithic period. This latter view is probably to be preferred, since it brings the four-legged vessels and other contemporaneous finds from Elateia into the Late Neolithic, like their counterparts elsewhere.

The relationship between the inhabitants of Greece in the Early Ceramic Neolithic and those in the Mesolithic and putative Aceramic Neolithic is still somewhat uncertain (Weinberg 1970:571–72; Milojčić -v. Zumbusch and Milojčić 1971:139–41), and the possibility of some chronological overlap between levels at sites where pottery was in use and Aceramic Neolithic levels has already been mentioned. The putative Aceramic levels at Argissa, Sesklo, and Souphli are followed without apparent hiatus by Early Ceramic levels, although at Gediki a sterile sandy layer 0.06 m deep intervenes (Theochares 1962:75). Similar plants and animals, clay sling bullets, and studs ("earplugs") occur both in these Aceramic and in Early Ceramic contexts. In general, the earliest pottery appears "fully formed and competent" (Weinberg 1970:591) rather than showing signs of experiment, although Theochares (1963:42–43) claims to have found some rather primitive vessels at Sesklo. The Early Ceramic levels at Knossos seem to represent a development from the Aceramic ones (Evans 1971). Sheep, goats, and emmer wheat appear abruptly at the Franchthi cave, whether or not there was an Aceramic period, but the excavator reports that the relevant levels, which appear to follow the Mesolithic without a break, "seem to show evidence of both continuity and change" (Jacobsen 1981:308).

There seems to be a fairly general consensus that a

Neolithic way of life did not come about independently in Greece, but rather that it was the result of some sort of diffusion from more advanced centers of the Near East. Physical movement of at least some animals and plants was probably involved, since domesticated forms of animals appear suddenly and the earliest plants, some of which are not known in a wild form in Greece, are very similar to those that appeared earlier in the Near East (J. Renfrew 1973:203). However, wild oats and barley are now known from Upper Palaeolithic levels at the Franchthi cave (Hansen and Renfrew 1978; Jacobsen 1981:306), and the situation may have been very complex. Whether new people came in significant numbers is impossible to determine, for the apparent increase in population could be due not only to immigration but also to increases in groups already present. In any case, despite the view of Theochares (1973:34–35), it is likely that at least some newcomers were involved. The new way of life probably spread in a similar way to Southeastern Europe (Nandris 1970; Garašanin 1982b:82–83). If such diffusion was via Anatolia, it did not involve the introduction of such complex architecture and household and religious furnishings as are found at Çatal Hüyük (Mellaart 1967).

The transition from the Neolithic period to the Bronze Age was not a simple process in the Aegean (see, for example, Treuil 1983:515–19 *et passim*). The impact of the new metallurgical technologies, which have recently been discussed by Treuil (1983:182–90), McGeehan-Liritzis (1983), and Muhly (1985a), was undoubtedly a significant factor in the changes that took place. Copper artifacts of Late Neolithic or equivalent date are known from a number of Aegean sites (Branigan 1974:97–98; Phelps, Varoutakas, and Jones 1979), including Dikili Tash (Period I: Séfériades 1983:647) and Sitagroi (Phase II: Renfrew 1970:298) in Macedonia, and the Kitsos cave in Attica (Lambert 1981:425–27). Copper metallurgy is itself attested before the end of Late Neolithic II in Phase III at Sitagroi in Macedonia (Renfrew 1970:300) and at Kephala in Keos (Coleman 1977). Silver and gold metallurgy may have accompanied copper metallurgy (Muhly 1985a:111–12), or perhaps even preceded it (Gale and Stos-Gale 1981b:176–77, 1981a:176–80); silver mines at Ayios Sostis in Siphnos were evidently exploited as early as Early Cycladic I (Wagner et al. 1980; Gale and Stos-Gale 1981: 201–2), and perhaps even earlier, to judge by a tanged arrowhead of Late Neolithic type found nearby (Wagner et al. 1980: pl. 1). (See further discussion of early copper metallurgy in addendum.)

The material culture of Late Neolithic Greece seems fairly similar to the contemporaneous ones of Southeastern Europe, and the development of metallurgy in Greece may have been influenced by that of the Balkans in the late Vinča period. Copper artifacts first occur there in the

fifth millennium B.C., and copper mining is attested on a substantial scale already before the end of the fourth millennium B.C, if not considerably earlier (Jovanović 1979; Muhly 1985a:109). Gold was also worked in the Balkans in the fifth millennium B.C., as shown by the finds from Varna (e.g., Gimbutas 1977). Both the types of artifacts and perhaps also the technical characteristics of Aegean Late Neolithic metallurgy (McGeehan-Liritzis 1983) are compatible with a hypothesis of some interrelationship between Greece and the rest of Southeastern Europe.

Whether European copper metallurgy was essentially independent from that of the Near East, as was first suggested by Renfrew (1969), is still an open question. Metallurgical developments generally occurred earlier in the East than in the West (Gale and Stos-Gale 1981a:176–80; Muhly 1985a:116), and Anatolia may have played a more important role in transmitting Eastern ideas than is yet attested (see De Jesus 1980 for a recent summary). The early appearance of tin bronze (De Jesus 1980:133, 150) also suggests that Anatolia may have been metallurgically precocious. In any case, such influences as did occur probably resulted from the diffusion of ideas rather than the widespread movement of peoples or artifacts. It is becoming increasingly clear that the exploitation of sources of ore and development of technical processes for metallurgy generally proceeded in accordance with local conditions and requirements in each region and that there is no need to postulate immigrants or invaders from either Southeastern Europe or Anatolia to account for the changes in Greece.

In the Balkans the initial use of copper was followed without great cultural changes by a flourishing Eneolithic stage, which is partly contemporaneous with the latest stages of the Neolithic and partly with the initial stages of the Early Bronze Age in the Aegean. In Greece, by contrast, widespread circulation of the new material seems initially to have been accompanied by, and perhaps to have contributed to, a severe breakdown in the traditional patterns of Late Neolithic civilization. When the radical realignments that followed were complete, Thessaly had lost its position of leadership in favor of Central and Southern Greece and the islands. The expansion of seaborne trade was surely an important factor in these realignments, and the demand for metal objects was probably a great stimulus to such trade. Although there are many sources of copper ore in the Aegean (Branigan 1974:59–66; McGeehan-Liritzis 1983; Gale and Stos-Gale 1984:259–70), apparently only a few were exploited. Since the extraction of metal from ore is highly complex (cf. De Jesus 1980:21–50) and requires large quantities of fuel, metallurgy must generally have been a more organized and centralized activity than any of the crafts that preceded it and must have necessitated specialized workers and craftsmen. The production of bronze in the Early Bronze Age would have been a further stimulus for trade. According to Branigan's tabulations (1974:73–74), bronze artifacts are slightly more common than unalloyed copper ones in the Cyclades, Crete, and the Troad, even in the first two phases of the Bronze Age, and thereafter the proportion of bronze to copper artifacts rises steadily. The arsenic for arsenical bronze, although it may have been present in some copper ores themselves or available nearby as an arsenate (Gale and Stos-Gale 1981b:13, 1981a, and references there cited), was not present in every source. The tin in tin bronze, which superseded arsenical bronze during the last phase of the Early Bronze Age and the Middle Bronze Age, almost certainly came from outside the Aegean, although its exact source is still a mystery (Branigan 1974:64–65; Franklin, Olin, and Wertime 1978; De Jesus 1980:51–56; Muhly 1985b).

Beginning in the Early Ceramic Neolithic, houses were generally constructed of mud-brick with stone socles; wattle and daub also occurs, as, for instance, at Nea Nicomedia (see Weinberg 1970:577–78). Houses probably had gabled roofs, to judge by surviving models, and were generally rectilinear in plan and freestanding. The "megaron house" plan is so far first attested in the Middle Neolithic, as, for example, at Sesklo, and another distinctive house type known as the "Tsangli house" also occurs in the Middle Neolithic in Thessaly (Weinberg 1970:590–91). Before the end of the Middle Neolithic the hill at Sesklo was enclosed, at least in part, by boundary walls (Theochares 1973: fig. 178). Ring walls of Late Neolithic date at Sesklo (e.g., Theochares 1973:fig. 186; Papathanasopoulos n.d.:37) and Dimini (e.g., Theochares 1973: fig. 185; Papathanasopoulos n.d.:40–41) suggest that both sites were fortified "acropoleis," although Chourmouziades (1979) has argued that the arrangements at Dimini were for workshops and storage rather than defense.

Neolithic burials were generally simple interments in pits (Chormouziades 1973), although cremation occurred in Thessaly from Early Neolithic times on (Gallis 1982). The earliest graves constructed of stones are those at Kephala in Keos (Coleman 1977), which date to the Late Neolithic II phase.

Summaries follow of the regional cultural sequences within the various geographical divisions or regions of the Aegean already mentioned. The regions are considered in the following order: Thessaly, Central Greece, the Peloponnese, Northwest Greece, the Cyclades, Western Macedonia, Central and Eastern Macedonia and Thrace, the Eastern Aegean, and Crete. Absolute dating will be discussed region by region and summarized at the end.

I begin with the Neolithic sequence in Thessaly (figs. 3, 4) since it is the best documented, thanks especially to Theochares and to Milojčić and his colleagues, and provides a useful chronological yardstick. Thessalian terminology is very complicated. Tsountas (1908), followed by Wace and Thompson (1912), originally developed a bipartite scheme in which "Thessaly A and B" are represented respectively by the sites of Sesklo and Dimini. Milojčić (especially 1959) subsequently modified and amplified this by using terms such as *Frühkeramikum*, *Protosesklo*, *Vorsesklo*, *Sesklo*, and so forth. Weinberg (e.g., 1970) and Theochares (e.g., 1962, 1973) have in turn made efforts to bring Milojčić's divisions into accord with the chronological picture elsewhere in Greece. I here use Weinberg's terms, and figure 3 shows how they may be tentatively equated with those of Milojčić and his colleagues. Although none has produced a complete sequence, there is sufficient overlapping among the many excavated sites to permit a general summary.

The Early Neolithic period is subdivided into three phases. The most completely published sequence is that from Otzaki (Milojčić -v. Zumbusch and Milojčić 1971), and a detailed summary of the first phase at Sesklo has recently appeared (Wijnen 1982). The pottery of Early Neolithic I (*Frühkeramikum* or "Early Pottery") is exclusively monochrome, and the shapes include bowls with ring feet and everted or slightly offset lips and jars with low collars or flaring necks. The earliest pottery of Central Greece and the Peloponnese is generally similar. Painted designs first occur in Early Neolithic II (*Protosesklo* or "Early Painted"). During Early Neolithic III (*Vorsesklo* or "Developed Monochrome"; also recently called the "Magoulitsa culture"), painted decoration declines or disappears at most sites, and in northern Thessaly its place is partly taken, as at Otzaki Magoula (Milojčić-v. Zumbusch and Milojčić 1971), by finger pinching and impressions made with fingernails and other instruments. Some of the impressed decoration resembles the cardium-impressed ware of the Adriatic, although the cardium shell was probably not actually used in Greece (Milojčić-v. Zumbusch and Milojčić 1971:78; Weinberg 1970:586). Two stages of the Early Neolithic III phase have recently been distinguished and termed the "earlier and later Magoulitsa culture" (Milojčić -v. Zumbusch and Milojčić 1971:146–47).

On the basis of her excavations at Achilleion, Gimbutas (1974a:283–84) proposes to include the "Pre-Sesklo" stage, by which she evidently means Milojčić's *Vorsesklo* stage, in Middle Neolithic rather than Early Neolithic. This change in terminology, even if desirable for Thessaly, would in my view be a step backward, since the transition from Early to Middle Neolithic in Thessaly would no longer correspond closely to that elsewhere in the Aegean. Hence the assignment of *Vorsesklo* to Early Neolithic, in accordance with the views of Weinberg and Theochares, is here retained. It is not yet clear just when the transition from Early to Middle Neolithic occurred in terms of the sequence of "Phases" distinguished in pre-liminary reports on Achilleion (e.g., Gimbutas 1974a; see further below).

In the Middle Neolithic (i.e., the *Sesklozeit* or *Sesklo-kultur;* formerly "Thessaly A"), painted decoration returns in profusion and a ware with a curious scraped decoration (*ausgewischte Ware*), in which an outer coating of red or yellow-brown slip is scraped off in places to produce patterns (Wace and Thompson 1912:A3; Mottier 1981:33–36), also appears. The sequence at Otzaki, where three phases were distinguished, has recently been published in detail (Mottier 1981: esp. 37–38). In the early phase, imitations of cardium impressions and bowls with offset lips attest to some continuity from Early Neolithic, but Red-on-White painted ware and cups with broad, flat handles (*Bandhenkeltassen*) are new. In the middle phase, bowls with a sharp angle at the midpoint and bowls with a fine groove outside below the lip are characteristic; bell-shaped bowls with flat bottoms first appear, and Scraped ware and a ware with painted areas set off by bands of comblike impressions become common. The late phase is the heyday of the Red-on-White ware, particularly with large "baroque" flame patterns. Scraped ware and the painted ware with comblike patterns are also frequent, as are "fruitstands" with high conical feet, especially in a smaller, thinner-walled variety than heretofore. Bowls with flaring walls also occur now for the first time.

The Middle Neolithic sequence at Otzaki is probably more or less representative of Thessaly as a whole and should be taken to supersede earlier attempts to subdivide the Middle Neolithic. Three phases, for instance, were earlier proposed by Theochares (1962:65), the earliest that of the Solid style of painted decoration, the second that of the Linear style, and the third that of the predominance of Scraped ware. The distinction between the Solid style and the Linear style, however, appears valid only for Tsani in western Thessaly, and it is not certain that this Linear style is earlier than the last phase of the Middle Neolithic elsewhere (Mottier 1981:41, n. 137). On the other hand, detailed publication of the material from Sesklo, where the sequence is somewhat different from Otzaki, may necessitate some adjustments. At Lianokladhi in the Spercheios Valley, which is intermediate between Thessaly and Central Greece, the earliest Neolithic finds (i.e., Stratum I; Wace and Thompson 1912:171–77) include a variant of Scraped ware. This has a white undercoating beneath a thick red paint which was scraped off to produce patterns. According to Mottier (1981:48–49), these finds are probably contemporaneous with the second and third phase at Otzaki, although they are sufficiently different that they should be assigned to a group of their own.

The Middle Neolithic is also characterized by an un-usual housetype with a nearly square plan and internal buttresses (the so-called Tsangli house; e.g., Wace and Thompson 1912:115, fig. 64; Milojčić 1959: abb. 2–4) and by the first certain appearance of the rectangular free-standing building known as the "megaron house" (Weinberg 1970:591). The "Tsangli house" has roughly contemporaneous parallels in Layer 2B at Can Hasan in Anatolia (French 1963: fig. 1), although full publication of the finds from both Otzaki and Can Hasan is necessary before detailed comparisons can be made.

Radiocarbon determinations from Sesklo (P-1679) and Argissa (GrN-4145) and for Phase I at Achilleion suggest that the Early Ceramic Neolithic began in Thessaly no later than about the middle of the seventh millennium B.C. The thirty-three determinations for the Early and Middle Neolithic from Achilleion will become particularly significant when the cultural sequence from that site is fully published. Even though they were run by different laboratories, the Achilleion determinations present a very consistent picture and suggest that occupation continued there without a break and on much the same scale for more than a thousand years. The transition from Early to Middle Neolithic in Thessaly is still hard to pin down chronologically, in part because it is not yet clear just where it comes in the Achilleion sequence. Five determinations for Middle Neolithic Sesklo suggest that the period had begun there no later than ca. 5600 B.C. The many determinations for Phase III at Achilleion would suggest a somewhat earlier beginning; it is not yet clear, however, whether this phase is to be assigned in its entirety to the Middle Neolithic or whether it straddles the Early and Middle Neolithic. In any case, a tentative estimate of ca. 5700 B.C. for the beginning of the Middle Neolithic seems reasonable on present evidence. The end of the Middle Neolithic is similarly difficult to estimate, but probably occurred before the end of the sixth millennium B.C., to judge by the evidence from elsewhere in the Aegean.

There is a bewildering profusion of terms and divisions for Thessaly in the Late Neolithic period (see fig. 3). The earliest stages are represented by the Dimini period or sequence (*Diminizeit*), which includes much material formerly described as "Thessaly B." The Dimini sequence has been subdivided by Milojčić (especially 1959:19; cf. Hauptmann 1981: abb. 7) into four stages, *Dimini I–IV.* In general there is continuous development throughout the four stages, and ceramic decoration becomes ever more varied and complex.

In the first stage (*Dimini I-Tsangli-Stufe*), Black Burnished and other dark burnished pottery appears in Thessaly for the first time, generally in shapes with angular profiles and often decorated with white-painted stripes, incision, or pattern burnishing. Although the painted pottery still shows some connections with Middle Neolithic prototypes, the use of matt black paint is new. "Fruit-stands" may have very high, narrow, elegantly flaring feet. In the second stage (*Dimini II-Arapi-Stufe*) spiral motifs first appear, shapes and decoration become more complex, and polychrome decoration is more frequent. The development of the third and fourth stages is best attested at Otzaki (Hauptmann 1981: esp. pp. 141–44). The third stage (*Dimini III-Otzaki-Stufe*) has been subdivided into two groups, A and B. White-painted decoration is predominant in group A, and "crusted" red and white paint, applied after firing, appears for the first time. So-called "rhyta" with oblique mouths, ring bases, and incised and polychrome decoration (e.g., Milojčić et al. 1976:pl. 16, nos. 13–15; Hauptmann 1981:pl. 31, no. 3) also occur in group A. The shape is probably related to the four-legged "rhyta" found in Central and Southern Greece and the Adriatic coast and is probably a forerunner to the Rachmani "rhyta," and possibly also the "scoops" of Central Greece and Keos. Group B represents a transition to Milojčić's fourth stage.

In the fourth stage (*Dimini IV-Klassische Dimini-Otzaki C*) the ingenuity and complexity of the painted decoration reach a climax, although the shapes receive less attention. Individual motifs, among which meanders and spirals are frequent, are often contained within a framework. Dark-on-light patterns predominate, and shallow bowls with incurving lip, two-handled jars with conical necks, and "fruitstands," often with scalloped rims, are the common shapes. Incision sometimes closely imitates painted patterns.

It has recently been claimed (Milojčić et al. 1976:13) that there was an "Ayia Sophia phase," characterized especially by complex white-painted patterns, intermediate between the third and fourth stages. Such material has not yet been sufficiently well documented in Thessaly, however, to establish that it belongs to a separate chronological phase. If it really existed, the "Ayia Sophia phase" would have been contemporaneous with Late Neolithic I in the Cyclades, given the similarities of the white-painted pottery to that of Saliagos.

Although there is general agreement that the Dimini sequence just outlined follows the end of the Middle Neolithic without a break, there are uncertainties about its duration and dating. Direct evidence is almost completely lacking, and the chronological issues are greatly obscured by the scarcity of radiocarbon determinations from Late Neolithic and Early Bronze Age Thessaly. Milojčić and his collaborators and successors in Thessaly tend to subscribe to a low chronology in which the Dimini sequence is regarded as synonymous with the Late Neolithic period, and the following cultural stages, termed "Chalcolithic," are considered contemporaneous with the Early Bronze Age in Central and Southern Greece (e.g., Hauptmann 1981:137; Weisshaar 1979b:390, 1982a: fig.

3). A higher chronology such as is given below, however, in which the Dimini sequence is assigned to Late Neolithic I, seems to me more in accord with the network of radiocarbon dating now available for the Aegean as a whole.

There are some indications that the Dimini sequence did not continue into the Late Neolithic II phase as the term is used here. Its painted wares have general parallels in Central Greece, the Peloponnese, and the Cyclades, and recent work suggests that they went out of fashion in those regions in Late Neolithic II. The situation in Thessaly is similar, since the Dimini sequence is followed by cultural stages such as the "Rachmani period," in which painted wares are almost completely absent. The decline of painted wares probably took place throughout the Greek peninsula and the Cyclades at roughly the same time.

The few radiocarbon determinations from Late Neolithic Thessaly also tend to support the assignment of the Dimini sequence to a Thessalian Late Neolithic I phase. Two radiocarbon determinations from Milojčić's third or fourth Dimini stage from Sesklo (P-1671) and Argissa (H-?) have a maximum 1σ range of 4560–4395 B.C. and suggest that the *Dimini IV* stage lasted into the latter half of the fifth millennium B.C. They also accord well with the assignment, discussed below, of the Rachmani period to Late Neolithic II. Another determination from the second or third Dimini stage at Argissa (UCLA-1657D) has too great a range to be useful.

Foreign influence, whether from the Balkans (e.g., Grundmann 1932) or Anatolia (e.g., Weinberg 1970:599; cf. Hammond 1976:92–95), has often been claimed for the Late Neolithic dark burnished wares. Similar pottery from the "Late Balkano-Anatolian Complex" of the Central Balkans (Garašanin 1982b:116–29), particularly the Vinča group, is obviously related to that from the Aegean. Claims of invasion or immigration, however, cannot be sustained on the basis of such similarities, which may be the result of similar cultural trends. The chronological evidence is not yet precise enough even to determine which region took the lead. The use of "crusted" decoration both in the Balkans and Greece is probably a shared trend, as may also be the "megaron house," which, as just mentioned, appears in Greece already in the Middle Neolithic.

Late Neolithic II is in my view preferable to the term *Chalcolithic* for that phase of the Neolithic in Thessaly which follows the four Dimini stages. This phase is still very poorly attested. Milojčić (1959:24–26) tentatively placed a group of finds of the so-called *Larissa-Kultur* after the end of the *Dimini IV* stage, and Hauptmann (1981:75–110) has recently supported his position in considerable detail. No settlement stratum, however, can be conclusively assigned to this putative phase, and Dimini strata at many sites are immediately followed by those of the "Rachmani period." Although the evidence from Arapi (Hauptmann and Milojčić 1969:115) and Servia (Ridley and Wardle 1979:225) would be compatible with a hypothetical *Larissa-Kultur* earlier than the end of the Late Neolithic but after the *Dimini II-Arapi* stage, such a phase does not appear to occur at that time at Otzaki. A separate "Black Burnished phase" is also not attested in Central Greece (French 1972:15). Black Burnished wares like those assigned to the *Larissa-Kultur* evidently continued through much of the Late Neolithic, and although there are probably concentrations of such pottery toward the end of the final Dimini stage, or shortly thereafter in the cemetery of cremation urns at Souphli Magoula (Biesantz 1959), it seems better to omit a separate stage represented by the *Larissa-Kultur* from our present sequence. (See addendum for further discussion of the *Larissa-Kultur.*)

The "Rachmani period," or "culture," which is generally thought to follow the Dimini sequence, with or without an intervening Larissa stage, has become better known recently from excavations at Pefkakia on the coast near Volos (Hanschmann and Milojčić 1976:130–35, 145; Weisshaar 1979a, 1979b) and from the publication of material from Otzaki (Hauptmann 1981:111–39). The excavations at Pefkakia have yet to be fully published, however, and problems remain. This "period" is characterized by red, brown, and black monochrome wares, "crusted wares," horizontally pierced T-lugs (sometimes called "Elephant lugs"), and plastic decoration. It has been divided into three stages, or "phases," by Weisshaar (1979a, 1979b), of which the first, or early, stage can be tentatively assigned to Late Neolithic II. The early Rachmani stage probably developed without a sharp break from the Dimini stages of the Late Neolithic, to judge by its occurrence immediately above Dimini levels at a number of Thessalian sites (Hauptmann 1981:136) and the general continuity in pottery. For instance, Rachmani "rhyta," which have oblique mouths and handlelike projections at either side (e.g., Hauptmann 1981: pl. 47, nos. 3, 4), are clearly descended from the "rhyta" of Late Neolithic I. An early dating for the first Rachmani stage may also be suggested by imports at Pefkakia of Black-on-Red and Graphite Painted pottery from Thrace (Weisshaar 1979b). There are also similarities between the early Rachmani stage and Kephala in Keos, which may also be assigned to Late Neolithic II in the Cyclades. It is not yet clear whether the material so far assigned to the early Rachmani stage can be regarded as characteristic of the whole of Thessaly, or whether other cultural groups of Late Neolithic II date will eventually be identified there.

There are no radiocarbon determinations for Thessalian sites of the Late Neolithic II phase. The early Rachmani stage probably began before the end of the fifth millennium B.C., if it followed fairly closely upon the *Dimini IV* stage, and the imports from Northern Greece just mentioned are consistent with such a dating.

It must be noted here that the stratigraphy of the Rachmani sequence at Pefkakia as described in the preliminary reports poses a considerable problem for the chronology given here for Late Neolithic Thessaly and the Cyclades. Deposits of the middle Rachmani stage, which evidently followed the early Rachmani stage without a break, are said to contain sherds with Early Helladic *Urfirnis* glaze (Weisshaar 1979a:387, 1979b:114). Early Helladic *Urfirnis* is dated in Central and Southern Greece no earlier than Early Helladic II. Since it is difficult to believe that the early and middle Rachmani stages lasted as long as 600–700 years, it might seem that the early Rachmani stage is better regarded as contemporaneous with Early Helladic I rather than Late Neolithic II, and this is the position adopted by Weisshaar (1979a:390). A skeptical view about the Rachmani deposits at Pefkakia seems to me advisable, however, and particularly whether they represent a uniform and continuous sequence. (See addendum for further discussion of Pefkakia and the Rachmani culture.)

The site of Ayios Petros, now an islet but formerly joined to Kyra Panayia (Halonnesos), an island in the Northern Sporades, was evidently settled in Early and Middle Neolithic times (Theochares 1970; Efstratiou 1983), and a radiocarbon determination apparently from one of the latest Middle Neolithic levels (BM-2020) gave a dating of 5455–5210 B.C.

Central Greece is less well known than Thessaly (figs. 2, 4). The most complete published sequence of the earlier stages of the Neolithic is that from Elateia (Weinberg 1962), although it is important to remember that excavations there, as at most sites, were on a very small scale. A monochrome pottery continued as the exclusive type throughout the lowest meter of deposit and represented the first stage of the Early Neolithic period. The succeeding strata are characterized by the appearance of Red-on-White Painted, or "Chaironeia," ware, in which painted patterns are applied at first to the clay surface of the pot and later over a light slip. Although the Red-on-White Painted ware appears already in layers assigned to the Early Neolithic period (Weinberg 1962:172, 175–76), it continues well into the Middle Neolithic and thus parallels in a general way the painted ware of the Middle Neolithic *Sesklozeit* of Thessaly (cf. Mottier 1981:50–51). The later stages of the Middle Neolithic were apparently absent in the trenches excavated at Elateia because of Late Neolithic leveling operations. The Late Neolithic is characterized by Black Burnished, Matt Painted, and matt Black-on-Red wares and by four-legged "rhyta," which vary from the "rhyta" of the Late Neolithic I phase in Thessaly in having legs and a basket handle (Weinberg 1962: fig. 12). A large bothros in Trench 3 and perhaps a burnt building in Trench 1, which were originally dated by Weinberg to the Middle Neolithic, are now better dated to Late Neolithic, and apparently belong to the Late Neolithic I phase. Radiocarbon determinations are available only for the Early Neolithic; the four samples all indicate a dating in the seventh millennium or the first half of the sixth millennium B.C. Although further documentation of the Middle Neolithic is necessary in Central Greece, it was probably roughly contemporary with that in Thessaly.

The Late Neolithic of Central Greece has lately become better known from excavations at the Corycian cave near Delphi, the Kitsos cave near Laurion, and from the systematic study of various sites in Euboea.

The deposit in the Corycian cave (Pechoux, Amandry, and Touchais 1981) may represent seasonal or sporadic use, and the finds were not assigned to specific strata. Ceramic parallels with Thessaly and the Peloponnese suggest that people first made use of the cave only after the Late Neolithic was well under way. Thereafter, the cave evidently was frequented until quite late in the Late Neolithic, that is, Late Neolithic II as defined below, to judge by the high proportion of coarse wares and the use of plastic decoration. A few fragments of Early Helladic II "sauceboats," found with the Neolithic pottery, attest to subsequent visits to the cave and suggest that the stratigraphy may be slightly disturbed. Two radiocarbon determinations (Gif-2123, Gif-2124), which fall toward the end of the fifth millennium B.C., cannot be precisely correlated with any particular Late Neolithic stage.

The Kitsos cave (Lambert 1981) was more intensively occupied than the Corycian cave. The excavator dates its earliest use (*couche* 4c) to the Middle Neolithic; the pottery she cites (i.e., Lambert 1981:312, CP 29), however, seems rather to belong to an early stage of Late Neolithic, as is also suggested by two radiocarbon determinations for *couche* 4c (Gif-2538, Gif-2541). The middle stages of Late Neolithic (*couches* 3, 4a and b) are characterized by Black, Brown, and Gray Burnished wares, various Painted wares, and the use of Crusted Red and Incision, sometimes in combination with pointillé. Next comes a late stage of Late Neolithic (*couches* 1, 2) with "scoops," that is, vessels with oblique mouths, ring bases, and high-swung band handles with struts (e.g., Coleman 1977: pls. 36, 82), Pattern Burnishing, and Incised and Grooved decoration. The excavator suggests that Early Helladic types may also be represented in the latest Neolithic deposits, although the pieces she cites (Lambert 1981: 3U4, CP 1; 314, CP 35; 316, CP 42) could probably also be Neolithic. Ten radiocarbon determinations for the early and middle stages of the Late Neolithic, that is, from *couches* 4 and 3, including the two

from *couche* 4c, have a maximum 1σ range of ca. 5100–3800 B.C.

The study of several dozen sites in Euboea by Sampson (1980, with references) is an important recent contribution. Most of the sites are known from surface survey, but a few, for example, Varka Psakhnon, Seimen Mnema, and Votsika Psakhnon, have been tested by excavation.

As a result of this work, the Late Neolithic sequence in Central Greece is now known in considerable detail. An initial phase, Late Neolithic I, represented at Elateia, the Corycian and Kitsos caves, Eutresis (Caskey and Caskey 1960: group I), Varka Psakhnon in Euboea and in Athens on the south slope of the Acropolis (Levi 1930–31), is characterized by Black and Gray Burnished wares, by Matt Painted and other painted wares which correspond roughly to those of *Dimini I–IV* in Thessaly, and by four-legged "rhyta." Pottery groups 3 ("Bothros phase") and 4 ("Dhrakmani phase") of French (1972:8–15) are to be assigned to Late Neolithic I. This phase is followed by a second, Late Neolithic II, which is represented at the Corycian and Kitsos caves, Eutresis (the Caskeys' group II), Seimen Mnema and Votsika Psakhnon in Euboea, and in Athens on the north slope of the Acropolis and in the Agora (Immerwahr 1971, 1982) and which is characterized by a great increase in coarse wares coupled with a decline or absence of painted wares, by an increase in incised and grooved decoration, by a profusion of plastic decoration, by "scoops" (presumably a later development of the Thessalian "rhyta" with ring bases of Late Neolithic I, and perhaps also related to the four-legged "rhyta" just mentioned) and in the later stages by Pattern Burnished wares and rolled rims on bowls. Pottery group 6 ("North Slope phase") of French (1972:17–18) is to be assigned to Late Neolithic II. Late Neolithic II in Central Greece is probably contemporary with at least the earliest stage of the Rachmani period in Thessaly, as is suggested by many similarities of shape and plastic decoration; even the "scoops" have a counterpart in the Rachmani "rhyta" with projections at either side.

In Euboea the Early Helladic I phase followed Late Neolithic II without apparent break and with no great change in material culture. The red-burnished ware characteristic of Early Helladic I may have evolved from a brown-burnished pottery of Late Neolithic II (French 1972:17, 18). Although Sampson (1980:196) describes the earliest stages of Early Helladic I as "subneolithic" in character, the differences in the pottery are sufficient to make a distinction, and it is evident that there was no significant chronological overlap between types characteristic of Late Neolithic II and those characteristic of Early Helladic I.

In absolute terms, the Late Neolithic probably began in Central Greece about 5300 or 5200 B.C., as it did in the Peloponnese (fig. 4). To judge by the radiocarbon dates from the Kitsos cave, Late Neolithic I probably came to an end ca. 4300 B.C., and Late Neolithic II may have lasted until nearly the middle of the fourth millennium B.C.

In the Peloponnese there are important stratified remains at Lerna (Caskey 1957, 1958), Corinth (recently Lavezzi 1978), the Alepotrypa cave at Diros in the Mani (Lambert 1972; Papathanasopoulos n.d.: 42 and bibliography), and the Franchthi cave. The last is at present the most important site for chronological purposes since the relative sequence is virtually complete and the more than twenty radiocarbon determinations line up in fairly good stratigraphic order. It must be stressed, however, that none of these sites has yet been published in full detail, and the picture presented here is liable to change.

At least two phases in the pottery repertoire of the Early Neolithic may be tentatively distinguished in the Peloponnese. During the earlier phase, Monochrome wares predominate, including the so-called Variegated or Rainbow ware at Corinth (Lavezzi 1978:405) and Lerna (Caskey 1957:160) and Burnished Monochrome ware at the Franchthi cave (Jacobsen 1969:362, 1973:262–63). During the later phase several varieties of Red Patterned wares occur, and the Black Burnished pottery is technically so improved that it may be distinguished as a separate ware. A Plain Monochrome ware, sometimes called "spongy" (Jacobsen 1973:264 argues that the pitted surface often associated with this ware is due to cleaning in acid), also appears during this phase at the Franchthi cave and continues into the Middle Neolithic. The development in the Peloponnese from a simple monochrome pottery to more elaborately finished and decorated wares parallels in a general way that in Central Greece and Thessaly.

Estimates for the beginning of the Early Neolithic in the Peloponnese depend in part on the as yet unresolved question whether there was an Aceramic phase at the Franchthi cave. The radiocarbon determinations from the ambiguous levels overlap slightly with those from the subsequent, unequivocally ceramic levels. In any case, it is clear from the three unambiguous determinations for the Early Neolithic at the Franchthi cave (P-1525, P-1667, P-2093) that the period began no later than ca. 6500 B.C. Early Neolithic probably came to an end in the Peloponnese ca. 5700 B.C., to judge by the radiocarbon determinations for the Middle Neolithic at the Franchthi cave.

The Middle Neolithic in the Peloponnese, as elsewhere in Greece, was relatively short, perhaps lasting only about 400–500 years. The four radiocarbon determinations for the Middle Neolithic and the three for the transition from Middle to Late Neolithic at the Franchthi cave have a remarkably brief range. The period came to an end

ca. 5300 B.C., to judge by the dating of the beginning of Late Neolithic, and it may have begun about 5700 B.C. The pottery is characterized chiefly by the use of the shiny slip called *Urfirnis*, either as a monochrome coating or in patterns. There are several varieties and imitations of Neolithic *Urfirnis* ware, which has no relationship with the much later Early Helladic *Urfirnis*. The ceramic sequence at the Franchthi cave, which seems generally similar to that at Lerna and Corinth, can be divided into three phases (Jacobsen 1969:362–67, 1973:264–66). In the earliest there is little change from Early Neolithic except for the use of a finer fabric and a reddish slip which represents a variety of *Urfirnis*. In the second phase the slip becomes more shiny, thus evolving into a true *Urfirnis*, and its use for painted patterns becomes more frequent. In the third phase there is a decline in the Patterned *Urfirnis* and an increase in Burnished *Urfirnis*, a ware on which the slip in burnished, sometimes in patterns. Middle Neolithic *Urfirnis* is generally similar in both shapes and decoration to the contemporaneous Middle Neolithic painted wares of Central Greece and Thessaly, but there is no evidence that the interrelationship was a very direct one.

The Late Neolithic sequence in the Peloponnese (fig. 4) has become clearer as a result of work at the Franchthi cave (Jacobsen 1973:266–75) and Corinth (Lavezzi 1978), although there has been until now no uniform terminology. In general two phases can be distinguished, and, in keeping with the suggestions made above for Thessaly and Central Greece, it is here proposed to designate them Late Neolithic I and II rather than "Late" and "Final" Neolithic as in the preliminary reports on the Franchthi cave. To the arguments given earlier one may add that radiocarbon determinations indicate that Late Neolithic II in the Peloponnese lasted about 600 years. It seems inappropriate to describe such a long period of activity as "Final." Late Neolithic I is characterized chiefly by Black Burnished and Matt Painted wares, by other painted wares including Polychrome ware as found at Gonia (Blegen 1930–31), and by four-legged "rhyta" like those of Central Greece; Gray ware is significant also in the Corinthia. The predominant ware during Late Neolithic II is coarse, often with plastic bands decorated with finger impressions and knobbed or horned handles; other significant wares include Incised, "Crusted," and Red Pattern Burnished.

Radiocarbon determinations from the Franchthi cave and Halieis suggest that Late Neolithic I lasted from ca. 5300 B.C. to 4300 B.C. and Late Neolithic II to nearly the middle of the fourth millennium B.C.

Northwest Greece, as yet not well represented in the archaeological record, may have followed Thessaly quite closely but also shows influence from the more northern parts of the Adriatic coast. At Sidari in Corfu (Sordinas

1970) a layer containing early Monochrome pottery with a radiocarbon determination of 5720 B.C. (GX-0071; uncalibrated) was followed by one with Impressed ware dated to 5390 B.C. (GX-0072; uncalibrated). The former perhaps corresponds to Early Neolithic I elsewhere in Greece, but the latter owes something to the northern Adriatic and perhaps corresponds to the Early Neolithic III phase in Thessaly, where Balkan influences are also discernible. The Middle and Late Neolithic periods are as yet represented at only a few sites such as Astakos in Akarnania (Benton 1947), but so far no extensive sequence has been published.

Recent work has done little to change our picture of the Cycladic islands in the Neolithic era (Coleman 1974, 1977:98–111). Surface survey in Melos (Cherry 1979; Renfrew and Wagstaff 1982) failed to produce any evidence of Neolithic settlement, and the earliest sure indication of human activity, as represented by chipped stone industries, is no earlier than the Late Neolithic period (figs. 2, 4). This lack of evidence of early occupation is unexpected, for Melian obsidian had already been reaching the mainland since before the end of the Palaeolithic period. It suggests that people simply went to the island for raw material rather than that there was any real trade in obsidian (Renfrew 1973:180–86; Renfrew and Wagstaff 1982:182–221). Saliagos, an islet between Paros and Antiparos (Evans and Renfrew 1968), and other related sites continue to represent the earliest stage of occupation yet known in the islands and may be dated to the Late Neolithic I phase (Coleman 1974:333–35, 1977:99). Pottery with white-painted patterns generally similar to that from Saliagos has recently been found at Ayia Sophia Magoula in Thessaly (Milojčić et al. 1976:10) and is associated with a stage intermediate between *Dimini II* and *III*, that is, about the middle of Late Neolithic I. Somewhat similar white-painted pottery has also been increasingly attested from the Southeast Aegean (cf. Sampson 1984: figs. 1–3 with Evans and Renfrew 1968, pls. XX–XXI). Radiocarbon determinations from Saliagos date it to ca. 5000–4600 B.C. Given this chronological evidence, recent attempts either to lower the dating of Saliagos and make it contemporary with the Rachmani phase in Thessaly (Hauptmann 1981:133, n. 140 and Beil. 13) or to raise it to Early Neolithic (Hood 1982:725, 1984) can hardly be taken seriously.

Kephala in Keos and sites related to it (Coleman 1977) have close connections with the mainland of Greece and may be assigned to Late Neolithic II from such interconnections with Attica and Euboea as Pattern Burnished ware, Plastic decoration, and "scoops." Kephala was evidently roughly contemporary with the first Rachmani stage in Thessaly rather than with one or another of the Dimini stages, as earlier seemed possible (Coleman 1977:109); consequently, the well-known "scoop" found

at Sesklo must also be dated to the Rachmani period (cf. Hauptmann 1981:34). The radiocarbon determination from Kephala (P-1280), which would place it very close to the end of Late Neolithic II, still seems erroneously somewhat late (cf. Coleman 1977:110).

There was probably also a Late Neolithic II phase elsewhere in the islands of truly Cycladic character, although it cannot yet be well defined. Stone vessels found at Kephala in Keos but probably not manufactured there are close to, although not identical with, those known in the "Pelos group" of Early Cycladic I (Coleman 1977:5, 106). Since Kephala was not itself a direct cultural ancestor of Early Cycladic I, it is probable that there were other Late Neolithic II sites in the Cyclades culturally antecedent to Early Cycladic I at which such stone vessels were made. The stone-built tombs of Kephala are perhaps also the result of influence from a Late Neolithic II Cycladic culture antecedent to Early Cycladic I, since such graves are common in the Early Bronze Age Cyclades whereas they are so far unknown elsewhere in the Aegean in the Neolithic period. Although no specific sites can yet be assigned to this hypothetical Cycladic Late Neolithic II phase, a further hint of its existence is also to be seen in the *pseudo-cycladique* beakers from the Late Neolithic levels of the Kitsos cave (Lambert 1981:299–300; see also pl. XXXI, 1607), which have a general resemblance to the marble ones of Early Cycladic I (e.g., Thimme 1977:313). Some of the graves usually assigned to the "Pelos group" may even belong instead to this hypothetical Late Neolithic II stage. One should note that rolled rims like those on bowls of Early Cycladic I are known at the Kitsos cave already in the Late Neolithic period (Lambert 1981:301) and that the characteristic "Pelos group" jars with conical necks (e.g., Thimme 1977:341) are very similar in shape to those from Late Neolithic Thessaly (e.g., Theochares 1973: fig. 61). The main difference is that the Early Cycladic jars have lugs rather than handles.

Currently the Neolithic sequence in Western and Central Macedonia (fig. 2) is best represented at Servia in the Haliakmon Valley (Heurtley 1939; preliminary reports on more recent excavations, Ridley and Wardle 1979). The Early and Middle Neolithic finds are close enough to those from Thessaly to suggest that Servia is a Thessalian offshoot. Deposits at Servia V, a site about 0.5 km east of the main site, may belong to the Early Neolithic II and III phases. The Middle Neolithic deposit, the earliest at the main site, was some 1.5 m deep and has been divided into five phases; these can be tentatively related to the Thessalian sequence. Phases 1 and 2 may have been roughly contemporaneous with Thessalian Middle Neolithic I, Phase 3 with Middle Neolithic II, and Phases 4 and 5 with Middle Neolithic III. Both Monochrome and Painted wares are found throughout, the painted reaching a peak of excellence in Servia 3. The Late Neolithic has been divided into two phases, 6 and 7, which although they have a local character, correspond to the earliest Late Neolithic stages in Thessaly (Ridley and Wardle 1979:225), that is, to Late Neolithic I. Black Burnished and Gray-on-Gray are two of the characteristic wares; the excavators point out the similarity of the former to "Larissa" pottery of Thessaly, a fact that is at odds with the insertion of a "Larissa phase" near the end of the Late Neolithic (see above).

Other Neolithic sites of importance in Western and Central Macedonia include Nea Nicomedia (Rodden 1964, with references to earlier reports), which can be dated to Early Neolithic II, and possibly Early Neolithic III (Weinberg 1970:577, 586–87; Theochares 1973:39–40, 119); Basilika C (Grammenos 1984), which can be dated to the Middle and Late Neolithic; and Olynthos (Mylonas 1929), which can be dated to Late Neolithic.

Radiocarbon determinations for Nea Nicomedia and Servia suggest that Early Neolithic II began in the region about 6000 B.C. and that Middle Neolithic began as in Thessaly about 5700 B.C. The Middle Neolithic determinations from Servia seem compressed (Ridley and Wardle 1979:226), but are comparable to those from other regions. Both the two Late Neolithic determinations from Servia (BM-1107, BM-1887) seem somewhat too early but are in keeping with the apparently early character of the deposit and would allow a date for the beginning of Late Neolithic ca. 5300 B.C.

Neolithic culture in the Northeast Aegean is distinctive and has strong resemblances to the contemporary cultures of the Balkans (Bakalakis and Sakellariou 1981:27–40). The cultural sequence in Eastern Macedonia and Thrace cannot therefore be as closely related to that in Thessaly as the sequences just discussed. Three important sites, Sitagroi (Renfrew 1970, 1971), Dikili-Tash (Deshayes 1970, 1972, 1973; Treuil 1983:96–99; Séfériades 1983; cf. Weisshaar 1979b:125–27), and Dimitra (Grammenos 1984) have recently been excavated, but only preliminary reports have so far appeared. A fourth, Paradimi, has recently been published (Bakalakis and Sakellariou 1981), although well-stratified finds are not extensive. Other sites include Akropotamos (Mylonas 1941).

The earliest stage of the Neolithic yet attested in Eastern Macedonia and Thrace is probably that represented by Sitagroi I, Dimitra I, and the earliest levels at Paradimi. It is characterized by gray and black burnished vessels almost completely lacking in decoration, often with distinctive knobbed handles and sometimes with angular profile. The second stage is represented by Sitagroi II and Dimitra II and is characterized by a ware with curvilinear patterns in a matt paint, "black topped" bowls, and carinated bowls with grooved spiraliform decoration. Small

copper objects first appear at this stage. At Dikili Tash the first period (I) evidently corresponds with both Sitagroi I and II, although it may begin a little later than Sitagroi I (Séfériades 1983:639). The third and final Neolithic stage is represented by Sitagroi III, Dikili Tash II, Dimitra III, and Paradimi IV. During this stage a characteristic Black-on-Red ware occurs, Graphite Painted ware appears and becomes common, and copper metallurgy is attested by both artifacts and slag. A subcategory of the Black-on-Red ware is termed the "Galepsos style" (see most recently Séfériades 1983:657).

The levels represented by Sitagroi I and II and Dikili Tash I are described as *neolithique moyen* by Treuil (1983:97–98) and Séfériades (1983), and this is probably appropriate, given their northern orientation. They are to be associated especially with Karanovo II–III in Bulgaria and the Vinča culture in Yugoslavia (Séfériades 1983:673). In Aegean terms, however, they probably do not begin much if at all earlier than Late Neolithic I, as is suggested by the general similarity of the gray and black burnished wares with those elsewhere in Greece; the chronological chart of Séfériades (1983:674) equates Dikili Tash I with the Tsangli (*Dimini I*) and Arapi (*Dimini II*) stages in Thessaly, that is, with what is here defined as Late Neolithic I. Although the radiocarbon determinations leave open the possibility that such wares may have begun earlier in Eastern Macedonia and Thrace than elsewhere in the Aegean, the chronological picture is still not secure.

The series of twelve radiocarbon determinations from Neolithic levels at Sitagroi and the series from Dikili Tash (fig. 5, table 1) pose some problems of interpretation. Although each series is fairly consistent within itself, that from Dikili Tash tends to suggest consistently older datings. The determinations from Sitagroi, for instance, indicate that its first stage may have began ca. 5400 B.C. and its second stage ca. 4900 B.C., whereas those from Dikili Tash I suggest datings a few hundred years earlier.

This divergence is particularly marked between the series of determinations for Sitagroi III and that for Dikili Tash II, which appear on archaeological grounds to be contemporaneous. The dating of this stage is of particular importance because of the previously mentioned exports from the region to Pefkakia in Thessaly. The five determinations from Sitagroi III would suggest a beginning for the phase at ca. 4400 B.C. at the earliest. Since they are all from the earlier levels of Phase III (Renfrew 1971:279), they do not indicate a lower limit. They do suggest, however, that this stage lasted well into the fourth millennium B.C. The beginning of Phase IV at Sitagroi, which evidently belongs to the Early Bronze Age, cannot be dated much earlier than the last quarter of the fourth millennium B.C. and thus provides a *terminus ante quem* for Phase III. Phase III may have ended considerably earlier, however, if, as is possible on archaeological grounds, there was a break in time between Phases III and IV (Renfrew 1971: table 2, 1972:70).

The Dikili Tash determinations present a considerably different picture. The seven samples from period II suggest a beginning ca. 5000 B.C. and an ending no later than ca. 4000 B.C., and probably considerably earlier. The determinations from the following period, III, are of little help in estimating a *terminus ante quem,* since they are few and internally inconsistent.

In my view, the dating suggested by the Sitagroi series is more in accord with the chronological evidence from elsewhere in the Aegean than is that suggested by the Dikili Tash series and is therefore to be preferred. It is to be hoped, however, that full publication of the two sites will clarify the situation and permit more precise estimates of this important cultural sequence.

The Eastern Aegean is peripheral to our discussion, since its connections with Anatolia were generally closer than those with the rest of the Aegean. Attempts to relate the sequences in the Aegean islands to those in Western Anatolia (e.g., Sampson 1984) have so far been hampered by differences in terminology and the lack of absolute dates for both regions. None of the sites yet investigated is clearly earlier than the Late Neolithic in the Aegean, which equates roughly with Late Chalcolithic in Anatolia. Hood's view (1982:715–25) that the beginning of the recently published sequence at Emborio in Chios is contemporary with the Aegean Early Neolithic must be regarded with skepticism, considering the lack of radiocarbon determinations and other strong supporting evidence. Other sites such as Tigani in Samos (Felsch 1974) and Besika Tepe (Lamb 1932; recently reinvestigated: Korfmann et al. 1985) and Kum Tepe in the Troad (Sperling 1976) were probably first occupied not long before Troy I, the beginning of the stratified sequence at Troy.

The deposits of Kum Tepe I A and I B, which immediately precede Troy I, are often equated in general with Late Neolithic II elsewhere in the Aegean on the basis of a similar use of pattern burnishing (Coleman 1977:107) and rolled rims on bowls. Although the sequence at Poliochni in Lemnos is sometimes thought to begin earlier than that at Kum Tepe, it has recently and plausibly been suggested by Sperling (1976:358) that the first stage, *nero* (Bernabò-Brea 1964), was roughly contemporary with Kum Tepe I B and I C, that is, the time of Troy I and the immediately preceding stage. Since fruitstands like those from Poliochni *nero* were found at Pyrgos in Crete in a context probably no earlier than Early Minoan I (Vagnetti 1972–73:127, n. 10) and in tombs in Ano Kouphonisi in the Cyclades associated with the "Kampos group" (Zapheiropoulou 1984), which are probably not much, if at all, earlier than Early Cycladic II, it now seems just as likely that the earliest remains yet known in the Troad and

Lemnos are contemporaneous with the first stage of the Early Bronze Age in the Aegean rather than with the last stage of the Neolithic.

Before we turn to Neolithic Crete, some general remarks are in order. Most of the evidence for the local sequences and their interrelationships (figs. 2, 4) has already been discussed. The indications of trade and other interconnections, although scanty, provide a further perspective. Melian obsidian, although widely dispersed, is not of much chronological value, since it was traded or circulated as a raw material and was reaching the mainland already in the Palaeolithic period. Its common occurrence, however, at mainland sites during the Neolithic era perhaps shows that travel by sea was very extensive. In a few instances pottery found its way from one region to another. For example, probable Late Neolithic imports from Eastern Macedonia or Thrace to Thessaly have already been mentioned. Middle Neolithic Thessalian sherds have recently been found at Mesimeriani in the Chalcidic peninsula (Felsch 1976), and Late Neolithic Thessalian pottery of the Dimini IV stage has appeared in Western Macedonia (Hauptmann 1981:69 and n. 161). Middle Neolithic *Urfirnis* ware from the Peloponnese probably occurred in Middle Neolithic contexts at Pyrasos in Thessaly (Theochares 1959:52–54; but doubted by French 1972:45, n. 13) and in Central Greece (Weinberg 1962:179–82), while Late Neolithic Thessalian Gray-on-Gray ware has been found at Corinth (Lavezzi 1978:428). Similarities in pottery and other artifacts demonstrate further contacts from region to region. Such contacts may have been especially close in Early Neolithic I, when in Weinberg's view (1970:584) there was a "koine" from Thessaly to the Peloponnese, and in Late Neolithic I, when except for the Eastern Aegean and Crete similar pottery styles are found in all regions of Greece (Weinberg 1970:601; Hauptmann and Milojčić 1969:41–43).

The development of the Greek Neolithic probably proceeded *pari passu* with that in the Balkans, and there is some evidence for direct contact (recent discussions and references in Schachermeyr 1976; see also Garašanin 1982a and 1982b; Prendi 1982). Radiocarbon dating and its dendrochronological calibration have had a profound effect on our picture of the chronological relationships, and the higher chronology for the Balkans, advocated by scholars such as Neustupný (1968) and Renfrew (e.g., 1971), has come to be fairly widely accepted. The Early Neolithic of Yugoslavian Macedonia has much in common with Thessaly and Western Macedonia in the Early Neolithic II and III phases, as is attested by the recently excavated site at Anzabegovo, sometimes called simply "Anza," near Titov Veles within the Vardar-Axios drainage (Gimbutas 1976:68–70; Garašanin 1982b:87–94; cf. Theochares 1973:47 and 308, n. 37). Finger pinching and impressed decoration found on pottery of Early Neolithic III and thereafter in Thessaly was probably influenced from the Balkans (Milojčić 1959:10–12; Weinberg 1970:585–86) and may even represent some immigration to Greece, although the facts are too complicated to permit a simple hypothesis of invasion (Milojčić -v. Zumbusch and Milojčić 1971:150–51). In this connection one may note that at Anzabegovo the initial Aegean Early Neolithic orientation gives way to a Central Balkan orientation in the following "Starčevo" period represented by Anzabegovo II and III, and it is then that "barbotine" and impressed pottery seem most common (Gimbutas 1976:70–71, 113–16). Since similar impressed pottery is also found in the Adriatic and Sicily as well as in Northwestern Greece (Milojčić 1959:11; Garašanin 1982b:106–9), it is also possible that the Greek versions were inspired by contacts in that direction rather than from the Central Balkans. There are perhaps reminiscences of the Middle Neolithic pottery of Central Greece in Southern Italy and Sicily (Mottier 1981:51, n. 221).

The relationship between the Black Burnished wares of Late Neolithic Greece and the Balkans has already been mentioned. The four-legged "rhyta" of Late Neolithic I found at Tsangli in Thessaly (Wace and Thompson 1912: fig. 50, a), in Central Greece (Weinberg 1962: 190–95), and the Peloponnese (Jacobsen 1973:269; Lavezzi 1978:420–21, 430) probably indicate contact with the Danilo culture of the Adriatic coast, where similar "cult" vessels are common (Garašanin 1982b:109–12; Prendi 1982:194–97). There are possible ceramic imports of Dimini wares from Thessaly at Cakran in inland Albania (Prendi 1982:196–97). Corinth may already have been important in the exchange of goods and ideas between Greece and the Adriatic (Lavezzi 1978:432, with references in n. 117). The pottery from Servia in the Late Neolithic I phase is reported to show influences from Albania (Ridley and Wardle 1979:225), and the close relationship between the Central Balkans and Eastern Macedonia and Thrace has already been mentioned. Sitagroi I may correspond fairly closely with Veselinovo-Karanovo III, and the Graphite Painted ware of Sitagroi III is very similar to that of Karanovo V and VI and of the Maritsa and Gumelnitsa cultures (Renfrew 1970:300). Possible contacts between the Aegean at the time of the first Rachmani stage in Thessaly and Bulgaria in the Eneolithic period have also recently been discussed by Weisshaar (1982b) with particular reference to the Eneolithic cemetery at Varna. His chronology seems unreasonably compressed, however, since he equates the first Rachmani stage with Kephala, Early Cycladic I, Early Helladic I, Sitagroi III, Troy I, and the cemetery at Varna! Such compression is conceivable only if the radiocarbon determinations now available for the Aegean in Late Neolithic II and Early Helladic I and for Varna (see Gimbutas 1977:44) are completely disregarded. In general, Late Neolithic influences from the Balkans seem not to have extended south beyond Thessaly. The Aegean area, for its part, evidently exported Spondylus shell ornaments to the Balkans (Renfrew 1973:186–87; Shackleton and Renfrew 1970).

Anatolian and Near Eastern influences on the Aegean were probably also considerable in Neolithic times, but the lack of information about early sites in Western Anatolia makes them difficult to pinpoint. As Weinberg (1970: *passim*) observes, the development of the Aegean Neolithic was similar to that of the corresponding periods in the Near East, and this was surely in part the result of some contact. Weinberg's claims of immigration at specific times, on the other hand, generally seem insufficiently supported: for example, that the first pottery users came to Greece from Central Anatolia, that the "Tsangli house" and Middle Neolithic painted pottery decoration were brought by people from the Near East, and that the Middle Neolithic "megaron house" came with immigrants from Anatolia. Mellaart (1975:247) has also expressed doubts about the connection posited by Theocharis and Weinberg (e.g., 1970:587) between the Early Neolithic white-filled incised pottery of Nea Makri in Attica and the pottery of Mersin in Southern Anatolia.

Recent work at Knossos (Evans 1964, 1968, 1971) has considerably amplified our knowledge of the Cretan Neolithic (fig. 2), as has publication of the Neolithic material from Phaistos (Vagnetti 1972–73). The Knossos sequence is continuous, lacking only part of the latest Neolithic stage, and shows that life continued without interruption and with little influence from abroad. Sixteen radiocarbon determinations line up in fairly good stratigraphic order and suggest that the Ceramic Neolithic followed immediately, or at least closely, upon the Aceramic. Only the later stages of the Cretan Neolithic are yet represented elsewhere than at Knossos. At Phaistos the deposit is contemporary with the latest Neolithic of Knossos (Vagnetti and Belli 1978), which was there largely obliterated by later building. Painted pottery was never adopted in Crete, and the Cretan phases which have been recognized do not correspond closely with those in the rest of the Aegean until the very end of the Neolithic. Early Neolithic I, Knossos strata IX–V, extended probably from the early sixth millennium B.C. to about 5000 B.C. Although Early Neolithic II, Knossos IV, and Middle Neolithic, Knossos III, were represented by considerable depths of deposit, the radiocarbon determinations suggest that they were brief forerunners to the Late Neolithic and lasted in all only about five hundred years, from ca. 5000–4500 B.C. Late Neolithic is represented at Knossos by Strata II and I, to the latter of which the houses excavated by Sir Arthur Evans probably belonged (for doubts see Vagnetti and Belli 1978:132), and by a very poorly attested stage which follows Stratum I and which may be equated with the Neolithic deposit at Phaistos (Evans 1971:113–14). Knossos II and I are dated by three radiocarbon determinations to the later fifth and early fourth millennium. A further determination, BM-716, described as "Final Neolithic" (Burleigh and Matthews 1982:159) and presumably therefore coming from the stage at Knossos that follows Stratum I, gave a date of 4135–3375 B.C. Since this stage may be close in time to the beginning of Early Minoan, this determination suggests that Early Minoan may have begun well before the end of the fourth millennium B.C. Warren (1976:206, n. 9) has concluded that the three fragments of stone bowls of possible Egyptian manufacture found in the houses excavated by Sir Arthur Evans at Knossos are "valueless as chronological evidence," although others (e.g., Vagnetti and Belli 1978:160) continue to cite them.

The Cretan Neolithic has a number of traits in common with the Eastern Aegean and the Troad, such as "trumpet" lugs, horned and wishbone handles, and pointillé decoration, but there is no exact correspondence and the Cretan examples are mostly earlier than the parallels so far available (Evans 1968:273–74). Extreme conservatism is apparent until near the end, when the stage represented at Phaistos, called variously "Late Neolithic," "Final Neolithic," and "sub-Neolithic," exhibits some characteristics that suggest increased contact with the rest of the Aegean (Vagnetti 1972–73:126–28). The "crusted" red decoration characteristic of this stage at Phaistos can be compared with that of Thessaly, Central Greece, the Peloponnese, and the Cyclades, but since it occurs there in both Late Neolithic I and II phases, it is of little chronological significance. One of the vessels from the "Final Neolithic" at Knossos has parallels in shape in Late Neolithic I Thessaly (cf. Evans 1971: pl. 3, with Milojčić et al. 1976: pl. 14, no. 11, and Hauptmann 1981: Beil. 1, no. 23) and Central Greece (Sampson 1980: fig. 73, no. 712; see Lambert 1981:313, CP 33). Other characteristics of the latest Neolithic stage such as primitive jugs and Pattern Burnishing look forward to Early Minoan (Vagnetti and Belli 1978), and it is even possible that some of the material assigned to "Final Neolithic" may be more conveniently placed in Early Minoan I. There is little evidence so far to suggest that there was a sharp cultural break at the end of the Cretan Neolithic and the beginning of the Early Minoan period, although the relevant sequence is still very poorly attested.

The radiocarbon determinations for the Ceramic Neolithic (see fig. 5 and table 1) are generally in keeping with the cultural evidence that developments proceeded at a more or less constant pace throughout the Aegean, except perhaps in Crete. The Aegean Early Ceramic Neolithic can be tentatively dated in general terms ca. 6400–5700 B.C., the Middle Neolithic ca. 5700–5300 B.C., Late

Neolithic I ca. 5300–4300 B.C., and Late Neolithic II ca. 4300–3700 B.C. Treuil (1983:136) places the beginning of the Late Neolithic in the Aegean region a little later, ca. 4900–4700 B.C., but this does not take into account the radiocarbon determinations for the Middle Neolithic and the Middle-Late Neolithic transition, particularly those from the Franchthi cave, which are considerably earlier. Although others might draw the limits a little differently, I doubt they would vary from those given here by more than a few hundred years.

Early Bronze Age

After consideration of the three main cultural regions, Cycladic, Minoan, and Helladic, traditionally distinguished in discussions of the Bronze Age, we turn to Thessaly, Macedonia, Thrace, and the Eastern Aegean, which, though peripheral, are of considerable influence and importance. Three phases have been recognized in each of the main regions, and these are roughly, but not necessarily exactly, synchronous from region to region. The Early Bronze Age way of life, when fully established, was significantly different from that of the Neolithic, but there was a long and gradual transition which is still very obscure. The chronological picture is still very inexact, and, in contrast to the Neolithic, there are relatively few radiocarbon determinations. Consideration of absolute chronology therefore follows the discussion of the relative chronology in each of the regions. The introduction of metallurgy to Greece has already been discussed (see above under "Ceramic Neolithic").

The former widely held view was that speakers of an Indo-European language ancestral to Greek entered Greece at the end of the Early Bronze Age, bringing with them the Middle Helladic culture. This interpretation was based on archaeological evidence that suggested a significant cultural break at that time, coupled with the recognition that mainland civilization gradually evolved from the Middle to the Late Bronze Age, at which time Greek is securely attested in the Linear B tablets. Excavations at Lerna in the 1950s, however, showed that the change from Early Helladic to Middle Helladic was not so abrupt as had been supposed, and suggested to some that at least the initial events connected with the "coming of the Greeks" might better be recognized in the burnings and cultural changes that brought an end to the Early Helladic II period in the Argolid (Caskey 1960). Further excavation and study have tended to confirm the view that the differences between Early Helladic III and Middle Helladic are less significant than was earlier believed. "Minyan" ware, for instance, already occurs in quantity in Early Helladic III (Howell 1974; Rutter 1983a). Hence, although significant changes must still be recognized at some sites such as Eutresis (Goldman 1931:231–36; Caskey and Caskey 1960:167), few scholars would now postulate a substantial group of newcomers at the beginning of the Middle Helladic period. The theory of widespread immigration or invasion at the end of Early Helladic II, on the other hand, is not universally supported by the evidence now available. The transition from Early Helladic II to III was not catastrophic at all sites, and there is increasing evidence that some of the architectural and ceramic changes had already begun to occur sporadically in Greece before the end of Early Helladic II and were thereafter gradually adopted rather than that they occurred abruptly throughout Greece. The impetus for the changes that took place at or near the end of Early Helladic II probably came from Anatolia, to judge by the Anatolian pottery shapes found in Euboea, the Cyclades, and Thebes.

Although the northern regions of Greece are as yet less well known than the southern ones, there is little evidence that invaders or immigrants came to Southern Greece by land from the north, either from the northern regions of Greece or by way of them from the Balkans. There was probably considerable continuity and perhaps chronological overlap in the northern regions of Greece between the Late Neolithic and Early Bronze Age cultures. The impetus for change appears to have come to Thessaly from Southern Greece and to Macedonia from Western Anatolia. Once started, the Early Bronze Age cultures in the northern regions of Greece appear to have developed without a break, and, although similarities with the Balkans suggest considerable interaction, there is no indication of large-scale immigration or invasion. The Middle Bronze Age may have come about in Thessaly as a result of influence from Macedonia (Hanschmann and Milojčić 1976:217–22). In Macedonia the transition to the Middle Bronze Age was probably gradual, and influence from Southern Greece may have been as important as that from anywhere else. There are almost no new sites founded in the Middle Bronze Age in Macedonia, and the termination of occupation at many Early Bronze Age ones suggests that some depopulation may have occurred (Heurtley 1939:xxii–xxiii).

As seen from the perspective of this apparent cultural continuity throughout much of Greece, the "northern" features usually cited as evidence for newcomers seem either equivocal or of no great significance. The "megaron house," for instance, is now known in the Aegean from at least the Middle Neolithic. Recent attempts to connect such buildings with northern intruders when equipped with curved ("apsidal") ends (e.g., Zanotti 1981:276–83) seem to me unconvincing, especially since such "apsidal" ends are now apparently known in Early Helladic II. "Minyan" ware, despite past views, is now often thought to originate in Greece itself (e.g., French 1974:51–54; Howell 1974:79), perhaps Central

Greece (Rutter 1983a:349). Tumulus burial is first attested at a time contemporaneous with Early Helladic II at Lefkas (Dorpfeld 1927, the "R" group of graves), and thereafter it occurs sporadically throughout the Bronze Age Aegean (Hammond 1976:110–16; Simpson and Dickinson 1979:429). The occasional use of such an elaborate manner of burial seems more likely the result of influence than invasion. Incised flasks with possible Balkan connections from Middle Helladic sites (Hood 1974), if really northern imports (Zerner 1978:180–86), and occasional sherds of Corded Ware from Aegean Early Bronze Age contexts (see below) may signify nothing more than casual contact, such as is attested also by the reported discovery of an Aegean "sauceboat" at Zlotska Pećina (Neustupný 1968:24).

As possible alternative scenarios to widespread immigrations or invasions, one may imagine either that Indo-European speakers were in Greece already during the earlier phases of the Early Bronze Age and perhaps somewhat earlier (cf. Renfrew 1974), or that they came gradually to Greece during the later stages of the Aegean Early Bronze Age, perhaps having set out originally by sea from Anatolia. In any case, the archaeological evidence is insufficient at present to confirm or deny such suppositions.

Mention should be made here of a controversy concerning the later part of the second Early Bronze Age phase and the earlier part of the third Early Bronze Age phase in the Cyclades and on the mainland. Recent discoveries and studies have led to the recognition of a number of distinctive cultural assemblages characterized by Anatolian influences in the Cyclades (as at Kastri in Syros and in Phase III at Ayia Irini in Keos), Central Greece (as at Thebes), and Euboea (as at Lefkandi I). Two divergent chronological views of these assemblages have recently been argued. One, represented especially by Rutter (1979, 1983a, 1983b, 1984; see fig. 6a), holds that in the islands they are best assigned to the later part of Early Cycladic II as "Early Cycladic II B" and in Central Greece to the later part of Early Helladic II. The other view, that of Barber and MacGillivray (1980; Barber 1983, 1984; MacGillivray 1983, 1984; see fig. 6b), holds that in the islands these assemblages are best assigned to the earlier part of Early Cycladic III as "Early Cycladic III A" and in Central Greece to an early part of Early Helladic III. Full publication of the Early Bronze Age sequences at Phylakopi in Melos, Tiryns, and Lerna is necessary before final judgments may be made on this controversy. Meanwhile, since Kastri in Syros has always been assigned to Early Cycladic II (e.g., Caskey 1971a:795–96) and since Barber and MacGillivray have so far failed to demonstrate convincingly that a redating is necessary or worthwhile, I here adhere to the previously accepted chronological schema for the islands.

Toward the end of the Early Bronze Age and the beginning of the Middle Bronze Age the Aegean came increasingly into contact with Egypt, Cyprus (Coleman, this vol., chap. 11, pt. 2), Anatolia, and the Levant (e.g., Dietz 1971; Branigan 1974:119–23). Daggers and other metal objects are the chief evidence for this, but Minoan pottery and imitations of Cycladic "duck vases" (most recently Rutter 1985) are also attested in Cyprus. Contacts with the Balkans other than those already mentioned are indicated by resemblances between the Aegean and Albania in the Eneolithic and Early Bronze Age, particularly as represented at Maliq II and III (Prendi 1982:201–4, 211–14). Small anchorlike objects of terracotta, common in Early Bronze Age Greece and also found in the Balkans, Italy, and the Western Mediterranean (Weisshaar 1980), are further evidence of interconnections of some kind, although not necessarily close and sustained contact. The same is true of bossed bone plaques from Early Bronze Age Troy and Lerna, which have counterparts in the Central and Western Mediterranean (Evans 1956; Caskey 1960:297; Holloway 1981: esp. 17–19).

Early Cycladic

The Cyclades have received much scholarly attention during the past ten years. Major works by Renfrew (1972) and Doumas (1977) have appeared, and many other scholars made significant contributions to a volume connected with an exhibition in Karlsruhe (Thimme 1977). The workshop on Cycladic chronology held in London in 1983 (MacGillivray and Barber 1984) has already been mentioned. Despite this attention, Early Cycladic civilization is still very imperfectly known because of the scarcity of stratified settlements and the lack of radiocarbon determinations. Phylakopi in Melos and Ayia Irini in Keos are the only settlements where more than one phase is plentifully represented. Excavations recently carried out at Phylakopi (Renfrew and Wagstaff 1982:35–38; Evans and Renfrew 1984) have provided some evidence to supplement that from the old campaigns (Atkinson et al. 1904). The results are not yet fully published, but preliminary reports (especially Evans and Renfrew 1984) suggest that, contrary to earlier belief (e.g., Caskey 1971a:794), the site was occupied for part of Early Cycladic II, although it probably still lacks a complete Early Cycladic sequence. Ayia Irini in Keos was occupied during parts of at least two phases of Early Cycladic, although questions still remain about the dating of Period III, the latest Early Bronze Age stage (Caskey 1971b, 1972; Wilson and Eliot 1984).

I here follow the system of phases for the Early Cycladic period, which I myself and others have argued elsewhere (Coleman 1974, 1979; Weinberg 1977; Barber

and MacGillivray 1980; see also Doumas 1983:28–29) is preferable to the "cultures" proposed by Renfrew (1972, 1979b). Theoretically, it might be possible to retain both phases and "cultures." Renfrew's chronological charts (e.g., 1977:21) project the "cultures" onto a chronological framework of "EBA 1, 2, and 3" phases. In my view, however, the division into "cultures" is both arbitrary and confusing, for many scholars refer to the "cultures" as if they were essentially chronological despite Renfrew's intentions to the contrary.

Much of the material that can be assigned to Early Cycladic I and II comes from tombs, and these can hardly be expected to present a coherent chronological picture. Grave goods, if there are any at all, tend to be very sparse and of a specialized nature, and consequently the chronological limits of the Early Cycladic phases are poorly defined. One must remember this especially in connection with the marble figurines and other objects which are found almost exclusively in tombs.

Early Cycladic I probably represents a continuation of a previous Late Neolithic II culture in the islands which is not yet well attested. Only two excavated settlements, neither fully published, have been assigned to the Early Cycladic I, or "Pelos," phase: the lowest level at Phylakopi, below the first city (Atkinson et al. 1904:82–85), now designated "phase A 1" (Renfrew and Wagstaff 1982:36–37; Evans and Renfrew 1984) and Grotta in Naxos (Kondoleon 1949). Doumas (1972:115, 1977:31), however, doubts that either is earlier than Early Cycladic II. Given such uncertainty about settlements, our picture of Early Cycladic I must depend at present on which groups of tombs we assign to it. Most tombs of the long-recognized Pelos group clearly belong, although there is a possibility that some go back to the Late Neolithic II phase. The Lakkoudes group recently distinguished by Doumas (1977:15–16) is also to be dated to Early Cycladic I, although his view that it represents the earliest stage of this phase is not strongly supported. More difficult is the small Plastiras group, named from a cemetery in Paros (Doumas 1977:96–100), the stone vessels of which are compatible with an Early Cycladic I date. The figurines, however, are of a rare type, with naturalistic features and hands meeting below the breast, and have more in common with the "naturalistic" figurines of Early Cycladic II than with the schematic ones of Early Cycladic I. Although I think that we should continue to include the Plastiras group in Early Cycladic I, as is now customary, we should be alert for further evidence which might change the picture. I argue below that the "Kampos group," which is often assigned to Early Cycladic I, if it really is a coherent group at all, is more conveniently dated to Early Cycladic II. There are no unequivocal imports to or exports from the Cyclades in Early Cycladic I.

The Early Cycladic II, or "Syros," phase can be divided into two stages. The earlier, Rutter's Early Cycladic II A, is represented by excavated settlement material from several sites: Phylakopi in Melos, phase A 2, and possibly also the preceding phase A 1, if the view of Doumas mentioned above is correct (Renfrew and Wagstaff 1982:37; Evans and Renfrew 1984); Pyrgos in Paros (Tsountas 1898:168–75); Mount Kynthos in Delos (see recently MacGillivray 1980); Panormos in Naxos (see Doumas 1977); and Ayia Irini in Keos, Period II or pottery phase B (Caskey 1971b:368–72, 1972, 1979). The later stage, Rutter's Early Cycladic II B, is represented by the excavated settlement material from the Kastri fort at Chalandriani in Syros, which has come to be called the "Kastri group" (Bossert 1967); Mount Kythnos in Delos (MacGillivray 1980); and Ayia Irini in Keos, Period III or pottery phase C (see references above and Wilson and Eliot 1984). A large number of tombs of this phase are also known (see lately Doumas 1977). Crafts and trade took great strides forward in this phase throughout the Aegean, and an "international" spirit prevailed for which Cycladic seafarers may have been largely responsible. Early Cycladic II is characterized especially by "naturalistic" folded-arm figurines, by open-spouted bowls known as "sauceboats," by flat-bottomed vessels with low walls known as "frying pans" (Coleman 1985; Thimme 1977: nos. 400–406), and by the use of stamped spirals and concentric circles. Glazed and Patterned wares are also common. Contrary to the view of Renfrew (1972:183–85), Early Cycladic II developed directly from Early Cycladic I (Coleman 1979a, 1979b; Barber and MacGillivray 1980:155). Many pot shapes show continuity, including footed jars and pyxides, both rounded and cylindrical (Coleman 1974:341); clay beakers of Early Cycladic II date have also recently been published which are clearly related to Early Cycladic I prototypes in marble (Kondoleon 1970: pl. 193, gamma; Zapheiropoulou 1970b: fig. 6, 1970a:429).

A problem is posed by the so-called Kampos group, which was first distinguished by Bossert (1965) on the basis of the cemetery at Kampos in Paros (Varoucha 1925–26). A rich grave from Louros in Naxos (Papathanasopoulos 1961–62: 132–34) and tombs from Ano Kouphonisi (Zapheiropoulou 1970a, 1970b, 1983, 1984) and Ayioi Anargyroi in Naxos (Doumas 1977:100–120) have also sometimes been associated with this "group," which is often thought to date to Early Cycladic I or to a transitional stage at the end of Early Cycladic I and the beginning of Early Cycladic II (e.g., Coleman 1974:341, 1979b:65; Barber and MacGillivray 1980:145; Matthäus 1980; Zapheiropoulou 1984). In discussions at the workshop on Cycladic chronology in London in June 1983, however, serious doubts were raised whether the material is sufficiently homogeneous and belongs to a short

enough time span to constitute a true group (cf. Renfrew 1984). At any rate, regardless of whether we continue to recognize a "Kampos group," most if not all the material mentioned above is probably best assigned to the Early Cycladic II phase (Doumas 1976:70, 1977:25; Coleman 1985:197). Most of the "frying pans" assigned to the "Kampos group," for instance, are decorated with rows of triangular impressions known as *Kerbschnitt* (see Coleman 1985), which otherwise does not occur earlier than Early Cycladic II, and stamped spirals such as on a jar from Ayioi Anargyroi (Doumas 1977:108, no. 1) and on a "frying pan" from Ano Kouphonisi (Zapheiropoulou 1970b: fig. 5; Coleman 1985: no. 45) would also be unusual or unique in Early Cycladic I. The tombs of Ayioi Anargyroi produced a folded-arm figurine (Doumas 1977:113, no. 6), a type generally thought to date exclusively to Early Cycladic II. Bottle-shaped vessels like those from Kampos, Ano Kouphonisi, and Ayioi Anargyroi are found in Crete in contexts which, although somewhat uncertain, may well be of Early Minoan II date. "Fruitstands" with slightly bulging stems from Ano Kouphonisi (Zapheiropoulou 1984: fig. 3c; Warren 1984: fig. 3a) are similar to those found at Pyrgos and Ayia Photia in Crete in similar contexts (Xanthoudides 1918: fig. 5, no. 3; fig. 10, nos. 74, 78; Warren 1984: fig. 3); the same type occurs in Poliochni *nero*, which may therefore be roughly contemporaneous. "Frying pans" of Kampos type are also found in Early Helladic II contexts in Attica and Euboea (Coleman 1985; see below), and a figurine with curtailed arms from an Early Helladic II grave at Ayios Kosmas (Mylonas 1959:80, no. 3, from Grave 4) resembles those from the Louros grave. If we assign the material usually associated with the "Kampos group" to Early Cycladic II, the Cycladic sequence will come more into line with Crete and the mainland and all Cycladic "frying pans" so far known will conveniently fall into the same phase (Coleman 1985:197).

The striking Anatolian influences associated with the "Kastri group," which most scholars regard as falling toward the end of Early Cycladic II, have received much recent comment. At issue are one- and two-handled tankards, beak-spouted jugs, shallow bowls, sometimes wheel-made (Caskey 1972: C36), and two-handled tankards of Trojan type (*depa amphikypella*) found at Kastri in Syros (Bossert 1967) and Period III at Keos (Caskey 1972: Group C; Wilson and Eliot 1984). Bronze artifacts from Kastri are also of Anatolian types, and the metal itself may have come from Northwest Anatolian sources (Stos-Gale, Gale, and Gilmore 1984). Barber and MacGillivray (1980; Barber 1983, 1984; MacGillivray 1983, 1984) have recently proposed that the "Kastri group" be assigned to "Early Cycladic III A" rather than Early Cycladic II. As supporting evidence they cite the stratification at Keos, where a stage showing Anatolian influence (Period III) follows one with characteristic Early Cycladic II types. Rutter (1979, 1983a, 1983b, 1984) argues, however, that similar influences occurred on the mainland in the "Lefkandi I assemblage" before the end of Early Helladic II and that it therefore seems preferable to continue to assign the "Kastri group" to Early Cycladic II. As mentioned above, the view of Rutter appears better to me, at least until further evidence is forthcoming.

Early Cycladic II can be generally correlated by imports and exports as well as numerous similarities with Early Minoan II (Doumas 1976; Sakellarakis 1977), with at least part of Early Helladic I, and with Early Helladic II (Caskey 1971a:796–97; Weinberg 1977). Folded-arm figurines were exported to Crete and copied there, not only in Early Minoan II, but also, it is claimed, in Early Minoan III (Tholos C at Archanes: e.g., Sakellarakis 1977:148), suggesting the possibility that Early Minoan III may have begun before the end of Early Cycladic II. The number of Cycladic finds from Tholos C at Archanes (Sakellarakis 1977) is remarkable, as is the similarity between the tombs of Ano Kouphonisi and Ayia Photia (Davaras 1972; Warren 1984:60), although the published evidence seems insufficient to confirm claims that the latter site represents a Cycladic colony.

Extensive "Cycladic" finds at Ayios Kosmas (Mylonas 1959:155) and Marathon (Marinatos 1970:350) have also led to suggestions that they were Cycladic trading posts or colonies. As for Crete, the claims are difficult to substantiate. The similarity of tomb types to those in the Cyclades is an equivocal point, since we have little evidence about "standard" Early Helladic burial practices. Artifacts with Cycladic connections are generally found in tombs, and, as Weinberg has pointed out (1977:143), the finds from the tombs at Ayios Kosmas, despite their contemporaneity, differ considerably from those made in the settlement and may represent specialized tomb offerings. Although there are a few indisputable Cycladic imports, only scientific analyses, which have not yet been carried out, could show where the rest of the Cycladic-like artifacts found on the mainland were actually made. Thus we must entertain the possibility that mainland funeral customs were generally similar to those of the Cyclades and developed parallel to them, rather than supposing that these sites and others like them were Cycladic colonies.

Recent discussions have raised serious questions about the definition and nature of the Early Cycladic III phase. A hotly disputed question, besides the controversy over terminology already mentioned, is whether there is a fairly widespread hiatus, or "gap," in our evidence of the Early Cycladic sequence. Rutter (1984 with references) has lately argued that there was such a gap, corresponding in his chronological scheme with the Early Cycladic

III phase (see fig. 6a), and that this gap represents a time of disturbance and change. Barber and MacGillivray (each 1984, with references; see fig. 6b), on the other hand, argue that the sequence as currently attested was continuous, and that whether on not there was a hiatus at Phylakopi, the "Kastri group" represents a stage chronologically intermediate between the finds generally accepted as belonging to Early Cycladic II (Early Cycladic II A in Rutter's scheme) and the material assigned to the first city at Phylakopi (I-ii or phase B; Early Cycladic III B in the scheme of Barber and MacGillivray and Middle Cycladic in the scheme of Rutter).

The stratification at Phylakopi is apparently not decisive on this point. As mentioned above, it has now become clear that the site was occupied during Early Cycladic II, the stage distinguished by the material grouped under "I-i" by MacKenzie (Atkinson et al. 1904:243–48; cf. Barber 1974, 1984:89; Barber and MacGillivray 1980) and assigned to "phase A 2" by the current excavators (Renfrew and Wagstaff 1982:36–37; Evans and Renfrew 1984). It has also been increasingly recognized that Phylakopi I as defined by the early excavations (i.e., I-ii and iii or phase B) is at least partly contemporaneous with the Middle Bronze Age elsewhere in the Aegean (Renfrew 1972:192; Barber and MacGillivray 1980:152; Barber 1984; MacGillivray 1984; Rutter 1984). This chronological equation is attested by the occurrence in levels of Phylakopi I of types such as the spouted askoi known as "duck vases," which are apparently found elsewhere in the Western Aegean almost exclusively in Middle Bronze Age contexts (Dietz 1974:139; Merrillees 1979; Walter and Felten 1981: nos. 393, 395; Rutter 1985). Some hiatus in occupation in the areas tested at the site therefore seems possible between Phylakopi I-i and I-ii or, in terms of the recent excavations, phase A 2 and the following phase B (Evans and Renfrew 1984:66). The possibility of a gap is further supported to some extent by the apparent absence from the Phylakopi sequence of any material of the "Kastri group," which might be expected to fall between the earlier Early Cycladic II material represented by group "I-i" (or "phase A 2") and the next attested material. The sequence at Ayia Irini in Keos provides further support, since there was certainly a break in occupation between Periods III and IV, that is between the time of the "Kastri group" and well after the beginning of Middle Cycladic (Overbeck and Overbeck 1979; Overbeck 1984:108–9; Wilson and Eliot 1984:85).

I have already explained why I think Rutter's assignment of the "Kastri group" to Early Cycladic II is to be preferred. Given the clear chronological overlap between the first city at Phylakopi and the Middle Bronze Age elsewhere in the Aegean, the assignment of Phylakopi I to the Middle Cycladic period also seems reasonable. Although Barber's point (1983:79) that Phylakopi I was formerly taken to define the later part of Early Cycladic is well taken, the recent excavations will almost certainly entail some chronological readjustments and there is therefore no real hindrance to reassigning the material associated with Phylakopi I to Middle Cycladic to bring it roughly into line with the rest of the Aegean (Rutter 1983b). Such reassignment poses no methodological problem under the assumptions about terminology and chronology put forward at the beginning of this chapter.

Rutter's concept of a gap in our present evidence during the time we may conveniently call the Early Cycladic III phase therefore seems attractive. Presumably it would not reflect a time of complete depopulation in the islands, since the arts and crafts of the early Middle Cycladic period, as at Phylakopi I, generally represent a continuation of those of Early Cycladic rather than a real cultural break. The major innovation of the latter period is that settlements are larger and apparently fewer (Cherry 1979:43–46; Renfrew and Wagstaff 1982:136–40). The final publication of the recent excavations at Phylakopi may yet produce additional evidence, and the recently published sequence at Aigina (Walter and Felten 1981) also provides some hints as to how the apparent gap may be filled (Rutter 1983b:71, 1984).

Early Cycladic interconnections with the Eastern Mediterranean (Höckmann 1977a) are attested by a seal from Amorgos with parallels in Syria (Thimme 1977: nos. 453, 454), by a model shrine or granary from Melos (Thimme 1977: no. 360) with parallels in Palestine, and by resemblances between Cycladic figurines and those from Anatolia. Some interaction between the Early Bronze Age Cyclades and the Western Mediterranean may also have occurred (see recently Höckmann 1977b), although, as argued by Renfrew (1979a; see also Renfrew and Whitehouse 1974), the evidence is often overstated. The western provenience of two Cycladic beaked jugs supposedly found in Minorca is doubtful (Topp and Plantalamour 1983, with references).

Early Minoan

Recent excavations have added much to our knowledge of the development of Early Minoan Crete and, inasmuch as excellent discussions of the cultural sequence and chronology have been published lately by Branigan (1970), Warren (1976, 1980), and Cadogan (1983), I may here be brief.

Details of the sequence of the latest stages of the Neolithic and the first phase of the Early Minoan period are still very obscure because of the lack of well-stratified sites from the time of transition. Although there is agreement that the earliest deposits at Phaistos belong to a late stage of the Neolithic, or "Final Neolithic," finds some-

times assigned to the Neolithic period from Partira, the Eileithyia cave at Amnisos, a well at Phournoi, and burials at Ayios Nikolaos at Palaikastro (e.g., by Vagnetti and Belli 1978; Warren 1980:489) are possibly of Early Minoan I date (Cadogan 1983:508). These disputed finds play a significant role in the dating of the beginning of Early Minoan I and the question whether Early Minoan I developed fairly directly from the preceding Late Neolithic culture (Branigan 1970:196–202, with discussion of other possibilities), or whether it may have begun with immigrations from Northwestern Anatolia (Warren 1974).

Undisputed stratified or isolated settlement deposits of Early Minoan I date are found at Knossos and Debla, and some tombs can also be certainly attributed (Warren 1980:489). The tholos tomb occurred, probably for the first time, although it is argued by Vagnetti and Belli (1978:135) that tombs of this type at Levena and Trypiti are to be dated earlier, in the "Final Neolithic." Minoan seal stones were also evidently first produced in Early Minoan I (Pini 1981:422), although they are not found in any great number until Early Minoan III/Middle Minoan I times. Painted pottery (Ayios Onouphrios ware and Levena ware, its light-on-dark counterpart) and pattern burnished "Pyrgos" chalices appear for the first time. Bottlelike jars and "fruitstands" like those of the Cycladic "Kampos group" were found in the Pyrgos cave in what is often assumed to be an Early Minoan I context (Xanthoudides 1918), but the stratigraphy was uncertain; similar jars recently found at Ayia Photia could equally well belong to Early Minoan II as Early Minoan I, since the large cemetery there was used in both periods (Davaras 1972). The Cretan evidence does not therefore contradict my view that the material of the "Kampos group" should generally be dated early in Early Cycladic II.

Early Minoan I corresponds roughly to the period of Troy I and probably the stage that immediately preceded it in Northwestern Anatolia (Warren 1980:493; Cadogan 1983:512).

Early Minoan II, which develops from Early Minoan I without a break, is well represented by architectural remains, particularly those recently excavated at Myrtos (Warren 1972b), Debla (Warren and Tzedhakis 1974), and Knossos (Warren 1972a; Wilson 1985), as well as the long-known site of Vasiliki, recently reexamined by Zoes (1976 and later reports in the Greek journals). Many tomb deposits are also ascribed to this phase. Warren (e.g., 1980:490) has distinguished two stages in eastern Crete and Knossos, and these can also be detected to some extent at other sites. Gray or Black Burnished ware and Painted ware with hatched decoration of the "Koumasa style" are typical of Early Minoan II A; Vasilike ware (mottled by differential firing; Betancourt 1979) and painted wares without hatched decoration are typical of

Early Minoan II B. A very early stage of Early Minoan II A has recently been identified at Knossos (Wilson 1985). The manufacture of stone bowls, which became such a distinctive element of Minoan craftsmanship in the Palatial periods, began in Early Minoan II A (Warren 1980:490).

Early Minoan II was a phase of considerable cultural exchange with the other areas of the Aegean. Interconnections with the Cyclades have already been cited. "Sauceboats" of Early Helladic or Early Cycladic II type have been found recently in Early Minoan II A levels at Knossos (Warren 1972a) and in less well stratified contexts in caves at Platyvola and Lera (Rutter and Zerner 1984: 75 and 81, I, A, 2 and 3 with references). Cretan exports elsewhere in the Aegean (Branigan 1970:186–89; Warren 1984), which include two foot amulets and a seal (Wiencke 1981; Rutter and Zerner 1984:81, I, B), are less common than imports. The cultural influence exerted on Crete by her neighbors at this time may well have been stronger than that which she exerted on them. Kythera has been claimed as an exception to this hypothesis, on the grounds that an Early Helladic II settlement there was apparently followed by an Early Minoan II colony (Coldstream and Huxley 1972:272–77; Coldstream 1974). Rutter and Zerner (1984:75–77), however, have recently suggested that the Early Minoan material in Kythera may have been brought by seasonal visitors and that there was no permanent settlement until Middle Minoan I A.

A number of stratified deposits of the Early Minoan III phase can now be recognized in Eastern Crete and at Knossos (Warren 1980:490–91; Betancourt 1982:183–84; Cadogan 1983:508–9), and this phase must therefore be regarded as a chronological reality, despite earlier doubts (summarized in Zoes 1968). It may have been a short period during which some sites were abandoned (Cadogan 1983:509) and Crete had little outside contact with the mainland (Rutter and Zerner 1984:76–77) or the Cyclades (MacGillivray 1984:73; Warren 1984).

Early Minoan III pottery is characterized by White-on-Dark ware (Betancourt 1982), which includes spirals in Eastern Crete. The appearance of polychrome decoration is generally taken to mark the beginning of Middle Minoan I A (Cadogan 1983:508–9). White-on-Dark ware continues in use, however, and occurs together with polychrome decoration. Since polychrome pottery probably began earlier at Knossos than elsewhere, some scholars have been led to postulate a greater or lesser overlap between "Eastern Early Minoan III" and "Central Middle Minoan I A" (Warren 1980:491). Although the actual situation is clear, it is preferable to avoid such a paradox of terminology (cf. Renfrew 1972:53–55). The most convenient way would probably be to regard Middle Minoan

I A as beginning everywhere at the time when polychrome first appears at Knossos; the vessels with white-painted designs in Eastern Crete, which precede the adoption there of polychromy but are nevertheless contemporary with the earliest polychrome pottery at Knossos, could then be regarded as pottery "of Early Minoan III type" dating to the Middle Minoan I A phase.

As already noted, Cycladic folded-arm figurines occur in Crete in tomb deposits dated by some scholars to Early Minoan III (Doumas 1976); the examples from Tholos C at Archanes (Sakellarakis 1977), which include one of ivory, are particularly noteworthy. Further publication of the archaeological contexts of these figurines will show whether they are to be taken as indicating a chronological overlap between Early Minoan III and Early Cycladic II; an overlap is not, in any case, likely to have been of long duration. A mainland Minyan bowl found at Knossos in a Middle Minoan I A context and originally dated to Early Helladic III (Hood 1971) has lately been reassigned to Middle Helladic I (Rutter and Zerner 1984:81, II, A, 1). Since Middle Minoan I A pottery is found in early Middle Helladic contexts at Lerna (Caskey 1960:299; Rutter and Zerner 1984) and in equivalent levels at Pefkakia in Thessaly, it is clear that the Early Bronze Age ended at roughly the same time in both regions.

Egyptian stone bowls found in Crete from Early Minoan II on (Warren 1980:493–97; Cadogan 1983:512) attest to a small-scale but steady relationship starting at least as early as the middle of the third millennium B.C. An Egyptian stone bowl with inscriptions connecting it to the Fifth Dynasty Pharaoh Userkaf comes from Kythera (Coldstream and Huxley 1972:273–77; Coldstream 1974:35; Cadogan 1983:512), but its exact provenience is unknown. A silver cylinder seal from an Early Minoan II tomb at Mochlos is an eastern import and related to the Early Dynastic II–III styles in Mesopotamia (Pini 1982). None of the Egyptian or Levantine scarabs yet found in Crete (Ward 1971:92–95; Warren 1980:494–95; Cadogan 1983:513) is necessarily earlier than Middle Minoan times.

Although the Middle Minoan period lies outside the scope of this chapter, it is worth noting that interrelationships between Crete and the mainland (e.g., Rutter and Zerner 1984), the Cyclades (e.g., MacGillivray 1984:73), Cyprus (Coleman, this vol., chap. 11, pt. 2) and the rest of the Eastern Mediterranean (e.g., Warren 1980:494–97; Cadogan 1983:513–16) increase considerably starting at or soon after the beginning of Middle Minoan I. These interrelationships probably went hand in hand with a great expansion of Minoan trade and influence, and perhaps also settlement abroad, which was probably related, in turn, to the building of the first palaces in Crete in Middle Minoan I B.

Early Helladic

The Early Helladic sequence has also been the subject of a recent and well-illustrated summary (Hanschmann and Milojčić 1976:155–84). As seen from the perspective of recent discoveries, the Early Helladic civilization was primarily a phenomenon of Central Greece and the Peloponnese. In the peripheral regions such as Thessaly and Macedonia, Early Bronze Age culture had more in common with the Balkans and Anatolia than did its more distinctive southern offshoot.

Until recently the development from Late Neolithic to Early Helladic has been unclear. Relatively few Early Helladic settlements overlie Late Neolithic ones, and it seemed possible that there was significant population decline in at least some parts of Greece. Recent work already mentioned above (Sampson 1980) shows that this was certainly not the case in Euboea, where twenty-three Early Helladic I sites have been identified. The people evidently moved often from one place to another, for although twenty-three sites are also listed for Late Neolithic II, Sampson's "Final Neolithic," only three were occupied in both phases. The Early Helladic I phase followed the Late Neolithic II without apparent break and no great change in material culture. Sampson (1980:196) describes the earliest stages of Early Helladic I as "subneolithic" in character and notes a steady development. There may also have been fairly continuous development from the Late Neolithic to Early Helladic at Eutresis, although the evidence from the earlier levels is not very extensive.

Eutresis in Boeotia is a key site for the Early Helladic sequence, inasmuch as all phases are represented (Goldman 1931; Caskey and Caskey 1960; for a useful diagram of the stratigraphy see Hanschmann and Milojčić 1976: Beil. 26). Neolithic remains (the Caskeys' Groups I and II) were found scattered in cavities in virgin soil. These are followed by an Early Helladic I deposit nearly 2 m deep (the Caskeys' Groups III–V and part of VI), which is followed in turn by deposits of Early Helladic II (part of the Caskeys' Group VI and Groups VII and VIII) and Early Helladic III (the Caskeys' Group IX). There is no evidence of a break in continuity between Early Helladic I and II. The pottery of Early Helladic I is characterized by Red Slipped and Burnished wares, and the shapes include hemispherical bowls, broad-mouthed "jugs," collar-necked jars with handles or lugs at the shoulder, and globular pyxides. The Early Helladic II pottery of Eutresis, like that throughout the area of Early Helladic culture, is characterized by saucers, "sauceboats," jugs, and askoi in Slipped and Burnished (Caskey and Caskey 1960:146) and *Urfirnis* wares and by coarse pans and hearths with stamped rims. Early Helladic III, which suc-

ceeded Early Helladic II at Eutresis without signs of violence, is rather different. The wheel is used for some of the smaller vessels; the glaze is of a different quality from that of Early Helladic II and is differently applied; light-on-dark Ayia Marina ware is found in considerable quantity; and there are rare examples of dark-on-light Patterned ware. Characteristic Early Helladic III shapes are tankards, one-handled cups, jugs (some beak-spouted), and two-handled jars.

Early Helladic I is also attested in the Corinthia, as recently at an important site near Perachora, which produced at least two Early Helladic I strata (Fossey 1969). Palaia Kokkinia near Piraeus (Theochares 1951) appears also to have a significant Early Helladic I level, although the stratigraphic evidence is insufficient for certainty. Otherwise, Early Helladic I finds have rarely been isolated stratigraphically from those of Early Helladic II. The scarcity of known Early Helladic I settlements might perhaps be explained if life were unsettled and people moved frequently during that time, as is suggested by the evidence from Euboea, since short-lived sites are hard to identify from surface indications.

Finds in Early Helladic I levels of pottery usually supposed to be of Early Cycladic II type, including "frying pans" and/or lids and other pieces decorated with *Kerbschnitt* (e.g., Goldman 1931: fig. 94:4) and stamped concentric circles or spirals (e.g., Goldman 1931: fig. 97 and pl. III, 2; Theochares 1951: fig. 26; possibly Fossey 1969: fig. 6 from Perachora Phase Z), have been much discussed as possible chronological indicators (Coleman 1985, with references). Earlier scholars tended to regard them as imports from the Cyclades. Bossert (1960) argued on the basis of differences in the stamped decoration, on the other hand, that many of these pieces were actually made on the mainland and that the use of stamped decoration may have begun earlier there than in the Cyclades. Renfrew (1972:536–37) has further suggested that there was a mainland type of "frying pan" with distinctive incised decoration. Weinberg (1965:301–2, 1977), by contrast, has continued to regard the pieces in question as actual imports and to argue that, since they were found in the lowest Early Helladic I levels during the earlier excavations at Eutresis (Goldman 1931:80–82) and in Group IV during the later ones (Caskey and Caskey 1960: IV, 13, 14, 18, 19), they provide evidence that Early Cycladic was well under way before Early Helladic I began.

Weinberg's general chronological point now seems to me to be sound, despite my earlier views to the contrary (Coleman 1974:342). Although many of the pieces with stamped decoration found on the mainland in Early Helladic I contexts may have been made there (Coleman 1985:201, 218–19), the shapes tend to be those with close parallels in the Cyclades, such as "frying pans," pyxides, and jars with suspension lugs. Given the extensive contacts these ceramic similarities attest, it is unlikely that there was a great lag in time from one area to another in the appearance of stamped decoration. Stamped decoration is first attested in the Cyclades on pottery associated with the so-called Kampos group, most or all of the material of which, as discussed above, is best assigned to Early Cycladic II. Since the first examples of stamped decoration occur on the mainland in Early Helladic I, it follows that Early Cycladic II began before the end of Early Helladic I.

Important recent finds have added much to our knowledge of Early Helladic towns and architecture. At Akovitika in Messenia (Themelis 1970; Karagiorga 1971) there is a complex of buildings, one of which resembles the well-known "House of the Tiles" at Lerna (e.g., Caskey 1955, 1960). Houses with similar plans at Aegina have also been recently published (Walter and Felten 1981:12–22), and the site, like Lerna, may also have been fortified in Early Helladic II (p. 22). An Early Helladic town at Lithares in Boeotia has a broad street flanked on either side by groups of rooms with party walls (Spyropoulos and Tzavella-Evjen 1973); it is dated primarily to Early Helladic I and II according to the excavators.

"Sauceboats" and saucers with ring or flaring feet and inturned rim are generally regarded as the hallmarks of Early Helladic II, but it should be noted that these vessels are not always found in Early Helladic II contexts such as tombs. The earliest type of "sauceboat" at Lerna has parallels in the Cyclades (Caskey 1960:290), where the shape is often thought to have originated.

Early Helladic II can be correlated in general with Early Minoan II and with Early Cycladic II (Caskey 1971a; Renfrew 1972:204–5), and the people of that phase were full participants in the "international" spirit of the day. Relations with the Cyclades were particularly close: common features include fortifications, "sauceboats," and the use of glaze paint, and the many Cycladic imports and imitations have already been mentioned.

Anatolian influences similar to those that occurred in the Cyclades toward the end of Early Cycladic II as dated above are also evidenced in Euboea at Lefkandi (Popham and Sackett 1968) and Manika (Papavasileiou 1910) and in Central Greece at Thebes (Konsolas 1981: Group B). The influences fall within what Rutter (1979) has defined as the "Lefkandi I assemblage," which is characterized by tankards, jugs with tall cutaway necks, shallow bowls, and, at Lefkandi, the extensive use of the potter's wheel (cf. also Papavasileiou 1910: pl. 8, upper, no. 2 from Manika). Two megaron houses found at Thebes (Demakopoulou 1975) should probably also be associated with the "Lefkandi I assemblage" and provide prototypes for

the Early Helladic III ones of Lerna IV. A megaron house with apsidal end found at Mourteri in Euboea (Sampson 1978) and others at Pefkakia in Thessaly (see below) are probably also roughly contemporary.

Early Helladic III represents a phase of considerable, but not wholesale, change. Its inception apparently occurred peacefully at some sites such as Eutresis and possibly Aegina, although it may have been marked by the burning of Early Helladic II settlements in the Northeastern Peloponnese (Caskey 1960:299–301). Early Helladic II predecessors have already been mentioned for the Early Helladic III megaron houses, which once seemed a striking innovation. Aegina has produced an impressive series of fortifications in the tradition of those of Early Helladic II (Walter and Felten 1981). The dark burnished ware known as "Minyan" first occurs in Early Helladic III (Rutter 1983a); there is a characteristic patterned ware in dark-on-light and light-on-dark varieties, and a curious incised and impressed ware is also found in the earlier stages (Rutter 1982). Otherwise, changes in the pottery repertoire are generally limited to a few shapes (Rutter 1979:9–10); "sauceboats," saucers, and jugs with short neck and cutaway mouth almost completely disappear and are replaced by tankards, two-handled bowls, one-handled cups, and cylindrical "ouzo cups." Rutter (1979) has recently argued in detail that the new shapes are the result of influence from the West Anatolian tradition, as represented by the "Lefkandi I assemblage." His view that Early Helladic III pottery as a whole shows a mingling of the Anatolian tradition with that of Early Helladic II seems reasonable.

That the change from the second to the third phase of Early Helladic was not so abrupt as has often been supposed is suggested by the existence at Tiryns, and possibly other sites in the Argolid, of levels in which Early Helladic II types such as "sauceboats" and saucers are found together with Early Helladic III types such as Patterned ware and two-handled bowls (Weisshaar 1981:1982b). It is not yet clear, however, whether these levels, described by Weisshaar as an *Ubergangsphase*, represent a true chronological stage rather than one that overlaps with Early Helladic II or III elsewhere.

Chronologically, Early Helladic III can be equated generally with Early Minoan III and with the as yet poorly defined Early Cycladic III phase in the islands.

The transition to Middle Helladic appears to have been peaceful at Lerna (Caskey 1960:298–99) and Aegina (Walter and Felten 1981), although at some other excavated sites such as Eutresis (Caskey and Caskey 1960:167) there is evidence of burning. The megaron houses of Early Helladic III continue into Middle Helladic. The intramural burials at Lerna are apparently a new feature (Caskey 1973:136), but other Middle Helladic burial practices, such as cist graves, pithos burials, and tumuli, are found also in Early Bronze Age Greece (e.g., at Lefkas; Caskey 1971a:792). New ceramic features, such as Matt Painted ware and ring-stemmed goblets, have no clear external ancestry and may well have come about as a result of development or interaction within the Aegean itself. Imported pottery in early Middle Helladic levels at Lerna (Rutter 1983b:72; Rutter and Zerner 1984) suggests an intensification of contact with Minoan Crete. In general, despite the changes, the archaeological evidence does not seem to me sufficient by itself to support a theory of large-scale immigration at this time from outside the Aegean such as advocated by Caskey (1971a, 1973) or Gimbutas (e.g., 1974b).

Early Bronze Age in Thessaly, Macedonia, Thrace, the Eastern Aegean, and Anatolia

An important step toward understanding the Early Bronze Age in Thessaly and Macedonia was taken with Hanschmann's publication of the Early Thessalian material from Argissa and discussion of its relationship with the neighboring regions (Hanschmann and Milojčić 1976). As in other regions, the earliest stages of the Early Bronze Age are obscure. Problems with the Rachmani sequence, or "period," have been discussed above. Its earliest stage is probably to be assigned to Late Neolithic II. During the middle and late Rachmani stages at Pefkakia, on the other hand, there are imports of "sauceboats" and other glazed pottery (e.g., Weisshaar 1979a:387, 390), which, taken at face value, suggest a chronological overlap of the later part of the Rachmani sequence with Early Helladic II. It is therefore possible that the early Rachmani stage overlaps chronologically to some extent with Early Helladic I. (See addendum for further discussion of the Rachmani culture.)

Pottery of the first phase of Early Thessalian, as the Early Bronze Age sequence in Thessaly is designated by Milojčić and his colleagues, is also found together with late Rachmani material at several sites (Hanschmann and Milojčić 1976:142–54), and it too may therefore overlap with Early Helladic II. Although the precise origins of Early Thessalian are not clear, many of its distinctive features may be due to influence from the Early Helladic culture of Central Greece at a time when Early Helladic I was passing into Early Helladic II (Hanschmann and Milojčić 1976:153, 224). The Early Thessalian sequence as currently defined cannot therefore have begun earlier than the beginning of Early Helladic II, ca. 2800 B.C. at the earliest.

Early Thessalian II as defined by Hanschmann and Milojčić (1976), which develops directly from Early Thessalian I, is characterized by increased intercourse with Southern Greece, the Cyclades, and Anatolia. External contact is especially evident at the coastal site of Pef-

kakia, where megaron houses "of Trojan type" and imported pottery such as *depa amphikypella* and Early Cycladic "frying pans" have been found (Milojčić 1974; Aupert 1975:659; Touchais 1977:593, fig. 182; Hanschmann and Milojčić 1976:133). Early Thessalian II can be equated with the later stages of Early Helladic II and Early Cycladic II.

The third phase of Early Thessalian follows the second without violence or apparent break. Although some imports and influences continue from Southern Greece, the predominant influences are from Western and Central Macedonia. Early Thessalian III ended at many sites with violent destructions which are thought to have been brought about by immigrants from Macedonia (Hanschmann and Milojčić 1976:225). Early Thessalian III overlaps with Early Helladic III, but perhaps ended somewhat earlier, since the earliest Middle Thessalian pottery also has links with Early Helladic III (Hanschmann and Milojčić 1976:225).

The sequence in Western Macedonia is still imperfectly documented, and the work of Heurtley (1939), especially at Kritsana in the Chalcidice, thus remains of considerable importance. Hanschmann has recently restudied Heurtley's finds in the museum at Thessaloniki (Hanschmann and Milojčić 1976:195–217) and divided the Early Bronze Age in Macedonia into three phases. These developed without drastic interruption, and there was probably a gradual penetration from the coast inland and to western Macedonia, where the Neolithic cultures lasted longer. Early Macedonian I, to which Hanschmann assigns Kritsana I and II, is characterized by bowls with "trumpet lugs," that is, tubular horizontal lugs that splay out at either end. According to her, this phase preceded Early Thessalian I but may have overlapped slightly with Early Helladic II. New forms in Early Macedonian II, as represented by Kritsana III and IV, include bowls with thickened or markedly incurving lips, and the potter's wheel now comes into sporadic use. Early Macedonian II was probably contemporary with both Early Thessalian I and a good part of Early Thessalian II (Hanschmann and Milojčić 1976: chart on 221). Early Macedonian III is more widely attested than the earlier phases, particularly in Northern and Western Macedonia. The latest levels at Kritsana, V and VI, represent only the first part of Early Macedonian III; the later part is abundantly represented at Ayios Mamas, Saratse, and Vardaroftsa. New forms at the beginning of this phase include horizontal handles placed on the shoulder of bowls; in the later stages, at Saratse and Vardaroftsa, kantharoi occur that are very similar in shape and sometimes in fabric to "Minyan" ware kantharoi of southern Greece (e.g., Hanschmann and Milojčić 1976: pls. 85:8 and 86:7). Early Macedonian III may have been contemporary with the later stages of Early Thessalian II and the whole of Early Thessalian

III (Hanschmann and Milojčić 1976: chart on 221). The earlier part of Early Macedonian III may also have been at least partly contemporary with Early Helladic III, to judge by the discovery of an Early Helladic III Patterned sherd in Kritsana VI (Heurtley 1939:170, fig. 43).

At Servia in inland Western Macedonia the Early Bronze Age levels, like the earlier ones, have much in common with the Thessalian sequence (Ridley and Wardle 1979:217–24). Phase 8 apparently corresponds to Early Thessalian I (cf. Ridley and Wardle 1979: fig. 14 with Hanschmann and Milojčić 1976: Beil. 6:24). Phases 9 and 10, the finds from which have not yet been distinguished from one another in the preliminary report, correspond to Early Thessalian II and III and have imports that link them with Early Helladic II and III (Ridley and Wardle 1979:220).

In Central and Eastern Macedonia the Early Bronze Age sequences at Dikili Tash (Deshayes 1970, 1972; Séfériades 1983) and Sitagroi (Renfrew 1970, 1971), for which there are many radiocarbon determinations, have not yet been published in detail, but preliminary correlations can be made with the Troad and with Hanschmann's schemes for Thessaly and Western Macedonia. There was probably a break between Sitagroi III, which appears to date to the time of Late Neolithic II elsewhere in the Aegean, and Sitagroi IV, which represents the earliest stage of the Early Bronze Age identified at the site. Dikili Tash IIIA, described by the excavators as representing the "Early Bronze Age I" stage, was roughly contemporaneous with Sitagroi IV (Séfériades 1983:639). Cups with single high-swung handles from Dikili Tash (Deshayes 1970: fig. 12, 1972:201, lower right; Séfériades 1983: fig. 43) and Sitagroi (Renfrew 1970: pl. XLI, above) attest to connections between this stage and Early Thessalian I (Séfériades 1983:659; Hanschmann and Milojčić 1976: pl. 8:1–4, 7) and suggest that it began no earlier than the beginning of Hanschmann's Early Macedonian I. This "Early Bronze Age I" stage is regarded as earlier than Troy I by Deshayes (1970:43, 1972:200) and as contemporary with the earlier part of Troy I by Renfrew (1971:280). The latter view is to be preferred, since similar cups with high-swung handles are found in the *azzuro* levels at Poliochni (Bernabò-Brea 1964: pl. X, b, e–g), which are probably contemporaneous with the earlier part of Troy I.

Sitagroi V, which follows Sitagroi IV without a break, has been further subdivided. The earlier levels (i.e., VA) are probably contemporary with Dikili Tash IIIB (Séfériades 1983:639). This stage may be equated with the later part of Troy I, to judge by the bowls with internally thickened rims and other ceramic features of Dikili Tash IIIB (Séfériades 1983:663–64). The later levels of Sitagroi V (i.e., VB) evidently represent a stage during which there is no evidence for occupation at Dikili Tash. They were probably roughly contemporary with the later part of the Early Bronze Age sequence at Troy, that is, Troy II–IV, and there are also probable connections with Early Macedonian III (Hanschmann and Milojčić 1976:214, n. 938).

Early Bronze Age Thrace is so far very poorly attested, although surface indications suggest that it was widely settled (Theochares 1971).

Fragments of Corded Ware, perhaps imported from southern Russia or the eastern part of the Balkans, have appeared at ten Aegean sites, mostly in Northern Greece, but including Eutresis and Ayia Marina in Central Greece. Hanschmann, in one of the most recent discussions of these finds (Hanschmann and Milojčić 1976: 231–35), notes that they may be divided into an earlier group, which dates to the first half of Early Helladic II, and a later group, which dates to Early Helladic III. There are recently published examples from Dikili Tash IIIB (e.g., Séfériades 1983: figs. 66, 67), which presumably belong to her earlier group. Somewhat similar cord impressions occur on the rim of a recently published bowl of Early Helladic III date from Lerna which was probably made locally (Rutter 1982: no. 24).

The Troad still provides the best yardstick by which we may relate the Eastern Aegean and Western Anatolia to the sequences already discussed. As already mentioned, recent publications (e.g., Sperling 1976) suggest that Kum Tepe I A and I B precede the earliest settlement at Troy and that the first stage (*nero*) at Poliochni in Lemnos began about the same time as Kum Tepe I B. The Kum Tepe I A–B sequence was probably largely contemporaneous with the earlier stages of the Early Bronze Age in the Cyclades and Crete (see above).

Imported Aegean sherds found in Troy I, which is contemporary with Kum Tepe I C, particularly those from "sauceboats" and Patterned ware, must date to Early Cycladic–Early Helladic II. Hence, despite other recent views to the contrary (e.g., Easton 1976:150–52), we must follow Weinberg (1965:303) in postulating a chronological overlap between Troy I and Early Cycladic–Early Helladic II. This equation is further supported by the imported Patterned sherds from the second (*azzurro*) phase at Poliochni (Bernabò-Brea 1964:584–85), which is evidently contemporary with the early part of Troy I. Troy I probably began earlier than Early Cycladic–Early Helladic II, although we cannot yet be sure just when in Aegean terms. The Anatolian influences that occurred in the islands and on the mainland of Greece toward the end of Early Cycladic–Early Helladic II and that are attested by the *depa amphikypella* found at Kastri in Syros, Ayia Irini in Keos, Orchomenos in Boeotia, and Pefkakia in Thessaly and by other ceramic features such as the use of the potter's wheel, may be dated in Anatolian terms to the time of Troy II–III.

Imports connecting Lerna and Troy suggest that Early Helladic III was in part contemporary with Troy IV (Caskey 1960:297). The import or local imitation of a "duck vase" in Troy IV (Blegen, Caskey, and Rawson 1951:136) suggests that it may also have been partly contemporaneous with the early Middle Bronze Age elsewhere in the Aegean, since such vessels were widely circulated at that time (Rutter 1985; see above). A Middle Minoan I A jar found on Samos in a context transitional between Troy IV and V (Isler 1973; cf. Warren 1980:498–99) is in keeping with this view. Troy V must therefore belong wholly to the Aegean Middle Bronze Age, as argued already by Easton (1976:158–61).

"Red cross bowls," vessels with red crosses painted on the inside, once seemed to indicate a close correlation between Anatolia and Greece (Weinberg 1965:305–6). Now, however, they are recognized as very imprecise chronological indicators. Such vessels are found throughout Anatolia (Korfmann 1983: fig. 1), and, although they are often thought to be characteristic of the Troy V period, it has recently been shown by Korfmann (1983) that they have a longer history, beginning in the Anatolian Late Neolithic or Chalcolithic period. In Greece such crosses are first attested in Early Helladic II, as at Lerna (Caskey 1960:290), and continue into Early Helladic III (Blegen, Caskey, and Rawson 1951: 227).

Excavated sites in the islands of the Eastern Aegean such as Poliochni in Lemnos, Thermi in Lesbos, Emborio in Chios, and Tigani and the Heraeum in Samos follow the sequence in the Troad fairly closely and for the most part have closer relationships with Anatolia than the rest of the Aegean. Some correlations are provided, however, by occasional imports and local imitations in Poliochni (Bernabò-Brea 1964:650–52, 1976:279, 303–4; cf. Renfrew 1972:209), Thermi (Lamb 1936:177–78), Tigani (Heidenreich 1935–36:169–70; Felsch 1974:132), and in level IV of the Heraeum at Samos (Milojčić 1961:48–49). These correlations are in general agreement with the chronological picture in the Troad.

A cemetery at Iasos on the Carian coast is especially noteworthy for its Aegean character (Levi 1961–62, 1965–66). Instead of the usual West Anatolian pithos burials, all of the eighty-five tombs excavated are stone cists that closely resemble Cycladic ones, and Doumas's recent work in the Cyclades (1977) shows that the incidence of multiple burial was also similar in both places. The grave goods include two beakers and a bowl of marble (Levi 1965–66: figs. 170, 171), perhaps imported from the Cyclades, and many jars with conical necks reminiscent of those of the "Kampos group." The latest tombs are probably contemporary with late Troy I or early Troy II, which as argued above is contemporary with Early Cycladic II. The evidence from Iasos is therefore consistent with our assignment of the "Kampos group" to Early Cycladic II.

"Absolute Chronology"

The absolute dating of the beginning and earliest stages of the Early Bronze Age (figs. 2, 4) is problematic, since we still lack any relevant radiocarbon determinations from the Cyclades and have only a few from Crete and the mainland (see table 1 for a complete listing). Although the end of the Late Neolithic period provides a rough *terminus post quem* for the Early Bronze Age, it cannot itself be precisely estimated in any of the various regions. On the basis of current evidence, including the single determination from Late Neolithic II Kephala, one may guess that Early Cycladic started ca. 3700 B.C. The latest Neolithic determinations from Knossos suggest that Early Minoan may have begun about the same time. Early Helladic probably began a little later, to judge by the two radiocarbon determinations for Early Helladic I at Eutresis. The radiocarbon determinations from Sitagroi IV suggest that the Early Bronze Age probably began no later than ca. 3100 B.C. in Thessaly and Macedonia.

The second phase of the Early Bronze Age in Crete and on the mainland, which were probably roughly coterminous, can be somewhat more confidently dated. Although there are some discrepancies from site to site, the radiocarbon determinations indicate that this was probably a long phase, lasting from about 2900 B.C. to about 2400 B.C. Early Cycladic II must have begun somewhat earlier, perhaps by ca. 3100 B.C., if the view expressed above that it overlapped somewhat with Early Helladic I is correct.

Early Minoan III and Early Helladic III, which were probably also roughly contemporaneous, represent a considerably shorter time than the preceding phase and probably came to an end ca. 2100 B.C. Such a dating is suggested by the radiocarbon determinations both from this phase and from the early stages of the Middle Bronze Age.

The datings just given are based exclusively on a consideration of the radiocarbon determinations given in table 1. It is encouraging to note that they differ from those proposed for Early Minoan by Warren (1980:499), which also take the Egyptian interconnections into detailed account, only in that Warren has Early Minoan I and III begin a little later and brings Early Minoan III to an end fifty years earlier. Cadogan (1983) is in substantial agreement with Warren, although he dates the beginnings of Early Minoan I and II slightly later. The considerably later datings proposed by Betancourt and Lawn (1984, especially fig. 7) depend on a very restricted number of determinations and appear to represent the latest possible estimates. The chronology here proposed leads to somewhat later datings for the earlier part of the Trojan sequence than those advocated by Easton (1976: 161–65).

Since there are as yet no determinations from Early Bronze Age Thessaly, absolute dating is there dependent on the correlations already discussed with the more southern parts of the Aegean and with Macedonia. Early Thessalian I perhaps began ca. 3100–2900 B.C. and Early Thessalian II ca. 2650 B.C. Early Thessalian III probably dates ca. 2400–2150 B.C. Three radiocarbon determinations from Servia in Western Macedonia are in general accord with this dating for Thessaly, at least in the older parts of their ranges. The Kritsana sequence for Central Macedonia lacks radiocarbon determinations, and it therefore must be dated by means of the correlations with Thessaly already discussed. Fifteen determinations allow the sequence from Sitagroi in Eastern Macedonia to be fairly closely dated, but, until the finds are more fully published, the implications for the absolute chronologies of other sites and regions are unclear. Sitagroi IV, which stands at the head of the Early Bronze Age sequence at that site, probably began ca. 3100 B.C., and Sitagroi Vb, the final level, probably ended ca. 2150 B.C. The radiocarbon determinations for the Early Bronze Age levels at Dikili Tash are very inconsistent with one another and hence are less useful than those from Sitagroi (cf. Séfériades 1983:639). Absolute dating for the Troad and the Eastern Aegean is treated in detail by Mellink in chapter 9 of this volume. The chronological correlations with the rest of the Aegean as already discussed suggest that Troy I came to an end ca. 2600 B.C.

Addendum

Brief mention should be made of some of the many publications that have appeared in the two years or so since this chapter was submitted. My comments follow more or less the same order as the chapter itself.

A report has appeared on the recent progress of dendrochronological investigations in the Aegean (Kuni-

holm and Striker 1987). Floating sequences of rings have been recorded for the Bronze Age and earlier in Greece and Anatolia. Although "absolute" dating so far extends back only as far as A.D. 1073, new techniques, such as "wiggle matching," may eventually lead to dating of these sequences to within ca. 25 years (Kuniholm, pers. comm.).

With regard to the terminology of the Late Neolithic period see Coleman (1984, 1987). Hauptmann (1986) continues to use the term *Chalcolithic* for what is here called Late Neolithic II.

A paper by Deilaki-Protonotariou describing an Aceramic Neolithic settlement at Dendra in the northeastern Peloponnese was recently given at a symposium in Athens; a summary was provided to participants (Deilaki 1987). The remains consist of the floors of small huts, more or less semicircular in plan, cut into bedrock. The finds are reported as similar to those of the Thessalian Aceramic stage; no pottery was found except for some later intrusions in one hut.

Three volumes of the final publication of the excavations at the Franchthi cave in the Argolid have now appeared or are about to appear (Jacobsen and Farrand 1987; Perlès 1987; Van Andel and Sutton 1987).

There is much new evidence on the Late Neolithic period, all tending to support its division, as presented in this chapter, into two phases, the earlier dating ca. 5300–4300 B.C. and the later ca. 4300–3700 B.C. The evidence includes lengthy series of radiocarbon determinations from Pefkakia in Thessaly and Mandalo in Western Macedonia and two determinations from Ayios Dhimitrios in the Western Peloponnese.

The important series of ten radiocarbon determinations from Pefkakia in Thessaly, soon to be published (Weisshaar, forthcoming *a*), was made available to me through the kindness of H.-J. Weisshaar. The series, which includes six determinations from the *Diministratum* at the site and four covering the Early, Middle, and Late Rachmani levels, may be listed in schematic form with calibrations according to the CRD system in use in this volume:

Period	Lab No.	Reported Date b.p.		CRD 1σ B.C.
		5568 ±	5730	
Dimini (LN I)	Pta-1397	5760 ± 45	5933	4595–4545
	Pta-1404	5650 ± 55	5820	4560–4425
	Pta-1395	5750 ± 40	5962	4590–4545
	Pta-1398	5720 ± 45	5892	4580–4530
	Pta-1396	5740 ± 55	5912	4585–4540
	Pta-981	5670 ± 65	5840	4565–4430
Early Rachmani	Pta-1405	5630 ± 50	5799	4555–4420
Middle Rachmani	Pta-465	5510 ± 65	5675	4435–4350
Late Rachmani	Pta-436	5520 ± 80	5685	4450–4335
	Pta-435	5770 ± 70	5943	4725–4550

The series displays remarkable internal consistency. The determinations from the *Diministratum,* which here presumably represents the latest stage of the Late Neolithic I phase, offer welcome confirmation for my estimate of ca. 4300 B.C. for the end of Late Neolithic I. The determinations from the Rachmani levels also tend to confirm the hypothesis that the Rachmani stages follow immediately after the Late Neolithic I Dimini phase and that they therefore represent the Late Neolithic II phase in Thessaly.

On the other hand, the Rachmani determinations also pose considerable problems for a dating of the later Rachmani stages to the second half of the fourth millennium B.C. and even later, as has been argued by the excavator on the basis of the reported finds of Early Helladic pottery in levels of the Middle and Late Rachmani stages. Although such a late dating has recently been supported by Hauptmann (1986), the possibility that the Early Helladic pottery might have been intrusive has been voiced by several scholars (e.g., Renfrew in Renfrew, Gimbutas, and Elster 1986:478–79; Zachos 1987a:134; Coleman 1987). The problems may be resolved when all the details of the Pefkakia stratigraphy are made available. Meantime, it appears to me highly probable that the whole Rachmani sequence falls within Late Neolithic II (fig. 4; see Coleman 1987).

Nineteen radiocarbon determinations from Mandalo in Western Macedonia have also been made available to me in advance of publication through the kindness of A. Papanthimou-Papaefthimou (Papaefthymiou-Papanthimou and Pilali-Papasteriou 1987; Kotsakis, Papanthimou-Papaefthimou, and Pilali-Papasteriou, forthcoming). Mandalo is a small mound ca. 20 km west of Classical Pella. The excavators have distinguished four stratigraphic phases: the three earliest, Mandalo IA, IB, and

II, evidently followed one another without any long chronological hiatus and fall within the Neolithic period; the latest phase, Mandalo III, dates considerably later than Mandalo II and belongs to the Early Bronze Age. There are as yet few finds from Mandalo IA. Mandalo IB is characterized by monochrome pottery, often with incised decoration; Mandalo II by copper artifacts and evidence for metalworking and by increases in black burnished ware and painted decoration. Neolithic Mandalo appears generally to belong to the cultural sphere of southern Yugoslavia and Albania; Mandalo IB and II are described as having affinities with Maliq II, Šupljevac, Bakarno-Gumno I–II and Crnobuki I–II (Kotsakis, Papanthimou-Papaefthimou, and Pilali-Papasteriou, forthcoming). How these stages at Mandalo may be related to the Aegean sequence is not yet clear, although affinities with the Rachmani culture have also been mentioned. The eighteen radiocarbon determinations which are assigned to strata are shown in the table below.

These determinations suggest that the whole Neolithic sequence at Mandalo, with the possible exception of the IA phase, falls within Late Neolithic in Aegean terms. They also indicate that Mandalo II is to be dated ca. 4350–4000, a result of great importance because of the existence of metalworking. The evidence from Mandalo, when taken together with the radiocarbon determinations from Sitagroi III, shows conclusively that copper metallurgy was practiced in Northern Greece before the end of the fifth millennium B.C.

A problem in the Late Neolithic sequence of Thessaly has recently been solved: the position of the "Larissa culture" (*Larissa-Kultur*). Material attributed to this stage, the most distinctive of which is a variety of black burnished ware, had been assigned either to an advanced stage of Late Neolithic I or to the beginning of Late Neo-

Period	Lab No.	Reported Date b.p.		CRD 1σ B.C.
		5568 ±	5730	
Mandalo IA	HD 9792–9597	6630 ± 100	6829	5675–5325
Mandalo IB	HD 9793–9601	5710 ± 145	5881	4735–4420
	HD 9788–9562	5600 ± 65	5768	4550–4410
	HD	5535 ± 65	5701	4445–4380
	HD 9786–9555	5440 ± 55	5603	4420–4115
Mandalo II	HD 9787–9555	5490 ± 55	5655	4430–4335
	HD 9789–9563	5430 ± 65	5593	4415–4110
	HD 9790–9595	6410 ± 190	6602	5525–5185
	HD 9794–9602	5460 ± 95	5624	4430–4115
	HD 9791–9596	5290 ± 65	5449	4170–3905
	HD	5464 ± 53	5628	4425–4305
	HD 9995–9834	5342 ± 104	5502	4395–3910
	HD	5417 ± 44	5580	4415–4105
Mandalo III	HD	4304 ± 96	4433	3155–2870
	HD	4125 ± 40	4249	2890–2640
	HD	4130 ± 65	4254	2890–2640
	HD	3920 ± 40	4038	2550–2320
	HD	3855 ± 65	3971	2420–2290

lithic II (fig. 3). New finds and analysis by Gallis (1987; cf. Hauptmann 1986:21–23), however, have shown that the "Larissa culture" is actually contemporaneous with the earliest stage of Late Neolithic I, that is, the Dimini I–Tsangli stage (fig. 4).

An important doctoral dissertation on the Late Neolithic and Early Helladic periods at Ayios Dhimitrios in the Western Peloponnese has been completed (Zachos 1987a). The earliest levels at the site, which are characterized inter alia by Pattern Burnished and Crusted wares, date to the Late Neolithic II phase. Partly on the basis of the Ayios Dhimitrios finds, Zachos is able to show that this phase was widespread throughout Greece; he lists forty-nine other Late Neolithic II sites in the Peloponnese alone (Zachos 1987a:5–10).

Two radiocarbon determinations are available for the Late Neolithic II phase at Ayios Dhimitrios (Zachos 1987a:305):

Lab. No.	Reported Date b.p.		CRD 1σ B.C.
	5568 ±	5730	
HD-10020	5400 ± 35	5562	4405–4100
HD-10163	5330 ± 75	5490	4360–3920

These, together with typological considerations (Zachos 1987a:112–35), suggest that both Ayios Dhimitrios and Kephala in Keos are to be dated early in the Late Neolithic II phase.

In Southern Greece, Pattern burnished ware of Late Neolithic II date has been recognized in connection with evidence of mining and metallurgy at Ayios Sostis in Siphnos (Gropengiesser 1986:3, and forthcoming). Similar ware has also been identified on the Velatouri hill in the area of the mines at Thorikos in Attica (Spitaels 1982) and, together with metal finds, in the Cave of Zeus in Naxos (Zachos 1987b). The accumulation of such evidence throughout Greece suggests that metalworking may have been fairly common in Late Neolithic II (cf. Spitaels 1982:43). It has also been recently suggested that there may have been an accessible source of tin in the Taurus Mountains in Southern Anatolia (Yener and Özbal 1987); the availability of such a source would help explain the widespread use of tin bronze in the Mediterranean region beginning toward the end of the second millennium B.C.

Figure 4 shows the relationships of the sequences in Central Greece and the Peloponnese, Thessaly, and the Cyclades when this recent information is taken into account.

Detailed investigations of the cultural sequence of Eastern (Turkish) Macedonia have been undertaken by Özdoğan (1987). His excavations in the Yarımburgaz cave (Özdoğan 1985, 1987) have produced a long Neo-

lithic and Chalcolithic sequence that, when fully published, will be of great value for our understanding of the development of the Neolithic in the Northern Aegean.

The first volume of the results of excavations at Sitagroi in Eastern Macedonia has appeared (Renfrew, Gimbutas, and Elster 1986). The table of radiocarbon dates (p. 173) includes one determination not listed above (Bln-1102 from Sitagroi IV). The excavators advocate somewhat earlier datings than proposed in this chapter (see especially Renfrew, Gimbutas, and Elster 1986:173, table 7.3). The later datings are preferable, in my opinion. The excavators are still in doubt whether there was a break in occupation between Sitagroi III and IV, although the table just cited shows them as continuous. It still seems likely to me that there was a considerable hiatus at the site. Sherds with corded decoration were found in Sitagroi Va and Vb (Renfrew, Gimbutas, and Elster 1986:484). Renfrew (Renfrew, Gimbutas, and Elster 1986:483) also mentions a series of six radiocarbon determinations from Early Bronze Age levels at Pentapolis, an Eastern Macedonian site near Serres.

A detailed discussion of the Neolithic period in the Dodecanese has recently been published by Sampson (1987); it includes much new material.

A book-length study on the exploitation of Melian obsidian has appeared (Torrence 1986). For Early Cycladic sculpture see the collection of essays in Fitton (1984) and a book by Getz-Preziosi (1987). A book on the Cyclades by Barber (1987) has not yet come into my hands.

A new book by Betancourt (1985) is likely to become a standard handbook for Early and Middle Minoan pottery; it includes much stratigraphical and chronological information. An article by Yule (1983) is a useful summary of Bronze Age scarabs found on Crete, beginning in Early Minoan III; the author states (p. 366) that twenty of the forty-six published examples are of Minoan manufacture. The Early Minoan II A house in the West Court at Knossos has now been published in final form (Wilson 1985).

An article by Fossey (1987), which has been made available to me in advance of publication through the kindness of the author, gives new radiocarbon determinations from Early Helladic II levels at Lake Vouliagmeni near Perachora and makes some important observations about "absolute" dating. The new determinations have been inserted in the tables in this chapter. Fossey's dates for Early Helladic II are 100–200 years earlier than those given in this chapter.

For a recent colloquium on Early Helladic architecture see Hägg and Konsola (1986). Volumes on the settlement of Lithares in Boeotia (Tzavella-Evjen 1984), which dates to Early Helladic I and II, and on the extensive Early Helladic settlement and cemetery of Manika in Euboea (Sampson 1985) have also appeared. The later stages of the Early Helladic I phase, which was absent at Lerna, will become better known in the Argolid thanks to reports by Dousougli (1987) and Weisshaar (forthcoming *b*), which were made available to me in advance of publication through the kindness of the authors. Interconnections between the mainland of Greece and the Northeast Aegean are suggested by the presence in this material of bowls with incised patterns on internally thickened rims (e.g., Weisshaar, forthcoming *b:* figs. 2, 3, 23), which resemble those from Troy I (e.g., Blegen et al. 1950: ills. 234, 238, 253–57).

The results of a colloquium in honor of J. L. Caskey, on the end of the Early Bronze Age in the Aegean, have been published (Cadogan 1986). Among the papers is one on Western Anatolia by Mellink (1986) which argues that a stage in the Anatolian sequence with one-handled tankards and lentoid flasks precedes one with two-handled tankards, wheel-made plates, and *depa* (Mellink 1986:145–52 and pl. 16). Since the so-called "Lefkandi I assemblage" includes all these shapes, it may represent a considerable span of time. Perhaps a compromise is therefore possible between the position of Rutter and that of Barber and MacGillivray in which part of the "Lefkandi I assemblage" may be dated to Early Helladic–Early Cycladic II B and part to Early Helladic–Early Cycladic III A. More *depa* and other Trojan imports found in Early Thessalian II levels at Pefkakia in Thessaly have been published by Podzuweit (1979).

For the transition between Early Helladic III and Middle Helladic see also Rutter (1986) and Pullen (1987).

Part 2
Cypriot Chronology from the First Occupation until the End of the Middle Bronze Age

Outline

Introduction

The vigorous efforts of early researchers such as Myres (e.g., 1914) to establish a sequence of prehistoric cultural development in Cyprus were hampered to some extent by the dearth of excavated habitation sites. This situation was greatly improved by the excavations of Gjerstad and his colleagues of the Swedish Cyprus Expedition in the years between the two world wars. Beginning in the 1930s, further basic contributions were made by Dikaios through his excavations at Erimi, Khirokitia, Sotira, and elsewhere. Since the island achieved independence in 1960, prehistoric Cypriot archaeology has made great progress, thanks in particular to the work and encouragement of the Department of Antiquities and its present director, Vassos Karageorghis. The contributions to the *Swedish Cyprus Expedition* by Dikaios (1962), Stewart (1962), and Åstrom (1972) are basic reference works and there are also admirable summaries of parts or all of the periods considered here by Catling (1970, 1971, 1973), Karageorghis (1982), Peltenburg (1982b), and Merrillees (1985). Recent work has greatly expanded the evidence available for relative chronology, and many new radiocarbon determinations have put absolute dating on a much firmer footing than heretofore. There are still hindrances, however, to a fully detailed knowledge of the chronological sequence. Chief among these is the almost complete absence of deeply stratified sites at which sev-

In the summer of 1982 a version of this chapter was circulated to a special seminar in Cypriot chronology at the Cyprus American Archaeological Research Institute in Nicosia. I should like to thank the participants, especially Paul Åström, James Carpenter, Alain Le Brun, E. J. Peltenburg, Stuart Swiny, and Ian Todd, for their valuable comments and criticism, both then and in subsequent communications. I should also like to thank Drs. Peltenburg, Swiny, and Todd for making unpublished information from their excavations available to me, Yechiel Lehavy and James Carpenter for advance notice of radiocarbon determinations from Dhali-Agridhi and Episkopi-Phaneromeni, respectively, James Weinstein for much useful criticism and advice, particularly about Egyptian and Near Eastern chronology, Jane Barlow and Kenneth Schaar for helpful discussions of the significance of the Alambra material, and Marcia Mogelonsky for careful reading and comments.

Text submitted February 1984
Text revised May 1986

eral phases or periods are represented. There are no true "tell" sites in Cyprus representing long periods of occupation; rather people chose to abandon their settlements every few hundred years, probably moving thereafter to other locations nearby for reasons that remain obscure (Catling 1963:131–32). Thus surface survey, even within a relatively small area, often yields a great multiplicity of sites of various prehistoric periods (e.g., Swiny 1981; Todd 1982:61–66).·

The "absolute" dating put forward here (fig. 2) is based on calibrated radiocarbon determinations. The calibrations are according to the recently published collaborative system called Calibrated Radiocarbon Dates (CRD), and, except where otherwise stated, individual determinations are cited with a 1σ range; see table 1 for complete information and the appendix for the table of 1σ calibrations.

The location of sites mentioned in this chapter is shown on the map (fig. 1).

Although certain stone implements have been mentioned as evidence for human activity in Cyprus prior to the Neolithic period (e.g., Stockton 1968; Vita-Finzi 1973; Baudou and Engelmark 1983:7, 8), many scholars remain skeptical. Pre-Neolithic visits, and perhaps even occupation, would not necessarily be a great surprise; the occurrence of Melian obsidian in mainland Greece bears witness to seafaring in the Mediterranean already in the Palaeolithic period (Coleman, this vol., chap. 11, pt. 1). Since Cyprus is visible on a clear day from the mainland coasts to the north and east, its existence would have been known from very early times (see addendum).

Neolithic

Dikaios's numerical terminology for the Neolithic period, though it long served as a basic framework, has tended to fall out of use in recent literature because of the complexities and uncertainties raised by new excavations and studies. Consequently, more general terms such as Aceramic Neolithic, Early Ceramic Neolithic, and Late Ceramic Neolithic seem appropriate (fig. 2), at least until there is wider scholarly consensus concerning the development of Neolithic culture in the island. The oldest evidence of widespread human presence in Cyprus is represented by an Aceramic Neolithic phase, Neolithic I in Dikaios's terminology, best known from excavations at Khirokitia (Dikaios 1953; Stanley Price and Christou 1973; Le Brun et al. 1984). The initial settlements occur throughout the island, except in the extreme southwest. Sites recently excavated at Cape Andreas-Kastros on the extreme northeastern tip of the island (Le Brun 1981) and at Kalavasos-Tenta near the south coast, sometimes also called Tenta-Mari or Mari-Tenta (Todd 1987), have much in common with Khirokitia and suggest that the culture

of the Aceramic was fairly uniform. Buildings with a circular plan, often referred to as "tholoi," and finely carved vessels of andesite are significant cultural elements. Chipped stone tools of obsidian from Anatolia and carnelian beads probably from southern Palestine (Stanley Price 1977b:74; Todd 1986a:15–17) attest to overseas contact. Aceramic Cyprus shares general characteristics with Anatolia and the Levant (Stanley Price 1977b), although neither the skeletal types, nor the round buildings, nor many of the artifacts of stone can be exactly paralleled elsewhere. A recently discovered wall painting at Kalvasos-Tenta could be related to those of similar date from the Near East and Çatal Hüyük in Anatolia (Todd 1982:47–48).

There are thirty-one radiocarbon determinations for the Aceramic phase, not counting three doubtful ones (see table 1). Taken together they have a wide range and might suggest an earlier limit in the eighth and a later in the sixth millennium B.C. (fig. 2). The Aceramic surely lasted no later than the end of the sixth millennium, since none of the dates that can yet be calibrated (i.e., the latest ones) has a limit later than 5000 B.C. It probably came to an end no later than ca. 5500, and possibly earlier still. The earlier limit is still very uncertain. The earliest determinations, which tend to have a high standard deviation and are all from Kalavasos-Tenta, must be regarded with caution because they do not line up consistently in stratigraphic order (Todd 1985c:10). It is probable, however, that the Aceramic Neolithic was a long-lasting phase. The recent excavators at Khirokitia have distinguished four stages of construction in addition to initial deposits immediately above bedrock, and some of these stages are further subdivided chronologically. At Kalavasos-Tenta three major periods of building have been identified (Todd 1985c: 1956). Todd has also noted (1985c:11) that much closer parallels for the material culture of the Cypriot Aceramic period can be found in the Levant in the eighth millennium B.C. than in the sixth. In any case, more work is necessary, particularly full study and publication of the recent finds from Kalavasos-Tenta, before an accurate estimate of the duration of this phase is possible.

A hiatus in the archaeological record following the Aceramic phase has long been suspected (e.g., Catling 1970:547–48), and recent excavations and radiocarbon determinations tend to confirm its existence. To help fill the gap Dikaios (1962:180–81) had postulated a "Neolithic I b" phase represented by a layer of occupation with painted pottery stratified above one of the Aceramic phases at Troulli on the north coast. Recent excavations at Philia-Drakos A (Watkins 1970, 1973), Vrysi (Peltenburg 1975, 1982c), and Dhali-Agridhi (Lehavy 1974) suggest that the term Neolithic I b is inappropriate for this phase, since painted pottery like that at Troulli begins much later than the Aceramic Neolithic (Peltenburg 1979), in what is here called the Late Ceramic Neolithic. Furthermore, the painted pottery is perhaps preceded by a phase in which only a monochrome Dark-Faced Burnished ware is found. This ware, the earliest pottery so far known in Cyprus, has been recognized only at a few sites such as Dhali-Agridhi and at Philia-Drakos A, where it occurred stratigraphically earlier than pottery with painted patterns. Two radiocarbon determinations of 5810–4765 B.C. (GX-2847A) and 4885–4405 B.C. (P-2769) from a deposit with Dark-Faced Burnished ware at Dhali-Agridhi have a wide latitude. Probably we should not put much weight on the earlier determination, since the two barely overlap and since at Philia-Drakos A Dark-Faced Burnished ware is followed almost immediately by Late Neolithic painted wares which probably do not date before ca. 4450 B.C. The phase characterized by Dark-Faced Burnished ware was probably fairly short, to judge by the apparent scarcity of this ware (Watkins 1973:39). Thus there is still considerable merit in the arguments most recently advanced by Stanley Price (1977a) for a time of significant population decline, if not abandonment of the island, between the Aceramic Neolithic and the Early Ceramic Neolithic phase represented by Dark-Faced Burnished ware. Present evidence suggests that the hiatus lasted from ca. 5600 B.C. to ca. 4800 B.C. (fig. 2).

A Late Ceramic Neolithic phase marked especially by pottery with painted and combed decoration immediately preceded the Chalcolithic period in Cyprus. The evidence from Philia-Drakos A suggests that the decorated pottery was a development of the Dark-Faced Burnished ware (Watkins 1981:11; Peltenburg 1978:71), and, despite considerable population increase during this Late Ceramic Neolithic phase, there is now no need, as Peltenburg shows (1978:71–74), to suggest any close relationship with the Beersheba culture of Palestine (Dikaios 1962:198) nor that the pottery was derived from Anatolia (Mellaart 1975:132). Although there is considerable cultural uniformity, two groups can be distinguished on the basis of pottery (Peltenburg 1978): a southern group best represented at Sotira (Dikaios 1961; Stanley Price 1979), which is characterized by combed decoration, and a northern group best represented at Vrysi (Peltenburg 1975, 1982c), which is characterized by painted decoration. Philia-Drakos A, in the central plain, belongs to the northern group (Peltenburg 1978:67). Similar settlements of closely set but often freestanding one-room houses with rounded corners are found in both groups. Although the term "Sotira culture" is used by Peltenburg (1978) for the two groups, it might be preferable in the interests of a consistent, islandwide terminology to refer these already recognized groups and future discoveries of contemporaneous material to a more generally applicable

Late Ceramic Neolithic chronological phase (fig. 2). The term "Neolithic II," which was used by Dikaios to designate the latest stage of the Neolithic, has been almost completely abandoned.

Twenty radiocarbon determinations for the Late Ceramic Neolithic from Sotira, Vrysi, Philia-Drakos A, and Kalavasos Site B fall, with only two exceptions, within a span of ca. 4450–3650 B.C. The two exceptions, Birm-182 and Birm-337, are described by the excavator (Peltenburg 1978:65) as "atypically high" and can probably be discounted.

A Ceramic Neolithic deposit at Kalavasos-Tenta was originally reported to have included sherds of Dark-Faced Burnished ware together with Neolithic painted wares (Kromholz 1981:18–21; Todd 1985c:12). Since the deposit was apparently water-laid (Todd 1985c:12), doubts may be expressed that it represents a single chronological phase. Although a radiocarbon determination of 4975–4550 B.C. (P-2780) might suggest that the Ceramic phase at Kalavasos-Tenta was contemporary, at least in part, with the Early Ceramic Neolithic phase of Dark-Faced Burnished ware, it cannot be considered reliable. Most, if not all, of the pottery seems to belong to the end of the Ceramic Neolithic (Kromholz 1981:32).

Chalcolithic

The Chalcolithic period in Cyprus is somewhat inappropriately named, since it continues until ca. 2500 B.C. (fig. 2), a time considerably later than the Chalcolithic periods of neighboring Anatolia, Syria, and Palestine. The period is best attested at present in southern and southwestern Cyprus, particularly at Erimi (Dikaios 1936; Heywood et al. 1981), Kalavasos (Todd 1981; Kromholz 1981; Todd 1985a:86–87), and at several sites just west of Paphos (Kissonerga-Mylouthkia, Kissonerga-Mosphilia, and Lemba-Lakkous: Peltenburg 1981, 1985a, and 1985c, with references to other reports). Surveys suggest, on the other hand, that Chalcolithic settlements were common throughout the island.

The Cypriot Chalcolithic is characterized by settlements of round houses with central hearths, as at Erimi and Lemba-Lakkous, and by curious linked underground chambers at Ayious near Kalavasos. Burials in pits are found in separate cemeteries, as at Souskiou-Vathyrkakas (Maier and Karageorghis 1984:24–34), and possibly also within settlements, as at Kissonerga-Mosphilia (Peltenburg 1985a:56–61). Graves at Lemba-Lakkous were probably extramural (Peltenburg et al. 1983:15). Red-on-White Painted ware is the most distinctive pottery, although there are also monochrome wares. The cruciform figurines of picrolite which occur in the southwestern part of the island are also worthy of note. No one site has yet produced a complete Chalcolithic sequence, and some chronological uncertainties remain. The recent series of twelve radiocarbon determinations from sites near Lemba suggests that the period was a long one during which there was considerable development and change. There is sufficient similarity between the Late Ceramic Neolithic and the Chalcolithic (Watkins 1981:15–16), particularly in the pottery (Kromholz 1981), to posit considerable continuity, although some Chalcolithic features, such as the types and groupings of the circular buildings, are not yet attested in the Late Ceramic Neolithic.

Dikaios (1962) originally distinguished two stages, Chalcolithic I and II, represented respectively by Erimi and by Ambelikou-Ayios Georghios near Morphou Bay. Recent work, especially that at Lemba, suggests that these divisions present a somewhat inaccurate picture of the development of the period (Watkins 1981; Peltenburg 1981) and possibly of the chronological position of Ambelikou-Ayios Georghios (Gjerstad 1980; but see below). Peltenburg (1981) has recently made use of a tripartite scheme in which the earliest stage is designated as "transitional" from the Late Ceramic Neolithic and the others as "middle and late Erimi," thus providing a useful and flexible framework, at least until recent finds are more fully studied and published. Ultimately, a more generally applicable and consistent terminology is desirable. The term *Chalcolithic III*, proposed by Merrillees (1966) and used at least once since (Swiny 1981:65), refers to a group of material, otherwise called the Philia culture, which is probably better assigned to the Early Bronze Age.

The pottery sequence for the Chalcolithic is fairly well established for the south coast, although further study of the recently excavated sites near Lemba and Kalavasos may necessitate some modification of the picture derived from Erimi. Although much work needs to be done, it is becoming increasingly clear that there was a gradual transition in Cyprus from the Chalcolithic culture to that of the Early Bronze Age, perhaps lasting a couple of centuries (Peltenburg 1981:38, 1985a:62).

The chronological position of an important site at Ambelikou-Ayios Georghios, which was investigated in 1942 and originally considered to belong to the "Chalcolithic II" phase (Dikaios 1962:141–49), has recently come into question. Gjerstad (1980), after reexamining the records and the finds, has suggested that the earliest deposit cannot be dated much, if at all, before the beginning of the Early Bronze Age and that the fragments of a curving wall, which he thinks may belong to an apsidal rather than a round building (1980:11), must also be dated to Early Cypriot. Since Gjerstad's redating is not entirely convincing (Peltenburg 1982a:58), however, we can only regard this material as somewhat chronologically uncertain until it has been further examined and discussed.

Radiocarbon determinations from Kalavasos-Ayious, Erimi, Kissonerga-Mylouthkia, and Lemba-Lakkous, with one exception, have an extreme range from 3875 to 2180 B.C. and support a dating of ca. 3650 B.C. for the beginning of the Chalcolithic and ca. 2400 B.C. for its end (fig. 2). The exception, BM-1543, gave a somewhat older dating, but Peltenburg (1981:34) suggests that supporting evidence is needed before it is accepted. These determinations indicate that Chalcolithic Cyprus was probably not influenced by the Khirbet Kerak culture of Northern Palestine and Syria (Peltenburg 1981:36), as was once thought possible, since features formerly thought to point to such a relationship, such as omphalos bases and red and black finishes, can now be shown to occur earlier in Cyprus than in the Khirbet Kerak culture. Two picrolite figurines have general counterparts in EB 1 and EB 2 Beycesultan (Vagnetti 1979). Other correlations with Tarsus and the Levant are as yet not precise enough to be of much chronological significance (Peltenburg 1981:36–38). Claims that Cypriot Red-on-White pottery was found at Ugarit (Ras Shamra) in level IVC can be discounted on both chronological and petrological grounds (Peltenburg 1985b). From a chronological point of view, anthropomorphic or pithecomorphic terra-cotta figurines and vessels from Western Cyprus (e.g., Karageorghis and Vagnetti 1981) are better compared with similar objects from Early Bronze Age Anatolia and the Cycladic islands (e.g., Bossert 1983) than with earlier examples from the Balkans (Karageorghis and Vagnetti 1981:55).

Copper objects are small and utilitarian, such as chisels and hooks (Peltenburg 1981: fig. 6, 1982c:42–43). Although there is as yet no direct evidence that copper was actually extracted from ore on the island itself during the Chalcolithic period, it is hard to imagine that all such simple objects were imported, or that Cyprus would lag many centuries behind Anatolia and the Levant in the exploitation of its own abundant copper sources. It has been suggested by Peltenburg (1982a:54–56) that native copper may have been first recognized as useful as a consequence of the exploitation of picrolite for figurines, since the two minerals are similar in appearance.

Claims that trade between Cyprus and northern Syria is mentioned in documents from Ebla at a time corresponding to a late stage of the Chalcolithic or an early stage of the Early Bronze Age (e.g., Pettinato 1981:226) must be regarded with caution, since they appear to depend primarily on the equation of the word *kaparum* with copper and its etymological derivation from "Cyprus."

Early and Middle Bronze Ages

Cypriot Bronze Age culture, once established, appears to develop continuously and without abrupt change. This long-lasting cultural continuity is in marked contrast to the popular conception that from early times the island was subject to frequent interferences or invasion from abroad. The present evidence suggests that there were few changes of any sort that can be attributed to external factors. Despite this apparent continuity, however, the reconstruction of a sequence of cultural development for the Early and Middle Cypriot periods has been beset by major difficulties. Underlying all of these is the dearth of excavated settlement sites and our consequent inability to assign specific and convincing bodies of material to the various phases that have been proposed. Cypriot chronology has of necessity depended largely on the evidence from tombs, particularly those of the north coast cemeteries of Vounous (Schaeffer 1936; Dikaios 1940; Stewart and Stewart 1950) and Lapithos (Gjerstad et al. 1934; Herscher 1975).

The inadequacy of tombs for the establishment of a chronological sequence is generally well known. In Cyprus, even though many of the rock-cut tombs that are characteristic of the earlier phases of the Bronze Age were in use for a considerable period of time, stratified sequences are very rare because of the seasonal action of groundwater and other disturbances. Tombs with single burials, the contents of which might be assumed to have been deposited on one occasion, have rarely been identified by excavators, and even those so identified cannot be regarded as certain, since the skeletal remains have rarely been studied and appearances can be deceptive. Furthermore, the tomb contents are limited, and some pots and figurines were probably made especially for funerary use.

Given such meager chronological evidence, the traditional divisions, Early Cypriot I–III (Stewart 1962) and Middle Cypriot I–III (Åström 1972), are based largely on assumptions about the stylistic development of the pottery rather than on stratigraphic grounds. In general such assumptions are often accurate. In the case of Early and Middle Bronze Age Cyprus, however, some are almost certainly erroneous, and the pottery classification is itself proving to be problematic for the assignment of new finds. The problems with the traditional chronological scheme have lately become so acute that I can only suggest that it be set aside, at least for the present, and that an attempt be made to construct a new chronology in its stead (see Barlow and Coleman 1982; Coleman 1985b:137–38, 1985a). Since an established system should not be lightly discarded, some further brief comments are in order.

At the outset, it is sometimes questioned whether the traditional scheme is applicable to the whole of Cyprus. The geography of the island, and the proximity of neighboring lands to its northern and eastern coasts, tended to promote local cultural variation. Changing economic and social conditions, on the other hand, caused the local varieties to differ in different ways as time went on. Hence, although the cemeteries of the north coast apparently belonged to a single cultural province, and although the south coast has been proposed as another (Herscher 1976, 1981), it is not clear that these were primary distinctions during all phases. Gjerstad (1980:13–14), for instance, has recently reiterated the importance during both Early and Middle Cypriot of a boundary running north-south, and pottery of the Karpass peninsula, the center of production of Red-on-Black ware in the later part of Middle Cypriot (Merrillees 1979b:118–23) often has an individual character. Since the traditional phases were based on a fairly narrow range of shapes and decoration in North Coast cemeteries, they are often insufficiently broad to accommodate such diversity. The various stages of White Painted ware, for instance, serve as the most important indicators for the traditional phases; yet White Painted ware hardly occurs in southwestern Cyprus during Middle Cypriot.

The traditional phases relied on a classification of pottery into a succession of stages within wares (e.g., Red Polished I–IV; White Painted I–V). This scheme, quite apart from doubts about its theoretical validity (Merrillees 1978:17–28), sometimes poses problems in practice. For instance, although the boundaries of a few of the subgroups, such as White Painted II, are fairly clearly and accurately defined, other subgroups, especially Red Polished II and White Painted III and IV, are much more vague. Furthermore, Åström altered the definition of several subgroups and reassigned many pots since the scheme was first set forth by Gjerstad (Coleman 1985b:139). Consequently, assignment of new finds to subgroups is often somewhat arbitrary. In addition, some of the traditional assumptions about these subgroups are proving to be inaccurate or inconvenient. For instance, the chronological succession of White Painted II, III, and IV now appears somewhat doubtful (Coleman and Barlow 1979:165), and the decision to make the appearance of White Painted II the primary indication of the beginning of Middle Cypriot may lead to an inconveniently early dating.

Recent excavations at Alambra, an important settlement in the south-central part of the island, furnish a case in point (Coleman 1985b, with references). We encountered such great difficulties and paradoxes in trying to assign the site to one or another of the traditional phases that we have introduced the concept of an "Alambra phase" of the Middle Cypriot as a convenient and temporary way of referring to the chronological phase to which the site belongs.

Such a reconsideration of Early and Middle Cypriot chronology as is here proposed will be a slow and collaborative task, given the insufficiency of our present evidence. Greater reliance should probably be placed in the future on the development of pottery shapes rather than on "wares" as hitherto. Technological distinctions may also be useful. The goal will be to establish a new sequence of phases firmly tied to specific strata at specific sites, as is the case with the proposed Alambra phase, and prior assumptions should give way to new evidence. The ultimate scheme, for instance, may have some form other than the traditional tripartite one. I myself have tentatively proposed a four-stage sequence for Early and Middle Cypriot (Coleman 1985a) which circumvents the necessity to make clear-cut distinctions between periods and phases when the stratigraphic evidence is insufficient. Whether or not this new system is adopted, we must recognize that the present system has become a straitjacket and start over from the beginning if Cypriot chronology is ever to have a secure footing.

In the summaries that follow, the main lines of development, so far as they are presently understood, are indicated by reference to specific sites. When possible, the traditional phases are also mentioned as a guide to the general scholarly literature.

Early Cypriot

Early Cypriot is known largely from tombs. Although various settlements that have been tested by excavation, such as Ambelikou-Aletri and Alambra, have been attributed to Early Cypriot from time to time, only three now qualify. Two of these, Philia-Drakos B (Dikaios 1962:150–51) and Kyra-Alonia (Dikaios 1962:152–55), are in the Ovgos Valley near the Morphou Bay; the third, Sotira-Kaminoudhia (Swiny 1985a, 1985b), is near the south coast and is currently being excavated. All three have been attributed to the "Philia culture" and date near the beginning of Early Cypriot. Significant architectural remains are known only from Sotira-Kaminoudhia. The rectangular and subrectangular structures that predominate there are in marked contrast to the round buildings of the Chalcolithic and represent the earliest known stage of an architectural tradition exemplified later at Alambra, Kalopsida, and Episkopi-Phaneromeni.

The beginning of Early Cypriot is best recognized in influences from Anatolia, and perhaps Syria, such as the occurrence of flat-bottomed jugs, beaked spouts, incised spindle whorls, and perhaps the use of incised decoration in general. Although these influences are strong enough to suggest to some (e.g., Catling 1971; Gjerstad 1980) the possibility of immigration or invasion, they could

also in my view have been due merely to contact between Cypriots and their neighbors. In any case, if new people came to the island, they must have been limited in number, since Sotira-Kaminoudhia and the earliest Ovgos Valley sites (Watkins 1981:18) show considerable continuity with the preceding Chalcolithic.

A stage called the "Philia culture" is taken by many (e.g., Dikaios 1962:190–91) to stand at the beginning of the Early Cypriot sequence, although an alternative view (Stewart 1962:269–70) holds that it was a local variant that overlapped chronologically with the rest of Early Cypriot. This "culture" is named after the village of Philia in the Ovgos Valley, near which the sites first associated with it, such as the tombs of Philia-Vasiliko, sometimes recently and more accurately called Philia-Laxia tou Kasinou, and the settlement of Kyra-Alonia, are located. Pottery and metal types associated with the "Philia culture" are found also on the south coast, for instance at Sotira-Kaminoudhia (Swiny 1985a, 1985b). An important cemetery at Vasilia near the north coast was also attributed to the "Philia culture" by Stewart (1962:216, 269–70), although both Stewart and Swiny (1985a:23, 24) doubt that it could be as early as the other sites. Since the pottery associated with the "Philia culture" exhibits some of the new features already mentioned, such as flat-bottomed jugs and incised decoration, it would seem most convenient to assign it and the tombs in which it is found to the beginning of the Bronze Age rather than to "Chalcolithic III," as proposed by Merrillees (1966; cf. Bolger 1983:60; Swiny 1985b:116). Chronological uncertainties still remain, however, concerning the relationship between the "Philia culture" and other Early Cypriot sites.

Two of the three excavated settlements of the "Philia culture," Philia-Drakos B and Kyra-Alonia, yielded only small numbers of finds, and Sotira-Kaminoudhia has yet to be published in detail. Nevertheless, it has been noted at all three sites that the "Philia culture" pottery is found together with pottery and objects of Chalcolithic types such as Red-on-White Painted ware (e.g., Swiny 1985b:120). This suggests not only that there was some chronological overlap between the final stage of the Chalcolithic culture and the initial stage of the Early Cypriot culture but also that some artifacts assignable to the "Philia culture" may be among the earliest manifestations of Early Cypriot. It has still not been demonstrated, however, that the "Philia culture" as a whole represents an entirely separate chronological stage rather than a local group contemporaneous with other local Early Cypriot groups. Jugs from north coast tombs not assigned to the "Philia culture" are somewhat similar in shape (e.g., Stewart and Stewart 1950: pl. LV, a–c; cf. Dikaios 1962: fig. 8, 21–28), for instance, and there is no stratigraphic evidence to show that the earliest interments in these tombs are later than those at Philia-Vasiliko. The very separateness of the "Philia culture" from Early Cypriot in general may in fact be questioned. The rock-cut tombs assigned to the "Philia culture" conform to general Early Cypriot burial practices, and, given the absence of excavated Early Cypriot settlements other than those of the "Philia culture," there is simply no evidence at present that "Philia culture" settlements differ significantly from Early Cypriot norms. Under the circumstances, therefore, it would seem prudent to regard the separate existence of the "Philia culture" as tentative until it can be further defined, thus rendering moot the issue of its chronological position as a whole.

The traditional scheme of stylistic development, "Early Cypriot I–III," still provides some guidance for the north coast tombs even though it can probably no longer be considered generally valid for the island as a whole. The "ECII" phase, however, may be imaginary, even for the north coast tombs (Hennessy 1973:5), if, as seems likely, Red Polished II ware had no independent chronological existence. That the distinction made by Stewart (e.g., 1962) between "ECIIIa, b and c" has any chronological, as opposed to stylistic, significance is extremely doubtful.

The extent and nature of Early Cypriot culture outside the Morphou Bay region and the north coast is still uncertain. Many tombs formerly attributed to Early Cypriot on the grounds that they contained no White Painted ware must now be dated to Middle Cypriot, particularly those at Margi, Kition, and Kalavasos (Barlow and Coleman 1982). Sotira-Kaminoudhia and related sites in the south (Swiny 1981: table 1, group 1) perhaps had a fairly close relationship with the Morphou Bay region.

The beginning of Early Cypriot is fixed approximately by the radiocarbon determinations for the preceding Chalcolithic culture, which came to an end ca. 2400 B.C. (fig. 2). Even if there was some overlap, as Peltenburg suggests (1981:38), it seems unlikely that Early Cypriot cultural styles and types began earlier than about 2600 B.C. The Lemba dates make the high chronology of Mellaart (1974) untenable (Peltenburg 1981:36–38). The new ceramic and other features that mark the beginning of Early Cypriot culture are paralleled at Tarsus in the Early Bronze II phase (see recently Swiny 1985a:20–22), although the correlations are not specific enough to indicate whether the foreign influence occurred in Cyprus during the time of EB II Tarsus (Watkins 1981:19) or just after it was destroyed, as is often supposed (e.g., Catling 1971; cf. Peltenburg 1981:38). An imported jar from one of the oldest tombs at Vounous (Stewart and Stewart 1950:237) may date as late as 2200 B.C., that is, Early Bronze Age IV in Palestinian terms (e.g., Amiran 1973; in this chapter I follow the system of terminology for the Levant as proposed by Gerstenblith 1983:2–3), although

the type may occur earlier in Syria itself, where the jar was probably made (see Holland 1977:51). Despite the suggestion of Merrillees (1979a) that local imitations of Aegean "duck vases" in Red Polished ware are to be dated near the end of Early Cypriot, one in White Painted ware (Åström 1972: fig. V, 5) is surely Middle Cypriot and the Red Polished examples may be roughly contemporaneous. Recent work (Coleman, chap. 11, pt. 1) suggests that most if not all of the Aegean models of these "duck vases" are probably no earlier than the Middle Bronze Age.

There is no observable break between Early and Middle Cypriot, and a convenient boundary, that is, one that would correspond roughly to the beginning of the Middle Bronze Age in neighboring regions, has yet to be established. White Painted II pottery (Åström 1972:172; Catling 1973:165) is hardly sufficient as a general indication of Middle Cypriot, since it perhaps begins earlier than Middle Cypriot, to judge by the finds from Alambra (Barlow and Coleman 1982), and at any rate does not occur throughout the island. Precise definition must await the excavation of a habitation site dating late in the Early Cypriot period. Pottery shapes rather than fabric or decoration will probably provide the most widely applicable criteria for the inception of Middle Cypriot, and the occurrence of a bowl with high-swung horizontal handle has been tentatively suggested as one possibility (Barlow and Coleman 1982). A recently published tomb deposit from Psematismenos near the south coast, for instance, although assigned by the excavator to the Middle Cypriot (Todd 1985b), is probably better dated earlier, to judge by the pottery shapes. In any case, however it may eventually be defined, the end of Early Cypriot will presumably continue to correspond fairly closely to the end of the Early Bronze Age in Cilicia and northern Syria (Negbi 1972) and the end of Early Bronze IV in Syro-Palestine (Saltz 1977: chart on p. 66; see further below).

Copper objects found in Early Cypriot tombs are larger and more elaborate than those so far known from Chalcolithic contexts, and include daggers and axes (Stewart 1962:243–53). A few objects of arsenical copper occur before the end of Early Cypriot, but tin bronze is evidently lacking (see S. Swiny 1982 for a recent summary). Some of the daggers have parallels in the Kfar Monash hoard from Palestine, which consequently is to be dated to Early Bronze II in Palestinian terms (Watkins 1975). Copper was surely smelted on the island by Early Cypriot times, although the dearth of settlement finds has precluded the discovery of direct evidence for such metallurgy. Early Cypriot metallurgy was probably influenced to some extent by Anatolia, and imported bronze objects from Crete (Catling and Karageorghis 1960; Catling and MacGillivray 1983:5–6) and Byblos (Branigan 1966) in late Early Cypriot or early Middle Cypriot tomb deposits further attest foreign interconnections. A large alabaster bowl from Vasilia (Stewart 1962:259) is a possible import from Egypt.

Middle Cypriot

The settlement of Alambra is important for an understanding of the end of Early Cypriot and the beginning of Middle Cypriot inasmuch as the many finds it has produced date to a relatively short time span (Coleman 1985b, with references). Alambra is characterized by houses with rectilinear plans, sometimes sharing party walls, and by Red Polished ware in shapes such as shallow bowls with high-swung handles which appear to represent fairly developed forms as compared with those of Early Cypriot. Two groups of White Painted ware, Groups A and B, are both decorated with "geometric" rather than "linear" motifs as defined by Åström (1972:275) and Johnson (1982:64, n. 49); neither the "White Painted III–IV Pendant Line Style" nor the "White Painted IV–VI Cross Line Style" occurs. Since these finds cannot be easily accommodated by the traditional scheme, we are temporarily referring to the time that the excavated part of the settlement was in use as an Alambra phase, and this probably falls at or near the beginning of Middle Cypriot. Objections raised by Merrillees (1985) to the concept and dating of an "Alambra phase" have been dealt with elsewhere (Coleman 1985b:138–40; cf. Barlow 1985). I reiterate here my conviction that it would be erroneous and misleading to assign Alambra to one or another of the traditional phases of Middle Cypriot, given the lack of a stratified sequence and the chaotic state of the traditional system.

The settlement of Ambelikou-Aletri near Morphou Bay (Diakaios 1946; Gjerstad 1980: pl. V; Merrillees 1984), although previously assigned to "Early Cypriot III," is dated by Merrillees to "Middle Cypriot I." It is probably roughly contemporaneous with the Alambra phase (Barlow and Coleman 1982). The tomb at Lapithos which contained a Minoan bridge-spouted jar (806A; Grace 1940), although often dated to "Early Cypriot III" (Åström 1979:56–58; Catling and MacGillivray 1983:3), is probably also of similar date (cf. Merrillees 1979a:21–23; Kehrberg 1982); I have argued elsewhere (Coleman 1985a:137) that the local White Painted pottery found in this tomb is contemporaneous with the other finds rather than later, as is often suggested (e.g., Åström 1972:183; Merrillees 1979a:22; Catling and MacGillivray 1983:3). The "tomb of the seafarer" at Karmi, which contained another imported vessel of early Middle Minoan date (Stewart 1963), is probably not much later. A White Painted imitation of Aegean "duck vases" has already been mentioned, and it probably also dates early in

Middle Cypriot. A Red Polished Cypriot jug found at Knossos in a deposit predominantly of Middle Minoan I A with some Middle Minoan III B "intrusions" (Catling and MacGillivray 1983) cannot, in my view, be dated more precisely than late Early Cypriot or early Middle Cypriot. Red Polished sherds found at Ugarit (recently Merrillees 1981:47, nos. 3, 4) also have too great a time range to be useful for chronological purposes.

Two radiocarbon samples from the settlement at Alambra have been dated to 1990–1695 B.C. and 1975–1640 B.C. respectively (ETH-210 and ETH-206); they suggest that Middle Cypriot did not begin until early in the second millennium B.C. but hardly allow for a more precise estimate. A radiocarbon determination on a charcoal sample from Ambelikou-Aletri of 2180–1940 B.C. is probably not to be given too much weight, for it is the only determination from that site and was only recently processed, although the sample was actually collected in 1942.

The uppermost levels of a house excavated at Kalopsida by Gjerstad (1926; cf. Åström 1966 and Barlow 1985) clearly belong to a later stage near the end of Middle Cypriot, designated "Middle Cypriot III" in the traditional chronology. The house, which has many rooms and is roughly square in plan, was evidently part of a town, providing a prototype for the urbanization of Enkomi in the Late Bronze Age. Similar buildings in Area A at Episkopi-Phaneromeni on the south coast (Carpenter 1981) are dated on the basis of the Proto-White Slip found within them to Late Cypriot I A, but may have been first inhabited before the end of Middle Cypriot. Fortifications were in use by the time of the Kalopsida house, if not earlier, at sites such as Krini on the south side of the Kyrenia hills (Karageorghis 1960:298), Kafkallia on the Ayios Sozomenos plateau (Overbeck and Swiny 1972), and Nitovikla in the Karpass peninsula (Åström 1972:3–5). Red-on-Black wares (Åström 1972:108–18) begin at this time, and there is a considerable variety of White Painted pottery with "linear" patterns, which had evidently replaced the "geometric" ones. Internal and external evidence attests considerable exchange with neighboring lands of the eastern Mediterranean before the end of Middle Cypriot (Åström 1972:240–56; Saltz 1977:57–59; Johnson 1982). A late Middle Cypriot jug of White Painted IV "cross line style" was found at Kommos in Crete in a Middle Minoan II–III floor deposit (Shaw 1984:154). In general, however, exports from Cyprus to the Aegean are rare until the Late Bronze Age (see Portugali and Knapp 1985:77).

There was probably at least one phase intermediate between the Alambra phase and the time represented by the Kalopsida house. At present, however, few substantial remains, except perhaps for the tomb deposits traditionally assigned to "Middle Cypriot II" (Åström 1972), can be suggested to fill the gap. Material from an earlier building examined in limited soundings beneath the Kalopsida house is difficult to date (Coleman and Barlow 1979:165–67; Coleman, Barlow, and Schaar 1981:86, n. 1; Barlow 1985), and the pottery now available from strata older than the house has apparently been somewhat disturbed since the excavation (Åström 1972:164–65), so that not too much weight can be given it. The very badly preserved habitation in Area G at Episkopi-Phaneromeni (Carpenter 1981:60) may possibly fit here, but there is as yet no detailed publication. Computer-assisted studies of White Painted pottery by Frankel (e.g., 1974), while important in other ways, are of little chronological value since they cannot independently distinguish chronological development of the motifs from regional variation.

External contacts fairly early in the Middle Cypriot period are attested by imports such as the previously mentioned Minoan vases from Lapithos and Karmi, a Syro-Cilician jug from Ayia Paraskevi near Nicosia (Merrillees and Tubb 1979), and two Syro-Palestinian pithoi of Middle Bronze I date from Vounous (Merrillees 1974:75–76, 1977:43–44). The lack of "geometric" White Painted patterns on Cypriot imports into Palestine and the predominance of the "White Painted III–IV Pendant Line Style" and the "White Painted IV–VI Cross Line Style" (Johnson 1982:68–70; Gerstenblith 1983:70–72) suggest that "linear" patterns replaced "geometric" ones before the end of the Middle Bronze I period in Palestine, that is, before ca. 1750 B.C. according to Gerstenblith (1983:106). Cypriot bichrome ware (Åström 1972:171; shown to be Cypriot in Artzy, Asaro, and Perlman 1973) and its local imitations are probably not found in Palestine before the Late Bronze Age (Wood 1982), and it may be questioned whether Bichrome began much earlier in Cyprus itself. The end of Middle Cypriot is to be correlated roughly with the end of the Middle Bronze Age in Palestine and thus with the end of the Second Intermediate period in Egypt, but no exact correspondence has been demonstrated (Saltz 1977:59).

The "absolute chronology" of Middle Cypriot (fig. 2) depends almost entirely on these external correlations. The only radiocarbon determinations yet available, apart from those from Alambra and Ambelikou-Aletri, are a uselessly early one from a tomb at Kalavasos-Panayia church and those from Area A at Episkopi-Phaneromeni. Although the latter site should date somewhere near the boundary between Middle and Late Cypriot, the five determinations do not present a consistent picture and tend in general to be too early. Whether this is so because of long-lived samples, contamination, or error, they provide us with little guidance. Pottery of late Middle Cypriot character has been found in Second Intermediate contexts at the Hyksos capital of Avaris (i.e., Tell el-Dab 'a: Bie-

tak 1979: pl. xxxiii), and Tell el-Yahudiyeh ware was imported to Cyprus before the end of Middle Cypriot (Kaplan 1980:75–80) and thereafter imitated in the island (Negbi 1978); otherwise, no imports from or direct links with Egypt have yet been identified.

In general terms, Middle Cypriot, whatever the difficulties of defining its beginning, should correspond to the Middle Kingdom and Second Intermediate period in Egypt, and the Middle Bronze Ages in Palestine, Anatolia, and the Aegean. Since its absolute dating must at present depend on these correspondences, it is subject to the same uncertainties, in particular whether high, middle, or low Near Eastern chronologies are preferred. Details of these Near Eastern chronologies are discussed elsewhere in this volume (Stager, chap. 2; Porada et al., chap. 5; and Mellink, chap. 9). As far as Cyprus is concerned, Åström (1972) has advocated a very low dating and has assigned to Middle Cypriot a span of only 250 years, from 1800 to 1550 B.C. Although this low chronology has been followed by many, it has recently been criticized by Dever (1976:34–35, n. 104) and Saltz (1977), who dates the beginning of Middle Cypriot to ca. 2000/1950 B.C. Åström (1979:60–61) has replied to some of these criticisms. Several scholars have recently chosen a middle course and dated the beginning of Middle Cypriot to ca. 1900 B.C. (e.g., Merrillees 1977). Since the end of Middle Cypriot corresponds roughly to the end of the Second Intermediate period in Egypt, most place it ca. 1600/1550 B.C. Merrillees (e.g., 1977:42–43), on the other hand, has argued that Late Cypriot I A began during the Second Intermediate period and that the end of Middle Cypriot must therefore be placed ca. 1650/1625 B.C. His position is based on claims that pottery usually attributed to Late Cypriot I A, such as Base Ring ware, "White Painted VI soft triglyphic style" juglets, and Proto-White Slip, has been found in contexts of the Second Intermediate period. The Second Intermediate period context of many of Merrillees's examples, however, is open to question (Oren 1969:145–49; Gittlen 1981:49–50), and in any case one must reiterate that the sequence of types in Cyprus is not yet securely based on settlement stratification.

Much more study on the interrelationships between Cyprus and neighboring lands is needed, particularly if the island's identification as Alasia, as mentioned during this period in documents from Babylon (Millard 1973) and Mari (Dossin 1939: 111), is to be accepted. Recent clay analyses (Artzy, Perlman, and Azaro 1981) suggest that much if not all of the pottery of Cypriot types found at Ugarit, including wheel-made pieces, was manufactured in Cyprus, and a detailed publication of all the Cypriot pottery found at Ugarit would be an important contribution. Above all else, however, further well-controlled excavations of settlement sites on the island itself are essential to a full understanding of these formative stages of the impressive Late Bronze Age civilization of Cyprus.

Addendum—September 1987

Excavations began in 1987 at the Preneolithic site of Akrotiri-Aetokremnos, near the southernmost edge of the Akrotiri peninsula (Simmons, 1988; cf. Swiny, 1988). Pigmy elephant and hippopotamus bones are found there together with chipped stone tools. The seven radiocarbon determinations so far available (Simmons, 1988, p. 21, table 1) are all from shell or bone. Five are significantly earlier than the earliest determinations for the Oceanic Neolithic, the three earliest clustering around 10,500 B.P. The evidence thus suggests that people first came to Cyprus in the Upper Palaeolithic or Mesolithic period and that dwarfed species of elephant and hippopotamus were still in existence at that time.

The dating of the earliest Aceramic Neolithic occupation remains problematic. Todd (1986a) has argued on the basis of the radiocarbon determinations from Kalavasos-Tenta that initial Neolithic settlement of the island may have taken place as early as 7500 B.C. (5730 year half-life). Le Brun (1986), on the other hand, holds that it did not take place until ca. 6000 B.C., or a little earlier in terms of the 5730 year half-life. The Tenta determinations are further discussed in the first volume of the final publication of the excavations (Todd, 1987). Although lack of consistency with the stratigraphic order continues to pose problems, Todd suggests that the site may have been first used in the eighth millennium B.C., on the basis of two determinations from the lowest levels (Todd, 1987, 177). Most of the occupation attested in the archaeological record at Tenta dates to the sixth millennium (Todd, 1987, 178).

Eight new radiocarbon determinations from the Aceramic Neolithic period at Khirokitia have also been published (Le Brun, 1988). Although the series also exhibits some anomalies in comparison with the stratigraphic record, it is significant that none of the determinations is earlier than ca. 6300 B.C. (5730 year half-life). Le Brun's dating of the beginning of the Aceramic Neolithic is therefore probably to be preferred on the basis of currently available evidence.

A volume on the excavations at Kalavasos-Tenta has been announced (Todd 1987).

The first volume of results of work at the Chalcolithic site of Lemba-Lakkous has now appeared (Peltenburg et al. 1985).

The "Philia culture," which is regarded above as the first stage of the Early Bronze Age, is discussed in an article that provides new information about the site of Sotira-Kaminoudhia (Swiny 1986b). A few deposits at that site contain pottery of both Chalcolithic and "Philia culture" types, which Swiny apparently regards as evidence for a gradual transition from the Chalcolithic to the Early Bronze Age. Parallels between "Philia culture" types and material from Early Bronze Age II Tarsus suggest that the final stage in the transition may have occurred ca. 2400 B.C. (Swiny 1986b:40).

Volumes on the excavations of Middle Cypriot tombs at Kalavasos-Panayia church (Todd 1986b) and Middle and early Late Bronze Age remains at Episkopi-Phaneromeni (Swiny 1986a) have been published.

Interconnections between Cyprus and Europe from the later part of the Early Cypriot period to the end of the Late Bronze Age have been discussed by Flourentzos (1986 and previous works there cited); the main evidence cited for such interconnections is brush or comb models or representations, and knot-headed pins.

Several papers given at a recent colloquium on "absolute chronology" (Åström 1987b) are of importance for the dating of Middle Cypriot; one, by Åström (1987a), reports the discovery of a Cypriot "pendant line style" jug in level Ib at Kültepe. Also of relevance for this period is the theory that the Late Minoan period began ca. 1700 B.C. and that the eruption of Thera took place ca. 1625 B.C. (Betancourt 1987). The scientific evidence so far available is strongly in favor of such datings (see, e.g., Baillie and Munro 1988). Such a high Minoan chronology is likely to lead to earlier datings for Middle Cypriot than here proposed.

An initial report on clay analyses of pottery from Middle Cypriot Alambra has appeared (Barlow and Idziak, 1988), and further studies on Alambra and other sites are forthcoming (e.g., Barlow, 1989; Barlow in final excavation report on Alambra, forthcoming). These analyses are providing new, scientifically based classifications of Middle Cypriot Pottery.

Twelve

Radiocarbon Chronology of Prehistoric Italy

Donald Freeman Brown, Emeritus, Boston University

Outline

The aim of this chapter is to construct a time scale on the basis of radiocarbon dates for the various cultures of Italy from the beginning of the Neolithic period to the end of the Bronze Age.

The dates used are based on a radiocarbon half-life of 5,568 years. Table 1 gives the laboratory numbers, dates B.P. 5568, dates B.P. 5730 (corrected with the formula B.P. × 1.03), dates B.C. (B.P. 5568 minus 1950), the CRD (Calibration of Radiocarbon Dates) 1 σ B.C., and *Radiocarbon* references. Not all available dates have been used; some samples give such erratic dates that they must for the time being be rejected.

The locations of radiocarbon-dated sites are given on figure 1, accompanying which is an index of the numbered sites. Figure 2 is a chronological chart based on the radiocarbon dates presented on table 1.

In the text, the name of each site is followed in parentheses by the name of the province in which it is located. As the ninety-one provinces are named after their capital cities, reference to a political map of Italy will give a fairly precise idea of site locations.

Since the publication of *Chronologies in Old World Archaeology,* 1965 edition, there have been several changes in our thinking about Italian prehistory. As more radiocarbon dates have accumulated, there has been in-

creasing confidence in their validity and general value for chronological reconstructions; as yet there have been few attempts to apply them to either large parts of or the whole of Italy.

In place of migration and invasion as well as the heavy dependence on the *ex oriente lux* theory, increased emphasis is now on local and regional development of cultures, with attention directed to ecological factors that have both mandatory and permissive influences on culture change.

There has been a tendency to relinquish systems of fairly rigid and supposedly well-marked time periods such as Early, Middle, and Late Neolithic, Eneolithic, and Early, Middle, and Late Bronze Age, each characterized by specific culture traits which changed abruptly from one period to the next. We are now aware that some traits appeared earlier than their assigned period, for example, copper before the Eneolithic, that others persisted into the succeeding period, and that some diagnostic ones were not accepted by all cultures of a given period. The present view of cultural succession is one of gradual changes, some slower, some more rapid. In this chapter, therefore, the cultures are presented in chronological or-

In gathering the radiocarbon dates and other source material for this chapter, I am most grateful for the aid of my daughter Linda Engelmann and Robert W. Ehrich.

Text completed September 1986

der as indicated by the radiocarbon dates, rather than by rigidly defined time horizons.

Italy is divided for convenience into two areas: central and southern Italy (regions south of the Po Valley) on the one hand, and northern Italy on the other. The cultures under consideration are presented in chronological order as follows:

Northern Italy	*Central and Southern Italy*
Impressed Ware	Impressed and Red-Painted Ware
Fiorano-Sasso	Fiorano-Sasso
Square-Mouthed Pottery	Trichrome and Ripoli
Lagozza	Diana
Remedello	Rinaldone and Gaudo
Polada	Conelle-Ortucchio
Apennine	Apennine

The Bonu Ighinu and San Michele cultures of Sardinia.

Impressed and Red-Painted Ware Culture, Central and Southern Italy

The sites of the Impressed and Red-Painted Ware culture are distributed mainly from Sicily and the Aeolian Islands north through the peninsula to the province of Ancona on the eastern side; they are very rare on the western side. In Latium and Tuscany is a *ceramica dentellata*, which may well be related to the Ligurian style of impressed ware.

There is some question as to whether impressed ware preceded the red-painted ware in this area. Sites do exist with nothing but impressed ware, but in radiocarbon-dated sites the impressed ware is regularly accompanied by *figulina* ware with red-painted decoration or occasionally with no paint.

The reliability of the dates for the earliest sites is uncertain. Casa S. Paolo (Bari) has produced a radiocarbon date of 5950 B.C., but the artifacts represent a much later period of the Neolithic. In the Grotta della Madonna (Cosenza), which has many levels of occupation, level H yielded impressed and red-painted wares with a date of 5605 B.C., with the possibility of contamination from a Mesolithic layer immediately below.

Of normal reliability is a group of radiocarbon dates from sites in which as a rule there is an association of impressed and red-painted pottery. An exception is the site of Rendina (Potenza) which has, according to the excavator, M. Cipolloni, no painted ware in its three phases of development. The first two are characterized by a ditched enclosure, hut foundations, and early impressed pottery of Molfetta style (typical impressed ware of southern Italy); the third and latest phase is represented by C-ditches, hut foundations, and later impressed Guadone-style ware. Radiocarbon dates of two samples from C-ditch No. 4 are 5160 and 4830 B.C. Two other samples for the "last level" of ditch No. 14 are 4950 and 4580 B.C., but no indication of pottery style or type of

ditch is given. The range for the site as a whole is 5160 to 4580, with sigmas of 140 and 150. The village thus belongs in the early stages of the Impressed Ware culture.

In the Foggia area, of numerous sites with ditched enclosures the earliest is Scaramella, with a date of 5050 B.C. and another of 4590 B.C. Six other Foggia sites with radiocarbon dates (see table 1) range in date from 4630 down to 4190 B.C. Thus the Impressed and the Red-Painted Ware culture may have lasted from around 5200 to 4200 B.C.

Stratigraphic evidence occurs in the Grotta dei Piccioni (Pescara). Here, in level VI with a date of 4297 B.C., impressed and red-painted wares occur. In level V, dated to 2820 B.C., the pottery includes Ripoli-style trichrome of the succeeding period.

Through the courtesy of Albert Ammerman, I have permission to add radiocarbon dates from two of his excavations at Acconia (Catanzaro), both of which contain impressed ware of Stentinello type, such as is found in Sicily. At Piana di Curinga, there are four dates: 4980, 4760, 4680 (this with a sigma of 350), and a rather anomalous 2740 B.C. At his other site, Bevilacqua, the dates are 4980 (with a sigma of 320) and 4480 B.C. All of these dates except one are compatible with those of sites containing the usual impressed style; furthermore they give a good basis for dating the Stentinello ware of Sicily, generally conceded to be the first pottery of that island.

Impressed Ware Culture, Northern Italy

As in central and southern Italy the earliest Neolithic culture in northern Italy is that which produced impressed pottery. The sites center in Liguria, with extensions to the east as far as the province of Trento. While the southern impressed ware has similarities with impressed wares across the Adriatic in Yugoslavia, the northern ware appears to be an outpost of the early impressed cardial ware that ranges from Spain through southern France to Liguria.

The dating of the northern Italian sites rests on three carbon-dated sites: the cave of Arene Candide (Savona), Arma di Nasino (Savona), and the rock shelter of Romagnano III (Trento). The excavations at Arene Candide have yielded in a general way the succession of cultures in the north, although they refer mainly to that of Liguria. The lowest Neolithic levels at Arene Candide have produced the earliest impressed ware in that area, with dates ranging from 4920 to 4270 B.C. Romagnano III has impressed pottery layers ranging from 4530 to 3860 B.C. Unfortunately dates from the site of Arma di Nasino do not follow the expected progression of cultures. The radiocarbon date for level X with impressed ware is 4030 B.C. and is questionable, but level IX with pottery of the Square-Mouthed Pottery culture, which normally follows the impressed ware, has five radiocarbon dates ranging from 4520 to 4005 B.C. Further difficulties occur in the higher levels (Lagozza culture). The range of dates for impressed ware in this area consequently must be placed at 4920 to 3860 B.C.

Fiorano-Sasso Culture

Central and Southern Italy

Named by Radmilli, who excavated the first site in central Italy at Sasso Furbara (Roma), the Fiorano-Sasso culture was found to have extensions north to the Po Valley and beyond. In central Italy the Grotta dell'Orso (Siena) has produced Sasso ware with a radiocarbon date of 4130 B.C. At Tre Erici, below Luni (Viterbo), Sasso ware with some *figulina* was found in level 10, which is dated to 3445 B.C. To the east at Ripabianca (Ancona) some Fiorano traces are found in association with the earlier impressed and *figulina* wares. The three radiocarbon dates from this site, 4310, 4260, and 4190 B.C., slightly extend the range established by the two other sites. Thus for central Italy the range is 4310 to 3445 B.C.

Northern Italy

The Fiorano sites occur in the eastern part of the Po Valley and as far north as Trento. For the type site, Fiorano Modenese, there is no radiocarbon date. Romagnano III (Trento), level T4, has a date of 4110 B.C. Chiozza di Scandiano (Reggio Emilia) has produced Fiorano ware in association with some square-mouthed ware datable to 4050 B.C. These dates conform well with the range for central Italy.

Square-Mouthed Pottery Culture, Northern Italy

No traces of the Square-Mouthed Pottery Culture are found in central Italy. In the north its distribution is from Arene Candide in Liguria east to the provinces of Trento and Verona, and south to Reggio Emilia.

From the site of Molino Casarotto (Vicenza) came three series of radiocarbon samples—the first two from Birmingham and the third from Rome. The first series produced the earliest dates, ranging from 4520 to 4175 B.C.; the other two gave dates of 3980 to 3575 and 4010 to 3190 B.C. The first series is similar to that of Arma di Nasino IX (Savona), which has a range of 4520 to 4005 B.C. for five radiocarbon dates. As mentioned above, Chiozza Square-Mouthed ware dates at 4050 B.C. From Grotta Aisone (Cuneo) is a single date of 3875 B.C. For the Square-Mouthed Pottery levels at Arene Candide are two dates produced by the La Jolla laboratory—3990 and 3750 B.C.—and two from Rome, 3515 and 3385 B.C. Compatible with these are dates from Monte Rocca (Ve-

rona) with 3720, 3570, 3420, and 3120 B.C. Romagnano III, 13–17 (Trento), gives dates of 3610, 3580, and 3520 B.C., and Isolino Virginia (Varese) gave 3584 and 3376 B.C.

With regard to Molino Casarotto, there is a note in *Radiocarbon* 15:11 that the second series (Birm. 261–67), dated 1970, represents six samples from the same site as the first series (Birm. 172–77), dated 1969. Both series are internally consistent, but the 1970 group is dated considerably later, with calibrated dates ranging from 5080–4750 to 4555–4325 B.C. This fits well with the third series in *Radiocarbon* 16:359–61 (Birm. 764–66a) and indicates that the square-mouthed pottery from Molino Casarotto is definitely later than Fiorano and conforms with the long-accepted relative and stratigraphic evidence. This means that for some reason the 1969 first series is unreliable and should be ignored, as should the 1969 Rome dates of Arma di Nasino in *Radiocarbon* 10. The apparently valid Molino Casarotto second series and third series compare favorably with the other square-mouthed pottery determinations listed as *R* 102, *R* 103, and *R* 95 and following in the table of radiocarbon dates (see table 1).

The range of dates for the Square-Mouthed Pottery extends from about 4000 down to 3120 B.C.

Trichrome and Ripoli Cultures, Southern Italy

The Trichrome and Ripoli cultures which produced these polychrome wares developed in the area of the red-painted and plain *figulina* pottery, extending from the province of Teramo on the Adriatic side south to that of Cosenza, and on the west side to Capri and the Aeolian Islands.

The type site for the Ripoli style is the group of hut foundations at Ripoli (Teramo), first excavated in the middle of the nineteenth century. Radiocarbon dates for three of the huts are 3680, 3610, and 3160 B.C. Fitting this sequence are two dates from a hut foundation at Fossacesia (Chieti), 3480 and 3470 B.C. In the Grotta dei Piccioni (Pescara), layer V contained Ripoli ware dated at 2820 B.C.

Excavations in Scaloria cave (Foggia) in 1979 revealed Ripoli-style painted ware in a level dated at 4170 B.C., or some five hundred years before the earliest dates for this culture, and hence is quoted here for information only. However a date of 3530 B.C. obtained from an earlier excavation of the cave conforms with the other available dates for trichrome wares.

Finally, the Serra d'Alto ware, called "fine painted ware" by T. Eric Peet early in the century, appears in level G of the Grotta della Madonna (Cosenza) dated at 3605 B.C., above layer H containing impressed and red-painted pottery. Serra d'Alto ware also occurs on the island of Lipari at the Castello, a very important stratified site. The date for this ware was 3250 B.C. The Serra d'Alto stratum lay below one containing Diana pottery and above one containing trichrome ware of Capri style.

Plain *figulina* ware occurs at the site of Petescia (Rieti), dated to 3448 B.C. and at Tre Erici level 10 (Viterbo), 3445 B.C.

For the Ripoli, trichrome, and Serra d'Alto wares, the radiocarbon dates do not allow us to arrange them in a chronological succession. It is likely that the different styles represent regional aspects of the developed painted ware.

The polychrome wares range from 3680 to 3160 B.C., excluding the aberrant date of 2820 from the Grotta dei Piccioni and that of 4170 B.C. from Scaloria.

Diana Culture, Southern Italy

Sites of the Diana culture are found in southern Apulia, Calabria, Sicily, Malta, and the Aeolian Islands. Radiocarbon evidence for the dating of Diana ware is limited. The earliest date, 3160 B.C., is from level F in the Grotta della Madonna (Cosenza) which overlies a Serra d'Alto level. The other dates come from Lipari, one from the acropolis, 3050, the other from Contrada Diana, 2935 B.C. The range of dates is 3160 to 2935 B.C. On Malta, however, a Diana-type ware appears in the Red Skorba phase and lasts to the beginning of or into the Zebbug phase, for which there are two dates, 3190 and 3050 B.C., rather early for the end of Diana ware.

Lagozza Culture, Northern Italy

Named after the type site Lagozza di Besnate (Verona), the Lagozza culture is found principally in the lake and moraine area of Lombardy and is related to the Chassey culture of France and the Cortaillod culture of Switzerland. Black polished pottery frequently labeled "Lagozza" is also found sporadically farther south in the Italian peninsula, but may not be valid evidence of a substantial spread of this culture to the south.

The earliest radiocarbon date comes from the Lagozza level of Arene Candide (Savona)—3125 B.C. This deposit lies immediately above the Square-Mouthed pottery layer. At the type site of Lagozza there are five dates from two laboratories ranging from 3030 to 2630 B.C. Reinforcing these dates are two from Monte Covolo (Brescia), level 20 at 2840 B.C. and level 13 at 2290 B.C., as well as Romagnano III (Trento) with a single date of 2860 B.C. Alleged Lagozza ware occurs in the Grotta dei Piccioni (Pescara), layer V, 2820 B.C.

There is thus a range of dates from 3125 to 2630, or to 2290 if the Monte Covolo date is accepted.

Rinaldone and Gaudo Cultures, Central and Southern Italy

The Eneolithic or Copper Age begins with a number of cultural changes. The use of copper, traces of which appear earlier, became more common, principally for daggers, many of which were copied in flint and accompanied by triangular-tanged points of flint. Though the principal sites are collective burials in oven-shaped tombs, the radiocarbon dating comes from caves and habitation sites.

The area of these cultures extends mostly on the western side of Italy, from the province of Pisa to that of Salerno.

The earliest date for the Copper Age in the south comes from a site that does not belong to the culture in question, but gives a possible initial date for the Gaudo culture. In level E of the Grotta della Madonna (Cosenza) with a date of 2820 B.C. there is pottery of Piano Conte style. On the island of Lipari the Piano Conte culture is stratigraphically dated to the beginning of the Copper Age. In the Grotta della Madonna the Piano Conte level lies above level F containing Diana ware, the last phase of the Neolithic.

A cemetery of the Gaudo facies at Buccino (Salerno) has a small series of radiocarbon dates ranging from 2580 to 1970 B.C., with one aberrant date of 1030. A date of 2356 B.C. comes from level III in the Grotta dei Piccioni (Pescara). In the stratified shelter of Romita di Asciano (Pisa), a single date of 2298 B.C. is given for level 10, one of three Eneolithic levels. A Bell Beaker sherd occurred in this group of levels. Finally, for level 8 of Tre Erici (Viterbo) there are three dates: 2075, 2005, and 1850 B.C.

The range of dates runs from 2820 to 1850 B.C. if the Grotta della Madonna is included, otherwise from 2580 to 1850 B.C.

Remedello Culture, Northern Italy

The Copper Age began in this region with the spread of Bell Beaker influences from the west into Liguria, the Remedello culture area of the Po Valley, west central Italy, Sardinia, and western Sicily.

The majority of the sites are cemeteries of trench graves furnished with copper and flint daggers, copper and polished stone axes, tanged triangular flint arrowheads, but little pottery. Radiocarbon dates come from stratified cave deposits.

The Grotta del Pertusello (Savona) in Liguria has a radiocarbon date of 2440 B.C. for a Beaker layer, and in level VI of Arma di Nasino (Savona) two samples have dates of 2270 and 1815 B.C. Farther east, at Monte Covolo (Brescia), level 8 gives a date of 2000 B.C., and level 6, 1860 B.C., but the standard deviations of 320 and 210 are too large for precise dating of these strata. A date for level 4, containing Early Bronze Age material, is 1890 B.C., earlier than that of level 6. Finally, Buca della Sabbia (Como), containing an archaic facies of the Copper Age, but no beakers, is dated at 1730 B.C. (R-1001, *RC* 18:324), rather later than expected.

The range of dates is from 2440 to 1815 B.C., paralleling fairly closely that of the Rinaldone culture to the south.

Conelle-Ortucchio Culture, Central Italy

The apparent gap of six hundred years between the end of the Copper Age and the beginning of the Bronze Age is reduced somewhat by radiocarbon dates from the Conelle-Ortucchio culture, which foreshadows the Apennine culture, especially in its pottery. The site of Ortucchio (L'Aquila) has a date of 1416 B.C., and Le Conelle (Ancona) 1315 B.C. A number of other so-called Proto-Apennine sites exist which anticipate Apennine pottery forms in one way or another, but none has radiocarbon dates. The problem points up the need for more radiocarbon dates from sites of this type and, as Whitehouse suggests, a greater refinement in the classification of sites and cultures.

Polada Culture, Northern Italy

The latest culture before the full Bronze Age in northern Italy is the Polada culture, found chiefly in the lake area north of the Po River. The pile dwelling at Lago di Ledro (Trento) has produced three dates: 1709, 1360, and 1187 B.C. Bande di Cavriana (Mantova) gave a single date of 1545 B.C.; Barche di Solferino (Mantova), 1391 B.C.; and Polada (Brescia), 1380, 1295, and 1270 B.C. The range is 1709 to 1187 B.C. In contrast to central Italy the gap between the Copper Age and the full Bronze Age is here only a hundred years, thanks to the existence of the Polada culture.

Apennine and Related Cultures, Northern, Central, and Southern Italy

The Apennine culture succeeded the Conelle-Ortucchio culture in the south, while the related Peschiera and Terramara cultures developed from the Polada in the north. Radiocarbon dates are unavailable except for one quoted in Radmilli (1962), for the Terramara of Castioni dei Marchesi (Parma), 2944 ± 105 B.P. or 994 B.C. These cultures were the last developments of the Bronze Age and were followed by those of the Iron Age.

The earliest date for the Apennine culture comes from the excavations at Luni (Viterbo) where a series of seven samples gives dates from 1245 to 825 B.C. At Ancarano di Sirolo (Ancona) there are three dates: 1240, 1190, and 1150 B.C. A single date of 1150 B.C. comes from Porto Perone (Taranto). Other dates are Narce (Viterbo) 1055, 1040, and 960 B.C.; Grotta Misa (Viterbo) 1080, 920, and 750 B.C. Finally, for the Milazzese culture, which has Apennine ceramic imports, the site of Capo Graziano on the Aeolian island of Filicudi has a date of 1050 B.C. for a late phase of the village.

The Apennine culture developed gradually into a "sub-Apennine" phase, with radiocarbon dates extending down into the Iron Age, which is not under consideration in this chapter.

Bonu Ighinu and San Michele Cultures, Sardinia

No attempt is made here to give the entire succession of cultures in Sardinia. One Early Neolithic site and two later cultures which have recently been radiocarbon dated will be considered.

The Early Neolithic occupation of Sardinia is represented by Grotta Filiestru, Mara (Sassari), with a date of 4700 B.C., which falls near the middle of the Impressed-Ware levels at Arene Candide in Liguria.

The Late Neolithic Bonu Ighinu culture is dated by a sample from a stratified deposit at Sa' Ucca de su Tintirriòlu, Mara (Sassari)—3730 B.C. From the same site are two radiocarbon dates for the succeeding San Michele culture, attributed to the Eneolithic period—3140 and 2980 B.C. In addition there are two dates from the Grotta del Guano, Oliena (Nuoro) for this culture—2950 and 2880 B.C. All of the above dates, ranging from 3730 to 2880 B.C., are several hundred years earlier than those of the Late Neolithic and Eneolithic cultures in Italy, a discrepancy difficult to account for.

Conclusion

The picture of cultural succession presented here both in text and in the tables is an artificial one. It does not allow for what really occurred: gradual transitions from one culture to its successor, including the survival of cultural traits in later cultures. Furthermore, the gaps between successive cultures as seen on figure 2 and table 1 are doubtless the result of incomplete radiocarbon data and the failure to search for and recognize sites that would fill gaps.

Nevertheless, with the growing importance of radiocarbon dating, it should be useful for prehistorians to have a body of such data, however incomplete, as a guide to future research strategies. For a more detailed discussion of the problems raised here, see Ruth Whitehouse

(1978) on Italian prehistory and radiocarbon dating, a primary source. Barker (1981) adds detailed analyses of cultural development and change in central Italy, with considerable reliance on radiocarbon dating. Phillips (1975), covering the whole western Mediterranean, again makes good use of this type of dating. Finally, for a still broader perspective, there is Trump's (1980) reconstruction of Mediterranean prehistory. In these sources one can find many references to individual excavations that yielded radiocarbon dates.

Thirteen

The Iberian Peninsula, 6000–1500 B.C.

Antonio Gilman, California State University Northridge

Outline

Over the past twenty years, understanding of the later prehistoric cultural sequences of the Iberian Peninsula has been transformed by the increasing number both of absolute dates from secure contexts and of stratigraphic excavations of settlements. Before this new information became available, the scarcity of fixed chronological points made any reconstruction of sequences dependent on prior conceptions of the historical processes which would have governed the events to be dated. Most prehistorians believed that one or another form of influence from the eastern Mediterranean had caused the principal changes in the Iberian cultural succession, and they adopted chronologies consistent with the Orient's supposed temporal and processual priority. Now there are well over 260 absolute dates available from almost one hundred sites with Neolithic, Copper, and Bronze Age components. Within the broad outlines made possible by these determinations, more detailed sequences have been established by the careful stratigraphic excavation of multiple component sites such as Cerro de la Virgen, Zambujal, and Montefrío.[1] As a result, it is now possible to construct a sequence of events in later prehistoric Iberia which in its large lines can stand on its own without appeal to the similarities that exist between Spanish and Portuguese cultural assemblages and their counterparts from other areas in Europe and around the Mediterranean.

In Iberia, as elsewhere in Europe, calibrated radiocarbon determinations have greatly lengthened the time span of each of the major phases of the later prehistoric se-

quence. The start of the Neolithic now falls at the beginning of the sixth millennium B.C. The Copper Age is well under way by the late fourth millennium. The beginning of the full Bronze Age is now set back to the later third millennium. As Renfrew (1973) has indicated, these new dates make continued adherence to an orientalist account of Iberian culture history untenable. The entire sequence must be reinterpreted in terms of an autochthonous evolutionary process. At the same time, the greater length of the sequence and the uneven distribution of absolute dates within it make it clear that gaps exist in almost every area of the peninsula. In the past, gaps in local sequences have been filled in by hypotheses of local archaism, but, as the discovery of a new Bronze Age culture in the southern Meseta within the past ten years indicates, they are equally likely to reflect the unevenness of archaeological research. As is to be expected, the new chronological evidence raises as many questions as it answers.

6000–4500 B.C.: Late Epipalaeolithic and Earlier Neolithic

The Earlier Neolithic Impressed Ware complex is well represented in eastern Spain and extends into coastal areas of Portugal (Guilaine and Ferreira 1970). The continuation of Epipalaeolithic assemblages into the sixth and fifth millennia is documented in the interior of eastern Spain, in Portugal, and in northern Spain. (Fig. 1 defines the principal geographic subdivisions of the Ib-

Richard Harrison and Robert Ehrich made useful criticisms of the first draft of this chapter. All remaining mistakes are mine, however. Robert Provin prepared figures 1 and 2.

Text submitted May 1984
Addendum submitted May 1987

erian Peninsula used in this chapter.) Other areas of the peninsula have no archaeological remains that can with any confidence be assigned to the period between 6000 and 4500 B.C. Although open-air settlements are not unknown—for example, Vale Pincel (Silva and Soares 1982) or Guixeres de Viloví (Baldellou and Mestres 1981)—almost all Earlier Neolithic sites are caves and rock shelters. This probably reflects a pattern of relatively short-term occupations which left neither sizable architecture nor thick settlement deposits. Accordingly, Earlier Neolithic sites have passed unnoticed unless they are in rock shelters or caves, where archaeologists will seek them out.

Fortea Pérez's (1973) review of early Holocene assemblages from eastern Iberia indicates that these fall into two main types: in the *Complejo Microlaminar* the predominant tool category is the backed bladelet; in the *Complejo Geométrico* microliths such as trapezes are the characteristic elements. Although in western Europe and northern Africa industrial complexes of broadly similar character succeed one another in time, Fortea Pérez argues that in Iberia both lasted until the Neolithic because lithic series of both facies have been found together with pottery. The only Epipalaeolithic assemblages in the eastern half of the peninsula with reliable radiocarbon dates later than 6000 B.C. (in radiocarbon years), Nacimiento in Andalusia and Botiquería dels Moros in Bajo Aragón,[2] are both of the geometric facies. The post-6000 B.C. Epipalaeolithic assemblages from the basal levels of the Muge shell middens in Portugal—Moita do Sebastião, Cabeço de Amoreira, Cabeço de Arruda—are also of geometric character. At Zatoya in Navarra the level 1 "Neolithic" assemblage, which dates to the sixth millennium, consists of forty-six plain sherds and a lithic series of the geometric facies. The radiocarbon evidence that has become available since Fortea Pérez's synthesis suggests, in short, that the Epipalaeolithic assemblages of immediately pre-Neolithic times are of the geometric facies and that the validity of the associations between ceramics and lithic series of the microlaminar facies at sites such as Mallaetes deserves careful reconsideration. Late radiocarbon dates from the Asturian middens at Coberizas and Bricia indicate that in northern Iberia foraging economies also continued well after 6000 B.C.

Like their counterparts of the Impressed Ware complex elsewhere around the western Mediterranean, Earlier Neolithic assemblages from Iberia are differentiated from their Epipalaeolithic predecessors and contemporaries by pottery decorated with a variety of incisions and impressions, by domesticated animals and plants, and by an inventory of ground stone artifacts. Until recently, the received wisdom on the origins of this complex has been that it was brought from the Near East by seafarers moving along the northern coasts of the Mediterranean (see

Childe 1957:265–67; Savory 1968:65–78). While some of the domesticates (wheat, barley, sheep) exploited in the Earlier Neolithic in Iberia clearly are of Near Eastern derivation, three aspects of the evidence now available make it necessary to envision the adoption of Neolithic arts as part of a complex process of acculturation (Arnaud 1982; Guilaine 1976; Lewthwaite 1981). First, there are clear continuities between Epipalaeolithic and Neolithic lithic series and rock art (Beltrán Martínez 1982; Walker 1977). Second, the complex of Neolithic arts characteristic of Iberian Impressed Ware sites does not appear as a ready-made group: the earliest dated assemblages are, if anything, as diverse as their successors. Third, the range of dates for Impressed Ware assemblages now extends back to a period too early for direct eastern Mediterranean connections to be plausible. At several sites (Dehesilla, Santiago, and Nerja in Andalusia; Verdelpino, level 4, in the Meseta; Fosca, levels 1 and 2, in Valencia), Earlier Neolithic materials are dated to the sixth millennium B.C., beyond the range of tree ring calibration. Some difficulties attend these early determinations. Thus, the thirteen dates published by Pellicer and Acosta (1982) from Dehesilla, Santiago, and Nerja are part of a series of thirty Gakushuin determinations; the other seventeen have not as yet been published because they are considered archaeologically unacceptable. The only Neolithic elements in the otherwise Epipalaeolithic assemblage from level 4 of Verdelpino are nineteen undecorated potsherds. The closest analogues to the style of pottery from Fosca are from eastern Andalusia, but a millennium later. The acceptability of these early dates is enhanced, however, by the existence of equally early dates for contexts of similar character in southern France, Corsica, and Algeria (see Guilaine 1979).

The material recovered from the deeply stratified site of Cariguela forms the backbone of Navarrete Enciso's (1976) synthesis of the Impressed Ware Neolithic in eastern Andalusia. Materials from the earlier phases of the Neolithic have a high proportion of comb-impressed sherds, while later phases have more incised and red-burnished (*almagra*) pottery. As we have seen, the Early Neolithic at Nerja, with impressed pottery, has produced dates in the early sixth millennium. At Zuheros assemblages similar to the later phases at Cariguela are firmly dated to the late sixth/early fifth millennium. A similar typological sequence is documented in the Spanish Levant at Or, where the earlier layers, with a predominance of cardium-impressed pottery, are dated to the mid-sixth millennium (cf. the similar assemblage at Can Ballester 1, level 3), while an upper layer, where cardial wares are supplemented by pottery decorated with a variety of incisions and impressions, dates to the early fifth millennium. In Catalonia and Alto Aragón there is an analogous succession. Components with cardial ware at Parcó and

Chaves have dates ranging from the mid-sixth to the early fifth millennium, while "Epicardial" components, with a variety of incised and noncardial impressed wares, at Toll, Can Sadurní, Frare (level 5), and Puyascada,[3] are somewhat later. That some of the earliest sites (e.g., Fosca) do not fall in with the general pattern of Impressed Ware ceramic development is the principal reason that some workers (e.g., Guilaine 1980; Aparicio Pérez 1982) do not accept their dates.

4500–3250 B.C.: Later Neolithic

Most of the radiocarbon and thermoluminescent age determinations that are the reference points of Later Neolithic chronology in Iberia come from Portugal and Catalonia. In Portugal the dated contexts are chambered tombs. In Catalonia the dates come from cave occupations and open-air burial and settlement contexts. The scatter of dates from other parts of Iberia derives from contexts that represent continuations of the patterns of the previous period. The extreme rarity of open-air settlements that can on any grounds be plausibly attributed to the Later Neolithic suggests the continuation of a relatively mobile settlement pattern.

Collective burials in Iberia are found in natural caves and in a variety of artificial chambers, and their associated grave goods make it clear that this rite was a common one in the peninsula from the Neolithic into the Bronze Age. Since chambered tombs are highly salient features of the archaeological record, much discussion has been devoted to their origins and to their development over the millennia during which they were built and used. As Daniel (1962) makes clear, two contrasting positions dominate the older literature: an orientalist one, which proposes that the earliest tombs are complex, corbel-vaulted passage graves and sees simpler megalithic forms as crude local adaptations of religious ideals derived from the eastern Mediterranean; and an occidentalist one, which proposes that the larger and more elaborate tomb types were developed locally from simpler prototypes. (Because chambered tombs were designed to be reused, proponents of both positions defined tomb architecture as the critical evidence for their comparative analyses.)[4] The absolute dates now available for Iberian chambered tombs make it clear, as Chapman (1981b) points out, that both the orientalist and occidentalist accounts must be reconsidered. Indeed, the implications of the dates are so far-reaching that some traditionalists (e.g., Kalb 1981) believe that they simply should be ignored.

Both thermoluminescent and radiocarbon determinations make it clear that in Portugal construction of megalithic tombs was well under way in the later fifth millennium B.C. The TL dates from the small passage graves of Poco de Gateira 1 and Gorginos 2 are confirmed by the earlier radiocarbon dates from the Outeiro de Anta 3 megalithic cist. For the early to mid-fourth millennium we have a TL date for the Carenque 2 rock-cut tomb and radiocarbon dates for the large passage graves of Carapito 1, Castenairos, and Seixas. Two independent lines of chronological evidence converge to place the megalithic tombs of the Alentejo culture far too early to make an eastern Mediterranean inspiration for their construction plausible.

The early dates for Portuguese megaliths confirm the autochthonous character of the Iberian chambered-tomb tradition, but they do not support the simple-to-complex developmental sequences put forward by the traditional occidentalists. Each of the various tomb types is shown to have a very long life. The Outeiro de Anta 3 cist seems to have been in use for two millennia. Rock-cut tombs, which mostly yield Copper Age grave goods, were in use in the early fourth millennium. Most corbel-vaulted tholoi also yield material of the earlier third millennium, but some have grave goods of Neolithic character (e.g., Folha da Amendoeira: Leisner and Leisner 1959). Thus, the available evidence does not suggest that a broadly applicable scheme of megalithic architectural development will be arrived at with any ease. As matters stand, passage graves are as early as the megalithic cists from which they would have arisen. Tholoi and rock-cut tombs (supposedly late forms) occur only a little later. If a tomb contains chronologically diagnostic grave goods, we may be able to say when it was used; but, on the basis of what we know, it is difficult to assign the numerous tombs of all constructional types with impoverished inventories to any particular phase of the peninsula's prehistory.

In Catalonia the Montboló facies of the Neolithic follows epicardial Impressed Ware assemblages, from which it is distinguished only by its pottery (undecorated wares, vertical tunnel lugs) (Petit i Mendizábal and Rovira i Port 1981). At Toll, Montboló materials are stratigraphically above the epicardial component and are dated by several radiocarbon determinations to the later fifth millennium. Layer 3 at Font del Molinot also has a date for the Montboló facies in this time range. The next phase of the Neolithic is the Fosa group, which mostly consists of single burials in pits in the open air (with grave lots showing affinities to the Chassey of southern France) (Llongueras i Campaña 1981). At Toll, materials of Fosa character are found stratigraphically above the Montboló component and are radiocarbon dated to the transition from the fifth to the fourth millennium. A hearth near the large Fosa cemetery of Bòbila Madurell has produced a date in the earlier fourth millennium. A time span between 4100 and 3500 B.C. corresponds well to that of Chassey analogues in southern France.[5]

Elsewhere in the peninsula, assemblages radiocarbon dated to between 4500 and 3250 B.C. represent continuations of the cultural patterns of the previous millennium. The materials from the uppermost layers at Nerja and Verdelpino are of Impressed Ware character. In Cantabria the Marizulo date comes from a geometric Epipalaeolithic context, while the dates from Tarrerón and Lloseta are from middens with scanty "post-Asturian" remains.

Many prehistorians have proposed that in southeastern Spain there existed a Later Neolithic "Almeria culture" of open-air villages and simple chambered tombs, partly contemporary with the Impressed Ware "Cave culture" and ancestral to the Copper Age Los Millares culture. Many of the southeast's simpler megaliths have yielded material similar to that from Alentejo tombs in Portugal. Some settlement sites in the southeast have artifact inventories that include supposedly archaic elements, such as the geometric microliths from El Gárcel (Gossé 1941) or the almagra pottery found at the base of the deposits at Terrera Ventura. The hypothesis that a culture analogous to the Alentejo culture arose in southeast Spain in the early to mid-fourth millennium is plausible, but, in the absence of modern excavations of "Almerian" sites which would produce dates from reliable contexts,[6] it is difficult to exclude the possibility that many of the localities attributed to the "Almerian" may simply be Copper Age sites with relatively impoverished inventories.

3250–2250 B.C.: Copper Age

Recent excavations of settlements in two regions of Iberia, central Portugal and southeast Spain, provide the stratigraphic basis of the chronology of Iberia during the Copper Age (the "Bronce I" of Spanish prehistorians). These two regions also provide the bulk of the absolute dates available for this period. The sequence documented in Portugal and in eastern Andalusia/Murcia is confirmed by a scatter of dates and by the composition of closed (but mostly unstratified) assemblages from elsewhere in the peninsula. The chronology of the Copper Age is clearly documented in southeast Spain and central Portugal because these regions have an abundance of deeply stratified, often fortified settlements. The long-term occupation of these villages was based on intensive systems of agriculture (see Gilman 1976). There is also clear evidence of increasing social inequalities both within and between communities (see Chapman 1981a), and it is the luxuries used to display differential rank (metal implements, fine pottery such as Beakers, ivory combs and buttons, and so on) that constitute the chronological diagnostics used to link up archaeological contexts from the various areas of the peninsula. Indeed, apart from the appearance of bifacially flaked points in replacement of geometric microliths, it is a variety of finery and ritualia

that defines the Copper Age as such, since sites without them retain a Neolithic character.

In the Tagus estuary region of central Portugal the Neolithic–Copper Age transition occurs shortly after 3000 B.C. The thermoluminescent determination for the Neolithic layer C at the Penedo de Lexim settlement is confirmed by the radiocarbon date for the west chamber at the Praia das Maças tomb (which was sealed off by a tholos with Copper Age materials).[7] The Vila Nova de São Pedro (VNSP) culture, which follows the Neolithic in the Tagus estuary, is characterized by a wide variety of luxury goods (Spindler 1981a), the trappings of an emergent elite. At the fortified type site, two main phases of construction were recognized (Paço and Sangmeister 1956), the earlier one (VNSP 1) with channeled, pattern-burnished copos as the diagnostic pottery type, the later one (VNSP 2) with Maritime Beaker pottery. This sequence has been confirmed by the careful stratigraphic excavations at Zambujal (where the VNSP 1–2 transition occurs in the third building phase of its elaborate fortifications), as well as by the stratification of grave goods in the tholos chambers of Praia das Maças and Pai Mogo 1 (Spindler and Gallay 1972). The second phase of construction at Zambujal is radiocarbon dated to the earlier third millennium, which accords with the TL date for the VNSP 1 layer A at Penedo de Lexim. Phases three and four at Zambujal (with Maritime Beakers) are radiocarbon dated to about 2400 B.C.[8] The Palmela Beaker complex, which Harrison (1977) places after the Maritime Beaker phase of the VNSP culture on typological and associational (but not on stratigraphic) grounds, has no absolute dates clearly associated with it, although the radiocarbon determination from the Praia das Maças tholos might be appropriate.

The diagnostic elements that define the Portuguese Copper Age sequence are mainly found in the Tagus estuary region, and outside that area archaeological contexts can be referred to one or another of its phases only if they contain imports from the Tagus or materials for absolute dating. The late fourth millennium TL dates for the Comenda da Igreja passage grave are appropriate for its mostly Neolithic inventory, but the mid-third millennium TL dates from the tholos and megalithic passage grave at Farisoa, which also yielded Alentejo culture materials, may reflect not the contextual problems often present in collective burial chambers but the marginality of the tombs' users to the network of elite exchange centered on the Tagus. By contrast, the Sta. Justa settlement, with an inventory of generalized Copper Age character (some metal, phalange idols, etc.), can be placed in the VNSP 1 phase because of its copos sherds and its radiocarbon dates, most of which are concentrated in the earlier third millennium. In the absence of a better understanding of the chronological changes in the more ordinary elements of archaeological assemblages, however, it is difficult to arrive at a comprehensive picture of the periodization of the Copper Age in areas where the presence of VNSP-type fossils is sporadic. Toward the end of the Copper Age in southern Portugal the long tradition of collective burial gives way to individual interment in cists. Cists of the Ferradeira horizon (Schubart 1975b) contain tanged daggers, Palmela points, V-perforated buttons—elements of the Beaker complex which are also sometimes found in Early Bronze Age contexts.

In southeast Spain the Copper Age succession is similar to that in Portugal: an early phase, Los Millares 1 (LM 1), with a variety of luxury goods, ritualia of metal, ivory, and so forth, is followed by a phase in which Beakers are added (LM 2). These are first of the Maritime, then of the Ciempozuelos style (whose center of distribution is on the Meseta: Harrison 1977). This sequence, long proposed on typological-developmental grounds (e.g., Blance 1971 [orig. 1960]), has been confirmed by excavations in deeply stratified settlements. At Cerro de la Virgen, a first phase of occupation with plain wares only is succeeded by a second phase with abundant Beaker materials, mostly of the Ciempozuelos type (although some Maritime pieces are also found). At Montefrío over five meters of cultural deposition begin with materials of Impressed Ware character and continue with plain wares, which are supplemented in the later deposits by a few Beaker pieces, first of the Maritime, then of the Ciempozuelos type. At Hornos de Segura (Maluquer de Motes 1974) two layers with undecorated pottery only are followed by one with some Ciempozuelos sherds. At Terrera Ventura, Beaker materials are found at the summit of the Copper Age deposits. The LM 1–2 sequence is clear enough where elements characteristic of the Beaker complex are present, but as Harrison (1977) indicates, the Beaker sumptuary assemblage is scarce in eastern Andalusia and Murcia, so that many Copper Age sites that are in fact late might, by their contents, seem early. Other elements of the Los Millares culture are mostly found in collective tombs, whose open contexts are not amenable to chronological ordering (see Chapman's [1975] critique of the Leisners' [1943] seriation of the southeast's megalithic tombs). Thus, integration of settlement and burial materials into a common sequence presents difficulties. Dating for reliable Copper Age contexts without Beakers (El Malagón settlement, Los Millares tomb 19 and settlement, Terrera Ventura, El Barranquete tomb 7, El Tarajal settlement, all radiocarbon dated; the upper, Copper Age levels at Carigüela, TL dated) covers the entire time span from late fourth to late third millennium.[9] Contexts with Beaker materials (Vir-

gen 2 and Montefrío, whose sample comes from the levels with Ciempozuelos fragments) fall after 2500 B.C. Thus, the available dating evidence places the LM 1–2 transition well in step with VNSP 1–2.[10]

Outside central Portugal and southeast Spain, Copper Age materials are too scattered to permit the construction of local sequences, although occasional diagnostic elements permit individual contexts to be tied into the periodization established in the better-known regions. In western Andalusia the later third millennium radiocarbon date from the Pisotilla passage grave accords with its generally Copper Age character. The rich Carmona Beaker materials (Harrison 1977), which have both habitation and mortuary contexts, are not as yet dated. They suggest, however, that by the end of the Copper Age the lower Guadalquivir, like the Tagus estuary and southeast Spain, was also an area of intensive Mediterranean agriculture.[11] On the Meseta there are settlement and burial finds of Copper Age date, but these are mostly undated and unstratified. The contents of closed finds indicate that the Maritime and Ciempozuelos Beaker groups are separate and presumably diachronous styles (Harrison 1977).[12] In Cantabria the Los Husos I cave produced a radiocarbon date in the mid-third millennium for a collective burial layer with a Maritime Beaker sherd. In the Spanish Levant, Copper Age contexts consist primarily of collective burial caves, open contexts with materials of Millaran character (Tarradell 1962). The only radiocarbon determination is from the settlement of Ereta del Pedregal, which was occupied in the mid-to-late third millennium. In Catalonia too most Copper Age materials come from funerary contexts—collective burials in caves and megaliths as well as individual interments. The dates from Coll and Frare, level 4, are for collective burials with entirely Neolithic inventories and fall in the mid-to-late fourth millennium. Closed finds enable three separate Beaker complexes to be identified: Maritime, Pyrenean, and Salamó (Harrison 1977). Frare, level 3, with a Beaker of Pyrenean style, dates to the mid-third millennium. The model of progressive regional differentiation used by Harrison to organize the Beaker phenomenon suggests that, here as elsewhere, Maritime Beakers, which are found throughout the peninsula, are earlier than the Pyrenean and Salamó styles, which have more restricted geographic distributions. In the absence of absolute dating evidence, Catalan contexts without diagnostic elements such as Beakers may fall anywhere from Late Neolithic to Bronze Age.

2250–1500 B.C.: Early Bronze Age

In the Early Bronze Age, contrasts in what the archaeological record makes available from the northern and southern portions of the peninsula are, if anything, stronger than in previous periods. In the south and east the regional groups defined by Tarradell (1965)—the El Argar culture of southeast Spain, the *Bronce valenciano* culture of the Spanish Levant, and the cist burial complex of southern Portugal, to which must now be added the Motillas culture of the southern Meseta (Molina and Nájera 1978)—represent well-defined continuations of the pattern of settlement based on intensive Mediterranean agriculture during the Copper Age. Other regions of the peninsula lack well-defined cultural complexes in the instances that any occurrences at all can be reliably assigned to this time period.

In southeast Spain the Copper-Bronze Age transition is marked by changes in settlement patterns (villages are removed to easily defensible positions on hilltops) and house forms (round to rectangular). Instead of the Millaran practice of collective burial in chambered tombs or caves, the dead of the El Argar culture are interred individually under house floors with goods expressing personal wealth and status (weapons and ornaments of bronze and silver, special pottery like the characteristic chalices, and so on) instead of Millaran ritualia. On the basis of a seriation of grave lots from the type site of El Argar itself, Blance (1964, 1971) subdivided the Early Bronze Age into two phases: the earlier Argar "A" characterized by burial in cists with items such as halberds and V-perforated buttons; and the later Argar "B" characterized by burials in large jars with items such as four-riveted daggers and silver ornaments. (See Schubart 1975a for changes in ceramic vessel form corresponding to the Argar A–B distinction.) Lull (1982) notes statistical weaknesses in these grave lot seriations, and, indeed, the distinction has proven hard to apply to settlement contexts. Thus, Argar "B" contexts at Monachil are radiocarbon dated practically as early as the Argar "A" at Cerro de la Virgen. Detailed analysis of the finds from such deeply stratified settlements as Monachil and Fuente Alamo (Schubart and Arteaga 1978, 1980) is necessary for a secure periodization of the Early Bronze Age in southeast Spain (see Torre Peña 1978). Be that as it may, radiocarbon establishes clearly the time span of the Argaric. Determinations from secure contexts, the Argar "A" deposits at Cerro de la Virgen and the basal levels at Monachil and Cuesta del Negro, place the beginning of the period in the later third millennium.[13] El Picacho and Cabezo Negro were occupied in the first half of the second millennium. The upper, Late Bronze Age component at Cuesta del Negro is dated to the later second millennium. A time span of 2250 to 1500 B.C., considerably earlier than the 1700–1300 B.C. span traditionally proposed on the basis of central European and eastern Mediterranean parallels (cf. Schubart 1973), seems to be indicated.

The *Bronce valenciano* of the Spanish Levant (i.e., Alicante, Valencia, and Castellón provinces) is a relatively impoverished variant of the Argaric, in which metal and other fine goods are less abundant and burials are placed not underneath house floors but on the slopes below the hilltop settlements. The dates from Terlinques and Serra Grossa place the beginning of the Bronze Age perhaps even earlier in this region than in eastern Andalusia and Murcia, and the upper level of the Mas de Abad settlement has a date showing that the BV was still in existence toward the end of the second millennium. In spite of an abundance of sites with radiocarbon determinations, an accurate reflection of the large number of sites known from this period (Tarradell 1962), the monotonous undecorated ceramics, and the scarcity of any distinctive artifact categories have impeded periodization of the BV's thousand-year time span.

In the newly discovered Motillas culture of the southern Meseta, the defensive preoccupations characteristic of the Spanish Early Bronze Age are expressed not just in the placement of settlements on hilltops but through the construction of forts, around which villages may cluster. The artifacts resemble those from the BV: they are broadly Argaric in character, but with less of its metalwork and fine pottery. (Indeed, one hilltop Bronze Age site in the southern Meseta, Encantada, is assigned to the BV by its excavators.) Radiocarbon dates available from Encantada, Romeros, Morra del Quintanar, Parra de las Vegas, Virgen del Espino, Recuenco, and Azuer establish the contemporaneity of the Motillas group with its counterparts to the south and east. Chronological subdivision of the Motillas culture remains to be worked out.

In western Andalusia there is little archaeological material that can be assigned with confidence to the Early Bronze Age. Harrison (1977) has suggested that the Carmona Beaker group lasted until the mid-second millennium, but no dated contexts are available to confirm this. The recent burial finds at Setefilla indicate an Argaric presence on the Guadalquivir in the early second millennium, and, as the recent discovery of the Motillas group suggests, one should not exclude the possibility that more extensive finds of classic Bronze Age character may yet be found. For the present, the miscellaneous extant finds of possible Bronze Age data from the Lower Guadalquivir have been grouped by Bübner (1981) into a "Los Alcores culture" of dubious validity. In southern Portugal the *Südwest-Bronzezeit* (SWB) (Schubart 1975b) continues the practice of cist burial established during the Ferradeira phase of the final Copper Age. The only radiocarbon dates, from Atalaia, present a scatter of ages that must be considered anomalous, but the cists (smaller than their Ferradeira predecessors) sometimes contain axes and riveted daggers of Argaric type among their generally scanty goods. Settlements belonging to the SWB have not been identified. In central Portugal closed contexts that would enable reliable description of Early Bronze Age assemblages have not been excavated, but a variety of materials of post–Copper Age character have been grouped as a VNSP 3 phase of the Tagus estuary sequence.[14]

Elsewhere in the peninsula a scatter of radiocarbon dates and type objects (mostly metalwork of Argaric character) shows that various nondescript artifact series were being produced during this period. In Cantabria the sepulchral caves of Pajucas, Gobaederra, and Guerrandijo, with materials of Copper Age character (e.g., bifacially flaked points, replaced by metal elsewhere), have radiocarbon dates in the second millennium. In the northern Meseta the habitation caves of Atapuerca, Asno, and Vaquera, with very undistinctive artifact series, and the open-air site of Los Tolmos, with ceramics of post-Ciempozuelos character and metal items of Argaric affinities, also have Bronze Age radiocarbon dates. In Catalonia a hearth at Bòbila Madurell, level 2 at Frare, and the uppermost deposits at Toll have Bronze Age dates, and a scatter of diagnostic elements from other sites (e.g., Roca del Frare: Harrison, Martí-Jusmet, and Giró 1974) indicate that megalithic tombs and sepulchral caves continued in use. As Tarradell (1963) indicates, the vast bulk of the assemblages assigned to the second millennium by radiocarbon dates and type fossils would not be out of place in earlier contexts. Since Catalonia is one of the better canvased regions of the peninsula, one may interpret the contrast between north and south during this period as a reflection not of the differential incidence of research, but of real divergences in life ways.

Discussion

The chronological periods we have just reviewed are summarized in figure 2. The various subdivisions are made possible because of the mutual consistency of dates from stratigraphically ordered or culturally homogenous settings. Dates for Impressed Ware and for Beakers, for Millaran and for Argaric, and so on, form clusters. At the same time, the chronology based on evidence internal to Iberia corresponds well with dates for analogous cultural manifestations elsewhere in Europe: the dates for Impressed Ware assemblages agree with those for similar series from other parts of the western Mediterranean; dates for early megaliths in Portugal and Brittany are about the same; Beakers in Iberia are of about the same age as in other parts of Europe. If internal cultural coher-

ence and interregional consistency are marks of archaeological validity, the new chronological sequence for Iberia, difficult as it may be for some traditionalists to accept, is certainly in its broad lines an accurate one.

The greater length of the chronology accentuates the thinness of our knowledge in many regions. Prehistorians, who will find it more difficult to fill in the larger blanks that they now face with survivals, influences, or other such constructs, must solve these problems by fieldwork. Programs such as those of the University of Granada and the German Archaeological Institute have shown how much can be discovered within a relatively short time by systematically designed and adequately funded research.

The new chronology accentuates the pattern of increasingly unequal cultural development which creates increasing contrasts between the various areas of the peninsula over time, at the same time that the new chronology obviates the traditional explanation of those contrasts, namely, the differential incidence of influences from the east. Rethinking the detailed problems of Iberian prehistory in terms of evolutionary processes has barely begun. Such a rethinking must take as its starting point the temporal and regional contrasts in settlement and subsistence strategies which the new chronology places in stark relief.

Addendum—May 1987

Since I submitted the text of this chapter three years ago, about 150 new radiocarbon dates have come to my attention for the time span treated here (6000–1500 B.C.). Some of these have been published in *Radiocarbon* (González Gómez, López González, and Domingo García 1985;[15] Evin, Maréchal, and Marien 1985; Delibrias, Guillier, and Labeyrie 1986), but most are found scattered in the literature. (I have also encountered about ten older dates which I had missed earlier.) The new determinations do not alter significantly the general picture I outlined then. Soares and Cabral (1984) provide a useful summary of available dates from Portugal, and Jorge (1985) discusses the context and significance of a wealth of new dates from recent excavations in northern Portugal. In that area, the recovery of samples from carefully controlled stratigraphic contexts confirms the antiquity of the construction of megalithic collective tombs and documents the existence of a distinctive Copper Age complex, stylistically distinct from its VNSP contemporary in the Tagus estuary region.

Part Three

Africa

Fourteen

The Maghreb, 20,000–4000 B.P.

David Lubell, University of Alberta, Edmonton
Peter Sheppard, University of Auckland, New Zealand
Antonio Gilman, California State University, Northridge

Outline

Introduction

The traditional view of the later prehistoric sequence in the Maghreb (see fig. 1) holds that there are clear "cultural" distinctions between the two major industries (the earlier Iberomaurusian and the later Capsian). Some authors take the view that contemporaneous variability within these industries represents "ethnic" distinctions among the human groups who made them. Furthermore, the skeletal remains of these groups are said, by some, to indicate that biological (population) differences among Iberomaurusian and Capsian groups were of sufficient magnitude to require different origins.

These interpretations of the later prehistory of the Maghreb are well expounded in a series of major publications by Balout (1955), Camps (1974), Camps-Fabrer (1966), Chamla (1968, 1970, 1978), Ferembach (1962), Tixier (1963, 1967), and Vaufrey (1955). More recent reviews (Gilman 1974; Lubell 1984; Lubell, Sheppard, and Jackes 1984) have challenged the traditional view on both theoretical and empirical grounds. Rather than arguing for distinctive "cultures," or "invasions" of different populations with particular biological characteristics *and* ethnic traditions (i.e., a "splitter's" view), these papers have interpreted both old and new data as indicative of cultural continuity within the Maghreb from 20,000 to at least 4000 B.P. In this chapter we concentrate on the chronological evidence, which offers considerable support for the continuity hypothesis. Our task has been made much easier by several overviews of Maghreb (Camps 1968, 1975; Camps, Delibrias, and Thommeret

Text submitted May 1984

1968, 1973) and North African (Close 1980) chronology which have appeared in recent years.

The Basic Framework

The Late Pleistocene and Holocene in the Maghreb is divided into two major prehistoric periods: the Epipalaeolithic and the Neolithic.

The Epipalaeolithic is dated to between about 20,000 and 7500 B.P. It includes a number of industries called, in roughly chronological order, Iberomaurusian, Capsian (both Typical and Upper), the Southern Tunisian Bladelet Industry, Columnatian, Elassolithic, and Keremian. In all likelihood, the eastern Oranian and Libyco-Capsian of Cyrenaica described by McBurney (1967) should be added to this list. While the evidence is equivocal in certain aspects, there is little doubt that both are, in some manner, eastern variants on the theme of the Iberomaurusian and the Capsian, respectively.

All the Epipalaeolithic industries are based primarily on the production of blade or bladelet blanks for the manufacture of a wide range of formal tools (there are 112 types in the typology developed by Tixier 1963). Many of these types are characterized by backed retouch (or blunting) on one or more edges. The distinction among industries is based on differential frequencies of these types as well as on techniques of manufacture, geographic location, and chronology (see Lubell, Sheppard, and Jackes 1984 for an overview of the industrial definitions).

It is generally agreed that all these industries contain the implements of a hunter-gatherer (or forager, see Lee 1979) tool kit. There is no unequivocal evidence (contra

Saxon et al. 1974; Saxon 1976) for either food production or domestication of plants and animals by Epipalaeolithic groups in the Maghreb. Iberomaurusian sites, which prior to ca. 13,000 B.P. are found only along the Maghreb littoral, contain the remains of wild mammals (primarily *Ammotragus lervia,* the Barbary sheep) and both marine and terrestrial molluscs (see Saxon et al. 1974). Capsian sites, which generally postdate the Iberomaurusian, are known only from interior regions in the eastern half of Algeria and southern Tunisia. They almost always contain huge numbers of land-snail shells (hence the name "escargotières" for these sites) in addition to the bones of hartebeests (*Alcephalus buselaphus*), aurochs (*Bos primigenius*), zebras (*Equus mauritanicus*), two species of gazelle (*Gazella dorcas* and *G. cuvieri*), and various other smaller mammals (especially lagomorphs) as well as reptiles and birds. Little or nothing is yet known of the plants that were almost certainly eaten and used by these groups. The numerous fragments of both decorated and plain ostrich eggshell also attest, in all likelihood, to their use as containers, to the consumption of their highly nutritious contents (see Lee 1979), but not to the eating of the animals themselves.

Neolithic industries replace Epipalaeolithic ones beginning about 7500 B.P. They fall into two broad regional groups: a Mediterranean Neolithic, with a coastal distribution in Algeria and Morocco, and a Neolithic of Capsian Tradition (NCT), with a distribution in the eastern Maghreb and the interior. The advent of the Neolithic in the Maghreb is defined typologically, by the presence of pottery and ground stone tools. The chipped stone industry exhibits broad similarities to that of previous periods—the Tixier typology for the Epipalaeolithic is easily applied to Neolithic assemblages—but new types, notably sidescrapers and bifacially flaked points, are added to the repertoire. The two regional groupings are distinguished by their ceramic styles and by the generally more nondescript character of the Mediterranean lithic series. Each has several subgroupings of a regional character with distinctive lithic or ceramic traits.

Just as there is substantial continuity between Epipalaeolithic and Neolithic with respect to stone working, just so there is continuity in the overall settlement pattern. Sites are temporary occupations in rock shelters or in the open air, with no indications of permanent structures. Very often Upper Capsian escargotières have a Neolithic component at their summits. The absence of long-term settlements suggests that mobile economic strategies continued into the Neolithic. Information about economic patterns is limited, however. Palaeobotanical remains are generally absent from the archaeological record (which in itself suggests the absence of storage strategies). At the NCT site of Grotte Capéletti

(Roubet 1979), where plant remains were found scattered through the deposits, no domesticates occur; the food items are acorns and wild grapeseeds. Continued hunting of hartebeests, zebras, and gazelles is widely attested, but domestication of sheep (*Ovis aries,* exotic to the Maghreb) is clearly indicated both at Grotte Capéletti and at the Mediterranean Neolithic site of Mugharet el 'Aliya (Gilman 1975), where domesticated pigs are also found. The small cattle (*Bos ibericus*) reported from many Neolithic sites may or may not have been under close human management. The available artifactual and ecofactual evidence indicates that after 7500 B.P. the inhabitants of the Maghreb borrowed selected Neolithic arts (sheep herding, ceramics) from neighboring regions, while otherwise maintaining an adaptation that had proven successful since the Late Pleistocene and which continued to prove successful until protohistoric times.

The Chronology

It is beyond the intended scope of this chapter to discuss at length the chronology of pre-Holocene industries of the Maghreb. However, since we are convinced there is continuity between the Iberomaurusian and later Epipalaeolithic assemblages, we must briefly review the former. On the basis of a number of dates from sites in Morocco (Taforalt, Grotte des Contrabandiers, Pointe d'El Majni) and Algeria (Tamar Hat), it is now clear that the Iberomaurusian *sensu lato,* with its very high frequencies of backed bladelets and scanty geometric microliths, began by at least 20,000 B.P. and certainly lasted until 11,000 B.P. (table 1). There are a few dates (e.g., El Haouita Terrasse, El Hamel level E) that may indicate "survivals" into the early Holocene, but these may simply reflect associational problems or other dating anomalies (table 2). The earlier dates are all from sites along the Atlantic and Mediterranean coasts at which there are long stratigraphic sequences, frequently spanning over 20,000 radiocarbon years. Interior sites, such as El Onçor and Es Sayar, date to the end of the Pleistocene or the early Holocene, and there is little or no depth to their deposits. The available palaeoenvironmental data, while still too sparse for complete reliability, do suggest the possibility that higher elevation interior regions were less attractive than coastal ones for human occupation between 20,000 and 10,000 B.P. (see Ballais and Roubet 1981–82). There is also a possibility that massive erosion during the late Pleistocene destroyed almost all interior sites, but we are not yet convinced that this is so (see discussion in Lubell, Sheppard, and Jackes 1984, and the recent article Coudé-Gaussen, Olive, and Rognon 1983). Two recent dates (SMU 655 and SMU 738) on hearths in situ in alluvial deposits of the Wadi Mezeraa near Cheria in eastern Algeria suggest that there was also some occupation of this part of the interior toward the end of the Pleistocene. While there were no diagnostic artifacts present, we are confident in these dates and are sure they do not relate to Capsian occupations. Suffice it to say that we can find no clear evidence for a chronological "hiatus" (see Tixier 1963) between the Iberomaurusian and later industries (see table 1), and that our recent review of the technological, typological, geographic, and palaeoanthropological data (Lubell, Sheppard, and Jackes 1984) presents a strong case in favor of continuity.

There are hundreds of known Capsian sites in eastern Algeria and southern Tunisia (for example, see Grébénart 1976). A number were excavated in the late nineteenth and the first half of the twentieth century, but it is only since the late 1960s that any concerted attempt has been made to deal with problems of stratigraphy and palaeo-economy (see Camps-Fabrer 1975; Lubell et al. 1975, 1976, 1982–83). Camps (1974) reviews the long history of research and the conflicting interpretations of Capsian chronology prior to and after the advent of radiocarbon dating.

It was at first thought that the Typical Capsian, with its larger tools and numerous burins, preceded the Upper Capsian, generally characterized by smaller tools, notched and denticulated pieces, and geometric microliths. Camps (1974) and Camps and Camps-Fabrer (1972) have defined three phases and five regional facies of the Upper Capsian. Both Typical and Upper Capsian assemblages contain high frequencies of backed bladelets. Prior to 1973, radiocarbon dates suggested that the two industries were contemporaneous (see Camps, Delibrias, and Thommeret 1968, 1973; Camps 1975; Grébénart 1976). However, work by Lubell and colleagues since 1972 at Ain Misteheyia and Kef Zoura D in the Télidjène basin, eastern Algeria, suggests that while the two may be contemporaneous in broad terms, when found in the same site the Typical Capsian will be stratigraphically and chronologically earlier than the Upper Capsian (table 3). We suspect this may also be the case at Relilai (see Grébénart 1976). In addition, the two industries are associated with different kinds of mammals and invertebrates (larger, grassland species for the Typical and smaller, more arid-adapted ones for the Upper). At both Ain Misteheyia and Kef Zoura D, the typical Capsian dates earlier than 8000 B.P., while the Upper Capsian does not begin until about 8000 B.P. when there is also a change in the technology (possibly primary pressure flaking for bladelet production), which has now been identified at several other sites (e.g., Medjez II, site 12; see Lubell, Sheppard, and Jackes 1984; Sheppard 1983, 1987) at about the same time. Thus, we hypothesize that the typological distinctions that exist between the Typical

and Upper Capsian are, in all probability, a reflection of different (and changing) environmental conditions, available resources, and perhaps style (the last is dealt with at length by Sheppard 1983, 1987).

Contemporary with the Capsian, but found in neighboring regions, are a number of other industries that appear to be local continuations of the preceding Iberomaurusian (Columnatian, Keremian, Elassolithic). There are no data that would allow us to investigate the differences (if any) in the palaeoeconomies of these industries. On the basis of typological and technological characteristics, as well as the geographical location of sites, we have proposed that the Columnatian, Keremian, and Elassolithic (with their emphasis on very small stone tools, high frequencies of end scrapers, and [among the geometrics] lunates) should be grouped into a Western tradition centered on the Hodna Basin in Algeria; the Capsian would be an Eastern tradition, with its main locus centered around the modern towns of Gafsa in Tunisia and Tebessa in Algeria (Lubell, Sheppard, and Jackes 1984).

It should be pointed out that there are striking similarities between the Keremian and a contemporaneous industry from the Nile Valley, the Arkinian (see Schild, Chmielewska, and Więckowska 1968), just as there are strong parallels between the Iberomaurusian and some of the late Palaeolithic Nilotic industries (Phillips 1975; Wendorf and Schild 1976). The cultural implications of these similarities are not at all well understood, but it is plausible to envisage some degree of contact or some similarity of response to similar conditions (our preferred hypothesis) during the Late Pleistocene and early Holocene. Research by Close (1977; Close, Wendorf, and Schild 1979) suggests that there were separate but similar, roughly contemporaneous traditions in the Nile Valley, Cyrenaica, and the Maghreb. Further work is required to clarify their interrelationships.

In the coastal regions of the western Maghreb, the few earlier Holocene assemblages that have been isolated are of an impoverished Iberomaurusian character (Camps 1974:263–64; Gilman 1975:70–75). After about 7500 B.P. ceramics are added to this lithic substrate to form the Mediterranean Neolithic (table 4). This falls into three regional groups—coastal Algeria (centered on Oran), northern Morocco, and Atlantic Morocco—clearly distinguished from each other in their ceramic styles (Gilman 1974, 1975). In northern Morocco it is possible on stratigraphic grounds to distinguish two chronological phases within the Mediterranean Neolithic. The earlier one is dominated by cardial-impressed and channeled wares similar in their general character to the Impressed Wares characteristic of the earliest Neolithic of Italy, southern France, and the Iberian Peninsula from 8000 to 6000 B.P. A later phase in northern Morocco is characterized by incised, punctated, and red-slipped wares without typological parallels around the Mediterranean or in northern Africa. The incised and channeled wares of the Oran facies (Aumassip 1971) are also of Impressed Ware character, and radiocarbon dates from Kristel Jardins, Cimetière des Escargots, and Deux Mamelles confirm the typological parallels. The comb-impressed and incised wares of Atlantic Morocco are dated to after 4500 B.P. (W 1510 is the more reliable of the El Kiffen determinations [Gilman 1975:111]; the GrN 2805 date from Dar es Soltan is taken from below the Neolithic layer) and are cross-dated to the later Neolithic in northern Morocco. Importation of Beaker pottery and various copper and bronze pieces into the western Maghreb from Iberia (Harrison and Gilman 1977) occurs during this later phase of the Mediterranean Neolithic.

The NCT falls into several regional facies whose characteristics are delineated by Camps (1974). In the interior of northeastern Algeria and Tunisia, the central focus of the Capsian, the Neolithic represents in artifactual terms simply the supplementing of ostrich eggshell containers by a little scantily impressed pottery and the addition of bifacially flaked points, sidescrapers, and ground stone tools to the lithic series (Roubet 1968, 1979). A sparse assemblage from the base of Grotte Capéletti has a radiocarbon determination (ALG 37) as early as the eighth millennium B.P. but most dates for the classic NCT range from the seventh to the fourth millennium. Little change in artifact assemblages is apparent over this long period: assemblage composition is stable over the Capéletti stratigraphy (Roubet 1979:492); the Ouled Zouai series, with a late radiocarbon determination (MC 208), is generally similar to the much earlier Damous el Ahmar assemblage (Roubet 1968:122). Camps (1974:292) suggests, however, that decoration disappears from the pottery after 5500 B.P.

In the Saharan regions south of the classic Capsian zone, three facies have been identified that combine Neolithic features with lithic series of continuing Epipalaeolithic character. Assemblages of the El Hadjar group (Aumassip 1972) lack pottery, but have "Neolithic" sidescrapers and bifacially flaked points. The Ain Guettara and El Bayed groups, distinguished from one another by the abundance and types of bifacial points, have ceramics resembling those of the central Saharan Neolithic (impressed decoration, often rocker-stamped, covers the entire body of the vessels). With the exception of the surface-collected Izimane sample (Gif 1655), radiocarbon dates from these three facies fall in the eighth and seventh millennia B.P., somewhat earlier than the dates for the classic NCT to the north. East of the classic Capsian zone in the Saharan Atlas, sites of NCT composition also date to the eighth and seventh millennia. Here some of the pottery shows Saharan affinities (e.g., rockerstamping at Ain Naga: Grébénart 1969), but most is decorated with the channels and incisions characteristic of the Oran group of the Mediterranean Neolithic (Cadenat 1966). Two sites, Rhar Oum el Fernan and Oued Saida, have yielded Beaker sherds (Harrison and Gilman 1977), thus indicating that the Neolithic in this area lasted at least until the end of the fifth millennium B.P. Assemblages attributed to the NCT, with a similar range of dates, are found as far east as Cyrenaica (at the Haua Fteah: McBurney 1967) and in the western Sahara, where they are too dispersed spatially, chronologically, and functionally to be placed in a systematic comparative context.

Conclusion

Lithic series from the Maghreb show strong continuities from 20,000 to 4000 B.P. The Iberomaurusian, with a littoral distribution in the Late Pleistocene, leads directly into a variety of early Holocene industries in the western Maghreb and into the Capsian, with two main functional/chronological variants, in the eastern interior. These cultures in turn begin after about 7500 B.P. to add selected Neolithic arts, idiosyncratically interpreted, to their repertoires. This transition, chronologically more precisely controlled than the earlier one, clearly reveals the essentially acculturative processes of change that are involved. The Neolithic appears earlier along the Mediterranean coast and in the northern Sahara, where direct access to Neolithic information sets was available, and only gradually penetrates the Capsian interior. It is only in the final stages of prehistory, in the course of trade with Iberia, that unequivocal intrusions into this isolated and welladapted world occur.

Fifteen

Neolithic Chronology in the Sahara and Sudan

T. R. Hays, North Texas Archaelogy Center

Outline

Environmental Setting
Cultural Chronology

The Sahara
The Sudan
Summary

In the past it was assumed that the appearance of the Neolithic in Africa resulted from a diffusion or diffusions from the Near East. In recent years, however, it has appeared that the development of a "Neolithic" way of life in the Sahara and Sudan may have occurred without influence from outside areas. Numerous recent studies indicate that prehistoric populations utilizing Neolithic artifact traits occupied large areas of the central Sahara and Sudan as early as the seventh millennium B.C. This chapter describes the cultural chronologies for the Sahara and Sudan during this "Neolithic" period. Since culural sequences for North Africa and sub-Saharan Africa are presented by other contributors to this volume, this chapter discusses only those sites located approximately between north latitudes 15 degrees and 30 degrees which exhibit Neolithic traits (see fig. 1).

Pertinent archaeological sites are characterized by the presence of microlithic tools, bifacial arrowpoints, pottery, and grinding stones, and in some cases polished stone axes and gouges, as well as bone points (harpoons). In addition, numerous localities in the Sahara containing rock art have been attributed to this "Neolithic" period.

Although the term *Neolithic* or "New Stone Age" originally denoted the presence of ground and polished stone tools and pottery (Daniel 1963), many prehistorians now consider the presence of domesticated plants and animals to be more important. A resolution passed at the 1965 Wenner-Gren African Symposium suggested that the application of the term *Neolithic* to isolated pieces or to groups of artifacts possessing one or more characteristics of Neolithic industrial complexes (grinding and polishing of stone, pottery, grindstones), but without any indica-

Text submitted July 1984

tion of domestication or agricultural activity, is unjustified and should be discontinued (Bishop and Clark 1967). This resolution reflected the position taken by prehistorians working in the Near East where the appearance of domesticates occurred earlier than Neolithic artifacts. Thus, in the Near East aceramic or prepottery Neolithic levels at Jericho, Hacilar, and Çatal Huyuk (Kenyon 1960; Mellaart 1967) were followed by pottery-bearing levels.

The criterion of domestication may be valid for the Neolithic in the Near East, but it does not hold for Africa. It is significant that there is no evidence for a preceramic Neolithic in Saharan Africa or the Sudan. Ceramics and ground stone artifacts appear earlier than does evidence for domesticated plants and animals, and in fact in some of these areas domestication did not occur at all. Some groups continued to practice a hunting and gathering economy, but developed the technological artifact traits usually associated with the Neolithic.

As a result, the term *Neolithic* can be quite confusing in describing archaeological occurrences in the Sahara and Sudan. The main problem is that Neolithic artifact traits appear in Africa well before the economic traits of domesticated plants and animals. Arkell attempted to deal with the problem by calling the material at Early Khartoum "Mesolithic" because it lacked domesticates, while the "Khartoum Neolithic" assemblage at Esh Shaheinab contained them (Arkell 1949, 1953; Arkell and Ucko 1965). Arkell was unhappy with the term *Mesolithic* as applied to an African site and later suggested calling the cultural manifestations "Early Khartoum" and "Khartoum Neolithic" (Arkell 1969). Shinnie, however, countered that "Khartoum Neolithic" should not apply to the Neolithic at Esh Shaheinab and suggested that "Shaheinab Neolithic" be used following the normal practice of using the name of the "type site" (Shinnie 1971).

If one follows the recommendations of the Burg Wartenstein Conference on Nomenclature, the term *Neolithic* in Africa would apply only to food-producing societies (Bishop and Clark 1967). However, many prehistorians working in the Sahara continue to use the term for sites with only neolithic artifact traits. These problems have been discussed in several publications (Hays 1971b, 1975b, 1976; Krzyzaniak 1978; Smith 1980b; Barich 1980). Nonetheless, such titles as "Neolithic of Sudanese Tradition" and "Saharo-Sudanese Neolithic" continue in use (Camps 1974, 1975).

Because of the lack of evidence for domestication associated with the earliest ceramic-bearing sites in Saharan Africa and Sudan, other terms have been suggested such as "Sub-Neolithic" (Bailloud 1966) and "para-Neolithic" (Hays 1975b). More recently, Clark (1980) used the terms "Pre-pastoral Neolithic" to describe the Saharan assemblages generally referred to as "Older Neolithic" by French prehistorians.

The concept of a Pre-pastoral Neolithic emphasized the lack of data for domesticated plants and animals at early sites in the region. Domesticated grains have not been found in the Saharan sites. Only a single pollen grain of a "cereal" found at Méniet and dated after 5400 B.P. (Hugot 1963) and two pollen grains of cultivated millet recovered at Amekni (Camps 1969) are known from the central Sahara. In the eastern Sahara in southern Egypt, there may be evidence for the presence of domesticated barley and wheat seeds at a ceramic site dated to 8100 B.P. (Wendorf and Schild 1980).

The term *Pre-pastoral Neolithic* also implies that when food production did occur in Saharan Africa, stock raising was emphasized over agriculture. Rock paintings in Tassili and elsewhere indicate that cattle pastoralists were widespread across the Sahara (Beck and Huard 1969). When early evidence for a food-producing economy does occur in the Sahara and the Sudan, it is usually in the form of pastoralism, based on the remains of domesticated cattle, goats, and sheep (Clark 1962). The beginning of pastoralism in the Sudan may be represented by the 2 percent of goats at Shaheinab (Arkell 1953). Full pastoralism dominated by cattle is evident at Kadero by 5300 B.P. (Krzyzaniak 1982), although millet and sorghum were utilized as well. Although cattle pastoralists are present in the central Sahara at least by 5500 B.P. (Barich 1978), the use of domesticated animals began later than the appearance of ceramics and ground stone. Here we consider both the "Pre-pastoral Neolithic" and the "Pastoral Neolithic." The radiocarbon dates cited refer to the originally reported ones with a half-life of 5,568 years. (For calibrated dates see vol. 2, table 2.)

Environmental Setting

The topography of the Sahara Desert includes a plateau extending from western Sudan to the highlands of the central Sahara. This crescentic plateau joins the savanna zones at either end and was a zone of movement for plants, animals, and man during times of climatic change (Hester 1968). In more moist periods, there was a northward advance of the tropical savanna-type Ethiopian flora and fauna (Clark 1962, 1967; Gabriel 1981).

There is ample evidence that the present Sahara Desert experienced climatic amelioration during the early Holocene. Two cooler and more moist climatic "Subpluvial" periods indicated by geological data are dated by radiocarbon to ca. 9000–7500 B.P. and ca. 6500–4000 B.P. (Faure 1966). Lacustrine deposits containing fossil pollen show a shift after 4000 B.P. from a Mediterranean savanna steppe climate to a dryer one characterized by subarid tropical plants.

A cooler, moister phase produced the upper (710 m) lake at Adrar Bous in Ténéré before 8100 B.P. (Delibrias and Dutil 1966; Servant, Ergenzinger, and Coppens 1969; Servant, Servant, and Delibrias 1969). By ca. 7000 B.P. the drier conditions prevailed, the lake decreased, and sand dunes occurred on the lake margins. These dunes stabilized between 6000 B.P. and 4000 B.P., and the "Tenerian Neolithic" people settled around the 700 m lake at Adrar Bous (Delibrias and Hugot 1962; Williams 1971). Other areas in the Sahara with lake deposits give similar evidence for two lake levels. This changing climate produced a transition from a Mediterranean environment to a drier one characterized by subarid tropical plants and animals. The spread of Ethiopian-Sudanic flora into the southern Sahara is based on analyses of fossil pollen recovered from diatomites (Faure, Manguin, and Nydal 1963), and the lacustrine deposits at Ténéré dated ca. 5200 B.P. contain mostly pollen of tropical plants (Acacia, Balanites). In the Acacus hills (Fezzan), pollen of a swamp plant occurs as well as Acacia and Balanites between 7600 to 5800 B.P. (Mori 1965). In the higher elevations of the Hoggar, Mediterranean species of cypress, pine, olive, and hackberry are dated at about 5500 B.P. (Quezel and Martinez 1958, 1962).

In general, the evidence suggests a cool period with an open woodland and savanna in the Sahara followed by a drying trend. The decrease in moisture caused a slow decline in Mediterranean flora in the lower elevations and the formation of recent sand dunes in isolated basins at altitudes below 1,000 m. Interdunal swamps containing tropical (Ethiopian) fauna were present in these basins during the subsequent "Neolithic pluvial" (Rognon 1967). This last wet phase produced a connection of the basins with the highlands, and their junction allowed an intermingling of Mediterranean flora and Ethiopian fauna which is still evident in some isolated areas (Clark 1967; Hall 1971).

The sequence of events during the "Neolithic wet phase" may be summarized as follows. Conditions much more moist than at present occurred during the seventh millennium, and again between 5500 and 2300 B.C. the Sahara was comparatively moist, corresponding to the "Saharan Neolithic" occupation. "Savannah woodlands may have been present on some of the better-watered highlands, and good pastures were probably available seasonally on the remaining uplands and in most of the wadi systems" (Butzer 1966:79). After ca. 2300 B.C. the climate became hyperarid in the Fezzan, and probably in Tassili and the Hoggar as well.

Cultural Chronology

The Sahara

The "Neolithic" assemblages from Saharan Africa have been grouped into a "Neolithic of Capsian Tradition" and a "Neolithic of Sudanese Tradition." The sites in the northern Sahara and Maghreb containing "Neolithic" artifact traits appear to derive from the Epipaleolithic Capsian. These "Neolithic of Capsian Tradition" sites, which rarely contain pottery and grinding stones but abundant arrowpoints, are associated with snail shell mounds and large amounts of ostrich egg shell. The interpretation is that these people continued an Epipaleolithic hunting and gathering way of life and only acquired "Neolithic" artifact traits from neighbors to the south (Camps, Delibrias, and Thommeret 1968). Thus, it is the central and southern Sahara that contains the earliest evidence of the "Saharan Neolithic."

The basis for the "Neolithic of Sudanese Tradition" terminology was the presence at Méniet in the Hoggar of pottery with decorative motifs similar to those described for sites near Khartoum (Hugot 1963). Numerous sites across the southern Sahara from Sudan to Mauritania have been so classified (Camps, Delibrias, and Thommeret 1968).

The "type site" for what Hugot (1963) called the "Neolithic of Sudanese Tradition" was the assemblage at Esh Shaheinab, north of Khartoum in Sudan (Arkell 1953). This large open site adjacent to the Nile River contained bones of fish, wild animals, and domestic dwarf goats. This occupation was preceded by a "Khartoum Mesolithic" (Arkell 1949) which had pottery and ground stone but no domesticates. In both occupations the settlement pattern consisted of sites located near the river, but whether they were seasonal or represented a semisedentism could not be ascertained with certainty. Significantly, the "neolithicization," attested by the presence of

domesticated goat, was accompanied by few artifact changes beyond the addition of burnishing of pottery and of stone gouges, and with no change in settlement pattern (Arkell 1972).

Méniet, in the Immidir region of Hoggar, is described as a "village" composed of more than one site (Hugot 1968), all of which were located at four rock shelters near a large lagoon formed by an ancient river. Numerous grinding stones, as well as pottery of good quality, were present. The excavations at Méniet established three levels of occupation, the earliest of which was dated ca. 5400 B.P. The later, middle layer contained the only evidence for domestication: a single pollen grain identified by its size as a cereal grass. Hugot (1968) suggested that domesticated wheat or barley was present at this time at Méniet.

Amekni, some 250 km southeast of Méniet, also contained evidence of a Pre-pastoral occupation, with sites in rock shelters at the base of a granite rock outcrop overlooking the Wadi Amekni, an ancient river. Subsistence resources included fish of the Nilotic type, buffalo, gazelles, oryx, wild sheep, and pigs. Numerous grinding stones and bedrock mortars suggest the use of cereal grasses. Two pollen grains from a lower level (1.4 m) dated earlier than 6800 B.P. were identified as cultivated millet (Camps 1969). If the occurrence of these separate pollen samples is accepted as proof of domestication, it must have been an incipient domestication that did not greatly affect the quantity of food resources.

Although the introduction of plant domestication had little impact in the Sahara, the use of domesticated animals was important. The rock art of the Sahara depicts herds of apparently domestic cattle as well as scenes of tropical wild animals. The paintings are assumed to represent scenes known to the painters, including cattle herders who lived between ca. 4000 and 2000 B.C. Although most of the rock art is not accurately dated, a few radiocarbon determinations tend to place domesticated cattle and styles of rock art in this time period. Lhote (1961) distinguished four periods or styles for the rock paintings of Tassili: Hunter (6000–4000 B.C.); Herder (4000–1500 B.C.); Horse (1500–600 B.C.); and Camel (600 B.C. on).

We have few archaeological remains of the Hunter or "Têtes/Rondes" period. The earliest level at rock shelters at Titerast-n-Elias corresponds to the "Têtes/Rondes" style and is dated ca. 7400 B.P. The style itself is normally associated only with wild fauna (Lhote 1969). Campsites of the Herder or "Bovidien" period are also located in the rock shelters, but at this time there is evidence of stone wall enclosures, sometimes built against the sides of the shelter, the floors containing potsherds, grinding stones, arrowpoints, and decorated ostrich egg shell. Two radiocarbon dates place the "Bovidien" style at Jabbaren to ca. 5500 B.P. and at Sefar ca. 5020 B.P. (Lhote 1961). Associated with these sites are bones of cattle, sheep, and goats, all apparently domesticated, the conclusion being that the "Têtes/Rondes" paintings were made by Pre-pastoral groups while the "Bovidien" paintings depicted scenes familiar to Neolithic cattle herders. This interpretation is substantiated by sites containing ceramics associated with the "Têtes/Rondes" style but without evidence of domestication as reported from Ennedi (Delebo) to the east and dated ca. 7200 B.P. (Bailloud 1969).

Not far from Tassili, in the Acacus Mountains of the Fezzan, other sites have yielded data concerning the early presence of cattle herders in the Sahara. The settlements in this area, some of which were quite large, were in rock shelters near the old water course of Wadi Teshuinat. Excavations at Uan Muhuggiag produced a stratified sequence, with evidence suggesting the use of grass huts for habitation and with cultural debris consisting of pottery, stone tools, and food remains. The earliest date for the pottery was ca. 7400 B.P. Level VIII, dated ca. 5950 B.P., contained the skull of the short-horned domesticated *Bos brachyceros* (Mori 1965). At the same site a rock painting in the "Bovidien" style underlay deposits dated to ca. 4730 B.P. Another site, Uan Telocat, level III, dated at 6754 B.P., contained cultural material similar to the pastoral level at Uan Muhuggiag, and Mori suggests this date as the beginning of the pastoral period. As at Tassili, the "Bovidien" paintings depict large herds (twenty, fifty, or one hundred animals) of cattle with domestic traits, such as spotted coats and a variety of horn shapes (Mori 1964).

Also in the Acacus Mountains, Barich (1974) reports early dates at Ti-n-Torna East. The lowest level, layer 4, does not contain pottery. Level 3, however, does contain ceramics and is radiocarbon dated at 8640 B.P. and 8540 B.P. As was true at other sites, this early pottery is unburnished and decorated with the "dotted wavy line" motifs of the Early Khartoum style.

Some of the best evidence for the occurrence of domesticated animals has been recovered in the Air Massif. At Adrar Bous a series of sites was related to both a ceramic "Subneolithic" and a cattle-herding "Neolithic." Several small surface sites from the margin of a high lake level contained ceramics, microliths, bone harpoons, and the bones of fish, aquatic, and terrestrial mammals and were dated ca. 7310 B.P. Smith (1976) has designated these as the "Kiffian Microlithic." Later sites in the same area corresponded to the Shaheinab-related "Tenerian Neolithic" (Hugot 1962; Clark 1971). These were mainly open sites, widely distributed around Adrar Bous and extended into the present Ténéré Desert to the east. At the time of occupation these sites must have bordered a large lake and swampy depression, and were both denser and

more extensive than those with the earlier industry. Circles of stone may have formed the foundations of shelters, but without any evidence of permanent dwellings—a pattern suggesting a long-term seasonal occupation (Clark 1971). One of these sites, Agoras-n-Tast, produced an almost complete skeleton of *Bos brachyceros* which gave a bone date of ca. 5750 B.P. (Carter and Clark 1976).

One area near the Sudan has recently become very important in reconstructing the climatic and subsistence base of the developing Neolithic in the Sudan and the Sahara. During the past few years several investigations in the Western Desert of Egypt have attempted to understand the late prehistory of the eastern Sahara. Of particular interest is the area near Nabta Playa about 100 km west of Abu Simbel (see fig. 1). Several sites around these ancient lakes have provided an extraordinary picture of cultural development from the Terminal Paleolithic through Late Neolithic. There is evidence of a settled ceramic-using occupation, beginning as early as 8200 B.P., possibly also with domesticated plants and animals (Wendorf and Schild 1980).

In addition to the archaeology, a detailed paleoclimatic sequence for the period from 9000 B.P. to 5800 B.P. is now available. Well dated by radiocarbon determinations, this sequence indicates three moist periods separated by two short periods of intense aridity (see table 1).

The Early Neolithic, associated with Playa II, contains a few sherds comparable in decorative motif to some atypical sherds from Early Khartoum (Banks 1980). The lithic assemblage shows marked continuities with the earlier local Terminal Paleolithic and shows no relationship to the Khartoum Mesolithic in the Nile Valley. Since only a single bovid bone was recovered, the presence of domestic cattle is problematic, nor did caprovid remains appear (Gautier 1980).

With the onset of the major pluvial period at 7700 B.P., peoples of the Middle Neolithic occupied the playa, making mat-impressed ceramics comparable to the dotted–wavy line pottery of the Late Khartoum Mesolithic (Banks 1980). Furthermore, they already had domestic cattle in addition to sheep and goats (Gautier 1980).

By 6300 B.P. the Late Neolithic sites at Nabta contained ceramics unrelated to the Khartoum Horizon Style, but comparable with that described for the Abkan Ware Group M (Nordstrom 1972) on the Nile near the Second Cataract (Banks 1980). Domestic cattle persisted, together with some domestic sheep and goats (Gautier 1980; see vol.2, fig. 3).

The Sudan

The type sites for the Sudanese Neolithic and for the Saharan Neolithic are the Khartoum Hospital site and Esh

Shaheinab (fig. 2). Arkell (1949) first described the earliest ceramic-bearing site in the Sudan as "Early Khartoum" for the Khartoum Hospital site, listing its characteristics as "Wavy Line" pottery and microlithic stone tools consisting mostly of backed crescents or lunates of quartz.

Some large crescents were of rhyolite, and the numerous ground stone artifacts included sandstone half rings. Bone harpoons, barbed on one side with grooves around the base, were abundant. Quantities of potsherds represented large bowls of well-fired unburnished brown ware decorated with combed impressions. Characteristic decorative motifs were "Wavy Line" and "Dotted Wavy Line." Faunal remains included reed rat, Nile lechwe, and water mongoose, indicating an environment three to four times wetter than today, with the high Nile probably 10 m higher than at present. Arkell considered this Early Khartoum site to be the "Khartoum Mesolithic" for there was no evidence for the use of domesticated plants or animals (Arkell 1949).

Arkell (1953) later described a "Khartoum Neolithic" site, Esh Shaheinab, located about 45 km north of Khartoum and situated on an old terrace 5 m above the present Nile flood level. Faunal evidence suggested an annual rainfall of about 500 mm, making the surrounding country a savanna and forest. Although wild animals predominated, bones identified as domestic dwarf goat also occurred (Bate, in Arkell 1953).

Lithic artifacts are similar to Early Khartoum, but with some additions. Two important new tool types were the bifacially flaked and polished celt and the bifacially flaked gouge with polished back. Bone tools included the bone harpoon, now with a hole drilled in its base, bone celts, and also barbless shell fishhooks. Pottery was burnished and decorated with "Dotted Wavy Line" motifs and with "impressed vee-and-dot patterns" (Arkell 1953).

Although changes in the surface treatment and design motifs on pottery form the central argument for viewing the Khartoum materials as an evolutionary development, Arkell reported only a single site (El Qoz) where the whole sequence occurs, and even here the stratigraphy appears to have been somewhat disturbed (Arkell 1953:97). Nonetheless, he proposed an evolutionary sequence of cultural development from a "Mesolithic" to a "Neolithic" stage, with its origin in the Khartoum area.

There were no radiocarbon dates for Early Khartoum, but Arkell did not think 7000 B.C. was too early (Arkell and Ucko 1965). Although two radiocarbon dates available from Esh Shaheinab averaged 5100 B.P., Arkell (1975) thought them too young, but recent radiocarbon determinations have corroborated them (Haaland 1979a, 1979b).

In the 1960s, several new sites outside of the Khartoum area were reported (see fig. 2). Early Khartoum pottery motifs appeared in the area around the second cataract, some 750 km north of Khartoum (Shiner 1968b; Geus 1978). Later research south of Nubia and south of Dongola uncovered more sites with similar pottery (Marks, Shiner, and Hays 1968), and even more recently others at Tagra and Shabona, near the White Nile south of Khartoum, have been reported (Adamson, Clark, and Williams 1974; Brandt, 1980). Finally, at a short distance north of Khartoum are the sites of Sarurab, Islang, and Saggai, which are similar to Early Khartoum (Mohammed-Ali 1982, 1984; Khabir 1981; el Anwar 1981; Caneva 1983).

The cultural chronology of the Nile Valley in the northern Sudan is based to a great extent on research during and following the Nubian Monuments Salvage Campaign. The earliest site with pottery in the northern Sudan was Abka near Wadi Halfa, dated to ca. 8260 B.P. (Myers 1960; Shiner 1968a).

A later pottery-bearing industry near the second cataract, designated the Khartoum Variant (Shiner 1968b), is dated at ca. 6540 B.P. These sites appeared to be generally related to the Late Khartoum "Mesolithic" in techniques of ceramic decoration and design motifs, characterized by unburnished comb-impressed ware. The lithic tool assemblages of the Khartoum Variant do not show close affinities with the Khartoum area, particularly in the variety of their lunates and ground stone artifacts. The presence of a high percentage of concave sidescrapers of Egyptian flint suggests cultural connections with the north rather than the south (Hays 1974).

The Dongola region is located about 350 km south of the Second Cataract and that much nearer to Khartoum. Its Karmakol industry shows striking parallels with the Late Khartoum Mesolithic, primarily in decorative techniques and in design motifs on the pottery (Hays 1971a). The ground stone tools and lunates are similar in the two areas although the large crescents known from Khartoum are absent. Unfortunately, radiocarbon dates are lacking for the Dongola area sites.

The cultural sequence seen near Khartoum does not appear farther to the north or south along the Nile. There are Late Khartoum Mesolithic–related ceramics at Wadi Halfa (Shiner 1968a) and Debba (Hays 1971a), but no Khartoum Neolithic–related ceramic assemblages have been found there. In contrast, the Debba area has A-Group-related wares (Marks, Shiner, and Hays 1968), and in Wadi Halfa, Abkan ceramics occur (Nordstrom 1972). A similar lack of Khartoum Neolithic sites has been reported to the south along the White Nile (Brandt 1980).

South of Khartoum are the sites of Tagra, Guli, and Shabona. Bone harpoon fragments were found at Tagra and Guli where pottery of the Early Khartoum style also was recovered. Radiocarbon dating of shell produced ages of 8100 B.P. for Tagra and 5480 B.P. for Guli (Adamson, Clark, and Williams 1974).

The site of Shabona lies on an old terrace of the White Nile, its cultural remains comprising ground stone and chipped stone artifacts, which include lunates, scrapers and drills; as at Early Khartoum, there are uniserially barbed bone points (Clark 1973). The ceramics from Shabona are apparently part of the Early Khartoum tradition, with unburnished cord-impressed pottery being characteristic. A radiocarbon date on shell from the site indicates an age of ca. 7000 B.P. (Brandt 1980).

One of the primary difficulties in assessing the Neolithic chronology of the Sudan has been the lack of well-stratified sites. Most are single component sites, or, if two cultural components do occur, they appear somewhat mixed. One site, however, that may elucidate the clouded picture of cultural development in the Sudan during the Neolithic period lies outside the Nile Valley.

The Sudanese Neolithic site of Shaqadud (Sheq el Dud) is a rock shelter located about seventy-five miles northeast of Khartoum and some thirty-five miles east of the Nile River (see fig. 2). The artifact inventory, from a surface survey, was reported as predominantly typical of the "Khartoum Neolithic" as excavated by Arkell at Shaheinab (Otto 1963). However, later inspection outside the rock shelter indicated the distinct possibility of at least 2 m of cultural deposits containing ceramics representative of the full range of cultural development in Sudan (Marks et al. 1980). Ceramic motifs included unburnished wavy line and dotted wavy line, burnished dotted wavy line, and sherds with triangular impressions, burnished redware, ripple ware, and black-top wares. From exploratory trenches made by Otto it became apparent that *in situ* stratified cultural deposits in the midden would yield evidence for cultural development from "Khartoum Mesolithic" through "Khartoum Neolithic" to something similar to A-Group at the Second Cataract. In addition, there was also a later ceramic ware not previously described (Marks et al. 1980).

Recent excavations at Shaqadud by the author, A. E. Marks of Southern Methodist University, and A. Mohammed-Ali and Y. Elamin of Khartoum University have yielded a radiocarbon-dated chronology for the appearance of the different ceramic wares. The midden contains up to 3 m of stratified cultural deposits which can be divided into three main periods. The upper zone contains a post-Shaheinab "Neolithic" (pre-Meroitic) which is comparable to much of the material in the cave. The middle zone represents the Shaheinab-related Neolithic dating to ca. 5500 B.P. In the lowest zone the ceramics are unburnished and fall within the range described for Early Khartoum, although true wavy-line pottery is rare.

The earliest radiocarbon date in the sequence is ca. 7400 B.P. (Marks et al. 1983).

The cave deposits represented a continuation of the cultural sequence. Combined with the midden, an almost complete stratigraphic sequence occurs from the very earliest ceramic occupation almost to Meroitic. The lowest levels of the cave may equate with the just post-Shaheinab A-Group-like materials along the central Nile. The later ceramics are similar to those called "Pan-Grave" illustrated by Arkell (1953). Radiocarbon dates indicate the cave was occupied between 4000–3600 B.P. (Marks et al. 1982).

The earliest ceramic-bearing sites in the eastern Sudan occur at the Atbara River near the town of Khashm el Girba (see fig. 2). Named the Saroba Group, these sites are usually fairly small and are located both near the river and on the savanna (Shiner et al. 1971). Their ceramics, consisting mainly of mat-impressed wares, belong within the Khartoum Horizon Style (Hays 1971a, 1976). The stone technology favored flake production and has a significant backed tool component, including geometrics. No polished stone artifacts were recovered, but ground stone was present. Faunal remains at the Pre-Saroba site include mainly fish, small mammals, and birds, and none of the animals is domestic. A radiocarbon date of 6200 B.P. is available for the Pre-Saroba sites (Hays et al. 1983). Recent radiocarbon dates on two Saroba sites indicate an age of ca. 5600 B.P.

Significantly, there is no evidence near the Atbara of a later cultural manifestation of the Shaheinab type. The Saroba Group appears to be followed by a people with very large and complex village sites of the Butana Group, which were first thought to date to ca. 2400 B.C. (Shiner et al. 1971). Artifacts, particularly pottery, suggest a transition from the Saroba Group. Several recent radiocarbon dates indicate the sites were occupied between 5400 and 4400 B.P. (Marks et al. 1983).

Along the Nile Valley in Sudan, peoples practicing a full Neolithic economy succeeded the Shaheinab Neolithic. Recent excavations at Zakyab (Haaland 1978) and Kadero indicate that domestic animals totaled 88 percent of the mammalian fauna, with long-horned cattle accounting for about 79 percent of the domestic forms (Krzyzaniak 1980).

Kadero, described as a settlement and burial ground, lies 18 km north of Khartoum and 6 km east of the Nile River (fig. 2). In contrast to Esh Shaheinab, its artifact assemblage contained few backed bladelets and crescents, and no harpoons or shell fishhooks, both typical at Shaheinab, have appeared there. In addition, there is a sharp increase over the Shaheinab assemblage in sandstone grinders, suggesting a greater exploitation of plant resources (Krzyzaniak 1978). Plant impressions on pottery first were identified as domestic millet and sorghum (Klichowska 1978). More recent reexamination, however, suggests the impressions were from wild plant seeds (Haaland 1981).

Most of the ground stone artifacts such as gouges, celts, and maceheads, which seem more frequent at Kadero than at Shaheinab, were made of rhyolite. The flaked stone tools consist mainly of scrapers, groovers, and borers made of quartz and chert. The pottery at Kadero generally resembles that from Shaheinab, except that Dotted Wavy Line decorative motifs are rare (Krzyzaniak 1978). It is mainly decorated with impressed designs made with a toothed implement, of which rocker stamp impressions forming a zigzag pattern or straight dotted lines are the most common. Decoration usually covers the entire body of the pot, the most characteristic patterns consisting of combinations of dots and triangles, generally arranged in horizontal concentric bands. Zigzags of dotted or continuous lines and bands of multiple lines of closely spaced dots are also common, and incised, horizontal lines and semicircular panels occur frequently (Chlodnicki 1980).

In addition to the typical Shaheinab sherds, at Kadero is a greater quantity of pottery with alternately hatched and plain chevron patterns, and hatched bands with closely spaced comb impressions. Similar wares have been reported at Omdurman Bridge (Arkell 1949:99–106, pls. 94–100), in the "protodynastic" burials at Esh Shaheinab (Arkell 1953:82–89, pls. 40–43), and from El Kadada (Geus 1979). A black-top redware also occurs at Kadero (Chlodnicki 1980).

Unfortunately, few other sites containing similar economic and artifactual traits such as at Kadero I and II have been excavated in the Sudan. Although the excavations at Geili have not been published in detail, there is good indication that this site is contemporary with Kadero. Pottery styles are similar, including the dotted rocker stamp motif, some "ripple ware," and a redware with black triangles along the rim (Caneva 1980). Positive identification of domesticated animal forms is lacking, but most of the faunal remains came from fishing and hunting. While the upper levels of Geili appear to be similar to Kadero and Shaheinab, the lower levels are more like Early Khartoum. No radiocarbon dates for either level, however, are as yet available.

In the area north of Khartoum the Kadero Neolithic is followed by groups of people with traits first described at the Second Cataract as Abkan and A-Group (Nordstrom 1972). The site of El Kadada about 200 km north of Khartoum has yielded an artifact assemblage described as similar to the A-Group of the Second Cataract (Geus 1976). A preliminary report describes the presence of numerous sandstone grinding tools, flaked quartz and chert

artifacts, bone harpoons, and shell fish hooks, but significantly with no gouges occurring. A large quantity of potsherds, mostly black ware, was reported. Black "ripple ware" pottery occurs and black-incised pottery, sometimes with white filling, is in abundance. The radiocarbon date of ca. 4630 B.P. indicates the contemporaneity of El Kadada with the Classic A-Group assemblages in Lower Nubia (Geus 1982; see vol.2, fig. 3).

Summary

This chapter has presented an overview of the cultural chronology in the Sahara and Sudan during the Neolithic period. The discussion considered sites containing "neolithic" artifact traits, both with and without evidence of domesticates. Radiocarbon dates for these sites fall generally between 9000 and 5000 B.P. During this time period two periods of climatic amelioration changed the desert into a grassland containing rivers and lakes. These two moist periods produced an environment for plants and animals that is now found only several hundred kilometers to the south. The perennial water of the lakes and the herds of large game animals attracted populations of hunters, who settled near the water sources. These early hunters made Neolithic artifacts such as grinding stones and ceramics, and left images on rocks of the animals they hunted. Rock art in the Sahara depicts buffalo, giraffes, antelopes, ostriches and other animals now found in East Africa. Fish and aquatic mammals also were plentiful. These hunting groups were widespread across the now desert areas of the central Sahara and Sudan, yet were similar in many respects. Many lived in rock shelters near ancient rivers or settled around the margins of now extinct lakes. Hunting and fishing were probably the basis of the subsistence economy, but the presence of numerous grinding stones attests to the importance of plants to the diet.

These scattered populations used the same kinds of microlithic artifacts, but it has been shown that they were not the same lithic industry (Maitre 1971; Hays 1971b, 1974, 1976). Nonetheless, the ceramic decorative motifs were quite similar. It was these similarities that led researchers to speak of a "Neolithic of Sudanese Tradition," a "Sahara-Sudanese Neolithic," and others. An intensive examination of the ceramic technology from these disparate groups, however, indicated that their similarities in pottery making were limited primarily to decorative motifs. The conclusion was that the widespread use of similar techniques of pottery decoration should be viewed as an example of a "Khartoum Horizon Style" rather than a diffusion or migration of people (Hays 1971b, 1976; Hays and Hassan 1974).

The appearance of ceramics in non-food-producing societies in the Sahara and Sudan does not follow the pattern seen in the Near East, where domestication of plants and animals occurred prior to pottery making. It has been pointed out elsewhere that sedentism is a more important criterion for the usefulness of ceramics than domestication. In several parts of the world, ceramics can be correlated with sedentary life-styles, but not always with domestication (Hays 1971b; Sutton 1974). Thus, it appears that an adequate and predictable food source was available to the Saharan hunters and fishers which allowed a degree of sedentism in which ceramics were useful (Hays 1976, 1980). The pottery vessels could have been used for cooking as well as for the storage of wild grains. Whatever the reason, well-made pottery of the Khartoum Horizon Style is widespread across the Sahara and Sudan by eight thousand years ago. This ceramic technology is contemporary with the earliest pottery in the Near East and must be viewed as an indigeuous African development (Camps 1969; Hays 1971b).

Considerable evidence indicates that there is a cultural continuum from the pre-Neolithic hunters to the later Neolithic herding groups. At numerous sites in the Sahara and Sudan the artifacts of the pastoral societies suggest an evolutionary change. Pottery became burnished, but design motifs show relationships with the earlier ceramics. Some new stone tool types are added, such as gouges, but the lithic tradition continues (Hays 1975b; Smith 1976; Wendorf and Schild 1980). In a few stratified sites the succession is quite clear (Bailloud 1969; Barich 1980; Marks et al. 1982).

The site of Shaqadud has provided the first stratified radiocarbon-dated chronology for the Neolithic in Sudan. The cultural materials from Shaqadud suggest that the cultural sequence first described by Arkell may be correct. It is important to note, however, that the Khartoum Neolithic (Shaheinab-related) sites in Sudan cover a short span of time. Several recently radiocarbon-dated sites in central Sudan indicate less than one thousand years for the Khartoum Neolithic compared with about three thousand years for the Khartoum Mesolithic. Future research is needed to explain this phenomenon.

The Neolithic pastoralists raised cattle, sheep, and goats, but should not be considered nomadic. Although numerous small camp sites have been found in the eastern Sahara (Gabriel 1976, 1981), the most common settlement pattern follows that of their sedentary predecessors (Smith 1980b). These pastoral societies apparently flourished in the Sahara until about four thousand years ago, when the present-day drying trend began. As the desert advanced, the populations began to move their herds to the better-watered areas. Some groups in the eastern Sahara moved to the Nile Valley (Wendorf and Schild 1980), while those in the central Sahara moved to the south (Smith 1980a). By ca. 2000 B.C., when the present configuration of the desert prevailed, the former inhabitants had been forced to leave. From that time on, human occupation of the Sahara was sparse and in Sudan was centered near the Nile and Atbara River valleys.

Sixteen

The Chronology of Africa South of the Sahara, 8000 B.C.–A.D. 1000

Creighton Gabel, Boston University

Outline

The area covered in this chapter includes the following parts of sub-Saharan Africa: Ethiopia, Somalia, Uganda, Kenya, Tanzania, the Congo basin, southern Africa, and the various countries of the Guinea Coast between Guinea and Gabon (fig. 1). The organization is broadly geographical and is geared toward major techno-economic changes and the distribution of larger-scale cultural "traditions." In this respect, local chronologies, where they exist at all, vary a great deal in quality and detail, and while the upper portion of the time frame included here is recent, it is entirely prehistoric for the regions in question. In general cultural-chronological terms, it encompasses the so-called Later Stone Age (herein restricted to terminal food-collectors), "Neolithic" food-producers, and the earlier Iron Age (up to about A.D. 1000). The later Iron Age, which is still poorly understood in a number of areas and then sometimes more in terms of oral history and historical linguistics than as a result of archaeological research, is largely excluded except for purposes of comparison.

In contrast with many other Old World areas, the prehistory of Africa is characterized by some rather unusual features. In long-term perspective, it incorporates almost all of the verifiable evidence for the emergence of humankind, and the very late survival of hunter-gatherers, both archaeologically and ethnographically, is likewise notable. There is a lot less concrete evidence for the Neolithic and then mainly in parts of West Africa and the East African Rift, otherwise with only a hint of it here or there. Also, its duration seems seldom to have exceeded 1,000–2,000 years. There is no Bronze Age outside North Africa, and where copper or gold was utilized, it seems always to have been in contexts where iron was

Text submitted March 1982

already being worked. Finally, the prehistoric period ended only with the advent of Arabs or Europeans, in no case before the tenth to late fifteenth centuries and sometimes as late as the nineteenth century. One may add that most of the major technological and economic changes in sub-Saharan Africa, from the inception of agriculture onward, have been conventionally viewed as introductions from external sources, even though the postulated stimuli for change have yet to pattern out satisfactorily. As further evidence accumulates, less diffusionistic explanations may prove warranted, as is now true for example in explaining the development of traditional African art.

At pre–Iron Age horizons the criteria for identification and classification remain more techno-cultural than otherwise. In terms of connections with historical populations, a relationship between certain aspects of the Later Stone Age in southern Africa and subfossil groups broadly similar to modern San (Bushmen) or Khoikhoi (Hottentot) seems likely, although even this may be less straightforward than once thought. Neither the Pygmies nor any of the other recent hunter-gatherers have been convincingly linked with specific prehistoric materials, either archaeological or osteological. Some of the relatively widespread ceramic traditions of the Early Iron Age may reflect movements of particular ethnolinguistic groups such as the Proto-Bantu, but it is mainly in the later Iron Age that one can begin to correlate archaeological data more certainly with known ethnic populations.

In an area with so little historical time-depth, archaeological chronologies depend very heavily on radiocarbon results even for recent centuries, and only in the last decade or so have these become available in any quantity. One of the first published syntheses for sub-Saharan Africa (Clark 1962) included less than fifty dates, and hardly any of those from East or West Africa. Ten years later, the number had increased seventeenfold (Gabel 1972:20), and at present new radiocarbon dates for West Africa alone average about a hundred per year (Calvocoressi and David 1979:1). To these are being added some thermoluminescence (TL) dates, in spite of continued concern about their accuracy. Additional progress is being made with obsidian-hydration, archaeomagnetic dating (Henthorn, Parkington, and Reid 1979), and radiocarbon dating of carbons extracted from iron alloys (van der Merwe 1978).

In many parts of the continent no adequate regional chronologies exist, reflecting differences in the amount and intensity of research. Field surveys in some nations such as Togo and Gabon are just now being undertaken, and there are large regions of others about which we know little. That a number of countries are either not mentioned, or only scarcely so, implicitly acknowledges that their prehistory is still in the ground.

The Later Stone Age

Loosely equivalent to the European Mesolithic, partly in time and partly in shared artifact types and lithic techniques, hunting-and-gathering economies comprising the Later Stone Age (LSA) are found over much of the area in question. Many of the industries show strong microlithic attributes which presumably reflect expanded use of composite tools and weapons. As in northern Europe, some examples of still-hafted specimens or ones with adhesive material visible on them have been recovered. Where circumstances have permitted, bone or, less commonly, wood artifacts such as digging sticks, bow fragments, arrows, linkshafts, staves, and so forth have survived, as occasionally have pieces of cordage or even leather. Poisons used by some modern African hunters are attested as far back as the third millennium B.C. in Zambia, where both linkshaft arrows and remains of poison-producing plants occurred in one site (Fagan and van Noten 1971:51). Ground stone axes or hoes, bored stones, and grindstones are fairly common, although all are distributed somewhat irregularly in time and space. Bodily ornament generally consisted of such items as beads of shell or other materials, but at least some of the naturalistic and schematic rock art of eastern and southern Africa is attributable to these peoples. Pottery is known from a number of LSA contexts, probably mostly later ones, the primary exception being in the northern Rift where ceramics appeared in the early Holocene. Subsistence was based on variable mixes of hunting, gathering, fishing, or shellfish collection, and especially around the Rift lakes and along the Cape coast one sees the first convincing evidence of aquatic foods being used in quantity, a trend that began as early as the Upper Pleistocene in the latter area.

In general, archaeological vestiges of the LSA suggest quite stable, long-term, and effective adaptations based on a relatively simple material culture. Only the rock art provides a hint of more complex behavior, both aesthetic and symbolic. Remarkably, in spite of the widespread presence of potentially domesticable plants and animals (Jewell 1969), there seems to have been no effort, or perhaps incentive, to experiment with cultivation or stockkeeping. In the end, life-styles appear to have changed or terminated primarily through the impact of technologically and economically superior intruders or neighbors. Even so, some food collectors persisted into recent centuries, especially in more difficult or marginal regions.

Most of the recognized industrial complexes, or "traditions," based on similarities or differences in lithic assemblages, reflect artifact types, technical modes of manufacture, or type frequencies. Some broadly similar industries extend over very large geographical areas and therefore can scarcely represent single cultural or ethnic groups. At the same time, variability among grossly similar assemblages within particular regions raises the question of whether this has to do with temporal or ethnic distinctions, specific activities, kinds of raw material available, random idiosyncracies, or some combination of these factors (Nelson 1973; Deacon 1972, 1976:168ff.).

What has emerged is that microlithic industries in at least some parts of the continent first appeared much earlier than once thought. Initially, the radiocarbon dates themselves were considered anomalous, but it is now clear that there were a number of such "early LSA" developments. Most are concentrated in an area from Lake Victoria southward toward the Zambezi (table 1), although Border Cave in eastern South Africa shows a comparable trend between about 36,000 and 31,000 B.C. (Pta-704, LJ-2892) (Hall and Vogel 1980). This may prove to be a more widespread phenomenon and in any case implies that at least some Africans developed composite implements, including the bow and arrow, at an early date.

The various expressions of the "Wilton" industrial complex, featuring geometric segments, other small backed pieces, convex or short end-scrapers, and *outils écaillés*, represent the epitome of microlithic emphasis. Bored stones, polished axes or adzes, and/or grinding tools appear in a number of instances but not consistently. Where it occurs, pottery is usually late and seems to reflect contact with Iron Age groups. Simple bone artifacts like awls and points are fairly common, but only at the Gwisho sites in Zambia (Fagan and van Noten 1966) and at some Cape sites such as Melkhoutboom (Deacon 1976) have wooden ones been preserved in quantity.

The "Wilton" designation has without much question been overextended to include similar lithic industries all the way from the Cape to the Horn. Not all are of the same age nor could they possibly represent the same, or even related, populations. Only from Zambia southward is there anything approaching a convincing association with a particular physical type (so-called large Khoisanoid). Some regional variation in lithic type-frequencies may indicate differences in food procurement or, in some cases, seasonal activities (Carter 1970; Parkington 1972). Based on the ratios of scrapers to backed segments, viewed as projectile armatures, Deacon (1972) has inferred a woodland small-game-trapping and root-and-bulb collection pattern in the interior Cape, contrasting with an open grassland big-game-hunting one in parts of Zimbabwe and Zambia. The Cape also furnishes evidence of a shift from the latter type of exploitation toward the former during the transition from late Pleistocene to Holocene, and it is there also that the earliest signs of maritime resource use are seen: first of mollusks, penguins, and stranded sea mammals during the Upper Pleistocene, then subsequently of fish and flying birds as well (Klein 1977:121). The later Holocene versions of this appear in coastal midden sites with characteristically informal tools that have been termed either "coastal Wilton" or "Strandlopers" (Sampson 1974: 403ff.). Both pottery and domestic sheep appear in some of these sites during the very first centuries A.D., long before the Iron Age commenced there (see below). It has never been quite clear whether the occupants of this littoral area represent a separate techno-cultural tradition or just one aspect of an inland maritime pattern of seasonal transhumance. Even though this life-style persisted until contact times, early European accounts are themselves confusing on the subject.

The so-called Smithfield industries of interior South Africa are no longer seen as a single cultural continuum. "Smithfield A," based on large flakes and circular scrapers, has been incorporated into a more widespread complex of the terminal Pleistocene and very early Holocene, variously known as "Oakhurst," "Pre-Wilton," or "early LSA." "Smithfield B," featuring long end-scrapers on blades, and "Smithfield C," microlithic but with more emphasis on scrapers than the Wilton, are much later than Smithfield A and often postdate the Wilton. A number of sites, in fact, are protohistoric. The "Smithfield N" variant of Natal, with high frequencies of concave-edged scrapers, has never been adequately dated.

Patterning of radiocarbon dates in South Africa and Zimbabwe (J. Deacon 1974) suggests the Wilton, preceded by more macrolithic industries, began to appear

about 6000 B.C. or so. An absence of dated Smithfield B/C sites during the earlier Wilton period may indicate that the distinctions between Smithfield and Wilton are something of a fiction based on type frequencies. They may have been no more than regional manifestations of the same industrial complex in the South African interior. In addition to the more informal coastal assemblages, some Wilton occupations on the Cape at inland sites (e.g., De Hangen Shelter at A.D. 1465–1860) were as late as much of the Smithfield farther north (table 2). (Laboratory numbers for specific dates cited, if not in the text, are found in the appropriate sections of tables 2–4. For additional dates the reader is referred especially to the continuing series of annotated radiocarbon reports appearing in the *Journal of African History,* the most recent of which are included in the reference list up to the time of writing this report.) In the Transvaal, large flake-and-scraper industries continued until the early part of the present millennium, only then being replaced by Smithfield.

As remarked above, Zambia seems part of an area where microlithic trends began earlier than in some neighboring regions. The local version of the Wilton, however, is later and concentrated in the south and west, whereas the partly contemporary Nachikufan industry is found to the north and east and in nearby Malawi. Because of its distribution in less open country and certain aspects of its tool kits such as concave scrapers, polished axes and adzes, and grindstones, the Nachikufan may represent an adaptation to woodland environments, while the Wilton may reflect one of hunting herd animals in grasslands and open woodland.

Dates for the Zambian Wilton generally fall after 3000 B.C. and sometimes substantially later, although perhaps due to differences in soils and vegetation cover such groups seem to have given way more quickly than the Nachikufan to Iron Age herders and farmers, at least in the south (Miller 1969). A few dated sites or assemblages with ceramics indicate overlap with Iron Age peoples in the early centuries A.D., but only in the drier southwest did Wilton hunter-gatherers last much longer. At Kandanda and other sites along the Kalahari frontier they seem to have persisted as late as the mid-fifteenth century A.D. (Phillipson 1977b:249; table 2).

There has been some debate as to whether the Nachikufan represents a single continuum. Miller (1971) has divided it into four phases: Nachikufan I, IIA, IIB, and III.

Nachikufan I, with larger scrapers, choppers, bored stones, and grindstones, is placed at 14,765–8870 B.C. Nachikufan IIA, at 7750–5370 B.C., emphasizes backed flakes and includes polished stone axes, while Nachikufan IIB (3680–2880 B.C.) has a high proportion of geometric microliths and concave scrapers. Nachikufan III, with an earliest date of 1550 B.C. at Leopard's Hill Cave, lasts until about A.D. 1650–1750 elsewhere. Backed microliths predominate but are associated with some of the other types from earlier horizons. The latest occurrences include both pottery and iron, and evidence of smelting was found at two sites. Evidence of similar LSA survivals has been cited in other parts of eastern Zambia as well (Phillipson 1976b).

Miller's total of seventeen dates from five sites seems a rather slim basis for establishing a chronology of almost seventeen thousand years, and furthermore the real distinction may lie between Nachikufan I and the other facies, with the differences among the latter being less developmental than activity-based (Sampson and Southard 1973). Phillipson (1976b:204–5) argues that Nachikufan IIB/III, the Wilton in the south and west, what he terms the Makwe industry of eastern Zambia, and the Kaposwa industry at Kalambo Falls (Clark 1974:107ff.) in the far north are all no more than local variants stemming from the earlier Nachikufan and related industries of the "early LSA" (table 1).

A possibly related industry is the Tshitolian of southern Zaïre and northern Angola. This includes foliate and tanged points, trapezoidal segments, backed blades, and, sometimes at least, heavier tools such as core axes, choppers, and the like derived from a presumed Lupemban ancestry. Clark (1970:175) notes considerable variability in artifact types according to the local environments in which the Tshitolian is found, especially gallery forest as contrasted with open grassland. Miller (1972), in discussing the differences, concludes that activity variants, ecological factors, and ethnic distinctions all may have played some role.

A number of dates have been published for the Tshitolian, and these range from the final Pleistocene up to the first or early second millennium A.D. (table 2). Unfortunately, many occurrences are surface sites or otherwise have dubious radiocarbon sample associations. Mixed sites seem common enough to cast some doubt on reported inclusions of Iron Age material with some of the later expressions.

Thus far comprising an isolated phenomenon in central Africa are the Ishango middens of Lake Edward in eastern Zaïre (de Heinzelin 1957). Here clumsily made quartz tools occurred in conjunction with barbed bone points and very fragmented human remains. The harpoons, except for a single example from Gamble's Cave in the Kenya Rift, constitute the southernmost occurrence of a weapon type found all the way across northern Africa. Extrapolated radiocarbon results suggested an age between 6000 and 9000 B.C., like some sites with such points in northern Kenya, although van Noten (1981b:562) mentions the presence of some extinct

fauna, which makes the earliest radiocarbon date of 19,050 B.C. (W-283) even more interesting.

Sites of "Wilton" type are present throughout much of former British East Africa, represented earliest at Kisese II Shelter and at Nasera (Apis) Shelter in Tanzania and later in open sites, middens, or overhangs in Uganda and Kenya as well. The level of investigation and description of these is generally of a lower order than that for southern Africa. In the most detailed synthesis carried out thus far the investigator (Nelson 1973) was unable to isolate clear-cut geographic or temporal patterns of variability.

Very early dates for Wilton horizons at Kisese (8870 B.C., NPL-36; 12,810 B.C., NPL-35) and Nasera (5150 and 6150 B.C., coll. sample ISGS-427) are not, in the latter case at least, incompatible with some in South Africa and Zimbabwe. Most of the remainder are quite recent, and a number are within the time span of the Pastoral Neolithic or Early Iron Age, from about 1600 B.C. to the seventh century A.D. (see fig. 2).

Centered exclusively in the Kenya and Tanzania Rift is the "Upper Kenya Capsian" (Eburran), initially recognized by Louis Leakey during his excavations at Gamble's Cave. The earlier "Lower Kenya Capsian" at Gamble's Cave, with its obsidian-backed blades, seems to have been the antecedent of this microlithic version. Dates from Kenya suggest that the earlier variant goes back to at least the eleventh millennium B.C. and was succeeded by the Upper Capsian early in the seventh millennium (Sutton 1972:3–4; Bower et al. 1977), although there are higher dates for the latter at Olduvai Gorge (Leakey et al. 1972; table 1).

Recent work in arid northern Kenya, around Lake Turkana, has brought to light a number of sites inhabited by semisedentary fishermen employing barbed bone points and in some cases producing pottery similar to the "Wavy Line" ware of Early Khartoum (Robbins 1972, 1974; Phillipson 1977c; Barthelme 1977). Dated sites include Lothagam (5610 B.C., UCLA-1247E) and comparable ceramic sites in the same district at 6470 (N-1100), 6010 (N-813), 4250 (N-812), and 3070 B.C. (N-814) (Sutton 1972:18; Soper 1974:179). At Lowasera on the southern end of the lake, Phillipson (1977c) recovered evidence of similar occupations by a fishing population beginning in about the eighth millennium B.C. and continuing until about 3000 B.C. (based on a somewhat inconsistent radiocarbon series, HEL and GX). Pottery may have been introduced there by about 6000 B.C. Whether all of this has any implications for connections with the Nile corridor is not yet clear. The hunting and fishing settlement at Early Khartoum is undated, although an age as early as 7000 B.C. has been suggested (Arkell and Ucko 1965:148). In any case, pottery in the Early Khartoum style appears by 6000 B.C. at Nabta Playa in southern

Egypt in association with livestock (Wendorf et al. 1976:112).

Sutton (1974) has argued that the Rift sites, extending down to Ishango and Gamble's Cave, along with similar ones from the Nile westward across the Sahelian/Saharan belt, represent an "aquatic" complex in which sedentism began early and possibly helped set the stage for food production. This was possibly a response to moister conditions and higher lake levels from the seventh or eighth millennium B.C. to about 2000–3000 B.C., after which environmental deterioration favored a change to pastoralism. In fact, new dates for the Turkana area, from sites with both ceramics and livestock, now indicate such a shift from about this time (see below).

In northern Somalia and parts of Ethiopia, Wilton-like assemblages appear to succeed the regional Hargeisan blade industry, while elsewhere in these countries an otherwise similar industry (Doian) incorporates bifacial and unifacial points. All of these remain poorly dated, and little has been done to define them further since Clark (1954) first outlined their characteristics on the basis of work done before and during World War II.

A variety of regional microlithic industries occurs across West Africa, where archaeologists, perhaps wisely, have refrained from classifying them in broad taxonomic groups. These are just beginning to come into chronological focus, both from new excavations and reexcavation of previously known sites. Some assemblages include only microliths; others have bored stones, flaked or polished axes or hoes, and/or ceramics as well. Some expressions may be related to the introduction of food production, but there is little direct evidence of this except in the case of sites belonging to the Kintampo group in western Ghana, discussed below.

Reexcavation of Rop Shelter in central Nigeria (Eyo 1972; Rosenfeld 1972) produced evidence of an earlier, aceramic, and less microlithic level, followed by one with pottery and geometric segments. Dutsen Kongba Shelter (York 1974), also near Jos, has three microlithic phases, the second with pottery and dated as early as the third through fifth millennia B.C. Iwo Eleru (Shaw 1978:45ff.), the most important site in the southern forest zone of Nigeria, seems to reverse the Rop sequence, with a more microlithic facies preceding a less microlithic one. Both pottery and ground stone axes appear here at a horizon dated about 3620 B.C.

Comparably early ceramics were recovered during reexcavation of Bosumpra Cave in Ghana (Smith 1975), in levels with microliths and polished stone tools from 3269 B.C. to about A.D. 1200. Likewise, a midden on the coast near Tema, with a "small flake industry" and pottery (Dombrowski 1977), is dated at 3908 B.C. (N-2982) and 2230 B.C. (Gif-4241). Some microlithic occurrences such as that at Akyekyema Buor Shelter (A.D. 1265) and the latest horizon at Bosumpra indicate a possible survival of this technology into the early part of the present millennium.

Other dated ceramic sites, some perhaps close to the time when food production was actually being introduced, include Rim in Upper Volta (1680–890 B.C., N-1250–N-1263) and Yagoua, Cameroon (2060 B.C., Gif-3424) (Calvocoressi and David 1979:7); Yengama Cave (Coon 1968) and Kamabai Shelter (Atherton 1972) in Sierra Leone with dates, respectively, of 2200 and 1500 B.C. (TL dates) and from about 2560 B.C.; Sopie Shelter (Gabel 1976) in northeastern Liberia (1450 B.C.); and the Kintampo sites in Ghana (ca. 1500–1000 B.C.). Only the last, however, have yielded evidence of domestication and then mainly of stockkeeping.

At the recent end of the LSA spectrum in the subcontinent, as information already presented will have made obvious, either low dates or mixed assemblages indicate overlap with agricultural populations (fig. 2) which was sometimes of significant duration (Miller 1969; Gabel 1974; Phillipson 1977b:247ff.), mute testimony to the adaptive viability of hunting-and-gathering economies in the sub-Saharan tropics. Of no less interest is the relative timing of displacement, ranging from near-immediate in some contexts to very late in others, that is, from later Iron Age to the present. No doubt this reflects ecological circumstances such as conditions more (or less) suitable for herding or cultivation; differences in the land requirements or land use of intrusive herders or farmers; forms of behavior such as raiding or stock theft conducive to conflict; development of mutual dependencies as seen among modern Dobe San and Herero or the Pygmies and their agricultural neighbors; or some combination of such factors. Certainly some of the indigenous food collectors must have been acculturated as well; the Khoikhoi herders of South Africa and the Sandawe farmers of northern Tanzania are probable recent examples.

Neolithic Economies

In only a few regions, primarily in parts of East and West Africa, is there concrete evidence of domestication in pre–Iron Age contexts. Its earliest history in sub-Saharan Africa has proved difficult to reconstruct. Few sites have produced appropriate floral or faunal material by which one might judge either the time at which various cultigens or livestock appeared or their respective geographical distributions in the precontact period (Shaw 1972, 1976). J. R. Harlan's (1971) concept of diffuse, or "noncentered," agricultural origins in Africa, if correct, may help explain why the evidence has been so elusive. In his view, there was not one particular nuclear zone of early domestication but a series of areas stretching from West Africa to Ethiopia in which different crops were developed and emphasized.

In lieu of extensive archaeological remains, there has been a tendency to rely heavily on ethnobotanical information and recent distributions of cultigens and their wild relatives. Apart from providing no real chronological indicators, the inherent difficulty with this is that four major crop complexes contributed to the present picture: (1) Southwest Asian: wheat, barley, and associated vegetables; (2) Southeast Asian: banana, plantain, sugarcane, taro, and certain species of yam and rice; (3) American: maize, manioc, peanuts, tobacco, cacao, and others; and (4) an impressive array of presumptively indigenous African crops. The last includes grains such as pearl millet, finger millet, sorghums, fonio, teff, and Guinea rice (*Oryza glaberrima*) as well as cowpea, "Kafir potato," earthpea or Bambara groundnut, Guinea yams (*Dioscorea cayenensis* and *rotundata*), rizga, yam pea or bean, geocarpa bean or groundnut, ensete or false banana, piasa, okra, cress, watermelon, fluted pumpkin, yergan or egusi, kola, coffee, roselle, oil palm, shea butter tree, castor, kat, nug, safflower, akee apple, ambary, and possibly cotton. Except for the American crops, unless one takes Precolumbian transatlantic contact seriously, the appearance of none of these complexes is securely dated, and the use and distribution of many plants have certainly gone through substantial change even in recent centuries. Therefore, with the possible exception of those cultigens such as ensete, kat, nug, teff, and rizga that are largely or entirely restricted to Ethiopia, contemporary distributions must be held somewhat less than fully reliable insofar as actual areas of origin are concerned.

Sheep and goats, which lack suitable wild ancestors on the African continent, must have been introduced from western Asia or the Mediterranean, as were horses and camels at a later date. Longhorn cattle of *Bos primigenius* type were indigenous to northern Africa as well as to Eurasia, and it is to these that the earlier cattle of North Africa, and possibly of pre–Iron Age East Africa, owe their antecedents. The present cattle of eastern and southern Africa, including Madagascar, are generally of humped varieties with a marked zebu (*Bos indicus*) strain that must have been introduced from southern Asia. When this took place is no more clear than it is for the Southeast Asian crop types, or for chickens, which must have come from the same area. Rock paintings of humpless cattle in Ethiopia and in Kenya (Mt. Elgon) may indicate their presence in eastern Africa before the Iron Age, but there is no means of dating the art. Donkeys, used as far south as Tanzania by people like the Maasai, may have been domesticated in Northeast Africa.

Some facies of the West African Later Stone Age may represent either semiagricultural economies similar to those suggested for the Nile Valley before the introduction of Southwest Asian crops and livestock (Clark 1971) or the beginnings of food-producing systems stimulated by displacement of those from the Sahel as a result of failing moisture in the second or third millennium B.C. Unfortunately, there is little botanical evidence to document the inception of agriculture, whatever the processes involved. The occasional association of LSA assemblages with food species such as oil palm, atili (*Canarium schweinfurthii*), or African lotus (*Celtis*), which may have been used in wild form, or the inclusion of stone blades with "sickle gloss," as at Iwo Eleru (Shaw 1978:49), are not by themselves sufficiently indicative of cultivation.

The major exception to this is the "Kintampo culture" of western Ghana (Flight 1976), known from fifteen to twenty sites in the forest/savanna ecotone, which some think was one of the critical environmental settings for early agricultural development in the African tropics (Harlan et al. 1976:18). Diagnostic artifacts include polished axes and bracelets, curious scored stone "rasps," pottery, grooved stones, and pieces of burned clay with pole impressions on them. Trade in axes, if not also the stone bracelets, seems well attested. Dates generally fall in the middle of the second millennium B.C. (table 3), or just about the time when many authorities believe influences from the north would have been intensified.

The largest Kintampo site is that of Ntereso, where barbed bone points occurred in association with fish bone and shellfish. Dwarf goats, along with more numerous antelope remains, and possible but still unconfirmed millet (*Pennisetum*) impressions on pottery rims were reported, but the site is controversial in that iron artifacts also were recovered, a presence in this area which seems inadmissable at so early a date. Saharan-type bifacial points from Ntereso, known from no other Kintampo site, are seen by some like Clark (1976:64) as proof of Saharan influences, and the stone bracelets and barbed points could be seen in the same light.

More reliable evidence of domestication comes from the "K6" site, where a so-called Punpun phase featuring pottery, hunting, and snail collection gives way after 1620 B.C. to a local version of the Kintampo culture. In the latter, both dwarf goats and small cattle have been positively identified along with cowpeas, atili, and oil palms (Carter and Flight 1972), but it is unclear whether these or any other plants were being cultivated.

Though barely pre–Iron Age, LSA populations appear to have been at Daima and at other sites such as Kursakata and Bornu-38 in northeastern Nigeria with a combined fishing and cattle-herding economy, if not also cultivation, living in semipermanent settlements that shifted with changing lake levels. These are dated around the fifth through tenth centuries B.C. (Connah 1981:76ff.;

table 3). Botanical evidence of cultivation, however, appears only in the ninth century A.D. (Connah 1976:341; I-2368), and the same crop, sorghum, has been identified at Niani in Guinea about the same time (A.D. 860, Kl-293). Both occurrences are well within the Iron Age, as are virtually all of the unmistakable cultigens from archaeological contexts south of Ethiopia and the Sahel (Shaw 1976:114).

On the Guinea Coast, cattle and ovicaprids must have been introduced from outside, and the same is probably true of the major cereals and a number of other crop types. Possibly this was part of a displacement process that began about 2000 B.C. and increasingly involved experimentation with local plants in the savanna and forest/savanna mosaic, where economically useful ones such as yams, rice, cowpeas, oil palms, and the like were added or substituted. The forest itself, in the south, may have added little except akee apples and kola nuts, a stimulant and trade item (Harlan et al. 1976:15).

Meantime, the best case for pre–Iron Age food production in East Africa is represented by the so-called Pastoral Neolithic, formerly the "Stone Bowl Culture." Dates in southern Kenya and Tanzania fall mostly between 1000 and 0 B.C., overlapping the very first part of the Early Iron Age (see fig. 2; tables 3 and 4). Aside from the characteristic stone bowls and platters, artifacts include a variety of ceramic types, percussion-flaked tools, and ground stone axes. Burials were commonly placed under stone cairns in the manner still followed by some pastoralists in the Horn, but multiple cremations have been found at Njoro River Cave and Keringet in the central Kenya Rift. Cattle of indeterminate type and ovicaprids occur in association with variable quantities of game remains, but even the larger settlements have thus far not produced definite evidence of cultivation.

One recent field survey in the central Kenya Rift (Bower et al. 1977) identified several distinct ceramic styles, which probably reflect both regional and temporal differences. Of these, Nderit (previously "Gumban A") and Kansyore seem to be the earliest. At one site, Salasun, surprisingly early occurrences of the two were reported: Kansyore-like ware at 4645 B.C. (GX-4469A) and Nderit-like ware at 5305 B.C. (GX-4422A). That such results may not be as unacceptable as first thought is indicated by some more recently published ones from the Lake Turkana area (Mgomezulu 1981:437), relating to sites with ceramics similar to Nderit ware as well as ovicaprids and cattle. These include site GaJi4 with dates as early as 1995 B.C. (SUA-637) and 2630 B.C. (GX-4642II); FwJj5 at 2050 B.C. (GX-4643); and GaJi2 at 2210 B.C. (SUA-634) and 2020 B.C. (P-2609). Other new dates from Serengeti Park in Tanzania (site HeJel) include one of 4234 B.C. (GX-5641), associated with both types of livestock. Prior to this, other Pastoral Neolithic sites

had been reported elsewhere in Turkana (Phillipson 1977b:71–73) and in the southern Afar Rift of Ethiopia (Clark 1976:86), which apparently date back to at least the second millennium B.C.

Judging by these results, there appear to have been movements of (Proto-Cushitic-speaking?) pastoralists throughout the Rift Valley by at least the second or third millennium B.C., and perhaps even earlier. (A recent critical survey of relevant dates, however, suggests that most or all of those prior to about 2000 B.C. are in error; Collett and Robertshaw 1983.) In spite of the fact that the highest dates (Salasun, Serengeti) we have at present are in the south, it seems likely on the basis of the animal domesticates that these new influences stemmed from Northeast Africa or, perhaps, the eastern Sudan.

Ethiopia presents a peculiar problem not only because of its location between the Sudan and southern Arabia but because of N. Vavilov's (1926, 1951) well-known citation of this area as an important center of domestication. His assumption that variability in certain crop types is to be viewed as a function of time depth, rather than one of environmental diversity and cultural practice, is now viewed critically (Harlan 1967:185ff.). Still, the present confinement of some crops to that country suggests that it may have been the scene of some significant steps in plant domestication, possibly including certain other cultigens of broader distribution and importance. The issue is confused somewhat by the addition at some point, probably in the pre-Axumite period, of plow agriculture and Near Eastern crops. The presence of barley and chickpeas, and less certainly of small stock, is attested, for example, at Lalibela Cave in northern Ethiopia (Dombrowski 1970) about 500 B.C. (Y-2434). Potentially earlier cultivation of finger millet farther east at Gobedra Cave (Phillipson 1977a) has been bracketed at 2,000–3000 B.C. within a radiocarbon series ranging from 8160 B.C. (P-2238) to 856 B.C. (BM-115). Beyond this slim evidence we have only hypotheses that variously invoke Sudanese, Arabian, or internal influences and remain to be tested.

The frequent association of pottery with polished stone axes or hoes in the "Leopoldian" of western Zaïre as well as in the "Uelian" and "Ubanguian" of northern Zaïre and the Central African Republic may be indicative of the spread of food-producing economies into Equatoria during the first or second millennium B.C. (Maret, van Noten, and Cahen 1977:493–95). However, since no firm evidence of cultivation has been forthcoming, any real evaluations of these must be held in abeyance.

Additional consideration of pre–Iron Age food production takes us to the southern tip of the continent, where there have been increasing discoveries along the Cape coast of pottery and sheep in "Strandloper" sites that clearly antedate the local Iron Age (Schweitzer and Scott

1973; Deacon, Brooker, and Wilson 1978; Schweitzer and Wilson 178; Sandelowsky, van Rooyen, and Vogel 1979). The earliest ceramics appear at Nelson Bay Cave (A.D. 20, GrN-5703) and Die Kelders (10 B.C., GX-1687). A date of 100 B.C. (SR-166) at Bonteberg is apparently suspect, as is one of A.D. 70 (Pta-1865) for both pottery and sheep at Byeneskranskop. However, both pottery and ovicaprids occur at Hawston around A.D. 50–90 (Pta-834, -835), and some sheep have been subsequently identified in the earliest ceramic levels of Nelson Bay Cave and at Die Kelders, although both cattle and more abundant sheep remains are found at the latter from about A.D. 350.

Sheep and pottery are reported as slightly later at Boomplaas Cave (about A.D. 250, UW-338) and Diepkloof (A.D. 460, GaK-4595). In Namibia, there seems to have been a parallel phenomenon. Pottery has been dated at Eros Shelter at A.D. 205 (GrN-5297), and less certainly at Apollo 11 Cave about A.D. 280 (Kn-I-870). Sheep occur at Mirabab Shelter as early as A.D. 400 (Pta-1535).

The source of neither the ceramics nor the animals has been determined. Early Iron Age influences via either Angola, Botswana, or Mozambique are usually cited, but the pottery is dissimilar to most Iron Age wares and the dates above are at least in part too early for the Iron Age even in Zambia and Zimbabwe (Inskeep 1976:36). One might dismiss the pottery as a local development, but the sheep must have come from an external source. Whatever the answer, these finds seem to complicate severely the long-accepted scenario of Bantu peoples arriving in the far south in recent centuries and introducing the first crops, livestock, metals, and ceramics as a single, integrated complex.

Some time ago, both pearl millet and finger millet were identified from deposits at Shongweni Cave near Durban (Davies 1975) dated as early as 1920 B.C. (Pta-823). More recent assessments, based on radiocarbon dating of the plant specimens themselves, suggest a more likely age of ninth to eleventh centuries A.D. (Hall and Vogel 1980:439; Pta-1951, -1948).

Early Iron Age

The beginnings of iron metallurgy in sub-Saharan Africa are rapidly coming into focus, although there are still important questions as to how it was established and in what exact contexts, for the technological, social, economic, and demographic patterns associated with its inception remain rather obscure. Nor is it clear whether the ritual behavior that so permeated metallurgical activities in recent times had its origins at this period.

The concept of an independent origin for African ironworking has been entertained from time to time but seems somewhat unlikely. One argument against it is chrono-

logical, for no African site thus far has produced evidence of ferrous metallurgy nearly as early as its initial appearance in western Asia and the Mediterranean. Furthermore, it was not preceded by lengthy experience with nonferrous metals as in Eurasia, and it would be difficult to attribute acquisition of appropriate pyrotechnic skills to ceramic experience since African pottery has traditionally been made in open wood fires rather than incharcoal-burning kilns (Shaw 1978:85).

Most treatments of the subject, therefore, have leaned toward external stimuli. Among the sources and routes of diffusion suggested have been (1) Nilotic: from Egypt via Meroe and then southward and westward across the Sudan; (2) south Arabian: via pre-Axumite Ethiopia along the "Sabaean Lane"; (3) Carthaginian: either southward across the Sahara or by sea to West Africa; or (4) Indian/Indonesian: by sea to the coast of eastern Africa. None at the moment is satisfactorily documented, nor of course need there have been only one such source.

Egypt's potential role is diminished by the fact that while iron may have been worked there, as opposed to being only imported, sporadically from about 1350 B.C. locally produced objects do not appear with any regularity until nearly seven hundred years later (Trigger 1969:34). Yet the earliest dates for ironworking in areas as far south—and as far apart—as Nigeria and Lake Victoria are nearly as high and certainly so if they are recalibrated to bring them in line with historical dates in Egypt (table 4). At the same time, available dates for smelting at Meroe in northern Sudan, whose own role in the presumed diffusion process has probably been overrated, include only one (514 B.C., Birm-97) that antedates the fourth century B.C.

It is possible that intrusions of Semitic-speaking peoples onto the northern plateau of Ethiopia from southern Arabia during the early to middle first millennium B.C. may have included the introduction of iron, which was already known in the latter area, but we have no archaeological evidence for this. Nor is there any indication how, or if, it might have spread farther south. Likewise, although Carthage was established by the Phoenicians in the eighth or ninth century B.C., it lay on the northernmost tip of Africa. To account for its potential role in the dissemination of ironworking to West Africa would require a traverse of the entire Sahara or long-distance sea voyages beyond Gibraltar, for neither of which is there much evidence. That copper metallurgy was being actively conducted in the western Sahara by the early second millennium B.C. (Sutton 1982:296, 313) may or may not have had anything to do with the beginnings of ferrous metallurgy, and a single date of 678 ± 120 B.C. (DaK-145) for iron smelting in southeastern Niger (Calvocoressi and David 1979:10) is interesting but hardly enough on which to build a firm case.

With respect to a possible influx of metallurgical techniques from southern Asia, we are still as much in the dark as we are regarding the various food products thought to have come from that same direction. Furthermore, the earliest East African furnaces were cylindrical-shaft types built of bricks and quite unlike Indian bowl furnaces, for example.

At present, then, no sufficiently clear patterning of dates or other evidence exists to warrant the selection of any single outside source or major diffusion route(s) related to the adoption of this complex technology in the sub-Saharan areas lying north of the equator. On the other hand, in the Lake Victoria region, as in Nigeria, there are indications of its possible establishment in the mid-first millennium B.C., while to the south, as far as the Transvaal, increasingly numerous radiocarbon dates suggest rapid introductions of metallurgy within a period of about A.D. 200–450 (table 4).

The earliest attested smelting in West Africa occurs on the Jos Plateau of Nigeria in the context of the Nok "culture." Associated are the oldest known examples of West African plastic art, consisting of many stylized but expressive terra-cotta heads and figures, mostly human (Shaw 1981). These pieces reflect a vigorous aesthetic tradition and modeling technique that can hardly represent an incipient phase of development. Their time range is usually judged to be from ca. 500 B.C. to A.D. 200, although there are now some thermoluminescence dates in the fifth and sixth century A.D. as well.

The first excavated Nok settlement was at Taruga, where evidence of ironworking consisted of iron objects, tuyeres, and several cylindrical-shaft furnaces. Published radiocarbon dates range from 591 to 280 B.C., and some provisional TL dates are said to fall within the expected time range, the earliest apparently being one of 555 B.C., although this was from the eponymous Nok site (Calvocoressi and David 1979:10).

West of the Nok area at Yelwa, another early art tradition was brought to light during salvage operations connected with construction of the Kainji Dam. These terra-cottas, while distinctive in their own right, bear some stylistic similarities to Nok. Dated from about the second century B.C. to A.D. 800 (Shaw 1978:96–98), they help close the chronological gap between Ife and the earlier art traditions, supporting to some degree the generic relationship suggested some years ago (Fagg and Willett 1962). At one of the Yelwa sites almost two hundred iron ornaments, axes, projectile points, and fishhooks also were recovered.

All other West African sites with evidence of metallurgy are dated in the second to fifth centuries A.D. or later. This, somewhat surprisingly, includes the Nigerian Sudan, where, for example, the one site (Daima) with a good Stone Age/Iron Age stratigraphic sequence may not have had iron before about A.D. 600. In Ghana, the earliest smelting furnace has been dated to about A.D. 180 (N-2140) (Posnansky and McIntosh 1976:165).

Although Ife probably reached its zenith in southern Nigeria sometime around the twelfth century A.D., there is one site, Orun Oba Ado, from which several dates in the sixth to tenth centuries (BM and M) have been obtained (Willett 1971). These may indicate a rather earlier origin and not one that was initially tied to the formation of the Mali trade empire farther north, as many had previously speculated. Similarly, the Igbo Ukwu finds in eastern Nigeria (Shaw 1970) seem to reflect another early aspect of regional or interregional trade, accumulation of wealth, and development of more complex societies in the latter part of the first millennium A.D. Although the original investigator (Shaw 1975) accepts the ninth-century dates, others (e.g., Posnansky 1973a) are inclined to reject them because they also predate the rise of Mali and its commercial influences.

In East, central, and South Africa, the standard and almost classic explanation of Iron Age origins has been framed in terms of a rapid and large-scale "explosion" of Proto-Bantu peoples from a single homeland, of disputed location, into and throughout the southern third of the continent (Oliver 1966; Posnansky 1968). This concept, which may indeed be at least partially correct, is a traditional migrationist hypothesis in which movements of a specific linguistic and physical group are seen as concomitant with the introduction of ceramics, iron, livestock, and cultivation. Such a convenient and orderly packaging of these diverse components, however, may be oversimplified, and some of the following questions have been raised: Were Bantu languages always associated with the spread of Early Iron Age cultural traits, or were other linguistic groups (Cushitic, Sudanic, Nilotic) responsible for introducing some of them? What was the degree of correlation between Proto-Bantu speakers and a particular racial population? Was southern, or even much of central, Africa solely the preserve of non-Negro (Khoisanoid) peoples before the Iron Age? Were Bantu-speaking groups already established in some of these areas before the Iron Age? Did ceramics, iron, cattle, ovicaprids, and cereal crops initially appear as components of a single complex, or were they introduced at different times and places and from different sources? Were the postulated movements of Proto-Bantu really rapid and large scale, or were they perhaps slower and involving only small groups such as clans or craft specialists?

All these queries have been posed without any consensus having been reached. Ultimately each aspect of the total constellation will have to be examined on its own merits. Perhaps it would be advisable to treat early Bantu dispersal and Early Iron Age origins as separate phenomena (Inskeep 1976:36), although many still regard their conjunction as an attractive possibility, if not a likelihood.

In any case, the critical time period seems to be the final centuries B.C. and the very first centuries A.D. Within that span, a number of regional ceramic traditions have been recognized, among which, to varying degrees, there is a sort of family resemblance (Huffman 1970; Soper 1971; Phillipson 1976a). Information on subsistence and settlement is often sketchy, but relatively small, semisedentary to sedentary villages practicing cultivation and husbandry of cattle or at least small stock seem typical. However, Early Iron Age sites with remains of game are more common than those with livestock (Phillipson 1977b:147), and actual remains of domesticated plants are not very numerous. Iron objects or other indications of metal use are often encountered, although it is not always possible to prove they appeared simultaneously with ceramics and domestication. Copper came into use occasionally at this time, mainly in the area between southern Zaïre and the Transvaal. The earliest radiocarbon dates associated with copper working are from Kanshansi in the Zambian Copperbelt (Bisson 1974): A.D. 400 (N-1286), 630 (N-1283), 760 (N-1284). Gold attained more importance later, primarily in Zimbabwe and its immediate environs. Truly interregional trade was mostly a later development, although there is some spotty evidence for it, in the form of glass beads or marine shells, during the later part of the Early Iron Age.

In East Africa, three primary and regionally distinct ceramic traditions have been recognized: Urewe (formerly "Dimple-base Ware"), Kwale, and Lelesu, but these display sufficient stylistic similarity to suggest a common origin. Urewe sites, first recognized in the Central Nyanza District of western Kenya (Leakey, Owen, and Leakey 1948), are now known throughout the Interlacustrine area from Uganda to Ruanda. Most dated occurrences fall in the first three or four centuries A.D., but substantially earlier horizons, if the radiocarbon dates are valid, have been revealed in the Buhaya region of western Tanzania where Peter Schmidt has excavated smelting and forging sites along Lake Victoria. At one of these, Kataruka, radiocarbon results include some from the late seventh to mid-fifth centuries B.C. as well as others in the first two centuries A.D. (Schmidt 1975; table 4). Van Noten (1981a) also reports a similar site at Rurembo, Ruanda, at 230 B.C. Even if the highest dates are somewhat in error, perhaps because the smelters were utilizing old wood for charcoal manufacture (Schmidt, pers. comm.), the Urewe tradition is still likely to rank as the earliest Iron Age in eastern or southern Africa. In Buhaya as in Ruanda, iron was smelted in brick-built furnaces, and in the former area a remarkably high-grade steel was

being produced no later than the first century or so A.D. (Schmidt and Avery 1978).

The Kwale sites of southeastern Kenya and northeastern Tanzania (Soper 1967a, 1967b) fall in about the same period as the later Urewe dates (A.D. 0–300) and also have yielded evidence of ironworking. Somewhat similar pottery has been found in the Kenya Eastern Highlands, especially at Gatung'ang'a (Siiriänen 1971), although there it seems to be nearly a millennium later. Comparably late Urewe-type ware has also been described in southern Uganda (Posnansky 1973b), suggesting that some of these Early Iron Age ceramic styles were characterized by great longevity. The same is true of certain central and southern African pottery traditions like those at Kalambo Falls in Zambia, Ziwa/Gokomere in Zimbabwe, and Phalaborwa in eastern Transvaal, for which dates also range over a period of seven hundred to a thousand years.

The third regional variant, Lelesu, is the least well defined and, at this point, is not securely dated. It occurs across northern Tanzania, bridging the Urewe and Kwale areas. Not much is known of the Early Iron Age in the rest of Tanzania except for the Uvinza region near Lake Tanganyika, where a distinctive mid-first millennium pottery has been identified at old saltworks (Sutton and Roberts 1968). This geographical gap is unfortunate in that it makes it difficult to ascertain more clearly the possible links between the East and south-central African materials.

Brief mention should be made of the large cemeteries at Sanga and Katoto in southern Zaïre (Nenquin 1963; Maret 1977), since some of the pottery in these richly equipped graves has been seen to correlate with that of Urewe. However, while there may be some relationships, the available radiocarbon dates go back no further than the eighth to tenth centuries (Hv-6609, 6611, 6619), and most are later still. The location of these sites on the upper Lualaba coincides with that of the Proto-Bantu "homeland" as proposed by M. Guthrie (1962), just as the Nok area falls within Greenberg's (1972) postulated center of Bantu origin far to the northwest.

At the extreme southern end of Lake Tanganyika, Early Iron Age occupation at Kalambo Falls began about A.D. 345 and continued with little change, at least in ceramic styles, for six hundred to a thousand years (Clark 1974:57). The pottery resembles that of Uvinza, implying connections farther north. In the Copperbelt of Zambia, just to the southwest, the Chondwe Early Iron Age sites fall near the middle to late part of the first millennium A.D. (Phillipson 1977b:132). Similar pottery, called Kapwirimbwe ware, appears in settlements with traces of extensive ironworking around the present capital, Lusaka, from about the fifth century (Phillipson 1968).

Extensive work of D. W. Phillipson and J. O. Vogel in the Southern Province led to recognition of the so-called Dambwa tradition, which was established in the Victoria Falls area and upstream along the Zambezi by the sixth to seventh centuries. Settlements are typically small and apparently were based on a combination of hunting, cultivation, cattle keeping, and herding of small stock. Dambwa pottery is most similar to certain Zimbabwian wares, and an influx of settlement from that direction is thought probable (Phillipson 1977b:125).

Still earlier Iron Age occupation of this area, however, is suggested by sporadic finds of channel-decorated pottery similar to that of Kalambo Falls (Clark and Fagan 1965), with dates in the first or second century A.D. and even earlier (table 4). The presence of metal is indicated only by a few pieces of bog iron at Machili, clearly transported by human agency but perhaps not for actual ironworking.

The Kalundu sites just north of the Zambezi on the Batoka Plateau represent another Early Iron Age group, whose large and more permanent-looking habitation areas belong to about the fifth to ninth centuries A.D. (Fagan 1967; Phillipson 1977b:136–37). Cowries from Kalundu itself reflect intermittent and probably indirect contact with the Indian Ocean coast. Iron in the same site was relatively scarce, but small amounts of copper also were found and hunting accounted for well over half the faunal remains.

In Malawi, earlier investigations (Robinson 1970, 1973) had suggested that Early Iron Age occupation began in about the third century A.D., and this has been confirmed by additional dates (Mgomezulu 1981:449). So-called Mwabulambo ware from the north resembles that of Kalambo, while Nkope ware in the south is stylistically closer to the Kwale ceramics of East Africa.

In Zimbabwe, Huffman (1971) outlined a three-phase development of the Early Iron Age (but see also Summers 1970; Phillipson 1977b:114ff.). Whereas Huffman classifies it all as "Stamped Ware," Phillipson prefers to call it "Gokomere/Ziwa" after the two best-known regional variants. Dates range from the late second century to around A.D. 800–1000. The Zhizo variant (formerly "Leopard's Kopje I") in the Matopos area of southwestern Zimbabwe seems to be late first millennium. This, together with archaeological evidence of recent LSA survivals, may indicate that herders and farmers were quite late in occupying this part of the country.

During the later part of the Zimbabwian Early Iron Age, mining and smelting of copper and gold began, as did that of copper in Zambia. Trade may have begun to increase somewhat, as attested by glass beads, and some simple stone structures or terracing and more defensive siting of settlements are in evidence. The beginnings of the major and more complex stone architecture (e.g., Great Zimbabwe, Khami, Inyanga), however, lie no further back than the tenth to twelfth centuries, or less.

In South Africa, the earliest Iron Age settlements are, expectedly, in the north. At Silver Leaves in the northeastern Transvaal, Kwale-like pottery occurs in conjunction with iron slag and *Pennisetum* millet about A.D. 250–330 (Klapwijk 1974), and the Klein Afrika site, with Gokomere-like ware (Prinsloo 1974), is of comparable age (A.D. 330). West of Pretoria, the Broederstroom site (Mason 1973) includes hut floors, furnaces, and remains of sheep, goats, and cattle. There are also Indian Ocean shells and a single copper artifact, the latter a little surprising since radiocarbon dates are A.D. 430–90. The settlement is remarkable for its size of over ten acres. The pottery is said to be distinct from that at Silver Leaves, with closer affinities to Malawian ware.

Perhaps the most unusual find in this area has been at Sterkspruit in the Lydenburg area, where several terracotta heads, two of them hood masks, were recovered with pottery similar to that of Broederstroom (Inskeep and Maggs 1975). These are unique in southern Africa and, indeed, in all of Bantu Africa. Radiocarbon determinations place them in the fifth to sixth centuries.

Other very early Iron Age dates have recently been obtained from a pair of sites on the east coast near the Tugela River mouth, Enkwazini and Mzonjani. Possibly related to Silver Leaves, these fall in about the late third to early fifth centuries A.D. Dates previously obtained from Castle Cavern in Swaziland show that ironworking was established there no later than 400–500 A.D. And although most of the material is later Iron Age, fairly extensive iron and copper working in the Phalaborwa district of eastern Transvaal (van der Merwe and Scully 1971) may extend back to the eighth century (A.D. 770, Y-1636).

As is apparent from this brief chronological sketch, there is no very clear progression of Early Iron Age dates such as might imply a slow and regular north-to-south diffusion of these new technologies and economies. Apart from the earliest Urewe dates, one gets the impression of quite rapid transmission of new ideas over much of the area between Lake Victoria and the Transvaal, during a period possibly as brief as a couple of centuries.

Epilogue

Although the Later Iron Age is beyond the scope of this survey, one can say that there were both continuities and differences with the earlier period. In a number of areas, from about A.D. 1000 on, it was clearly a time of significant cultural change: state formation or at least some semblance of centralized political authority at the regional or tribal level; growth of interregional trade; extended metallurgical technology; more complete dependence on produced food and, in some places, improved agricultural methods, including water control; and, probably, the establishment of some of the more complex belief systems that prevailed at the time of contact. For several regions it was also a time of tribal movements, shifting political allegiances, and organized warfare. If sometimes only indirectly, external influences were stronger, especially via the Islamic presence to the north and along the Indian Ocean. Repercussions from these spheres, as later from European ones, no doubt stimulated alterations of lifeways even for some peoples quite far from the actual contact zones, a result particularly of growing commerce in gold, ivory, and slaves, all of which had an impact way beyond the purely economic level.

This later part of the Iron Age brings us close to the time of European colonialism and exploration and as such is essentially protohistoric in nature, permitting the use of nonarchaeological data for reconstruction. Ethnographic and documentary evidence, together with oral traditions and historical linguistics, even when these are incompletely illustrative, allow us to look backward in time with more facility and confidence. Along the Guinea Coast, many small states and indigenous urban centers arose during this period, epitomized by Ife, Oyo, and Benin in southern Nigeria; Dahomey (a country recently, and somewhat confusingly, renamed Benin); and the pre-Ashanti Akan kingdoms of Ghana. Unfortunately, the roots of these are not yet archaeologically well known, partly because so much of the information is based on graves, shrines, and art works. Our knowledge is also scant regarding the development of the central African savanna kingdoms and those of the Interlacustrine region of East Africa. Southward, Great Zimbabwe was apparently the religious and administrative center of a powerful chieftaincy or state that owed at least some of its prosperity in the fifteenth and sixteenth centuries to trade relations with the Arab coast, and it may well not have been an isolated phenomenon.

In summary, according to most contemporary scholarly interpretations, the seeds of precolonial political integration, military power, technological advance, and organized trade in East, West, central, and southern Africa may have been locally sown but were substantially nourished by external stimuli. On the other hand, the intimations of earlier cultural complexity in the Nok area, in eastern Nigeria, in Buhaya, in the Sanga area, and perhaps elsewhere—as archaeological research progresses—may yet lead to another paradigm in which more weight is accorded autochthonous change and development that drew largely on indigenous resources.

Addendum

Since the manuscript for this chapter was submitted, quite a number of new dates have been published. Most, however, do not significantly alter the overall chronological picture as presented in the preceding pages, but rather serve to amplify or extend it. The few results discussed below are mainly ones that relate to major technological or economic changes within the portion of the continent under review. All dates are given in radiocarbon years B.C., A.D., or B.P.

With regard to the "early Later Stone Age," new dates are available for Nasera Rock in Tanzania, where two levels displaying a LSA technology but no microliths ("Naseran Industry") are placed at about 22,500 B.P., while one with microliths is about a thousand years later: 19,750 ± 600 B.C. (ISGS-445A) and 19,650 ± 400 B.C. (ISGS-445B) (Robertshaw 1984). Overlying this is an Eburran ("Capsian") microlithic industry with dates of 20,510 ± 500 B.C. (ISGS-449) and 16,330 ± 645 B.C. (GX-6618A). At Mwambacimo, on the southern edge of the Zambian Copperbelt, are additional dates for the Nachikufan I industry that agree quite well with those previously reported, although covering a slightly broader time range: 16,130 ± 180 B.C. (Pta-2453), 10,950 ± 110 B.C. (N-3434), 10,050 ± 90 B.C. (N-3435), and 7,880 ± 90 B.C. (Pta-2454) (Musonda 1984).

Reexcavation of the K6 Rockshelter in Ghana has provided four new dates (McIntosh 1986) that generally confirm those obtained earlier for the Kintampo LSA (or "Neolithic"): 1750 ± 90 B.C. (UCR-1691), 1655 ± 100 B.C. (UCR-1693), 1600 ± 127 B.C. (UCR-1692), and 1545 ± 100 B.C. (UCR-1690). All samples consisted of oil-palm seed husks. The transition represented seems to be associated with a change from high-forest fauna to types of wild animals (and goats) reflecting savanna woodland or cleared areas. Farther north at Daboya, on the White Volta in northern Ghana, P. Shinnie and F. Kense obtained another series of dates for Kintampo materials. Preliminary reports suggest these may be even earlier, although it appears there are some problems still to be resolved (McIntosh 1986:423). Daboya also seems to be the earliest site in Ghana with definite evidence of iron use, at 60 ± 140 B.C. (GX-6133) (Sutton 1982).

A recent review of pre–Iron Age herders in South Africa lists seventy-seven dates (from thirty-six sites in the Cape and Namibia) associated with sheep and/or pottery (Klein 1986; fig. 2). Twenty-four of the samples relate to ceramics only, although in some instances the faunal data may be too inadequate to determine whether livestock were also present. Strikingly, the only reliable dates from the northern Cape are around 1100–1200 B.P., in spite of the fact that sheep, at least, must have been introduced from that general direction. Nonetheless, it seems safe to assume that sheep and pottery were present in the southern and western Cape at or just after 2000 B.P. Of potential interest in this regard is a date in the late first millennium B.C. (2140 ± 60 B.P., Pta-3072) from Bambata Cave in southeastern Zimbabwe in a level containing Early Iron Age pottery, an LSA assemblage, and probable sheep remains (Walker 1983).

With respect to the inception of metallurgy, the following results seem to be of particular interest.

Recent investigations of occupation mounds in the southern Sudan have produced, at one site, a large group of iron objects dated at 810 ± 70 B.C.—two or three centuries prior to the earliest known ironworking at Meroe (Robertshaw 1984). Also relevant to this transition in eastern Africa are a number of early dates from Burundi and Ruanda (de Maret 1985), which are within the Urewe Early Iron Age area. All are associated with EIA pottery, and two samples were from furnaces. In Burundi, one of the latter, at Mirama III, was dated at 530 ± 85 B.C. (Hv-11142). The remaining Burundi dates are Muguba V: 1210 ± 45 B.C. (Hv-11141); Rwi-

yange: 1230 ± 145 B.C. (Hv-11144) and 905 ± 285 B.C. (Hv-12130); and Mubuga X: 10 ± 115 B.C. (Hv-12128). In Ruanda, charcoal from a slag furnace at Gasiza was dated at 685 ± 95 B.C. (Hv-11143), while another sample, associated with EIA ware at Kabacusi, was almost two hundred years earlier (865 ± 165 B.C., Hv-12123). Additional dates in the early first millennium A.D. also have been reported.

Also of some import is a dated sample from Lubumbashi in southernmost Zaïre that was associated with EIA pottery and iron (A.D. 385 ± 55, Hv-10591) (de Maret 1982). One of the sherds was covered on one side with copper slag. This appears to confirm the evidence for copper smelting on the Zambian side of the Copperbelt in the early fifth century. Together, these sites represent the earliest clear indication of copper use south of the equator.

In Nigeria, the controversy over the age of the Igbo Ukwu finds seems not to have been resolved by the release of three new dates in the tenth, eleventh, and thirteenth centuries A.D. (McIntosh 1986). The question of possible pre-Arab trade that might relate to acceptance of Shaw's four ninth-century dates remains an open one.

Part Four

Continental Europe and the British Isles

Seventeen

The Archaeological Chronology of Northwestern Europe

Homer L. Thomas, Emeritus, University of Missouri
Ralph M. Rowlett, University of Missouri, Columbia

Outline

The Early Neolithic Cultures
The Western Neolithic Cultures

The Mature Neolithic Cultures
The Chalcolithic Cultures

The large number of archaeological excavations in France and the British Isles during the last two decades has drastically revised the chronology of northwestern Europe between the end of the Mesolithic and the beginning of the Bronze Age (see fig. 1). Although this field activity has been accompanied by the construction of numerous regional or diachronically limited chronologies, except in the most general terms there have been few attempts to project a chronology for the whole northwestern European area. This trend in the building of archaeological chronology, or rather chronologies, for the diverse regions of northwestern Europe has resulted in the neglect or rejection of the diffusion process in explaining culture change (Renfrew 1973). Culture change, which in the past described culture periods and also often explained their character and relationships, is now interpreted in terms of systemic models of culture, frequently local or at best regional in scale. Explanation in terms of culture continuity has led to the increasing "particularization" in the chronology of cultural development in northwestern Europe (Clarke 1968).

However, the seemingly diverse and highly regionalized cultures of northwest Europe during Neolithic and Chalcolithic times still display many common characteristics. While some of these may well be due to parallel development arising from a common heritage extending back through the Mesolithic into the Palaeolithic, others are so distinctive that they demand an explanation of culture relationships within, and in some cases beyond, northwest Europe. Needless to say, any chronological study of the area must depend on regional surveys of the

Text submitted September 1984
Text revised April 1986

thousands of finds that have accumulated in the course of the past 150 years. Increasingly, recent surveys such as the monumental reviews of French archaeological work edited by Jean Guilaine (1976) and of British prehistory edited by Colin Renfrew (1974) demand emphasis. For Switzerland, there is the somewhat older but excellent survey published by the Schweizerische Gesellschaft für Ur- und Frühgeschichte and edited by R. Wyss (1969). These surveys, together with reports of the excavation of major sites and the vast numbers of radiocarbon dates now available for northwestern Europe brought together in the *Bulletin de la Société préhistorique française* (Delibrias and Evin 1975; Delibrias, Evin, and Thommeret 1982), and the recent surveys for France (Guilaine 1976:871–87) and Britain (Renfrew 1974:128–36, 164, and 223–25), make possible the projection of a tentative archaeological chronology for northwestern Europe.

The Early Neolithic Cultures

The earliest neolithic of northwestern Europe is known from two cultures, one with a distinctive pottery decorated with cardium-shell impressions found in the Mediterranean area of southern France, and the other with a pottery usually named for its vessels covered by an incised curvilinear-band decoration, linear *Bandkeramik,* which is found scattered across northern France. These two cultures, which are usually designated as the Cardial Ware and linear *Bandkeramik* cultures, developed during the time of the Atlantic climate characterized by moist-warm conditions, which had induced a forested environment. Both occurred in lands occupied by Mesolithic peoples, whose cultures were destined to survive well into Neolithic times. In the British Isles, Mesolithic culture persisted much later than on the Continent because here the beginning of the Neolithic cannot be placed much before a mature Neolithic appeared in France and the southern Low Countries.

The Cardial Ware culture is known from a relatively large number of sites located in the regions of Languedoc and Provence in southern France, not only in the immediate coastal lands but also in upland areas of the interior. At sites such as the Abri Chateauneuf-lès-Martiques (Bouches-du-Rhône) (Escalon de Fonton 1976) and the Grotte d'Unang (Vaucluse) (Paccard 1979), it occurs immediately above Mesolithic and below Chassey occupations, thus establishing its relative chronology. Among the numerous radiocarbon dates available for Cardial Ware sites, calibrated dates such as 4750 ± 100/5745–5365 B.C. (Gif-2990) and 3740 ± 130/4730–4415 B.C. (Gif-2756) for layers 47 and 40 at La Baume Fontbregoua (Var) place this culture in the last half of the sixth and first half of the fifth millennium B.C. Radiocarbon dates available for the succeeding Chassey culture support placing the Cardial Ware culture before the middle of the fifth millennium B.C. While the two radiocarbon dates from Cap Ragnon and Île de Riou in the Bouches-du-Rhône are high for Cardial, the plainware found in level C20 at Camprafaud (Hérault), dated 5950 ± 150 (Gif-3030), leads to speculation about the existence of a Pre-Cardial culture comparable to the Earlier Neolithic of Iberia (Gilman, this vol., chap. 13; Guilaine 1980). Given the long duration of the Cardial and Epi-Cardial Ware culture, one can regard as plausible preliminary attempts to phase its development at sites such as Grotte IV at Saint-Pierre-de-la Fage (Hérault) (Arnal 1977) (see table 1).

Dating the beginning of the Cardial Ware culture to sometime in the middle and last half of the sixth millennium places it at the time when similar cultures appear along the Mediterranean coasts of Spain, Italy, Yugoslavia, and Greece. However, the significance of these correlations for problems concerning the origin and development of the Cardial Ware culture of southern France falls outside the scope of this chapter on the archaeological successions of northwestern Europe (Camps 1971; see fig. 3).

Not long after the Cardial Ware culture arose in southern France, the Linear *Bandkeramik* culture developed in central Europe (see Wells, this vol., chap. 19; Ehrich and Bankoff, this vol., chap. 21). It is possible that this early Linear *Bandkeramik* reached easternmost France, where it is known from the excavations at Reichstett (Bas-Rhin) (Thévenin et al. 1977), at about the same time it reached the southern Netherlands. In any event the subsequent westward movement of this culture into northern France can hardly date before its settlements in Dutch Limburg (see Thomas and E. Rowlett, this vol., chap. 18). Typological comparisons suggest that it was a mature culture

of the Middle Rhine, and especially one associated with the Plaidt group at the confluence of the Rhine and Moselle, that spread westward into northern France. Unfortunately, this western Linear *Bandkeramik* cannot be fixed stratigraphically in relation to either the preceding Mesolithic or the subsequent Neolithic (Bailloud 1979:39–41). Calibrated radiocarbon dates such as those ranging from 4630 ± 400/5675–5260 B.C. (Ly-1828) to 3780 ± 170/4920–4440 B.C. (Ly-2552) for Cuiry-les-Chaudardes, Les Fontainettes (Aisne), and of 3650 ± 120/4555–4400 B.C. (Gif-3354) for Chichery (Yonne) place this culture in the late sixth and early fifth millennia. These calibrated dates, together with others from northern France (see table 1), are in agreement with those for Linear *Bandkeramik* sites of the French Rhineland, which in turn agree with those farther east (see Wells, chap. 19; Ehrich and Bankoff, chap. 21) in placing this culture between 5300/5200 and 4500 B.C. (see fig. 4).

During the time of the Cardial culture, smaller Neolithic groups can be detected in the south of France. In the eastern Pyrenees, there was the Montobolo group, whose plainware has led some to link it with the Plain Ware culture of Iberia (Gilman, chap. 13), a connection justified by a calibrated radiocarbon date for Montobolo. On the other hand, it is difficult to trace the source of the Neolithic component of the Pyrenean group. In the west of France, there are Neolithic sites in the Charente-Maritime and Vendée, whose impressed wares are thought to have been inspired from southern France, but others point to Iberian centers. Calibrated radiocarbon dates justify placing the Pyrenean and western French groups in this period. Beyond the south of France, except for the still poorly defined group in the west, the lands of central, northwest, northern, and eastern France were still in the hands of Mesolithic groups, despite the penetration of Linear *Bandkeramik* groups across northern France. While there are few sites with radiocarbon dates in France, except for the famous Mesolithic kitchen midden at La Torche in Brittany (4020 ± 80/5085–4730; GrN-2201) (Vogel and Waterbolk 1963:176), there are comparable ones for the late Tardenoisian Birsmatten-Basishöhle (Canton Bern) in Switzerland (Guyan 1953; Gfeller, Oeschger, and Schwarz 1961) and late Tardenoisian Maarheeze in the Netherlands (Vogel and Waterbolk 1963).

Beyond the English Channel, new interpretations of the development of the Mesolithic postulate a similar late continuation of the Mesolithic into the beginning stages of the Neolithic. Calibrated radiocarbon dates for the earliest Neolithic of the British Isles (see table 1) indicate that the Mesolithic survived well into the fifth millennium in England and perhaps even later in Scotland and central and southern Ireland (see fig. 2).

The Western Neolithic Cultures

Traditionally the Neolithic in northwestern Europe began with the Windmill Hill (England), Chassey (France), and Cortaillod (Switzerland) cultures. Today, the discovery of the earlier Cardial and Linear *Bandkeramik* cultures, together with increasing evidence for regional successions, has not only robbed them of their traditional roles, but has also forced a drastic revision of our concept of their relative chronological status. It is now clear that all three belong to the maturing of the early Neolithic and represent decidedly regional aspects of its development.

The Chassean culture must be traced separately in southern and northern France. The southern Chassey centered in Provence and Languedoc, but also extended westward as far as Saint-Michel-du-Touch (Haute-Garonne) and northward through Ardèche into southern Burgundy and Franche Comté (Phillips 1982). Successions at sites such as the Grotte de Camprafaud (Hérault) (Rodriguez 1976), La Baume Fontbrégoua (Var) (Courtin 1973), and Escanin 2, Les Baux (Bouches-du-Rhône) (Montjardin 1966) indicate that it was separated from the time of Cardial Ware culture by a "transitional" period designated as Epi-Cardial or Early Chassey and Middle Neolithic. A calibrated date of 3740 ± 130/4730–4415 B.C. (Gif-2756) for level 40 at La Baume Fontbrégoua indicates that an "Early to Middle Neolithic" with a late Cardial industry must be placed in the first half of the fifth millennium B.C., a dating supported by calibrated dates from other sites (see table 1). A number of calibrated radiocarbon dates such as the date 3660 ± 130/4570–4375 B.C. (Gif-2755) for level 33 at La Baume Fontbrégoua and 3590 ± 100/4540–4345 B.C. (MC-498) for layer C11 at Font-Juvénal (Aude) place the early southern Chassey in the last half of the fifth millennium.

Its connections with cultures in the Italian peninsula further justify this dating of the southern Chassey culture. Although more recent archaeological work casts doubt on the phasing of Chassey development projected by J. Arnal and C. Burnez (1958), they were probably right in connecting Chassey with Arene Candide levels 24–14 on the basis of square-mouthed vessels, despite Bernabò Brea's (1946:60–130, 1956:246–47) contention that only the later Lagozza levels 13–9 paralleled the Chassey. The correlation of Chassey with the Chiozza-Matera horizon in Italy based on the Arene Candide 24–14 connections is further supported by incised decoration in the Matera style in Chassey contexts such as that of La Perte du Cros (Galan 1967:42–44; see fig. 3).

During the last twenty years, archaeological discoveries in northern and eastern France demonstrate that the Linear *Bandkeramik* culture developed into the distinctive Cerny variant. Although there is little stratigraphy in the north, the excavations at Montagne de Lumbres (Pas-de-Calais) showed that traces of northern Chassey seem to postdate a Cerny occupation. In the Cerny sites, the flint industry indicates contact with an older Mesolithic population, but more important for chronology are the techniques of pottery decoration, which include the use of punches suggestive of Rössen practice and of buttons showing southern Chassey influence (Bailloud 1979:61–73). Although in the past radiocarbon dates for the Cerny group have seemed either too high or too low, two from the Cerny occupation at Sablins near Étaples (Pas-de-Calais), 3710 ± 120/4570–5520 B.C. (Gif-3701) and 3740 ± 120/4580–4425 B.C. (Gif-4024), along with other recent radiocarbon dates (see table 1) make it contemporary not only with southern Chassey, but also with Rössen of eastern France (Hurtrelle and Piningre 1978).

The westward movement of Rössen into Lorraine and Franche Comté, together with its penetration into northern Switzerland and the spread of its influence into northern France, provides a check on culture correlations during the last half of the fifth millennium B.C. (Raquin, Sainty, and Thévenin 1972). The archaeological connections of pottery from levels Xb and IX of the Grotte de la Baume at Gonvillars (Haute-Saône), which is strategically located in the Belfort Gap, provides a cross check supported by a calibrated date of 3430 ± 250/4435–3900 B.C. (Gif-468) for level Xb. Although derived from late Linear *Bandkeramik*, the pottery forms are similar to those of the Cerny group of the Paris Basin and the Rössen of Wauwil type, which also occurs in the Egolzwil culture of Switzerland (Pétrequin 1970 1974). The Egolzwil culture, which is now firmly established as preceding the Cortaillod, is present at settlements such as Egolzwil III (Vogt 1951:193–215). Its relative chronology is fixed by pottery imports and copies from the Rössen which had penetrated northern Switzerland. Given the Rössen connections of Egolzwil and Cerny and the connections of Gonvillars, together with the fact that Linear *Bandkeramik* was followed by Cerny in northern France and by Rössen in western Germany (see Wells, chap. 19), there is a basis for establishing the chronology of the Middle Neolithic in northern France, northern Switzerland, and western central Europe. These correlations are also supported by radiocarbon dates. The radiocarbon measurements for material from Egolzwil III (K-115, 116, 118, and 121) give an average date of 2940 ± 90/3865–3550 B.C. (Tauber 1960:6–7). Today these seem low in view of those from Cerny sites and others from Rössen sites (see Thomas and E. Rowlett, chap. 18), as well as from Cortaillod, the successor of the Egolzwil (see Wells, chap. 19), all pointing to the second half of the fifth millennium B.C. This dating would fit with placing the Linear *Bandkeramik* culture in the later sixth and first half of the fifth millennium B.C. It must be noted that cultures of the Rhine Basin, which belong to central Europe, have been considered only when this area is important for establishing chronological horizons in northwestern Europe (see fig. 4).

In western France, the pottery occurring in early Neolithic contexts found from the Garonne northward into Brittany is now thought to date to the time of the Cerny Ware (L'Helgouach 1971, 1976). In Brittany this pottery, which is designated as Carn Ware, has been found in unmixed context only in the central tomb of Île Carn near Ploudalmézeau (Finistère). It has a calibrated date of 3390 ± 250/4425–3885 B.C. (Gif-414).

The related passage graves of Barnenez (Finistère), which are without datable associated finds, belonged to the same period, to judge from a series of calibrated radiocarbon dates ranging from 3800 ± 150/4760–4430 B.C. (Gif-1309) to 3150 ± 140/3990–3770 B.C. (Gif-1116). Calibrated radiocarbon dates ranging from 4030 ± 150/5195–4710 B.C. (Gsy-47B) to 2650 ± 200/3655–3035 B.C. (Gsy-47A) suggest that the settlement at Le Curnic (Finistère) could have been occupied at this time. Here, as at so many other sites, its probable date is suggested by two that range between 3560 ± 250/4555–4100 B.C. (Gif-345) and 3390 ± 60/4375–3920 B.C. (GrN-1966). These are close to the calibrated date of 3245 ± 300/4350–3785 (Gsy-64) for twig charcoal from the passage grave of Île Bono in the Sept-Îles archipelago (Côte-du-Nord) (see table 1). Similar megalithic tombs and a related pottery, the Cous ware, occur to the south of Brittany along the Atlantic coast of France. Calibrated radiocarbon dates of 3850 ± 230/4975–4435 B.C. (Ly-966) and 3530 ± 170/4455–4105 B.C. (Ly-1699) for tumuli E and F respectively at Bougon (Deux-Sèvres) belong to the same time as those of Brittany (see table 1). By and large, these radiocarbon measurements and their calibrations indicate that the Early Neolithic not only of Brittany (Primary Armorican Neolithic) but also of the Atlantic coast of western France equates chronologically with the Cerny culture of northern France (see fig. 4).

The beginning of the Neolithic in the British Isles is now represented by a few sites found in eastern England and northeast Ireland. These, which are assigned to the Early Neolithic by H. Case (1976:9), must mark the rise of an agrarian way of life in a land still dominated by a late Mesolithic people. Calibrated radiocarbon dates from Bromme Heath (Norfolk), which range from 3474 ± 117/4420–4090 B.C. (BM-679) to 2217 ± 78/2930–2640 B.C. (BM-755), are low (Wainwright 1972). However much higher dates are reported for samples from an occupation at Ballynagilly (Co. Tyrone) in Northern Ireland, which range from 3795 ± 90/4735–4530 B.C. (UB-305) to 2960 ± 90/3870–3640 B.C. (UB-301) (see table 1) (ApSimon 1971). The dates reported from Ballynagilly fall within limits suggesting that this occupation belongs to the second half of the fifth millennium. Thus the beginning of the Neolithic in the British Isles would go back to the time of the Cerny of northern France, the penetration of the Rössen into eastern France, and the early southern Chassey of southern France (figs. 2, 4). Unfortunately, the archaeological evidence is insufficient to connect developments with those of the Continent.

The Mature Neolithic Cultures

In northwest Europe, the Neolithic achieved maturity during the fourth millennium according to calibrated radiocarbon dates or during the late fourth and early third on the basis of uncalibrated ones. Although a widespread regional differentiation of cultures characterized this maturity, much of their "particularism" was probably due to internal development, which was influenced in part by their adaptation to changing environmental conditions during the transition from the Atlantic to the Sub-Boreal climate. In northern France and many parts of the British Isles the thinning out of forests, attributed just as much to human activity as to climatic change, may explain the widespread differentiation of culture (Evans 1975:142–47). In southern and southwestern France, a very diverse topography may be equally important in explaining the development of local culture groups. Countering this "particularism" was the rise of a megalithic mortuary architecture along the Mediterranean and Atlantic coasts of France and the Atlantic coastal fringes of the British Isles.

In southern France, the southern Chassey culture continued through much of the fourth millennium (see fig. 3). Many archaeologists have currently abandoned attempts to recognize phases of the long development of the southern Chassey culture from the stratigraphic evidence of sites such as Roucadour (Lot) and La Madeleine (Hérault) and from typology (Arnal and Burnez 1958:14–36). It is clear, however, that earlier sites equate in time with Arene Candide 24–14 and the Chiozza-Matera horizon of the Italian peninsula. Radiocarbon dates, together with archaeological connections consisting of similar plain pottery and *flûte-de-Pan* handles, suggest that the sites of the later southern Chassey may also date to the early Lagozza horizon, now dated to the first half of the fourth millennium B.C. (see Brown, this vol., chap. 12). Calibrated radiocarbon dates of 3150 ± 130/3990–3770 B.C. (Gif-1485) for the late southern Chassey occupation of Grotte de Camprafaud (Hérault), and of 2910 ± 90/3800–3520 B.C. (MC-495) for layer 7a of Font-Juvénal (Aude) support this correlation (see table 1).

During the last half of the fourth millennium, the southern Chassey culture gave way to a group of distinct local cultures (see fig. 3). The Chassey tradition persisted in what might be called Epi-Chassey in the Basses-Alpes, where sites such as the Abri II de Saint Mitre have occupations dated to the last half of the fourth millennium. At Saint Mitre, the Chassean occupation of layer 3, which has a calibrated date of 2400 ± 150/3355–2875 B.C. (MC-201) has an arrowhead of Lagozza type, perhaps datable to the late Lagozza horizon. While this time is poorly defined in Provence, the Ferrières culture, which is characterized by a distinctive incised pottery, took the place of the Chassey in eastern Languedoc. The calibrated date of 2400 ± 130/3355–2875 B.C. (Gif-1360) for an occupation at the Grotte des Pins at Blandas (Gard) indicates that Ferrières belongs to the later fourth millennium. In western Languedoc there was the Saint Ponien group, which has calibrated dates of 2400 ± 140/3355–2875 B.C. (Gif-1157) for level 10 at Camprafaud (Hérault) (Rodriguez 1970) and 2620 ± 300/3645–3015 B.C. (Gif-1541) for hearth 22 at Saint-Etienne de Gourgas (Hérault), placing it in the same period as the Ferrières culture (see table 1) (Guilaine and Roudil 1976:271). On the *causses* (plateaux) of the Cevennes, there were comparable groups, such as the Treilles group of the Grand Causses and the Crosian group of Quercy (Clottes and Costantini 1976:284–86), the dating of which is established by a calibrated radiocarbon date of 2650 ± 130/3560–3150 B.C. (Gif-1517) for level IV at Grotte I des Treilles near Saint Jean et Saint Paul (Aveyron) (Balsan and Costantini 1972). To the north in the Massif Central, there were the various groups of the "Pasteurs des Plateaux," one of which is dated to this time by the calibrated dates of 2800 ± 300/3785–3355 B.C. (Ly-82) and 2430 ± 280/3370–2865 B.C. (Ly-196) for an occupation at Le Rond du Lévrier (Haute-Loire) (Daugas 1976; see table 1).

During the time of these post-Chassey groups, the chronology is further complicated by the rise of megalithic mortuary architecture. The passage graves of the Gard and Hérault, the rock-cut hypogea of the Arles region, and perhaps the earliest derivative gallery graves had their beginnings in these times. Here we can note only that their use continued into the subsequent Chalcolithic, when distinct regional groups developed in the uplands beyond the Mediterranean coast of France (Courtin 1976; Guilaine and Roudil 1976).

The Chassey cultures of eastern, northern, and western France cannot be divided into phases because stratigraphic evidence is lacking (see fig. 4). What little stratigraphy exists simply indicates that the Chassey was earlier than the Seine-Oise-Marne culture. Today their relative chronology must rest largely upon their external connections, more often than not supported by radiocarbon measurements (Bailloud 1979:101–7).

The eastern Chassey culture, long known from excavations at Camp de Chassey (Saône-et-Loire), arose in Burgundy, Franche-Comté, the Savoy, and in western Switzerland. Recently published radiocarbon dates for the Camp de Chassey, which have calibrated ranges of 3750 ± 150/4735–4420 B.C. (Ly-1772) to 3430 ± 160/4425–3915 B.C. (Ly-1771) (see table 1) suggest that the early phase of eastern Chassey was contemporary not only with early southern Chassey, but also with the Cerny and Augy-Sainte-Pallaye of northern France.

The mature eastern Chassey culture has tenuous connections with the Cortaillod culture, which helped establish its relative chronology. These are indicated by the assemblage of level 5 at the Grotte de Souhait (Ain), which has a flint industry with Cortaillod elements, but a pottery interpreted as "Chassean" (Desbrosses, Parriat, and Perraud 1962). At the site of "Sur le Grand Pré" near Saint Léonard (Canton Wallis) (Sauter 1957:136–49), which has Cortaillod, Chassey, and Lagozza connections, soil formed from the decomposition of wood has a calibrated date of 2800 ± 100/3670–3370 B.C. (B-232). This date agrees not only with those from the Chassey of northern France, but also with those from the Cortaillod culture of Switzerland, such as dates ranging from 2890 ± 110/3790–3510 B.C. (B-116) to 2440 ± 80/3355–2910 B.C. (B-114) for the settlement of Burgäschisee near Seeberg (Canton Bern) (Sauter and Gallay 1969; Strahm 1977; see Wells, chap. 19).

Today, it is clear that by the time of the mature eastern Chassey, Cortaillod had spread into the Jura and beyond into eastern France, where its influence played a part in the formation of the Middle Neolithic Burgundian culture, which has pottery displaying Chassean, Cortaillod, and Michelsberg traits. At the *oppidum* of Myard near Vitteaux (Côte d'Or), the Middle Neolithic Burgundian culture is dated by calibrated radiocarbon dates ranging from 3225 ± 135/4140–3790 B.C. (Gif-2342) to 2820 ± 135/3665–3355 B.C. (Gif-2343) (see table 1). Following the recent excavations in eastern France, it is increasingly clear that the dominance of the eastern Chassey culture in the last half of the fifth millennium gave way in the fourth before the penetration of the Cortaillod and Michelsberg cultures and the development of the Middle Neolithic Burgundian culture, now found along with a mature eastern Chassey culture (Thévenot and Carré 1976).

The Chassey culture of northern France, which arose in an area previously occupied by the Cerny, has long been known from sites such as Fort Harrouard (Eure-et-Loire), the Camp de Catenoy (Oise), and Champigny-sur-Marne (Seine) (see fig. 4). Calibrated radiocarbon dates, such as 2450 ± 125/3365–2895 B.C. (Gsy-97) for Fort Harrouard, 3190 ± 140/4120–3780 B.C. (Ly-149) and 2590 ± 140/3395–2025 B.C. (Ly-148) for La Brèche au Diable near Soumont-Saint-Quentin (Calvados), and 3170 ± 130/4110–3775 B.C. (Gif-2919) and 2340 ± 100/3150–2865 B.C. (Gif-2918) for Jonquières (Oise), place the northern Chassey in the fourth millennium (see table 1). The habitation site of Montagne de Lumbres (Pas-de-Calais), which yielded pottery with Chassean and Michelsberg traits, has samples with calibrated dates ranging from 3340 ± 200/4355–3895 B.C. (Gif-5055) to 2520 ± 200/3390–2905 B.C. (Gsy-49). In the past, connections between northern Chassey and Michelsberg rested almost entirely on the presence of the distinctive *plat à pain* of the Michelsberg culture at sites such as the Camp de Catenoy and Fort Harrouard (Philippe 1927; Bailloud 1961b). Now there are Chassey sites in the eastern Paris Basin, often called Middle Neolithic sites, such as Noyen-sur-Seine (Seine-et-Marne), which have a northern Chassey pottery found in direct association with a Michelsberg pottery (Mordant 1977; Mordant and Mordant 1978; Bailloud 1979:415). Beyond, in northeast France, there are the Michelsberg sites of Étaples (Pas-de-Calais) and Estrun (Nord) (Bailloud 1976; Leman and Leman 1973).

The Michelsberg culture, which occupied the lands flanking the Rhine in western Germany and extended into southern Belgium, eastern France, and northern Switzerland, has connections important for establishing the relative chronology of the Michelsberg in relation not only to the Chassey, but also to the cultures of central Europe. At Entzheim in Basse-Alsace, there is evidence for the contemporaneity of Late Rössen and Rhenish Wauwil and Bishheim groups with early Michelsberg (I) (Schmitt 1974; Lüning 1971), while in southwestern Germany Michelsberg (II) is found with Schussenried at Ehrenstein in Württemberg. In turn the Schussenried culture is known from isolated finds of its pottery in the Aisne region (Arnal and Burnez 1958:68) and from the lowest levels of the Camp de Château (Jura) (Bailloud and Mieg de Boofzheim 1955:126), suggesting contemporaneity with the early Michelsberg and with the Chassey culture of both northern and eastern France. These correlations are supported by radiocarbon dates of wood samples from the early Michelsberg (II)–Schussenried settlement at Ehrenstein (see Wells, chap. 19). Thus Michelsberg equates in time with northern Chassey, and both cultures fall in the horizon immediately following the Cerny of northern France and the Rössen of eastern France and western Germany. The Michelsberg culture also penetrated northern Switzerland, where it is known from a great number of older finds in the Bodensee and Aar Valley areas. Here its chronological position is best determined at sites such as Thayngen-Weier (Canton Schaffhausen) (Guyan 1955; Winiger 1971), where it appears in association with Cortaillod (younger Cortaillod, as defined by von Gonzenbach 1949) as well as Pfyn elements. Wood samples have a calibrated range of 2960 ± 100/3870–3640 B.C. (K-540) to 2740 ± 180/ 3675–3335 B.C. (B-44) (see Wells, chap. 19). This agrees fully with the Cortaillod and northern Chassey dates. Lüning (1968:99–100) maintains that the Michelsberg component of Thayngen-Weier belongs to a mature Michelsberg (III–IV) phase and was contemporary with the Pfyn culture of northeastern Switzerland, the Bodensee area, and Liechtenstein (Lüning 1968:145–50; Winiger 1971:103–8), where it is an element in the upper level of Lutzengütle. Scollar (1959:97) equates the Pfyn culture with Jevišovice C2 in Moravia (see Ehrich and Bankoff, chap. 21). Jevišovice C2 may in turn be equated with the Bohemian Siřem phase of the Funnel Beaker culture or its chronological equivalent, and through it with the late Baalberg and early Salzmünde phases of central Germany, whose beginning may be dated about 3500 B.C. Together these connections and radiocarbon dates of the eastern and northern Chassey of France, the Cortaillod of Switzerland, and the Michelsberg culture indicate that their development occupied much of the fourth millennium.

In Brittany and along the Atlantic coast of France, the evidence for the earliest Neolithic consists of passage graves with associated Carn and Cous pottery, which probably date to the time of the Cerny culture of northern France. Recent archaeological work suggests that development in the fourth millennium during the time of the northern and eastern Chassey fell into two phases usually assigned to the Secondary Neolithic (see fig. 4). In Brittany, the first is characterized by Chassean pottery found in association with passage graves with transepted chambers, such as Keriaval at Carnac (Morbihan) and compartmented chambers as at Kerleven (Finistère), where charcoal gives a calibrated radiocarbon date of 2875 ± 125/3785–3505 B.C. (Gsy-111) (Le Roux and L'Helgouach 1967). A calibrated date of 3030 ± 150/3905– 3650 B.C. (Gsy-89) for cist Y at Mané Miguel (Mont Saint-Michel) at Carnac (Morbihan) suggests that this was also the time of the Breton long mounds. Another calibrated date of 3125 ± 140/3970–3765 B.C. (Gif-1870) for cairn III at Landela on the Île Gaignog (Finistère) indicates that older passage graves continued in use for burial (Giot 1976). Yet calibrated dates ranging from 3210 ± 190/4150–3775 B.C. (Ly-421) to 3050 ± 130/ 3910–3655 B.C. (Gif-1345) for the passage graves of La Hougette at Fontenay le Marmion (Calvados) indicate a continuation of circular chambers typical of the earliest Neolithic of Brittany (Verron 1976:390–91). There is a comparable date of 2840 ± 220/3805–3365 B.C. for similar context in Tumulus F at Bougon (Deux-Sèvres), which has a Chassean vase support decorated in the Bougon style, which is similar to the vase support decorated in the Er Lannic style found at Kerleven. These sites, together with many other related ones, define the culture of Brittany and west central France during the first half of the fourth millennium (see table 1; L'Helgouach 1976:366–69).

In the interior of the Atlantic West of France, this was the time of the early Matignons and Peu-Richard cultures, which is indicated by a calibrated radiocarbon date of 3050 ± 140/3910–2655 B.C. (Gif-1732) for the lowest level of the Matignons settlement at Roquefort (Gironde), as well as by a comparable date of 2840 ± 250/3805–3365 (Gif-313) for La Garenne de Saint-Hippolyte (Charente Maritime), a camp of the early Peu-Richard culture (see fig. 3). The pottery of both these cultures has a Chassean basis, but now with a new decorative element. Burnez and Case (1966:193–97) have noted that Matignons pottery is vaguely like that of Lyles Hill and Sandhills in Ireland and of Vlaardingen in the western Netherlands. Further similarities are found in Los Millares pottery, and close analogies in the pottery decorated in the Er Lannic style of southern Brittany suggest that megalithic graves, such as at Bougon along the west-central coast of France, date to the time of the early Matignons and Peu-Richard cultures (Joussaume 1976).

During the second half of the fourth millennium, the second phase of development in Brittany and the Atlantic West of France was characterized by a further transformation of culture traditions. In Brittany, change can be noted in the later megalithic graves of Kerugou (Finistère) and Goërem (Morbihan), which now have new types of plan and construction (L'Helgouach 1965:166–73, 1970). In this period a new type of tomb with lateral entrance appears in the Côtes du Nord, to judge from Kerugou-like pottery found in the tomb at Crec'h Quillé (L'Helgouach 1967). These tombs, which have their closest analogies in the *hunebedden* of the northern Netherlands and the *Hunenbetten* of northwest Germany, yield collared flasks such as those of the tomb at Kergüntuil (L'Helgouach 1965:236, 245–48), which were current in the north at the time of these graves (see Thomas and E. Rowlett, chap. 18).

In west-central France, this was the time of the late Matignons and Peu-Richard cultures. There are calibrated radiocarbon dates of 2620 ± 300/3645–3015 B.C. (Gsy-32) for the later occupation at Les Matignons (Charente) and 2485 ± 200/3380–2890 B.C. (Gsy-71) for the late Peu-Richard occupation at Camp de Briard (Charente). The late Peu-Richard occupation at La Sauzaie (Charente Maritime) has calibrated dates ranging from 2550 ± 140/3385–2990 B.C. (Gif-1557) to 2410 ± 120/3180–2895 B.C. (Gif-2610), a range supported by the Kerugou similarities of its pottery. Calibrated radiocarbon dates of 2750 ± 140/3665–3355 B.C. (Ly-1195) for a late burial in Tumulus E at Bougon (Deux-Sèvres), 2400 ± 130/3355–2875 B.C. (Gif-1589) for the *dolmen angoumoisin* at L'Anse de la Répub-

lique at Talmont-Saint-Hilaire (Vendée), and dates ranging from 2730 ± 130/3660–3350 B.C. (Gif-3676) to 2690 ± 130/3650–3165 (Gif-4180), probably for the later use of "La Ciste des Cous" at Bazoges-en-Pareds (Vendée), indicate a persistence of megalithic traditions in west-central France (see table 1; Joussaume 1978, 1976).

By the beginning of the fourth millennium, the Neolithic culture of the British Isles was established throughout the islands and had begun to differentiate into a series of regional groups with distinctive pottery styles. Today these regional groups, which Case (1976:13) has assigned to a Middle Neolithic, are recognizable on the basis of their type of site and pottery associations. Geographically, these regional groups may be divided into two sections—one situated in the lowland zone of south and east Britain, the other in the highland zone of west and north Britain (see fig. 2; Fox 1947:28–50).

Within the southern lowland zone, causewayed camps, long barrows, long mortuary enclosures, and traces of habitations have yielded pottery indicating at least four regional groups. In southwest England, there was the Hembury group which has been defined on the basis of pottery found in the atypical causewayed camp with a rare gate and hut at Hembury (Devon). Calibrated radiocarbon dates ranging from 3330 ± 150/4145–3795 B.C. (BM-138) to 3150 ± 150/3990–3770 B.C. (BM-130) place Hembury in the early fourth millennium. A calibrated date of 2960 ± 150/3880–3530 B.C. (BM-73) for the earliest occupation at Windmill Hill (Wiltshire) suggests that the Windmill Hill group was equally early. The same is true of the Abingdon group of the Thames Valley, in view of calibrated dates of 3110 ± 130/3960–3755 B.C. (BM-351) and 2960 ± 110/3870–3640 B.C. (BM-350) for Phase II in Area C at the causewayed camp of Abingdon (Berkshire). Calibrated radiocarbon dates of 3145 ± 49/3940–3785 B.C. (BM-770) for charcoal from shallow pits at the habitation site of Eaton Heath (Norfolk) and 3230 ± 150/4140–3790 B.C. (BM-134) for context yielding a Mildenhall pot in the long barrow of Fussell's Lodge (Wiltshire) place the Mildenhall group which centered in East Anglia in the same period (see table 1).

The lowland zone of northeastern Britain, which extended from Lincolnshire northward into eastern Scotland, has long barrows and habitation sites that yield pottery in the Heslerton, Towthorpe, and Grimston styles. These pottery styles have little significance for chronology because of their widespread interpenetrating distributions. However, calibrated radiocarbon dates of 3080 ± 90/3910–3760 B.C. (NPL-73) for the long barrow on Seamer Moor (Yorkshire) and 3010 ± 150/3895–3645 B.C. (NM-189) for the long barrow at Willerby Wold (Yorkshire) suggest that the Middle Neolithic of northeast Britain began as early as it did in the southern lowland zone (see table 1; Smith 1974; Megaw and Simpson 1979:78–112).

In the highland zone of western and northwestern Britain, the Middle Neolithic is characterized by a megalithic architecture that began in this period. In southwestern England, there is the Severn-Cotswold group, known from monuments such as West Kennet (Wiltshire) and Wayland's Smithy (Berkshire) (Corcoran 1969). While the early Middle Neolithic date of Wayland's Smithy is a matter of speculation, the Windmill Hill Ware of the first phase of West Kennett seems to tie it to this period (Piggott 1958). Although it is difficult to establish the chronology of the portal dolmens of north Wales (Powell 1973), the megaliths of the Clyde and southwest Scotland seem to have begun in the early fourth millennium. This is indicated not only by the calibrated radiocarbon date of 3160 ± 110/3965–3780 B.C. (Q-675) for the chambered tomb at Monamore on the island of Arran (Buteshire), but also by plain round-bottom vessels typical of the Middle Neolithic found in the segmented chambered tombs at Cairnholy (Kirkcudbright) (Piggott and Powell 1948–49) and Beacharra (Argyll) as well as at Monomore (Scott 1969). In Northern Ireland there are numerous court cairns (De Valera 1960), which have wedge-shaped mounds similar to those of the Clyde and Severn-Cotswold groups. On the other hand, their internal structures are much more complex in plan. Most of the court cairns date to the Late Neolithic, but the date of related types of megaliths in western England and southwest Scotland suggests that their beginnings extend back into Middle Neolithic times. However, calibrated carbon dates for pre-cairn habitation occupation of what became court cairn sites, such as the dates of 3095 ± 95/3920–3765 B.C. (UB-535) and 2980 ± 80/3875–3645 B.C. (UB-534) for charcoal found with Western Neolithic pottery in the black habitation layer below the dual court cairn at Carnanbane (Co. Londonderry), indicate a persistence of settlement usage through much of the early fourth millennium. Of course this persistence into the Middle Neolithic can also be traced at Ballynagilly (Co. Tyrone), which has a range of calibrated dates extending from 2960 ± 90/3870–3640 B.C. (UB-301) to 2885 ± 55/3690–3535 B.C. (UB-625) (see table 1).

Although this is not the place to discuss either the origins or relationships of the cultures of the British Neolithic, it must be noted that the pottery of the southwest (Hembury) group dates to the same time as the comparable Chassey pottery, while the pottery of eastern and northern Britain was characterized by open-shoulder bowl forms similar to those of the contemporary Michelsberg culture (Piggott 1961). The long barrows of the lowland zone belong to the same period as those of Brittany (Giot 1960:36–42), complicating the problem of

correlations between British and Continental cultures. At much the same time, megalithic tombs spread along the western coasts of France and Britain. Today, the causewayed camp has contemporary analogies not only in the Michelsberg camps, but also in those of the Matignons and Peu-Richard cultures of western France. Whatever their importance may be for the origin and development of British cultures, these similarities between the British Isles and the Continent provide broad support for assigning the Middle Neolithic to the first half of the fourth millennium.

The second half of the fourth millennium was characterized by the maturity of the Neolithic traditions of the British Isles. This age, which Smith (1974) has called the mature Neolithic and Case (1976) designates as the Late Neolithic, is known from the later causewayed camps and long barrows of the lowland zone and the fully developed megaliths of the highland zone. In southern and eastern Britain, this was the time of the widespread and diverse Peterborough pottery found in association with causewayed camps, late long barrows, and habitation sites. At Ebbsfleet (Kent), an early variety of Peterborough pottery designated after this site as Ebbsfleet ware has a calibrated radiocarbon date of 2710 ± 150/3660–3340 B.C. (BM-113). A somewhat later calibrated date of 2580 ± 50/3390–3020 B.C. (BM-74) is provided by a charcoal sample from the primary silt in the ditches of the causewayed camp at Windmill Hill (Wiltshire). The calibrated dates of 2970 ± 150/3885–3540 B.C. (BM-149) and 2750 ± 150/3665–3355 B.C. (BM-150) for the Neolithic camp at Hazard Hill (Devon) and 2760 ± 115/3660–3365 B.C. (BM-205) for the causewayed camp at Knap Hill (Wiltshire) indicate that the causewayed camp must be placed in the second half of the fourth millennium. Similar datings are available for the later long barrows such as at Nutbane (Hampshire), where a sample found in a pit of the second forecourt building has a calibrated date of 2730 ± 150/3660–3350 B.C. (BM-49). The presence of Peterborough pottery in the secondary context of long barrows of eastern England indicates that such burials were still being made in the Late Neolithic, an attribution supported by calibrated dates of 2460 ± 150/3370–2900 B.C. (BM-191) and 2370 ± 150/3180–2855 B.C. (BM-192) for the long barrow at Giants Hills (Lincolnshire). Further excavation and analysis will probably reveal a regional differentiation of culture during the Late Neolithic, now characterized as a diverse "Peterborough" style, similar to the "particularism" of culture found not only in France but also in Scotland and Ireland (see table 1).

The Late Neolithic of the highland zone of western and northern Britain was characterized by the persistence of megalithic traditions. In the Severn-Cotswold group of southwest England, the presence of Peterborough pottery in the fills marking the final phase of transepted galleries, such as at West Kennet (Wiltshire) (Piggott 1958), indicates that their final use belongs in the time of the Late Neolithic. By this time the megalithic tomb must have been well established in the Dyfed and Gwyneed groups of south and north Wales as well as on the Isle of Man and in the Peak district, but unfortunately assemblages surviving in these tombs are inadequate for chronological purposes. In southwest and western Scotland, this was the time of the late segmented galleries of the Clyde, such as at Carn Ban, and the rise of the megalithic in the Hebrides. The increasing regional diversity is manifest in the Beacharra, Achnacree, and Rothesay pottery styles of the southwest and the Hebridean style of North Uist and Harris and perhaps the Unstan style of the north (Henshall 1972:164–87; Scott 1964; Corcoran 1972).

In Ireland there was a similar regional differentiation of culture. Although this was the time of the complex court cairns of the north, whose age is indicated by the calibrated radiocarbon date of 2445 ± 55/3190–2935 B.C. (UB-241) for the court cairn of Annaghmare (Co. Armagh), it was also the period when an increasing diversity of types characterized the megalithic culture that was spreading through Ireland. This is reflected in the diversity of their associated pottery, such as pottery of the Ballyalton and Dundrum bowl types. Settlements of the center and north, such as Townleyhall (Co. Lough), which has a calibrated radiocarbon date of 2730 ± 150/3660–3350 B.C. (BM-170), are characterized by Sandhills pottery, while those of the southwest yield Limerick ware. This latter pottery style is best defined by pottery from the lower Pre-Beaker level of a house at Knockadoon near Lough Gur (Co. Limerick), which has calibrated dates of 2740 ± 240/3675–3335 B.C. (D-41) and 2460 ± 240/3375–2880 B.C. (D-40) indicative of a Late Neolithic time (see table 1; Herity and Eogan 1977).

The Chalcolithic Cultures

The latest Neolithic of northwestern Europe is increasingly recognized as the time when the use of copper for tools and ornaments was spreading, and thus such terms as *Chalcolithic* and *Copper Age* become more and more common. Many archaeologists have called this the Beaker Age, in the belief that peoples associated with the Beaker culture diffused the use of copper. This, however, is not the place to deal with either the nature or the origin of the Beaker cultures (Harrison 1980). Whatever the ultimate solution for these problems may be, the widespread appearance of the beaker marks the beginning of a new age.

In France, culture transformation was widespread. In the south, the late Post-Chassey developed into a series of Chalcolithic cultures which interacted with contem-

porary Beaker and megalithic elements (see fig. 3). Among these was the Couronnian of Provence, which is dated to the first half of the third millennium by a calibrated radiocarbon date of 2290 ± 100/3035–2780 (MC-714B) for its type site of Collet-Redon at La Couronne-Martigues (Bouches-du-Rhône). It was contemporary with rock-cut chamber tombs with collective burials, to judge from the calibrated date of 2150 ± 140/2910–2530 B.C. (lower layer) (Gif-1620) and 2090 ± 140/2885–2400 B.C. (upper layer) (Gif-857) for the Roaix hypogeum (Vaucluse). Maritime Beakers come from related hypogea such as Fontvieille (Bouches-du-Rhône) and La Balance, Avignon (Vaucluse), which has a calibrated date of 2150 ± 120/2890–2540 B.C. (Gif-705). The later Bas-Rhodanian Bell Beaker has a calibrated date of 2010 ± 175/2870–2180 B.C. (Gif-116) at Grotte Murée (Basses-Alpes) (see table 1; Courtin 1974, 1976:265–66).

The Fontbouisse culture, which centered in eastern Languedoc, belongs to the early and middle third millennium, judging by calibrated radiocarbon dates of 2190 ± 120/2910–2630 B.C. (Ly-554) for the Grotte de Boucoiran (Gard) and 1930 ± 180/2655–2120 B.C. (Gif-191) for Grotte Pravel (Gard) (Guilaine and Roudil 1976:275–76). Again there is evidence of contemporaneity with both megalithic and Bell Beaker cultures, for the Bas-Rhodanian Bell Beaker is present at sites such as Saint Côme-et-Maruéjols (Gard) which has a calibrated date of 1940 ± 140/2645–2165 B.C. (Ly-422) (see table 1). Beyond, in southern France, were numerous local megalithic groups characterized by small dolmen chambers and menhirs. By the late middle third millennium, the Bell Beaker culture had formed distinct regional groups not only in the Lower Rhône, the Bas-Rhodanian, but also in Catalonia and the eastern Pyrenees, the Pyrenean. In the late third millennium these diverse elements coalesced into a Chalcolithic culture destined to continue well into Early Bronze times, when this region fell under the dominance of the Rhône culture.

In northern France, the northern Chassey was replaced by the Seine-Oise-Marne (SOM) culture, largely known from its gallery graves (*allées couvertes*) and rock-cut tombs (hypogea) (Bailloud 1979: 139–340). It is impossible to divide its development into phases. However, tanged daggers and beads brought by Bell Beaker trade establish its chronological position. Some archaeologists maintain that SOM influence extended eastward into Westphalia, but today the development of the gallery graves of Hessen and Hannover-Braunschweig is best explained in terms of central and northern Europe (Schrickel 1976) (see Thomas and E. Rowlett, chap. 18). Calibrated dates for SOM sites in northern France, such as 2090 ± 180/2905–2315 B.C. (Ly-703) for Porte-Joie (Eure), 2550 ± 50/3370–3050 B.C. (Gro-4676) for Les

Roches, Videlles (Seine-et-Oise), and 1800 ± 150/ 2410–1955 B.C. (Gsy-114) for Les Mournouards, Le Mesnil-sur-Oger (Marne), place this culture in the third millennium (see table 1).

Along the Loire and in western France, older traditions gave way to others related to the SOM. One close to SOM arose along the Loire, where the earlier Angevin galleries were replaced by the elongated Loire galleries. To the south, the Vienne-Charente culture had many elements, such as flat-based pottery, tying it to the SOM. Along the coast in western France and in the Dordogne, the earlier Peu-Richard and Matignon cultures were replaced by the Artenacian culture, which can be traced eastward into the Causses (Roussot-Larroque 1976: 346–50; Joussaume 1976:361–63; and Clottes and Costantini 1976:289–91). This culture, which has generalized connections with the SOM, is now dated to much the same time by calibrated dates such as 2310 ± 140/3155–2765 B.C. (Gif-3009) for Camp Allaric (Vienne) and 2200 ± 130/2955–2545 B.C. (Gif-2743) for Camp de Pierre dure (Charente-maritime) (see table 1).

The SOM culture extended eastward through Champagne into Belgium and southeastward into northern Burgundy, but in southern Burgundy it gave way to the Saône-Rhône culture, which occupied lands extending east to the Jura and western Switzerland, and southeast into Savoy. The assemblages of sites like tumulus I at Vertempierre near Cagny (Saône-et-Loire) (Thévenot 1961) and Ouroux-sur-Saône (Saône-et-Loire) (Thévenot, Strahm, and Gallay 1976) show a persistence of eastern Chassey elements, but now with bell beakers of both Rhenish and Mediterranean derivation. Although these beakers indicate only a date in the third millennium for the Saône-Rhone culture, it can be dated in Switzerland to the early middle third millennium (see Wells, chap. 19). Furthermore, the Bell Beaker culture played a major role in the transition to the subsequent Rhône culture of the Early Bronze Age.

In eastern France and Switzerland, the Cortaillod culture gave way to the Horgen, a succession assured by the stratigraphy of sites such as Egolzwil 2 (Canton Lucern) (Itten 1970) and Chalain in the Jura (Pape 1978; Bailloud 1961). In northeastern Switzerland, the Horgen occurs in strata immediately above the late Pfyn at Zürich-Rentenanstalt, but there is only limited stratigraphic evidence for its displacement by a mature Corded Ware culture at sites such as Zürich-Utoquai (Strahm 1969:108). Calibrated radiocarbon dates such as 2150 ± 60/2880–2635 B.C. (Gro-949) for the Horgen level at Escalon in the Jura and 2510 ± 120/3370–2970 B.C. (B-779) and 2220 ± 250/3045–2535 B.C. (B-778) for the closely related Lüscherz group at Vinelz on Lake Biel (Canton Bern) indicate that it belongs to the early and middle third

millennium, the time of the earlier phases of the closely related SOM culture (Strahm 1978). Dates for the subsequent Corded Ware culture, which displaced the Horgen, are dealt with elsewhere, in the chapters on south Germany (see Wells, chap. 19) and northern Europe (see Thomas and E. Rowlett, chap. 18).

The SOM culture penetrated westward into Brittany, where its distinctive *allées couvertes* are found throughout the Armorican peninsula at sites such as Kergus (Morbihan) and Kerbannalec (Finistère) (L'Helgouach 1965:259–300). Diverse SOM elements found in association with late burials in older passage graves such as at Barnenez (tomb D) (Finistère) and Kercado (Morbihan) (L'Helgouach 1965:113–14) suggest that there was a widespread displacement of the older megalithic tradition. Yet the diverse late megalithic graves of the Conguel and Kersidal groups of Morbihan have a pottery whose vessel shapes turn up without decoration in the dolmen at Taizé (Deux-Sèvres), along with bell beakers (L'Helgouach 1976:371), which suggests that the megalithic tradition persisted into the third millennium.

A further transformation of the culture of Brittany was brought about by the Bell Beaker culture. Its beginning is marked by the appearance of Maritime Bell Beakers in sites such as the *allée couverte* at Kerbors (Côtes-du-Nord). The Lower Rhenish Corded Beaker found in a secondary burial at Goërem (Morbihan), which has a calibrated radiocarbon date of 1910 ± 200/2650–2020 B.C. (Gif-329), probably belongs to the time of the formation of the distinctive Armorican Bell Beaker culture. This culture, which is found along the south coast of Brittany, belongs to the last half of the third millennium. Its beakers are similar to those of Iberia rather than the British Isles, Netherlands, Rhineland, and central Europe (L'Helgouach 1976:371). The coalescence of the diverse elements of Breton culture led to the formation of the transitional culture of the so-called first series of Armorican barrows that mark the transition to the Early Bronze Age (L'Helgouach 1976).

The influence of the Bell Beaker culture is found mainly along the coasts of France, where there are concentrations in southern France and in Brittany. They are of course also found beyond these areas, in the Dauphiné, the eastern Pyrenean uplands, and the valley of the Garonne, and then along the west coast. To the north they are reported in coastal areas bordering the English Channel and also in the SOM tombs of the southwest Paris Basin. While most of the beakers from south, southwest, west, and northwest France tie to bell beakers of the Mediterranean, those found in northern Burgundy, in the Jura area and Alsace, belong with the beakers of the Rhine Basin. Their origins and development are still obscure, making it premature to project a Beaker chronology (Treinen 1970; Lanting and van der Waals 1976). (For some of these problems see the later section on the British Isles and Thomas and E. Rowlett, chap. 18).

In the British Isles, the Late Neolithic "Peterborough" culture continued into the Copper or Chalcolithic Age, but everywhere are indications of widespread change resulting from the intrusion of Beaker peoples, reflected not only in the influence of Beaker pottery styles on late Ebbsfleet pottery and the new Mortlake pottery style of Peterborough ware, but also in the abandonment of causewayed camps, long mounds, and many of the megalithic chamber tombs of the west (Smith 1974:111–17; see fig. 2). At Windmill Hill, for example, the silting deposits in the upper part of the ditch produced not only Mortlake Ware, but Rinyo-Clacton (Grooved Ware) and Maritime/International Bell Beakers (E). At West Kennet, the final fill contained similar wares, but so far no material dated by radiocarbon samples.

Some idea of their dating may be gained from radiocarbon determinations for Rinyo-Clacton sites, which occur in southern England (East Anglian, Wessex, and Dorchester groups), northwest England (Ronaldsway group), and Scotland (Southern and Orkney groups). Today, the Rinyo-Clacton culture, which was named for the sites of Rinyo on the island of Rousay in the Orkneys and of Clacton-on-Sea in East Anglia, is often designated as the Grooved Ware culture because of the distinctive decoration of its pottery. Most of the calibrated radiocarbon dates for this culture are for samples from associated henge monuments found in southern England. A date of 2490 ± 150/3375–2910 B.C. (BM-129) for the henge monument of Arminghall (Norfolk) should mark an early phase of the East Anglian group. Those for Durrington Walls, a henge of the Wessex group, ranged from 2050 ± 90/2670–2505 B.C. (BM-400) to 1900 ± 90/2430–2165 B.C. (BM-397), and are probably indicative of its lower limits (Wainwright and Longworth 1971:55–71). Unhappily there are no radiocarbon dates for Woodhenge, where Rinyo-Clacton was associated not only with Peterborough but also with International Bell Beaker (E). (All beaker designations are in Clarke's system [1970]). Whatever its cultural attribution, the first phase of Stonehenge is marked by associated Rinyo-Clacton wares and dated by two radiocarbon dates, calibrated as 2180 ± 105/2905–2625 B.C. (I-2328) for the construction of the ditch, and 1848 ± 275/2555–1960 B.C. (C-602) for Aubrey Hole 32. Together these dates suggest that the beginning of the Rinyo-Clacton as well as International Beaker (E) and the widespread abandonment of Late Neolithic camps and tombs could have taken place as early as the late fourth millennium, and certainly not later than the first quarter of the third (see table 1).

Calibrated radiocarbon dates for the tombs of the Boyne culture of Ireland, ranging from 2585 ± 105/3385–3135 B.C. (UB-361) to 2465 ± 40/3355–2955 B.C. (GrN-5463) for Newgrange (Meath), and from 2310 ± 160/3155–2765 B.C. (D-43) to 2130 ± 160/2900–2525 B.C. (D-42) for Tara (Meath), indicate that this culture is roughly contemporary with the Rinyo-Clacton Grooved Ware. Bone pins of the Ronaldsway group of Rinyo-Clacton similar to those of the Boyne passage graves support this. Chronologically not only the Boyne culture but also the Rinyo-Clacton and the latest cultures in the Neolithic tradition with pottery in the Mortlake style parallel the Late Neolithic in Brittany, where the megalithic graves of Conquel and Kerbors are of the same period as the SOM culture, also datable to the late fourth/early third millennium. Generalized associations of the International Bell Beaker with these cultures in both Brittany and the British Isles suggest that they too must go back to this horizon. In Ireland this was when Kilhoyle wares of the Final Neolithic appeared in wedge-shaped galleries of the north and in reused tombs of the west and southwest (Herity and Eogon 1977:80–101). In wedge-shaped galleries such as Kilhoyle (Londonderry), Bell Beaker sherds were found with Kilhoyle vessels.

In the wedge-shaped grave at Dunteige (Antrim), the pottery is comparable with late Beacharra ware. Furthermore, Beacharra pottery comparable to late Ballyalton bowls from derivative Irish court cairns and portal dolmens occurred in a habitation site at Townhead near Rothesay (Bute) and has a calibrated date of 2120 ± 100/2880–2535 B.C. (GaK-1714). Townhead also yielded Achnacree bowls with heavy rims like those of Mortlake type (Piggott 1954:319). This late impressed ware occurs at Glenluce (Wigtownshire), Hedderwick (East Lothian), and Grandtully (Perthshire), where two calibrated dates, 2130 ± 190/2925–2395 B.C. (GaK-1398) and 1970 ± 100/2640–2305 B.C. (GaK-1396), place it in the early middle third millennium (Smith 1974:116–17). The European or International Bell Beakers (E) found at both Hedderwick and Glenluce may well be equally early (Clarke 1970:531–32). It is usually assumed that the appearance of bell beakers along the coast of southwest Scotland and northwest to the Hebrides marks the end of the megalithic tradition. Much the same can be said of the megalithic culture in Wales and the Severn-Cotswold group of western England, in which the Bell Beaker (E) marks the last phase of both Notegrove and West Kennet (Piggott 1958).

The traditional Abercromby (1912) and, more recently, the Clarke model (1970) have failed to explain the development of the Beaker culture in the British Isles. In 1977, H. Case proposed a developmental scheme, with the Early style of beakers as true bell beakers, the Middle style as beakers in association with early wrist guards having attachment holes and with tanged daggers, and the Late style as beakers found with riveted knives, late wrist guards, amber and jet buttons, and also with flint knives and daggers. Most of the Late Beakers are distinguishable by their emphasis on panel/metope decoration (Case 1977). The Early style is datable to the late fourth and early third millennium, thanks to the external connections of its European or International Bell Beakers (E). With the Middle style, appearing alongside derivative International style beakers, which begin to develop an incipient zonal decoration, is a new type with allover-corded decoration, the AOC Beaker. Examples of the derivative Bell Beaker with incipient zonal decoration occur in association with tanged daggers and simple wrist guards at Mere Barrow and Roundway in Wiltshire (Clarke 1970: figs. 130, 132). At Windmill Hill, this type occurs with AOC Beakers in the upper silting that marks the end of the causewayed camp. The beakers with incipient zonal decoration are reminiscent of the one found at Ede-Ginkelse (Guelders) associated with a tanged copper dagger, arrow points, and a wrist guard (Lanting and van der Waals 1976:33, fig. 25), as well as another from Odoorn (Drenthe) (De Laet 1958:102) in the Netherlands. Analogies for the AOC Beakers such as that from Garderen (Guelders) come from quite a different assemblage consisting of a type H battle-ax, a dagger made of Grand Pressigny flint imitating a tanged dagger, a flint ax, and numerous amber beads (Lanting and van der Waals 1976:20–21, fig. 11). The International Bell Beaker and their derivatives as well as the AOC Beaker are datable in the Netherlands and Belgium to the middle of the third millennium by numerous radiocarbon dates. Whatever their origin, these two types of beaker occur in southern and eastern England and can be traced northward into eastern Scotland. Although there are no diagnostic radiocarbon dates, it is tempting to place these beakers also in the middle of the third millennium.

There are also beakers with a pronounced zonal decoration for which Clarke (1970:84–117) sought a Middle Rhenish inspiration. These occur at sites such as Farleigh Wick (Wiltshire) and Devil's Dyke (Sussex) (Clarke 1970: fig. 167) as well as other sites, showing a widespread distribution across southern England. Northern versions of these can be traced through Yorkshire into eastern Scotland, as well as westward and northwestward to Wales and the Lake District. The somewhat later de-

velopment of the Zoned Beaker from the Incipient Zoned Beaker in the Middle Rhine Basin suggests that these belong in the late middle third millennium.

The Late Beakers, which were characterized by extraordinarily complex decoration, often involving triangular and sometimes metope decorative motifs, appear together with riveted daggers at Shrewton (Wiltshire), Dorchester XII (Oxfordshire), and Lilburn (Northumberland) (Clarke 1970: figs. 549, 128, and 550), in southern and eastern England. Late Beakers with similar associations occur at Fernworthy (Devon) and at Glenforsa (Argyll) (Clarke 1970: figs. 886 and 676) in southwestern England and western Scotland. Although there were widespread regional differences in beaker shape and decoration, there is no space in this brief chapter on chronology to enter into this question. However, the sheer diversity of shape and decoration, together with regional particularism, argues for a development within the British Isles. Yet in a general way these Late Beakers distantly recall the Veluwe Beakers of the Netherlands which are firmly dated to the last quarter of the third millennium. Such Late Beakers have been found at Fifty Farm (Suffolk), where the habitation site is dated $1850 \pm 150/2425–1995$ B.C. (BM-133), Antofts Windypit (Yorkshire), where a burial is dated $1800 \pm 150/2410–1955$ B.C. (BM-62), and Chippenham (Cambridgeshire), where another burial is dated $1850 \pm 150/2425–1995$ B.C. (BM-152), all the dates indicating that the Late Beakers belong to the last third or quarter of the third millennium. Calibrated radiocarbon dates for the second and early third phases of Stonehenge, $1620 \pm 110/2145–1790$ B.C. (I-2384) and $1720 \pm 150/2320–1875$ B.C. (BM-46), suggest that the famous monument was begun in the time of this extraordinary pottery.

The presence in these Late Beaker graves of flint daggers like those from Amesbury (Wiltshire) and Garton Slack (Yorkshire) (Clarke 1970: figs. 890 and 778) reminds one that this was also the time of the flint daggers of the cist graves of Late Neolithic Scandinavia (see Thomas and E. Rowlett, chap. 18). The Barbed-Wire Beakers, which occur with Late Beakers at Winchester (Hampshire) and other sites (Clarke 1970: figs. 222 and 223), probably reached Britain in Late Beaker times, and, once there, developed into the extraordinarily decorative Barbed-Wire forms, illustrating once more the native creativity of this period which immediately preceded that of the Wessex Bronze Age.

Eighteen

The Archaeological Chronology of Northern Europe

Homer L. Thomas, Emeritus, University of Missouri
Elsebet S.-J. Rowlett, Museum of Anthropology, University of Missouri, Columbia

Outline

Northern Europe, as here treated, comprises parts of Belgium and the Netherlands, Germany north of the Main, and Scandinavia (see fig. 1). During the past twenty years, there has been little substantive change in the broad chronological outlines of the Neolithic cultures of the north European plain and Scandinavia. Despite the established successions of the Neolithic cultures of Denmark (Becker 1947, 1961b), Schleswig-Holstein (Schwabedissen 1958, 1962, 1966), eastern Germany (Unvezagt 1958:173–203), and the Low Countries (De Laet and Glasbergen 1959), there have been major shifts in the interpretation of relationships between specific cultures. However this has not led to new culture or artifact designations as it has in the British Isles and other quarters of northwestern Europe.

These shifts in the cultural relationships of northern Europe have come about not so much because of radiocarbon dating, but rather as a product of archaeological fieldwork. Many new excavations have yielded an increasing amount of evidence for cultural distributions, forcing reconsiderations such as those of the Single Grave and Funnel Beaker cultures. As in northwestern Europe, chronologies are increasingly projected without using external connections, owing in good part to the growing predominance of culture continuity in archaeological interpretation. However, many chronological connections are still valid and suggest that the chronology and development of the cultures of northern Europe demand consideration not merely of culture continuity but also of external influences.

Unfortunately there are few general surveys of recent work, such as are available for northwestern Europe.

Text submitted September 1984
Text revised April 1986

However, there are numerous monographs and articles concerning individual cultures or regions, which are noted here when they are relevant to chronological problems. Fortunately the radiocarbon dates for the Neolithic of northern Europe as well as for central and northwestern Europe have been brought together relatively recently by Wolfgang Pape (1979).

The Earliest Neolithic Culture

The earliest Neolithic culture of northern Europe was introduced by settlers who spread westward and northwestward through the loess lands of south-central Europe and brought with them the Linear _Bandkeramik_ culture, so named because of the distinctive curvilinear band decoration of its pottery. Their expansion involved three distinct movements, one of which penetrated through the loess lands along the Upper Danube to those of the upper and central Neckar basin. Somewhat later they pushed into the middle Rhineland. The second movement, of great importance for northern Europe, came via the loess lands of Moravia and Bohemia to central Germany and from there to the Main Valley and then on to the lower Rhine and Meuse areas of West Germany, Belgium, and the Low Countries (Sielmann 1972). A third movement explains the appearance of Linear _Bandkeramik_ elements at sites such as those along the lower Oder and Vistula valleys, indicating a penetration almost to Szczecin on the edge of the Baltic Sea. Calibrated radiocarbon dates for the Limburg sites of the Netherlands show that the Linear _Bandkeramik_ settlers had reached the northwestern limits of their region as early as the late sixth millennium B.C. Calibrated dates from Sittard are 4150 ± 140/5250–4920 B.C. (Gro-320), 3840 ± 190/4960–4430 B.C. (Gro-422), and 4250 ± 150/5305–4955 B.C. (Gro-

423). Other dates which fall close to these are from charcoal samples from Linear *Bandkeramik* contexts at Geleen and Elsloo (see table 1). Charcoal samples from Westeregln in Kreis Stassfurt and Zwenkau near Leipzig gave calibrated dates of 4190 ± 100/5255–4940 B.C. (Bln-92) and 4210 ± 70/5240–4975 B.C. (GrN-1581) respectively for central German Linear *Bandkeramik*. Together, calibrated dates place the Linear Bandkeramik in the last half of the sixth and earliest fifth millennium. The broad range of the calibrated radiocarbon dates makes it impossible to use them to establish the absolute chronology of the successions for the Maas (Modderman 1970), lower and middle Rhine (Dohrn-Ihmig 1976), lower Main (Meier-Arendt 1966), Rheinhessen (Meier-Arendt 1976), and central Germany (Hoffmann 1963; Zápotocká 1972; Meier-Arendt 1976), which have replaced the five-phase system of Quitta (1960).

To the west of the Rhine and Maas are the derivative Linear *Bandkeramik* groups in Belgium and northern France. The long known Omalian group of the Liège area is now assigned to the Limburg group of Belgium, the southern Netherlands, and western Germany. Calibrated dates for the Belgian sites of Omal (Liège) (4205 ± 75/ 5250–4975 B.C.; HV-9284; De Laet 1982:206) and Blicquy-Porte Ouverte (Hainaut), (4335 ± 195/5460– 5000 B.C.; HV-9278; De Laet 1982:206) place it in the late sixth, earliest fifth millennium, a dating in agreement with its archaeological attribution to Moddermann's phase II along the Maas in Dutch Limburg (see table 1). It is also linked by pottery similarities to the late Linear *Bandkeramik* of the valley of the Aisne and the Paris Basin, where there are comparable calibrated dates at Berry-au-Bac and Cuiry-les-Chaudardes (see Thomas and R. Rowlett, this vol., chap. 17). There are comparable calibrated dates for the Blicquy group of western Hainaut, which differs from the Limburg groups, but which also had connections in northern France (see fig. 4; De Laet 1982:212–22).

The fifth millennium brought increasing divergence of development within the *Bandkeramik* tradition. During the late sixth millennium the Stroked Ware culture arose during the Šárka phase of the Linear *Bandkeramik* culture of central Germany and Bohemia (see Ehrich and Bankoff, this vol., chap. 21). This culture occurs not only in southern Germany (see Wells, this vol., chap. 19), but also along the lower and upper Main in Franconia. Calibrated dates for Stroked Ware are few in number, but exist at Zwenkau in central Germany where they range from 4050 ± 115/5110–4855 B.C. (H-224/223) to 3890 ± 120/4935–4555 B.C. (K-555) (see table 1). Archaeological connections link it to the Hinkelstein culture of the Rheinhessen, Rhein-Main, and Württemberg areas as well as to the time of the widespread Grossgartach of the upper Rhine Valley, the Rhine-Main basin, Rhenish

Hesse, and the middle and lower Rhine valleys (Meier-Arendt 1972:58–63). The Grossgartach, which must be regarded as a derivative of the Linear *Bandkeramik* culture of the Early Neolithic of southern Germany, is assigned to the Middle Neolithic (see fig. 4).

During the last half of the fifth millennium, the Rössen and subsequent Bischheim cultures brought an increasing cultural uniformity to Germany south of the north German plain. Again there is a lack of radiocarbon dates for firmly fixing Rössen's absolute chronological position. Among the three of four which exist, the calibrated date for Inden in the Rhineland has a range of 3990 ± 200/ 5195–4560 B.C. (KN-330), suggesting that its beginnings overlapped the end of the Stroked Ware culture, a correlation supported by archaeological connections. The calibrated date of 3350 ± 200/4415–3875 B.C. (Gro-433) for Wählitz is suggestive of its time span, within which one must place its numerous local groups (Goller 1972).

The Bischheim culture succeeded the Rössen in Franconia, Rhenish Hesse, the Rhine-Main basin, and the middle and lower Rhineland. At Hüde in Kreis Grafschaft Diepholz, calibrated dates for Bischheim range from 3615 ± 85/4550–4350 B.C. (Hv-814) to 3225 ± 155/4140–3790 B.C. (Hv-1230), which makes possible only its general assignment to the last half of the fifth millennium. Attribution to the last quarter of the fifth millennium is partially supported by a calibrated date of 3410 ± 160/4420–3905 B.C. (Bln-231) for grain from a storage pit at Kmehlen in central Germany. It has been thought by some to belong to the Baalberg-Gatersleben culture, but probably belongs to the Gatersleben culture which derives from the southeast but has indirect connections with Bischheim. While the Bischheim culture gave way to the Michelsberg culture in west and southwest Germany, the Gatersleben lasted until the rise of the Funnel Beaker cultures (see fig. 4; Baumann 1965).

In the past, it has been argued that the Linear *Bandkeramik* culture occupied lands abandoned by its Mesolithic population at the end of the Boreal climatic period (Waterbolk 1962:234–35). Recent investigations have shown that not only was there a very late survival of the Mesolithic Tardenoisian (Rozoy 1978:596–97), but also that in the Low Countries in the valleys of the Meuse, the Rhineland, and the Schelde there was contact between the Mesolithic and Linear *Bandkeramik* peoples, which is attested by their flint industries (De Laet 1982:207–8).

During the time of the Linear *Bandkeramik*, Stroked Ware, Rössen and Bischheim cultures, much of northern Europe was still occupied by Mesolithic peoples: Schleswig-Holstein and Mecklenburg by those with the Ellerbek culture, while southern Scandinavia was in the hands of people of the Post-Maglemosian and Ertebølle traditions (see fig. 2). Contacts between the Neolithic peoples to the south and the Mesolithic peoples of the north are limited until the latest phases of the Ertebølle and Ellerbek cultures. In the north, pottery first appears in late Ertebølle (D II), with calibrated dates of 3160 ± 100/3965–3780 B.C. (K-1535) for the upper layers of Ertebølle (Tauber 1973:94) and 3420 ± 100/4410–3930 B.C. (K-750) for the late Ertebølle occupation of Christianholm (Tauber 1964:217), suggestive of a correlation with Rössen and Bischheim (see table 1). Similar dates come from the Ellerbek occupation at Rude (Schleswig-Holstein) (Barendsen, Deevey, and Gralenski 1957:911; see table 1). At Rude, as well as at the type site, Ellerbek near Kiel, there is a Mesolithic assemblage, but it is accompanied by conical-based pottery, domesticated animals, and perhaps some elements of agriculture, if one can trust the grain imprints found on a few pottery sherds. Calibrated dates indicate that this late phase of Ellerbek, which Schwabedissen (1962:260–63) called Proto-Neolithic, was contemporary with Rössen and Bischheim (see fig. 3).

The Early Neolithic Cultures

The full development of the Neolithic on the north European plain and in southern Scandinavia came with the Funnel Beaker (*Trichterbecher*) culture, which appears in its earliest form in southern Scandinavia, northern Germany, Czechoslovakia, and Poland. There have been many attempts to explain its origin, of which three are important. The first seeks an origin in eastern Europe (Becker 1954:155–65, 187–92; 1961b:599–600); the second derives it from the local north European Mesolithic (Jażdżewski 1936, 1965:81–83; Troels-Smith 1953:43–43; Schwabedissen 1958:35–42, 1962:260–65); and the third connects it with the Lengyel culture of the middle Danubian basin (Neustupný and Neustupný 1961:59). However, none of these interpretations is necessary for establishing the relative or absolute chronology of the Early Neolithic of northern Europe.

In Scandinavia (see fig. 2), the beginning of the Funnel Beaker culture can be established by the finds at Store Valby, unfortunately not dated by either radiocarbon or pollen-analytical determinations. The chronology must still rest on indirect evidence from sites such as Mulbjerg (Mul I) on Zealand. Here Store Valby pottery, which defines the beginning of phase A pottery of the Funnel Beaker culture, is associated with Ertebølle pottery. The average of the radiocarbon determinations on a variety of samples from Mulbjerg (K-123, 124, 125, 126, 127, 129, 131, and 132) places its occupation about 2820 ± 80/3675–3480 B.C. Pollen-analytical studies indicate that it dates after the decline of the *Ulmus* curve and before the spread of *Plantago lanceolata*, that is,

above the Atlantic/Subboreal boundary. The Mulbjerg date is in agreement with the Uppsala dates of 2740 ± 170/3665–3350 B.C. (U-47) and 2605 ± 140/3520–3040 B.C. (U-46) for samples from the Early Neolithic level at Vätteryd in Skåne, which is fixed by pollen-analytical analysis immediately above or later than the Atlantic/Subboreal boundary. On the basis of radiocarbon determinations, Godwin (1961:288) estimated that the Atlantic/Subboreal boundary should be placed ca. 3000 B.C. When this date is calibrated for the Bristlecone correction, it becomes a period ranging from 3885 to 3650 B.C., a range that supports the Mulbjerg and Vätteryd dates. Since Mulbjerg is an Ertebølle and not a Funnel Beaker A site and has a complicated stratigraphy, it is extremely difficult to date (Tauber 1960:7–8). The calibrated date of 3370 ± 210/4420–3880 B.C. (U-48) for charcoal and hazelnuts from the mixed Ertebølle–Early Neolithic site at Elinelund 71 in Skane probably gives a better dating for the beginning of the Funnel Beaker A culture in Scandinavia than Mulbjerg and Vätteryd, notwithstanding the usefulness of these latter sites in placing the Early Neolithic in relation to the climatic development of the north. Furthermore, the Elinelund date is supported by a date of 3310 ± 100/4165–3885 B.C. (K-923) for the habitation layer at Konens Høj (Jutland) and 3190 ± 115/3995–3790 B.C. (H-29–146) for the early Funnel Beaker level at Heidmoor in Schleswig-Holstein, despite the fact that neither occupation can be attributed to a specific phase of the Funnel Beaker culture (see table 1).

Unfortunately, the beginning of the Funnel Beaker culture is difficult to establish in northern Germany and the northern Netherlands. The isolated Funnel Beakers found here cannot be separated into A and B types, although, considered together, they are closer stylistically to the A types (Becker 1961b:591–92). Interpretation of the initial development of the Funnel Beaker culture on the north European plain is further hampered because outside Poland it is largely known from finds of single vessels, which in Scandinavian terms are attributable only to early Funnel Beaker, that is, to an A/B phase (see fig. 3). However, to the south, in Czechoslovakia, Neustupný (1961b:317–18) has postulated a Funnel Beaker A phase, based largely on a depot of pottery at Bozice (for a later dating see Lichardus 1976). This same depot, together with a few single vessel finds, was used by Zápotocký (1957:206–35) to establish his Funnel Beaker I phase, which was the equivalent of the A/B phase. Complications arose when attempts were made to correlate development in Czechoslovakia with that of the north European plain and southern Scandinavia, because central Germany had to be taken into account. Here Mildenberger (1953) postulated a Funnel Beaker development characterized by the succession of the Baalberg and Salzmunde cultures, while Fischer (1961:416–17) held that there was an early Baalberg culture and a late Baalberg culture, which paralleled the Salzmünde culture (see fig. 4). Many misunderstandings that persist until today arose from the fact that Neustupný equated his second Funnel Beaker phase (B) with Baalberg, while Zápotocký correlated his phase II (C) with Salzmünde (see fig. 4). Unfortunately, there are few archaeological finds with which to resolve this complicated problem of correlations. These are important for evaluating theories of origin, which, however, do not concern us here. What little field evidence there is for determining the beginnings of the Funnel Beaker culture consists of the cultural associations and a calibrated radiocarbon date of 3410 ± 160/ 4420–3905 B.C. (Bln-231) for grain from a pit sunk into a Linear *Bandkeramik* house at Kmehlen (Kreis Grossenhain), which was found with sherds of very early Funnel Beaker pottery (Baalberg type) and Gatersleben pottery. In central Germany, this find of the late fifth, early fourth millennium suggests that it is possible that early Baalberg not only goes back to Funnel Beaker A times, but also overlaps the end of Stroked Ware of the last half of the fifth millennium in the same way that Funnel Beaker overlaps Ertebølle in the north. During the early fourth millennium, the development of the early Funnel Beaker culture would have paralleled the early Michelsberg culture of western Germany, the Lengyel culture of western Hungary, and the Tiszapolgár culture of eastern Hungary and Slovakia (see Ehrich and Bankoff, chap. 21). The subsequent development of the Funnel Beaker must be traced separately in southern Scandinavia, the northern Netherlands, and northern and central Germany as well as in Poland (see Bogucki, this vol., chap. 20) and Czechoslovakia (see Ehrich and Bankoff, chap. 21).

In southern Scandinavia, the Funnel Beaker culture has been divided into four phases (A–D), the earliest in association with Late Ertebølle, the latest extending into the period of the passage graves that mark the beginning of the Middle Neolithic (see fig. 2). Following phase A, best defined by the assemblage at Store Valby, phase B is characterized by finds from the settlement at Havnelev in Zealand and by the single burial found in an oval pit or earth grave at Virring in Jutland (Mathiassen 1940:3–16; Brøndsted 1960:147–48). There is a calibrated radiocarbon date of 3060 ± 100/3900–3665 B.C. (K-1659) for a sample from a primary feature of a long barrow at Lindebjerg in northwest Zealand. This date, along with calibrated dates of 2960 ± 90/3870–3640 B.C. (K-3124) and 2860 ± 70/3675–3510 B.C. (K-3125) for phase B context at Rude in Jutland, suggests that phase B probably belongs in the latter part of the first half of the fourth millennium B.C. (see table 1). Various relations can be established within southern Scandinavia. B-type pottery turns up in Ertebølle sites such as Strandegaard, indicat-

ing that a late Ertebølle culture still lingered on and, indeed, in terms of other sites, continued perhaps to Middle Neolithic times. The dwelling places of southern Scandinavia have yielded Funnel Beaker pottery, but it is often difficult to distinguish whether it belongs to the A or B phases (Becker 1961b:590). Except for the baking plates of phases A and B, which are similar to those of the Michelsberg culture, traits with secure external connections are hard to find.

Funnel Beaker C phase is known from a vast number of finds that indicate the rise of at least three regional groups in Denmark and three or four in Sweden. This is the period of the *dysse* or dolmen which was generally covered by a round barrow or, if there is more than one tomb, by a long barrow. The *dysse* consists of small chambers, either square, rectangular, or with five or six sides. Until World War II the *dysse* was ascribed to outside influence, but Becker (1947:264–69) has shown that it could have evolved out of the use of boulders in flat cist graves. Since the *dysse* may not be a Western creation, external connections must be established by finds such as the copper disks of Salten in Jutland and the stone axes with splayed blades found at various sites in southern Scandinavia (Becker 1947:fig. 54). The Salten disks are like those from Brześć Kujawski of the Lengyel culture, the Stollhof hoard of the Bodrogkeresztúr culture, and the Romanian Hăbăşeşti hoard of the Linear *Bandkeramik* group. Although current in southeastern Europe in much earlier times, the disks did not reach northern Europe until the time of the Bodrogkeresztúr culture (Driehaus 1961). The collared flasks that appeared in phase B, the knob-hammer axes, which are certain in phase C, and the thin-butted stone axes are important not only for internal connections, but also for connections with the Funnel Beaker or derivative Funnel Beaker cultures of the northern Netherlands and northern and central Germany. A calibrated radiocarbon date for charcoal found below the stone pavement of the passage grave at Vroue, Jutland, 2620 ± 100, ranges from 3390 to 3155 B.C. (K-1566), along with calibrated dates of 2900 ± 100/3795–3515 B.C. (K-919) for the *dysse* at Konens Høj in Jutland and 2630 ± 90/3395–3160 B.C. (K-?) for C context at Sarup in Fünen, place the Funnel Beaker C phase in the last half of the fourth millennium (see table 1). This agrees with available dates for the Lengyel and Bodrogkeresztúr cultures (see Ehrich and Bankoff, chap. 21).

In the northern Netherlands and northern and central Germany, the early Funnel Beaker culture (A/B), which had so much in common with the Funnel Beaker culture of phases A and B, developed along markedly regional lines during the time of Scandinavian Funnel Beaker C culture (see figs. 3 and 4). Until the 1950s it was thought that the megalithic graves found in the northern Netherlands, northwestern Germany, Schleswig-Holstein,

Mecklenburg, and occasionally in central Germany were related to the passage graves of later Middle Neolithic Scandinavia. Dehnke (1940:175–80) assumed a parallel development between northwestern Germany and Scandinavia from a common Funnel Beaker A/B culture, while Sprockhoff (1938:20–24) held that the distinctive megalithic grave of northwest Germany evolved in and spread from Holstein. In the middle fifties, the work of Lüüdik-Kaelas (1955:71–73) showed that the early megalithic graves of the northern Netherlands lacked the distinctive ladle and developed footed bowl of the Middle Neolithic passage graves of southern Scandinavia, but possessed handled jugs and/or collared flasks which are typical of Funnel Beaker C but are absent in the Middle Neolithic of the north (Bakker 1980; Knöll 1981).

In the northern Netherlands the early megalithic grave is well known from the numerous *hunebedden* of the province of Drenthe. In the famous tombs at Drouwen (*Hunebed* D-19) and Bronnegger (*Hunebed* D-25) are elongated burial chambers with side entrances covered by mounds. At Drouwen, the burial chamber yielded not only a spoon, a low-footed bowl, and a collared flask, but also copper fragments (Giffen 1927:83–96). A similar grave at Buinen (*Hunebed* D-28) (De Laet 1958:84–88) yielded two copper spirals, which have excellent connections with the Jordanów culture and clearly support an attribution to the time of Funnel Beaker C. The high-footed bowl of Drouwen is entirely comparable to those of the Jordanów and Salzmünde cultures, further securing the archaeological correlations of these graves. Calibrated radiocarbon dates of 2640 ± 80/3400–3160 B.C. (GrN-2226) for a similar grave at Odoorn (Drenthe) and 2430 ± 75/3355–2905 B.C. (GrN-4201) for a settlement at Angelslo (Drenthe) provide further supporting evidence (see table 1).

The closely related *Hunenbetten* of northwest Germany, Schleswig-Holstein, and Mecklenburg probably began in Funnel Beaker C times. The earliest, such as Tosterglope I and Haassel, both in Lower Saxony, yielded a pottery with early *Tiefstich* decoration entirely comparable to the decoration of the so-called Drouwen style. As in the northern Netherlands, this pottery in the Haassel style comes from both flat graves and megalithic chamber graves, along with funnel beakers and flasks, but not the distinctive footed bowls or spoons found in the tombs of the Netherlands (Dehnke 1940:68, 149). Extending into Mecklenburg, the somewhat simpler type of burial chamber is covered by a trapezoidal mound. In turn, these Mecklenburg mounds are comparable to the wedge-shaped or trapezoidal mounds of Kujavian type that extend eastward from the Oder into Poland. Here a calibrated radiocarbon date of 2675 ± 40/3520–3355 B.C. (GrN-5044) for a settlement pit at Zarębowo (Wielkopolskie) places it in the time of the Funnel Beaker C

graves in northwestern Germany and in the northern Netherlands. This pit has an assemblage of the Wiórek phase of the Funnel Beaker culture, which can be equated with Funnel Beaker C. It is important to note that pottery found at the settlement of Wiórek has Salzmünde connections, while spirals similar to those of Buinen in the Netherlands and the Jordanów cemetery turn up in the Kujavian barrow at Lesniczowka, which is also datable to the Wiórek phase (see Bogucki, chap. 20). This circle of connections is completed by the Mecklenburg megalithic graves, the pottery of which is similar to that of late Baalberg in shape and decoration, and should date to early Salzmünde times (Bakker, Vogel, and Wiślański 1969:9–10, 214–15). Although the origin of these diverse megalithic types falls outside the scope of this chapter, these connections suggest that the *dysse* of southern Scandinavia, the *hunebedden* of the northern Netherlands, the *Hunenbetten* of northwest Germany, Schleswig-Holstein, and Mecklenburg, and the Kujavian barrows of Great Poland date to the Funnel Beaker C horizon and may well represent regional developments within this culture.

The construction of the relative chronology of the Funnel Beaker culture not only of northern Germany but also of southern Scandinavia depends on the interpretation of the chronology of central Germany. Here the Baalberg culture is of particular importance because of its connections with other cultures. Unfortunately, its chronological position within central Germany and its specific relationships with Bohemia and Moravia are difficult to establish. Mildenberger (1953:49–51) assumed that it must correlate with Funnel Beaker C in the north, and that the Salzmünde culture succeeded it. On the other hand, Fischer (1951:104, 1961:416–17; see also Preuss 1961:405–13 and Driehaus and Pleslová 1961:370–72) holds that the Baalberg culture continued into a late phase that paralleled the Salzmünde culture. These interpretations are based on the geographic distribution of these central German cultures and on the stratigraphy of their burial tumuli. At Baalberg itself, the Funnel Beaker material comes from a ground grave in a tumulus with later burials of the Walternienburg, Globular Amphora, and Corded Ware cultures (Höfer 1902:15–49; Mildenberger 1953:23–25). The beginning of the Baalberg culture overlapped late Rössen and Gatersleben, which had replaced Linear *Bandkeramik* in central Germany (Lichardus 1976). The contemporary Bohemian Baalberg group can be linked with the Schussenried culture, which overlaps early Michelsberg in western Germany (Neustupný 1961b:314–16). The Michelsberg culture, which by then had displaced both Rössen and Stroked Ware in the upper and middle Rhine basin, expanded not only northward into the lower Rhine basin to penetrate the southern Low Countries, but also eastward into Bohemia. During early Michelsberg II times, Michelsberg elements reached central Germany, where they occur in the context of Jordanów-related cultures. It was only in its late phase, when the Michelsberg culture dominated the whole of the Rhine basin, that it moved in force up the Main Valley and into Bohemia. Late Michelsberg is found as a distinct culture in Bohemia, where it is connected with Siřem or later Baalberg groups (Scollar 1959:97–100; see Ehrich and Bankoff, chap. 21, for discussion of Siřem phase), confirming the earlier tie between Baalberg, Schussenried, and early Michelsberg. The Salzmünde culture and presumably later Baalberg may connect with late Jordanów, which has two-handled tankards, cylindrical ribbon bracelets, spectacle spirals, and small disks with embossed ornament that must derive from the southeast at the time of the Bodrogkeresztúr culture (Childe 1958:123). Similar connections of the Scandinavian Funnel Beaker C phase would support an equation of the C groups in southern Scandinavia with Salzmünde and later Baalberg in central Germany. This web of interrelations suggests that the Scandinavian Funnel Beaker B phase connects through earlier Baalberg to the Schussenried and early Michelsberg cultures, whereas the Scandinavian Funnel Beaker C phase links through Salzmünde and later Baalberg to later Michelsberg, late Jordanów, and Bodrogkeresztúr. Unfortunately, it is difficult to correlate the development in central Germany with that proposed for Bohemia and Moravia by E. F. Neustupný (1956:66–69, 1961:441–57) and Zápotocký (1957:206–35; see also Driehaus 1959:53–64, and below see Ehrich and Bankoff, chap. 21).

There are several calibrated radiocarbon dates for Schussenried, early Michelsberg, Rössen, and Salzmünde important for the above synchronisms for the Funnel Beaker culture. Although the early Baalberg connections are primarily important for the dating of Funnel Beaker A, the Ehrenstein calibrated dates of 3250 ± 140/4150–3800 B.C. (H-125–107) and 3190 ± 130/4120–3780 B.C. (H-61–148) for Schussenried and early Michelsberg permit the beginning of the Funnel Beaker B phase to go back before the middle of the fourth millennium. The Ehrenstein dates are also supported by the Wählitz date of 3350 ± 200/4415–3875 B.C. (Gro-433) for the Rössen culture, which overlapped the early Baalberg. On the other hand, the calibrated dates for a Salzmünde site in central Germany suggest that the Funnel Beaker B phase could have come to an end by the middle of the fourth millennium. Two charcoal samples from the ditch before the palisade of the Salzmünde settlement on the Dölauer Heide near Halle give dates of 2830 ± 100/3675–3485 B.C. (Bln-64) and 2680 ± 100/3545–3345 B.C. (Bln-53), indicating that the Funnel Beaker C phase occupied the last half of the fourth millennium. This dating is supported by a calibrated date of 2725 ± 110/3650–3360 B.C. (H-566–592) for a sample from the

settlement of Ćmielów, usually assigned to Funnel Beaker C (see Bogucki, chap. 20). These calibrated dates (see table 1), which are supported by connections of the Funnel Beaker C phase of Scandinavia, the later Baalberg and Salzmünde cultures of central Germany, the Siřem culture of Bohemia, the Jordanów culture of western Poland, and the Bodrogkeresztúr culture of Hungary agree with those of Vroue, Konens Høj, and Sarup for the Funnel Beaker C phase in southern Scandinavia, supporting the attribution of this phase in the Netherlands, northwest Germany, and central Germany as well as southern Scandinavia to the last half of the fourth millennium.

The Middle Neolithic Cultures

In northern Europe, the Middle Neolithic brought a further cultural regionalization which led to marked differences between southern Scandinavia, the Netherlands, northwest Germany, and central Germany. In Scandinavia, the Middle Neolithic began with the appearance of the Megalithic passage grave, which was long thought to be an introduction from the west because of its excellent Portuguese and Breton prototypes (Daniel 1959:55–59). The relative chronology of the Scandinavian Middle Neolithic rests on the pottery from a series of short-lived settlements in Denmark. Troldebjerg and Klintebakke define Middle Neolithic Ia and Ib, while Blandebjerg, Bundsø, Lindø, and Store Valby characterize Middle Neolithic II–V (see fig. 2). The pottery of each of these settlements, fixed typologically in relation to the preceding and subsequent settlements, can be used to date finds associated with pottery from passage graves and occasionally from hoards (Becker 1961b:585–94).

The famous Danish hoard of Bygholm near Horsens in Jutland has long been used to establish the beginning of the Passage Grave period, for it is securely fixed to Middle Neolithic Ia. This hoard consists of four stone axes, two copper arm spirals, and a copper dagger with a midrib on one side, similar to those found in Portuguese megalithic tombs. Unhappily, the Bygholm hoard is far from diagnostic, since the Portuguese connection is difficult to fix chronologically, and the arm spirals might well have been current as early as Funnel Beaker C.

The beginning of the Middle Neolithic in Denmark is ambiguous because Middle Neolithic Ia, which is defined by pottery from the settlement of Troldebjerg (Winther 1935), is still associated with *dysse*, not passage graves. The passage grave began in Middle Neolithic Ib when pottery such as that found in the settlement of Klintebakke was current (Becker 1961b:588–89; Berg 1951). Unfortunately, this is transitional in character, consisting partly of Funnel Beaker types—now classified as D phase—and partly of new ones such as a footed bowl and a broad ladle. In this pottery we see the beginning of densely furrowed decoration. There are few types that can be connected with similar ones outside Scandinavia, but the footed bowl is similar to the Middle Danubian footed bowl. The pottery in the so-called Grand Style of Middle Neolithic II has its closest similarities with that of the Walternienburg of central Germany. External relations are equally limited for Middle Neolithic III. Its pottery decoration and more rounded profiles have been explained as Bell Beaker influence. Connections for Middle Neolithic IV and V are even more tenuous (Ebbesen 1975).

The Passage Grave culture of Sweden closely follows the Danish pattern, although Early Neolithic elements tended to linger longer than in Denmark. There is little that is important for external chronological connections except that the tanged and barbed arrowheads from the Fjärrestad passage grave (Lüüdik-Kaelas 1952:165–75) date to Middle Neolithic III, provided that these points represent an intrusion of Bell Beaker influence.

Internal development is difficult to follow in Sweden because of the rise of sub-Neolithic cultures, which can now be dated as early as the first stages of the Middle Neolithic at sites such as Hennige Bro (Thomas 1961:810) and Jonstorp (Bagge 1951b:50–51). These cultures, which have been called Dwelling Place, Pitted Ware, and Secondary Neolithic, occur in southern, central, and western Sweden and in southern Norway, and represent the assimilation of Neolithic elements by late Ertebølle peoples (Thomas 1961:809–13). Thomas regards the Pitted Ware A/B culture which spread through Scandinavia during the late Passage Grave period as Secondary Neolithic, but Becker has argued that it represents an intrusion from the Russian woodlands (Becker 1950:153–263). In any event, these cultures and those of the Arctic north, which cannot be dealt with here, are not of major importance in determining the relative position of the Scandinavian Passage Grave culture in the chronology of northern Europe.

Aside from the passage graves, which have obvious western European connections, several synchronisms place the early Passage Grave period within the framework of a wider European chronology. The form of the first southern Scandinavian passage graves is like those of Portugal and Brittany, and their connection with western Europe is reinforced by the dagger of the Bygholm hoard. Unhappily, however, these similarities are so general that they have little chronological value. The early passage graves of Brittany are now dated by calibrated radiocarbon determinations to the fifth millennium, but this is of little value for fixing the beginning of the Scandinavian passage graves. The dating of the Passage Grave period must rest on archaeological synchronisms. The similarity of the Middle Neolithic II pottery to that of the Walternienburg, which immediately followed the Salz-

münde or derived, along with the Salzmünde, from the Baalberg (Preuss 1961:408), suggests that Middle Neolithic I must be tied to later Salzmünde times, since Funnel Beaker C must be connected with early Salzmünde on the basis of the Siřem-Jordanów synchronism and southeastern connections. The long accepted equation of Walternienburg with Middle Neolithic II would fit well into the relative chronology of central and northern Europe, for Walternienburg gave way to the mature Corded Ware culture of central Germany, and the related Single Grave culture became widespread in Scandinavia during the subsequent Middle Neolithic V, following what must have been brief Middle Neolithic III and IV periods. The Corded Ware cultures, which extend across the whole of central Europe and southern Scandinavia and should form a convenient chronological horizon, may be as early as the late fourth millennium, judging by radiocarbon determinations for material found in Corded Ware context in the Netherlands. However, in view of the long period covered by the Corded Ware cultures, such dates are of little value in fixing the chronology of the Middle Neolithic.

Within southern Scandinavia, there are several radiocarbon dates for Middle Neolithic I, but only one for its subsequent development (see table 1). Calibrated radiocarbon dates of 2440 ± 120/3355–2910 B.C. (K-718) for Tustrup, 2480 ± 120/3365–2930 B.C. (K-717) for Ferslev, 2590 ± 110/3385–3135 B.C. (K-1601) for Fovlum, and dates ranging from 2700 ± 100/3575–3350 B.C. (K-1766) to 2580 ± 100/3380–3045 B.C. (K-1769) for Herrup, all in Jutland, place Middle Neolithic Ia at the end of the fourth/beginning of the third millennium. Unfortunately, the calibrated dates of 2610 ± 100/3390–3150 B.C. (K-1568) and 2480 ± 100/3365–2930 B.C. (K-1567) for the passage grave at Vroue (Jutland) and 2540 ± 120/3375–3020 B.C. (K-978) for the passage grave at Katbjerg (Jutland), which are dated to Middle Neolithic Ib, only reveal the inherent limitations of the use of radiocarbon determinations in the separation of periods with short time spans. The calibrated dates available for the subsequent periods of the Middle Neolithic, such as those ranging from 2350 ± 100/3155–2870 B.C. (K-1571) to 2260 ± 100/3005–2765 B.C. (K-1574) for the late graves of the passage grave at Vroue and 2360 ± 100/3160–2875 B.C. (K-1789) for the stone packing grave at Øster Ristofte (Jutland), come only from contexts datable to Middle Neolithic V (see table 1). These calibrated dates, together with Swedish passage grave dates, indicate that the Middle Neolithic was of short duration, which fits very well with current concepts (Becker 1981). Furthermore, they are supported by archaeological synchronisms, with supporting radiocarbon dates, with northern and central Germany.

The Funnel Beaker tradition continued on the north

European plain, but now gave rise to distinct regional cultures. In the northern Netherlands, northwest Germany, Schleswig-Holstein, and Mecklenburg, these cultures are characterized by megalithic graves destined to last until the domination of the mature Corded Ware culture. Their development is traceable through two successive stages that paralleled the Passage Grave culture of Middle Neolithic Scandinavia and the late Salzmünde and Walternienburg cultures in central Germany. To the southwest, these cultures were bordered by the Michelsberg culture of the southern Low Countries and the Rhineland (see Thomas and R. Rowlett, this vol., chap. 17). In the western Netherlands (see fig. 3), this was the time of the Vlaardingen culture, which had inherited the dune areas of the west from the earlier Hazendodonk and still earlier Swifterbank cultures. Calibrated radiocarbon dates ranging from 2470 ± 120/3365–2925 B.C. (GrN-4114) to 2300 ± 75/3040–2785 B.C. (GrN-2304) for the type site of Vlaardingen in South Holland and calibrated dates as late as 2140 ± 50/2875–2620 B.C. (GrN-4906) for Voorschoten, South Holland, suggest that the Vlaardingen culture began during the late fourth millennium during the time of the Funnel Beaker C cultures (see table 1). Such a dating would explain the presence of later undecorated collared flasks at Vlaardingen sites. On the other hand, the later ranges indicate that the Vlaardingen culture continued until the dominance of the Beaker cultures. Although the Vlaardingen culture had its principle connections to the west, its later phases would have been contemporary with the Havelte phase of the late Funnel Beaker culture of the northern Netherlands (Kooijmans 1974:10–26; see table 1). To the east in East Germany and Poland, the late Funnel Beaker cultures were gradually displaced by the emergence of the Globular Amphora culture during the late fourth and early third millennium (see Bogucki, chap. 20).

In the northern Netherlands, the development of the late Funnel Beaker culture is defined by the succession of the Early and Late Havelte styles of pottery that succeeded the Drouwen style (see fig. 3). The Early Havelte stage has a calibrated radiocarbon date of 2470 ± 55/3355–2955 B.C. (GrN-1824) at Anlo in Drenthe. A range of calibrated dates, 2365 ± 60/3150–2895 B.C. (GrN-5765) to 2195 ± 100/2915–2635 B.C. (GrN-2370), for Angelslo, also in Drenthe, places the Late Havelte stage somewhat later in the early third millennium (see table 1). In synchronous *Hunebedden,* the relative chronology of this succession is attested by the pottery of lower and upper pavement B of *hunebed* D-25 at Bronnegar (Giffen 1927:231–71).

In northwestern Germany, the development of the *Hunenbetten* culture is marked by the Early and Developed styles of *Tiefstichkeramik,* for which the relative chronological position is tied by its Developed-style pottery to

that of the Walternienburg culture (see fig. 3). The cemetery at Pevestorf (Kreis Lüchow-Dannenberg, Lower Saxony) has yielded early burials of a Globular Amphora b culture which show connections with Bernburg, in part contemporary of Walternienburg, and the "East Harz amphora" group of the Corded Ware culture (Voss 1965:361–68). A calibrated radiocarbon date of 2430 ± 100/3355–2905 B.C. (Hv-582), together with these connections, suggests that both Globular Amphora and Corded Ware elements were already in eastern northwest Germany by the time of the Developed *Tiefstichkeramik* (see table 1 and fig. 3).

Phasing of the megalithic graves in Schleswig-Holstein and Mecklenburg is more difficult to determine, but pottery from graves such as at Lont in Schleswig-Holstein show relationships with the Scandinavian Middle Neolithic Ib period (see fig. 3). At Rugge, near Flemsburg, a *Hunebett* yields a stone double ax with excellent Scandinavian Middle Neolithic IV analogies, and pottery with Globular Amphora connections (Dehnke 1940:23–24; Davidsen 1972). In Mecklenburg, burials yield primary graves with globular amphorae of the Mecklenburg-Pomeranian subgroup and then secondary burials with pre-Mansfeld Corded Ware, which should also be datable to these times (Preuss 1976). Dating is indicated by calibrated dates at Gnewitz and Serrahn.

The traditions of the central German Funnel Beaker culture continued from the late fourth into the early third millennium, their development traceable in the succession of the late Salzmünde and Walternienburg cultures (see fig. 4). The late Salzmünde, known from fortified settlements such as Salzmünde and Halle-Heide in Province Saxony, is marked off from early Salzmünde by its pre-Walternienburg cups with *Tiefstich* decoration (Fischer 1969). Fischer (1961) has argued that its pottery decoration was the inspiration for the feather-bundle motif on amphorae like the one from Hefta (Province Saxony), which mark the beginning of the Corded Ware culture in central Germany. Furthermore, sherds of Corded Ware come from Salzmünde itself and should date before its destruction. The northwest German *Hunebetten* connections of Salzmünde pottery suggest that Corded Ware was as early in central Germany as it was in the northern Netherlands, to judge from a calibrated date of 2545 ± 60/3370–3050 B.C. (GrN-6295) for a single grave of the "Protruding Foot Beaker" group of the Corded Ware culture at Hikken in Drenthe (see table 1). During the succeeding Walternienburg culture of Saxony and Thuringia and the related Bernburg, Schonfeld, and Elbe-Havelland cultures of the northern province of Saxony and of Brandenburg, older traditions continued despite an increase of both Corded Ware and Globular Amphora elements. Archaeological connections tying the Walternienburg culture to the time of the Developed *Tief-*

stichkeramik of the late megalithic of northwestern Germany and to the "Grand Style" pottery of the passage graves of Middle Neolithic II of southern Scandinavia are in part fixed chronologically by a calibrated radiocarbon date of 2155 ± 100/2895–2545 B.C. (Bln-838) for a Bernburg context at Dölauer Heide near Halle (Province Saxony) (see table 1). In central Germany, the stratigraphy of many of the barrows, such as those at Bohlen-Zeschwitz and Burgorner, indicates that the Walternienburg and Corded Ware cultures might well be contemporary (Mildenberger 1953:26–27). This correlation is supported by the location of Walternienburg settlements on heights that were probably fortified, suggesting that they existed in troubled times.

The Single Grave and Corded Ware cultures, which occur throughout much of central and northern Europe, form a cultural horizon of great importance, but because they developed over such a long period, caution is required when relating this horizon to chronological problems (see figs. 2–4). As suggested above, the appearance of these cultures as intrusive elements in the late megalithic graves of the northern Netherlands, northwestern Germany, Schleswig-Holstein, and Mecklenburg and in contact with the Salzmünde and Walternienburg cultures is probably indicative of their beginning phases. In southern Scandinavia, the presence of a widespread Single Grave culture is not indicated before the time of the passage graves of Middle Neolithic V (Becker 1981:109–16). Eventually these cultures, which were everywhere characterized by their single burials, generally under tumuli, and with corded pottery, and battle-axes, came to dominate all of central and north Europe.

On the north European plain, Corded Ware cultures extended from the Netherlands eastward across Germany into Poland. Although there are many theories concerning their origin, few have any direct bearing on either the chronology of these cultures or the archaeological chronology of the region. Whether they came from the outside or evolved within the region, present evidence suggests that in their earliest phases they were limited factors in the areas in which they were to become dominant. In general European terms, Corded Ware begins at about the time of or shortly after the onset of the Globular Amphora episode, which must be linked to eastern Europe (Ehrich and Bankoff, chap. 21; Bogucki, chap. 20). Once formed, the Corded Ware culture developed along regional lines. Distinct regional groups arose in central Germany in Saxo-Thuringia, northern Germany, the Netherlands, the Rhine basin, and in southern Scandinavia.

In central Germany, the relative chronological position of Corded Ware is established by the sequence of Baalberg, Walternienburg/Bernburg, Globular, Amphora, and Corded Ware burials in the Baalberg barrow; of Bern-

burg, Corded Ware, and Aunjetitz (Únětice) in the Helmsdorf barrow; and of Baalberg, Corded Ware, Globular Amphora, and Aunjetitz burials in the Defflinger barrow, together with similar sequences of burials in more than thirty other such barrows in central Germany (Mildenberger 1953:23–47). As indicated above, its beginnings probably go as far back as the time of Salzmünde, while its full development, designated as Kalbsrieth, took place in Walternienburg times (Fischer 1958:192–96). In the later Mansfeld phase, it became dominant in central Germany. Calibrated radiocarbon dates of 2115 ± 100/2880–2535 B.C. (Bln-533) for a grave at Dornburg, 1990 ± 100/2645–2310 B.C. (Bln-65) for a grave of the barrow of Dölauer Heide, and 1880 ± 100/2425–2155 B.C. (Bln-166) for a grave of barrow III at Forst Leina place the Mansfeld phase in the middle third millennium. There is a further date of 2055 ± 65/2660–2525 B.C. (Bln-942) for a sample from Quedlinberg in the central province of Saxony belonging to the late Schonfeld (II) culture, which equates archaeologically with the Mansfeld phase (Wetzel 1976:28; see table 1). In the late third millennium, the Corded Ware culture gave way to the Proto-Aunjetitz or Proto-Únětice, which lasted until the beginning of the Early Bronze Age (Lüning 1980).

In northwestern Germany and Schleswig-Holstein, Corded Ware pottery marks the final phase of the *Hunenbetten*. Although there are instances of earlier correlations, much of the Corded Ware clearly ties to that of the Mansfeld phase of central Germany (Struve 1955:41–44). Once established in northwestern Germany, the dominant Corded Ware groups had many external connections useful for constructing their chronological position. At Logabirumerfeld (Lower Saxony), there is a net-decorated beaker typical of the Lower Graves of the Single Grave culture of Denmark. On the other hand, the All-over-Corded beaker found in a ground grave at Holzhausen (Oldenburg) is similar to those of the middle Corded Ware phase in the Netherlands (Pätzold 1958), confirmed by a calibrated radiocarbon date of 2150 ± 110/2890–2540 B.C. (H-556-483) for this grave. These correlations are supported by the calibrated radiocarbon date of 2090 ± 80/2865–2525 B.C. (GrN-4058) for the tumulus at Katenbaker Heide (Oldenburg), which has a Protruding Foot Beaker. In the late third millennium, a transitional Late Neolithic culture prepared the way for the rise of the Early Bronze Age. This culture was characterized by a *Kummerkeramik* in northwestern Germany, *Fischgratenbechern* in Schleswig-Holstein, and *Wickelschnurkeramik* in Mecklenburg and Brandenburg (Clarke 1970:140–43). At Amelinghausen Lower Saxony, a Type I flint dagger found with degenerate Corded Ware marks this transitional age. Farther north a Type I flint dagger occurs with a *Fischgratenbecher* both at Jordkirch and Bredenbek in Schleswig-Holstein. These connections argue for equating this transitional age with the Late Neolithic of southern Scandinavia and are supported by a calibrated radiocarbon date of 1680 ± 80/2185–1875 B.C. (GrN-3518) for a *Kummerkeramik* burial at Wildeshausen in Oldenburg/Lower Saxony (see table 1).

In the Netherlands and northern Belgium, this age of the Beaker cultures went through three periods of development. Protruding Foot Beakers (Ia) characterized by a slender S-profile, a small protruding foot, and a cord-impressed decoration restricted to the neck of the vessel characterized the first period. These early beakers designated as Ia by Lanting and van der Waals (1976; see also van der Waals and Glasbergen 1955; Glasbergen and van de Waals 1961) were thought to be derived from the Corded Ware beakers of central Germany, but today are given a more generalized origin within the Corded Ware culture. Calibrated radiocarbon dates of 2545 ± 60/3370–3050 B.C. (GrN-6295) for Hijken, 2260 ± 40/2935–2785 B.C. (GrN-6724) for Nordbarge, both in Drenthe, and 2215 ± 55/2905–2760 B.C. (GrN-6129) for Ede in Gelderland place the early period of these beakers in the late fourth and early third millennium B.C. The middle period is marked by a proliferation of beaker types in the Corded Ware tradition: Ib beakers decorated with grooved lines, Ic–d beakers ornamented with herringbone patterns, often with either grooved or cord-impressed lines, and ZZ beakers with horizontal bands of zigzags separated by grooves. It must be noted that their distinctive decoration is applied quite differently from those in other Corded Ware traditions such as during the Mansfeld phase of the Corded Ware culture of central Germany. At Eext, in Drenthe, a Ib beaker is dated 1995 ± 40/2640–2390 B.C. (GrN-6349), while at this site ZZ beakers are dated 2195 ± 30/2890–2655 B.C. (GrN-6787) and 1935 ± 65/2430–2305 B.C. (GrN-939). At De Eese, also in Drenthe, a Ie beaker has a calibrated date of 1920 ± 55/2425–2295 B.C. (GrN-6687). Together, the ranges of these calibrated radiocarbon dates place the variously decorated beakers of the middle period, which are often found with battle-axes, in the middle of the third millennium. During the same period the decoration spread from its neck to the whole surface of the beaker, giving rise to the All-over-Ornamented (AOO) (2IIa–b) beaker. Calibrated radiocarbon dates of 2190 ± 70/2895–2645 B.C. (GrN-851) for the AOO beaker found at Anlo in Drenthe and 2030 ± 60/2650–2515 B.C. (GrN-4908) for one found at Voorschoten in south Holland, where a habitation also yielded sherds of Ia, Ib, and Id beakers, place the AOO beakers in the same period as the developed Corded Ware beakers (see table 1).

In the middle of the third millennium, Bell Beakers

appear in the Netherlands and the Rhineland. Typologically, the Bell Beakers that Dutch archaeologists designate as Maritime Bell Beakers (2Ia) seem already developed or locally modified types as compared to Bell Beakers from either Brittany or the south of France (Treinen 1970:67–75, 263–95). Calibrated radiocarbon dates ranging from 1960 ± 30/2435–2320 B.C. (GrN-2518) to 1900 ± 50/2420–2190 B.C. (GrN-3097) for Vlaardingen in south Holland (Glasbergen, Groenman van Waateringe, and Hardenberg-Mulder 1967) and from 2144 ± 240/2935–2505 B.C. (IRPA-3) to 1945 ± 40/2435–2310 B.C. (GrN-6646) for Mol in East Flanders (Beex and Roosens 1962, 1963) suggest that they too date to the middle period of these beaker cultures. For purposes of chronology, it is important to note that Bell Beakers with an incipient zone decoration (2Ib) occur at Ede-Ginkelse in Gelderland and Odoorn in Drenthe with tanged daggers, an association typical of the Middle-style Beakers of the British Isles, which are also datable to the middle of the third millennium (see table 1; also Thomas and R. Rowlett, chap. 17).

The development of the Bell Beaker led through the zoned Bell Beaker (2Ic) to the distinctive Veluwe Beaker, which can be dated to the late third millennium on the basis of calibrated dates of 1685 ± 40/2170–1900 B.C. (GrN-5131) for Molenaarsgraf in Limburg, 1925 ± 35/2435–2300 B.C. (GrN-7099) for Wageningen in Gelderland, and 1870 ± 35/2410–2170 B.C. (GrN-6155) for Bennekom in Drenthe. The Veluwe beaker dominated the eastern Netherlands, continuing down to the eve of the Early Bronze Age. In the northern Netherlands, Barbed Wire beakers appear in the late Beaker period, an attribution supported by calibrated dates of 1670 ± 65/2155–1890 B.C. (GrN-852) and 1645 ± 85/2165–1860 B.C. (GrN-1977) for the Barbed Wire beaker at Anlo and 1720 ± 35/2185–1950 B.C. (GrN-6367) for the one at Eext, both in Drenthe (see table 1). Further supporting evidence is provided by the contemporaneity of Barbed Wire Beakers of the Late Beaker period in the eastern British Isles (see Thomas and R. Rowlett, chap. 17). The time of the Veluwe Beaker was also that of the Pot Beakers, which tie, on the one hand, to those in eastern England, where one at Fifty Farm, Cambridgeshire is dated by a calibrated determination to 1850 ± 150/2425–1995 B.C. (BM-155) (see Thomas and R. Rowlett, chap. 17, table 1), and on the other to the *Kümmerkeramik* of northwestern Germany at much the same time.

In the Rhineland, the Corded Ware culture appeared at approximately the same time as in the Netherlands. It is found in the central German uplands from Hesse to Westphalia and in the lower, middle, and upper Rhine as well as the Main valleys. Stratigraphic evidence from Eschenz-Insel Werd in Canton Thurgau, Bodman in Bodensee, and Wilcheringen in Canton Schaffhausen indicates that it displaced the Michelsberg culture (Scollar 1959:96–97). The development of the Corded Ware culture is less well defined in the Rhine Valley and its associated uplands than in either the Netherlands or central Germany. Recent studies, such as that of the Main-Tauber area (Wamser 1981), suggest that the "Beaker" culture was characterized by an intense geographic "particularism" that is not yet fully understood. Until this is possible, it will be necessary to use broader geographical groupings such as the *Westdeutsche Becher* group of Sangmeister, the "Southwest" German group of Sangmeister and Gerhardt (1965), and the "West" and "East" Swiss groups of Strahm (1981). All these investigations point to the existence of an early period of Corded Ware development, which was characterized by a relatively uniform Corded Ware culture, often assigned to what is called an *Einheits-Horizont*. The later development was complicated by influences of other cultures as well as by the Bell Beaker complex. Any analysis of this difficult problem falls outside the scope of this chapter, but it can be noted, for instance, that the occurrence of a developed Bell Beaker with an AOO Beaker at Altlussheim (Müller-Karpe 1974: pl. 516, H 6 and 10) suggests that in terms of Dutch development the maturity of Beaker development probably belongs to the middle of the third millennium. During the late third millennium, cultural development in the Rhineland was caught up in those currents of culture change spreading across southern central Europe that led to the formation of an Early Bronze culture.

In Scandinavia, the recent work of Davidsen (1978) has demonstrated that the passage graves of Middle Neolithic V, identified by the pottery of Store Valby, were not restricted to the Danish Isles (Becker 1954), but extended throughout Denmark. This means that the Lower Graves of the Single Grave culture became common not in Middle Neolithic III but in V, an assumption clearly supported by calibrated radiocarbon dates. With Middle Neolithic V limited to the early third millennium, calibrated dates of 2130 ± 100/2885–2535 B.C. (K-1843) for Gabøl and 2200 ± 100/2915–2635 B.C. (K-1582) for Vester Nebel, both in Jutland, now place the Lower Graves of the Single Grave culture in the early middle third millennium. The Ground Graves fall in the middle of the third millennium through calibrated dates of 1950 ± 120/2560–2295 B.C. (K-1284) for Kobberup, 2050 ± 100/2670–2505 B.C. (K-1451) for Gammelstrup, and Upper Graves possibly belong in the late middle third

millennium with calibrated dates of 1940 ± 100/2555–2285 B.C. (K-1138) for Gasse Høje and 1910 ± 100/2435–2175 B.C. (K-2067) for Myrhøj, all in Jutland. This chronology, together with the new concept of development of the Single Grave culture in Denmark, fits very well with central German development, where increasing evidence suggests that the full displacement of older traditions (Walternienburg, etc.) did not take place until the Mansfeld phase of the Corded Ware culture, which is also datable to the middle of the third millennium. A Bell Beaker level at Heidmoor in Schleswig-Holstein suggests that they too were current in the north during the third millennium B.C. (see table 1).

In southern Sweden, the Middle Neolithic was an age of great complexity, making it difficult to separate passage grave, Single-Grave, and Pitted Ware elements. Assuming that the displacement of the passage grave took place at much the same time in Sweden and Denmark, we may consider the Swedish and Norwegian Boat Ax culture to have been contemporary with the Bottom Grave phase of the Single Grave culture of Denmark. Unfortunately, the so-called boat-ax variety of this period, which many authors have linked to copper versions in eastern Russia, is not specifically useful for chronology. Finds from Fagervik III–IV are more helpful, suggesting that the Early Swedish Boat Ax culture came into contact with Pitted Ware as the latter reached its late classic B/C and Final C phases (Bagge 1951a:57–118; Becker 1980). We can thus regard the Early and Late Swedish phases of the Swedish Boat Ax culture as parallel to the Ground and Upper Grave phases of the Danish Single Grave culture.

The Late Neolithic Cultures

In the late third millennium the diverse cultural elements of the Single Grave and the Boat Ax cultures together with lingering Pitted Ware elements coalesced into the Cist Grave culture of the Late Neolithic. The dating of the beginning of the Cist Grave culture, which was to last until the Early Bronze Age, is indicated not only by the calibrated carbon date of 1610 ± 120/2135–1755 B.C. (K-1204) for a cist grave at Gaev Bakke, Jutland, but also by the connections of its flint daggers and *Wickelschnurkeramik* to daggers and pottery of similarly dated finds in northwest Germany, Schleswig-Holstein, and northern Germany.

Nineteen

The Neolithic Chronology of Central Europe: Southern Germany, Switzerland, and Austria

Peter S. Wells, University of Minnesota

Outline

Early Neolithic
Middle Neolithic
Late Neolithic

Eneolithic
Early Bronze Age
The Synchronic Chart

This discussion presents an up-to-date account of the principal defined cultural groups of the Neolithic period, from the beginnings of agricultural economy to the development of a full Early Bronze Age, and of their relative and absolute chronologies, in the lands just north of the central and eastern Alps (fig. 2). Within this area, researchers have been exceptionally active throughout this century. As a result the material of the Neolithic period is very rich, and numerous small regional cultural groups have been identified, as well as larger, interregional ones. It is impossible in an essay of this scope to cover all of the local developments or to discuss all of the salient aspects of the major groups. This is a broad and general outline of the cultural patterns particularly as reflected in recent studies. I emphasize the citation of principal recent works on the various groups in order to lead one into the full literature on each.

The region can be divided into three main natural geographical zones from south to north. In the south are the Alps, which cover the southern half of Switzerland, the southernmost edge of Bavaria in Germany, and all of eastern and central Austria. In the middle another zone extends from the French border in western Switzerland across the whole of southern Germany and into upper and lower Austria, variously designated as the Alpine Foreland or the Swiss-Bavarian basin or plateau. North of this zone in southern Germany are the Central Uplands from the Danube northward to the Main and beyond, and here the area of our concern ends.

Of these three zones, that of the Alps was very sparsely

Text submitted January 1982

populated during the Neolithic period (Pittioni 1954:174; Drack 1969b). Hence our discussion centers on the cultural developments north of the high mountains. The chronological chart (fig. 1) reflects the general patterns of the regional groups from west to east throughout our area.

In the study of the Neolithic period, as in that of other prehistoric phases, it has been general practice to designate material cultural assemblages that share features as "cultures" (see particularly the discussion in Lüning 1972). For example, the earliest groups of Neolithic peoples in central Europe shared common house types, pottery forms and decoration, stone tool shapes, and the like, and all are considered parts of the Linear Pottery culture. Several points need to be made about this traditional approach to Neolithic culture history. The definition of archaeological cultures is largely arbitrary and depends on the notions of the one or more investigators working at the time that the sequences are defined. Two individuals might divide a region very differently depending on their perceptions of similarity and difference, and on their own training and early experience. Thus, the archaeological cultures as they are defined are constructs of modern investigators, not necessarily entities that would have been recognized by the persons living at the time.

The significance of archaeologically defined cultures in terms of political, social, ethnic, or linguistic entities is unclear (Lüning 1976a:33). For the central European Neolithic period, definitions of cultural groups have been made principally on the basis of pottery forms and ornamental styles, although other categories of material culture, such as flaked and polished stone tools, bone and antler implements, and copper objects are often important in drawing similarities between assemblages. The greater the number of resemblances between material cultural groups, the closer the presumed relationship between the people who made the objects. To what extent differences and similarities in material culture reflect other kinds of cultural relationships is difficult to determine at present—close similarities can result from regular interaction between communities in the form of trade or sharing of ideas as well as from ethnic affiliation, for example (see Ehrich 1950).

The names given to the various Neolithic cultural groups do not designate equal quantities. Some, such as Michelsberg, encompass a wide range of typological, geographical, and chronological diversity, while others, such as Cham, are much more specific regionally and chronologically. Investigators often disagree as to when a group should be considered as a separate "culture" and when it should be regarded as a subgroup of a larger entity. In the central European literature there has been much discussion of these issues (see references in Lüning 1976a and Meier-Arendt 1977).

Most recent research on the Neolithic period of central Europe has concerned itself principally with typological, chronological, and technological problems involving the definition and interrelations of the material cultural groups (Lüning 1976a:31–33). Change over time has been viewed mainly in a cultural evolutionary way, and investigators attempt on the basis of typological changes to distinguish the formation of new groupings, defined by pottery and other material aspects, from older ones. Since these groupings are modern constructs, the significance of such attempts to trace cultural evolution in pottery types is very questionable. Little work has been done on examining change from perspectives other than pottery typology (some of the potentially productive directions in which such attempts might be made are illustrated in Uerpmann 1977 and Lüning 1978).

A major problem with the current cultural evolutionary approach, aside from the arbitrary nature of the groupings, is the tendency to represent the development through time as running from one sharply defined stage to another. In a recent study of radiocarbon dates of Neolithic sites Pape (1979) has shown that "cultures" defined on the basis of pottery typology overlapped chronologically a great deal more than has generally been supposed (see also Sangmeister 1973). As more determinations become available, a much clearer picture of the relationships between the different groups is likely to emerge (Lanting and Mook 1977:i).

The boundaries of our area are modern political ones and not those of prehistoric cultural geography. All of the principal groups discussed here are also represented in other areas. Those in the western part of Switzerland such as Saône-Rhône show strong material cultural similarities to those in the Jura and in the Saône Valley regions of eastern France. Those in southwestern Germany often extend into Alsace across the Rhine. Southern German groups such as Rössen and Michelsberg are also well represented in the Rhineland and other parts of northern Germany. Those in upper and lower Austria such as Lengyel and Baden frequently have strong connections in Bohemia, Moravia, Slovakia, and Hungary, while groups in Burgenland and Styria share features with those in Hungary and Slovenia.

For general overviews of the sequences in the separate countries treated here and of current research, see particularly Lüning (1976a) and Meier-Arendt (1977) for southern Germany, Drack (1969b) for Switzerland, and Pittioni (1954) for Austria.

Early Neolithic

The earliest appearance of Neolithic cultural groups in central Europe is currently dated to 5500–5250 B.C. (calibrated) or slightly earlier (Quitta 1967:265, fig. 1; on the Mesolithic background and its absolute dating see Oeschger and Taute 1978). This first Neolithic appearance is that of people manufacturing Linear Pottery and polished stone tools and having domesticated plants and animals (Lüning 1976a:37). The earliest phase of Linear Pottery represented in our area is concentrated at sites in the middle and lower Neckar basin and along the Danube in Bavaria (map in Quitta 1960: fig. 3, after p. 164). The particular morphological and decorative features that characterize the earliest pottery of this tradition are discussed by Quitta (1960:164–66) and Meier-Arendt (1972). Although the mechanisms of transmission are unclear, it is generally thought that pottery forms and designs that constitute the Linear Pottery tradition were introduced into central Europe from regions to the east where pottery had been in use for some time before. Most authors suggest connections with the Starčevo-Körös and early Vinča groups of the middle Danube area (Quitta 1960:166–67; Lichardus 1972; Meier-Arendt 1972; Menke 1978:32), but Ehrich (1976:183–84) points out some problems with this thesis. It has been proposed that in parts of central Europe, particularly in the mountainous zones, a Neolithic economy developed without pottery, contemporary with the Linear Pottery earlier phases in the non-Alpine regions (Menke 1978:51).

Characteristic features of the Linear Pottery tradition are round-bottomed ceramic vessels with decoration formed by incised lines, often in spirals and meanders and often with impressed lines and dots inside the bands.

The stone tool inventory includes chipped flint and polished wedges, especially the asymmetric "shoe-last celts" (*Schuhleistenkeile*). Associated with these particular pottery and stone forms are long houses represented by long, thin, rectangular foundations of postholes with a posthole trench at one end (Modderman 1972). Settlement of Linear Pottery groups was preferentially on the easily cleared and well-drained loess soils of central Europe. The Linear Pottery tradition is well represented in southern Germany (Meier-Arendt 1972), in lowland parts of Austria (Pittioni 1954:128–43; Lenneis 1976; Trnka 1980), but only rarely in northern Switzerland (Drack 1969a:67–68, 79).

For a period of about half a millennium, according to the radiocarbon dates, the Linear Pottery was the only ceramic and Neolithic tradition in central Europe. A number of typologically defined regional subgroups have been recognized, particularly in the later phases (Müller-Karpe 1968:117–21), including the Hinkelstein and later Grossgartach groups in southwest Germany (Meier-Arendt 1969, 1975), in Austria the Music-Note (*Notenkopf*) and later Stroke-Ornamented and Zseliz forms (Lenneis 1979a, 1979b), and, particularly in eastern central Europe, the Stroke-Ornamented pottery group.

Radiocarbon determinations suggest that the latest phases of the Linear Pottery tradition date to around 4415–4315 B.C. (calibrated) (see table 1; also Quitta 1967:265, fig. 1). Subsequent traditions of the later Neolithic are generally traced typologically to later phases and subgroups of the Linear Pottery, with some introduction of new features, particularly from eastern Europe.

Middle Neolithic

The principal material cultural tradition of the later Neolithic in the central part of our area is the Rössen, with radiocarbon dates in neighboring regions ranging from about 5000 to 3900 B.C. (calibrated) (Pape 1979:32). Characteristic are pottery vessels with flat bottoms (as opposed to the rounded bottoms of the Linear Pottery) and with bands of deeply impressed strokes which were often filled with a white paste. Common forms include globular vessels, flat bowls, and beakers. Burial practice was predominantly inhumation with both flexed and extended positions. Shoe-last celts occur in Rössen, as in the earlier contexts, and limestone bracelets and shell jewelry are also common (Meier-Arendt 1974:4; distribution maps in Drack 1969a:79; Goller 1972:239, fig. 71).

The Rössen tradition is viewed as principally an indigenous development of the later Linear Pottery subgroups in the greater southwest German area. Closest connections in the material assemblages are drawn between Rössen and the chronologically preceding Grossgartach group, which is in turn considered to have developed out of that of Hinkelstein (Meier-Arendt 1969, 1975). A series of specific similarities in the pottery and stone tools suggests a direct development from Grossgartach to Rössen (Meier-Arendt 1974:10), but some new elements also appear in the Rössen tradition which were not present in Grossgartach, leading investigators to seek other sources for them, as, for example, in the Stroke-Ornamented groups (Goller 1972).

During the Middle Neolithic of central Europe, communities throughout the Swiss Alpine Foreland first became fully Neolithic in the economic sense (Müller-Karpe 1968:134; Drack 1969a:68). Pottery of Rössen tradition occurs in Swiss settlements of the earliest Neolithic phases there, in early Cortaillod layers and associated with Egolzwil material (Drack 1969a:68).

During the later phases of the Rössen tradition and after its end in southwest Germany and neighboring regions a series of local pottery styles emerged which has given rise to a number of regional subgroup designations, such as Bischheim in the northern part of the upper Rhine Valley (Goller 1972:244, fig. 72), Schwieberdingen centered on the middle Neckar (Lüning 1969b), Aichbühl in the upper Danube-Federsee area, and Goldberg in the Nördlinger Ries (Lüning 1969a). These local subgroups appear to parallel the earlier phases of the Cortaillod development in Switzerland, including the material at Egolzwil (Sauter and Gallay 1969, with map on p. 65) and to overlap chronologically with the earlier phases of the Michelsberg tradition of the Late Neolithic. At the same time, the Lutzengüetle group appeared in the northeast corner of Switzerland, with typological connections to the Aichbühl and later Schussenried of southwest Germany (Drack 1969a:69, 81). In Bavaria, particularly lower Bavaria, and in upper Austria, the Münchshöfen group developed at about this time (Süss 1976), characterized by conical ceramic vessels with two small handles, conical beakers, and bottle-shaped vessels, and by decoration executed in strokes and incisions. Münchshöfen ceramic forms show close connections with the Lengyel tradition to the east, while stone tools show continuity of traditions from the local Linear Pottery and Rössen forms (Süss 1976). These various local groups of Switzerland, southern Germany, and upper Austria overlap chronologically with both the Rössen and the Michelsberg traditions.

In eastern Austria the Lengyel tradition makes its appearance around 4900 B.C. (calibrated) at the time of the later phases of the Linear Pottery groups (Ohrenberger 1969; Ruttkay 1979). This material cultural group, characterized by footed bowls, round bowls, amphorae, ceramic figurines, and decoration of lugs, linear double spirals and meanders, concentric semicircles, and zigzag lines, is well represented throughout much of eastern Europe. Its development is a long one over about a millennium, into the latter part of the Late Neolithic (Ruttkay 1976).

Late Neolithic

The Michelsberg tradition of the late Neolithic (Lüning 1967) is a widespread and long-lasting one of some seven hundred years duration, with radiocarbon dates ranging roughly 4500–3750 B.C. (calibrated). Michelsberg is well represented throughout southern Germany and into northern Switzerland (Lüning 1969a). Characteristic pottery forms are tulip-shaped beakers and flat round ceramic plaques known as "baking plates." These and other ceramic forms, common among which are handled jugs, dippers, and coarse vessels of various shapes, carry little decoration.

In the west of Switzerland, Michelsberg is contemporary with later phases of the Cortaillod tradition, represented at lakeside settlements showing a large utilization of fish resources. Cortaillod pottery is characterized by round-bottomed forms with dark polished surfaces generally without decoration, as in the Michelsberg (for discussion and literature on Cortaillod see Sauter and Gallay 1969; Stöckli and Sauter 1976).

A local development at this time in southwest Germany is the Schussenried group, characterized by handled jugs of many sizes, bearing incised linear patterns including filled bands and triangles (Lüning 1976b).

The earliest dated copper objects in west-central Europe belong to this period, at the end of the Rössen tradition and beginning of the Michelsberg sequence. Excavations at Schernau near Kitzingen in lower Franconia yielded a small ring and an awl of copper in a settlement pit dated at 4125–3880 B.C. (calibrated) (KN-726). Lüning (1973) notes that on the basis of the pottery the site cannot be ascribed to either the Bischheim or Schwieberdingen groups, although there are similarities to both, but suggests instead that it represents part of a small local Late Rössen–Early Late Neolithic group. The first regular occurrence of metals in our area consists of the flat axes of the Altheim-Pfyn-Mondsee groups and the beads of late Cortaillod (see Primas 1976).

Late in the Michelsberg sequence is a series of local developments that share many features and are regarded as special facies of the Michelsberg tradition, in particular the Pfyn group in Switzerland and in the Lake Constance region and the Altheim group in Bavaria (Driehaus 1960). Their most important common feature is the presence of copper objects and equipment for melting and working copper. The Pfyn group is characterized especially by handled jugs, deep pots, and wide-open bowls with flat bottoms (map in Drack 1969a:81). The contemporaneous Altheim group in Bavaria is marked by mainly undecorated pottery with gentle profiles and flat bottoms, and finer vessels with handles including bowls, cups, and jugs. In both Pfyn and Altheim, and in the contemporary Mondsee group of upper Austria and Land Salzburg, flat copper axes and copper awls occur, representing the use of metal on a regular basis.

The Mondsee group of upper Austria and Land Salzburg, closely connected to Bavarian Altheim, is characterized by vessels with white inlaid paste decoration (Willvonseder 1963–68). Common forms include handled vessels, pear-shaped vessels, animal figures of pottery, and spoon-shaped crucibles. Decoration consists of zigzag lines, rhomboids, concentric circles, and triangles. With respect to evidence for metalworking, the Mondsee group is connected with Altheim, Pfyn, and late Cortaillod. Particularly in Pfyn and Mondsee contexts, ceramic crucibles are a characteristic part of the cultural assemblages, along with copper axes and awls (Drack 1969a:74). The crucibles make it clear that these communities were actively producing metal objects, and not just importing them from outside or hammering native copper. This development marks the beginning of the so-called Copper Age.

Overlapping with the later phases of Pfyn-Altheim-Mondsee is the Baden group in eastern Austria, with sites concentrated in the border lands of Hungary and Slovakia (map in Pittioni 1954:178, map 5). Characteristic ceramic forms include high-necked beakers, handled cups, and bowls with high band handles, all often decorated with vertical and horizontal grooves.

In Bavaria the Cham group is thought to have been a successor of the Altheim (Schröter 1976:252), with radiocarbon dates ranging from about 3050 to about 2350 B.C. (calibrated).

All of these regional developments at the end of the Michelsberg sequence are considered to mark the beginning of the Eneolithic or Copper Age, since the first regular evidence for the working of copper metal occurs in this context.

Eneolithic

Subsequent to the main Michelsberg development, including the Swiss subgroup Pfyn, and partly overlapping with the later phases of Cortaillod in Switzerland, is the Horgen tradition, characterized in particular by high, bucket-shaped vessels of coarse and undecorated pottery. In the west of Switzerland, Horgen settlement deposits often occur stratigraphically above those of Cortaillod. In the north and east, Horgen assemblages overlie those of Pfyn (Itten 1969:84). The radiocarbon dates make the relative positions of the three groups clear (see table 1; Pape 1979). Unlike the earlier groups mentioned for

Switzerland, Horgen is a widespread tradition encompassing the entire Alpine Foreland region of the country and extending into southwest Germany (map in Itten 1969:93). The origins of its particular material cultural features are often sought in France (Itten 1969:94, 1970).

Following the Late Michelsberg subgroups is the very widespread tradition known as Corded Ware, sometimes referred to by its most characteristic stone form as the Battle-Ax people. This tradition is marked particularly by elegant beaker-shaped vessels decorated with string impressions and by finely worked polished stone axes with perforations and frequently with imitation casting-seams modeled in the stone. The Corded Ware tradition is best represented by its burials, although in Switzerland settlements are well known. Burial was under a small tumulus, generally an inhumation in a flexed position, although local variations occur. The appearance of the Corded Ware groups at about 2500 B.C. (calibrated) (Strahm 1979) marked a major departure from earlier cultural developments in central Europe. Local variations in material culture became relatively minor, and a fairly uniform assemblage of pottery and stone forms became common throughout central Europe (Pittioni 1954:238–46; Strahm 1969:97; Pleslová-Štiková 1976). Copper production is well represented in Corded Ware contexts.

Some local groupings are still identified within the Corded Ware complex, as for example the Saône-Rhône group in the extreme southwest corner of Switzerland and in the Saône and Doubs regions of eastern France (Strahm 1975; Strahm and Thévenot 1976). The Saône-Rhône group, recently defined and incorporating a number of previously delineated groups such as the Auvernier, is characterized by large, barrel-shaped vessels with horizontal lugs below the rim. Decoration is rare, and the characteristic pottery is coarse rather than fine. Metal daggers and awls are present.

Following the Corded Ware complex and with considerable chronological overlap indicated by the radiocarbon dates (Pape 1979:29, fig. 18) is the Bell Beaker tradition, which Harrison (1980:17) characterizes as a part of the Corded Ware. Characteristic forms of the Bell Beaker assemblages are ceramic beakers shaped like inverted bells and footed bowls. These vessels are ornamented with horizontal bands filled with strokes, and both forms often bear a polished red surface. Also characteristic are polished stone wrist guards, copper daggers, and the practice of flexed inhumation burials.

The Bell Beaker phenomenon appears to be not so much a cultural tradition in its own right, as were the groups discussed from the earlier phases of the Neolithic, but rather a specific set of characteristic elements that occur within other cultural contexts of the time (Shennan 1976). The Bell Beaker assemblage is best represented in its burial aspect and is abundantly present in southern Germany (Schröter 1976) and rather less so in Switzerland (Strahm 1969, 1976; Gallay 1976) and Austria (Pittioni 1954:251–67; Toriser 1976). Of particular importance in the chronological position and in the economic and social interpretation of the Bell Beaker phenomenon is the frequent occurrence of metal objects in the graves, particularly copper daggers (actually knives) and awls.

Early Bronze Age

The Early Bronze Age communities of central Europe overlap considerably in time with those of the Eneolithic period, and all evidence points to a continuity of population and of material cultural traditions. The chronological overlap is apparent in two principal respects, in the radiocarbon dates and in the evidence for interaction between communities bearing the traditions. (For the radiocarbon dates see table 1 and Pape 1979:29, fig. 18.)

The local development of the Early Bronze Age patterns in the individual regions within our area from the Eneolithic Corded Ware and Bell Beaker groups has been outlined by various authors (e.g., Strahm 1971:21–22; Schröter 1976:253). Although new bronze objects and especially new quantities of the new metal characterize the Early Bronze Age (by definition), many of the other material aspects of the human groups continue largely unchanged. Among the graves at Straubing in lower Bavaria, the continuity of ceramic and stone forms is clear in the Bell Beaker and Early Bronze Age graves (Hundt 1958). Wrist guards, V-perforated buttons, arrowheads, and daggers, and the orientation of burials, attest to the continuity between the Bell Beaker groups and those of the Early Bronze Age (Schröter 1976:253). Similar connections in the material culture can be drawn between the Eneolithic and Early Bronze Age groups of Switzerland (Strahm 1971:21–22).

There is also considerable archaeological evidence for interaction between communities possessing Eneolithic assemblages and those of the Early Bronze Age (discussion in Strahm 1969:112–14; Gallay 1971:159). Here again we must be aware that the nature of the human populations who made and used the material objects recovered by archaeologists remains very unclear to us. The radiocarbon dates suggest that groups using the material assemblages which we know as Corded Ware, Bell Beaker, and Early Bronze Age were living at the same time for a period of several centuries (Pape 1979:29, fig. 18). How these different human populations were related to one another ethnically, linguistically, economically, and politically is unclear but of great importance. As more information is collected about the ways of life and economic activities of these groups, we should be able to develop a clearer picture of the nature of the similarities and differences between the various traditions and communities. In any case, it is becoming increasingly clear from the results of radiocarbon determinations that we must reckon with a much greater degree of chronological overlap of different material cultural traditions than has been thought until now.

The Synchronic Chart

Figure 1 is a very simplified rendition indicating only approximate relative chronological positions of the major traditions and some of the smaller groups discussed in the text. In each case, I have placed the name of the group roughly in the middle of its chronological duration. Along the right are calibrated dates in years B.C. The figure has two principal shortcomings of which the reader should be aware. First, it suggests regional groupings on only a very coarse level. Within every local region of central Europe, the interrelations of material groupings are very complex. The figure glosses over most of this local level variation. Second, the figure does not indicate how long different traditions can be recognized in the archaeological record. The degree of overlap between groups should be apparent from the radiocarbon dates presented in table 1. Readers should also refer to the histograms of radiocarbon dates in Pape (1979).

For other perspectives on the relative positions of these and other, smaller, groups see particularly the synchronic charts in Pittioni (1954:274), Lüning (1969a:8, fig. 1), Mauser-Goller (1969:103), Strahm (1969:112), Sangmeister (1973:396, table 1), and Meier-Arendt (1977:62, fig. 11; 112, fig. 42).

Twenty

The Neolithic and Early Bronze Age Chronology of Poland

Peter I. Bogucki, Forbes College, Princeton University

Outline

This chapter presents a comprehensive cultural chronology for the area corresponding primarily to the present-day territory of the Polish Peoples' Republic, from the initial appearance of Neolithic food-producing communities to the beginning of the Bronze Age. The area under consideration includes the territory from the Odra (Oder) River on the west to the Pripet Marshes on the east, from the Baltic coast on the north to the Carpathian and Sudeten Mountains on the south. In addition, cultural developments in the east Baltic area will be discussed, especially as they relate to the Polish materials. The materials from this large expanse of central Europe will be compared with those found in adjacent areas, particularly to the south and west. The information presented here should thus interdigitate with that found in other chapters in this volume and form part of an overall radiocarbon-supported chronology for central Europe.

In this chapter, uncalibrated dates with a 5568 year half-life and general millennium figures derived from them are indicated by the use of a lowercase b.c., while calibrated dates are indicated by a capitalized B.C. This convention, widely followed in recent British practice, makes it possible to distinguish calibrated from uncalibrated dates at a glance.

Natural and Cultural Areas

The natural zones of the area considered here have had a marked impact on its culture history. The bedrock geology is not so important as the Pleistocene and post-Pleistocene sediments which divide the area into well-defined natural areas.

In the north, a narrow plain lies along the Baltic coast and separates it from the Pomeranian-Masurian lake belt (see fig. 1). Early in the Holocene, this plain was probably somewhat wider, but the Subboreal rise in the Baltic sea levels led to its present configuration. The Pomeranian-Masurian lake belt stretches from East Germany into European Russia and is a product of the Baltic terminal moraine of the Weichsel glaciation, where the hollows in the sand and gravel hills have filled with water. To the south of the lake belt is the zone of glacial meltwater valleys, the result of water from the ice front and the rivers blocked by it running west to the North Sea. There are two main meltwater valleys, running roughly along lines from Toruń to Eberswalde and Warsaw to Berlin, along with an additional short one from Glogów to Leipzig. The meltwater valleys are separated from each other by broad interfluves covered, for the most part, with boulder clays. Central Poland, to the south and east of the Warsaw-Berlin Valley, is covered with glacial outwash, mostly sands and gravels of marginal fertility. On the southern edge of the central Polish outwash plain are

The author thanks J. A. Bakker (Amsterdam), S. Milisauskas (Buffalo, N.Y.), and R. W. Ehrich (Fitzwilliam, N.H.) for many helpful criticisms of an earlier draft of this chapter, although not all of their comments were incorporated into the final version. Much of the discussion of the Early Neolithic in Poland has grown out of conversations with R. Grygiel (Łódź). Errors in content and judgment, of course, remain the responsibility of the author. Peggy Hoffman was of great assistance in typing the final version of the manuscript.

Text submitted June 1984
Text revised May 1986

the Świętokrzyskie (Holy Cross) Mountains, part of the mineral-rich Tertiary mountain system of central Europe which functioned as a source of raw materials in prehistoric times, especially flint and iron. Between the present-day cities of Kraków and Częstochowa is a north-south belt of *karst* landscape that was also important as a prehistoric flint source. Forming a broad belt across the southern tier of this area are the loess-covered uplands of Małopolska (Little Poland) and Upper Silesia. The loess, which ranges up to 100 m thick in places, was deposited during the Pleistocene when this area was an ice-free corridor from central Europe to the Ukraine. The loess belt grades into the mountain soils of the Carpathian foreland to the south. Finally, the peaks of the Carpathian Mountains form a striking natural southern boundary to the area under consideration. To the southwest, the Sudeten Mountains form a slightly less impressive barrier.

The southern wall of mountains is not impenetrable, however. The Moravian Gate, where the Odra River runs between the Sudetens and Carpathians, functioned as a major prehistoric avenue of communication. The Kłodzko Valley through the Sudetens also appears to have been an important route. Even the high Carpathians were passable, such as in the Poprad Valley, which allowed Slovakian radiolarite and Hungarian obsidian to reach sites in southern Poland.

It is possible to define four natural regions within this area, the borders of which generally coincide with those between prehistoric cultural units. Region I includes Pomerania, Wielkopolska (Great Poland), Kujavia, and lower Silesia. Region II lies east of the Wisła (Vistula) and north of the Western Bug, encompassing the Masurian lake district and the plains of eastern Masovia and stretching up into the east Baltic forests. The glacial outwash zone of central Poland forms region III. Region IV is the area south of the southernmost advance of the ice sheets and includes the loess uplands of Upper Silesia, Małopolska, and southeast Poland, as well as the Sudeten and Carpathian forelands (see fig. 1).

The Earliest Food-Producing Communities North of the Carpathians

The first appearance of Neolithic communities north of the Carpathians occurs with the entry of the Linear Pottery culture into this area in the last half of the fifth millennium b.c. This culture is distributed across central Europe and is best known for its wide dispersal of very similar pottery types and villages with longhouses, as well as its rapid spread between Slovakia and eastern France. The earliest Linear Pottery is thought by many to be linked with the Starčevo-Körös-Criş complex of southeast Europe (Quitta 1960; Tringham 1971), although this view is not shared by all (Ehrich 1976).

Quitta (1960) has referred to the earliest Linear Pottery as "Krumlov" ware, which is distributed as far west as the Main in Germany. In Poland, Krumlov ware had been unknown until the early 1970s, when Romanow excavated the site of Gniechowice near Wrocław in Silesia. Romanow's results are still unpublished, but it appears from secondary sources (Kulczycka-Leciejewiczowa 1979:48) that he found some very early Linear Pottery that corresponds to Quitta's Krumlov ware. Although Kulczycka-Leciejewiczowa has identified Gniechowice-type early ceramics at sites in the Kraków area as well, Gniechowice remains the only site in Poland where a number of individual features contain only the early material.

The most probable route for Linear Pottery through the Carpathians is via the Moravian Gate (fig. 1). From there, communities spread out to occupy two main areas of the southern Polish loess: the Wrocław plain and the uplands of Małopolska and southeast Poland. The actual distribution of Linear Pottery settlement, when viewed on such a scale, may simply reflect the irregular distribution of archaeological fieldwork. The areas with the densest concentrations of Linear Pottery sites are those closest to the cities of Kraków and Wrocław. Few Linear Pottery sites are known from the Polish side of the Moravian Gate itself, although there are a number of them just across the border. The loess hills of the Moravian Gate do not differ substantially from the loess uplands elsewhere in southern Poland, except that they lie at a greater distance from archaeological research centers.

The major initial Linear Pottery occupation of the south Polish loess took place during its second main "horizon" across central Europe, characterized by "Ačkovy" ceramics in Czechoslovakia and "Flomborn" ware in western Europe (Meier-Arendt 1972). In Poland, ceramics of this horizon are called the "Zofipole" type, after a site near Kraków. Zofipole ceramics are also known from several sites in southeast Poland. Like Flomborn and Ačkovy, this ware has simple curvilinear incised lines, often in interlocking S patterns. Compared with later Linear Pottery wares the Zofipole ceramics are usually thicker and the incised lines wider.

The succeeding "classic," *Notenkopf,* or "music-note" phase of Linear Pottery saw a further expansion of settlement and the development of larger settlements in areas settled previously. The characteristic ornament now consists of incised lines relieved by round punctates at their ends or at intersections with other lines. Curvilinear patterns still prevail, although more complicated than those of Zofipole ware. Sites of this phase are found in both the upper Odra and Wisła valleys as well as in parts of Kujavia, Wielkopolska, and Pomerania in region I. The lowland sites mark the first appearance of Neolithic communities on the North European Plain. The *Notenkopf* sites of southern Poland and those in the lowlands are coeval, as indicated by radiocarbon dates from Strzelce, Brześć Kujawski, Olszanica, Niemcza, and Strachów as well as by identical ceramics. The central Polish outwash plains of region III remain practically devoid of Linear Pottery sites, and they do not appear at all in region II, the east Baltic forests.

The final step in the development of Linear Pottery north of the Carpathians was the appearance of ceramics linked to the Želiezovce and Šarka styles of Czechoslovakian Linear Pottery. The Želiezovce style is a continuation of the *Notenkopf* motif, except that the formerly round punctates became lozenge-shaped indentations. In addition, the curvilinear patterns of incised lines gave way to angular patterns of straight lines. The Šarka style consists of lines of punctates that either parallel or interrupt continuous incised lines or that form patterns independent of the incised lines. In the latter form, they anticipated the motifs of Stroke-Ornamented Pottery of the early fourth millennium b.c.

True Želiezovce ceramics occur primarily in the upper Wisła Valley (Kulczycka-Leciejewiczowa 1979:68). Along the lower Wisła in Kujavia, a ware related to Želiezovce is found, with similar angular patterns of incised lines but without the lozenge-shaped punctates. Šarka-style ceramics, on the other hand, appear primarily in Silesia along the upper Odra. The typological differentiation of the main drainages of this area in late Linear Pottery suggests that their ceramic traditions were influenced from two different directions, for Šarka ceramics are mainly encountered in Bohemia and Moravia, and Želiezovce ware occurs in Slovakia. This differentiation is part of an overall regionalization of Linear Pottery which takes place across central Europe at this time.

The first half of the fourth millennium b.c. saw a further fragmentation of the Linear Pottery tradition. In the Odra Valley, the Šarka ware was replaced by the Stroke-Ornamented Pottery culture (*Stichbandkeramik, Kultura Wstęgowa Kłuta*), which takes its name from the bands of short strokes, usually in two to six parallel rows, that decorate its pottery. The angular patterns of these bands are reminiscent of the incised lines on late Linear Pottery. There is a greater variety of vessel forms, with pear-shaped and zoomorphic ones appearing along Linear Pottery forms. A good discussion of Stroke-Ornamented Pottery in English is available (Kopacz 1974).

On the upper Wisła, in region IV, the early fourth millennium b.c. (mid-fifth millennium B.C. calibrated) saw a replacement of Želiezovce Linear Pottery by a culture known by a variety of names, the most common being Lengyel or Lengyel-Polgár. Trans-Carpathian influences manifest themselves in the form of tall footed vessels, painted decoration, and other traits characteristic of the Lengyel cultures of the middle Danube and the Polgár culture of the Tisza drainage. The ceramics of the upper Wisła drainage were not influenced from a single direction at this time, however. In addition to the southern elements, a high frequency of stroked decoration on Lengyel vessel forms indicates that there were influences from the west and southwest as well. Polgár influence, I suggest, was minimal during the first centuries of the fourth millennium b.c. and was really only felt later, especially after copper artifacts started to appear north of the Carpathians.

In region IV, the earliest Lengyel phase saw the appearance of two foci—the Samborzec group found on the uplands west of the Wisła and the Malice group located farther east in the Wislok and San drainages. Both groups occur in the area around the city of Kraków. Stroked decoration appears on Lengyel vessel forms in both groups, but in the Samborzec group, red painted decoration, a characteristic of early Lengyel phases south of the Carpathians, is found on some vessels. The patterns of stroked and painted decoration are reminiscent of the angular incised lines of late Linear Pottery. In the Malice group, painting occurs less frequently, and other decoration is confined to occasional bosses, lugs, and fingernail impressions. The chronological relationship between Samborzec and Malice is unclear. Kamieńska (1973) suggests chronological priority for Samborzec, which seems reasonable because of the higher frequency of stroked ornamentation. The absolute dating of these groups is based on typological connections to radiocarbon-dated Stroke-Ornamented Pottery and Lengyel materials in other areas which indicate that both date to the period 4000–3900 to 3700–3600 b.c. (5000–4700 to 4550–4400 B.C. as calibrated).

In Silesia, Stroke-Ornamented Pottery is succeeded by the Janówek group of the Lengyel culture, known from Janówek and other sites in the Wrocław area (Wojciechowski l973). Janówek ceramics are characterized by red-and-white linear painted decoration. The vessel forms correspond to some found in Moravian-Slovakian Lengyel painted ware. In addition, there is a minor amount of stroked ornament. Farther up the Odra, directly astride the Moravian Gate, some Lengyel assemblages have been found that lack painted decoration. J. K. Kozłowski has called these the Ocice group, after the site of Racibórz-Ocice, and has distinguished two phases of uncertain duration (Kozłowski 1972:77). Since no radiocarbon dates exist for these groups, the chronological relationship of Janówek and Ocice is unclear, but the Ocice group appears to be the later of the two.

The unpainted Ocice Lengyel ceramics are similar to those found on the upper Wisła following the Samborzec and Malice groups. In Małopolska, the Pleszów group is possibly coeval with Janówek, with some red and white painted pottery and perhaps some stroked decoration.

This group is characterized by tall-footed and s-profile vessels, usually ornamented with small conical bosses. The Pleszów group was succeeded by the Modlnica group, which is synchronized with Ocice on the basis of the total lack of both painted and stroked decoration.

Coeval with the Modlnica group, the earliest materials of the Lublin-Volhynian Lengyel group appear in the loess plateau east of the Wisła and near Lublin. This group is difficult to date, since most sites are poorly known. Based on stratigraphic observations in Volhynia (Zacharuk 1971), its beginning can be synchronized with the middle phase or the early part of the late phase of the Tripolye culture in the Ukraine. The Lublin-Volhynian group shows affinities both to Modlnica and to the Tiszapolgár culture south of the Carpathians (Kulczycka-Leciejewiczowa 1979). In this case, it is probably correct to speak of a "Lengyel-Polgár" culture.

All middle Lengyel regional groups in southern Poland can be dated to the mid-fourth millennium b.c., although only one radiocarbon date is available. The conventional wisdom, based on dates for cultures preceding and succeeding them, is to place them between 3700 and 3300–3200 b.c. (4550–4425 and 4150–3900 B.C.), but with no real idea of the temporal dimensions of each group. This would synchronize them roughly with other Lengyel groups like Brodzany-Nitra, with the Tiszapolgár culture of the Tisza drainage, and the Gatersleben, Aichbühl, and late Rössen cultures of central and southwest Germany (see Wells, preceding chapter; Lichardus 1976).

The final Lengyel phase is characterized by several foci across the southern tier of Poland and two more in the Polish lowlands. Although there are important subregional differences within the south Polish groups, one can identify the Jordanów (Jordansmühl) group of Silesia and the Złotniki-Wyciąże group on the upper Wisła as representing the final Lengyel phase in southern Poland. Farther east, the Lublin-Volhynian white-painted ware persisted to a late date.

The Jordanów group is best known from the work of Seger (1916) at the Jordanów cemetery. Its characteristic ceramic form is a squat urn with two large handles. Footed bowls and other Lengyel forms also appear. Incised decoration reappears but only on the urns in bold patterns of incised lines, usually in groups of three to five parallel strokes. Unlike Linear Pottery decoration, the Jordanów lines are generally short incisions of several centimeters, arranged in chevron patterns similar to those characteristic of the Rössen culture in Germany. Among the grave finds are many copper ornaments which, along with those of the Brześć Kujawski group in the Polish lowlands, represent the earliest use of copper north of the Carpathians. The copper itself appears to have come from the Tisza area (Dziekoński 1962).

On the upper Wisła, the Złotniki-Wyciąże group has numerous ties with the Tisza Valley and in particular to the "epi-Polgár" Male Zaluzicé–Lažňány group in Slovakia. The vessel forms, especially the "milk jugs" (*Milchtöpfe*), exhibit Polgár influences. Here, indeed, one can speak of a Lengyel-Polgár culture, which was definitely not true of the earlier Lengyel phases in southern Poland.

The dating of these late Lengyel groups in southern Poland seems problematical, since most available radiocarbon dates fall in the first centuries of the third millennium b.c. Whereas it had been thought that these groups did not continue beyond 3000 b.c., it now appears that they persisted somewhat later, to about 2800/2700 b.c. (ca. 3600–3400 B.C.). Certain areas thus appear to have had terminal Lengyel occupations coeval with early Funnel Beaker settlement in adjoining areas. At Racibórz-Ocice, a late Lengyel pit cut into a Funnel Beaker pit, while in Jordanów cemetery there is the well-known grave 28, which contains both Funnel Beaker and Jordanów elements (Wiślański 1979c; Driehaus 1960; Lichardus 1976). Much needs to be done in southern Poland to clarify the relationships between late Lengyel and the Funnel Beaker and Baden cultures.

In the lowlands of region I, two different chronologies for the fourth millennium b.c. have recently been developed, one by Czerniak (1980) and the other by Grygiel (1980). Both sequences are similar save for their terminology, but since articles using both have recently appeared (Czerniak and Piontek 1980; Grygiel and Bogucki 1981; Bogucki and Grygiel 1981), a concordance between them would be useful.

Czerniak sees the Early Neolithic cultures of the Polish lowlands (= Linear Pottery, Stroke-Ornamented Pottery, and Lengyel in southern Poland) as parts of an overall entity which he calls the "Band Pottery culture" (*Kultura Ceramiki Wstęgowej*). He divides this into an early stage (= Linear Pottery) and a late stage, which lasts from about 3900 (4750–4700 cal.) to about 2900 (3700–3625 cal.) b.c. and is divided into three phases. As such, the "Band Pottery culture" is *not* equivalent to the German *Bandkeramik*, which refers strictly to Linear and Stroke-Ornamented Pottery. Grygiel, on the other hand, follows a traditional division of the lowland Early Neolithic into Linear Pottery (see above) followed by early and late Lengyel. In his view, Early Lengyel in the lowlands is really a blend of Stroke-Ornamented Pottery and Lengyel elements, much like the Samborzec and Malice groups on the upper Wisła. (It is also possible to consider the Early Lengyel materials from the lowlands as a variant of Stroke-Ornamented Pottery [Bogucki 1982].) The late Lengyel Brześć Kujawski group has a number of distinctive elements, such as bone armlets and a ceramic inventory which suggests a breakdown of north-south connections. This group corresponds to Czerniak's phases

IIb–IIIb, while Grygiel regards Czerniak's IIIc as a form of epi-Lengyel that is transitional between Brześć Kujawski and the later cultures of the third millennium b.c. The following presents a comparison of the Czerniak and Grygiel chronologies for the fourth millennium in the Polish lowlands.

B.C.	Grygiel		Czerniak		B.C.
					5250–4975
4200					
					5200–4925
4100	Linear Pottery		Early Band Pottery		
					5050–4850
4000					
					4750–4700
3900		I		a	
					4575–4550
3800	Early Lengyel	II	Late	I	
				b	4550–4425
3700		III			
					4450–4400
3600				a	
				II	4400–4300
3500		I	Band	b	
					4375–3950
3400	Late Lengyel	II		a	4150–3900
3300	(Brześć Kujawski Group)				
3200		III	Pottery	III b	3975–3875
					3900–3775
3100					
3000				c	3875–3650

Relatively little is known about regions II and III at the time when the Early Neolithic cultures appeared in regions I and IV. The outwash plains of central Poland and the Masurian lake region both supported relatively large Mesolithic populations which clearly did not disappear the moment that food-producing communities occupied neighboring areas. The available data suggest that the Linear Pottery and Lengyel cultures had little direct impact on the indigenous foraging populations in the areas of marginal fertility and grazing potential, at least until the mid-fourth millennium b.c. Even when pottery began to appear in regions II and III, it occurred together with traditional Mesolithic stone tool types, primarily of the Janisławice culture (Nowak 1981:364–65).

In the extreme northwest corner of Poland and in neighboring parts of what formerly was East Prussia, a number of problematical assemblages occur which have been called the "Serowo culture," after the site of Serowo (formerly Zedmar). Until 1969, most data on these came from amateur excavations conducted prior to World War II. The apparent typological connections of the Serowo material with the other early pottery of the east Baltic zone (e.g., Sarnate, Narva) were emphasized (Gross 1939). However, controlled excavations in 1969 at Serowo (Dolukhanov, Timofeev, and Levhovskaia 1975) have shown that these materials are instead much later, related to later "Forest Neolithic" groups of the east Baltic zone. A radiocarbon date of 2239 ± 50 b.c. (2920–2775 B.C.) supports this conclusion.

The chronology of the late hunting-gathering and incipient food-producing cultures farther to the northeast along the Baltic in Latvia and Estonia has been thoroughly discussed in English by Zvelebil (1978). Here, it should only be noted that this area did not become integrated with the culture history of areas to the south and southwest until the very end of the third millennium b.c. (ca. 2550–2500 B.C.), with the appearance of corded pottery. Until then, it was populated by groups who persisted in their hunter-gatherer lifeways even though they adopted some Neolithic traits like pottery. As such, they had much in common with the communities inhabiting the Masurian lake belt (region II) and the central Polish outwash (region III).

Increasing Cultural Complexity

The final centuries of the fourth millennium b.c. saw the extension of Neolithic occupation into some areas not previously settled. This phenomenon can be observed when settlement patterns are observed on a regional level, and a more accurate statement would be that Neolithic settlement extended into previously vacant ecological zones within regions I and IV. It was only later that real Neolithic settlement appeared in most of areas II and III. The expansion into new ecological zones is accompanied by a change in material culture which marks the appearance of the Funnel Beaker culture (*Trichterbecherkultur, Kultura Pucharów Lejkowatych*). The conventional abbreviation TRB is used below.

The fact that it possesses a different artifact inventory and is found in ecological zones different from those of the Linear Pottery and Lengyel sites has led TRB to be characterized as a "northern" culture (e.g., Childe 1957) that resulted from the "acculturation" of indigenous foragers by the Linear Pottery and Lengyel populations or by the "dilution" of Neolithic communities by local Mesolithic groups. Fundamental to this model was the idea that the new ceramic-using agricultural way of life was so superior that the Mesolithic groups readily accepted it. Efforts were then often made to find a TRB "heartland." Such attempts have proven relatively unprofitable. It now seems more productive to regard TRB as the expansion of earlier Neolithic communities into previously unexploited lowland zones, which resulted in interaction with some local Mesolithic groups. In the upland zones of region IV, TRB settlement took place on the loess interfluves, a zone where there was minimal Mesolithic settlement due to its low degree of natural productivity. To consider the TRB communities of this area as the result of the acculturation of a large local Mesolithic population makes little sense.

The role of "Danubian" Neolithic traditions in the origin of TRB is often underestimated, and the antecedents of Polish TRB can be profitably sought in the local late Lengyel (or Lengyel-Polgár) assemblages of southern Poland and Kujavia, just as western TRB probably has its roots in the late fourth millennium Rössen and Gatersleben cultures (see Lichardus 1976). Rather than treat TRB as a unified cultural entity with a single core area (like the Linear Pottery culture), one can view it as reflecting a process of settlement extension and local adaptation which took place across much of north-central Europe, perhaps in concert with local Mesolithic groups.

Archaeologists have recognized two major territorial divisions of Polish TRB, the so-called eastern and southeastern groups (Jażdżewski 1936; Bakker, Vogel, and Wiślański 1969; Wiślański 1979c). The area of the eastern group corresponds generally to region I, while materials of the southeastern group are characteristic of region IV (fig. 1). The separation between these groups appears rather sharp (Wiślański 1979c) and reflects the directions of cultural connections during the late phases of the Lengyel culture (another argument for a late Lengyel root of Polish TRB.)

The earliest eastern TRB materials are those of the Sarnowo phase (Wiślański 1979c), found in the same parts of Wielkopolska and Kuyavia as the Brześć Kujawski group. Sarnowo ceramics are similar to Becker's A/B and C styles of Danish TRB (Becker 1947; Skaarup 1973). A/B ceramics in Denmark date mostly from the period 3050–2800 b.c. (3875–3500 B.C., and earlier dates from Ringkloster and Konens Høj are questionable (Tauber 1972; Skaarup 1973). The more southerly A/B and Sarnowo materials have slightly earlier dates: Rosenhof at 3250 ± 70 (4120–3855 cal.), Schönermark at 3155 ± 70 (3900–3785 cal.), and Sarnowo at 3620 ± 60 (4460–4400 cal.) b.c. The dates from Rosenhof and Schönermark suggest some temporal priority of the north German A/B ceramic over those of Denmark, but the Sarnowo date is several centuries earlier than all other TRB dates. Much has been made of this, since it would establish a contemporaneity between Lengyel and TRB which lasted several centuries and would make the Polish lowlands a leading contender for the TRB "heartland" (Bednarczyk and Kośko 1974).

The single Sarnowo date is far from secure. The sample is associated with Barrow 8 in a complex of TRB long barrows in the Zgłowiączka Valley (Gabałówna

1970). Its description (Vogel and Waterbolk 1972:69) reads as follows: "*Finely dispersed charcoal fragments* in a dark pit filling under Kujavian long barrow, stratigraphically older than central grave of the barrow. Associated with sherds of Sarnowo phase (Becker A/B) of the TRB culture. Barrow may be assigned to the Wiórek phase. Comment: earliest date so far for A/B pottery; *terminus post quem* for barrow" (emphasis mine).

Bakker, Vogel, and Wiślański (1969) considered the sample to be of "B" quality, and the description of its occurrence would arouse suspicion in anyone who has ever collected samples for radiocarbon dating. The Sarnowo date *cannot* be considered reliable, and until more dates are available, there is no evidence that the earliest Polish TRB materials are earlier than 3200/3100 b.c.

Even if the earliest date for the appearance of Sarnowo TRB should be 3200/3100 b.c. (3970–3770 B.C.), it would still indicate some overlap between the latest Lengyel and earliest TRB in both areas I and IV. As noted above, the TRB and late Lengyel materials usually occur in discrete ecological zones. In area IV, the TRB sites are on the interfluves, with Lengyel sites primarily on floodplains and river terraces. In the lowlands, the earliest TRB sites generally occur on the *edges* of areas of Lengyel settlement, while *later* ones are often in the same general locations as Linear Pottery and Lengyel sites.

The A/B ceramics from Sarnowo are much like the later products of the Brześć Kujawski group. Many A/B vessel forms, with the exception of the beakers themselves, have analogs in late Lengyel assemblages. The flint work from Sarnowo differs from that of Brześć Kujawski and shows some similarities to the late Mesolithic Janisławice group. Although this difference, has been cited as evidence for a Mesolithic component in A/B TRB (Niesiołowska 1973, 1981), others have pointed out similarities between A/B flintwork and that of the Linear Pottery culture in Kujavia (Lech and Młynarczyk 1981).

Whether or not A/B sites in region I represent the habitations of a discrete population with an "ethnic" identity separate from that of the Brześć Kujawski group remains uncertain. It should be remembered that the A/B sites are very small, with only limited samples of pottery. They might well represent the initial settlement of Lengyel groups in new ecological zones, rather than an "acculturated Mesolithic" population living side-by-side with agriculturalists.

In area IV, the situation is somewhat more complex. Here, the earliest TRB material is somewhat later than A/B, except for the ceramics of a single pit at Wrocław-Pracz (Wojciechowski 1981). As in region I, there is a shift into new ecological zones (Kruk 1980) and some stratigraphic evidence suggesting that Lengyel groups persisted after the beginning of TRB. At Kraków-Mogiła 62, a Wyciąże-Złotniki pit cut through a TRB feature (Kaczanowska 1976), while in Silesia at Racibórz-Ocice, an Ocice pit intersected one containing a small, "atypical" TRB assemblage (Kozłowski 1972; Wiślański 1979c). The lack of Mesolithic settlement on the loess interfluves argues against the "acculturated Mesolithic" hypothesis of TRB origins in region IV. Rather, the change to TRB ceramics, which show resemblances to late Lengyel wares, appears correlated with the economic changes described by Kruk, and it is possible that more conservative communities inhabiting valley bottoms continued to manufacture ceramics in the Lengyel tradition past 3000 b.c. (ca. 3700 B.C.). The TRB flint industry of region IV shows strong connections with that of Lengyel rather than with any Mesolithic industries (Lech and Młynarczyk 1981), another point in favor of local TRB development in region IV.

The second, or Wiórek, phase of the eastern TRB, named after a site near Poznań, is marked by the appearance of collared flasks among the vessel forms (Jażdżewski 1936). During this phase, the first Neolithic occupation of areas not previously settled by the Linear Pottery and Lengyel cultures took place in the lowlands, such as the Pomeranian coast, parts of the Masurian lake district (region II), and central Poland (region III). Recently, Wiórek has been subdivided into early and late stages, based on the progressive increase of decoration on rims and necks. The early stage has also been called the Pikutkowo phase (Niesiołowska 1967), while the late one retains the name of Wiórek. No radiocarbon dates are available for Early Wiórek/Pikutkowo, which has typological connections with the earlier A/B materials, although stratigraphic data show it to be later (Wiślański 1979c). Materials of this phase also exhibit similarities to the Baalberg group of East Germany and to the earliest TRB ceramics of the southeast group (Kruk and Milisauskas 1981). Baalberg elements also appear in the developed (or late) Wiórek ceramics, particularly in the rim modes and vessel forms. Pikutkowo and Wiórek can be synchronized with EN C in Denmark. The northern elements are strongest in northwestern Poland (Wiślański and Czarnecki 1970) but are noticeably weaker in Kujavia and Wielkopolska. The end of Wiórek in region I can be placed at approximately 2700 b.c. by radiocarbon dates from Zarębowo and Radziejów. Considering the analogous materials from other areas noted above, a time span from 3100/3000 to 2700 b.c. (ca. 3900 to 3400 B.C.) for Pikutkowo and Wiórek is probably appropriate.

The well-known "Kujavian" unchambered long barrows, which occur in most parts of region I, belong primarily to the Wiórek phase (Chmielewski 1952; Bakker, Vogel, and Wiślański 1969). The custom of building such tombs had appeared in the Sarnowo phase and disappeared at the end of Wiórek (Wiślański 1979c). In parts of Pomerania, the custom continued somewhat longer in the Łupawa group (see below), but the later tombs are slightly smaller, no longer than 35 m long instead of ranging between 40 and 150 m (Jankowska 1981).

The Wiórek phase of eastern TRB was succeeded by the Luboń phase, again named by Jażdżewski (1936) after a site near Poznań. Just as collared flasks are diagnostic of Wiórek, two- and three-strand cord marking, vertical incised lines radiating from the base of the vessel appeared, presaging the decoration of the Baden cultures which appeared slightly later south of the Carpathians and in parts of region IV. The Luboń phase can be synchronized with Bronocice III in southeast Poland (see below), Salzmünde in Bohemia and East Germany, and Boleráz in Slovakia.

Several local Luboń groups can be distinguished. These include the Ustowo group at the mouth of the Odra (Siuchninski 1981), the Łupawa group of central and eastern Pomerania (Jankowska 1981), and the Radziejów group of Kujavia (Kośko 1981). In their overall lack of decoration, the Ustowo ceramics contrast with Lubon pottery from elsewhere in region I. The Łupawa group has a number of idiosyncratic elements, especially in the flint industry and burial rite. The Radziejów ceramics contain the prominent proto-Baden elements mentioned above. Only two radiocarbon dates are available for these Luboń groups, which, together with dates for parallel materials from southeast Poland, indicate that this phase falls between 2700 and 2500 b.c. (ca. 3500–3200 B.C.). Jażdżewski (1981) believes Luboń to have lasted somewhat longer.

In region IV, the chronology of the southeast TRB is well supported by radiocarbon dates from Ćmielów (Bakker, Vogel, and Wiślański 1969), Niedzwiedz (Burchard 1973), and Bronocice (Kruk and Milisauskas 1981). The periodization of southeastern TRB follows roughly that of the eastern group presented above, with the difference lying in the lack of an initial phase analogous to Sarnowo.

Kruk and Milisauskas have published the first systematic TRB chronology for southeast Poland. They base their chronology primarily on data and radiocarbon dates from Bronocice, a multicomponent TRB settlement in the loess uplands of Malopolska (Milisauskas and Kruk 1978), where they have distinguished five occupation phases. Three of these are TRB and two are related to the Baden culture (see below). Bronocice I ceramics are characterized by funnel beakers, collared flasks, bagshaped, flat-bottomed vessels (Sackgefässe), and cups with ansa lunata handles. Decoration parallels Early Wiórek/Pikutkowo in region I and is also similar to early Baalberg materials from Bohemia and Moravia. On the basis of several radiocarbon dates, Bronocice I has been assigned to between 3200–3100 and 2900 b.c. (ca. 3900 to 3700–3625 B.C.), which would fit other dates for the TRB "collared flask horizon" (Bakker 1979) elsewhere in central Europe. Bronocice II saw a decrease in, but not a disappearance of, collared flasks. Shouldered funnel beakers, *Sackgefässe,* amphorae with lugs, and cups also appear. Decoration is primarily stamped in vertical and slanted patterns. Bronocice II is coeval with developed Wiórek in region I, late Baalberg, and some of the Jevišovice C2 material in Moravia, which would fit in the period between 2900 and 2700/2600 b.c. (3700–3625 to ca. 3350 B.C.). Bronocice III materials are similar to those of phase II. Cups are abundant, many with *ansa lunata,* as are pitchers and conical bowls. Collared flasks are completely absent by this time. There is an overall decrease in ceramic ornamentation, contrasting with the baroque Lubon ware in region I. Stamped chevron and herringbone motifs are common, and the three-strand cord marking characteristic of Lubon appears on a few sherds. In addition, ceramic forms and decoration reminiscent of the earliest Baden materials south of the Carpathians appear in Bronocice IIIb, which Kruk and Milisauskas synchronize with a period between layers C1 and C2 at Jevišovice. In general, Bronocice III is coeval with early Salzmünde in Bohemia and Luboń in northwestern Poland, thus dating to between 2700/2600 and 2500 b.c. (ca. 3525 to 3350–3025 B.C.).

Jażdżewski (1936) believed that the TRB ceramics of southeast Poland corresponded only to developed Wiórek and Luboń in northwest Poland. The study of material from Ćmielów, Gródek Nadbużny, and Bronocice along with many radiocarbon dates has shown that TRB occurred in southeast Poland earlier than previously thought, coeval at least with Early Wiórek/Pikutkowo. There is still an overall lack of materials corresponding to A/B-Sarnowo TRB, although some TRB sherds with similarities to A/B pottery have been found at Turkowice near Zamość (Kruk and Milisauskas 1981), still suggesting some chronological priority for TRB in region I.

Large areas of Poland and the east Baltic zone, including most of regions II and III, were devoid of TRB settlement during the first half of the third millennium but instead have yielded many sites of the Pit-Comb Ware Complex (*Ceramika Dołkowo-Grzebykowa*). This complex, which is not really a single "culture," represents foraging populations which continued Mesolithic lifeways in areas of marginal fertility but high natural productivity. As such, this complex has been called the "Forest Neolithic," "Ceramic Mesolithic," and "Subneolithic," although none of these terms is completely satisfactory. Although pottery appears on these sites, Mesolithic tool traditions, particularly those of the Janisławice culture, continued with little change (Niesiołowska 1973; Nowak 1981). Pit-Comb Ware sites are usually thin oc-

cupations with limited inventories. Often sherds of this complex are found on sites of other cultures, especially in the border zones between the natural regions outlined here.

Although there are a number of radiocarbon dates for Pit-Comb Ware in the east Baltic region (for a list, see Zvelebil 1978), none has yet been published for Poland. The east Baltic dates indicate that Pit-Comb Ware first appeared there around 3000 b.c. (3870–3660 B.C.) or shortly thereafter, but on the basis of typological comparisons, Wiślański (1979b) believes that the Polish Pit-Comb Ware is somewhat later, not before 2500 b.c. At Bronocice, however, Pit-Comb sherds were found in several pits, one of which also contained materials of the Lublin-Volhynian group of the Lengyel culture and others which could be dated to Bronocice III (TRB) and IV (Baden). Thus, it appears that Pit-Comb Ware initially appears in regions II and III sometime before 2500 b.c. and perhaps as early as 3000 b.c. The question of its duration is discussed below.

The Late Neolithic and the Corded Ware Problem

The final stage of Polish TRB saw the appearance of two relatively distinct cultures which temporally overlap somewhat with it. The first of these, the Globular Amphora culture (*Kultura Amfor Kulistych*), is essentially a lowland phenomenon, with some penetration into regions II, III, and IV. The second, the Baden culture (*Kultura Ceramiki Promienistej*), is confined primarily to the river terraces and uplands northeast of Kraków in region IV, although there is also some Baden influence in late TRB assemblages in the lowlands of region I as well.

The earliest Globular Amphora assemblages appeared on the Polish and German plains at approximately 2500 b.c. (3350–3025 B.C.), roughly the same time as the latest TRB and earliest Baden assemblages in southern Poland, but not in area IV until approximately two hundred years later (Wiślański 1979a). In parts of regions II and III, Globular Amphora materials also mark the first appearance of communities with agriculture and stock herding. Some have emphasized the differences between Globular Amphora and TRB to show that the former was not indigenous to this area (Gimbutas 1980). This view is not shared by many, however, and most view Globular Amphora as a local development in which TRB played a major role (Wiślański 1979a) or even as a subgroup (Jankowska 1977) or phase (Ebbesen 1975) of TRB itself.

Wiślański (1966, 1979a) has divided Globular Amphora into three phases. Materials of the earliest (I) are confined to region I, primarily in Kujavia and Wielkopolska, and are characterized by stamped and punctate ornamentation liberally applied around rims and necks.

Cord marking rarely appears, but when it does, it is the Luboń three-strand type. Characteristic Globular Amphora I vessel forms include globular and wide-mouthed amphorae in addition to other late TRB forms. For this phase, there are two radiocarbon dates. That from Zarębowo dates a pit containing both TRB and Globular Amphora sherds (Bakker, Vogel, and Wiślański 1969), while the second, from a grave at Chodzież (Prinke 1977), dates typologically late Globular Amphora I materials and should mark the transition to phase II. It is not unreasonable to assign a span of 2500–2300 b.c. (3350–3025 to 3000–2875 B.C.) to Globular Amphora I.

Globular Amphora II saw a "standardization" of main vessel forms (perhaps an illusion as the sample is composed largely of grave goods) and an increase in the amount of cord marking, which occurs on about 20 percent of decorated sherds. Stamped ornament is most frequent, with zigzags and chevrons as common motifs. The dating of Globular Amphora II is problematical, as there are two divergent dates from the same grave at Klementowice near Lublin. Wiślański (1979a) places this phase in the period 2300–2200 b.c. (3000–2875 to 2900–2750 B.C.), and synchronizes it with "classic" Baden and probably the earliest Corded Ware in region IV.

A peak in the density of ornament, especially of cord marking, occurred in Globular Amphora III. The ornament lost its previous "refinement" and became increasingly "baroque." Cord marking became the standard technique of decoration, occurring in parallel bands around rims and in chevron and semicircular patterns suspended beneath these bands. No dates are available for Globular Amphora III, but Wiślański (1979a) believes it to have lasted until about 2000 b.c. (ca. 2500 B.C.), coeval with much of Corded Ware as the high degree of cord marking would suggest.

In region IV, beyond the main area of Globular Amphora settlement, Baden elements appeared in the second half of the third millennium b.c. The culture is centered on the middle Danube area, and its influence is most strongly felt in parts of Poland close to the main trans-Carpathian corridors. Baden pottery in southern Poland is sufficiently different from the Baden materials south of the Carpathians for Kruk and Milisauskas (1981) to refer to it as "Baden-like." The reason for this distinction is that in its "core" area, Baden follows epi-Lengyel and epi-Polgar assemblages (e.g., Boleráz, Jevišovice C2), while north of the Carpathians there is the added element of TRB.

Godłowska (1979) has divided Polish Baden into three phases. The earliest is closely connected with late TRB in southeast Poland and Boleráz in Slovakia. At several TRB sites such as Niedzwiedz (Burchard 1973) and Bronocice (Kruk and Milisauskas 1981), Baden traits have appeared in TRB contexts, as did the Baden-influenced late TRB ceramics of region I. Burchard synchronizes the Niedzwiedz materials with Jevišovice C1 and Ohrozim in Moravia, while Kruk and Milisauskas equate the earliest Baden at Bronocice with the period between Jevišovice C2 and C1, that is, earlier than C1. Radiocarbon dates indicate a span of 2600–2500 b.c. (3375–3025 B.C.) for this phase. In Silesia, similar "proto-Baden" influence is found at late TRB sites coeval with Luboń TRB in region I (Bukowska-Gedigowa 1975).

While the earliest Baden in region IV can be considered "proto-Baden," the succeeding "middle" phase connects more closely with "true" Baden from south of the Carpathians. According to Godłowska, this phase is characterized by numerous cups with *ansa lunata,* although these are rare in the Bronocice IV assemblage corresponding to this phase, and by *Sackgefässe* with tapering sides and flat bottoms. In addition to the characteristic incised lines, bands of fingernail impressions are often found below the rims, frequently in conjunction with applied strips of ornament.

The late Baden in the upper Wisła basin has also been called the Zesławice-Pleszów group (Godłowska 1979). A new element in the ceramic inventory is a conical cup with *ansa lunata.* Paralleling Globular Amphora III, there is a marked increase in the density of ornamentation on late Baden vessels. This phase can also be synchronized with "classic" Baden in Slovakia and Hungary, corresponding to phases III and IV of Baden according to Němejcová-Pavúková (1981).

In southeast Poland, the absolute chronology of Baden has been greatly improved by the recent series of radiocarbon dates from Bronocice (Kruk and Milisauskas 1981). Although the "proto-Baden" elements that occur with late TRB ceramics can be dated as early as 2600 b.c. (3375–3175 B.C.), the beginning of actual Baden, or "Baden-like," ceramics is later, ca. 2500–2400 b.c. (3300–3000 B.C.). The latest Baden assemblages probably end by about 2200–2100 b.c. (2900–2700 B.C.).

The final centuries of the third millennium b.c. saw the spread of a complex of cultures characterized by cord-marked pottery across a large area of Europe (see Buchvaldek 1980 for a review of this phenomenon.) The perceived unity of the Corded Ware complex is taken by some to indicate a wave of invaders from the east that overran Europe (e.g., Gimbutas 1977, 1980). This wide view of Corded Ware links it with the Single Grave culture in north Germany and Denmark and the Battle-Ax culture of the circum-Baltic area. Others hold a more limited view and insist that more traits than just simple cord marking are diagnostic. Machnik (1979a), for instance, considers the Corded Ware culture to be characterized by elongated beakers, amphorae with two or four handles, axes with asymmetrical cutting edges, and single contracted inhumations under barrows, in addition to cord-marked pottery. Historically, this view of Corded Ware has had more adherents since the concept was introduced by Klopfleisch in 1883. Since this chapter treats Corded Ware within only the area of modern day Poland, see the other chapters in this section, by Wells, Gimbutas, Ehrich and Bankoff, and Thomas, R. Rowlett, and E. Rowlett, for a discussion of this complex in other areas.

The Corded Ware culture in Poland has several phases, which Machnik (1979a) correlates with Corded Ware "horizons" in Europe. The oldest of these is related to the "Pan-European" horizon, based on scattered finds from destroyed barrows in parts of southern and northern Poland. As in other parts of central Europe, Corded Ware I ceramics occur in two basic forms, beakers and amphorae. There are two variants of beakers, wide-mouthed with cylindrical necks and S-profiled with flaring necks, both decorated above the neck with cord impressions or with stamped and incised herringbone designs. Amphorae generally have egg-shaped profiles with or without cylindrical necks. The decorative motifs on the amphorae are the same as on the beakers, and it should be emphasized that cord decoration is by no means universal. Although no radiocarbon dates exist for Corded Ware I in Poland, some from elsewhere in central Europe (see Behrens 1981) suggest a dating of ca. 2300–2200 b.c. (ca. 2900–2800 B.C.), making it coeval with Globular Amphora II in region I and middle Baden along the upper Wisła.

Machnik relates Corded Ware II in Poland to the "central European" horizon. Like the first phase, Corded Ware II finds occur in two zones, the Baltic coast and Masurian lake region and on the loess uplands of southern Poland. Kujavia and Wielkopolska still show no Corded Ware occupation at this time, and the vigorous Globular Amphora culture persists in these areas. Also at this time, two cultures (or groups) that show mixtures of Globular Amphora and Corded Ware arose: the Rzuczewo culture along the Baltic coast and the Złota culture of the loess area near Sandomierz. Settlements with pure Corded Ware II components have yet to be identified in Poland, although several clusters of burials are known from this phase in the Kraków region, Silesia, western Pomerania, and southeast Poland. All share similar artifact inventories, little changed from the earliest phase save for some details.

The two Corded Ware variants mentioned above, Rzuczewo and Złota, deserve special mention, for these are the only sites in Poland where settlement and economic data are available for this period. Prior to World War II, the Rzuczewo culture (*Haffküstenkultur* in German) was identified by Kostrzewski at Rzuczewo near Gdansk and by German archaeologists on the coast of East Prussia (Kostrzewski 1930; Killian 1955). Its settle-

ments have yielded many house plans and rich faunal remains. Rzuczewo is considered to have both Corded Ware and Globular Amphora ceramic elements, thus presenting an argument for a temporal overlap of the two larger cultures. There is a wide range of vessel forms, usually variations on beakers but also amphorae of various sorts. The beakers seem to be closer to Corded Ware forms while the amphorae are more like those of Globular Amphora (Machnik 1979a). Other vessels are also reminiscent of Globular Amphora shapes, and in addition, there is a coarser utility ware. Other traits include flint and stone axes, large quantities of amber artifacts, and rich (but unstudied) chipped stone and bone industries. Until recently, the chronology of Rzuczewo was known only by analogy with Corded Ware and Globular Amphora, but two radiocarbon dates have recently become available (Wiślański 1978). Conventional wisdom has placed Rzuczweo between 2200 and 2000 b.c. (2900–2500 B.C.), coeval with Corded Ware II. The radiocarbon dates, however, suggest that it began earlier, although it might have lasted until about 2000 b.c. or later.

The Złota culture, the other main congener of Corded Ware in Poland, is known primarily from the settlement and cemetery complex at Złota, also excavated prior to World War II. Thirty-one sites of this culture are now known (Krzak 1976), all clustered in an area 50 km in diameter around Złota. This culture consists of a mixture of Corded Ware and Globular Amphora elements, much like Rzuczewo, but with the sporadic appearance of Baden-like pottery as well. In addition to Baden radial incised lines on some pots, Złota ceramic decoration is predominantly of cord impressions and stamping on the upper half of vessels. Parallel wavy lines of cord impressions around rims are especially characteristic. The Złota graves are unusual in that they have a distinctive "niche" in which the inhumation is laid. No radiocarbon dates are available for Złota, but Machnik synchronizes it with Rzuczewo and the older Corded Ware, later Globular Amphora, and late Baden in the upper Wisła basin. The reader should consult Krzak's 1976 English-language monograph for a discussion of the finer subdivisions of Złota.

In the final phase of Corded Ware, a number of local clusters appeared. These include the Kraków-Sandomierz, Silesian, lower Odra, and Wielkopolska-Kujavy groups. As with the earlier phases, the last is also known exclusively from grave finds. A settlement at Łask, near Poznań, which Kostrzewski identified as Corded Ware, is more likely to date to the Early Bronze Age (Machnik 1979a). Two other settlement contexts containing Corded Ware, at Zarębowo and Nowiny, occur on sites with Globular Amphora and TRB components. Machnik (1979a) suggests that there may be Corded Ware camps on locations previously occupied by Globular Amphora settlements. Several radiocarbon dates for late Corded Ware groups indicate dates of approximately 2100–1850 b.c. (2675–2300 B.C.) for this phase. The 1850 b.c. date, however, does not mean the end of cord marking and represents a relatively arbitrary separation between Corded Ware and a number of Corded Ware–derived groups of the Early Bronze Age.

Up to this point, I have treated the Late Neolithic of this area as a local development, but it is not completely so. The Bell Beaker "culture" appeared in parts of region IV coeval with late Corded Ware and Globular Amphora, especially in Upper Silesia and Małopolska. It is clearly intrusive, with vessel forms, ceramic decoration, and most other traits completely unlike the local materials. With the exception of a few vessel forms, it is identical with Bell Beaker pottery found elsewhere in central Europe, primarily in Bohemia and Moravia (Machnik 1979b). Although no radiocarbon dates are available for Bell Beakers in Poland, this culture is conventionally placed between 1900 and 1800 b.c. (2425–2125 B.C.), immediately preceding the earliest Únětice materials in Silesia (Machnik 1977).

A final word is in order about Pit-Comb Ware, the complex of Forest Neolithic groups inhabiting much of regions II and III. In its late stages, several local groups have been distinguished, going under the names of the Niemen culture and the Sokołówek and Linin groups (Kempisty 1973). Any chronology of these can only be in the most general terms, but the Pit-Comb Ware complex appears to have persisted on the fringes of the farming cultures all during the Late Neolithic and into the Early Bronze Age (Wiślański 1979a).

Continuity and Discontinuity in the Early Bronze Age

As one might expect with any arbitrary temporal division, the beginning of the Bronze Age is filled with a variety of cultural units that actually represent the continuation of Neolithic cultures, the only difference being the appearance of bronze metallurgy. These groups fit into two categories: those that represent an extension of the Corded Ware culture into the Bronze Age and those that are related to the central European Únětice (Aunjetitz) culture group, including the Únětice culture proper in Silesia. In general, the area where Únětice and its congeners appear corresponds to region I, while all other areas have Early Bronze Age cultures developed from local Corded Ware groups.

The late Corded Ware of southeast Poland (i.e., the Kraków-Sandomierz group) is followed by the "epi-Corded Ware" Chłopice-Veselé culture, which forms the last phase of the Corded Ware tradition with some bronze artifacts. This culture is known from a number of settlements as well as inhumations (Machnik 1977). The most common vessel form is a muglike cup with a handle set well below the rim. Other vessel forms include amphorae with a single handle and a tall tapering neck as well as bowls. Chłopice-Veselé ceramic decoration represents the extreme in cord marking. Whereas late Corded Ware vessels are usually decorated only above the neck, Chłopice-Veselé pots have cord marking all over, in radial lines reminiscent of the incised Baden lines. Chłopice-Veselé flintwork is somewhat different from that of the earlier Corded Ware, utilizing mostly flakes instead of blades (Machnik 1977). This difference, however, may be due to the fact that Corded Ware tools come only from graves, while Chłopice-Veselé flints come from settlement contexts as well.

The dating of Chłopice-Veselé has been aided by several radiocarbon dates and a number of connections with other Early Bronze Age groups, such as Csepel in Hungary (Machnik 1977; Bukowski 1980). It is at least partly synchronous with the earliest phase of Únětice (proto-Únětice), although there are few direct links between the two cultures. The radiocarbon dates place the Chłopice-Veselé culture in the relatively short period between 1850 and 1750 b.c. (2300–2000 B.C.).

The Mierzanowice culture (Machnik 1977; Bukowski 1980) is a development from Chłopice-Veselé in Małopolska. Before World War II, it was also called the Tomaszów group of Corded Ware. As with Chłopice-Veselé, this culture is known from both settlements and graves. Mierzanowice vessel forms are basically the same as those of Chłopice-Veselé, although minor details such as handle placement are different. Decoration is still predominantly cord marked, although to a lesser extent than seen in Chłopice-Veselé. A plainer utilitarian ware occurs in Mierzanowice settlements, along with a rich flint industry (Kopacz 1976). Machnik's chronology of Mierzanowice recognizes two phases, the earlier coeval with the second phase of Únětice and the later with Únětice III and IV. On the basis of several radiocarbon dates, he places Mierzanowice between 1750 and 1600 b.c. (2100–1850 B.C.).

Farther east on the Lublin uplands and coeval with the appearance of Mierzanowice in Małopolska, the Stryzów culture developed from Chłopice-Veselé. Previously known as the Stryzów group of Corded Ware, it has been studied best at the eponymous site of Stryzów and at other settlements. Relatively few graves are known. Common Stryzów forms are S-profiled pots, amphorae, and bowls, continuing Corded Ware traditions. A characteristic of many smaller vessels is a thickening around the rim. Stryzów pottery has a density of cord marking reminiscent of Chłopice-Veselé, in straight, wavy, and zigzag lines. In the absence of radiocarbon dates, Machnik dates Stryzów between 1750 and 1600 b.c. (2100–1850 B.C.) on the basis of similarities to Mierzanowice (Machnik 1977).

During these developments in southeast Poland, this period in western and northwestern Poland saw the appearance of the Únětice culture and related groups. Únětice and its congeners, unlike the epi-Corded Ware groups farther east, show few connections to the previous Late Neolithic groups in Silesia and western Poland, with the exception of Bell Beakers whose vessel forms are quite similar to those of proto-Únětice. The formation of Únětice was a complex process with included elements of several central European cultures, especially Bell Beakers. The focus of its origin appears to have been in Bohemia and Saxo-Thuringia, to the southwest of the area under consideration here. By the time it appeared in Poland along the upper Odra, it had already undergone some degree of development.

In Poland, Únětice is divided into five phases (Sarnowska 1969; Machnik 1977). The first, proto-Únětice or Únětice I, is characterized by handled beakers and jugs with a paucity of surface decoration, contrasting sharply with the baroque Chłopice-Veselé pottery. Shallow bowls, sometimes with four feet, also form a large part of the ceramic inventory. In Únětice II, tall, handled jugs became prominent, decorated with incised ornament in zigzags and festoons. In the third and fourth phases of Únětice, vessels became lower in height and handles became common on all forms. Decoration commonly consists of several parallel incised lines around the neck or waist of a vessel. Únětice V, also called "classic" Únětice, is the peak of Únětice development, with a wide variety of vessel forms which are rarely decorated. The profiles of the vessels are sharp, almost angular, and are usually concave above the shoulder and convex below. As such, they are markedly different from the rounded profiles of Mierzanowice and Stryzów pottery.

Bronze artifacts are very common from Únětice III onward and include pins, torcs, spirals, bracelets, and an occasional flanged ax. In "classic" Únětice, the assortment of bronze forms is especially rich, and gold and amber ornaments are also frequently found.

During Únětice III and IV, two offshoots of this culture appeared in parts of Region I. These are the Iwno culture of Wielkopolska and Kujavia and the Grobia-Śmiardowo culture of Pomerania. Both have the same range of vessel forms characteristic of Únětice III and IV, with some variations in decoration. Iwno vessels have somewhat more decoration, in the form of parallel and zigzag incised lines, while Grobia-Śmiardowo pottery has just the opposite trend, toward less surface decoration. Metal forms are similar to those mentioned for "classic" Únětice.

There are several radiocarbon dates from Polish sites for Únětice and its congeners which indicate that it starts at about 1900 b.c. for proto-Únětice and lasts through 1500 b.c. (a span from 2400 B.C. to 1700 B.C. at its greatest possible duration). The Iwno and Grobia-Śmiardowo cultures, coeval with Únětice III and IV, probably fall between ca. 1750 and 1500 b.c. (2100–1700 B.C.). The Únětice and related cultures are succeeded by the Middle Bronze Age Tumulus culture group, which is beyond the scope of this discussion.

It is necessary to emphasize the differences between Únětice and its relatives on the one hand and the Corded Ware–derived Early Bronze Age cultures of southeast Poland on the other. These manifest themselves in virtually all aspects of the artifact inventory. Vessel forms and decoration differ markedly as to the frequency and variety of bronze forms, which are relatively scarce in southeastern Poland. Another important difference is the evidence for social stratification. Whereas in Únětice a number of very rich graves, such as the Łęki Małe tumulus and the Leubingen mortuary house, have been discovered, the Mierzanowice and Stryzów burials are simple inhumations, usually in cemeteries, with relatively few grave goods. There is a distinct lack of interaction between Únětice and the coeval cultures of southeastern Poland (Machnik 1977; Bukowski 1980), and it appears that there was a very real cultural separation between the Early Bronze Age cultures of western and eastern Poland. In this case, it seems possible to recognize true "ethnic" differentiation in the archaeological record, especially since no direct links can be made to a common Corded Ware heritage for Únětice as they can for the eastern cultures.

Conclusion

This chapter has presented a radiocarbon-supported chronology for the part of east-central Europe corresponding to modern Poland during the period 4500–1500 b.c. (5500–1700 B.C.). The data presented in the text are summarized in figure 2, which is a chronological chart for all four of the regions defined at the beginning of this chapter. Table 1 contains all radiocarbon dates known to the author for sites in this area up to November 1982.

Throughout this discussion, I have treated most cultural developments as strictly local phenomena, with the different cultures and phases within cultures smoothly progressing along. Such an approach is different from the traditional view taken by some European archaeologists, who have viewed culture change as the product of migrations and invasions. Given the types of communities that are represented by these archaeological cultures, namely small-scale village farming settlements, there is no need to invoke mass movements of people to account for the changes in the archaeological record. Rather, a close examination of the evidence indicates that there was gradual, but sustained, change throughout the period considered here, and the archaeological "cultures" described above are almost arbitrary divisions of a continuum from the earliest farming communities of the Linear Pottery culture to the stratified societies of Únětice. Future research will continue to blur the distinctions among these groups and will strengthen the overall picture of gradual development and change.

Twenty-One

Geographical and Chronological Patterns in East Central and Southeastern Europe

Robert W. Ehrich, Peabody Museum, Harvard University
H. Arthur Bankoff, Brooklyn College, City University of New York

Outline

Geographical Setting

The area covered in this chapter comprises the political entities of Czechoslovakia, Lower Austria, Hungary, Romania, Yugoslavia, Bulgaria, and Albania. Geographically it includes the drainages of the upper Elbe, flowing northwestward to the Baltic, the middle and lower Danube system flowing to the Black Sea, those of the Yugoslav and Albanian coasts to the Adriatic, and the Vardar of south Yugoslavia and the Marica (Maritza) of Bulgaria to the Aegean (see fig. 2).

South of Moravia, Lower Austria westward to its general division from Upper Austria in the Enns, Salzach, and Traun tributaries of the Danube (Pittioni 1961; Ehrich 1976) opens via the Vienna Basin to the Hungarian lower lands to the east and to the Little Alföld plain connecting with the lower Moravian Plain to the north.

The Middle Danubian basin includes the entire Danubian drainage from the edge of Upper Austria and the eastern Alps to the Danubian Gorge or Djerdap which

separates it from the Lower Danubian drainage. The latter lies mostly between the Transylvanian Alps which form its northern border and the Stara Planina range to the south.

Bohemia, the northwest corner of our area, is diamond shaped, framed on the southwest by the hills of the Bohemian Forest which separate it from the Upper Danube, on the west by the Erzgebirge, on the northeast by the Sudetens, and along the southeast by the Czecho-Moravian Heights. The upper Elbe system provides its

We herewith express our deepest thanks for many kindnesses and much help from numerous colleagues, not only those who gave generously in conference of their time and knowledge but also those who made available as yet unpublished information, called our attention to published works hitherto unknown to us, and often sent or gave critically needed volumes and offprints.

Many have tried to guide us through the welter of materials, but what we have done with it remains our own responsibility. It is, of course, too much to hope that any specialist in the area will be completely happy with all of our results. However, this chapter may at least help to serve as a general guide for the nonspecialist.

Among those to whom we are particularly indebted are the following, whose countries and names we list alphabetically: *Austria:* The late

Revised August 1987

only drainage. Its northern part is, for the most part, a loess-covered basin with rolling hills, its southern part a deeply trenched plateau.

East of Bohemia, Moravia, the valley of the southward-flowing Morava, provides a corridor of easy access to the north European plain and separates the Sudeten ranges from the Carpathians. On the north a low watershed separates the headwaters of the Morava from those of the Oder. On the south the Morava joins the Danube, and its lowland connects with the Little Alföld plain as well as Lower Austria.

The northern Carpathian arc not only furnishes the political boundary between Poland and Slovakia, but is a watershed between the north European plain and the Middle Danube. In western Slovakia the broad valleys of the Vah and Hron rivers curve flatly westward to enter the Danube before it bends sharply south at the Danube knee and divides the hilly country of Transdanubia on the west from the Great Hungarian Plain to the east. Eastern Slovakia, on the other hand, is cut by the dendritic pattern of the upper Tisza, which rises in the Ukraine and collects the westward flowing waters of the Someş, Körös (Criş), and Maros (Mureş) from the Transylvanian basin as it runs southward parallel to the Danube before joining it some twenty-five miles above Beograd. The Alföld or Great Hungarian Plain extends eastward from the Danube to the western hills that border Transylvania.

The Carpathian arc encloses the Transylvanian basin on its north and east and returns westward as the Transylvanian Alps, which mark the northern edge of the Lower Danube plain. Irregular massifs loosely plug Transylvania's western side, through which the major rivers all flow west to the Tisza. Only the upper Olt in the southeast penetrates the wall of the Transylvanian Alps, and the Bistrica cuts through the eastern wall to join the Siret. East of the Carpathians the Siret and the Prut wheel southward around the mountains to define the Romanian

provinces of Moldavia and the eastern part of Muntenia, which were formerly described as the Romanian portion of Bessarabia.

On the west the eastern Alps mark the edge of the middle Danubian basin. The headwaters of the Sava and the Drava rise here and run eastward to join the Danube, the Drava reaching it above Osijek and the Sava at Beograd. The major tributaries of the Sava join it from the south, and this one system covers approximately one-half of Yugoslavia.

Along the western side of the southern tier the Dinaric Alps and Albanian Mountains isolate the Adriatic drainage from the interior, except for the Drim system, which rises in the Kosovo-Metohija and in eastern Macedonia. From here eastward to the Vardar and Morava valleys the Sava tributaries of the Krka, Bosna, Drina, and lesser streams drain the south part of the Yugoslav basin. The Crna in the southwest traverses the plain of Pelagonia, which opens toward Greek Thessaly, and flows eastward to join the southward-running Vardar below Titov Veles. East of the Vardar and the northward-flowing Yugoslavian Morava, which joins the Danube, the mountains screen off the Struma and Strumica in the south and the Timok to the north of them.

Bulgaria to the east is divided roughly into the southern or right-bank plain of the lower Danube, watered by streams from the Stara Planina to the south, and below the Stara Planina is the Rhodope Massif and the valley of the Marica, which flows to the Aegean (see fig. 2).

In other papers Ehrich (e.g., 1970a, 1970b, 1987) has called attention to the persistences and reappearances of culture areas and culture boundaries within this area and also as a principle in culture history. The role of geographical boundaries, river systems, and interior contact areas is critical to understanding the culture history of the region.

Some Archaeological Considerations

The strong correlations between geographical and cultural patternings (e.g., Ehrich 1970b; Sherrat 1982) may seem deceptively simple, but the actual complexity of synthesizing is often obscured by the fact that the literature is in eight or more languages. Even the same rivers and cultures may have different names in neighboring countries, for example, Körös (Hungarian) and Criş (Romanian), while in English at least two Morava rivers, one in Czechoslovakia (German March) and the other in Yugoslavia, present a possible source of confusion.

Whether or not one agrees with them in detail, several summary works now provide more comprehensive introductions, as do separate studies of particular cultures and periods, as well as relationship patterns discussed in site reports, published symposia, and various articles.

Richard Pittioni and Elizabeth Ruttkay, Vienna; *Bulgaria:* Georgi Il. Georgiev and Rumen Katincarov, Sofia; *Czechoslovakia:* Miroslav Buchvaldek, Prague; Bohuslav Chropovský, Nitra; Evžen Plesl and Emilie Pleslová-Štiková, Prague; *England:* John Chapman, University of Newcastle on Tyne; *Hungary:* Ida Bognár-Kutzián; Nándor Kalicz; János Makkay, Pál Patay, and Pál Raczky, all of Budapest; *Romania:* Eugen Comşa; Vladimir Dumitrescu; Silvia Marinescu-Bîlcu; Petre Roman; Alexander Vulpe, Bucharest; and the late Nicolae Vlassa, Cluj; *Yugoslavia:* Aloyz Benac, Sarajevo; Draga and Milutin Garašanin, Beograd; Jovan Glišić, Priština; Borislav Jovanović and Nikola Tasić, Beograd.

In the United States we are deeply grateful to Homer L. Thomas for his constant assistance and for sharing his wealth of information, to Bela Maday for a translation from the Hungarian, and to Nancy Lambert Brown for putting the synchronic chart into respectable form.

We also express our appreciation to Norman Hammond who, when in the United States, made available to us copies of the advance proofs of the pertinent sections of the second edition of the *Cambridge Ancient History.*

Despite their fundamental imprecision, the increasing numbers of radiocarbon determinations help bring the picture into better focus, although unevenness in the degree of excavation, publication, the number of determinations available, variations between the results from different laboratories and in the reliability of the samples lead to some discrepancies and lacunae in the overall coverages. Since the literature for this area contains many charts giving relative chronologies of greater or lesser scope, we emphasize what seem to be acceptable equations, using key calibrated radiocarbon dates, averaged and usually with ranges, as reference points and controls. (For individual dates see tables 1–7.)

In this chapter we concentrate on cultural sequences, distributions, radiocarbon determinations, and on bibliography in which many items provide extensive further references.

The writers are thoroughly aware that pottery groups by themselves do not constitute separate cultures. However, ceramic inventories do express complex patterns of learned behavior, and close similarities between pottery groups or wares usually indicate peoples who are in actual contact with each other or who have a shared cultural heritage. As in almost any classification, the greater the number and intensity of similarities, the greater is the degree of presumed relationship (e.g., Ehrich 1950, 1965a:3–4). In Europe many cultures are customarily described by reference to their ceramics, for example, *Bandkeramik* or Linear, Stroked Ware, Corded Ware, Bell Beaker people, and so forth. When we use these terms, we refer to peoples with such pottery and to their cultures.

Some Geographical Archaeological Applications

In Bulgaria, the central area along the Danube is no longer considered a potentially distinct north-central region. The division now seems to be simple northwest or western, with essentially western or west-related complexes, southeastern with a dominating role by the Marica (Maritsa) and Tundža (Tundzha) rivers of the Thracian plain, and northeastern with varying relationships to the Romanian and steppe spheres to the north and east and with others to the south.

As the first major site in which stratification was well established (Georgiev 1961), the mound of Karanovo with its successive levels has served as the key to interpreting both the Marica drainage and the relatively level nearby Thracian plain. Several other sites, such as Yassatepe (Jasatepe) and Kapitan Dimitrejovo, have been fitted into the Karanovo sequence. Georgiev's (1961:49) numbering of the strata as reported in the 1965 edition is now universally accepted.

Strata at the site of Čavdar at the northern edge of the Sofia basin, and at some other sites, not only confirm the Karanovo stratigraphy but have also produced radiocarbon dates that have a wide application. We incorporate the individual phases of the Karanovo sequence in our discussions of the various chronological equations.

For Romania, since the Körös and Maros drain most of Transylvania westward, cultures of the earlier periods moved upstream from the west, and southeastern Transylvania mostly reflects the impact of Muntenia on the upper Olt. Eastern, and later northern, Transylvania shows strong influence from beyond the Prut, that is, the Dniester-Bug area, via Soviet Moldavia and ultimately from Romanian Moldavia. Along the Danube Valley south of the mountains, cultures from the west traversed Oltenia to the Olt, which forms the boundary between Oltenia and Muntenia. Cultural development in these two provinces differed from each other.

To the west the Yugoslav Adriatic drainage serves as part of the littoral culture area, the cultures of which are generally distinct from those of the plateaus east of the ranges (Ehrich 1970a, 1970b). Only the Drim system of Albania provides any ingress for coastal culture elements to penetrate as far as the Kosovo-Metohija area in which cultures moving eastward along the Drim and northward along the Vardar systems, and Danubian elements moving southward by the Ibar and Sitnica tributaries of the Western Morava, met and to some extent mingled (J. Glišić, pers. information).

For the chronological equations that follow, the data are uneven with regard to geographic coverage, cultures, and periods.

The total procedure is, of course, one of building up a series of relative chronologies and then checking their validity through the medium of calibrated radiocarbon dates, both within our general area and beyond its geographical limits by reference to related cultures. Since radiocarbon coverage is spotty and since some determinations are unreliable because of faulty attribution, contamination, inconsistencies between laboratories, irregularities in the process, and the like, the best one can hope for is to anchor the various networks of relationships roughly in time by establishing, to some degree at least, some acceptable reference points.

In this context, the calibrating of the radiocarbon determinations to adjust them to the dendrochronological time scale has been of inestimable value in standardizing and establishing comparable results. For the most part we have been able to use the reported 5568 half-life b.p. dates when calibrating, but in those instances in which only B.C. dates are given, we have converted them back to what must have been their original b.p. determinations, and where the standard deviations are not given we have assumed a ± of 100.

For our tables of calibrated averaged dates in the text we have used the following formula: arithmetical average of the reported dates b.p. $\pm$ the average 1σ divided by the square root of the number of dates averaged. We have then used the resulting b.p. date for entry into the calibration tables given in the appendix (see also "Concerning the Radiocarbon Dates" in the introduction to this volume). In this process we have made use of those dates for which the combined sigmas are approximately equal to or larger than the differences between the b.p. dates averaged or in a stepped series between the pairs within them, and we have eliminated those dates that are obviously out of range. We give the individual dates for our area in tables 1–7. Dates from outside our area are as noted.

In constructing our series of temporal equations we have to a great extent eliminated discussion of specific intrasite and intersite relationships which are either treated in some detail in the sources cited or in the items referred to in their bibliographies. We have used only such cultural traits as the Danilo-Kakanj cult vessels and the much later graphite-ornamented Karanovo VI–Gumelniţa–Early Sălcuţa–Krivodol–Bubanj I pottery to establish specific chronological and geographic relationships. In general the three deeply stratified sites of Karanovo, Vinča, and Obre stand out as landmarks.

Although we are dealing with chronological horizons, we avoid this term in favor of *temporal equations* in order to avoid confusion with the summary maps for which Homer Thomas uses *horizons* to denote more general equivalencies and a greater order of exactitude. In the interests of brevity we have selected only a very few sites or strata by which to label each temporal equation, although many others of equal importance are included in the equations themselves.

Since the following general comments span more than one temporal equation, it seems better to include them at this point rather than to try to do so piecemeal under the separate discussions.

There seems to be general agreement that the older pattern of existing cultures was gradually disrupted by incursions of nomadic and seminomadic peoples, originally from the steppes to the east, who moved westward for the most part by stages. Gimbutas for some years (e.g., 1980a:1, 1982:18) has identified the original groupings, our equations I–V, as Old Europe, with the eastern influxes beginning in our equation V. She has divided these last into three general Kurgan Waves which she labels Kurgan I 4400–4200 B.C., Kurgan II 3400–3200, and Kurgan III 3000–2800. She interprets these waves as probably more or less signifying movements of Indo-European-speaking peoples who gradually came to dominate the European scene. She envisions a survival of existing cultural elements with an overwash of and integration of the new cultural patterns with those of the old, with varying degrees of admixture in the amalgam. Her formulation has by no means met with universal or complete acceptance. (For other views see, e.g., Anthony 1986; Thomas 1982; Ecsedy 1979:55, 56.)

In this regard Kalicz (1980:247, also fig.2, p. 248, and fig.3, p. 259) stresses that between the Balaton and Balaton-Lasinja cultures there are marked differences in culture content and in affiliations with contemporary groups, the patternings of which show marked differences throughout the area. He attributes this change to "a chain reaction instigated by a wave of Kurgan movement" (p. 267). The major impact of the eastern steppe peoples appears in the cultures of temporal equations V, VI, and VII.

Temporal Equations

Temporal Equation I (Earliest Period)

Gura Baciului–Anzabegovo I–Karanovo I–Thessalian Early Neolithic II or Proto-Sesklo Horizon, and a suggested revision of the Thessalian Early Neolithic terminology

As of 1965, with the possible exception of Karanovo I, the Starčevo culture horizon with Karanovo II and Starčevo-related cultures appeared to be the earliest Neolithic in southeastern Europe. However, since then, evidence of an earlier occupation has appeared. Between its distinctive pottery and the wares of later Starčevo levels at various sites there seems to be no relationship. Thus the continuity suggested by calling this culture either Pre- or Proto-Starčevo is misleading, and we therefore refer to it as the Gura Baciului–Anzabegovo I–Karanovo I horizon. To this belongs the bottom layer at Veluška Tumba (Simoska and Sanev 1975), formerly called Pelagonian and thought to be later Neolithic, Anzabegovo I (Gimbutas 1976 and M. Garašanin [pers. information]), Vršnik I (Garašanin and Garašanin 1961), Cîrcea I near Craiova on the Jiu River in Wallachia (Nica 1977), Gura Baciului near Cluj in western Transylvania on the Little Someş drainage (Vlassa 1972), Donja Branjevina at Odžaci in the Yugoslav Bačka (Karmanski 1968, 1975), and Gălăbnik in the upper Struma (Pavúk and Čochadžiev 1984). Recently I. Paul has been excavating a settlement of this period at Ocna Sibiului (Triguri) in the upper Olt drainage of southeastern Transylvania. Although Dumitrescu (1983a) mentions three strata there, it is unclear whether all three belong to this period or represent a succession. No further information is currently available (pers. comm. from M. Garašanin, E. Comşa, and A. Vulpe).

Generally the levels of this period occur independently. Only at Donja Branjevina does the excavator claim that the pottery appeared in association with Starčevo material, particularly the so-called altars. Although some skepticism has been voiced as to the manner of excavation, it also seems quite possible that this admixture may have resulted from a disturbance of the earlier level and a backfill during subsequent Starčevo, or even later, times. The five sherds painted in this style from Szarvas 23 (Makkay 1981) may well have a similar history of contamination.

The distinctive pottery clearly links some of these sites and relates them to Proto-Sesklo of Thessaly (e.g., M. Garašanin 1982c). Since Veluška Tumba on the Pelagonian plain is in the Crna drainage, which is a component of the Vardar system but with the plain also opening toward Thessaly and eastern Macedonia, and since Anzabegovo lies near the end of the Ovče Polje which bypasses the Iron Gate or Gorge of the Vardar, such a southern origin, also possibly working northward in west Bulgaria, would seem reasonable.

The generally accepted recognition of this early period renders obsolete the currently popular trend toward seeing a local transformation from the Mesolithic to the Neolithic in the Iron Gates of the Danube from the Epipaleolithic or Mesolithic from Schela Cladovei to what is clearly the Starčevo period (see also Dumitrescu 1983a). Also a direct transition from Mesolithic to Neolithic in Tier III to the north in east-central Europe, where the Linear ceramic group is still later, that is, Late Neolithic in our southern equation but still the earliest Neolithic in Tier III (Ehrich 1990) and western Europe is beyond belief.

Thus Starčevo-Körös-Criş and Karanovo II and III become Middle Neolithic. The somewhat later incised *Bandkeramik* I of north and northwest Hungary, west Slovakia, Austria, Moravia, Bohemia, and West Germany as well as Poland would become Late Neolithic, as do Karanovo IV and Vinča A and B (Vinča-Tordos). Other cultures throughout the area are also similarly elevated on the terminological scale.

One must remember, however, that these broad classificatory terms have been for convenience only in the construction of general sequences and equations in large areas, so that one might incorporate much more specific groups and relationships as outlined below. They have no intrinsic meaning of their own. The examples given merely identify the major patterns of the broader framework.

Now, although the *Bandkeramik* or Linear wares represent the oldest Neolithic population in central Europe, where they are still called Early Neolithic, they equate with the Vinča-Tordos or Late Neolithic farther south. For this reason we abandon the Early, Middle, and Late Neolithic designations and formulate our discussion in terms of temporal equations, relapsing only with regard to specifically local or regional sequences.

At Anzabegovo and at Gălăbnik I strata of the Gura Baciului–Anzabegovo I–Karanovo I–Thessalian Early Neolithic II "Proto-Sesklo" horizon underlie levels of the Starčevo and Karanovo II Neolithic complexes. A brief summary of key calibrated radiocarbon dates follows.

Ten radiocarbon dates reported from Anzabegovo Ia and Ib overlap and fall so closely together that we can treat them as from a single stratum. These include two dates that are lower than expected but exclude two others for which the reported dates fall above the range of the calibration tables, and a third within the range but that could be from either Stratum I or II.

Three dates from the early Neolithic at Veluška Tumba fall within a very narrow range, with a very similar one from the nearby site of Tumba.

In Bulgaria a series of nine dates at Čavdar is assigned to the Karanovo I period, while fourteen from Azmak and two from the hospital at Stara Zagora, while partly within the same range, may average slightly later. (For the Čavdar report equating Čavdar I–III with Karanovo I–III see Georgiev 1981:107–8.)

Site	No. of Dates	Range B.C.	Average B.C.
Anzabegovo I	9	6400/5715–5550/5250	6075–5555
Veluška Tumba	3	6025/5500–5965/5470	5960–5485
Tumba	1		5810–5395
Čavdar	9	6330/5730–6000/5485	6125–5590
Azmak	14	6300/5640–5325/5065	5760–5390
Stara Zagora	2	6425/5665 and 5915/5460	

We thus have some anchor dates to which we can relate other sites and strata of this horizon as, for example, Odmut (see below).

Furthermore, since the assemblages from Gura Baciului, Anzabegovo I, and Karanovo I equate with the so-called Proto-Sesklo of Thessaly, it seems appropriate at this time to try to resolve a matter of very considerable confusion. Starting with an early and a late phase of Sesklo, as initially designated at Otzaki Magula, Milojčić subsequently determined a third phase falling between them, which he labeled Pre-Sesklo (*Vorsesklo*). Still later at Argissa a fourth phase appeared falling between Early Sesklo and Pre-Sesklo, which he inserted as Proto-Sesklo (e.g., Milojčić 1959).

Although this sequence is now semisacrosanct by usage, John Coleman, Marija Gimbutas, and Homer Thomas join us in recommending the following substitutions in terminology in order to make sense out of this semantic monstrosity:

A change from Late Sesklo to Thessalian Middle Neolithic; a change from Pre-Sesklo to Thessalian Early Neolithic 3; a change from Proto-Sesklo to Thessalian Early Neolithic 2; and a change from Early Sesklo to Thessalian Early Neolithic 1.

Any new subdivisions requiring insertion into this scheme can be incorporated by adding subordinate letters to these numbered phases.

Temporal Equation II

Starčevo-Körös-Criş–Karanovo II–III–Thessalian Early Neo-lithic 3 (Pre-Sesklo)

During this period some geographic regionalization appears, although Neolithic sites still do not occur in the northern part of our area.

The Starčevo-Körös-Criş complex is essentially Middle Danubian, with some penetration to the east. The Starčevo group in the south is characterized by a much higher proportion of painted wares, while in the Körös (Hungarian) and Criş (Romanian) assemblages painted pottery of this period is relatively rare. Much, although not all, of the other pottery is virtually indistinguishable. According to Kosse (1979) in Hungary at least, the Körös people depended more on sheep and goats and wild game whereas the Starčevo people relied more heavily on cattle. Although this last seems a difference based on local adaptations to microenvironments, the ceramic inventories do seem to reflect two large regional branches of a single major culture (see also Dumitrescu 1983a).

With regard to the Körös-Criş complex Dumitrescu (1982:27, pers. comm. in 1984) thinks that although Starčevo and Criş are often mentioned as two related cultures, they actually form a single one with varying elements. In a general broad level of classification he is undoubtedly correct, although those who prefer to see distinctions can justifiably argue that they constitute major regional variants. On his map 2 (1982:18–19) Dumitrescu shows its distribution eastward through Transylvania except for the northern part, its mountains, and southern Moldavia, Muntenia, and the Dobrudja, which constitute the southeastern fringe below the mountain wall.

Geographically the heart of the Starčevo culture would seem to be in the Banat-Bačka plains north of the Danube. Southward it extends up the Morava to its watershed with the Vardar and down the Vardar at least to the Ovče Polje and the Svetoniskolska River at Anzabegovo, Vršnik near Turini and Rug Bair in Macedonia (Gimbutas 1976; Garašanin and Garašanin 1961; Galović 1964). Westward a few sites, including Gornja Tuzla, suggest a rather thin population or lack of exploration of the southern Sava drainage, with its westernmost manifestation appearing in the two bottom layers at Obre I (Benac 1973a, 1979; Gimbutas 1974a) in the Bosna Valley, where it seems to be peripheral and impoverished. There is no current evidence that it extended over the watershed of the Dinaric Alps to the Adriatic drainage, which seems to have belonged to a littoral culture area (Ehrich 1970b).

To the north it seems to extend up the Tisza as far as the Körös junction, and westward along the southern part of the Danube-Tisza plain (Makkay 1982: maps 1–3; Kalicz and Makkay 1977) to southern Pannonia where some eleven sites are now known in the Drava drainage between Lake Balaton and the Drava, a not surprising route of penetration. (N. Kalicz reported three of these sites in a paper read at the IUPPS Congress at Nice in 1976; also further personal information from him and from J. Makkay.)

Starčevo wares have also appeared between the Sava and Drava rivers at Vinkovci (Dimitrijević 1969b, 1979b) and Sarvaš (Schmidt 1945) as well as at other sites near the boundary between Syrmia and Slavonia.

Eastward the Starčevo variant extends beyond the Danube Gorge along the north lower Danubian plain (Dumitrescu 1982: map 2, pp. 18, 19), and some occurrences are reported to the south of it in northwest Bulgaria on the upper Struma. East of the Timok, the closely related complex found at Kremikovci (Georgiev 1975) and variants at Gradeschnitza (Nikolov 1974) occur eastward to the Sofia basin, and in caves along the northern slopes of the Stara Planina (M. Garašanin 1982; map 6, on p. 76; G. I. Georgiev, pers. information).

On the Adriatic coast the earliest Impresso Wares may begin during this period, although for the most part they seem to equate with early Vinča (Batović 1979). Since the stratifications at Anzabegovo (Gimbutas 1976) and Vršnik (Garašanin and Garašanin 1961) confirm each other quite well, Ehrich (1954, 1965c) still knows of no justification for describing a Starčevo I phase as being without painted pottery (see Arandjelović-Garašanin 1954; M. Garašanin 1982c). Since there are unquestionably two levels assignable to the Starčevo horizon at both sites (Garašanin 1982c; Gimbutas 1976), and since Horizon I at Gălăbnik is already late Starčevo while some Starčevo elements seem to appear in Horizon II, suggesting an equation with Anzabegovo-Vršnik II (Pavúk and Čochadžiev 1984), one can distinguish two major phases, and probably two subphases for each. For his periodization Garašanin follows that of Arandjelović-Garašanin as preferable to others (e.g., Dimitrijević). However, this scheme was erected on the basis of some misconceptions with regard to the type site of Starčevo itself (Ehrich 1977; Ehrich and Garašanin, final report in prep.), and there seems little justification for applying it across the board.

Starčevo levels occur at stratified sites appearing as Anzabegovo II and III, Vršnik II and III, Gălăbnik, probably II and certainly III, and at the bottom of Vinča as Ia, Obre I, levels I and III, and Gornja Tuzla and also as equated at Karanovo II and III. In addition to radiocarbon dates from Yugoslavia and Bulgaria there are a few Körös dates from Endröd, Szarvas, and Méhtelek in Hungary, and a few Criş determinations from Romania.

Despite a growing acceptance of the settlement at Lepenski Vir as Neolithic (e.g., M. Garašanin 1979, 1983; Jovanović 1969, 1971, 1974, 1984), since the excavator's initial erroneous ascription of it to the Mesolithic period is still being perpetuated by some (e.g., Srejović 1978, 1979: chart, p. 36; Evans and Rasson 1984) and is also being used to document an absolutely nonexistent (see Dumitrescu 1983a) cultural transformation within the Danube Gorge (also rejected by M. Garašanin 1978), a few comments are necessary.

1. The highly distinctive, complex, and close architectural similarities between the settlements at Padina, which is demonstrably of Starčevo Neolithic character (Jovanović 1969, 1971, 1974, 1984, and pers. comm.), and Lepenski Vir argue strongly for their contemporaneity.

2. The paucity of domestic animal remains (Clason 1980) is of no significance, for the terrain would support neither foraging, the growing of fodder, nor the growing of crops. Such livestock as do appear must have been driven in and then slaughtered or butchered outside the immediate area and the parts carried in.

3. As originally described by Jovanović (1969:31–32), although Mesolithic graves were found underneath and around the houses at Padina, there is no evidence that associates them with the settlement, and they seem earlier. Živanović (1976:518) describes the skeletons as being of Cro-Magnon type, which is also characteristic of the Mesolithic. Jovanović (1969:32) refers to a Europoid Mesolithic type followed by a more Mediterranean Neolithic one in the area, the elements of which are mentioned by Živanović.

4. Three radiocarbon dates from graves ascribed to the oldest Padina Mesolithic when calibrated average 5592 ± 60 B.C. (Jovanović 1969:32; Živanović 1976). One as Middle Mesolithic is calibrated as 5800–5390 B.C., and a third, purportedly from the youngest Mesolithic, as 4735–4555 B.C. seems clearly too young and is probably aberrant. The dates of the others fall within the Starčevo range and may or may not be reliable.

From the houses at Padina three dates, one from each of the three Starčevo phases B1, B2, and B3, fall so closely together that the presumption that the different terraces represent separate occupations seems less likely than that they were contemporary; a fourth date from B3, the so-called oldest, is far too young (Jovanović 1984:163).

The ascription of Lepenski Vir to the Mesolithic thus is without cultural or chronological foundation. The averages of the three apparently reliable dates from Padina and the three from Lepenski Vir fall close together and overlap and conform well with Anzabegovo I and also II or early Starčevo, while the other Starčevo period dates equate with Anzabegovo III and Starčevo itself as late Starčevo. Interestingly, the three dates from Vlasac that fall within the range of the calibration tables lie within the range of Starčevo period dates, whereas the two outside this range fall five hundred to six hundred years earlier (see table 7).

A basic list of averaged calibrated B.C. dates for this period is as follows:

Site and Level	Dates	Range B.C.	Average B.C.
YUGOSLAVIA			
Anzabegovo II	8	6185/6515–5875/5400	5995–5550
Anzabegovo III	4	5745/5365–5565/5260	5605–5305
Obre I and II	2	5865/5395–5740/5380	5785–5400
Starčevo	10	5970/5490–5515/5250	5705–5365
(Essentially late Starčevo. From bone collagen. Excludes an aberrant experimental date from pottery.)			
Padina settlement phases B1–3	3	6210/5615–6140/5580	6170–5610
Lepenski Vir	3	6060/5515–5845/5430	5950–5475
HUNGARY (Körös)			
Endröd, Méhtelek (combined)	8	5695/5435–5515/5220	5715–5370
BULGARIA (Karanovo II/III period)			
Stara Zagora	9	5970/5490–5575/5240	5735–5380

Temporal Equation III

Vinča–Karanovo IV–Linear Incised Ware (Bandkeramik)

Marked regionalization and diversity appear during this period. Our three major reference points are the two deeply stratified sites of Vinča on the middle Danube and Karanovo in the Marica-Tundža drainage. The third consists of the more or less unstratified flatland occupation sites of the Linear Incised or *Bandkeramik* wares in northeast Hungary, across Slovakia to lower Austria, Moravia, Bohemia, and other areas to the north and west (e.g., see this vol., Bogucki, chap. 20; Wells, chap. 19; and Thomas and R. Rowlett, chap. 17).

Since the excavations at Vinča took place before the advent of radiocarbon dating (e.g., Vasić 1932–36; Filip et al. 1969:1589) and at Karanovo (Georgiev 1961; Filip et al. 1969:577) before it could be put to practical use, the rough equations derived from them have rested on relative data. Further, because of some confusion in the reliability of its interpretation, much of the Vinča sequence was at least partly unraveled by reference to styles and to other sites. As of this writing a control excavation at Vinča is under way. The floating chronology thus arrived at, as in other areas, has been the subject of controversy between those favoring a high chronology and those supporting a low one. Throughout Europe and the Middle East the new calibrated radiocarbon evidence generally favors the high chronology.

The Vinča Complex

Vinča lies on the right bank of the Danube across from Starčevo, some 11 km downstream from Beograd. Since the material from the excavations of Vasić between 1908 and 1932 was reported by depth rather than by stratum, considerable confusion resulted. Childe (1929) recognized an early and a late period in the Vinča Neolithic-Eneolithic sequence, and in 1939 Holste proposed a four-part periodization from A to D. This is still fundamental despite the addition of subphases, and despite M. Garašanin's more recent subsuming of Vinča A-B1 as Vinča-Tordos (Turdaş) and B2-D generally as Vinča-Pločnik (e.g., Garašanin 1982c:118), in some sense reverting to Childe's Vinča I and Vinča II (see also Garašanin 1979; synchronic chart, p. 212.)

The origins of this culture are far from clear. One school sees it primarily as the result of diffusion from Anatolia (e.g., M. Garašanin 1979, 1982c as the leading exponent of this traditional view), while others (e.g., Chapman 1981; Markotić 1984) give much greater weight to local development and internal spread. (For a discussion of these differing points of view see Chapman 1981:1–5.) Some characteristic Vinča elements do appear at Starčevo, while at Vinča Starčevo pits underlie the Vinča deposits, and some Starčevo elements seem to survive into Vinča A.

Both Chapman and Garašanin stress regional differences, with Chapman particularly seeing variation in rates of ceramic change.

Based on uncalibrated B.C. dates eked out by some relative data such as imports, Chapman (1981:18) arrives at a series of general dates for the separate periods by rough brackets for Vinča itself. When calibrated at 1σ CRD B.C., these are:

Vinča A 5275/5040—5265–5010
Vinča B 5275/5010—5195–4920
Vinča C 5195/4720—4950–4560
Vinča D 4950/4560—4135–3895

Thus, although traditionally the four periods were considered to be of roughly equal length, Vinča D now appears to be much longer than any of the other three.

Against this scale Gomolova Ia (5095–4690), representing the Vinča-Tordos (B1/B2) transition to Vinča C or early Pločnik, falls into place and Gomolova Ib (4575–4520) fits comfortably into Vinča D. However, although Babska Ib ceramically seems Vinča C, its radiocarbon

dates fall in the Vinča D range in Šumadija, as is also true of Gornja Tuzla VI. Other equations (Dimitrejević 1979b:268; Chapman 1981:20) are as follows:

Sopot-Lengyel Ib = Vinča B
Sopot-Lengyel II = Vinča C
Sopot-Lengyel III = Vinča D

Gimbutas and Garašanin both describe Anzabegovo IV as early Vinča, and three dates from that level fall clearly together (Gimbutas 1976:29, 30), yielding a range of 5255/4730–5280/5025 with a CRD 1σ average of 5240–4925. This could indicate a date of either Vinča B or C, although it is generally considered as B2. Chapman follows Gimbutas in considering it Vinča B, and Markotić also shows it as such on his map (1984:pl. 72). Since most discussions seem to bracket Vinča A with B1, and Vinča B2 with C, Markotić (1984:14) suggests combining them into two phases of approximately equal length, with durations of 340 and 310 years respectively, while phase D would be approximately 550 years long.

However, in this instance available radiocarbon dates, when calibrated and averaged, add some degree of confusion. In the following list four miscellaneous dates classed as Vinča are so close and intertwined with seven others from Hungary, variously described as early Vinča, Körös-Vinča, and Vinča A, that we have combined them in a single series. The total ranges seem to be within acceptable limits.

On the other hand, the determinations identified as Vinča B fall within the Vinča A range or very slightly later, as do the three dates ascribed to Vinča C. Whether these anomalies reflect inadequacies or errors in sampling, identification, or other factors will have to await further research and additional dates.

The seven determinations for Vinča D from Yugoslavia do follow the earlier ones but are not as low as one would expect, suggesting that they may belong to the earlier part of the period. The two dates from Hungary are considerably later and may indicate a total duration of perhaps eight hundred years for Vinča D.

For the series the major cultural break is between Vinča C and Vinča D.

Dates Classed as	No.	Range B.C.	Average B.C.
Vinča A	11	5405/5195–5210/4895	5315–5090
Vinča B	6	5635/5180–5210/4895	5235–4955
Vinča C	3	5280/4985–5055/4710	5200–4915
Vinča D	7	5220/4695–4590/4430	4950–4705
Vinča D	2	4347/3870 (Hungary)	4160–3885

Geographically the distribution of the Vinča culture conforms well with that of Starčevo, although with some exceptions. Chapman (1981:fig. 63) shows his early "A

"+ B" sites mainly concentrated along the Tisza to the lower and middle Maros (Mureş), along the Danube east to Ostrovul Golu, and west along the Sava to Vinkovci, southward up the Morava to Drenovac with outliers on the upper Morava and the Vardar drainage at Anzabegovo and Zelenikovo. Markotić (1984:pl. 72) somewhat less equivocally shows Vinča A sites only along the Tisza, with three "A + B" on the upper Mureş, again with a few on the Danube and no Phase A but a few Phase B sites along the Morava. Between the Drina and the lower Bosna, there are only late Vinča sites, mostly D but with some C. Markotić (p. 197) thus thinks that the Vinča culture originated in the Mureş area, where the earliest settlements seem to exist, and then spread west and southwest into the Banat, Syrmia and Slovenia, eastern Croatia and northern Bosnia, and parts of Montenegro, southward into Serbia and ultimately into Greece, where he identifies the Larissa culture with Vinča D, and eastward into western Bulgaria, Oltenia, and Muntenia. Although both he and Chapman reject Garašanin's "Balkano-Anatolian hypothesis," Chapman more cautiously seems to admit a greater number of links but not general origins.

For Romania Dumitrescu (pers. comm. 1984) considers his 1983 contribution as reflecting his more recent thinking when compared to his 1982 article. Most of the basic data are the same and both are useful summaries. Generally sites of the Starčevo-Criş culture occur throughout the country except for Muntenia and the southern part of Moldavia. After that the cultural unity breaks up and the patterning becomes much more complex for both the Neolithic and the Eneolithic (see Dumitrescu 1983a: map, pp. 80–81).

In Moldavia to the east of the Carpathians the Criş people seem to have persisted until the advent of those with Linear pottery, who came around the mountains. In Transylvania Vinča-Turdaş does not appear east or north of the Mureş (Maros), and for the rest, with very few exceptions, immediate successors seem to be generally lacking.

In discussing Transylvania, Vlassa (1963) reminds us that the Turdaş material on which the Vinča-Turdaş association is based was unstratified and thus that any phasing from the site is based on typology alone. Since erosion has rendered a control study impossible, he conducted excavations at Tărtăria on the middle Mureş. Here he describes the lower part of the thin oldest layer as Turdaş, probably Vinča A, and its upper part as equating with Vinča B, Tisza 1, and east Slovakian Linear. The next two levels he labels Turdaş-Petreşti and Petreşti-Turdaş, reflecting the differing prevalence of their elements. Petreşti seems largely a local development. He describes the latest level as earliest Coţofeni.

The questions concerning the disputed provenience of

the Tărtăria tablets are still not settled, but they are no longer considered to reflect the Mesopotamian Protoliterate. Although some still think the pit in which they were found was Coţofeni in date, the current trend is to accept it as from the Turdaş layers and to consider the tablets as belonging with the corpus of pottery marks of that period (e.g., Makkay 1976b; Winn 1981). A second unequivocal find of such material is necessary to resolve the issue. Formerly the tablets were thought to be key elements in establishing chronological relationships, but they have lost much of their importance in this regard.

Along the north bank of the Danube below the Transylvanian Alps and east of the Romanian Banat, where it is at home, Vinča-Turdaş penetrates as far as the Jiu, beyond which lies the derivative Vădastra complex reaching to the Olt River, the division between Oltenia and Muntenia.

On his maps of the four Boian phases (Comşa 1974:31, fig. 9, Bolintineanu phase; 33, fig. 10, Giuleşti phase; 38, fig. 11, Vidra phase; 42, fig. 12, Transitional phase) Comşa shows the earliest settlements beginning in central Muntenia on the Argeş-Dîmboviţa drainage and scattered to the east as far as the Buzau. In the subsequent Giuleşti phase the settlements are much more thickly distributed in this area and are also clustered in the southeast corner of Transylvania, reaching across the southern edge of Moldavia. In the third or Vidra phase there are again fewer sites, mainly concentrated in the lower Argeş and Dîmboviţa area which generally seems to be the nexus for this culture, but with a thin scattering south of the Danube in northeast Bulgaria. His fourth map continues much the same distribution north of the Danube with a separated group to the east along the Black Sea coast and numerous sites in northeast Bulgaria south of the Danube in the upper Tantra, Beli Lonu and Kamčin drainages, and reaching southward into the Tundža River system. Since this last phase is transitional to Gumelniţa, it equates with Karanovo V, now usually designated as the Marica (Maritsa, Maritza) culture and considered by Todorova to be early and middle Eneolithic (Todorova 1978: maps 7 and 8, table 33).

For her late Neolithic (map 6) Todorova equates Vinča A2 with Linear III, and for her early Eneolithic (map 7) Vinča B with Petreşti, Vidra (Boian III), Linear and early Marica, and Pre-Cucuteni I, II-Tripolye A1. For relative chronological equations within Bulgaria see her table 1, and for wider correlations her table 33.

Although she bases the periods of her synchronization tables 1 and 3 on radiocarbon dates, calibrated according to the Suess system, she does not use individual determinations and one must utilize specific dates from other sources in order to confirm or invalidate her equations. In this regard her generalized maps by period also give rough synchronizations. The reader should be warned that certain misspellings on her table 33 could lead to confusion.

Westward from the area of its major concentration, known sites of the Vinča culture thin out (Markotić 1984: pl. 72), with the Korenovo group appearing in the west Syrmian–east Slavonian area. Dimitrijević (1979b: 312, 360) equates Korenovo with classic Linear II and III, but as not necessarily earlier than Željezovce, and with Vinča B1. Generally Vinča A and B sites do not seem to extend farther west and south in any strength to the lower Bosna, where Vinča C and D sites are represented.

Except for the upper reaches of the Drava and Sava systems, late Vinča appears throughout Syrmia and parts of Slavonia with sites clustering in the open lands of the lower Bosna. Of twelve sites plotted on his map (1981:421, and identification table p. 493), Chapman identifies only one as early Vinča.

Obre, the Middle Bosna, and the Adriatic Drainage

Ehrich (1970a, 1970b) has pointed out the role of the Dinaric Alps in providing a marked but not impermeable barrier that generally separates the coastal lands of the Adriatic on the west from the mountainous plateaus and basins to the east of them. Cultural penetration seems to have been largely by way of the Neretva, with elements moving from west to east.

For the Adriatic slope and shore, Batović (1966, 1979) indicates a clear sequence beginning with Impresso-Cardial wares followed in turn by the Danilo and Hvar/Lisičići phases, all of which belong with a littoral culture subarea of the north Mediterranean sphere.

On the middle Bosna south of the gorges that close off the lower plain which is dotted with late Vinča sites is a totally different series of archaeological culture groups. For these the two stratified sites of Obre I and Obre II, excavated jointly by Yugoslav and United States teams, together provide a sequence of eight levels with some clear relationships not only with the coast but also more or less indirectly with Italy to the west and eastward as well.

A series of radiocarbon dates (Gimbutas 1974a:16) establishes the Obre sites as an anchor point with wide implications (for which see Benac 1973a, 1973b, 1979).

Since the authors differ somewhat in terminology and interpretation, it seems best to start with the four levels of each site from the discussion of the Yugoslavian team's more extensive excavations.

Obre Site I, levels I and II, consists of two major components: a primarily inland one of Starčevo (so-called Starčevo III) and a strong Impresso-Cardial one from the Adriatic coast. Site I, level III can be described as early

Kakanj in which Starčevo painted ware and Impresso wares disappear, barbotine ware continues, and rhytons replace the characteristic Starčevo "altars." Rhytons, often described as cult vessels, are of coastal Danilo type. Obre I, level IV can be designated as Kakanj II, or developed Kakanj, in which barbotine ware disappears, as do Danilo-type rhytons.

Significant for the purpose of comparative dating, only the cult vessels of level III relate to the Danilo culture, and it is this type only that was discussed as Middle Neolithic in relation to the Elateia bothros by Weinberg in the 1965 edition. The bothros is now considered by some to be Late Neolithic or Sesklo III, as in Coleman's chapter in this volume, or terminologically perhaps more consistently as Thessalian Middle Neolithic as we propose in this chapter under temporal equation I. In any event it is only the Obre I, level III and Danilo cult vessels that seem to have spread southward and eastward and are also apparently of the type cited by Bray (1966) as appearing in the Peloponessos. The rhytons of Obre I, level IV are a Bosna Valley Kakanj development and do not seem to have been diffused.

Obre Site II, level I contains some Butmir elements which appear with those of Kakanj, Danilo, Lengyel-Pannonian, and other components with two late rhyton legs and late Kakanj hollow legs like those from the younger Kakanj at Arnautovići. In a Danilo group of eleven painted sherds, four are of Italian Ripoli type, while the spiral decoration on others is characteristically Danilo/Smilčić.

Although Benac considers this layer to be transitional to Butmir, Sterud and Sterud (1974) see a sharp break between level I as Kakanj and level II as the earliest in the Butmir sequence.

Obre II, level II represents a complete break with the Kakanj complex, and there is no evidence of Danilo contact. There are, however, some Hvar/Lisičići relationships, which are important for cross-dating. Obre II, level III is later Butmir, and Obre II, level IV is represented by intrusive Kostolac pits which are much too late for comment at this juncture.

Although there seems to be general agreement as to the content of the various strata, differences in interpretation have led to some confusion in labeling.

Benac in 1979 considered Obre I, level II as Proto-Kakanj, with levels III and IV as early and full Kakanj. Both here and in Obre II, level I, we may have somewhat parallel cases in that Obre I, level II is probably a Starčevo layer with intrusive elements penetrating its upper portion from above, while Obre II, level I, as analyzed by the Steruds, would be Kakanj III, with a similar penetration of Butmir and other elements downward into its later levels, or by imports from contemporary Butmir sites. Either or both cases of admixture could have resulted from trampling during the muddy season, but neither seems to represent a local developmental transition.

In grouping her radiocarbon dates Gimbutas (1974a:16) combines Obre levels I and II into a single IA (Starčevo) unit, whereas Benac (1973a:420) designates them as Starčevo/Impresso I and II. For Obre II, Gimbutas identifies two major phases divided into subphases that are much earlier than the Kostolac pits and labels them as Butmir I, II, and III. Like Benac and in contradistinction to the Steruds, she considers Obre II, level I as Butmir Ia and Ib and as transitional rather than as a defined Kakanj III.

For the purposes of this chapter it seems best to refer to the Obre periods and phases by site stratification, with the following cultural designations: *Obre I:* Phases I and II Starčevo-Impresso, Phase III Early Kakanj, Phase IV Developed Kakanj; *Obre II:* Phase I Developed and Late Kakanj (Benac and Gimbutas—Butmir I), Phase II Butmir I (Benac and Gimbutas—Butmir II), Phase III Butmir II (Benac and Gimbutas—Butmir III), Phase IV Kostolac.

Our equations and averages of the Obre radiocarbon dates follow; for the individual dates see table 7.

Suggested synchronisms for Obre I (Benac 1973a:418–27, with comparative tables on pp. 425–26) and for Obre II (pp. 182–86) are as follows (see also Benac 1979):

Obre II, level III. Our Butmir II (Benac Butmir III) = Lisičići/Hvar II = Diana/Bellavista = Larissa/Rakhmani = Vinča D1 = Sopot Lengyel II/III.

Obre II, level II. Our Butmir I (Benac Butmir II) = Danilo IV–Hvar Lisičići = Serro d'Alto/Diana = Dimini IV/Larissa = Vinča C = Sopot Lengyel II = Lužianky/Lengyel = Petreşti/Turdaş (Petreşti A-B).

Obre II, level I. Our Kakanj III (Benac Butmir I) = Kakanj III = End of Capri/Ripoli/Scaloria = Dimini II/III = central Greece Neolithic = Vinča B2 = Sopot/

Lengyel Ib = Željezovce/Lengyel = Turdaş/Petreşti (Petreşti A/A–B).

Obre I, later level IV. Kakanj II = Dimini II/III = Arnautovići/Kakanj III = Danilo II/III = Capri Scaloria.

Obre I, level IV. Kakanj II = Gornja Tuzla V = Sopot/Lengyel IA = Vinča A2 = Boian B = Sesklo III (?) (our Thessalian Middle Neolithic) = Dimini I/II = Danilo II = Adriatico/Capri I.

Obre I, levels III/IV. Kakanj = Boian A.

Obre I, level III. Our Kakanj I = Danilo I = Adriatico I/II/Stentinello/La Quercia = Gornja Tuzla VIa = Vinča Al = Boian A = (*Vorsesklo*) Sesklo I and II (our Thessalian Early Neolithic 3).

Obre I, levels II/III. Late Starčevo = Leţ III (Criş III).

Obre I, levels I/II. Starčevo III/Cardium Impresso = Gornja Tuzla VIb = Starčevo "spiraloid" = Leţ II = *Vorseslklo* (Barbotine, "*Nagel*," cardium) = Adriatico I/Cardium Impresso.

For a summary of calibrated dates from Gimbutas (1974b:16) when averaged, see the table below.

Since Obre I and Obre II are different sites, the close association of the dates from Gimbutas's Obre I, level IV, phase C and Obre II, level Ia suggests at least a partial contemporaneity of occupation during Kakanj III.

Odmut

From the Piva district in northwestern Montenegro, Srejović (1974:5; *RC* 19:473) gives ten purportedly Mesolithic dates from the rock shelter at Odmut. Six of these are earlier than the CRD tables and cannot be calibrated. The remaining four yield an average of 6080–5530 B.C. Marković (1974:10) describes Odmut III as early Neolithic with Starčevo elements as well as with traits of Crvena Stijena III–Smilčić type. Three close radiocarbon

Sites	Level	*Our Period*	Gimbutas	No.	*Range* B.C.	*Average* B.C.
Obre II	III	Butmir II	(III)		(No dates given.)	
Obre II	II	Butmir I	(IIb)	4	4935/4555–4725/4550	4725–4550
Obre II	II	Butmir I	(IIa)	3	4950/4705–4935/4695	4935–4695
Obre II	I	Kakanj III	Butmir I			
			Ib	3	5075/4870–5015/4725	5055–4735
			Ia	6	5200/4915–4730/4440	5210–4930

(Here Ib seems to be the upper part of the stratum in which the later elements occur.)

Sites	Level	*Our Period*	Gimbutas	No.	*Range* B.C.	*Average* B.C.
Obre I	IV	Developed Kakanj	C	2	5300–4965	5265–5030
Obre I	III	Early Kakanj	B	1		5470–5235
Obre I	I–II	Starčevo/Impresso	A	2[a]	5865–5380	5785–5400

a. One determination has been omitted as being too early to be averaged with the other two dates.

dates from this layer yield a calibrated average of 6005–5500, with a range of 6060/5515–5965/4750.

Not only do these two averages approximate each other, but the first set coordinates well with Anzabegovo I, Veluška Tumba, and Čavdar (Karanovo I) and also with Anzabegovo II (8), Padina (3), and Lepenski Vir (3), while the dates for Obre I, levels I–II, fall only slightly later.

Since Batović (1979:634) equates Starčevo II with Obre I, levels I–II and late Impresso, it seems logical to assign Odmut I to our temporal equation I and Odmut II to our temporal equation II.

Although later dates for the late Neolithic and Eneolithic (*RC* 19:473) are not well enough identified for use, an Eneolithic date from level VI (Lab. no. Z 37) with no further comment gives a calibrated date of 3065–2860, and an Early Bronze Age one (Marković 1974:11), when calibrated, falls at 2205–1890. This is later than 2300 B.C. and is as it should be.

Albania

In Albania, although numerous sites are known, the number of those with significant excavations or adequate surface exploration remains relatively thin, and no radiocarbon dates seem available. The following summary is generally based on Prendi's article of 1982, supplemented by the somewhat more detailed breakdown of the Middle and Late Neolithic in the comparative table for the Adriatic zone by Batović (1979:634).

In northern Albania the Drim River system cuts through the mountains to the coast and provides access to the Metohija and Kosovo regions of inland Yugoslavia, with some elements recognizable at Rudnik near Kosovo (Prendi 1979:3; J. Glišić, pers. information), while upstream to the south the Shkumbi, Semeni, and Vijosë drainages lead toward Greece.

Early Neolithic

Southeast: The site of Vashtëmi is described as a single site with three horizons.

Equation I: Relationships with early Vršnik = Anzabegovo I = Veluška Tumba = Nea Nikomedeia. Some elements are similar to Proto-Sesklo (our Thessalian Early Neolithic 2), others to Pre-Sesklo (our Thessalian Early Neolithic 3).

Equation II: Some impresso and barbotine with limited links to Starčevo II/a = Kremikovci Ia = Karanovo I.

Northeast: Kolsh I is later than Vashtëmi. Kolsh I = Starčevo IIb = Vršnik II–III = Anzabegovo II–III = Kremikovci Ib.

Northwest: Blaz II = Kolsh I = Cardium Impresso = Smilčić I = Zelena Pećina III.

Middle Neolithic

Northeast: The Cakran group. Some items are found in Kolsh II with Vinča material. Its rhytons correspond to those of Danilo and Kakanj I. Barbotine is still in use and relates to Cakran and Elateia. A rough equation is Cakran = Danilo I = Proto-Kakanj (our Kakanj I or Obre I, level III) = Elateia II = Dimini I or Dimini-Tsangli.

However, although Prendi indicates that the Cakran material has not been sufficiently studied to support more detailed equations, the Batović table (1979:634) suggests the following: Cakran I = the end of Starčevo as at Obre I, levels I and II = La Quercia I = Pre-Sesklo (our Thessalian Early Neolithic 3.

Cakran Late I, II, most of III = Danilo I–III = Obre I, levels III–IV and Obre II, early level I (Kakanj III).

Cakran II = Sesklo I–II = Vinča A–B2 = Danilo = Kakanj = Scaloria, Ripoli II.

Cakran III = Sesklo III–Dimini I = Sopot II = Kakanj III (Butmir I or Obre II, level I).

Late Neolithic

Southeast: The Maliq-Kamnik group, phase IIa, seems related to Dimini, while Ib contains resemblances to Vinča *Bandkeramik* and shows close links with the Dimini Otzaki group. Generally this phase is transitional to the Eneolithic of Maliq II.

Eneolithic

Although some slight variations indicate two phases, Maliq IIa and IIb, they are not sufficiently distinctive to treat separately. Significant traits for Maliq II include some copper tools and some graphite pottery decoration.

Along the Adriatic, Maliq II = Hvar II/III = Obre II, levels II, III (Butmir II, III, our Butmir I, II).

In Italy, Maliq II = Ripoli I–III = the end of Diana = Serra d'Alto = Rivoli Chiozza.

To the north, Maliq II = Sopot III.

Eastward, Maliq II = Šupljevac–Bakarno Gumno–Crnobuki in Pelagonia = possibly the Hisar phase in Kosovo = Vinča C–D = Sălcuţa = Krivodol = Bubanj Hum I and also has some analogies with the late Neolithic in Greek Macedonia and Rakhmani.

Early Bronze Age, ca. 2100/2000–1800 B.C.

Maliq IIIa = Armenokhori in Pelagonia = Kostolac = the Aegean Early Bronze Age.

Maliq IIIb = Armenokhori–late Early Bronze Age. There are significant similarities to Early Bronze Age features in Macedonia at Servia, Kritsana, and Ayios Mamas, and in Epirus to Argissa Magoula III which provides a good parallel with Thessalian Early Bronze Age III, thus equating it with the Belotić–Bela Crkva group.

Middle Bronze Age, ca. 1800–1500 B.C.

Maliq IIIc = Middle Helladic II–III and Late Helladic I.

Late Bronze Age

Maliq IIId 1–3. Urnfield elements and Mycenaean elements from the twelfth century B.C., sometimes in graves with Late Helladic IIIc.

The Linear (Bandkeramik) *Complex*

Although some accept this complex as derived from the earlier Starčevo-Criş cultural grouping, such an interpretation seems highly unlikely. Although one may speak of a very broad, shared technocomplex, its general identification appears to rest on the use of stone tools, handmade pottery, spiral decoration, and the like. The sites show no internal development from one complex to the other; their geographic distributions, except perhaps at their fringes in northeastern Hungary, appear mutually exclusive, and in a detailed comparison of traits and elements there is no adequate complexity of resemblances either in quality or in number, while the total differences seem overwhelming and do not support such a derivation.

In those areas where Linear-*Bandkeramik* appears, it constitutes the earliest Neolithic culture. Despite its late dating as compared with the areas farther south, it is still usually termed Early Neolithic where it is at home. Bogucki's dating of late Linear in this volume is considerably later than that for Czechoslovakia.

In general one can distinguish three major subcomplexes of the Linear-*Bandkeramik* culture. Szatmár, the earliest, and the following Alföld-*Linearkeramik* (ALK) occur in the lower lands of northeast Hungary, reaching to the base of the foothills (Kalicz and Makkay 1977; Makkay 1982, and for the ecology see Kosse 1979; Sherratt 1982). In Lower Austria also there is now evidence for an early Linear phase preceding music-note pottery (Ruttkay, Wessely, and Wolff 1976).

A second, marked by the so-called music-note type of pottery decoration, is found from Lower Austria eastward and northward into Moravia, through the Moravian Gate and into Poland along the Oder and Vistula rivers, thence eastward north of the Carpathians and then southward into Moldavia and the Ukraine, where it is later than the surviving Criş and earlier than Pre-Cucuteni (Marinescu-Bîlcu 1974:140–41; Chapman 1981:21; Dumitrescu 1983a). West of Moravia its settlements occur thickly in Bohemia, up the Danube and down the Rhine.

(See Wells, chap. 19; Thomas and R. Rowlett, chap. 17; and Bogucki, chap. 20, in this vol.)

The third, Želiezovce (Zseliz) complex, is primarily concentrated in western Slovakia, but occurs in Transdanubia as earlier than Lengyel and, more rarely, usually as imported fragments in Music-note contexts, in the eastern fringes of Lower Austria, scattered in Moravia, but with a large group in southern Poland around Krakow (Bogucki, chap. 20, this vol.). Scattered finds are reported in the Tisza and Vinča complexes (Filip et al. 1969:1669–70; Dumitrescu 1983a; Comşa 1974).

Variants equating chronologically with Želiezovce are the spectacular ceramics of the Bükk culture of central north Hungary, centered around the Bükk Mountains, and the distinctive Šarka ceramics of Bohemia, represented at some fifty sites, which are thought to be at least partly transitional to the stroked ware that follows.

A reduction of their summary as given in table 2 by Kalicz and Makkay (1977) for their study of the Linear-*Bandkeramik* in northeastern Hungary (also Makkay 1984) yields the following equations:

1. In the northeasternmost part of Hungary: Older Szatmár = Körös.
2. Throughout northeast Hungary: Later Szatmár = Late Körös/Proto-Vinča.
3. Across the northern Alföld: Early Alföld Linear (ALK) = Vinča A = early Late *Bandkeramik* (Transdanubia) = Barca III (eastern Slovakia).
4. Szákálhat = Zseliz or Želiezovce (western Slovakia) = Zseliz-Music Note (Transdanubia) = Vinča B1/B2 = Szilmeg (north central plain) = Bükk I, II, III (north-central Bükk Mountains).
5. Sopot-Bicske (Transdanubia) as derived from Vinča B2 = Vinča C.
6. Tisza (northern Alföld) = Herpály (southern and eastern Alföld) = Vinča C-D.

In Yugoslavia the dot-filled ribbon motif of Vinča and the long houses at Gomolava (pers. information from H. T. Waterbolk) strongly suggest a connection between Linear wares and early Vinča.

Averages for the calibrated radiocarbon dates for Czechoslovakia by Pavlů and Zápotocká (1982:21) are as follows; this list is entirely of the so-called early Neolithic period.

Culture	Bohemian Phase	No.	Range B.C.	Averages B.C.
Linear	IVa Middle Šarka	2	4755–4415	4575–4525
	III-IV Early Šarka	1		5275–4960
	IIa, b, and c	7		5235–4960
	Ic	6	5430/5045– 5275/4970	5305–5075
	Ib	2	5520–5225	5520–5235
	Hungary			

| Alföld Linear | 7 | 5350/5085–5210/4925 | 5270–5025 |
| Szákálhat | 11 | 5395/5205–4545/4365 | 5205–4925 |

The earliest Bohemian phases 1b and 1c may equate with the Szatmár complex in Hungary, for which we have no radiocarbon determinations. In averaging we have deleted BM 563 from IIb as being aberrantly early, and since the dates for some of the subphases fall very close together, overlap, and give irregular internal results, we have combined them. Even so, the averages for the Linear phases and the determination for phase III-IV, labeled early Šarka, belong with them. The two middle Šarka dates, however, are considerably later and equate not with the two Stroked Ware culture dates of 4925–4555 B.C. and the two Lengyel IV ones of 4935–4695 B.C., but with two Stroked Ware dates of 4745–4560 B.C.. Three post-Jordanów (Bajč-Retz) dates average 4115–3880 B.C. and are still later.

In Hungary the seven dates designated Alföld Linear (ALK) compare well with the Bohemian Linear Ic through early Šarka as given above, as does another labeled young ALK or Bükk or Zseliz, while a "developed" Linear falls some seventy-five years earlier. Eleven Szakálhát dates, late in northeastern Hungary, again equate with the Czech Linear II and early Šarka.

Two Romanian Linear dates from Tîrpeşti in Moldavia, (Dumitrescu 1974a) calibrated at 5320–5060 B.C. and 5280–4980 B.C., again fit well with the Bohemian presumably Music-Note dates.

Other dates for this complex are three from south Germany (a fourth excluded as being far too late) with a calibrated average of 5190–4905 B.C., and four from Austria (a fifth again being excluded as inconsistent) averaging 5080–4880 B.C.. (For the individual dates, see Wells, chap. 19, this vol.)

For Poland (Bogucki, chap. 20) an average for two calibrated Linear dates is 5280–5050 B.C., with a total range of 5305–5000 B.C.

In Bulgaria four dates of the Hotnica culture from Kačica, Veliko Turnovo, have a narrow total range of 5265/5000–5250/4975 B.C. and an average of 5260–5000 B.C., thus falling in the same range as the Linear ones. Although we do not have dates for Karanovo IV, the dates for the Karanovo II and III-Starčevo equation should be somewhat earlier than the Linear ones, and for Karanovo V those of the Marica culture are slightly later, thus bracketing Karanovo IV and presumably equating it with the Linear complex and with Vinča-Turdaş.

For the west, Thomas and R. Rowlett (chap. 17, this vol.) give fourteen *Bandkeramik* dates from a single site in Aisne and five from another. Eliminating one determination as far too late but adding four others from the Rhineland, the average for the twenty-two calibrated

dates is 5200–4915 B.C. The range for all these dates is 5675/5260–4920/4400 B.C. However, by eliminating the two highest dates and the lowest one remaining, the maximum range falls to 5390/4990–5050/4560 B.C., a reduction of some 445 years.

Thus the dates from Hungary, Austria, Czechoslovakia, Poland, south Germany, the Rhineland, and north and northeast France would seem to confirm the long-held hypothesis that the Linear-*Bandkeramik* expanded very rapidly throughout its whole area and was of relatively short duration.

For this horizon, then, radiocarbon determinations seem to support the rough equations of Vinča-Turdaş = Karanovo IV = Boian = Linear = Obre I, levels III, IV and Obre II, level I.

Temporal Equation IV

Tisza (Theiss) Boian–Karanovo V (Marica)–Lengyel–Stroked Ware

In the northern Alföld the Linear pottery was followed by the Herpály culture, which occupied the lowlands eastward to the Tisza and slightly beyond. In its southern part the Tisza (*Theiss*) complex followed Vinča-Tordos and apparently derived in part from both it and from the incised ware complex to the north. Eastward the Petreşti group occupied central and southern Transylvania, while east of the Carpathians the late stages of Criş survived until the arrival of the westward extension of the Pre-Cucuteni people from the Dniester into Russian and Romanian Moldavia and the northeastern corner of Transylvania (Dumitrescu 1982: map, p. 19; Ellis 1984: comparative table, pp. 10, 11, 31, and maps, pp. 18, 19, 29), and until the end of the linear wares in northern Moldavia.

Along the lower Danube south of the Carpathian Alps, the Tisza culture extended eastward across Oltenia as far as the Vădastra group on the lower Olt drainage. Beyond the Vădastra area, the Boian group characterized Muntenia, its latest, or Vidra, phase extending southward into the Tundža drainage, while the Marica culture with three phases, formerly designated Karanovo V (Todorova 1978), occupied the Marica and lower Tundža valleys. Unfortunately we have no specific radiocarbon dates for the Marica or Karanovo V culture at this time, and these two chronological positions must be fixed relatively. In northwest Bulgaria both Vădastra and some Vinča settlements came southward from across the Danube, while Vinča C/D (Vinča-Pločnik) persisted in the southern Danube and Sava drainages (Garašanin 1979).

Farther west in Hungary, the Lengyel complex, recognizable by its distinctive pottery, developed through four phases in Transdanubia (Dombay 1960: map, p. 11), spreading northward and appearing in the Burgenland

and in Lower Austria (Ruttkay 1981, 1983), the Little Alföld, in southwestern and central Slovakia as Ludanice (Lengyel IV), northward along the eastern side of the Czechoslovakian Morava, or eastern Moravia, into Poland and Silesia. Its later unpainted Polish Jordanów phase also appeared in Bohemia.

In Bohemia the incised Linear or *Bandkeramik* wares passed through the late Linear Šarka phase and were followed by the late Stroked Ware or *Stichbandkeramik* which has strong affiliations with the early Rössen and with cultures beyond the Erzgebirge or Ore Mountains to the west (see Wells, chap. 19, and Thomas and R. Rowlett, chap. 17).

Leading equations: Late Šarka = Early Stroked = Lengyel IV = Boian IV = Early Varna culture. In western and central Slovakia, Lengyel III = Tisza in eastern Slovakia.

Identification	No.	Range B.C.	Average B.C.
Early Stroked	2	4975–4435	4925–4555
Lengyel IVa	4	5190/4900–4745/4420	4935–4695
V	2	4920–4490	4745–4560
VI	6	5100/4835–4415/3955	4565–4435
(Transdanubia; from Kalicz and Raczky 1987:29)			
Tisza	16	53665/4965–4545/4410	4985–4730
Csőshalom	5	4960/4515–4550–4390	4745–4560
Boian IV	10	5110/4855 –4555/4395	4740–4560
Sava-Varna Transition & Early Varna	5	5085/4730–4935/4553	4935–4695
Varna culture	8	5085/4730–4445/4325	4560–4430
Poljanice II/III	2	5100/4815–4735–4555	4595–4545
IV	2	4725–4540	4595–4545
Polish Stroked	1		4750–4430
(See Bogucki, chap. 20, this vol.)			
Karanovo VIa and KGK	26	4975/4565–3935/3660	4550–4420
Herpály	28	4745/4560–4430/4335	4575–4540
Vinča B	3	5015/4555–4575/4420	4595–4545
C	3	5280/4985–4565/4365	5015–4725
D	1	5200/4750–4575/4525	4760–4685

In the above list of averages, Early Stroked equates with Lengyel IVa, Tisza, the Sava-Varna Transition and Early Varna, Poljanice II/III, and apparently with Vinča B-C. The reversal by which the Vinča B dates appear earlier than those of Vinča A may be the result of insufficient sampling, geographic distribution variation, or perhaps misattribution of the sample.

As given here, Lengyel V and VI appear progressively later than Lengyel IV. Lengyel V = Csőshalom = Boian IV = Vinča D.

Ruttkay's eleven dates for her Moravian Austrian Lengyel group (Ruttkay 1983:52–53), when averaged, seem

to coordinate well with the two dates for Lengyel V and the five from Czőshalom.

Lengyel VI = the Varna culture = Poljanice IV = Karanovo VIa and Herpály.

As a whole, the dates listed generally fall between 5,000 and 4,500 B.C.

Temporal Equation V

Lengyel–Varna (Goljama Delčevo)–Karanovo VI–Gumelniţa

The chronological relationships of this period are quite complex. To keep oriented, one must bear in mind the basic geography that was operative in the distribution of the preceding cultures and also in the following ones. Thus the Lengyel tradition continues in Transdanubia with extensions as far as western and south-central Slovakia, eastern Moravia, and northward into Poland, westward into Lower Austria, the Burgenland, and Bohemia. (See for example the symposium on the Lengyel culture, Študijné Zvesti 1969; see not only the article by E. Neustupný but other papers as well.)

For Slovakia, the cleavage between west and east continues (Pavúk and Šiška 1981) and remains anchored to the major river systems, which in south-central Slovakia flow west to enter the Danube above its so-called knee, whereas the tributaries of the Tisza drain eastern Slovakia, the cultures of which are, not surprisingly, extensions of or derived from northeastern Hungary.

Since there are several suggested equations in greater or lesser detail and completeness, and since these tend to vary slightly, it seems best to pull together what we can in a general pattern, leaving further references for detailed analyses in the bibliographies of the works cited, and to use the calibrated but uneven radiocarbon dates to act as checkpoints within the suggested network.

We start then with Bognár-Kutzián's equation for her Early Copper Age (1972:207–8). She divides the Tiszapolgár culture into two phases and four groups with Lucska, the most northerly, extending into eastern Slovakia; Basatanya, concentrated in northeastern Hungary; Tiszaug along the Tisza River; and Deszk clustered around the Maros junction, with a few outliers toward the Danube. She shows her earlier phase primarily clustered along the northern part of the Körös system drainage (map 35, p. 191).

For the Early Copper Age she lists the following extended equation: Tiszapolgár AB = Gumelniţa late A2 and early B1 (Late II and early IIIa–Karanovo VI 2) = Sălcuţa II and early III = latest Vinča-Ploćnik = Cucuteni A 3–4 = Tripolye latest A, B1-early Pitgrave Kurgan (Sredni Stog II) = late Petreşti = Sopot-Lengyel, latest III = latest Lengyel, including unpainted and Brodzany type = earliest Ludanice = late Rössen = beginning Gatersleben. To this we add Sitagroi III in

Greek Thrace (Renfrew 1971; Renfrew, Gimbutas, and Elster 1986:173).

Dimitrijević (1979a), Kalicz (1980), and Makkay (1976a) describe the Balaton-Lasinje I sites as derived from Vinča and as occupying the territory between the Sava and Drava rivers, following their upper waters into the eastern Alps and reaching into central Slovenia as the first settlers there. In Transdanubia their sites are later than the Lengyel ones, and the two cultures differ markedly. Kalicz equates Lasinje I with Lengyel-Ludanice in Slovakia, Bodrogkeresztúr, Jordanów, Münchshöfen, Bubanj-Hum Ia, and Sălcuţa (Kalicz 1980, fig. 2, pp. 248, 249; Makkay 1976a:270).

Two dates for Stroked Ware V (Pavlů and Zápotocká 1982) fit Bohemia into the pattern. Of sixteen Lengyel dates cited by Bogucki (chap. 20, this vol.), eleven are within this range when averaged and five are somewhat later, equating with Bayč-Retz (Pavlů and Zápotocká 1982:21) and suggesting two phases. In West Germany on the upper Danube near Ulm, Ehrenstein also belongs in this later phase and is actually a part of the Michelsberg complex, as is Schussenried, which extends into Bohemia, where Michelsberg elements also appear in late Jordanów (Jordansmühl) contexts.

According to PDČ (1978:245–46), Late Rössen parallels Michelsberg II in West Germany and is the earliest correlation in Bohemia, in which Michelsberg III and IV mostly appear. Classic Michelsberg does not appear as an entity but does appear with late Jordanów, and above all with Schussenried.

Kalicz (1980:250, and map, fig. 3, p. 279) sees marked archaeological differences between Lasinje II-III and the preceding Lasinje I. Their geographical distributions differ significantly, although both sets of sites occupy unfavorable areas of the eastern Alps and Slovenia. Neighboring culture areas to the west are the Altheim, following the Münchshöfen and Schussenried, the Baalberg to the north, and the Lažňány and Hunyadi-halom or Sălcuţa IV on the east. See also Makkay's table equating the cultures of the southern Vojvodina and the southern Alföld with Transdanubia (Makkay 1976a:270).

On the basis of graphite ornament on pottery as well as some other elements, Karanovo VI in eastern Bulgaria, Gumelniţa to the north in Romania, Sălcuţa in Oltenia and the eastern Banat, Krivodol in northwestern Bulgaria, Bubanj-Hum I and II in the Morava River basin around Niš and southward as well as on the Timok, at Šuplejevac and Bakarno Gumno in Pelagonia and at Maliq II and III in Albania (e.g., Garašanin 1982:148), are all associated and are considered by many as variants of a single widespread culture complex.

There is a consensus that the Cucuteni and Tripolye sequences run more or less parallel and are very closely related, although there are some differences as to how their phases match up in detail (e.g., see Bognár-Kutzián 1972; Ellis 1984; Gimbutas, chap. 22, this vol.). On a general and simplified scheme, Ellis (1984:31) shows (1) late Pre-Cucuteni II slightly overlapping with Tripolye A, which predominantly equates with Pre-Cucuteni III; (2) Cucuteni A = Tripolye B 1–3; (3) Cucuteni AB = Tripolye B II; (4) Cucuteni B = Tripolye CI 1.

For her western Black Sea coastal strip, Todorova (1978: table I, p. 183) shows the Varna culture as contemporary with Karanovo VI, Gumelniţa, Krivodol II, and early Sălcuţa.

With regard to the twenty-seven individual dates grouped as Karanovo VI-KGK below, the total potential range is 5040–3660 B.C. as shown. However, eliminating the two highest and the one lowest date in the series results in a total range of 4765–3950 B.C., some 565 years less.

Marija Gimbutas has recently made available three radiocarbon dates from Poduri in Romanian Moldavia (see chap. 22). These yield an averaged date of 4935–4695 B.C., which accords well with Early Stroked and Lengyel. Although this is somewhat earlier than our averaged Gumelniţa A2 dates from Cascioarele with which she would equate them, the Poduri dates fall within their range.

Among the averaged calibrated dates with which this note is associated, thirteen Gumelnita A2 dates from Cascioarele give a range of 5040/4555–4390/3915 B.C., with an average of 4460–4410 B.C.

Identification	No.	Range B.C.	Average B.C.
Gumelnita A2 (Cascioarele)	13	5040/4555–4390/3915	4460–4410
Sitagroi III	5	4755/4545–3975/3285	4425–4320
Polish Lengyel			
Phase I	11	4565/4435–4360/3790	4405–4095
Phase II	5	4150/3775–3860/3490	3895–3765
(See Bogucki chap. 20)			
Bayč-Retz	3	4385/3940–3890/3760	4120–3875
Epilengyel	2	4135–3630	3910–3760
Varna culture, final phase	2	3945/3775–3900/3665	3905–3775
Michelsberg			
Ehrenstein III	7	4145/3895–3995/3790	4115–3880
Ehrenstein IV	12	4420/3905–3910/3760	3980–3865
Schussenried	8	4420/4090–3955/3795	4140–3890
(See Wells, chap. 19, this vol. and Pape 1979)			
Tiszapolgár	8	4400/4075–3865/3495	3960–3795

In the above list Ruttkay's two Epilengyel dates (1983:55) accord well with or overlap Polish Lengyel, phase II, Bayć-Retz, the final phase of the Varna culture, Michelsberg (Ehrenstein III, IV and Schussenried), and Tiszapolgár. Early Stroked fits chronologically with late Lengyel, Boian IV, Varna, Tiszapolgár, and Polish Stroked, all of which fall in the first half of the fifth millennum, while the averages for Czechoslovakian Lengyel, Karanovo VI (KGK VI), Gumelniţa A2, Goljama Delčevo, Bub (Varna), and Sitagroi III in equation V all fall between 4575 and 4320 B.C. The ranges of course are wider and more variable. Also, at Sitagroi in Greek Thrace a chronological and cultural break is said to occur between phases III and IV.

In two papers Makkay (1976b and 1985) raises a question concerning the goldwork from the Varna cemetery as a chronological marker. In the first he stresses that the production of goldwork in east-central Europe, as appearing in the Bodrogkeresztúr and Gumelniţa cultures of the middle Eneolithic period, apparently ceased before the Baden period and thus seems to reinforce the inclusion of the Varna culture in this equation. In his second article he finds similarities between several Varna gold objects and some dated approximately fifteen hundred years later. Since calibrated radiocarbon dates generally confirm a middle Eneolithic dating of ca. 4500–4000 B.C. and earlier, one is temporarily at a loss to find a satisfactory and definitive explanation. It seems highly unlikely that the similarities persisted over so long a time when none have appeared in the interim. This leads to the suspicion that the resemblances are not sufficiently complex and numerous to justify an assumption of relationship.

Temporal Equation VI

Bodrogkeresztúr-Cucuteni–Pitgrave Kurgan–Late Sălcuţa, Gumelniţa, and Karanovo–Jordanów–Jevišovice C2–TRB/C.

This period is one of continuities and discontinuities in that some traditions persist or end and others, of longer or shorter duration, appear.

Working without benefit of radiocarbon determinations, Bognar-Kutzián's equations span a wider time frame with somewhat less precision than is now possible (Bognár-Kutzián 1972:207–9).

For her Middle Copper Age she gives the following rough equation: Bodrogkeresztúr AB = Ludanice = Lažňány in northern Transylvania = Lasinja = Cucuteni AB and B, Tripolye B II and Cy II = the Pitgrave Kurgan culture = Sălcuţa Late III and IV = Gumelniţa late BI and BII (Late IIIa and IIIb-Karanovo late VI 2 and its following hiatus = earliest Ezero = Cernavodă I = Bubanj-Hum Ia = Hisar Ia in the Kosovo Metohija =

Jordanów = Jevišovice C 2 = Funnel Beaker C = Gatersleben. Most of these fall between 4000 and 3500 B.C. in the calibrated radiocarbon framework.

Today calibrated radiocarbon dates suggest that Balaton-Lasinje 1 = late Early Bodrogkeresztúr B and lasts at least until late Boleráz, and in eastern Bulgaria Pevec falls in the hiatus between Karanovo VI and VII.

In this series Bodrogkeresztúr occupies much the same territories as Tiszapolgár in northeastern Hungary, but with some westward extension across northern Hungary as far as the Danube. The Lažňány group, although appearing in eastern Slovakia, essentially fills the geographical gap in Transylvania between the Bodrogkeresztúr complex and Cucuteni to the east and also along the north.

To this point there is general agreement that we have been dealing with localized or essentially indigenous cultures, after which there occurred westward movements of what were essentially steppe peoples, some of whom had already, to some extent if only temporarily, settled down.

Of the few radiocarbon dates available for this equation we have the following:

Identification	No.	Range B.C.	Average B.C.
Early TRB			
Lower Austria	2	3890–3660	3880–3665
Bohemia	7	3885/3665–3385–3125	3665–3505
(Balaton Lasinje II–III)	(2)	3865/3550–3675/3485	3685–3505
Bodrogkeresztúr	2	3839–3485	3865–3550
(Confirmatory dates from the west as given by Pape 1979)			
Mondsee	4	3880/3530–3670/3370	3660–3485
Baalberg	2	3875/3490	3795–3640
Salzmünde	2	3675/3345	3670–3500
Upper Austria	Ruttkay (1983)		
Mondsee	17	3880/3650–3045/2790	3525–3360
Lower Austria	3	3380/3155–3375/3145	3375–3155

In Bohemia, of the seven radiocarbon dates attributed to the Early Funnel Beaker culture, the four from Makotřasy are ascribed to the later part of Early Baalberg (Pleslová-Štiková 1976, 1980) and the remaining three seem also to belong in the early Baalberg range. In extension of our equation, Ottoway (1976:117) refers to a consensus that the Austrian Mondsee is coeval with the Altheim, Baalberg, and Salzmünde cultures of south Germany, and also with the Pfyn-Cortaillod cultures of Switzerland (see Wells, chap. 19, this vol., and also Pape 1979).

The two TRB dates from Lower Austria (Ruttkay 1983:55) are slightly earlier than the seven from Bohemia, and her seventeen dates labeled Mondsee (pp. 54–55), when averaged, fall about 150 years later than those given by Pape.

Temporal Equation VII

Coţofeni-Ezero-Cernavodă–Karanovo VII–Usatovo Folteşti-
Baden-Kostolac-Řivnáč-Cham–Vučedol/Zók–Globular
Amphora–Corded Ware–Bell Beaker

After the Bodrogkeresztúr phase a series of regional variants with slightly differing time relationships appeared in Hungary and some of them spread fairly widely. These are subsumed under the name of Baden but include (1) Boleráz, earliest Baden which is related to Cernavodă and equates with Jevišovice C I, falling beyond Cannelated and Ludanice; (2) Úny, described as Hungarian cannelated; (3) Viss in northeastern Hungary, belonging with Pećel described as a Baden phase in the Carpathian Basin, and (4) Bošáca, along the Moravian Slovakian border in the eastern Morava and the west Slovakian Vah valleys. Its older phase = young cannelated with Kostolac elements = early Jevišovice B.

In the northwest, Bohemia again served as a nexus for a variety of peoples with varying cultures and as a focus for wide correlations. Thus the Řivnáč culture of north-central Bohemia has close relationships with the Cham group of Bavaria (Pleslová-Štiková 1968b, 1969:15–24). Cham appears in southern and southwestern Bohemia (PDČ: Map 2), and Ottoway's nine Cham oldest dates (Ottoway 1986:735) are almost identical with the single Řivnáč date from Homolka. At Homolka the presence of Vučedol elements and imported sherds of Globular Amphora vessels gives further cross ties. At other sites there are some signs of partial contemporaneity between the middle Corded Ware and Řivnáč people on the one hand and perhaps the later Corded Ware and Bell Beaker people on the other (e.g., Pleslová-Štiková 1974: 172–77).

Both Corded Ware and Bell Beaker sites appear in considerable strength in the loess of north Bohemia (PDČ: map 3). They appear to have been, at least to some degree, contemporary. There does not, however, seem to have been much contact between them. The Řivnáč and Cham sites, although earlier, may have overlapped with early Corded Ware. Since the Corded Ware people sem to have been predominantly pastoralists, the Řivnáč people were settled farmers, and the Bell Beaker people, known mostly from graves, have been thought to be either propectors or traders, the three groups may well have exploited somewhat separate economic niches in the same territory.

Although the Corded Ware traces from the north are almost nonexistent in Moravia, Bell Beakers are numerous and striking and closely follow the Danube to below its knee and southward as far as Csepel Island below Budapest. These west Hungarian occurrences are relatively numerous and occur in pits that indicate settlements as well as in graves, but Kalicz-Schreiber (1976:21) states emphatically that in Hungary the Bell Beaker complex does not represent a self-contained culture, but that it appears as a recognizable component in a mixed context consisting mainly of Makó elements which continued into Proto-Nagyrév and Early Nagyrév times. By Late Nagyrév Bell Beakers disappear. Shennan (1976:231–39) pursues a somewhat similar line for Bohemia and Moravia. However, the repeated association of Bell Beaker traits—nonceramic and ceramic—in recognizable clusters brings into question Shennan's attempt to explain this complex in industrial trade terms or as societal preference or demand.

One may well continue to regard the Bell Beaker complex, here at least, as probably indicating an ethnic group of people dispersed in small units that were absorbed by the already resident populations. The truth may, of course, lie somewhere between these two views. In any case, over a wide area Bell Beakers provide a useful marker that has broad implications for establishing chronological relationships.

Baden and Kostolac have appeared as separate entities in northwestern Yugoslavia, with Kostolac slightly later. However, they frequently appear together and then are termed Baden-Kostolac, implying some contemporaneity but with Kostolac apparently surviving later. This is also true in the Danube Valley of western Romania. Although Kostolac occurs in Transylvania, it also appears in the overlying pit at Obre on the middle Bosna, indicating a very wide geographical range.

The gap between our Baden and Vučedol dates reflects a hiatus found at both Sarvaš and Vučedol itself (Schmidt 1945), where Vučedol phases I and II are lacking and only phases III and IV appeared.

Although we have been using the term Vučedol to avoid confusion, it is now customary to refer to the general culture as Vučedol-Zók. The site of Vučedol lies in Croatia and that of Zók in southern Hungary, the combined term representing linguistic differences, Serbo-Croatian and Hungarian, in the designation of a single culture.

To the east the Ezero culture occupies Bulgarian Thrace (Garašanin 1982a). Despite a series of twenty-eight dates from the eponymous site identified by levels (Georgiev et al. 1979), the radiocarbon dates do not accord with the sequence given. Even when Quitta combined them (1978) into two major groups labeled A (twelve dates) and B (fifteen dates), when calibrated and averaged, there is still no distinction between them.

Farther north the Cernavodă groups seem essentially nomadic, moving westward from the Dobrudja and lower Danube to Oltenia and subsequently farther west over a considerable period of time, as did some of the Usatovo Foltești-Gorodsk groups established northwest of the Black Sea. Five closely grouped dates attributed to the Usatovo culture, one from Usatovo itself and the other four from Majaki, have a calibrated average date of 3165–2915 B.C., and virtually identical are two dates from Mikhailovka I (Gimbutas 1980b:277, 282; for her Kurgan II period see her map on p. 275).

Ecsedy (1979:56) agrees that the Corded Ware peoples were part of this westward movement traveling across the north, but sees their origins in the forested steppe in that they do not have Kurgan burials and also that their remains are lacking in the truly forested zone.

Although there seem to have been indigenous changes, the existing Neolithic cultures apparently came to an end in the middle Danubian and Carpathian basins as the result of invasions, both primary and secondary, by peoples of the steppe who moved westward from the east and southeast. Despite several attempts to deal with chronological aspects, cultural impacts, and the like, specifics of the disintegration of the Neolithic patterns are far from clear (*Godišnjak* 1983).

For the most part there is general agreement that the incursions and influxes were of people of the Cernavodă complexes. Unfortunately we have almost no radiocarbon dates, and culturally the Cernavodă sites are small, scattered, and briefly inhabited, while most of those excavated have been cursorily sampled. A further difficulty is that the designations Cernavodă I, II, and III represent separate groups occupying different territories but the boundaries of which more or less coalesced in the Cernavodă area. Although these are to some extent identifiable, the sequence and details of their movements are vague. There is some question as to whether Cernavodă II represents merely a variant of ceramic style or a subcultural difference. In any event, a shared stylistic pottery complex that appears in different sites would apparently indicate a recognizable group, however small.

Although the Cernavodă groups almost certainly came from the north Pontic Steppe and settled temporarily before moving voluntarily or being pushed farther to the west, there are questions as to their temporal relationships, for example, whether the movement of Cernavodă II preceded that of Cernavodă III, took place at the same time with Cernavodă III surviving later, or whether Cernavodă II arrived after Cernavodă III but did not last as long. It is virtually impossible to arrive at answers to questions of appearances and survival until an adequate corpus of radiocarbon determinations exists.

In reexamining the Bubanj-Hum material, M. Garašanin reports two important gaps—one between Bubanj-Hum Ia and his new Bubanj Ib, into which he would intercalate Sălcuţa IIc(?)-IV and Cernavodă I, and a second

gap between this stage and the incursion of Baden-Kostolac into which he would insert the evolution of Cernavodă III-Boleráz and Classic Baden. His sequence would then read Bubanj-Hum Ia, Sălcuţa II?-IV, Bubanj Ib, the evolution of Cernavodă III-Boleráz-Classic Baden and Baden-Kostolac (M. Garašanin 1983:25).

In the same volume, writing on Romania, Roman (1983:117–23) thinks Cernavodă I = Cucuteni AB and B = Decea Mureşului = end of Usatovo-Gorodsk = oldest eastern Globular Amphora = Sălcuţa IV and Pevec in Bulgaria in the hiatus after Karanovo VI. Second, Cernavodă III-Boleráz = Coţofeni = Baden. (For the Coţofeni group see also Roman 1976 and for the Baden culture in Romania see Roman and Németi 1978.)

In a series of maps he shows the following distributions: (1) Cucuteni in Moldavia and Cernavodă I in Muntenia, Oltenia, and eastern Transylvania; (2) Sălcuţa in Oltenia and northwestern Bulgaria; (3) Cernavodă III in Muntenia and Oltenia, Globular Amphora in Moldavia, and Boleráz in northern Transdanubia; (4) Early Coţofeni essentially in Transylvania, Cernavodă II in southeast Muntenia, Foltești in Moldavia, and Ezero in Bulgarian Thrace; and (5) Glina III in Muntenia, Schneckenberg on the upper Olt and southeastern Transylvania, Makó and Nyírség east of the Tisza, and Jamna in south Russia, and eastern Muntenia.

For further comments on the Eneolithic migrations of the Pit Grave steppe groups into the Carpathian basin, the Danube Valley, and the Balkan region see Tasić 1982–83, particularly his map (p. 17) and table (p. 19).

Identification	No.	Range B.C.	Average B.C.
Baden	4	3395/3025–3150/2370	3360–2995
Baden (Lower Austria)	3	3380/3155–3375/3145	3375–3155
Bošáca (late cannelated)	1		3370–2950
Sitagroi IV	7	3395/3145–3170/2885	3355–2980
Coţofeni (with Kostolac and Vučedol	7	3375/3145–3170/2910	3175–2935
Cernavodă	3	3375/3025–3045/2790	
Ezero A, XIII–IX	13	3370/2950–2900/2615	3150–2900
Ezero B1, VIII–IV	15	3390/3155–2905/2540	3165–2915
Mikhailovka I	2		3155–2895
Usatovo-Majaki	5	3360/2910–3055/2885	3165–2915
Bernburg (Pape)	5	3390/3150–2920/2640	3165–2905
Kostolac (Pape)	4	3580/3035–2910/2580	3030–2875
Řivnáč	1		3025–2950

Cham (Ottoway *RC*)	9	3370/3145– 2930/2800	3040–2885
Vučedol (*RC* 21:1)	8	3155/2970– 2890/2540	2945–2790
Globular Amphora, Germany, etc.	9	3365/2895– 2410/2115	2925–2790
Ocher Grave	3	3845/2790– 2895/2525	2910–2630
Cham Hienheim (Pape)	3	3160/2900– 2910/2530	2880–2630
Sitagroi Va	3	3160/2875– 2405/2155	2875–2620
Middle Corded (Pape)			
Swiss	5	2925/2730– 2895/2645	2895–2665
Auvernier France	9	2935/2645– 2655/2320	2870–2545
Saale	6	2880/2635– 2320/2090	2665–2535
Corded (Buchvaldek)	4	2655/2530– 2415/2245	2550–2385
Bell Beaker			
Hungary (Csepel)	4	3025/2775– 2415/2175	2670–2535
France	14	3365/2930– 2650/2020	2670–2540
Sitagroi Vb	5	2655/2525– 2410/2160	2560–2505
Netherlands	28	2900/2650– 1995/1695	2425–2315
Italy	9	3360/2910– 3055/2880	2320–2090
Early Bronze Age			
Únětice	1		2320–2135
Nagyrév	2		2225–1985
Odmut VII	1		2205–1890

Temporal Equation VIII

Early Bronze Age

We must emphasize that the major cultural break falls between the disintegration of the basic localized Neo-lithic patterns and the influxes of the Eneolithic peoples from the east which occurred in the various regions between 3250 and 2900 B.C. Although the Bronze Age is beyond the limits of this chapter, there is a strong continuity between the Eneolithic and Bronze Age cultures, modified mainly by the widespread adoption of full bronze technology and the variety of bronze products, improved farming practices, and better modes of transportation, particularly by horse, and the changes attendant upon them (see Shennan 1986).

On our table 2 the individual calibrated dates from Ezero range from 3390/3155 to 2900/2615 and the one from Celei Sucidava falls within that range. Their categorization as Early Bronze Age may well result from a difference in classification, or perhaps an Early Bronze Age appeared in southeastern Europe earlier than it did in the east central zone.

Traditionally given as somewhat later, Neustupný (1976:112–14) now sees the Bell Beaker culture ending and the Early Bronze Únětice and Nagyrév cultures beginning about 2300 B.C. and possibly lasting to somewhere between 2100 and 1850 B.C. In some areas the Early Bronze Age may have ended sooner. Based on relative relationships as well as on occasional radiocarbon determinations, a rough date of 2300 B.C. for the changeover from the late Eneolithic to the Early Bronze Age would seem to be acceptable for the entire area. Thus we close our discussion at that point.

Addendum—June 1987

Received too late for discussion are a review article on the Neolithic of Romania (Comşa 1987) and the first volume of the report of the Divostin excavations (McPherron and Srejović 1988).

Twenty-Two

Chronologies of Eastern Europe: Neolithic through Early Bronze Age

Marija Gimbutas, University of California, Los Angeles

Outline

The Earliest Agriculturalists North of the Black Sea

The Dniester-Bug Culture

The stratigraphy of systematically excavated sites documents an extended period of autochthonous experiments in animal and plant domestication by hunter and fisher groups who had occupied the area from the Mesolithic (Markevich 1974; Danilenko 1969). Stratigraphy and radiocarbon dates have verified a sequence of three prepottery and five ceramic phases, from ca. 6500 B.C. to ca. 5500–5200 B.C. Four radiocarbon dates are known from Soroki (see table 1). The earliest layers of the site were about 20 cm thick; phase 1 was separated from phase 2 by a sterile layer.

The two earliest Neolithic levels (Soroki II$_{3-2}$) lack pottery but contain bones of domesticated cattle and pigs, wild wheat seeds (*Aegilops cylindrica*), and small grind-

ing querns. Domestication of pigs and cattle was probably accomplished independently by the Dniester-Bug population, and wild wheat was gathered some five hundred years prior to contacts with Starčevo (Criş) agriculturalists. High percentages of fish bones (roach of the carp family, eel, and pike), recovered from the earliest villages, indicate that the availability of fish may have provided the initial impetus toward a settled way of life. Throughout the duration of the Dniester-Bug culture, farming was a secondary aspect of an economy based on fishing and the hunting of aurochs, red and roe deer, and boar. Soroki II$_1$ (the second phase with pottery), ca. 5800–5500 B.C., contains einkorn wheat, the most commonly cultivated species in southeastern Europe. A series of sites of the Pottery Neolithic phases have yielded emmer wheat and spelt, in addition to the dominant einkorn wheat; their existence was established by the impressions of husks, ears, and grains in the ceramics. Further evidence is the use of straw as pottery temper (Janouchevitch and Markevitch 1971). The small PrePottery vil-

Text submitted May 1984
Final revision February 1988

lages of semisubterranean dwellings are located on the narrow bank between the river and the steep slope of the lowest terrace. The Pottery Neolithic settlements included above-ground houses (see table 2).

The indigenous equipment of the Dniester-Bug population was notably different from that of Starčevo and Karanovo agriculturalists. Polished stone tools were rarely produced; rather, antler was employed in a variety of ways, including the manufacture of axes, probably used to prepare the ground for planting. A gradual microlithization of flint tools is observable. Small chips set in bone or antler handles were used as points, scrapers, and knives. Burins and perforators were also microlithic.

The earliest coarse ceramics were large, pointed, or flat-based pots, constructed of clays tempered with vegetable matter and decorated with linear incisions (fig. 1:I). The influence of the Starčevo culture is visible around the middle of the sixth millennium in the appearance of fine, well-fired, plain (gray or buff) and painted wares (see fig. 1:II). The superseding of Starčevo elements by central European Linear Pottery styles marks the end of the independent Dniester-Bug culture.

North Pontic Neolithic Groups

The earliest Neolithic stage north of the Black Sea is represented by the Matveevo group northeast of the Sea of Azov (Krizhevskaya 1978). The settlements belong to settled fishermen with incipient pig and sheep/goat domestication. The analysis of animal bones has shown 85 percent wild forest fauna, 5 percent domesticated animals, and 10 percent probably domesticated animals. Only tiny bits of poorly fired pottery, tempered with concretions of limestone, were discovered. Clay was also used for figurines and for other purposes (clay daub was found).

Two radiocarbon dates obtained from the charcoal of Matveevo place this stage in the second half of the seventh millennium B.C.

Lab No.	Reported Date b.p.	CRD 1σ B.C.
GrN 7199	7505 ± 210	5780 ± 210 (estimate)
LE 1217	7180 ± 70	6290–5705

Next in importance is the Rakushechnyi Yar site in the lower Don basin, district of Rostov (Belanovskaya 1978; Telegin 1981). Cultural deposits were nearly 5 m thick and consisted of twenty-three horizons; all except the upper two are assigned to the Atlantic climatic period. Of the six culture layers, the four lower strata (VI–IIIb) belong to the local Neolithic; the upper (IIIa–I) belong to the Eneolithic (Srednii Stog II and Yamna) culture. Two radiocarbon dates were secured for the lower Neolithic layers (V–IV):

Lab No.	Reported Date b.p.	CRD 1σ B.C.
Bln (no number)	6070 ± 100	5220–4905
KI 955	5790 ± 105	4755–4545

The upper layer (IIIa) is dated by a single radiocarbon date:

Lab No.	Reported Date b.p.	CRD 1σ B.C.
Bln (no number)	4360 ± 100	3180–2895

The radiocarbon dates from the Neolithic strata of the Rakushechnyi Yar are more than a thousand years later than those of Matveevo. Connecting links between the two are missing. However, the culture seems to represent a local development. Fishing continued essential to the economy; animal husbandry was more advanced, including cattle, sheep/goats, pigs, dogs, and horses (probably domesticated). Cultivated plants have not, as yet, been discovered. Thick-walled pots, tempered with vegetable matter or crushed shells, were flat-based. Houses were built of timber uprights covered with clay daub. Flint workshops included long-blade tools. Bone was extensively used for fishing tools.

Related Neolithic layers, with pottery and domesticated animals, are known from the Crimean caves and the islands of the Dnieper rapids, but unfortunately, no radiocarbon dates for these are available.

The Crimean Neolithic is subdivided on a typological basis into six phases, named after excavated sites: (1) Ash-Bash; (2) Zamil-Koba; (3) Tash-Air (6th layer); (4) Kaya Arasi; (5) Tash-Air (5th layer); (6) Dolinka.

Several caves, Tash-Air, Zamil Koba, and Kaya Arasi, are significant for reconstructing the history of animal domestication north of the Black Sea. All three have stratified deposits with Upper Paleolithic material at the base and are overlain by Mesolithic strata. Above the Mesolithic, two Pottery Neolithic layers included a large number of pig bones, in which wild and domesticated species were mingled. Crimean cave sites also yielded bones of domesticated dog and cattle (at Kaya Arasi: Formozov 1962:109). The dark gray or black pottery, pointed-based and thick-walled, was tempered with crushed limestone or sand, and decorated by impression and incision. The flint industry includes geometric microliths.

The lower Dnieper Neolithic is known from the series of sites south of Dniepropetrovsk, where the stratified sites of Surskii and Shulaev indicate a development parallel to that of the Rakushechnyi Yar Neolithic strata. An earlier layer at Shulaev yielded about 20 percent domesticated animals (dogs and cattle), while the upper layers in both Shulaev and Surskii contained nearly 40 percent domesticated animals: cattle, dogs, pigs, and sheep (Danilenko 1969:179). The Dnieper transgressions into the lowest layers, and deposits of paludinae shell, indicate damp conditions. The end of this culture was caused by a gradual takeover of the lower Dnieper basin by the descent of the Dnieper-Donets people from the north.

The Dnieper-Donets Culture

The earliest phases of the Dnieper-Donets culture are found in the middle Dnieper basin. From there the Dnieper-Donets people descended to the shores of the Sea of Azov and spread eastward to the upper Donets area (see fig. 2) marked by the distinctive practice, without close parallel elsewhere, of collective burial in trenches, in which the dead, of massive Crô-Magnon type, lay in an extended position. The large cemeteries (some containing over one hundred skeletons) of the late phase of the culture suggest a settled way of life. Habitation sites revealed subsistence based on hunting, fishing, shellfish collecting, and domestication of cattle, pigs, sheep/goats, horses, and dogs. The present knowledge of this culture stems from finds at two hundred localities (Telegin 1968), although the village structure and architecture are unknown. Early Dnieper-Donets sites yielded large pointed-base pots with vegetable temper; a flat-based, bulbous, rimmed vessel is characteristic of later sites.

The chronology is built on the relationship between the Dniester-Bug and the Early and Classical Cucuteni cultures.

On the basis of parallels with the Dniester-Bug culture, the beginning of the Dnieper-Donets culture should be sought in the sixth millennium.

Early Cucuteni (i.e., "Pre-Cucuteni") and Early Classical Cucuteni potteries coincide with the middle period of the Dnieper-Donets culture and place it within the first half of the fifth millennium B.C. The latest Dnieper-Donets sites have been shown to parallel the Cucuteni AB and B phases, and should consequently be dated ca. 4000–3500 B.C. (see table 6).

On typological grounds, the Dnieper-Donets chronological sequence consists of at least eight phases labeled by site names: Igren 8, Bondarikha, Yosipivka (Osipovka), Mariupol, Mikol'ske, Grini, Zasukha, and Pustinka (see table 3). There are only a few radiocarbon dates (see table 3a).

The Dnieper-Donets culture is subdivided into three periods, A, B, and C. Period A is characterized by cemeteries of pit hollows and row trenches which contained from one to ten or eleven ochre-colored skeletons. Microlithic flint tools, fish, and deer teeth are usual grave gifts. Pottery vessels were not found in graves. Annular beads of shell and agate appeared in the A2 subphase. The most likely date for this period is 5500–5000 B.C.

Period B is characterized by large collective pits, subrectangular in shape, filled up with skeletons and covered with powdered ochre. Because of the repetitive use of the grave pits, the skeletons of the previously buried dead were usually destroyed and the skulls were moved into a distant corner of the pit, or were reburied in a separate pit. Fish and deer teeth were not as frequent as in *Period A* graves. Annular beads and plates made of boar tusk were numerous. Pottery vases were usual finds. A few radiocarbon dates for *B2* cemeteries in the Dnieper rapids region place this phase into a period of 5000–4500 B.C.

Period C, approximately 4500–4000 B.C., is a stage marked by disintegration and evident decline of the culture. The collective burial in grave pits gradually vanished and an alien burial practice was introduced. Steppe people of a different physical type (less broad-faced) came into this area and the Dnieper-Donets people were either pushed northward or assimilated by the invaders. The last phase is known only from the northern territories of the Upper Dnieper, Pripyat, and Nemunas basins.

In northeastern Poland and southern Lithuania, the "Nemunas" branch of this culture was assimilated before or around 3000 B.C. by the central European Globular Amphora culture.

The Cucuteni Culture

Affiliated with, and periodically stimulated by, its southern neighbors, the Boian variant of the East Balkan tradition, the Cucuteni culture of Moldavia and the western Ukraine formed the northerly outpost of Old European civilization. Ethnically, the Cucuteni culture was a medley of the indigenous inhabitants (Dniester-Bug and Linear Pottery) and infiltrating Boian Mediterraneans. Since the forest-steppe environment necessitated a shifting agriculture, there accrued no accumulation of large mound deposits such as are found in Bulgaria and southern Romania. Habitation sites are located on the terraces in the middle and upper basins of the Siret, Prut, Dniester, and Boh (southern Bug) rivers, and during the latter half of the culture, in the middle Dnieper area (see fig. 3).

Discovery, Name, and Early Chronological Classifications

Among the earliest discovered sites were (1) Cucuteni in northern Moldavia, first reported in 1889, and later systematically excavated in 1909 and 1910 by Hubert Schmidt (Schmidt 1932); (2) Sipintsi (Schipenitz) in what was formerly Bucovina, reported by J. Szombathy in 1893 and published by Kandyba (1937); and (3) Tripolye (in Ukrainian, Tripilye) on the middle Dnieper, reported by Khvojko (1899). The baked clay floors of large houses, the bichrome and trichrome vases, and the hundreds of female figurines found during these early excavations soon aroused international interest.

Since its discovery, two names for the culture have been in use: "Tripolye" in Russia and "Cucuteni" in Romania. Both terms took root, and both terms continue after a century of research to be applied to one and the same culture.

The stratified site of Cucuteni in the middle Prut Valley was of utmost importance in the consequent research of this culture, and its name certainly deserves to designate it. During the excavations at Cucuteni of 1909–10, Hubert Schmidt came upon traces of two consecutive strata. The lower, or A stratum, contained trichrome pottery, and the upper, B stratum, included bichrome. Soon thereafter, Schmidt discovered another site in the same area (Dîmbul Morii) with pottery showing a style intermediate between Cucuteni A and B. The label "Cucuteni AB" was given this new phase. After Schmidt published his book *Cucuteni in der Oberen Moldau, Rumänien* in 1932, the knowledge of the Cucuteni A, AB, and B strata constituted a benchmark for all further chronological studies. In the excavations of 1936, 1938, 1940, 1951, and later, thousands of square meters of Cucuteni AB settlement were revealed at Traian by Vladimir and Hortensia Dumitrescu (H. Dumitrescu 1952–59; V. Dumitrescu 1945).

New light was thrown on an even earlier phase by the excavations of Radu Vulpe in 1936 and 1948 at Izvoare, near Neamţ in the basin of the upper Siret, Moldavia. There Vulpe discovered a stratum with monochrome, incised pottery which preceded Cucuteni A and was thereupon called "Pre-Cucuteni" (Vulpe 1957). Finds of Pre-Cucuteni character also appeared at other sites such as Traian-Dealul Viei (or Zăneşti), Traian-Dealul Fîntinilor, Larga Jijiei (V. Dumitrescu 1959), and Tîrpeşti (Marinescu-Bîlcu 1974), and the early stage was divided into Pre-Cucuteni I, II, and III. The Romanian archaeologists continue to use the term "Pre-Cucuteni," although it does not designate a culture preceding the Cucuteni. The Pre-Cucuteni phases should be understood as Early Cucuteni.

On typological and stratigraphic grounds Dumitrescu (1963) has defined four phases of Cucuteni A: A_1, A_2, A_3, and A_4. To the first two, Cucuteni A_1 and A_2, belong two strata of the Izvoare site, II_1 and II_2 (Vulpe 1957), and of the Frumuşica site, the latter excavated by R. P. C. Matasă (Matasă 1946); also a large village of Truşeşti, north of Iaşi in Moldavia (Petrescu-Dîmboviţa 1963), and other sites. A number of other great sites belong to Cucuteni A_3, which equates to Hubert Schmidt's Cucuteni A, among them one of the layers of the very prominent stratified site of Hăbăşeşti, excavated in 1949–50 (V. Dumitrescu 1954). Other sites with related but somewhat more advanced materials (e.g., Ruginoasa, Draguşeni, and Fedeleşeni) are assigned to Cucuteni A_4. The Cucuteni

AB phase has been subdivided into early and late: $A–B_1$ and $A–B_2$ (Dumitrescu 1963).

The Cucuteni B period is also an extended, long-lasting phase. Excavations in the 1960s of habitation sites (Petreni, Valea Lupului, and others) made possible the division of the period into three subphases: B_1, B_2, and B_3 (Dumitrescu 1963). These were represented, for example, when the resumption of the excavation of the Cucuteni site by Petrescu-Dîmboviţa in 1961–65 revealed six phases: A_2, A_3, AB_1; AB_2, B_1, and B_2 (Petrescu-Dîmboviţa 1965). Thus, in the seventy-five years of spade work in Romania following Schmidt, the chronology of the Cucuteni culture expanded from the two originally identified A and B periods into twelve distinct phases: Pre-Cucuteni I–III, $A_{1–4}$, $AB_{1, 2}$, $B_{1–3}$.

A number of villages in the Moldavian and Ukrainian SSR have been excavated before and after World War II; some yielded more than one stratum; for example Nezvisko (Chernysh 1962), Darabani (Passek 1949), Polivanov Yar (Passek 1951; Popova 1978), and others. Tatiana Passek produced a monograph in 1949 on the chronological classification of the Tripolye culture: phases A, B, C, with two subphases (Passek 1949). There, Tripolye A equates with Pre-Cucuteni II and III; BI equates with Cucuteni A, and BII is synchronous with Cucuteni AB; C_I corresponds to Cucuteni B. For the classification of the southern sites Passek introduced the Greek letter γ, to parallel C. Since it unnecessarily complicates the system, I have deliberately omitted it from the discussion.

Tripolye C_{II} comprises the Gorodsk-Usatovo stage, a Cucuteni-Kurgan melange during which the Cucuteni culture continued in a degraded form as the culture of a subjugated people. Radiocarbon dates for this phase are given in table 7. The two phases of the cemetery of Vikhvatintsi, still undoubtedly Cucuteni, apparently belong to a phase preceding the Usatovo, CII. Twenty years later, Passek's period C was subdivided by Movsha into six phases: Tripolye $BIII_1$, $BIII_2$, $BIII_3$, CI, CII, CII_2 (Movsha 1972). Tripolye $BIII_{1–3}$ correspond to Cucuteni $B_{1–3}$; Tripolye C became post-Cucuteni B. In all, Soviet scholars have succeeded in distinguishing fifteen phases on stratigraphic and typological grounds of the Tripolye culture (including the radiocarbon phases of mixed Cucuteni-Kurgan character; see table 4).

Radiocarbon Dates

Table 5 lists the available dates (Cucuteni and Tripolye fused as a single culture).

In the basins of the upper Siret, the upper Prut, and the upper Dniester, the earliest Cucuteni ("Pre-Cucuteni") sites follow the "Music Note" phase of the Linear Pottery culture. At Tîrpeşti, on the River Siret, the Linear Pottery stratum yielded two radiocarbon dates: Bln 801, 6245 ± 100 b.p. (5310–5035 B.C.) and Bln 800, 6190 ± 100 b.p. (5280–4980 B.C.), indicating the end of the sixth millennium B.C. (fifty-second through fifty-first centuries B.C.).

Pre-Cucuteni II (Tripolye A_1) radiocarbon date has been obtained from the shrine of Poduri "Dealul Ghîndaru," district of Bacău: Bln 2804, 5820 ± 50 b.p. (4750–4560 B.C.). The Pre-Cucuteni III (Tripolye A_2) stratum above the shrine yielded the date: Bln 2803, 5880 ± 150 b.p. (5040–4555 B.C.). The succeeding layer, assigned to the transition between the Pre-Cucuteni and Cucuteni A periods, yielded a slightly later date: Bln 2782, 5780 ± 50 b.p. (4730–4550 B.C.) (Monah et al. 1986; Monah 1987). In calibrated chronology all three should be placed within the forty-eighth through forty-sixth centuries B.C. The animal bone date from Luka-Vrublevetskaya, a Tripolye A site, is obviously too late. Tîrpeşti date GrN 4424 is synchronous with Novye Ruseshty I, a Tripolye A settlement. This Tîrpeşti sample was described by Dumitrescu as being either "Pre-Cucuteni" III or Cucuteni A_1–A_2.

Typologically, Pre-Cucuteni is contemporary with middle and late Boian and early Gumelniţa of southern Romania:

Pre-Cucuteni III   Gumelniţa A_1–A_2 Boian 5 (late Spanţov)
Pre-Cucuteni II   Boian 4 (Vidra, early Spanţov)
Pre-Cucuteni I   Boian 3 (Giuleşti)

The radiocarbon dates for Karanovo V and early Karanovo VI (Boian–early Gumelniţa) place the Early Cucuteni between ca. 5100 and 4600 B.C. (cf. Ehrich and Bankoff, chap. 21).

Table 6 lists the sites in order of stratigraphy and typology, with their radiocarbon dates.

The Classical period is the best dated. The five phases (Cucuteni A_1, A_2, A_3, A_4, AB_1) belong in the period between the forty-sixth and the fortieth centuries B.C., each phase lasting ca. 140 years.

Cucuteni A_3:   44th–43d centuries B.C.
Cucuteni A_2:   45th–44th centuries B.C.
Cucuteni A_1:   46th–45th centuries B.C.

The Late Cucuteni phases belong in the period between the thirty-ninth and thirty-fourth centuries.

Simplified Classification and Relative Chronology

For the nonspecialist, I propose a simplified version of chronological classification:

III.   *Late Cucuteni* (Cucuteni *B*, Tripolye C_1), ca. 4000–3400 B.C.

II.   *Middle or Classical Cucuteni* (Cucuteni *A* and *AB*, Tripolye *B*) ca. 4600–4000 B.C.

I.   *Early Cucuteni* (Pre-Cucuteni, Tripolye *A*) ca. 5100–4600 B.C.

The three main periods, I–III, coincide with the three stages of ceramic styles as well as with the three periods of evolutionary development of Cucuteni villages and architecture.

Early Cucuteni is characterized by excised, white encrusted ceramics, closely analogous to the Boian ware of southern Romania. The earliest bichrome pottery, a red- and white-painted ware, points to the beginning of the Classical Cucuteni. This was soon succeeded by trichrome wares, painted white or red with black bordering, which mark the apex of Classical Cucuteni ceramic art (Cucuteni A_2, A_3). Vases, painted dark brown on orange-red, and pictorial representations of mythical images are typical of Late Cucuteni (fig. 4).

A steady population increase is indicated by the size of villages, which grew from ca. 30–40 houses in the Early Cucuteni to 100–200 houses in the early Classical, and to 1,500 at the beginning of Late Cucuteni (Dobrovody, Maidanetske, Tallyanki, and other towns) (Shmaglii, Dudkin, and Zin'kov'skii 1973; Shishkin 1973). Late Cucuteni is an urban stage. Site territories covered up to four hundred hectares.

Villages and towns were founded on river terraces— Early Cucuteni, occasionally on low ones; Classical and Late Cucuteni always on wide, secondary terraces. One or two ditches and a rampart protected the village on the inland side. Architecture shows a development from modest, somewhat flimsy huts in Early Cucuteni to three- or four-room houses and two-storied buildings in the Classical and Late Cucuteni. The houses ranged from 8 to 30 m in length, large enough for twenty to thirty people. The interior was divided by partitions into two or three rooms, each with a hearth and a clay oven. Walls of wicker work up to 2 m high, supported by vertical beams and daubed with clay, were built above a specially prepared wood or clay platform, over which was superimposed a fired, clay floor. A pitched roof was supported by a longitudinal row of posts.

Latest Cucuteni (Tripolye CII) is a period of dissolution for the Cucuteni culture, one caused by the increasing pressure from the steppe during the Mikhailovka I phase of the North Pontic Maikop culture and the infiltration of the Funnel-Necked Beaker culture of northwestern Europe as far east as the Dniester basin and Volynia (Movsha 1985).

The Neolithic and Eneolithic of the Middle Volga–Southern Urals Region

The Neolithic

Recent work in the forest-steppe and the northern edge of the steppe between the middle Volga and lower Ural suggests early beginnings of the Neolithic economy there. About fifteen sites yielded domestic fauna. Of these, horses (55.3 percent) predominate, followed by cattle (27.6 percent) and ovicaprids (17 percent). The morphology and the age-slaughter pattern of the horses from Vilovatoe and Mullino II indicate domestic horses. Petrenko hypothesizes that from this earliest stage of horse domestication the horse was exploited both for meat and for riding (Petrenko 1984:70–71). The radiocarbon dates are 5720 ± 160 b.c. from Mullino II and 5600 ± 200 b.c. from Berezki (Matyushin 1982; Petrenko 1984). The calibration would place them in the second half of the seventh millennium B.C. This shows that the Neolithic of the Volga-Urals is as early as the Aegean Neolithic and that it predates the North Pontic Neolithic. The Near East must have been the source of this economy, except for the horse which most likely was domesticated in the middle Volga forest-steppe region, at the forest edges and close to the rivers. The presence of the domesticated horse in the seventh millennium B.C., not suspected heretofore, is of the greatest significance for the understanding of the following cultural development of south Russia.

The Volga-Urals culture referred to as "Eneolithic" in Soviet literature developed from the Neolithic culture in the same territory between the middle Volga and the lower Ural and extending to the Caucasus Mountains and the Caspian Sea in the south. The Eneolithic is subdivided into three periods: early (or "Samara"), middle (or "Khvalynsk"), and late (or "early Yamna") (Vasil'ev 1981).

The Early Eneolithic Samara Culture

The early Eneolithic is called the "Samara culture." The name derives from the cemetery of S'ezzhee on the bank of River Samara, the tributary of middle Volga, district of Kuibyshev (Vasil'ev and Matveeva 1976). This cemetery revealed the earliest evidence of the horse cult: remains of horse sacrifices and miniature figurines of horses carved out of bone plate (fig. 5). A large sacrificial area in which two skulls of horses were found was above the richest graves in pits. Graves were intensively sprinkled with ochre. A child's grave in a deep pit below the sacrificial remains was equipped with the long flint dagger of an adult person (fig. 6:1), two figurines of double-headed oxen or bulls made of boar's tusk (fig. 5:3, 4), three spoon-shaped objects with sculptured heads of ducks at ends, laminae and pendants of shell, a necklace

of shell beads, animal teeth, and two large polished gouges and adzes of stone. The unusually rich grave gifts, some of which clearly had a symbolic meaning (the weapons and tools of an adult person in the grave of a child of one and a half to two years old, as well as the figurines), suggest a ritual burial. Flint and bone daggers of this cemetery are truly formidable weapons (fig. 6). Some of the bone daggers with flint or quartzite blades set in along both sides were as long as 56 cm. Such weapons are not known to the world west of south Russia. Pots from the sacrificial areas were tempered with crushed shells. The predominant shape was a truncated egg (fig. 7). The decoration was in horizontal bands or zigzag lines over the upper part or over the whole surface, executed by stabbing, stamping, comb impressions, and by pitted or button design below the thickened rim. Similar pottery is known from a number of sites between the lower Don on the west, the middle Volga in the north, and the lower Ural region in the east.

There are no radiocarbon dates for the S'ezzhee cemetery. The chronology rests on stratigraphy and typological comparisons. It precedes the Khvalynsk period, dated by radiocarbon to the first half of the fifth millennium B.C. The hypothetical date for the Samara period is the end of the sixth millennium B.C., or the period around 5000 B.C.

The Middle Eneolithic Khvalynsk Culture

The middle period of the Eneolithic is represented by the cemetery of Khvalynsk, located on the bank of the Volga, district of Saratov (Agapov, Vasil'ev, and Pestrikova 1979; Vasil'ev 1981:22–42). One hundred fifty-eight skeletons were unearthed in pit graves; singly the skeletons were buried or from two to five or more in one grave. The dead were placed lying on the back with contracted legs and knees upward. Twelve graves were covered with stone cairns. As in S'ezzhee, sacrificial areas were unearthed with remains of horse, cattle, and sheep bones. Grave goods included metal artifacts (rings and spiral rings), pendants of boar's tusk, bone and shell beads and bracelets, a shaft-hole ax with side lugs, a sculpture of a schematized head of a horse, probably a scepter, bifacially retouched flint points, arrowheads, daggers, stone adzes, and bone harpoons. A very similar inventory was brought to light in the rich grave of an individual discovered in 1929 at Krivoluchie, district of Samara (Gol'msten 1931) (fig. 8). In the south, related burial rituals and grave equipment came to light at Nal'chik, in the region of Kabardino-Balkaria, central northern Caucasus (Kruglov, Piotrovskii, and Podgaetskii 1941). Furthermore, related materials are known from sites to the Sea of Azov on the west and the River Ural on the east. The similarity of grave goods in sites separated by thousands of kilometers suggests an unprecedented mobility and intertribal relationship.

The radiocarbon dates for the Khvalynsk period are from the early fourth millennium b.c. (analyzed by the Laboratory of the Ural Institute of Education). Calibrated they belong to a period before the middle of the fifth millennium b.c. (Vasil'ev 1981:63). Dates themselves are not published by Vasil'ev. He also mentions that samples analyzed in Kiev are even higher.

The Late Eneolithic Early Yamna Culture

The late Eneolithic is the early Yamna culture characterized by a wide spread of kurgans, low earthen barrows above pit graves. Before this period earthen mounds were not universal; more often graves were covered by a stone cairn or remains of sacrificial activities. On the steppe, earthen mounds above the graves emerged during the Khvalynsk period. The kurgan is a feature of the steppe (Merpert 1974:131). In all respects the late Eneolithic is a continuation from the Khvalynsk period. The continuity of the material culture is best documented by excavations in the same areas where Khvalynsk sites existed previously, for instance, by the excavation of a settlement of Alekseevo near Khvalynsk (Vasil'ev 1981:44–50). Continued in production were the egg-shaped pots tempered with crushed shell and the stone tool kit dominated by gouges and adzes and typical weapons—bifacially retouched spear points and arrowheads and long daggers. The type site is Repin on the bank of the lower Don (Sinitsin 1957:32–35). This settlement yielded the greatest number of pots and horse bones. Horse bones constituted 80 percent of all domesticated animal bones.

This is a period of rising mobility. Contacts with the west, with the Cucuteni and the Karanovo VI cultures, place it in the middle of the fifth millennium b.c. or soon thereafter.

The swift horse cut traveling time by a factor of five, nullifying whatever territorial boundaries had existed previously. These developments largely affected the exploitation of steppe resources and virtually all other aspects of life. Riding provided the ability to strike across great distances, instigated trading capacities, the accumulation of wealth, the looting of cattle and horses, a rapid rise of social differences, and warfare and violence. Once the steppe was conquered, it inevitably became a source of out-migration.

The Kurgan Culture

Kurgan (a term introduced by the author in 1956) is the archaeological blanket term for the seminomadic pastoralists from the south Russian steppelands. The Russian word *kurgán* (itself a Turkic loanword) means literally a "barrow"; hence, the technical term *Kurgan* refers to the

tumuli which are a characteristic feature of the burial practices of a culture, and is extended to designate the people of that culture as well. Chronologically the term is applicable to a time span comprising two millennia, from ca. 4500 to ca. 2500 b.c. This period saw three Kurgan thrusts into east-central Europe: at ca. 4400–4200 b.c., at ca. 3600–3400 b.c., and at ca. 3000–2800 b.c.

The "Kurgan tradition" is characterized by an economy, essentially pastoral with subsidiary agriculture; by a patriarchal and hierarchial society with prominent hillforts as tribal centers; by small, transient villages of semisubterranean houses; by horsemanship; by distinctive burial rites including hutlike structures built of stone or wood, covered either by a cairn or an earthen mound; and by horse and weapon cults and sun-oriented symbolism.

I divide this tradition into four periods, Kurgan I–IV (table 7). This chronology, based on contacts with the west, radiocarbon dates, stratigraphy, and typology, does not represent the evolution of a single group of people, but rather several groups of steppe peoples differing spatially and diachronically but sharing a common tradition. Kurgan I and II people were from the Volga forest-steppe and steppe; Kurgan III (Mikhailovka I–Maikop), developed in the north Pontic area influenced by the Caucasian and Mesopotamian cultures; and Kurgan IV (Yamna) people were again from the Volga steppe (table 7).

Kurgan I: First Wave into East-Central Europe

The Kurgan people first entered European prehistory in the mid-fifth millennium b.c. when they appeared in east-central Europe. The chronology is built on contacts with Cucuteni A_3 and Karanovo VI. The lower Dnieper basin (the Dnieper-Donets culture) was infiltrated before the middle of the fifth millennium b.c. The Dnieper-Donets culture was gradually replaced by a Kurgan culture, called "Srednii Stog II" (SS II).

In the Dnieper rapids region a stratified site with an earlier Dnieper-Donets settlement, Srednii Stog I, is overlain by a new cultural complex, Srednii Stog II, whose people practiced single burial in flat or in cairn-covered shaft or cist graves; the body was supine, either contracted or extended, and usually supplied with flint daggers and beakers with pointed bases. In contrast to the vegetal temper characteristic of the earlier Dnieper-Donets ceramics, the pots are tempered with crushed shell; the stamped pitted or cord-impressed decoration about the neck and shoulders presents a solar motif (fig. 9). The skeletal remains, moreover, are dolichomesocranial, taller statured, and of a more gracile physical type than those of their predecessors in the substratum (Zinevich and Kruts 1968). Local evolution cannot account for such abrupt changes; our task, then, is to seek neighboring cultures typologically similar to SS II for a possible source of this contrasting stratum. Such a parent culture is to be found in the steppe region of the lower Volga and lower Urals of the Khvalynsk period of the first half of the fifth millennium B.C. The earliest SS II sites in the lower Dnieper basin may date from a period earlier than the middle of the fifth millennium B.C.; the rest are contemporary with the early Yamna period.

The Srednii Stog II complex is an extension of the Volga-Ural pastoralists into the north Pontic. The hundred or so sites in the lower Dnieper-Don interfluve are primarily cemeteries. Settlements are found on high and wide riverbanks. Such was excavated at Liventsivka I on the lower Don at the confluence with Mertvii Dinets near the town of Rostov-na-Donu (Bratchenko 1969). This hilltop settlement yielded a stratigraphy of five superimposed cultural layers. The lowest (earliest) layer included Srednii Stog II pottery.

In graves, the typical skeletal disposition is supine, legs flexed or extended, arms alongside the body, the whole dusted with ochre. The grave pits are rectangular, retaining traces of bark floor-covering. The grave goods show the influence of the local substratum and are enriched by trade objects from the west (Telegin 1973). High-class male burials included bifacially worked spearpoints, triangular flint arrowheads, and formidable long flint daggers, usable on horseback (fig. 10). Exceptionally rich male graves include thousands of *pectunculus* or other shells (originally attached to disintegrated leather or woven belts); copper bead and animal tooth necklaces; shell and copper pendants; spiral arm rings and finger rings of copper; long, thin, spiral-headed copper pins; and copper tubes. The copper came from the Aibunar or other mines in central Bulgaria of the Karanovo VI period via barter with the Cucuteni people (of the Cucuteni A_{3-4} period).

Antler cheek pieces and the depiction of bridle equipment on stone sculptures is fairly convincing proof of horsemanship. At Dereivka, in the lower Dnieper steppe, fifty-five horses were counted within a settlement of three dwellings, representing 68 percent of the total number of domesticated animal remains. The radiocarbon dates for the Dereivka settlement are as follows:

| UCLA 1466A | 5515 ± 90 BP | 4450–4335 B.C. |
| UCLA 1671A | 4900 ± 100 BP | 3865–3550 B.C. |

Following the penetration of the Dnieper rapids region, Kurgan incursions struck Romania, Bulgaria, and east Hungary. We can trace the spread of the domesticated horse from the Volga steppe north of the Caucasus Mountains to east-central Europe by antler cheek pieces, stylized horse-head sculptures, by actual horse bones, and by remains of horse sacrifice.

In nine of the western Kurgan I burials (Fedeleşeni and Berezivka, Moldavia; Obîrşeni and Salcuţa IV, southern Romania; Székelyvaja, Transylvania; Casimcea and Suvorovo in Dobrudja; Rzhevo, Bulgaria; and Suvodol, Macedonia), stone scepters in the shape of a horse head analogous to those from Kuibyshev on the Volga, Arkhara in the northern Caucasian steppe, and Terekli-Makhteb in northern Dagestan were found (Gimbutas 1977; fig. 11). On the basis of stratigraphic and typological evidence from Obîrşeni, Fedeleşeni, and Berezivka, the scepters are dated to the Cucuteni A_{3-4} (Tripolye B1) period: forty-fourth to forty-second centuries B.C. The Casimcea burial also yielded, besides a scepter, several axheads, spearpoints, and flint daggers of the type found in SS II graves. The Suvorovo burial, classified as a "suttee" grave, has close parallels in the SS II sites of Yama and Aleksandriya in the lower Dnieper region. Luxurious grave goods such as copper rings, bracelets, and pendants of Karanovo VI type, shell artifacts made from *spondylus* imported from the Aegean, and daggers made of Carpathian obsidian or flint were found west of the Black Sea in the sites of Casimcea in Dobrudja and Czongrad in Hungary. Close parallels are known from the SS II sites of Petro-Svistunovo and Chapli in the lower Dnieper region. In addition, the Kurgan at Kainari, Moldavia, included grave goods synchronous with Cucuteni A_3: forty-fourth through forty-third centuries B.C. (Movsha 1972:16, 17).

Domestic horse bones appeared in the Gumelniţa (Karanovo VI), Cucuteni A_3, and Tiszapolgár (northeastern Hungary and Moravia) sites with Kurgan Wave Number 1 (Bökönyi 1978:25ff., 1987). The evidence for a horse sacrifice—a horse skull cut from the neck—was found in 1986 in a Tiszapolgár pit in Tiszaföldvár, northeastern Hungary (Bökönyi 1987).

Kurgan II

This period is late Srednii Stog II in the lower Dnieper basin, contemporary with Cucuteni AB–B_1 (Tripolye B_{II}–C_I) around 4000 B.C.–early fourth millennium B.C. Along the western coast of the Black Sea, in Dobrudja, Cernavoda I culture emerged, typified by fortified sites on high river terraces, subterranean dwellings, and gray crushed-shell tempered pottery, unmistakably related to the Kurgan wares.

The Cucuteni civilization survived the first Kurgan Wave intact. Its ceramic tradition continued undisturbed, although Kurgan elements within Cucuteni settlements (1–10 percent of Cucuteni A and AB pottery) indicate some sort of interaction between the two groups. This intrusive shell-tempered pottery (referred to by some as "Cucuteni C") is identical to that of the SS II sites of the lower Dnieper. Petrographic analysis showed that all Cucuteni and SS II samples were of similar mineralogical composition. This indicates that both peoples exploited similar clay types, but the respective technology was very different: the Cucuteni ware was well fired, completely oxidized, and with no temper, whereas the Srednii Stog II ceramics were low-fired and contained tremendous quantities of crushed shell, organic residues, and plant material. The SS II pottery was fired in a reducing atmosphere at a temperature of approximately 500°–600°C. The possible firing temperature of Cucuteni A and B ceramics on the other hand lies between 850° and 1000° (analysis by Linda Ellis: Ellis 1984).

The density of Cucuteni sites indicates no massive dislocations in the wake of the First Wave of relatively small groups of Kurgan infiltrators; nor is there evidence for an amalgam of the two groups throughout these six hundred to eight hundred years of coexistence, at least not until the mid-fourth millennium B.C.

Kurgan III

The Mikhailovka I Phase of the Maikop Culture North of the Black Sea and the Caucasus

This period is synchronous with the transformation in central Europe from agricultural to pastoral/agricultural economy, from a society matricentric and matrilineal to a patriarchal one (as reflected by Ezero-Baden and Globular Amphora cultures) accomplished by the first and subsequently the second infiltration into east Europe of peoples from north of the Black Sea (Gimbutas 1979, 1980). The Old European copper metallurgy was replaced now by circumpontic metallurgy related to the Caucasus and the Near East (Chernykh 1980).

The home base of the Second Kurgan Wave is the remnants of hillforts and the hundreds of kurgans with cromlechs and mortuary houses in pits built of stone slabs, stones, or wood (fig. 12) that are concentrated north of the Caucasus and the Black Sea: in the Crimea, the lower Don, lower Dnieper, Ingul, and Ingulets valleys. Royal or other important male burials share a characteristic monumental style: tumuli are surrounded by stones or orthostats, then by an outermost ring of stones, and under the kurgan is a stone- or wood-lined pit, sometimes topped by a stone cupola or earthen mound covered with stones. In the grave goods we find evidence of vehicles, silver spirals, and daggers of arsenic copper. Associated with burials are sacrifices of oxen and horses. Skulls of these animals were placed in pairs (two ox skulls, two horse skulls). The central grave of one kurgan (no. 4) at Novoalekseevka, district of Kherson, was surrounded with a ring of oxen skulls and leg bones. The skulls were laid in pairs. In another kurgan (no. 6), two oxen skulls with the foreheads touching each other were placed at the

feet of a child under which lay a skeleton of an adult. Children's and youths' burials associated with oxen and horse sacrifices could have been sacrificial. Thus, for instance, in grave number 14 of the same kurgan a skeleton of a youth was found between the two skulls of horses (Zbenovich and Chernenko 1973).

Large apsidal houses (with apsis used for storage), exclusively on hilltops, are an architectural innovation. The features spread now over western Anatolia (Troy I–II), northeastern Greece (Sitagroi V), Bulgaria, and Romania (Ezero culture), northwestern Yugoslavia, eastern Hungary, and Slovakia (Baden culture), and Poland, eastern Germany, and northeastern Romania (Globular Amphora culture). Moreover, apsidal houses, probably not unconnected with east-central European, emerged in Palestine during the thirty-fourth through thirty-third centuries B.C. (Best 1976).

Typical royal burials are known from Tarnava, northwestern Bulgaria (Nikolov 1976). To the same tradition, though of a later date, belong the Mala Gruda royal grave at Tivat on the Adriatic coast and other related graves in Hercegovina (Govedarica 1987) as well as the Steno tumuli on the island of Leukas, west of Greece, assigned to the Early Helladic II period (Dörpfeld 1927).

Known from the end of the nineteenth century, the royal tomb at Maikop in the northwestern Caucasus is the richest and the most familiar of this culture. And although it dates from the first half of the third millennium B.C. (contemporary with Troy II and Early Helladic II)— thus to the later part of the culture—the place name has become eponymous for the whole north Pontic culture which began soon after the middle of the fourth millennium B.C. The beginning phase of the Maikop culture is best represented by the lowest layer of the Mikhailovka hillfort in the lower Dnieper basin (Lagodovs'ka, Shaposhnikova, and Makarevich 1962).

The Mikhailovka hillfort on R. Pidpil'na, a tributary of the lower Dnieper, was undoubtedly a strategic Kurgan center. The finds from its lowest horizon, Mikhailovka I, show affinities with those from Crimean and north Caucasian stone cists on the one hand and with the Usatovo kurgans near Odessa on the other. The chronology of this phase is based on radiocarbon dates from Mikhailovka I:

Lab. No.	Reported Date b.p.	CRD 1σ B.C.
Bln-629	4400 ± 100	3360–2910
Le-645	4340 ± 65	3160–2900
Bln-630	4330 ± 100	3170–2885

The two upper layers of Mikhailovka belong to the Yamna culture of the Volga origin.

Mikhailovka I ceramics are typified by the globular amphorae with rounded or flat base and cylindrical neck wound with cord impressions; semiglobular tureens and braziers also occur. Some vases were stabbed, pitted, and beaded about the mouth, neck, and shoulder (fig. 13). Four-legged braziers were ornamented with the solar motif. The ceramic was tempered with crushed shell or limestone and sand, usually of grey color and with a well-polished surface. Parallels are known from the northern and central Caucasus, and from the Kuro-Araks basin in Transcaucasia (stratum E in Khizanaant Gora and in Amiranis Gora: Kushnareva and Chubinishvili 1970: fig. 21:6).

In the lower Dnieper basin, on both sides of the river, kurgans with several kinds of burial rituals were found, but considered to be roughly contemporary. In addition to the diagnostic burial in grave pits covered with stone slabs and surrounded with one or two stone rings, in a number of kurgans graves were found in oval, boat-shaped, or rectangular pits including extended skeletons (Nikolova and Rassamakin 1985). Their chronology is indicated by the deposition in graves of Cucuteni-Tripolye figurines of the Tripolye CI_1 period. The figurines were highly schematized, with no arms or legs, had flat backs and large faceless cylindrical heads marked with groups of parallel lines or tri-lines. This type is known as latest Tripolye, "Serezliivka," type (Passek 1949: fig. 98:11). Graves also yielded rounded or biconical pots, some with polished surface, and made of the same kind of clay as the figurines, with no temper of crushed shells. Such items in graves speak for the continuity of Tripolye traditions during the Mikhailovka I period. These graves seem to represent the last flutter of the great culture before its merge with the Kurgans.

Usatovo in the steppe region around Odessa, Gorodsk on R. Teterev, west of the middle Dnieper, and Folteşti I in Moldavia form a complex representing an amalgam of Kurgan and Cucuteni traditions. Kurgans line the highest ridges along the rivers of the area, with the best sites being located at Usatovo near Odessa (Lagodovs'ka 1946, 1953) and Tudorovo in Moldavia (Melyukova 1962). Near the settlement and tumuli at Usatovo is a contemporaneous cemetery of the indigenous latest Cucuteni (Tripolye CII) culture: simple, unmarked pit graves, arranged in rows. Contrasting burial rites of the Cucuteni and Kurgan populations are paralleled by differences in their respective habitation sites. Cucuteni dwellings were on wide river terraces. The Kurgan people located their semisubterranean dwellings on spurs, dunes, and steep hills along rivers. The houses at Gorodsk are typical: small, about 5 m in length, and with a round hearth in the center (Passek 1949:194–275). Household goods are definitely not Cucutenian (Movsha 1970). Potsherds, recovered mainly from hearths, show a rough corded pottery, pitted and stabbed.

Table 8 lists the radiocarbon dates obtained by analyses of charcoal and animal bone from the Gorodsk, Danku, Usatovo, and Mayaki sites.

Kurgan IV

The Yamna ("Pit grave") Culture of the Volga-Dnieper Steppe

The Yamna pastoralists of the Volga steppe are related to Kurgan I (early Yamna) and are distinct from the Maikop complex. Their western thrust is identified by hundreds of graves in Romania, Bulgaria, Yugoslavia (south Banat), and eastern Hungary.

Diagnostic features of prominent male burials are deep pits; timber hut construction within the grave pit, roofed with oak or birch beams (fig. 14); floor covering of mats, bast, or ashes; grave walls hung with rugs; predominant western orientation of the dead; and supine skeletal position with contracted legs (lateral in later graves). Ochre was scattered with the dead. Round and low barrows, usually no higher than 1 m, were surrounded by stone rings or ditches. Stone cists and cromlechs common in the north Pontic Mikhailovka I complex, are not characteristic of Yamna grave architecture. Important males were equipped with a hammer-headed pin of bone or copper, a round copper plate, spiral hair-rings or earrings of silver or copper, chains or necklaces of copper wire tubes and canine teeth, flint arrowheads, tanged daggers of arsenic copper or flint, awls, flat copper axes, and stone "battle-axes." About 75 percent of Yamna graves had no grave goods.

The Mikhailovka hillfort yielded the best stratigraphy: Mikhailovka I was overlain, after a hiatus, by two layers (1.20 m thick) of the Yamna culture, Mikhailovka II and III. Tall beakers with rounded bases, decorated with horizontal cord impressions, comb-stamped herringbone design, rows of pits or incisions, and cord-impressed or incised hanging, and striated triangles are typical of the Yamna layers. This type of pottery is well evidenced in the Yamna graves in the lower Dnieper–lower Volga basins. The habitation area had been constantly enlarged. Final habitation of this hillfort extended over an area of 2 ha. The fortification—ditches and stone walls of flat fieldstones, about 2 m high—belongs to this last phase. Houses were rectangular, with stone foundations dug in the ground, consisting of two or three interconnected rooms.

In Moldavia and the western Ukraine, Yamna kurgans are stratigraphically situated above the Usatovo-Folteşti settlements and graves. Most of the calibrated radiocarbon dates for the Yamna graves west of the Black Sea range shortly after 3000 B.C. (table 9).

Yamna graves from the lower Dnieper, Don, and lower Volga steppe date from the same and also from a later period. A number of earlier Yamna radiocarbon dates from the Ukraine and southern Russia are given for comparison (table 10). The chronological link is obvious. Table 11 includes radiocarbon dates from later Yamna graves, most of which are secondary graves in barrows.

The East Baltic Area

This section covers the time span from the developed Mesolithic during the Boreal period through the Neolithic, developed from local Mesolithic during the Atlantic times, to the arrival of the Corded Pottery people from the southwest and the Comb-Marked Pottery people from the east in the middle of the third millennium B.C.

Mesolithic and Pottery Neolithic of Settled Fishermen: The Kunda and Narva Cultures

A distinct cultural upsurge in the east Baltic began during the Mesolithic when the climate warmed in the Boreal period and when deciduous forest spread through the east Baltic region, developing favorable conditions for fishing. The population associated with the descendants of the final Magdalenian culture and related to the Maglemose culture of northwestern Europe became increasingly settled. The Mesolithic culture, called Kunda, continued into the Neolithic "Narva" stage—a Pottery Neolithic of settled fishermen (Jaanits 1968; Rimantienė 1971, 1979; Zagorskis 1967). A number of sites were occupied from ca. 7000 to ca. 2500 B.C. The cultural continuum is attested by a number of radiocarbon dates from Kunda, Narva, Sārnate, Osa, Pieštiṇa, Kääpa, Šventoji, and other sites (table 12).

The richest peat bog sites of the Narva culture, with an exceptional preservation of wooden artifacts (fishing tools, dugouts, oars, troughs, ladles, sculptures of water birds, snakes, elks, and owl goddesses), fabrics of linden bast, fishing nets as well as amber ornaments, are Šventoji in western Lithuania (Rimantienė 1979, 1980) and Sārnate in western Latvia (Vankina 1970), both near the Baltic Sea.

The cultural situation changed drastically with the appearance of totally new cultural complexes: the Pit- and Comb-Marked Pottery food gatherers and the Corded Pottery food producers.

The Pit- and Comb-Marked Pottery Culture

Just before the arrival of the Corded Pottery people came the hunter/fisher folk, called Pit- and Comb-Marked Pottery people, considered to have been Finno-Ugric speakers. They entered Finland, Estonia, and Latvia; offshoots reached western Lithuania (Gurina 1961). The campsites of the Pit- and Comb-Marked Pottery people were contemporary with those of the Narva group (table 12). After the Corded Pottery people entered the same territories, the Finno-Ugric stock gradually retreated to the north and stabilized in Estonia and Finland.

The Corded Pottery Culture

The sites of the first agriculturalist stockbreeders along the southeastern coast of the Baltic Sea (the Baltic "Haff-küstenkultur" or "Rzucewo" group) precede those of the more northern and eastern territories. Southeast Baltic ceramic ware is typologically close to that of the "Common European Corded Pottery Horizon," but there are no radiocarbon dates of the earliest phase. Dates from Lithuania and Latvia are from the mid-third millennium B.C. (table 12).

The Baltic "Haffküstenkultur" group (Rzucewo) is known from a series of villages near the Baltic Sea, some fortified, with above-ground houses standing close together. The most prominent sites are Succase (Suchacz) and Tolkemit in former east Prussia, and Rzucewo in the Vistula delta. The former, a village of some twenty houses, is assumed to have spanned three or four habitation horizons (Ehrlich 1940). Small, permanent villages have also been discovered in western Lithuania: Šventoji, Bùtingė, Šarnelė, and Nida (Rimantienė 1979, 1980). A full range of domesticated animals was present. Remains of domesticated plants are poorly documented except for hemp. At Šventoji and Šarnelė (Lithuania) both hemp seeds and cords were found. Agricultural tools—saddle querns, pestles, flint sickle blades—and grain impressions on pottery are known only from the later settlements of this culture.

A similar spread of new culture groups is apparent in the upper Dnieper–upper Volga basins—the cultures known as the "Upper and Middle Dnieper," the "Fat'yanovo" (upper Volga), and the "Balanovo," on the Volga in eastern Russia (Krainov 1972; Bader 1963; Bader and Khalikov 1976). Here, as elsewhere, the Corded Pottery/Battle-Ax people spread along the rivers and established their hillforts on high riverbanks or promontories. Their dead were buried under barrows 1–2 m high, as in Poland. Their social structure, economy, and armament must account for their success in overcoming the local hunters and fishers of Byelorussia and central Russia (the Volosovo culture) whom they probably absorbed. The same pattern of the social structure as in central Europe is evidenced in all these newly acquired territories. A number of exceptionally rich burials in isolated barrows, higher than the rest, witness the importance of prominent males, probably tribal or district leaders, a good example of which comes from Moshka in the upper Dnieper basin (Artemenko 1964).

The later cultural development in these areas is not pursued, except to state that it was gradual and continuous during the Bronze and the Iron Age. The territories between the Baltic Sea in northern Poland and central Russia are strewn with river names of Baltic origin.

Belorussia and Central Russia: Upper Dnieper–Upper Volga Basins

Radiocarbon dates show the beginning of the Neolithic period in the upper Volga basin to be as early as the sixth millennium (table 13:1, 3, 4) and to continue throughout the fifth (table 13:2, 5, 6). "Neolithic" is applied here for the culture of hunters and fishermen with pottery and polished stone tools. It follows the Swiderian Mesolithic and

is synchronous with the early Narva culture. Pollen analyses suggest the second half of the Atlantic period, the time of climatic optimum, warm and humid, when the Russian plain was covered with forests of deciduous trees.

The Pit- and Comb-Marked Pottery culture layers overlie (at Sakhtysh I, Yazykovo I, and Ivanovskoe III) the earliest Neolithic deposits without any sterile layer between them. The majority of the radiocarbon dates falls within the first half of the fourth millennium B.C.

The latest horizon, called Volosovo, immediately follows the horizon of Pit- and Comb-Marked Pottery culture, although radiocarbon dates indicate a parallel existence of the two (Krainov 1972) (see fig. 15).

Part Five

East and Northeast Asia

Twenty-Three

China

Kwang-chih Chang, Harvard University

Outline

The area of China (ca. 3.7 million m²) is less than 10 percent smaller than that of Europe (4.1 million m²), yet China's prehistoric and early historic chronology must be described within a single chapter, in contrast to Europe's nine. This was possible in the previous editions of this volume because the archaeological data were scarce and absolute dates prior to 841 B.C. were largely unknown. Since the early 1960s when the previous version of this chapter was prepared, the situation has drastically changed, first by the vast amount of new archaeological research throughout China, which has built up a number of regional chronologies of prehistoric and early historic cultures, and second by the publication, since 1972, of several hundred radiocarbon dates from throughout the area. Since the 1960s seventeen radiocarbon laboratories have been set up in China, and four of them routinely process archaeological samples.[1] The results thus far have already revolutionized Chinese archaeology, and one may anticipate continuous adjustments of the chronological picture in the years ahead.

To discuss thoroughly the data and the outstanding issues of prehistoric and early historic archaeology of China as a whole would require much more space than is available. This treatment, therefore, will be highly selective. I list in the tables only those radiocarbon dates that have been reported with full or at least adequate archaeological information,[2] and I discuss only the following regions of China for which radiocarbon dates and cultural

Text submitted 1982
Text revised 1983

stratigraphies combine to furnish a reasonable chronological framework: the Yellow River basin of north China, the northern borderlands in Inner Mongolia and southern Manchuria, the lower Yangtze Valley, the middle Yangtze Valley, the southeastern coast, and the southwest. I conclude with some general remarks pertaining to China as a whole.

The Yellow River Basin

The chronological watershed in northern Chinese history occurs in 841 B.C., the first year of the Gonghe regency under the Zhou dynasty.[3] Historical events and dynastic reigns after 841 B.C. can be related to an absolute yardstick of years, as the ancient Chinese historian Sima Qian was able to do in his *Shiji* (*Historical Memoirs*) under "Shier zhuhou nianbiao" ("Annual Tables of the Twelve State Lords"), compiled around 100 B.C. Before that date, however, Sima, in his "Sandai shibiao" ("Table of Reigns of the Three Dynasties"), could only relate such events to a succession of reigns, the durations of which in absolute numbers of years were for the most part obscure.

Major efforts on the part of modern Chinese historians to date events in ancient history prior to 841 B.C. have been concentrated in two interrelated projects. The first is the determination of the absolute number of years each of the ten kings of the Zhou dynasty reigned prior to 841 B.C., namely—starting from the beginning of the dynasty—kings Wu, Cheng, Kang, Zhao, Mu, Gong, Yi(1), Xiao, Yi(2), and Li. The second project focuses on the determination of the year in which King Wu of Zhou, in the eleventh or twelfth year of his reign, conquered the Shang dynasty. Since this event marks the beginning of the Zhou dynasty, it suffices to mention that the Zhou conquest date is very much an unsettled question in ancient Chinese historiography. No fewer than eighteen different years have been chosen by various authors for this single important event: 1122, 1116, 1111, 1076, 1075, 1070, 1067, 1066, 1057, 1050, 1049, 1047, 1045, 1030, 1029, 1027, 1025, and 1017.[4] These dates are based on bits of textual evidence pertaining to the conquest in late Zhou literature. They are often conflicting and variously interpreted. One of them could be right, but historians are not agreed as to which, and I cannot favor any one of them to the exclusion of others in the light of internal evidence.

Archaeologically based cultural periods before the Zhou conquest of approximately 1100 B.C. in north China include the following: (1) Peiligang and related cultures; (2) Yangshao culture; (3) Dawenkou culture; (4) Longshan and related cultures; (5) Erlitou culture; and (6) Shang civilization. I discuss each of the cultural periods below with regard to its main chronological issues.

Peiligang and Related Cultures

Discovered in 1977, the Peiligang culture (named after the type site in Xinzheng, Henan) is now the earliest known Neolithic culture of north China. Distributed in the central part of Henan along the eastern foothills of the Songshan Mountains, the Peiligang culture is characterized by millet farming, pig and dog breeding, pit-house dwelling, and an artifact assemblage characterized by querns and grinding stones, stone sickles, and brown and gray pottery with plain or incised surface and several types including the short-legged *ding*-tripod (Henan Kaifeng Cultural Relics Commission 1979). Table 1:1–13 lists radiocarbon dates on samples from Peiligang and several adjacent sites in Henan, which place this culture firmly in the sixth millennium and probably in the late seventh millennium B.C. (The single sample of an eighth millennium B.C. date, ZK-572, must await corroboration. The calibrated ranges in this and subsequent tables have been calculated according to Klein et al. 1982.)

Neolithic cultures similar to Peiligang both in cultural inventory and in chronology have been found widely in north China. In southern Hebei, sites classified as the Cishan culture have yielded three radiocarbon dates (table 1:14–16), again in the upper sixth and lower seventh millennium B.C. range. To the west, similar assemblages have occurred at isolated sites along the Wei River valley (table 1:17–19) as far west as the Dadiwan site in Qin'an in eastern Gansu; Dadiwan's two radiocarbon dates (table 1:17–18) again fall in the same range. To the

east, the so-called Beixin culture of Shandong, described under the Dawenkou culture, also resembles Peiligang but appears to be later in time.

These earliest known Neolithic cultures of the Yellow River basin in north China have brought this area's agricultural prehistory much closer to its beginnings than suspected twenty years ago, but their sites appear to be fully sedentary villages with a very heavy farming focus. We await future archaeological work to bring us back further along the sequence to the beginnings of northern Chinese agriculture. On the other hand, the Peiligang and related cultures of the Yellow River basin appear to be the source from which the Yangshao in the west and the Dawenkou culture in the east may have sprung.

Yangshao Culture

Characterized by red pottery painted with dark decorative patterns, the Yangshao culture of millet farmers who lived in villages of semisubterranean houses derived its name from Yangshaocun, first excavated in 1921, but distributed in the whole of the middle Yellow River valley from Gansu-Qinghai to Hebei. A large series of radiocarbon determinations has dated it (table 2) to the two millennia after about 5000 B.C., except for Gansu where it began somewhat later and lasted much longer. Yangshao apparently descended from Peiligang and its related cultures, and was subsequently transformed into the later neolithic complexes.

The chronological picture within Yangshao culture has proved in recent years to be complex and is still far from clear. A series of regional and local chronologies has emerged not only from the radiocarbon dates but also from stratigraphy and typology. In *southern Hebei* and *northern Henan* two phases are well defined—an earlier Hougang phase (table 2:1–2) and a later Dahecun or Qinwangzhai one (table 2:3–13), respectively placed in the late fifth–early fourth and the mid- to late fourth millennia B.C. In *central* and *western Henan* is a newly discovered and still inadequately defined early phase of Yangshao culture as represented by the remains at Shuangmiaogou (in Dengfeng) in central Henan in the Songshan Mountains area (table 2:14–17). This is followed by the much better known Miaodigou phase of the early to mid-fourth millennium B.C. (table 2:18–24), a phase widely seen not only in Henan but also in Shanxi and eastern Shaanxi. In *eastern Shaanxi* the earlier Yangshao phase at Banpo (table 2:25–29) and Jiangzhai (table 2:30–32) is well known from the extensive and well-reported excavations at these sites and is firmly dated to the whole fifth millennium B.C. This was followed by a new Shijia phase (table 2:33–34), a contemporary of Miaodigou at mid-fourth millennium B.C. In *western Shaanxi* virtually the whole Yangshao sequence is represented at the Beishouling site from its earliest strata of around 5000 B.C. (table 2:38–39), through its middle strata stretching throughout the fifth millennium (table 2:40–46), to its uppermost layers (table 2:47) of the early fourth millennium. The earliest Beishouling much resembles Peiligang culture and could serve as a link between it and the Dadiwan remains to the west, and the middle Beishouling is comparable to Banpo and Jiangzhai. At Dadiwan itself in *easternmost Gansu*, following its earliest phase just mentioned, are remains classified as Wei River phase (table 2:49–50) and as Shilingxia phase (table 2:51–54), in the late fifth and fourth millennia respectively. The Shilingxia phase, newly established, is sometimes regarded as transitional between Miaodigou to the east and Majiayao to the west.

Farther west in *eastern Gansu* and *eastern Qinghai* we are in the classical Gansu Yangshao domain, and the long-established sequence of Majiayao-Banshan-Machang is now well confirmed by radiocarbon chronology. Majiayao is placed in the late fourth and early third millennia B.C. (table 2:55–61), Banshan in the middle and late third millennium B.C. (table 2:62–66), and Machang in the late third and early second millennia B.C. (table 2:67–73).

Dawenkou Culture

Identified in 1959 with the excavation of the type site, Dawenkou culture, located in the eastern part of north China (mainly Shandong and northern Jiangsu), is now known to be a major neolithic culture that paralleled Yangshao culture to its west. Like Yangshao, Dawenkou has polished stone celts and characteristic Chinese ceramic types such as *ding* and other tripods and *dou* and other pedestaled bowls, but both its artifactual assemblage and a number of its customs as exhibited in archaeological remains are highly distinctive. Its pottery is often painted, but its geometric designs are unique, and many of its ceramic types, such as the *ding* tripod with shallow bowl and long legs, small-necked jars with loops on the shoulders, *gui*-type water pitcher, and cup on very tall stem, are all characteristic. The artifactual assemblage is rich in bone and ivory carvings, water deer tooth pendants, and jade ornaments. The graves were conspicuously furnished, and the human skulls show evidence of head deformation and tooth extraction (Shandong University Department of History 1979).

Thirty-one radiocarbon dates are now available from seven Dawenkou sites (table 3:8–38). As Xia Nai (Shandong University Department of History 1979:7) states, "Dawenkou culture lasted a long time, approximately two thousand years from 4300 B.C. through about 2300 B.C." A number of studies characterize the internal development of Dawenkou culture, which is usually divided into Early, Middle, and Late stages. Throughout its

long sequence, from about 5000 to 3000 B.C., Dawenkou must have been in close contact with Yangshao but the two distinctive traditions were apparently maintained throughout. This parallel but separate development of the Yangshao and Dawenkou cultures may relate to the topography of the Yellow River basin in early Holocene times when the western highlands and the Shandong highland were separated by a low-lying area, for the most part marshy or even submerged under water (Ding 1965).

The Beixin culture, centering in the Tengxian area of western Shandong, has been recently identified as probably ancestral to Dawenkou. Its dating to the earlier parts of the fifth millennium B.C. (table 4:1–7) placed Beixin culture in between the earlier Peiligang, which it resembles in many ways, and the later Dawenkou. As to the other end of Dawenkou, there is general agreement that it gave way to the Shandong Longshan culture. Dawenkou influence is also regarded as being in part responsible for the rise of Shang civilization (Chang 1976).

Longshan and Related Cultures

In the Yangshao culture area, around 3000 B.C. Yangshao culture gave way to the Longshan characterized by gray and black pottery and increasingly ranked society. Several regional phases are distinguishable: those in central and northwestern Henan (table 4:1–4), in northern Henan and southern Hebei (table 4:5–19), in eastern Henan (table 4:20–27), and in southern Shanxi and central Shaanxi (table 4:48–63). In the Dawenkou culture area, the Longshan culture appears to begin somewhat later, perhaps in the middle of the third millennium B.C. (table 4:28–37), in Shandong (table 4:38–47), and in Lüda, across the Gulf of Chihli. Farther west, in Gansu was the Qijia culture, radiocarbon dated to the late third and early second millennia B.C. (table 4:64–69). The Qijia culture is the first Chinese prehistoric culture with a well-established occurrence of copper tools and ornaments, although similar finds have also been reported from Yangshao sites in Shaanxi, Gansu, and Qinghai.

The Erlitou Culture

Ever since the 1959 discovery of the Erlitou site in Yanshi, near Luoyang in northwestern Henan, the positions of the site and of the larger culture the site represents have become a major problem in Chinese archaeology. In view of its geographical area, mainly southern Shanxi and western Henan, which is identical with the attributed geographic area of the Xia people whose dynasty preceded Shang, and in view of the radiocarbon dates of the main sites (table 5), which, at approximately late third and early second millennia B.C., again coincide with those of the traditional Xia, students of early Chinese history are increasingly convinced that Erlitou culture *is*

Xia. This, however, cannot yet be established for two reasons. The first is that no written data from Erlitou sites have as yet come to light to identify them with Xia. The second is that all of the major sites are still being excavated, and no detailed excavation reports are as yet available. So far, three sites or groups of sites are considered to represent the core of the culture, namely, Erlitou itself; Gaocheng in Denfeng, Henan; and Dongxiafeng in Xiaxian, Shanxi. Erlitou has four major strata and fifteen radiocarbon dates so far (table 5:25–39). Gaocheng, a very small site, has yielded three radiocarbon dates (table 5:22–24). Dongxiafeng, on the other hand, has provided a series of twenty-one radiocarbon dates (table 5:1–21). Unfortunately, very little of the excavations at Dongxiafeng has been published, and we have no reliable data on which to tie the twenty-one dated samples to the site's stratigraphy, which apparently began in the Longshan period and lasted through the Erlitou and Shang periods. We are not told which of the twenty-one samples are Erlitou.

Shang Civilization

Stratigraphically, the known remains of Shang civilization are grouped into Middle Shang (represented by Zhengzhou) and Late Shang (represented by Yinxu, Anyang). Using the traditional chronology of 1766–1122 B.C., we would expect Middle Shang to be about 1550–1350 B.C. and Late Shang to be about 1350–1100 B.C. The available radiocarbon dates of Middle Shang (table 6:10–12) and Late Shang (table 6:1–6) are not very far off, but their ranges of confidence are so wide that they do not settle the chronological controversy mentioned earlier.

The Northern Borderlands

Among the several dozen radiocarbon dates available from Manchuria and Inner Mongolia, thirty-two are selected to make up table 7. These pertain to important chronological issues of the northern borderlands of the Yellow River basin and can be firmly resolved on the available evidence. First, several sites in Liaoning that have yielded combed and rocker-stamped pottery are shown to be at least as early as the earliest Yangshao, possibly beginning around 5000 B.C. The same ceramic tradition persisted in the area of southern Manchuria and Inner Mongolia until the second millennium B.C. (table 7:1–13), although evidence of continued contact with Yangshao and Longshan cultures to the south is clear in the sequence. Second, by the second millennium the area witnessed the lower Xiajiadian culture (table 7:14–16), which had primitive metallurgy and showed evidence of interaction with Shang civilization to the south. Third, the increased number of radiocarbon dates from the sites

of the Kayao (table 7:17), Tangwang (table 7:18–22), Siwa (table 7:23), Shajing (table 7:24–32), and Nuomuhong (table 7:33–34) cultures of Gansu and Qinghai has reinforced the chronological assessments that had been based on earlier radiocarbon dates, stratigraphy, and typology (Chang 1977).

Early Neolithic Cultures of South China

It has long been expected that some day very early ceramics would be brought to light in south China, for very early pottery had long been a part of the Hoabinhian cultural inventory in Indo-China (Gorman 1969), and an early Holocene dating of a coarse cord-marked pottery horizon had long been suggested for Taiwan (Chang and Stuiver 1966). In fact, throughout south China coarse and early-looking pottery had been found in scattered localities, especially in the limestone caves in the southwest. However, partly because of a traditional bias for the cultural superiority and chronological priority of the Yellow River basin and partly because extensive excavations were lacking, scholars had not suspected any great antiquity for these seemingly primitive remains. In the early batches of Chinese radiocarbon dates published in the mid-1970s were two samples from Xianrendong (in Jiangxi Province) and from Zengpiyan (in Guangxi Autonomous Region) (table 8:1, 14–15) that dated to around ten thousand years before the present. In dealing with these dates, Chinese archaeologists took a very careful and skeptical attitude, wondering if the limestone environment was not in some way responsible for the exaggerated antiquity of the samples (Xia 1977; An 1979:401). In an effort to settle this issue more definitively, physicists at the radiocarbon laboratories of the Institute of Archaeology and at Peking University undertook an extensive experimental project to test the effect of limestones and of molluscan shells on wood, bone, and charcoal samples insofar as the latter's radiocarbon determination was concerned. The conclusions are that "wood, all other terrestrial plant and bone collagen have the same unaffected ^{14}C-concentration, just like atmospheric carbon dioxide" and that "these samples do give a correct and reliable ^{14}C-age, no matter whether they are from limestone" (C-14 Laboratory, Peking University, and C-14 Laboratory, Institute of Archaeology 1982). These laboratories have also published a number of new radiocarbon dates from the cultural layers of three ceramic sites, namely, Zengpiyan in Guilin, Baozitou in Nanning, and west bank of Zuojiang in Nanning, all in Guangxi (table 8). The first site is in a limestone cave, but the other two are shell middens in the open.

If these conclusions concerning the reliability of these early dates are accepted, we are faced in south China with one of the earliest ceramic cultures in the world, just as many archaeologists had expected. Zengpiyan could begin as early as 10,000 B.C., with the other sites not far behind. All of them are characterized by coarse cord-marked and incised pottery, associated with mollusk collecting and hunting-fishing.

The Lower Yangtze River Valley

Throughout Chinese history the lower Yangtze River valley—from southern Jiangsu to northern Zhejiang, including Shanghai, the Lake Tai shores, and Hangzhou Bay—has been one of the richest areas and often the richest area of China in both natural and cultural resources. In recent years its archaeology is proving that the same is also true for Chinese prehistory.

From at least 5000 B.C., about the same time that Yangshao culture farmers were planting their millet and breeding their pigs, there were already farmers in this area planting rice, breeding pigs and water buffaloes, and harvesting the very abundant water plants and water vegetables grown in the area's many rivers and lakes.

The earliest neolithic culture in the lower Yangtze is the Hemudu culture south of the mouth of the Zheijiang River. In 1973 the remains of a timber village brought to light not only crops and animals but also art objects of ivory and bone and a ceramic assemblage characterized by distinctive types of black and gray ware with cord marks on the surface reminiscent of the cord-marked pottery dated to south China's early Holocene. A series of twenty radiocarbon dates (table 9) from the site's fourth and third strata—the two that typify Hemudu culture—firmly places that culture in the fifth millennium B.C.

In the lower Yangtze River valley following Hemudu—and at least in large part developed from it—are the Qingliangang (divided into the earlier Majiabang and the later Songze phases) and the Liangzhu cultures. A large series of radiocarbon dates places the former (table 10) in the late fifth to mid-fourth millennia B.C. and the later (table 11) in the fourth and third millennia B.C. range. The Qingliangang and Dawenkou had many cultural items in common, including ceramic types, and Liangzhu and Longshan pottery types are again closely similar. Their respective chronological positions do no violence to their formal similarity and the presumption of their close interaction.

The Middle Yangtze River Valley

Neolithic cultures in Jiangxi (table 12:1–2), in the Lake Dongting area of Hunan and Hubei (table 12:3–14), and along the Yangtze in western Hubei and eastern Sichuan (table 12:15–24) date to the late fourth and early third millennia B.C., roughly contemporary with late Qingliangang and early Liangzhu to the east and late Yangshao and early Longshan to the north. Within this long stretch

of the Yangtze River, several regional types are recognizable, especially the Qujialing (table 12:3–14) and Daxi (table 12:15–24) cultures. The dating of the Daxi culture has been reinforced by a small series of thermoluminescence dates from the Guanmiaoshan site in Zhijiang, Hubei (Institute of Archaeology Laboratory 1982). It is noteworthy that the thermoluminescence series includes two early Daxi dates around 6000 B.C. (TK20: 6430 ± 515). These make the single early Daxi radiocarbon date (table 12:15) somewhat more believable. Future chronological data from this area will bear close watching.

After Qujialing and Daxi, in the middle Yangtze came an ill-defined Hubei Longshan culture (table 12:25) and then metal cultures comparable in date as well as in style to the northern Shang and Zhou dynasties. In table 12 we give several groups of available radiocarbon dates that are of some special interest. The Wucheng site of northern Jiangsi is often compared with Middle Shang of Zhengzhou in cultural style, although its bronze culture appears much less developed. The Wucheng dates (table 12:26–30) tend to bear out its middle Shang status. The Tonglü-shan copper mines are a series of extensive underground shafts, from which numerous remains throw light on the mining technology of Bronze Age China. The radiocarbon dates from the mines (table 12:31–39) scatter throughout Shang and Zhou. Jinancheng (table 12:40–50), Leigudun (table 2:51–52), and Changsha (table 12:53) are three important sites of the broadly defined Chu civilization of eastern Zhou. Their radiocarbon dates are a confirmation more of the reliability of the dating laboratories than of the dating of Chu, since the chronology of the Chu sites is well known from textual sources.

The Southeast Coast Cultures

Only at isolated spots in the southeast coast area are prehistoric cultures—those prior to the latest Zhou period when historical cultures came to the Pearl River delta area—known from extensive excavations, among them Tanshishan of Fujian, Fengbitou and Yuanshan of Taiwan, Shixia of Guangdong, and Shenwan (Sham Wan) of Hong Kong. Generally, three stages are apparent. The earliest, characterized by cord-marked and comb-impressed pottery, date from the fourth millennium B.C. and earlier (table 13:1–11). The next, best known from the Shixia culture, is assigned the third millennium B.C. (table 13:12–20). The next two millennia, the second and the first, saw the gradual spread of metal use and the "geometric" style of ceramics, eventually leading to the late Zhou and Han dynasty sites. In Taiwan, however, because of the island's geographic position, the same prehistoric traditions that it earlier shared with Fujian persisted into the first millennium B.C. (table 13:21–31).

The Southwest

Southwest China (Sichuan, Yunnan, Guizhou, and Guangxi) is still at an early stage of archaeological development, but the area's prehistory is clearly of the utmost significance because of its location between the rest of south China and Southeast Asia. In tables 14 and 15 are selected radiocarbon dates that make two points. Table 14 lists thirty-two radiocarbon dates, an unusually and almost unnecessarily large series, from the neolithic site of Karuo in Changdu, eastern Tibet. The approximately 3500–2000 B.C. dating of a neolithic site in this remote and high (3100 m above the sea) area of China is somewhat surprising, and it means that another potentially rich chapter in the prehistory of Tibet is waiting to be opened. Table 15 lists nine dates from the bronze- and copper-yielding sites of Yunnan. Both Haimenkou and Dapona have yielded "primitive" copper artifacts and are expected to be early, but the three available radiocarbon dates have failed to confirm this. Additional dates from these sites are eagerly awaited.

General Observations

The 492 radiocarbon dates used in this chapter represent the bulk of the available ones so far published and include virtually all those associated with the prehistoric and early historic cultures of China with which we are familiar since the beginning of ceramics. These constitute the difference between this chapter and its previous edition. The resultant chronology is now much more reliable and more complex than that of 1965, not only the year of the previous edition of this book but also, ironically, the year in which radiocarbon samples were first processed in both Peking and Taipei. (The Taipei dates were published almost immediately, but those of Peking had to wait until 1972 because of the intervening Cultural Revolution.)

Figures 1 and 2 indicate the chronological framework into which the bulk of the prehistoric and early historic cultures can now be placed (cf. An 1981).

Pottery now appears in the Chinese archaeological record much earlier than previously expected: before 9,000 B.C. in south China, between 6,000 and 7,000 B.C. in north China, and before 5,000 B.C. in Inner Mongolia, as the record now stands. The earliest southern Chinese pottery was predominantly cord-marked, but that of the earlier northern Chinese and Inner Mongolian was combed, comb-impressed, rocker-stamped, and infrequently cord-marked. There is good evidence that this earliest northern Chinese pottery was associated with the cultivation of millets (*Setaria italica;* see Huang 1982), but the southern Chinese pottery was primarily associated with hunting, fishing, and mollusk collecting, while the agricultural activities of its makers can only be conjectural

(Chang 1967). On the surface, a case might be made for the diffusion of ceramics from the south to the north, since the earliest pottery sites are in the south and the latest are in the north, but any such diffusionist hypothesis would be premature. Recognition of the Peiligang and related cultures results from archaeological activities of only the last five years, and their precedent cultures are being actively sought. In addition, still earlier pottery occurs in Japan, comparable in latitude to the northern part of East Asia rather than south. Therefore, for the time being at least, additional interdisciplinary field research in the various regions of China and concentrated in these early horizons is much needed and would be potentially more rewarding than any current speculation about their cultural interrelationships.

From the Peiligang group, the 6000–7000 B.C. dating of both foxtail millet (*Setaria italica*) and rocker-stamped pottery is of comparative interest. The millet, as the major staple, continued into later northern Chinese prehistory, but after 5000 B.C. rocker stamping declined in the Yellow River basin but persisted strongly in the northern borderlands of Inner Mongolia, southern Manchuria, and adjacent regions in the north.

At about 5000 B.C., the area of China saw at least five major foci of neolithic cultures. The first, from north to south, is the comb-ceramic Xinle culture of Inner Mongolia. The second, now covering the whole middle Yellow River valley, consists of the Yangshao, of Henan, Hebei, Shanxi, Shaanxi, and Gansu. The third, east of Yangshao, in the lower Yellow River valley, is the Beixin and (somewhat later) the Dawenkou cultures of Shandong and northern Jiangsu. The fourth focus is the Hemudu culture of the Hangzhou Bay area. The fifth and final known focus is the Dapenkeng culture of the southeastern coastal areas. The three foci of the north were probably derived from the Peiligang group of cultures, and the fourth and fifth foci were both probably descended from the early neolithic culture of south China as represented by Zengpiyan and Xianrendong. Yangshao, Beixin-Dawenkou, and Hemudu were cultures with very heavy agricultural emphasis, with Yangshao depending on millets (*Panicum miliaceum* as well as *Setaria italica*) and Hemudu on rice (*Oryza sativa*).

The five known neolithic cultures of the fifth millennium B.C. were each characterized by distinctive features, but compared among themselves they can be grouped in various ways according to different degrees of similarity and diversity. In their archaeological manifestation, Yangshao, Beixin-Dawenkou, and Hemudu are more advanced than Xinle and Dapenkeng, but the latter two could be described as more ecologically specialized. Xinle was a culture of the northern steppes, and Dapenkeng one of coastal and estuarian waters. Each of the five cultures exhibits some evidence of cultural interaction with its neighbors, but no exclusive interaction sphere beyond that of the five cultures is apparent.

Such an interaction sphere, however, appeared toward the fourth millennium B.C. when an increasing list of cultural manifestations became widely shared by a greater number of cultures. Late Yangshao of western north China, Late Dawenkou of eastern north China, Hongshan of Inner Mongolia, Qujialing and Daxi of middle Yangtze, Qingliangang of lower Yangtze, and Shixia and early Fengbitou of the southeastern coast are linked together by so many conspicuous cultural traits and complexes (particularly in ceramic typology) that, *in contrast with other contemporary cultures* in the adjacent areas, a common sphere of interaction is strongly indicated. I have for a long time referred to the cultural entity involved in this interaction as "Lungshanoid," because many of the shared characteristics resemble those of the Longshan cultures. When the term was first coined (Chang 1959), cultural diffusion from a nuclear area in north China was thought to be the prime agent to account for the similarity. Now, with twenty years' additional data to better our understanding of the various "outlying" regions as well as of the nucleus, we see the similarity more in terms of increased interaction between a number of regional centers, each spreading out in varying directions (Chang 1981). This larger sphere of interaction, formed around 4000 B.C., was the area in which the historical Chinese civilization developed.

At the beginning, the historical Chinese civilizations took the form of a number of local cultures, in which several local political entities (tribes or states) were involved. This formative process clearly begins around 3000 B.C., when the various regional Longshan cultures and their local phases took form in the archaeological record. In the Yellow River basin alone, seven Longshan regional phases are recognizable: Gansu Longshan (Qijia), Shaanxi Longshan (Kexingzhuang), Shanxi Longshan, western Henan Longshan (Wangwan), northern Henan Longshan (Dahan), eastern Henan–western Shandong Longshan (Wangyufang), and eastern Shandong Longshan (Rizhao). Recent studies of both archaeology and textual history increasingly point to the probability that each of these local Longshan cultures eventually developed into one of the major cultural and political groups prominent in Chinese ancient history. For example, it is almost certain now that the historical Xia dynasty developed out of the western Henan Longshan, the Shang out of the northern and eastern Henan Longshan, and the Zhou out of the Shaanxi Longshan.

Recent developments in Chinese archaeology once more confirm the traditional adage of the archaeological discipline that chronology is at the base of any study of process.

Addendum—February 1987

Since the submission of this chapter, there have been many new radiocarbon determinations. The new information does not, however, alter the material enough to warrant substantial revisions. For an account of these recent variations, readers may refer to my volume titled *The Archaeology of Ancient China* (4th ed., Yale University Press, 1987).

Twenty-Four

The Neolithic Cultures of Siberia and the Soviet Far East

Henry N. Michael, Museum Applied Science Center for Archaeology,
University Museum, University of Pennsylvania

Outline

Foreword

In any terms, the territory under survey in this chapter is vast. The three major subdivisions of what is loosely called "Siberia"—Western Siberia, Eastern Siberia, and the Soviet Far East—comprise almost one-half of the Soviet Union's 22.4 million km².

The physical map of the territory shows clearly the diversity of the landscape. Western Siberia is a vast plain stretching between the Urals and the Yenisey River. The east part of Eastern Siberia, between the Yenisey and Lena rivers, is the mineral-rich pre-Cambrian shield of the Central Siberian Plateau or Srednesibirskoye ploskogore. (In this chapter the system of transliteration from Russian is that recommended by the United States Board on Geographic Names, with the exception that the Russian "soft sign" has not been transliterated as an apostrophe and, wherever appropriate, the letter *y* has been inserted between two vowels.) The southernmost and eastern parts of Eastern Siberia are a jumble of mountains which become more complex as one progresses eastward. The boundary between Eastern Siberia and the northern part of the Soviet Far East is formed by the continental divide separating the Arctic and Pacific drainages. The southern part of the Soviet Far East, the Maritime Province or Primorye, includes the left drainage of the lower Amur and the right drainage of the Ussuri.

One of the unifying features of this extensive territory is that the major rivers, among them some of the longest in the world, drain into the Arctic Ocean. The one exception is the Amur, which flows to the Pacific. The general south-north drainage facilitated movements of people and ideas even during the Paleolithic era.

The radiocarbon dates here cited come from eleven Soviet laboratories. Since some of these laboratories are relatively new and have not been cited in Western publications, they are listed as follows:

GIN	Geological Institute of the Academy of Sciences of the USSR, Moscow
IM	Geochemical Laboratory of the Institute for the Study of Permafrost, Yakutsk
Kril	Laboratory for the History of Siberian and Far Eastern Forests of the Institute of Forests and Wood, Siberian Branch of the Academy of Sciences of the USSR, Krasnoyarsk
LE	Radiocarbon Laboratory, Institute of Archaeology, Leningrad Section of the Academy of Sciences of the USSR
Le	Radiocarbon Laboratory of the Radium Institute, Leningrad
LG	Laboratory for Quaternary Geochronology of the All-Union Geological Research Institute, Leningrad
LU	Radiocarbon Laboratory of Leningrad University
MAG	Radiocarbon Laboratory, Magadan (Soviet Far East)

Text submitted March 1983

Helen Schenck and Nicholas Hartmann, both of the Museum Science Center for Archaeology, have employed their considerable skills in redrawing the maps and photographing the tables of artifacts respectively. To both go my profound thanks.

Ri   Radiocarbon Laboratory, Riga

RUL   Laboratory of Archaeological Technology of the Institute of Archaeology, Academy of Sciences of the USSR, Moscow

SOAN   Geochronological Laboratory of the Institute of Geology and Geophysics, Siberian Branch of the Academy of Sciences of the USSR, Novosibirsk

Introduction

During the Holocene, changes in climate and in the flora of northeastern Asia also witnessed changes in the nature and density of the human population. Even with the increasing populational density, the number of inhabitants remained very small, although they occupied vast spaces that had been empty during the Paleolithic. For every known Paleolithic site in northeastern Asia there are at least a hundred Neolithic ones. Neolithic sites, although present even in the remote parts of northeastern Asia, such as the interiors of the Taymyr and Chukot (Chukchi) peninsulas, are densest in the taigas of the Angara and Lena basins, around Lake Baykal, in the Chita region, along the Amur, and in the Primorye.

The nonagricultural Neolithic economy of the territory is principally one of hunting and fishing. Emphasis on either depends to a degree on the climate and landscape. Thus between the Urals and the Yenisey River we find cultural remains of semisettled fishers and hunters, with the emphasis on fishing increasing in the Ob Valley and the regions immediately to the west. On the Yenisey, this western Siberian culture came in contact with the hunters and fishers of the Cis-Baykal, among whom the hunting of forest animals gained in dominance. In the tundra and wooded tundra of Eastern Siberia, including the Taymyr Peninsula, the lower reaches of the Olenek and Lena rivers, and farther east to the Bering Strait, are cultural remains of nomads who combined deer hunting with Arctic lake fishing. In the valleys of the Lena south of the Arctic Circle and its principal tributaries, the Vilyuy and Aldan, we again find the remains of semisettled fishers and hunters.

At present we have a good many radiocarbon dates from Neolithic sites in the USSR, all of which are based on the 5568 half-life rather than on the generally accepted 5730 half-life in the West. Up to 1982 none of those published in the Soviet Union had been calibrated, although in the near future calibration apparently will be adopted (V. M. Masson, pers. comm., November 1981).

In this chapter, radiocarbon dates and dating in general are cited as published in Soviet sources. Calibration adjustments appear in the discussion and in its summary parts.

Generally, the oldest Neolithic sites in the Soviet Union occur in the south—Central Asia, the Trans-

Caucasus, southern Ukraine, and the south of "Siberia." The radiocarbon dates in these areas reach slightly beyond 7000 b.p., or barely into the sixth millennium B.C.

In the wooded zone, as opposed to the steppe or wooded steppe, the oldest Neolithic sites appear somewhat later, the earliest about 6000 b.p.

For the Siberian wooded zone, the most consequential dates are the sixty odd ones for the Yakutian sites of Sumnagin I, Ust-Timpton, and Belkachi I. The earliest in the Neolithic series are from layers XVI–IX of Sumnagin I which date to 6000–5800 b.p. These dates fit sequentially between the earlier preceramic cultures of Sumnagin and the overlying layers of the Middle or Developed Neolithic. The Middle Neolithic of the wooded zone dates to between 5000 and 4000 b.p. To this period also belong the Neolithic sites of the far north, both in Europe and Siberia.

As in western Europe, the advent of radiocarbon dating has changed interpretations by Soviet archaeologists. Thus, for example, pottery was thought to have appeared in the wooded zone of Soviet Europe about 5000 B.P., but even uncalibrated radiocarbon dates put it at 6250–6150 b.p.

Okladnikov (1968:95) outlined and named the principal cultural areas of "Siberia" (see fig. 1). Modified by Dikov (1979), this scheme can be used for a presentation and periodization of the various cultures.

The Trans-Ural

During the Neolithic the so-called Eastern Uralian culture, which developed out of the local Mesolithic, occupied the territory of the wooded Trans-Ural and the adjacent territory of Western Siberia. It is difficult to establish a precise chronological span for this Neolithic culture because of the paucity of firm dates. The majority of present-day investigators adhere to the traditional chronology established by Chernetsov (1968:41; Chernetsov and Moszyńska 1974:7–33) and Bader (1970:162), whose chronology puts the beginning Neolithic in this area at 6100–5900 B.P. and its end at about 4200 B.P. Starkov (1970:8) would adjust this to about 4500 B.P.

Today, the stratigraphy and topography in a number of Holocene sites in the Trans-Ural permit the application of geology, palynology, and radiocarbon dating (see below).

The Mesolithic sites of this area are tied to the first elevated floodplain terrace (3–8 m in height). Among them are the sites of Istok II and III which are at 3 m, Sukhrino at 5 m, Kamyshnoye at 6 m, and Vyyka at 8 m. (For location of some of the sites mentioned in this section, see maps I and II in Chernetsov and Moszyńska 1974.)

Palynological studies at Istok II indicate a beginning dominance of pine (52 percent) and birch (35 percent);

there are also linden (6 percent) and elm (4 percent). The first appearance of elm in a nearby bog was dated to 8210 b.p. (6260 ± 150 B.C.), analogous to the Gorbunovo peat bog and Istok II, mentioned above, and to other sites as well. On this basis the Mesolithic site of Istok II belongs in the first half of the Atlantic, that is, in the span of the fifth millennium B.C. (Khotinskiy 1978:163, 1970).

Keeping in mind that Istok II is late Mesolithic in date, the Early Neolithic sites of the Trans-Ural fall at the end of the fifth or the beginning of the fourth millennium B.C. Such sites as Evstyunikha, Sumskaya III, Makhtyli, and Ipkul XIII existed in a moderately humid climate, which toward the end of the Early Neolithic, about the middle of the fourth millennium B.C., changed to a dry one, and the location of the sites during the Middle Neolithic, eleven of which are associated with the lowest banks or shores of rivers and lakes, confirm this. Thus the Yurinskaya site is located on a shore almost level with marsh; the cultural levels of Strelka are within the lowest parts of the Gorbunovo peat bog, as are other lake sites. The river sites are usually at the very edges of the low elevated floodplain terraces, and today are covered with driftwood and sapropel or gravel, sometimes of considerable depth. The present position of these levels indicates humidification of the forested and forest-steppe areas of the Trans-Ural at the beginning of the third millennium B.C., according to a radiocarbon date of 4800 ± 200 b.p. from a Strelka driftwood sample. With elevated water levels we encounter the so-called shore sites, such as Beregovaya I and II, and Chashchikha I and II at the Gorbunovo peat bog, which had been established on the new shores of the lake. The riverine sites retreat to the 6–8 m elevated terraces (Starkov 1978:91).

The phase of intense humidification, agreed by most to have taken place at the end of the Atlantic, apparently did not last long, for the sites of the following archaeological period are again located at the level of the bogs and marshes and indicate the beginning of the Boreal phase. In the Trans-Ural this warm, humid period is also characterized by the increase in broad-leaved trees, for the palynological studies at Istok II indicate the increase of elm (4 percent) and linden (16 percent).

The radiocarbon dates of 4630 ± 100 b.p. (Mo-390) and 4360 ± 200 b.p. (Mo-1), for the boundary horizons or "Grenz-horizonten" (Zeuner 1958:64) of the Ayat and Gorbunovo peat bogs respectively, fix the end of the Neolithic at about the middle of the third millennium B.C.

However, the climatic conditions of the Subboreal are arguable (see Zeuner 1958). Some view this period as essentially xerothermic and place the formation of its boundary horizon within that time span (Neyshtadt 1968; Predtechenskiy 1957). Others (e.g., Prokayev 1960) point to the appearance of extensive areas of wooded steppe in the south of the central Urals. According to this second view, the Subboreal consisted of a succession of humid and cool periods (Zubakov 1972:181). Archaeological data gathered over the years in the Trans-Ural suggest an extreme instability of Subboreal climate, and thus there could have existed successions of humid and dry phases (Starkov 1978:92).

Toward the end of the Neolithic and particularly during the Eneolithic there is a population movement into the far north of Western Siberia that is tied to the driest phase of the climatic optimum of the Atlantic and the Neolithic sites of the Arctic Trans-Ural: Chest-tyy-yag, Sortynya I, Bugrasyam-vad, and others date to this time (see Chernetsov and Moszyńska 1974, particularly chaps. 1 and 2). During the Early Subboreal a second wave of migration reached as far north as the Yamal Peninsula. Considering the normally marshy aspect of this part of Western Siberia, this migration would seem to have been possible only during a rather dry period, and it is also then that the formation of the middle cultural level at Gorbunovo takes place. This level is characterized by Early Bronze Age ceramics and is conventionally dated to the first half of the second millennium B.C.

As implied above, the Neolithic and Bronze Age sites of Western Siberia reflect a complex history of local population movements from the fourth to the second millennium B.C. The people who occupied the wooded steppe between the taiga and the steppe proper had ancient ties with the successors to the Mesolithic cultures of the grasslands and deserts of Central Asia who left sites characterized by geometric microlithic artifacts. In the Middle Neolithic of the wooded steppe there is naturally much in common with that of Central Asia, specifically with the people who represented the Kelteminar culture (see fig. 1). In general terms this is also true of the Trans-Uralian cultures. Some investigators even propose a separate "cultural-ethnic community," a large group of related tribes who at that time occupied the Cis-Ural region, the Urals, and the southern reaches of Western Siberia. Okladnikov (1968:104) thinks them the ancestors of the Ugrians, bordering on the west with the ancestors of Finnic groups of eastern Europe, and in the south with the early Iranian-speaking Indo-Europeans of Central Asia. Later, from this cultural-ethnic community, there develops the Early Bronze Age Afanasevo culture.

A second group of Neolithic peoples in the northern and eastern taiga of the Ob basin seems to be culturally closer to those of Soviet northeastern Europe in the upper Volga-Oka drainage and Karelia where sites contain the typical pit-comb ware, most obviously expressed in vessels with pointed bottoms and with comb ornamentation in zonal, straight-lined, geometric patterns (see, e.g., Molodin 1977).

In addition to these two zones of contact between Central Asia and northern Europe, there was a third one between the southern part of Western Siberia and the Yenisey and Angara basins to the east (see below).

Eastern Siberia

The territories of Eastern Siberia and extreme northeastern Asia were characterized during the Neolithic by a transition from the Mesolithic, which, among other things, resulted in the formation of cultures with net-impressed pottery (Michael 1958:12). In other regions of Siberia and the Soviet Far East, and in parts of Western Siberia, as well as in the Amur basin, the Early Neolithic was characterized by other types of ceramics.

Yakutia

Because of the presence of multilayered sites and a large series of radiocarbon determinations from Yakutia, it is here that a reliable chronology may be established and used as a standard for the dating of neighboring areas (see Mochanov 1969a, 1969b, 1969c, 1969d; Mochanov et al. 1970; Mochanov and Fedoseyeva 1975; Mochanov 1977).

The Early Neolithic culture of Yakutia, named the Syalakh by Mochanov, evolved out of the prepottery Mesolithic Sumnagin culture (figs. 2 and 3). The most expressive trait of the Syalakh is its pottery. The vessels are like an inverted mitre in profile, with a net-impressed surface. The slightly thickened rim is ornamented with a belt of pits, or in other cases a collar of clay applied to the upper part of the vessel and incised at regular intervals.

The stone artifacts include prismatic cores, knifelike blades, angle and side gravers, end scrapers, insert or side blades, and punches. There are also leaflike arrowheads on blades. All of these preserve the Mesolithic tradition. Innovations are expressed in the bilateral working of some of the tools and in the polishing of adzes and axes.

Uncorrected radiocarbon dates indicate a transition from the Mesolithic to the Early Neolithic in Yakutia at about 6000 b.p., with the Syalakh culture lasting about one thousand years.

On the Taymyr and Chukot (Chukchi) peninsulas, materials from Glubokoye I and Abylakh for Taymyr, Ust-Belaya for Chukotka (see fig. 8), agree typologically with the Syalakh culture of Yakutia. Unlike Khlobystin (1978), however, Mochanov (1969c) earlier dated Ust-Belaya to the Middle or Developed Neolithic, represented in Yakutia by the Belkachi culture (see below). In any event this correlation testifies to the wide extent of the Early Neolithic over the northernmost reaches of northeastern Asia.

In the Evenki nomadizing zone ("Evenkia") of the Early Neolithic, Tura I best exemplifies the material culture. It is however more akin to the Isakovo and Serovo cultures of the Angara basin than to the Syalakh.

In Yakutia the Belkachi culture characterizes the Middle Neolithic (Mochanov 1969a, Mochanov et al. 1970; Mochanov and Fedoseyeva 1975; see fig. 4). Uncalibrated radiocarbon dates bracket it between 5000 ± 100 b.p. and 3900 ± 100 b.p.

The pottery of the Belkachi culture is not only well represented at the type site but also at other sites in the Aldan and middle Lena basins such as Kullaty, Shestakovka, Kapchagay II, and Uolba (fig. 4). The ware is cord decorated and of three types: (1) egg-shaped with a straight, simple rim with perforations; (2) egg-shaped with a thickened, bulging, appliqué rim with incised or comb-impressed ornamentation; (3) egg-shaped with a thickened, flat appliqué rim with horizontal comb impressions (Mochanov 1969c:166). The lithic inventory is typical of the Middle Neolithic, with the artifacts bilaterally retouched and polished.

The Belkachi culture was not only very widespread but also influential in the formative processes of neighboring cultures. The Gromatukha culture of the Zeya basin apparently shows direct influence, since the headwaters of the Aldan and Zeya tributaries are very close (Mochanov 1969c:181; Okladnikov and Derevyanko 1977:8, and elsewhere). To the west, during the Early Neolithic, groups traveling eastward through the valleys of the Podkamenaya ("Stony") and Nizhnaya ("Lower") Tunguska rivers seem to have occupied the upper Vilyuy drainage. Their successors during the Middle Neolithic were much influenced from the east as shown by Belkachi ceramics and stone implements (Mochanov 1969c:182). The Belkachi culture also strongly affected the Chukot Peninsula. At such sites as Ust-Belaya and Chikayevo and others in the Anadyr basin, many artifacts could not be traced to local "roots" but had full analogies in the Middle Neolithic of Yakutia. The typical corded ware was also present, suggesting not merely contact but also direct occupation by Belkachi culture-bearing people.

In Yakutia the Late Neolithic is represented by the Ymyyakhtakh culture (fig. 5), conventionally radiocarbon-dated as 3900 ± 100 b.p. to 3100 ± 100 b.p.

The characteristic pottery of this period has admixtures of animal hair or fish scales in the clay. It is egg-shaped or globular. Its surface, worked with an appropriately prepared paddle, has ribbed or wafflelike impressions, the latter sometimes described as "pseudo-textile" (Michael 1958:85), and thus differs radically from the corded ware of the Middle Neolithic.

These Ymyyakhtakh ceramics occur over the entire area of Yakutia, in the Evenki nomadizing zone, the Taymyr and Chukot peninsulas (see fig. 5), and, analogous pottery appears on both the western and eastern shores of Lake Baykal.

The finishing of stone artifacts reaches new heights. The raw materials are more diversified and include quartzite, slate, nephrite, flint, chalcedony, diabase, sandstone, and others. There are single and double prismatic cores, blades, and flakes. Elongated triangular arrowheads with a straight or notched base are frequent and have a fine bilateral retouch. Except for their size, spearheads have the same form and workmanship. Knives are oval with an almond-shaped cross section and the end scrapers are small, trapezoidal, or triangular with fine retouching over the entire surface.

As compared with the Belkachi culture there is a sharp decrease in tools made from blades. Lateral and angle burins on blades are rare; they are replaced by multifaced ones with corelike or retouched handles. Most of the blades, used primarily as inserts, are unretouched.

Small rectangular adzes and miniature elongated triangular chisels hexagonal in cross section represent the polished tools of slate and nephrite. Perforated nephrite discs served as ornaments, while notched pebbles of diabase and quartzite were net weights.

Generally the stone tools are less diverse than in the Belkachi culture, explainable perhaps by the slow but steadily increasing appearance, toward the end of the era, of bronze tools with which the groups to the south of Yakutia were already familiar. The importation of such bronze tools must have influenced the manufacture of certain lithic ones, which in specific cases became less common or disappeared from use.

The Lake Baykal Region

In the late 1940s Okladnikov (1950) developed the periodization of the Neolithic cultures of the Angara basin and the Cis-Baykal. Michael (1958) has consolidated and interpreted these early works in English.

Geographically, in contrast with the Yakut Neolithic which is concentrated in the center of Eastern Siberia, the Angara basin cultures were subject to influences from Western Siberia.

Although primarily concerned with the Neolithic and Bronze Ages of the Angara basin, Okladnikov briefly examined both the predecessors and successors to these periods, recognizing nine sequential stages for the area: (1) The Late Paleolithic-Mesolithic; (2) the aceramic Khina; (3) the Early Neolithic Isakovo; (4) the Serovo; (5) the Middle Neolithic Kitoy; (6) the Glazkovo, during which the first metal artifacts appear; (7) the Shivera, which witnesses the development of *local* copper and bronze metallurgy; (8) the fully developed Bronze Age; and (9) the Early Iron Age. (For a discussion of the chronology for this periodization, see Michael 1958:25–33 and his table 3.)

Okladnikov's periodization was based on a comparative study of grave goods from mound burials. Since his pioneer work, some of these grave goods have been correlated with multilayered habitation sites such as Gorelyy Les in the Angara basin and Ulan-Khada and Iterkhey on Lake Baykal. This engendered a challenge of Okladnikov's periodization (see below).

The Isakovo pots differ from those of Syalakh in that they are neither ornamented nor embellished with applied fillets or ridges. The vessels from the burials have a paraboloid form, although at Ulan-Khada, contemporary ones probably had a more complex profile, the recovered sherds suggesting a slightly constricted neck. Stone artifacts associated with Isakovo ceramics are usually made from knifelike blades, a fact not previously evident from grave goods alone.

In his early works, Okladnikov (1950) dated the Isakovo phase to the fourth millennium B.C. On the basis of the contemporary Syalakh culture, this would seem borne out by the *uncorrected* radiocarbon dates for the latter. This problem is discussed later in this chapter with the application of correction factors to the radiocarbon dates.

Today, the periodization of the Angara basin–Lake Baykal region Neolithic is open, for apparently there has not been a full correlation of the burial mounds, on which the earlier periodization was based, with materials from the multilayered habitation sites, many of which were excavated relatively recently. As seen above, Okladnikov's sequence was Isakovo-Serovo-Kitoy-Glazkovo. Gerasimov (1955) countered with a different sequence: Kitoy-Serovo-Glazkovo, in which Okladnikov's Isakovo and Serovo were presented as one stage, but the scheme has been rejected (see Okladnikov 1976:149ff.). Khlobystin (1965, 1969, 1978) views Kitoy not as a stage in the development of the Cis-Baykal Neolithic, but as an independent, local culture, participating with the Serovo in the formation of the Eneolithic Glazkovo culture. Thus his sequence is the prepottery Khina, Serovo (combined later with Kitoy), followed by Glazkovo.

In evaluating the role of the Kitoy, Khlobystin writes:

> To the Kitoy Culture was assigned the distinctive pottery with cord impressions, with a rim most often thickened with a triangular in cross-section appliqué, with small perforations at the very edge. Such pottery is decorated with lines made with the stab-and-drag technique, and rarely, with comb impressions. It was represented in Layer IX of Ulan-Khada and lay between layers with net-impressed and early Glazkovo ceramics. . . . I shall call it pottery of the Posolsk type since it was found in greatest quantity in sites near Posolsk, on [the southeastern shore of] Lake Baykal. (Khlobystin 1978:96; also see Khlobystin 1969 for a more detailed description)

Khlobystin's claim that the Kitoy remains were a separate ethnocultural phenomenon and not a stage in the evolutionary scheme of the Cis-Baykal Neolithic received support from an analysis of the paleoanthropological materials. Studies of the skulls by Mamonova (1973) indicate that the Kitoy population was of a quite different physical type from the Serovo and Glazkovo peoples, who are similar to each other. Mamonova also pointed out that mixing between the Kitoy and Glazkovo types was minimal.

Reexamining old materials and comparing them with those recently acquired have to some degree changed the interpretation of the history of cultural developments in the south of Eastern Siberia.

When Vitkovskiy excavated burial number 1 of the Kitoy mound in 1881, he found a vessel, mitrelike in form, with impressions of a large-eyed net on its surface. (For details see Michael 1958:25ff.) Another net-impressed vessel was found by Okladnikov in 1972 when he excavated a Kitoy burial on Cape Burkham of Olkhon Island in Lake Baykal. The burial was dated to 5720 ± 50 b.p. (Le-1076), which suggests that the Kitoy culture began in the Early Neolithic.

Khlobystin claims that a direct relationship between the Serovo and Glazkovo is reflected in the general agreement of their lithic and bone inventories, and also in their net-impressed pottery. Further evolution of Serovo ceramics results in a smooth-walled pot ornamented with comb impressions. Khlobystin mentions a radiocarbon date for Serovo burial number 2 (Khlobystin 1978:97) as 3990 ± 80 b.p. (Le-513), although in his definitive and concluding work of 1976, Okladnikov did not mention it. Khlobystin sees this date as confirming the Serovo-Glazkovo relationship and also takes as supporting evidence the concurrence of physical type mentioned above.

The ethnocultural processes in the Angara-Baykal region were probably much more complex than hitherto supposed; this is suggested in part by the widespread occurrence of Posolsk ceramics over the region. In addition Savelev and Medvedev (1973:60) have isolated a specific Ust-Belaya type of pottery, which Khlobystin recognizes as early Glazkovo on the basis of Ulan-Khada materials.

Khlobystin correlates his Posolsk pottery with that of Belkachi despite its difference in profile by a thickened rim and more stab-and-drag linear ornamentation (for illustrations see Savelev and Medvedev 1973:61–62). He dates it by uncorrected Belkachi radiocarbon dates to the third millennium b.c., that is, coeval with the late Serovo burial. As for the origin or origins of the Posolsk and Ust-Belaya pottery ornamentation, he sees considerable influence of the Baykit culture, the type site of which is located on the Nizhnaya Tunguska River, penetrating to the east from Western Siberia. The ornamentation of the Baykit pottery is like that of the Neolithic pottery of

the Trans-Ural. Analogous ware from a site near the conjunction of the Polovinka and Pyasina rivers on the Taymyr Peninsula was dated by a sample from the cultural level to 4060 ± 120 b.p. (Le-1017), agreeing with Andreyev's dating of the Baykit pottery to the third millennium B.C. (Andreyev and Fomin 1964:4, and fig. 27).

A recent (November 1982) publication by A. K. Konopatskiy takes up anew the question of succession of Neolithic phases. The work contains enough additional information and radiocarbon dates to warrant supplementing and modifying some of the conclusions arrived at earlier in this section.

Konopatskiy's work deals with the early cultures of Lake Baykal and emphasizes those of Olkhon Island and the nearby shore of the mainland. These areas contain a number of Paleolithic, Neolithic, Bronze Age, and Iron Age sites that have been discovered and excavated or examined in the 1970s.

To the Neolithic belong the habitation sites of Ubugun, Elgen (Ilige), Ivanov vzvoz ("rise"), Vostochnyy Kurkut Bay, and Shamanskiy Cape. There are also ritual interments of elk bones at Tudugu, the Kulgana burial, and burial mounds at Khoturuk and Shamanskiy Cape (see fig. 6).

Earlier we have reviewed the various suggestions for the periodization of the Lake Baykal–Angara basin area and have concluded that the question of periodization is still open. Konopatskiy's new data tend to tighten the periodization, although there are some problems (see below).

Of the thirty-five radiocarbon dates published by Konopatskiy, twenty-nine pertain to stages of the Neolithic and Bronze ages although he questions five of the latter (see table 1). The Bronze Age dates are included for the purpose of comparison of the various stages of cultures of the Cis-Baykal (table 2) and more specifically for the comparison of the Angara basin, Olkhon, and upper Lena groups of sites (table 3).

In perusing the tables, one becomes aware that all of the dates emanating from the SOAN (Siberian Branch of the Academy of Sciences) laboratory are reckoned from A.D. 1970 rather than A.D. 1950, the latter commonly accepted in the West. Also, the USGS-109 date is so treated, whereas Le- and GIN- dates refer to A.D. 1950.

These new dates certainly throw additional light on the historical processes that took place in the Cis-Baykal area, including the temporal relationships.

Khlobystin (1978:96) thinks that corded ware may have been present in the southern area earlier than in Yakutia. At the time the only radiocarbon dates seemingly associated with this early phase of the Neolithic were those from layers VII and VI of Gorelyy Les. Based on a 5568 half-life they were 8444 ± 124 b.p. (Ri-51) and 6695 ± 150 b.p. (Ri-50) respectively (Savelev and Goryunova 1974; Veksler and Putans 1974). At the time these dates were rejected as too early, but recently published dates from Olkhon Island and nearby mainland shores of Lake Baykal seem to confirm the greater antiquity of the Neolithic in the very south of Eastern Siberia. These dates are from the fifth and fourth cultural levels respectively of the multilayered site of Sagan-Zaba and place them at 8775 ± 40 b.p. (SOAN-1574) and 7630 ± 45 b.p. (SOAN-1573).

Acceptance of the Gorelyy Les and Sagan-Zaba dates would indicate a very early start of the nonagricultural Neolithic in the Cis-Baykal region, as early in fact as the Neolithic of the southwestern European Russian Plain or the Trans-Caucasus (see Dolukhanov 1982, particularly p. 345). It should be noted that in his comparison of Neolithic stages (table 2) and regions (table 3), Konopatskiy does not utilize these four dates, thus implying that they are not acceptable to him. Obviously more research will have to be done if the suggested greater antiquity of the Baykal Neolithic is to be supported.

In a temporal and areal comparison of the Cis-Baykal cultures, in which Konopatskiy utilizes sixteen of the radiocarbon dates, the principal divergent one seems to be SOAN-1665, which comes from a Kitoy complex. The date 4380 ± 15 b.p. overlaps practically all of the Serovo dates and almost reaches the earliest Glazkovo date. Konopatskiy suggests that the charcoal sample that came from a Kitoy site flooded by reservoir water for several decades prior to its excavation may have been affected by the percolating water.

Another problem of a lesser degree is posed by the juxtaposition of SOAN-790 and Le-1076. Both came from the same half-rotted planks covering the same Olkhon Island Kitoy burial. Konopatskiy assigns the divergence to different techniques employed by the two laboratories. I would add that the difference could be caused or at least enhanced by the planks being fashioned from dendrochronologically different parts of trees. A plank fashioned from the outer part of a tree trunk should date younger than one made from wood near the pith of an old tree, and, as is known, subarctic conifers grow very slowly and often contain several hundred tree rings.

The Neolithic cultures of the Yenisey, typified by ceramics with comb-impressed patterns, similar to those of the Western Siberian Neolithic, may be dated to the second half of the third–beginning of the second millennium B.C. These established themselves on territory previously occupied by cultures of Eastern Siberian origin or which at least were strongly influenced by them. The multilayered site at Kazachka where Western Siberian Neolithic ceramics lay above net-impressed ones (Savelev et al. 1976) supports this. At this time, the basins of the two Tunguska rivers were a contact zone in which were located the cultures of Yakutia, the Angara basin, and

Western Siberia. The latter two were much more successful in leaving their imprint.

The developed Middle Neolithic of the Taymyr Peninsula contained two other types of ceramics beside the Baykit ones mentioned above: the Belkachi at Khatanga in the east of the Taymyr Peninsula, and net-impressed with a thickened rim at such sites as Maymekhe I and II. By analogy with the Belkachi culture, these ceramics date to the second millennium B.C. (Khlobystin 1975).

The Belkachi culture also penetrated from Yakutia to the Chukot Peninsula where there are sites with corded ware. However, the ceramics may not have reached this locality until the beginning of the Bronze Age. For instance, in an Ust-Belaya (fig. 6) cemetery burial—not to be confused with the Ust-Belaya site in the Angara basin—a bronze graver and needle accompanied the corded ware. A radiocarbon date of 2680 ± 95 B.P. (LE-187) was obtained from the upper level in which the artifacts were found.

In the middle Lena and Aldan basins, sites assignable to the Late Neolithic Ymyyakhtakh culture appear at the beginning of the second millennium B.C. However, the penetration of this culture into the Evenki nomadizing zone and the Arctic takes place only toward the end of the second millennium B.C., when the manufacture of bronze articles was practiced in *most* of Eastern Siberia. At the site of Abylakh I on the Taymyr Peninsula, which by ceramic and lithic content belongs to the Ymyyakhtakh culture, a radiocarbon sample associated with a bronze melting site in the upper cultural level yielded a date of 3100 ± 60 b.p. (LE-790). Traces of bronze melting occur in lower Lena sites and some Yakutian ones, all associated with waffle-impressed pottery. In some Ymyyakhtakh burials there are copper objects, and thus one cannot classify the Ymyyakhtakh culture as Neolithic in its entirety but must regard its final stages as introductory to the Bronze Age. In this connection the northern Siberian sites with waffle ceramics are datable to the middle of the first millennium B.C. and are associated with quite different cultures (Khlobystin 1978:98).

Waffle-impressed ceramics are present in Chukot Peninsula sites, for instance, Chirovo Lake, which has a radiocarbon date of 2800 ± 100 b.p. But here, in the extreme northeast of Asia, because of no workable copper deposits, the Neolithic Age persisted in some sites until about 500 B.C.

In the Cis-Baykal area the earliest copper objects come from the Glazkovo culture. The date of a charcoal sample from Level VII of Ulan-Khada, obtained during the 1963 excavations, was 3660 ± 60 b.p. (LE-883), which fixes the initial stages of the Glazkovo, although from ceramics in lower levels, the initial Glazkovo may have belonged to the Neolithic. The radiocarbon date, however, agrees with Okladnikov's much earlier dating (Okladnikov 1950; Michael 1958). The more recently acquired radiocarbon dates, which were published by Konopatskiy (1982), place the beginning of the Glazkovo some four hundred years earlier (see table 3).

Thus in the nonagricultural Neolithic of Eastern Siberia, including the Evenki nomadizing zone, we have the following periodization based on Soviet sources and supported by uncorrected, 5568 half-life radiocarbon dates:

Stage	Dating (b.p.)	Cultures
Early Neolithic	6500–5200	Isakovo, Syalakh, Kitoy
Middle Neolithic	5200–4200	Serovo, Kitoy(?), Belkachi, Posolsk, Baykit, Western Siberian comb-impressed, Maymekhe
Late Neolithic	4200–3400 to 3200	Early Glazkovo, early Ymyyakhtakh

Insofar as present information can take us, in the Trans-Baykal there are analogies to the Cis-Baykal and to Yakutia expressed in the early Neolithic Muklin, the Middle Neolithic Chidansk, and the Late Neolithic Budulansk cultures.

The Soviet Far East

The southern part of the Soviet Far East consists mainly of the two large areas of Khabarovsk *kray* and Primorskiy *kray* (Primorye) and the two smaller Amur *oblast* and Sakhalin *oblast* which still are of considerable size. These four administrative territories comprise somewhat less than 1.5 million km².

The Amur Basin

Until very recent times the archaeology of the middle Amur basin was limited and of no great extent. The first systematic investigations of the Amur and of the Maritime Province (Primorye) began in the mid-1950s. These resulted in a number of monographs mostly dealing with the Primorye (Okladnikov 1959, 1963a, 1965; Shavkunov 1968; Andreyeva 1970; Okladnikov and Derevyanko 1973).

Over the past twenty-five years further work in the Amur basin and the Primorye has changed the concepts about the economy and type of settlement of the Neolithic population. Whereas in Eastern Siberia one encounters a nomadic or seminomadic population, living in light portable dwellings, the fishing peoples of the Soviet Far East had adopted solid semisubterranean buildings associated with fish-drying sheds and storage rooms and, for the summer, small houses on piles. Such typical complexes were discovered at Suchu on the Amur, in the Rudnaya River valley in the Primorye, and in other localities. This settled life affected the social organization, for the construction of the houses implies close cooperation of large

groups. The settled life also affected art, as appearing in the complex and expressive pottery ornamentation. In general, the ornamental style of the Neolithic peoples of the Amur tended toward curvilinearity and ribbon patterns.

The first general works on the origins of this unusual culture proposed vigorous contacts with northern and northeastern China and the Japanese Islands. Since these were not unidirectional, the influence of the Amur peoples was also reflected in the culture of the donors (Okladnikov 1954:246).

Contact with cultures south of the Primorye appears in the Paleolithic, at sites such as Osinovka and on the Peschaniy and De Fries peninsulas. At Osinovka, Okladnikov traces the method of manufacture and the form of chopping tools to the Paleolithic of China and even farther south to Indo-China and Burma (Okladnikov 1958:109–10).

Fieldwork in the Amur basin resulted in a threefold division of diverse Neolithic cultures: (1) In the upper Amur basin is an extension of the Trans-Baykal Neolithic (Okladnikov 1962:5–6, 1964:112–80). (2) On the middle Amur are four Neolithic cultures identified below and including the Novopetrovka Blade culture which is analogous to that of the cemetery site near Angangxi in Dongbei (Manchuria). (3) The cultures of the lower Amur are typified by such sites as Suchu I, Kondon, and Sheremetyevo on the Ussuri River (see below).

In the Primorye the Neolithic cultures developed in their own way. The Early Neolithic is typified by the middle cultural level at Osinovka which contained pottery with curvilinear or spiral-ribbon and comb-impressed vertical zigzag ornamentation of the so-called Amur weave. The following stage is represented by habitation sites of the Kirovskoye type, and the final one by sites like Gladkaya I, which contains pottery with a meandering pattern and obsidian tools.

There are indications that in the Amur basin and the Primorye the Neolithic peoples were not simple settled fishers and hunters. The presence of querns and hoes may indicate incipient agriculture (Okladnikov 1962:7).

The excavations of 1961–65 enabled an updating of the periodization and chronology of the middle Amur basin (Okladnikov 1966:32–41).

The distinctive Gromatukha culture is assignable to the Early Neolithic of the basin. Among its stone implements, adzelike tools made from knapped river pebbles predominate. A similar technique of preparation is known to the southeast of the Cis-Baykal in northern Mongolia, and in a Mesolithic site near Khabarovsk to the east. Together with this old technique is a new one—the removal of knifelike blades from prismatic cores and of microblades from end-scraper-like cores. Despite these new elements, tools made from pebbles and special blanks from which large, leaflike blades and dart heads were made, were dominant.

The second distinctive culture, the Novopetrovka, was characterized by an accomplished technique of working lamellar cores and a widespread utilization of the knife-like lamellae for making work tools such as knives, punches, arrowheads, gravers, and scrapers. Derevyanko (1965, 1969, 1970b) first described the Novopetrovka culture. The type site near the village of Novopetrovka yielded several dozen cores and hundreds of lamellar blades. Some of the cores closely resemble Upper Paleolithic wedge-shaped ones, worked on one side only. Others are of the so-called Gobi type, with one edge shaped by a row of parallel, narrow facets, with the other side reduced to a wide cutting edge. In subsequent years, many Gobi cores have been found in middle Amur sites and in the extreme of northeast Asia generally, indicating widespread contacts between Mesolithic and, later, Neolithic peoples. The presence of Gobi cores in Neolithic cultures is regarded as a Mesolithic survival or tradition. Since no pottery was found at Novopetrovka during the early excavations, Derevyanko labeled it Mesolithic (Derevyanko 1965:137), but in the 1965–66 excavations of Novopetrovka II, pottery was found.

From the dune site of Sergeyevka comes another manifestation of the Early Neolithic. In addition to the stone implements in the lower of two cultural levels, comprised of small lamellar blades, insert blades, prismatic cores, unilaterally flaked adzes, and large sidescrapers, was a characteristically thin-walled pottery with paddle "pseudo-textile" impressions. The upper cultural level revealed more advanced stone working with fine bilateral retouching and pottery decorated with oblique rows of comb-punctate design similar to that from the Angara-Baykal area to the northwest.

Since the finds in the upper cultural level at Sergeyevka are analogous to those of Gromatukha on the Zeya River, we see the development of three horizons: the Mesolithic (Novopetrovka I) and two sequential Early Neolithic ones, the first represented by Novopetrovka II and the lower cultural level at Sergeyevka, the second by the upper level at Sergeyevka and by Gromatukha.

The other two cultures of the middle Amur are Late Neolithic. These are the Osinovo Lake or Voykovo culture and the Lower Amur culture , so named because it was thoroughly influenced from that direction. In these cultures the knifelike blades disappear, but the bilateral working of knives, insert blades, and arrowheads prevails.

The discovery and excavation of the multilayered site near Voznesenovka in the lower Amur basin played an important role in establishing the Neolithic periodization and chronology of that area. The two lower horizons represent the Early Neolithic. The stone tools are characterized by bilateral creeping retouch. Two types of ceramics are present: (1) pottery with a graceful stamped pattern, often represented by overlapping triangles, or a pattern made with a paddle tightly entwined with cording (this ware is often raspberry in color and burnished), and (2) straight-walled, truncated cone-shaped pots with a principal ornamentation of various combinations of comb impressions. The contents of these two lower levels at Voznesenovka have analogies in the habitation sites of Malyshevo and the Amur Sanatarium site in Khabarovsk. Thus, this cultural-chronological Early Neolithic stage has been named the Malyshevo culture (Okladnikov 1963a).

Ceramics with stamped rhombic ornamentation forming the "Amur weave" typify the Middle Neolithic of the lower Amur. The second level at Voznesenovka also yielded miniature rings of white, opaque nephrite, arrowheads beautifully finished with bilateral retouch, and a well-fired clay pear-shaped rattle ornamented with a pitted pattern and containing small stones inside. This complex is close to that of the habitation site near the village of Kondon, 120 km north of Komsomolsk-on-Amur, hence the Middle Neolithic Kondon culture, dated at Kondon to 4520 ± 25 b.p.

The third or Late Neolithic level of Voznesenovka contained pottery ornamented with vertical zigzags fashioned with comb punctates or perhaps a roulette and also sherds with spiral ornamentation. Here too belong the remarkable "masks" fashioned on shallow-profiled slipped vessels, and polished slate tools gradually replace bilaterally retouched ones (Okladnikov and Derevyanko 1977:23–26 passim).

On the basis of his survey of sites of the lower Amur, particularly those at Kazakevichevo near the mouth of the Ussuri, Larichev (1961) suggested that the lower Amur Neolithic began at 3100–2900 B.C. and ended in the second millennium B.C.

Kamchatka

The Early Neolithic in Kamchatka appears toward the end of the postglacial climatic optimum and is well represented in the burials and fire pits of Layer IV of the much-studied Ushki sites (fig. 7, sites numbered 1–4), as well as those on the west coast of Kamchatka (fig. 7). Comparative palynological studies of Layer IV and Layers V–VIII of Ushki I indicate a greater extent and density of forests for the Layer IV period (Shilo, Dikov, and Lozhkin 1967).

Apparently the Early Neolithic culture of Kamchatka preserved only weakly some of the Paleolithic-Mesolithic traditions. Prismatic cores, some with one striking platform, were seldom used, and blades, when struck from them, were used mostly unretouched. Arrowheads are broader, the narrow ones having gone out of use. Scrapers on broad blades continue, as do end scrapers on flakes. The most obvious loss then was the working of wedge-shaped cores, their place taken by various types of prismatic- and cone-shaped ones. Often the knifelike blades struck from them are larger than before. The form is strongly geometric, and sometimes all the edges are retouched. Macroblades prevail over microblades. Among the innovations is a series of arrowheads, rhomboid in cross section, with a triangular-in-outline tang and oblique retouch.

This complex of artifacts has no equivalents elsewhere in northeastern Asia, although its individual elements are widespread in Asia and even reach into the Arctic regions of North America (Dikov 1979:110).

The closest analogies to the Ushki Early Neolithic complex are found in Chukotka in the Amguema River valley at Site 3 (fig. 7, no. 80). Here conical cores and arrowheads with rhomboid cross section were found. The aceramic Site 3 is probably the oldest in the Amguema Valley.

On the basis of analogies in Layer VIII of the Aldan basin site of Belkachi I (dated 6000–5000 B.C.) to the unpolished scraperlike adzes, prismatic cores, a whole series of conical cores including pencil ones worked on all sides or unilaterally, knifelike blades with or without retouched edges, from Layer IV of Ushki II, Mochanov suggested that the Mesolithic Sumnagin culture (see fig. 2) had spread eastward to Kamchatka (Mochanov 1969c:124ff. and tables 1, 3, 10, 12). However as distinct from the Sumnagin culture, the Ushki complex contains bifacially worked knives and arrowheads, and these elements seem more probably derived from the relatively recently uncovered Maltan complex in the upper Kolyma basin (Dikov 1979:110). Also, the dating of the Ushki complex in Layer IV, originally estimated by Dikov (1977:123–24) as between 4000–3000B.C., is closer to that of Maltan than Sumnagin. Subsequently, the radiocarbon date of Ushki Layer IV of 4200 ± 100 B.C. (MAG-132) confirmed Dikov's estimate. He notes further that few elements in the Ushki Late Mesolithic or Early Neolithic complex were derived from the preceding local Paleolithic.

The contents of Layer IV of Ushki I and II as described above may be termed the First Ushki Neolithic culture of the area, and Layer III of these sites the Second Ushki Neolithic (Dikov 1979:113).

Although there is considerable likeness between the contents of Layers IV and III among small and very large knifelike blades, sometimes also very long blades with retouched edges, leaflike blades worked bifacially, and gravers on knifelike blades occur. Thus the rest of the

lithic inventory of Layer III must be regarded as new, possibly endogenous in small part, like the tanged blade points, but is most probably exogenous (Dikov 1979:115).

Dikov reviews in some detail analogies with the innovations in Layer III with regard to the chronology of comparable sites and cultures, giving particular attention to tanged and tangless arrowheads that are triangular in cross section or that are "filelike." He sees the tanged ones as endogenous since there are no analogies in nearby regions. Triangular cross-sectioned end points range far to the west into northern Scandinavia, throughout the northern tier of Siberia, including Chukotka, and to the south as far as Japan (Dikov 1979:115–18).

From his survey Dikov concludes that the most direct contacts during the Second Ushki Neolithic culture were with Chukotka and Yakutia to the north, and he points out the lively activity of movement and exchange that took place over the subpolar zones of the Old World.

Previous to his 1979 survey of the pertinent literature, Dikov (1977:242) had dated the Second Ushki Neolithic culture to the beginning of the second millennium B.C. on basis of a sample from nearby Klyuchi 3 (no. 13 on fig. 7) of 3875 ± 350 b.p. (MAG-4).

At approximately 2000 B.C., toward the end of the warm period, the Neolithic of Kamchatka takes on a fully developed aspect. Not only do ceramics and polished axes appear but also an assortment of flat, thinly retouched knives, scrapers, arrowheads, and spearheads. Dikov recognizes two regional Middle Neolithic cultures on the peninsula: the South Kamchatka and the Central Kamchatka ones, the former preceding the latter (Dikov 1979:120). However, since the cultural complexes of sites in the two regions are basically similar, he unites them as the Tarya culture, after a well-known site on the Tarya Peninsula near Petro-Pavlovsk Kamchatskiy, but as having a southern variant (see fig. 7).

Despite local variations, viewing the contents of the Tarya culture as a whole, it is one of the representative cultures of Kamchatka and, genetically speaking, one that may be divided into two uneven parts: (1) artifacts representing a continuation of earlier, local Kamchatka types, and (2) artifacts making their first appearance during the Middle Neolithic of Kamchatka. The overwhelming majority of artifacts belongs to the second group and includes retouched insert blades that are sometimes only partially retouched, and triangular-shaped straight-based, bifacially retouched knives, flake knives not fully retouched, and also polished knives of argillaceous slate.

There are many new forms of end scrapers and sidescrapers. Some of the former, with or without tangs, are on curved or straight blades. There are various combinations of scraper cutters, scraper punches, pear-shaped or trapezoidal scrapers bifacially worked, sidescrapers on flakes, large massive sidescrapers, notched spoke-shaves on knifelike lamellae, and a massive scraperlike polisher.

Projectile points are quite numerous and varied: bilaterally retouched leaf-shaped arrowpoints, spearpoints, and dart points, tanged or triangular either with a straight base or curved one. Only a few projectile points on retouched flakes have been found.

There are new types of gravers: angle gravers on blades or flakes, center gravers, lateral gravers with a retouched handle, and corelike gravers. Punches also have retouched handles.

The adzes of the Tarya culture are altogether new. Most characteristic are the polished, unilaterally convex ones in the form of an elongated triangle with a subtriangular cross section, although they also occur in a shortened and broader form and are sometimes irregular in outline. Partially polished adzes, also triangular in form and with both wide surfaces convex, are frequent. Polished adzes also occur in more or less rectangular form, slightly narrowing toward the heel; rarely are they rectangular in cross section. Unpolished adzes are rare.

Of final importance are the ceramics, although not numerous in Tarya sites, and querns. Space restrictions do not allow for illustrations of these artifacts. However, Dikov describes and comparatively illustrates stone artifacts from Kamchatka, Chukotka, and the northern shores of the Okhotsk Sea (Dikov 1979:291–325), which the interested reader can consult.

After extensive comparison and correlation of several of the key artifacts in the Tarya culture, comparisons that include the Ust-Belaya culture of Chukotka (see below), the Sakhalin culture (Kozyreva 1967), the Kurile Islands, the Cis-Baykal, the Yakutian Belkachi culture, and the Primorye, Dikov (1979:125–26) concludes that they fit into the chronological frame of the second and first millennia B.C. There are several radiocarbon dates that confirm this estimate. At Elizovo (no. 42 on fig. 7) a charcoal sample yielded 3900 ± 100 b.p. (GIN-183), and at Kultuk-Ushki III (no. 5) there were three dates from samples of a troughlike wooden vessel: 2070 ± 190 b.p. (Mo-354), 2160 ± 290 b.p. (MAG-5), and 2440 ± 80 b.p. (RUL-607). The Elizovo date points to the earlier onset of the southern Kamchatka variant of the Tarya culture.

Dikov (1977:242) also lists several additional dates for the southern variant: the lower cultural level at Mishenaya (fig. 7, no. 43) with 2160 ± 92 b.p. (MAG-32), Kirpichnaya III (no. 44) with 2390 ± 70 b.p. (MAG-103), and Avacha (no. 46) with 2990 ± 100 b.p. (Kril-252).

It seems obvious then that the Tarya culture was exposed to vigorous exchange with north and south, with the stronger influence apparently from the north.

Chukotka

As in Kamchatka the oldest traces of post-Paleolithic man in Chukotka date to the Mesolithic or Early Neolithic, that is, to the period of postglacial warming. Also, they occur in the interior of the large peninsula rather than on its shores. Prior to this, the very few manifestations of Paleolithic man in Chukotka are in the Inaskvaam River valley, and possibly at Chikayevo in southern Chukotka (Dikov and Kolyasnikov 1979). No doubt more will appear, for the ice-free corridor of Chukotka must have been a major avenue of Paleolithic man's approach to northern North America, where several Upper Paleolithic sites have already been discovered. The earliest Holocene finds lie in the lowlands of the Anadyr River on the Krasnoye Lake spits and on Osinovskaya spit (fig. 7, nos. 63, 68–70), and also on the shore of Lake Tytyl in the headwaters of the Malyy Anyuy River, and on a hillock near Ust-Belaya (fig. 7, no. 72).

Some of these sites can be correlated with dated sites elsewhere in extreme northeastern Asia. For instance, the conical and prismatic cores and broad scrapers from Tytyl I are like those from the Mesolithic layer at Maltan (fig. 7, no. 170), the radiocarbon date of which is 7490 ± 70 b.p. (MAG-183). The end scraper on a broad flake from Tytyl II correlates with those from the Mesolithic Sumnagin culture of Yakutia (q.v.), as do the Ust-Belaya partially retouched lamellar arrowheads (Mochanov 1977:246–48; see fig. 8).

Another Chukotka Late Mesolithic or Early Neolithic site without pottery is located near Lake Iunigytkhyn (Dikov and Katenin 1979)—its lithic content is like that of similar dated sites.

The contents of the "102 km" site on the Amguema River tract (fig. 7, no. 80) correlate well with the aceramic Level IV of Ushki I in the Kamchatka River valley, which has been dated to 6150 ± 100 b.p. (MAG-132). The objects from the cache and site on Lake Elgygytgyn are somewhat later.

The dates of the interior sites of the Chukot peninsula and of those in other parts of the Asiatic Arctic, Alaska, and Greenland with its pre-Eskimo Sarkak culture suggest that during the fourth and third millennia B.C. hunters of herd animals occupied this region, and that most hunting groups, whose stone-working techniques largely reflect the Mesolithic, did not use ceramics (Dikov 1979:133).

There are a few fragments of thin-walled net-impressed pottery among the earliest remains of the mixed Neolithic–Bronze Age site of Ust-Belaya (fig. 7, no. 72) and in a burial at this site with charcoal dates of 2860 ± 95 b.p. (RUL-187) and 2920 ± 95 b.p. (Kril-244). The introduction of the later corded ware is seen near Kameshki (site no. 58). As described above, net-impressed pottery appears in the Aldan Valley during the fourth millennium B.C., corded ware in the third (Mochanov et al. 1970). From the dates given above for the presence of pottery in Chukotka, the time lag is obvious, like the similar delay in the Cis-Baykal where the net-impressed pottery of the Serovo culture also dates to the third millennium B.C. The lithic content of the Chukotka sites shows a considerable influence of Yakutia on the Neolithic of Chukotka, particularly during the second millennium and the beginning of the first millennium B.C. It is during this period that we see the development of both the Northern Chukot Middle Neolithic and the already mentioned Ust-Belaya culture, which to a high degree are similar and have the same economic basis.

The earliest remains of the characteristic hunting-fishing Northern Chukot Neolithic culture were discovered in the tundras near the Arctic Ocean. Dikov assigns to this culture several sites, some already mentioned in describing the spread of the Belkachi culture of Yakutia. These are the Chirovaya Lake sites (fig. 7, no. 51), the Yakitikiveyem River site (no. 186), the Ayon Island sites (nos. 160–64), the Amguema River sites (nos. 79 and 81), and those on Lake Ekityki (no. 185). In 1977 two additional sites were discovered on the shores of Lake Tytyl in the headwaters of the Malyy Anyuy River (IV on fig. 7). Several characteristics unite these sites, particularly arrowheads that are often large and long, worked on both sides, with one side more convex than the other or triangular in cross section and also flat arrowheads with rounded point and tanged base. The ceramics are smooth-walled, made of clay mixed with deer hair, the outside covered with pseudotextile impressions similar to the Late Neolithic pots of Yakutia.

The enumerated campsites were geographically oriented to the seasonal migrations of deer. They were used repeatedly and sometimes were sites of burials as at the Ekiatap River junction with the Amguema (fig. 7, no. 95) or of permanent kiln-ovens for smoking fish and with pits for the storage of meat, as at Chirovaya (no. 51).

Chirovaya, a principal site of the Northern Chukot Neolithic, was dated by Okladnikov (1953) to the end of the second–beginning of the first millennium B.C. However, the abundant new finds at this locality allow a fuller comparison with other cultures, particularly those of Yakutia, and therewith adjust its dating to the beginning of the second millennium B.C. This also applies to the Amguema sites (nos. 79 and 81), although one of them yielded an aberrant date of 6665 ± 100 b.p. (GIN-182). The Chirovaya date of 2800 ± 100 b.p. establishes the upper limit for the culture.

In the early 1950s, Okladnikov thought that Chirovaya represented the lower Lena culture of Late Neolithic and Early Bronze Age hunters and fishers within the interior of Chukotka. Now that abundant new materials are available, his hypothesis becomes more credible. The ceramics are most expressive of this. The working of pot surfaces at Chirovaya is like that of the lower Lena sites, resulting in a pseudotextile pattern. In form, the Late Neolithic vessels in northern Chukotka, although also round-bottomed, always have an everted lip differentiating them from the essentially straight-walled Ymyyakhtakh vessels, which incline slightly toward the mouth. The northern Chukotka adzes are not as finely worked as the rectangular Ymyyakhtakh ones, and some of the arrowheads, as mentioned earlier, are elongated and massive and not of the Lena type. Thus we may regard the Northern Chukotka culture as a locally distinct variant of the Late Neolithic of the lower Lena, or as an independent culture that, together with the Lena culture, forms one cultural region (Dikov 1979:139).

After Okladnikov discussed the relationship of the lower Lena and Northern Chukotka cultures, Mochanov (1969c) assigned the Chirovaya site to the Belkachi culture and thus to the third millennium B.C. Dikov objects to this, saying that despite the numerous analogies between them, the Northern Chukotka culture differs importantly from the Belkachi one. A basic attribute of the Belkachi stage is its corded ware, whereas the Northern Chukotka culture, particularly at Chirovaya, contains false textile or "waffled" pottery, thus indicating cultural rather than genetic ties.

The Ust-Belaya Culture

The Ust-Belaya culture is distributed over the wooded tundra area of the Chukot Peninsula. To it belong the middle Anadyr River sites of Uvesnovaniya (fig. 7, no. 57), Vilka (nos. 59 and 60), in part the mixed site of Chikayevo (no. 74), and the Omrynsk (no. 73) and Ust-Belaya cemeteries, the latter constituting an important archaeological base with its unmixed burials. All of these sites are located at river crossings, reflecting the spring and fall migrations of the northern wild deer, and also the hunting, fishing, and gathering economy of the peoples involved.

The extensive lithic complex consists of various cores, flakes, and lamellar blades, projectile points, knives, scrapers, gravers, punches, axes, and adzes (figs. 8 and 9). The contents of the unmixed burials allow a chronological division into earlier and later periods (see figs. 1 and 2). Burials of the later period contain bronze gravers and smooth-walled pottery with paddled ribbing.

When the Ust-Belaya contents are compared with those of other sites, it becomes evident that the two periods or stages mentioned above belong to one culture. This is confirmed particularly by the burials in the partial cremation of the corpse and the similarity in grave goods, including ceramics. However, the possibility of a two-stage division at Ust-Belaya indicates to some degree its duration and helps in dating it.

The earlier limit of the culture is dated by several types of artifacts, including ceramics, which are typical of the Ymyyakhtakh culture, which as we have seen belongs to the middle of the second millennium B.C. Also, the association of waffle ceramics with paddle-stroked ribbed pottery and stepped adzes like those of the third millennium Belkachi culture led Dikov to set the oldest limits of the Ust-Belaya culture at the very beginning of the second millennium B.C. (Dikov 1979:147).

The later limit reaches to the end of the second–beginning of the first millennium B.C. The principal indicators here are the bronze gravers mentioned earlier and a bronze needle rectangular in cross section found in a burial. Judging by the dating of the Bronze Age in neighboring Yakutia, these bronze objects could not be earlier than the end of the second millennium B.C. Of considerable significance to this dating is a walrus ivory toggled harpoon head recovered from a burial. The harpoon, an early Eskimo type according to Collins (1937), is not slotted for the insertion of a point and has an open socket. It is closely similar to the rare pre-Dorset and Dorset points of Greenland and Baffin Island in sites from the end of the second and beginning of the first millennium B.C. (Bandi 1969). This type of point also appears in Alaska at Kachemak I and in the Norton complex (Giddings 1964) of like date. The Norton complex also contained a stone arrowhead with side notches and a tanged scraper, both characteristic of early Eskimo sea mammal hunting and dated to the first half of the second millennium B.C. (Bandi 1969).

In light of the above, the chronological brackets of the Ust-Belaya culture span the period from about 1250 B.C. to about 500 B.C. Charcoal samples from a burial mound of the early stage of Ust-Belaya yielded dates of 2865 ± 95 b.p. (RUL-187) and 2920 ± 95 b.p. (Kril-244).

Worth noting here is the 1975 find of the Paleo-Eskimo site of Chertov ovrag (Devils' Ravine) on Wrangel Island (Dikov 1976, 1978). Although its stone artifacts are similar to those of other Paleo-Eskimo sites, they lack polished tools. Of greatest interest and importance in dating the culture was a large walrus ivory toggled harpoon head of archaic form, much like those of northern Greenland's Independence culture of the second millennium B.C. The stonework of Chertov ovrag shows many similarities to that of the Paleo-Eskimo cultures of northern North America, including Independence and Cape Kruzenstern, the latter dated 4000 b.p. Thus we have a maritime culture on Wrangel Island that precedes in time those of Okvik and Old Bering Sea. Charcoal from a fire pit at Chertov ovrag has a confirmatory date of 3360 ± 155 b.p. (MAG-198).

Radiocarbon Dates and Calibration

As mentioned at the beginning of this chapter, all Soviet radiocarbon dates here cited are on the basis of the 5568 half-life of C-14. Conversion to the more generally accepted 5730 half-life adopted by the International Radiocarbon Conference held in Cambridge, England, in 1962 has thus far not been followed by Soviet archaeologists, nor have correction or calibration factors been used. Several calibration curves and sets of tables have been developed since the mid-1960s. Although those most often used by archaeologists are by Clark (1975), MASCA by Ralph, Michael, and Han (1973), and by Suess (1970), there were at least nine other schemes, some of them superseded by "improved" ones from the same laboratory, some calculated independently. Although these calibration curves and tables agree in a gross way, their proliferation has caused confusion among some users or would-be users; for these reasons a Workshop on Calibration of the Radiocarbon Time Scale was held at the University of Arizona in Tucson, 28 January to 2 February 1979 (Michael and Klein 1979).

The principal goals of the workshop were to examine the existing calibration schemes and to produce one based on precisely dated wood samples and representing a consensus of the laboratories involved in calibration. The results were presented to the Tenth International Radiocarbon Conference, held in Heidelberg and Bern, by Klein et al. (1980) and were accepted. The task of developing the calibration curve and tables was carried out mostly by Klein during 1980 and 1981 and is known as Calibration of Radiocarbon Dates–82 (CRD-82). For curve and tables see Klein et al. (1982) and Klein's tables in the appendix of this publication.

It is well known that the application of calibration to radiocarbon dates has caused an archaeological revolution, particularly in the chronological interpretation of the Neolithic and Bronze ages of eastern and southeastern Europe (Neustupný 1969; Renfrew 1973). While the nonagricultural but pottery-making Neolithic cultures penetrated into the steppes, forests, and tundras of northeastern Asia somewhat later than they had in Europe, the calibration of the conventional radiocarbon dates on which the chronology and periodization of many are based will push the beginnings of the Neolithic of this region further into antiquity; the ending of it will be chronologically affected to a lesser degree.

Table 4 expresses the differences between the 5568 and 5730 half-lives of the Neolithic dates, and also the results of their calibration with the CRD-82 system.

Figure 10 expresses graphically the differences between 5568 half-life dates and the CRD-82 ones for the well-documented Neolithic of Yakutia.

In those cases in which radiocarbon dates are unavailable or very scarce, correlations must be with analogies to neighboring regions where such dates do exist. In table 4 one must interpret the unevenness in the quantity of samples for the different regions and recognize that although all stages of the Neolithic may be present at a given site, there may not be a radiocarbon date or dates for each of them. In this very brief survey of the Neolithic of northeastern Asia, I have tried to point out widely distributed mutual influences of many of the cultures involved. Thus, for instance, the well-dated ones of Yakutia and Kamchatka can serve as reference points for establishing relative as well as absolute chronologies for those not represented or only partly represented by radiocarbon dates.

To emphasize the continuity and sequential nature of the radiocarbon dates, table 4 includes dates from the Mesolithic strata of some of the sites. Unlike those from Neolithic levels, some of the Mesolithic dates remain uncalibrated. Although currently the dendrochronological span reaches from present to 6700 B.C. (8686 B.P.), because of the paucity of wood in the few hundred years prior to 6700 B.C., calibration studies have been carried only to 6350 B.C. (8300 B.P.). Since at this point the calibration factor for radiocarbon dates calculated with a 5730 half-life is about +600 years, radiocarbon dates older than 5750 b.c. (7700 b.p.) cannot be calibrated. Numerous radiocarbon dates exist for eras preceding and subsequent to the Mesolithic-Neolithic ones. The succession of these dates is for the most part orderly and logical, but there are a few aberrant ones.

This survey points out the inadequacy of conventional, uncalibrated radiocarbon dates in interpreting the chronological span of a given culture, particularly in the B.C.

era. Differences of uncalibrated 5568 half-life dates and their CRD-82, 1σ calibration (table 4 and fig. 5) make it clear that the Neolithic in the taiga of Eastern Siberia began some one thousand years earlier than indicated by the uncalibrated dates. Similarly the Middle Neolithic started about seven hundred years earlier and the Late Neolithic about six hundred years earlier. The figures cited above are based on the midpoint of averaged dates so that they may be compared with the 5568 half-life laboratory dates. Actually a more cautious statement should be in terms of time brackets, namely, that the Early Neolithic started from 1200 to 800 years earlier, the Middle Neolithic from 900 to 500 years earlier, and the Late Neolithic from 750 to 400 years earlier. The few radiocarbon dates we have from Western Siberia indicate a slightly earlier start of the Neolithic there.

Thus the dating must be adjusted as shown below.

Since more recent dates are less affected by it, calibration does not affect all regions in the same way. Because of the nature of the calibration curve and the tables derived from it, there is less of a discrepancy in those areas where Neolithic techniques were introduced later. Thus in Kamchatka the difference for the start of the Early Neolithic is five hundred years, while in Chukotka it is only an insignificant one hundred years.

As more radiocarbon dates become available and as the calibration factors are extended further into antiquity, some refinements in the above dates may be necessary, but in a rough way even these preliminary figures emphasize the necessity of adjusting our thinking about traditional chronologies of the Neolithic Age in northeastern Asia.

Stage	Calibrated Dating		Uncalibrated Dating	
	b.p.	(b.c.)	b.p.	B.C.
Early Neolithic	7350–5950	(5400–4000)	6500–5200	(4550–3250)
Middle Neolithic	5950–5000	(4000–3050)	5200–4200	(3250–2250)
Late Neolithic	5000–3500	(3050–1550)	4200–3200	(2250–1250)

Twenty-Five

Korean Archaeological Sequences from the First Ceramics to the Introduction of Iron

Sarah Milledge Nelson, University of Denver

Outline

Early Village Period
  Osan-ni
  Tongsam-dong
  Suga-ri
  Sangno Daedo
  Amsa-dong
  Misa-ri

Si Do
Chitam-ni
Kungsan-ni
Sopohang
The Megalithic Period
Addendum

Until the last decade or so, the number of papers on Korean archaeology in Western languages was so small that Korea was simply ignored in any compendium of world archaeology. China and Japan were and are better known in the West, and perhaps for that reason Korean archaeology is widely believed to be a subset of Chinese and/or Japanese developments. Korea is seen as a bridge between the two, or sometimes as a barrier (e.g., Chard 1974:103), but rarely as important in its own right. There are of course commonalities with nearby areas, as well as variability within the Korean peninsula. Yet it is clear that an indigenous cultural pattern which owes little to China developed in Korea before the adoption of Buddhism in the early centuries A.D., despite the hegemony of the Han dynasty over parts of northern Korea from 108 B.C. to A.D. 313. Ties with Japan, especially between southeastern Korea and southwestern Japan, are far more numerous and much earlier, but with the possible exception of the very earliest ceramics, the direction of "influence" appears to be from Korea to Japan (Im 1982c), not the other way around. As more elements such as megaliths and bronze were added to the cultural inventory, the divergence became even more marked. The early Korean states show artifacts and burial patterns that bespeak a self-conscious difference from their neighbors rather than an identity with them (Nelson 1982b). Even now, after twelve centuries of strong Chinese influence on the upper class, there is a core of culture that is essentially Korean (Osgood 1954).

Text submitted May 1985

Chronological studies in Korean archaeology have been traditionally based on typological classifications more than on either stratigraphy and seriation or radiocarbon dates (Lee 1984), with a few recent and notable exceptions (Lee 1987, 1978; Han 1978; Choi 1982). Im (1984a) has attempted to combine stratigraphy, typology, and radiocarbon dates to create an overall understanding of a given time period. But until recently the radiocarbon dates have been too few to allow distinctions between regional and temporal types, and the concept of functional types has been slow to develop. Most chronological sequences proposed for Korean prehistory are either very general or are built on fragile typological schemes that are not grounded in stratigraphic sequences. The logic underlying such sequences tends to be largely implicit rather than explicit. For the most part, diversity is viewed in a linear temporal fashion, without regard to other possible interpretations. Additionally, there is often an assumption of multiple waves of migration into Korea from the north. Although it is not totally unfounded, for it is based on tradition and ancient documents along with similarities between archaeological sites in Korea and Manchuria, yet used as a basis for interpretation rather than as a hypothesis to be tested with archaeological data, the migration theory tends to distort rather than to clarify.

Local typologies that have been worked out by Westerners have proved to be either too complex for useful comparison with other sites (Sample 1974) or designed for other purposes (Nelson 1975). For chronology building, Korea needs a system of typological pottery designations that falls between the broad scale of "undecorated" Mumun and "comb-pattern" Chulmun pottery, which has guided temporal interpretations in the past, and the minute scale implied by names like Pusan Appliqué. Such a classification is in the process of development, but the names are not yet standardized, nor are there any standardized type descriptions of the emerging wares. This chapter therefore depends heavily on the radiocarbon dates and stratigraphic sequences, using them to judge the adequacy of various pottery types as chronological markers. Radiocarbon determinations are presented as calibrated dates with one standard deviation, as presented in the tables. The chapter sketches out the known sequences and attempts to describe the ceramic wares as they appear in the Korean literature. For the earlier stage, called here the Early Village period, I follow but expand on the work of Im (1984a), and for the later one, which I call the Megalithic period, I use a variety of sources.

Korean prehistoric archaeology can be divided into four stages: Paleolithic; the Early Village period, formerly called Chulmun, which features pottery with incised designs and other surface-roughening techniques, "Neolithic" in the broad sense; the Megalithic period, sometimes called Bronze Age or the Mumun period, which is marked by stone cist graves, megaliths, bronze, and rice cultivation as well as undecorated pottery; and the Wonsamguk period, which contains iron and several new pottery types including well-fired hard gray pottery, along with a variety of new burial forms. Thanks to radiocarbon dates, and some recent carefully excavated sites, this sketch can be filled in with many details. Although the outline has been clear for some time, the dating of both the Early Village and Megalithic periods has been pushed back considerably, as the result of a reasonably consistent series of radiocarbon dates.

The periodization of Korean archaeological assemblages has varied markedly over the years. The terms *Neolithic, Bronze Age,* and *Iron Age,* although they have been used occasionally, have more often been considered inappropriate for Korea because the congruence of specific pottery styles with various technological stages is inexact and disputed. On the other hand, to use pottery styles as period markers, for example, Chulmun as analogous to Jomon in Japan, with the cord-marked designation standing for a lengthy time period, has become increasingly muddled, since there is Chulmun period pottery that is not comb-marked, while undecorated or Mumun pottery occurs in several different contexts. This division between the Chulmun and Mumun wares dates back to Fujita (1948, cited in Sample 1974:4), who described these wares as two kinds of Neolithic pottery with different selection of site locations—Chulmun located on the coasts and riverbanks and Mumun on hillsides. Attention next was paid to the question of which was earlier

and was eventually settled in favor of Chulmun when bronze artifacts were noted to be consistently associated with Mumun ware. However, as more sites have been excavated and more detail is known, these terms have become less useful. For example, the misuse of the term *Chulmun* has been appropriately criticized by Im (1984a:11). While I agree with the critique, I find the substitution of the term *Neolithic* equally unsatisfactory. The previous terminology having become Procrustean in the extreme, I propose to call the time period about 6000–2000 B.C. the Early Village period, and the era 2000–300 B.C. the Megalithic period. Although these are not entirely new terms, they are not customarily used as designations for primary divisions. Their use here will serve to differentiate major changes in both technology and ceramic complexes while avoiding terms loaded with unintended meanings. Some archaeologists may dispute my dating ranges, especially with regard to the boundary between Early Village and Megalithic periods, but I believe that radiocarbon dates substantiate my view, as detailed below.

I have dealt with neither the Paleolithic sites nor the Wonsamguk, or proto–Three Kingdoms, period in this chapter. Tables 1 and 2 present all the known dates for the Early Village and Chulmun periods respectively. In the tables, sites are assigned to a period on the basis of their contents rather than their dates. In a general way the periods are sequential, but not surprisingly there is some overlap. By and large these overlaps have been explained not as transitional periods with evolution in place, but as holdouts for a time of the previous "people" against new immigrants. In a standard interpretation, the Chulmun makers are characterized as Paleoasiatics, the Mumun as the Eastern Barbarians (Tong-I in Korean) mentioned by the Chinese from their earliest writings, and sometimes more specifically as Ye-Maek (e.g., Kim J.B. 1975; Kim 1983; Sohn, Kim, and Hong 1970; Choi 1984). The Wonsamguk pottery and iron are seen to have been brought by Chinese immigrants fleeing from Han dynasty taxation, as recorded in the Hou-Han-Shu, and from the actual Chinese presence in the north of Korea in the Nangnang (Lelang) and related commanderies from 108 B.C. to A.D. 313.

In Korea, cultural traditions begin with a culture hero named Tangun who has been equated with the Early Village period. Tangun is the offspring of a bear and a sky god, and the legend reflects a forest environment at a time when people were beginning to make use of cultivated plants. The next culture hero is Kija, who appears in Chinese writings as Chitzu, an agnate of the final king of the Shang dynasty in China. Kija is said to have left China for Korea with a large retinue toward the end of the second millennium B.C. and to have taught the people sericulture and other civilized arts. Kija's descendants ruled until about 200 B.C., when yet another conquerer, this time from the northern Chinese state of Yen, overthrew them. The Chinese Han state conquered part of northern Korea in 108 B.C. and founded four commanderies, of which the most important and continuous was Nangnang. In the meantime, the state of Chin is described in southern Korea, as well as, somewhat incompatibly, the three Han states: Mahan, Chinhan, and Pyonhan. Out of these grew the southern historical kingdoms of Paekche and Silla, while the kingdom of Koguryo arose in the north and eventually drove out the Han Chinese commanderies.

Early Village Period

The assumption that the pottery-making early villagers were immigrants stems from two sources: a definite hiatus in radiocarbon dates between preceramic and ceramic sites, and an expectation that the ceramic technology must have come from elsewhere—an unexamined assumption that the presence of pottery necessarily means either diffusion or migration, with independent invention not considered as a possibility. The model that seems to underlie cultural reconstructions appears to be that of an empty peninsula, peopled from the north. Driven by some unknown impulse, they came and settled along Korea's coasts and rivers to become fisher/foragers, bringing pottery but little other technology with them (Kim 1983). Recent archaeological finds strengthen the model of settlement by people who already possessed ceramic technology, but the earliest settlement is in the southeast along the coasts (Im 1982a), destroying the already weakened presumption of northern immigrants as the first village dwellers.

Sites of the Early Village period (fig. 1) for which a series of radiocarbon dates exists are few: Osan-ni, Tongsam-dong, Suga-ri, and Amsa-dong. Stratified sites without radiocarbon dates are also rare: Sangno Daedo has well-reported stratigraphy but only one date; Sopohang contained four distinct layers; and other sites in the north, described as having horizontal stratigraphy, have no radiocarbon dates at all. A recent paper (Im 1984a) weaves together the stratigraphic sequences from Osan-ni, Tongsam-dong, and Sopohang with a typological scheme supported by radiocarbon dates and stratigraphy from the west coast region, and anchors these sequences in time by means of radiocarbon dates. Stressing the clusters of similar sites found in various regions, Im concludes that a single typological sequence for all of Korea is inappropriate. He presents separate sequences for the west coast, the east coast, and the south coast and shows that similar pottery styles in these regions did not necessarily occur at the same time. However, Im sees major shifts, although different ones, in each region at about 3500 B.C. and calls this Middle Neolithic. Late Neolithic

occurs from 2000 to 1000 B.C. While Im's paper is a sound beginning, the data exist for a finer grained examination of these local sequences. Therefore I discuss the major sites in some detail and proffer some further conclusions.

Osan-ni

The site of Osan-ni is a convenient place to begin, for it contains the earliest radiocarbon date so far known for the Early Village period (Im 1984b, 1982b). The site is situated on the central east-coast, not far above the thirty-eighth parallel. On the shore of an ancient lake cut off from the sea by sand dunes, the site appears to have been a typical small village with coiled pottery and a combination of chipped and polished stone tools. Two areas, designated Locality A and Locality B, were excavated. According to the radiocarbon dates, the two localities are approximately contemporaneous in their lowest levels, but have fundamentally different pottery styles. So far the problems raised by this circumstance have not been dealt with directly in interpreting the site (e.g., Im 1982b, 1984b); instead all flat-based pottery has been lumped together and treated as one entity. The Yungkimun relief-decorated pottery of Locality B, however, is found at other east coast sites and could be an important chronological marker, while the combination of impressed and incised rim bands in Locality A is so far unique in Korea as are some of the associated stone tools. In the future the Locality A sequence could be of great importance to understanding the development of the Early Village period, and pending further investigation it should be seen as distinct.

Locality B is marked by flat-based, wide-mouthed pots with relief decoration in linear patterns around the rim. This was a small excavation, which produced no identifiable living floor, but of four whole or reconstructible pots, three were Yungkimun and one impressed, and the few potsherds were mostly incised or impressed. Five shanks of composite fishhooks, three broken rectangular stone knives, two chipped triangular projectile points, a broken stone chisel, one chipped and one polished stone ax, a whetstone, and a quern with grinding stone were found (Im 1982b). Only one date comes from Locality B, with a wide error placing the layer between about 6000 and 5600 B.C.

The excavated area at Locality A is much larger. Three distinct artifact-bearing layers were separated from each other by sterile sand. The lowest level, Layer V, was further subdivided into seven microlayers containing dwelling floors, some of which overlapped. Five determinations from this layer, and one from just below in Layer VI, fall between 6200 and 4100 B.C. If the two dates with very large standard deviations are disregarded or considered to be in the middle of their range, the stratum probably dates from 5400 to 4300 B.C. In Layer V both jars and bowls are represented, and the pottery decoration is complex and well executed. The pottery industry is well developed without simpler local antecedents, and it thus appears that the ceramic tradition must have roots elsewhere. As mentioned above, the pottery is all flat based, a characteristic of pottery from northeastern sites as well as at Osan-ni. One common shape is a neckless globular jar with a pair of loop handles below the rim. Decorative motifs consist of lines and dots in bands extending not more than halfway down the body. Decorative techniques are limited to impression and incision, with impression more common, although both can occur on a single pot. Neither these pottery shapes nor these designs have been found at any other site in Korea. Associated stone tools are similar to those at Locality B, with the addition of some scrapers, an obsidian saw, and several polished artifacts shaped like plumb bobs with a groove for a string around the top. These have not been reported elsewhere in Korea. One piece of obsidian was identified by X-ray fluorescence as having originated at Paektu-san on the northern border of Korea.

Layer III, the middle artifact-bearing layer, was very similar to Layer V, the major difference lying in the somewhat larger bases of the pottery. The upper level, Layer II, contained classic Chulmun pottery with pointed bases, and also a few flat bases and some Yungkimun sherds. Pebble net sinkers were prominent in this layer. At the top of the site was a small area with sherds from the Megalithic period, discussed below.

The radiocarbon dates suggest that the Yungkimun from Locality B may be the earliest kind of pottery at Osan-ni. The Locality B date, 5895–5635 B.C., is earlier than all but the problematical ones from House 1 in level V at Locality A. There are no dates from other Early Village levels, but the Megalithic period pottery level is dated at 1785–1355 B.C., providing an upper limit to the Early Village time range. Thus the sequence appears to be flat-based Yungkimun in the sixth millennium B.C., followed by flat-based impressed and incised ceramics down to perhaps 4000 B.C. Following this was Chulmun incised pottery with pointed bases, which disappeared around 2000 B.C.

Tongsam-dong

On a large island in Pusan harbor in southeastern Korea, the site of Tongsam-dong is a shell mound with alternating layers of shell and soil. The site is large, extending over approximately 2500 m². and it appears to be complicated by horizontal as well as vertical stratigraphy. Twenty-three radiocarbon dates, from four different laboratories and four separate excavations, help establish

time boundaries for various styles. The earliest date, 5050–4560 B.C., is from L. L. Sample's 1963 excavation at the site and is derived from the level she designated as Mokto, described as dominated by pinched pottery with rounded or pointed bases (Sample 1967:377). The pinched pottery is not known elsewhere in Korea, but a type from the same layer, called Mokto Appliqué, appears to be the same as the Yungkimun found at Osanni. In an earlier layer designated Chodo, which had no datable materials, Sample characterized the ceramics as "sophisticated," with decorative patterns "in a variety of techniques including punctate, incision, and appliqué" (Sample 1967:376). The few bases found were flat, and the illustrated sherds are similar to those of Locality B at Osan-ni. The Seoul National University (SNU) excavation also found Yungkimun sherds with analogous radiocarbon dates, ranging from 4950–4540 B.C. to 4115–3800 B.C. in a level the SNU team designated Layer V. Thus Yungkimun can be seen to exist at Tongsam-dong from about 5000 to 4000 B.C. Beginning at about 4000 B.C., the earliest radiocarbon date being 3885–3650 B.C., incised pottery became more common. Sample divided this into two periods, the earlier of which she called Pusan and the later Tudo. Some sherds of each grouping appear to be closely similar to classic Chulmun of the west coast, but the layers contain other kinds of pottery as well. Dates range down to 2415–2130 B.C., except for Sample's date for the Tudo level which everyone, including Sample (1974:102), believes to be too late. The uppermost levels belong to the Megalithic age, with dates beginning around 2000 B.C.

Thus, to simplify this complex data, it appears that Yungkimun at Tongsam-dong is the earliest ceramic, as it probably is at Osan-ni. In both locales it appears as a well-made pottery without simpler antecedents. The flat-based dotted motifs of the next stage at Osan-ni are not found at Tongsam-dong; instead there is overall pinched pottery. At both sites, however, Chulmun pottery appears after 4000 B.C. and lasts until 2000 B.C.

Suga-ri

To judge by both its radiocarbon dates and its pottery styles, another shell mound on the southern coast, Sugari, lacks the earliest stages that are found at Tongsam-dong and Osan-ni. Three dates from Layer V range from 3355 B.C. to 2655 B.C. The vessels are wide-mouthed pots with pointed or rounded bases. Allover incised patterns are common, with rows of short slanted lines, "herringbone" patterns, or crossed slanting lines creating diamonds. Two decorated loop handles were not unlike those from Osan-ni.

Two dates from Layer III are 3015–2865 B.C. and 2930–2640 B.C. The pottery is similar to that of Layer V, but often only the upper half of the pot is decorated. Plain pots are found throughout.

Layer I contains pottery with a few short slanted lines around the mouth and/or with doubled-over rims. This kind of treatment is associated with the Megalithic age, and its two dates at this site are 1700–1545 and 1430–1225 B.C. Spindle whorls are found, and chipped stone tools continue even in this level.

The authors of the report (Chung, Im, and Shin 1981) have concluded that sites on the southern Korean coast represent five time periods. The earliest, which they call Incipient, is marked by flat-based vessels that are either plain or appliquéd. The lowest level at Tongsam-dong is given as an example, along with Sinam-ni A, Tade-po, and Yongsan-dong. The Early period has pointed or rounded bases and is either undecorated or has impressed grooves, like Sample's Pusan period at Tongsam-dong. The Suga-ri site begins in the Middle period, when the pottery has bold grooves, like Sample's Tudo period. The Late period has a variety of incised styles, and in the Final the pottery is decorated only on the upper half, or is entirely plain with a doubled-over rim, a style associated with the Megalithic period. This scheme is an excellent reconstruction for the south coast and fits well with the known radiocarbon dates. However, it is specific only for the southern coast and cannot be generalized for the whole of the peninsula.

Sangno Daedo

One of the deepest stratified shell mounds that has been excavated, Sangno Daedo has ten distinct levels (Sohn 1982). A very early date of 5540–5195 B.C. comes from Level V, in which the pottery has mostly rounded bases, although a few are flat. Both round and flat bases are found throughout, and neither is therefore a time marker at this site. Incising is the dominant decorative technique, with the familiar diamond pattern and rows of short slanted lines. Appliquéd sherds are found in lower levels, and the stone tool inventory in the lowest includes some microliths (Chang 1981). Thus, this site may ultimately turn out to have the earliest pottery yet excavated in Korea. Unlike other excavated shell middens, pottery is not well represented at this site, but the small amount that does exist fits into the general chronological framework, although appearing to be earlier here.

Amsa-dong

The Amsa-dong site is near the Han River in central western Korea. The site has been surface collected often since its exposure by a flood in 1925, and it was partially excavated over several field seasons by various institutions. Regrettably, no comprehensive report has ever been published. From fragmentary reports (Kim 1970; Kim 1962)

it can be ascertained that at least twenty dwelling floors have been excavated, similar in plan to those at Osan-ni. The oldest date is 5300–5020 B.C., making it somewhat younger than Osan-ni and Sangno Daedo, but placing Amsa-dong within the framework of the earliest Early Village sites. Four houses have been dated, ranging from the early fifth millennium to the middle fourth millennium B.C. Im Hyo-jai's excavation (1982a:91) was the first to demonstrate clear stratigraphy at the site. Layers 4, 5, and 6 contained Chulmun pottery with overall decoration in Layers 5 and 6, but the decorated area diminished in Layer 4. The pottery is classic Chulmun ware, with incised allover designs and rounded to pointed bases. Some pottery has rows of concentric dots pendant from the rim design in a "wave pattern," but Im's excavation did not make clear whether this is ceremonial pottery, a time marker, or has some other distinction. The stone tool inventory was largely created by chipping pebbles of preselected appropriate shapes into such tools as net sinkers and hoes. There are also grinding stones with querns, ground stone axes, whetstones, and a few chipped triangular projectile points.

Misa-ri

The nearby site of Misa-ri has a Megalithic age layer above two Chulmun layers (Im 1981). Its only date of 3895–3640 B.C. indicates contemporaneity with Amsa-dong, and its pottery styles are demonstrably the same (Nelson 1975). A dwelling and associated stone tools are also like those of Amsa-dong.

Si Do

The four radiocarbon dates from the west coast island of Si Do are all much later than those of Amsa-dong and Misa-ri, although Chulmun sherds are associated with all four of them (Han 1970). Im (1984a) explains the dates, which have a 1σ range from 1450 to 1015 B.C., as late types of Chulmun, with decoration only on the upper half of the vessels. It is notable that this shell mound site dates so much later than other west coast island sites such as Sanyu Do at 3675–3510 B.C., Oi Do at 2870–2545 B.C., and Soya Do at 2420–2290 B.C., which are also shell mounds. Taehuksan Do, off the southwest coast, dates to 1900–1660 B.C., falling in between. Im (1984a) considers Soya Do and Oi Do to be Middle Neolithic, while Si Do is Late Neolithic in his scheme. In terms of area of decoration, there is a progression from overall decoration to only a remnant pattern near the rim.

Chitam-ni

Farther north near the Taedong River is the site of Chitam-ni, famous for being the first discovered Early

Village site in which cultivated grains were found. Two areas of the site were excavated. Area 1 had pottery with overall incised designs, including herringbone and bands of short slanted lines, as well as a few sherds with handles, found in a large dwelling about 7 m square. Area 2 contained smaller houses and classic Chulmun-style pots sunk into the floor for storage in which grain identified as millet was found. Other potsherds had pendant concentric semicircles formed with punctates in the wave pattern style found at Amsa-dong. Associated artifacts included polished projectile points and objects designated as sickles and plowshares, which have not occurred at any sites in the south (To and Hwang 1959). On the basis of the grain and the agricultural implements, Area 2 is considered to be later than Area 1. Therefore the wave pattern is believed to be a later style (Kim W.Y. 1975; Im 1984a).

Kungsan-ni

Farther north along the west coast is the shell mound site of Kungsan. In the B layer of the mound which was composed largely of clam shells, House 2 contained pottery with round or pointed bases, polished stone axes, polished triangular projectile points, antler hoes, and sickles made of boars' tusks, as well as querns and grinding stones. This was separated by less than 50 cm of clay from a shell layer preponderantly of oysters. The pottery in the oyster layer had flat bases, pendant concentric circles in the wave pattern, and stone hoes rather than antler hoes. Otherwise the stone assemblages were similar. This is further evidence that the wave pattern might be a later style.

Sopohang

On the northeast coast the shell mound of Sopohang has been excavated at least twice, but there are no reported radiocarbon dates (Kim and So 1972). The mound is made up of oyster shells with much bone and other refuse mixed into it. Two areas were excavated, both of which had dwellings. The vessels in the lower levels of Phases I and II were flat-based pots with incised lines and impressed dots (Henthorn 1968) which Im (1984a) believes are contemporaneous with Level V of Locality A at Osan-ni. Although the decorative details are different, Im finds them "comparable." Above this, vessels are decorated with relief designs. Squared spiral designs and polished ware become more common, which Im (1984a:18–19) would also equate with levels at Osan-ni.

For the Early Village period, a general date of 6000–2000 B.C. is consistent with the radiocarbon dates, although there were a few sites that lasted well into the next millennium. Time differences within the period are marked by local pottery changes, but not by peninsula-wide horizon styles—at least not until the spread of Chulmun ware. Chulmun Pottery appears to have originated in the regions of the Han and Taedong rivers in the sixth millennium B.C. and to have diffused to cover Korea by 3000 B.C. Perhaps this diffusion was the result of the success of millet farming which is known to have begun by this time in the sites of west-central Korea.

The Megalithic Period

It is difficult to find a neutral term to designate the next stage in Korean archaeology, although there are several characteristics that make it distinct from the Early Village period. Names applied have included the Mumun period after the plain pottery, the Dolmen period because of the estimated ten thousand megalithic monuments that were presumably erected during this time, and the Bronze Age, reflecting the fact that some stone cist burials, which are frequently associated with dolmens and almost always have Mumun pottery in them, also often contained objects made of bronze (Kim J. B. 1975). The dating estimates vary, depending on which characteristic is seen as primary. Although few "dolmens" have been dated, they are closely associated with the dominant pottery styles and appear to be contemporaneous. Furthermore, dolmens are supplanted by mounds of earth and/or stone as grave markers in the Wonsamguk period, so they seem to define a particular stage in Korean prehistory. Because a definite change in the dominant ceramics is also clearly visible in the archaeological record, I here follow general usage and consider appearances of varieties of Mumun as the "type fossil" for this period. At many sites megaliths, bronze, cist graves, and rice agriculture were also present, but it is not yet certain whether these traits were present at the beginning of the period or whether they appeared later. Although there are some tentative answers, the known group of radiocarbon dates is too small to establish firmly any single point of view. The best that can be done is to note the earliest appearances of these various traits and perhaps to infer their preceding presence or absence. Sites are distributed more evenly over the peninsula than in the preceding period (fig. 2).

As mentioned earlier, the term *Mumun* was originally applied to any undecorated pottery. However, since plain pottery sherds and even whole vessels were increasingly found in the Early Village period, the definition of Mumun narrowed and became more precise. The term now covers several types of relatively plain pottery, including Plain Coarse Ware which was the original Mumun; Paengi or top-shaped pottery largely found in the northwest; Karak pottery with a flower pot shape and a row or two of incision on or below its doubled rim, named after its type site on the Han River near Seoul; Gongyul pottery, featuring a series of punctates near the rim and a scalloped lip, and Ichunggu, the folded-over double rim which, combined with a rounded base, is most often found in the south and east. Small burnished orange globular jars and long-necked black vessels are also found in this stage but are not limited to any particular area. With this crude division, it is possible to explore the radiocarbon dates for clues to the range and temporal spread of these types. First I present some data from sites already familiar—Osan-ni in the east and Tongsam-dong in the south. The small site of Kumgok-dong adds to the regional picture. Moving north and west, I examine two recently excavated village sites near the Kum and Han rivers and then consider North Korean sites for additional insights.

The earliest radiocarbon dates for any variety of Mumun are associated with the double-rim type known as Ichunggu. These dates are associated with sites on the east and south coasts, beginning around 2000 B.C. A group of dated strata with this pottery style includes Osan-ni, Tongsam-dong, and Suga-ri whose Chulmun layers have already been described, as well as Kumgok-dong, Namdongmyong-ni, and Tongnae in the southeast.

Stone tools associated with the Mumun level at Osan-ni are not described in the site report, since most of the layer had eroded away leaving only a small remnant at the highest point. The pottery included Mumun coarse ware and Ichunggu styles as well as some horn-shaped handles. The associated date is 1785–1355 B.C. (Im 1982b, 1984b).

At Tongsam-dong, the uppermost layer in Sample's excavation, which she called Yongdo, contains a type named Yongdo Smoothed, which appears to fall within the range of Ichunggu. In the same layer was Yongdo Coarse, which appears to be Mumun plain coarse ware. Some flake tools, a hoe, a grinding stone, and several shell bracelets complete the assemblage, with a date of 1885–1645 B.C. (Sample 1974).

Suga-ri's upper levels, Layers I and II, contained Ichunggu ware along with some flaked stone tools and biconical spindle whorls. One or two bands of short slanted lines below the rim appear to be the only decoration, and all the bases found are rounded rather than flat (Chung, Im, and Shin 1981).

Kumgok-dong is a rock shelter on a hill above Pusan which, in its major habitation layer, produced a few sherds of classic Chulmun pottery, a great deal of Ichunggu ware with small dots or dashes below the rim fold, and a few undecorated sherds with no decoration. Most of the bases were rounded or pointed. Chipped stone tools occurred, along with a diamond-shaped elongated projectile point with a central tang, and a small chisel (Kim and Jong 1980). The date of this layer is

2120–1865 B.C. In general, then, on the south and east coasts, Mumun appears to have begun about 2000 B.C.

The plain pottery of the western sites tends to be rather later but is associated with rice, bronze, polished stone daggers, stone cists, and dolmens, none of which has been found in the early southeastern shell mounds. However, semilunar knives, which in Korea seem to be associated with rice cultivation, were discovered at Osan-ni and Tongsam-dong around 2000 B.C. The styles of Mumun in the west are also different, although the folded rim appears in both areas.

The Gongyul style of Mumun ware, with holes pierced below the rim and often a serrated lip, is found near the Han River. The best reported site is that of Hunam-ni on the South Han River about 80 km from Seoul (Seoul National University 1974, 1976; Kim, Im, and Choi 1973; Im 1978). Here the radiocarbon dates exhibit a wide range, with House 7 dated 15 B.C.–A.D. 430, which is probably an error; House 14 with four dates ranging from 410 to 10 B.C. perhaps relating to the Wonsamguk layer in this house; House 3 dated at 850–405 B.C.; House 8 at 910–420 B.C. including three dates with large sigmas; and House 12 dating 1660–1040 B.C. There are obvious problems of interpretation here, but generally the site is referred to as approximately 800 B.C. (e.g., Choi 1984). Neither the form nor the content of the variously dated dwellings appears to differ significantly, except for the Wonsamguk age-level above one of the house floors at the foot of the hill. Perhaps the houses do represent a very long and stable adaptation at this site, or perhaps some of the dates are greatly in error.

In addition to the Gongyul style at Hunam-ni there are Karak-style pottery and small burnished red jars. Both chipped and polished stone tools were still in use, and semilunar stone reaping knives with two holes are added to the stone tool inventory. The projectile points are of two styles—one with a diamond-shaped cross section and a stem, the other hexagonal in cross section with a sharply incurved base. Several polished stone daggers, which are commonly found in stone cist burials, were found on house floors. Spindle whorls, net sinkers, and beads complete the assemblage. This was the first Mumun site to produce actual grains of rice and other domesticated grains. The rice, of the japonica variety adapted to northern climates, was found in House 12, belonging to the second millennium B.C. The question of the beginning of rice cultivation in Korea has been specifically addressed by Choe (1982), Kim (1982), and Nelson (1982a) in related papers. Yasuda and Kim (1980) believe they have found nonarchaeological evidence for rice cultivation as early as 1500 B.C.

The same long-term stability noted at Hunam-ni appears to be evinced at Naepyong-ni on the north Han

River. Radiocarbon dates are 1265–1045 B.C. for a dwelling floor that contained pottery with a beveled edge and incised in widely spaced bands around the rim. Dates of 815–765 B.C. and 415–380 B.C. were associated with house floors having standard coarse Mumun pottery.

Farther south, near Puyo, the large village site of Songgung-ni also contained rice grains and Mumun pottery. Two dates were 870–785 B.C. and 820–585 B.C. Nearby was a stone cist burial, containing an early type of bronze dagger known as Liaoning and a bronze chisel fashioned from the stem of a broken dagger, a polished stone dagger, eleven polished stone projectile points, two comma-shaped jade pendants called magatama, and seventeen tubular beads. This important site thereby links Mumun pottery, polished stone knives, rice, stone cist burial, and Liaoning bronze daggers by the ninth century B.C. (National Museum of Korea 1979). The only other dated site with bronze is a wooden coffin from Taegong-ni, which is 820–585 B.C. A fine-lined bronze mirror was found here, adding this kind of locally produced mirror to the early complex.

Among the dolmens, yet another element of the Megalithic period, three major styles have been identified (Whang 1981). Often called the northern style because they are more common there, some dolmens have a large above-ground rectangular chamber made of stone slabs with a very large capstone up to 10 m long. This type of megalithic monument presumably contained burials, as did one excavated in Manchuria (Mikami 1961), but most of them have been looted and contain nothing. A second style has a large, thick capstone placed on short uprights, while the third consists of a large stone placed directly on the ground. Both of these latter styles are called southern dolmens and always cover a subterranean burial. Most of the burials are in the form of stone cist graves, but jar burials and pit burials are also found under dolmens. The contents of the cist graves are similar to the burial described at Songgong-ni. Cist graves also occur without dolmens, leading some authors (e.g., Rhi 1976) to argue that they antedate the dolmens. Few dolmens have been dated, so this remains a moot question, but these few fall within the range of Mumun sites. The dolmen at Yangsu-ri is dated to 2665–2140 B.C., which puts it on the early side; Oksong-ni contained a Mumun living floor beneath a dolmen dated 830–745 B.C.; and Sangjapo-ri dates rather late—390–160 B.C. Again, a very long and stable adaptation is implied if we are to believe all these dates.

The top-shaped pottery, so named because the globular body rests on a very narrow, flat base, occurs exclusively in the north. This ware is found at sites in Hwanghae and South Pyongan provinces in the west of the peninsula, associated with semilunar knives, spoked maceheads, stone discs with central perforations, grinding stones, spindle whorls, stepped adzes, and projectile points with a diamond-shaped cross section, as well as polished stone daggers of similar shape without a handle. No radiocarbon dates have been published from any of these sites. However, carbonized rice at the site of Honam-ni near Pyongyang was found in a layer identified as having late Chulmun pottery. Rice was also found at the earliest Paengi ware level. This level is cross-dated to 1500 B.C. (Choe 1982:524).

At Simchol-li, dolmens were associated with the dwelling sites containing the same kinds of artifacts. Both northern and southern dolmens occur, but cist coffins are reported only under the southern type. The site of Soktal-li has associated stone cist burials, but it is not known if they had dolmens for cover stones (Pak and Yi 1965). The Sinhung-dong site, with an otherwise identical artifact assemblage, also contained a bronze button (Kim 1978).

Most of the known dwellings of the Megalithic period are rectangular, semisubterranean with a central hearth not lined by cobbles, and on the whole are somewhat larger than the Early Village dwellings. However, a few very long houses have been excavated, such as Yoksam-dong near Seoul (Kim and Lim 1968) and Chinpa-ri near Pyongyang (Kim 1978). These contain artifacts like those of other sites and do not seem to represent any different adaptations.

From the distribution and dates of Mumun styles it appears that the sequence goes from south to north rather than appearing first with the Paengi pottery in the northwest, as is commonly assumed (e.g., Choi 1984; Han 1983). This fits with the suggestion of Kim Byung-mo (1981) that the Korean Megalithic originated under southern influences, not northern ones. In addition to those in Korea and Japan, dolmens also occur in Manchuria and in Shandong, China, but since they are undated, they could represent the end of a wave of dolmen building as well as its beginning. Nowhere else in Asia are dolmens as numerous as in Korea; perhaps Korea is after all the point of origin, if diffusion must be assumed. However, dates are completely lacking from the north. North Koreans claim that rice is found as early as 1500 B.C. (Choe 1982), and bronze by 2000 B.C. (Kim WY 1981), but how these estimates relate to the stone cist burials and dolmens is unclear.

The question of bronze as part of the original Megalithic culture is still arguable. Actual radiocarbon dates are no earlier than 1000 B.C. However, because early Korean bronze resembles the Karasuk culture far more than it does Shang dynasty bronzes of China, it is usually asserted that Korean bronze derives from the Minusinsk basin by way of the Liaodong peninsula. Jeon (1976) reports that early Korean bronze, found in North Korea, dates from the tenth century B.C. and contains a large admixture of zinc. Bronze artifacts have been found clustered around many of today's major cities, which probably were central places then as well as now. One grouping is in the vicinity of Pyongyang, which became the capital of Wiman's state, and perhaps even earlier served as an important center. Another set of bronze discoveries is on the east coast north of Wonsan, in the region where the Ye-Maek are believed to have settled. Bronzes have been found near the Han River, near the Kum River, in the far southwest, and near the present cities of Taegu and Kyongju in the southeast. In all of these areas, known chiefdoms arose at least by 300 B.C.

New burial forms marked by mounds rather than dolmens, as well as iron smelting and earth fortresses, are characteristics of the final prehistoric phase of Korean archaeology. The radiocarbon dates are far too few to determine a chronology on that basis, and the finds are too complex to discuss within the context of this chapter. However, the dates do show that about 300 B.C. the Megalithic period came to an end, supplanted by new cultures and perhaps partly by new inhabitants.

Addendum—March 1987

Only a few additional radiocarbon determinations have been published, and these are congruent with the sequences presented here.

Part Six

South and Southeastern Asia

The Indus Valley, Baluchistan, and Helmand Traditions: Neolithic through Bronze Age

Jim G. Shaffer, Case Western Reserve University

Outline

We were often confined to sinking those sondages which are supposed to provide stratigraphic answers and which graduate students and others delight in arranging on charts, but which are generally unreliable for what they are supposed to do and certainly worthless for any real effort to resolve the culture history of the site, let alone a region. I am certain that others besides myself would say in common "if only we had been permitted to complete what we started." (Fairservis 1978:x)

Since the 1965 edition of this volume, numerous surveys and excavations as well as new techniques have made for a more complete and complex archaeological picture. More important, this research has fundamentally changed many theoretical perspectives on cultural developments. Although Dales (1965c) and others attributed a large degree of cultural autonomy to the region discussed in this chapter, major cultural developments such as food production and urbanization were thought to reflect diffusion from Western sources. However, excavations at Mehrgarh indicate that food production developed autonomously in this region sometime before 6000 B.C. There-

fore, the Mehrgarh data provide a chronological and cultural basis from which subsequent developments may reflect local, rather than diffusionary, cultural processes. Recognition of this factor has refocused attention on the unique archaeological traits in this region and generated the possibility that the sequence and nature of cultural developments may not mirror those found in other areas (see Shaffer 1982b for discussion).

This has necessitated restructuring the data, with a new framework articulating older data with the new and sometimes different types of information gathered by recent research. The framework is based on four heuristic archaeological concepts—tradition, era, phase, and interaction system—originally developed for New World

This chapter benefited greatly from critical suggestions and/or additional information supplied by the following scholars: George F. Dales, Walter A. Fairservis, Louis Flam, Jonathan M. Kenoyer, Philip L. Kohl, C. C. Lamberg-Karlovsky, Richard H. Meadow, Margaret B. McKean, Rita P. Wright, and, most especially, J.-F. Jarrige and M. Rafique Mughal. Robert W. Ehrich not only helped editorially but also assisted in clarifying the major heuristic concepts used in this chapter. Although the above individuals, and many others as well, have contributed directly and indirectly to the contents of this article, the author accepts sole responsibility for the interpretations presented here.

Text submitted June 1984
Text revised October 1985

archaeology but which have been modified to fit local contingencies.

The central concept of this chapter is the cultural *tradition* (Willey and Phillips 1958:37). A tradition refers to persistent configurations of basic technologies and cultural systems within the context of temporal and geographical continuity. This concept facilitates a stylistic grouping of diverse archaeological assemblages into a single analytic unit, while limiting the need for establishing the precise nature of cultural and chronological relationships that link assemblages but imply that such relationships exist. Three cultural traditions are defined here: those of Baluchistan, Helmand, and the Indus Valley.[1]

Traditions are subdivided into *eras* which group archaeological units, or phases (see below), that share a few, very general cultural characteristics. Such units do not have fixed boundaries in time and space, and more than one may coexist contemporaneously within a tradition. These are not developmental stages, and not all are found in every tradition. The term *era* as here used is much like Steward's formulation in 1949 (also 1955:178–209) in that eras form a sequential series proceeding in the same order and connoting changes in general cultural organization within the areal traditions. They are not necessarily contemporary with the eras of other traditions. The four used here are (1) Early Food Producing—an economy based on food production and an absence of ceramics; (2) Regionalization—distinct artifact styles, essentially ceramics, which cluster in time and space, and interaction networks which link dispersed social groups; (3) Integration—a pronounced homogeneity in material culture distributed over a large area reflecting an intense level of interaction between social groups; and (4) Localization—comparable to regionalization except that there is a more generalized similarity in artifact styles, indicating continued, but altered, presence of interaction networks.

Eras may have one or more *phases*. A phase represents "an archaeological unit possessing traits sufficiently characteristic to distinguish it from all other units similarly conceived, whether of the same or other cultures or civilizations, spatially limited to the order of magnitude of a locality or region and chronologically limited to a relatively brief interval of time" (Willey and Phillips 1958:22). *Phases* thus may be applicable to the area of a major cultural tradition as a whole, or more commonly to separate sequences within its geographical subareas. This is the smallest analytical unit; and its major feature is a diagnostic ceramic style located at one or more sites during a particular time. The interplay of these heuristic concepts takes concrete form on figures 2, 3, and 4.

The final concept employed here is that of the *interaction system(s)* (after Caldwell 1965; Binford 1965). Interaction systems refer to various avenues of social communication existing within and between social groups which may crosscut both traditions and phases (see also Lamberg-Karlovsky and Tosi 1973; Shaffer 1972, 1974b, 1978b, 1982a, and 1982b). This communication is reflected in a widespread distribution of similar cultural traits and artifacts, intrusive and indigenous within a relatively brief time period. Thus these systems not only may adumbrate social interrelationships for which we have no specific information as to their nature, but they are also highly important in establishing relative chronologies when radiocarbon determinations are inadequate and in reinforcing those dates that do exist.

The Indus Valley Tradition

Geographical Area

The geographical area of the Indus Valley corresponds to the "Greater Indus Valley" (Mughal 1970, 1973), which is essentially the arid, or arid-savanna, alluvial plain of the Indus River system.[2] This extends from the Himalaya Mountains in the north to the Arabian Sea in the south, incorporating the coastal regions from the Iran-Pakistan border eastward to, and including, Saurashtra. To the west it is bordered by the Baluchistan mountains and on the east by the Thar Desert and the Ganges-Yamuna Divide. The summer monsoon rainfall pattern combines with spring melting of highland snows to produce late summer–early fall floods.[3]

The Tradition

The Indus Valley Tradition[4] (see figs. 2 and 5) dates from pre-6000 B.C. to at least 1500 B.C. and perhaps later. Food production based on domesticated barley, wheat, rice, and millet and on cattle, sheep, goats, and water buffalo was the adaptive strategy. Except for local exploitation of riverine and marine resources, the importance of hunting and gathering declines through time. Sedentary settlements ranged from small villages to large urban centers. Pastoral nomadism may also have been an adaptational component (Possehl 1979b; Shaffer 1972, 1974b, 1978b).

Buildings were constructed with mud and fired bricks, pisé, stone, and combinations of these materials. Most settlements have examples of public architecture, such as plazas, platforms, streets, and multiroom nonhabitational structures, and hydraulic features, such as wells, drains, and tanks. At urban centers such structures are more numerous and larger in scale, and enclosing walls are built around at least part of the settlement.

Artifacts are technologically and stylistically sophisticated, suggesting various degrees of craft specialization in even the earliest phases. Pottery includes handmade, wheel-made, and mold-made vessels in a wide variety of vessel forms, the most diagnostic of which are everted rim globular jars, flanged/double rim jars, and the dish-on-stand. Vessels are decorated with a variety of colored and textured slips, and incised and painted motifs. Painted decoration includes monochrome, bichrome, especially black-on-red slip, and polychrome patterns utilizing a wide variety of geometric, zoomorphic, and floral motifs, the most diagnostic of which are intersecting circles, "fishscales," peacocks, humped cattle, fish, and pipal leaves. Other characteristic terra-cotta objects are bangles, miniature cart frames and wheels, zoomorphs, especially humped cattle, anthromorphs, triangular and ovoid cakes, and, more rarely, stamp seals.

Using steatite, or chlorite, and a variety of semiprecious stones, lapidary craftsmen made many of this Tradition's diagnostic artifacts such as etched and long-barrel carnelian beads, cubical weights, and Harappan stamp seals. Except for milling stones, flint blades, and microliths, other types of stone tools are relatively rare (see Cleland 1977 for discussion). Ivory, indigenous to this area, and shell (see Kenoyer 1983 for discussion) artifacts, especially personal ornaments, are also characteristic of this Tradition.

One of this Tradition's most impressive traits in its later phases is the quantity, quality, and variety of metal objects. The most frequent metals used were copper and bronze, followed by smaller quantities of silver, gold, and electrum. Although a variety of personal ornaments were made, the outstanding feature was the large quantity and widespread distribution of functional tools. Also in these later phases was the large-scale production of blue faience personal ornaments.

The full range of cultural systems responsible for the development and maintenance of these technologies continues to elude us. At present only the economic system can be partially reconstructed. Beyond a food-producing subsistence economy there existed a distributional or trading system that linked the microeconomies of subregions within this area. Existence of this system is indicated by the distribution of artifacts made from nonlocally available materials like marine shell, metals, semiprecious stones, and intrusive ceramics. However, ethnographic studies (e.g., Harding 1967) indicate that such systems are usually focused on the movement of such important commodities as food, textiles, and wood. Given the vicissitudes of an arid environment and a food-producing economy, this distribution of usable commodities may have been very important. While details of this system cannot yet be delineated, it did exist from at least the Regionalization Era on, incorporating both large and small settlements, penetrating neighboring cultural traditions in varying degrees, and playing a crucial role in the development of this one. Moreover, this system was probably only one of many such organizational cultural

systems such as kinship, politics, and religion which facilitated interaction between contemporary dispersed social groups.

The widespread material cultural homogeneity in the Harappan Phase of the Integration Era suggests that such interaction systems were most intense during that period. One indicator of this intensity is the widespread use of Harappan script. Formative elements of the script first appear in the Regionalization Era, and by the Integration Era it is quite sophisticated and distributed throughout the area. A common script implies the ability and need to communicate information across time and space as well as a certain degree of historical and cultural continuity. The distribution of materials with limited sources of origin, and cultural homogeneity, together with a common script indicate interaction between dispersed social groups in this area, and that the common cultural pattern here called the Indus Valley Tradition was the result of social communication generated by such interactions.

Early Food-Producing Era

Throughout the entire area discussed in this chapter, in only one site, Mehrgarh, are there adequately excavated occupations relating to the Food-Producing Era. Despite the small sample we assume that these data reflect a basic representative cultural pattern. Mehrgarh is located in the Kachi plain on the geographical border between the Indus Valley and Baluchistan. Although subsequent phases defined at Mehrgarh are most strongly affiliated with the Baluchistan Tradition, this initial phase reflects a cultural pattern presently believed applicable to both the Baluchistan and Indus Valley Traditions.

Mehrgarh Phase

The definition of the Mehrgarh sequence is changing as research continues at the site (Jarrige 1977, 1981a, 1985, and in press a, b; Jarrige and Lechevallier 1979, 1980; Jarrige and Meadow 1980; Lechevallier and Quivron 1981; Lechevallier, Meadow and Quivron 1982; Meadow 1981, 1982). Only the earliest occupations, Period IA, are pertinent. The excavators ascribe these early occupations to the very beginning of the seventh millennium B.C. (see also Kachi Phase discussion).

Period IA, with 7+ m of deposits, is purely aceramic. Preliminary testing revealed habitation debris, various lithic and bone tools, hearths, possible mud-brick structures and numerous burials, adult and subadult, which were in simple pits, sometimes stained with red ochre, and which possessed ornaments and/or offerings. The quality of workmanship, quantity of objects involved, and the fact that some were made from marine shells, lapis lazuli, and turquoise, which are not locally available, suggest considerable economic investment in non-utilitarian objects, which were taken out of circulation via a major religious activity. These imported materials indicate either long-distance travel and/or interaction with other groups to obtain these commodities. Young goats were used as grave offerings for some adults, indicating this animal's cultural importance in a society that still practiced a significant degree of hunting.

Domesticated plants in the earliest occupations are evidenced by grain impressions of two-row hulled and six-row barley, einkorn, emmer, and bread wheats. Wild animals were still economically significant during Period IA, the most important of which were gazelle followed by deer, sheep, goats, cattle, and various other species. Significant numbers of domesticated goats were, however, present along with a rare example of domesticated cattle.

Many essential traits of this Tradition became established during this Phase. The most important of these were a food-producing economy, sedentary villages with mud-brick architecture, and the development of lapidary and shell-working crafts. Moreover, the use of imported materials may show limited interaction with other social groups. Furthermore the burial context of many imported objects suggests they had significant cultural value and argues that the interaction system responsible for their distribution may have been equally important.

Regionalization Era

The dating of the Regionalization Era is very imprecise. Its earliest phase, Balakot, dates to ca. 4000–3500 B.C., leaving a 2000-year gap between the Balakot and Mehrgarh Phases. At present no archaeological complex in this Tradition can be attributed to this intervening period, thus reflecting our still very limited data concerning the early phases of this Tradition. Another major problem is that the two earliest Phases, Balakot and Amri, ca. 3500 B.C., appear already well developed. Moreover, both Phases demonstrate at least some degree of cultural affiliation with the Baluchistan Tradition. Clearly there is a significant degree of cultural interaction between social groups of both Traditions during these early periods. Determining the nature of these interactions will be a critical aspect of future research. This Era ends at ca. 2500 B.C. with the development of the Harappan Phase in the Integration Era. However, in some subregions social groups demonstrating characteristics of this Era persisted and were contemporary with Harappan groups.

Balakot Phase

The Balakot Phase has been identified only in the early occupations at Balakot (Dales 1974, 1979a, 1979b, 1981, 1982), a site near the Makran coast northwest of Karachi. Radiocarbon dates suggest a chronology of ca.

4000–3500 B.C., but the ceramics may indicate a later terminal date of ca. 3200–3000 B.C.

Most of the redware pottery is wheel-made or a combination of wheel- and mold-made, with the most common vessel form being the earliest examples of everted rim globular jars. Painted motifs in black, brown, and rarely red and green are applied to a cream/white slip. The basic decorative scheme is a combination of simple and wavy horizontal bands. However, complex "Nal"-style (DeCardi 1965) floral and zoomorphic motifs are present, including polychrome examples. The late pottery of this Phase closely resembles that of the Amri Phase, and painted and incised abstract marks on the pottery—potter's or owner's marks—may represent a formative stage in the development of the later Harappan script. Similar markings have been identified on pottery from the Amri and Kot Diji Phases. Among other terracotta objects were the earliest examples of bovid figurines.

Stone tools (Cleland 1977), a variety of semiprecious stone and shell (Dales and Kenoyer 1977; Durante 1979; Kenoyer 1983) beads, and amorphous copper/bronze objects are also present. Habitation structures were found along with mud-brick paved areas, possibly the earliest examples of platforms in this Tradition.

The economy was based on food production, with limited amounts of gazelle hunting and shellfish gathering. Cattle were the major domesticated animal, along with small numbers of sheep and goats (Meadow 1979, 1982). Plant remains were few in number and poorly preserved. The most common plant identified (J. West quoted in McKean 1983:18–21) was six-row barley, followed by jujube and rare examples of chickweed and vetches. Pollen data (McKean 1983) supported these identifications and added *Cucumis,* a gourd or melon, to the list of economically important plants.

The sophisticated ceramic industry and the few metal objects suggest that some degree of craft specialization may have been present. Interaction with other contemporary complexes is indicated by the presence of lapis lazuli beads, similarities in vessel forms, the resemblance to Amri-style pottery in the late occupations, and the similarity in abstract signs on the pottery. The data are, however, still too limited to evaluate the significance or nature of these interactions.

Amri Phase

Amri Phase sites are located mainly in the lower Indus River valley, or Sind. Surveys (Krishna Deva and McCown 1949; Flam 1981a, 1981b, 1982; Majumdar 1934; Mughal 1972) have located numerous sites, but most information is based on the Amri excavations (Casal 1964, 1979). Providing an absolute chronology for the Amri

Phase is difficult. The resemblance to Amri-style pottery noted for late Balakot Phase pottery suggests a post-4000 B.C. date. Jarrige (in press a) has noted the presence of possibly intrusive wheel-made black-on-red pottery in the earliest Amri occupations which resembles Mehrgarh III and IV–V pottery. In addition, Jarrige sees parallels between the Amri and Mehrgarh III bone and lithic industries. Jarrige, therefore, dates the beginning of the Amri phase to the mid-fourth millennium B.C., which is consistent with the evidence from Balakot. At the same time, small quantities of Hakra Phase, ca. 3200–2700 B.C., pottery are found in the earliest occupation, Amri IA, and small quantities of Kot Diji Phase, ca. 2700–2300 B.C., pottery may be identified throughout occupations of this Phase (Mughal 1970:84–87). Finally, two radiocarbon dates from the middle occupations, Amri IB–C, suggest a range between ca. 3500–3300 B.C. At present a very tentative chronology of between ca. 3600–3000 B.C. and perhaps later is proposed for the Amri Phase.

The distinctive, mainly handmade, monochrome and bichrome decorated pottery occurs in a variety of vessel forms, including the first examples, albeit rare, of the dish-on-stand. A variety of complex geometric motifs are present, and in Amri ID is found the first use of "fishscale," intersecting circles, and humped bovid motifs as well as red slip.

Among the contiguous rectangular mud-brick buildings in Amri IB–D were examples that had their interior space divided into small rectangular compartments. Somewhat similar architectural features can also be found in the Kachi and Kili Gul Muhammad Phases of the Baluchistan Tradition at Mehrgarh.

Although the economy was based on food production, hunting and fishing were locally important. Cattle were the major domesticated animal, along with lesser quantities of sheep and goats. Domesticated plants were probably present. Hunted species included various caprids, rhinos, bears, pigs, land tortoises, and turtles; shell middens associated with some sites indicate riverine and marine resources were exploited. Fairservis (1975:208–16) proposes three economic patterns for this Phase, based on agriculture, pastoralism, and fishing, which he feels accounts for its more variable settlement pattern of very small dispersed sites versus larger, more nucleated sites on the alluvial plain. Recently, Flam (1981a:184–88, 1984) defined an "acro-sanctum/lower town"–type settlement for this Phase, which he perceives as a predecessor to the Harappan "twin mound" urban settlement; however, this type has yet to be substantiated by excavation.

A degree of craft specialization is suggested by the pottery, but the limited sample for other artifacts precludes speculation about local levels of production. The presence of metal and semiprecious stone artifacts in the Amri Phase suggests some degree of involvement in the interaction systems responsible for distribution of these materials. Other such indicators are Hakra- and Kot Diji–type pottery at Amri; Amri-style pottery at Balakot; similar abstract signs on pottery in Amri, Balakot, and Kot Diji Phases; similarities in vessel forms, individual decorative motifs, and other artifacts such as terra-cotta bangles, humped bovid figurines, and triangular cakes. Indeed, many cultural characteristics of this Tradition were apparently emerging by ca. 3000 B.C.

Hakra Phase

Definition of the Hakra Phase has been possible only since Mughal's (1981, 1982, in press) Bahawalpur surveys. Hakra Phase occupations can now be defined at Sarai Khola I (Halim 1972; Mughal and Halim 1972), Jalilpur I (Mughal 1972, 1974), at sites near the Indo-Pakistan border (Dalal 1980, 1981; Sharma 1982), and in the Swat Valley (Stacul 1969) where it is represented by Periods I and III–IV of the general sequence for that area. Most sites represent single occupations, but a few do show stratigraphically later Kot Diji, at Sarai Khola, Jalilpur, and Ghaligai (Stacul 1969), and Harappan Phase occupations. Therefore, Mughal concluded that Hakra precedes both the Kot Diji and Harappan Phases, and in the absence of available dates he estimated a chronology of ca. 3500–3000 B.C. Recent dates from Sarai Khola I and the earliest levels at Ghaligai indicate a time range of between ca. 3200–2700 B.C. At the same time, one can make some comparisons with the Burzahom (Kaw 1979; Sankalia 1974:298–304; Stacul 1969, 1979; Tusa 1979) material from Kashmir which dates to the late third millennium B.C. In addition, during Period IV of the Swat Valley sequence, intrusive Punjab Phase pottery, which dates ca. 2100–1300 B.C., is associated with Hakra occupations dated between ca. 1800–1400 B.C. Based on this information and the presence of Hakra pottery in the Amri Phase, an estimated chronology for this Phase in the central Indus Valley is between ca. 3300–2700 B.C. However, the Swat Valley and Kashmir data indicate that in these northern mountainous regions Hakra Phase groups persisted into the mid-second millennium B.C.

The greatest concentration of known sites is in Bahawalpur in the north-central Indus Valley. The Bahawalpur and Sarai Khola data are discussed separately from that of the Swat Valley, which merits individual treatment. Mughal describes most Bahawalpur sites as small, temporary settlements, perhaps of pastoral nomads. Outside of Bahawalpur such sites may lie buried under the thick alluvial deposits of the Indus River. On the other hand, Mughal also found larger, permanent settlements of up to 26 ha which have not yet been identified outside of Bahawalpur. At present, Hakra Phase settlement data are too limited to evaluate.

Hakra Phase pottery includes wheel- and handmade redwares and limited quantities of graywares. Some wheel-made vessels, especially everted rim globular jars, resemble later Kot Dijian Phase pottery in form and decoration. Jars and bowls decorated with geometric comb-incised motifs, "Hakra Incised," also occur. The bowls are similar to those found in Kot Diji Phase occupations like Fabric D at Kalibangan I. Sharply carinated S-shaped jars with external glossy black slip, "Hakra Black Burnished," and bowls with basket-impressed bases are comparable to types associated with Burzahom materials. Other terra-cotta artifacts included bangles, humped bovid figurines, and the first female figurines.

Abundant geometric microliths are reported from Hakra sites. At Sarai Khola I a variety of bone points/punches and spatulas was found as well as a single stone celt. No architectural features have been recognized, but the stone tools associated with the Gumla I (Dani 1970–71) ovens suggest that they may be contemporary with this Phase.

Meadow (in press) identified cattle and sheep/goats/gazelles at Jalilpur I, but the small sample precludes interpretation. Some degree of craft specialization is suggested by the sophisticated ceramic industry, rare metal objects, and the kilns located at some smaller settlements. Metal and shell objects and Hakra pottery in the Amri Phase suggest some degree of interaction with other social groups. In addition, small quantities of black-on-buff pottery at Hakra sites suggest, according to Mughal, that some interaction occurred with Baluchistan Tradition groups.

The early Swat Valley sequence, Periods I–III, is based on the Ghaligai rock-shelter excavations (Stacul 1969, 1981). Period IV is found at Ghaligai as well as at Aligrama I–II (Tusa 1979), early Damkot (Rahman 1968–69), a site designated as Loebanr III (Stacul 1979), Bir-kot-ghundai (Stacul 1981), and at a few other sites (Stacul 1979:661). A degree of cultural continuity links these periods with later developments, Periods V–VI, which are not discussed here due to their late dates and possible Iron Age affiliations.[5]

The Ghaligai excavations present some interpretative problems. The depth of excavations, 12 m, and the structural-stratigraphic characteristics of rock shelters result in a very limited sample for the early periods. Furthermore, rock shelters are favored locations for pastoral nomad camps which may account for the discontinuities noted at Ghaligai. The existence of Hakra Phase pastoral nomadic camps was suggested for sites in Bahawalpur, and this may be the case for Ghaligai also. Thus, the "sudden" appearance of Kot Diji Phase–type occupations in Period II, followed by the reappearance of Hakra occupations in Period III, may reflect shifting sea-sonal pastoral nomadic camp sites rather than major cultural changes affecting the entire Swat Valley. The presence of such pastoral groups may also account for the intrusive Punjab Phase pottery found in Period IV.

Period I pottery is a handmade, mainly red-brown ware, with coarse sand temper, and sometimes coated with a thick red or brown slip. A few burnished grayware sherds also occur. Other noteworthy artifacts are shouldered stone hoes and pointed bone tools. Period II pottery, however, is a wheel-made, occasionally burnished, red-buff ware. Simple geometric black-on-red slip motifs are found as well as a single example with incised motifs. Except for a few unusual vessel forms this pottery corresponds in form and decoration to Kot Diji Phase pottery. Period III witnessed the return of a handmade pottery assemblage. These gray and brown/buff wares are very similar to the handmade Hakra pottery found in Balhawalpur and Sarai Khola I. Vessel forms are very like those known at other Hakra sites except for sharply carinated and pedestal bowls. Stone and bone tools are similar to those in Period I except for a single stone macehead.

Much more is known about Period IV due to the additional data from Loebanr III, Aligrama I–II, Bir-kot-ghundai, and other sites. Although a greater range of variation occurs, most pottery is similar to that from Period III except for limited examples of wheel-made vessels. At Loebanr III and Bir-kot-ghundai, intrusive Punjab Phase black-on-red slip pottery occurs with its characteristic zoomorphic motifs. Other artifacts include polished stone celts or axes, green jade beads, various bone tools, faience objects, a shell bangle, and a copper point and hook. At Loebanr III large oval pit houses and storage pits are found which have their closest parallels in the Burzahom pit houses. In the late occupations stone walls and square rooms are found but no complete buildings are yet exposed. The Kherai cemetery with its rectangular, stone-slab-covered burials may date to this period (Stacul 1979); its inhumations and cenotaphs contained pots and, in some cases, gold earrings.

Little is known about the Period I–III economy except that hunting is mentioned as important; wheat is present in Period II and barley in Period III (Stacul 1981). In Period IV at Loebanr III and Aligrama (Costantini 1979), barleys, some wheats, as well as oats and rice are found, but the most plentiful plant is the lentil. The field pea and grape also occur. The faunal remains (Compagnoni 1979) are dominated almost entirely by domesticated cattle, followed by lesser numbers of sheep-goats and pigs. These economic data in conjunction with the establishment of new settlements and other changes in the archaeological record suggest that significant cultural changes were taking place in this very late example of the Hakra Phase in the Swat Valley. Clearly the Hakra Phase represents a complex, multidimensional development in the Indus Valley Tradition about which little is presently known.[6]

Kot Diji Phase

Characteristic Kot Diji, hereafter KD (see table 1), Phase occupations have been located in Bahawalpur,[7] Gumla II–IV, Jalilpur II, Kalibangan I,[8] Kot Diji Levels 4–16 (Khan 1965), Rahman Dheri (now Rehman Dheri) I–III (Duranni 1981; F. Khan 1979), Sarai Khola IA–II, at various Siswal sites (Suraj Bhan 1975; Shaffer 1981), and at Ghaligai during Swat Valley Period II. At Jalilpur, during Periods I–II, a gradual transition from Hakra to KD Phase–type potteries was defined, unlike Sarai Khola I–II where the change was more abrupt. However, at most sites the initial occupations were Kot Dijian, which in some instances, as at Kot Diji and Kalibangan, were succeeded by Harappan occupations. The Jalilpur data, and to a lesser extent the Sarai Khola and Bahawalpur data, imply a direct cultural relationship between Hakra and KD Phases. Unfortunately a similar transitional sequence linking KD and Harappan Phases has not yet been found. Still there is an emerging consensus, largely reflecting Mughal's (1970, 1973, 1980) research, that such a direct cultural relationship exists. The identification of pottery with traits characteristic of both KD and Harappan Phases at Gumla IV, Rahman Dheri III, perhaps Amri II, and similar pottery at Mehrgarh VIIC (Jarrige, in press b) attests to the existence of a relationship between these two Phases which future research will have to define more precisely. Several radiocarbon dates available for the KD Phase suggest a chronology of ca. 2700–2300 B.C. However, KD Phase pottery was found in the Amri Phase, and Rahman Dheri I dates to the beginning of the third millennium B.C. Moreover, in some cases, such as the eastern Punjab (Shaffer 1981) and Rahman Dheri III, local KD Phase groups may have persisted into the early second millennium B.C. Taking into consideration all these factors, a basic time range of ca. 2800–2300 B.C. is proposed for the KD Phase, with the proviso that significant regional variations existed including KD Phase settlements that were contemporary with the Harappan Phase.

KD pottery demonstrates a degree of regional diversity which in the future may warrant definition of new or subphases. Most pottery is a wheel-made redware that occurs in a wide variety of vessel forms, the most important of which are everted rim globular jars, dish-on-stand, and the first flanged/double rim jars. Monochrome, bichrome, and polychrome decorative schemes involving a wide variety of simple and complex geometric, zoomorphic, and floral motifs are found. A great deal of variation in decorative schemes and vessel forms can be found in KD Phase pottery which may reflect contemporary regional groups and/or temporal differences. Among other terra-cotta artifacts are found the earliest examples of miniature cart frames and wheels, and a wide variety of female figurines.

Other artifacts associated with this Phase include a variety of stone and copper/bronze tools and personal ornaments made from semiprecious stones, shell, and ivory.

Adequate architectural data are available only for Kalibangan I (Lal 1979), which had several features foreshadowing developments in the Harappan Phase. At Kalibangan, mud-brick buildings were oriented toward the cardinal directions and arranged along streets. Individual structures had rooms arranged around a central courtyard containing domestic features, and water drains were constructed with fired bricks. A large, parallelogram-shaped, mud-brick wall with exterior buttresses enclosed the settlement. While similar Harappan Phase–type architecture will be found at other KD Phase settlements it should be noted that at some, such as Sarai Khola II, there is little resemblance to the Harappan.

Although the plant remains have not been published, both the importance and state of agricultural development are indicated by the plowed field found below the first KD Phase occupation at Kalibangan I. Meadow (1982, in press) identified cattle, sheep-goats, and/or gazelles at Jalilpur II. Moreover, the size and age of the cattle suggested they had been kept for dairy products, traction, and breeding as well as for meat. The sheep/goat evidence indicates that they were mainly a meat source.

The sophisticated ceramic, lapidary, shell, and metal industries clearly suggest various degrees of craft specialization. Existence of regional stylistic variations in KD pottery may indicate the presence of local production centers, and the same may be true for other crafts, as for example the massive number of unfinished semiprecious stone beads and lumps of raw materials found at Rahman Dheri. The present concentration of KD Phase settlements in the central and north-central Indus Valley may mean that except for ceramics materials such as lapis lazuli, turquoise, shell, and copper were not locally available. Obviously KD groups were participating in the interaction systems responsible for their distribution and for other types of cultural information. The extent and intensity of this participation is indicated by examples of KD pottery in Sind, Kashmir, Baluchistan, and southern Afghanistan (Shaffer 1978a, 1978b), by ceramic and other artifact similarities linking KD, Hakra, and Amri Phases, and by the use of abstract signs as potter's or owner's marks similar to those identified in Balakot and Amri contexts, and now bearing a direct resemblance to Harappan script characters (Durrani 1981). One dimension of these interaction systems is indicated by a canopied-cart-and-driver motif on a pot found in Banawali I (Bisht and Asthana 1979), a KD settlement in the eastern Punjab. This motif—the presence of minature cart frames and wheels, and bull figurines, combined with Meadow's suggestion that cattle were used for traction—suggests that such vehicles facilitated the distribution of materials and cultural information.

Important settlement pattern changes between Hakra and KD occupations were found in Bahawalpur. The number of permanent settlements almost doubles in the KD Phase, while "camp sites" decrease significantly. Sites associated with industrial activity denoted by kilns increase significantly during the KD Phase. Moreover, three size categories of KD sites were defined: (1) the majority, under 5 ha; (2) 5–10 ha; and (3) over 10 ha, the largest being 27 ha. These data indicate an increased intensity and diversity of KD cultural activities during the KD Phase. The differentiation in site sizes suggests that various social and economic activities were not uniformly distributed among social groups and that perhaps urban centers were present.

Integration Era

Since pronounced cultural homogeneity is a major characteristic of the Integration Era, it contains only the Harappan Phase which not only had its most intense distribution in the central and north-central Indus Valley, but affected the entire Indus Valley and its bordering regions to varying degrees. The Harappan Phase reflects the autonomous development of a complex, urban civilization.

Harappan Phase

Available dates (Agrawal 1982a, 1982b; Agrawal and Kusumgar 1974; Brunswig 1973, 1975; Dales 1973a) indicate ca. 2500–2000 B.C. for the Harappan Phase. At the same time it should be noted that occupations with pottery having both KD and Harappan Phase characteristics have been recognized at several sites,[9] that Harappan and KD Phase occupations have overlapping dates at some sites such as Kalibangan I–II, that some KD settlements such as Rahman Dheri III are contemporary with the Harappan, and that Harappan artifacts have been found in some Regionalization Era occupations, such as the Siswal B sites in the eastern Punjab. Although some (e.g., Dales 1973a:164) feel that these conditions may indicate major chronological problems, the position taken here is that some degree of chronological and stratigraphic overlap is to be expected since the Harappan phenomenon represents a phase in a continuous cultural tradition, while the absence, or limited frequency, of Harappan artifacts at contemporary sites with other types of occupations probably reflects varying degrees of partici-

pation in the Harappan Interaction System. At present, there seem to be no significant cultural discontinuities that separate the Harappan Phase from earlier, indigenous developments.

Major excavations relating to this Phase include Allahdino (Fairservis 1982; Hoffman and Cleland 1977; Hoffman and Shaffer 1973), Balakot, Banawali (Bisht 1976, 1982; Bisht and Asthana 1979), Chanhu-daro (Mackay 1943), Harappa (Vats 1940; Wheeler 1947), Kalibangan, Lothal (Rao 1973, 1979), Mohenjo-daro (Marshall 1931; Mackay 1938; Dales 1965a, 1965b; Dales and Kenoyer 1986), and Surkotada (Joshi 1972). A wealth of descriptive detail is available for this Phase, and the interested reader should consult recent summaries (see n. 4; Agrawal 1982b; Fentress 1976; Possehl 1982).

Harappan pottery (see Dales and Kenoyer 1986 and Shaffer 1974a for recent analysis) is distinguished by its quantity, range of vessel shape and size variation, black-on-red decorative style, extensive use of the peacock motif, and a basic homogeneity throughout its distribution (see Manchanda 1972 for catalog). Its homogeneity provides a striking contrast to the rich regional styles of the previous Era, but some traits, such as certain vessel forms and individual decorative motifs, link Harappan pottery with earlier styles. Harappan pottery has its most intense distribution in the central Indus Valley, while away from this area, as in the eastern Punjab, its frequency is more restricted, being usually found at larger sites where it is associated with Regionalization-style pottery. Other terra-cotta objects correspond to those found in the previous Era, especially the KD Phase, although stylistic changes occur.

An important change has been noted (Cleland 1977; Hoffman and Cleland 1977) for the lithic industry, where pointed and cutting tools are replaced by metal tools to a significant degree. Harappan copper/bronze metallurgy, and to a lesser extent silver and gold, is most impressive for the quantity and variety of objects, and for their widespread distribution in a variety of cultural contexts. Lapidary crafts were highly developed, and many of this Tradition's characteristic artifacts such as etched and long-barrel carnelian beads, cubical "weights," and steatite stamp seals were manufactured in quantity and widely distributed, as were shell and faience objects.

Excavated sites revealed complex, mud and/or fired brick structures, sometimes with stone foundations. Multiroom habitation (Sarcina 1978–79, 1979) and nonhabitation units were grouped into large blocks separated by streets. Although some main thoroughfares intersect at right angles, the so-called grid pattern of Harappan settlements has been overemphasized (Jansen 1979). Monumental/public architectural units such as enclosing walls, streets, platforms, hydraulic features, and large nonhabitational and nonindustrial buildings, along with industrial areas are most intense at large urban sites like Harappa and Mohenjo-daro, but qualitatively similar features are found at small settlements such as Allahdino.

The Harappan subsistence economy was very complex and involved a number of crops (for recent summaries see McKean 1983; Visnu-Mittre and Savithri 1982), including wheats, barley, rice, dates, cotton, melons, peas, seasame, chick-peas, and millets. Rice and cotton represent significant additions to the economy, but at present it is impossible to determine their place of origin and relative economic contribution. At Balakot (Meadow 1979), during the Harappan occupation, emphasis on cattle over sheep and goats continued, and water buffalo and nilgai appear. Increased use of shellfish and fish during this Phase was noted at Balakot. Use of marine resources, the definition of a shell bangle industry at Balakot and other sites (Dales and Kenoyer 1977; Kenoyer 1983), and the widespread inland distribution of marine shell all suggest that the exploitation of marine resources were important and may help explain Harappan settlements located along the coast (Dales 1962).

The sophistication of Harappan material culture clearly indicates the presence of full- and part-time craft specialists, and craft activities are also reflected in the Bahawalpur settlement pattern. The number of Harappan sites quadruples compared to the KD Phase, and almost all are permanent settlements. "Camp sites" have their lowest frequency—6 percent—in this Phase. Almost half the settlements are classed as industrial involving the pyrotechnology of ceramics, fired bricks, and metallurgy, while one-fifth of the remainder also bear evidence of such activities. The three previous site size categories persisted into this Phase, and one, Ganweriwala, approached the dimensions of Mohenjo-daro and Harappa. Clearly cultural-economic activities were differentially distributed across the landscape, and urban centers were present. The intensity of settlement and industrial activity during the Harappan Phase in Bahawalpur cannot be duplicated in any other region or phase associated with this Tradition, suggesting that it was a major focus of cultural and economic activities.

The Bahawalpur data contrast sharply with information from other areas. In Sind (Flam 1981a, 1981b, 1982, 1984), Harappan Phase sites are less numerous, smaller, and more widely dispersed, probably reflecting more dispersed agricultural resources. Although even the small settlements like Allahdino have all the Harappan characteristics, some regional stylistic variations do appear in the pottery. In Saurashtra (Possehl 1980), numerous Harappan small "camp sites" suggest the presence of pastoral nomads, but at larger nucleated settlements like Lothal, Rangpur, and Surkotada, Harappan artifacts and features are associated with regional ceramic styles of Black-and-Red Ware, Lustrous Red Ware, and a distinctive regional

decorated pottery type at Surkotada. Furthermore, no Saurashtra urban site approaches the dimensions of those in the central Indus Valley. The Saurashtra data appear to be somewhat analogous to the eastern Punjab pattern noted previously.

Social groups in the central Indus Valley played a vital role in the development and maintenance of the Harappan Phase. It is possible that this area was a central, but not the only, industrial region for the manufacture of many, but not all, characteristic ceramic, lithic, shell, and metal Harappan artifacts. Once processed, these goods were distributed throughout the Indus Valley via the Harappan Interaction System.

The Harappan Interaction System refers to all avenues of intersite communication that were responsible for the distribution of Harappan Phase characteristics throughout the Indus Valley. It represents an intensification and formalization of similar ones already present in the Regionalization Era. Its extensiveness is reflected not only in the materials involved, such as semiprecious stones, metals, shells, and ceramics but also in the functional nature of the artifacts, from shell bangles to bronze points. No doubt other, more perishable commodities like food, wood, and textiles were also involved. Other matrices of social communication and trade must have been present to account for the homogeneity in noncommodity-type traits such as architecture and the use of a common formalized script (Fairservis 1983).

The structure of this interaction system is partially discernible. For example, given the alluvial plain location of Bahawalpur, it is doubtful that the intense industrial activity noted there could have been sustained by local resources except, of course, for clay. Thus, if metal and semiprecious stones were processed there, they must have come from elsewhere. Raw material source areas have usually been attributed to Baluchistan or the Iranian plateau (e.g., Lamberg-Karlovsky 1972). Critical reviews of the evidence (Chakrabarti 1977b; Shaffer 1982a), however, indicate Harappan objects and/or sites are rare even in neighboring Baluchistan, and at the same time, artifacts from western areas are very rare in a Harappan context. Alternatively, Harappan settlements in the eastern Punjab would have provided direct, or indirect, access to mineral deposits in the Himalayas and north Rajasthan, while Saurashtran settlements would have had access to deposits in Gujarat and south Rajasthan. Indeed, Possehl (1980:70–77) interprets Lothal as a "Gateway City" that focused on the production of finished and semifinished objects traded out of the community. He also suggests that many commodities may have been obtained by interaction with hunting-gathering, or pastoral nomadic, groups as at Langnaj and Bagor, and/or agricultural groups like Ahar located in western India. Likewise, Harappan coastal settlements such as Balakot,

Sotka-koh, and Sutkagen-dor may have played a roll in obtaining and processing such local resources as dried fish, shell, or other materials. Clearly multiple commodity sources were available within the larger Indus Valley area even if they were broadly dispersed.

Existence of full- or part-time specialists concerned with distributional activities is postulated on the intensity and extensiveness of this interaction. Coastal and riverine transport was possible, and the use of carts has already been mentioned for the previous Era. Another important factor that may have facilitated distribution and communication was the camel, the bones of which were identified at Mohenjo-daro and Harappa, with photographs revealing a camel skeleton excavated by Wheeler at Mohenjo-daro (Meadow 1984b and 1986). Although the camel may (Compagnoni and Tosi 1978) or may not (Meadow 1984b and 1986) be native to the Indus Valley, it first appears in the archaeological record during this period. Camels can carry or pull a much larger load more efficiently than cattle, need less water, and have more versatile foraging capacity. The appearance of the camel and the development of the Harappan Interaction System may be coincidental, but the cultural and economic impact of this animal must have been very significant (Shaffer 1988).

Shortugai

Information about Shortugai is still very limited (Francfort 1981; Francfort and Pottier 1978; Gardin and Lyonnet 1978–79), but the nature of the finds deserves special discussion. Shortugai is a Harappan settlement on the Amu Darya in north Afghanistan and is the only known Harappan settlement west of the Baluchistan–Indus Valley margin. Artifacts, especially the ceramics, associated with Shortugai I–II are characteristically Harappan, and the few available dates suggest it is contemporary with this Phase in the Indus Valley.

Shortugai's location near lapis lazuli deposits in northeast Afghanistan has suggested to some (e.g., Kohl 1978) that this settlement was associated with a lapis lazuli trade. However, lapis lazuli objects are relatively rare in the Indus Valley, and Fairservis (pers. comm.) seriously questions many identifications of this stone in the Harappan Phase. Furthermore, definitely Harappan artifacts are rare in central Asian sites and central Asian objects have yet to be identified in the Indus Valley. An alternative explanation may be that if, as Meadow (1984b) suspects, the Bactrian camel was present in the Harappan Phase, and if the camel was important in maintaining the Harappan influence (Shaffer 1988), then obtaining a source of these animals may have played an important role in establishing the Shortugai settlement. Unfortunately, until more is known about the archaeology of Afghanistan, Shortugai remains a controversial enigma.

Localization Era

The Localization Era is not well known, and the few available dates indicate a time period of ca. 2100–1300 B.C. Previously it was thought that a significant cultural discontinuity separated protohistoric Bronze Age from early historic Iron Age developments in South Asia. However, excavations at Bhagwanpura (see Punjab Phase below) defined a stratigraphic-cultural overlap of these periods. Although the picture is not complete, it is increasingly obvious that this Tradition represents a cultural continuum stretching from perhaps 7000 B.C. into the early centuries A.D. Recognition of this continuum within the context of this Era implies a possible independent development of iron technology (Chakrabarti 1974, 1977a; Shaffer 1984a) and necessitates fundamental rethinking about present concepts regarding the Indo-Aryan invasions into the subcontinent (Shaffer 1984b).

The bulk of information for this Era focuses on ceramic data. What appears to have happened is that characteristic Harappan decorative elements and vessel forms were blended with regional ceramic styles that had persisted in varying degrees. By the end of this Era in some regions there appears to have been a transition from this Harappan-related pottery into the gray and redwares characteristic of Painted Gray Ware groups which persist into the Iron Age. Harappan-style shell, semiprecious stone, metal, and faience objects were still made and distributed while, at the same time, other characteristic artifacts such as stamp seals, triangular cakes, miniature cart frames and wheels, perforated pottery, cubical weights, and fired bricks either disappeared or, like script characters, became rare. Mud-brick buildings are known, but few have been excavated. In some regions these mud-brick buildings were associated with semicircular, mud, thatch, and post structures. Little is known about the subsistence economy but a basic resemblance to that of the Harappan Phase may be assumed. Several Harappan settlements including urban centers were abandoned, and many new, generally smaller, ones were established. Although many scholars (e.g., Ghosh 1973) contend that urban centers disappeared entirely, the discovery of large sites with pottery from this Era (Mughal, in press; Shaffer 1981; Suraj Bhan and Shaffer 1978) may yet challenge these ideas. Together these factors indicate that the Harappan Interaction System had undergone a major disruption, structural change, or both, and no longer was the major integrating force. Whether the causes for these changes were natural, such as coastal uplift, changes in river drainage patterns, and increased desiccation, or cultural, or perhaps a combination of both, cannot yet be determined.

Punjab Phase

Settlements of the Punjab Phase are found in the central and north-central Indus Valley and include Cemetery H at Harappa, Mitathal IIB (Suraj Bhan 1975), Bhagwanpura IA–B (Joshi 1976, 1977, 1978a, 1978b; Joshi and Madhu Bala 1982), and others such as Siswal C–D sites (Shaffer 1981). Chronological data are limited but a suggested range would be ca. 2100–1300 B.C. The terminal date is based on the presence of Painted Gray Ware–type pottery in Bhagwanpura IB. At Atranjikera (Tripathi 1976) a *single* early date for this type of pottery ranged between 1300–1000 B.C. A series of TL dates from Bhagwanpura suggests that the transition to Painted Gray Ware pottery took place between 1500–1000 B.C. Although presently difficult to substantiate, this terminal date fits the chronological pattern for this Era.

Pottery from this Phase is generally referred to as Late Harappan, or Cemetery H, which is a very distinctive black-on-red slipped pottery. The vessel shapes, decorative schemes, and individual aspects of the motifs, however, betray their Harappan origin although the style of execution is distinctive. In Bhagwanpura IB some Late Harappan vessel forms were made in grayware, a few Late Harappan motifs were found on Painted Gray Ware pottery, and typical Painted Gray Ware types of red and gray potteries were found associated with Late Harappan pottery. Moreover, semicircular, mud, thatch, and post structures similar to those known from other Painted Gray Ware sites were associated with mud-brick buildings. Bhagwanpura is the first well-defined ceramic and stratigraphic link connecting the Late Harappan, Punjab Phase, with the Painted Gray Ware complex. Finally, the limited examples of pottery with white paint/slip found associated with this Phase are probably intrusive Jhukar Phase examples.

The most important information on settlement pattern comes from Bahawalpur (but see also Dikshit 1982; Madhu Bala 1978; Shaffer 1981; Suraj Bhan and Shaffer 1978). The number of sites decreases from those of the Harappan Phase by almost two-thirds, and most of these represent new settlements. Exclusively industrial sites decreased, while the number of "camp sites" increased. Persistence of the three site-size categories suggests that urban centers were still present. Mughal's (in press) settlement data indicate that the Punjab Phase more closely resembles that of the KD Phase than the immediately preceding Harappan Phase.

Jhukar Phase

The Jhukar Phase is found mainly in the Sind with excavated occupations identified at Amri, Chanhu-daro, Jhukar (Majumdar 1934), and Mohenjo-daro. At these sites Jhukar and Harappan Phase pottery overlap, and a great deal of stylistic similarity may be recognized (see Dales and Kenoyer 1986 for discussion). Jhukar Phase occupations can be defined, however, which are stratigraphically later than the Harappan Phase. Only a single radiocarbon date is available which ranges from 2165 to 1860 B.C., but this Phase was probably contemporary with others from this Era.

Most information concerning this Phase is limited to objects of material culture, and especially to the black-on-red slip ceramics which are distinguished by the occasional use of white paint or slip as a background and the limited use of zoomorphic motifs. Stamp seals continue but they are circular, made from terra-cotta or faience, have no script, and are geometric or, more rarely, zoomorphic in pattern. Mud-brick architectural units were not as substantial as in earlier Phases.

Rangpur Phase

The Rangpur Phase (see Possehl 1980; Possehl and Rissman, chap. 27, this vol., for discussion) is located only in Gujarat where it is best exemplified by Rangpur IIB–III (Rao 1963) and Lothal B (Rao 1973, 1979). At both sites the Rangpur Phase is stratigraphically later than the Harappan, but only a few dates from Lothal B are available. However, because of the presence of Rangpur Phase pottery at Ahar and Navdatoli in western India, Possehl (1980) would date these developments between ca. 2100–1380 B.C.

Most Harappan artifacts disappear and Lustrous Red Ware, hereafter LRW, occurs for the first time. LRW is a fine redware that is red slipped and polished, often to a high luster. The black motifs are strikingly similar to those found on Cemetery H pottery. However, the vessel forms are so different from those of Cemetery H that one should not overemphasize this stylistic similarity. Moreover, nothing like LRW has yet been found in the Jhukar Phase. The black-on-red decoration, some individual motifs, and basic similarities in vessel forms all indicate Harappan affinities. Another ware of this Phase is Black-and-Red Ware which is sometimes decorated with simple white motifs. However, the known geographical distribution of Black-and-Red Ware is so great, from Gujarat to the Ganges Valley (see H. N. Singh 1982), that it is not possible to determine whether this type was locally manufactured.

In the Saurashtra region, Possehl (1980) has made some initial observations on changes in settlement pattern. Here the initial occupation by Harappan groups established several small settlements in riverine regions as well as the only known urban center of Lothal. By the advent of the Rangpur Phase many Harappan sites including Lothal were abandoned, but there was an increase in smaller settlements with Rangpur IIB–C type pottery. Rangpur III settlements were even fewer in number and still smaller. Possehl attributed these changes to a resurgence of pastoral nomadism and dry farming which may have been associated with the availability of domesticated millet. This proliferation of smaller settlements following the abandonment of Harappan Phase sites somewhat parallels the situation already noted for the Punjab Phase except for the continued presence of a few large-size settlements there. Clearly the demise of, or structural changes in, the Harappan Interaction System affected all regions.

The Baluchistan Tradition

Geographical Area

The Baluchistan area[10] in western Pakistan and southeastern Iran consists of several northeast-southwest mountain ranges separated by narrow alluvial valleys. Although there are some perennial rivers, most of its moisture comes from summer and winter rains and sometimes snow. A rugged mountainous topography, narrow alluvial valleys, and bimodal distribution of moisture distinguish Baluchistan from the arid plateau regions to the west and the monsoonal Indus River alluvial plain to the east. Although geographical conditions are not determinative factors, they contributed to the development of a distinct cultural tradition.

The Tradition

The Baluchistan Tradition[11] (see figs. 3 and 6) dates roughly between pre 6000–1300 B.C. Food production was based on domesticated plants, particularly barley and wheat, and on cattle, sheep, goats, and water buffalos. Hunting and gathering may have been regionally and periodically important, but generally declined through time. Although the predominant archaeological site is the small agricultural village, urban centers and quite possibly pastoral nomad camps (Shaffer 1974b, 1978b) were also present.

Architectural units show a great deal of regional variation. Public/monumental buildings have been recognized at only a few sites, but the large size of many sites suggests that such buildings were probably present.

The most common lithic tools were milling stones, ground stone balls, and flint blades, microliths, and scrapers. The large variety of semiprecious stone beads and pendants, alabaster bowls, and steatite/chlorite beads, pendants, stamp seals and, rarely, bowls demonstrates that lapidary crafts were highly developed. Likewise, marine shells were imported and manufactured locally into personal ornaments. Metallurgy was equally well developed and includes a variety of copper/bronze personal ornaments and tools. Although the quantity and quality of these objects vary from one settlement to another, the general impression is that of a variety of part- and perhaps full-time craft specialists.

The most impressive craft activity, and a major feature of this Tradition, was the ceramic industry. The high quality and rich, decorative diversity of Baluchistan pottery have few parallels in the Bronze Age world. Pottery was predominantly a red-buff ware, but regionally, as in the Quetta Valley and Kachi plain, graywares were produced in significant quantities. Wheel-made pottery appears early and quickly becomes the dominant technique, but handmade and mold-made techniques persisted. A wide variety of vessel forms occurs, some of which like cannisters are unique to this Tradition. Vessels were treated with a variety of colored slips as well as textured slips, including a distinctive variety known as "Wet Ware." Monochrome, bichrome, and, more rarely, polychrome decorative schemes are found that utilize a rich variety of geometric, zoomorphic, and floral motifs. Graywares, like Faiz Muhammad Graywares, were made from a finer paste, turned on a fast wheel, fired to a higher temperature, and decorated with black or red motifs painted directly on the vessel surface. Other important terra-cotta objects include bangles, animal and human figurines, and rare stamp seals.

The sophisticated material culture associated with this Tradition indicates a considerable development of craft activities. For example, Mehrgarh became a regional ceramic production center, and no doubt others were present. The existence of such centers implies a relatively sophisticated economic organization capable of coordinating commodity production and distribution. The persistence throughout this Tradition of regional ceramic styles suggests an economic organization efficient at local levels. At the same time, the distribution of some commodities such as marine shells, certain semiprecious stones, and intrusive ceramics indicates that interregional distribution systems were also present and were an important part of multiple interaction systems which linked several of the areas. However, this interregional interaction was never intense enough to homogenize the various Phases into a single cultural system. Unlike the Indus Valley Tradition, where regional phases were integrated into a single Harappan cultural phase, the social groups in this Baluchistan Tradition maintained strong regional identities reflected by the persistence of regional ceramic styles. Thus, the Integration and Localization Eras never appeared in the Baluchistan Tradition.

Some interaction did take place between social groups of this Tradition and those belonging to the Indus Valley (see nn. 7 and 10) and Helmand Traditions. However, given the present data it is difficult to evaluate the nature, intensity, and cultural significance of these interactions between Traditions. The sporadic finds of Harappan artifacts throughout Baluchistan, excepting the major Harappan occupations at Dabar Kot, Nowsharo, and Pathani Damb (DeCardi 1964:25; Fairservis 1959:308–28; Jarrige, in press b; Mughal 1972:137–44), indicate some degree of contact between them. Likewise Baluchistan Tradition artifacts have been located at a few sites of the Indus Valley Tradition. Still, given their geographical proximity there is surprisingly little evidence of interaction. Whether this reflects significant ethnic differences or only an inadequate archaeological sample cannot yet be determined.

On the other hand interaction with the Helmand Tradition in southern Afghanistan was quite intense during a relatively brief period in the Quetta Valley. Indeed, cultural similarities are so pronounced that one cannot discount the possibility of a direct cultural intrusion.

Raw material procurement may have structured and maintained these intra- and intertraditional interactions. However, whether this resulted from detailed distribution network or networks or was the result of casual but regular exchanges between various social groups including pastoral nomads is not now known. Since it is unlikely that such intergroup interaction focused exclusively on commodity movement, to some extent social, political, and religious behaviors must have been involved.

Early Food-Producing Era

The Early Food-Producing Era of the Baluchistan Tradition is best known from Mehrgarh IA, or the Mehrgarh Phase of the Indus Valley Tradition. Our present level of knowledge suggests that development of a food-producing economy as exemplified by Mehrgarh IA data represents a sequence of cultural events common to both Baluchistan and the Indus Valley—the Mehrgarh Phase thus serving as the initial phase for both Traditions. Although our most comprehensive data are from Mehrgarh, Fairservis (1956) was the first to identify a nonceramic cultural occupation associated with domesticates in Kili Gul Muhammad I. His sample was very small but the Mehrgarh data have validated his interpretation of that important sequence.

Some caution should be exercised in evaluating the economic data from Mehrgarh within the context of the Baluchistan Tradition, for its location on the Kachi plain may have affected its representativeness. Given its close proximity to the monsoonal Indus Valley areas, the moisture conditions at Mehrgarh may have differed from the rest of Baluchistan, resulting in a higher ratio of some domesticated species like cattle and the presence of others such as water buffalo. Thus Mehrgarh may not reflect precisely the situation in all other Baluchistan regions. Likewise, the few late dates for Kili Gul Muhammad I,

ca. 4600–3900 B.C., may indicate that this Phase regionally persisted for a longer period of time.

Regionalization Era

The Regionalization Era incorporates all archaeological phenomena subsequent to the Mehrgarh Phase until the early Iron Age, or ca. post 6000–1300 B.C. The broad chronological and geographical range of this Era and the cultural diversity definable within it make it a somewhat unwieldy heuristic category. Matters are further complicated by the absence, or very limited amounts, of data available for many regions. At the same time, this persistent cultural diversity imparts to this Tradition a major characteristic distinguishing it from neighboring ones.

Kachi Phase

The Kachi Phase has been defined on the bases of Mehrgarh IB–IIA (see previous citations, especially Lechevallier and Quivron 1981 and Jarrige 1985, in press a and b). Its major features are the introduction of pottery, the first substantial mud-brick buildings, evidence for craft activities, a commitment to an agricultural economy, and the first copper artifact. The stratigraphy and some aspects of the material culture indicate a degree of cultural continuity with the previous Mehrgarh Phase, or Mehrgarh IA.

The chronology for this Phase is very complex and related to that for the Mehrgarh Phase. Mehrgarh IA was dated to the seventh millennium B.C. by the excavators, with actual dates ranging between ca. 8200–4100 B.C., but these dates have a more central range of ca. 5300–4800 B.C. Given the extensive deposits, 7+ m, associated with Mehrgarh IA, the much earlier date proposed by the excavators may indeed prove justified. The dates for Mehrgarh IB range between ca. 4990–4430 B.C., with a central range of ca. 4950–4550 B.C. Unfortunately no dates have been published for Mehrgarh IIA. Given this information plus the stratigraphic and cultural continuity linking Mehrgarh IA–IIA, the date tentatively proposed here for the Kachi Phase is ca. 5000–4300 B.C. rather than that of the excavator's sixth millennium B.C. chronology for these developments. Thus the previous Mehrgarh Phase would date possibly as early as 7000 B.C. and most certainly within the range of post 6000–5000 B.C.

One, of the most important archaeological developments of this Phase is the initial appearance of pottery (Jarrige, in press a and b). The first pots were medium to large handmade bowls constructed with a coarse paste. These were manufactured by coating both sides of baskets, some of which had already been coated with asphalt, with clay and then firing the vessel at a low temperature. In a few cases the external vessel surface was coated with a dark red slip. Jarrige (in press a) thinks that pottery was locally developed at Mehrgarh in response to a need for containers more efficient than asphalt-coated baskets. Also found were unfired clay animal and human figurines.

During this Phase the settlement size and complexity of Mehrgarh increased. Several square, mud-brick buildings divided into small compartments, or cells, some less than 1 m², were constructed in conjunction with buttressed terracing walls. The small compartment size, absence of habitation debris, and the presence of grain impressions indicate these buildings were used for grain storage. Areas outside the buildings had debris reflecting domestic and craft activities like lapidary and shell working.

Several graves (Lechevallier and Quivron 1981) were associated with this Phase. In Mehrgarh IB each was associated with a mud-brick wall or platform. Grave goods included stone tools and vessels, cakes of red ochre, and strings of beads made from marine shells, turquoise, lapis lazuli, and other stones. A single cylindrical copper bead was found in a child's grave.

Significant changes took place in the subsistence economy. Faunal evidence (Meadow 1981, 1982, 1984a) indicates that by Mehrgarh IIA wild animals had been almost entirely replaced by domesticates and, moreover, that the major domesticated animals were cattle, followed by lesser numbers of sheep and goats. Plant remains (Costantini 1984) are clearly dominated by naked six-row barley, with lesser amounts of hulled six-row barley, two-row barley, einkorn, emmer, and bread wheat. The other plants identified were jujube and dates. Quite clearly these developments suggest an extensive commitment to an agricultural economy which is reflected in the other characteristics of this Phase.

Kili Gul Muhammad Phase

Kili Gul Muhammad, hereafter KGM, Phase occupations can be identified at Kili Gul Muhammad II–III (Fairservis 1956), Mehrgarh IIB–III,[12] Surab I–II (DeCardi 1965), Sur Jangal I–II, Rana Ghundai I–III, Early Dabar Kot, and possibly Early Periano Ghundai (see Fairservis 1959 for discussion of these sites). The KGM and subsequent Kechi Beg Phases are the only ones identified in both north and south Baluchistan.

Chronological data are limited to four dates—two each from Mehrgarh IIB and Rana Ghundai—with a very wide range, 5975–3345 B.C. A few examples of late KGM phase–style pottery were found in the Amri Phase, which dates ca. 3600–3000 B.C. Likewise, KGM Phase–style pottery is found in Mundigak I–II, a Helmand Tradition site, which must date pre-3000 B.C. At Mehrgarh the excavators date Period III between 4000–3500 B.C. At the

same time several cultural traits link the Kachi and KGM Phases. Taking these factors into consideration, the time period for the KGM Phase proposed here is ca. 4300–3500 B.C.

The Kachi Phase coarse pottery is replaced in Mehrgarh IIB by a redware pottery made from a finer paste, fired to a higher temperature, and made with a turning device. Initially these pots were burnished but undecorated; however, later examples were decorated with simple painted geometric motifs. By late Mehrgarh IIB a thin, burnished, red-buff ware decorated with more complex motifs sometimes executed on a red slip was found. This decorative style evolves in Mehrgarh III to include friezes of complex geometric and zoomorphic motifs. The early black-on-red slipped pottery resembles Fairservis's (1956:256) Kili Gul Muhammad Black-on-red Slip, and later examples compare to his (Fairservis 1959:365–67) Jangal Painted. Stylistic parallels also exist between this pottery and the Togau Ware defined by DeCardi (1965:128–34). By the end of Mehrgarh III a greenish gray ware with finger-impressed surfaces appears which may represent early examples of "Wet Wares" (Fairservis 1956:269–70). The quantity and quality of Mehrgarh III pottery, and the presence of ceramic industrial areas, indicate significant development of this craft activity.

Other craft activities were also undergoing intensification (Jarrige, in press b). Although only a few fragments of copper rods and pins were found, the discovery of crucibles with melted copper ore adhering indicates a degree of local production by Mehrgarh III. Particularly interesting was a fragment of a copper compartmented amulet, or stamp seal, found in one of the Mehrgarh III graves, but most burials had few grave goods. Numerous lapidary and shell workshop areas were found throughout this Phase. Moreover, the use of lapis lazuli, turquoise, carnelian, and marine shells in these craft activities indicates communication with areas outside Baluchistan.

The compartmented buildings similar to those in the Kachi Phase continued, and again these appear to have functioned as granaries with workshop areas located outside. Excavations at sites other than Mehrgarh were too limited to define structures.

The subsistence economy was similar to that of the Kachi Phase. However, oats and large quantities of wild or cultivated cotton seeds were found. The high incidence of six-row barley and possible cotton cultivation suggests that some type of irrigation system may have been present. Cattle remained the major domesticated animal, followed by sheep and goats.

Kechi Beg Phase

Kechi Beg, hereafter KB, Phase occupations can be identified at Kili Gul Muhammad IV–Damb Sadaat I (Fairservis 1956), Surab III, late Sur Jangal III, Rana Ghundai III–IV, Mehrgarh IV–V, and possibly Dabar Kot and Periano Ghundai. At Kili Gul Muhammad and Mehrgarh, although this Phase was stratigraphically later, it demonstrated continuity with the KGM Phase. Only two dates are available from Damb Sadaat I, and these agree basically with Jarrige's estimated chronology for Mehrgarh IV–V of ca. 3500–3000 B.C. However, KB Phase–style pottery in Pirak I–II (Jarrige, Santoni, and Enault 1979), which dates significantly later, suggests that KB Phase–related groups may have persisted considerably later.

The appearance of polychrome pottery characterizes this Phase, although KGM-style pottery continues. Mehrgarh IV (Jarrige 1977:74–94 and previous citations) had three major styles of decorated pottery: monochrome with black motifs; bichrome with motifs in two colors; and polychrome. Polychrome with brown, plum, red, and white motifs involved complex geometric patterns covering large vessel areas, whereas the other two styles are similar to KGM pottery except for more intricate geometric and more stylized zoomorphic motifs. Greenish gray Wet Wares are found in larger quantities and include fragile goblets and carinated jars.

In Mehrgarh V, polychrome motifs become much bolder and are restricted to bowls and small vessels, and monochrome decorations replace bichrome ones. Concomitant changes in firing techniques allowed the production of homogeneous red and reddish gray wares, and the decoration on reddish gray wares changes from geometric to naturalistic motifs, foreshadowing later ceramic developments. Other terra-cotta objects remain unchanged except for female figurines, which undergo increasing stylization.

Terra-cotta, bone, and steatite stamp seals with geometric motifs appear for the first time in this Phase and with some frequency. The number of stonecutting tools declines, and Jarrige (1981a:111) suggests that this may indicate an increasing importance of copper/bronze tools, even though only a few such tools were found. No workshop areas were located, but there is no evidence of a decline in craft activities.

Architectural structures, defined only in Mehrgarh IV, represent a complex series of rooms and open areas associated with habitation activities.

Although no plant and animal remains have been reported, no drastic changes from the KGM Phase are anticipated.

Damb Sadaat Phase

Damb Sadaat, hereafter DS, Phase material, first found in Damb Sadaat II–III, is best represented by Mehrgarh VI–VII. Several characteristics, especially ceramics, link it with the KB Phase at Mehrgarh. At Damb Sadaat the KB and DS Phase relationships are not as obvious, which probably reflects the more limited excavations. At both sites the DS Phase is stratigraphically later than the KB Phase. Mehrgarh was abandoned after Period VII which the excavators estimate to be about 2600 B.C. Five dates from Damb Sadaat II–III range from 3650 to 2395 B.C., with a central range of ca. 3000–2600 B.C. Therefore a suggested chronology for the DS Phase is ca. 3000–2500 B.C. However, there are some ceramic similarities linking this Phase with the KD Phase settlement of Rahman Dheri II–III, which dates ca. 2500–2000 B.C. Thus, it is possible that the DS Phase persisted into the second half of the third millennium B.C. and would have been, in part, contemporary with the KD and Harappan Phases of the Indus Valley Tradition.

During the DS Phase, Mehrgarh became a local ceramic production center as evidenced by extensive kiln remains (C. Jarrige and Audouze 1978). Continuity and change characterize this pottery when compared to that of the previous KB Phase at Mehrgarh. For example, Mehrgarh V polychrome persisted into but disappeared by the end of Mehrgarh VI. Likewise, a major decorated pottery was a monochrome red-buff ware with motifs similar to those of Mehrgarh V but with a tendency toward more naturalistic zoomorphic and floral motifs, including rather elaborate friezes, as well as complex hatched and solid geometric motifs. This pottery comes in a variety of vessel forms including pedestal and stemmed vessels and at present appears to be a local production of Quetta Ware (Jarrige 1985 and in press b). Quetta Ware, as defined by Fairservis (1956:255–56, 259–61, 321–26), incorporates most motifs and vessel forms found at Mehrgarh except that at Damb Sadaat motifs were occasionally applied to a white slip. Fairservis found an initial Damb Sadaat II decorative emphasis on solid geometric motifs, with occasional use of hatched zoomorphic and floral motifs. In Damb Sadaat III this shifts to linear and curved geometric motifs. By Mehrgarh VII utilitarian- and luxury-type potteries were mass-produced in a variety of vessel forms including several stemmed examples. Wet Wares were also present in limited quantities. The most spectacular pottery was Faiz Muhammad Grayware (Fairservis 1956:263–65; but see also Wright 1984) found at both Mehrgarh and Damb Sadaat. Mehrgarh decorated graywares have been described by Jarrige and Lechevallier (1979:520) as having high quality and a rich variety of zoomorphic, floral, and geometric motifs that are sometimes arranged in very naturalistic friezes. Open bowls, however, have more typical "Quetta"-type motifs. The origin of these graywares is probably in the fine reddish-gray wares first made in Mehrgarh V. Finally in Mehrgarh VIIC, the last occupation, Quetta Ware and Faiz Muhammad Grayware were found associated with a group of pottery having both KD and Harappan Phase characteristics (see n. 9).

Naturalistic animal and human figurines were mass-produced in this Phase. In Mehrgarh VII, standing male and seated female figurines were made with legs and arms separated from the body, beaklike noses, and goggle eyes, with both sexes resembling the "Zob mother-goddesses" found throughout Baluchistan. Square and circular terra-cotta compartmented stamp seals and a single one with a zoomorphic motif occurred.

Stone artifacts were like those of previous Phases, including a variety of semiprecious stone beads, steatite compartmented stamp seals, and alabaster bowls. Metal objects were rare, but copper/bronze tools and personal ornaments were identified. The sophisticated material culture, identification of work areas, and the location of objects in various stages of manufacture associated with this phase betray the existence of part- and full-time specialists.

The only Mehrgarh VI architectural features were a series of habitation rooms and open work areas. The earliest public/monumental architecture, a large mud-brick platform, was found in Mehrgarh VII. North of the platform was a narrow mud-brick wall with pilasters attached to a room complex. Overlooking this platform was another series of mud-brick, rectangular, habitation rooms. Here, in a corridor separating two rooms, lay an adult burial in a clay box with grave goods. A series of infant burials in clay boxes, some with grave goods, came from deposits above Mehrgarh VII. A large number of adult graves and cenotaphs with central Asian–style objects were found at Mehrgarh, but their stratigraphic context has not yet been published.[13]

Rectangular mud-brick habitation structures were identified in Damb Sadaat II, and a large mud-brick platform in Damb Sadaat III. The platform, the only public/monumental architecture, was associated with stone drains, a mud-brick bench, and spur walls connecting it with other areas of the site. Below the platform, in a small hollow, were a human skull and female figurines.

The subsistence base was like that of previous Phases except for a decreased importance of cattle.

DS Phase social groups maintained extensive communication with other groups. The KD-Harappan Phase–style pottery in Mehrgarh VIIC clearly indicates some link with the Indus Valley Tradition. Intrusive DS Phase–style pottery in other Baluchistan Phases and Nal Phase–style pottery in the DS Phase occupations demonstrate contact between social groups in this Tradition. Likewise, lapis lazuli and turquoise indicate contact with groups to the west, and marine shells with groups to the south. Finally there is a pronounced cultural similarity linking DS Phase groups with those in southern Afghanistan belonging to the Helmand Tradition (see below for

discussion). This information, together with the evidence that Mehrgarh had become a regional production center, argues for the intensification of interaction systems which linked various Baluchistan Tradition Phases during this period.

Nal Phase

Nal occupations are found mainly in south Baluchistan (DeCardi 1983), where the Surab sequence (DeCardi 1965) is a major stratigraphic reference. No dates are available for Nal occupations, therefore a chronology must be constructed based on their stratigraphic positions and intrusive potteries. Surab III, which had both Nal and KB potteries, is later than the KGM occupations, Surab I–II, at the site. By Surab IV Nal pottery is dominant and associated with intrusive DS pottery. Intrusive Nal pottery has been identified in the DS Phase at Mehrgarh. At Sohr Damb (Hargreaves 1929) a Nal occupation and cemetery reportedly lay below a Kulli Phase occupation, but methodological problems compromise this data. Fairservis (1975:189–94) found Nal and Kulli pottery together in Niai Buthi I, whereas Niai Buthi II was a Kulli occupation dated to ca. 2320–2090 B.C. A Nal occupation, also with intrusive DS pottery, was found below an early Kulli one, dated to ca. 2635–2300 B.C., at Nindowari (Jarrige 1983). Stratigraphic information from Baluchistan indicates (1) Nal is later than the KGM Phase; (2) some overlap occurs with the KB Phase; (3) Nal and the DS Phase are contemporary; and (4) Nal is earlier than the Kulli Phase. However, the early occupations of the Balakot Phase, ca. 4000–3500 B.C., had pottery that strongly resembled Nal. All these factors suggest a date of ca. 3300–2500 B.C. for the Nal Phase with the possibility it may date even earlier or slightly later.

Most information about this Phase relates to its distinctive, wheel-made, decorated pottery (DeCardi 1965; Fairservis 1975:158–59). Although several vessel forms are known, the most distinctive is the ring-based canister. A variety of geometric, zoomorphic, and floral motifs are known, many of which are distinguished by the use of colored pigments to fill out a motif.

Rectangular structures of mud-brick with stone foundations occurred in the Nal occupations at Sohr Damb and Nindowari I, and at Sohr Damb a variety of stone tools, beads, and copper/bronze objects were associated with them. However, at Sohr Damb most Nal pottery was found in fractional burials which may be later than the structures. Fairservis (1975:171–72) has associated some of the water-control systems in southern Baluchistan with this Phase.

Kulli Phase

Kulli sites lie mainly in the southeastern and southern fringes of Baluchistan. Information concerning this

Phase is based on excavations at Mehi (Stein 1931), Niai Buthi, Nindowari (Casal 1966; Jarrige 1983), Sohr Damb, and Fairservis's (1975:185–202) work in Las Bela District. Kulli and Nal pottery were found together in Niai Buthi I and Nindowari II, but Kulli occupations were stratigraphically later than Nal at Niai Buthi II, Nindowari III, and possibly Sohr Damb. Intrusive Harappan artifacts were found in Nondowari III and intrusive Kulli artifacts in the Harappan occupation at Balakot. Furthermore, many stylistic analogies exist between Kulli and Harappan Phase artifacts. Two single dates from the Kulli occupations at Nindowari and Niai Buthi range between ca. 2635–2090 B.C. All current evidence indicates a chronology of ca. 2500–2000 B.C. for this Phase, making it contemporary with the Harappan.

Kulli pottery is a wheel-made red-buff ware with black-on-red slip decorations, although black-on-buff slip examples occur during its early stages at Niai Buthi I and Nindowari II. The diagnostic decoration is a central frieze of naturalistic animals, especially humped bovids, with elongated hatched bodies and exaggerated eyes. A variety of vessel forms is known but the most important forms are the dish-on-stand and a straight-sided jar which has affinities with the Nal canister. Terra-cotta bangles, miniature cart frames and wheels, and animal and human figurines were made in quantity. Other artifacts included shell bangles, semiprecious stone beads, and steatite or alabaster bowls. Copper/bronze tools and personal ornaments are also found.

Architectural data relate mainly to the unparalleled public/monumental structures located at Las Bela and Nindowari. These were grouped into distinct rectangular units enclosed by stone walls. Building materials included large stone slabs, mud and fired bricks, and clay plaster. At both sites were found large clay platforms with stone substructures that presented a steplike profile, with ramps or stairs connecting various levels. At Nindowari a large stone structure divided into small cells may have been a granary. Jarrige (1983:49; also Raikes 1965) thinks that a large number of *gobarbands,* stone structures related to a terrace-type agricultural system, may date to this Phase (but see Possehl 1975).

Stratigraphically there appears to be some link between Nal and Kulli Phases. However, the ceramics are so different that it is difficult to postulate what the cultural relationship might have been. That Kulli and Harappan groups were interacting is indicated by the two Harappan seals found in the Nindowari granary, and by the Kulli pottery and figurines in the Harappan occupation at Balakot. At the same time, Kulli artifacts are absent at such Harappan sites as Mohenjo-daro and Harappa. Although this Phase is most intriguing (e.g., Dales and Flam 1969), too little is presently known to understand its cultural position within this Tradition.

Periano Phase

The Periano Phase has been found only in northern Baluchistan, where it is recognized by its distinctive pottery. In Rana Ghundai III–IV, Ross (1946) found an overlap between Periano and KB pottery. Fairservis (1959:302–6) reanalyzed the Rana Ghundai sequence and found Periano pottery to be the dominant type in his level C, indicating it was later than KB and possibly contemporary with the DS Phase. A few sherds of DS Phase pottery can also be found among the surface collections. Surface collections at Periano Ghundai and Dabar Kot (Fairservis 1959; Mughal 1972) revealed a possible association of Periano and Harappan Phase potteries. Based on this data an estimated chronology for this Phase would fall between ca. 3000–2300 B.C., but until sites are excavated this is mere speculation.

The diagnostic potteries for this Phase are Periano Painted and Faiz Muhammad Painted as defined by Fairservis (1959:367–68, 373–74) in the Zob and Loralai regions. Periano Painted has black-on-red slip decoration whereas Faiz Muhammad was black-on-gray. Periano motifs are mainly geometric and similar to those on the DS Phase Quetta Ware and Faiz Muhammad Grayware. These ceramic data suggest some type of cultural connection linking the DS and Periano Phases. Harappan artifacts and stylistic traits like Periano pottery with double or flanged rims may indicate contact with the Indus Valley Tradition, but also suggest limited analogies with Mehrgarh VIIC (see n. 9). Until more data are available, only the possible existence of this Phase may be noted.

Bampur Phase

The Bampur Phase occurs only in southwestern Baluchistan. Although this area was explored by Stein and other early researchers (see Miragliuolo 1979 for discussion), our knowledge is based on DeCardi's (1970) Bampur Valley excavations supplemented by the Damin Tomb material (Tosi 1970) and Miragliuolo's (1979) survey work.

Six occupational periods were recognized by DeCardi (1970), which were grouped into two units, Bampur I–IV and V–VI, for comparative analysis. Based on the ceramics, Tosi (1970) and Lamberg-Karlovsky (Lamberg-Karlovsky and Tosi 1973) think the Bampur area was strongly influenced from the Seistan basin, such as at Shahr-i Sokhta. Since they correlated Bampur I–IV with Shahr-i Sokhta II–III and Bampur V–VI with Shahr-i Sokhta IV, this would date the Bampur Phase between ca. 2800–2200 B.C.

Chronologically these correlations seem reasonable, but the degree of cultural affiliations between these two areas was not as intense as argued. Parallels in motifs and vessel forms certainly exist, but they are neither the dominant nor the most distinctive elements of Bampur pottery. The vessel form parallels are very general, and those among the motifs reflect the use of only simple geometric patterns. While some degree of communication existed between these two areas, the Bampur Phase is very distinctive.

Bampur pottery is predominantly a wheel-made redware, which, along with small quantities of grayware, occurs in a variety of vessel forms. Painted decorations were black linear or nonlinear geometric motifs executed on a cream-buff or, less frequently, red slip. Floral and zoomorphic designs, especially snakes and insects, occur with increasing frequency in the later occupations. A major decorative feature was the use of cordons either as a border for the decorative motifs or as a major design element in the form of an undulating line centrally located in the panel. The more finely made and burnished grayware was occasionally decorated with black linear motifs.

In Bampur V–VI, ceramic changes do occur, but they are not radical, and a basic continuity exists. Of particular significance was a grayware "canister" collared jar decorated in a style similar to that of the Umm an-Nar pottery in the Oman peninsula. A limited number of grayware sherds were found with incised patterns that appear to be local imitations of decorated steatite/chlorite bowls on the Iranian plateau (Kohl 1978).

DeCardi's limited excavations uncovered no significant architecture and yielded only a few nonpottery artifacts. A few fragmentary copper/bronze artifacts were found along with a stamp seal, possibly depicting a camel. Also found were stone tools, a compartmented stamp seal, and a shell pendant.

Pirak Phase

The Pirak Phase, identified only at the Kachi plain site of Pirak (Jarrige, Santoni, and Enault 1979), as defined here, consists of Pirak I–II. Pirak III with its Iron Age affiliations will not be discussed. However, significant cultural continuities link Pirak I–III, and in a more comprehensive discussion Pirak III would be included. Although DS and Harappan Phase pottery occurred in Pirak's lower levels, the excavators contend that they are not directly related to the major occupational sequence and are also not discussed here (but see Shaffer 1984a). Chronological data are limited but an estimated time range for this Phase, Pirak I–II, would be ca. post 2000–1300 B.C.

Most Pirak pottery is handmade, coarse, red-buff ware coated with a clay wash that fired white. Monochrome and bichrome decorated varieties occur, both of which emphasize geometric motifs. Pirak decorated pottery, particularly bichromes with their intricate geometric decorations, are very like KB Phase pottery except that they are handmade. This similarity highlights the possible uniqueness of Mehrgarh's KB-DS Phases when that site became a local ceramic production center. The Pirak material suggests that the KB Phase persisted for a long period even on the Kachi plain and demonstrates the strong regional character of cultural developments in this Tradition.

Contemporary with this pottery were small quantities of a wheel-made red/pink ware and, in late Pirak II, a grayware that has a coarse paste, heavy vegetable temper, and a carbonized core suggesting a low firing temperature, or a short firing time. This ware was occasionally decorated with simple geometric motifs sloppily executed in plum paint. Except for its paste this pottery is very similar in vessel forms and decorations to the red and gray wares associated with the early Iron Age Painted Gray Ware culture (Tripathi 1976) in northern India. The Pirak sequence appears analogous to that at Bhagwanpura in the Punjab Phase of the Indus Valley Tradition since both indicate a continuous cultural sequence linking the Bronze and Iron Ages in South Asia.

Associated with this Phase are the earliest examples of terra-cotta horse, camel, and "horsemen" figurines. Examples of these animal figurines in later occupations have painted decorations suggesting trappings, and several are perforated for the attachment of strings and wheels. Other artifacts include terra-cotta stamp seals, stone beads, decorated bone points, and shell bangles. An elephant tusk fragment came from Pirak I, and in Pirak II were two decorated ivory combs. A new diagnostic stone tool in this Phase was the serrated sickle blade which may indicate domestic rice cultivation. Examples of copper/bronze tools and compartmented stamp seals were infrequent despite evidence of local ore production.

Rectangular mud-brick buildings were found throughout this Phase, and in most instances they appeared to be part of larger undefined structures. Most buildings were habitations, but one of them had a series of circular silos while another appeared to have functioned as an animal pen. Structures in Pirak IB were associated with a large courtyard area containing platformed fireplaces, large numbers of animal bones, and a crucible. This courtyard complex may indicate the presence of a copper-smelting cottage industry. The only examples of public/monumental architecture are found in Pirak I. One, a large mud-brick platform with water channels, lay west of the main building area but its function remains unknown. Another was a large mud-brick wall that may have enclosed several smaller buildings.

Direct evidence of craft activities was limited. The handmade pottery done in a style of considerable antiquity and the large number of unfired figurines are suggestive of local potters, and the quantity of bone points argues for local production of this item as well. The single elephant tusk fragment indicates that ivory was locally worked. Numerous copper/bronze fragments, limited metal artifacts, and the crucible suggest that metallurgy might have been an important aspect of Pirak's craft activities. Certainly iron smelting was a key Pirak III activity.

The traditional crops were barley, wheat, and, to a lesser extent, oats, but the main one was domesticated rice. Indeed, Pirak is the earliest site where rice was the major crop, and this may represent a significant shift in agricultural practices. At present rice appears to have been introduced from the east, from Gujurat and the Ganges Valley, but the mechanisms of its introduction remain unknown. Given the Kachi plain ecology, it is doubtful that rice cultivation was possible without an irrigation system, but none has yet been identified. Equally interesting at Pirak were large amounts of millet and limited quantities of sorghum. Like rice, these too were probably introduced from the east. Their cultivation indicates that agriculture was cyclically organized, with semiannual harvests in the spring and autumn. The Pirak agricultural systems were very complex and represented a significant change from past practices.

Important changes in animal husbandry were also recorded. Cattle, followed by sheep and goats, continued as the most important subsistence animals. However, camel and horse bones and their figurine representations leave little doubt as to their domesticated status. The domesticated camel was present in this region during the Harappan Phase, but the Pirak figurines indicate that it had achieved a new and important cultural status among Pirak Phase social groups. Since the rarity of camel bones suggests that this changed status was not related to dietary shifts, it must reflect its increasing importance as a beast of burden. Whether this change reflects increased camel use in commodity transport or the appearance of modern-style pastoral nomadism (Jarrige, Santoni, and Enault 1979:405) remains to be determined. Osteological data were inconclusive as to the species, but figurines indicate the predominant animal was the Bactrian camel although dromedaries may have been present.

The Pirak data furnish the earliest firm evidence for the domesticated horse in South Asia, and, like the Bactrian camel, this was introduced from central Asia. The rarity of bones and the presence of "horsemen" figurines indicate that the horse's function was human transport. Given these factors it is not surprising that horse and camel figurines were similarly decorated, suggesting they had similar cultural importance.

Clearly the Pirak Phase is critically important to understanding the integration of the Baluchistan Tradition into the Iron Age/Early Historic period. At Pirak the KB

Phase–style pottery provides a link with Bronze Age developments, while the Iron Age–style Painted Gray Ware pottery indicates that a cultural continuity persisted into the Iron Age which is clearly represented by Pirak III. At the same time, important changes occurred in the subsistence economy, and in the means of transport and communication between social groups. It is difficult to evaluate this Phase until more data are collected and the Bhagwanpura excavations published. Still the Pirak and Punjab Phases definitely indicate that a cultural continuum links the Bronze and Iron Ages in this region and that the Baluchistan and Indus Valley Traditions contributed directly to the formation of Early Historic cultures. The previous concept of a "Dark Age" in South Asian archaeology is no longer valid.

The Helmand Tradition

Geographical Area

Located in southern Afghanistan, this area is north of the Baluchistan Mountains, south of the Hindu Kush, and is bordered on the west by the Seistan basin. Major geographical features are the stony western Dasht-i-Margo and the sandy Registan deserts.[14] These arid conditions are ameliorated only by the Helmand River system which drains the Hindu Kush Mountains and flows southsouthwest into the few lakes and marshy regions of the land-locked Seistan basin. The Helmand system supports a low desert-type vegetation and tamarisk scrub environment in the mountain alluvial fans, on the alluvial plains near Kandahar, and along the Helmand River as it snakes southwestward between the deserts. Most precipitation results from winter storms in the mountains and accompanying lowland spring floods. Although agriculture is limited by available water, this area is a major winter pasturage for pastoral nomads who range into Baluchistan and central Afghanistan during spring and summer. In addition, recent geological surveys located significant deposits of lead, copper, silver, gold, iron, and alluvial cassiterite tin in the adjacent Hindu Kush Mountains, where some of these metals were mined in antiquity.

The Tradition

The Helmand Tradition (see figs. 4 and 7) dates between ca. 4000–1900 B.C. Our knowledge is based on excavations at Deh Morasi Ghundai, Mundigak, and Said Qala Tepe, as well as on surveys of the Seistan basin (Dales 1972, 1973b; Fairservis 1961; Hammond 1970). Another major site, Shahr-i Sokhta, is located in Iranian Seistan and treated elsewhere in this volume, but some discussion is necessary here. Compared to Baluchistan and Indus Valley Traditions the data are very limited.

Wheat, barley, sheep, goats, and cattle were the major

domesticates, but grapes, date palms, flax, and camels were identified at Shahr-i Sokhta (Caloi et al. 1977). Unlike the other Traditions, water buffalo, cotton, and rice have not yet been identified. Sheep and goats predominate over cattle, and the constellation of domesticates resembles that associated with Southwest Asian rather than South Asian cultural complexes, in part reflecting more arid conditions. Although agriculture was the primary subsistence pattern, pastoral nomadism and/or other types of transhumance strategies may have been present.

Habitation structures were single- or multiple-room rectangular mud-brick buildings. At Mundigak, in the Shahr-i Sokhta phase, examples of public/monumental architecture, designated as a "palace" and "temple," were both enclosed by a series of large elaborate walls. These buildings were constructed of mud and fired bricks and stones. A contemporary, mud-brick public/monumental structure was found at Said Qala Tepe.

Part- and full-time specialists were present. The potter's craft was well developed, and even in the earliest occupations wheel- and handmade red-buff wares were made. Handmade pottery occurs throughout the Tradition in varying quantities and in only a few vessel shapes. A heavy carbon exterior coating on most handmade vessels suggests it was a common utilitarian ware. Basket-impressed pottery was made from a similar paste, and early wheel-made pottery occurs in only a limited variety of vessel forms. Decorations were restricted to simple geometric monochrome motifs.

Later wheel-made wares were characterized by a greater variety of vessel shapes, and decorated examples demonstrated an increasing use of complex geometric motifs. Monochrome patterns predominate, but more complex decorative schemes were executed on a buff/white slip. Floral and zoomorphic motifs appear in the later occupations, and by the Shahr-i Sokhta Phase this pottery represents a regional variation of "Quetta Ware" as found in the DS Phase in Baluchistan.

Associated with the "Quetta Ware" were decorated graywares that appear to be local variations of Faiz Muhammad Graywares also found in the DS Phase. A limited quantity of vessels with polychrome geometric decorations also occurs. Intrusive sherds from various Baluchistan and Indus Valley Tradition Phases are encountered throughout this Tradition, and at Shahr-i Sokhta I, possible Namazga III–style pottery from Turkmenistan is present. Other terra-cotta objects included beads, house models, and animal and human figurines.

Stone tools are generally nondiagnostic, except for an extensive projectile point series at Mundigak. However, a well-developed lapidary craft is indicated by numerous semiprecious stone beads and pendants, alabaster bowls, steatite/chlorite compartmented stamp seals, and other artifacts. Lapidary workshops were identified at Shahr-i

Sokhta and probably were present at Mundigak (C. Jarrige and Tosi 1981). Shell artifacts were present, bone implements numerous, and bone handles were used for some copper/bronze tools. The metallurgical craft is highly developed, with numerous types of personal ornaments, stamp seals, and tools, including rare shaft-hole axes and adzes found mainly at Mundigak. Also at Mundigak two copper/bronze artifacts incorporated the use of iron, and at both Mundigak and Said Qala Tepe several iron ore nodules were found. Although this use of iron does not indicate a full iron technology, it certainly suggests that craftsmen knew the metal (Shaffer 1984a).

Although the subsistence economy was based on food production, no evidence of an Early Food Production Era has appeared. However, until this area has been adequately explored, the possible existence of a cultural phase comparable to but not identical with the Mehrgarh Phase must be entertained.

The Regionalization Era is represented by the Mundigak and Helmand Phases. Many artifacts, especially ceramics, suggest a strong Baluchistan Tradition cultural affiliation. The Mundigak phase wheel-made, red-buff wares have many parallels with early KGM Phase pottery, especially in individual decorative motifs and vessel forms. At the same time, rarity of KGM black-on-red slip–type decorations suggests treating it independently. Likewise, ceramic parallels link the Helmand Phase red-buff ware with late KGM and KB Phase potteries. Again, however, rarity of KGM black-on-red slip and KB bichrome–style decorations suggests the Helmand Phase should be separately treated. Also present in this Phase, at Shahr-i Sokhta I, were a few examples of Namazga III–style pottery which is absent in the Baluchistan Tradition. Although strong cultural affiliations link the Helmand Tradition's early phases with Baluchistan's KGM and KB Phases, there is sufficient evidence to suggest treatment as a separate cultural tradition.

The Integration Era is synonymous with the Shahr-i Sokhta Phase and Interaction System. Major features of this Era are the appearance of urban centers and public/monumental buildings, increased craft activities, widespread material culture homogeneity, and the appearance of differential social-economic statuses. The widespread cultural homogeneity and distribution of various imported commodities and metals indicate an intense level of interaction between social groups. Like the Harappan Interaction System the nature and structure of this Interaction System remains unknown, but existence of differential social statuses and the nature of Mundigak's public/monumental buildings suggest that the two systems were differently organized.

Recently much discussion has centered on the possible cultural influence exerted by Turkmenistan groups on this Tradition. Noting parallels between these areas in human figurines, certain metal artifacts, stamp seals, burial customs, and most especially motifs on painted pottery, many scholars (e.g., Biscione 1973; Lamberg-Karlovsky and Tosi 1973; Masson and Sarianidi 1972:94–96; Tosi 1973 but see also Tosi 1983a) have argued that what is called here the Shahr-i Sokhta Phase reflects direct cultural diffusion from Turkmenistan. Since Quetta Ware and Faiz Muhammad Grayware styles of pottery characterize both Shahr-i Sokhta and DS Phases, such interpretations have implications for Baluchistan as well. Fairservis (1975), on the other hand, has always maintained that these developments were essentially indigenous, a position now partially supported by the Mehrgarh sequence. Jarrige (in press a and b) has noted that most nonceramic parallel traits used to support the diffusionist position can now not only be identified as having considerable antiquity in the Balulchistan area but that they also occur in a sequence demonstrating cultural continuity stretching back to a nonceramic Neolithic. Given the strong cultural connections linking early phases of the Helmand and Baluchistan Traditions there is no reason to suspect a Turkmenistan origin for these traits. Painted pottery motif similarities are confined mainly to "solid"-style geometric decorations found on Quetta Ware and Faiz Muhammad Grayware. These decorations are relatively infrequent compared to the more "open"-style geometric decorations, which, along with zoomorphic and floral motifs, have no Namazga III stylistic counterpart. Namazga III pottery is also handmade from a coarse, vegetable-tempered paste, whereas Quetta Ware and Faiz Muhammad Grayware are wheel-made with a non-vegetable-tempered fine paste. Likewise, vessel shapes, except for a few examples in Shahr-i Sokhta I (Sarianidi 1983), are very different. Moreover, no pottery comparable to Faiz Muhammad Grayware has been identified in Turkmenistan. Finally, the Mehrgarh pottery appears to reflect a continuous developmental sequence from the very earliest stages of ceramic production through Quetta Ware. The Mehrgarh sequence and the close cultural relationships linking the Helmand and Baluchistan Traditions have raised serious questions about the extent of Turkmenistan influence on cultural developments in these regions during this period. Until the Shahr-i Sokhta and Mehrgarh excavations are fully published, and Mehrgarh III–VII better dated, the extent and degree of Turkmenistan influence will remain unresolved.[15]

The Localization Era of this Tradition is very unclear. Except for Shahr-i Sokhta, all known settlements are abandoned. Shahr-i Sokhta itself, during this era, reverts back to a small agricultural village with cultural parallels to the late Bampur Phase. Mundigak is "reoccupied" in Period V, and at least one public/monumental building built, but the associated material culture is very different from that of the Shahr-i Sokhta Phase. Indeed, Mundigak

V's closest parallels are with the central Asian Chust culture (Masson and Sarianidi 1972:164–65), and no similar material is found elsewhere. Apparently the Shahr-i Sokhta Interaction System was completely disrupted by the beginning of this Era, but the conditions responsible for this situation remain unknown. Given our limited data it would be unwise to suggest that this Tradition came to an end, but it is obvious that in the Helmand basin significant cultural changes occurred during the early second millennium B.C.

Regionalization Era

The Regionalization Era is represented by the Mundigak and Helmand Phases and dates between ca. 4000–2800 B.C. Archaeological evidence indicates that these early settlements were established by groups with a strong Baluchistan Tradition cultural affiliation. Indeed, some intrusive sherds indicate direct or indirect interaction between these groups and those in Baluchistan. Only two sites with Helmand Phase occupations are known, but their locations on the eastern and western fringes of the Helmand basin suggest the entire area could have been settled by widely dispersed groups.

Mundigak Phase

The Mundigak Phase is represented only by the early occupations at Mundigak, Period I$_{1-3}$ (Casal 1961; see also Shaffer 1978a). Based on ceramic parallels and one acceptable date, TF 1129, the chronology for this phase would be ca. 4000–3500 B.C. Unfortunately the excavated area was small, limiting available data. For example, Mundigak I$_{1-2}$ had no architectural features although Casal suggests the possibility of tents, and in Mundigak I$_3$ the remains of only two pisé walls were found.

Although small quantities of handmade ware are found, most pottery is a wheel-made red-buff ware occasionally decorated with simple painted geometric motifs that persist into later phases. Two possibly intrusive sherds were found with repetitive, small, solid zoomorphic motifs similar to those found on KGM pottery. In general, this pottery is similar to early KGM pottery. Among the other artifacts was a copper/bronze blade fragment. Faunal remains were not properly sampled but domesticated sheep, goats, and cattle were present. No mention was made of botanical remains from this Phase.

Helmand Phase

Occupations representing the Helmand Phase are Mundigak I$_4$–II and Shahr-i Sokhta I (Tosi 1968, 1983b), of which those at Mundigak are the most extensively excavated. Available dates and ceramic parallels with the KB

461

Phase suggest a time span of between ca. 3500–2800 B.C.

Mundigak buildings are rectangular mud-brick units clustered into blocks separated by open areas often containing ovens or kilns. Most appear to be habitations; however, some may have been used for storage or as work areas. The only "public" structure is a stone-lined well.

Both wheel-made and handmade red-buff wares are present in varying quantities throughout this Phase. Among wheel-made pottery a few new vessel forms are introduced. The monochrome decorations are restricted to linear or hatched-filled geometric motifs. Vessel forms and decorative motifs are comparable to, but not identical with, late KGM-KB Phase pottery in Baluchistan (see also Tosi 1983b). At Mundigak intrusive KGM and KB Phase pottery and perhaps even KD Phase (Mughal 1970:300) pottery are found. On the other hand, at Shahr-i Sokhta I the only intrusive potteries are a few possible Namazga III and Nal-style sherds (Amiet and Tosi 1978; Sarianidi 1983; Tosi 1983b).

Stone tools from this and subsequent Phases are non-diagnostic except for the flint projectile points found at Mundigak. Lapidary crafts are, however, well developed and represented by alabaster bowls, a limited quantity but wide variety of semiprecious stone beads, and steatite compartmented stamp seals. Cylinder seals and sealings are found in Shahr-i Sokhta I (Amiet 1983; Amiet and Tosi 1978). Shell and copper/bronze objects are also present.

Although communication between Helmand Phase social groups and those in other Traditions is shown by the ceramics and intrusive commodities such as marine shell, lapis lazuli, and turquoise, its intensity and structure are unknown.

The basic economic data (Caloi et al. 1977) are from Shahr-i Sokhta, but are still not completely published. A limited amount of hunting and fishing was practiced. However, the major emphasis is on domesticated animals, mainly sheep followed by smaller quantities of goats and cattle. Domesticated barley is the most common plant, followed by wheats, melons, cucumbers, grapes, and possibly flax.

Integration Era

The Integration Era is characterized by the Shahr-i Sokhta Phase and Interaction System. Occupations of this Phase may be identified at several sites which are characterized by a material culture homogeneity betraying a high level of social group interaction. Indeed, the interaction level seems as intense as that of the Harappan in the Indus Valley. This system extends throughout the Helmand basin and incorporates, to a degree, the DS

Phase in Baluchistan. However, the nature of the cultural relationships linking Shahr-i Sokhta and DS Phases remains unknown at present. During this Era new settlements are established, urban centers develop, craft activities are intensified, and socioeconomic differences in society appear. At present these traits appear linked to the development of the interaction system but just how is not known. By the end of this Era all sites are abandoned except Shahr-i Sokhta, and the final occupation there is different from this Phase.

Shahr-i Sokhta Phase

Shahr-i Sokhta, hereafter SiS, Phase occupations are represented by Shahr-i Sokhta II–III, Mundigak III–IV, Said Qala Tepe I–IV (Shaffer 1971, 1972, 1978a, 1978b), and Deh Morasi Ghundai I–III (Dupree 1963). The best series of dates for this Phase is from Shahr-i Sokhta, which indicates a time range between ca. 2800–2300 B.C.

Architecturally the SiS and Helmand Phases were much alike. At Shahr-i Sokhta several large, complex, multiroom buildings with numerous internal features were found, and comparable buildings existed in early SiS occupations at Mundigak. During Mundigak III_4 a retaining terrace wall was constructed and the area behind it filled to increase surface area for Mundigak III_{5-6} buildings. In Said Qala Tepe II, ceramically similar to late Mundigak III, a large mud-brick wall of unknown function was constructed. By the end of Shahr-i Sokhta II that settlement covered about 45 ha, which, along with ample evidence for industrial activities, suggests that it functioned as an urban center. Mundigak III and Said Qala Tepe were much smaller, only about 3 ha, and were probably agricultural villages; however, evidence for limited industrial activity was found at Mundigak.

In Shahr-i Sokhta III, similar buildings were found and the settlement size expands to approximately 80 ha. Mundigak habitation units were like previous examples. During Mundigak IV, on Mound A, previous buildings were leveled and Casal's "palace," a large multiroom complex with an exterior wall faced with decorative columns, was constructed. To the east, in another area of the site, another large and massive building, Casal's "temple," was also constructed; it had exterior walls faced with decorative triangular-shaped columns. Its interior was divided into nonhabitational small rooms, and in one area Casal interpreted an architectural feature as a shrine. The remains of two, possibly three, large walls with bastions and regularly spaced buttresses enclosed a large segment of the settlement, including these two public/monumental buildings. Mundigak's architecture has no parallel at any other site in the Traditions discussed here. Exactly why such architectural features should be found at Mundigak is unknown. Even with all these architectural developments Mundigak remained a rather small, 32 ha settlement, reflecting a very modest-sized urban center. C. Jarrige and Tosi (1981) suggest these developments at Mundigak relate to important commodity procurement and processing activities for the Shahr-i Sokhta Interaction System. At the same time, the nature and degree of Mundigak's public/monumental architecture suggest that other cultural factors were involved.

Both continuity and change characterize the ceramics when compared with the Helmand Phase. Wheel-made ceramics show greater vessel diversity but also include previous forms. Geometric decorations become increasingly complex during this Phase, and some examples are executed on a white/buff slip. In general this pottery is similar to the "Quetta Ware" encountered in the DS Phase of the Baluchistan Tradition. In Mundigak III$_5$–IV$_1$ floral motifs become more frequent and zoomorphic ones are occasionally found. The most striking examples of these motifs occur on small pedestal/stemmed jars with incurving walls found in Mundigak IV$_1$. These pedestal/stemmed jars are stylistically similar to the Mehrgarh VII graywares. Mundigak IV$_{2-3}$ pottery is characterized by an increasing quantity of redware with predominantly geometric black-on-red slip motifs, which are similar to the earlier SiS pottery and perhaps comparable to the late Mehrgarh VII pottery. At Mundigak and Said Qala Tepe Faiz Muhammad Graywares and Wet Wares are found in limited numbers. However, the Shahr-i Sokhta graywares appear to be a local variety of Faiz Muhammad Graywares. A small amount of polychrome pottery with solid geometric motifs also occurs. Limited numbers of intrusive sherds include examples of KD, Nal, and possibly late Amri-style pottery.

Terra-cotta animal figurines are varied and abundant, and human examples increased as well. In late Mundigak occupations and at Deh Morasi Ghundai "Zob style" figurines similar to those in the DS Phase are found.

Qualitatively there is little change in stone tools, and projectile points continue only at Mundigak. Lapidary craft objects increase significantly throughout this Phase. A wide variety of alabaster vessels and semiprecious stone and shell beads is found. Compartmented stamp seals increase in number and variety and, except for a few ivory and metal examples, are manufactured from steatite/chlorite. Metallurgical activities also intensified during the SiS Phase, and the range of copper/bronze tools, found mostly at Mundigak, expands significantly. Late occupations have a greater number and variety of metal personal ornaments and stamp seals. Iron "buttons," possibly smelted, were identified on two objects. In the Shahr-i Sokhta cemetery (Piperno 1977; Piperno and Tosi 1975), lapidary, shell and metal objects, stamp seals, and

certain types of stone tools and vessels, and pottery are differentially distributed among the graves, indicating significant socioeconomic differences within that population.

Again the best economic data come from Shahr-i Sokhta. The subsistence economy is similar to the Helmand Phase, with indications of an increasing emphasis on grapes, flax, and goats; dates are also present. There is also evidence (Compagnoni and Tosi 1978) for the use of the domesticated camel.

The existence of the Shahr-i Sokhta Interaction System is recognizable in the many similarities linking these sites. Present evidence also suggests that the degree of cultural interaction linking the SiS and DS Phases was intense and regular. At the same time, architectural and ceramic differences between Mundigak and Shahr-i Sokhta suggest that their respective cultural roles in this System differed. For example, there is more evidence of interaction with Baluchistan and Indus Valley Traditions at Mundigak. Besides Baluchistan affinities for the zoomorphic motifs and Zob-style figurines, intrusive pottery from Nal, Amri, and KD Phases is present at Mundigak, whereas at Shahr-i Sokhta only a few Nal-style sherds appear in the earlier occupations and cemetery (Amiet and Tosi 1978). To what extent, if any, this greater degree of interaction with these Traditions contributed to Mundigak's position in the Interaction System is unknown. At present Mundigak is unique and one of the most problematical sites in any Tradition discussed here.

The Shahr-i Sokhta Interaction System, which integrated Helmand Tradition social groups with those in the DS Phase of Baluchistan, is poorly understood. That it existed is beyond doubt. The pronounced similarities in such a wide range of artifacts across such a large geographical area through time can only be accounted for by intense and regular communication between the social groups involved. No doubt commodity procurement and distribution played an important role in this communication (see C. Jarrige and Tosi 1981), but other avenues of cultural communication were surely just as important. In these respects the Shahr-i Sokhta Interaction System resembles the Harappan one of the Indus Valley, and it is interesting to note that both Systems have some evidence for domesticated camel. Important differences, however, suggest that the two Systems were fundamentally different in structure. First, Mundigak with its peculiar architectural features and disproportional relationship to its agricultural resources (C. Jarrige and Tosi 1981) cannot be duplicated in either Tradition. Second, interaction with the Baluchistan Tradition appears to be greater in the Shahr-i Sokhta Interaction System than in the Harappan. Finally, burials associated with differential wealth at Shahr-i Sokhta suggest that society was structured in a fundamentally different way from those in the Indus Valley Tradition, where such burials have not yet been found. Beyond these general observations data are too limited to make detailed reconstructions or comparisons. By the end of the SiS Phase this Helmand System was terminally disrupted, and settlements, except for Shahr-i Sokhta, were abandoned.

Localization Era

Existence of the Localization Era is only tentatively proposed here, for it is represented by only the Seistan Phase, or Shahr-i Sokhta IV. Mundigak V bears little similarity to its previous Phases and suggests a later cultural intrusion possibly from central Asia. Perhaps the second millennium B.C. cultural developments in the eastern Helmand basin will be clarified by publication of the Sibri excavations (see n. 11), but until these developments are better defined discussion here will be limited to the Seistan Phase.

Seistan Phase

The stratigraphic relationship between the SiS and Seistan Phases has yet to be determined, and both cultural changes and continuities link these Phases. The Shahr-i Sokhta dates suggest a chronology of ca. 2200–2000 B.C.

During this Phase Shahr-i Sokhta's settlement area shrank to about 5 ha, and it again represents a small agricultural village. Architecturally there is continuity with the previous Phases although new techniques do appear such as the use of different size mud-bricks. The major structure, the "Burnt Building," is a complex multiroom structure covering almost 600 m² and is the largest building found in any Phase at the site. Despite its size there is no architectural feature or associated artifact to suggest that this building is anything more than a large habitation structure.

Seistan Phase ceramics do undergo significant changes. Although previous red-buff wares continue, new vessel forms are introduced that reflect new manufacturing techniques such as the fast wheel. The previous painted grayware is replaced by incised graywares. Indeed, painted pottery in general undergoes a drastic frequency decline, which is attributed (Tosi 1983b) to increasing craft industrialization. Among the few painted vessels the motifs differ from those of previous Phases and may be compared to those in the late Bampur Phase, Baluchistan Tradition, and the Umm an-Nar and Yahya IVB pottery (Tosi 1983b). Other terra-cotta objects, including figurines, are rare.

Metallurgical production continues but with decreased intensity, although a few new tool types are introduced and the number of personal ornaments increases. More striking is the absence of lapidary craft activities. Not only are many stone artifacts absent but so are the semiprecious stones frequently found in the previous Phases. Even steatite artifacts, including stamp seals, are absent from this Phase. These developments suggest that many commodities were no longer available, or in demand, after the demise of the Shahr-i Sokhta Interaction System.

No significant changes in the subsistence economy are reported except for yet another slight increase in the frequency of goats relative to sheep.

The Seistan Phase does not, however, appear to reflect a radical cultural change from the SiS Phase. Stratigraphic, architectural, ceramic, and other material cultural continuities link the two. The Seistan Phase then is not characterized so much by the introduction of new traits as it is by the disappearance of previous ones. Concomitantly Shahr-i Sokhta changes from one of the larger urban centers on the Iranian plateau to a small village. Quite clearly the disruption of the Shahr-i Sokhta Interaction System had a significant impact on cultural developments in the Helmand basin (see also Dales 1977). During this same period, ca. 2300–1900 B.C., the Harappan Interaction System is also undergoing major structural changes. Whether these two phenomena are related is a major topic for future research, but it is clear that major cultural changes during the beginning of the second millennium B.C. were occurring throughout the area considered here. Furthermore, these changes provided a background for the emergence of Iron Age/Early Historic cultures in these areas.

Twenty-Seven

The Chronology of Prehistoric India:
From Earliest Times to the Iron Age

Gregory L. Possehl, University Museum, University of Pennsylvania
Paul C. Rissman, University Museum, University of Pennsylvania

Outline

Several general treatises on the chronology of prehistoric India already exist (see Lal 1963; Mandal 1972; Agrawal and Kusumgar 1974, 1979; Ramchandran 1975), and most of the recent general works on the prehistory of India and the other South Asian countries contain lists of radiocarbon dates (see B. Allchin and R. Allchin 1968, 1982; Fairservis 1971, 1975; Sankalia 1974; Possehl 1979; Agrawal 1982a and 1982b).

The geographic scope of this chapter is for the most part restricted to the consideration of prehistoric materials that come from the modern nations of India and Sri Lanka (figs. 1, 2, and 3). Prior to the partition of the South Asian land mass, sometimes referred to as the subcontinent, there was little ambiguity in the meaning of the word *India*. The creation of Pakistan in 1947, as well as independent Bangladesh, Burma, and Sri Lanka, however, demands that we use a vocabulary that is more explicit. In this chapter, *India* thus designates the modern nation state of the same name. *Ancient India,* the *subcontinent,* and *South Asia* refer to the former encompassing geographic entity.

The chronology of the prehistoric eras of the subcon-

tinent has reached a point where some of the gross outlines of time/space relationships are beginning to emerge. This is due to the advances in radiocarbon dating, in terms of both the number of dates and their quality. Despite this progress we still cannot present a coherent chronology for all regions of India during all of the prehistoric eras. A few regions are reasonably well known through all or most of these millennia, but most of the outline is a variable mosaic with quite different qualities. In some instances only one period is known for a region. Such is the case, for example, in Gujarat state in which the Bronze Age Harappan occupation floats in a context of almost totally unknown eras prior to and following it. Although the resulting picture may be marked by more unevenness of chronological insight than by clarity, there remains a great deal that can be said.

A few words on the major gaps in this picture are in order, for they will be largely passed over in the body of the text. Northeastern India, including the mountainous states of Sikkim, Assam, Meghalaya, Arunachal Pradesh, Nagaland, Manipur, Mizoram, and Tripura, is a virtual blank for prehistoric chronology. The same is largely true for the deep south of the peninsula, especially Kerala. But these gaps in our knowledge are useful

Text submitted July 1987

to prehistorians since they clearly mark areas within which they can carry out productive research, the results of which could yield important insights beyond the chronological information that is the focus of this essay. For example, the mountainous states of India's northeast have been thought by some (Sauer 1969; Gorman 1969, 1971) to be areas for understanding the origins of food production in monsoon Asia. Little-known Orissa and Bihar are mineralogically rich and may have played significant roles in the development of major technological innovations, especially metallurgy.

Little is said of the Harappan Civilization in this essay. Our colleague Jim Shaffer has covered this topic in his contribution to this volume (chap. 26). We do have a few things to say about the Gujarati aspect of the Indus Civilization, but principally as it impinges on an understanding of what is going on in surrounding regions during the second and third millennia B.C. Even though it penetrates deep into India the interesting Harappan material in northern Rajasthan, Punjab, Haryana, and western Uttar Pradesh will be no more than mentioned, and then only in reference to other chronological issues.

Sites mentioned in this text have been located on a series of maps accompanying the text. These are nowhere near a comprehensive set of documents. The map coverage for prehistoric India is quite uneven. Most of the site reports have some kind of orientation map, at least for the individual site. These are useful, but tedious to employ. (Good map coverage for larger bodies of material can be found in Joshi, Madhu Bala, and Jassu Ram 1984; Schwartzberg 1978; and Sankalia 1974).

The present mosaic of regions and chronology inevitably fails to give a satisfying sense of knowing the subcontinent in prehistoric times. Nonetheless, the past fifteen years have seen giant strides forward in our understanding of prehistoric India, and it is around these accomplishments that one can develop a thesis. By focusing on these achievements this presentation also takes on a natural structure, for we can discuss particular chronological topics in some detail, rather than having to present a less meaningful miscellany. One area of such progress is in the chronology of the Indian Paleolithic.

The Chronology of the Paleolithic of India

The Lower and Middle Paleolithic

We can present one radiometric date for the Lower Paleolithic of India. This is a thermoluminescent determination from the Sihawal Formation near Baghor II in the Son Valley of northern Madhya Pradesh (fig. 4) at 103,800 ± 19,800 B.P., Alpha 899 (Clark and Williams 1986). This date comes to us as a part of the interdisciplinary work conducted jointly by G. R. Sharma of the University of Allahabad and J. Desmond Clark of the University of California, Berkeley. The Sihawal formation is the oldest Quaternary formation in the middle Son Valley. It is composed of a basal conglomerate of colluvial-alluvial sandstone cobbles in a matrix of mottled gray and yellow-brown clay. The gravels contain Lower Paleolithic bifaces, some of which are relatively fresh, others of which are strongly abraded. The Cambridge University team working in the Potwar plateau of Pakistan reports a radiometric date of ca. 2 million years in association with a tool or tools (Bridget Allchin, pers. comm., 6 July 1987).

Until recently there was nothing substantial in the hominid fossil record of the Indian subcontinent (Kennedy 1973, 1980, 1984a, 1984b). However, Arun Sonakia of the Geological Survey of India has discovered parts of a fossilized human cranium in the village of Hathnora on the northern bank of the Narmada River in central India (Sonakia 1984, 1985; Kennedy 1985). This is in the vicinity of Hoshangabad (fig. 4), a region with numerous Paleolithic sites, some of which were originally studied by H. DeTerra and T. T. Patterson (1939). Sonakia's preliminary reports on this find indicate that it was found in situ associated with a Middle to Upper Pleistocene cemented gravel and conglomerate. He notes that the specimen "bears a number of similarities to Asian *Homo erectus*" (1985:615). Kenneth A. R. Kennedy has been more cautious, referring to it as "*Homo* sp. indet." (1985:615).

Uncalibrated radiocarbon dates of the Indian Middle Paleolithic are presented in table 1.

A Note on the Radiocarbon Half-life and Calibration

Dates in the body of this chapter are presented in three ways: (1) uncalibrated dates b.p. (Before Present) using the 5568 radiocarbon half-life, (2) dates given B.C. (Before Christ) calculated on the 5730 half-life, and (3) calibrated dates B.C. (Before Christ) using the unpublished 1σ tables of Klein, Lerman, Damon, and Ralph (see the appendix of this vol.; also Klein et al. 1982). Only the calibrated dates are expressed as a range.

Discussion of the Indian Middle Paleolithic

As can be seen from the dates in table 1, the Middle Paleolithic flake industries of India are spread throughout the subcontinent. Good stratigraphic successions are available at a number of sites, especially Bhimbetka, the Belan and Son Valleys, and Nevasa (fig. 4). Bridget and Raymond Allchin (1982:47–57) have noted a basic difference between the Middle Paleolithic of central and peninsular India, as compared to that of the Indus plains and the Thar Desert, north of Gujarat. In central India, extending through the Vindhyas up to the Ganges plains, there is a strong line of continuity out of the Lower Paleo-lithic core biface technology. The use of Levallois technique is documented, along with other flake-producing technology. This body of material has been called the Nevasian (Sankalia et al. 1960:102–14). The Middle Paleolithic to the west of the Aravalli Hills and north of the Saurashtran peninsula is a far more diverse body of material. These industries can be divided into "lesser regional groups, and into what appear to be the outcome of a series of marked local traditions" (B. Allchin and R. Allchin 1982:51). The diversity of these industries can be exemplified by reference to the so-called Late Soan of DeTerra and Patterson (1939) as compared to that of Sanghao Cave in northwestern Pakistan (Dani 1964).

On the Son River the Allahabad/Berkeley team under the direction of G. R. Sharma and J. Desmond Clark uncovered evidence for two phases of the Middle Paleolithic. At an excavation in the Rehi Nala, a northern tributary of the Son River, they found fresh flake tools which included small subtriangular and cordiform hand axes. A later Middle Paleolithic component has been found adjacent to the site of Baghor I (fig. 4).

The age of the Son Valley Middle Paleolithic can be estimated from a radiocarbon determination taken from carbonate in the clays of Gerwa well near the Baghor sites (fig. 4), which gave an age of ca. 25,000 B.C. Since the carbonate is postdepositional, Clark and Williams (1986:30) suggest that the Middle Paleolithic may well be 40,000 or 50,000 years old in this area.

Work by Deccan College under the direction of V. N. Misra at Didwana in north-central Rajasthan (figs. 4 and 5) has yielded some further insights into the chronology of the Middle and Upper Paleolithic (dates are b.p. uncalibrated):

> A few C-14 dates on pedogenic carbonates and TL dates on fossil sand sheets of the 16 R locality at Didwana indicate that the Middle and Upper Palaeolithic industries (there) date to around 100,000 B.P. and 20,000 years B.P. respectively. The region seems to have been deserted during the terminal Pleistocene (ca. 20,000–10,000 B.P.) due to intensely arid climate when the dune building activity was strong and the lakes became saline. High fresh water lake levels during 6,000–4,000 B.P. suggest considerable increase in rainfall when Mesolithic populations flourished throughout the desert. (Misra and Rajaguru 1984)

The Indian Upper Paleolithic

Indian Upper Paleolithic blade and burin industries are just emerging as reasonably well defined entities. The key sites and radiocarbon determinations can be found in table 2. Critical works on this material are by Paddayya

(1973), Allchin, Goudie, and Hegde (1978), G. R. Sharma et al. (1980), and G. R. Sharma and Clark (1983).

The stratigraphic order of the Indian Middle Paleolithic, of the blade and burin industries of the Upper Paleolithic, and of the widespread Indian microlithic industries has been established at Bhimbetka (Agrawal 1982a:31–49), in the Belan Valley (Sharma et al. 1980), and in the Son Valley as well (G. R. Sharma and Clark 1983; Clark and Williams 1986).

The Upper Paleolithic of the Son Valley

Three Upper or Epipaleolithic sites found by the Allahabad/Berkeley team in the Son Valley may be mentioned here. At Rampur, not far from the Baghor sites in figure 5, an industry of small blades and burins is associated with Beta-4792, 9920 ± 120 B.C. It is also likely that there is an association between such diminutive tools and Beta-4793, 24,300 ± 420 B.C., at the base of the Baghor formation at Rampur (Clark and Williams 1986:30).

At Baghor III on figure 5 (Clark and Dreiman 1983; Clark and Williams 1986), tools similar to those at Rampur were found: small blades of near microlithic proportions, retouched blades in the form of triangles, awls, borers, lunates, and so forth. The excavators use the dates from the Rampur area to infer a date for Baghor III, rather than PRL-714, 4710 ± 180 b.c. (5575–5210 B.C.).

Baghor I (fig. 5; Kenoyer et al. 1983b; Clark and Williams 1986) is apparently somewhat later than Rampur and Baghor III. It is a multiactivity site that may be remarkably preserved. Tools include an assortment of blade types as well as triangles and awls. Location and typology strongly suggest to Clark and Williams (1986) that Baghor I belongs to the period between the Rampur/Baghor III assemblages and the Mesolithic site of Baghor II (see figs. 7, 8 and below).

A shrine at Baghor I may indicate an astoundingly long period of cultural continuity in the Vindhyas, possibly extending from 10,000 B.C. to the present (Kenoyer et al. 1983a; Clark and Williams 1986).

Upper Paleolithic Phase in the Belan Valley

Another insight into the Indian Upper Paleolithic may be derived from the cemented gravels below the Neolithic mound of Mahagara (fig. 5) (G. R. Sharma et al. 1980). The Allahabad team obtained two radiocarbon determinations for the lowest Gravels III, with a purely Upper Paleolithic tool industry. These determinations (TF-1245 and PRL-86) give a tentative date for this formation at ca. 24,000 to 17,000 B.C. This is in general agreement with the dates that the Allahabad/Berkeley team reported from the Son Valley. The possible presence of sheep and/or goat remains in these gravels is potentially of great significance and is discussed below.

The Transitional Phase of Cemented Gravels IV at Mahagara

Mahagara Cemented Gravels IV, with the beginnings of the microlithic tool-making technology, as well as more sheep/goat remains, has five radiocarbon determinations, although two of them come from shell. The consistency of these dates (see Mahagara Gravels IV in table 2), which range from ca. 12,000 B.C. to 8,000 B.C., are important since this chronology is consistent with the dates for similar materials at Baghor I and III. It is clearly too early to begin to draw conclusions about chronology, but the dates in hand offer a sound start.

Faunal Remains from the Mahagara Gravels III and IV

The presence of sheep/goat remains at Mahagara from Upper Paleolithic times through the Neolithic is extraordinary. If the identifications are correct the animals must have been domesticated to be even present there.

Zooarchaeologists have developed several criteria to assist them in judging whether animals in a particular collection are domesticated or wild. S. Bökönyi gives six of these (1969:221). For him one of the surest ways to establish domestication is to find a situation in which "species appear that have no wild ancestors in that particular region, at least since the Pleistocene" (1969:221).

The wild sheep and goat populations nearest to Mahagara are in the Himalayas, 250 miles to the north, or in the mountains of Baluchistan and Afghanistan, 1,000 miles to the west. There is no reason to believe that these ranges were significantly different in the early Holocene. This information is available in some detail in Ellerman and Morrison-Scott (1966) and has been summarized in Schaller (1977:45–82). These distances are considerable and in both instances involve the crossing of major riverine systems, the Indus or the Ganges, for the animals to have reached Sharma's site.

K. R. Alur's preliminary report on the faunal remains (Alur 1980) indicates that there was a reasonable amount of sheep/goat material, even in the Upper Paleolithic. He reports the presence of molars, mandibles, and metacarpal condyles of these animals. All of these are identifiable body parts. The mandibles and metacarpal condyles even offer the opportunity of differentiation between sheep (*Ovis*) and goats (*Capra*).

The potential importance of these materials is very great, for we are dealing with the possibility of domestication at a very early date, perhaps prior to 20,000 B.C. However, the research in and around the Belan Valley is still in a very early stage, and the ambiguities probably reflect problems inherent at the beginning of any large research program.

Industries of the Holocene
Microlithic Technology in the Holocene

The Mahagara Gravels IV indicates that there may be a gradual transition between the Upper Paleolithic blade industry and the maturity of a full microlithic technology. This is also true at other sites: Chopani Mando I (fig. 6; G. R. Sharma et al. 1980:36) and Baghor I (fig. 5) on the Son River. Typologically the microlithic industries of India appear to be remarkably similar to those of the Near East and Europe. The general types, including crescents, lunates, trapezoids, triangles, backed blades, microburins, fluted cores, and the like are certainly shared.

Integrated microlithic tool kits have a very long history in India and surrounding countries. Early dates at ca. 25,000 and 20,000 B.C. have been very recently reported, and not fully evaluated, for the site of Batadombalena Cave in Sri Lanka (Deraniyagala 1984 and below). Baghor II in Madhya Pradesh has the following uncalibrated date: PRL-715, 6380 b.c. Other sites may date to the Medieval period. Table 3 lists dates available from microlithic sites. These have not been differentiated from one another in any significant way because this introduction is intended only to give a sense of the geographic range for microlithic technology in India and the period of time involved. Site locations are found on figure 6.

Sites with Microlithic Technology

The dates in table 3 give a summary of sites in India with a predominantly microlithic industry and some chronological control. The dates are wide ranging, from 10,000 B.C. to medieval times. Some sites have clear associations between Chalcolithic or Iron Age pottery and the small stone tools. Bagor in Rajasthan (V. N. Misra 1973a) is one of these, and Langhnaj is another. Jerome Jacobson worked on a complex of sites in Madhya Pradesh with these kinds of associations (Jacobson 1970:396–423). The rock shelter/cave complex at Bhimbetka is another astoundingly rich area.

Microlithic tools with the specific typological attributes noted above were made in peninsular India well into historic times by substantial numbers of people. A warning must be noted about the use of the terms *microlithic* and *mesolithic*. In many instances an author is attempting only to convey a sense that the industry is composed of small stone tools. There are a number of such diminutive industries. One of these is the Chalcolithic short-blade industry associated with sites of the Posturban Phase of the Harappan Civilization in Gujarat. Fine examples of "true" microliths survive into historical periods in India, just as they apparently did in other parts of the world (B. Allchin 1966:26, 35, 49). Jacobson (1970:22) has noted that there have been reports from India of microliths made from bottle glass (B. Allchin 1966:102; Gordon and Gordon 1943:95; Todd 1939:42). None of these comes from reliable contexts, but given the other evidence it is not impossible that microliths were made from such material.

Three Aspects of Indian Microlithic Sites

The Mesolithic, Early Food Production, and Interactive Trade and Barter

The different contexts of microlithic technology in India are important since each has some chronological significance. A discussion of this can begin with a consideration of three different forms of settlement and subsistence that have an association with a microlithic stoneworking technology: the Mesolithic aspect, the Early Food-Producing aspect, and the Interactive Trade and Barter aspect.

Sites of the Mesolithic aspect generally occur in small caves and open settings. Tools are frequently abundant and associated with the remains of wild mammals, shells, and an occasional ground stone implement. Ring stones or "maceheads" are the most common of the latter type.

The *Mesolithic* is a much abused concept. We understand that the term is properly used to refer to Old World archaeological assemblages that fall within the Holocene and lack evidence for food production or an accommodation with surrounding food-producing peoples. In India Mesolithic peoples made proper microliths: lunates, crescents, triangles, microblades, and the like. But it is also true in India that many people who ought not to be called Mesolithic made such tools. There is no necessary correlation between these tools and a particular form of settlement and subsistence. Confusion over the definition of the Mesolithic—settlement and subsistence versus typology—has muddled much writing on Indian sites with microlithic technology. Some authors seem to imply, or even state, that if a tool assemblage contains microliths it is thereby "Mesolithic" by definition. We feel that this equation has little utility since it raises questions such as the percentage of microliths necessary to classify a body of material as "Mesolithic." Also, it may bring very diverse assemblages into conjunction. Is the Harappan village of Allahdino a Mesolithic site because it has a few microlithic tools? (Hoffman and Cleland 1977). Third, and most important, a focus on typology may actually mask the rich, historically significant aspects of the peoples who made and used these tools. As will be seen, these folk were involved in a diversity of sociocultural settings and economic activities. They were, in fact, playing key roles in regional economies. Dwelling on

tool typologies is not likely to be the most profitable way to understand these aspects of the human career.

In this essay, *microlith* and *microlithic* refer to tools that were made by some of the diverse communities of ancient India. The tools themselves are of limited importance to understanding the sociocultural and economic settings of these peoples. They are, however, a kind of proxy that allows us to communicate efficiently about this diverse class of archaeological data.

Microlithic tool technology was employed by many peoples involved with the development of food production in India. This can be seen at places like Koldihwa or the Mahagara Neolithic (see below) where there is evidence for some attention being devoted to cultivation. However, another process, especially in western India, involved the integration of domesticated animals, principally sheep and/or goats, into economies that would otherwise be classed as hunting and gathering. The later history of these peoples seems to have involved increasing sedentism in some cases, leading to the establishment of village farming communities. A certain amount of indigenous "experimentation" with the control and increased productivity of local flora and fauna may also be a part of this story.

Sites of the Interactive Trade and Barter aspect have the classic microlithic technology associated with variable faunal and floral assemblages. At times domesticated plants and animals are a part of the picture, although this is not exclusively the case. Of interest in sites of this aspect is the presence of technologically sophisticated materials such as copper/bronze, iron, and glass. Other materials such as carnelian beads, sea shells, and steatite also occur. Coins are known from some of these sites. Pottery is generally present and usually can be tied to the ceramics of surrounding village farming communities. Trade and interaction between these sites and surrounding communities, at times some distance away, can be inferred from these ceramics and the known source areas for the "exotic" materials found at these small settlements.

Microliths are also found in many of the early village farming communities throughout the subcontinent. But a more frequent stone tool manufacturing technology is one based on the crested guiding ridge and the production of long "ribbon" blades. Cores produced by crested ridge technology are rare in sites of any of the Microlithic aspects.

Chronological Significance of the Three Aspects of the Microlithic

There is much misunderstanding concerning the date and nature of sites with microlithic assemblages. Some of the most recent reconstructions of India's past (e.g., Sankalia

1974; Fairservis 1975; Agrawal 1982a) confront one with the "Mesolithic" model for all of the diverse contexts in which a microlithic technology occurs in India. Implications that the dates at hand are incorrect are themselves in error, for a satisfying model of prehistoric life in India can be generated which encompasses both the available chronological information and the material culture.

A Survey of Sites with Microlithic Technology

Of the many sites in India with a predominantly microlithic technology, few are adequately reported and fewer still have been excavated (see fig. 6). It is therefore impossible to determine where most of them would fit within our tripartite typology. A broad survey of these sites is called for, nonetheless, if only because it is possible to estimate the dates for some of them.

Northeastern India

One of the best known microlithic sites in India is Birbhanpur in Bengal (Lal 1958). The site has what Prof. Lal calls a nongeometric microlithic industry. Reports on flora and fauna are not available. Study of the soil and geology of the site concludes that "the geochronological evidence adduced here, although inconclusive so far as the absolute chronology of the site is concerned, places this microlithic culture in the comparatively mild and dry phase following the lateritic weathering, and though it would be difficult to fit this phase firmly into the acknowledged time-scale of climatic chronology without further geological investigation, the probability is that it may be assignable to the beginnings of the Holocene" (Dr. B. B. Lal in Prof. B. B. Lal 1958:48). A later study of the Birbhanpur soils supports this conclusion (Lal and Lal 1961).

A provocative report on a site known as Selbalgiri-2 in the Garro Hills of Assam mentions microliths in association with pottery (*Indian Archaeology: A Review* 1967–68a:7 and 1967–68b:8). Tools include lunates, trapezoids, points, and arrowheads. There is no chronological information.

Central India

In Madhya Pradesh, V. S. Wakankar and V. N. Misra have developed an archaeological sequence in the Bhimbetka area. In this hilly tract of some ten square kilometers, over eight hundred caves and rock shelters have been found. According to D. P. Agrawal (1982a:66), "most of them have habitation from Acheulian to the Mesolithic period." Some have a microlithic tool kit unassociated with ceramics and metals. In stratigraphic terms this directly follows the Upper Paleolithic of the area. Studies of the Bhimbetka fauna and flora are lamentably absent,

and preservation of this material is said to be very poor (V. N. Misra, pers. comm.), but the microlithic aspect just noted is followed by strata in which microliths are associated with Chalcolithic and Iron Age pottery, metals, glass, and other materials associated with the historical ages (Wakankar and Brooks 1982; V. N. Misra, Nathpal, and Nagar 1977). The dates for Bhimbetka on table 3 do not allow us to discriminate between these various associations at the site complex. Moreover, one of the excavators, V. N. Misra, has expressed some doubt about the quality of some of the samples (V. N. Misra in Agrawal et al. 1978:235).

Bombay

Farther south, in the region around the present city of Bombay, there has been some exploration, but little systematic excavation. K. R. U. Todd pioneered the archaeological work in the area (Todd 1939, 1950). He was followed by S. C. Malik (1959) and D. P. Agrawal and S. Guzder (1972). Bridget Allchin (1966) has also summarized much of the material. The significant sites are Pali Hill near Bandra and Yerangal Point, both on Salsette Island, now incorporated into the Bombay peninsula (Todd 1950: fig. 1; Malik 1959:27).

The shores of Bombay, once a chain of islands connected by tidal flats, must have been an exceptionally rich and attractive environment for a hunting and gathering population, and many of the sites from this area may relate to the Mesolithic aspect, but studies of fauna and flora are wanting. There are no absolute dates for these sites, although D. P. Agrawal has suggested an early chronology for some of them. It seems, he observes, that there are no sites between present sea level and +5 m. This suggests that coastal sites were destroyed by mid-Holocene sea levels which were much higher (Agrawal, Avasia, and Guzder 1973).

Some of the sites on Salsette Island also relate to other aspects of the Indian microlithic. For example, a wide range of beads including agate, carnelian and jasper, some of which may have been etched, were reported from Pali Hill, Yerangal, Hog Island, and some other sites (Todd 1950:7).

South India

In the deep south of peninsular India, a number of sites seem to relate to the Mesolithic aspect of the microlithic tool-making tradition. In Karnataka, formerly Mysore state, the site of Sanganakallu (Sankalia 1969; Ansari and Nagaraja Rao 1969) has been well excavated. Based on the stratigraphic position of the microlithic industry there and some soil analysis, Sankalia (1974:246) has suggested that it dates broadly to between 9,000 and 3,000 B.C. The same may be true for Kovali in Bijapur District of Karnataka (Pappu 1970, 1974:264). Over thirty sites with microlithic industries are known from the Shorapur Doab in Karnataka (Paddayya 1973). There is no way to date securely all of them or to know whether any of the inhabitants were raising domesticated animals, but some of the settlements are stratified under the Southern Neolithic. This indicates that the tools predate the middle of the third millennium B.C. (see below for the chronology of the Southern Neolithic).

The broadly conceived investigation of the famous site of Nagarjunakonda (Subrahmanyam 1975:46–71) also produced evidence that people made and used microlithic tools there. There are two specific localities, plus a number of surface collections, on which there are full reports, although fauna and flora are omitted. Once again the microliths, at least in part, predate the introduction of pottery and the Southern Neolithic.

In Tinnevelli District of Tamil Nadu (Madras), eleven microlithic sites have been located on the sea coast, among dunes and coastal shallows. The following are the most important: Megnanapuram, Kuttampuli, Kuthankuli, Sawyerpuram, Kattalankulam, Kullatur, and Puttan Taruvai (Sankalia 1974:241; Zeuner and Allchin 1956). The sites are on either side of the mouth of the River Tambrapani in red-weathered sand dunes known in Tamil as *teris*. The dunes have been studied by Frederick Zeuner, Bridget Allchin, A. V. N. Sarma, and a team led by D. P. Agrawal. Thus we now have some dates for the various sea terraces and some idea that these sites were occupied during the early Holocene. Sarma's publication (1976:186–90) has a fine discussion of the dates themselves. D. P. Agrawal has the following to say about the chronology of the *teri* sites:

> Due to older transgressions of the sea, there are three terraces of sand dunes at 1.5 m, 6 m, and 15 m quite inland from the present day coast. The dunes obviously must have formed during arid conditions, but man occupied them only during wetter conditions as indicated by weathering and the sand. Even the microliths are stained red by the hydrated ferrix [*sic*] oxide, a product of weathering. Zeuner assigned the 6 meter terrace, from which most of the microliths derive, to ca. 4000 B.C. (Zeuner and Allchin 1956). We have 14C dated the +5 m sea level transgression for the western coast of India to ca. 5000 B.C. (Agrawal and Guzder 1972). On the eastern board [of India] also a large number of samples were dated which confirm this date, but no report has come-out yet. (Agrawal 1982a:75).

Sri Lanka

A few words about Sri Lanka are in order here, since South India has just been mentioned. First, a well-formed microlithic tool kit has been documented at Batadombalena Cave (also known as Batadomba). This may be as early as 28,000 B.C., well before this technology appears elsewhere in the world (Deraniyagala 1984:107). This very early date may be corroborated by a TL date of 26,000 B.C. for ancient sand dunes at Bundala, Sri Lanka, in which microlithic tools also have been found (Deraniyagala 1984:105). At Beli-lena Kitugala the claim has been withdrawn for a microlithic industry dating to as early as 10,000 B.C. associated with "possibly domesticated cereals" (Agrawal, Krishnamurthy, and Kusumgar, in press: 3) or the seeds of millets (Protsch and Weninger 1984:194). S. U. Deraniyagala has informed the authors that the dates are seemingly acceptable but that the seeds have "been conclusively identified by M. D. Kajale as granules from the charred epicarp of the edible wild breadfruit *Artocarpus nobilis*" (Deraniyagala, pers. comm., 1985).

Beli-lena Athula, another site with microliths, has a date of TF-1094, 6420–5420 B.C. Wild seeds and fruits have been reported there (*Indian Archaeology: A Review* 1980–81a:110). The site of Bellan Bandi Palassa has a thermoluminescence date of 4550 ± 700 B.C. from fired rock crystal (Wintle and Oakley 1972). So little is known of this site that it is difficult to fit it into a larger scheme.

There is considerable archaeological research taking place in Sri Lanka. We are confident that in the not-too-distant future a great deal more will be known about its prehistory.

The Mesolithic Aspect
The Belan and Son Valleys

For approximately ten years G. R. Sharma, of the University of Allahabad, developed a program of exploration and excavation on the southern edge of the Ganges alluvium, including the flanks of the Vindhyan Hills to the south. Much of this work centered on the valleys of the Belan and Son rivers, which enter the Ganges Valley from the state of Madhya Pradesh (fig. 7). Several important sites were also found on the Gangetic plain itself. The Allahabad team was joined by a group from the University of California, Berkeley, headed by J. Desmond Clark. (Reports are available in G. R. Sharma et al. 1980, and G. R. Sharma and Clark 1983.)

Foundations in the Mahagara Cemented Gravels III and IV

We have already noted that the Allahabad team's dating of the Mahagara Cemented Gravels III, with Upper Paleolithic tools, to ca. 24,000–17,000 B.C., is a reasonable conclusion. It is also congruent with research in the Son Valley.

The Mahagara Cemented Gravels IV, with the beginnings of the microlithic tool-making technology, has five radiocarbon determinations, two of them from shell. Their consistency, which ranges from 12,000 B.C. to 8,000 B.C., is important for judging their reliability, and for their general agreement with the date from nearby Baghor II.

The Allahabad/Berkeley team also worked in the Son River valley, not far from the Belan. They discovered a number of sites that document occupation in the area from Lower Palaeolithic times on. One of these is known as Baghor II.

Baghor II

Baghor II sits on a ridge of Late Pleistocene alluvium known as the Baghor formation (Sussman et al. 1983:161). Microlithic tools and other debris are well concentrated on its surface. In 1980, excavations there uncovered a single component settlement that apparently was used repeatedly by a hunting-and-gathering population. A single radiocarbon determination calibrated at 8645–7645 B.C. (PRL-715) supports the team's contention that the site is early. Unfortunately the fauna was not well preserved, and no flora has been reported. The excavators summarize this extremely important site in the following way:

> Baghor II is a primary context early Mesolithic habitation site occupied during the early Holocene on a repeated semi-permanent basis. The lithic assemblage is fully microlithic, characterized by an informal and numerically minor shaped tool component which, despite the unprecedented presence of geometric microliths in similar assemblages from the middle Son and adjacent regions, places the Baghor assemblage in an early phase of the Indian Mesolithic tradition. (Sussman et al. 1983:186)

Baghor II is one of the best possibilities in India to be a true "Mesolithic" site, even though there is only one radiocarbon determination. As the excavator's narrative makes clear, the tools are typologically appropriate to this determination.

Ghagharia Rock Shelter

Four kilometers east of Baghor I is Ghagharia rock shelter, one of four in the vicinity. Tools in the basal levels are much like those of Baghor II (Clark and Williams 1986). There is a later "Mesolithic" which follows stratum I and is in turn followed by Neolithic, Chalcolithic, and Iron Age levels.

The Allahabad University Sites

G. R. Sharma's team has excavated four sites that may have the same "Mesolithic" character noted at Baghor II: Sarai Nahar Rai, Mahadaha, Chopani Mando Period I, and Lekhahia I, Phase Two. The Sharma publication (G. R. Sharma et al. 1980) presents various aspects of these sites as techno/typological equivalents, although at one point they suggest that Mahadaha is slightly later than Sarai Nahar Rai (Sharma et al. 1980:117).

Sarai Nahar Rai

This site is located on the alluvium of the Ganges, on the shores of a now dry oxbow lake 15 km southwest of Pratapgarh in Uttar Pradesh. It is presented as a single occupation settlement of approximately two thousand square meters (Agrawal 1982a:167). Fragmentary architecture, in the form of hearths and floors surrounded by postholes, marks the habitation (Sankalia 1974:239; G. R. Sharma 1973:139–41). Agrawal reports the presence of bones of sheep, goats, buffalo, cattle, and elephants (1982a:67). Thirteen burials were found within the settlement, their heads pointing to the west. This population is reported to have been very tall, with some men and women over six feet in height (Kennedy 1984). Two dates from Sarai Nahar Rai are calibrated to 1140–854 B.C. and 8900–7900 B.C. (table 4).

Mahadaha

Mahadaha, also near the shores of a former oxbow lake on the Ganges alluvium, is 31 km northeast of Pratapgarh in Uttar Pradesh. A summary of the site can be found in G. R. Sharma et al. (1980:77–131). There are three areas: a "Lake" area, a Butchering Complex, and the Cemetery/Habitation area.

The "Lake" area seems to have been a trash dump, active when the oxbow lake near the habitation was at a higher level. It was rich in microliths, querns, rubbers, burnt clay lumps, ochre, and the like, as well as the bones of sheep/goats, cattle, gaurs, hippos, antelopes, deer, turtles, birds, and fish.

The Butchering Complex was littered with animal bones, some with signs of cutting. Bone and antler tools and ornaments, some in the process of being fashioned, were found here. There is apparently little difference between the "Lake" area and the Butchering Complex in the species represented.

The Cemetery/Habitation area contained fifteen graves with seventeen individuals. Grave goods included microlithic tools, bone points, and bone ornaments. Sixteen hearths complement the interments in this area and suggest additional functions for this portion of the site. Dates for Mahadaha are given in table 4. The calibrated range for three dates is 1385–885 B.C. and 2675–2515 B.C.

The Allahabad team's arguments for accepting the very early chronology for Sarai Nahar Rai and Mahadaha are based on the typology of the material culture. The dates, and their internal inconsistency, argue against this. What we may have, for Mahadaha at least, are signs of the kind of accommodation between a hunting-gathering population and later food producers that have been suggested for the Interactive Trade and Barter aspect of the Indian Microlithic tradition.

Lekhahia I

Lekhahia I is located on the Kaimur River in Mirzapur District of Madhya Pradesh, some 19 km southeast of Mahagara. (For the best summary see Sankalia 1974: 237–38.)

The site has been divided into four phases, each apparently with two "natural" layers. Uppermost Phase Four is the latest material.

Phase Four (Layers 1 and 2). This stratum contains geometric microliths and pottery. The tools are reduced in size from those of Phase Three.

Phase Three (Layers 3 and 4). The tool industry of this phase consists of geometric microliths, including triangles and trapezes. Pottery includes dull red and dull gray wares, at times impressed. The impressed pottery is said to be identical with that from the Mahagara Neolithic (G. R. Sharma et al. 1980:137). Calibrated date TF-417, 2135–1755 B.C., comes from Phase Three (see table 4).

Phase Two (Layers 5 and 6). Geometric microliths are found in Phase Two. There is no pottery.

Phase One (Layers 7 and 8). The lowest phase has nongeometric microliths and Upper Paleolithic tools, but no pottery. There is one radiocarbon determination: TF-419, 3035–2780 B.C. (table 4).

There are no reports on animal bones from Lekhahia I.

Chopani Mando

Chopani Mando is a three-period site on the floodplain of the Belan Valley, 77 km southeast of Allahabad City. It is approximately 150 by 100 m. The excavations there are summarized in Sharma et al. (1980:33–76).

Period III. The latest period at the site is called Protoneolithic or Advanced Mesolithic. Up to thirteen round or oval huts were found along with four hearths. The floors of the huts were "littered with a large number of microliths and stone pieces" (Sharma et al. 1980:37). Fragments of flat querns, mullers, and ring stones occurred with redware pottery.

G. R. Sharma reports that from Period III come the bones of cattle and sheep/goats as well as carbonized wild rice (Sharma et al. 1980:75).

Period III is the only occupation with ceramics. These include a Red Ware, and a Khaki or Brownish Gray Ware. Some of these sherds are decorated with a set of impressed designs (Sharma et al. 1980:65–68). While these designs differ in detail from the ceramics of the Vindhyan Neolithic (see below), the tradition of decoration is the same. The agreement between radiocarbon determinations for the Vindhyan Neolithic and BS-129, at 3385–3135 B.C. (table 4), for Chopani Mando III may thus be significant.

Period IIB. Subperiod IIB contains geometric microliths which are said to be nearly identical with those from Sarai Nahar Rai (G. R. Sharma et al. 1980:71–72). There are five circular huts. The animal bones were too fragmentary for identification.

Period IIA. Subperiod IIA is an earlier architectural level with two huts like those of IIB. Nongeometric microliths are also reported.

Period I. This earliest settlement at Chopani Mando is termed Epipaleolithic. The tool assemblage contains two aspects: one with thick, broad, elongated blades, points, and scrapers and the second with tools like those just noted, but smaller. On the basis of typological similarities to Mahagara Gravels IV, Sharma and his team date it to ca. 17,000 B.C. (Sharma et al. 1980:72).

Early Food-Producing Aspect

The Vindhyan Neolithic

Important evidence relating to the beginnings of sedentism and food production in northern India comes from recent work in the Belan and Son valleys. Taken together this material forms a distinctive cultural assemblage that can be called the Vindhyan Neolithic. Some consideration was given to the proper place for the presentation of this important new material when this essay was planned. The excavators who have made these discoveries have stressed two things that lead us to the present organization of our work. First, there are clear lines of technotypological continuity between Vindhyan Neolithic sites and settlements of other kinds, which can be described as Mesolithic in charactger. Second, these sites seem to contain a significant microlithic component in their worked stone inventory. Since reports on much of this work are preliminary in nature, judgments of this kind may well change in the future.

Significant chronological information on these early food producers is also in hand, thanks to J. Desmond Clark. We begin with a brief review of two sites in the Son Valley: Kunjhun II and Kunjhun River Face.

Kunjhun II

At Kunjhun II the Allahabad/Berkeley team found an eroded settlement with cord-impressed pottery, dished grinding stones, and stone axes (Clark and Williams 1986). The cord-impressed pottery is quite distinctive and apparently of the type found at Mahagara and Koldihwa (G. R. Sharma et al. 1980: pl. MGR.XII and XIII). It may also have a typological relationship to the ceramics of Chopani Mando III (see above). In any event, it is now seen as an important marker for the Vindhyan Neolithic.

Excavations at Kunjhun II produced evidence for the heat treatment of chalcedony, agate, and chert. Heat-treated nodules were worked into tools on the spot. Kunjhun II was also a butchering station as shown by a good collection of large mammal bones, some of which had been split to retrieve the marrow. The animals included the *gaur* as well as a large- and medium-sized deer and an antelope (Clark and Williams 1986). There are a number of locations like Kunjhun II in the Son Valley.

Kunjhun River Face

A step trench at the river, 500 m north of Kunjhun II, was named Kunjhun River Face by the Allahabad/Berkeley team. The excellent collection of the Vindhyan Neolithic ceramics includes the Cord Impressed Ware, which was the most common type. Other ceramics include the Black Burnished Ware and Red Slipped Ware of the Vindhyan Neolithic. Chipped stone and faunal remains were also recovered. Three dates available from the Kunjhun River Face are in table 4 and calibrate to a range of 3530–3335 to 1565–1265 B.C.

The dates and material from Kunjhun River Face are very much in keeping with the material from G. R. Sharma's Neolithic site at Mahagara in the Belan Valley.

Mahagara Neolithic

Situated in the Belan Valley 3 km southwest of Chopani Mando is the Neolithic habitation mound of Mahagara. It will be recalled that this site sits on Gravels III and IV of the Belan Valley. (The best summary of Mahagara is found in G. R. Sharma et al. 1980:133–200.)

The site has 2.6 m of habitation debris and as many as seventeen stratigraphic levels. Architecture is represented by floors 4.3–4.6 m in diameter, surrounded by postholes. The huts were arranged in curvilinear patterns, not in lines. A cattle pen was also located (G. R. Sharma et al. 1980:146). Pottery includes the distinctive Cord Impressed Ware, Burnished Red Ware, Burnished Black Ware, and a Rusticated Ware. Ground stone querns, mullers, adzes, celts, and chisels were found. A microlithic chipped stone industry utilized chert and chalcedony.

Rice is reported from the Mahagara Neolithic, but the publication on the site (Sharma et al. 1980:182) does not state clearly that it is domesticated. K. R. Alur's report notes the presence of sheep/goats, cattle, horses, deer, and wild boars. The sheep/goat remains are all from domesticated stock. Alur considers the cattle bones to be generally the remains of domesticated animals, but some wild species also seem to be present (Alur 1980:220).

There are four radiocarbon determinations for the Mahagara Neolithic in table 4, with calibrated ranges of 1770–1545 to 1670–1375 B.C. The dates from Mahagara and Kunjhun River Face are clearly in agreement, indicating a date for the Vindhyan Neolithic at between about 4000 and 1200 B.C. This chronology also agrees with one of three dates from the site of Koldihwa.

Koldihwa

Koldihwa is ca. 85 km southeast of Allahabad on the Belan River, opposite Mahagara. It is approximately 500 by 200 m in size (Sharma et al. 1980:135). The site has three periods: Iron Age, Chalcolithic, and Neolithic.

There is no real evidence for architecture at the site, although burnt clay lumps showed the impressions of screens. The material inventory includes the Cord Impressed and associated wares of the Vindhyan Neolithic, as well as ground stone celts, a Neolithic blade industry, and microliths (Sharma et al. 1980:135). Remains of rice in pottery have been identified by Vishnu-Mittre and Tetzu Chang as domesticated (Sharma et al. 1980:135–36).

The Allahabad team has used three radiocarbon determinations to date the Koldihwa Neolithic in table 4. PRL-223, from the Koldihwa Neolithic/Chalcolithic interface, agrees with dates for the Vindhyan Neolithic from Mahagara and Kunjhun II. This strongly suggests that the two earlier dates from Koldihwa (PRL-100 and PRL-101) are either aberrant or indications of an earlier, unreported occupation at the site. The Sharma team occasionally quotes PRL-224 adjusted to 7080–6080 B.C. as a Neolithic date, but the stratigraphic association of this sample is very uncertain since it was originally published as coming from an Iron Age pit (Agrawal et al. 1977:231).

Similarities in material culture, especially the ceramics, further suggest a close temporal and cultural relationship between Kunjhun II, Kunjhun River Face, Mahagara, and Koldihwa. The presence of the Vindhyan Cord Impressed Ware at Lekhahia I, Phase Three, ties this occupation to the complex as well. Chopani Mando III, with an impressed ware and wild rice, has a radiocarbon determination that calibrates to 3385–3135 B.C., within the temporal limits of the Vindhyan Neolithic.

The Allahabad/Berkeley team has demonstrated that the Belan and Son valleys, along with the plains of the Ganges, have important material relating to the development of food production in north-central India and possibly all of Asia. The sites they excavated are rich in the sense that there is generally an architectural matrix within which artifacts can be studied and the preservation of organic material is good, possibly excellent. The strong lines of continuity are also important. Chronological relationships have been summarized in figure 8.

More on Early Food Producers and Indian Microliths

Somewhat different evidence for early food production in India comes from the site of Bagor (not to be confused with the Baghor sites discussed above) in Rajasthan and the Adamgarh complex of caves and rock shelters in Madhya Pradesh. Here the adaptations that led to a food-producing economy involved the development of a pastoral economy, with little evidence for agriculture and sedentism.

Bagor Phase I

Bagor is in Rajasthan to the east of the Aravalli Range. The site is stratified within what is now a fossil sand dune called the Mahasati Mound, which sits above the Kothari River, a tributary to the Banas. The Bagor sequence contains three phases (V. N. Misra 1973a). Lowest Phase I is a purely microlithic settlement. In Phase II the microlithic technology continues and is complemented by the introduction of copper (bronze?) tools and pottery. In Phase III the microlithic technology is accompanied by iron and glass artifacts. Only Phase I is of interest to this discussion of early domestication. Phases II and III, however, form a part of the Interactive aspect of the Indian microlithic.

Faunal remains from Phase I include a predominance of sheep/goat bones (65 percent) as well as those from the zebu, buffalo, pig, antelope/gazelle, deer, hare, fox, and mongoose (Thomas 1975). This assemblage did not change through the three phases, although the absolute number of bones declines in Phase II.

The sheep/goat remains from all three phases of Bagor are thought to have been domesticated because of their distance from native areas, the age profile of the sample, and indications of a controlled diet implied by a lack of tooth wear. The zebu (*Bos indicus*) is also thought to have been domesticated (Thomas 1975:325).

Radiocarbon dates from Bagor I (table 4) are in the main stratigraphically consistent, although all samples were taken from the carbonate fraction of bone. Calibrated they range from 5355–4955 B.C. to 3955–3775

B.C. An examination of table 4 will show that the Bagor Phase I dates are reasonably close. While further work and more dates are definitely needed from Bagor, and from other sites in the region, there is some reason to now look at the beginnings of the food-producing economy in this part of India as starting with the integration of sheep/goats, and perhaps cattle, into hunting and gathering subsistence economies in the fifth, possibly the sixth, millennium B.C. The earlier date is suggested by the work at Adamgarh Cave.

Adamgarh Cave

Adamgarh is located near the town of Hoshangabad in central India, just south of the Narmada River. The site is not far from where the archaic *Homo sapiens* was recently found. Excavations in 1960–61 by R. V. Joshi (*Indian Archaeology: A Review* 1960–61a:13; Joshi and Khare 1966; Joshi 1978) were undertaken while Joshi was with the Archaeological Survey of India. The work was published when he moved to Deccan College (Joshi 1978). The site is a complex of rock outcrops covering an area of about 12 ha. Joshi excavated eighteen separate trenches in this area. What he found is much like the evidence from Bhimbetka ca. 100 km to the north. Both the Lower and Middle Paleolithic are in strata below microlithic levels that appear to have a "Mesolithic" character. Those nearest the surface are generally disturbed to some degree and contain Chalcolithic, Iron Age, and Medieval pottery, as well as iron and glass.

In trench ADG-1 Joshi found some 30 cm of disturbed material over 50–70 cm of relatively undisturbed black soil containing a significant number of microliths. In the underlying lateritic clays were Lower and Middle Paleolithic tools. ADG-1 yielded potsherds to a depth of 85 cm. Iron extended down to 11 cm and glass bangles to a depth of 20 cm. Broken ground stone "maceheads" and hammer stones were also found.

Joshi recovered over five thousand microliths in trench ADG-10 from levels that contained neither glass nor iron. Pottery, unlike that from Chalcolithic or other known contexts, was apparently found throughout this cut, although never in much quantity (Joshi 1978:44).

Faunal remains from Adamgarh include the dog, *Bos indicus, Bubalus bubalis, Ovis vignei, Capra hircus aegagrus,* and *Sus scrofa,* as well as deer, an equid, hare, and other assorted mammals and reptiles (Bhola Nath 1967). The dog, sheep, and goat are said to have been domesticated.

The association of the microliths and domesticated animals may derive further significance from an associated radiocarbon determination of TF-120, calibrated to 6410–5705 B.C. (table 4) derived from shell taken from

ADG-10 at a depth of 15–21 cm (Agrawal and Kusumgar 1968:131–32). A second date for Adamgarh Cave is from Trench ADG-2: TF-116, calibrated to 1100–805 B.C. (table 4). This sample was taken from uncharred bone excavated at a depth of −190 cm (Agrawal and Kusumgar 1968:132). This would be within the stratigraphic contexts that yielded Middle or Lower Paleolithic tools from this cut (Joshi 1978:44). The dating team notes at the end of their report that "dating of collagen (organic fraction) from other bone from Adamgarh can alone confirm the chronology of this Mesolithic Culture" (Agrawal and Kusumgar 1968:132). To date this has not been done.

The calibrated date TF-120 at 6410–5705 B.C. (table 4) for Adamgarh is not unreasonable, if the chronology for early domesticated animals at Bagor is anything near correct. This is not to say that the chronology, even of Bagor, is secure. But it does provide a somewhat different problem orientation for future fieldwork since it is possible that central and western Indian hunter-gatherers were integrating domesticated animals into their subsistence economy as early as the sixth millennium B.C. The full exploration of this adaptation has only begun. It will, however, demand that research programs pay increasing attention to organic remains. While some faunal studies have been undertaken, flora remains are almost untouched.

Neither Bagor nor Adamgarh Cave show evidence for the use of domesticated plants, although the inhabitants of these sites seem to have integrated domesticated animals into their subsistence regime. This is not the case at all of the early, transitory sites in western India that are associated with the Indian microlithic technology. For example, a mix of plants and animals seems to be present at such sites in the Belan Valley. We believe that well conceived and executed research strategies, with the intensive use of flotation and an explicitly developed sampling strategy, would produce similar evidence in other regions of the subcontinent.

Interactive Trade and Barter Aspect

The single remaining aspect to this discussion is the relationship between these small, transitory, even ephemeral, sites and surrounding, contemporary villages and towns. The origin and development of the sedentary village farming community have not yet been addressed in this essay, but are discussed in the following section. However, by the beginning of the third millennium B.C. village farming communities are found all through western India from the Himalayan foothills south to Malwa (figs. 2, 6, and 9). These are characterized by permanent settlement, long-term storage, and a dependence on agriculture as the predominant component in the subsistence regime, although sheep/goats and cattle are present.

A wide range of sophisticated goods may also be found in the towns and villages of western India at this period: copper and bronze tools, ornaments and weapons, ornaments of gold and silver, beads and other baubles fashioned from a wide range of "exotic" stones such as lapis lazuli, carnelian, agates, steatite, and rock crystal. Seashells may also be present. Not every site exhibits the entire range of materials, but their overall distribution, especially metals, is reasonably broad.

The emergence of the kind of interactive accommodation suggested here also seems to be present in the area dominated by the Vindhyan Neolithic. The mix of settlement and subsistence systems which may be present in this region after ca. 4000 B.C. is what one would expect under these circumstances of regional cultural integration (see fig. 7).

The archaeological map of western India in prehistoric and protohistoric times appears much like a mosaic of clusters of sites with several different forms of adaptation: settled farming communities, hunter-gatherers, hunter-gatherer-pastoralists, even agricultural peoples who may have been highly mobile for significant parts of the year when they relied on domesticated animals for their survival. At times these clusters of similar sites seem to be the sole occupants of a "territory." In other instances the spatial distribution overlaps with evidence for different forms of adaptation within the same region; however, the niches being exploited are distinctively different. This mosaic is, of course, incomplete. But evidence for the simultaneous existence of various forms of adaptation is compelling, in spite of the chronological ambiguities that have already been noted. It is also clear that these peoples did not live in isolation from one another. A study of the material suggests interaction and, by implication, interdependence between these variously adapted entities.

Some Evidence for Interactive Trade and Barter

Bagor Phase II

Phase II at Bagor marks the first appearance of pottery in abundance as well as the introduction of copper. The microlithic technology continues, as does the mixed subsistence system.

V. N. Misra says the following about the ceramics of Phase II:

> Some affinities are noticeable between Bagor pottery and that of the Ahar culture in Mewar . . . and the Kayatha culture of Malwa. . . . The surface treatment of the Bagor pottery is similar to that of the red ware of the Ahar culture. . . . Some of the shapes . . . are common

to the two cultures. In decoration the Ahar pottery . . . like that of Bagor, is characterized by incised designs. . . . The presence of a few unpainted black and red ware sherds at Bagor also provides a hint of some link with Ahar. The large neckless jar at Bagor is also exactly paralleled in the period I pottery of Kayatha. (V. N. Misra 1973a:103)

The Ahar, or alternatively Banas, "culture" sites are farming settlements clustered in the Banas River valley, directly adjacent to Bagor. Kayatha sites are located slightly farther south (see Wakankar 1967: pl. 24). The Ahar sites date to 2600–1500 B.C. (see below). The relevant periods at Kayatha (I and II) and other sites in its vicinity date to 2450–1700 B.C. Citations for the comparison of the most important of these ceramics, the incised redwares, are as follows: Bagor (V. N. Misra 1973b: fig. 22); Ahar (Sankalia, Deo and Ansari 1969:77–86); and Kayatha (Ansari and Dhavalikar 1975:46, 47, 56, 57, 64, 66, 67).

The exact source of this kind of formal similarity in the archaeological record is, of course, always difficult to trace with certainty. But V. N. Misra's suggestion, that it indicates that the inhabitants of Bagor had some kind of contact with settlements of the Ahar and Kayatha Complexes, is a good one (V. N. Misra 1973b:305). Gilund, a site with the full inventory of Ahar ceramics, is only 30 km south of Bagor.

A notable feature of Bagor Phase II is the occurrence of copper arrowheads in burials. These are typologically very similar to those illustrated from Mature Harappan contexts (V. N. Misra 1970a:225).

The two relevant radiocarbon determinations for Bagor (table 5) at this point are TF-1009, 3395–3160 B.C. for the Period I/II transition, and TF-1005/1006, 2645–2310 B.C. for Period II proper (table 5). They support the notion that Bagor had substantial contacts with the Harappan Civilization as well as with the Ahar and Kayatha Complexes (see below).

Ganeshwar/Jodhpura

Ancient copper tools have been discovered in abundance in Rajasthan and adjacent areas (see fig. 9 and Agrawala 1978, 1979, 1980; Agrawala and Kumar 1982). Excavations at the site of Ganeshwar in Sikar District produced over a thousand copper implements including arrowheads, spearheads, bangles, celts, chisels, fishhooks, and the like (Agrawala and Kumar 1982: pls. 11–1 through 11–7). These tools were found in association with a "microlithic" stone tool kit and incised ceramics. Typologically the metal tools are definitely Harappan, although the Ganeshwar specimens may have somewhat greater stylistic variation than the Harappan inventory usually

admits. Celts like those found at Ganeshwar, while they are of Harappan type, have also been found at places like Ahar (Sankalia, Deo, and Ansari 1969: 199–203, pl. 22 and fig. 122), Kayatha (Ansari and Dhavalikar 1975: pl. 25), and Navdatoli (Wheeler 1959: pl. 25), possibly expanding the arc of interaction between sites in Rajasthan and those to the southeast.

Agrawala and Kumar (1982) refer to the ceramics from Ganeshwar, and a second site known as Jodhpura, as OCP or Ochre-Colored Pottery. This has a close typological affinity with the incised wares from Ahar and Bagor. The OCP presents us with a complex, imperfectly understood problem. The pottery from places like Ganeshwar, Jodhpura, Bagor, and the Ahar and Kayatha Complexes all overlap in their typology, principally in the red-to-buff incised wares (for Ganeshwar compare Agrawala and Kumar 1982: pl. 11.8 with citations given above for the Bagor ceramics). There are two radiocarbon determinations from Jodhpura (table 5) that are associated with the incised ware in question. They calibrate to PRL-277, 850–755 B.C., and PRL-278, 2895–2515 B.C. The lack of agreement between the two determinations does not provide us with information that will independently date Jodhpura and, by inference, Ganeshwar. The typological ties to the incised wares from other sites already noted, especially Bagor II, suggest that these places, and others like them in northern Rajasthan, belong to the first half of the third millennium B.C.

No fewer than eight other sites, unfortunately more poorly known than Ganeshwar, have also produced copper tools of the distinctive types mentioned above. Some of these tools have inscriptions in Indus script. The sites are listed in Agrawala and Kumar (1982:130–31) and appear on our figure 9.

All of these sites, as well as those of the Ahar Complex, are near the well-known Khetri Copper Belt (Agrawal 1971:147–48). For example, Ganeshwar is near old copper mining activity at Dariba, Ahuirwala, and Baleshwar (Agrawala 1978). Copper mines at Matoon and Umara are only ca. 20 km from Ahar (Agrawala and Kumar 1982:131). It is therefore perfectly reasonable to presume that the Khetri Belt was *one* of the sources of Harappan copper. Moreover, it was people who once inhabited places like Ganeshwar, Jodhpura, Bagor, Pugal, and possibly Ahar who were most probably active participants in the production and distribution of this metal.

The significance of this reconstruction for the chronology of prehistoric India lies in the fact that the dates at hand are not inconsistent or incorrect, nor are we dealing with "mesolithic survivors" at places like Bagor and Ganeshwar. Rather we are confronted with sophisticated populations at these sites, and others like them. They may have lived in small groups, possibly organized on "band" or simple lineage principals, but they seem to have played an important role in a regional economy. This ultimately involved the integration of peoples including hunter-gatherer-herders, settled farming peoples like those of Ahar and Kayatha, and possibly even the urbanized elite of the Indus Civilization.

Lothal and Langhnaj

Additional evidence for this kind of economic relationship among the peoples of western India during the second and third millennia B.C. is available from the sites of Lothal (S. R. Rao 1973, 1979) and Langhnaj (fig. 3; Sankalia 1965). This has been discussed in two places (Possehl 1976, 1980:67–80) and therefore need not be reviewed in detail here. Lothal's position on the southeastern border of the Mature Harappan Civilization suggests that its inhabitants were involved in the maintenance of relations with other kinds of people across the "border." Economics would certainly have been an area of strong interest given the craft and commercial character noted at Lothal.

Langhnaj is a site with an abundant microlithic industry. Located some 100 km north of Ahmedabad in Gujarat state, it has a radiocarbon determination number TF-744, calibrated to 2440–2160 B.C. (table 5). There are also three thermoluminescence dates from the dunes at Langhnaj (Singhvi, Sharma, and Agrawal 1982); however, the report on them deals with TL technique aimed at dating geological formations, not habitation sequences. Associated with the radiocarbon determination is a copper knife of high purity, Black and Red Ware pottery, and beads of Harappan type. H. D. Sankalia has recently taken issue with these two pieces of evidence, but in his report on the Langhnaj excavations he notes that stone disc beads were found at the excavation (Sankalia 1965:41). Such stone disk beads are perfectly legitimate Harappan types. Moreover he makes special note of the presence of Black and Red Ware sherds from "fairly low levels" (1965:44). This is at odds with his more recent statement (Sankalia 1982:4).

Possehl (1980:67–80) offers the reconstruction of Langhnaj's place in the second millennium regional economy of western India. This paper suggests that Langhnaj and other sites like it were inhabited by peoples who were involved in some kind of economic exchange with the Harappans at settlements like Lothal. The Langhnaj subsistence regime seems to have been based on hunting and gathering since no domesticated species were found there. The mobility of peoples of this type would have brought them into regular contact with the kinds of raw materials that the craftsmen of Lothal

needed to keep their "factories" busy. These materials would have been exchanged for Harappan products like the copper knife and disk beads recovered from Langhnaj. This remains a viable hypothesis. The evidence from Bagor and Ganeshwar tends to make this proposition even more tenable.

Additional evidence, and interesting chronological information, comes from the dune site of Kanewal located about 165 km south of Langhnaj, in Kheda District, at the head of the Gulf of Cambay (Mehta, Momin, and Shah 1980). Kanewal has an occupation level with a transitory settlement following one of the phases of the Gujarati Post-urban Harappan within which Lustrous Red Ware was used. The transitory settlement has a proper microlithic tool kit and no formal architecture.

Settlement surveys in Gujarat, summarized in Possehl (1980), have demonstrated a strong line of continuity for the Post-urban Phase Harappans there. The stratigraphic sequence at Kanewal offers reasonably conclusive evidence for the geographic and chronological overlap of the Post-urban Harappan with hunter-gatherer-(herders?) in this region.

Some Inferences from Biological Anthropology

A recent paper by Kennedy, Chimet, Disotell, and Meyers (1984) shows in a broadly suggestive way some major lines of "cleavage" among various early South Asian populations. Three population clusters emerged from their multivariate analysis: (1) a group of hunter-gatherers that includes Langhnaj, Sarai Nahar Rai, and Mahadaha among other sites; (2) a western population dominated by Harappans, but including the later inhabitants of Timargarha (Dani 1967), but excluding Lothal; and finally (3) the ancient populations found at Lothal and Langhnaj.

The suggestion that the Lothal population shared many biological features with that of Langhnaj has been made before (Possehl and Kennedy 1979). This analysis by Kennedy and his colleagues is the most rigorous support for this proposition. We infer from this juxtaposition of features that the inhabitants of Langhnaj, Lothal, and doubtless other sites in their region were sharing their people as well as goods.

Although this model of the Interactive, Trade and Barter aspect of the Indian Microlithic Technological Tradition was not originally derived from a study of the ethnographic record in India, it shares much with this scene (Roy 1912; Gardner 1965, 1972; Fox 1969; and Sinha 1972). Hunter-gatherer agriculturalist exchange is an extremely important cultural and social relationship with considerable value for explaining the past (Possehl and Kennedy 1979; Peterson 1978:346–48).

The Development of the Sedentary Village in India

The Indus Valley

Jim Shaffer's contribution to this volume outlines the development of village farming communities in the Greater Indus Valley. Recent excavations at Mehrgarh have documented these beginnings as within the seventh millennium (Jarrige 1979, 1981, 1982, 1984a, 1984b, 1986; Jarrige and Lechevallier 1979). The Mehrgarh sequence serves to confirm the work done by Walter Fairservis in Quetta (1956). A strong thread of continuity allows us to trace the path of cultural change and development from these foundations to the emergence of Indus urbanization at ca. 2500 B.C. based on calibrated dates. A transitional period of perhaps 150 years has been proposed by Possehl (1986:93–99) as a critical time of rapid change which immediately preceded the emergence of the Urban form of the Harappan tradition at ca. 2500 B.C. It is within this short period of time that many, but not all, of the distinctively Harappan, urban features of this early civilization seem to have been fashioned. This transitional period is documented within the two building phases of Amri II (Casal 1964:39–42).

This short period of rapid cultural change preceding the emergence of the Urban Phase of the Harappan Civilization rests on some four thousand years of cultural development in the region. Our proposal does not conform to the once popular view that the roots of the Indus Civilization were shallow, that the Indus Valley had somehow lagged behind Mesopotamia and Egypt (e.g., Piggott 1950). On the contrary, the roots of the Indus Civilization are deep, but the pace of cultural change was varied, in the Indus Valley as elsewhere.

To the east of the Greater Indus Valley, village farming communities first appear in the very early third millennium and seem to have emerged within a series of complex and poorly understood cultural environments in Gujarat (Somnath), Mewar (Ahar), Kashmir (Gufkral), and the central and southern Indian hills and plains. Peoples, such as those at Bagor and Adamgarh, whose subsistence adaptation drew on both wild and domesticated resources, were very much a part of this sociocultural context.

In some respects much of this early village-farming-community material is well studied. Since the material inventory is known, and since there has been a fair amount of survey, something can be said of settlement patterns. In some instances the ceramics are sufficiently well studied so that an exercise in ceramic "philately" is no longer necessary. To lend order to this discussion we have chosen, more or less arbitrarily, to move from north to south, pausing to discuss the Kashmir Neolithic, the village farming communities in eastern India, the Banas "culture" and Kayatha, as well as settled farming communities in central and southern India.

The Kashmir Neolithic

The Archaeological Survey of India has conducted major excavations at two early food-producing sites in the Vale of Kashmir: Burzahom and Gufkral (table 6). Burzahom lies 25 km northeast of Srinagar and was originally reported by H. DeTerra and T. T. Patterson (1939:233–34). The survey's excavation team, headed by T. N. Khazanchi, began work in 1960. The best reports have appeared in *Indian Archaeology: A Review* (1960–61b:11, 1961–62a:17–21) and authored by Pande (1970, 1973).

Burzahom

Of the three periods at Burzahom—Neolithic, Megalithic, and Historic (fig. 3)—only the Neolithic material is of immediate concern. There are two architectural levels to the Neolithic period, here designated Phases IA and IB. The earliest settlers cut pit dwellings into the loess on which the site is built. These are replaced by mud-brick buildings and others that are built of stone rubble in Phase IB.

The ceramics are handmade coiled pots which are generally gray, brown, even black in tone. They are frequently burnished and sometimes incised (*Indian Archaeology: A Review* 1961–62a: figs. 5, 6, and 7). Mat impressions often appear on the bottoms of the pots.

The bone tool industry is unusually rich, especially for a South Asian site. Bone awls, needles, spatulas, and elaborate harpoons are present along with other implements (*Indian Archaeology: A Review* 1961–62a: fig. 8).

Ground stone implements include adzes, axes, and chisels along with flat rings on a fine-grained stone. Of unusual interest are flat, rectangular knives with two holes near the center of the top, apparently used in hafting. In another geographic context these might be called *ulus* (*Indian Archaeology: A Review* 1960–61a: pl. XVIII).

Reasonably unambiguous animal burials include the remains of dogs, wolves, the barasingha (a local ungulate), and the Himalayan ibex. There is one very fine dog burial in Phase IB (Agrawal 1982a:105).

Of particular interest at Burzahom is a pot from Period IB with classic Kot Dijian features on which is painted one of the "horned dieties" as seen at Kot Diji (Khan 1964: fig. 16) and Gumla (Dani 1970–71: fig. 1a). The Burzahom pot has been published in several places (including Agrawal 1982a:102; Sankalia 1974:353). When excavated it contained over nine hundred beads of carnelian and banded agate (B. M. Pande, pers. comm.).

This pot is important when considering the economic relationships between the plains of India and Pakistan and the mountains to their north. There is a long list of products found at Pre-urban and Urban Phase Harappan sites on these plains, which are likely to have come from the Himalayas (see Fentress 1976:306–9 for a tabulation of these and other products).

We do not believe that this pot has great chronological significance, for similar vessels and fabrics have recently been found side by side with Mature Harappan materials at Manda (J. P. Joshi and Madhu Bala 1982:187) and Ropar, incorrectly "Rupar" (Y. D. Sharma 1982:161). It is becoming increasingly clear that the diagnostic materials that define M. Rafique Mughal's (1970) "Early Harappan" occur in contexts contemporary with the Mature, Urban Harappan, at least in the eastern "domain" of the civilization (Possehl 1982b: fig. 3).

Gufkral

The chronology of Burzahom is now interwoven with that of another site known as Gufkral (fig. 3), also located in Kashmir, ca. 42 km southeast of Srinagar. A. K. Sharma's (1982:19) excavations there revealed the following cultural sequence:

Period III	Historic
Period II	Megalithic
Period IC	Late Neolithic
Period IB	Early Neolithic
Period IA	Aceramic Neolithic

In the Aceramic Neolithic, Sharma found that the inhabitants of Gufkral had dug pit houses into the loess, just as in Period I at Burzahom. In addition the ground stone inventory of this occupation shares some features with Burzahom in that there are ground stone celts and an unfinished ring stone. Querns are also present, along with a rich bone tool inventory (A. K. Sharma 1982:21 and pls. II and III).

The animal remains from Aceramic Gufkral include both wild and domesticated sheep and goats. In addition, the inhabitants hunted cattle, red deer, the Himalayan ibex, and other local species (A. K. Sharma 1982:21).

Although the plant remains of Period IA have not yet been systematically reported, A. K. Sharma has noted the presence of both wheat and six-row barley, along with a lentil (1982:22).

Period IA at Gufkral seems to represent a settlement earlier than the initial period at Burzahom. The two sites are, however, a part of the same cultural tradition. This becomes even clearer in Gufkral IB with the introduction of ceramics like those of Burzahom IA (A. K. Sharma 1982: pl. II).

Animal remains from Gufkral IB indicate that the inhabitants were still predominantly hunters. The domes-ticated goats, however, show a reduction in size and a short-horned *Bos* makes an appearance. A domestic fowl (*Gallus sp.*) is also present. The common pea (*Pisum arvense*) was added to the inventory of cultivars (A. K. Sharma 1982:32).

In the final Neolithic settlement of Period IC at Gufkral, hunting was very much reduced as a subsistence activity. The sheep, goats, and cattle are all said to be domesticated, and pigs were added to the resource base (A. K. Sharma 1982:23). All food grains found in IB were also present in Period IC.

Based on a comparison of the ceramics, and the fact that Gufkral IA seems to be aceramic, we propose a rough equivalence between Gufkral IB and the initial Burzahom settlement. Gufkral IC then equates to Burzahom IB. This relationship is not clarified by a consideration of the radiocarbon determinations given in table 6.

Dates and periods for Gufkral are in A. K. Sharma (1982:24–25). The chronology of Burzahom given here is after D. P. Agrawal and Sheela Kusumgar (1974:68). We have not found it possible to assign specific periods to all of the dates from Burzahom; therefore the material in table 6 is somewhat selective.

For the initial "Aceramic" phase of the Kashmir Neolithic we must disregard BS-358 and assume on stratigraphic grounds that Period IA at Gufkral predates BS-359, 2660–2385 B.C. On this basis we estimate the date for the Aceramic phase at ca. 2800–2500 B.C. Phase IB at Gufkral and Phase IA at Burzahom can then be placed at approximately 2500–2000 B.C. The final occupation of the Kashmir Neolithic, Gufkral IC, and Burzahom IB can then be estimated at ca. 2000–1500 B.C. It may be that the end date of 1500 B.C. will be extended by additional research. These dates are, of course, very tentative, and we suggest that the breaks between "periods" occur at approximately 500-year intervals to emphasize this fact.

Material very similar to the Gufkral/Burzahom collections is available from Ghaligai Cave Period III (Stacul 1967; Shaffer, this vol., chap. 26) and Loebanr III (Stacul 1977; Shaffer, chap. 26), both in Swat, Pakistan. The chronology suggested above does not conflict with the estimated dates for these two sites (Shaffer, chap. 26).

Further typological parallels appear in the Neolithic levels of Sarai Khola, near Taxila in northwestern Pakistan (Halim 1972). M. Rafique Mughal's analysis of the Sarai Khola ceramics contains a discussion of these ties and of parallels with the Neolithic of north China (Mughal 1972:36).

There are also general typological similarities between the Kashmir Neolithic and materials from southern Siberia, in the vicinity of Lake Baikal. These have been summarized in English by Henry N. Michael (1958). The chronology for these far-flung materials does not rule out the possibility that the mountains and plains of the subcontinent represent the southwestern edge of what would otherwise be a northeastern Asian cultural tradition. There are, however, immense unsolved problems associated with such a proposition, for the typological parallels are far from being well established. Moreover, we are still in search of a model to explain the broad geographical expanse of the north Asian cultural configuration, if in fact the typological studies provide us with sufficiently compelling evidence for true historical connections.

Settled Communities in the Eastern Ganges

The chronology of the early village farming communities in the Indian states of Punjab, Haryana, northern Rajasthan, and western Uttar Pradesh has been covered by Jim Shaffer in this volume and elsewhere (Shaffer 1981). Farther afield, settled farming communities on the eastern Gangetic plain in eastern Uttar Pradesh, Bihar, and Bengal have not received much attention from the archaeologist. We have already discussed the materials from the Belan Valley. There are, however, additional sites.

Sohgaura

Excavations at Sohgaura in Gorakhpur District of far northeastern Uttar Pradesh have yielded two radiocarbon determinations for a Chalcolithic period. These are given in table 7.

Soghaura seems to fit with an emerging body of material from Bihar and West Bengal, documenting the establishment of settled farming communities (Arara, Bahiri, Barudih, Bharatpur, Mahisdal, and Chirand) in this region during the middle of the second millennium B.C. The radiocarbon determinations for these sites are also given in table 7.

Arara and Bahiri

These two sites (fig. 7), recently worked on by Dilip Chakrabarti, seem to represent late prehistoric settlement in West Bengal. The Black and Red Ware of Arara may relate to ceramics at other Neolithic/Chalcolithic settlements such as Bharatpur, Mahisdal, and Chirand.

Chirand

The most significant Neolithic/Chalcolithic site in Bihar is the mound of Chirand near the confluence of the Ghagra and Ganges rivers (fig. 7; Narain 1970; Verma 1970–71; Sankalia 1974:304–5; *Indian Archaeology: A Review* 1981–82:27–30). The site has three main periods: III, Iron Age; II, Chalcolithic; and IA/B, Neolithic.

During the whole of the Chirand Neolithic the inhabitants lived in small dwellings. In Phase IA there is some suggestion of round houses, possibly small pit-houses with bamboo screens around them. In IB there is a mud-brick wall.

The worked stone inventory includes polished celts and microliths. The ceramics include a Gray Ware with both burnished and unburnished surfaces, and a Black and Red Ware. There is also a rich bone industry, ground stone querns, balls, and pestles.

Verma (1970–71:22) cites evidence for the cultivation of wheat, barley, rice, *masoor* (*Lens esculenta*), and *moong* (*Phaseolus aureus*), all from the Neolithic levels. The evidence for rice comes in the form of husks in pieces of burnt clay, as well as charred grains. These reports are, however, not yet fully satisfactory.

Radiocarbon determinations indicate that Chirand I may date to the beginning of the second millennium (ca. 2200–1500 B.C.). It should be noted that TF-445, 1990–1695 B.C., came from a pit filled with microliths and sealed by the Neolithic IA deposit (Agrawal and Kusumgar 1969:189). Sankalia has observed that there may be earlier important material at the site (1974:304).

Chirand II may date to something on the order of 1500–800 B.C. Agrawal (1982a:245) has noted the presence of iron in period IIB.

Bharatpur

At this site in Burdwan District, West Bengal, the Archaeological Survey of India conducted excavations during the field seasons of 1971–72, 1972–73, and 1973–74. Short reports can be found in *Indian Archaeology: A Review* for these years. In Period I (the rest of the site is Iron Age and later), the following is reported:

> Ceramic industries, associated with the earliest culture includes the characteristic painted and plain black-and-red ware and buff-on-red wares. The shapes represented in the different wares were found to be similar to those from the earliest deposits of Mahisdal and Pandu Rajar Dhibi. The design repertoire was essentially linear, such as wavy lines in groups, vertical and horizontal bands and oblique strokes. Among other finds mention may be made of: objects of bone and antler; neolithic celts; microliths; and beads of semiprecious stones. The use of copper was scarce. (*Indian Archaeology: A Review* 1972–73:36)

Mahisdal and Pandu Rajar Dhibi

Two more early farming communities in the eastern Ganges Valley are Mahisdal (*Indian Archaeology: A Review* 1963–64c: 59–60; B. Allchin and R. Allchin 1968:198–99) and Pandu Rajar Dhibi (Dasgupta 1964; *Indian Archaeology: A Review* 1961–62c:59–62, 1962–63b:43–46, 1963–64d:61–62, 1964–65b:46–48).

Mahisdal is located in Birbhum District (fig. 7). Period I has small, simple huts of plastered reeds. Pottery includes a white-painted black and red ware, as well as an unpainted variety, and a red ware, sometimes with black paint. As noted above, the forms complement those of Pandu Rajar Dhibi, especially the spouted bowls. A stone blade industry is associated with at least one copper celt. A mass of charred rice was also found in Period I.

Pandu Rajar Dhibi is in adjacent Burdwan District of West Bengal (fig. 7) with ceramics much like those of Mahisdal. A radiocarbon date of 1012 ± 120 b.c. that has no apparent laboratory designation was run by neither the Tata Institute nor the Physical Research Laboratory (D. P. Agrawal, pers. comm.).

Given the radiocarbon dates, it is possible to date these early villages of the Mahisdal/Pandu Rajar Dhibi type to approximately 1500–600 B.C.

Barudih

This is an early village farming community in Singhbhum District of Bihar. Not much is known of the site (*Indian Archaeology: A Review* 1963–64a:9), but the dates given above place it within the same chronological horizon as Chirand, Bharatpur, Mahisdal, and Pandu Rajar Dhibi.

Sonpur

The K. P. Jayaswal Research Institute, Patna, carried out excavations at the mound of Sonpur in Gaya District of Bihar for at least five seasons, most of them during the 1960s. It is clear that there is early material there, comparable to that from the places just discussed, but there has not yet been a sufficiently clear exposition of it to make a chronological judgment (see *Indian Archaeology: A Review* 1961–62d:4–5, 1970–71:5–6).

Early Village Farming Communities in Mewar and Malwa

In the western regions to the south of the Ganges Valley, village farming communities emerge as a broad horizon within the first half of the third millennium B.C. Two considerations should be kept in mind: (1) the settled farming community is only one of the major forms of adaptation that food producers in India made at this time; and (2) the emergence of settled communities along the eastern borders of the Greater Indus Valley just when the Urban Phase of the Indus Civilization takes form is not necessarily unrelated.

The Banas and Kayatha Complexes

In southwestern Rajasthan, in the vicinity of the Banas River and its tributaries, a region known as Mewar, the initial phase of agricultural settlement develops in the middle of the third millennium. Banas material has been substantially brought to light at Ahar (figs. 10 and 11), near the modern city of Udaipur (Sankalia, Deo, and Ansari 1969). There is also an important survey report on an exploration of the Banas and Berach valleys (Misra 1967).

Ahar

Although Period I at Ahar has been divided into three subperiods—a, b, and c—there is a basic continuity of material throughout. A distinctive Black and Red Ware with white paint occurs in all three subperiods. Found elsewhere, it is a useful chronological aid. Ahar I is notable for the virtual absence of stone tools. The needs of the inhabitants in this regard were apparently met by copper implements, which are abundant. Copper mines in the vicinity of Ahar were mentioned above.

Radiocarbon determinations for Ahar I are given in table 8. Date TF-37 should probably be disregarded in this series because of its inconsistency with the others. A chronology for Ahar I is reasonably reconstructed as follows: Period Ia, 2600–2150 B.C.; Period Ib, 2150–1950 B.C.; and Period Ic, 1950–1500 B.C. or later.

Kayatha

Kayatha lies ca. 285 km southeast of Ahar on the Malwa Plateau (figs. 10 and 11), a fertile area drained by the River Chambal and its tributaries. Two separate excavations have taken place there: the first by V. S. Wakankar (1967), the second by a Deccan College team (Ansari and Dhavalikar 1975). The long series of radiocarbon determinations from this site are difficult to organize by period due to inconsistency in reporting. There has been some selection of dates in table 9.

Three periods at Kayatha are of concern here. Period I has a unique ceramic assemblage (Ansari and Dhavalikar 1975:4) with "Kayatha Ware" which has designs in purple painted over a deep brown slip. There is also a Buff Ware with painting in red as well as a Red Incised Ware.

Kayatha was apparently abandoned between Periods I and II. Period II ceramics show strong parallels with Ahar Ib and Ic. These are so close that the excavators have suggested that the site may have been settled by peoples from Rajasthan during this time (Ansari and Dhavalikar 1975:6). The predominant evidence appears to be the presence of the distinctive Ahar white-painted Black and Red Ware. But Ahar-style Red Slipped Wares also occur in quantity and with some variations in tan, orange, chocolate, and brown, all burnished in Aharian fashion. Only a few sherds of the purple-painted Kayatha Ware occur in Period II (Ansari and Dhavalikar 1975:6). There are seven dates for Kayatha II, including one for the Period I/II transition given in table 9.

Period III at Kayatha is marked by the introduction of Malwa Wares. This is a well-known ceramic corpus known from Navdatoli, Apegaon, Songaon, Inamgaon, and a host of other sites in central India. The pottery of Kayatha III is generally orange to buff in fabric and painted black, at times deep purple, but different from the Kayatha Ware. Most of it is wheel-thrown. The Ahar Black and Red Ware continues on from Period II. We note here that this ware occurs only in the earliest phase of occupation at Navdatoli. Dates for Kayatha III are also found in table 9.

We propose the following summary chronology for Kayatha:

Period III	Malwa period	1700–1400 B.C.
Period II	Banas period	1950–1700 B.C.
Period I	Kayatha period	2450–2000 B.C.

The Foundations of the Central Indian Chalcolithic

We have already noted the presence of Malwa ceramics in Period III at Kayatha. This complex is extremely important and widespread throughout the states of Madhya Pradesh and Maharashtra in the second millennium B.C. It is earlier than the so-called Jorwe culture throughout large parts of this same region. Together the Malwa and Jorwe materials are known as the Central Indian Chalcolithic. In recent years archaeologists have found materials preceding the Central Indian Chalcolithic at sites such as Songaon, Bahal, and Daimabad.

Songaon

At Songaon (figs. 10 and 11; Deo and Majumdar 1969, incorrectly "Sonegaon") a stratum resting on virgin soil was associated with a distinctive Blotchy Gray Ware in the following stratigraphic series (Deo and Majumdar 1969:5):

Period III	Late Jorwe Ware, Black and Red Ware, Red Ware
Period IIb	More Jorwe Ware than Malwa Ware
Period IIa	More Malwa Ware than Jorwe Ware
Period I	Blotchy Gray Ware and Coarse Red Ware

The one radiocarbon determination for Period I is as follows: TF-384, 1890–1655 B.C. (table 10).

Two points concerning this ceramic inventory are that (1) S. B. Deo, who worked at Ahar with the Deccan College team, notes that the Black and Red Ware of Period III is different from that of Ahar I (Deo and Majumdar 1969:5); (2) the Blotchy Gray Ware shares typological similarities with the Gray Ware of the so-called southern Neolithic (see below). The radiocarbon determination for

Period I, TF-384, calibrated to 1890–1655 B.C., is perfectly in keeping with this association (see Deo and Majumdar 1969:6 for a correction to Agrawal and Kusumgar 1968:139, where TF-384 is associated with Period II).

Bahal

There are no radiocarbon dates for Bahal (fig. 10). The Blotchy Gray Ware occurs there, and it is presumably the chronological equivalent of Songaon I.

Apegaon

At Apegaon, Deo, Dhavalikar, and Ansari (1979) did not find a Gray Ware in pre-Malwa context, however a distinctive ceramic christened "Ramatirtha Ware" occurred (fig. 10). This is a typological equivalent to the Savalda Ware found in the Tapti Valley (Sali 1970). Radiocarbon dates are presented in table 10.

Daimabad Period I

At Daimabad in Ahmednagar District of central Maharashtra (fig. 10), S. A. Sali of the Archaeological Survey of India has uncovered a five-period sequence of prehistoric occupation (Sali 1986, 1982:177; see table 10 for radiocarbon dates).

Period V	Jorwe Complex	1500–1100 B.C.
Period IV	Malwa Complex	1700–1500 B.C.
Period III	Buff and Cream Ware Occupation	1800–1700 B.C.
Period II	"Late Harappan" (equivalent to Post-urban Phase Rangpur IIB/C?)	1900–1800 B.C.
Period I	Savalda Occupation	2000–1900 B.C.

In addition to the Savalda Ware, which equates with Ramatirtha Ware of Apegaon I, there is a Period I Blotchy Gray Ware at Daimabad (M. K. Dhavalikar, pers. comm.). This ceramic has not been sufficiently well studied to propose equivalences with other wares in Maharashtra and Madhya Pradesh, however it does resemble the Gray Wares of the Southern Neolithic of peninsular India (B. Allchin and F. R. Allchin 1968:168).

The Post-urban Harappan material of Daimabad II is quite convincing. Sturdy redware fabrics like those from Rangpur IIB or IIC are present. The inhabitants of Daimabad II also used mud-bricks for house construction. An extended supine burial in a brick-lined grave, a terracotta "seal" with a well-formed Harappan "letter," and a potsherd with an Indus inscription all make the case (Sali 1982: pls. 15.1–15.6). The Buff and Cream Ware occupation is not well understood at this time.

In reviewing the Daimabad dates in table 10 we find a convincing match in the C-14 chronology between Daimabad I, Apegaon I, and Songaon I, suggesting a date of

2000–1900 B.C. for this material. The Buff and Cream Ware levels at Daimabad III have been given a date of ca. 1900–1800 B.C., which is not out of line with PRL-655.

The date of 2195–1750 B.C. (PRL-426) for Daimabad II is in keeping with what is known of the Harappan chronology in neighboring Gujarat (see below). The second date is several hundred years younger than would be expected, especially given the absence of Lustrous Red Ware at Daimabad.

Recent work in the Tapti Valley, one of the traditional passes through the Western Ghats between the lowlands of Gujarat and the uplands of the Deccan plateau, has shown that there are a number of sites with Post-urban Phase Harappan materials. (Dhavalikar, pers. comm.). Deccan College excavated one of the sites during the 1984–85 field season. Sali's earlier work there (1970) also demonstrates the presence of his Savalda Complex, along with Post-urban Phase Harappans.

The Harappans in Gujarat

An Overview of the Chronology

A chronology for the Harappans is available in several places (Agrawal 1964, 1965, 1966, 1982a; Fairservis 1975; Possehl 1980; Shaffer, this vol., chap. 26).

Large-scale excavations at Mature Harappan sites in Gujarat have been conducted at Lothal (Rao 1973, 1979, 1985), Rangpur (Rao 1963), and Surkotada (Joshi 1972). Smaller excavations were undertaken at Desalpur (Soundara Rajan 1984) and Pabumath by the Gujarat State Department of Archaeology (*Indian Archaeology: A Review* 1977–78:21, 1978–79:67–68, and 1980–81:14). These are all sites with the "classic" inventory of Urban Phase Harappan materials: inscribed seals, as well as distinctive Harappan ceramics, metalwork, beads, architecture, and the like. Radiocarbon determinations from Lothal and especially Surkotada (table 11) can be used to suggest that the Urban Phase Harappans settled Gujarat, including Kutch, in ca. 2400–2300 B.C.

In 1980, Possehl presented maps showing the distribution of sites from three phases of the Gujarati Harappan (1980:57–59), ranging from the Urban Phase (Rangpur IIA) through the Lustrous Red Ware Period (Rangpur III). These maps showed an Urban Phase penetration of Gujarat through Kutch, proceeding on to Rangpur, Koth, and Lothal. These latter sites were then thought to be on the southeastern border of the Urban Phase Indus "state." In the succeeding Rangpur II B–C phase there appeared to have been a very significant increase in the number of sites in this region, especially Saurashtra (also noted in B. Allchin and R. Allchin 1968:182–83). This was thought to have been related to the introduction of *bajra* (*Pennisetum typhoideum*), *jowar* (*Sorghum bicolor*), and

ragi (*Eleusine coracana* and *E. indica*) into the Indian subsistence economy (Possehl 1980:8–9).

The Lustrous Red Ware Period (Rangpur III) was well represented in Saurashtra, although there appeared to have been a drop in the number of settlements from the time of Rangpur II B–C. Lustrous Red Ware had been found in the highlands surrounding Gujarat, at Ahar, Navdatoli and Chandoli, and it was from these places, and Lothal B, that a tentative chronology for the Harappan Tradition in Gujarat had to be fashioned (Possehl 1980:40–44). In 1980 there were very few radiocarbon determinations for the Rangpur II B–C and III periods. It is somewhat surprising to see how little has changed in this regard.

The ceramics of Lothal B and Rangpur II B–C have generally been seen as comparable and representative of the initial Post-urban Phase in Saurashtra. Possehl has listed 120 sites (1980:60) with what he considered Rangpur II B–C ceramics, and more have been discovered since then as reported in the yearly installments of *Indian Archaeology: A Review.*

The reinvestigation of Rojdi, a Harappan site in Rajkot District, has somewhat altered the chronology of the Harappans in Gujarat. The pottery from Rojdi is clearly of the Harappan tradition, but it lacks the key Urban Phase ceramic markers: the classic goblet, beaker, S-form jar (with the possible exception of one rather atypical example in *Indian Archaeology: A Review* 1958–59:20, fig. 9, B, 2), and the teacup with a perforated handle. Rojdi has not yielded a single sherd with the Indus black-on-red painting style. The site has also failed to produce any of the Harappan stamp seals or the other Urban Phase Harappan paraphernalia of daily life as found at Mohenjodaro, Chanhudaro, or the other sites against which one might measure such cultural dimensions. With the exception of one or two possible examples, Rojdi is also devoid of Lustrous Red Ware.

The New Chronology for the Harappans in Gujarat

The material inventory of Rojdi initially suggested that the history of the site was to be found within the Post-urban Phase, with a possibility that the settlement was founded in the later part of the Harappan Urban Phase. However, new radiocarbon dates (table 11) place most of the occupation within the time period of the Urban Phase Harappan.

Frank Herman, the person charged with the primary analysis of the Rojdi pottery, has examined a portion of the full ceramic corpus. His work suggests, at least in a provisional way, three ceramic phases at the site (Rojdi A, B, and C). The earliest Rojdi A is quite similar to the

Urban Phase pottery of Rangpur IIA, but the distinctive Indus painting style is absent and some of the key vessel forms of the Urban Phase Harappan are variants of what we know of from places like Mohenjodaro, Chanhudaro, or even Surkotada (e.g., the goblet and S-profile jar). Rojdi C, the upper levels of the site, has pottery that is characteristic of the early Post-urban. Rojdi B is late Urban Phase, possibly transitional to the Post-urban.

The new radiocarbon dates from Rojdi A and B (table 11) seem to compare well with those from Lothal A and the three phases of occupation at Surkotada (table 11) and are fully congruent with the chronological data for the date of the Urban Phase in Sind and Punjab (Shaffer, this vol., chap. 26), even recognizing the fact that there seems to be a complex cultural mosaic of cultures in the vicinity of 2600 to 2400 B.C. in the southern Indus Valley.

While the bulk of the occupation at Rojdi falls within the Urban Phase, the material inventory of Rojdi A and B is clearly not of the Mature Harappan, at least as we know it from Mohenjodaro, Chanhudaro, and other sites in Sind, or even Lothal and Surkotada, within Rojdi's region. This material inventory is also shared between Rojdi and a very large number of settlements in Saurashtra. Many, if not most, of the 120 sites associated with Rangpur II B–C listed in Possehl (1980:89–119) would fall into this category, for example.

Rojdi A and B, and many other sites in Saurashtra, and possibly north Gujarat as well, appear to represent a new regional expression of the Harappan Urban Phase. We propose to call this new regional *Urban Phase* manifestation the "Sorath Harappan," drawing on one of the ancient names for Saurashtra. The Post-urban Phase in Gujarat might then be called the "Sorath Post-urban Harappan." The Sorath Harappan of Urban Phase times is stylistically divergent from the Harappan Tradition as it is known from the Urban Phase sites in Kutch and Sind/Punjab; but it is clearly a part of this larger cultural whole. If judged from the most preliminary evaluation of the Sorath Harappan it also appears to be less internally differentiated than what we know of the Urban Phase Harappan elsewhere.

The Sorath Harappan

Sites of the Sorath Harappan are generally quite small. In fact, Rojdi at ca. 7 ha is the largest settlement that is known, if one rules out places with obvious signs of lateral stratigraphy. The average site size can be estimated at 5.3 ha (Possehl 1980:65), suggesting little range in settlement dimensions as well. Second, the material inventory of the sites is simple, if compared to sites in other Urban Phase regions. There are no stamp seals and very little writing (one sherd from Rojdi has an inscription).

Ornaments are not abundant; architecture is not elaborate, although there are foundations at the site of Somnath that may be those of a public building. There are circumvallations around some settlements, including Rojdi. Human remains from the entire range of Indus sites in Gujarat are rare, giving us little by way of an insight into the Sorath Harappan from this important data set. The ceramics for the Sorath Harappan present us with a challenge, one that will eventually lead to a far more crisp definition of this assemblage than is available today.

The discovery of the Sorath Harappan gives us a potential insight into another of the problems faced within the Saurashtran Chalcolithic sequence. This came from the site of Somnath, at Prabhas Pathan on the south coast of the peninsula.

The Mound of Somnath at Prabhas Pathan

In the early and mid-1970s, Deccan College and the Gujarat State Department of Archaeology began the reinvestigation of the site of Somnath (*Indian Archaeology: A Review* 1971–72, 1975–76b, 1976–77b; Sankalia 1972). This site had been excavated at an earlier date, for which there is a modest final report (Nanavati, Mehta, and Chowdhary 1971). In the course of the renewed excavation, eight radiocarbon determinations were secured. These are given in table 11.

The Period I, Pre-Prabhas dates are the earliest for a fully food-producing economy in Gujarat. In fact, excepting the dates from Bagor in Rajasthan (V. N. Misra 1973a) and Adamgarh Cave in central India (R. V. Joshi 1978), sites with a herding component integrated into an otherwise hunting and gathering subsistence economy, the Somnath dates are the earliest for a food-producing economy within the bounds of the present Indian nation. They certainly antedate the Banas culture of southern Rajasthan, along with the Kayatha, Malwa, and Jorwe complexes of central India and their suggested predecessors (Dhavalikar 1970). In fact, to the excavators they seemed to be unacceptably early when the dates initially appeared (Agrawal 1982a:193).

The Pre-Prabhas ceramics from Somnath are not Early Harappan in style. Vessel shapes, especially the smaller jars, bowls, and dishes, have an "affinity" with ceramics found in the Indus Valley. A more complete statement on this matter will have to await the appearance of a final report; however it is safe to say that the Pre-Prabhas ceramic vessel forms have a general "affinity" with that of the Harappans. The same is true for the fabrics of the Pre-Prabhas period, which tend to be dense red and buff wares.

The dates from Rojdi and the emergence of the Sorath Harappan have been so surprising that archaeologists with an interest in Gujarat should begin a complete re-thinking of their position on the synthesis of Harappan material there. Within such a restructuring the probable validity of the Somnath Period I dates should be accepted. New intensive exploration should also be directed toward the isolation of other sites with the Pre-Prabhas component, promoting the investigation of these early farming and herding peoples of Gujarat.

Surkotada

The Urban Phase Harappan is represented in Gujarat at a number of sites (Lothal, Pabumath, Desalpur), but probably most clearly at Surkotada in Kutch District. Dates are given in table 11.

Period IA. The Harappans at Surkotada founded their settlement on virgin soil. They created a "citadel" by building a massive rubble-faced wall of mud-bricks and clay lumps around their settlement, which was initially ca. 60 by 120 m. The significant ceramics of Period IA are the typical Harappan Black on Red painted ware as well as the unpainted redware. Vessel forms include the S-shaped jar, beaker, goblet, dish on stand, perforated jar, and cup with perforated lug handle. A red-slipped Polychrome Ware and a Polytone Cream Slipped Ware are present, along with a "Reserve Slipped Ware" which Joshi compares to materials from Mohenjodaro and Mesopotamia (J. P. Joshi 1972:124). Beads of steatite, lapis, carnelian, faience, and terra-cotta occur, as do copper rings, bangles, and a spearhead.

Period IB. During the middle period at Surkotada the "citadel" wall was renovated in a way that reduced the internal living space of the site. The Harappan Black on Red Ware continues, but in reduced frequency. A painted Coarse Red Ware, which began in the middle of Period IA, makes up some 70 percent of the total ceramic inventory of this occupation. Other wares also carry forward from Period IA, but only sporadically. Beads of agate, carnelian, steatite, and terra-cotta are recorded along with a heavy copper celt.

Period IC. The final period at Surkotada saw the almost complete reconstruction of the "citadel," with the addition of a "Lower Town," bastions, and a remodeled periphery wall. J. P. Joshi has noted the occurrence of a thick ash layer at the close of Period IB, and he speaks, rather darkly, of the "advent . . . of a people using a white painted Black and Red Ware" (1972:131). The intramural architecture of the site is impressive and rather well preserved during this period.

The typical Harappan wares continue as before, with the Indus pointed-bottom goblet having "a new lease on life" (J. P. Joshi 1972:133). The painted Coarse Red Ware of IB persists, but has been replaced by a very coarse, handmade redware as the predominant ceramic,

apparently up to 70 percent of the total. There are a few decorated red or cream sherds as well as an unpainted Black and Red Ware that might have parallels with Lothal. The most interesting ceramic is the white-painted Black and Red Ware of the Ahar style (J. P. Joshi 1972:134). This never occurs in much quantity, only 4.5 percent, but is unmistakable. Distinctively Gujarati Harappan forms are also made in this ware (see J. P. Joshi 1972: fig. 12, no. 16).

A Summary Chronology for the Harappans in Gujarat (also see fig. 12)

Rangpur III	Late Post-urban Phase, Lustrous Red Ware	1700–1400 B.C.
Rojdi C, Lothal B, and Rangpur IIB/C	Early Post-urban Phase	2000–1700 B.C.
Rojdi A/B, Lothal A, Surkotada I, and Rangpur IIA	Urban Phase	2400–2000 B.C.

The Central Indian Chalcolithic

Malwa

A mature phase in the prehistory of western India emerges with the beginnings of the Malwa Complex in the region of the same name. The principal ceramic of this complex "culture" is a black- or brown-painted redware, which may shade into orange or buff. There are also a Cream Slipped Ware and two principal varieties of Bichrome Ware. Ahar-type white-painted Black and Red Ware is present at some sites as well.

The Malwa peoples cultivated wheat and barley and some rice. *Ragi,* a millet, comes from the Malwa levels of Daimabad (*Indian Archaeology: A Review* 1980–81b:106). Two forms of gram—lentils and the grass pea—are also documented. The Indian jujube, a collected plant, appears as well. Cattle, pigs, sheep, and goats were the mainstays among the domesticated animals, and there is evidence for the hunting of local wild ungulates.

Malwa houses were either small circular affairs about 3 m in diameter, or rectangular, 3.5 by 2.5 m on the average (Agrawal 1982a:223). Floors were formed of rammed earth and gravel which was carefully plastered with mud and lime. There are often many applications of this floor plaster within a single house, indicating prolonged use. The walls surrounding these floors, which can be well preserved, were formed of split bamboo, or other light building material. These were formed into screenlike affairs that may have been covered with mud daub. They were held in place by small posts driven into the perimeter. The conical, thatched roofs of the round houses were complemented by gabeled coverings of the rectangular buildings.

The two Malwa sites about which we know the most are Navdatoli (Sankalia, Subbarao, and Deo 1958; Sankalia, Deo, and Ansari 1971) and Inamgaon (Sankalia 1977a; Sankalia, Ansari, and Dhavalikar 1975) (figs. 10 and 11). Other excavated sites, in alphabetical order, are Apegaon (Deo, Dhavalikar, and Ansari 1979), Daimabad (Sali 1986, 1982), Dangawada (Wakankar 1982; *Indian Archaeology: A Review* 1978–79:70–71, 1979–80: 54–55), Eran (*Indian Archaeology: A Review* 1960–61c:17–18, 1961–62c:24–25, 1962–63a:11–12, 1963–64b:15–16; U. V. Singh 1962), Nagda (*Indian Archaeology: A Review* 1955–56: 11–19), and Songaon (Deo and Majumdar 1969). There is also Malwa material at Kayatha.

Navdatoli

One of the best known of the Malwa Complex sites is Navdatoli. Dates for the four phases there are found in table 12.

There is a small amount of Lustrous Red Ware, as in Rangpur IIC and III, in all four of the Malwa phases at Navdatoli. This series of radiocarbon determinations gives a calibrated chronology for the Malwa occupation at Navdatoli as follows: Phases I and II, 2000–1600 B.C.; Phase III, 1600–1500 B.C.; and Phase IV, 1500–1400 B.C.

These dates generally agree with those from the Malwa occupations at Kayatha, Daimabad, and Barakhera, and Period II at Apegaon with a Malwa/Jorwe overlap. Dates for these sites are in tables 9, 10, and 12.

Dangawada

A recently excavated site known as Dangawada in Ujjain District of Madhya Pradesh (figs. 10 and 11) has five dates for the Malwa material of Period IB (*Indian Archaeology: A Review* 1979–80:54–55) given on table 12.

Eran

An eastern extension of the Malwa Complex seems to be present at the site of Eran (figs. 10 and 11), ca. 300 km northeast of Navdatoli (*Indian Archaeology: A Review* 1960–61c: 17–18, 1961–62c: 24–25, 1962–63a:11–12, 1963–64c:15–16; Singh 1962). The following is a short review of the stratigraphy of Eran:

Period IV	Medieval sculpture and coins.
Period III	Red Polished Ware and a black-painted redware. Coins of the western Kshatrapas and Nagas.
Period IIB	Predominance of redware, disappearance of Black and Red Ware. Iron, coins.

Period IIA	Black and Red Ware different from Period I. Northern Black Polished Ware (?). Iron.
Period I	Malwa ceramics, white-painted Black and Red Ware. Copper.

There are some differences among the various sources for the periodization of the radiocarbon determinations from Eran (compare Ramachandran 1975:37–40; Agrawal and Kusumgar 1974:115; Agrawal, Kusumgar, and Singhvi 1983:3, and the various date lists published in *Radiocarbon*). We have adhered to the information given in *Radiocarbon* when compiling table 12. A summary of this chronology is discussed below.

Inamgaon

At the large, extensively excavated site of Inamgaon, a Deccan College research team has reported the following sequence and summary chronology (figs. 10 and 11):

Period III	Late Jorwe	1200–900 B.C.
Period II	Jorwe	1500–1200 B.C.
Period I	Malwa	1700–1500 B.C.

The occupation of the site begins with Malwa material. This is comparable to that found at other sites already discussed. The scale of the Deccan College excavation has produced, however, by far the largest set of data. Radiocarbon determinations for Inamgaon I are given in table 12.

Summary

Radiocarbon dates suggest that the appearance of Malwa material at Inamgaon differs little from the time horizon of 1700 B.C. found in other parts of central India. Navdatoli may deviate from this chronology, but the radiocarbon determinations from this site are not internally consistent with respect to stratigraphy. Kayatha III also has dates that might indicate a somewhat earlier beginning for the Malwa Complex in the northern part of its range. But moving the beginnings of the Malwa back to 1800 or 1900 B.C. does not fit well with dates for Period I and II at Kayatha. These dates cast some doubt on the suggestion that the Malwa Complex began in the northern part of its range and spread to the south.

The Jorwe Complex

The Jorwe Complex directly follows, in fact emerges from, the Malwa material. The principal ceramic, the "Jorwe Ware," is a hard-fired redware with black paint on a red slip. A jar or pitcher with a nearly vertical spout rising from a carinated body is a hallmark vessel form, along with open bowls (see Sankalia et al. 1960:212–22 for good illustrations, some in color).

Jorwe settlements occur in virtually all parts of Maharashtra, save for the coastal lowlands known as the Konkan. The sites are closely associated with the well-known Black Cotton Soils which form above the bedrock Deccan Trap. These loams are good for dry farming because of their water retention properties. They are, however, very hard when dry and consequently difficult to plow, thus explaining some preference for Jorwe settlements to be located in riverine alluvial areas with looser soils. The list of cultivars used by the Jorwe folk differs little from the Malwa assemblage; however, better recovery techniques employed at the Jorwe site of Inamgaon (Kajale 1977) have given us a more detailed view of the plant economy.

According to D. P. Agrawal (1982a:235) the average Jorwe settlement was on the order of 2–3 ha, with "main centers" of 20 ha. The principal excavated sites are Jorwe (Sankalia and Deo 1955), Nevasa (Sankalia et al. 1960), Chandoli (Deo and Ansari 1965), Prakash (Thapar 1967), Songaon (Deo and Majumdar 1969), Inamgaon (Sankalia 1974:473–99; Sankalia, Ansari, and Dhavalikar 1975; Sankalia 1977a), Apegaon (Deo, Dhavalikar, and Ansari 1979), and Daimabad (Sali 1982). The site of Khed in Ahmednagar District also has two dates (Agrawal et al. 1977:231). At Inamgaon there is ceramic evidence for a Late Jorwe Phase.

Radiocarbon determinations for Jorwe sites are given in table 13. Based on these dates and an overall view of the Jorwe Complex, it is possible to give calibrated dates for the Early Jorwe as 1500–1200 B.C. The Late Jorwe immediately follows this and lasts into the first millennium B.C., although there are no radiocarbon determinations with readings this late. One of the principals in the excavations at Inamgaon summarizes the stratigraphy as follows:

> the earliest settlement at the site, that of the Malwa Culture—which flourished from ca. 1600–1400 B.C.—is . . . extensive. The size of the habitation increases during the Early Jorwe Period, but it again shrinks in the Late Jorwe Period. It is important to note that whereas almost all of the chalcolithic sites in the Tapti and the Pravara-Godavari valleys were deserted around 1000 B.C. habitation at Inamgaon continued until ca. 700 B.C. (Dhavalikar 1977:46–47)

The centuries encompassing the Late Jorwe are critical in central India. Following this period there is a transition from the chalcolithic village farming community to the Iron Age and to the Indian Megaliths. No iron has yet been found in a central Indian Chalcolithic site. Those occupied during the Late Jorwe period do admit such a possibility, since iron dated to ca. 1000 B.C. has been found at Hallur (Nagaraja Rao 1971:14, 91–92). More is said of the Iron Age following a discussion of the early food-producing communities in South India.

The Southern Neolithic

Settled agriculture in South India begins in the second half of the third millennium with the appearance of what is now called the Southern Neolithic (fig. 13). These materials are "neolithic" in the sense that there is evidence for agriculture and stock raising, pottery, ground stone, and village farming communities. Copper, bronze, and gold seem to occur in all but its earliest horizons.

It has already been noted that ceramics like the Blotchy Gray Ware, found at pre-Malwa sites like Daimabad, Songaon, and Bahal on the Deccan, have a resemblance to Southern Neolithic ceramics. This corresponds in time with the earliest stages of the Southern Neolithic. It seems, then, that at the end of the third millennium and the beginning of the second millennium these food producers inhabited a substantial part of peninsular India. In the north (Madhya Pradesh and Maharashtra) their ceramic assemblage was replaced first by the Malwa and then by the Jorwe Complexes. There is, however, some evidence for continued interaction between these regions throughout the second millennium (Dhavalikar 1970 and below).

Settlements of the Southern Neolithic found in virtually all of Karnataka (formerly Mysore), southwestern Andhra Pradesh, and northern Tamil Nadu are associated with the granite hill slopes and riverine settings of the region. The sites are small and many seem to be temporary, possibly forest herding camps, with a food economy based on cattle, millets, and pulses. A curious feature of some settlements is the presence of mounds of dung with evidence of periodic, large-scale burning (Zeuner 1959; F. R. Allchin 1963).

There has been a fair amount of excavation at settlements and ash mounds of the Southern Neolithic. In alphabetical order the principal sites are Brahmagiri (Wheeler 1947–48), Hallur (Nagaraja Rao 1971), Hemmige (Hanumantha Rao and Nagaraju 1974), Kodekal (Paddayya 1973), Kupgal (Majumdar and Rajaguru 1966), Maski (Thapar 1957), Paiyampalli (*Indian Archaeology: A Review* 1964–65c:22–23, 1967–68a:26–30), Palavoy (Rami Reddy 1976), Piklihal (F. R. Allchin 1960), Polakonda (*Indian Archaeology: A Review* 1975–76a:5, 1976–77a:10), Sangankallu (Ansari and Nagaraja Rao 1969), Tekkalakota (Nagaraja Rao and Malhotra 1965), Terdal (*Indian Archaeology: A Review* 1965–66:34), Tirumukkudal Narsipur (*Indian Archaeology: A Review* 1961–62e:35–36, 1964–65c:32), and Utnur (F. R. Allchin 1961). Bridget and Raymond Allchin (1982:287) have organized a three-period synthesis of the

Southern Neolithic which we have used to organize the radiocarbon chronology given in table 14.

Period I of the Southern Neolithic

Period I of the Allchin scheme has only ash mound sites associated with it. These seem to represent forest stations where cattle and possibly other animals were kept or captured from the forest by means of drives (F. R. Allchin and B. Allchin 1974:71–77). The periodic burning of the dung has ethnohistoric parallels, and F. R. Allchin has a fascinating study of this material (1963). The presence of querns, stone rubbers, and the like indicates the probability of cultivation. Ground stone axes are present along with a chipped stone industry that has strong techno-typological ties to the preceding period of settlement which was dominated by sites with microliths (B. Allchin and F. R. Allchin 1968:166). The ceramics of Period I are handmade graywares, which may run to buff-brown. Both red and black slips are attested with some painting in purple. These wares resemble the Blotchy Gray Ware of Songaon, Bahal, and Daimabad. There is no metal in the Allchins' Period I.

Period II of the Southern Neolithic

Period II marks the introduction of significantly more substantial settlement, and ash mounds are complemented by purely domestic sites. These latter may consist of houses, sometimes round wattle and daub affairs with plastered floors. They are likely to be found on the tops of granite hills, or on terraces cleared on their slopes. The ground stone industry continues as in Period I, with a profusion of axes, and continuity in the chipped stone can be noted as well. Copper and bronze appear for the first time as in the Piklihal Upper Neolithic (F. R. Allchin 1961:107–8), Tekkalakota I (Nagaraja Rao and Malhotra 1965:75), and Hallur Ib (Nagaraja Rao 1971:10). Karnataka is famous as a gold-mining state, and it is perhaps not surprising that two gold ornaments can be attributed to Tekkalakota I, along with copper implements (Nagaraja Rao and Malhotra 1965:75). Period II ceramics differ little from their Period I counterparts. The Allchins mention the introduction of spouted and perforated vessels and the roughening of exterior pottery surfaces as possible signs of contact with more northern reaches of the peninsula.

Period III of the Southern Neolithic

The settlement patterning of Period III is quite stable, but there are significant changes in the ceramics. The unburnished gray and buff-brown wares disappear. A dull red-ware with black painting appears in quantity. Spouted vessels and jars with severely constricted necks are also a part of the new inventory. The new features, plus something approaching the Jorwe Black on Red Ware, may indicate contacts with the north (Agrawal 1982a:111). Agrawal also makes the point that the Black and Red Ware of the Indian Megalithic seems to have been derived from Southern Neolithic Period III ceramics. Metal, especially copper and/or bronze, appears in some quantity (see references above) in both ornaments and tools. The flat axes or adzes are of particular interest in that they are indistinguishable from tools found at Jorwe sites, or even at places like Ganeshwar, or possibly at Harappan sites (see above).

A summary chronology for the three phases of the Southern Neolithic is as follows: Phase III, 1600–1000 B.C.; Phase II, 2000–1600 B.C.; and Phase I, 2500–2000 B.C.

The Transition to the Megaliths of the South Indian Iron Age

We close this chapter with a short review of one of the most perplexing problems in South Asian archaeology: the emergence of the Megalithic Complex of South India (see table 14 for transition dates).

M. S. Nagaraja Rao has kindly given us information that may clarify this situation. Continuity between the Neolithic and Megalithic periods can be seen in ceramics, especially the Hallur white-painted Black and Red Ware. This is found at places like Komarana-Halli, 12 km east of Hallur, and at Tadakana-Halli, 4 km west of the site. Komarana-Halli also has multispouted vessels, like those found at Hallur.

Nagaraja Rao informs us (pers. comm.) of a TL date of ca. 1000 B.C. for Komarana-Halli. This is congruent with dates from the transitional period at Hallur (TF-570, TF-573, and TF-575 given above) which calibrate to ca. 1400–1100 B.C. Period II at Hallur has produced a number of iron implements.

The dates for the transition from the Southern Neolithic to the Megalithic from Payampalli and Palavoy which have just been presented should also be considered. While they are very early for a traditional view of this problem, there is no reason to dismiss them out of hand.

There is, then, strong evidence for continuity between the Neolithic and Iron Age in the southern reaches of the peninsula. The evidence also suggests that we should look for the causes of the transition within South India rather than across the seas.

Concluding Statement

There has been a great deal of research on the prehistoric communities of India and surrounding countries. Many recent discoveries are important and intriguing, but the chronology within which these findings can be placed is far from clear. It is not that there is a simple lack of precision in the dating. Some areas, such as the mid-Ganges plain and the Belan Valley, still have significant internal inconsistencies in their prehistoric chronologies. In other parts of the country, such as Malwa and the Deccan pla-teau, there has been a great deal of careful research, and the "skeleton of history" is much clearer. However, in the construction of a chronology there remain more questions than sound answers, and these call for a continued dedication to carefully conceived, problem-oriented field research.

Twenty-Eight

Radiocarbon and Chronology in Southeast Asia

Bennet Bronson, Field Museum of Natural History
Joyce C. White, University of Pennsylvania

Outline

The first radiocarbon dates for archaeological materials in Southeast Asia came from Harrisson's excavations at Niah Cave in Sarawak, East Malaysia, in the late 1950s. Prior to this, conclusions about the later prehistoric chronology of the region had been based largely on comparisons of chance-found museum artifacts and on inspired guesswork by a handful of scholars who were sometimes unacquainted with the methods and theories of archaeologists working elsewhere in the world. The publication of the initial series of Niah dates (Vries and Waterbolk 1958:1555) therefore marked the beginning of a revolution. Its effects are still being felt.

The more publicized side of this revolution has to do with the extension backward in time of traits and institutions formerly thought to be quite young. Niah itself, with its early absolute dates and modern-looking lithics, fauna and human remains established that *H. sapiens sapiens* was not, as had frequently been proposed, a recent immigrant to the region. Niah also encouraged prehistorians to reconsider the significance of the boundary between the Holocene and Pleistocene in tropical Southeast Asia. This boundary is now acknowledged to be less visible and perhaps less significant than in regions farther north.

An equally dramatic pushing-back of previously accepted dates resulted from two Thai projects of the 1960s:

Text submitted December 1984
Text partially revised March 1986

Gorman's excavations at Spirit Cave in 1966, which suggested that horticulture might have been present by about 10,000 B.C., and those of Solheim, Parker, and Bayard at Non Nok Tha in 1966 and 1968, which yielded indications of bronze metallurgy in the third or even fourth millennium B.C. The Spirit Cave dates for horticulture have not yet been confirmed by other excavations. However, those from Non Nok Tha have been both supported and contradicted by further data from Non Nok Tha itself and from several other sites.

To be sure, there are also chronological markers that have not been pushed back appreciably by the advent of absolute dating. Among these are the dates for the first appearance of true states and cities in the region and of evidence for contact with the urban civilizations of such areas as China, India, and the Middle East. Although a number of research programs have focused on those topics, the current state of knowledge is not greatly different from that of the preradiocarbon era. Most current specialists would agree with their predecessors of the 1930s that extensive outside contact did not occur before the last few centuries B.C. and states and cities not before A.D. 100–200 (see fig. 1).

The vigorous controversy ignited by the dates for Southeast Asian bronze is discussed briefly elsewhere in this article. For the moment it is sufficient to point out that the disagreement has led to a sharp intensification of research in Thailand, particularly in its northeastern Khorat Plateau. Gorman and Charoenwongsa's well-

491

known Ban Chiang excavations of 1974 and 1975 have been followed by other major and minor northeast Thailand projects, many of them focused to some degree on the problem of dating the appearance of bronze. This concentration of research has led to a concurrent concentration of radiocarbon dates. Approximately one-fourth of all Southeast Asian radiocarbon determinations known to exist are on samples from northeast Thailand.

Archaeological research in Vietnam has also been affected by the bronze controversy, but the main interest of Vietnamese prehistorians has been directed toward the more general themes of reinterpreting and extending the fieldwork of the colonial period, toward confirming or disproving the hypotheses thus generated, and toward questions of the chronology of local cultural developments with respect to China. These efforts have produced evidence for the existence of complex social organization during the Dong Son and earlier periods, well before the Chinese conquest of 110 B.C. They have also produced, for northern (but not central or southern) Vietnam, a considerable number of radiocarbon determinations. While the total of published dates does not approach the total for northeast Thailand, the Vietnamese have tested only a small number of samples from each site, so that more sites have been at least partially dated. Because of this and because of the amount of fieldwork done there during both the colonial and postcolonial periods, northern Vietnam has the most mature archaeological chronology of any area in the region.

The Philippines is the only other part of Southeast Asia for which a moderately large number of well-distributed absolute dates are available. Here, however, the primitive state of archaeological research prior to and for some time after independence has meant that recent researchers have had to begin almost from scratch in deriving basic relative sequences. Many dates are therefore difficult to connect with others, and a satisfactory outline of Philippine prehistory has yet to be produced in spite of a steady improvement in the quantity and quality of fieldwork done there over the past two decades.

The situation in the rest of the region is similar to or worse than that in the Philippines. In Malaysia, virtually all radiocarbon dates have come from only three site localities in or near the eastern part of that country: Niah in Sarawak, Kota Batu in Brunei, and Madai in Sabah; most of the excavating at the first two was performed in the 1950s with inadequate stratigraphic controls. Little of the fieldwork done in west Malaysia during the past thirty years has been published, and very few absolute dates exist.

In Indonesia, the bulk of research has until quite recently been conducted on the same lines as in Vietnam, toward checking the fieldwork and hypotheses of archaeologists of the colonial period. Because the hypotheses in question, being based largely and sometimes exclusively on armchair research, are rather less satisfactory than in Vietnam, progress has been slow. The considerable amount of fieldwork now under way will undoubtedly lead to new syntheses. But for the moment, no useful outline of post-Pleistocene prehistoric sequences exists for any part of the country except Sulawesi and Timor. Only a handful of radiocarbon dates is available for the large and strategically located islands of Java and Sumatra. There are none for Kalimantan, Indonesian Borneo.

Archaeological research in Burma is moderately active but isolated; only two sites are known to have been radiocarbon dated. In Cambodia, which contains several well-known prehistoric sites and an astonishing density of monuments of the historic period, research has been completely halted since 1972. Only one site for which absolute dates exist has been adequately published. In Laos, no scientific excavation and very few scientific explorations have ever been performed. Despite its key location with respect to many of the issues currently of most interest to prehistorians working in Vietnam, Thailand and China, Laos remains a blank spot on the archaeological map (see figs. 2, 3).

The available data for constructing a regional chronology for Southeast Asia are therefore very uneven in quantity and quality. Publications are both few and short. In all parts of the region there is an acute scarcity of reports characterizing assemblages in sufficient detail for them to be compared with finds from other sites. A further difficulty in at least some areas is an apparent tendency for sites to be more culturally independent than in most other parts of the world. In places like Thailand, for example, stylistic horizons during the prehistoric period have been exceedingly hard to define. It is not uncommon for two sites separated by a few tens of kilometers and covering the same time span to yield collections of artifacts that seem so different in style that the sites cannot be convincingly linked.

This may of course be partly an effect of small sample size and of limitations in methods used to analyze those artifacts, but we believe that it also reflects in some degree an ancient sociocultural reality. Unusually complex mosaics of economically specialized and interdependent but culturally autochthonous communities still exist in the hilly areas of Thailand, Laos, Burma, Vietnam, and southwestern China. If such patterns existed in ancient times as well, they would help to explain the general feeling among Southeast Asia specialists that detailed area- and region-wide chronological syntheses are not yet possible, even in places as seemingly well explored as northeast Thailand.

We at any rate do not propose to offer such a synthesis. In what follows we have subdivided the data on the basis of the simple presence or absence of what seem to be useful chronological markers: flaked or polished stone, pottery, bronze, iron, objects showing at least indirect contact with the literate civilizations of China and India, and locally produced inscriptions. The resulting "periods" are not held to be in any sense stages of cultural development or levels of socioeconomic integration (see fig. 1). While developmental themes are briefly discussed below in the appropriate places, we feel that it is premature to attempt to make these the basis of a region-spanning chronological outline of the kind that is usual in archaeologically better known parts of the world.

Early Lithic Period

Although outside the proper scope of this chapter, a true Southeast Asian paleolithic in the European or African sense of the term has been slow in coming to light. In Java, fossils of Early Man are quite abundant in terms of the amount of fieldwork thus far devoted to finding them. Unfortunately, although these are associated with several more or less distinctive fossil faunas, artifacts that can be proved to be contemporary with them have thus far been hard to find (Bartstra 1982).

This is true of most other parts of the region as well. The only areas that have produced convincing associations of extinct animals and artifacts are northern Vietnam for the late Pleistocene and northern Thailand for the middle Pleistocene; several sites in the latter area now seem to be fairly well fixed to an age of at least 600,000 years (Sorensen 1976b; Pope et al. 1981). Most of the other Southeast Asian "Paleolithic" assemblages mentioned in the older literature are now regarded either as doubtful or as belonging to the Pleistocene-Holocene interface.

The dated lithic implements that most resemble those of the earlier Paleolithic of western Eurasia are the large hand-axe-like core tools found at least occasionally at Niah, Tingkayu, and Hagop Bilo in Borneo and at sites of the Son Vi complex in northern Vietnam. The tools of these last, characterized by "chopper-chopping tools" but with an admixture of hand axes (Solheim 1983b:11; Boriskovsky 1968:83), bear strong similarities to the post-Pleistocene Hoabinhian implements found in the same area but apparently do sometimes occur with extinct fauna and with carbon samples dating to the Pleistocene; it is unclear to the present writers whether the majority of Sonviian implements are typologically distinct from those of later industries.

Undated assemblages of chopper-chopping tools, made mostly on cores or pebbles, include the well-known "Anyathian" of Burma, the "Patjitanian" or "Pacitanian" of Java (which also includes hand axes; Heekeren 1972:35–38), the "Tampanian" of the Malay peninsula,

and the "Fingnoian" of Thailand. While some of these may be quite late or even nonartifactual (e.g., the Tampanian; see Harrisson 1975), some may prove to have genuinely early dates.

Other industries dating to the late Pleistocene include flake tools found at several sites in Island Southeast Asia: Tabon on Palawan, some phases at Niah in Sarawak, and Leang Burung 2 in Sulawesi. As the main date lists show, Layers II–V at Leang Burung 2 have produced a quite convincing series of dates older than 20,000 B.P. The associated fauna, however, is modern, and the implements themselves are not greatly different in form from assemblages at much later sites. A recently discovered flake industry of a vaguely similar type is that of the School Rock Shelter or Tham Lang Rongrien in southern Thailand. The 27,000 B.P. date from that site stands as the earliest plausible radiocarbon date for any site on the Southeast Asian mainland.

Later Lithic: Hoabinhian and Small Flake Industries

The lithic industries of the Holocene are more germane to the present review because of the strong tendency for Southeast Asian stone-working traditions to persist from early periods down to dates close to or even past the introduction of bronze and iron metallurgy in the same areas. It has thus far proved to be difficult to date such sites on the basis of the forms of stone tools; those made in 10,000 or even 20,000 B.P. may well exhibit many of the same rather indeterminate attributes as examples found in association with pottery in the fourth and third millennia B.C. While it seems likely that sophisticated analysis of large samples will eventually show distinctions that have chronometric utility, many prehistorians in Southeast Asia appear to share Fox's (1970:33) feeling that ancient stone knappers in the region often did not attempt to give their products distinct and recurring forms.

Between the later Pleistocene and the middle Holocene, Southeast Asia is divided by a persistent tendency for the peoples of the mainland to use large tools made on pebbles, cores, and flakes and for their insular contemporaries to use small tools made on flakes. This distinction should not be overstated—there are small flake tools on the mainland and core tools in the islands. Yet it remains a central theme for any discussion of the prehistory of the region.

The insular small-tool tradition makes an early appearance at Leang Burung 2 in Sulawesi and Tabon in Palawan (where some of the flakes used are actually quite large) before 20,000 B.P. By 10,000 B.P. it is solidly established at numerous sites, including Ulu Leang 1 in Sulawesi; Tianko Panjang in Sumatra; Uai Bobo 2 in Timor; Niah in Sarawak; Agop Sarapad, Agop Atas, and Tapadong in Sabah; Musang in Luzon; and perhaps Sohoton II in the Visayas. Many of these industries, especially those of southern and southwestern Indonesia, remain rather formless down through the time they are displaced by metal and polished stone. Others, however, have developed into true blade industries, sometimes with microliths, by 5000 B.P.

Assemblages with a substantial content of blades are found in an arc stretching from Timor in the far southeast (the lower levels at Lie Siri and Uai Bobo 2) through Sulawesi and Talaud Island in central and northern Indonesia (Batu Edjaja, Leang Burung, Ulu Leang, and Leang Tuwo Mane'e), to Palawan (Duyong), the Visayas (Buad Island, near Samar), and Luzon (Dimolit and Bato) in the Philippines. As at Dimolit, certain of these blade industries are not provably earlier than the use of pottery and might even, as at Pintu in northern Luzon, persist down past the time when metal and glass appear. This is undoubtedly true of some of the plain flake industries as well. Inspection of the notes that accompany the main date lists will reveal a number of instances of flake tools found in apparently primary association with glass, bronze, and iron.

The very different core, pebble, and large flake industries of the mainland, sometimes called "mesolithic" in spite of the absence of arrowheads and microliths, are more usually designated by the umbrella term *Hoabinhian* after several sites in the province of Hoa Binh in northern Vietnam, excavated by Colani (1927) in the 1920s. Numerous sites with large tools made entirely by flaking and with presumably Holocene associations have been located since then in the same area. Good series of dates from Tham Hoi, Sung Sam, and Hang Chua can be assumed to bracket this classic Vietnamese aspect of the Hoabinhian, with ten determinations between 11,365 and 9075 B.P.

The situation outside Vietnam is less neat. Industries called Hoabinhian occur in Burma, Thailand, Cambodia, Malaysia, northwestern Indonesia (in northern Sumatra, the only manifestation of the complex in the island area), and undoubtedly in Laos as well. They are typologically variable. Although the reviews by Matthews (1968), Gorman (1972), and Glover (1977a) define the Hoabinhian more tightly than did Colani and her co-workers, one is nonetheless struck by the great variety of forms— flakes ranging from large to quite small, pebble tools, bifacially and unifacially worked choppers and scrapers of many sorts, often with edge grinding in later levels— subsumed under the Hoabinhian rubric. It comes as no surprise to learn that a substantial time span is involved.

Vietnamese prehistorians limit the time span of the Hoabinhian by assigning the earliest large tool assemblages to the "paleolithic" Sonviian period and those with

at least some edge-ground implements to the Bacsonian, considered a transitional phase between the "mesolithic" and "neolithic." Specialists elsewhere in Southeast Asia have found such distinctions difficult to make. Accordingly, assemblages called Hoabinhian in Thailand, Burma, and Cambodia have dates that for aceramic contexts range from the tenth millennium B.C. at Tham Ongbah and Spirit Cave to perhaps the fourth millennium at Ban Dan Chumpol. For the pottery-associated Hoabinhian, dates may be even younger, extending down to the first millennium B.C. in the upper levels of such sites as Laang Spean in Cambodia and Gua Cha in Malaysia. On the evidence of Spirit Cave, edge grinding may appear somewhat after the beginning of the Hoabinhian, but even this feature is not yet well established as a time marker for subdividing the period.

It therefore seems best to regard the Hoabinhian as, at most, a diffuse tradition rather than as a complex with a precise cultural or chronological meaning. Like the small flake tradition of the insular area, the Hoabinhian of the mainland begins in the Pleistocene, flourishes in the first few millennia of the Holocene, and persists in a technological if not cultural sense in a number of areas down through the time of the introduction of pottery and even metal. The explanation for this apparent persistence may or may not lie in the parallel persistence of hunting and gathering lifeways in most parts of the region, where nonagricultural peoples (in northern Thailand, the Malay Peninsula, Sumatra, Borneo, and most of the Philippines) have continued to play specialized roles in local economies down to the present day.

The Nonpottery "Neolithic"

Defined by the simple presence of stone implements with overall grinding and polishing rather than in terms of agriculture or settled village life, the aceramic neolithic in Southeast Asia is either nonexistent or a short and unimportant stage in cultural development. Only two dated sites outside Vietnam are reported to produce neolithic implements but no pottery: Gua Kechil in West Malaysia and Phnom Loang in Cambodia. The indicated dates, in the third millennium B.C., are well within the time span associated with pottery and perhaps even with bronze elsewhere in the region.

Within Vietnam, recognizing an artifactual neolithic is rendered difficult by the presence of numerous assemblages of the Bacsonian type—essentially, of implements very like those of earlier periods but with edges (and sometimes faces) modified by grinding, a trait that in Thailand is considered a normal feature of the late Hoabinhian. Dates from the northern Vietnamese sites of Bo Lum, Tham Hai, Bo Nam, and Hang Dang place the Bacsonian proper in the period 10,000–7500 B.P. As this is considered to have developed quite smoothly into a full-fledged neolithic industry, it is possible that a series of Vietnamese cultures with fully ground and polished tools but without ceramics will eventually be established. These would constitute a convincing prepottery neolithic, especially if they could be dated to the eighth to sixth millennia B.P. However, as of the time of writing, few such sites have been proved to exist.

In Vietnam as in the rest of Southeast Asia, fully ground and polished tools on present evidence seem usually to coincide with the appearance of pottery and in fact are often found in association with metal. For all their prominence in the writings of an earlier generation of Southeast Asianists (summarized by Heekeren 1972: 154–206), "neolithic" stone adzes and axes now seem quite limited in their utility as chronological markers.

Agriculture

The previous impression that the quasi domestication of plants in Southeast Asia during the early Holocene has been securely demonstrated may need revising in the light of paleobotanists' reservations (Yen 1977) and the failure of new evidence to appear since the dramatic announcement of possibly cultivated plant remains at Spirit Cave in Thailand (Gorman 1969; Solheim 1972). A similarly cautious attitude may be advisable with regard to the early presence of goats and pigs on Timor in Indonesia (Glover 1971), although here the fact of at least human-assisted transportation can hardly be doubted, for Timor lies beyond Wallace's Line and is thus outside the zone where placental land mammals could have been found in prehuman times.

As of the moment, the earliest datable nonwild rice in Southeast Asia is represented by a questionable (Glover 1977b) late fourth millennium B.C. date from Ulu Leang 1 in Sulawesi and an early third millennium date from Ban Chiang in northeastern Thailand (Yen 1982). There is no reason to doubt that rice was grown in some parts of the region by then. In spite of various stratigraphic problems and morphological peculiarities in the rice grains themselves, the Thai and Sulawesi dates are younger than dates for rice at Hemudu near Shanghai in China (CPAM 1978), which, like Sulawesi but unlike Thailand, is well outside the area in which the domesticated grain is thought to have originated (Chang 1976). Moreover, earlier indications of rice in Southeast Asia exist and may soon be dated, as in the case of recent finds of carbonized grain at the classic Hoabinhian site of Som Chai in Vietnam (Pham Huy Thong, pers. comm.). Earlier excavators at Khok Phanom Di in eastern Thailand found large quantities of burnt rice and of rice grain impressions. Although the association between these and the very early radiocarbon dates reported for that site remains uncertain, it is likely that Higham and Bannaruag's current excavations there will clarify the problem.

The earliest dates for cattle, dogs, and chickens also come from Ban Chiang, in cultural levels dated to the fourth millennium. These, along with associated pigs, all appear to be domesticated (Higham and Kijngam 1979). When water buffalo appear in the Ban Chiang sequence around 1000 B.C., they seem already to be of domesticated size.

Few other convincing domesticates have been found in any Southeast Asian site, whether old or young. And yet the old arguments of Carl Sauer and others for the theoretical likelihood of very early domestication in the Southeast Asian tropics remain highly plausible. These arguments have in fact rarely been tested in the field. Only a handful of investigators have even attempted to employ modern sieving and flotation techniques at pre–Bronze Age sites. Considering that complex agriculture is now thought to have been established at Kuk in New Guinea by 6000 B.P. (Golson 1977) and that pigs have been found in convincing fifth millennium B.P. contexts at no fewer than three New Guinea sites (Kafiavana, Yuku, and Kiowa; White and O'Connell 1982:187), one finds it difficult to believe that a serious program of paleobotanical and paleozoological research in appropriate places will not find evidence of plant and animal domestication in some parts of Southeast Asia at comparable or earlier dates.

How early such dates might be in any particular area cannot yet be estimated. It seems reasonable to think that areas with fertile soils and extraordinarily dense present-day agricultural populations, like northern Vietnam and central Java, would have been particularly attractive to early farmers. However, such evidence as now exists comes from locations that are agronomically marginal. It also seems logical to look for farming in places where nonsubsistence technologies were relatively advanced. Yet, in spite of several attractive hypotheses (e.g., Kijngam, Higham, and Wiriyaromp 1980), the evolutionary association between agriculture and given types of artifacts or settlements remains undemonstrated and, in principle, far from invariable. Preceramic sites with farming are conceivable enough, as are nonagricultural villages or metal-using hunters and gatherers. The classic Near Eastern–European pattern of farming/villages/pottery/metals cannot yet be shown to be applicable anywhere in Southeast Asia.

The Premetal Ceramic Period

Assemblages with pottery and stone implements but without metal are comparatively common in the region. Moreover, the implements are often flaked, not ground. Of the forty-odd sites of this kind for which dates and descriptions are available, the sherd-bearing strata in about half of them yielded only flaked or edge-ground tools, while in the rest such strata produced at least some axes or adzes with fully ground surfaces, usually mixed with substantial numbers of tools made by flaking.

In geographic terms, ceramic sites with only flaked tools tend to be concentrated in Indonesia and Malaysian Borneo. Ceramic sites in the Philippines and on the mainland may produce only flaked and edge-ground tools or, as is especially common in Vietnam, a mixture of flaked and fully ground tools. In two of the dated "neolithic" Philippine sites, Sanga Sanga and Duyong, the edge-ground tools are of massive shell rather than of stone. In Thailand, ceramic-producing assemblages without metal may be rather more scarce than in the insular area. Of the eight instances for which direct or inferred dates exist, two (Khok Charoen and Ban Kao) fall within the chronological range of the Bronze Age, and three others (the lowest levels at Ban Tong, Ban Chiang, and Non Nok Tha) are not far outside that range. Only three (the uppermost strata at Spirit and Khao Talu Caves, and all strata at Khok Phanom Di) are securely premetallic.

The known dates for the appearance of pottery in the various parts of Southeast Asia may be somewhat misleading in view of the uneven distribution of research and the difficulty of dating the lower portions of several important ceramic sequences. Nonetheless, these known dates seem to form a coherent picture. Setting aside a few improbably early determinations, they are summarized in table 1.

That Padah-Lin has potsherds in all levels, including those with 13,400 and 11,250 B.P. dates, might cause the 7740 B.P. dates cited here to be viewed with skepticism. The pre-7000 date from Spirit Cave, on the other hand, is backed by two others, all from the same upper strata. There is little reason to question them. While a number of the other early pottery dates from the region are as problematical as those from Padah-Lin, the overall impression is that the technology of making containers from heat-hardened clay has considerable age in most of the Southeast Asian mainland and the nearby islands. One does not doubt that most of these areas will prove to have possessed pottery by the end of the sixth millennium B.C. Pottery in the more remote parts of the insular subregion may not be so old. A late limit of the third or second millennium B.C. is set by the above-quoted Uai Bobo and Ulu Leang dates and by the well-established (see Bellwood 1979:244–58) 1500 B.C. dates for the appearance of the Lapita complex, the first pottery in Melanesia.

The character of these early ceramics need not be discussed here. It is sufficient to say that Southeast Asian vessels of most periods tend to be well made, that decoration may be quite complex, and that there is thus far little reason to think that any particular decorative attribute (e.g., cord marking) is generally earlier than any other. Moreover, the relative independence of sequences at neighboring sites, a trait especially characteristic of Thailand, makes it difficult to generalize about even subregional or local trends in ceramic style. In no part of Southeast Asia familiar to the present writers is the prehistoric pottery well enough understood for stylistic or technical details to be a reliable guide to the chronology of newly discovered sites and those that lack datable carbon.

Villages

As the great majority of preceramic sites are very small—indeed, most are in caves or rock shelters—the issue of dating the inception of Southeast Asian village life does not arise until the ceramic period. Even then, the data are uneven. No candidate sites earlier than the Iron Age or the Protohistoric period have thus far been excavated in Burma, Cambodia, Malaysia, or Indonesia unless occasional periods of settlement within the enormous cave at Niah, which is large enough to hold a substantial number of dwellings, managed to reach village status.

Only three areas are known to have produced premetal settlements that might qualify as hamlets or villages, that is, as centers of habitation larger and more permanent than the camps of transient bands. The first is the Visayas and Luzon in the Philippines. There, a number of open-air sites exist which are either relatively large or furnished with substantial houses. These include Edjek and Dimolit, and perhaps Lal-Lo and Batungan as well; their dates extend from the fifth to the third millennia B.C. The second area with premetal hamlets is northern Vietnam, where the larger middens of the coastal Da But and Quynh Van cultures of the sixth to fourth millennia should qualify for that status and where more substantial settlements, notably Phung Nguyen itself (Khoach 1983), were in existence by the start of the second millennium and the Bronze Age.

The third area is central and northeastern Thailand. Only three of the dated villagelike sites there have not produced bronze or iron from their major deposits: Khok Phanom Di, Ban Kao, and Khok Charoen (Watson 1979). The two last are only of moderate size and are known or rumored to have yielded absolute dates well within the Bronze Age time range. The first, however, is both large and seemingly old, covering several hectares with shelly habitation refuse 5–10 m in depth and dated by seven radiocarbon samples to the period 6800–4520 B.P. Although these and four later dates from Khok Phanom Di are not in stratigraphic sequence, their number and the character of associated finds—the absence of metal and the unfamiliar appearance of the ceramics, in an area where many later ceramic assemblages are known to archaeologists—lend them credibility. If the dates are valid, Khok Phanom Di is the earliest large settlement yet discovered in Southeast Asia.

A number of the Bronze Age sites in northeastern Thailand, including Non Nok Tha, Ban Tong, and probably Ban Chiang, have premetal components. Some of these undoubtedly represent hamlets or villages, although only tiny portions of their surfaces have as yet been seen. Other later sites in the same area, including Ban Chiang, are extensive enough to qualify as substantial villages. However, it is not until the Iron Age that any Thai site can be considered a possible town.

The most plausible candidates for proto-urban status among dated Thai settlements are Non Chai, which covers several tens of hectares, and Phimai during the Black Ware phase (best dated at Ban Tamyae), which was even larger. Both sites appear to have reached their maximum extension in the last few centuries B.C. Several other medium- and large-sized Thai sites, among them Ban Chiang Hian and Chansen, have produced dates and materials that seem to fall into the same time range. These too might be considered possible prehistoric towns if not for their massive overburden of protohistoric and historic deposits and the consequent difficulty of estimating their extent at earlier periods.

We should note in passing that the masking effect of later deposits is a serious problem with regard to the majority of the several hundred moated and walled sites in central and northeast Thailand, eastern Cambodia, and southern Vietnam located by French and British military aerial photographers in the 1930s and 1940s (Williams-Hunt 1950) and by Thai geographers and archaeologists in the 1960s and 1970s (Vanasin and Supajanya 1982; Kijngam, Higham, and Wiriyaromp 1980). The smaller and more circular of these have often been assigned to the Bronze or Iron Age or even to the neolithic, and many (like Ban Chiang Hian and Chansen) do contain prehistoric deposits. But we know of none that do not also produce artifacts of protohistoric or historic date. Considering that the only townlike feature of most such sites is the surrounding earthwork and that none of these earthworks has yet been shown through excavation to predate the nearby protohistoric or historic deposits, we feel that it is premature to speculate about the chronology and development of prehistoric settlement hierarchies.

Bronze Age

The date of the first use of tin bronze in Southeast Asia continues to arouse much controversy. The original announcements of third or even fourth millennium B.C. dates for the northeastern Thai sites of Non Nok Tha (Solheim 1968) and then Ban Chiang (Chin You-di 1975) attracted widespread publicity in the world press. Skepti-

cism and support seem originally to have been based more on a priori positions, often chauvinistic, than on close analyses of data. More recently, however, closely reasoned critiques (Loofs-Wissowa 1983; Higham 1983) and defenses (Bayard and Charoenwongsa 1983; Solheim 1983a; Bayard n.d.[a]), both based on real archaeological evidence, have begun to appear.

A brief discussion of the relevant sites and finds will be found in the appendix. Because one of the present authors is currently working with data from the largely unpublished and critically important excavations at Ban Chiang and because the Bronze Age of northeast Thailand has not been summarized elsewhere, the inclusion of such a discussion seems appropriate even though it is unavoidably somewhat more detailed than other parts of this review.

Available dates for the first appearance of bronze in various parts of Southeast Asia are listed in table 2; as before, a few dates that seem impossibly early have been omitted.

Several of these dates require further comment. The one from Musang, from shell associated with a bronze or brass needle, may be too early. The accepted dates for early bronze in the Philippines, based on finds from Duyong and other caves in Palawan that cannot be directly dated, are in the 700–600 B.C. range (Fox 1970:121–34). The dates from Samrong Sen and Pejaten are unique for their areas and from contexts that are stratigraphically unclear. Stratigraphic problems may also exist with respect to the earlier bronze dates from Niah in Sarawak, and even the otherwise plausible date from Hang Gon in southern Vietnam is considerably earlier than other dates from that site. No dates at all are available for prehistoric bronze in several other subdivisions of the region (e.g., central Philippines, western and northern Indonesia, West Malaysia, or Burma).

Thus, the case for early bronze in Southeast Asia—that is, bronze early by traditionally accepted Southeast Asian or Chinese standards—depends almost entirely on evidence from central and northeastern Thailand and from northern Vietnam. This evidence, however, is not negligible in quantity. Of the Bronze Age dates tabulated in tables 6 and 7, twenty-three (from five sites in Thailand and four sites in Vietnam) are earlier than 1500 B.C.

Several conclusions may be drawn. Bronze was certainly in use in the northern parts of the Southeast Asian mainland well before 1000 B.C. It was almost certainly in use before 1500 B.C. But whether this can be pushed back past 2000 B.C. is likely to be a matter of opinion and of careful reviews of the stratigraphy and associations of individual samples. In terms of interregional comparisons, this means that the development of bronze technology in northern Southeast Asia is not demonstrably out of phase with its development in China, where bronze now is beginning to be found with some regularity at sites in the Erlitou and even late Long Shan or Lungshan periods (e.g., at Meishan, with crucibles and two radiocarbon dates between 2290–2005 B.C.; Second Henan Archaeological Team 1982).

The situation in other parts of Southeast Asia appears on present evidence to be quite different, but the present evidence is very scarce. Only in the Philippines has enough material been excavated and dated for one to be fairly sure that numerous early bronze-using sites are not waiting to be found there. While it seems logical to expect that the remoter parts of eastern and northern Indonesia will turn out to have been similarly late in turning to metallurgy, no good reason exists for thinking this is true of Malaysia or of the southern and western parts of Indonesia, where Bronze Age sites have rarely been looked for, much less excavated and dated.

The same logic applies with even more force to Burma, Laos, and Cambodia. In none of these is bronze likely to be late. Whereas data on early metallurgy in those countries are as scarce as in the insular subregion, their geographical proximity to Vietnam and Thailand and their access to similar mineral resources suggest that methods for smelting and fabricating copper alloys should be as early there as anywhere in the region.

The Dong Son Problem

A famous issue relative to the Bronze (and Iron) Age is that of the so-called Dong Son culture, a group of sites in northern Vietnam once thought by an earlier generation of prehistorians to be the first users of metal in the region and, indeed, the initial bearers of advanced culture to other Southeast Asian peoples. The supposed spread of Dong Son influence was traced primarily by the presence at sites as far distant as eastern Indonesia of a distinctive type of large bronze drum but was variously believed also to be detectable through such evidence as genetic traits, decorative motifs, religious concepts, and the use of copper alloys.

We have not attempted to review the extensive literature that has accumulated around the problem of the origin and diffusion of the Dong Son drums, culture, or style (see, e.g., Heekeren 1958 and papers in Barnard 1972 and Smith and Watson 1979). Like many other current Southeast Asianists, we feel that the cultural and stylistic aspects of Dong Son can be meaningfully discussed only within a Vietnamese and southern Chinese context.

The drums themselves are a more widespread phenomenon but would appear on present evidence to be simple trade items, made at several centers and shipped throughout the region over a long span of time. Many are found with iron as well as bronze, and the great majority prob-

ably represent the Iron Age or Protohistoric period rather than a preferrous Bronze Age. A few dates exist for charcoal and wood samples found in association with bronze drums at Sungai Lang in Malaysia and Tham Ongbah in Thailand, and with drums and other objects in the Dong Son style at Go Chien Vay, Go Mun, Lang Ca, Lang Vac, and Viet Khe in Vietnam. The dates in question (see the entries for those sites in tables 6 and 7) cover almost a millennium, from the sixth to fifth century B.C. (at Go Chien Vay and Viet Khe) to at least the end of the second century A.D. (at Sungai Lang).

Iron Age

The chronology of the first appearance of iron, summarized in table 3, clusters more tightly than that of bronze. For the insular subregion, dates in the 300–100 B.C. time range seem reasonable and are what most specialists would expect. The somewhat earlier results from Painted Cave at Niah in Sarawak and from Sungai Lang in West Malaysia come from samples of wood from large trees, while the association between the carbon and the iron is none too clear in the case of the sample from Pejaten on Java.

The earlier dates from Thailand and Vietnam, on the other hand, are rather more surprising. Some may be inclined to question them in view of the usually accepted eighth- or seventh-century origin of iron metallurgy in China. And yet, as table 4 shows, they are supported by a number of other dates in the same time range from neighboring sites. While we ourselves are skeptical about the tenth- and ninth-century dates from Ban Chiang, Ban Puan Phu, and Ban Tong, we can see no archaeological reason for rejecting all the rest and are therefore inclined to entertain the possibility that iron in several parts of the northern Southeast Asian mainland came into use at much the same period as in China, between 700 and 500 B.C.

The Go Chien Vay date in table 4 is important because it is said to be from an occupation layer that contains not only Dong Son bronzes but *cast* iron. Assuming that this term (the French *fonte*) is not used erroneously by the author (Tan 1980:131), it represents the first appearance outside China of an iron-making technology that was eventually, in the sixteenth to nineteenth centuries, to transform world industry. However, there is no evidence that the cast-iron process passed beyond Vietnam to the rest of Southeast Asia in early times. Iron in most of the region was probably smelted by lower-capacity bloomery methods similar to those recorded in several parts of Southeast Asia during the nineteenth and early twentieth centuries A.D. (see Harrisson and O'Connor 1969: 307–53).

The Protohistoric Period

The concept of protohistory is not readily applicable except in Burma, Cambodia, and central and southern Thailand and Vietnam, where several centuries separate the earliest evidence for close contact with India and China from the first indigenous inscriptions (usually, in Indian scripts). In northern Vietnam, a fully historic period with locally written chronicles follows very soon after the initial contact with the literate cultures of China in the third or second centuries B.C. In northeast Thailand, a number of the site components listed here as "Iron Age" are undoubtedly protohistoric in terms of date and direct or indirect evidence of contact with history-writing peoples, but data to demonstrate this are currently lacking. It may be that the inland parts of the mainland remained relatively isolated from expanding Chinese and Indian cultural influence until the sixth or seventh century A.D.

In the peninsular and island subregion, the only early sites known to have been in contact with either India or China are Tengku Lembu on the Malay Peninsula (Sieveking 1962; Bronson 1979:330) and Buni on Java (Walker and Santoso 1980); both, with vessels similar to those of the first to second century A.D. at Arikamedu in South India, remain undated. One occasionally also sees references in this connection to the Han dynasty (second century B.C.–second century A.D.) glazed vessels collected by Orsoy de Flines (1972) for the Central Museum in Jakarta and believed by him to have been found in Sumatra and Borneo. However, since the late 1930s when Flines bought his Han vessels, not a single further sherd of Han ceramic has been found by archaeologists anywhere in Indonesia or adjacent countries. It has come to seem more and more probable that Flines was sold newly imported antiques by a clever art dealer.

The key mainland sites showing definite extraregional contacts in levels earlier than the first local inscriptions are Oc Eo (Malleret 1959–63) in southern Vietnam, Beikthano in Burma, and Chansen, Don Tha Phet, and U Thong (also called "Tha Muang"; Loofs 1979) in central Thailand. The only hard dates from the first, Oc Eo, are numismatic: two Roman coins of the second and third centuries A.D. The other four sites have produced the radiocarbon dates listed in tables 6 and 7. All appear to have been active in the first few centuries A.D.

In a technical sense, certain of the Chinese porcelain-producing sites of the Philippines, East Malaysia, and northern and eastern Indonesia could be counted as protohistoric, since local literacy in those areas probably lagged some centuries behind the first appearance of the imported wares. We have nonetheless labeled these sites in the main tables as "historic," feeling it to be unnecessary to enter too far into the complex problems of the history of local scripts and of the massive eighth- to eighteenth-century Southeast Asian trade in exogenous stoneware and porcelain.

Cities and States

The earliest true cities in the region are probably those of northern Vietnam, where the pre-Chinese center at Co Loa already had urban characteristics and where historical sources record the establishment of provincial capitals soon after the Chinese conquest of 110 B.C. (Davidson 1979c:311). The earliest outside northern Vietnam might be Oc Eo, Beikthano, or U Thong, all of which possess such urban traits as buildings in permanent materials, fortifications, evidence of long-distance trade, substantial populations, and considerable size. Since many other as yet undated sites of similar type are known in mainland Southeast Asia, it is likely that one of these will eventually be shown to have temporal priority.

No such sites, however, are known from insular Southeast Asia. In fact, settlements with evidence of relatively large, dense populations do not seem to appear until well into the second millennium; even the famous temple centers of central Java like Prambanan and Borobudur, epigraphically dated to the eighth to tenth centuries A.D., are of a distinctly nonurban character. The earliest recognizably urban center in Java is the fourteenth- to fifteenth-century site of Trowulan, the capital of the empire of Majapahit. While cities of some sort must have existed before this somewhere in the island subregion, they have not yet been found.

The problem of pre- and protohistoric states in Southeast Asia has only begun to be addressed by archaeological field research. MacDonald (1980) and Kijngam, Higham, and Wiriyaromp (1980) have assembled evidence showing that social stratification and settlement heirarchies had developed to at least a moderate extent in northeast Thailand by the first millennium B.C. These presumably indicate a corresponding level of political development. Vietnamese archaeologists (Davidson 1979c; Khoach 1983) have proposed and partially demonstrated that complexly organized political units existed in the Red River area by the middle and perhaps early Bronze Age. Some of these, which might be associated with the mythical kingdom of Van Lang, may have achieved the status of true states some centuries or decades before the imposition of Chinese control during the Han dynasty.

Outside northern Vietnam, however, the evidence for autochthonous state development remains very thin. Most specialists in the archaeology of Southeast Asia would probably subscribe to the conclusions reached by the historians and epigraphers of the 1930s and 1940s, as summarized by Coedès (1968) and Hall (1968), that the region cannot be shown to contain true, identifiable states until very shortly before these are first noticed by Chinese chroniclers in the first few centuries A.D.

The Historic Period

The historic dates in tables 6 and 7 need little comment except to point out that no systematic effort has been made to use radiometric techniques to check epigraphically and art historically derived dates for the monumental Hindu-Buddhist sites of Burma, Thailand, Cambodia, Vietnam, and southwestern Indonesia. While the dates derived by these more traditional methods are in the main convincing, a number of problems remain that could be best addressed by radiocarbon dating, including the vexing question of the total time span of the monumental centers and their chronological relationship to residential areas within and outside the zones where the temples and other large buildings are concentrated.

The historic dates for nonmonumental sites within the above countries and for areas like the Philippines where the Hindu-Buddhist complex never penetrated are on samples associated with imported small finds, mostly porcelains and stonewares from China and mainland Southeast Asia. These often represent economies and social organizations that are relatively noncomplex. The main problem they pose is their close resemblance to sites of much earlier periods. In fact, almost any recent village site that happened to lack glazed ceramics and was outside the limited areas of Thailand and Vietnam where local earthenwares of various periods are to some extent recognizable might well be assigned to the Iron or Bronze Age. This undoubtedly helps to explain some of the apparently very late dates for prehistoric Southeast Asian settlements.

Appendix: The Bronze and Iron Ages of Northeast Thailand

The chronology of northeast Thailand is still only partially understood and cannot yet be discussed in terms of well-defined and dated ceramic horizons of wide applicability. The uncertainty of cross dating among assemblages is exacerbated by the paucity of published sequences, problems in the interpretation of stratigraphic and chronometric data, and a tendency toward idiosyncrasy in the ceramic assemblages of individual sites. At this stage the region's chronology can best be approached through discussions of individual site sequences and tentative parallels suggested between them. We thus begin with the site of Ban Chiang, which has to date the most comprehensive sequence in terms of chronological depth and evidence for the course of cultural development for the area. All dates cited in the text are calibrated.

Ban Chiang is a cemetery and habitation site on the northern Khorat Plateau on the Songkram River watershed which drains into the Mekong River. A preliminary six-phase chronology (Gorman and Charoenwongsa 1976) was based on field impressions of the burial ceramic sequence and the radiocarbon determinations from the first season (1974) of the University Museum, University of Pennsylvania/Thai Fine Arts Department excavations. The report was written prior to the bulk of the laboratory analysis conducted in 1977–79, and circumstances prevented publication of revisions prior to Gorman's death in 1981.

While a full revision of the Ban Chiang mortuary sequence is in preparation by White, an interim chronological framework incorporating revisions in the relative and absolute chronologies was developed for an exhibition of the Ban Chiang materials (White 1982). This interim chronology broadly divides the Ban Chiang sequence into an Early Period (ca. 3600–1000 B.C.), a Middle Period (ca. 1000–300 B.C.), and a Late Period (ca. 300 B.C.–A.D. 200). In the 1975 excavation, Early Period burials were generally confined to the lower grayish soil stratum and most commonly were supine, with one or more pots placed toward the head or foot of the grave. A few adults were found in flexed position, and several infants were buried in large pots. Middle Period burials were found above the gray stratum in the reddish soil stratum. These characteristically had several pots of distinctive carinated styles shattered over supine skeletons. In Late Period burials, red-painted pottery was placed intact over the supine bodies.

Most of the available dates derive from burial contexts. In the absence of a well-defined soil stratigraphy, available dates from the few hearths were difficult to relate to the cultural sequence based on grave goods. The dating strategy attempts to calibrate the burial ceramic sequence from date ranges consistently associated with particular ceramic types. Dates from charcoal collected from layers, pits, and possible hearths complement the burial-associated dates.

The base of the sequence is dated by two fourth millennium B.C. dates, P-2265 (3915–3340 B.C.) and P-2452 (3785–3355 B.C.). These are dates from charcoal collected from basal levels of the cultural deposit and may date from the early occupation of the site.

Several types of ceramics from basal graves were not associated with bronze grave goods and thus may predate the appearance of bronze at the site. The most distinctive style has a surface treatment of intricate designs comprised of incising, comb pricking, and rocker stamping. Either associated with or overlying these Early Period densely incised wares and other related types are several dates: P-2245 (2205–1685 B.C.), P-2266 (3680–2910

B.C.), P-2271 (2205–1685 B.C.), P-2263 (3365–2535 B.C.), P-2242 (2550–1950 B.C.), P-2451 (2215–1690 B.C.), and P-2456 (2340–1755 B.C.). These ranges basically accord with Gorman and Charoenwongsa's (1976) estimate of ca. 2000 B.C. and possibly older for the densely incised vessels.

Stratigraphically above the densely incised pottery are several styles, including beaker types and other cord-marked forms, that generally do not have incised designs. The earliest grave-associated bronze artifacts were found in burials with ceramics of these types. These styles are estimated to date in the first half of the second millennium B.C., ca. 2000–1500.

The upper phase of the Early Period is characterized by globular cord-marked pots of medium to small size which occasionally have incised and painted designs on the shoulder. Associated radiocarbon samples indicate that this ceramic type dates in the mid to late second millennium B.C.: P-2261 (1865–1365 B.C.), P-2246 (1405–1240 B.C.), P-2454 (1865–1365 B.C.), P-2272 (1430–865 B.C.), and P-2240 (1675–1220 B.C.). Two samples are relevant to the interface between the Early Period burials in the gray soil stratum and the Middle Period burials in the red stratum: P-2634 (930–825 B.C.) and P-2455 (1115–875 B.C.).

The sherd scatters over Middle period burials are often derived from two types of carinated wares: a cream to whitish variety often with a simple painted design under the rim, and a peach to buff variety with a painted and incised band on the shoulder. Iron bangles and iron spearpoints with bronze hafts appeared in association with this type of burial. Two carbon samples were associated with scatter burial 19 which cuts into a burial with one such spearpoint: P-2664 (420–380 B.C.) and P-2665 (795–585 B.C.). This latter date supports the possibility that iron appeared in the region within the first half of the first millennium B.C. (vide Bronson 1979:334–35).

Associated with Late Period ceramics are two dates: P-2241 (190–10 B.C.), and P-2244 (195–20 B.C.). Some Late Period graves also included carved baked clay rollers, opaque glass beads, high tin wire necklaces, as well as iron tools and bronze bangles. The most recent date from the site, P-2406 (A.D. 35–570), associated with a nondiagnostic pot, suggests that the Late Period may extend into the first few centuries A.D.

A few other northeast Thai sites have yielded chronometric dates within a time range comparable to the Ban Chiang sequence, but only one has been fully reported in the literature (Higham and Kijngam 1984). These sites are discussed beginning with those closest to Ban Chiang in Udon Thani Province on the northern Khorat Plateau, followed by sites to the south and west in the Mun-Chi drainage basin and in the eastern foothills of the Petcha-

bun Mountains. Parallels can only be suggested, given the incompleteness of available data and the problem of the idiosyncratic nature of excavated assemblages.

Ban Tong, 5 km southwest of Ban Chiang, and Ban Phak Top, 26 km west-southwest of Ban Chiang, were tested by William Schauffler (1976) of the University of Pennsylvania in 1975 and produced a total of sixteen radiocarbon dates. These dates have not received extensive comment by the excavator, but some observations can be made. A possible fourth millennium date from Ban Tong, P-2419 (3365–2800 B.C.), tends to support comparable dates from Ban Chiang which suggest initial settlement of the area prior to 3000 B.C. Bronze fragments were recovered from as low as layer 16 in the test square and iron fragments as low as layer 3. Bronze-bearing layers 8 through 16 yielded several dates spanning the second millennium B.C. Burial 1 produced a large broken pot with a painted and incised rim similar to some Ban Chiang Middle Period pots. An associated date of 915–765 B.C. (P-2723) supports the Ban Chiang dating for this period.

Ban Phak Top is renowned for the looting of densely incised pottery comparable in surface treatment to pots found in lower levels of Ban Chiang. Although the excavator has not commented on the ceramic sequence for the site, a date from the basal level, P-2407 (2435–2310 B.C.), may support a third millennium date for this pottery style. Bronze objects appeared as far down as layer 7, which bore a date of 1645–1430 B.C. (P-2732), but Schauffler remarks (1976:29) that while his excavations recovered no burial-associated bronze, looters of the site claimed to have found burials with both bronze and black incised pottery.

Ban Na Di, located 20 km southwest of Ban Chiang, has the most published data of any site in northeast Thailand. When the thirteen dates from this site were originally published (Higham 1981; Higham and Kijngam 1982a), the excavators compared the Ban Na Di sequence to the preliminary Ban Chiang sequence. In the monograph on the site (Higham and Kijngam 1984), the excavators revise their comments in light of the revisions in the Ban Chiang chronology of White (1982).

The settlement at Ban Na Di dates back at least to the mid-second millennium B.C. on the basis of R-9345/5 (1690–1230 B.C.) from a small hearth in layer 8 found about 25 cm above sterile soil. Bronze was present from the earliest levels. The excavators at first suggested a correspondence between level 8 and lower level 7 of Ban Na Di, with the former phase II at Ban Chiang. However, the absence of the highly characteristic densely incised pottery at Ban Na Di suggests that the site postdates this ceramic phase. Since the beaker types and other shapes estimated to date between 2000–1500 B.C. at Ban Chiang are also absent, it seems likely that the basal layers and earliest burials at Ban Na Di correspond to the late Early Period at Ban Chiang, which is characterized by globular cord-marked pots with everted rims. These date generally in the mid to late second millennium B.C. as do the basal levels at Ban Na Di.

A "family resemblance" is evident between Ban Na Di and Ban Chiang burial ceramics, but there are many distinctive styles at each site, and only a few clear typological equivalents. The characteristic decorative motif for the early Ban Na Di ceramics is a curvilinear appliqué commonly occurring on globular cord-marked pots with short everted rims. Appliqué bands are also present at Ban Chiang throughout most of the Early Period, but they are not found on the shapes comparable to those mentioned for Ban Na Di which dated to the latter half of the second millennium and first millennium B.C. This suggests that curvilinear or serpentine appliqué is not a regional temporal diagnostic indicator since it has been found on pottery dated over a span of more than one thousand years.

Of the various Ban Chiang Middle Period styles, only a couple of carinated styles are represented in the Ban Na Di assemblage. The lowest example appears in burial phase 1b from mid to upper level 7 which has a proposed date of 700–500 B.C. Most other examples come from level 6 burial phase 1c with a proposed date of 500–400 B.C. These dates are within the range of Ban Chiang Middle Period dates. Iron appears in two phase 1c burials, and one iron fragment was found in level 7. Thus iron appears at Ban Chiang and Ban Na Di at least by the mid-first millennium B.C.

The Ban Na Di excavations produced no burials comparable to Ban Chiang Late Period burials, but level 5 with a proposed date of 100 B.C.–A.D. 200 does show a marked increase in red-slipped sherds. Overall, therefore, there is considerable overlap in the Ban Chiang and Ban Na Di ceramic sequences and radiocarbon chronologies. Regional specialists differ somewhat in how they use the data to draw temporal boundaries, but this is to be expected given the variation in data bases.

To the southwest of Ban Chiang in Khon Kaen Province and along the foothills of the Petchabun Mountains, several sites, which date from approximately the same time range as sites of Ban Chiang tradition, have been excavated or tested. These include Non Nok Tha, Non Nong Chik, Don Klang, Non Khao Wong, Ban I Loet, and Ban Puan Phu. Details of the local chronology are not well understood, in part because Non Nok Tha, the most extensively excavated and dated site in this area, has for a variety of reasons an uncertain sequence. The Non Nok Tha chronology has received considerable comment (Bayard 1971, 1979; Smith 1979b; MacDonald 1980) which will not be reiterated here. Bayard (1977:64) has proposed a broad chronological framework as follows: an Early Period or Phu Wiang phase ca. 3500–2500 B.C., a Middle Period or Non Nok Tha phase ca. 2500 B.C.–A.D. 200, and a Late Period or Don Sawan phase ca. A.D. 1000 to the present.

Clear ceramic parallels between Non Nok Tha and the Ban Chiang area sites are notably rare. Possible exceptions include Early Period pots with incised and rouletted designs on their shoulders which perhaps are related to the early incised wares at Ban Chiang and Ban Phak Top. At all three sites these ceramics seem to date in the third millennium B.C. According to Bayard the earliest bronze at Non Nok Tha was found in Early Period layers and graves, for example, the socketed tool in burial 90 which produced a thermoluminescence date of 2620–2220 B.C. on an associated pot. Iron and water buffalo seem to be absent from the prehistoric levels, although there is some possibility that iron appeared toward the end of the Middle Period (Bayard 1979:31).

A few sites tested in the area have produced materials related to Non Nok Tha. Ten kilometers to the south Non Nong Chik produced dates well into the second millennium B.C. and also broadly comparable ceramics (Bayard 1977). Twenty-nine kilometers to the northeast of Non Nok Tha, Don Klang produced strikingly similar ceramics including incised wares in the lower levels (Schauffler 1976). Unfortunately those lower levels produced no dates, but an upper phase with glass beads and red lidded jars yielded several, approximately in the range of 500 B.C.–A.D. 200. These upper-phase ceramic types were not found at Non Nok Tha and thus may help to fill the gap between the Middle and Late Periods, and perhaps might push back the beginning of this gap by a few centuries. A ceramic lid virtually identical to those found at Don Klang was excavated from Non Khao Wong (Penny 1982:69) from a deep feature that also produced charcoal sample P-2943 (195 B.C.–A.D. 230). Other dates from this site, P-2944 (435–5 B.C.), and P-2945 (275 B.C.–A.D. 45), place the base of the deposit in the same general range as the upper phase at Don Klang.

The distribution of sites known to date from the first millennium B.C. seems to extend well beyond areas with the early settlements dating from the third and fourth millennia. The probable expansion of settlement seems to be accompanied by evidence for increased social and technological complexity, although the chronology and nature of these developments are under some debate by regional specialists. Surveys of the eastern Petchabun piedmont zone (Bayard 1980; Penny 1982) revealed open-air sites dating primarily to the first millennium B.C., for example, Non Khao Wong, Ban I Loet, and Ban Puan Phu.

Although a few sites in the more central parts of the Khorat Plateau drained by the Mun and the Chi rivers have produced basal dates in the second millennium B.C., for example, Ban Chiang Hian (Higham 1983), Non Chai (Charoenwongsa and Bayard 1983), and Non Yang (Suchitta 1982–83:91), current evidence suggests that the settlement of the southern half of the Khorat Plateau developed in large part after 1000 B.C. While the Ban Chiang Hian sequence supported by the Ban Kho Noi sequence in Mahasarakam Province suggests settlement prior to the appearance of iron and water buffalo in the area, ca. 500 B.C., there is a marked discontinuity in pottery style when both iron and water buffalo appear at these sites (Chantaratiyakarn 1983).

The lowest levels of the major occupations at Non Chai in Khon Kaen Province and Non Dua in Roi Et Province date from about 500 B.C. and also show evidence of iron and ceramic parallels with levels 6 and 7 of Ban Chiang Hian. Red-slipped or -painted pottery is often mentioned as occurring in deposits of this time period and is paralleled in the Ban Chiang Late Period of ca. 300 B.C.–A.D. 200. In Khorat Province, however, the pre–Khmer Phimai black ware seems to date from the first millennium B.C. and possibly the early centuries A.D. (D. Welsh, pers. comm.; Solheim and Ayres 1979:68, 77). At Non Dua in Roi Et Province the phase I red-slipped wares are succeeded in Phase II, ca. A.D. 1–700 by the so-called Roi Et wares which have alternating bands of brown and white paint. Plain white ceramics characterize Phase III ca. A.D. 700–1000 (Higham 1977; Higham and Kijngam 1982b). At about this time, the southern portion of the Khorat plateau was incorporated into the Khmer Empire.

To summarize current understanding of the prehistoric culture sequence of northeast Thailand, two areas are known to have early village settlements and cemeteries dating from the third and fourth millennia B.C. Sites of the Ban Chiang cultural tradition are situated on the northern Khorat Plateau, north of the Dong Mun hills. Surveys primarily in the provinces of Udon Thani and Sakon Nakon (Kijngam, Higham, and Wiriyaromp 1980; Vallibhotama 1982–83) have located well over one hundred sites of this tradition in addition to those discussed above.

Although less well delineated, western Khon Kaen Province also seems to have an early settlement tradition possibly centered in the Phu Wiang area, with Non Nok Tha as the best-known site. The Phu Wiang tradition is probably broadly related to the Ban Chiang tradition in social and technological parameters, but ceramically it is somewhat distinct. Bronze artifacts, primarily bangles and tools, appear in both areas at least by the first half of the second millennium B.C. and possibly prior to 2000 B.C. Given the small number of sites excavated and the small proportion of each site excavated, it is still premature to conclude the basal date for bronze in the area.

By the first millennium B.C., settlement seems to expand into both piedmont areas and the more central parts of the Mun-Chi drainage basin. This was accompanied by technological and probably social developments. Between 1000–500 B.C., water buffalo and iron appear, and this may indicate intensification of rice production. Later glass beads and high tin bronze alloys appear. Burial rituals become more elaborate, for example, the Middle Period scatter burials at Ban Chiang, and it seems likely that social differentiation increased.

Within the first millennium B.C., differentiation in site size and function seems to develop at least in the southern Khorat Plateau. The prehistoric development of the region culminated in a hierarchical network of both moated and subsidiary sites during the first millennium A.D. (Kijngam, Higham, and Wiriyaromp 1980; Higham and Kijngam 1982b). At about 1000 A.D. the southern portion of the Khorat Plateau, along with much of the rest of mainland Southeast Asia, was incorporated into early historic Southeast Asian state systems.

Addendum

Although the broad outlines of this appendix have not substantially changed since submission, the reader interested in a detailed revision and discussion of the chronology for the site of Ban Chiang can see Joyce C. White, "A Revision of the Chronology of Ban Chiang and Its Implications for the Prehistory of Northeast Thailand," Ph.D. dissertation, University of Pennsylvania, 1986; University Microfilms, Ann Arbor. Updated chronologies for Thailand as a whole are presented in P. Charoenwongsa and B. Bronson, eds., *Prehistoric Studies: The Stone and Metal Ages in Thailand*, Thai Antiquity Working Group, Bangkok, 1988; and in C. Higham, *The Archaeology of Mainland Southeast Asia*, Cambridge University Press, Cambridge, 1989. An overview of Indonesian and Malaysian archaeology appears in P. Bellwood, *Prehistory of the Indo-Malaysian Archipelago* (New York: Academic Press, 1985).

Twenty-Nine

Summary

Homer L. Thomas, University of Missouri, Emeritus

The archaeological chronologies of these volumes concern the succession of cultures found in Europe, Asia, and Africa. They fall into four distinct groups with somewhat different diachronic ranges because of marked differences in the state of our knowledge of their development as well as distinct variations in the development of culture within these vast regions. The chronologies of cultures found in northern Africa, southwestern Asia, and Europe may be grouped together because of the existence of patterns of parallel development and/or direct and indirect interrelationships during the Neolithic, Chalcolithic, and Early Bronze Age. The chronologies of culture succession in India and southeastern Asia constitute another distinct group, much less well known archaeologically, the beginnings of which extend back only into the time of the later phases of the preceding group of cultures. Although the cultures of China and Korea go back to times as early as the earliest cultures of the first group, their development was distinct from that of the first and second groups. The fourth group of cultures found in Africa south of the Sahel had an equally early and independent development.

Although the third edition of *Chronologies in Old World Archaeology* brings the addition of chronologies for India and Southeast Asia and Africa south of the Sahel as well a revision and expansion of chronologies of East Asia, it still places strong emphasis on the succession of cultures in northern Africa, southwestern Asia, and Europe. In good part this is due to our much greater knowledge of these last three regions, resulting from the work of archaeologists extending back to the middle of the nineteenth century and in some areas as far back as the eighteenth century. These regions have also been the spawning grounds for much of the controversy over method and theory that has characterized recent years.

In this summary I attempt to give broader significance to these diachronic analyses of the regions of the Old World by relating them to one another by means of a synchronic synthesis. I do this by using maps representing the succession of culture horizons during the Neolithic, Chalcolithic, and Early Bronze Age. I give emphasis to the cultures of North Africa, southwest Asia, and Europe not only because they have similar time spans but at times share similar developments that mark them off from the cultures to the south of the Sahel in Africa and the cultures to the east in India and southeast Asia as well as in China and Korea. Although this summary must be brief, I hope that it will give a new perspective to the continuing controversy between the "Old" and "New" archaeologists. This is because the chronologies of this volume, particularly the chronologies for Greece, Anatolia, Mesopotamia, and Iran, indicate major revisions of absolute dating. As a result, most of the connections between the cultures of Europe, the Aegean, and southwest Asia can be interpreted just as easily in terms of older concepts of cultural interrelationships as by current models calling for independent or parallel development.

I have based the maps strictly on the information contained in the chapters themselves, whether or not my own interpretations differ. My assignment of the cultures to horizons has necessarily been subjective, but insofar as possible it is in accordance with radiocarbon dating and significant cultural correlations.

Horizon I, Figure 2

The Pre-Pottery Neolithic and Mesolithic

Many of the chronologies begin with the Aceramic or Pre-Pottery Neolithic, but a few like those for the Maghreb (Lubell, Sheppard, and Gilman), the Arid Zone or southwest Asia (Zarins), the Arabian Gulf (Potts), and the Aegean and Greece (Coleman) extend back into the Epipaleolithic and even the still earlier late Upper Paleolithic. However, while the Aceramic Neolithic dominated many parts of southwest Asia and extended northeastward into central Asia, eastward into Baluchistan, and westward as far as Greece, many of these lands were in part in the hands of peoples with a Mesolithic culture. Much of Africa, Europe, South and Southeast Asia, and eastern Asia were still at a Mesolithic stage.

The absolute dating of these Aceramic Neolithic cultures, which is made possible by calibrated radiocarbon dates, is important because it provides the means of defining the beginning of a series of culture successions used in this synchronic summary. The chronologies for Mesopotamia (Porada, Hansen, Dunham, and Babcock), Cyprus (Coleman), Anatolia (Mellink), and the Arid Zone (Zarins) place the Aceramic Neolithic in the eighth and seventh millennia B.C. In Mesopotamia, the Aceramic is dated from 7500 to 6500 B.C., while in central Asia (Kohl) it has a terminal date of 6500 B.C. Leaving aside the very late date for the Aceramic of Syria (Schwartz and Weiss), most of the chronologies for the Aceramic Neolithic of southwestern Asia place it in the late eighth and early seventh millennia. Available calibrated radiocarbon dates for the subsequent Pottery Neolithic, such as those for the Proto-Hassuna culture of northern Mesopotamia as well as for related cultures of Iran (Voigt and Dyson), Syria, and Anatolia, suggest that the Aceramic gave way to the Ceramic Neolithic during the middle of the seventh millennium. Elsewhere evidence from the Arid Zone, Baluchistan (Shaffer), and central Asia indicates a persistence of the Aceramic Neolithic well into the time when the Ceramic or Pottery Neolithic was current in much of southwestern Asia. On the other hand the Aceramic Neolithic developed relatively late in Greece (Coleman) and lasted probably as late as 6200 B.C. before giving way to the Pottery Neolithic.

Although the Mesolithic cultures lie outside the scope of this work, those like the Typical Capsian of the Maghreb, the B-Group of the Gulf, the Mesolithic of the Italian peninsula, and the Epipaleolithic of Iberia (Gilman) were destined to play significant roles in the development of the subsequent Neolithic. Unfortunately the present state of research does not permit us to define clearly the relations between the Mesolithic and subsequent Neolithic in northwestern, northern, central, southeastern, and eastern Europe.

Horizon II, Figure 3

The Pottery Neolithic and Mesolithic Cultures

In southwest Asia the Ceramic Neolithic (C.N.)/Pottery Neolithic (P.N.) belongs to the later seventh millennium B.C., although in some areas it did not displace the Aceramic Neolithic until the next millennium. The Proto-Hassunan of northern Mesopotamia is placed between 6500–6200/6000 B.C. (Porada, Hansen, Dunham, and Babcock), while in southern Iran the Mohammed Jaffar phase is dated before 6000 B.C. (Voigt and Dyson). In Central Asia Kohl places the initial Djeitun culture before 6200 B.C.

While the Ceramic Neolithic of Anatolia is left undated (Mellink), Schwartz and Weiss put the Ceramic Neolithic of Ras Shamra VB and Amuq A between 6000

and 5000 B.C. In adjacent Palestine Stager dates the contemporary Yarmukian culture between 6310 and 5690 B.C. To the south and east of Palestine, the Pre-Pottery Neolithic B culture persisted in the arid zone. Much the same is true of the B-Groups of the Arabian Gulf as well as the Mehrgarh Aceramic phase of Baluchistan (Potts; Shaffer). The Ceramic Neolithic which reached Greece as early as 6200 B.C. is defined by the early phase of the Early Neolithic I of Thessaly (Coleman). Cyprus remained in the hands of an Aceramic people (Coleman).

Although it is premature to speculate about the development and differentiation of these early Ceramic Neolithic cultures, it is now possible to establish the distinct existence of five or six of them. To the east of the Proto-Hassuna culture of northern Mesopotomia there were distinct ceramic Neolithic cultures in southern and western Iran, although some traits found at Ali Kosh of the Mohammed Jaffar phase in the south turn up at Tepe Guran and Tepe Sarab in the west. Assemblages from Hajji Firuz and Yanik Tepe indicate the existence of another distinct Ceramic Neolithic culture in northwest Iran, which possessed traits showing contact with the Proto-Hassuna culture of northern Mesopotamia. The Ceramic Neolithic of Palestine and Syria is characterized by a dark-faced burnished pottery, which distinguishes it from the Ceramic Neolithic cultures of Mesopotamia and Iran. Beyond the Taurus there were distinct Ceramic Neolithic cultures in southern Anatolia and Greece.

Beyond this broad zone of Ceramic Neolithic extending from the Aegean across southwestern Asia to central Asia, the Mesolithic cultures continued in the Terminal Paleolithic of the Sahara, the Epipaleolithic of Iberia (Gilman), and the late Epi-Gravettian of the Italian peninsula; changes were already being felt in the lands of the Maghreb, where the Typical Capsian developed under the impact of changing environmental conditions (Lubell, Sheppard, and Gilman). Much the same could be said of the Tardenoisian culture of Transalpine Europe.

Horizon III, Figure 4

The West Asian Pottery Neolithic and Its First Expansion

The early sixth millennium B.C. was characterized by Ceramic Neolithic cultures across the highlands of southwest Asia into central Asia. This was the time of the Hassuna and Samarra cultures of Mesopotamia, which fall between 6000 and 5500 B.C. (Porada, Hansen, Dunham, and Babcock). In Iran, regional sequences such as the Sefid, Surkh, and Chogha Mami Transition of the Deh Luran, the Mushki and Jari phases of Fars, later Hajji Firuz and Yanik Tepe of northwest Iran, and Tepe Sialk I, 3–5 of the western Iranian plateau date to much the same time span (Voigt and Dyson). In central Asia, calibrated radiocarbon dates enabled Kohl to place the Early and Middle Djeitun culture between 6200 and 5400 B.C. Here this was also the beginning of the Neolithic in the Kyzyl Kum and Zaravshan. Far to the southeast the Mehrgarh continued in Baluchistan. The same maturing of the Ceramic Neolithic, which was marked by a growing particularism characterized by relatively few interregional connections, occurs in the western areas of southwest Asia. In Syria, this was the time of Ras Shamra VA and Amuq B, which do have Hassuna connections, while in Palestine the Munhatta culture is dated by Stager to between 5900 and 5600 B.C. Generalized connections link Mersin XXIV–XX of Cilicia with Can Hasan IIB on the Konya plain, while calibrated radiocarbon dates assign Hacilar V–I to much the same time span as that of the Hassuna and Samarra cultures (Mellink). Although many would designate this horizon in southwestern Asia after the Hassuna and Samarra cultures, the widespread regional particularism as well as the persistence of old traditions in the P.P.N. B culture of the Arid Zone (Zarins) and the B-Group in the Gulf (Potts) warn against such usage.

Numerous calibrated radiocarbon dates indicate that the first half of the sixth millennium was the time of the second and third phase of the Early Neolithic of Thessaly and the latter part of the Early Neolithic of central and southern Greece (Coleman). During the first half of the sixth millennium, most of the cultures of southwestern Asia such as the Hassuna and Samarra cannot be phased; in Greece and beyond in southeastern Europe there is abundant evidence for two phases.

In southeastern Europe, the Gurk Baciului–Anzebegovo I and Karanovo I horizon can be archaeologically correlated with the Thessalian Early Middle Neolithic II, while the subsequent Starčevo-Körös-Criş and Karanovo II horizon can be equated with Thessalian Early Neolithic III. Ranges of calibrated radiocarbon dates for sites of Karanovo I indicate that it belongs to the earlier part of the first half of the sixth millennium, a dating that is supported not only by ranges of dates from sites of the Starčevo-Körös-Criş and Karanovo II horizon, but also by Thessalian dates indicating that the beginnings of the Neolithic in southeast Europe must be placed in the time of the early Hassuna and Samarra cultures.

New work in northern Africa now places the rise of the Saharan Neolithic, the "Neolithic of Sudanese Tradition," as early as 8000 B.P./6000 B.C. This Neolithic, which is defined by the "well-made pottery of the Khartoum Horizon Style," is found across the Sahara and Sudan (Hays). It is also thought that this was the source of the Neolithic elements found in the Neolithic of Capsian tradition in Libya as well as in the north Saharan Neolithic groups, which are known from sites with calibrated radiocarbon dates that place them in the first half of the sixth millennium (Lubell, Sheppard, and Gilman). One

wonders if this could also be the source of the Earlier Neolithic found at Cueva de Nerja, Santiago, and other sites in Iberia (Gilman).

Horizon IV, Figure 5

The West Asian Earliest Chalcolithic and the Mediterranean Cardial and Impresso Ware Cultures

Archaeological evidence indicates that established cultures of North Africa, southwest Asia, and central Asia continued down until the sixth millennium. This is true everywhere except in Iran, where cultures that began around 6000 B.C. have developments in some areas, such as in the Deh Luran area of Khuzistan, which can be subdivided into three phases on the basis of stratigraphic evidence. Unfortunately, it is difficult to correlate these phases with phases of regional successions in Iran or Mesopotamia. This is unfortunate because this was a period in which copper was becoming important as evidenced by the copper pins and tools found at Tepe Sialk I, 3–5 (Voigt and Dyson). The stimulus of the demand for copper must have led to the use and expansion of the already long-established obsidian trade routes.

While there was little change in southwest Asia, there were major culture changes in Greece, southeast Europe, and the lands and islands bordering the northern shores of the western Mediterranean Sea. Although there was little change on Crete and, as yet, with no evidence of permanent settlement in the Cyclades, there were marked changes on the Greek mainland and especially in Thessaly. In the latter area, Early Neolithic III is marked by the decline of painted pottery and the appearance of impressed ware and must be dated to a period of one or two centuries at the end of the Early Neolithic which lasted down to ca. 5600 B.C. (Coleman).

Much the same dating can be given to pottery impressed with the edges of Cardium shells, Cardial Ware, found along the Dalmatian coast of Yugoslavia (Ehrich and Bankoff). Comparable calibrated radiocarbon dates exist for the Impressed Ware culture of Sicily, southeast and eastern Italy, and western Liguria (Brown). Most archaeologists assign the Ghar Dalam culture of Malta and Impressed Ware culture of Sardinia and Corsica to this time. Calibrated dates for the Cardial Ware culture of southern France (Thomas and R. Rowlett) and eastern and southern Spain belong with them (Gilman). Calibrated radiocarbon dates for the Cardial and Impressed Ware cultures of the western Mediterranean indicate that they were not much later than comparable ones in Sicily, southern Italy, Dalmatia, and Greece.

The Starčevo-Körös-Criş and Karanovo II–III cultures of southeastern Europe (Ehrich and Bankoff), provided the basis for the extraordinary expansion of the Neolithic through central into western Europe during the last half

Summary

of the sixth millennium (Thomas and E. Rowlett). The
expansion of the neolithic into eastern Europe is correlated by some archaeologists with the Anzebegovo I,
Gurk Baciului, and Karanovo I cultures (Gimbutas) and
by other archaeologists with the Starčevo-Körös-Criş
cultures. Whatever its inspiration, the Neolithic of the
Bug-Dniester II culture marks the beginning of sedentary
life in eastern Europe.

Horizon V, Figure 6

*The West Asian Early Chalcolithic and the Expansion of the
European Neolithic*

The second half of the sixth millennium brought the consolidation of the Chalcolithic of southwestern Asia, the
formation of the Vinča A–B and related cultures of southeastern Europe, and the rise and expansion of the Linear
Bandkeramik culture of central Europe. Elsewhere in Europe and northern Africa there were changes, but not on
the scale of nor with the significance of those taking place
in southwest Asia, southeast Europe, or central Europe.
Unfortunately the present archaeological record does not
permit us to define contemporary developments in Africa
south of the Sahara and Sudan. To the east little is known
of developement in the Indus Valley and India beyond the
Mehrgarh culture of Baluchistan. Southeast Asia is even
less well known in these times. Although subsequent archaeological evidence suggests that one is on the eve of
the Neolithic of Siberia, it is only in north China that
archaeological excavation indicates that the Neolithic is
under way (Chang).

The Halaf culture has long been associated with the
beginning of the Chalcolithic of southwest Asia. Today,
the chapters of Porada, Hansen, Dunham, and Babcock
and of Schwartz and Weiss suggest that the Halafian period was not only much shorter than was formerly
thought, but also that it was much more complicated and
that the contributions of Voigt and Dyson indicate that
what took place in Iran was comparable and equally complex. A somewhat different and less well defined development occurred in Anatolia during Early and early
Middle Chalcolithic times (Mellink). At this point it is
difficult to relate these to the Middle and Late Djeitun
Transcaucasia culture of central Asia (Kohl) and to the
Eneolithic of Transcaucasia (Glumac and Anthony). It is
interesting that Coleman places the Middle Neolithic of
Greece in this time range. Although he argues against
external connections, a higher chronology for Anatolia
places the houses with internal buttresses of Can Hasan
IIa in the same horizon as those of Middle Neolithic
Thessaly.

Southeast European development was marked by
widespread regionalization. In Bulgaria this was the time
of Karanovo IV, while the Boian culture occupied the

lower Danubian Valley, and in Serbia, northern Bosnia,
eastern Croatia, southeast Hungary, western southern
Romania, and west Bulgaria the Vinča culture was dominant. This past brought the establishment of a tradition
that can be traced through four major phases, Vinča A,
B, C, and D, spanning a period of over one and a half
millennia. The early phases, Vinča A and B, sometimes
designated as Vinča-Tordos, can be correlated with the
Middle Neolithic of Thessaly. To the west there are indirect connections by date with the Kakanj culture of Bosnia (Obre I, levels III–IV, and Obre II, level I) and
through it with the Danilo culture of the Dalmatian coast.
These cultures in turn have Thessalian Middle Neolithic
ties. To the north the Vinča cultures can be equated with
the Linear *Bandkeramik* at Vinča A. Today, this enables
the correlation of the earlier Linear *Bandkeramik* of Poland (Bogucki), southern Germany and Austria (Wells)
and central Germany, the Rhineland and Low Countries
(Thomas and E. Rowlett) and is fully supported by the
ranges of radiocarbon dates. An increasingly complicated web of archaeological connections, again supported by calibrated radiocarbon dates, allows us to
equate the later phases of the development of Linear
Bandkeramik in the Lower and Middle Rhine valleys, the
Rhine-Main basin and central Germany with the Šarka of
Bohemia, the Želiezovce of Moravia and Slovakia, the
Zseliz and Szakálhát of Hungary (Ehrich and Bankoff),
all phases of the *Bandkeramik* tradition, dating to Vinča
B times. Beyond southeast Europe, the Music Note phase
of earlier *Bandkeramik* allows one to fix the time of the
last phase of the Bug-Dniester culture (Gimbutas). Cali-
brated radiocarbon dates given by Gimbutas for Cucuteni
A, together with evidence that Pre-Cucuteni succeeded
Linear-*Bandkeramik* (Music Note phase), suggest that it
belongs to the latter part of this horizon.

Archaeological connections supported by calibrated
radiocarbon dates not only enable us to establish the chronology of the first widespread Early Neolithic of southeast, central, and nearer eastern Europe, but also extend
to northern France. Here there was a mature Linear-
Bandkeramik culture that derived from the Middle Rhine,
a culture destined to continue in a late *Bandkeramik* form
that lasted well into the fifth millennium. Westward connections of the *Bandkeramik* culture also extend to the
Fiorano culture of northeast Italy, which had globular jars
with incised decoration explainable in *Bandkeramik*
terms.

Horizon VI, Figure 7

*The West Asian Middle Chalcolithic and the Regionalization
of the European Neolithic*

The consolidation of the Chalcolithic, which brought increasing trade and a wider use of copper, was followed

by the beginning of urbanization in the first half of the fifth millennium. Although this process has long been thought of in terms of Mesopotamia (Porada et al.), the same development can be traced in Iran (Voigt and Dyson) and Turkmenistan (Kohl) as well as in Anatolia (Mellink). Although the influence of the Ubaid of Mesopotamia spread in Syria (Schwartz and Weiss) and extended into southwest, western, and northwest Iran, development in much of Iran and all of Anatolia was marked by increasing regional particularism rather than Ubaidian influence. To the southwest, older traditions held in the continuing Wadi Rabah period of Palestine (Stager) and the lingering Pottery Neolithic of the Arid Zone (Zarins). At this time archaeologically known development began in Egypt with the Fayum A and Tasian cultures (Kantor).

In the Aegean and Greece (Coleman), older traditions persisted in the Early Neolithic II and Middle Neolithic of Crete as well as in the continuing Early Neolithic I of the Cyclades, and the Late Neolithic I of the Greek mainland, Thessaly, and Macedonia. Although Coleman has little to say of contacts with the east, he notes the northern connection of four-legged rhyta that point to trade between Greece and Dalmatia during Danilo and Hvar times. Contact between Late Neolithic I Greece and southern Italy has long been defined by the Trichrome Ware found in Sicily and south Italy (Brown). Beyond in the lands bordering the western Mediterranean Sea, older traditions persisted in the Sasso culture of central Italy (Brown), the Cardial culture of southern France (Thomas and R. Rowlett), the Epi-Cardial and Impressed Ware cultures of Iberia (Gilman), and the Neolithic of the Maghreb (Lubell, Sheppard, and Gilman).

In southeastern Europe, the first half of the fifth millennium was characterized by a widespread regionalization of culture development. Although older traditions continued in Vinča C, elsewhere new cultures arose. To the west, the Kakanj gave way to Butmir in central Bosnia, while the Hvar culture emerged on the Dalmatian coast. In the western Carpathian basin, southwest and central Slovakia, Moravia, Silesia, and Poland, the cultures of the Linear *Bandkeramik* tradition gave way to the Lengyel in the last centuries of the sixth millennium. Regionalization was intense in the eastern Carpathian basin, exemplified by the Herpály, Tisza, and Petreşti cultures. In the lower Danubian Valley, Boian continued into this period, but toward the middle of the fifth millennium gave way to the Gumelniţa culture (Ehrich and Bankoff).

The tradition of the Linear *Bandkeramik* culture continued in the Stroked Ware culture of Poland (Bogucki), Czechoslovakia (Ehrich and Bankoff), south-central Europe (Wells), and southern areas of northern Europe (Thomas and E. Rowlett). In the Rhineland and southwest Germany the Linear tradition gave rise to local groups such as the Hinkelstein and Grossgartach (Wells; Thomas and E. Rowlett). To the west the Linear tradition continued in a late phase found in northern France. In eastern Europe it arrived in Moldavia as Music Note and survived in a late phase to Pre-Cucuteni times and must also have played a role in the rise of the Tripolye A culture that was later to dominate the western Ukraine. Farther east the Pontic Neolithic reached its second stage of development in the Dnieper-Donetz II culture (Gimbutas).

Beyond these Neolithic cultures of Transalpine Europe were the Mesolithic cultures of the British Isles, Scandinavia, and much of woodland Russia. In the latter area there are indications that central Russia was beginning to achieve a Neolithic status (Gimbutas).

Horizon VII, Figure 8

The West Asian Middle Chalcolithic and the Mature Neolithic of Europe

By the last half of the fifth millennium, Mesopotamia (Porada et al.) and large areas of western and southern Iran (Voigt and Dyson) were on the eve of full-scale urbanization characterized by the beginnings of literacy. Metallurgical activity was widespread throughout southwestern Asia. To the north the rise of the Kelteminar I culture in the Caspian-Aral region came at the time of a mature Namazga I (Kohl), while the Kachi culture was replaced by the Kili Gul Muhammad culture in Baluchistan (Shaffer). Despite dynamic change in Mesopotamia and the lands to the north and east, older traditions persisted in the Eneolithic of the Transcaucasus (Glumac and Anthony) and the Late Chalcolithic of Anatolia (Mellink). In the northern Levant, Ubaid influence continued dominant in Syria (Schwartz and Weiss). To the south it is difficult to define the onset of the Chalcolithic in precise chronological terms (Stager), but the rise of the Beersheban and Ghassulian cultures may mark the start of the Chalcolithic in Palestine. In the northern Sinai, this probably came at the beginning of the Elatian culture (Zarins). The Arabian Neolithic of central and north Arabia (Zarins) as well as the Ceramic Neolithic of the Arabian Gulf as defined by the Qatar A and C–D groups (Potts) continued until the end of the fifth millennium.

This was the time of the early Late Ceramic Neolithic in Cyprus and the early Late Neolithic in Crete. In the Cyclades as well as in the Peloponnesus, central Greece, and Thessaly, these were the cultures attributed to Late Neolithic II (Coleman). Thessalian Late Neolithic II has Crusted Wares with interesting connections in the Balkans and was probably the period of the difficult-to-define Rachmani culture. While there is widespread evidence for culture change on the Greek mainland, the Ripoli and Trichrome, Sasso and Square Mouth cultures persisted in

Sicily and south Italy, central Italy, and north Italy respectively (Brown). On the other hand, there was a dramatic change in culture in the Iberian peninsula, where the rise of the Almerian and Alentejo cultures mark a distinct advance destined to lead to developments that were to define the coastal lands as distinct from the interior where the Impressed Ware tradition persisted into the next millennium (Gilman). In Portugal this change is marked by megalithic passage graves in the south and megalithic cists and rock-cut tombs in the center. South of Gibraltar the Mediterranean Neolithic and the Neolithic in the Capsian tradition continued in the Maghreb (Lubell, Sheppard, and Gilman).

The Cardial culture of southern France was displaced by the Early Chassey or as some would say, the Middle Neolithic. It did not completely displace the Cardial tradition, because Epi-Cardial elements still lingered in Provence. In western France, the Primary Neolithic of Brittany was characterized by the appearance here and along the west coast of France of the first megalithic monuments. Inland across northern France, the Cerny culture gave way to or was modified by Rössen elements in eastern France. The Middle Neolithic of the Haute-Saône and Burgundy was in many ways transitional like the Middle Neolithic or Early Chassey culture of southern France. Like the latter, it gave way to a mature Chassey culture. Beyond the English Channel in the British Isles, Bromme Heath in England and Ballynagilly in Ireland indicate a thinly scattered Early Neolithic.

The Hinkelstein and Grossgartach cultures of the Rhineland and southwest and west middle Germany, which derived from the Linear *Bandkeramik* tradition, now gave way to the Rössen culture, while the Stroked Ware culture of south Germany, central Germany, and Poland shattered and were followed by the further expansion of the Lengyel in Poland, the rise of the Gatersleben in central Germany, and the formation of the Aichbühl and Münchshöfen cultures in southern Germany (Thomas and E. Rowlett; Wells; Bogucki). Late groups of the Rössen culture such as the Bischheim lasted down until the initial spread of the Michelsberg culture. Perhaps of even greater importance are the connections between the Gatersleben, Aichbühl, and Münchshofen with the Lengyel cultures of east-central Europe and the Carpathian basin (Ehrich and Bankoff).

The Carpathian basin was dominated in the west by the late Lengyel culture and in the east by the Tiszapolgár culture. Although the beginnings of the Tiszapolgár go back to just before the middle of the fifth millennium, its connections with early Funnel Beaker suggest that it continued into the early fourth millennium. It has, furthermore, connections to the southeast with the Sălcuţa II–III and later Gumelniţa cultures and to the east with Cucuteni A and AB and Tripolye Late A to BII. In Bulgaria this

was the period of Varna and Karanovo-Gumelniţa. Vinča D continued in Serbia, and its indirect connections via Obre II, level III in central Bosnia permits us to place the mature Butmir culture and thus the continuing Hvar culture of Dalmatia in this horizon (Ehrich and Bankoff).

In eastern Europe, this was the time of the first expansion of the Kurgan culture, which is defined by the Khvalynsk complex in the lower Volga basin and Srednij Stog II in the lower Dnieper region. Both are equated with Cucuteni A3 and Karanovo VI (Karanovo-Gumelniţa) (Gimbutas). Change was not restricted to the steppe. Although the Narva culture continued in the Baltic area, the Pit-Comb Ware culture now becomes a well-defined entity in central Russia and eastern Poland (Bogucki).

Horizon VIII, Figure 9

The West Asian Late Chalcolithic, the European Copper Age, and the Middle Neolithic of North Europe

The first half of the fourth millennium brought an increasing concentration of culture development in the valleys of the Nile and Tigris and Euphrates. In Mesopotamia, the Early and Middle Gawran in the north and the Early and Middle Uruk in the south were characterized by the formation of urban centers which in the south are marked by the achievement of writing, an advance that has led some archaeologists to designate these times as Proto-Literate a (Porada et al.). In Egypt (Kantor) this was the time of the Amratian and Merimde cultures. Although Uruk elements penetrated into Syria (Schwartz and Weiss), the Chalcolithic with Beersheban and Ghassulian elements continued in Palestine and Jordan (Stager) and spread to central and north Arabia (Zarins). The same persistence of older traditions is indicated by the Qatar A and C–D groups in the Arabian Gulf (Potts).

The Chalcolithic of the highlands of southwestern Asia exhibits relatively little change. In Iran the further development of the Chalcolithic is now well defined in all areas except the northwest (Voigt and Dyson). There was relatively little change in central Asia where the Namazga I culture developed into Namazga II (Kohl). In Baluchistan, Kili Gul Muhammad continued its development, while the Nal culture appeared in the lower Indus valley (Shaffer). Much the same persistence of older traditions is to be found in Late Chalcolithic Anatolia (Mellink), while major changes took place in the Caucasus region. Here, the Eneolithic gave way to the Kura Araxes I culture in the Transcaucasus, while an Eneolithic one emerged in the north Caucasus (Glumac and Anthony).

Unfortunately, development cannot be phased in the Aegean or in Greece. This was the period of the continuing Late Neolithic of Crete, the Late Neolithic II of the Cyclades, Greek mainland, and Thessaly, and the Sitagroi III phase of eastern Macedonia and Thrace (Coleman). In contrast there were marked changes in the Italian peninsula and Sicily. The Diana culture replaced the Ripoli and Trichrome cultures in Sicily and the south while the Lagozza displaced the Square Mouth and Sasso cultures in north and central Italy and spread into the south (Brown). On the other hand little change occurred in the Iberian peninsula (Gilman) or in the Maghreb (Lubell, Sheppard, and Gilman).

In France there was no fundamental change in cultural traditions in the south, west, and Brittany. The Late Chassey developed out of Early Chassey in the south, while the Secondary Neolithic of the west and Brittany was marked by the elaboration of megalithic tombs (M). Real change occurred in the north, where the Chassey culture now became dominant. In the east there was widespread penetration of Michelsberg elements, except in Burgundy, where the influence of the Cortaillod culture gave rise to the Burgundian Middle Neolithic (Thomas and R. Rowlett).

The Middle Neolithic of the British Isles was characterized by the regionalization of the Neolithic tradition in the south and east and the transformation of the west by the megalithic. In the south were the Hembury, Windmill Hill, and Abingdon groups and the Mildenhall group in East Anglia. In the west, the megalithic is known from the early tombs of the Severn-Cotswold group, the scattered tombs of Wales, the Clyde group of southwest Scotland, and the first Court Cairns of northern Ireland (Thomas and R. Rowlett).

In northern Europe, the Funnel Beaker culture began in this period. It is defined by the Funnel Beaker A and B culture of Scandinavia, the Funnel Beaker A/B culture of the northern Netherlands and north Germany (Thomas and E. Rowlett), the Sarnowo and Pitkutkowo groups of western and north Poland, and the Bronocice I group of Małopolska (Bogucki). In central Germany, the Baalberg I group is usually equated with the Scandinavian Funnel Beaker B group (Thomas and E. Rowlett) and the Bohemian Funnel Beaker B (Baalberg) group (Ehrich and Bankoff). South of the Funnel Beaker area the greatest change was brought by the Michelsberg culture, which developed in the Rhineland and spread into eastern France, southern Belgium, southwest Germany and northern Switzerland, and Bohemia (Thomas and E. Rowlett; Wells; Ehrich and Bankoff). Everywhere it displaced older traditions except for the Schussenried in southwest Germany and the Cortaillod in central Switzerland (Wells).

In southeastern Europe (Ehrich and Bankoff), the long-established Sălcuţa and Gumelniţa cultures came to an end in the early fourth millennium. Many sites such as Karanovo now show a gap in occupation. Following this destabilization of cultures, which many archaeologists attribute to intrusions from the east, elements of older culture traditions coalesced into successors such as that of the Cernavodă I culture of southern Romania. Culture change in the Carpathian basin is marked by the displacement of the Lengyel culture by Balaton-Lasinja I and the transformation of the Tiszapolgár culture into Bodrogkeresztúr A. In the south the Bubanj IA culture arose in southern Serbia either through the transformation of older local traditions or from the fusion of local elements with displaced elements from the lower Danubian Valley. To the north, older traditions survived in the Lengyel-Ludanice group of Slovakia and the Jordanów culture of northeast Bohemia and Silesia.

The Cucuteni AB–B/Tripolye C1 culture continued to dominate the western Ukraine. On the Pontic steppe, the equation is with the Kurgan II culture which can be expressed in terms of late Srednij Stog, and the Narva culture continued in the Baltic states (Gimbutas). In the woodland zone the Early Pit and Comb Ware tradition continued in northeast Poland (Bogucki), while calibrated radiocabon dates suggest that the Neolithic of central and eastern Russia may be defined by the Volosovo and Volga-Kama groups.

Horizon IX, Figure 10

The West Asian Late Chalcolithic and Culture Change

The late fourth millennium was marked by the beginning of state formation leading to the rise of the historically known states of Gerzian Egypt and Late Uruk Mesopotamia. Literacy emerges to meet the needs of the developing states and the increasingly complex commercial systems. These developments are indicated not only by the archaeological evidence found in Egypt (Kantor) and Mesopotamia (Porada et al.) but also by the widespread distribution of evidence for Proto-Elamite found in southern and western Iran (Voigt and Dyson). Related changes characterized Early Bronze Ia Anatolia (Mellink), the Caucasus (Glumac and Anthony), central Asia (Kohl), and Baluchistan and the Indus Valley (Shaffer). In the Levant, Syria became increasingly linked to late Gawran and Uruk centers (Schwartz and Weiss), while Palestine (Stager) and Sinai (Zarins) developed more intimate relations with Egypt. On the other hand, the development of culture is difficult to define in northern Arabia (Zarins) and the Arabian Gulf (Potts), where archaeological sites are assigned roughly to the late fourth and early third millennium.

In Cyprus (Coleman), the Aegean and Greece (Coleman), the Italian peninsula (Brown), and Iberia (Gilman), culture development is viewed as occurring in place relatively free from external stimuli. One can only wonder how the lands of the Mediterranean escaped the influence of the emerging civilizations of Egypt and southwest Asia. It is perhaps a reaction to the past over-emphasis given to the role of trade, because archaeologists in the days before radiocarbon dating used limited evidence for culture contact as a basis for chronology. The vast amount of archaeological data unearthed in the last twenty-five years in combination with the proliferation of new methods and techniques for analysis and synthesis have made it possible for contemporary archaeologists to emphasize internal cultural development.

In northwest Europe, the archaeological record is characterized by widespread regional culture changes. In southern France, the Chassey gave way to cultures such as the Ferrières in the south and the Peu-Richard and Matignons in the west. While the Secondary Neolithic continued in Brittany, the northern Chassey differentiated along regional lines in the north and east. In the British Isles, the particularism of the times is marked by the Late Neolithic Peterborough and Ebbsfleet cultures of southern and eastern England. The megalithic continued to develop, evolving new tomb types and creating new pottery styles in the western British Isles as well as in Brittany and the west of France (Thomas and R. Rowlett).

Northern Europe was still dominated by the Funnel Beaker culture, but this once relatively uniform and widespread culture now broke into a series of regional subgroups. Distinct cultures are found in southern Scandinavia, the Netherlands, northwest Germany, Schleswig-Holstein, east Germany, and Poland. In middle and southern central Europe, the regionalization of the Funnel Beaker culture was conditioned by the absorption of older elements and influences from the southeast. It is only in these terms that one can understand the character of the Baalberg II and Salzmünde I cultures of central Germany, the Altheim culture of southern Germany, and the Pfyn II culture of northeast Switzerland and Liechtenstein. The now long-established Cortaillod culture continued in Switzerland, while the Michelsberg persisted in western and southwest central Europe (Thomas and E. Rowlett).

During the last half of the fourth millennium, south-central Europe is linked to the Carpathian basin via the Pfyn II and Altheim cultures and by Jevišovice C2 (Moravia), and the Balaton-Lasinja II–III (West Hungary) cultures. The late Funnel Beaker elements of Pfyn II, Altheim, and Jevišovice C2 equate chronologically with the Baalberg II and Salzmünde I groups of central Germany and the Funnel Beaker C culture of southern Scandinavia, which is assigned to the last half of the fourth millennium by numerous calibrated radiocarbon dates. Balaton-Lasinja II–III has ties on the one hand to the late Funnel Beaker culture of Bohemia and Moravia and on the other to Bodrogkeresztúr B. The Bubanj culture continued in southern Serbia, while the Cernavodă persisted in the lower Danubian Valley. (Ehrich and Bankoff.)

To the east in the western Ukraine, there was a survival of the Cucuteni-Tripolye tradition. On the Pontic steppe, this was the time of the second wave of expansion of the Kurgan culture, and the Narva cultures occupied the Russian woodlands (Gimbutas).

Horizon X, Figure 11

The West Asian Proto-Historic Cultures and the Rise of Beaker and Corded Ware Cultures in Europe

Much controversy still surrounds the absolute dating of the cultures of Egypt, southwest Asia, and the Aegean at the time of the transition from the late fourth to the early third millennium. At this point it becomes necessary to resolve the differences between chronologies for Egypt and Mesopotamia by historical chronologies and by dating secured by radiocarbon determinations. Resolution of the differences is not possible at this time because of the differing historical chronologies and the broad ranges of calibrated radiocarbon dates, which are not narrow enough to resolve these discrepancies.

Here the cartographic requirements necessitate a broad correlation in which equations between cultures often depend on overlapping phases. Thus the early phase of the Proto-Dynastic of Egypt (Kantor), which is dated 3100–2650 B.C., is equated with the Jamdat Nasr of Mesopotamia (Porada et al.), dated to 3100–2900 B.C. It is on this basis that Early Bronze II of Palestine (Stager), Ninevite V of Syria (Schwartz and Weiss), and late Gawra of northern Mesopotamia are placed in this time frame. The culture successions of Iran (Voigt and Dyson) can be tied to Mesopotamia. However, those of central Asia (Kohl), the Arabian Gulf (Potts), Baluchistan and the Indus Valley (Shaffer), as well as the Early Bronze IA of Anatolia (Mellink), and the Eneolithic and Kura-Araxes II of the Caucasus (Glumac and Anthony) must rest on calibrated radiocarbon dates.

The Chalcolithic of Cyprus (Coleman) as well as the Early Minoan I of Crete, the Early Cycladic I of the Cyclades, the Early Helladic of the Greek mainland and the Middle and Late Rachmani of Thessaly had their beginnings in the middle of the fourth millennium but, except for the Early Cycladic I, extended into the first century of the third millennium, justifying their inclusion in this horizon (Coleman).

Calibrated radiocarbon dates indicate that the Gaudo culture of southern Italy, the Rinaldone culture of central Italy, and the Remedello culture of north Italy (Brown) had their beginnings in the late fourth millennium. The Millares I and VNSP cultures of the Iberian peninsula (Gilman) have been placed in this horizon on similar grounds.

In northwestern Europe, the late fourth and early third millennia were marked by the transformation of older cultures and the first expansion of the Beaker culture. The

511

Ferrières culture gave way to the Fontbouisse, while the Pasteurs des Plateaux and the Crosian and Treilles groups appeared in the Causses and southern Massif Central. In western France, the Matignons and Peu-Richard were replaced by the Artenacien. Although the megalithic tradition lingered on in Brittany, the Bell Beaker culture appeared on the coasts. The Seine-Oise-Marne culture continued in the north, while the Eastern Chassey was replaced by the Saône-Rhône culture (Thomas and R. Rowlett).

The older traditions of the British Isles were transformed by the spread of the Grooved Ware complex, which is found in the south, east, western midlands, and the north. As in France, the Early Beaker culture appeared. One can only wonder about the origins of the Boyne culture of Ireland, which must be dated to these times by calibrated radiocarbon dates (Thomas and R. Rowlett).

A similar transformation took place in Scandinavia, where the Middle Neolithic developed within the Funnel Beaker tradition. On the north European plain there were related developments in the Early Havelte of the northern Netherlands, which is associated with Hunebbeden, and the Early *Tiefstich* of northern Germany, which occurs in association with *Hunenbetten*. The megalithic *Hunebedden/Hunenbetten* began in the preceding period and differs not only in type from the passage graves of the Middle Neolithic of Scandinavia but also in time. At the western end of the north European plain, the earliest Beakers, the protruding foot Beaker (Ia), appeared in the Netherlands, as did the Globular Amphora culture of east Germany and Poland at the eastern end. The Dutch Beaker Ia is related to the earliest Corded Ware beakers that occur in central Germany with the Salzmünde II culture. Along the Rhine the Michelsberg culture persisted and is still found from Belgium southward to southwest Germany and northern Switzerland (Thomas and E. Rowlett). In Switzerland, the Horgen culture replaced the Cortaillod, while the Cham culture pushed into Bavaria (Wells) and Bohemia (Ehrich and Bankoff).

In Bohemia the Řivnáč culture, was closely associated with the Cham group. The Mondsee, Vučedol A, and Kostolac A cultures of Austria, Slavonia, and northwest Serbia have connections probably best explained by trade in east Alpine copper. In the Carpathian basin, older traditions were either displaced or transformed by the Baden culture, the earliest phase of which is best represented by the Boleráz group. In Romania, the Cernavodă I culture gave rise to the Coţofeni culture in Oltenia and Transylvania the Cernavodă III culture in Muntenia and the Dobrudža, while the Ezero culture arose in Bulgarian Thrace (Ehrich and Bankoff).

Gimbutas associates the formation of the Usatovo and Gorodsk cultures of the western Ukraine and the Folteşti culture of Moldavia with the expansion of Kurgan II between 3400 and 3200 B.C. On the other hand she places the formation of the Cernavodă and Ezero cultures of southeast Romania and eastern Bulgaria, the Coţofeni culture of Romania, and the Baden culture of the Carpathian basin during the expansion of the Kurgan III culture between 3000 and 2800 B.C., while in the woodland zone of Russia the Pitted Ware people expanded.

Horizon XI, Figure 12

The West Asian Early Historic Civilizations, the Late Copper Age, and the Late Neolithic of North Europe

During the late Proto-Dynastic of Egypt (Kantor) and the Early Dynastic I(I–II) of Mesopotamia (2900–2600 B.C.) (Porada et al.), the cultural traditions of not only Egypt and Mesopotamia but also of most of southwestern Asia were characterized by a continuation of the established cultures. In the Levant, the Timnian II continued in the south, Early Bronze II in Palestine, and Late Ninevite V in Syria (Zarins; Stager; Schwartz and Weiss). A similar persistence of established cultures can be traced in western and southern Iran. Major changes occurred in the northwest, where Yanik E.B.I and Geoy Tepe K 2 occupations are characterized by intrusive Kura-Araxes elements from the south Caucasus area, while in northwest Anatolia, Troy I was founded (Mellink).

There was a similar continuity of culture in Chalcolithic Cyprus (Coleman), the Early Minoan II of Crete, and the Early Cycladic II of the Aegean. The same can be said for the succession of Early Helladic I and II on the Greek mainland and Thessalian I and II and Macedonian I and II in northern Greece (Coleman). The persistence of cultural tradition is also clear in the Italian peninsula, where Gaudo, Rinaldone, and Remedello all continued and in the Iberian peninsula, where the Millares I and VNSP I lasted until the rise of the Bell Beaker culture (Brown; Gilman).

Much the same characterized northwestern Europe, for here, as in southwestern Asia and the Mediterranean, there was a widespread persistence of cultures. There is, however, a subtle change, for Maritime Bell Beakers are now much more common along the coasts of southern and western France as well as in Brittany where they can be attributed to this horizon by calibrated radiocarbon dates. Grooved Ware sites still predominate in the British Isles, but Early Beakers are now more frequent (Thomas and R. Rowlett).

The same continuity of culture characterized northern Europe, where the Middle Neolithic of southern Scandinavia continued. The Early Havelte style became the Late Havelte style in the Netherlands, and the Early *Tiefstichkeramik* developed into the Late *Tiefstichkeramik* in north Germany. In central Germany, Salzmünde II was replaced by the Walternienberg-Bernburg culture, while the Michelsberg culture persisted in western and southwestern Germany (Thomas and E. Rowlett). Globular Amphora continued in east Germany and northern and central Poland, while Baden increased its hold on southern Poland (Bogucki). It could be argued that there was little change, but everywhere there is increasing evidence for Corded Ware in the Netherlands, northern Germany, central Germany, east Germany, and Poland. Corded Ware is now found in southern Germany and in Switzerland where it displaced the Horgen culture (Wells). Real change was to come to northern and central Europe in the early middle third millennium.

This was a period of relative stability in east-central and southeastern Europe. The Cham and Řivnáč cultures continued in the north, the Mondsee, Ljubljana (Laibach moor), Vučedol, and Kostolac in the west, and the Baden in the Carpathian basin. Much the same was true in the east and southeast, except that the Coţofeni culture, which had both Vučedol and Kostolac elements, spread through much of Romania. The Cernavodă III continued in southeast Rumania and the Ezero culture in eastern Bulgaria.

The third wave or expansion from the Pontic steppe took place between 3000 and 2800 B.C. as averaged. It occurred at the time of the Kurgan IV culture, which lasted from 3000 to 2500 B.C. Gimbutas associates this expansion with the spread of Corded Pottery of the so-called Pan or "common European horizon." Comb and Pit Ware continued in the Baltic states, and in central Russia change is marked by the appearance of corded pottery which is known from the upper and middle Dnieper, Fatjanovo, and Balanovo.

Horizon XII, Figure 13

The West Asian, Egyptian, and Mediterranean of the Mature Historic Civilizations, the European Late Copper Age, and the Late Neolithic of North Europe

The middle of the third millennium was the period of the Old Kingdom of Egypt (2540–2250 B.C.) (Kantor) and of the Early Dynastic III (2600–2334 B.C.) (Porada et al.). Influences from Old Kingdom Egypt penetrated the southern Levant in the time of Timnian II of Sinai (Zarins) and the Early Bronze III of Palestine (Stager), and extended as far north as the coast of Lebanon (Schwartz and Weiss). On the other hand, the influence of Early Dynastic III of Mesopotamia reached into western, southern, and southeast Iran. Northwest Iran at the time of Hasanlu VII had links with the Kura-Araxes III culture of the Caucasus, while Hissar III in the northeast had connections with centers of the Namazga V culture in Turkmenistan (Voigt and Dyson). Although the Namazga V culture dominated central Asia, the Kyzyl Kum and

Zeravshan cultures continued, and the Kelteminar was now in its third phase. New cultures such as the Pre-Chust Bronze culture of Fergana and centers like Shortugai I which maintained connections with the Harappan culture of the Indus Valley now appeared (Kohl). Connections may well have been made through such centers as Shahr-i-Sokhta II–III and Mundigak III–IV in the Helmand basin, while those of Periamo continued in northern Baluchistan, as did the Kulli ones in southern Baluchistan. The predominant culture of the region was, of course, the Harappan of the Indus Valley (Shaffer). Influences from both Mesopotamia and the Indus Valley occur in the Umm an Narr horizon, which extended from Kuwait to Oman in the Arabian Gulf region (Potts).

Mesopotamian influence extended northward through the Transcaucasus to Maikop (Glumac and Anthony) and penetrated northwestward to Alaca in central Anatolia and beyond as far as Troy. Mellink assigns the tombs at Alaca and late Troy I to Early Bronze II 2700–2400 B.C. and places Troy II in the period of Early Bronze IIIA (2400–2200 B.C.), which equates chronologically with the latest Early Dynastic and the Akkadian dynasty of Mesopotamia (Mellink).

Although Anatolian influence had reached Greece in the preceding period, it was during the middle third millennium that southwest Asiatic influence reached Cyprus (Coleman) and, to a very limited extent, Greece (Coleman). This was also the time of the Early Cypriote culture of Cyprus, the late Early Minoan II of Crete, the late Early Cycladic II of the Aegean, the Early Helladic II of Greece, and the Early Thessalian II, which had extensive connections with Helladic and Cycladic centers.

In the central and western Mediterranean there was widespread influence of the Bell Beaker culture. The older Gaudo, Rinaldone, and Remedello cultures continued in Italy, but now Bell Beakers appeared in Remedello centers (Brown). The older cultures, the Millares II and V.N.S.P. II, persisted in the Iberian peninsula, but the archaeological record makes clear that the times belonged to the Beaker folk. The Bell Beaker culture dominated central Spain and extended to west Andalucia and Valencia, while the variant Maritime Beaker group occupied central Portugal, the Palmela group southern Portugal, and the Pyrenean Beaker group Catalonia and Alto Aragon (Gilman).

Older cultural traditions lingered on in France, as in the late Fontbouisse and related groups in the south, the late Artenacian in the west, the Seine-Oise-Marne in the north, and the Saône-Rhône group in the east. The Beaker culture, which now began to regionalize, was still limited to the coasts except for a scatter through the Rhône Valley and in the territory of the S.O.M. culture, and there are now the distinctive Pyrenean and Rhodanian Beaker groups of the south and the Armorican Beakers of Brittany. Although the Beaker culture did not displace older traditions in the Iberian peninsula or France, it largely did so in the British Isles. Everywhere in England, Wales, Scotland, and Ireland this was the period of the Middle Beaker culture (Thomas and R. Rowlett).

The middle third millennium brought a dramatic and much disputed transformation of culture in northern and central Europe. In southern Scandinavia, the Single Grave culture of the late Middle Neolithic took over the land, while the Pitted Ware culture appeared in eastern Sweden and penetrated as far as eastern Jutland. The related Corded Ware culture now dominated north, central, and south Germany as well as Poland and Switzerland. In the Netherlands, it is known from Beakers of IB-e and AOO types. Along with the Corded Ware culture, Bell Beaker groups are found in the Netherlands, the Rhineland, and northern and southwest Switzerland. Although this is not the place to discuss their origin, they must have played an important role in laying the foundations for the rise of the Bronze Age in the subsequent period (Thomas and E. Rowlett; Wells; Bogucki).

In east-central Europe, the middle of the third millennium was characterized by the consolidation of Corded Ware culture in southern Poland (Bogucki) and Czechoslovakia (Ehrich and Bankoff) and the formation of the Čaka-Makó and Nyirség-Zatin cultures in the Carpathian basin (Ehrich and Bankoff).

In southern Serbia, Bubanj II probably developed in response to influences from the south. There was widespread stabilization of culture in Bulgaria and Romania, where the Coţofeni and Ezero cultures maintained older traditions despite the penetration of Troadic influence. Changes were in the making as Bell Beaker elements penetrated Bohemia and Hungary. The trade network associated with these groups, together with the continuing development of the Mondsee-Vučedol trade associated with the increasing exploitation of east Alpine copper, was laying the foundations for the Early Bronze Age.

In eastern Europe, Gimbutas brings her chronology to an end ca. 2500 B.C.

Horizon XIII, Figure 14

The Transitional Age of Southwest Asia and the Rise of the Early Bronze Age in Europe

In southwestern Asia, the last three centuries of the third millennium were marked by considerable political instability. This was the First Intermediate period of Egypt and the Akkadian and Ur III periods in Mesopotamia (Porada et al.). During Early Bronze IV, Palestine was invaded by the Amorites and Syria by the Hurrians (Zarins; Stager; Schwartz and Weiss). The stability of Mesopotamia

under the Akkadians was interrupted by the Guti invansions and never really recovered during the rule of Ur III. While there was considerable cultural continuity in northwest, west, southwest, and southeast Iran, well defined by the Elamite culture of Susa IV-VA-B, northeast Iran is marked by the intrusion of Namazga V elements (Voigt and Dyson). In central Asia, the Namazga V culture disintegrated, while stability continued to the east in such centers as Dashli and Hirdai in western Bactria and at Shortugai in eastern Bactria, which had begun in preceding Namazga V times (Kohl). Although those of the Helmand basin, like Shahr-i-Sokhta and Mundigak, are marked by destruction, established cultures such as the Kulli of southern Baluchistan and the Harappan of the Indus Valley continued (Shaffer). The Umm an Narr Horizon of the Arabian Gulf region lasted through this time, its sites and localities still maintaining connections with Mesopotamia and remaining in contact with the Helmand basin and southeastern Iran (Potts).

Cultural continuity also characterized the Caucasus, where the Kur-Araxes persisted in the south and the Maikop culture in the north (Glumac and Anthony). During Early Bronze IIIb, Cilicia and southeast Anatolia were again tied to Syria and Mesopotamia respectively and Cilician influence extended as far as Kultepe in the Konya plain. Archaeological evidence is more limited for southwest and western Anatolia, but archaeological data indicate that Beycesultan XIII–VI in the southwest had relations with the now impoverished cities of Troy III–V. At Alaca Huyuk and Alishar Huyuk (Mellink) are indications of a new tradition in central Anatolia.

On the island of Cyprus, the Early Cypriot culture continued its development and during this period established connections with Palestine (Coleman). On the island of Crete, Early Minoan III and, in the Cyclades, Early Cycladic III maintained older traditions. On mainland Greece, the Early Helladic tradition continued into its third phase, characterized by Minyan ware which many archaeologists would interpret as an influx or as intrusive. This same continuity characterized the Early Thessalian III and Early Macedonian III in the north of Greece (Coleman). Much the same concept of continuity appears in archaeological thought concerning Italy, where the Polada culture dominated the north (Brown), and Iberia, where the Argar culture of east Andalucia and the Carmona culture of west Andalucia define a locally evolving Early Bronze Age. Older traditions persisted in the third phase of the V.N.S.P. culture of central Portugal as well as in Post Beaker sites of the Meseta and the north (Gilman).

In northwest Europe, Early Bronze influences coming via the Rhône Valley from central Europe may well account for the rise of the Rhodanian, Rodezian, and

Quercy groups. Older traditions survived in Brittany and in the Seine-Oise-Marne culture of northern France. The British Isles were dominated by a Late Beaker culture which had sporadic connections across the North Sea with the Netherlands and northwestern Germany (Thomas and R. Rowlett).

Although older traditions lingered in the Cist Grave culture of the Late Neolithic of Scandinavia, the Veluwe culture of the Netherlands, and the Late Neolithic of northern Germany and northern Poland, the first phase of the Early Bronze Age was under way in middle and southern central Europe. Here one finds the Transitional cultures of the Rhineland, southern Germany, and Switzerland that derived from the Proto-Aunjetitz of central Germany, the Únětice I of Bohemia and Middle Poland, and the Chlopice-Veselé culture of Silesia, Little Poland, and Volhynia (Bogucki), which mark the beginning of the Early Bronze Age in central Europe.

The Proto-Únětice, now designated as Únětice I, dominated the northern border of east-central Europe. South of Czechoslovakia was the Gáta-Wieselberg culture of Transdanubia, often called Somogyvár-Vinkovci, which extended into Yugoslavia, and the Early Nagyrév culture of eastern Hungary. Southern Yugoslavia was dominated by the Bubanj III culture, which has excellent connections with Early Helladic III. Influences from Troy III–V spread into eastern Bulgaria and southeast Romania in sufficient strength to convert these regions to Troadic ways. In the lower Danubian Valley native traditions were still strong enough to permit the transformation of the Coţofeni culture into that of Glina III. To the north the Schneckenberg culture arose in eastern Transylvania. Beyond the Carpathians in Moldavia and the western Ukraine the lands were in the hands of the steppe "Ochre Grave" people.

These chronological studies do not cover eastern Europe during this period.

The twenty-two chapters utilized in the construction of the horizon maps (figs. 1–14) provide geographic contiguity and, proceeding from area to area, some degree of cultural relationships. For the most part there has been enough archaeological activity in them to provide identifiable sequences and intra-area relationships. There are unfortunately a few missing links in the chain, such as between the east Baltic–northern Woodland–west Siberian regions, with regard to the pit-comb ware and their distributions, an adequate corpus of east-central Asian material, and the like.

There seems to be no relationship between either northeastern Asia (Michael) or Korea (Nelson) with the areas mapped here. In India, although the northwest provinces reflect ties with the Indus Valley, the rest of the subcontinent seems a world apart. Southeast Asia is even more isolated, at least until the Bronze-Iron periods, and the early cultures are not yet sufficiently known to relate them back to India or north to China (Bronson and White). In sub-Saharan Africa there is again little to tie to the north and east.

For these six areas, despite the difficulties caused by inadequate cultural information, we have radiocarbon dates by which we can correlate what seems to be emerging within them with the equivalent chronological horizons of North Africa, the Mediterranean, the Near and Middle East, west-central Asia, and western, northern, central, and eastern Europe. One must also remember that, except for China and Korea, sedentary development really does not begin until after the middle of the third millennium B.C.

In the meantime one can only take the available radiocarbon dates, consider any parallels between the ethnographic present and the emerging archaeological patterns in a given area, and try to arrive at some understanding of probable developments, culture contacts, and borrowings.